Habitats and Ecological Communities of Indiana

Indiana Natural Science

Gillian Harris, editor

Habitats and Ecological Communities of Indiana
Presettlement to Present

Edited by John O. Whitaker, Jr., and Charles J. Amlaner, Jr.

Marion T. Jackson, George R. Parker, and Peter E. Scott, *Associate Editors*

Indiana University Press
BLOOMINGTON AND INDIANAPOLIS

This book is a publication of
Indiana University Press
601 North Morton Street
Bloomington, Indiana 47404-3797 USA

www.iupress.indiana.edu

Telephone orders 800-842-6796
Fax orders 812-855-7931

(Indiana State University Department of Biology and Department of Earth and Environmental Sciences and Indiana Department of Natural Resources Wildlife Diversity Program, Catherine "Katie" Gremillion-Smith, Project Manager; supported by State Wildlife Grant T-2-P-2, administered by the US Fish and Wildlife Service)

♾ The paper used in this publication meets the minimum requirements of the American National Standard for Information Sciences—Permanence of Paper for Printed Library Materials, ANSI Z39.48-1992.

MANUFACTURED IN CHINA

Library of Congress Cataloging-in-Publication Data

Habitats and ecological communities of Indiana : presettlement to present / edited by John O. Whitaker, Jr. and Charles J. Amlaner, Jr. ; Marion T. Jackson, George R. Parker, and Peter E. Scott, associate editors.
p. cm. — (Indiana natural science)
Includes bibliographical references and index.
ISBN 978-0-253-35602-4 (cloth : alk. paper) —
ISBN 978-0-253-00520-5 (e-pub : alk. paper)
1. Habitat (Ecology)—Indiana. 2. Habitat (Ecology)—Indiana—History. 3. Biotic communities—Indiana. 4. Biotic communities—Indiana—History. 5. Natural history—Indiana. I. Whitaker, John O. II. Amlaner, Charles J.
QH76.5.I6H33 2012
577.09772—dc23 2011030456

1 2 3 4 5 17 16 15 14 13 12

Published
with the
generous support
of the
Laura Hare
Charitable Trust

Contributors

BRANT FISHER and CATHERINE GREMILLION-SMITH (fish, aquatic habitats), Division of Fish and Wildlife, IDNR

MICHAEL A. HOMOYA (flora), Division of Nature Preserves, IDNR

BRUCE A. KINGSBURY (amphibians and reptiles), Department of Biology, Indiana University–Purdue University, Fort Wayne

JULIAN J. LEWIS (caves and cave invertebrates), Lewis & Associates LLC, Cave, Karst & Groundwater Biological Consulting

GEORGE R. PARKER (forest habitats and land use), Department of Forestry and Natural Resources, Purdue University

J. C. RANDOLPH (acreages), School of Public and Environmental Affairs, Indiana University

PETER E. SCOTT and STEVEN L. LIMA (birds), Department of Biology, Indiana State University

THOMAS P. SIMON and STEPHANIE L. WORDEN (fish, aquatic habitats), Aquatic Research Center, Indiana Biological Survey

JAMES H. SPEER and CHRISTOPHER M. GENTRY (soils), Department of Earth and Environmental Sciences, Indiana State University

QIHAO WENG (habitat land use, cover mapping), Department of Earth and Environmental Sciences, Indiana State University

JOHN O. WHITAKER, JR. (mammals), Department of Biology, Indiana State University

This book is dedicated to
the people who appreciate, enjoy, and protect
the natural environment in Indiana.
May their efforts be rewarded.

Contents

Acknowledgments

Michael Homoya would like to thank all of those who have helped to identify and preserve natural areas in the state, especially those affiliated with the Indiana Department of Natural Resources' Division of Nature Preserves. Since the inception of the Nature Preserves Act in 1967, there have been over 200 preserves, totaling over 30,000 acres, dedicated.

Our understanding of Indiana fish is due to a large number of people too numerous to list. Special thanks to John Whitaker, Jim Gammon, and Tom McComish for their leadership and to the late Shelby Gerking for his guidance and assistance in many technical aspects of early ichthyological investigation. Without the assistance of Charles Morris, Greg Nottingham, Andy Ellis, Doug Campbell, Ronda Dufour, Tony Brannam, Steve Wente, Stacy Sobat, Greg Bright, Jim Smith, Joe Exl, and Jim Stahl, we would never have accumulated the necessary data. Also, many thanks to those who have assisted in the management of our database. We especially appreciate the efforts of Ronda Dufour and Bonnie Bloomquist, who kept us moving forward in the modern age of electronic data acquisition.

Julian Lewis would like to thank Keith Dunlap, Indiana Karst Conservancy; Salisa L. Lewis, Lewis & Associates; and Arthur N. Palmer of the State University of New York for reading the manuscript and making suggestions for its improvement.

Bruce Kingsbury would like to recognize Joanna Gibson for her editorial review of the text relating to herpetofauna in each chapter and for her assistance with herp table construction. Alan Resetar and Mike Lodato provided valuable editorial input on the tables. Bruce would also like to thank the other authors of the book, particularly John Whitaker, for assistance in making the herpetofaunal contributions better.

Peter Scott and Steven Lima would like to thank the many birders and ornithologists who continually clarify the status of Indiana's birds through fieldwork and reviewing records, and the conservationists who save habitats important for birds.

Charles Amlaner would like to thank the Indiana Department of Natural Resources, and particularly Dr. Katie Smith, for supporting this project from its inception. Without the department's financial and logistical support, this almost 10-year project would never have been completed. Many knowledgeable people selflessly contributed invaluable amounts of time to see this comprehensive volume through to completion. And no one has contributed more time, energy, and talent to this entire project than John O. Whitaker Jr. Without his steadfast leadership, his vast knowledge of ecology, and his great depth of love for the state of Indiana, we would not have this wonderful compendium of knowledge about Indiana's natural resources and environmental history.

John Whitaker would like to thank all of the other authors for their patient and timely answering of his numerous questions and requests for additional information. George Parker has been of exceptional help in organizing the text, helping to make it flow better, and he has helped to edit the entire manuscript. Qihao Weng and Jim Speer provided excellent maps to accompany the text, and Sue Berta helped with administrative details. Katie Smith gave us the opportunity to write this manuscript and has provided us with many thoughtful questions and passages which improved the manuscript considerably. Also, she was patient when we took longer than anticipated in our writing. Linda Castor helped to organize, edit, and otherwise ready the maps and photos for publication. Angela Chamberlain spent many hours helping with final details, such as being sure that maps, figures, etc., were all correctly indicated in the text; her assistance was exceptional. Last, but certainly not least, our heartfelt thanks go to Laura Bakken, who managed to keep straight the numerous changes and corrections from numerous authors, often on older drafts. Without her excellent typing and organizational skills and her knowledge of biology, this project would have been much more difficult. I am sure that all of the participants benefited from her input.

Abbreviations

BOD	biological oxygen demand
CRP	Conservation Reserve Program
DNR	Department of Natural Resources
DOW	Division of Water
DSC	Division of Soil Conservation
ECBP	Eastern Corn Belt Plains
EPA	U.S. Environmental Protection Agency
ESA	Endangered Species Act
GIS	geographic information system
GLO	General Land Office
IBH	Indiana Board of Health
IDEM	Indiana Department of Environmental Management
IDNR	Indiana Department of Natural Resources
INESCA	Indiana Nongame and Endangered Species Conservation Act
IP	Interior Plateau
IRL	Interior River Lowland
NCSS	National Cooperative Soil Survey
NEPA	National Environmental Policy Act
NFHAP	National Fish Habitat Action Plan
NLCD	National Land Cover Data
NRC	Natural Resources Commission
NRCS	Natural Resources Conservation Service
ORSANCO	Ohio River Valley Water Sanitation Commission
SFRA	Sport Fish Restoration Act
STATSGO	State Soil Geographic database
SWG	State Wildlife Grant Program
USDA	U.S. Department of Agriculture
USFWS	U.S. Fish and Wildlife Service
USGS	U.S. Geological Survey

Introduction

The main objectives of this volume are to evaluate the present diversity and health of the state's wildlife and habitats and to summarize 2 centuries of ecological change. Our goal is to contribute to an understanding of Indiana's habitats and biodiversity and to help guide conservation planning for a broad array of wildlife, including nongame species. To achieve this, we have organized the book by habitats and historical periods. Using a GIS-based classification of habitats and land uses, we map, quantify (in terms of acreage), and describe 8 distinct habitats, along with their vascular plants, vertebrate fauna, and (for subterranean systems) cave invertebrates. To convey historical change, we describe (as best we can using the literature and current information on the distribution and habitat of organisms) the conditions prevailing at the century intervals of 1800, 1900, and 2000. The data for 2000 should serve as baseline information for future studies, as they reflect an evaluation of habitat and wildlife conditions in Indiana at the beginning of the new millennium. Various specialists treated the 5 vertebrate classes (amphibians, birds, fish, mammals, reptiles), vascular plants, cave invertebrates, soils, and other topics. Each author or pair of authors wrote a section for each relevant habitat and sub-habitat. Although this gives chapters a "written-by-committee" feel, the format allows one to readily see (a) how particular habitats vary in their importance for different taxonomic groups, and (b) how changes in habitat structure have affected them differently.

In addition, this book was written for two practical purposes: to help Indiana qualify for new federal wildlife conservation funds and to guide the state's use of such money. Prior to the year 2000, federal funding to states for wildlife management was mainly for game animals and federally listed endangered species. Then, through the Wildlife Conservation and Restoration Program (2000) and the subsequent State Wildlife Grant Program, matching funds for nongame animals of conservation concern became available through the U.S. Fish and Wildlife Service. Congress required states to first complete a Comprehensive Wildlife Strategy. Although flexibility was permitted in designing such documents, two requirements were (1) to summarize information on the distribution and abundance of animal species in a way that portrayed the diversity and health of the state's wildlife, including species with low and declining populations; and (2) to describe the location and condition of key habitats and community types essential to the conservation of wildlife. This national planning effort is a major conservation milestone.

The Indiana Department of Natural Resources commissioned a quantitative analysis of wildlife habitats, including a historical overview of changes in habitats and the fauna associated with them, especially vertebrates. This work was to take the form of a "useful reference book," in the words of the Comprehensive Wildlife Strategy (see below). Ecologists and geographers at Indiana State University were chosen to lead the effort, and this volume is the result. The focus on vertebrates was justified by the fact that vertebrate animals have been well studied since settlement days, so a synopsis of changes in their distribution and abundance was possible. In contrast, invertebrate species remain much less well known. However, in subterranean karst habitats of southern Indiana, the species are overwhelmingly invertebrates, to a much greater degree than in surface habitats. They are fairly well known, thanks to diligent cave biologists, and include many endemic species. For this habitat, therefore, invertebrates are featured. In addition, for all habitats, we will review the characteristic vascular plant species that, except for caves and aquatic systems, define the habitats more than anything else. Although this work was commissioned by the Indiana Department of Natural Resources, the information presented represents the opinions and analyses of the authors and not the IDNR.

The habitat classification used here was devised by biologists from the Indiana Department of Natural Resources working with D. J. Case and Associates (2005). It was influenced by the habitat-classification ability of spectral imaging procedures, such as LANDSAT, and specifically by the work of geographers at Indiana State University. A classification linked to spectral imaging and GIS databases means that habitat changes can be monitored using data from satellites.

Eight habitats were defined in the *Indiana Comprehensive Wildlife Strategy,* which is available online at the IDNR website (www.wildlifeactionplans.org/indiana.html). The strategy document presents them alphabetically: (1) agricultural habitats, (2) aquatic systems, (3) barren lands, (4) developed lands, (5) forest lands, (6) grasslands/prairie, (7) subterranean systems, and (8) wetlands. In this book, we have organized the classification so that the 6 (mostly) natural habitats are treated together, followed by the two man-made habitats (agricultural and developed). The strategy document also recognizes sub-habitats, such as row crops, cereal grains, and orchards within agricultural habitats. We will present information for sub-habitats when vertebrate wildlife species or vascular plants differ notably for these subdivisions and knowledge is sufficient.

Ours is hardly the first effort to characterize Indiana's habitats and biological diversity and to summarize changes since European settlement. Two previous books stand out. *Natural Features of Indiana* (Lindsey 1966), published on the sesquicentennial of statehood, provided an overview of bedrock and soil substrates, vegetation, and biological and cultural features. Its scope was broader than ours: besides taking a historical perspective and treating vertebrates, vascular plants, cave fauna, habitats, soils, geology, and agricultural history, as we do, there were chapters on insects, animal parasites, lower green land plants, plant diseases, fleshy fungi, and algae. Many notable scientists contributed, often in imaginative ways. Reading their accounts brings one closer to the natural and agricultural world of preceding eras than any later book can. The book remains valuable reading for any Indiana naturalist.

Thirty-one years later, *The Natural Heritage of Indiana* (Jackson 1997) appeared. Its scope was similar to Lindsey's volume, covering "terrain" (geology, soils, physiography) as well as "biota" (6 chapters on plants, 2 on invertebrates, 4 on vertebrates), and was of similar length (482 pages, compared to Lindsey's 600). There was some continuity in authorship (Gammon, Jackson, Lindsey, Minton, Mumford, Newman) between the two books, as there is between Jackson's volume and this book. *The Natural Heritage of Indiana* emphasized the state's 12 natural regions, which had been defined and mapped earlier (Homoya et al. 1985) based on a combination of physiography, watersheds, and biological distributions. It also explained how habitats and natural communities recognized by midwestern ecologists were distributed across natural regions. Historical changes in habitat quantity and quality were expertly summarized, and future ecological prospects for Indiana were pondered. The writing and a rich set of color photographs captured the imagination of a broad audience and inspired a 4-part film of the same name by Samuel Orr, shown on public television beginning in 2007.

Besides the descriptive accounts, authors compiled tables listing the characteristic species of each habitat, plus master lists of all regularly occurring species known statewide, including extinct and extirpated species. The tables, which are presented as appendixes following the last chapter, constitute much of this book. Each taxonomic or other category has a separate numbering sequence that begins with a different capital letter: general information, including habitat and land use acreage (G), soils (S), plants (P), amphibians and reptiles (H), birds (B), mammals (M), fish (F), and cave invertebrates (I). The tables include the scientific names of species and their common names, which are used (almost exclusively) in the text. A combination of maps and tables indicates the distribution and extent of each habitat and subhabitat in Indiana. Most of the maps were created by Qihao Weng and his graduate students in the Department of Geography, Geology and Anthropology, Indiana State University. Other maps, and the estimates of acreage, were developed by J. C. Randolph and his students in the GIS laboratory at the School of Public and Environmental Affairs, Indiana University at Bloomington. Finally, we have provided photographs of habitats, sub-habitats, endangered organisms, and poorly known cave invertebrates.

One of our goals was to evaluate wildlife's use of man-made habitats, as well as the modified natural ones. The principal man-made habitat, agriculture, still accounts for more than half of land use in Indiana, although total farmland acreage peaked about a century ago and is steadily declining. Thus, the conversion of prior habitat to agriculture has had huge impacts on flora and wildlife, and the present extent and types of agricultural habitats strongly influence wild species. Second, there are developed lands, consisting of residential, commercial, and industrial areas, transportation systems, etc. Such lands include urban forests and golf courses, structures relevant to wildlife such as cell and communications towers, and a vast network of paved roads, railroads, utility lines, and rights-of-way. To varying degrees, depending on the type of animal, wildlife species use these man-made habitats and are affected by them in myriad ways, which we will attempt to describe. A third man-made habitat is found in the coal-rich southwestern counties, which have been surface-mined for a century. Since the 1950s, large mined areas (many square miles in size) have been restored, usually as grasslands, using a handful of hardy Eurasian grass and legume species (Brothers 1990), which we will describe in chapter 5. These grasslands are relatively long-lasting because of the nutrient-poor soil and substrate and are surprisingly hospitable to native vertebrate wildlife, including former prairie species, which colonize them on their own.

The landscape ecology of habitats—especially the fragmentation of once-continuous habitats by agriculture, development, roads, and growth of human population—is critically important to wildlife. Unfortunately, a proper evaluation is beyond the scope of this work, although scattered comments will be found. Our main goals in analyzing each habitat are to identify all or most species that use it, especially the characteristic ones; to describe historic changes in abundance; and to highlight species that have disappeared, might be restored, or are at risk.

The descriptive portion of this book is organized as follows. Part 1, "A Statewide Overview: Land Use, Soils, Flora, and Wildlife," provides a broad perspective on settlement and habitat conversion in Indiana, the state's soils, and vascular plants and vertebrate wildlife. Part 2, "Natural Habitats: Changes over Two Centuries," treats the 6 major natural habitats, terrestrial and aquatic. For each, there is a general description of the habitat's spatial distribution and human impacts on it, followed by descriptions of characteristic plants, fish, amphibians and reptiles, birds, mammals, and (for subterranean habitats) cave invertebrates. Each account is organized historically, describing the situation in 1800, 1900, and 2000. Part 3, "Man-Made Habitats: Changes over Two Centuries," treats agricultural habitats and developed lands in the same manner. In part 4, "Species Concerns: Declining Natives and Invading Exotics," we first review the native plant and wildlife species that have been extirpated and those now or formerly listed as endangered or threatened at federal or state levels. Then, we summarize exotic species problems. Third, as a contribution to taxonomic history, we list the species that were scientifically described based on Indiana specimens. The conclusion provides a summary of the status of Indiana's habitats and wildlife and points out some areas for future research.

Part 1.

A Statewide Overview: Land Use, Soils, Flora, and Wildlife

This part begins with a statewide perspective on the history of land use and habitat alteration since presettlement times (chapter 1). Next, we describe the variety and geographic distribution of soils in Indiana (chapter 2). Finally, we describe the biological diversity of vascular plants and vertebrate animals at a statewide level, summarizing changes since presettlement times (chapter 3). With the exception of soils, which are treated only here, these chapters are broad overviews. More details are given in the subsequent chapters on different habitat types.

Arial view of Naval Surface Warfare Center at Crane. Photo by Scott Johnson.

Land Use and Human Impacts on Habitats

1

In 1800, the land we call Indiana was just being settled by immigrants, and many Native Americans still occupied much of the territory. Indiana would become a state a few years later, in 1816. At that time, David Thomas (1819) in *Travels through the Western Country in the Summer of 1816* provided an interesting look at the habitat. A dam and mill were being built in 1816 by Major Abraham Markle on Otter Creek, in what is now Vigo County. Thomas stated that everything to the north of the dam was Indian country. The mill burned in the 1930s, but the dam still exists (it has been repaired a few times). The dam is about a half-mile east of North Terre Haute, and is just above a major rock outcrop. It is situated in such a way that the water flowing over the dam provides a deep pool just below the dam and keeps the rock bare, providing bare rock habitat with some stones. Downstream are areas of progressively smaller rock fragments, then gravel, and finally the silt and sand bottom which forms most of Vigo County. The construction of this dam almost 200 years ago created a habitat which continues to have by far the greatest biodiversity of any stream in Vigo County (108 species of fish taken there to date), and one that could be unrivaled in the state. Indiana in 1800 consisted of 3 main habitats: forest (some 20.4 million acres) comprised 90% of the state; prairie (approximately 2 million acres) made up 10% of the state; and approximately 5.6 million acres of wetlands (25% of the state) were embedded within the forest and prairie.

The state has now greatly changed. Although Markle's dam is still present and still affects the habitats and fish of Otter Creek, most of the Native Americans are gone, the forest is much reduced, many of the wetlands have been drained, and only scattered fragments of the original prairie remain. Much of the land is now agricultural. Forest covers only 25% (4.3 million acres) of the land, and many kinds of development are progressively eating away at the remaining natural lands, and also at the farmlands.

Clearly, it is time, after 200 years of development by European settlers, with countless changes to the habitats and to the species present (introductions, increases, decreases, extirpations, extinctions) and ever-increasing rates of development (about 101,000 acres per year in Indiana in 2000), to document what was, what is, and where we might be heading from here, including how fast the changes are occurring. This should give future observers some baseline data for comparison.

1800. The 22,958,877 acres of land contained within Indiana have changed dramatically in the more than 200 years since 1800. They had undoubtedly been changed by several thousand years of Native American occupation prior to 1800, but our knowledge of this is limited. The early pioneers from the eastern United States found villages, camping places, dancing floors, burial grounds, earthworks, gardens, and large corn fields, particularly in the northern half of the state. The Native Americans also had an extensive trail system throughout the state (Parker 1997).

Native Americans practiced extensive agriculture in Indiana prior to European settlement with crop fields of several hundred acres found around villages during the military expeditions of the late 1700s (Whicker 1916). Crops were grown in natural openings, or in forest clearings created by deadening large trees and using fire to clear the understory (Latta 1938). New clearings were made as soil productivity declined. The process of clearing, burning, cropping, abandonment, and forest regrowth strongly influenced forest structure in localized areas of Indiana.

Native Americans also burned grasslands to attract and move game animals such as deer, bison, and elk (McCord 1970). The burning of grasslands releases nutrients, resulting in more succulent vegetation for 1–2 growing seasons. Such fires maintained prairies and savannas throughout much of the state, and also changed forest structure over large areas of the Indiana landscape by favoring the regeneration of fire-tolerant species, such as oaks and hickories.

While Native Americans were important in affecting the plant and animal communities in Indiana, their estimated population of 20,000 in 1800 indicates the yearly combined extent of their farming activities would have been small, and a total of considerably less than 100,000 acres was under cultivation statewide. However, their use of fire influenced much larger areas of the state. It is likely that, in 1800, the Indiana landscape was still recovering from the activities of the much larger Native American populations that were present in the 1400s and 1500s, prior to the decimation caused by diseases brought by early European settlers (Denevan 1992).

The French were active in the area beginning in the late 1600s, primarily as traders with the native peoples (Barnhart and Riker 1971). While French traders lived in villages such as Ouiatenon, near Lafayette, in the early 1700s, their first permanent settlement was at the site of the present city of Vincennes in 1732. These families kept large numbers of cattle and hogs in confined pastures and grew wheat, corn, rice, cotton, and tobacco on land close to the fort.

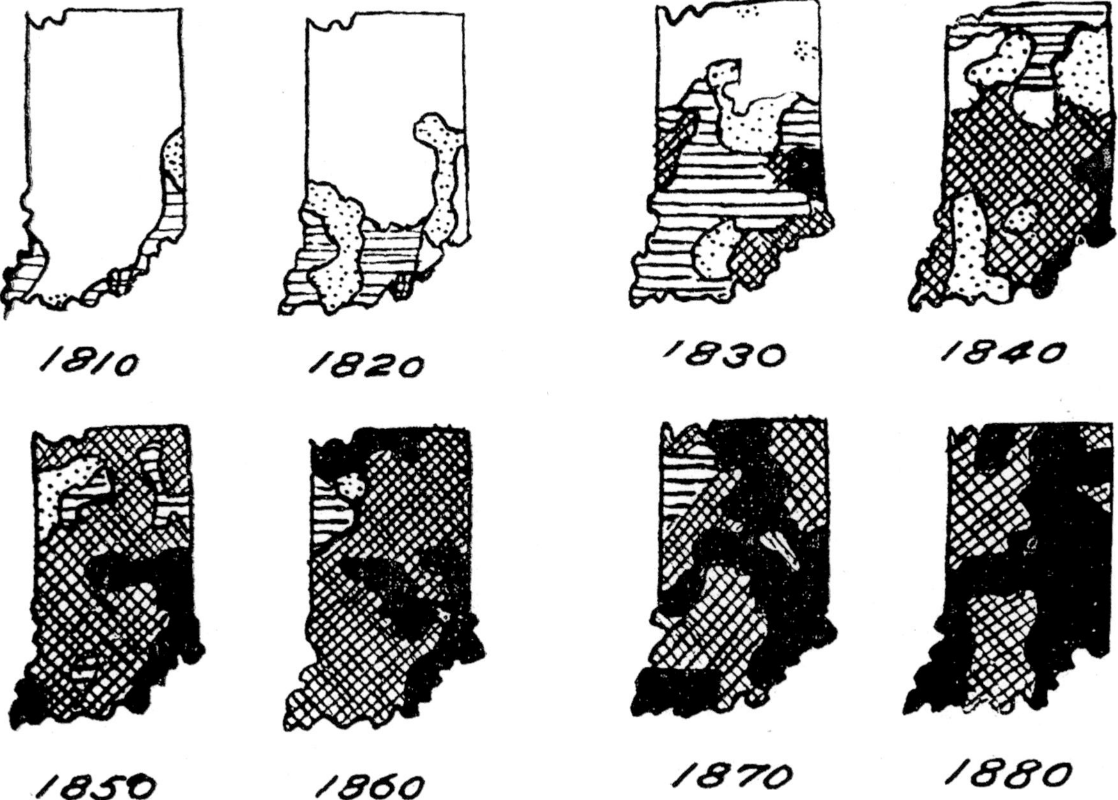

Map 1.1. Progress of settlement and density of population in Indiana in successive decades of the twentieth century. Reproduced by J. C. Allen & Sons from *Handbook of Geology*. From Latta 1938.

Settlement of Indiana Territory expanded rapidly from the Ohio River in the southeast following the American Revolution (Map 1.1; Latta 1938). Eighteen counties of southern Indiana were organized between 1795 and 1817. The white population grew from less than 5,000 in 1800 to 24,000 in 1810 and 147,178 in 1820. The new settlers adopted the natives' methods of clearing forests to make way for croplands. Each farm family could deaden about 9 acres of forest per year. Settlers also brought free-ranging livestock with them.

Most of Indiana Territory would have been in natural vegetation at the beginning of European occupation around 1800, but plant communities were in all stages of recovery from Native American activities, particularly fire. It is estimated that 20 million acres of forest, 2 million acres of prairie, and 1 million acres of glades, barrens, and savannas were present at that time. Embedded within these vegetation types (and part of this acreage) were some 5.6 million acres of wetlands.

It is difficult to determine the actual areas of different habitats in 1800 based on the limited information available, and even more difficult to determine the habitat conditions then. We know there were disturbances of forests through fire and clearing for crops, but their extent and location cannot be quantified except in a few instances, as mentioned above. The discussion below by land use category is based on both historical information and a projection of our current knowledge of habitats back in time. Maps of the distribution of habitats for presettlement Indiana have been developed using the General Land Office public land survey records of the early 1800s (Map 1.2) and visual observation of conditions across the state in the early 1900s (Map 1.3). Our current knowledge of soils was used to estimate the area of forest, grassland, and wetland complexes that would have been present in different regions of the state in 1800 (Map 1.4; Homoya et al. 1985).

1900. The period from 1800 to 1900 saw rapid changes in the habitats of Indiana. Widespread disturbance and exploitation of native fauna and vegetation occurred prior to 1860, and was followed by more permanent conversion of forests, wetlands, and prairies to croplands, cities, and transportation systems. The first wave of European settlers squatted on unpurchased lands, built cabins, cleared a few acres for corn and vegetables, and subsisted largely on wild animals. They settled along forested stream valleys, since these lands were considered to be the best for cropland: wetlands were difficult to drain, and prairies were hard to plow and thought to have inferior soils.

Clearing of forests by individual settlers took several years (Johnson 1978). Between 2 and 9 acres of land were cleared each year. First, small trees were cut and piled around large trees. The piles were then burned, killing the large trees, and crops were planted on plowed land between the stumps and standing dead trees. Standing dead trees would fall or be cut during a 3- to 4-year period and burned. Croplands

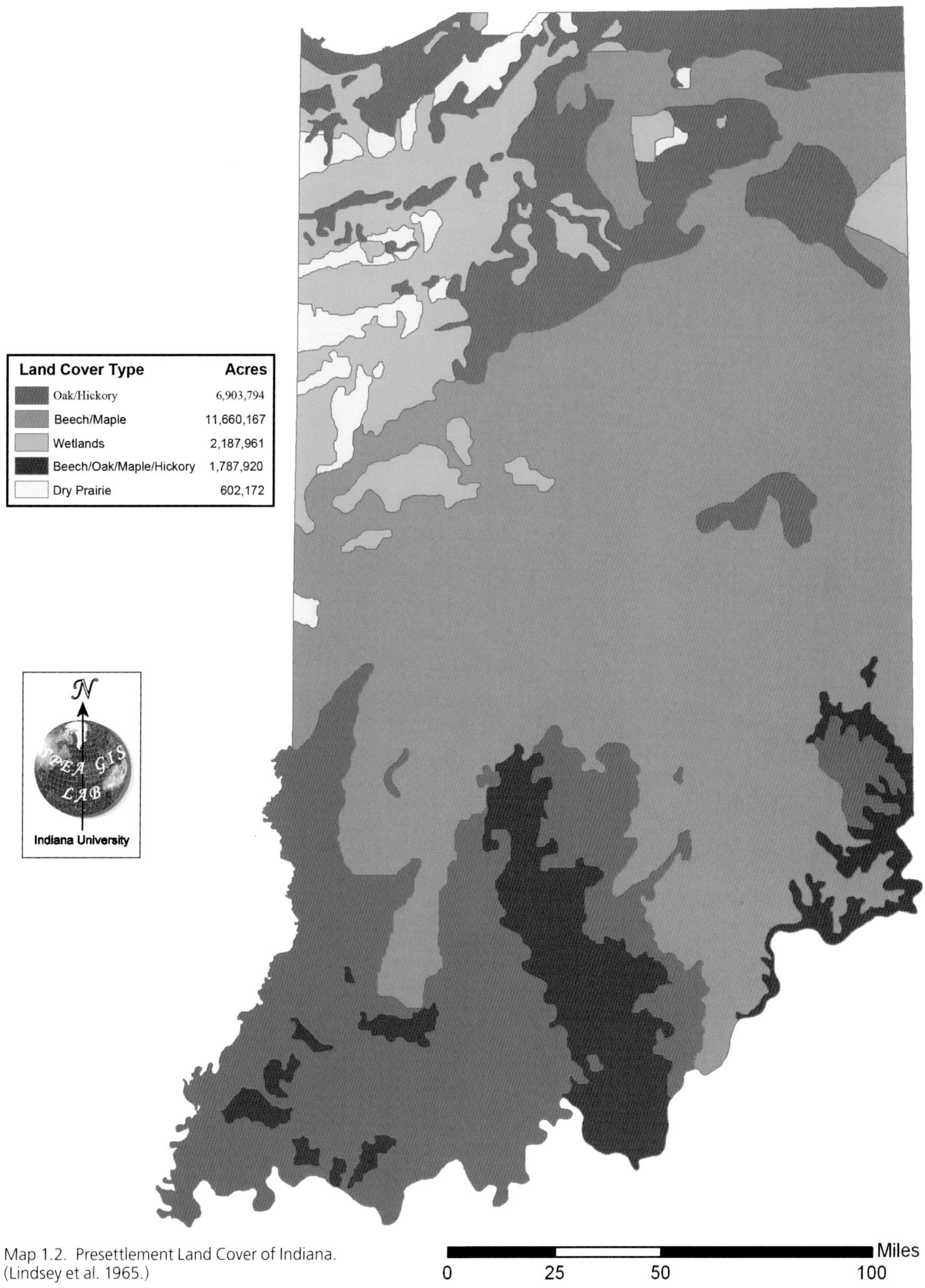

Map 1.2. Presettlement Land Cover of Indiana. (Lindsey et al. 1965.)

were abandoned after a few years as production declined and new lands were cleared. Abandoned croplands rapidly returned to native forest due to incomplete removal of native species and the small size of fields, allowing reseeding from surrounding forests. With the rapidly expanding human population, as much as 10 million acres of forest land may have been disturbed in this way prior to 1860.

With new technology and equipment, the clearing of forests, draining of wetlands, and plowing of prairies became widespread after 1860. Fourteen million acres of the state (61% of the total) were in farmland by 1880. By 1900, over 16.6 million acres of the 21.6 million acres in farmland had been improved (cultivated for crops) (U.S. Census Bureau 1900). Some commercial fertilizer and crop rotation with legumes

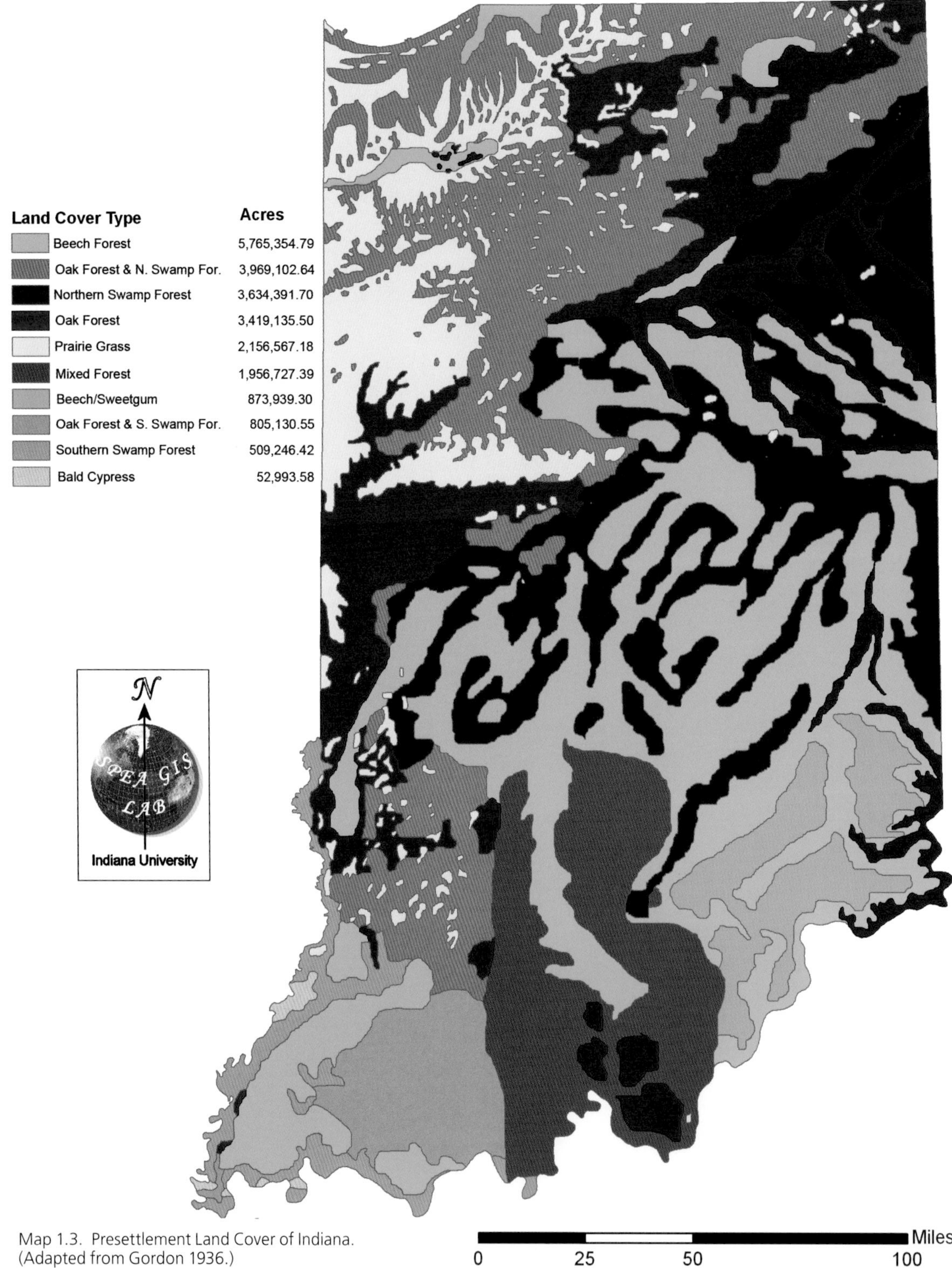

Map 1.3. Presettlement Land Cover of Indiana. (Adapted from Gordon 1936.)

allowed the permanent use of cleared lands for crops. Streamside forest had largely been removed (Freeman 1908), leading to declining water quality and destruction of habitat for aquatic species. Urban centers and transportation systems were set for continued expansion by the late 1800s (*Historical Atlas* 1876). Incorporated cities covered over 81,000 acres, and there were more than 11,600 mi of gravel road by 1901 (Indiana Department of Statistics 1901–1902).

While there is a substantial amount of data from the 1800s to characterize the habitats of the state, most of it is on the county level. The first agricultural census was completed in 1850, and a complete atlas of county maps was produced in 1876 (see one example in Map 1.5). This atlas includes the location of urban centers and transportation systems, and also shows the location of significant prairies and wetlands. Forest groves are shown in Benton County's map.

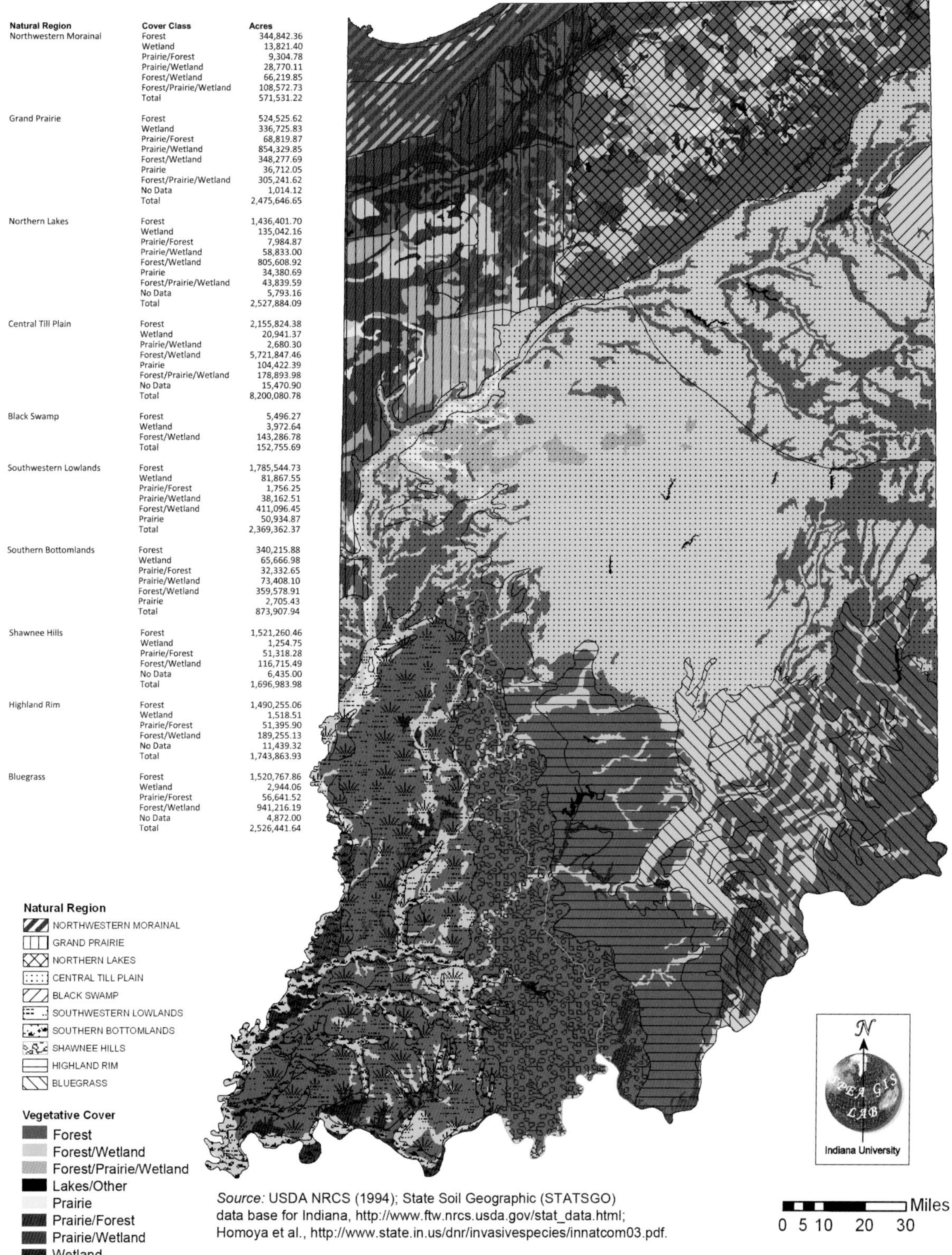

Natural Region	Cover Class	Acres
Northwestern Morainal	Forest	344,842.36
	Wetland	13,821.40
	Prairie/Forest	9,304.78
	Prairie/Wetland	28,770.11
	Forest/Wetland	66,219.85
	Forest/Prairie/Wetland	108,572.73
	Total	571,531.22
Grand Prairie	Forest	524,525.62
	Wetland	336,725.83
	Prairie/Forest	68,819.87
	Prairie/Wetland	854,329.85
	Forest/Wetland	348,277.69
	Prairie	36,712.05
	Forest/Prairie/Wetland	305,241.62
	No Data	1,014.12
	Total	2,475,646.65
Northern Lakes	Forest	1,436,401.70
	Wetland	135,042.16
	Prairie/Forest	7,984.87
	Prairie/Wetland	58,833.00
	Forest/Wetland	805,608.92
	Prairie	34,380.69
	Forest/Prairie/Wetland	43,839.59
	No Data	5,793.16
	Total	2,527,884.09
Central Till Plain	Forest	2,155,824.38
	Wetland	20,941.37
	Prairie/Wetland	2,680.30
	Forest/Wetland	5,721,847.46
	Prairie	104,422.39
	Forest/Prairie/Wetland	178,893.98
	No Data	15,470.90
	Total	8,200,080.78
Black Swamp	Forest	5,496.27
	Wetland	3,972.64
	Forest/Wetland	143,286.78
	Total	152,755.69
Southwestern Lowlands	Forest	1,785,544.73
	Wetland	81,867.55
	Prairie/Forest	1,756.25
	Prairie/Wetland	38,162.51
	Forest/Wetland	411,096.45
	Prairie	50,934.87
	Total	2,369,362.37
Southern Bottomlands	Forest	340,215.88
	Wetland	65,666.98
	Prairie/Forest	32,332.65
	Prairie/Wetland	73,408.10
	Forest/Wetland	359,578.91
	Prairie	2,705.43
	Total	873,907.94
Shawnee Hills	Forest	1,521,260.46
	Wetland	1,254.75
	Prairie/Forest	51,318.28
	Forest/Wetland	116,715.49
	No Data	6,435.00
	Total	1,696,983.98
Highland Rim	Forest	1,490,255.06
	Wetland	1,518.51
	Prairie/Forest	51,395.90
	Forest/Wetland	189,255.13
	No Data	11,439.32
	Total	1,743,863.93
Bluegrass	Forest	1,520,767.86
	Wetland	2,944.06
	Prairie/Forest	56,641.52
	Forest/Wetland	941,216.19
	No Data	4,872.00
	Total	2,526,441.64

Map 1.4. Historic Vegetative Cover and Homoya's Natural Regions. (Adapted from Gordon 1936.)

These maps have not been digitized so they are used only in a qualitative manner in this volume. The Twelfth Census of the United States (U.S. Census Bureau 1900) and the biennial reports of the Indiana Department of Statistics were the primary sources of information for characterizing the state in 1900. These reports provide data on farming activities and forest conditions for each county. Acreages of native habitats are not quantified except as unimproved farmland and lands not in farms in the Twelfth Census of the United States (U.S. Census Bureau 1900). The *Ninth Biennial Report* of the Indiana Department of

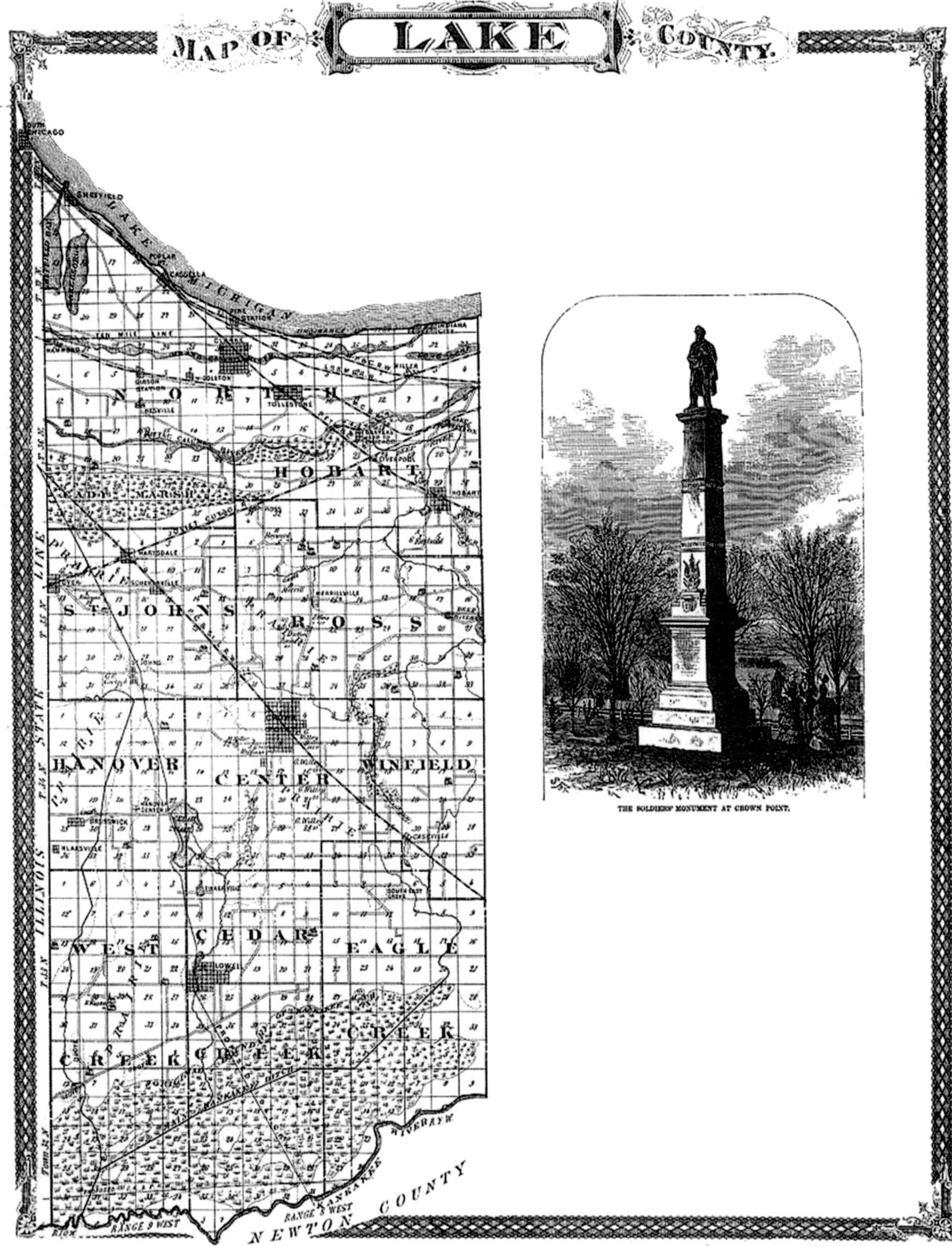

Map 1.5. Map of Lake County in 1876.

Statistics provides county acreage for the relative conditions of native forest in 1902. Forest covered about 3.8 million acres with most in poor condition due to logging, burning, and grazing by domestic livestock. Only 250,000 acres were considered first-grade forest at that time.

2000. The period from 1900 to the early twenty-first century was, in some ways, one of increasing awareness, protection, and improved management. Badly abused farmland abandoned in the 1920s and 1930s was largely transferred to public ownership. The average size of farms increased from 97 acres in 1900 to 250 acres in 2002 (U.S. Census Bureau 1900; U.S. Department of Agriculture 2002). Farms became more specialized with the development of fertilizers and pesticides in the 1940s and 1950s, which increased the land in crop production on farms. Total farmland decreased to just over 15 million acres, most of it (12.5 million acres) in cropland in 2002. About 41% of the cropland was planted using no-till methods to reduce soil erosion. The over 2 million acres of farmland not in crop production were in forest, pasture, and wet-

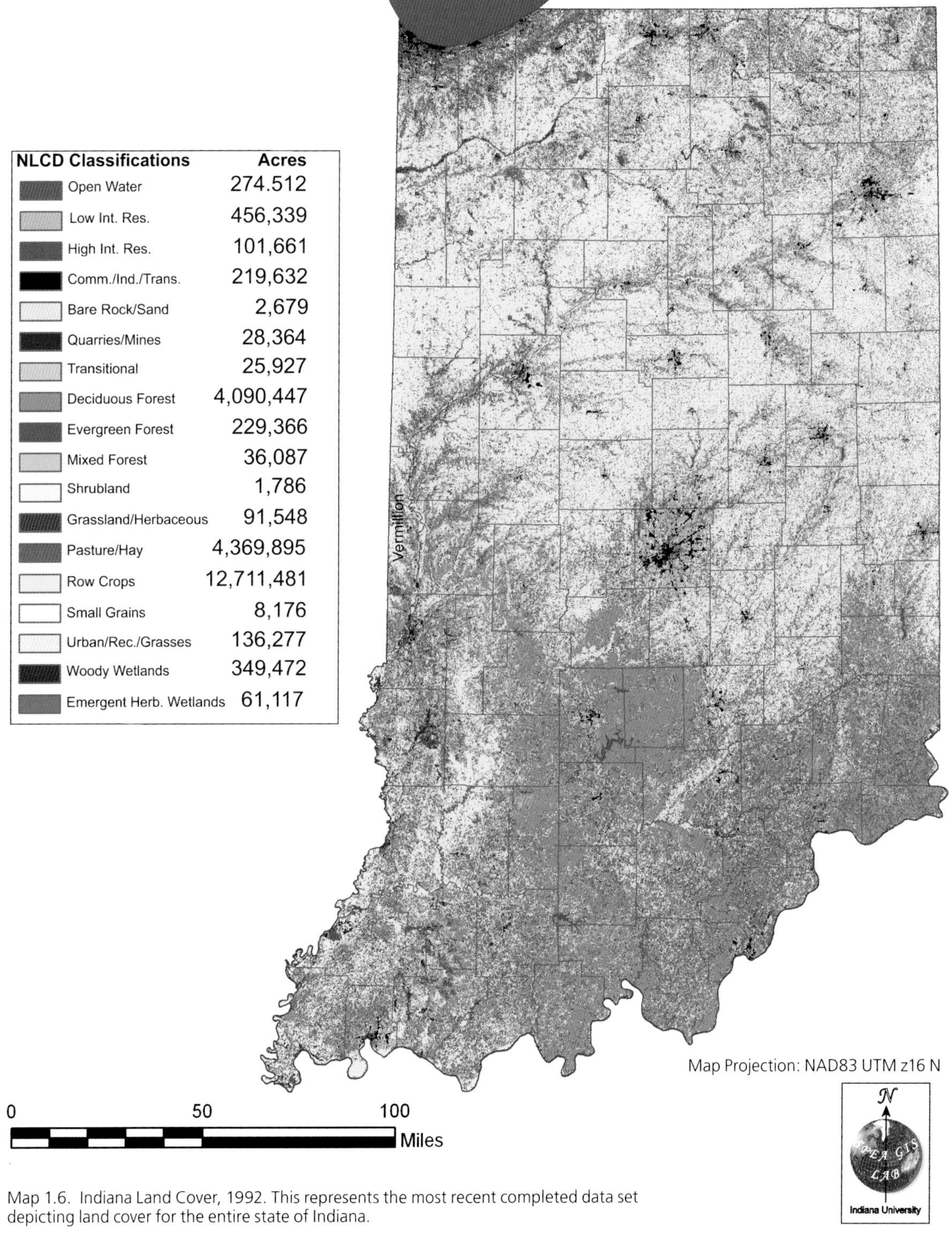

Map 1.6. Indiana Land Cover, 1992. This represents the most recent completed data set depicting land cover for the entire state of Indiana.

land habitats or regrowing via successional recovery. Conservation programs begun in the 1970s have subsidized farmers to remove some farmland from crop production to serve as buffers to soil erosion and to restore wetlands. Forest and prairie have been planted on former croplands through the federal Conservation Reserve Program (Allen and Vandever 2003).

There are several million more acres of land in non-farm use today than in 1900. Both private and public programs have purchased farms for recreation, to protect and restore native habitats, and to provide public services such as transportation systems. Almost 8 million acres were in non-farm use by 2002 with over 4.5 million acres in forest and about 1 million acres in wetland habitats. Urban areas cover about 1 million acres, and rural roads, railroads, and airport runways cover almost 800,000 acres (Indiana Department of Natural Resources 2000).

The foregoing paragraphs make use of an abundance of data that are available today thanks to computers and software for spatial analysis. There are

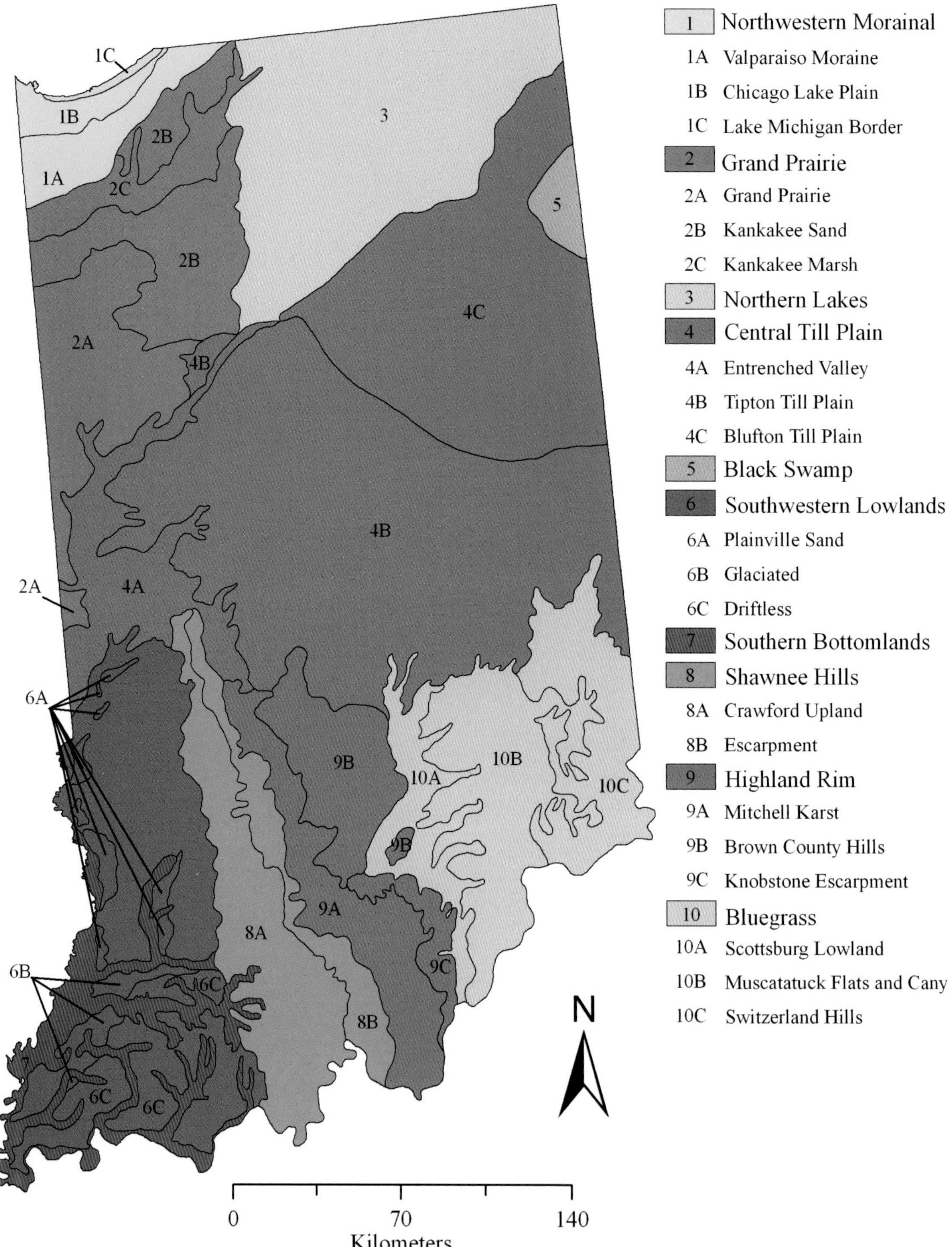

Map 1.7. Homoya's Natural Regions of Indiana.
Source: Map created by Christopher Gentry and James Speer, July 25, 2006. Data source: USDA/IDNR.

challenges, however, in summarizing data from multiple sources and understanding the inconsistencies between data sets. For example, different databases provide different acreages for the state and counties due to different methods of sampling.

The data for land use in 2000 presented above, and in subsequent chapters, come from several sources. First, we used the 1992 National Land Cover Data (NLCD), developed from thematic mapper™ data as part of a cooperative project between the U.S. Geological Survey and the U.S. Environmental Protection Agency (Map 1.6, Table G-1). The NLCD data were superimposed over the natural regions of Indiana (Homoya et al. 1985) to determine the area in different habitats by natural region (Maps 1.7, 1.8). Second, we used the U.S. Fish and Wildlife Service's National Wetlands Inventory (1995) to determine the area of various wetland types in each natural region.

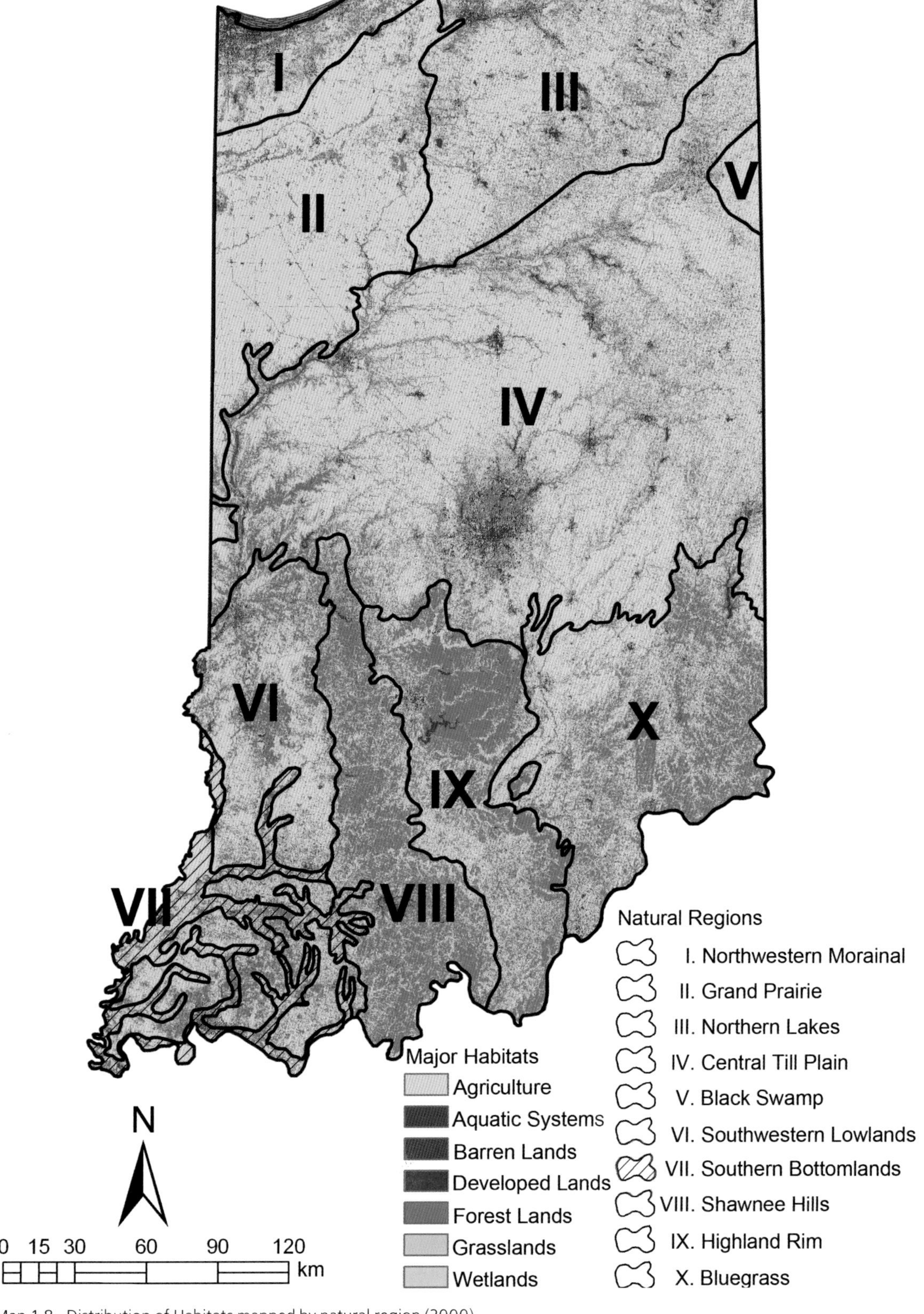

Map 1.8. Distribution of Habitats mapped by natural region (2000).

Third, the data on forest types by size, class, and region were based on the U.S. Forest Service's 1998 and 2003 surveys of the state. Fourth, the farmland habitats inventory used data from 2002, the nearest 5-year reporting interval as of this writing, as published by the National Agricultural Statistics Service (http://www.nass.usda.gov) in 2003–2004. Other sources of information will be referenced in the individual habitat chapters.

2 Soils

Soils are integral to any functioning ecosystem, providing the nutrients for plants and habitat for many vertebrate animals and insects, and multitudes of microorganisms. They require hundreds of years to develop and are good indicators of the climate, vegetation, and organisms involved in their formation. Therefore, knowledge of them provides suggestions for how best to use landscapes for productive agriculture or for the preservation and/or restoration of more natural conditions. Current soil characteristics indicate that most of Indiana was covered (in "presettlement" times, shortly before 1800) by beech/maple and oak/hickory forests, with smaller areas of dry prairie, savanna, and wetlands in the northwestern portion of the state.

Almost all of this book's information on soils is presented in this chapter, rather than being distributed among the 8 habitat chapters, as is the case for wildlife. We will first discuss how soils are identified and classified, and describe the national and state-level databases on soil distribution. We will then survey the soils of Indiana geographically from north to south, using the state's 10 natural regions, which were defined with some consideration of soil types (Homoya et al. 1985).

Soil identification and classification are conducted through the observation of soil horizons and distinctive soil layers in a pedon (the minimum sampling unit of soils, which is generally a 1 m^2 soil pit). Soil horizons include the O horizon, or organic layer at the surface; the A horizon, a mixture of organic and mineral matter; the E (eluviation) horizon, a leaching zone; the B horizon, where elements accumulate and clays develop; and the C horizon, the deepest part where the parent rock is being broken down and incorporated into the soil.

Characteristic soil layers are also used to identify soil types and are called epipedons if they are at the surface or diagnostic horizons if they are deeper underground. Soil types vary across the landscape with changes in slope, aspect, and moisture retention creating soil catenas. A catena is a change in soil type across a local area where the climate is constant, but changes in topography force changes in drainage and soil aeration. These in turn control the vegetation that will survive, producing distinctive changes across fine spatial scales, such as the transition from a cypress swamp to an oak/hickory stand with just a few feet of elevation change.

The U.S. Department of Agriculture (USDA), Natural Resources Conservation Service (NRCS), and National Cooperative Soil Survey (NCSS) have compiled soil information for all of the United States. The state soil geographic database (STATSGO) was designed for state- and regional-level analysis and management. It is compiled from soil survey data, and land remote-sensing satellite (LANDSAT) images are used to extrapolate this information to the landscape scale (National Cartography and Geospatial Center 1995). The coverage of this database for Indiana is complete, but multiple soil series are aggregated into unique map units. The resultant maps cover the whole state but do not have the finest resolution in soil characteristics, although distinct soil regions are maintained. The mapping scale of STATSGO is 1:250,000 and the minimum mapping unit area is 6.25 km^2. Guo et al. (2003) found that the STATSGO database had good spatial coverage across the United States and adequately represented the soil series present throughout, although it excluded rare soil series covering an area smaller than the minimum mapping unit. STATSGO reports all soil units on the map unit level, which aggregates similar soil series into soil associations that describe the general soil characteristics for each region (Map 2.1). Resource descriptions and management uses can be based on these map units.

The U.S. Soil Taxonomy (Soil Survey Staff 1999) classification system divides all soils into a nested hierarchy, allowing aggregation at varying spatial scales (Table S-1). Similar soil characteristics are used to aggregate the soil types so that higher-order classes represent similar characteristics of all of the subsequent categories. This is similar to the Linnaean classification system for all living organisms. The soil order is the broadest layer of this classification, with 12 orders representing all of the soils in the world. These are broken down into sub-orders, great soil groups, subgroups, associations, series, and families. Most management and field classification is based on the soil series level, which is analogous to the genus in organism classification. The soil series name, coupled with the textural class, is the soil type, which is analogous to the scientific name of an organism, e.g., Miami silt loam. This is the main identifiable unit of soils. There are some 19,000 soil series in the U.S. Soil Taxonomy system. These series are clustered together in common associations, making the system more manageable and demonstrating common co-occurrences of soil types.

Five main soil orders are found in Indiana. The state is dominated by Alfisols with the second most

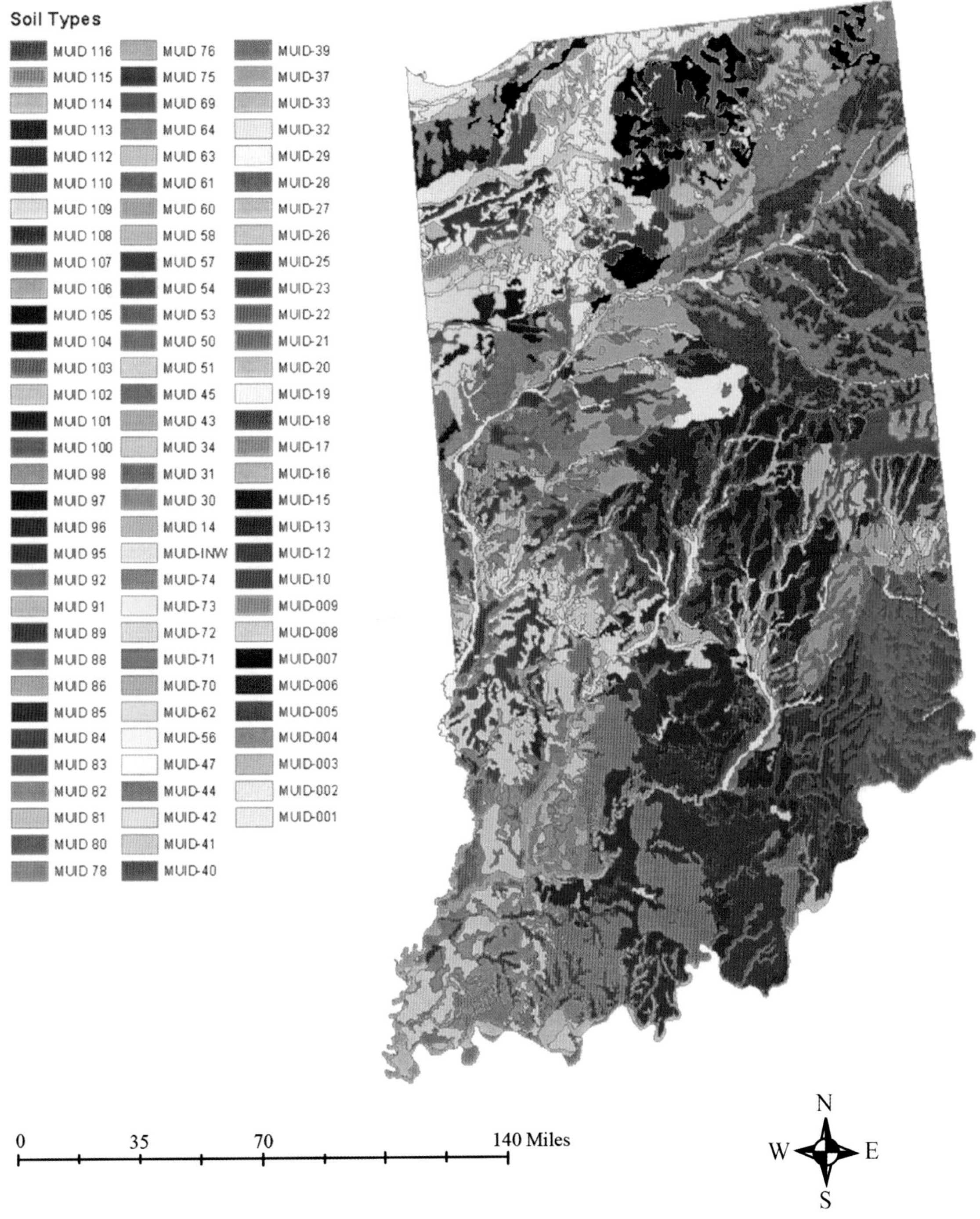

Map 2.1. Soil types of Indiana. For soil type names, see Maps 2.5–2.14.
Source: Created by Bruce T. Harper and James Speer; software: ArcGIS; data: IN, NRCS Dept.

common soil order being Mollisols, followed by Ultisols, Entisols, and Histosols (Map 2.2). Fifty-three soil series represent the majority of soil types found throughout Indiana (Table S-1). These are grouped into associations of 3 soil series that commonly occur together, and the map units from the STATSGO database are based on these soil associations. They developed in warm and humid climates and often supported hardwood forests prior to European settlement. Alfisols develop under dry deciduous forests and are characterized by some moisture retention and a high availability of base cations, such as calcium and magnesium. Mollisols develop under tall grass prairie and have a thick A horizon with much organic matter deep in the soil from root penetration. They have good nutrient retention and are excellent for modern agricultural uses. Ultisols are characterized by a well-developed clay layer in the B horizon and a low availability of base cations. Entisols are newly formed soils that lack distinctive soil horizons. Histosols develop

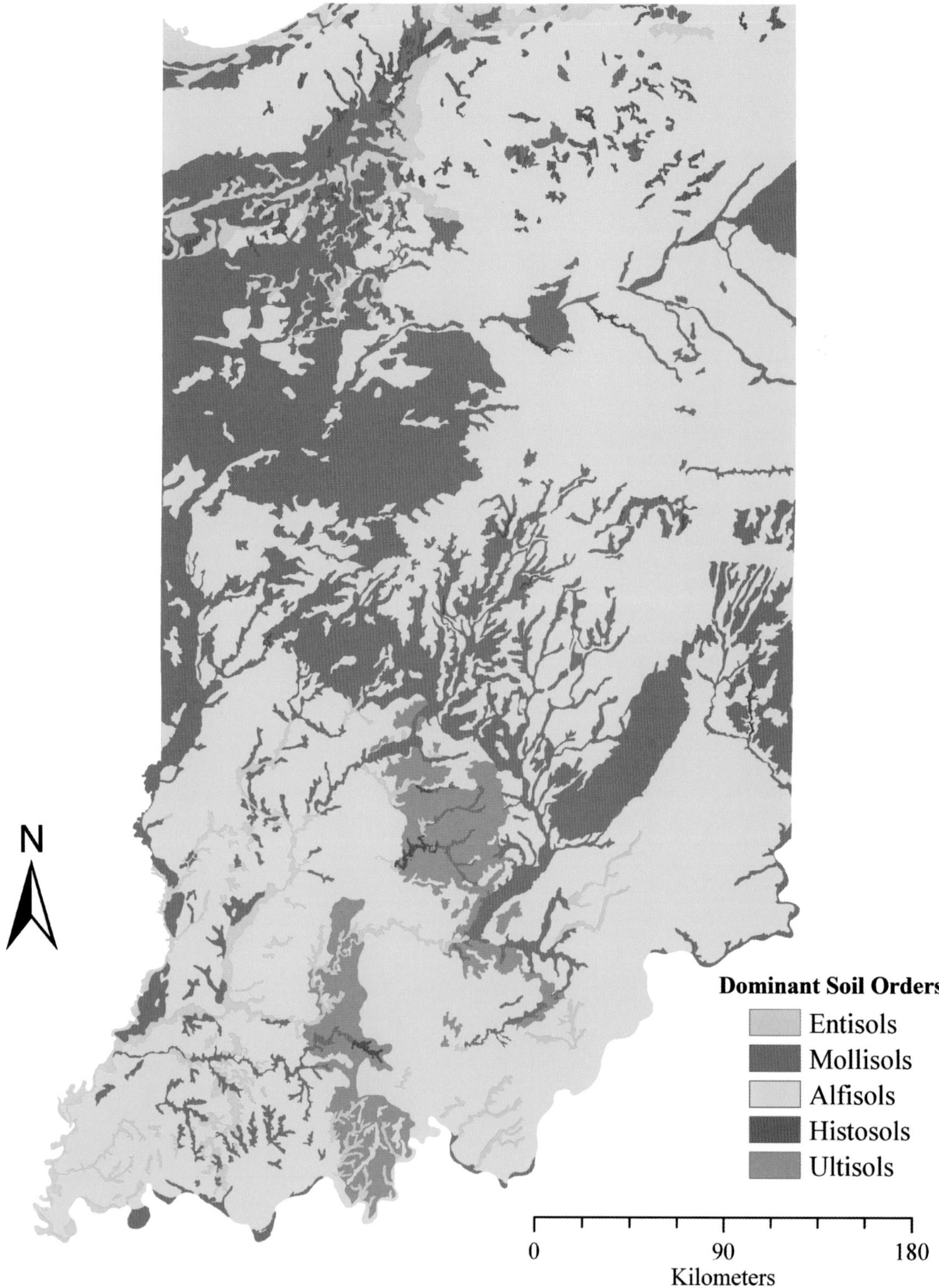

Map 2.2. Five soil orders represented in Indiana.
Source: Map created by Christopher Gentry and James Speer, November 10, 2005. Data source: USDA/IDNR.

under wet bog conditions with a thick O horizon of decomposing organic matter on top of the mineral-rich soil horizons.

In the next section, general soil conditions, land use, and original vegetation will be described for each of the 10 terrestrial natural regions of Indiana (Map 1.7; Homoya et al. 1985). The soils present were cataloged in each area by joining the STATSGO database with the natural regions using a geographic information system (GIS). A digital elevation model (Map 2.3) was used to examine the elevation and relief of each natural region, and a mosaic of satellite images (Map 2.4) was examined to understand current vegetation cover. The natural regions were then described

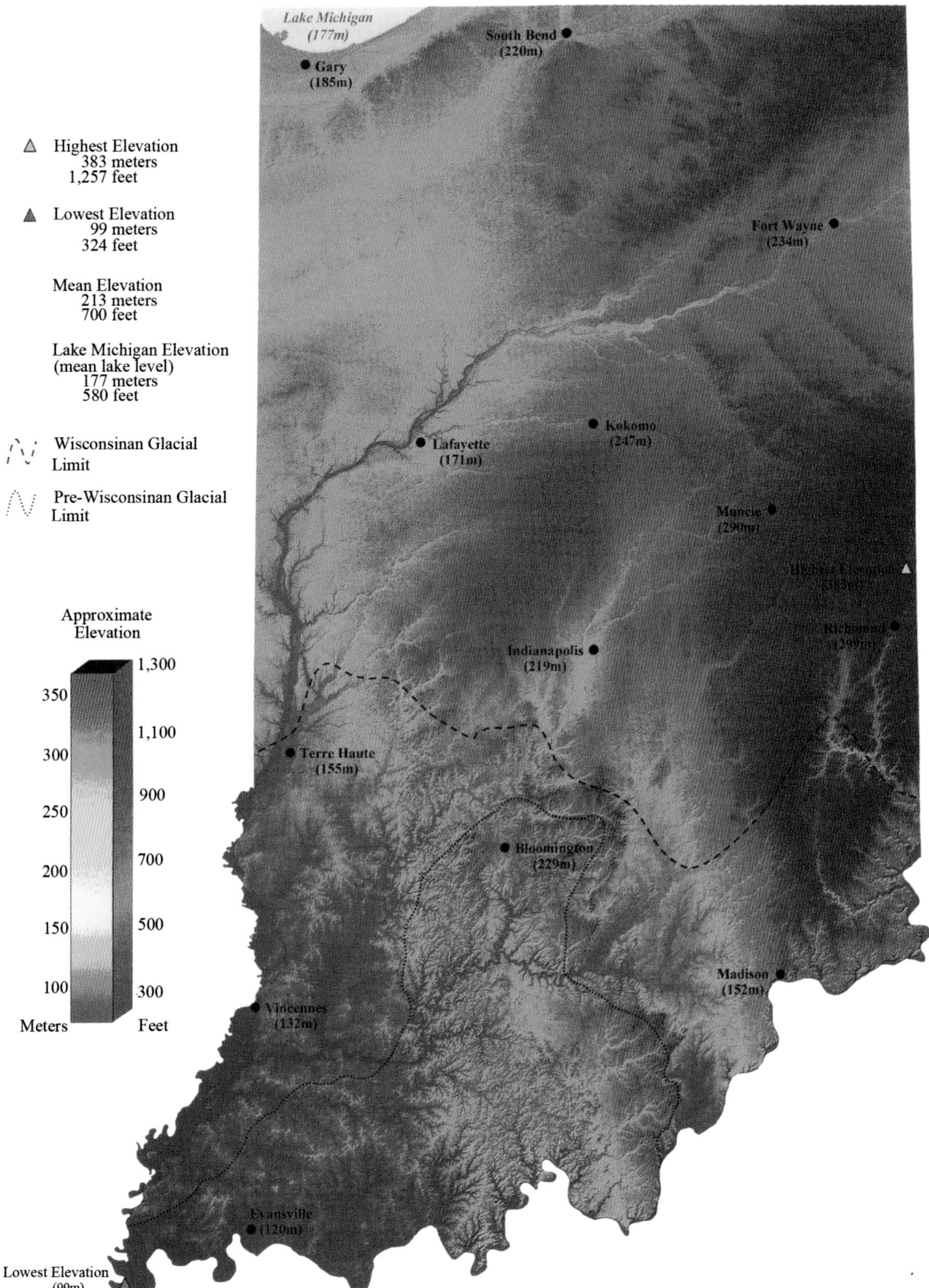

Map 2.3. Digital elevation map of Indiana showing changes in topography across the state. (From Wilson 2003).

This satellite image mosaic was created from nine images collected by the LANDSAT7 (EMT+) remote sensing system. The images were acquired in June 2000 and September and April 2001.

Dark green tones indicate forested areas, such as Hoosier National Forest in the south-central portion of the state and Jefferson Proving Grounds, the rectangular feature in the southeast.

Urbanized areas appear in light purple and blue tones, which are most noticeable around Indianapolis (center of the state) and the urbanized area around the Lake Michigan rim in the northwest.

Water appears in dark blue and black. The color of water features is a function of depth and the amount of suspended sediment, with shallower and more turbid water appearing in lighter tones.

Most of the agricultural areas were not covered in crops at the time the satellite images were acquired. The appearance of farm fields in this image is largely a function of soil moisture and vegetation cover, with more moisture and more plant cover contributing to darker tones.

The mosaic extends 5km over the Indiana border so that adjacent features are visible. County boundaries are overlaid for spatial reference.

Map 2.4. A composite image of Indiana from space, showing urban areas, agricultural land, and natural forest (from Wilson 2003).

based on the dominant soil associations and the characteristics of the soil series in those associations. Past vegetation conditions were also reconstructed using the distributions of modern soil orders and comparing them to maps generated from the General Land Office surveys (see Lindsey 1966; Map 1.2).

Soils of the Natural Regions

Northwestern Morainal Natural Region

The Northwestern Morainal Natural Region of Indiana is located around the southern margin of Lake Michigan (see Map 1.7). The three main soil associations, which cover 61.5% of the land area, are Blount-Glynwood-Morley; Morley-Markham-Ashkum; and Coloma-Spinks-Oshtemo (Figure 2.1; Map 2.5). The

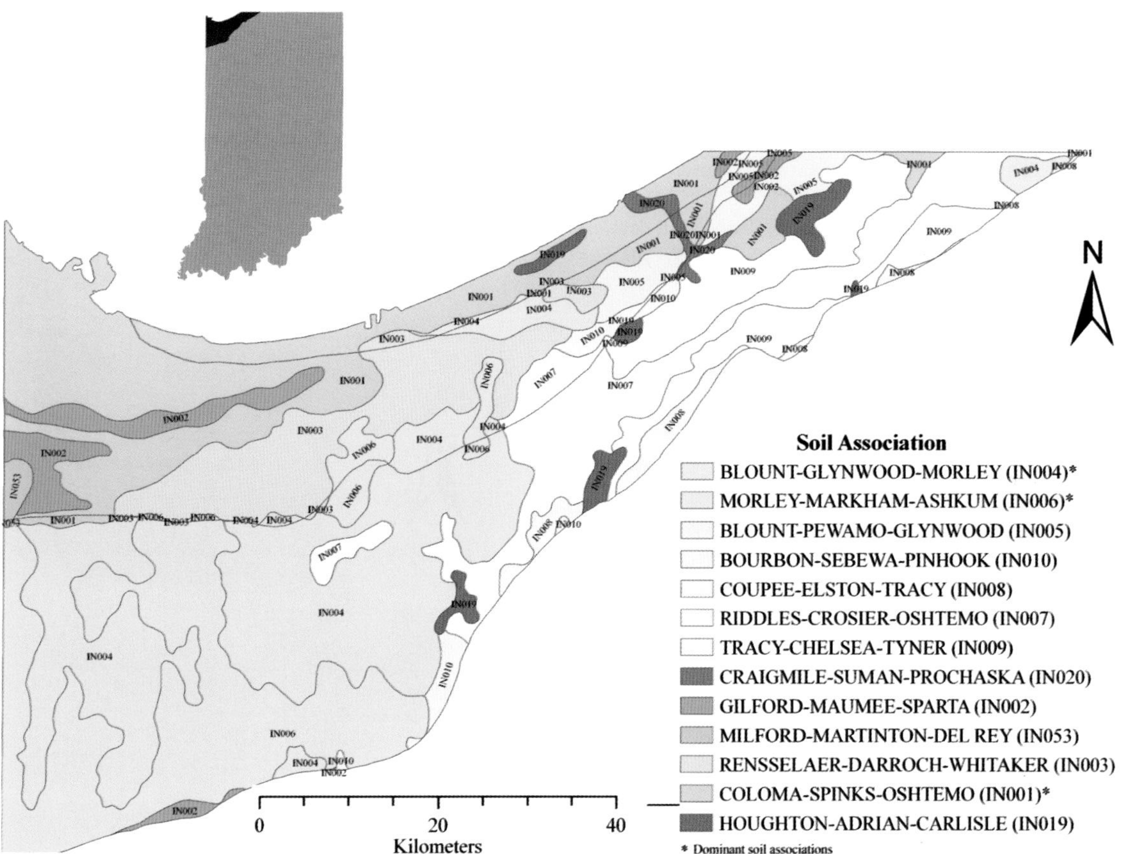

Map 2.5. Soils in Northwestern Morainal Natural Region.
Source: Map created by Christopher Gentry, Yiran Huang, and James Speer, November 10, 2005. Data source: USDA/IDNR.

Indiana Dunes National Lakeshore is dominated by the Coloma soil series, a Lamellic Udipsamment (layered because of sand dune formation) and a relatively young soil that has not had time for diagnostic soil horizons to form. Ecological succession acts to stabilize the dunes as the vegetation progresses from hydrophytic plants, to coniferous trees, then finally to oak/hickory forest (Cowles 1899). The region can be poor for crops because of the excessive drainage of some areas, but corn, soybeans, oats, and pasture can be supported on the Alfisols. Some Mollisols with their thicker A horizon and higher organic content provide excellent agricultural land. The native vegetation was oak/hickory forest with some areas of dry prairie interspersed with wetlands (Lindsey 1966). The area was probably dominated by northern red oak, white oak, green ash, bur oak, pin oak, eastern white pine, wild black cherry, red maple, slippery elm, shagbark hickory, tulip poplar, and black walnut (Neely 1987; Natural Resources Conservation Service 2002; Deniger 2003b; Calsyn 2004). See Qadir (1964) for stand tables for these soil series.

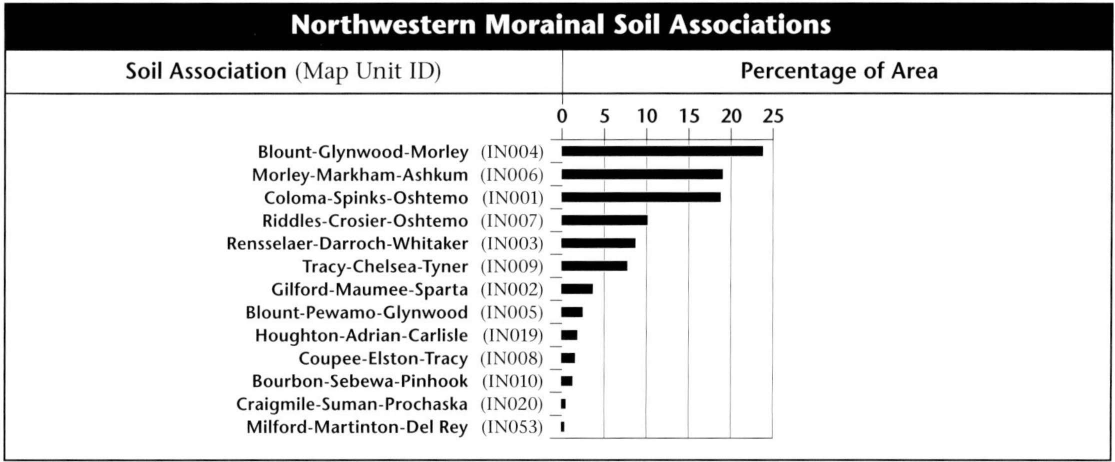

Figure 2.1.

Grand Prairie Natural Region

The Grand Prairie Natural Region, also located in northwestern Indiana, is bounded on the south by the Wabash River (see Map 1.7). It is primarily a flat plain at about 200 m elevation and is covered by glacial till. Three main soil associations occur in this region. The Gilford-Maumee-Sparta; Coloma-Spinks-Oshtemo; and Saybrook-Drummer-Parr associations cover 39.2% of the area (Figure 2.2; Map 2.6). This region is broken into very fine soil series distinctions based on microtopography. Much of it used to be in prairie grasses that produced Mollisols, a smaller area of Alfisols, and some Entisols. This area is productive for corn, soybeans, and occasional oat crops, with relatively little of the land in pasture. The Drummer soils series is so productive that it has been named the state soil of Illinois. The native vegetation used to be

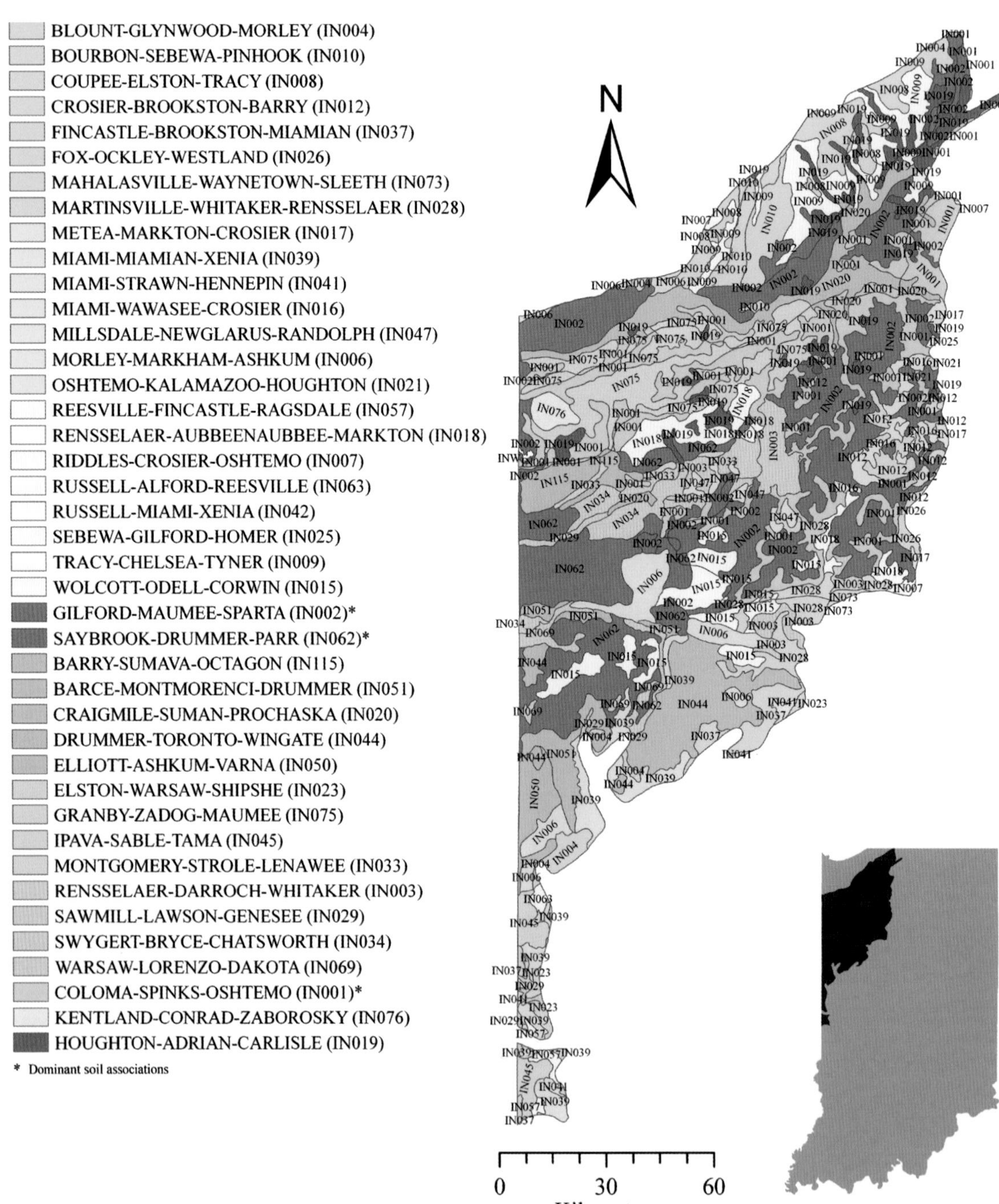

Map 2.6. Soils in Grand Prairie Natural Region.
Source: Map created by Christopher Gentry, Yiran Huang, and James Speer, November 10, 2005. Data source: USDA/IDNR.

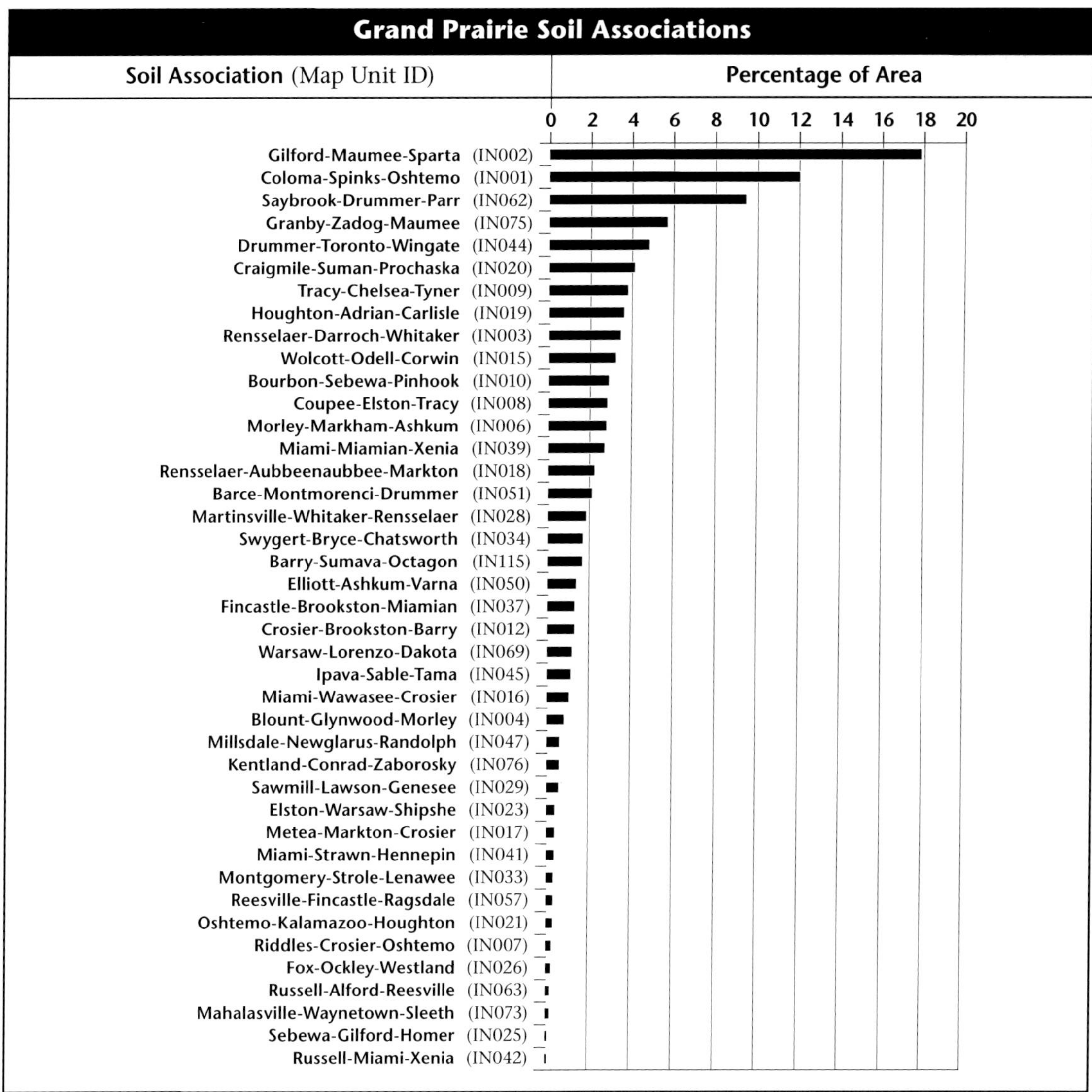

Figure 2.2.

extensive wetlands with patches of dry prairie but today this region supports white oak, northern red oak, pin oak, bigtooth aspen, red maple, silver maple, eastern white pine, black oak, and various hickories. The soils developed on glacial till, along with some eolian loess deposits. Many soils are sandy and deep with very good drainage (Treater and Walker 2001; Natural Resources Conservation Service 2002, 2003; Deniger 2003a; Wigginton and Clark 2003; Northwest Ohio Soil Survey 2005).

Northern Lakes Natural Region

The Northern Lakes Natural Region is located in the northeastern portion of Indiana (see Map 1.7). The topography is gently rolling at about 325 m elevation. Many or most of Indiana's natural lakes occur in this region. Most of the lakes are small and near the terminal moraines. The numerous outwash and lacustrine plains are often indicated by marshes (many now drained), which are broken up by low sand ridges or knolls. Large rugged moraines are numerous. Tamarack bogs, mostly small, occur across northern Indiana. The best-developed remaining bogs are Cowles Bog (Porter County) and Pinhook Bog (LaPorte County) in northwestern Indiana. The area was covered by Wisconsinan glacial advances and the Illinoian glaciation before that. The soils are a product of the deposition of glacial till interspersed with occasional moraines. The area's soils are highly variable, and 5 associations comprise 68.9% of the land area: Riddles-Crosier-Oshtemo; Blount-Glynwood-Morley; Miami-Wawasee-Crosier; Oshtemo-Kalamazoo-Houghton; and Crosier-Brookston-Barry (Figure 2.3; Map 2.7). The soils all have similar parent materials of glacial till except for the Houghton soil series, which is a Histosol located in depressions and developed from organic-rich deposits (i.e., a muck soil). The other soil orders are Alfisols with small areas occupied by Mollisols. These soils are deep and well-drained with varying available water capacity and permeability. Corn, soybeans, and pasture are primary in this region, while small grains (such as oats and winter wheat) are often grown. The native vegetation was primarily forest dominated by northern

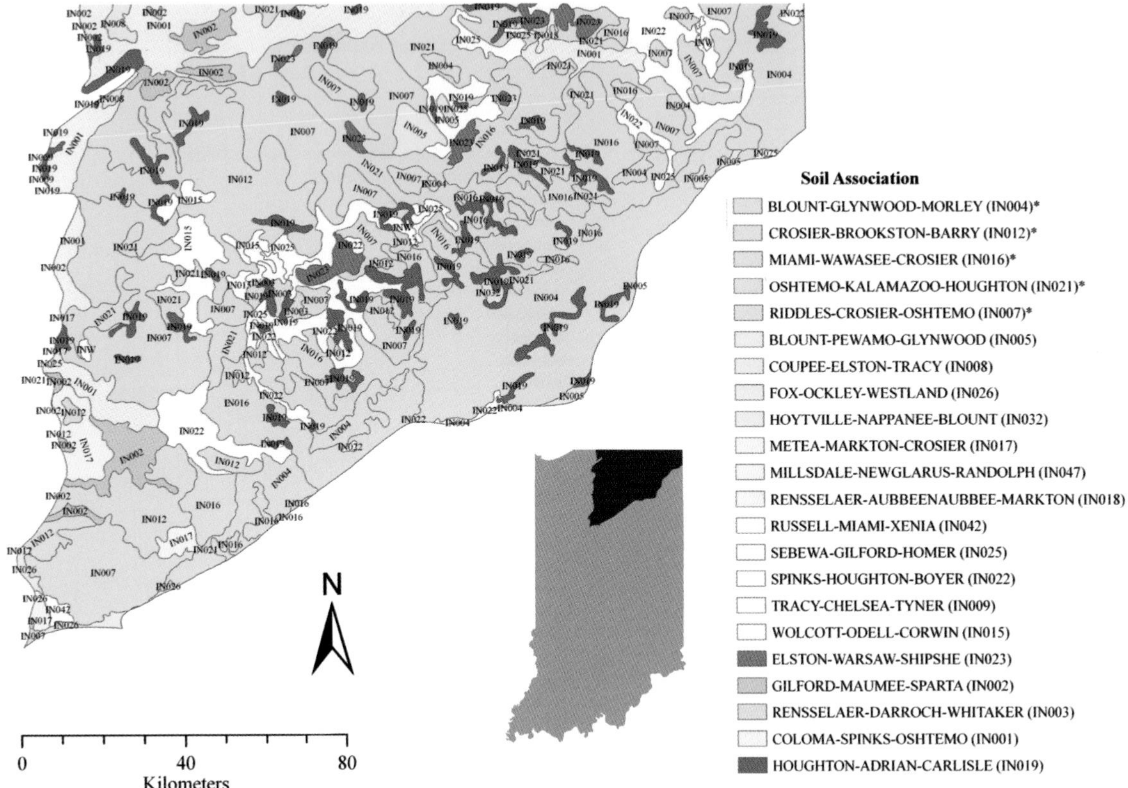

Map 2.7. Soils in Northern Lakes Natural Region.
Source: Map created by Christopher Gentry, Yiran Huang, and James Speer, November 10, 2005. Data source: USDA/IDNR.

red oak, white oak, tulip poplar, green ash, bur oak, pin oak, wild black cherry, slippery elm, black oak, eastern white pine, American beech, sugar maple, and hickory species (Neely 1987; Natural Resources Conservation Service 2002; Jackson 2004; National Cooperative Soil Survey 2005a, 2005b). Lindsey et al. (1965) reconstructed this region as being oak/hickory and beech/maple forest around 1816. These forest types are supported by the Alfisols that are common in this area.

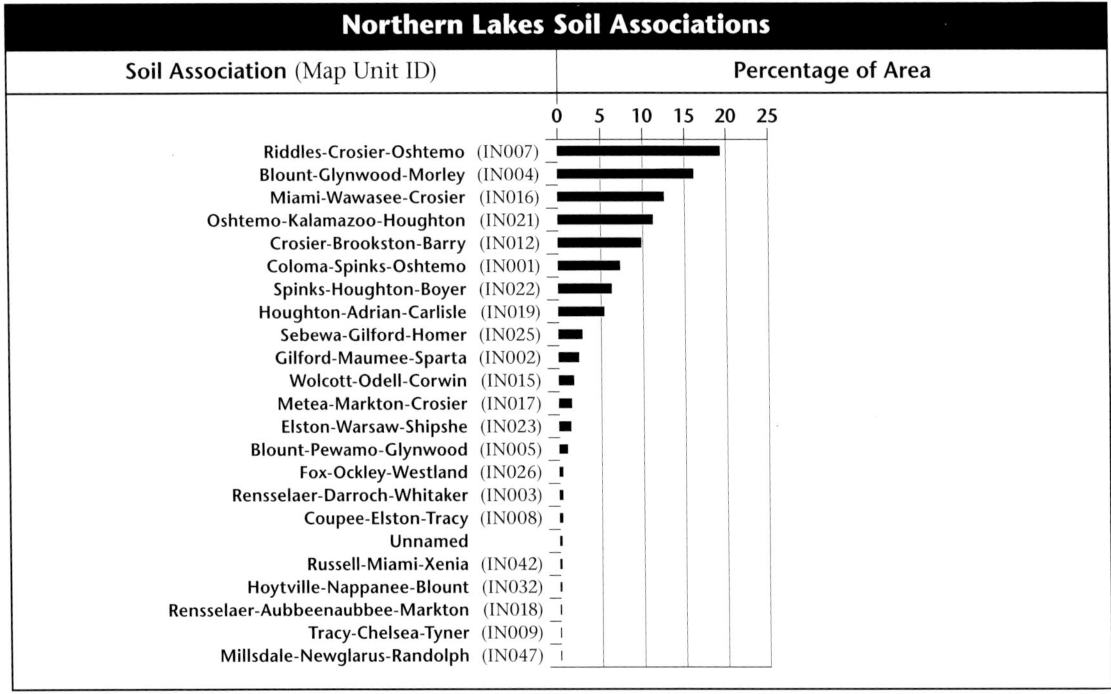

Figure 2.3.

Central Till Plain Natural Region

The Central Till Plain Natural Region covers almost half of Indiana (see Map 1.7). Although it is predominantly a flat to slightly undulating till plain, it also includes the state's highest point, located just north of Richmond at 383 m (1,257 ft). The till plain soils are derived from glacial till and some wind-blown loess that was deposited 12,000 years ago when the Laurentide ice sheet retreated, as the Wisconsinan glacial period ended and the Holocene interglacial began. The till plain is dissected by stream channels that separate individual flat upland areas. Five soil associations dominate the region, collectively comprising 61.3% of the area: Blount-Pewamo-Glynwood; Crosby-Treaty-Miami; Miami-Crosby-Treaty; Blount-Glynwood-Morley; and Fincastle-Brookston-Miami (Figure 2.4; Map 2.8). They are mostly Alfisols with some Mollisols. The widespread Miami soil series, prized for its ability to grow corn, is Indiana's state

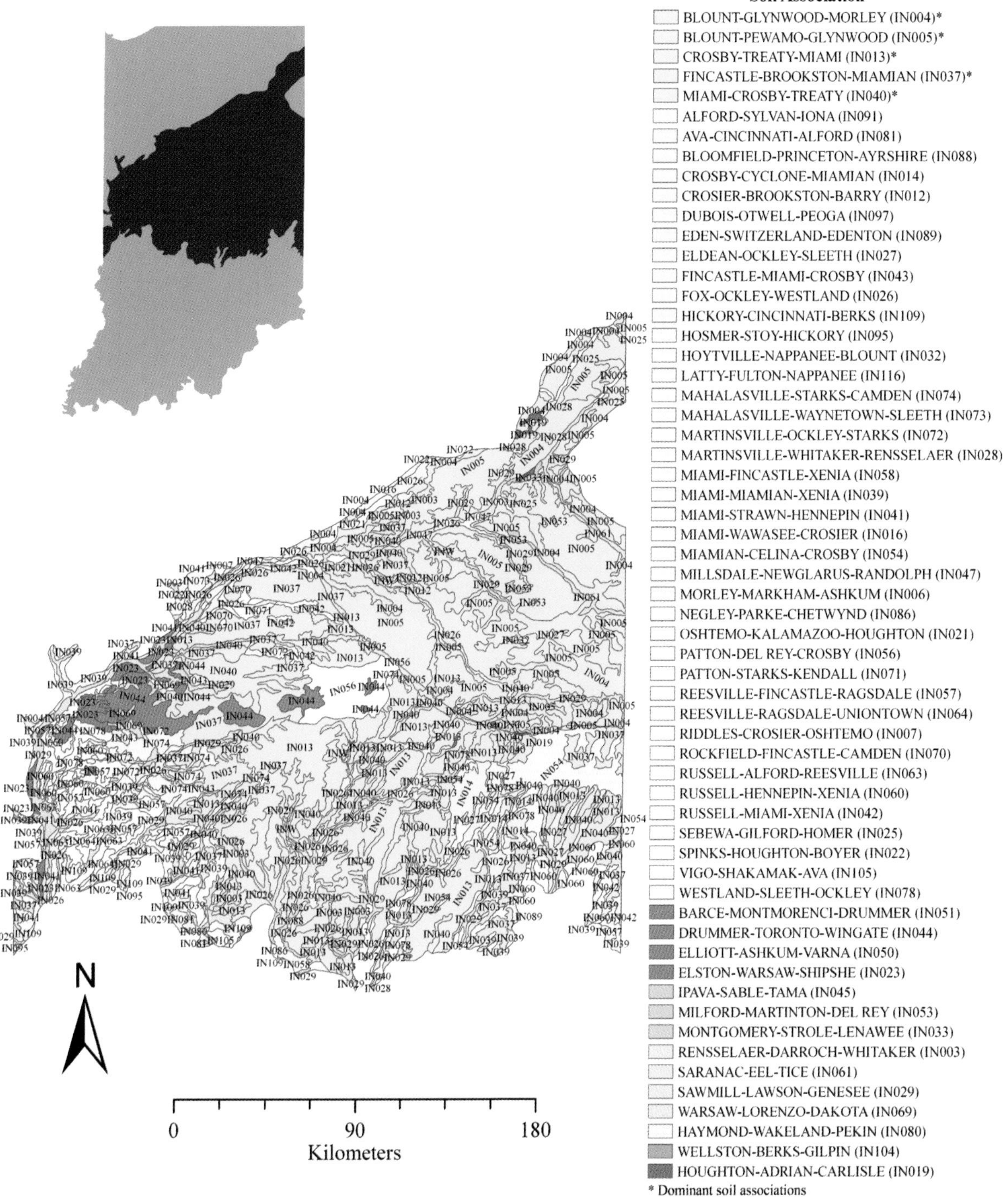

Map 2.8. Soils in Central Till Plains Natural Region.
Source: Map created by Christopher Gentry, Yiran Huang, and James Speer, November 10, 2005. Data source: USDA/IDNR.

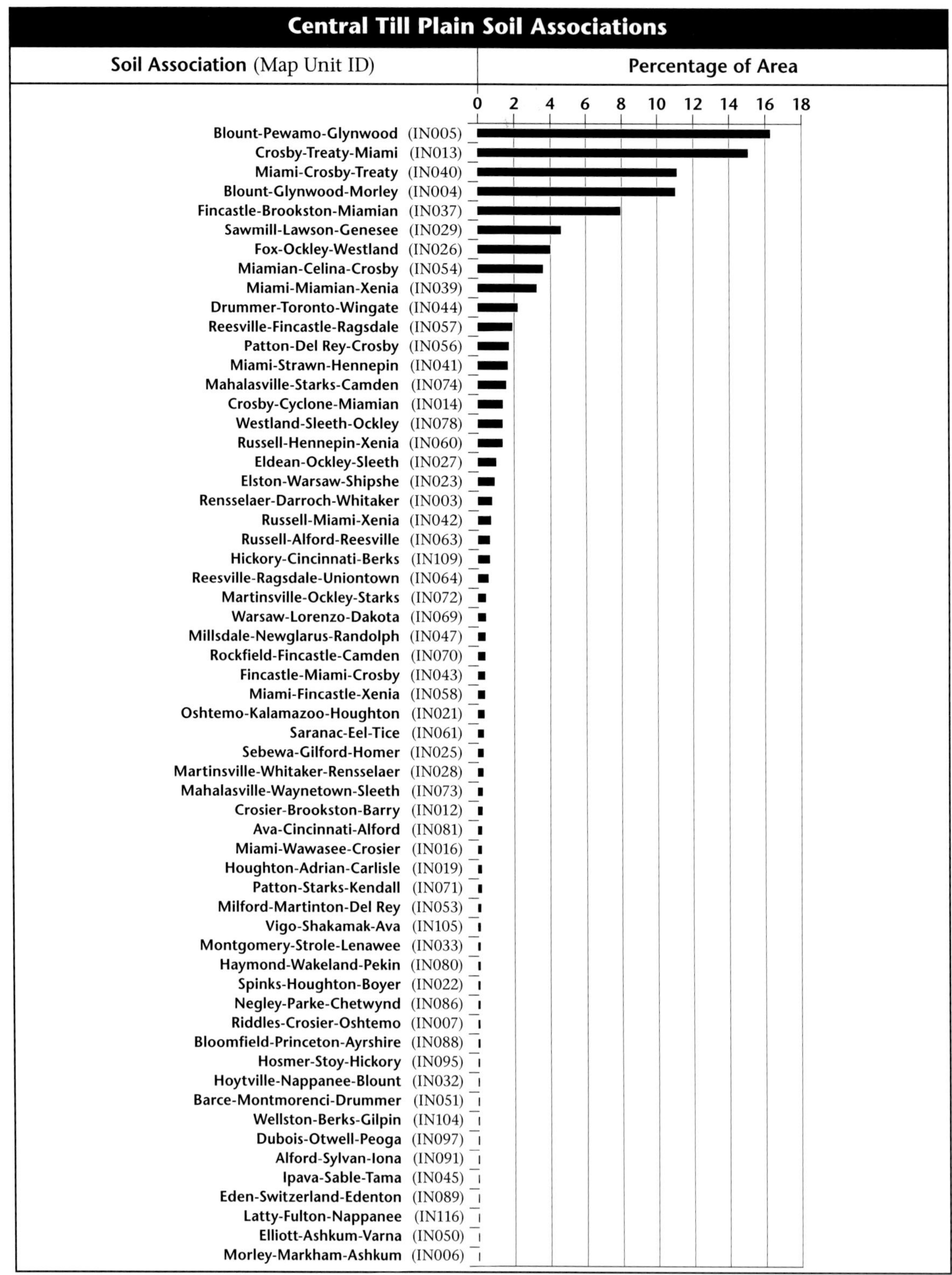

Figure 2.4.

soil. The original vegetation was mostly beech/maple forest. Today, the upland soils support white oak, sugar maple, tulip poplar, northern red oak, wild black cherry, black walnut, white ash, American basswood, and slippery elm, with the wetter soils supporting red maple, pin oak, American elm, bur oak, and swamp white oak. Most of this land is currently under agriculture with corn and soybeans being the main crops, plus wheat, oats, and other small grains. Lesser acreage is used for pasture and hay, or has been left in woodlands (Montgomery 1974; Neely 1987; Natural Resources Conservation Service 2002; Wigginton and Clark 2003).

Black Swamp Natural Region

The Black Swamp Natural Region is dominated (66.5% of the area) by the Hoytville-Nappanee-Blount and Blount-Pewamo-Glynwood soil associations (Figure 2.5; Map 2.9). These soils formed on Wisconsinan glacial till (deposited approximately 12,000 years ago) and lake sediments. They are very deep and poorly drained soils. Most are presently used for croplands growing corn, soybeans, hay, and some wheat. They range from Alfisols to Mollisols depending upon the presettlement vegetation cover. These soils were generally covered in hardwood forest that ranged from mesic sites with sugar maple, white oak, northern red oak, white ash, and American basswood to swamp forest with swamp white oak, bur oak, pin oak, American elm, black ash, cottonwood, red maple, and marsh grasses (http://soils.usda.gov).

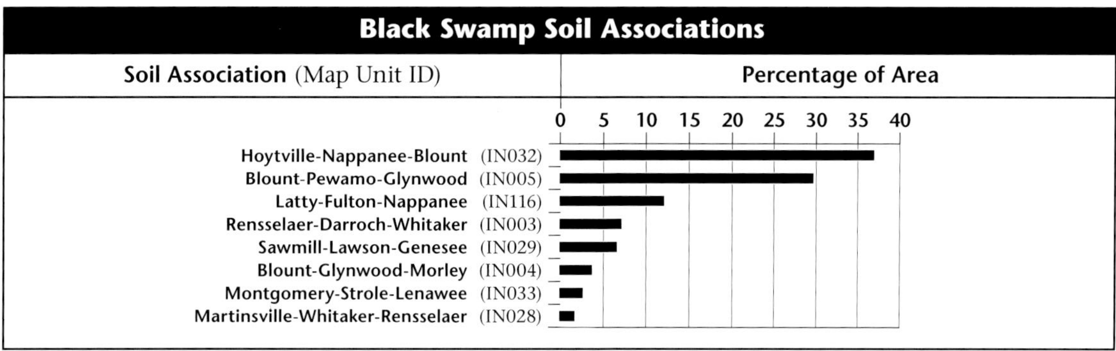

Figure 2.5.

Southwestern Lowlands Natural Region

The Southwestern Lowlands Natural Region is located in the southwestern portion of Indiana in the quadrant just north and east of the confluence of the Ohio and Wabash rivers. The soils are a complex mix with the 3 main soil associations—Hosmer-Zanesville-Stendal; Alford-Sylvan-Iona; and Ava-Cincinnati-Alford—accounting for only 35.8% of the soils (Figure 2.6; Map 2.10). The soils are predominant-

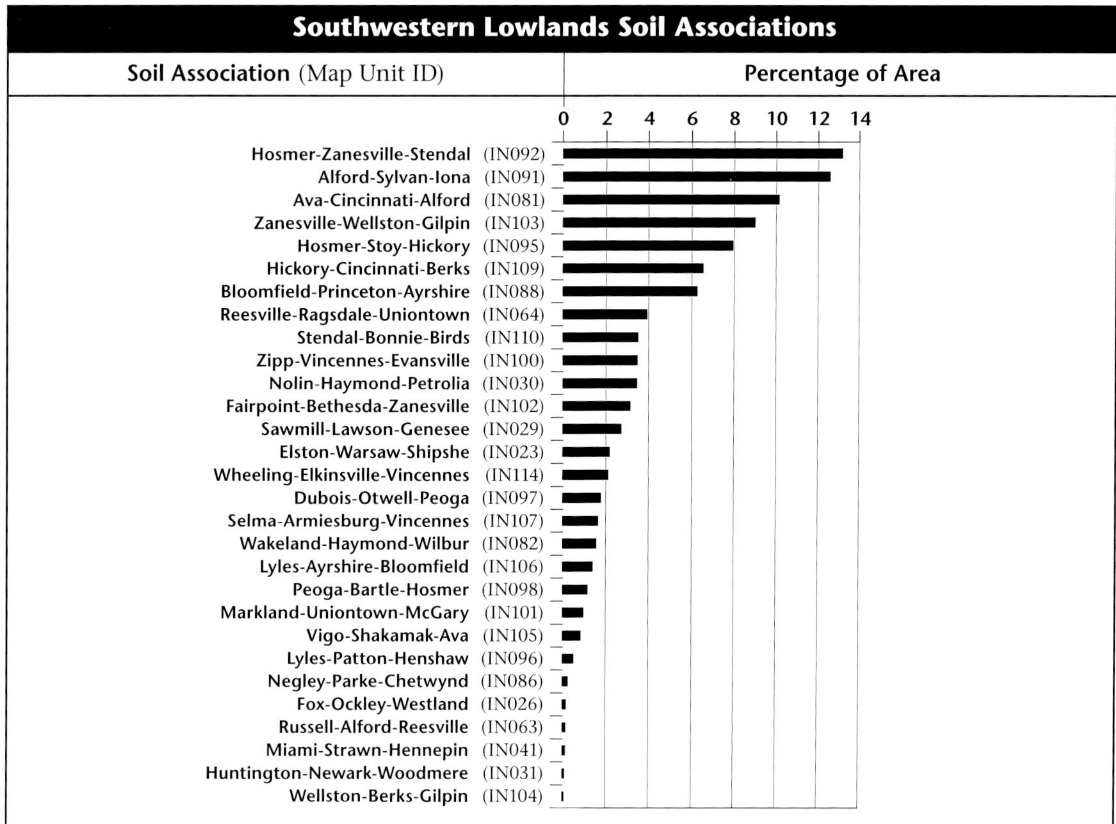

Figure 2.6.

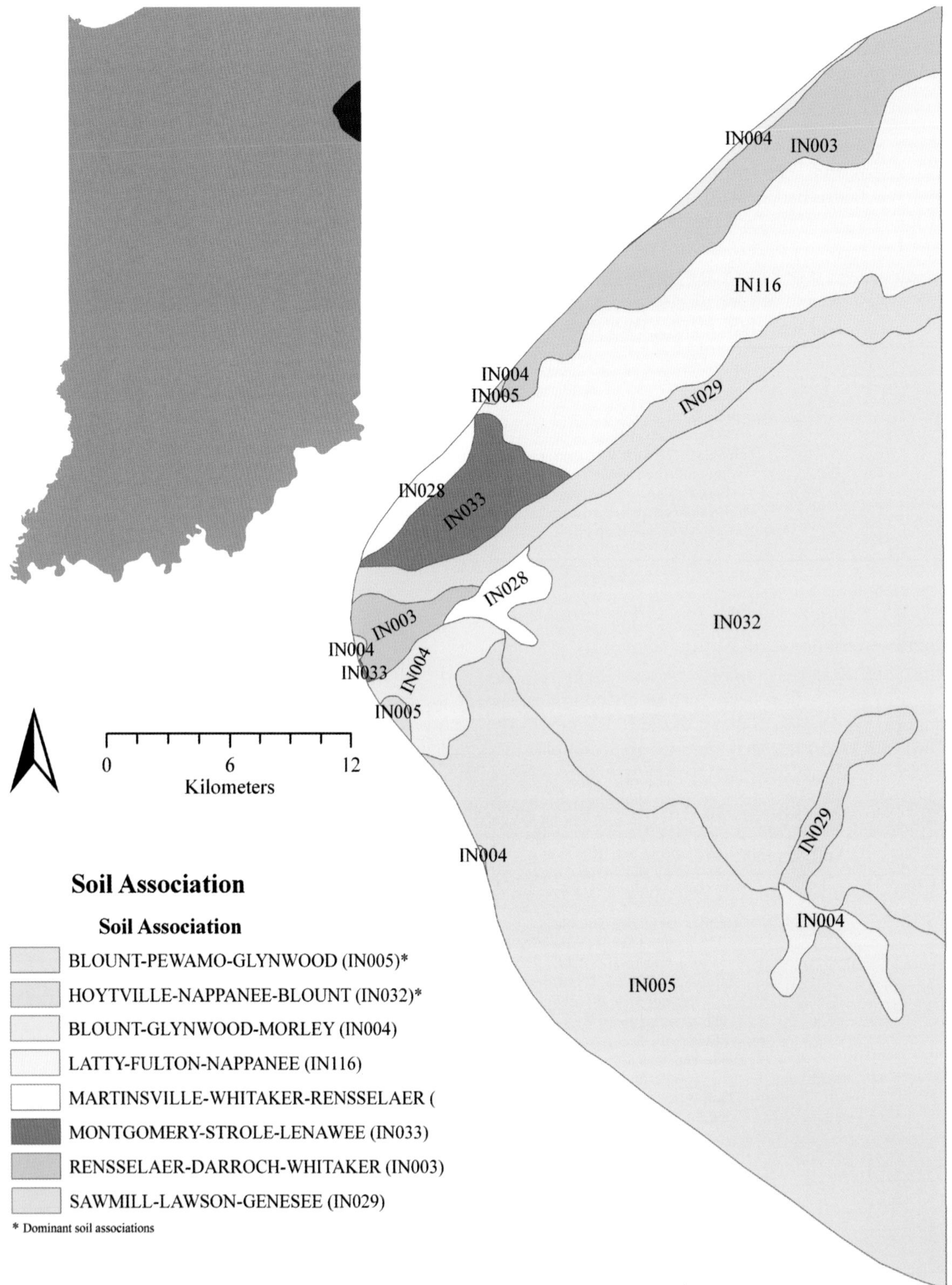

Map 2.9. Soils in Black Swamp Natural Region.
Source: Map created by Christopher Gentry, Yiran Huang, and James Speer, November 10, 2005. Data source: USDA/IDNR.

ly Alfisols and are on the mesic end of the moisture continuum. The parent material is alluvium and loess over sandstone, siltstone, and shale. Some zones have more than 1.5 m of loess accumulation.

Corn, soybeans, small grains, meadow, and pasture are all produced in this region. Soil erosion from surface runoff is a major hazard to agriculture in the area. Frost action destroys many deep-rooting plants, making the region uneconomical for alfalfa growth. The native vegetation was mixed hardwood forest composed of northern red oak, white oak, black walnut, wild black cherry, sugar maple, white ash, Virginia pine, eastern white pine, and tulip poplar (Kelly 1974; Wingard 1975; McCarter 1982).

Map 2.10. Soils in Southwestern Lowland Natural Region.
Source: Map created by Christopher Gentry, Yiran Huang, and James Speer, November 10, 2005. Data source: USDA/IDNR.

Southern Bottomlands Natural Region

The Southern Bottomlands Natural Region is a series of floodplains of the streams and rivers that course through the southwestern portion of Indiana. The lowest elevation in Indiana, 99 m (324 ft), occurs in this region at the confluence of the Wabash and Ohio rivers. These floodplains are dominated by Inceptisols that are poorly developed because of the frequent disturbance and deposition of alluvium from heavy floods. The Nolin-Haymond-Petrolia; Stendal-Bonnie-Birds; and Alford-Sylvan-Iona soil associations occupy 39.5% of the area (Figure 2.7; Map 2.11). All of the soil series have developed in the alluvium that covers the floodplains, where there is also some accumulation of loess. The organic matter and transported soils that accumulate on these floodplains have produced deep, well- to poorly drained soils

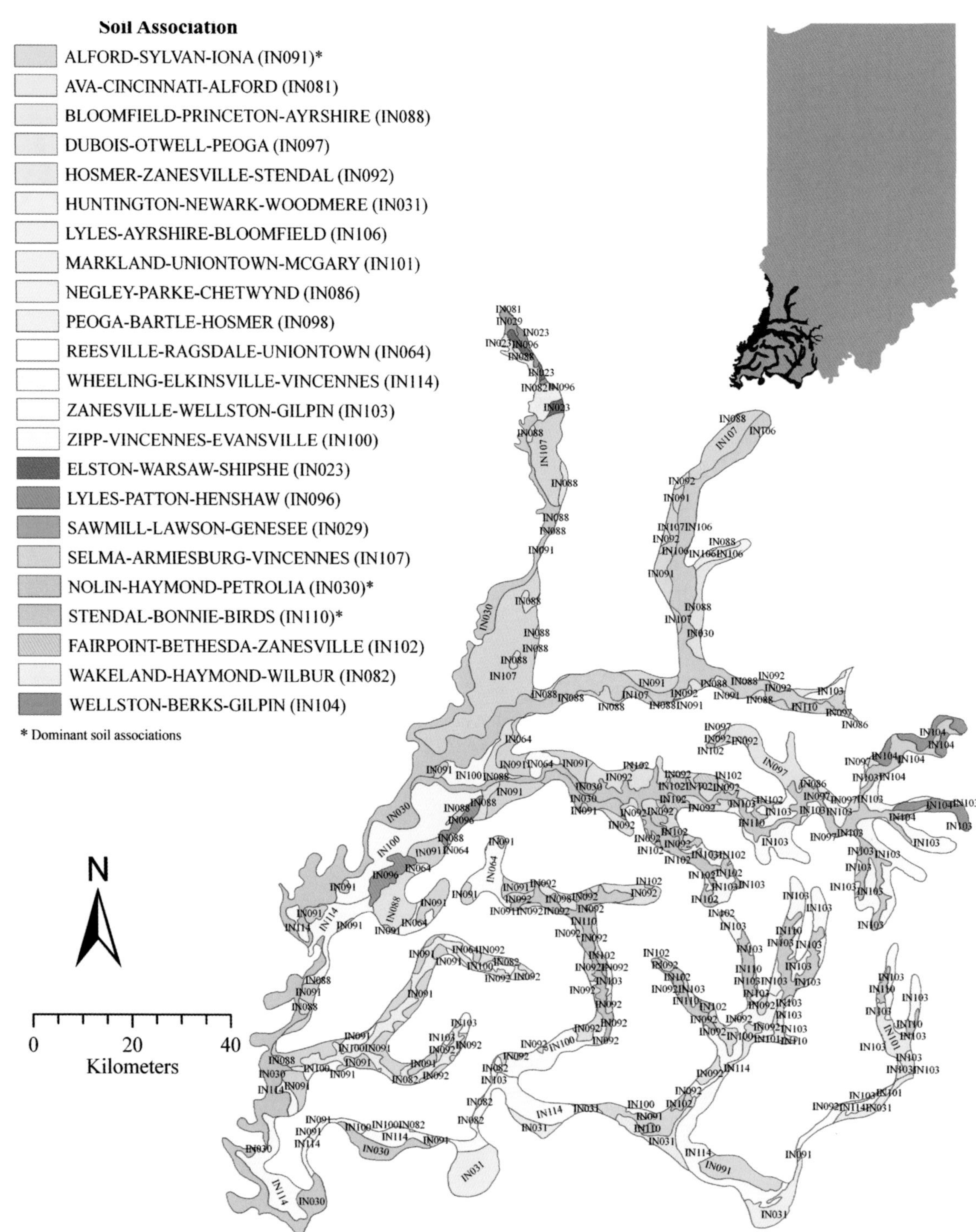

Map 2.11. Soils in Southern Bottomlands Natural Region.
Source: Map created by Christopher Gentry, Yiran Huang, and James Speer, November 10, 2005. Data source: USDA/IDNR.

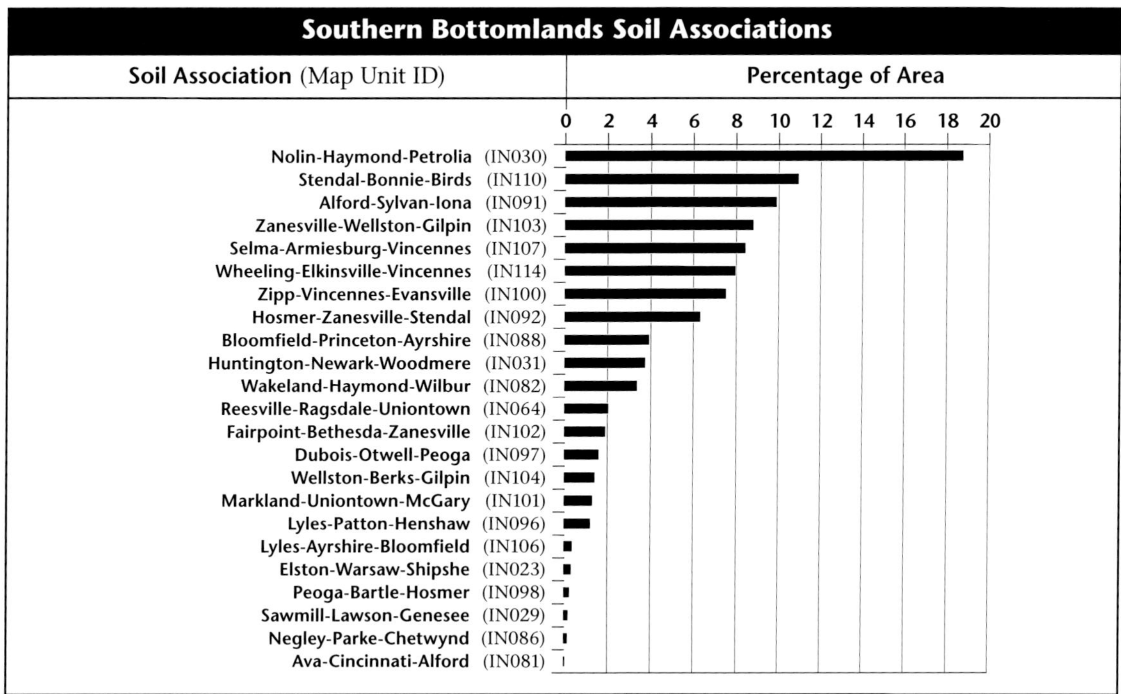

Figure 2.7.

that are excellent for agriculture. Frequent flooding, especially in winter and spring, reduces their potential as agricultural lands; however, with protection from flooding, these lands are good for corn, soybeans, small grains, and alfalfa. The native vegetation consisted of tree species that can withstand seasonal flooding, including bald cypress, black gum, bur oak, green ash, overcup oak, pin oak, red maple, shellbark hickory, silver maple, swamp white oak, and sweetgum (Kelly 1974; Wigginton and Marshall 2004).

Shawnee Hills Natural Region

The Shawnee Hills Natural Region is located in the highly dissected southern portion of Indiana between Greencastle on the north and the Ohio River between Tell City and Leavenworth on the south. It has a more

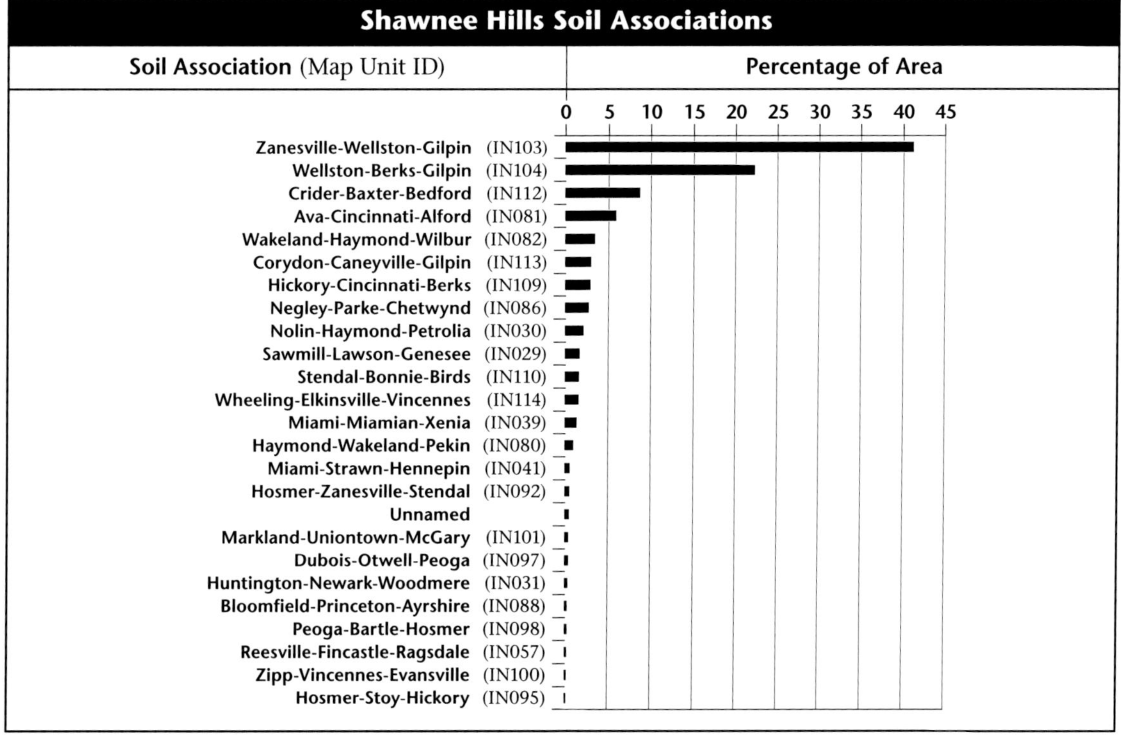

Figure 2.8.

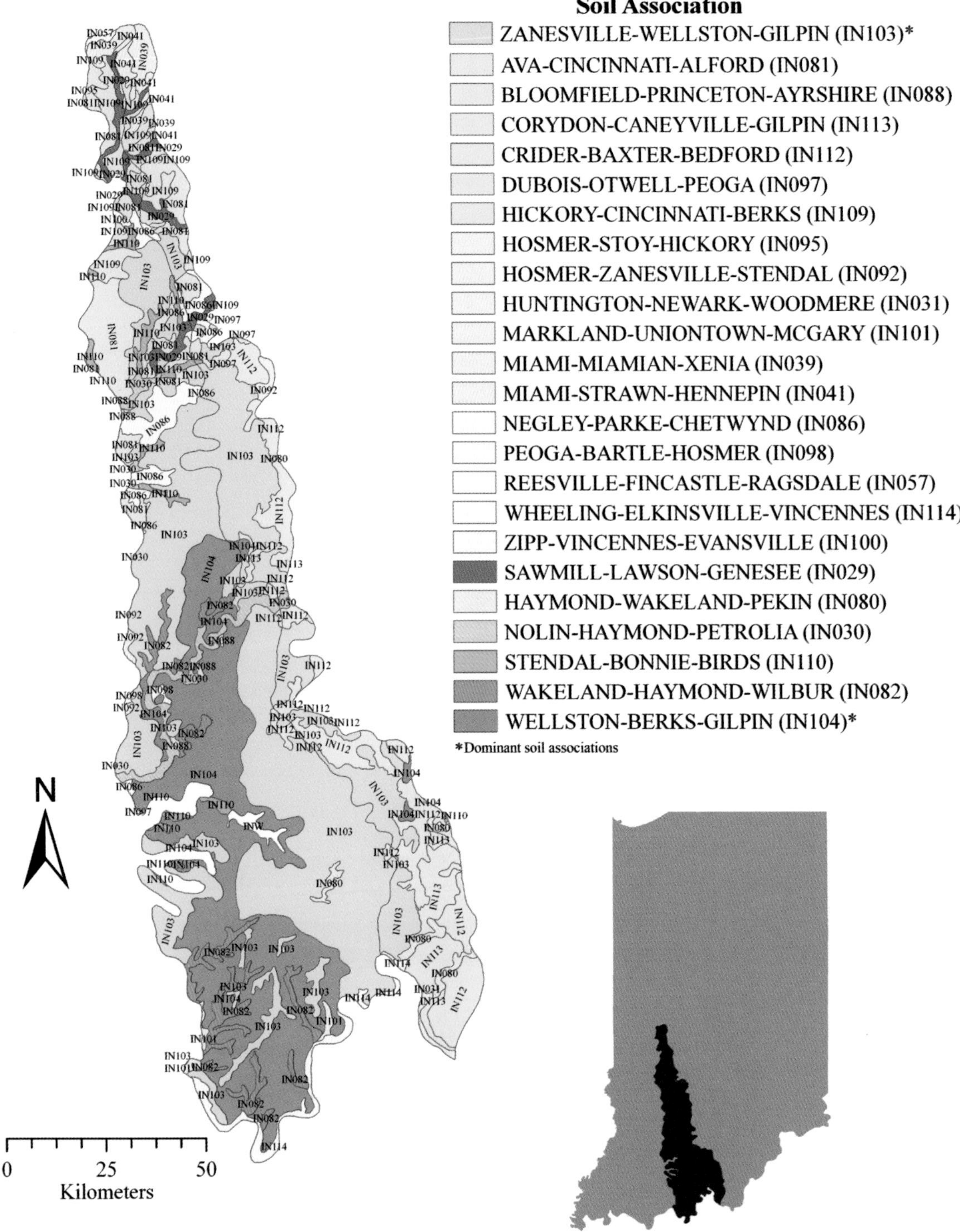

Map 2.12. Soils in Shawnee Hills Natural Region.
Source: Map created by Christopher Gentry, Yiran Huang, and James Speer, November 10, 2005. Data source: USDA/IDNR.

varied topography than most of the state due to many open ravines and sinkholes (see Map 2.3). This region retains extensive forest as a result of steep terrain that makes agriculture impractical in many areas. The original forest cover was oak/hickory interspersed with an important western mesophytic component, becoming beech/maple in the northern reaches of the area (see Map 1.2). Two soil associations (Zanesville-Wellston-Gilpin and Wellston-Berks-Gilpin) cover 63.3% of this region (Figure 2.8; Map 2.12). These soils are Ultisols and Alfisols, which formed under oak/hickory forests, and younger Inceptisols on steep and unstable slopes. The main trees supported in this region were white oak, a variety of hickories, and tulip poplar. The soils are moderately deep and well-drained, having formed on weathered sandstone, siltstone, and shale (Wingard 1975). The Shawnee Hills Natural Region is very rugged for Indiana and is not a good area for many crops.

Highland Rim Natural Region

The Highland Rim Natural Region is located along the relatively hilly terrain from the Bloomington-Nashville area south to the Kentucky border. This region is dissected into relatively steep valleys with prominent karst topography typified by many sinkholes, dissolution valleys, and a lack of surface water drainage. The bedrock is primarily limestone with some chert present. Weathered sandstone, siltstone, and shale are also parent materials for these soils, as is some wind-blown loess. The steep topography results in thin soils at many locations; often, there is exposed bedrock. The Crider-Baxter-Bedford and Wellston-Berks-Gilpin soil associations comprise 65% of this region (Figure 2.9; Map 2.13). Crider, the state soil of

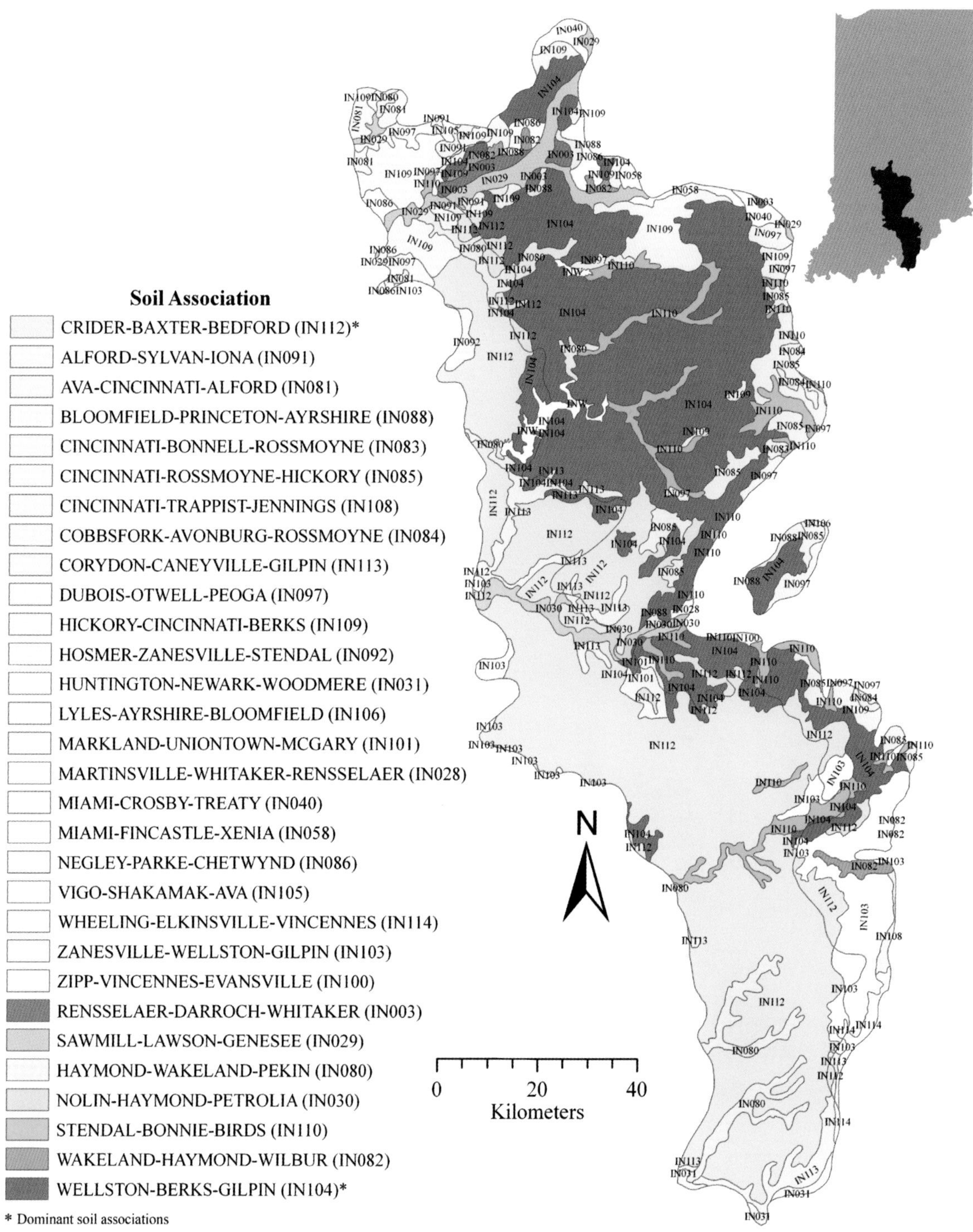

Map 2.13. Soils in HIghland Rim Natural Region.
Source: Map created by Christopher Gentry, Yiran Huang, and James Speer, November 10, 2005. Data source: USDA/IDNR.

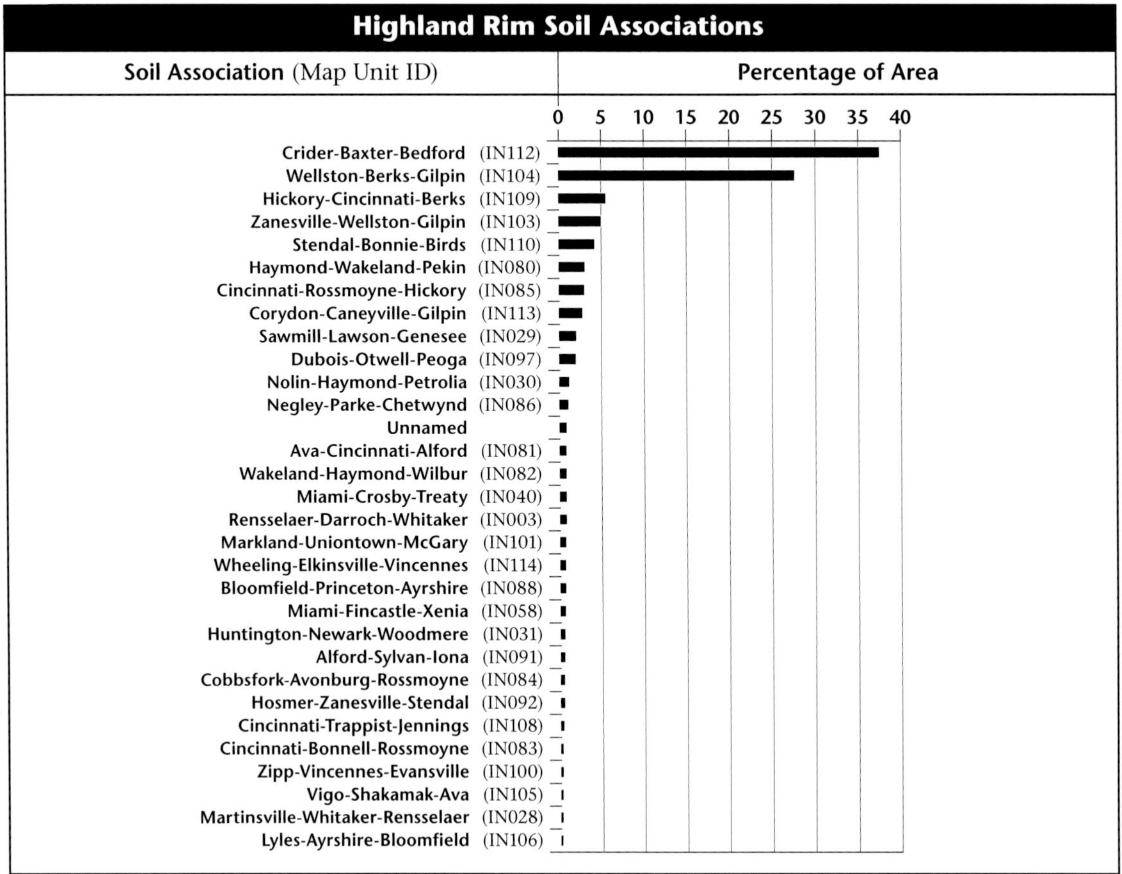

Figure 2.9.

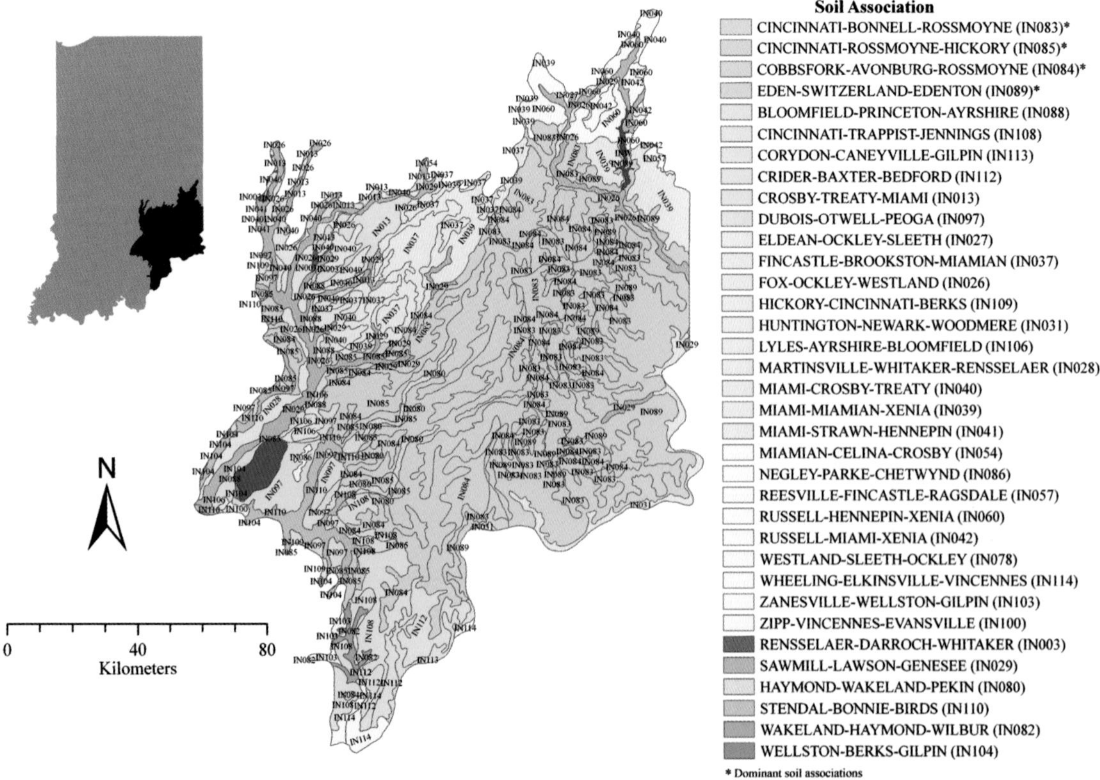

Map 2.14. Soils in Bluegrass Natural Region.
Source: Map created by Christopher Gentry, Yiran Huang, and James Speer, November 10, 2005. Data source: USDA/IDNR.

Kentucky, can support some row crops but predominantly supports pasture. Most of these soils are best suited for pasture or forest because of the steep slopes that lead to the quick runoff of surface water along with extensive erosion. The soils are moderately deep and internally well-drained in flat areas. The original forest in this region was mixed hardwoods dominated by northern red oak, Virginia pine, tulip poplar, white oak, and sugar maple. The soils are mainly Ultisols, which developed under deciduous forest, and Alfisols. Some Inceptisols are present on the steeper slopes (Gilbert 1971; Wingard 1975; Nagel 1998). Inceptisols are moderately developed soils, but they are largely without the well-developed diagnostic horizons that distinguish the other soil orders. They do characteristically provide moisture for vegetation growth for half the year, during the growing season. This soil order is fairly rare in Indiana.

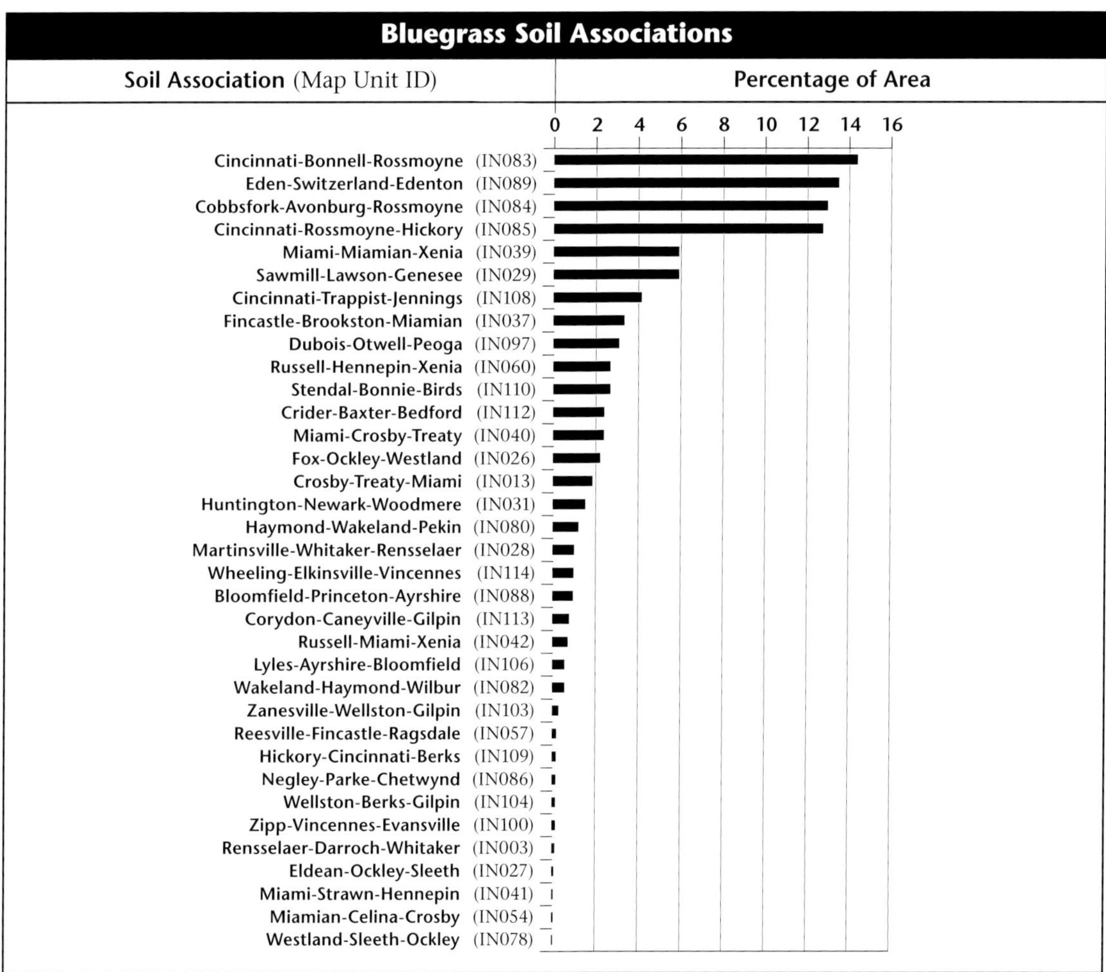

Figure 2.10.

Bluegrass Natural Region

The Bluegrass Natural Region, located in the southeastern corner of the state, has a complex soil distribution, including young soils presently developing in stream channels (Figure 2.10; Map 2.14). Its elevation range, from 100 to 300 m, includes some of the highest land area in Indiana (see Map 2.3). The region is dominated by a high elevation component to the east and a lower elevation component to the west. Alfisols predominate with 4 soil associations—Cincinnati-Bonnell-Rossmoyne; Eden-Switzerland-Edenton; Cobbsfork-Avonburg-Rossmoyne; and Cincinnati-Rossmoyne-Hickory—comprising 53.5% of the area. The soils are moderate to very deep and from poorly to well-drained. They developed mainly on Illinoian glacial till (deposited approximately 80,000 years ago) or wind-blown loess, with alluvium as a minor parent material. The Bluegrass Natural Region originally had beech/maple forest as the dominant vegetation type, with smaller areas of western mesophytic and oak/hickory forests. Upland sites are dominated by northern red oak, white oak, black walnut, wild black cherry, sugar maple, white ash, and tulip poplar. Moist bottomland sites have bald cypress, eastern cottonwood, hawthorn, and eastern red cedar. Corn, soybeans, small grains, hay, Christmas trees, and pasture are the major crops now grown, but much of the land is still in woods, since these soils are not prime farmland.

* * *

The parent material of Indiana soils is mostly limestone with some components of sandstone, siltstone, and shale. Three glacial advances largely leveled the state's northern portion, and deposited till and loess all the way to the southeast and southwest corners of the state. Especially in the north, the thick deposits and the microtopographic variations in slope and water retention strongly influence soil development. The glacial history means that soils are 12,000 years old or younger in the north, and no more than 80,000 years old in much of the south (except in the Shawnee Hills and Highland Rim regions).

Because of the generally deep, well-drained soils and relatively flat topography, agriculture is the main economic pursuit for Indiana with the majority of the crops being grown in the northern two-thirds of the state. These crops include corn, soybeans, winter wheat, oats, and alfalfa, while some land is in pasture. Indiana has a temperate climate, and its 35–45 inches of rainfall are rather evenly distributed throughout the year, resulting in well-developed soils and good growing conditions.

In 1816, the state was covered with eastern deciduous forests that were dominated by beech/maple or oak/hickory (Lindsey et al. 1965). Tall grass prairie and wetlands dominated the northwestern part of the state, which is reflected in the Mollisol and Histosol soils that are widespread in the Northwestern Morainal and Grand Prairie regions. The forests throughout Indiana were dominated by a combination of white oak, northern red oak, American beech, red maple, sugar maple, tulip poplar, ash, basswood, elm, and a variety of hickories. All of these species still exist in Indiana, although present-day trees rarely reach the great age and size that they did in the pre-European-settlement forests.

Vascular Plants and Vertebrate Wildlife

3

Vascular Plants

Because of the great diversity of natural communities and vegetation types found within the borders of Indiana, there is a corresponding diversity of vascular plant species. Floras published in 1881, 1900, and 1940 recorded native species in the state totaling 1,194, 1,400, and 1,838, respectively (Deam 1940). Charles C. Deam, Indiana's preeminent botanist of the twentieth century, was exceptionally thorough in his efforts to document the state's flora. He believed that the number of native species for Indiana would never surpass 1,900, yet the total now approaches 2,000 (K. Yatskievych, unpublished data). This has been the result of intensive and extensive fieldwork, so that the current list of all vascular plants in Indiana (Table P-1) now totals more than 2,900 species, subspecies, and varieties.

This total includes many introduced, alien, and adventive species that now reside in Indiana and are either reproducing or have sustaining populations in the state. Many, if not most, of these species introductions have occurred since Deam's exhaustive survey (Deam 1940). Perhaps another factor contributing to the increase in species number is the natural range expansions of certain species that entered the state in the late twentieth century, particularly those with wind-dispersed seeds. These additions, offset by the probable extirpations of species before they were documented, make it safe to say that the number of native vascular plant species known to occur in Indiana in the past two centuries has been approximated at 2,000. Of this number, 55 species are thought to be extirpated from Indiana (Indiana Natural Heritage Data Center 2005).

The number (and geographic area) of non-native plant species has clearly increased in the state since 1800, in terms of both species and individuals. The flora of 1881 included 140 non-native species; 177 were listed in 1900, and 302 in 1940. That figure jumped to nearly 800 in 2005. The latter is an indication of increasing globalization in trade and travel, which results in the purposeful as well as inadvertent introductions of species.

1800. With the vast numbers of natural communities and relative lack of invasive non-native species, the native flora of Indiana was at its most diverse and expansive at this time. The majority of the nearly 800 non-native species known in 2000 were not present, and the now-extirpated species would have occurred, some perhaps in large numbers, at least locally (e.g., western beard tongue and prairie white-fringed orchid). Species requiring high light intensities, such as those in prairies, barrens, fens, marshes, and open woodland, would have existed in great numbers due to the high frequency of fire on the landscape. Fire would have suppressed woody vegetation, thus reducing shade. In the graminoid communities, a myriad of grasses, sedges, and forbs would have dominated, including big bluestem, little bluestem, Indian grass, switchgrass, prairie cordgrass, northern dropseed, river bulrush, great bulrush, common tussock sedge, marsh blazing-star, downy sunflower, prairie dock, black-eyed Susan, and rattlesnake master.

In the woodland communities, some of the species most likely benefiting from canopy thinning and litter consumption by fire would have been woodland sunflower, forked panic grass, violet bush clover, crownbeard, soft agrimony, woodland brome, buffalo clover, nodding fescue, elm-leaved goldenrod, and early oak sedge. Running buffalo clover, a federal- and state-listed endangered species, was apparently widespread in southern Indiana in areas of moist alkaline soils.

Eastern red cedar is sensitive to fire and was greatly restricted to sites that did not readily burn (e.g., rocky, low-fuel sites). Once fire was controlled, it spread across pasture land and abandoned cropland. Black locust was primarily found in the southeastern part of the state until it was spread through planting for fence posts and as a home-site ornamental and honey source.

Land clearing, beginning in the early part of the nineteenth century, began the reduction in species and numbers of plants, especially those of prairie and wetland habitats. Some species were impacted significantly. It is clear that bald cypress, American larch (eastern), and arbor vitae (northern white cedar) probably disappeared from many areas before their occurrence could be documented.

1900. By 1900, most of Indiana had been cleared of natural communities. Huge tracts had been converted for agricultural pursuits, either for row crops or pasture. Consequently, many species declined. Sites not as suitable for farming were spared somewhat, but these were commonly disturbed by livestock. A few plant species are thought to have become extirpated by this time. Mare's tail was last collected in the state in 1880, false bugbane in 1889, early coral-root in 1897, and short-beaked bald rush in 1899. Most other native species probably persisted, albeit in greatly reduced numbers, in landscape remnants.

2000. Perhaps the greatest period of landscape alteration occurred in the early to mid-1900s, and consequently it might have been the nadir for numbers of individuals of most of Indiana's native flora. By 2000, much of the state was cleared or altered, although following the Great Depression some areas reverted to some semblance of their former natural state, providing for an increase in numbers of some native flora. This has been especially true for forest species. Almost no areas that were formerly prairie have reverted, and thus the state's prairie flora is among the most reduced in numbers. Most prairie species can still be found in the state, but in scattered, very small remnants. These are threatened by herbicides and by invasion by non-native species that were introduced for food or livestock forage in the twentieth century, especially Hungarian brome and tall fescue. Two lists of species of plants known from Indiana are given alphabetically in Tables P-1 and P-2. Table P-1 lists plants by common name, P-2 by scientific name.

Illustrative of the decline of plant species is the list of endangered, threatened, and rare species prepared by the Indiana Department of Natural Resources' Natural Heritage Data Center (Table P-13). Approximately 400 plant species are threatened with decline and possible extirpation in the state, and just over 50 species are thought to be extirpated.

Fish

The number of fish species thought to currently inhabit the various aquatic systems of Indiana is 200 (Table F-1). Eleven species—alligator gar, Alabama shad, popeye shiner, harelip sucker, blackfin cisco, shortnose cisco, shortjaw cisco, southern cavefish, crystal darter, stargazing darter, and saddleback darter—are now considered extirpated from the state. The Great Lakes form of the muskellunge is also extirpated, although a native population of the Ohio River form may still exist. Its current status is uncertain, and muskellunge is also now stocked extensively.

Although not officially listed as extirpated, several other species have not been seen in the state for years or only on a very limited basis, including lake chub, pallid shiner, pugnose shiner, bantam sunfish, and cypress darter. Several other species are very rare in Indiana and may only remain in a few locations. The redside dace is currently known from only two very small watersheds. The gilt darter, once found in many of the larger rivers of the state, is now restricted to a section of the Tippecanoe River. The last remaining populations of greater redhorse and lake sturgeon in the entire Ohio River drainage are now found in Indiana in the Eel River, in the upper Wabash River, and in the mainstem of the East Fork of the White River, respectively.

Portions of four major watersheds (Lake Michigan, Lake Erie, Kankakee River, and Ohio River) drain the Indiana landscape. Although the Ohio River drainage contains the greatest fish diversity and has the most unique species, there are characteristic species in the other drainages as well (Tables F-2 through F-5). Many species are restricted to Lake Michigan (Table F-2). The bigmouth shiner and weed shiner are only found in the Kankakee River drainage of Indiana (Table F-3). Regionally, the diversity of fish in Indiana is comparable to that of Illinois but greater than that of Michigan or Ohio. Fish diversity increases going south, as about 30 more species have been documented from Kentucky waters (Burr and Warren 1986) than from those of Indiana.

The introduction of exotic species has certainly added to the diversity of fish of Indiana. Twenty-two of the 211 species of fish known to inhabit Indiana waters are considered exotic (Table F-6). They have invaded Indiana waters through a variety of means. Some were the result of intentional stocking for sport fishing opportunities. Others migrated here through unnatural, man-made drainage connections or traveled in the ballast water of transoceanic vessels. Many exotic species have escaped from private waters, eventually making their way to Indiana. The unintentional—and, in some situations, intentional—stocking through aquarium release and the dumping of bait buckets has also been implicated. Many native species also inhabit areas of the state where they were not historically found, moving between drainages in many of the same ways that the exotics have arrived.

The current list of 211 species of fish from Indiana is the result of a rich legacy of ichthyological investigation in the state, starting with Rafinesque (1820) near the beginning of the nineteenth century. There have been several attempts to catalog the species of fish found in Indiana waters: Jordan and Gilbert (1877), Jordan (1878), Eigenmann and Beeson (1894), Hay (1894), Eigenmann and Beeson (1905), Meek (1908), Blatchley (1938), Gerking (1945, 1955), Simon et al. (1992, 2002). Many of the older accounts can be somewhat confusing, with the inclusion of erroneous species, the separation of species that later were combined, and species designations that were later split to represent multiple species. Many authors also hypothesized on species they thought should occur in Indiana, but had not yet been found.

1800. The exact number of fish species inhabiting Indiana waters by the beginning of the nineteenth century is not documented. Aquatic systems would have been in their most pristine condition at this time; native species should have been flourishing. Ironically, overall diversity was probably much lower than currently, as the introduction of exotic species had not occurred yet. Native species would have been at their maximum distribution, not relegated to the rather disjunct populations that many species now must maintain.

1900. Most of the 37 species of fish with type localities from Indiana were described by the beginning of the twentieth century (Table F-7). Including those species that were hypothesized from the state and later found, Eigenmann and Beeson (1894) documented around 155 species of fish from the state; Hay (1894) at the same time listed around 165. Hay, interestingly, included common carp, the earliest exotic species, which Eigenmann and Beeson did not. Great modifications to the landscape of Indiana had already occurred by the beginning of the twentieth century and its toll was seen on the aquatic systems. Most of the species now considered extirpated from Indiana (see Table F-1) were recorded for the last time in some of these early reports on the fish of the state.

2000. Nearly 50 years after some of the earliest attempts to document the fish of Indiana, Gerking (1945), in a statewide survey and extensive compilation of historical accounts, documented the presence of 170 species and an additional 16 subspecies; 40 species were also listed as hypothetical. Under current nomenclature and including those hypothetical species that have now been found, Gerking (1945) reported 189 of the 211 species currently known. This increase was due in large part to a better understanding of the lamprey species found in the state, to the discovery/inclusion of some additional native species (Alabama shad, gravel chub, pallid shiner, cypress minnow, ironcolor shiner, silverband shiner, weed shiner, greater redhorse, brook trout, northern studfish, banded sculpin), and in small part to the addition of exotic species (goldfish, rainbow smelt, rainbow trout, brown trout; sea lamprey was hypothesized).

Simon et al. (1992) listed 204 fish species from the state, although 4 were erroneously included. The increase in species since Gerking (1945) was mainly the result of the following exotic species becoming established in the state: alewife, grass carp, silver carp, rudd, white catfish, coho salmon, chinook salmon, Atlantic salmon, and striped bass. Several native species, including threadfin shad, largescale stoneroller, ribbon shiner, northern madtom, and blackspotted topminnow, were also recorded for the first time.

By Simon et al. (2002), the number of fish species in the state had grown to 209, with the arrival of several more exotic species, including bighead carp, threespine stickleback, white perch, and round goby. Striped mullet and inland silverside had also entered the state, although likely as natural range expansion upstream on the Ohio River. The current number of 211 was reached with the addition of the exotic oriental weatherfish and the recognition of the smallmouth redhorse as a unique species.

Amphibians and Reptiles

There have been 40 species of amphibians and 58 species of reptiles recorded from Indiana within the last 200 years (Table H-1). The state's herpetofauna is moderately diverse compared to that of surrounding states, and is influenced by several geographic and historic factors. While the southernmost parts of Indiana were not severely impacted by Wisconsinan glaciation, much of the state was impacted until about 12–15,000 years ago. With the recession of the glaciers, species invaded from the west and south, and perhaps also from the east. The diversity of herpetofauna in the southern parts of the state is greater than in the north. However, many species also occur only in the north, so diversity is not simply a matter of latitude. Instead, species diversity appears driven by which species invaded the north after the glaciers receded and, also, how the south has been influenced by more southerly fauna migrating along the Ohio River or from the Appalachians.

1800. The herpetofauna of Indiana into the mid-1800s was no doubt very similar to what it had been in presettlement time. Since no herpetofauna offered a resource to be harvested en masse in terms of food or for trade, they largely escaped any concentrated extraction efforts. However, the deliberate killing of poisonous reptiles (rattlesnake, copperhead) was pervasive, and surely impacted the numbers of such species, especially in the vicinity of settlements and along travel corridors. Also, the harvesting of certain species for food, for example, snapping turtles and bull- and green frogs, must have impacted these species as the wave of European settlement advanced.

1900. As human population growth and habitat alterations occurred at an accelerating pace during the 1800s, negative impacts on the state's herpetofauna greatly increased. The landscape was extensively modified for agriculture, and fire was suppressed. Despite these changes, the extirpation of species was likely rare, and in those cases where it did occur, it was perhaps due to Indiana being on the periphery of the species' ranges. Instead, most impacts were in the form of declines, perhaps setting the stage for future extirpations.

The alligator snapping turtle has likely been functionally extirpated from Indiana, with the most reliable records coming from along the lower Wabash River in the late 1800s (Minton 2001). Claims of observations continue, and although no doubt most of these are common snapping turtles, adventurous alligator snapping turtles may yet reach Posey County in southwestern Indiana. A sighting confirmed by M. Lodato from the White River near Martinsville (Minton 2001), and thus farther into Indiana, is a curious outlier to this pattern. Any observations, past or present, may have been wayward individuals from farther down the Ohio River, and successful reproduction in Indiana's rivers may not have been occurring.

The western mud snake once occurred in the floodplain forests of the larger southernmost rivers. No recent observations have been verified, and even dated records are obscure, but, like the alligator snapping turtle, this species may yet lurk in the state.

As infrastructural development became more pervasive, amphibians and reptiles faced a variety of challenges that went well beyond loss of habitat. Roads emerged as one of the greatest threats to amphibians and reptiles. Most obviously, they cause direct mortality to the animals attempting to cross them. Large snakes, gravid female turtles, and migrating salamanders are among the groups most impacted. However, even when herpetofauna avoid roads, they are impacted by the fragmentation of their remaining populations. Railroad tracks and the elevated structures they are built upon are another underappreciated barrier for many species. Most obviously, box turtles struggle to successfully navigate them, or at times manage to get over one rail, then not the second, and die in between. In addition, many aquatic turtle species seeking suitable terrestrial nesting locations will also be challenged by this barrier.

A growing number of other anthropogenic factors have come into play. Erosion-control fencing blocks the movements of many species, while the open netting style is a death trap for snakes, as is snow fencing. Many water control structures trap turtles, frogs, salamanders, and snakes. Diseases are transported about the landscape on tires, on boots, and even in pets released back into the wild. Collection for the pet trade was also an increasing threat, but it has been reduced by state regulations.

2000. Herpetofaunal declines continued in the late 1900s and into the twenty-first century. The patterns of habitat loss described above largely remain, and will likely persist or accelerate into the foreseeable future. The mysterious decline of Blanchard's cricket frog continues. Hellbenders are in dire straits. It is anticipated that the federally threatened northern populations of copperbelly water snake will be gone from the state in the next few years, and most populations of Blanding's and spotted turtles are in danger of extirpation in the next decade or two.

Toward the end of the twentieth century (perhaps most obviously in the 1970s), a dramatic decline was noted for Blanchard's cricket frog across the northern part of the state and through much of the remainder of their range around Lake Michigan. As is the case with many amphibian declines, the cause of the reduction is not well understood and is likely the result of a variety of factors. However, M. Lannoo (personal communication) has suggested that the decline is the result of the unavailability of annually reliable shallow wetlands, in concert with the variety of other insults impacting amphibians. Cricket frogs are virtually an annual species, as few live more than a year. Thus, as wetlands are removed, the adults may not be able to find reliable wetlands frequently enough to persist. A. Resetar (personal communication, 2004) proposed an alternative theory, suggesting that acid rain contributed to declines, and those populations that persist in the Great Lakes region are in a "base cation refugia" afforded by calcareous soils or even industrial waste. Skinner and Lehtinen (2006) tested this hypothesis in western Ohio and did not find support for the idea.

Many other species of amphibians and reptiles showed significant declines during the 1900s. Unfortunately, this is likely the case with most, if not all, forms as a consequence of habitat loss, pollution, collection, and the introduction of exotic species. It is noteworthy that most species of amphibians and reptiles that have been lost or have exhibited the most severe declines have been those associated with wetlands or with aquatic systems. The northern populations of copperbelly water snake have nearly disappeared, and the southern populations have also declined dramatically. To the north, the eastern massasauga, Blanding's turtle, and spotted turtle have all experienced serious decline. The status of Kirtland's snake and of Butler's garter snake is unknown. Although it may be locally abundant, the status of the northern leopard frog is also a concern. To the south, the stream-dwelling hellbender has disappeared from most of the watersheds within which it previously occurred.

Terrestrial losses have also been noted. Most eastern box turtle populations are disappearing or facing declines, and the range of the timber rattlesnake has collapsed to only a few areas within its former range in the state. Many private individuals have commented on the general decline of large snakes. "There aren't as many around as there used to be" is a common refrain. Others note that the frequency of road-killed snakes and turtles, an anecdotal measure of abundance and distribution, is much lower in the early twenty-first century than it was in the 1980s.

Surveys for crawfish frogs have revealed new localities for that species, and there is some evidence that they are capable of colonizing new habitats, such as restored surface mining areas and other restoration projects. Four-toed salamanders have also been found at several new locations. However, that species does not show any evidence of being a good colonizer.

Curiously, several species new to the state have been reported as recently as the late twentieth century. In some cases, this suggests that further exciting discoveries may yet await us, but in others we find that species may be expanding into the state, or are certain introductions. In 1993, the green salamander was found in southeastern Indiana on bluffs overlooking the Ohio River (Madej 1994). This species was very likely in the state all along but was undiscovered. Continued searching may well reveal it in other similar habitat along the Ohio River, but it is also likely that its distribution will not be extensive. The mole salamander was found in Posey County in 2004. This is another species that was certainly here historically, but that was missed, and it is unlikely that many additional populations will be found.

Other species appear to be recent arrivals. The green treefrog was confirmed in wetlands in Vanderburgh County around Evansville in 2003 by M. Lodato. Zack Walker (personal communication) indicated that they have also been found in Posey County. While it is surprising that the species was not observed previously, despite aggressive searches, the habitat of the Ohio River valley is certainly suitable. The species may be a rare example of one that is expanding its range. River cooters naturally occur in southern Indiana, but have recently been spotted in northeastern Indiana along the St. Joseph River. Whether these are the result of captive releases is not known, but it seems likely. This means of dispersal is true for many populations of red-eared slider discovered across Indiana since the late twentieth century.

While some of Indiana's immigrants are possibly from nearby native populations, others clearly are not. The common wall lizard (*Podarcis muralis maculiventris*) is an alien species established at the Falls of the Ohio, near New Albany. While it was officially documented in 2004 (Z. Walker, personal communication), it may have been established for some time. This lizard is native to Europe, and thus an obvious exotic. This population appears derived from the upstream Cincinnati population, which has been there for many years. From 2005 to 2007, unsuccessful efforts were made by the Division of Fish and Wildlife to eliminate the Falls of the Ohio population. With time, other herpetofauna may become established in the state, though with Indiana's moderately severe winters, such invasions will be somewhat constrained. Efforts are being made to extirpate the known population of wall lizards before its distribution expands.

Birds

The number of bird species recorded at least once in Indiana in historic times is 407, according to the Indiana Bird Records Committee (2005). This includes extinct or regionally extirpated species, which are discussed below in the century-by-century account of historical changes. The total also includes many species (approximately 100) that have occurred "accidentally" thanks to avian mobility, hurricanes, and migration errors; 1 or 2 such species are added each year. Indiana habitats are of little or no ecological significance to these accidental or casual species, so they are not considered here. However, rare species that occur regularly will be discussed, including those dependent on endangered natural habitats of the state. This account focuses on some 309 species that presently occur regularly, typically annually (Table B-1).

Within a north-temperate region like Indiana, the seasonal status of a bird species is typically described by one of the following categories: permanent resident (breeding), summer resident (breeding), migrant only, and winter resident. Indiana has many species in each of these categories. Some 158 species were confirmed as breeders during the 1985–1990 breeding bird atlas project (Castrale et al. 1998); approximately 45 are permanent residents, the rest are migrants that winter in the neotropics or in the southern United States. Forty-two species (excluding permanent residents) are most common in winter. There are 141 species that most commonly (or exclusively) occur as spring or fall migrants (see Table B-1). Numbers for these categories exceed the total of 309 regular species, because some of the breeding species are more common as migrants or wintering birds. The state is an important migration route for waterfowl and passerines (warblers, thrushes, sparrows, etc.) that breed in habitats of Canada and the bordering U.S. states.

Webster (1998) made an insightful biogeographic analysis of breeding bird distribution. He found significant geographic turnover in species presence when he compared 50 priority blocks (distributed over several counties) in the northwestern and southeastern corners of Indiana, which were separated by some 336 km: of 159 species found overall, 28% occurred in only one of the two regions. Bird distributions within the state did not correspond well with the natural regions mapped by Homoya et al. (1985) or with the physiographic regions of other authors. When Homoya et al.'s 10 terrestrial natural regions were collapsed into 6, there was more success in relating them to bird distributions. A common practice of ornithologists, begun by Butler (1898) and emphasized by Keller et al. (1986) and Brock (2006), is to evaluate the abundance and seasonal status of a species in three broad latitudinal bands (northern, central, southern). There is also a small longitudinal category of western, drier-country species.

1800. Anyone familiar with the present-day avifauna of Indiana would have little trouble recognizing the avifauna of the state if transported back to the year 1800. The majority of the 158 native breeding birds present today were also present at that time. The relative abundance of various species around 1800 would, however, be very unfamiliar to a present-day observer. Forest birds were found in abundance throughout Indiana with the exception of the prairie and savanna habitats in the northwest. These prairie habitats were intact and thriving, complete with greater prairie-chickens and a host of grassland birds large and small. Wetland avian communities were thriving and abundant, especially in the north. The Grand Kankakee Marsh in northwest Indiana was intact as one of the largest and most important wetland complexes in the Midwest. Many sandhill cranes and possibly whooping cranes and trumpeter swans bred in the Grand Marsh, as perhaps did several species of ducks which we now consider to be nonbreeders in Indiana. Marsh birds such as rails and bitterns were abundant throughout the north.

Perhaps most spectacularly, a present-day birder transported back to 1800 would find populations of ivory-billed woodpeckers, passenger pigeons, Carolina parakeets, and greater prairie-chickens. Common, present-day species of introduced birds, such as rock pigeon, European starling, and house sparrow, were not yet present, and would not be for a century or more. In short, in the year 1800, the avifauna of Indiana was probably about as rich and vibrant as it had been at any time since the end of the Pleistocene. This situation, however, would change dramatically in a few decades, reflecting the sweeping ecological impacts of European settlement.

1900. The first wave of habitat destruction following European settlement centered on forests, whose soils provided good agricultural land. Massive forest destruction began during the early 1800s and undoubtedly led to a corresponding loss of forest birds from much of the state, especially in the central and northern sections. Birds of the deep forested habitats, such as pileated woodpecker (Butler 1898), largely disappeared from the Central Till Plain and other areas that were similarly stripped clear of large forest tracts. Such forest bird species became largely restricted to southern Indiana by the end of the nineteenth century, although most were probably doing reasonably well where forest habitat remained. The passenger pigeon is a clear exception here, and was effectively (if not actually) extinct in Indiana and elsewhere by the end of the 1800s.

Wetland birds also suffered major losses in the 1800s. The destruction of wetland habitats was minimal at first, but accelerated toward the end of the century as small and large wetlands were drained for agricultural use. During the latter part of the 1800s, efforts began in earnest to drain the Grand Kankakee Marsh. The demise of the Grand Marsh resulted in the disappearance of whooping cranes, trumpeter swans, and the vast majority of sandhill cranes breeding in Indiana. Several species of ducks (e.g., American wigeon, redhead, green-winged teal) may have bred regularly, along with some shorebirds (Wilson's phalarope, lesser yellowlegs, solitary sandpiper) that very rarely (if ever) breed in the state at present. The general decay in wetlands toward the end of the 1800s also led to the loss of horned grebe and common loon as breeding birds in the state. Many other species of marsh birds once common in the north undoubtedly declined greatly as well. The wood duck population declined with the loss of old lowground forests, whose cavities served as nest sites for them. Canada geese largely had disappeared from Indiana as breeding birds by the end of the nineteenth century.

Prairie destruction accelerated during the end of the 1800s, but generally led to the extirpation of few if any avian species from Indiana, although the greater prairie-chicken was in serious decline. The saving grace for many grassland birds was the fact that nineteenth-century agriculture typically involved a great deal of pasture land and fallow fields, which provided much suitable habitat for grassland birds, perhaps with the exception of species like Henslow's sparrows, which require relatively undisturbed grasslands. The demise of grassland avian communities in Indiana awaited the development of "industrial" agriculture during the twentieth century.

Several species were ultimately extirpated from Indiana during the 1800s, often via a combination of habitat loss, direct hunting, and various other forms of persecution. As mentioned above, the list includes whooping crane, trumpeter swan, passenger pigeon, and perhaps a few species of ducks and shorebirds. Gone by the mid-1800s were Carolina parakeet and ivory-billed woodpecker. Wild turkey, swallow-tailed kite (whose levels were never well documented), and common raven were gone by the end of the century.

Many species of birds undoubtedly benefited from the great habitat destruction of the 1800s, especially those typical of edge, open, or successional habitats. Many such species are among the most familiar birds today in Indiana, including the common grackle, northern cardinal, song sparrow, American robin, American crow, barn swallow, eastern kingbird, bobwhite quail, and mourning dove. These species were undoubtedly present prior to European settlement, but were not as common as they were at the end of the century (or as they are at the beginning of the twenty-first century). Furthermore, the expansion of new species—barn owl, Bewick's wren, Bachman's sparrow, lark sparrow, dickcissel, savannah sparrow—into Indiana during the latter half of the nineteenth century was undoubtedly another byproduct of forest destruction and the sorts of habitats that were produced in its place.

The 1800s saw the arrival of the first Old World exotic species in the state. House sparrows first appeared in Indiana during the late 1800s and rapidly established throughout the state. House sparrow increases were favored on farms by the practice of storing loose hay in barn lofts. The edges of the hay mows simulated the thatched roofs of Old World houses, and were used extensively by house sparrows as nest sites. With the onset of widespread baling of hay, house sparrow numbers, and problems with them, declined. One result of the house sparrow's rapid increase appears to have been the great decline of cliff swallows, which was clearly evident by the end of the century; these swallows were closely associated with human habitation at the time and suffered from nest usurpation by house sparrows. Deliberate introductions of the only other Old World species to be introduced during this era, the ring-necked pheasant, began at the close of the nineteenth century and continued well into the twentieth century.

2000. Many of the trends begun in the 1800s continued into the twentieth century. Wetland-dwelling birds, in particular, continued to decrease as many of the wetlands not destroyed during the 1800s were drained. Almost all marsh birds, such as marsh wrens, many rails, both American and least bitterns, black terns, and sandhill cranes, were given status as threatened or endangered in the state in the 1970s. Black terns may effectively no longer breed in the state. Double-crested cormorants established a minor breeding presence in Indiana during the twentieth century, but this was relatively short-lived. Piping plovers had disappeared from Lake Michigan beaches by the mid-1900s.

Grassland birds experienced major declines during the 1900s with the advent of permanent row crop agriculture, which greatly reduced the area of the fallow fields and pastured grasslands that had sustained these species after the destruction of native grasslands. Greater prairie-chickens diminished rapidly and were largely extirpated by the mid-1900s. Many other species declined to very low numbers as breeders, including upland sandpipers, northern harriers, and short-eared owls (although the latter two species now winter in the state in large numbers). Bobolinks had plummeted as breeding birds by 1950, while red-winged blackbirds expanded their breeding habitat from marshes into upland grasslands, becoming the most numerous breeding bird there. Grasshopper sparrows and especially Henslow's sparrows also greatly declined in number. The only obligate grassland bird still in reasonably good shape at the end of the twentieth century was the eastern meadowlark, which can exist in marginal habitats to an extent greater than other grassland birds. Perhaps the most unexpected development during the twentieth century was the advent of large grasslands in reclaimed coal mines following the Surface Mining Control and Reclamation Act of 1977; such habitat is now a major refuge for grassland birds of all types in Indiana, and provides the only known nesting locations for short-eared owls in the state. Many grassland birds remain listed as threatened or endangered in Indiana.

The advent of permanent row crop agriculture led to an increasing lack of successional habitat during the twentieth century, as main habitat types became row crops and relatively mature forest. This lack of successional habitat may have led to the great decline in the bobwhite, the disappearance of Bachman's sparrow and Bewick's wren, and the near disappearance of the golden-winged warbler from the northern part of the state during the twentieth century. The loss of fence rows to expansive row crop agriculture also impacted species that formerly nested there or used fence rows as travel corridors.

Forested habitat reached its low point in both area and condition early in the twentieth century, and has increased somewhat since then (see chapter 4). Most birds of the deep forest still remain largely restricted to the southern half of the state, where the only relatively large tracts of forest remain. Ruffed grouse were originally widespread in the state, though local in the habitat patches that they prefer: dense young sapling growth in areas that are naturally opened or artificially clear-cut but are scattered within a largely forested landscape. They were doing well in the mid-twentieth century, but have become increasingly scarce since the 1980s, and are now restricted to a handful of counties in central and southern Indiana. Birds relatively tolerant of forest fragmentation, including neotropical migrants such as red-eyed vireos, Acadian flycatchers, and scarlet tanagers, are still found breeding in remnant forest fragments throughout Indiana. Research strongly suggests, however, that species breeding in smaller forest fragments experience very poor breeding success due to the combined effects of increased predation and cowbird parasitism (Robinson et al. 1995). At the beginning of the twenty-first century, it appeared that much of the forested habitat remaining in Indiana represented a reproductive sink for many neotropical migrant birds, with the likely exception of the larger tracts of forest in the Hoosier National Forest and the surrounding state land in south-central Indiana.

A few formerly extirpated species recolonized during the twentieth century. Some of these comebacks followed deliberate reintroductions, such as those of the Canada goose (which had essentially disappeared by the end of the 1800s) and wild turkey (reintroduced beginning circa 1955 after a several-decade absence). Intensive reintroduction programs also led to the reestablishment of breeding bald eagles (several dozen known nests at the end of the twentieth century) along major rivers and reservoirs, and of peregrine falcons in several urban areas in Indiana. Cliff swallows made an unassisted comeback in the latter part of the twentieth century after disappearing from the state earlier in the century; this recolonization probably reflected the proliferation of bridges away from human habitation (and house sparrows).

Several native North American birds established breeding populations in Indiana during the twentieth century. Bell's vireos spread from the west around 1940 and established a significant breeding presence mainly in western Indiana. Blue grosbeaks spread into Indiana around 1950 and increased substantially by the end of the twentieth century. Both herring gulls and especially ring-billed gulls established a breeding presence on Lake Michigan during the late 1990s, followed by double-crested cormorants in 2004. The federally endangered least tern established a sustained breeding colony in Gibson County in the mid-1980s. A species native to western North America—the house finch—also spread into Indiana by the 1970s; this did not reflect a natural range expansion, but was derived from birds from the West Coast that were released in New York during the 1940s.

Several now-familiar Old World exotic species became established breeders in the state during the 1900s, including rock pigeons (early 1900s), European starlings (1919), and ring-necked pheasant (established during the early part of the century after repeated introductions in several counties). The gray partridge was also introduced several times in northern Indiana during the 1910s, but the established population lasted only a few decades (gone by 1980). Mute swans became established breeders around 1970, and have increased slowly in numbers since then. The Eurasian collared dove arrived in Indiana during the late 1990s, and may ultimately increase substantially in urban areas.

Mammals

In the year 2000, 57 species of mammals were known to occur naturally in Indiana. Another 7 species occurred at the time of European settlement but are now extirpated, and there has been no attempt at reintroduction: bison, American elk, gray wolf, mountain lion, black bear, fisher, and porcupine (Table M-1). Three other species were extirpated and absent for decades, but have been reintroduced: beaver (extirpated about 1840), white-tailed deer (1891), and river otter (1942). Four species were introduced by humans: house mouse, black rat (soon extirpated; see below), Norway rat, and red fox. One species of bat, the gray myotis, has become resident since the time of settlement, expanding its range from Kentucky. It became established in Indiana about 1980, forming a maternity colony in a quarry at Sellersburg in Clark County; gray myotis also inhabited a second roost about 5 mi away in Charlestown Military Base (now a state park). The western harvest mouse has also become a resident, moving in from Illinois about 1969. One mammal on the state list, the silver-haired bat, is a migrant. It hibernates in southern Indiana and farther south, and then, like many songbirds, migrates northward through Indiana in the spring, has its young in the north, and migrates back south in the fall.

1800. Sixty-one of the 65 species of mammals represented by wild populations since the time of European settlement would have been present in 1800 (Table M-1). Prominent among these would have been several large herbivores, carnivores, and fur-bearing mammals that were hunted to extinction in the state, either very promptly (by the 1830s or 1850s) or over the next century. Most had statewide distributions. Bison occurred throughout the state and may have been most abundant in the southwest where great herds passed on the paths (traces) which extended from the prairies of Illinois into Indiana, crossing the Wabash near Vincennes, thence southeast to the Falls of the Ohio, where they crossed into Kentucky. These great herds were gone by about 1808. Elk also occurred throughout Indiana and disappeared by 1830. Even the white-tailed deer was hunted to extirpation by 1900, although it was reintroduced starting in the 1930s and even had to be controlled by the latter part of the twentieth century. Mountain lions and wolves were prominent in 1800 and helped to keep the deer in check at that time. Black bears were also present and were hunted by the early European settlers. Mountain lions, wolves, and bears were despised as livestock predators. The beaver was heavily trapped throughout its range, and much of the exploration of the country was by beaver trappers. However, the beaver was later reintroduced and, like the deer, had recovered to the point of being a pest in the latter part of the twentieth century. Other fur-bearers present with the early settlers but then extirpated were the fisher and river otter. The otter was reintroduced in the 1990s and is now doing very well in the state.

Although settler-farmers carried out most of the extirpations through hunting, trapping, and habitat destruction, the decline of fur-bearers such as beaver began during the fur trade era, well before U.S. colonist settlement and statehood. For example, the Fort Wayne trading post operated by the U.S. government purchased only about 20 beaver pelts from Native Americans between 1803 and 1806, which contrasts with an abundance of otter (103), bear (118), "cat" (136), deer (4,317), and raccoon skins (4,570) (Nichols 2008). "Cat" was likely a combination of mountain lion and bobcat.

Very early in the settlement period, two non-native species arrived with humans to share their buildings: the house mouse and the black rat. The coyote was present, but perhaps only in the northern part of the state.

1900. In 1900, about 55 species of mammals were present, reflecting a mixture of extinctions and introductions. By the end of the nineteenth century, several species had become extirpated, including the bison and American elk (wapiti) about 1830, the beaver about 1840, the black bear about 1850, the mountain lion about 1851, the fisher about 1859, and the white-tailed deer about 1891. Bison, elk, and deer were hunted for meat. Beavers were trapped for fur. Bears and mountain lions were hunted for meat and hides and/or to get rid of them as predators. Fishers and otters were probably over-trapped for fur.

Rather early in the settlement era, one introduced rat species replaced another. The black rat was present first, having arrived with the earliest European settlers and the house mouse. Norway rats entered North America about 1775, but the first reports for Indiana were in 1827 at Brookville, 1835 at Richmond, and 1840 at Vincennes. Apparently, soon after its appearance the Norway rat drove out the black rat, in about 1845.

The red fox arrived about 1855, from European stock. Although the species was apparently native in the northern part of North America (north of 40–45° N) earlier, it was absent in the mid-Atlantic United States, where it was introduced from England for hunting purposes about 1650–1750. Red foxes were not recorded at New Harmony in 1832 nor in Wayne County in 1844. In 1870, red foxes had been known in Franklin County only "in the last ten or 15 years" (Haymond 1870: 204). The species was unknown in Knox County before that date, but was common there by 1880.

Because they are such ecologically and historically important species, we will provide some detail on the demise of the beaver and the white-tailed deer. Evermann and Butler (1894b) stated that a beaver was taken near New Harmony "not many years ago" and that one was seen in the Wabash River near Lafayette in 1889. However, Hahn (1909) questioned both of these records and stated that the last definite record of the species in the state was at Vincennes in 1840. Beavers were reintroduced in 1935 into the Jasper-Pulaski and Kankakee fish and wildlife areas, using animals from Wisconsin and Michigan. By 1955, they were widespread and continued to increase into the twenty-first century, apparently little affected by a legal trapping season.

The white-tailed deer was common in the pioneer days but was gone by 1900. It is difficult to determine exactly when it was extirpated. Hahn (1909) gives some information. One European settler killed 370 in the fall of 1822 in Johnson County, and in 1834, 6 were killed in a day in Wells County. A drive in the 1840s in Warren County resulted in 160 deer being killed. Later deer reports were in 1859 in LaGrange County and in 1874 in Warrick County. There were probably none left in Franklin County in 1869, but some still existed in Allen County in 1880. The species disappeared between 1853 and 1867 in Noble County. One was killed in 1890 in Jasper County, and another was seen in 1891 in adjacent Newton County. The last deer seen in the state prior to extirpation was near Red Cloud in Knox County in 1893. A restocking program initiated 41 years later, in 1934, was very successful as today white-tailed deer are abundant or even overabundant in Indiana.

2000. The gray wolf was extirpated about 1908 through predator elimination, the porcupine about 1918, and the river otter about 1942 through over-trapping. (The otter was reintroduced in the 1990s.) Habitat reduction was another adverse factor as development proceeded in the twentieth century. By 1950, a total of 55 species of (free-ranging) mammals existed in the state.

The western harvest mouse moved into the northwestern portion of Indiana on its own about 1969. It spread and thrived, and by 2000 it occurred in at least 18 counties, extending from southern Lake County to northern Vigo County, and east to Marshall and Fulton counties.

About 1980, the gray myotis established a maternity colony in Clark County in a quarry at Sellersburg. The gray bat had occurred in Indiana previously as an accidental, but it has grown to a full-scale population. This colony grew from about 400 bats in 1982 to nearly 4,000 by the year 2000. It also inhabits a second roost about 5 mi away in Charlestown Military Base (now a state park). This appears to be one colony as bats have been radio-tracked while flying between the two localities.

In 1982, 2 shrews, the pygmy shrew and the smoky shrew, were added to the list of mammals known to occur in Indiana. They were found in the unglaciated hills of southern Indiana, where they were undoubtedly present at the time of settlement. As of 2000, 57 species of mammals occured naturally in Indiana.

Two additional species have been found in the state since 2000, bringing to 59 the number of species of mammals in Indiana. Armadillos now occur in Kentucky and southern Illinois, and 4 individuals have been found in southwestern Indiana in Pike, Vanderburgh (2), and Gibson counties. If winters remain mild, armadillos may increase in number and range. The additional species of bat was found in Indiana in the spring of 2009: the eastern small-footed bat, *Myotis leibii.* Three individuals were trapped at the entrance to Wyandotte Cave, where they were apparently hibernating. It is not known if this species had occurred in Indiana all along or if it just arrived; however, it had been expected for many years..

Part 2.
Natural Habitats: Changes over Two Centuries

In this part, we will begin our systematic review of Indiana's major habitats, using the 6 natural habitats defined in *Indiana Comprehensive Wildlife Strategy* (D. J. Case and Associates 2005): forest lands, grasslands, wetlands, aquatic systems, barren lands, and subterranean systems. Forest, grasslands, and wetlands were Indiana's three great original terrestrial habitats, accounting for roughly 20, 2, and 1.5 million acres, respectively, in 1800 (Parker 1997). Therefore, it makes sense to treat them first, since maintaining and restoring such habitats are fundamental conservation goals. It is also logical to group wetlands (swamps, marshes, and so on) with aquatic systems, namely, lakes (including Lake Michigan) and rivers, since there is much overlap in aquatic wildlife's use of these two habitats. Barren lands, which have rock or sand substrates and little vegetation, include both natural sub-habitats (cliffs, dunes) and man-made quarries. The subterranean systems of southern Indiana, which harbor many unique cave invertebrates, complete this series of habitats.

Habitat chapters are structured as follows. First, we will give a general description of the habitat's spatial distribution, the sub-habitats that comprise it, its acreage, human impacts on it, and often a description of vegetation associations. This will be followed by descriptions of characteristic plants, fish, amphibians, reptiles, birds, mammals, and (for one chapter) cave invertebrates. Each of these sections (general description, flora, herpetofauna, etc.) has a historical framework, describing the situation in 1800, 1900, and 2000. The entries for 1900 and 2000 summarize changes over the preceding century. After an overview of the whole habitat, the same organization will be repeated for each sub-habitat, when sufficient information is available. Since we have tried to avoid unnecessary repetition, depending on the habitat and taxonomic group, the reader will sometimes find the most information in the habitat overview, and other times more in the sub-habitat treatments.

Lupine. Photo by Scott Johnson.

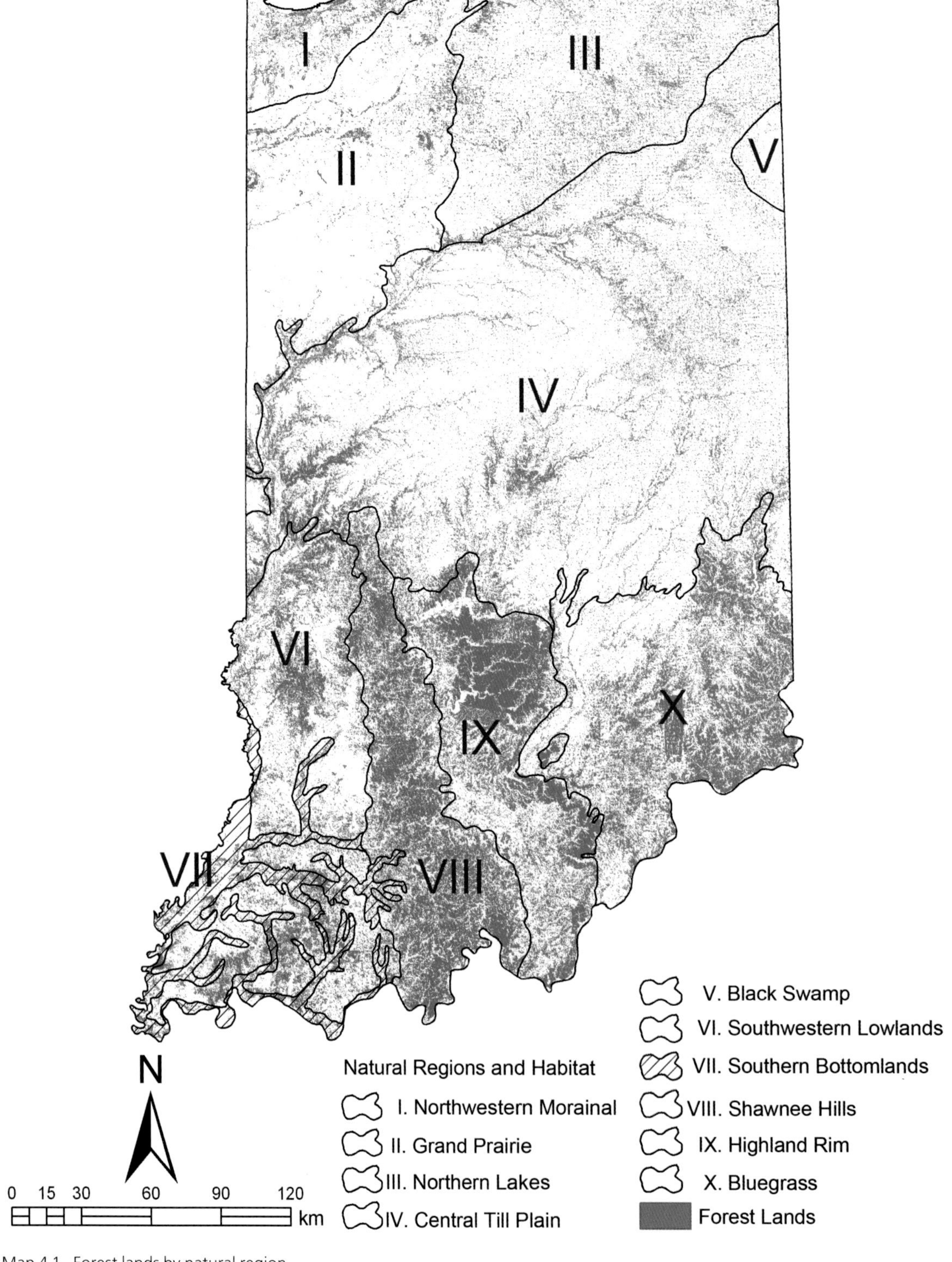

Map 4.1. Forest lands by natural region.

Forest Lands

The main natural habitat of Indiana has always been deciduous forest (Figure 4.1; Map 4.1). Prior to settlement by colonists from the young United States, some 20 million of the state's 23 million acres were probably forested. Indiana is part of the vast temperate deciduous forest biome of eastern North America, though near the western edge of it: Illinois was "the prairie state." As elsewhere in the biome, climate and soils dictate the forest and its predominant leaf type. Indiana's annual rainfall of 36–44 inches (91–112 cm) and a 5- to 7-month growing season favor trees and forest over other vegetation, and the state's mid-temperate latitude and rich soils favor deciduous broadleaf over evergreen needle-leaf species.

Forests are only superficially monotonous. The knowledgeable observer can catalog regional and local diversity in tree species associations almost endlessly. Only a subset, typically 20 to 30 species, of Indiana's "101 trees" (Jackson 2004) are present in a given forest parcel of 10 hectares or so. Species occurrences and relative abundances differ between upland and floodplain, between 38 and 41 N latitude, and are influenced by soil type, fire frequency, and other factors. Second, there is a structural diversity associated with forest age. Many forests begin with tulip (*Liquidambar*) saplings in an old field, and go through a characteristic series of vegetative phases: from old field to seedling/sapling, to pole stage, and finally to mature or high-canopy forest. This also happens constantly within mature forest when gaps are created. The early and mid-successional habitats are as important to certain wildlife groups as mature forest is to others.

All vegetation scientists who have tried, using various methods, to reconstruct presettlement habitat coverage agree that most of Indiana was forested,

Figure 4.1. Forest in Brown County State Park. Photo by James H. Speer.

with significant areas of prairie and wetland also occurring. Data are not sufficient to determine the actual acreage of forest in 1800 that was in various development stages or size classes. We know that areas were recovering from the clearing and burning of the Native Americans, and that large areas of forest savanna were present around prairies in the northwestern portion of the state. We used three different vegetation maps to estimate the distribution and area of vegetation types across the natural regions of Indiana.

Also of interest from pre-1800 are the tracks of the tornadoes that swept across Indiana prior to European settlement. Lindsey (1973) mapped these from his General Land Office (GLO) record studies. General "Mad" Anthony Wayne engaged Native Americans in such a blowdown in Ohio in the Battle of Fallen Timbers.

Starting in the mid-1800s, data on privately owned farmland were collected annually or biennially. These data did not distinguish forest types, and usually listed prairie and wetlands as waste lands or unproductive farmland. Forest surveys, which began only in the 1950s, provide data on forest type and size class. Numerous studies have been done on individual forests across the state since 1900.

1800. The General Land Office (GLO) survey done from 1799 to 1846 has been used to describe the state's early vegetation (Potzger et al. 1956; Lindsey 1961; Lindsey et al. 1965). Potzger et al. (1956) used records of 214,500 witness trees to characterize forest types in the early 1800s. They estimated that beech/maple covered about 40% of forested areas, primarily in the central and eastern sections; oak/hickory about 30%, in areas north and south of the beech/maple belt; and mixed forest (mixed mesophytic) covered the remaining 30%, primarily in the south-central portion of the state. Prairie and savanna were mostly found in the northwestern area of Indiana. The 16 prairie townships had only 10 witness trees each, on average, and were bordered by oak openings (savannas).

Lindsey et al. (1961, 1965), Schmelz and Lindsey (1970), and Crankshaw et al. (1965) refined Potzger's map by correlating soil types from county soil surveys with witness tree locations from the GLO survey (see Map 1.2). Soil maps were then used to map vegetation types, the procedure we followed in chapter 2. For individual tree species, earlier researchers calculated importance value, basal area, and density by soil type. For this book, Richard Thurau and J. C. Randolph (Indiana University) superimposed the Lindsey map over the natural regions of Indiana (Homoya et al. 1985) to estimate the area covered by different vegetation types for each natural region (Table G-13). Beech/maple covered over 11.7 million acres, primarily in the central and southeastern portion of the state. Oak/hickory covered over 6.9 million acres of the northeastern and southwestern areas. Mixed species forests (western mesophytic) were scattered over 1.8 million acres in the southern third of the state with the largest area in the south-central region where limestone soils are common. Both Potzger's and Lindsey's maps are fairly general and do not depict the diversity of site conditions found across the state.

Robert Gordon (1936) produced a potential vegetation map of presettlement Indiana based on field surveys in 1928 (see Map 1.3). Gordon's map should be viewed with caution, since his field surveys were done at the height of vegetation disturbance across the state (see the discussion below about Indiana in 1900). While his map is not necessarily an accurate depiction of all vegetation types, it does provide a better depiction of the great spatial variation of vegetation types within a region, as shown in the discussion below of vegetation pattern based on soil associations. Table G-14 gives the area of each vegetation type shown on Gordon's map by natural region.

We used the current soil conditions across the state to develop a presettlement vegetation map for each natural region. STATSGO soil associations were utilized to assign vegetation complexes to various regions of the state (see Map 1.4; Table G-15). Soil associations consist of 3 soil series that occur together, with each soil having different drainage and profile characteristics (Franzmeier et al. 1989; http://soils.usda.gov). For example, a given association could have a poorly drained soil spatially related to another soil that is well-drained with a thin surface horizon and a third that is a well-drained soil with a 7- to 10-inch dark surface horizon. This association would be mapped as a complex of wetland, forest, and prairie. Soil series within soil associations also have a common developmental history, i.e., the entire catena developed on the same landscape, over the same time period. While no attempt was made to assign a specific vegetation type to each of the habitats in the complex, they will be discussed as each natural region is described. For example, wetlands can take the form of wet prairie, marsh, or swamp (forested) depending on local conditions and past disturbance. Map 1.4 shows the great variation in vegetation that probably was present in Indiana in 1800. These complexes could be further refined in spatial scale and vegetation type by using individual soil series available for counties and the correlation data of species to soil type developed by A. A. Lindsey, W. B. Crankshaw, and S. A. Qadir (Crankshaw et al. 1965; Lindsey 1961).

The percentages of forest, prairie, and wetlands and the combinations of these within each natural region based on soil associations are summarized in Table 4.1. Further discussion of the natural regions is below.

The Northwestern Morainal Natural Region consisted of 6 vegetation types. Forest, much of it on sand dune soils, occupied 60% of the region. A complex of forest, prairie, and wetland covered 19% of the region, and the remaining 21% was covered by other combinations of 2 vegetation types. Many wetlands were open marsh or bog, and much of the forest was savanna, due in part to repeated fires set by Native Americans.

The Grand Prairie Natural Region included 7 vegetation complexes, with prairie/wetland the most common type.

Table 4.1. Vegetation Types by Natural Region in 1800

Natural Region	F	P	W	FP	FW	PW	FPW
Northwestern Morainal	60	—	2	2	12	5	19
Grand Prairie	21	2	14	2	14	35	12
Northern Lakes	58	1	5	—	32	2	2
Central Till Plain	26	1	—	—	70	—	2
Black Swamp	4	—	2	—	94	—	—
Southwestern Lowlands	76	2	3	—	17	2	7
Southern Bottomlands	39	—	8	4	41	8	—
Shawnee Hills	90	—	—	3	7	—	—
Highland Rim	85	—	—	4	11	4	—
Bluegrass	60	—	—	2	37	—	—

Note: Data presented as percentage of forest (F); prairie (P); wetland (W); complex of forest and prairie (FP); complex of forest and wetland (FW); complex of prairie and wetland (PW); and complex of forest, prairie, and wetland (FPW).

The Northern Lakes Natural Region was mostly covered by forest (58%) and forest/wetland (32%). Around 13% of the forest complex occurred on sand dune soils. Over 35% of the forest/wetland complex included poorly drained habitats with organic soils. Wetlands with organic soils covered 5.3% (135,071 acres) of the region. Wetlands included areas of both marsh and acid bogs (Swinehart and Parker 2001). More of the wetlands would have been forested in this region than in the regions already mentioned due to fewer Native American fires and a less favorable climate for prairie. Prairies were present, but not as common as in the previous regions discussed.

The Central Till Plain Natural Region covers over 8 million acres of central Indiana. It is relatively level, with large areas of forest/wetland soils (70% of the region). Most of the scattered wetlands in 1800 were small, forested depressions with poorly drained soils (Schmelz and Lindsey 1970). An additional 26% of this region was covered by forest without wetland.

The Black Swamp Natural Region was primarily forest/wetland (94%).

The forests of the Southwestern Lowlands Natural Region (76% of the land) commonly occurred on soils with a fragipan that restricted water movement and therefore rooting depth. These soils tended to be wet in the spring and drier in the summer and fall.

The Southern Bottomlands Natural Region had a more equal mix of forest (39%) and forest/wetland (41%) complexes. Here also, fragipans were common in the forested soils.

The Shawnee Hills Natural Region was primarily forested (90%). Forest composition varied based on physiography and whether the soils were derived from limestone or sandstone and shale (Van Kley and Parker 1993). Many soils, particularly on broad ridges, also had fragipans. Forest/wetland covered 7% and forest/prairie covered 3% of the region.

The forest complex covered 85% of the Highland Rim Natural Region. Forest composition varied across the region by physiographic position and whether the soils were derived from limestone or sandstone and shale (Van Kley and Parker 1993). For example, the Crider-Baxter-Bedford soil association (limestone soils) covers 44% of the forest complex on the western portion of the region. The forest/wetland complex occupied about 11% of the region. Forest/prairie complexes occupied 4% of the region.

Sixty percent of the Bluegrass Natural Region was covered by a forest complex. Forest composition varies in response to factors of physiography. Limestone soils are not as widespread in this region as in the previous two regions, and most of the soils have fragipans. The forest/wetland complex covered 37% of the region and forest/prairie covered 2%. The wetlands in this region were mostly forested.

1900. There were 3,838,042 acres of timber land in 1901 (Freeman 1908) with about 2.3 million acres recovering from harvest. The 1901–1902 biennial report of the Indiana Department of Statistics provides data on forest conditions by county (Table G-16). This report indicates that 250,080 acres of first-grade forest remained on farmland within the state. Over 2.7 million acres were classified as third-grade forest. First-grade forest on farms averaged 1.3% across all natural regions. The greatest percentage of first-grade forest occurred in the Shawnee Hills Natural Region with 2.1%. Third-grade forest varied from 7.8% in the Southern Bottomlands to 24.5% within the Shawnee Hills. Forest grades were not defined in the report, but it is likely that third-grade forest was in a severely degraded condition due to harvest, grazing, and/or burning. This report shows that individuals were concerned about forests, since trees were being planted throughout the state. However, the species being planted were primarily for on-farm use, such as catalpa for fence posts, or pines on worn-out lands in southern Indiana hill country. Data on tree species being harvested (Clark 1987) indicate that remnants of all forest types remained, but most had been heavily cut and probably grazed and burned.

Riparian forests were largely cleared for agriculture. The Eighth Annual Report of the State Board of Forestry states: "The amount of timber now standing along stream banks, together with its character and quality, is hardly worthy of consideration. Throughout the entire distance of three hundred and fifty miles traveled along the Wabash, but few first class wood lots were found. The prevailing scene is open pasture, cultivated fields and bare river banks" (Freeman 1908: 27). A description of the vegetation and environment along the Wabash and Tippecanoe rivers was published in 1961 based on data collected in the late 1950s (Lindsey et al. 1961). This study provides good information on the relation of plants to soil and hydrological regimes, but no data on the extent of native vegetation found along these rivers.

2000. The NLCD of 1992 recorded 4,343,879 acres of forest in Indiana. Forest cover ranged from 3.2% in the Black Swamp region to 56.4% in the Shawnee Hills region (Table G-1). The forest survey completed in 1998 divided the state into 4 units for inventory (Schmidt et al. 2000). The Northern survey unit includes the Northwestern Morainal, Grand Prairie, Central Till Plain, Black Swamp, and Northern Lakes natural regions. The Lower Wabash unit includes the Southwestern Lowlands and Southern Bottomlands natural regions. The Knobs unit includes the Shawnee Hills and Highland Rim natural regions, and the Upland Flats unit includes the Bluegrass Natural Region. Forests are divided into 11 general forest types (Table G-17) based on the dominant overstory species present. These types vary in species composition depending on site conditions, geographic location, and past disturbance. Oak/hickory, maple/beech, and elm/ash/cottonwood types are the most common, covering 85% of the forest land. Forest land in 2003 was estimated to exceed 4.5 million acres (Woodall et al. 2005). Forest area has increased by 52,500 acres since 1998 and 450,000 acres since 1950.

Remaining old-growth forests (forests with trees greater than 150 years of age and with little disturbance in the previous 100 years) were scattered across the state in 19 different stands covering 895 acres (average size: 47.2 acres) in 1997 (Spetich et al. 1997). Old-growth forest is expected to increase on publicly owned lands to 136,400 acres by 2060 if current management practices are continued. Most of this increase will be within the Highland Rim and Shawnee Hills natural regions, mostly within the Hoosier National Forest.

The chestnut tree, *Castanea dentata,* needs special treatment, as it is the only tree species which has been essentially extirpated from Indiana. It was once common throughout the hill country of southern Indiana, where it was a much-sought-after nut for human consumption. However, by the early 1940s nearly all had succumbed to chestnut blight, the pathogenic fungus *Cryphonectria parasitica.* The blight is believed to have arrived in North America from Asia about 1905 (Jackson 2004). It forms cankers or lesions which destroy the cambium of the lower trunk, essentially girdling and thereby killing the tree. The root system may remain alive for years, giving rise to numerous sprouts which also eventually die from blight. Today, even these are relatively few, although they are occasionally found in the knobs of southern Indiana. For all intents and purposes, this tree is gone from Indiana and from eastern North America, although the occasional tree still exists, such as one found by Linda Castor (Figure 4.2) in Clay County, Indiana, north of Cloverland. This is a full-sized tree (diameter at breast height [dbh] = 34.1) and produced hundreds of nuts in 2009, although a great proportion of them were infected with a beetle larva, probably curculionid. Geneticists are now working to develop resistant strains from surviving trees in the hope that, someday, chestnut trees might once again occur in the forests of southern Indiana and elsewhere.

Figure 4.2. Large chestnut tree with chestnuts in Clay County, Indiana. Photo by Terry L. Castor.

Flora

With most of Indiana's original landscape occupied by various forest communities, a significant portion of the state's flora can be found there. In addition to the tree species that comprise the canopy, a variety of shrubs and herbaceous species occur in the understory. Of particular note is the occurrence of spring ephemerals. These species develop quickly in the spring (usually March and April) as day length and temperature increase. By emerging while the overhead trees are leafless, the plants are exposed to higher light levels than are available after leaf-out. Because these plants have high light needs, they have only a short time to prosper. Many complete their flowering and seed set within a period of a few weeks and then go dormant as the forest canopy closes.

Each species of flora has its own soil, moisture, temperature, and light requirements, and thus, few species occur in all forest types, or range throughout the state. Nonetheless, some are quite common, particularly those tolerant of a wide variety of conditions, e.g., spring beauty, common wood sedge, and woolly blue violet. Others are quite rare, especially those with very specific habitat requirements. Typically, it is unusual variations in the forest environment that provide the most likely habitats for rare species, e.g., sites with extreme edaphic conditions.

With the exception of a few scattered areas, all of the forest in Indiana is composed of deciduous species. See Table P-3 for a list of the known and expected species of deciduous forests.

1800. At this time, the native flora of the state was perhaps at its zenith, both in numbers of individuals and in numbers of species. Natural communities were relatively intact, and the occurrence of invasive exotic species was minimal.

1900. Clearing, but not necessarily timbering, of forest lands brought a reduction of habitat for native species. Most of the species of the state that were present during 1800 probably were still present, but in diminished numbers. A few species that were documented for the state in forest environments and apparently extirpated by 1900 are early coralroot, yellow false foxglove, and cusped bluegrass. Most likely, others disappeared before their occurrence in the state could be documented.*2000.* With the advent of more powerful heavy machinery, particularly the bulldozer and power shovel, extensive drainage and clearing of Indiana's original forest lands had occurred by this time, especially on level or nearly level terrain. Although some previously cleared land has been reclaimed since the mid-1900s, the numbers of individuals of many forest species dropped as the percentage of original forest in the state continued to decline. In addition to clearing, many of the forests were grazed and trampled by livestock, an activity that was detrimental to most species depending on the severity and duration of occupation. Although this activity had declined considerably by 2000, the lasting impacts to compositional change are still evident in the sites that were severely grazed. Telltale signs are a lower diversity of native species and a higher frequency of exotics. Invasive exotic species have been and are a significant threat to the integrity of forest lands. A few of the more detrimental species include garlic mustard, Amur honeysuckle, and Nepalese browntop.

Fire suppression also has played a role in the reduction of certain forest species, especially those that prefer higher light levels than what occurs in dense shade. Dense shade and thick leaf litter accumulations, which are responses to fire suppression, can have deleterious effects on some forest species, especially those in the drier forest communities. Current trends to implement prescribed burning may help to reverse this condition.

A continuing threat to plant populations is the placement of houses and other structures in forest environments.

Forest species extirpated by 2000 include Allegheny vine, northern grape fern, American fly honeysuckle, short-horned rice grass, Hooker's orchid, and round-leaved orchid.

Amphibians and Reptiles

Given that most of Indiana was once covered with hardwood forests, it may not be surprising that forests can have very high herpetofaunal diversity. Species of amphibians and reptiles showing an affinity for forest are listed in Table H-2.

Most of Indiana's amphibians flourish best in closed-canopy forest. In particular, salamanders are most diverse in healthy, mature forests, where they may form a large proportion of the vertebrate biomass.

Many plethodontid salamanders do not require wetlands in which to lay their eggs, so they may be found far from wetlands or streams. Instead of heading for water, they lay their eggs in moist locations beneath woody debris, such as logs. Redback, zigzag, and slimy salamanders are classic examples of this breeding pattern. Other species of plethodontids do require access to streams, but not wetlands, to breed. Examples include the two-lined and ravine salamanders.

Ambystomatid salamanders may also be extremely abundant in forests, even though for much of the year they may prove difficult to find. These salamanders require access to wetlands in order to breed, so will be less abundant or disappear farther away from such habitats or in areas where porous soils preclude wetland formation. Ambystomatid salamanders emerge from their upland forest hideouts in late winter, and descend into ephemeral wetlands to breed. These migrations are often highly synchronized waves of particular species, with individuals sometimes numbering in the thousands. As forest fragments become smaller, or as the wetlands in an area are lost, these salamanders are among the first amphibians to disappear.

Many frogs can be abundant in forests as well, although the diversity is not as great as that of the salamanders. The American toad and the wood frog, aptly named, can be found quite some distance from wetlands, hopping about on the forest floor. Gray treefrogs also make their way deep into forest.

Although we link most turtles to wetlands, lakes, and streams, the eastern box turtle is quite at home in forests. The Blanding's turtle, generally associated with wetlands, can also spend significant time away from wetlands in forested habitats.

A wide variety of snakes live in forests. Across much of the state, the obvious species include the eastern garter snake and the northern ribbon snake. Less obvious is the diverse array of snake species that live secret lives under forest debris. The midland brown snake is one of the most abundant vertebrates in Indiana, though not readily seen due to its secretive nature and diminutive size. The western earth snake, northern red-bellied snake, and midwest worm snake are other not-so-obvious species. Although these snakes are small, there are also very large, but still rarely seen, forms. The timber rattlesnake and northern copperhead may be in full view, but blend into the leaf litter with their cryptic coloration.

Given the sun-warming needs of many snakes and lizards, gaps in the canopy at windthrows, rocky areas, or along forest edges are better places to find forms not mentioned above. The black rat snake, eastern milk snake, and racer are good examples of these. Such openings are better locations as well for lizards, such as the five-lined and broadhead skinks and the eastern fence lizard. Leopard frogs may also be abundant in areas of forest that do not have a closed canopy.

1800. The forest herpetofauna of Indiana were likely fully intact well into the 1800s. Population health for most species likely did not decline substantially during the initial forest clearing for farming.

1900. By the late 1800s and into the early 1900s, local extirpations of forest herpetofauna were likely common. The extensive clearing of forests not only caused direct loss of habitat, but began to impose another significant challenge: fragmentation of the remaining habitat. As roads began to crisscross the landscape, animals that were adapted to the previously continuous habitat were isolated into smaller and smaller forest pockets, often separated from critical resources such as breeding ponds and becoming increasingly susceptible to being killed on roads.

Aggressive drainage or deepening of shallow wetlands were another serious blow to amphibians, limiting opportunities to breed. Eastern box turtles declined initially simply from the loss and fragmentation of their habitat, then declined further as road mortality rose (especially for females) and as a consequence of collection for the pet trade. Forest snakes also declined. Species reliant on amphibians suffered the consequences of losses in prey, while larger, mobile species declined from road mortality and killing by people.

All snakes suffer from people's general antipathy toward them, and likely in many areas any snake found would be killed. The larger species, such as rat snakes and racers, received the greatest "attention," even after some fear of snakes subsided. This fact, compounded by lower densities and greater spatial requirements, would lead the larger species to be locally extirpated first.

2000. To date, no species of forest amphibian or reptile has been extirpated statewide. Nevertheless, local extirpations of forest amphibians and reptiles are likely ongoing for the same reasons as during the previous 150 years: forest removal, fragmentation, the imposition of barriers such as roads, and the removal of wetlands from the forest matrix.

Though documented cases of amphibian die-offs due to disease are unknown for Indiana, this is a growing concern across the United States and elsewhere. Both forest amphibians and forest reptiles are vulnerable.

The spread of the emerald ash borer in northeastern Indiana will likely highly modify the forests of the state. The most direct impacts to herpetofauna of this invasion—and the possible loss of all species of ash—will be on amphibians, and maybe particularly salamanders, as a consequence of the loss of canopy and the resultant increases in insolation and declines in humidity. Such impacts may be temporary, relieved ultimately by closure of the canopy by other species of trees.

The appearance of the common wall lizard along the Ohio River may pose a problem to native lizards via competition, and to reptiles in general via introduced disease.

Birds

One hundred fifty-six species, approximately half of Indiana's annually occurring birds, are characteristic of forested habitats (Table B-2). These species are about equally divided in their affinities for shrubland (pioneering forest) and mature forest, with a considerable number using both. Thus, the drastic changes since 1800 have benefited some birds and greatly reduced the populations of others. The core area for mature forest birds has been, since 1900, the southern half of the state, especially the hilly south-central portion. A key question for midwestern forest bird conservation is: how much habitat fragmentation can forest birds tolerate? Other issues include logging practices, and the amount of standing dead wood left in forests (which are important foraging and nesting sites for woodpeckers and cavity-nesting birds); changes in forest structure caused by invasive plants (abetted by frugivorous birds in some cases); and fire suppression and management.

1800. Birds of the mature forest were most abundant at this time, when large percentages of land were forested in most natural regions of Indiana. Forests of beech and oak experienced the thunder of untold numbers of passenger pigeons seeking the mast of these trees, especially in fall and winter. Wild turkey, another mast eater, was abundant. A score of other species that use mature forest and avoid early successional stages were at peak abundance, including red-bellied and pileated woodpecker, Acadian and great crested flycatcher, red-eyed vireo, wood thrush, ovenbird, Kentucky warbler, and scarlet tanager.

1900. Three large forest birds were extirpated from Indiana by 1900, the passenger pigeon, Carolina parakeet, and ivory-billed woodpecker. Extinction soon followed for at least 2 of them; the ivory-billed woodpecker may still exist in parts of the southeastern United States. Causes included market hunting, general hunting and persecution, and the clearing of forests. Wild turkey was also extirpated by 1900 (Mumford and Keller 1984) due to hunting and forest clearing, and the wood duck became very scarce. Pileated woodpecker was restricted to rugged forested land in southern Indiana. Northern bobwhite increased in the scrubby successional habitat that followed forest clearing. Bewick's wren colonized brushy areas near dwellings and became "the house wren" in the southern half of the state beginning in the 1870s.

2000. Various changes in species abundance occurred in forests, including increases as well as decreases. The wide range of avian responses was not surprising given the many changes to the state's potentially forested lands during the twentieth century. Pileated woodpecker adapted to second-growth forests, spread widely, and became common up to the edges of towns, following decades of limited distribution. Wild turkey, reintroduced at mid-century, became common throughout the state, apparently thriving in the mixture of forest and agricultural lands. Ruffed grouse, a forest species that needs openings, declined in range and numbers. Wood duck, which had been greatly reduced a century earlier, rebounded with protection from unregulated hunting and the installation of artificial nest cavities. Cerulean warbler, a small insectivore of the canopy that requires large mature forest in the breeding season, was in decline. It breeds mainly in the Ohio River valley and is a midwestern "poster species" for the generally threatened neotropical migrant guild (Hamel 1998). American crows changed their winter roosting habitats, leaving forests, scrub, and swamps (Butler 1898) for cities, but retained the behavior of roosting by the thousands (e.g., approximately 50,000 in Terre Haute in the winters of 1996–2005) and returning to forests in March or April to nest.

Two songbirds of the brushy pre-forest, Bewick's wren and Bachman's sparrow, were extirpated by 2000. The likely causes were loss of suitable habitat following the post-European-settlement expansion, perhaps exacerbated for Bewick's wren by competition with the house wren, which expanded southward. Both extirpated species were similarly affected across wide regions outside of Indiana, and Bachman's sparrow was at the edge of its range in Indiana.

Frugivorous birds influenced forest and shrubland composition by accelerating the invasion by exotic plants, especially bush honeysuckle, glossy buckthorn, Oriental bittersweet, and autumn olive, with bird-dispersed seeds.

Mammals

Thirty-seven species of true woodland mammals now occur; 7 extirpated species once occurred in the forests of Indiana; and 12 other species that occur in riparian corridors and plantations appear marginally in forests (Table M-2). Species predominantly limited to forests are the smoky and pygmy shrews, northern myotis, evening bat, red bat, and hoary bat. These bats roost in trees and thus are tied to forest habitats, although they may forage in open areas, like other bats. Five of the 6 shrew species in Indiana occur in forested habitats (least shrew being the exception), but the smoky and pygmy shrews have restricted distributions in the south-central unglaciated hill country. The masked shrew, southeastern shrew, and short-tailed shrew are often found in forests, but may also be found in more open areas. The eastern mole, though more familiar as a denizen of lawns and other open areas, is common in wooded areas.

All records of the southeastern myotis are from hibernating individuals in caves in the wooded areas of southern Indiana, but this species was probably extirpated in the state by about 1985. It has never been known to produce young in Indiana. The swamp rabbit occurs only in the river-bottom woods of the southwestern part of the state, now almost entirely limited to the Gibson County area. The eastern cottontail occurs throughout the state in many habitats, including woods. The 4 tree squirrels—the gray, fox, red, and southern flying squirrels—and the eastern chipmunk are closely associated with woods, whereas the woodchuck often hibernates in burrows in woods, but in the summer usually lives in fields. The squirrels feed heavily on nuts, acorns, and other large-seeded plants; and the fox, gray, and red squirrels often bury nuts. They return to retrieve them later when food is scarce. They find them mostly by going to good places to store them, then using olfaction. However, many stored nuts and seeds are never found and may sprout, thus adding trees to the forest, a good case of mutualism. At the time of European settlement, the gray squirrel was probably the common tree squirrel of Indiana forests; the fox squirrel inhabited savannas and more open areas and moved in as various forests were cut. The woodchuck has been declining in recent years, apparently mostly because of the increase in coyotes. The coyote is a predator on woodchucks and also a competitor for their burrows.

The most abundant mammal in woods throughout Indiana is the white-footed mouse. The beaver, muskrat, and otter are aquatic mammals that will enter woods adjacent to suitable aquatic habitat. The Allegheny wood rat is endangered and presently occurs only on the wooded bluffs along the Ohio River in Harrison and Crawford counties. Earlier, the species occurred farther to the north to at least Monroe County, but it is not known how long it has been absent from there. A decline in food resources is one of several hypotheses that have been suggested as contributing to the decline of the Allegheny wood rat. LoGiudice (2006) suggested that chestnuts may have been an important food source for wood rats and that the demise of the American chestnut tree was one of the factors leading to the demise of the wood rat. The southern bog lemming sometimes occurs in woods, and the meadow jumping mouse is quite often found in moist areas in forests with ample ground cover.

Although the coyote, long-tailed weasel, striped skunk, and white-tailed deer often venture into woods, the gray fox, raccoon, and bobcat are much more closely tied to woodlands. Among the extirpated species, the porcupine, black bear, fisher, mountain lion, and wapiti were closely associated with forests, whereas the bison and gray wolf were less so, though they often entered woodlands.

1800. All of the mammals listed in Table M-2 were present in forested areas in 1800, although the coyote was very uncommon. The bison and wapiti both were extirpated by about 1830, and the black bear, mountain lion, and fisher followed in 1850, 1851, and 1859, respectively. In addition, the white-tailed deer and the beaver were gone by the end of the century, but would be reintroduced at a later date.

1900. Extirpation of the gray wolf and porcupine occurred within the first two decades of the twentieth century. There was a last, questionable record of the wolf in 1908. The coyote remained at very low levels in the early decades of the century. The last known otter was taken at Hovey Lake in 1942, but otters were reintroduced at the end of the century. By 1940, beaver and white-tailed deer had been reintroduced, but both were still rare in most regions.

Between 1950 and 2000, there were some interesting developments. The coyote, beaver, and white-tailed deer became abundant throughout much of the state. The beaver became so abundant that it was often a nuisance; there was little trapping, in part because of low fur prices. The river otter, reintroduced in the 1990s, spread rapidly.

2000. The 3 reintroduced species—white-tailed deer, beaver, and river otter—are currently doing very well. The deer and beaver, in fact, are often pest species, along with the raccoon. The red squirrel is common in northern Indiana, and the southern flying squirrel is abundant in many wood lots throughout the state where there are adequate holes in trees. One can determine if this species is present by tapping on dead stubs that have woodpecker holes up to perhaps 20 ft high. If flying squirrels are present, they will poke their noses out, and if you continue to tap they will come out, climb to the top of the stump, and glide to another tree. Fox squirrels are common throughout the state especially in more open woods. Gray squirrels are common in more remote, heavily wooded areas, but appear to be increasing in west-central Indiana. The white-footed mouse is the most common woodland small mammal, but the woodland vole and short-tailed shrew are common burrowers in moist woodland soils.

Forests by Developmental Stage (Successional Stages)

Old-Field Communities

This pre-forest or early successional (seral) stage arises after forested lands are cleared and used for agriculture or other purposes, and then abandoned. They promptly enter an "old-field" condition with many herbaceous and woody species that are eventually replaced by forest species. Such areas often occur in Indiana when the ground is plowed but not planted or otherwise used, i.e., it is allowed to lie fallow. In that case, early seral stage grasses and forbs grow and the habitat is essentially old field or weedy field. These lands are generally classified as "non-stocked" in forest surveys (Schmidt et al. 2000).

1800. Pre-forest areas occurred on agricultural lands that had been abandoned by Native Americans and early European settlers. There were also some areas recovering from Native American fires, exposed sand dunes, and sandbars along streams. There is no way to determine the actual acreage, but it is likely these habitats only covered a few thousand acres or even less.

1900. There were likely huge areas of pre-forest in 1900 due to the amount of forest clearing that occurred in the late 1800s. Only 3.8 million acres of forest remained in Indiana of the original 20 million acres present in 1800. Data are not available to allow an estimate of the acreage in pre-forest.

2000. The forest survey of 1998 classified 32,000 acres as non-stocked forest land. The National Land Cover Data (NLCD) of 1992 classified 25,878 acres as "transitional" lands, which were defined as "areas transitioning between forest and agriculture, forest clearcuts, temporary clearing of vegetation, or changes due to natural events such as floods or fire" (Table G-1). Forest clear-cuts belong in the seedling/sapling stage, but were not separated in the data. The larger area estimated by the forest survey is probably closer to the actual area of this habitat found across the state since it is based on sampling on the ground while the NLCD estimate is based on satellite imagery.

FLORA. A pioneering flora can vary considerably depending on substrate conditions, available seed sources, and the kinds and degrees of disturbance that brought the site to non-forest conditions. Typically, the first species to appear are annuals, especially those that are wind dispersed. In addition, seeds present in the soil (seed bank) can sprout soon after disturbance. Some early successional annuals include horseweed, common ragweed, common evening primrose, foxtails, fireweed, field garlic, hairy crabgrass, common pepper cress, and fall panicum. See Table P-4 for a list of expected and known species of pre-forest areas.

Unless planted, the earliest successional areas typically are not manifested as grasslands, but sites adjacent to established grasslands—that can serve as seed sources—can develop into grasslands with time. Many old fields do eventually succeed into grasslands. Early colonizing native grasses include common purpletop, nimblewill, little barley, small love grass, fall witch grass, fall panicum, poverty oat grass, northern rush grass, and broom sedge. See Table P-4 for a list of expected and known species of early successional areas.

AMPHIBIANS AND REPTILES. Forest that is in pioneering stages will be more suitable for reptiles than amphibians, given the higher levels of incidental radiation and desiccation. Grasslands that are undergoing succession to shrub or forest will have a combination of species for grassland and forest. American toads and leopard frogs will use them. Snakes such as racers and black rat snakes will be attracted to such areas, as will garter and ribbon snakes. Timber rattlesnakes, northern copperheads, and a variety of the more diminutive species, such as northern brown snakes, will avoid them.

The community of herpetofauna will depend upon the site's history, as an area with a long history of being a grassland will have more related species than a grassy area that was once forest and is now being allowed to return to forest. Many salamander species are slow to colonize this habitat from more forested zones.

BIRDS. This early stage in ecological succession in Indiana typically starts with an abandoned agricultural field that transforms, over several years, into a brushy "old field" in which sapling trees and various shrubs dominate the vegetation. This section deals with the birds that can be found in such habitat up to the point where a closed-canopy pole forest is established, in which there is little herbaceous or ground-level vegetation. Such bird species are sometimes referred to as (forest) "edge species," and they represent a substantial subset of the "transitional" birds discussed later in this chapter.

A fairly large portion (approximately 45%) of Indiana's 309 annually occurring birds can be found in early successional or transitional forested habitats (Tables B-1 and B-2). Species typical of the very early stages of succession include northern bobwhite, eastern kingbird, common yellowthroat, field sparrow, song sparrow, and American goldfinch. The very early stages of succession might also include some obligate grassland birds (see chapter 5) when succession proceeds from an existing grassland, or when an abandoned agricultural field is not immediately dominated by forbs. However, such grassland birds will drop out as woody vegetation begins to dominate. Species typical of the brushier end of the spectrum include brown thrasher, catbird, northern mockingbird, eastern towhee, northern cardinal, and indigo bunting; several of the very early species mentioned above will also linger into the brushy stage. Nearly all of Indiana's diurnal raptors (except eagles and peregrine falcons) will hunt in such areas.

The birds typical of early successional habitat are common and thus familiar to people at least casually aware of birds. However, the brushier end of the old-field spectrum hosts several species that are much less common and/or limited to certain regions of the state, such as American woodcock, whip-poor-will, loggerhead shrike (south), Bell's vireo (west), blue grosbeak (south), blue-winged warbler, prairie warbler, golden-winged warbler (far north), and yellow-breasted chat. Some species now extirpated from Indiana were specific to successional habitats, most notably Bachman's sparrow and Bewick's wren.

Patch size and the landscape context within which such habitat occurs are not as important for these early successional birds as they are for the grassland, wetland, and mature forest birds discussed below. In other words, even relatively small, isolated patches (e.g., 3–4 acres) of successional habitat will likely be occupied by many such species. Some species may prefer early successional habitat in a relatively open context (e.g., loggerhead shrike, blue grosbeak) or forested context (whip-poor-will, blue-winged warbler), but most are landscape generalists.

Historically, Indiana had relatively little successional habitat at the start of the nineteenth century, although wind (major blowdowns) and fire presumably created a steady enough supply of such habitat to maintain populations of the birds that are adapted to it. The destruction of forested habitat that accelerated during the 1800s produced much habitat for these early successional species. The European pioneers felt that the landscape was becoming "civilized" when the cardinal and bobwhite first appeared. There perhaps was another peak in successional habitat during the twentieth century as marginal farmland was abandoned in some places (especially in the southern half of the state) and allowed to revert to forest. At the start of the twenty-first century, however, such early successional habitat is not very common. As a result, some species are much less common than they were several decades ago. Examples include prairie warbler and whip-poor-will (Nolan 1978). The decline in such habitat may also be partly responsible for the current rarity of loggerhead shrike and golden-winged warbler and the extirpation of Bewick's wren and Bachman's sparrow. However, as with transitional birds in general, the birds of early successional habitats can be considered a major beneficiary of the historical patterns of habitat destruction and alteration in Indiana.

A relatively persistent form of brushy vegetation, although it often grows up into a thin line of trees, is the fence row along county roads and between fields. Species listed above as typical of the "brushier end of the old-field spectrum" are found in fence rows. Robinson (1996) specifies fence rows as an important avian habitat in southern Illinois for migrant, nesting, and wintering passerines. In his habitat descriptions, species preferring fence rows are commonly associated with woodland edges and old fields with briar patches.

Early successional habitats (or successional habitats in general) are now relatively rare in Indiana given current agricultural practices. Very early successional habitats, such as recently fallowed agricultural fields, are usually dominated by a variety of non-native forbs. Most obligate grassland birds are not much attracted to such habitats, with the possible exception of dickcissel. Fallow fields with a mixture of grass and forbs may, however, attract a significant complement of grassland birds. For grassland birds, however, landscape context will be important when considering the value of successional habitat. Successional habitat surrounded by much grassland might prove attractive, whereas such habitat surrounded by forest or developed lands will attract few if any grassland birds, with the exception of non-obligate species, such as field sparrow and common yellowthroat. Small plots of such habitat (less than 50 acres) will also attract few grassland birds. Note, however, that successional habitats associated with forest or adjacent to it, with some woody plant invasion, may be important breeding habitat for species that are not currently common in the state, such as American woodcock, prairie warbler, northern bobwhite, whip-poor-will, and chuck-will's-widow. Indeed, a host of breeding bird species are attracted to shrubby successional habitat (Table B-2).

MAMMALS. The mammals of early successional areas are mainly those associated with grasslands, or perhaps more closely with dry grasslands, dry prairie, or even no-till lands, although many annual forbs are present in the latter habitat.

The pioneering forest is essentially shrubland and does not support many species of mammals, although almost any species might pass through this habitat. The species most expected would be the eastern cottontail rabbit, eastern chipmunk, white-foot-

Figure 4.3. Early succession, or sapling, forest. Photo by George Parker.

ed mouse, and predators searching for bird nests and small mammals, e.g., the coyote and red fox. The relatively low biodiversity may be due to the lack of permanence of the habitat and the low diversity of nesting situations.

Young or Seedling/Sapling Forest

Young forests are areas of regenerating forest in the seedling/sapling to pole-timber size (5 inches in diameter) classes (Schmidt et al. 2000), as indicated in Figures 4.3 and 4.4. About 29% of Indiana's forests are currently in this size class (Woodall et al. 2005).

1800. There is no way to estimate the distribution of size classes present within forests in 1800. The GLO survey data might be used to estimate a general distribution of forest size classes found across the state, but this was not done for this project. Observational accounts indicate that large areas were being disturbed across the state, leading to a mix of age classes and also influencing species composition. In 1809, William Johnson told of passing through a thicket of young hickories and oaks, each about as thick as a man's thumb, for 8 mi before coming to the Elkhart River, where he found an Indian village sitting on the edge of a prairie (cited in McCord 1970).

1900. There were 3.8 million acres of timber land in 1901 (Freeman 1908) with about 2.3 million acres of forest recovering from harvest. Forests were in all stages of recovery from the harvests that occurred during the 1800s. Indiana led the nation in hardwood lumber production in 1869, 1879, and 1899 and was second in 1889 (Clark 1987). Total production peaked at 1.3 billion board feet in 1899 in the state. A conservative estimate of 10,000 board feet per acre would mean 130,000 acres of forest were cut in 1899. Around 700 million board feet were cut annually from the state from 1869 to 1899, meaning that about 2.1 million acres were cut over that 30-year period. (The 2.1 million acre estimate is probably low since the volume per acre was likely less than 10,000 board feet.) At least 50% of this area was in early forest in 1900.

2000. The 1998 forest survey of Indiana found 240,300 acres of forest was in the seedling/sapling size class. This size class included 68,800 acres of oak/hickory, 36,000 acres of elm/ash/cottonwood, 73,600 acres of maple/beech, 36,400 acres of cherry/ash/tulip poplar, and 22,500 acres of oak/pine. Other types had less than 2,000 acres each.

FLORA. As the pioneer successional stage ages, perennial herbaceous species and woody species may infiltrate the site. Again, like the pioneer successional stage, species that are capable of wind dispersal are commonly the first to colonize. Depending on the site, examples include species of maple and ash, tulip poplar, eastern cottonwood, sycamore, river birch, trumpet creeper, and sweetgum. Expected herbaceous species include broom sedge, wild garlic, beggar's ticks, common purpletop, golden cassia, marsh fleabane, early goldenrod, black-eyed Susan, common milkweed, blackberry species, and tall goldenrod. See Table P-4 for a list of expected and known species of early forest areas.

Successional forests will vary greatly in species composition depending on their origin. Forests which originate from abandoned pasture land are likely to have tree species such as honey locust, osage orange, and other species whose seeds are spread by livestock or wind. Forests recovering from harvest are likely to retain the species that were present prior to harvest, and early successional species will be pres-

Figure 4.4. Sapling forest being burned. Photo by George Parker.

ent the first few years following harvest. Early successional species such as blackberry usually decline within the first 10 years as tree species grow and produce more shade.

AMPHIBIANS AND REPTILES. The species found within forests in the seedling/sapling stage will depend on the history of the site. Forests that are developing from abandoned agriculture land will have fewer species than will forests developing from forest harvest. Forest that is in early development will be used by herpetofauna much like the pioneering stage. It will be more suitable for reptiles than amphibians, given the higher levels of incidental radiation and desiccation. The salamander community will be poorly developed, likely lacking most species found in mature forest. American toads and leopard frogs will use such areas, as will snakes such as racers, black rat snakes, garter snakes, and ribbon snakes. Timber rattlesnakes, northern copperheads, and a variety of the more diminutive species, such as northern brown snakes, will avoid them.

BIRDS. The seedling/sapling to pole-timber stage is a productive feeding and nesting habitat for birds, inhabited by many species listed in the previous section, especially if shrubs are present. Likely species include black-billed and yellow-billed cuckoo (if wild black cherry saplings and tent caterpillars are present), downy woodpecker, eastern wood-pewee, black-capped or Carolina chickadee, tufted titmouse, blue-winged and prairie warbler, yellow-breasted chat, eastern towhee, song sparrow, northern cardinal, indigo bunting, and American goldfinch.

MAMMALS. The early forest is much like the pioneering forest, and does not support many species of mammals, although almost any species might pass through this habitat. The species most expected would be the cottontail, eastern chipmunk, and white-footed mouse. White-tailed deer use these areas for bedding and feeding.

Pole Stage

The pole stage includes trees that range between 5 and 11 inches in diameter (Figure 4.5).

1800. The GLO survey data might be used to estimate a general distribution of forest size classes found across the state, but that was not done for this project.

1900. If we assume that the 2.1 million acres of forest cut between 1869 and 1899 were allowed to regrow and reached pole size within 20 years, then around 700,000 acres were in the pole size class in 1900.

2000. There were 1,018,100 acres of forest in the pole size class in 1998 (Table G-18; Schmidt et al. 2000). This size class varied by forest survey unit from 188,100 acres in the Upland Flats unit to 365,200 acres in the Knobs unit. This size class varied by forest type with 339,300 acres in oak/hickory, 156,600 acres in elm/ash/cottonwood, 295,800 acres in maple/beech, 117,200 acres in cherry/ash/tulip poplar, 27,900 acres in oak/pine, 11,800 in oak/gum/cypress, 10,100 acres in shortleaf/Virginia pine, and 7,700 acres in white/red/jack pine.

FLORA. The pole stages of forest succession are typically quite dense, and thus deeply shaded. Consequently, many of the species associated with the pioneering and early forest stages disappear, as those species normally have high light needs. If the site was previously completely cleared of its original forest vegetation, the introduction of obligate forest species will likely be quite slow, if at all. Much depends on the proximity to existing forest (to serve as a seed

Figure 4.5. Pole stage forest. Photo by George Parker.

source), how much soil erosion occurred before the tracts were abandoned for agriculture, and time. See Table P-4 for a list of expected and known species of pole stage forests.

AMPHIBIANS AND REPTILES. The presence of these species will depend on the type of disturbance creating the forest. Pole stage stands originating from forest harvest may have similar species as uncut adjacent forests, whereas forests originating from abandoned agriculture or pasture are likely to be different in species composition. Pole stage forest lacks the understory that favors many amphibians. Salamanders will be slow to recolonize such areas, though they may do so on occasion, and thus the diversity of amphibian species will remain low. The canopy may be quite complete, so such areas may not have the attraction for snakes of the earlier successional stages.

BIRDS. Pole stage forest is not likely to be productive for birds because of the lack of understory vegetation, openings, and the feeding opportunities that trees with large trunks and branches provide. Typical species would be leaf-gleaning, fly-catching, or seed-eating birds that do not mind foraging in a rather dense array of leaves at middle to lower heights. These might include eastern wood-pewee, warbling and red-eyed vireo, blue-gray gnatcatcher, indigo bunting, Baltimore oriole, and American goldfinch. However, no bird species would reach peak abundance in this stage, and species diversity would be low relative to other forested or pre-forest habitats.

MAMMALS. Pole forest is much like early forest and does not support many species of mammals, although almost any species of Indiana mammal might pass through this habitat. The species that would most likely be found in this habitat are the same three: the cottontail rabbit, the chipmunk, and the white-footed mouse. The relatively low diversity is because of the multiple trees of about the same size, few tree species, and the lack of larger trees that might provide diverse nesting situations and continuous supplies of food.

Mature or High-Canopy Forests

There are 8 sub-types of mature forest, which are named based on the dominance of certain tree species. In addition to the 8 sub-types, plantations are included in this section. Most vertebrates that occur in one mature forest type occur in others; differences in relative abundance are beyond the scope of this book to describe. Thus, for the flora and each vertebrate group, we will give a single account for mature forest, which may include some comments on associations with particular mature forest types.

Mature forests (Figure 4.6) are dominated by trees greater than 11 inches in diameter (Schmidt et al. 2000). About 70% of Indiana forests are currently in this size class (Woodall et al. 2005). These forests vary in their structural condition and species composition depending on their past history of disturbance and their site condition. Most range from 80 to 120 years in age. A small percentage of forests in Indiana exceed 150 years of age (Spetich et al. 1997). The fol-

Figure 4.6. Mature forest. Photo by George Parker.

Figure 4.7. Oak/hickory forest. Photo by George Parker.

Figure 4.8. Beech/maple forest. Photo by George Parker.

lowing discussions of forest types by time period reflect the potential total area covered by each in all size classes, not the actual area in mature forest.

1800. There are no data which allow an accurate estimate of the area in mature forest in 1800. It is likely, based on the small number of people in the state, that most of the 20 million acres were in mature forest habitat. However, while the trees were relatively mature, it is likely that forest understories were more open, particularly in the northwestern portions of the state near the prairie-forest border, due to the repeated fires set by Native Americans.

Oak/pine: This forest type was restricted to areas where jack, white, and Virginia pine occurred in 1800. Jack and white pine were primarily found in the Northwestern Morainal Natural Region while Virginia pine was restricted to the southern part of the Highland Rim Natural Region.

Oak/hickory (Figure 4.7): Estimates of the land covered by this forest type vary since these forests are transitional to more shade-tolerant species. The timing and amount of land that had been disturbed by Native Americans prior to 1800 would have been an important factor in determining how much land was in oak/hickory versus beech/maple. Lindsey et al.'s presettlement map (1965) indicates there were 6,897,879 acres of oak/hickory (Table G-13). This is probably an underestimate since Lindsey et al. (incorrectly) characterized most of the Central Till Plain as beech/maple. Gordon's (1936) presettlement map indicates that 8,191,874 acres were oak/hickory forests of various types (see Map 1.3). Gordon's map accounts for more of the variation in habitat condition (soil drainage) than does Lindsey et al.'s map.

Oak/gum/cypress: This is a bottomland forest type that includes all forests in which tupelo, blackgum, sweetgum, wet-site oaks, and/or cypress comprise, singly or in combination, a plurality of the stand. Gordon's (1936) presettlement map shows 2,914 acres of bald cypress in the Southwestern Lowlands region and 49,736 acres in the Southern Bottomlands region. He also mapped over 4.1 million acres of northern and southern swamp forest across the state.

Elm/ash/cottonwood: These bottomland forests covered most of the major stream riparian areas in 1800, except around Native American villages and European settlements along the Ohio River and lower Wabash River. There are 4,168,573 acres of riparian habitat in the state, most of which were forested in 1800 (Table G-19). Riparian area varies from 25,270 acres in the Black Swamp region to 1,196,141 in the Central Till Plain region (Table G-19; Map 4.2).

Maple/beech (Figure 4.8): Lindsey et al. (1965) estimated there were 11,659,480 acres of this forest type in presettlement Indiana. Gordon (1936) estimated that this type covered 5,764,486 acres. Gordon's map reflects the variation in site conditions across the Central Till Plain better than Lindsey et al.'s map

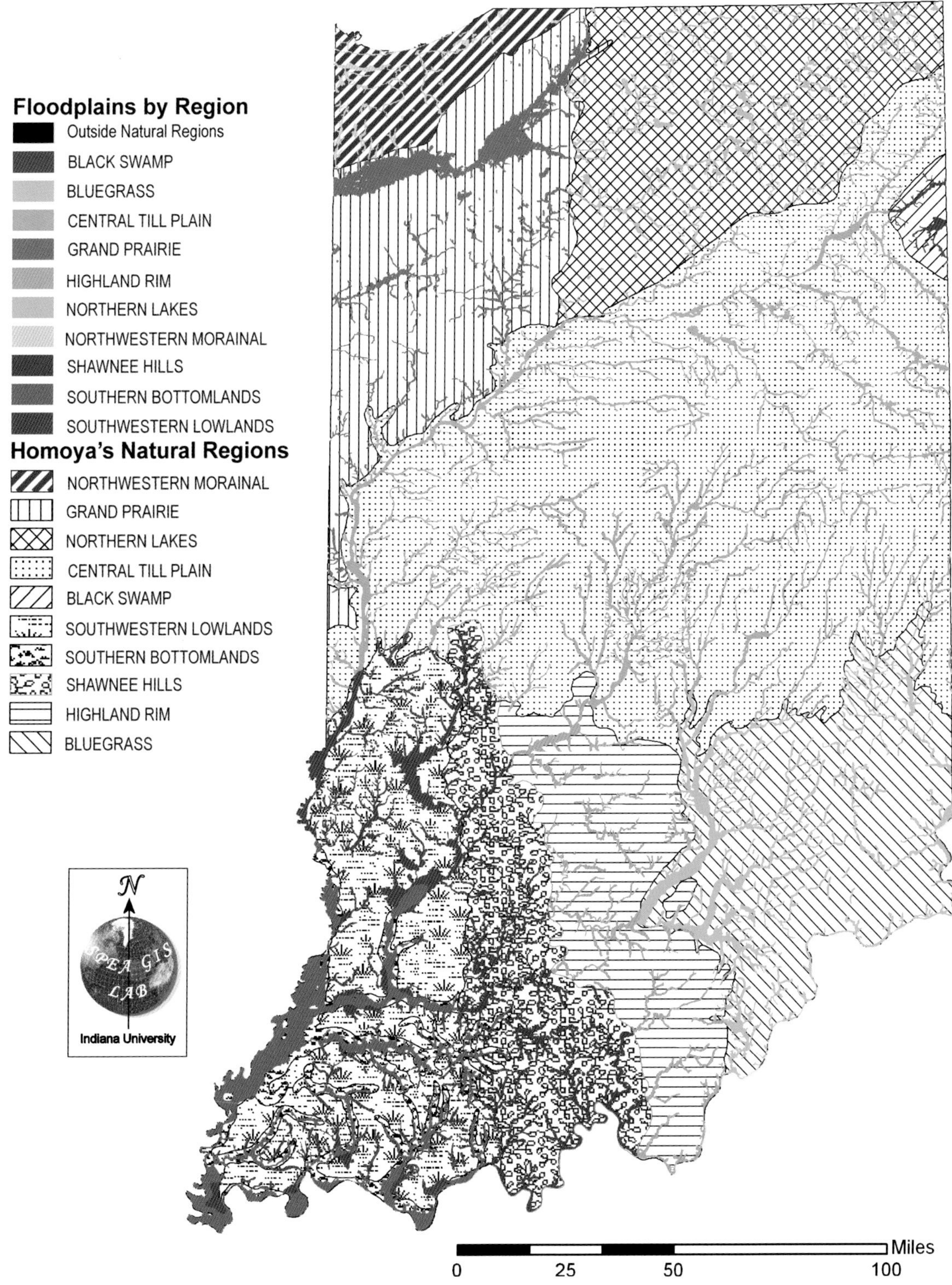

Map 4.2. Indiana floodplains identified by Homoya's Natural Regions.

does. While much of the Central Till Plain has the site conditions to support a beech/maple forest (closer to Lindsey et al.'s estimate), it is not known how much of the region was affected by Native American activities or other disturbances (e.g., tornadoes), resulting in seral oak/hickory forests, so the actual area in beech/maple was probably somewhere between the two estimates.

Cherry/ash/tulip poplar: This forest type is a successional variant of the beech/maple and mixed forest types shown by Lindsey et al. and Gordon (Tables G-13 and G-14).

Aspen/birch: It may be possible to estimate the area of aspen/birch forests found in 1830 using GLO survey data, but it was not done for this project. These are successional forests that colonize a variety of sites

Figure 4.9. Hemlock forest at Hemlock Cliffs, Crawford County. Photo by Ronald L. Richards.

following disturbance, so it is likely that the area covered in 1800 was less than found today.

Evergreen: Coniferous forests were limited to scattered areas of white pine and/or eastern hemlock (Figure 4.9) in the dunes of the Northwestern Morainal region, the western part of the Central Till Plain and Shawnee Hills regions, and Virginia pine in the southern part of the Highland Rim region. Scattered areas of eastern red cedar also occurred within natural regions south of the Central Till Plain. Eastern red cedar was restricted to steep, rocky sites not prone to fire. White pine was restricted to dune soils in the Northwestern Morainal region and a few isolated remnants in west-central Indiana. Shortleaf pine is not native to the state and was not present in 1800.

Plantations: There is no indication that European settlers or Native Americans planted trees in the early 1800s. There were plenty of trees for their needs, and they were more concerned with clearing forests to build homes and produce crops.

1900. Between 1 and 2 million acres of mature forest are believed to have been present in 1900 based on data in Table G-16, if the first- and second-grade forest acreage is used as an indicator. While some trees may have reached saw-timber size from the cutting in the mid-1800s, most were being cut as small saw timber and/or as poles for posts, poles, and railroad ties.

Oak/pine: These forests were heavily cut by 1900, probably reducing the pine component.

Oak/hickory: The area in this forest type was probably proportionally similar to that found today if harvest records are indicators (Clark 1987). Over 67% of the timber harvested in Indiana between 1869 and 1910 was oak species.

Oak/gum/cypress: This was similar to the area found in the state in the twenty-first century.

Elm/ash/cottonwood: Riparian areas were the first areas to be cleared for agriculture during the 1800s and had been largely cut or cleared by 1900 (Freeman 1908). Around 232 million board feet of lumber were cut in 1899 from sycamore, elm, ash, and gum (Clark 1987), which would amount to 23,200 acres, assuming 10,000 board feet per acre.

Maple/beech: While there are no estimates of forest by type in 1900, it is reasonable to assume that this type covered about the same area as we find today.

Cherry/ash/tulip poplar: Forest harvest tends to increase the amount of this forest type, so its acreage was likely similar to what is found in the twenty-first century.

Aspen/birch: There was probably more of this type than is found today, because this association invades heavily disturbed sites, which were ubiquitous in the 1800s.

Evergreen: Most coniferous forests were likely cut during the 1800s since no old stands are found in the state. White pine, Virginia pine, and eastern red cedar probably remained, but were cut for various forest products during the 1800s. Eastern red cedar was cut for posts during the 1800s, and periodic fires restricted its range.

Plantations: Some plantations were being established around 1900, but the total area was probably less than 1,000 acres (Freeman 1908). Plantations were largely for the production of posts with catalpa and black locust the main species planted. Table G-16 provides data on the number of trees planted in 1902 by county and natural region.

2000. The forest survey of 1998 (Schmidt et al. 2000) found 3,051,900 acres of forest in the saw-timber size class. This habitat varied from 364,800 acres in the Upland Flats unit to 1,271,300 acres in the Knobs unit. This size class varied by forest type with 1,195,700 acres of oak/hickory, 467,500 acres of elm/ash/cottonwood, 1,024,500 acres of maple/beech, 173,800 acres of cherry/ash/tulip poplar, 92,300 acres of oak/pine, 39,100 acres of shortleaf/Virginia pine, 22,200 acres of white/red/jack pine, and 29,700 acres of oak/gum/cypress.

Oak/pine: This type of forest has greatly increased since 1900 as hardwood species have invaded native and planted pine stands. There were 77,200 acres of this type in 1998 with over half (41,100 acres) in the Knobs unit of south-central Indiana (Table G-17). This type will decline in the future as hardwood species replace both planted and native pine species.

Oak/hickory: This type covers more forest land in Indiana than any other with over 1.6 million acres reported in 1998. This forest type currently dominates many sites due to disturbances in the 1800s but will gradually decrease as oak and hickory species are replaced by more tolerant species, such as sugar maple (Woodall et al. 2005). Oak/hickory forests vary greatly in species composition across the state and by site condition within a local area. For example, bur oak, swamp white oak, and pin oak occupy wet depressional habitats, while northern red, white, chinquapin, and shingle oak occur on better-drained upland sites on the Central Till Plain. This forest type is common in all forest survey units and natural regions with over half the acreage of this type found in the Knobs unit: 821,700 acres (Table G-17).

The association of oak and hickory species can occur in both moist and dry habitats. On dry sites, the common species are combinations of black, scarlet, white, chestnut, post, chinquapin, and blackjack oaks along with pignut and mockernut hickories. On moist sites, red, white, Shumard's, cherrybark, and shingle oaks can be found growing with bitternut, big shellbark, and shagbark hickories. Oak- and hickory-dominated forests were some of the most extensive types in the state, at least in the unglaciated hills of south-central Indiana, that is, the Shawnee Hills and Highland Rim natural regions. Oak- and hickory-dominated forests were likely a more common type in 1800 and 1900 than in 2000, in part because of the overall reduction of forest in the state due to clearing, and also because of a century of fire suppression. Fire suppression reduces light levels (by allowing the development of a dense mid-canopy) and thus degrades the site for oak and hickory regeneration. See Table P-5 for a list of species of this type.

Oak/gum/cypress: The forest survey of 1998 indicated that there were 42,800 acres of this forest type across the state, mostly in the Northern and Lower Wabash units. Forty-five percent of the oak/gum/cypress type occurs in the Northern unit, 34% in the Lower Wabash, 18% in the Knobs, and 3% in the Upland Flats unit.

Elm/ash/cottonwood: This type primarily occurs in riparian areas (Table G-17). These forests cover 660,100 acres across the state, or about 15.8% of the total riparian habitat. Forty-two percent of the elm/ash/cottonwood type is in the Northern unit, 25% in the Lower Wabash, 19% in the Knobs, and 14% in the Upland Flats unit.

Maple/beech: This type covered 1,393,900 acres of the forest land across the state in 1998 (Table G-17). Acreage varied by survey unit from 216,700 acres in the Upland Flats unit of southeastern Indiana to 537,000 in the Knobs unit of south-central Indiana.

Sugar maple and American beech forest was and is one of the more common forest types in the state. It occurs statewide, with the exception of the Grand Prairie Natural Region. The sites for the type are typically mesic, and thus the species found are ones that benefit from moist soil conditions and shade. Tree and shrub associates include tulip poplar, white ash, American linden, northern red oak, white oak, shagbark hickory, bladdernut, maple-leaved viburnum, and spicebush. Spring ephemerals produce some of their best displays in maple/beech forest. Some common ones include spring beauty, yellow adder's tongue, toothwort, harbinger of spring, and northern bitter cress. The flora of the maple/beech forest, aside from the introduction of exotics and the lesser extent in area of the type, probably has not changed considerably from 1800. See Table P-5 for a list of species of this forest type.

Cherry/ash/tulip poplar: These forests have wild black cherry, white ash, and tulip poplar comprising the majority of the stand. There were 327,400 acres of this forest type across the state in 1998. This type covered 147,600 acres of the Northern survey unit, with the remaining acreage about equally divided among the other three units, which had around 60,000 acres each.

The cherry/ash/tulip poplar forest type occurs on sites similar to those with maple/beech, and thus harbors a similar flora. It can occur in most parts of the state, with the exception of the Grand Prairie Natural Region. See Table P-5 for a list of species of this forest type.

Aspen/birch: This forest type includes stands where most of the stock is quaking aspen, bigtooth aspen, and paper birch. This type is transitional with 7,200 acres occurring across the state. It is found in the Knobs unit (4,800 acres) and the Northern unit (2,400 acres).

Quaking aspen and white birch forest is principally confined to the Chicago Lake Plain section of the Northwestern Morainal Natural Region adjacent to Lake Michigan. Quaking aspen has a considerable range across northern Indiana, but the white birch is quite restricted in the state, mostly to the Lake Michigan area. The sites are relatively level and on moist, acidic sand. Red maple is a common associate, as are cinnamon fern, New York fern, winterberry, Canada mayflower, and swampy dewberry. Some of the rare species found here are follicle sedge, swamp star sedge, running ground pine, and northern weak sedge. See Table P-5 for a list of species of this forest type.

Evergreen: The area of coniferous forest is much larger in the twenty-first century due to reduced fire and grazing, which allowed eastern red cedar and Virginia pine to expand into abandoned farmland. Pine trees were also planted over large areas of abandoned farmland and strip-mined lands in the 1930s–1950s to reduce soil erosion. Eastern red cedar, Virginia/shortleaf pine, and white pine are the major species currently found in the state. Jack pine is a minor species occurring on dune soils in the Northwestern Morainal region. Eastern hemlock is a minor species at various locations, mostly steep slopes and cliffs in the west-central and southern parts of the state. Coniferous forests (white pine, shortleaf/Virginia pine, and eastern red cedar) currently cover 118,400 acres, primarily in the Knobs, Lower Wabash, and Northern survey units (Schmidt et al. 1998). White pine was widely planted during the 1900s to control soil erosion on abandoned farmland, for Christmas tree production, and in conservation reserve plantings for wildlife habitat and soil erosion. It is also commonly planted in suburban habitats as an ornamental. White pine covered 29,900 acres (not including Christmas tree plantations) in the Northern, Lower Wabash, and Knobs units.

Shortleaf pine, along with loblolly pine, was planted on badly eroded, abandoned farmland in southern Indiana during the 1940s and 1950s. Virginia pine has expanded by colonizing abandoned pasture land in southern Indiana. Shortleaf/Virginia pine forest covered 51,000 acres, mostly in the Lower Wabash and Knobs units (primarily in the Highland Rim and Shawnee Hills regions). A mix of oak and pine covers another 77,200 acres. With the abandonment of pastures and reduced fire in the 1900s, eastern red cedar has become more abundant and widespread. This species covered 37,500 acres in the Knobs and Upland Flats units in 1998 (Table G-17). Mixed eastern red cedar/hardwoods covered an additional 79,800 acres in those units plus the Lower Wabash unit.

The occurrence of pine species anywhere in the state is likely in combination with one or more species of oak, except in sphagnum bogs, where white pine occurs alone. In addition to white pine and Virginia (scrub) pine, jack pine also is native to Indiana. Its range is quite restricted, occurring only in the dunes bordering Lake Michigan. There, it commonly associates with black oak, juneberry, witch hazel, sassafras, late low blueberry, and Pennsylvania oak sedge (Swink and Wilhelm 1994). In southern Indiana, the most common tree associate of Virginia (scrub) pine is chestnut oak. White pine might have any of several oak species growing with it, including red, white, and/or black oak. In 1800, pine species were likely more common in the oak/pine habitats, in that fire might have kept areas more open, providing more light for the pine species. Logging had reduced these species by 1900. See Table P-5 for a listing of plants in oak/pine forests.

FLORA. Mature forest is the only stage of the forest successional continuum that provides a suitable environment for a great variety of forest species. Since these communities are approaching stability, various forest strata are well developed, and a high diversity of obligate forest understory species are usually present. Diversity depends on site conditions, especially the edaphic, and is also influenced by topography and microclimate. As noted in the pole stage discussion, this diversity will be depauperate if the site was ever completely cleared of forest vegetation down to mineral soil. See Table P-5 for a list of the species of mature forests.

"Original" forests are those which have been in continuous forest and whose soils have been little disturbed. Thus, a site that was under cultivation for some time and then revegetated with trees would not be considered an original forest. Original forest composition varies greatly, depending on a number of environmental and geographic variables. In general, it is thought that the original forests of 1800 were the most diverse with native species, followed by those in 1900. In 2000, the original forest, if not too disturbed and too small in area, still maintains a high level of native species diversity, but forest fragmentation and the invasion of exotic species may be impacting diversity. See Table P-6 for a list of species of original forests.

At some sites where the canopy strata are so compact that little light reaches the forest floor, some species do not thrive or they disappear. For example, forest dominated by sugar maple tends to have fewer understory species than does oak-dominated forest with more open canopies. This is more likely in mesic forests situated in deep ravines. In drier upland sites, more light is typically available. Indeed, a great percentage of species in dry upland forests have fairly high light requirements, and thus light availability is crucial. Fire keeps canopy strata open, providing more light, at least to a degree that benefits species on the forest floor. In addition, fire consumes leaf litter, aiding forest floor species. See Table P-6 for a list of species of old forests.

Upland forest exists on well-drained sites throughout the state. Species associated with this type also require well-drained soils, and are usually specific to certain substrate types, e.g., sandy, acidic, alkaline, etc. The largest expanses of Indiana upland forest in the twenty-first century exist in the Shawnee Hills and Highland Rim natural regions. For species composition, see Table P-6.

White pine is rarely, if ever, canopy-dominant in Indiana. Its natural occurrence is quite restricted, confined mostly to the Big Pine Creek and Bear Creek watersheds in the west-central counties (Entrenched Valley section of the Central Till Plain Natural Region) and to the dunes and bogs adjacent to Lake Michigan (Valparaiso Moraine section of the Northwestern Morainal Natural Region). However, numerous white pine plantations exist throughout the state. The native white pine occurrences are mostly on well-drained substrates, such as steep, rocky slopes, or on deep sand. A few occurrences are in wetlands, including sphagnum bogs. The flora associated with white pine varies according to substrate. In the well-drained sites, the flora is similar to that found on sites dominated by hardwoods. However, where pine occurs on rock outcrops, plants of more northern affinities may be found, e.g., Canada blueberry, dwarf honeysuckle, checkerberry, wild sarsaparilla, and Canada yew.

Species of northern affinities also occur in the areas of white pine which border Lake Michigan and in the sphagnum bogs nearby. The last known population of Hooker's orchid was in a mature white pine stand in the dunes (Homoya 1993). In the bog habitat, white pine grows with American larch, highbush blueberry, black chokeberry, Virginia chainfern, pitcher plant, and poison sumac. See Table P-5 for species that could occur in white pine forests.

Native Virginia pine forests are restricted to the steep slopes and crests of hills in the southern Knobstone Escarpment section of the Highland Rim Natural Region. Shortleaf pine is not native to the state, although it probably exists in some pine plantations in the south. Virginia pine exists in plantations, as well as in abandoned fields, where it naturalizes. Thus, the occurrence of Virginia pine, including the plantations and naturalized sites, is possibly greater now than at 1800 or 1900. Sites with native Virginia pine are typically xeric, rocky, and acidic. Commonly associated species include chestnut oak, black oak, red maple, pignut hickory, late low blueberry, black huckleberry, cat brier, goat's rue, and poverty oat grass. See Table P-5 for a list of species in this forest type; and see also the listing under the oak/pine type in the same table for additional expected species.

In 1800, eastern red cedar was confined to steep bluffs and rock outcrops, as this fire-intolerant species was able to escape both wildfires and the shade of deciduous forests at these sites. Following European settlement, and the control of fire, eastern red cedar was free to colonize fence rows and fields throughout the state. Perhaps the oldest living trees in Indiana are red cedar. The large, twisted branches and trunks of those growing on exposed, dry cliff edges attest to their antiquity. Eastern red cedar is especially prevalent on limestone in the Shawnee Hills, Highland Rim, and Bluegrass natural regions. In the twenty-first century, red cedar is quite common, especially in the southern half of the state. Plants commonly associated with red cedar include blue ash, chinquapin oak, redbud, hop hornbeam, aromatic sumac, cat brier, dogbane, nodding wild onion, wild yam, and poverty oat grass. In the twenty-first century, Japanese honeysuckle and tree-of-heaven are two common invasive species that seriously compete with native vegetation on red cedar sites. Neither was present in 1800, nor even in 1900, at least outside of cultivation. See Table P-5 for a list of species in this forest type.

AMPHIBIANS AND REPTILES. When forest is well established, it takes on the microclimatic and structural aspects which make it attractive to many salamanders and frogs. Protection from direct solar radiation, elevated moisture levels, and the availability of moist refugia and many hiding places due to the prevalence of downed dead wood should encourage the full diversity of forest herpetofauna. Mature forest will also have areas with open canopy as the result of senescent tree death, windthrow, and other factors. Thus, even with a nearly complete canopy, mature forest will offer the canopy gaps attractive to some snakes and lizards.

Oak/hickory forest is a habitat that will have a high diversity of amphibians and reptiles, carrying the full array of species observed for any forests in the state. Species may segregate somewhat based on moisture levels and whether an area is on a ridge versus a ravine bottom.

The herpetofauna of maple/beech forest can be very diverse, such that most any forest amphibian and reptile will be found in this type. Salamanders will be particularly diverse, and reach high densities. Plethodontid salamanders, such as redback, zigzag, and slimy salamanders (Figure 4.10), will be found throughout the forest, given that they do not require wetlands in which to lay their eggs. Species such as the two-lined and long-tailed salamanders will occur in those areas where they might reach streams to breed. Depending on the location in the state, eastern newt; a plethora of ambystomatids, such as spotted salamanders, Jefferson's salamanders, blue-spotted salamanders, and smallmouth salamanders; and various hybrids of these species will occur where wetlands are available for reproduction. Gray treefrogs, American toads, and wood frogs can be quite abundant in maple/beech forest. Leopard frogs will be found closer to emergent wetlands. The eastern box turtle can be locally abundant in large tracts of beech/maple forest, as can the eastern garter snake, northern ribbon snake, and midland brown snake.

Figure 4.10. Slimy salamander. Photo by Bruce Kingsbury.

The herpetofauna of elm/ash/cottonwood forest can be very diverse, such that most any forest amphibian and reptile could be found in this type. In those areas where the forest is in a riparian zone, plethodontid salamanders like the redback, two-lined, northern slimy, and ravine salamander may all occur. Eastern newts and the ambystomatid salamanders, such as spotted, Jefferson's, blue-spotted, and smallmouth may also occur. In more lowland areas prone to flooding, many of these species will drop out. Gray treefrogs, American toads, and wood frogs can be quite abundant in elm/ash/cottonwood forest. Leopard frogs will also be found in lowland settings. The eastern box turtle can be locally abundant in large tracts of elm/ash/cottonwood forest, as can be the eastern garter, northern ribbon, and midland brown snakes.

BIRDS. Mature eastern hardwood forest, specifically upland deciduous forest, is a characteristic habitat for 104 species, including 2 species now extirpated (Table B-2). Hardwood forests dominated by oak and hickory may support higher bird densities than those dominated by maple and beech, but the avian species composition for both types is similar. Oak foliage supports many caterpillars attractive to birds (Marquis and Whelan 1994), and acorns are avidly sought by wild turkeys, red-headed woodpeckers, blue jays, and other species. Fire frequency is an important variable (Aquilani et al. 2003), and topography is important for at least one slope-nesting species, the worm-eating warbler. A few species nest only along streams (e.g., eastern phoebe, Louisiana waterthrush). Latitude has some influence on species composition: southern forests support substantial numbers of some species that are absent or rare in the north (e.g., Kentucky, hooded, and worm-eating warbler; see Webster 1998).

Common nesting species of mature hardwood forest include wild turkey, turkey vulture, red-tailed hawk, yellow-billed cuckoo, eastern screech-owl, great horned owl, barred owl, ruby-throated hummingbird, 6 woodpeckers (red-bellied, pileated, downy, hairy, red-headed, and northern flicker), eastern wood-pewee, Acadian and great crested flycatchers, red-eyed and yellow-throated vireos, blue jay, American crow, Carolina and black-capped chickadees, tufted titmouse, white-breasted nuthatch, Carolina wren, blue-gray gnatcatcher, wood thrush, ovenbird, Kentucky warbler, scarlet tanager, and brown-headed cowbird. In addition, many species whose primary habitat is floodplain forest or pioneering/transitional woods also have a presence in mature forest (often in gaps), and some are very common (indigo bunting, northern cardinal, eastern towhee). In Table B-2, a code "2" indicates species that use mature upland hardwoods as a secondary habitat (41 of the 104 total species).

Besides the 30 or so common nesting species, an almost equal number of uncommon or rare species also use mature hardwoods as their primary habitat. This includes declining or local species such as ruffed grouse (which needs clearings within forest), broad-winged hawk, and cerulean warbler. Nest parasitism by brown-headed cowbirds and nest predation by other animals are high in disturbed forests, and these burdens increase with the extent of forest fragmentation. Indiana data from the relatively unfragmented Hoosier National Forest contributed to a late twentieth-century analysis of the problem in midwestern landscapes (Robinson et al. 1995).

Among the U.S. Geological Survey's Breeding Bird Survey routes in Indiana, the one with the highest percentage of deciduous forest (97%; Hoosier, route no. 35900) indicates what extensive mature hardwood forest (with some significant pine stands) can support in south-central Indiana. The 25-mi route follows ridge roads east of Lake Monroe in Hoosier National Forest in Monroe and Jackson counties (U.S. Geological Survey 2006). The 10 most frequently detected species, in descending order, were red-eyed vireo, American crow, scarlet tanager, indigo bunting, Acadian flycatcher, ovenbird, tufted titmouse, pileated woodpecker, northern cardinal, and wood thrush. Seventy species were detected, including an impressive 18 species of warblers. The absence of open habitat was confirmed by low numbers of American robins, red-winged blackbirds, common grackles, and song sparrows.

Mature hardwoods are important for species migrating to and from breeding grounds in the mixed deciduous/evergreen forests of the U.S.–Canada border and in the boreal forest of Canada (see "Migration" column in Table B-2). Such species include the yellow-bellied sapsucker, blue-headed and Philadelphia vireos, ruby-crowned kinglet, 3 thrushes, and 15 warblers. Nonbreeders that winter primarily in mature upland forest, joining many permanent residents, include the yellow-rumped warbler, white-throated sparrow, and purple finch.

One extinct species, the passenger pigeon, and one long thought to be extinct, the ivory-billed woodpecker (apparently rediscovered in Arkansas in 2005–2006), once inhabited mature hardwoods forest. Indiana data for the woodpecker are shadowy, but there are many reports for the pigeon (Mumford and Keller 1984). The immense pigeon flocks, which ate acorns (acting as seed predators), broke branches, and nested in colonies probably had more of an impact on beech, oak, and hickory forests than any other single bird species. Although nesting colonies of pigeons were larger in Michigan, many pigeons nested singly or in colonies in Indiana (Butler 1898). Another iconic extinct species, the Carolina parakeet, inhabited floodplain forest more than upland forest (see the section "Forested Wetlands and Riparian Wooded Corridors").

Only a few species are so strongly associated with evergreen (conifer) forest that they are absent or rare in Indiana's extensive deciduous forests. Nesting species in this category are sharp-shinned hawk, long-eared owl, pine warbler, and black-throated green warbler. All but the pine warbler are localized or rare even within conifer forests (Castrale et al. 1998). One other nesting species, the chipping sparrow, is also characteristic of evergreen forest, but is mainly found in an alternative, vastly more common habitat: large mowed lawns with scattered trees. Wintering and migrant species with a strong affinity for conifers include the fairly common red-breasted nuthatch and golden-crowned kinglet, the uncommon northern saw-whet owl, and the rare red crossbill and white-winged crossbill.

Many birds of mature deciduous forest also inhabit mature conifer forest. These include various woodpeckers, flycatchers, chickadees, white-breasted nuthatch, tufted titmouse, thrushes, vireos, warblers, and sparrows. Most raptors—for example, red-tailed hawks, turkey vultures, and all owls—like to roost in conifer stands or in isolated conifers. Only species with notable affinities for evergreen forest as a secondary habitat are listed in Table B-2; the list of species that use conifers would be much longer. Remnant stands of eastern hemlock (in Shades State Park, for example) or pines sometimes attract nesting by a few warblers that breed mainly in the boreal evergreen forests of Canada: magnolia and Blackburnian warblers and the local but annual black-throated green warbler. One conifer, the eastern red cedar (juniper), can be an important source of "berries" for the frugivorous cedar waxwing, American robin, hermit thrush, northern mockingbird, and others. Field sparrows, among others, like to nest in red cedar.

MAMMALS. Mature forest has dead and dying trees, which present a greater diversity of nesting and hiding sites, leading to a greater diversity of mammal species. In reality, many of the species found here are quite abundant on the edges of the forests, rather than in them, because of a greater diversity of plant life and food there. The mammals most associated with old-growth forest are indicated in Table M-2. Many of the species indicated in this table occur throughout the state. However, the otherwise widespread masked shrew is absent in the south-central unglaciated hills, while the smoky and pygmy shrews occur only in those hills. The southeastern shrew occurs in the unglaciated hill country and in the southwest portion of the state. The southeastern myotis is listed in Table M-2, but was probably extirpated in the state as of about 1985. The silver-haired bat is only present during spring and fall migration. The pipistrelle is very uncommon or absent in the northern part of the state; the evening bat is found in southern Indiana, especially in the lower Wabash floodplain, but it is also found in a few other places in southern Indiana. The swamp rabbit is found only in the vicinity of northern and southern Gibson County, with a few in Posey County (Hovey Lake) and in southern Knox County to the north. The red squirrel occurs in the northern half of the state and the wood rat only along and near the bluffs of the Ohio River in Crawford and Harrison counties. The 7 extirpated species (at the end of Table M-2) were all present in the woods of Indiana in earlier times, but were gone before 1920.

Most of the forest mammals occur in most kinds of forest. However, some are more particular. Mammals expected in oak/gum/cypress forests are indicated in Table M-2. The southeastern myotis might have been present earlier, but it is probably not now. The silver-haired bat migrated through the area in the spring and fall. The swamp rabbit would be expected, but is now extirpated, or nearly so, in much of the area in which this habitat occurs. It presently occurs mostly in northern and southern Gibson County along the Wabash River. The river otter earlier occurred in this habitat before extirpation in 1942.

Red cedar forest also has a somewhat distinctive set of mammals. Although many of the mammals of forest systems could occur there, the most typical are gray squirrel, white-footed mouse, raccoon, and Allegheny wood rat. The wood rat today has a very limited distribution in Harrison and Crawford counties.

The 10 extant mammal species most likely to occur in pine forests are listed in Table M-2. The most common of these are short-tailed shrews (under pine needles), white-footed mice in the trees and on the ground, and red squirrels, which spend much of their time in conifer trees when available. Among Indiana's extirpated species, the porcupine and fisher were most closely associated with white pine forest. In 1800, the porcupine and fisher were still present and probably occurred in white pine forest. The fisher was extirpated about 1859. The porcupine was still present in 1900 and was not extirpated until about 1918.

Mammals of forested uplands are indicated in Table M-2, totaling 31 presently existing and 6 extirpated species.

1800. All 37 species indicated for mature forest (Table M-2) probably occurred in 1800. The coyote was uncommon, and mainly occurred in the north. The masked shrew probably occurred throughout the state except in the south-central unglaciated hills in 1800, whereas the smoky and pygmy shrews occurred only in those hills, although they were not discovered until 1982. The southeastern shrew occurred in the unglaciated hill country and in the southwest corner of the state to the west of the unglaciated hills. This distribution of shrews has changed little.

The southeastern myotis was a resident at least in winter in some caves in the south-central part of Indiana. The big-eared bat could have been a resident, but more likely was an accidental from Kentucky as is the case now. The silver-haired bat was present only during its spring and fall migration. The pipistrelle was probably uncommon or absent in the northern part of the state, and likely less common than today because there were few abandoned mines in some of the areas now occupied by this species. The evening bat was found in southern Indiana, especially in the lower Wabash and White River floodplains, but was probably in the bottoms associated with some other larger streams as well.

The swamp rabbit was found in the southwestern counties east through Warrick and possibly into western Perry County, north perhaps as far as southern Sullivan County or even southern Vigo County. The red squirrel occurred in the northern half of the state. The wood rat occurred primarily along the bluffs of the Ohio River in Crawford and Harrison counties, and probably for some distance north, perhaps to Orange County or even Monroe.

The extirpated species (the porcupine, gray wolf, black bear, fisher, mountain lion, wapiti, and bison) were all probably present in this habitat in 1800. The porcupine occurred mostly in the northern part of the state. The wapiti was probably quite uncommon in 1800.

1900. Probably all of these species (Table M-2) occurred in woodlands of Indiana in 1900, except for the black bear, fisher, mountain lion, wapiti, and bison, all of which had become extirpated during the nineteenth century, and the coyote was still probably not very abundant. The black bear, fisher, mountain lion, and wapiti all became extirpated between 1830 and 1860, and the gray wolf and porcupine would have been nearly gone, as they were extirpated from the state by 1908 and 1918, respectively. Most of these species were probably extirpated by over-hunting and -trapping, and by people killing "predators."

The white-tailed deer and the American beaver were extirpated from the state by 1900. They were hunted and trapped out, respectively. However, both of these latter species were reintroduced early in the twentieth century and would thrive late in that century. The silver-haired bat was present only during its spring and fall migration. The pipistrelle was probably uncommon or absent in the northern part of the state. The wood rat might still have occurred for some distance to the north (perhaps to Orange County) at this time.

2000. Many of the woodland species (Table M-2) are still in Indiana in the early twenty-first century. The southeastern myotis is listed in the table, but it decreased over several decades and was probably gone by the early 1980s. The reason for this is unknown. The big-eared bat remains a rare accidental from Kentucky. The pipistrelle is still very uncommon in the northern part of the state, but its numbers increased in the latter part of the twentieth century, perhaps as it dispersed into areas with abandoned coal mines which can be used as hibernacula. The evening bat is found in southern Indiana, especially in the lower Wabash floodplain and its major tributaries, from Vigo County south to the Ohio River, but there are outlier populations in hardwood forest along the Muscatatuck River, near the Indianapolis International Airport, and at Camp Atterbury. It now lives mainly in hollow trees whereas in the mid- to late twentieth century it had expanded its summer range to include buildings as maternity roosts. However, no evening bats have been known to use buildings as maternity roosts since 1995. The Indiana myotis is not really a forest species, but it has been slowly increasing in Indiana, whereas it has been decreasing range-wide. The Indiana myotis is more an edge species, roosting under loose bark usually in trees where the loose bark is in full sun. Their hibernacula, however, are mostly in caves in forest.

The swamp rabbit at the beginning of the twenty-first century occurs only in Wabash River bottoms, mostly in the Pearl Island and Long Pond areas of southern and northern Gibson County. The wood rat now occurs only along and near the bluffs of the Ohio River in Crawford and Harrison counties. The coyote has thrived in Indiana since the mid-1980s. (Coyotes generally do not call until they reach substantial populations, and they did not call earlier. Whitaker heard them calling in Indiana for the first time during the 1980s, and has heard them commonly since.)

The extirpated species were all gone by 1920. The table indicates their approximate year of extirpation in the state. Although the otter had been extirpated about 1942, it was reintroduced and is now increasing in number and range. The white-tailed deer and the American beaver, which were extirpated from the state by 1900, were reintroduced starting in the 1920s; both were thriving by the late 1970s and early 1980s.

The red squirrel occurs only in hardwoods in the northern half of the state. The Allegheny wood rat occurs only along the bluffs overlooking the Ohio River in Perry, Crawford, and Harrison counties. The meadow jumping mouse occurs in woodland clearings where ground cover is fairly heavy. Stands of impatiens are particularly good habitat for this species. The mink, muskrat, and beaver occur along lakes and streams in woodland situations.

Sub-Habitats

Forested Wetlands and Riparian Wooded Corridors

Bald cypress forests have been uncommon in Indiana, being restricted to the far southwestern part of the state in the Southern Bottomlands Natural Region. There are only a few current examples, perhaps the best of which is found in Twin Swamps Nature Preserve in Posey County (Figure 4.11). Bald cypress typically grows in deep swamps ponded continuously, or nearly so, and thus the co-occurrence with oak is not likely. The possible exception might be with overcup oak, and perhaps pin oak and swamp white oak. These are fairly tolerant of short periods of flooding, but not for the durations that cypress can tolerate. The same holds true for gum, unless the gum is water tupelo, a species that can grow in water that is as deep as cypress can handle, and for as long. However, water tupelo is not native to Indiana, nor has it naturalized in the state. Bald cypress was extensive in one area, Knox County, where over 20,000 acres formerly occurred (Ridgway 1872b). By 2000, almost all of that was gone, and today there are fewer than 10 occurrences of the type in the state (Indiana Natural Heritage Data Center 2005). Floristically, species diversity in cypress swamps is not particularly high, although some species are rather rare, e.g., featherfoil. Typical associates include swamp cottonwood, red maple, buttonbush, swamp rose, swamp beggar's ticks, and duckweed. See Table P-5 for a list of species in the oak/gum/cypress forest type.

The environment most conducive to the growth of elm, ash, and cottonwood is wet floodplain forest (Figure 4.12). Although in 1800 and 1900, American elm was a major forest component on floodplains, it is virtually missing today as a canopy tree due to the effects of Dutch elm disease and phloem necrosis. Elms still occur on floodplains, but usually as small saplings. A large, canopy-sized tree is very rare. The most common ash of floodplains is green ash, and the cottonwood is eastern cottonwood. All three of these species occur statewide. All species of ash are seriously threatened by the emerald ash borer (a beetle), and like the American elm, mature trees may essentially disappear from the landscape. The forest type commonly has silver maple, sycamore, and boxelder as associates. Other expected associated species include common wood reed, side-flowering aster, giant ragweed, poison ivy, and wood nettle.

In areas saturated with seepage, black ash can dominate. These seepage communities are known as forested fens. Associated trees, especially in northern Indiana, might include American larch, poison sumac, and yellow birch. Other depressional wetlands occur across the glaciated regions of the state with bur and swamp white oaks, red maple, and green ash as the dominant tree species. Black ash is also common in those wetlands.

1800. Forested wetlands were likely in a mature forest condition in the early 1800s, except for those impacted by tornadoes or where Native American villages occurred along the Wabash River. When European settlers arrived, they moved along rivers and streams, clearing lands for crops and cabins. This activity was mostly in the southern tier of counties along the Ohio River in the early 1800s (Latta 1938). There are 4,168,573 acres of riparian habitat in Indiana today (Table G-19), and most would have been forested in 1800. Riparian area varies by natural region from 25,270 acres (16.5%) in the Black Swamp to 1,196,141 acres (14.6%) in the Central Till Plain.

Figure 4.11. Bald cypress forest at Twin Swamp. Photo by Michael Homoya.

Figure 4.12. Bottomland woods. Photo by George Parker.

The understories of these wetlands were influenced by fires set by Native Americans prior to settler activities. Settlers continued the practice of burning and also introduced free-roaming livestock beginning in the early 1800s. Some of the oldest remaining trees in Indiana are found within these wetlands. For example, the Davis forest in Randolph County has bur oaks that are 350–450 years of age in the wet depressions while oaks on the surrounding uplands are mostly 150–200 years old (G. R. Parker, unpublished data). Current soil profiles indicate that forested wetlands were present in all natural regions with the most extensive areas occurring in the Northern Lakes, Central Till Plain, Black Swamp, Southwestern Lowlands, Southern Bottomlands, and Bluegrass natural regions. A minimum estimate of this habitat is probably 1,751,052 acres (not including the 4.2 million acres of riparian forest), based on Gordon's map. This estimate assumes that the oak and swamp forest complex is about 25% wetlands.

1900. Riparian habitats were the first areas cleared for agriculture in the 1800s. The area was probably similar to what is found currently, but in a degraded condition. Unimproved farmland in 1900 provides the best estimate of potential forested wetlands by natural region (Table G-3) when compared to the habitat potential based on soil associations (Table G-15). For example, the Central Till Plain had 1,528,242 acres of unimproved farmland in 1900. Over 5.7 million acres of this region was a forest and wetland complex in 1800 based on soil conditions, so it is likely that most of the unimproved farmland was forest with wetlands that were more difficult to drain, or forested woodlands that families decided to maintain as such. If 25% of these forests were wetlands, there were 382,061 acres of forested wetland in the Central Till Plain in 1900. Other regions had various mixtures of vegetation complexes that can be examined in a similar manner.

2000. The NLCD data from 1992 indicate that there were 342,618 acres of wooded wetlands across the state (Table G-1). This is probably an underestimate due to the difficulty in detecting small wetland depressions under forest canopies. For example, data for the Central Till Plain indicate that there were 93,257 acres of wooded wetlands (forest or shrub cover) and 654,639 acres of deciduous forest. Most of these deciduous forest woodlands have depressional wetlands (Lindsey et al. 1965) with as much as 25% being wetland (G. R. Parker, personal observation). This distribution of forested wetlands is true for all other natural regions except the Shawnee Hills and Highland Rim regions. The 1995 National Wetlands Inventory found 501,637 acres of palustrine forested wetland across the state (Table G-21). The percentage of these wetlands varies across natural regions from 25.8% in the Central Till Plain to 2.6% in the Shawnee Hills.

The elm/ash/cottonwood and oak/gum/cypress types primarily occur in riparian areas (Table P-6). These forests cover 702,900 acres across the state, or about 16.9% of the riparian habitat. Twenty-five percent of the Northern unit, 22% of the Lower Wabash unit, 8% of the Knobs unit, and 16% of the Upland Flats unit is covered by these forest types. Ninety-four percent of these forests are the elm/ash/cottonwood type. Forty-two percent of the elm/ash/cottonwood type is in the Northern unit, 25% in the Lower Wabash, 19% in the Knobs, and 14% in the Upland Flats. Forty-five percent of the oak/gum/cypress type occurs in the Northern unit, 34% in the Lower Wabash, 18% in the Knobs, and 3% in the Upland Flats.

Figure 4.13. Riparian corridor. Photo by James R. Gammon.

FLORA. Floodplain forest, also known as bottomland forest, exists in areas periodically inundated by overflow from streams and rivers. The flora of these areas is tolerant of temporarily saturated soils. In 1800, large areas of floodplain existed along the major rivers, especially in the Southern Bottomlands Natural Region and the Scottsburg Lowlands section of the Bluegrass Natural Region. In 2000, only small remnants of these once-expansive floodplains exist, often as narrow riparian corridors (Figure 4.13). A list of the species in these forests can be found in Table P-6.

Forested wetlands can exist as swamps and fens. All are discussed elsewhere, either in chapter 6 or by forest type, e.g., oak/gum/cypress and elm/ash/cottonwood. The Southern Bottomlands, Northern Lakes, Northwestern Morainal, and Central Till Plain natural regions had expansive areas of forested wetlands in 1800, but they exist only in remnants today. See Table P-6 for a list of species of this forest type.

Three areas of the state are known for flatwoods: the Muscatatuck Flats and Canyons section of the Bluegrass Natural Region, the Driftless section of the Southwestern Lowlands Natural Region, and the Central Till Plain Natural Region. Flatwoods are on relatively level terrain and are ephemerally wet from direct precipitation (not overflow from streams or rivers, or at least rarely so). Many of the same species that occur in floodplain forests also occur in flatwoods, as do species of mesic upland forests. This is because a flatwoods is a mosaic of level upland and slight depressions that seasonally contain standing water. An unusual type is the post oak flatwoods of the Driftless section of the Southwestern Lowlands Natural Region. This type gets quite dry during the summer and fall seasons, and has species that also occur on dry upland sites. Since 1800, almost all flatwoods have been cleared for agricultural pursuits. Species for this type can be found in Table P-6.

Wooded stream and river corridors are typically composed of floodplain forest species, such as the elm/ash/cottonwood type or the oak/gum/cypress type, discussed above. See Table P-6 for a list of species of this forest type.

AMPHIBIANS AND REPTILES. Forested wetlands are an important group of habitats for amphibians and reptiles. This is the case despite the fact that few Midwest herpetofauna are adapted specifically for them. Instead, the biodiversity is generated by multiple users with overlapping interests. There are many types of forested wetlands, the variety largely resulting from the duration and extent of the surface water. Truly permanent forested wetlands have always been relatively uncommon in the state, though the cypress sloughs in southwestern Indiana epitomize what many would think of as forested wetland. Instead, most forested wetlands are in river floodplains, components of what were once tremendously large, continuous corridors stretching along major rivers, such as the Ohio and Wabash, and also many more, like the White and Patoka.

In many respects, the composition of the herpetofaunal community in deeper, permanent forested wetlands is much like that of aquatic systems such as lakes and rivers. Likely amphibians include the pervasive green frogs and bullfrogs, and also mudpuppies and lesser sirens. Turtles that generally just get into the southern part of the state and that utilize these habitats include the false and Mississippi map turtles and the river cooter. If they are not already extirpated, these are the types of areas where we might see alligator snapping turtles, western mud snakes, and possibly the western cottonmouth.

The herpetofauna that need fish-free environments to breed will drop out in permanent wetland systems. This will also be the case even in many of the temporary wetlands, either because they only occasionally dry down, or because fish are routinely imported in floodwaters. Consequently, ambystomatid salamanders are generally absent from these habitats. Many frogs may not persist either until fishless wetlands suitable for breeding are available in the vicinity.

Forests which seasonally flood in the winter may harbor hibernating amphibians and reptiles, such as garter and water snakes and frogs. Often, these species are overwintering in abandoned crayfish burrows which, even when an area is not inundated, reach water by penetrating the water table below the surface. If such hydrological patterns are interrupted, as by winter drawdowns during land management efforts, the hibernating animals may be lost.

Many amphibians and reptiles hibernate in the mud of shallow wetlands, forested or otherwise, or in soils nearby where the water table is just below the surface of the ground. Examples of the former include many frogs, such as leopard frogs, green frogs, and bullfrogs, and many turtles, such as painted, spotted, and Blanding's turtles. Examples of the latter include garter snakes, water snakes, and even racers and, again, frogs. Access to the water table is often via abandoned crayfish burrows. Hibernating in water prevents desiccation and, perhaps counterintuitively, freezing. Winter disturbances of shallow wetlands, or areas nearby with the water table close to the surface, may have catastrophic effects that go well beyond direct mortality. Winter drawdowns may freeze all of the immobile hibernators that were once covered by an insulating "blanket" of water. Drawdowns may impact herpetofauna well up into the drainage if the water table is affected.

Snake diversity can be quite high, especially in those areas where river flooding does not rapidly move through the floodplain forest ("sheet flooding"). Wetland associates such as the midland water snake and diamondback water snake may be found in the forests not too far from open water. The copperbelly water snake may be hundreds of meters from water as it searches for frogs or transitions from one body of water to another. Garter snakes and ribbon snakes may also be numerous in forested wetlands. Even upland forest species such as racers, rat snakes, and kingsnakes may be found in forested wetlands after the water has withdrawn from some areas. For all of these species, patchy forest in terms of canopy cover will lead to the most snakes and the most species. Closed-canopy forests will tend to have fewer snakes in them.

In terms of herpetofauna, riparian corridors might best be thought of as some combination of lowland (often as floodplain), forest, and upland forest. There are no real riparian zone specialists. Consequently, one should also consult the "Mature or High-Canopy Forest" section above.

BIRDS. Floodplain and riparian forest are important avian habitats, in part because flooding sometimes preserves forested land from conversion to agriculture or residential development. However, along big rivers like the Wabash, the once-wide floodplain forest is usually a distressingly thin ribbon of trees. Ravine topography has been a better guarantee of riparian forest survival, but ravines are usually associated with small intermittent streams within upland forest. The majority of birds in floodplain forest also inhabit upland forest, but there are some distinctive species—a few found only in floodplain forest, and others that appear to have higher densities there than in upland forest. Table B-2 lists under "Floodplain/Wet Woods/Riparian Forest" a set of 71 species characteristic of the habitat, including 30 species for which it is the primary habitat. This list is similar to that given in chapter 6 for forested and shrub wetlands (Table B-4), but here "mature forest" (of relatively large, tall trees) is the overriding criterion; forested/shrub wetlands are a more open or a lower-stature habitat. Thus, more woodpecker species are listed for mature floodplain forest than for forested/shrub wetlands; alder and willow flycatchers are listed for the latter habitat only, and Acadian and great crested flycatchers only for the former.

Birds for which floodplain forest is (or was) a primary nesting habitat include 2 ducks (wood duck and hooded merganser), 3 herons (great blue, green, and the rare yellow-crowned night-heron), bald eagle, red-shouldered hawk, barred owl, the extinct Carolina parakeet (Mumford and Keller 1984), warbling vireo, house wren (Dailey 2003), and several warbler species (prothonotary, yellow-throated, northern parula, yellow, and Louisiana waterthrush). The warblers have distinct vegetation or habitat preferences within such forest (Mumford and Keller 1984; Castrale et al. 1998). For example, prothonotary warbler needs flooded trees with nest cavities. Yellow-throated warbler is strongly associated with sycamores, yellow warbler with willow and cottonwood, and Louisiana waterthrush with flowing tributaries or small rivers rather than extensive flooded bottomlands.

Southward-flowing rivers like the Wabash and White are important migratory corridors for forest birds (see chapter 7), although most species use upland forest as well. Migrant species abundant in wet bottomlands near Terre Haute include American redstart and yellow-rumped warbler; especially in fall, the habitat is rich in warbler species and is the most likely place to find rusty blackbird.

Riparian wooded corridors support many of the birds listed for forested wetlands. The difference is that some might not tolerate a narrow corridor of woodland, compared to a wider bottomland forest (a much rarer habitat). The nature of such corridors varies considerably, including cottonwood stands along Wabash River levees; wider, mixed-species forests along sluggish streams; and ribbons of young trees along streams through farmland, to give a few examples. Such corridors support plenty of nesting birds and are probably quite important for migrants, especially passerines. Breeding species of riparian corridors include wet-woods species, such as eastern phoebe, warbling vireo, Carolina wren, house wren, wood thrush, northern parula, yellow warbler, and yellow-throated warbler, and generalists, such as indigo bunting and northern cardinal.

MAMMALS. Mammals of the forested wetlands are indicated in Table M-2, although it is difficult to know whether some species should be included or not. It is partly a matter of how wet the forested wetlands are and for how long a period. Some of the more questionable species on this list are the opossum, coyote, white-tailed deer, and fisher.

Mammals present in the floodplain forest are very similar to those of the forested wetlands (Table M-2) and include those that can survive prolonged flooding. Flooding is usually restricted to short periods of the year, and many mammals move in and out. The most characteristic floodplain forest species are the masked shrew, essentially all of the species of bats of the state, swamp rabbit, white-footed mouse, beaver, muskrat, and black bear.

1800. All of the species of forested wetlands and riparian wooded corridors, including those indicated as extirpated today (Table M-2), were probably present in 1800, all of them throughout the state except that the southeastern shrew, southeastern myotis, and evening bat were probably found only in the southern part of the state, or at least were much more common there. The swamp rabbit would have been found in much of the Southern Bottomlands Natural Region. The coyote was probably not very common, but was more common in the northwest and west than in other parts of the state.

1900. The black bear, mountain lion, elk, and fisher were gone, and the gray wolf and porcupine were nearly gone. The beaver and white-tailed deer were gone, but they would later be reintroduced. The beaver and fisher were eliminated primarily by over-trapping and the deer and bear by over-hunting. The coyote was apparently fairly common at this time. The swamp rabbit still occurred in much of the Southern Bottomlands Natural Region.

2000. Except for the extirpated species, all species of forested wetlands (Table M-2) occurred at the beginning of the twenty-first century. The southeastern bat was probably extirpated by the mid-1980s. The southeastern shrew and evening bat were probably much more common in the southern part of the state. By the 1970s, much of the habitat of the swamp rabbit had been destroyed. The species in 2000 occurred primarily in the north (Long Pond area) and south (Pearl Island area) of Gibson County, with a few individuals in Knox County just north of and across the White River from Long Pond. A very few occurred in Posey County at Hovey Lake in 2000. The decrease was primarily because of loss of habitat, coupled with over-hunting. Although hunting was prohibited in the state as of 1985, the swamp rabbit is listed as endangered in Indiana, and the entire population is estimated at about 80 individuals. The species needs bottomland woods coupled with higher points which can serve as refugia during flooding. Most of the higher ground suited for refugia in the previously occurring habitat has been converted to farmland. Also, the construction of Gibson Lake destroyed the major swamp rabbit habitat in Gibson County.

The coyote was apparently scarce in the middle part of the twentieth century but became quite common throughout the state by the mid-1980s. The deer and the beaver, which had been extirpated by 1900, were reintroduced and attained large populations by the 1970s and 1980s.

Mammals of the flatwoods forest are very similar to those of the forested wetlands (Table M-2), but are limited to those that can survive flooding, which is usually of short duration (a week or two) but sometimes lasts for several weeks. Again, it is difficult to

Figure 4.14. Canebrake. Photo by William McCoy.

know whether some species should be included or not, as it is partly a matter of how wet the area gets and for how long it is flooded. The most characteristic flatwood forest species are the masked shrew, bats, swamp rabbit, white-footed mouse, beaver, and muskrat. Numerous species of mammals, practically all of the species that occur in woods, use the riparian wooded corridors (Table M-2).

Many of the species occur in riparian wooded corridors throughout the state. However, the southeastern shrew occurs just in the southwestern part of Indiana, and the masked shrew occurs throughout most of the state except in the south-central unglaciated hill country. The star-nosed mole occurs just in northeastern Indiana. All of the bats use riparian wooded corridors. The swamp rabbit occurs in the flooded bottoms of the Wabash River and to the east of the river in some areas. The red squirrel occurs in riparian wooded corridors in the north.

Canebrakes

"Canebrakes" are dense stands of cane, *Arundinaria gigantea* (Figure 4.14). Although not forest, canebrakes consist of a woody or semi-woody grass that once grew in dense stands, usually within lowground forests of southwestern Indiana. Canebrakes were very extensive along the Ohio River, lower Wabash, and some other spots in Indiana in presettlement days, according to early travelers and explorers, and General Land Office surveyors also noted them. Ridgway (1872b: 728) wrote, "In the 'hollows' parallel to the river, the small cane (*Arundinaria tecta*) formed dense brakes and grew 10 or 12 feet high, the canes matted with thorny 'green brier' (*Smilax* several species) and mixed with tall stinging nettles (*Urtica* and *Laportea*); or where the cane was scant or absent, the ground bristled with Equisetaceae."

FLORA. The flora of canebrakes is similar to that found in floodplain forests, although not as diverse as the latter in situations where the stands of cane are especially dense. Closely spaced canes do not allow for the light and space needed by most plants. Soils formed under stands of native cane were exceptionally fertile because of constant flooding and, being much easier to clear with fire than were forests, they were converted to farm fields very quickly following European settlement.

Today, canebrakes are essentially nonexistent, as the large-scale conversion of floodplain forests to agriculture all but eliminated them. Although giant cane is not rare in the far southern region of Indiana, only small colonies persist.

AMPHIBIANS AND REPTILES. Use of canebrakes by reptiles and amphibians is poorly studied. It is anticipated that canebrake stands would offer excellent cover for a variety of bottomland herpetofauna, but that the value of the stand would diminish as it became larger, much as is the case for extensive stands of cattails. Given that another name for timber rattlesnakes in the south is "canebrake rattlesnake," perhaps they use this habitat.

MAMMALS. Canebrakes produce very good cover, thus are used by many species of mammals, and the swamp rabbit (Figure 4.15) is a characteristic species of that habitat. Harrison and Hickie (1931) obtained the first swamp rabbits from Indiana

Figure 4.15. Swamp rabbit. Photo by NealyBob@PBase.com.

Figure 4.16. Swamp rabbit pellets on log in Gibson County. Photo by John O. Whitaker, Jr.

and thought that the species was closely confined to stands of cane. Swamp rabbits have been eliminated from most of their former range in Indiana, but still occur in Gibson County (Pearl Island and Long Pond) with outliers in Knox County and at Hovey Lake in Posey County. Swamp rabbits were hunted in southern Indiana until November 1985; they had been reduced by then to about 80 individuals through loss of habitat and hunting pressure. Swamp rabbits defecate on logs in winter (Figure 4.16), and we currently estimate their numbers by assessing the area covered by logs with pellets (1 rabbit per 10 acres). Swamp rabbits will feed upon cane although it is not a major food. Other mammals that would probably be most common in canebrakes are the opossum; masked, southeastern, and short-tailed shrews; white-footed mouse; and many of the larger mammals.

Plantations

There are 187,600 acres of forests that were initiated through planting in 2000 (unpublished forest inventory analysis data, U.S. Forest Service). These plantings include 25,300 acres of oak/pine, 43,100 acres of oak/hickory, 25,700 acres of elm/ash/cottonwood, 10,600 acres of maple/beech/birch, 46,400 acres of white/red/jack pine, 30,600 acres of loblolly/shortleaf, and 6,000 acres of exotic softwoods.

Figure 4.17. Pine plantation. Photo by IDNR–*Outdoor Indiana* magazine.

Pine plantations were not established until the 1930s. Areas were planted to pines on badly eroded farmland in southern Indiana to reduce soil erosion and on abandoned strip-mined lands (Figure 4.17). Black locust plantations were established on strip-mined lands in the 1940s–1980s, and several plantations for potential firewood were established on farmland in the 1980s and 1990s. Black walnut has been planted on farmland from the 1980s to the present time for potential wood products. There is no estimate of their area.

FLORA. Most plantations are of species utilized for wood products, reforestation, Christmas trees, windbreaks, wildlife use, or natural community restoration. Common species are white pine, red pine, loblolly pine, Scotch pine, white spruce, and an assortment of hardwoods, especially black walnut. The flora associated with plantations varies considerably and depends on the former use of the site and age of the plantation. As a general rule, plantations have rather low species diversity, at least when compared to the flora of a similar site with natural forest. Some plantations are highly manicured, while others are allowed to regrow with pioneering species. No table is

Figure 4.18. Walnut plantation. Photo by George Parker.

provided for this type, as the possibilities for species occurrence vary greatly.

AMPHIBIANS AND REPTILES. The utility of conifer plantations to Indiana's herpetofauna is expected to be limited, especially in those cases where silvicultural practices lead to forest floors lacking woody debris, and/or where the forest is composed of only one species. If succession has led to a more complex forest, and time has allowed the accumulation of woody debris, then plantations are not prohibitive to herpetofauna. In a twenty-first-century study comparing herpetofaunal community composition in secondary growth hardwood stands and in unmanaged, 40- to 60-year-old remnant pine plantations in Hoosier National Forest, the compositions were relatively comparable between the two habitat types (Gibson et al. 2005). Amphibian abundances and diversities were quite similar, though reptile abundances were significantly higher in the hardwood stands, particularly with respect to small, fossorial snakes. Thus, while creating conifer plantations does not benefit amphibians and reptiles, plantations are more habitable when less intensively managed, or when time leads to increased complexity in the canopy and on the forest floor.

MAMMALS. The mammals found in plantations are indicated in Table M-2. None of the extirpated species have been found there, since the plantations are so recent. However, all the other species probably occur in pine plantations throughout the state, except for the red squirrel, which occurs only in the northern part of the state.

Like pine plantations, other plantations, often of walnut (Figure 4.18) or black locust, are rather recent. Walnut or black locust plantations are often in fields, and the herbaceous vegetation may often dictate what mammal species occur. The young plantations often have much herbaceous vegetation covering the ground and thus have mammalian fauna similar to that of grassy or weedy fields. Likely mammals in young plantations of this sort are indicated in Table M-2. The specific community is probably determined by the geographic location and the plant community of the specific site. The masked and southeastern shrews probably do not occur often in plantations, unless the site is moist. Then, the southeastern shrew occurs only in the southwestern part of the state, and the masked shrew occurs throughout the state, except in the unglaciated south-central area. The plains pocket gopher and western harvest mouse occur only in the prairie areas of the northwest, with the harvest mouse having a much larger and still-growing range. Their dispersal seems to be slowed mainly by rivers. The harvest mouse occurs in at least 17 counties, the pocket gopher in about 3.

Transitional Forests: Open Woodland and Oak Savanna

In regions such as northwestern Indiana, where prairies were once extensive habitats transitional between grassland and forest occurred nearby. These included savannas, "grassy landscapes interrupted by scattered trees" (Figure 4.19), and woodlands, "similar to savannas but with greater canopy cover" (Grundel and Pavlovic 2007a). From a continental perspective, such areas are part of the Central Forest/Grassland Transition Zone ecoregion (Ricketts et al. 1999). Key natural factors generating the vegetation mosaic are a rain-

Figure 4.19. Savanna at Gibson Woods. Photo by Scott Johnson.

fall regime insufficient to support closed-canopy forest, sandy or calcareous substrates that drain quickly, and fire. Human impacts, of course, have been extensive, two of the main ones being the conversion of prairie to agricultural land and the suppression of fire. Although native tall grass prairie is largely gone, the transitional vegetation remains. A current classification of vegetation in the region (Grundel and Pavlovic 2007a) recognizes 5 categories, based on average densiometer-measured canopy cover and shrub density: open (20% canopy cover), savanna (20–50% canopy cover), woodland (50–90% canopy cover), forest (90% canopy cover), and scrub (no percentage given). A characteristic association is black oak/sand/savanna (Nuzzo 1986; Swink and Wilhelm 1994; Will-Wolf and Stearns 1999).

1800. Savannas occurred in areas surrounding prairies due to repeated fires and the presence of sandy or calcareous soil, which made them too dry to support forest. The largest area of savanna was in the eastern areas of the Grand Prairie Natural Region, which was maintained by Native American fires (Potzger et al. 1956; Gordon 1936). Savanna habitat was also present in the Northwestern Morainal, Northern Lakes, and Central Till Plain regions. Small glades and barren communities were scattered across the southern regions of the state from the Southwestern Lowlands on the west to the Bluegrass Natural Region in the southeast. Approximately 2,000 acres of land with the potential of supporting a post oak barrens are scattered across the purchase area of the Hoosier National Forest (Zhalnin 2004).

1900. Most of the savannas were heavily disturbed through livestock grazing and timber harvest or clearing by 1900. It is likely that most of the area present in 1800 (about 1 million acres) was still present in 1900 due to the grazing and burning that occurred in the 1800s.

2000. Greater fire protection and reduced livestock grazing allowed the development of woody understories over most of the savannas by 2000. Twenty-first-century efforts by public and private organizations have begun to restore savannas across the state.

FLORA. Woodland habitats, because of the relatively wide spacing of trees, allow for greater light levels to reach the understory. Consequently, many species with high light needs, such as those that occur in grassland environments, can coexist with trees. Most of this transitional type occurs in northwestern Indiana, on the edges of the Grand Prairie Natural Region. It also was important in the Northern Lakes Natural Region, the Northwestern Morainal Natural Region, the Southwestern Lowlands Natural Region, and to a lesser extent, the areas around the Big Barrens region of the Mitchell Karst Plain section of the Highland Rim Natural Region. In 2000, very little of the type exists in the state. Those that do are on either very sandy or rocky substrates (which are less suitable for agricultural pursuits). Major tree species are black oak, bur oak, white oak, and post oak (in the south only). For a list of species found in the type, see Table P-7.

AMPHIBIANS AND REPTILES. Savanna habitat will tend to have a herpetofaunal community most like grasslands (Table H-3) but, depending on the history of the site, may also have forest species (Table H-2). For example, in manipulated landscapes, areas that have been changed from closed-canopy forest to open woodland will likely not have as many grassland herpetofauna, given their inability to find the new habitat. As areas become more open, they will be more suitable for reptiles than amphibians, given the higher levels of incidental radiation and desiccation. Many salamander species are slow or are unable to colonize this habitat from more forested zones. American toads and leopard frogs will use such areas, and so will racers, black rat snakes, hognose snakes, garter snakes, and ribbon snakes. Timber rattlesnakes, northern copperheads, and a variety of the more diminutive species, such as northern brown snakes, will avoid them until the canopy fills in further.

BIRDS. The birds of the transitional gradient from open habitats to forest (referred to here as "transitional birds") are among the most common and familiar birds in the state. These transitional habitats cover a gradient of forest cover from largely treeless but nonagricultural areas to open oak savannas, to the partially closed canopy of woodland, to nearly closed-canopy forest (Grundel and Pavlovic 2007a, 2007b). This gradient of forest cover is more generally a gradient of ecological succession in this part of North America, one that is maintained by disturbances of various sorts (especially fire, but more recently other anthropogenic disturbances). As such, this grassland-to-forest transitional gradient is, from an ornithological perspective, intertwined with the old-field-to-forest transitional gradient (see "Old-Field Communities" section of this chapter; and Herkert 1998). Table B-2 lists the characteristic species of these categories in a single column ("Pioneering/Shrubland/Savanna/Open"), which is appropriate within the present larger context of forest lands, but field ornithologists can place most species more finely along the transitional gradient.

At the more open end are many species typical of early successional habitats, such as field sparrow, eastern kingbird, common yellowthroat, and American goldfinch. At the midpoint of the gradient, common species include red-tailed hawk, northern flicker, American robin, eastern bluebird, warbling vireo, indigo bunting, and Baltimore oriole. Many of the bird species often considered to be "edge species" can be placed into these two groups of birds. At the more closed-canopy end of the gradient, one may find species that are also found in forests, such as downy woodpecker, yellow-billed cuckoo, eastern wood-pewee, tufted titmouse, blue-gray gnatcatcher, and American redstart.

Overall, approximately 32% of the 309 breeding birds in Indiana can be found to some significant extent at some point in this gradient (Table B-2). The great majority of terrestrial birds that winter in Indiana can typically be found at some point in this successional gradient (as opposed to the deep forest).

The numerical status of transitional birds in Indiana reflects the fact that much of what remains of forested habitat mimics several points within the transitional gradient from open to forest. Isolated, open forest remnants are woodland- or savanna-like in many ways, especially in being largely edge habitat. Trees along a fence row adjacent to pastures mimic conditions at the more open end of the gradient. Suburban habitats are also woodland-like in many respects. Human activities in relatively forested areas, especially activities such as logging and the creation of wildlife openings, may also produce much suitable habitat for such species. Abandoned agricultural fields (old fields) along forest edges mimic the more open stages of the gradient.

1800. Most of Indiana was relatively heavily forested at the start of the nineteenth century. There were definitely openings in the forest made by Native Americans, but this period represents a (relative) low point in the populations of most if not all transitional bird species.

1900. The forest destruction that started in earnest during the first half of the nineteenth century must have been a boon to transitional bird species. By the end of the century, the ornithological landscape—dominated by transitional birds—would be very familiar to anyone from the early twenty-first century.

The transitional birds of the northwestern portion of the state (especially in the former prairie region), however, probably experienced a different scenario of ecological change during the nineteenth century. A prominent habitat in this area was the midwestern oak savanna, which in most respects is a blending of the prairie and forest habitats on dry sandy soil maintained by frequent fires. This habitat declined simultaneously with adjacent tall grass prairie habitat in Indiana during the 1800s, though from a somewhat different combination of factors, since it was not as arable, and was very much in decline by the end of the century. Hence, transitional birds in this portion of the state probably declined substantially.

2000. Transitional birds may have reached their peak density during the early part of the twentieth century. At that point in time, forest destruction had reached its peak and the lack of permanent row crop agriculture made the area in and around fragmented forest habitat more conducive to many sorts of transitional birds. The shift to permanent row crop agriculture during the mid-1900s undoubtedly had a negative impact on many transitional birds, but such species remained among the most abundant and recognizable species in Indiana.

Savanna destruction also continued into the twentieth century via a combination of habitat conversion to agriculture and fire suppression. However, even though most oak savanna habitat in Indiana was destroyed by the end of the century, there were no resulting statewide avian extirpations or near-extirpations. The reason is that few if any midwestern birds appear to be oak savanna specialists with the possible exception of the red-headed woodpecker (Temple

1998; Brawn et al. 2001; Grundel and Pavlovic 2007a). In other words, the species that inhabited savannas were those that focus on the more open end of the successional gradient rather than being savanna specialists per se. On a regional scale, however, populations of transitional bird species (along with wetland and grassland species) were undoubtedly near a historical low point in the northwestern portion of the state at the close of the twentieth century.

At the start of the twenty-first century, the transitional bird species of Indiana may be considered the major beneficiaries of habitat destruction in Indiana. A few such species, however, have declined over the last century. Among them is the red-headed woodpecker (U.S. Geological Survey 2006), which may be suffering specifically from the demise of the oak savannas and the persistent increase in maple trees at the expense of oaks in Indiana. The decline of golden-winged warbler and whip-poor-will in Indiana may reflect the lack of specific sorts of successional habitats (Castrale et al. 1998). Nevertheless, as a group, transitional birds are among the most abundant and characteristic bird species in the state.

MAMMALS. This is a transitional habitat including species of both woodlands and grasslands. Thus, most of the state's mammal species could occupy this habitat, depending on location and also on the amount of moisture in the area. Table M-3 lists 48 of 59 extant species, and 5 of 8 extirpated species, as using (now or formerly) such habitats. Historical changes from 1800 to 1900 to 2000 reflect the species extirpations, reintroductions, and range expansions chronicled for forest lands earlier in this chapter.

1800. All the mammals listed for this habitat (Table M-3) were likely found there in 1800, except for the western harvest mouse and red fox. The coyote was present, but perhaps only in the northern part of the state. By mid-century, 3 of these species had been extirpated, including the bison and elk about 1830, and the mountain lion about 1851.

1900. The mammals included all species listed (Table M-3) except for 6: the western harvest mouse, mountain lion, wapiti or American elk, bison, American beaver, and white-tailed deer. Five species had been extirpated, the bison and elk about 1830, and the mountain lion about 1851. The beaver (1840) and white-tailed deer (1891) were also gone, although both species were reintroduced later.

2000. The gray wolf was extirpated about 1908 mostly through predator elimination. Habitat reduction was another adverse factor as development proceeded. By 1950, the mammals in this habitat included all those listed in Table M-3 except the western harvest mouse, black bear, gray wolf, fisher, mountain lion, wapiti or American elk, and bison.

Grasslands

5

This chapter includes all grasslands, including the original tall grass prairie, which comprised more than 2 million acres, mostly in the northern half of Indiana; pasture; haylands; strip-mined land in southwestern Indiana; vegetated dunes; savanna; and agricultural land put into the various reserve programs. "Grassland" often includes more or less forbs or other nongrassy herbaceous plants.

Sub-Habitats

Original Prairie

An understanding of Indiana's native grassland community, the tall grass prairie, is essential to appreciating the changes to this habitat category in the past 200 years. The French word *prairie* means "meadow." But the "Indiana prairie" encountered by early European settlers was unlike any meadows they had ever experienced in the forested regions of Europe. Indiana's prairie was dominated by grass species, especially big bluestem (Figure 5.1), switchgrass, Indian grass, and in wetter sites slough grass, which all can grow to 10 ft tall or more. A human on horseback could be swallowed up in the vast sea of tall grass. Scattered among the grasses were perennial wildflowers and legumes, collectively called "forbs," such as blazing star, partridge pea, black-eyed Susan, and various sunflowers (Figure 5.2). Small trees and shrubs, such as hazelnut, occurred at grassland edges, especially along drainages.

To the early Europeans, the tall grass was unfamiliar and uninviting. They found the prairie difficult to navigate without landmark trees or clear vistas, and mistook the paucity of trees as a sign of soil infertility. There were hordes of insects and dangerous, fast-moving prairie fires. Attempts at cultivation were thwarted by dense sod. Only after John Deere invented the self-scouring, steel-bladed plow in 1837 would the tall grass prairie give way to large-scale agriculture. Thus, some of the most fertile soils in the world became available to feed a growing nation.

The North American prairie ecosystem formed after the Pleistocene glaciation, within the past 10,000 years. As the glaciers retreated, the climate became warmer and drier, and the grasslands developed under three major forces: climate, fire, and grazing. Although in most years the prairie region has adequate rainfall during the growing season, it is also subject

Figure 5.1. Big bluestem. Photo by James R. Gammon.

Figure 5.2. Prairie dominated by black-eyed Susan. Photo by IDNR–*Outdoor Indiana* magazine.

to prolonged periods of drought. During wet periods, trees advance into the grasslands along the prairie border, especially along stream courses, only to die out during drought periods.

Fire is important in suppressing woody vegetation. The prairie community is uniquely adapted to be maintained, not destroyed, by fire. Whether started by Native Americans or by lightning, prairie fires rapidly swept across vast areas, killing woody plants, removing thatch, and releasing nutrients, thereby promoting plant growth. Prairie plants are mostly herbaceous perennials with their growing points slightly below ground, protected from the heat of a fast-moving fire; thus, prairie plants survive fires unharmed. This same adaptation also left prairie plants largely unharmed by browsing animals. The prairie supported grasshoppers, small rodents, rabbits, elk, deer, and large herds of bison. Prairie grazers were often nomadic, moving on as the above-ground biomass was consumed, which allowed the grazed areas to soon recover.

The soils of the tall grass prairie are some of the most fertile in the world. A prairie can have more biomass below ground than above. Prairie plants produce a tangle of roots, rhizomes, bulbs, and corms. Unlike the European grasses used for lawns and pastures, prairie grasses have deep root systems. The roots of big bluestem and switchgrass can extend more than 7 and 11 ft, respectively. The roots of some prairie forbs extend even deeper. Deep roots are also advantageous to prairie plants during drought. Water infiltration and percolation are improved by extensive root systems, reducing runoff and providing a mechanism for aquifer replenishment. Prairie grasses can sequester large amounts of carbon in their underground biomass and in some areas are more appropriate for this purpose than are trees. As some of the roots, rhizomes, and other underground vegetative structures die each year, they contribute to the organic matter in the soil and add to the soil's fertility. Therefore, prairie plants build soil fertility in a way many shallow-rooted agricultural crops do not.

Native prairie grasses are often referred to as warm season grasses. Unlike the European grasses, warm season grasses do not green-up, that is undergo their greatest vegetative growth, in the early spring. Rather, they produce most of their above-ground biomass during the late spring and summer, after many European grasses have already gone to seed. In many ways, European and other non-native grasses found in lawns, pastures, and golf courses are not the functional ecological equivalent of native grasses. The prairie community may still be ideally suited to the climate of periodic droughts, but the factors of fire and grazing that maintain prairie are difficult to accomplish today. However, the art and science of prairie restoration continue to be refined, and restored grasslands provide a limited, fragile repository of the basic building blocks of this native ecosystem.

Original grassland (prairie, both wet and dry) made up a significant proportion of the state's vegetation in 1800 (see Map 1.3). Today, very little of the original prairie remains, although a great deal of grassland exists. For example, many of the abandoned strip-mined areas of southwestern Indiana have been restored to grassland communities.

Figure 5.3. Cultivated grassland. Photo by Qihao Weng.

1800. A vast area of prairie, wetland, and savanna was present in the northwestern region (Grand Prairie Natural Region) of the state at the beginning of the nineteenth century. The presettlement vegetation map (Map 1.2) developed by Lindsey et al. in 1965 indicates 601,664 acres of dry prairie in the state (Table G-13). Gordon's (1936) map (Map 1.3; Table G-14) indicates there were 2,155,876 acres of prairie in Indiana, with some prairie areas occurring in all but the Black Swamp and Bluegrass natural regions. The complexes of prairie with forest or wetlands shown on Map 1.4, based on soil associations that were predominantly derived under grassland vegetation, are probably a more accurate picture of the spatial pattern of grassland communities than is the Gordon map. The greatest area of prairie occurred in the Grand Prairie, Central Till Plain, Northern Lakes, Northwestern Morainal, and Southwestern Lowlands natural regions (see Map 1.4). Current soil profiles indicate that prairie also occurred in the Bluegrass Natural Region (Table G-15).

1900. The 1876 atlas shows many large areas of prairie remaining (Table G-22). Most were being grazed or cut for hay, and many were likely lost to agriculture by 1900.

2000. The Nature Conservancy estimates that only about 1,000 acres of original prairie remained in 2000, mostly as tiny remnants. The Nature Conservancy has since restored 5,400 acres of prairie. The Census of Agriculture (U.S. Department of Agriculture 2002) indicates that 18,381 acres of wild haylands occur on private farms within the state, but it is not known how much of this is in original prairie. The restoration of prairie habitat has greatly increased since the 1980s as part of the Conservation Reserve Program, which established native grasses on 28,448 acres. Planting varied from 857 acres in the Northwestern Morainal region to 7,026 acres in the Central Till Plain region. The National Land Cover Data (NLCD) of 1992 indicates there were 91,085 acres of grassland/herbaceous habitat across the state (Map 5.1; Table G-1). Much of this is probably cultivated grassland or old fields (Figure 5.3). The majority (almost 42,000 acres) is in the Grand Prairie region. The restoration of grasslands through public and private programs may allow partial recovery of plant and animal species that have declined over the past 200 years.

FLORA. Naturally occurring grasslands occurred primarily in northwestern Indiana, but examples, albeit very small in some cases, probably occurred in every county of the state. The Grand Prairie Natural Region is named for the predominance of naturally occurring grassland in northwestern Indiana. The prairies of northwestern Indiana were contiguous with grasslands in Illinois and the vast grasslands of the midwestern and western United States. Other areas of significant native grassland occurred in the Highland Rim, Northern Lakes, Northwestern Morainal, and Southwestern Lowlands natural regions. Grasslands created from the planting of pasture land, or in successional areas of old fields, are found throughout the state. The flora of these sites consists mainly of introduced species, typically of Eurasian origin, e.g., meadow fescue, tall fescue, and Hungarian brome.

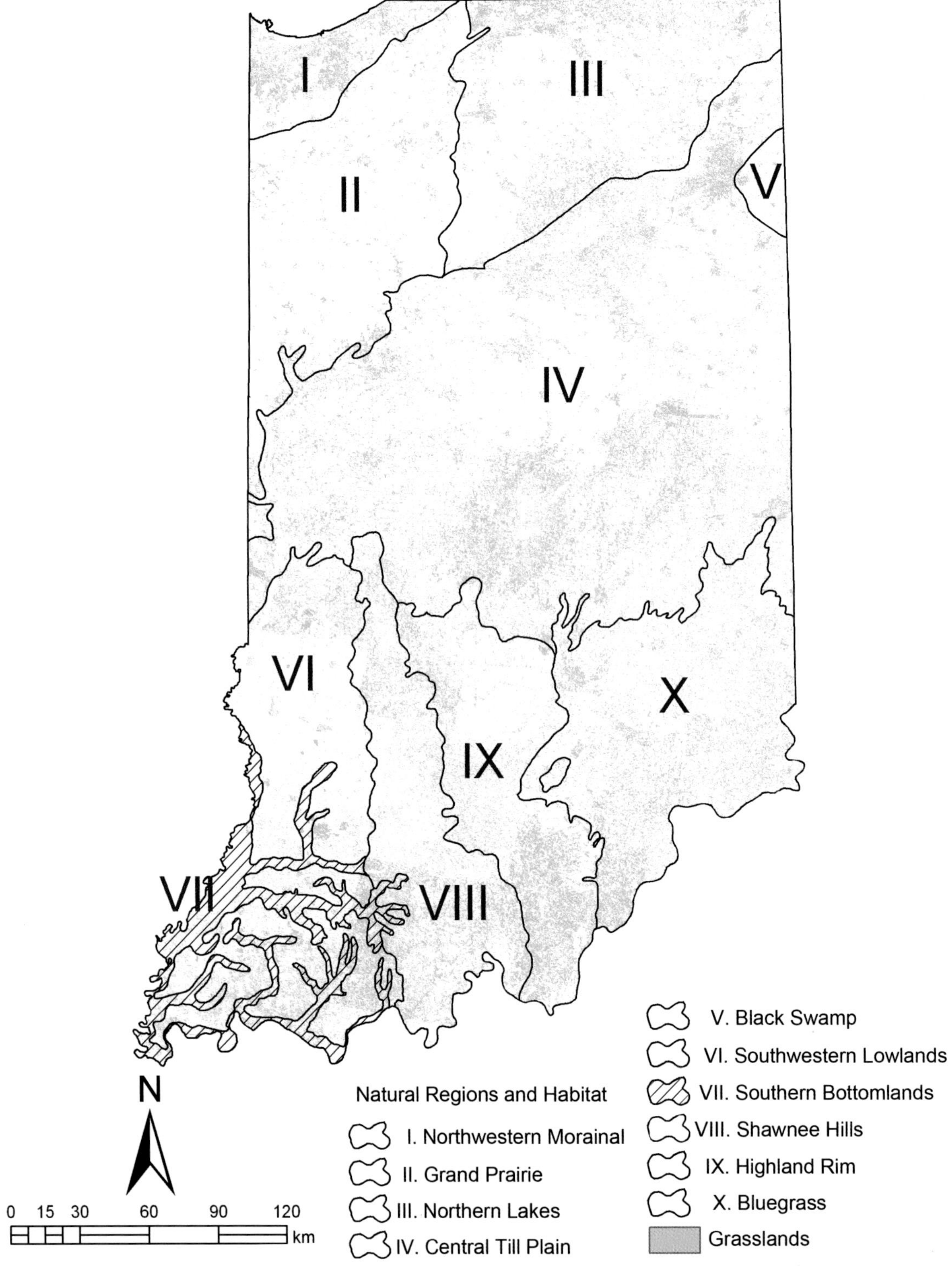

Map 5.1. Grasslands by natural regions.

Native prairie vegetation consists of a diverse assemblage of species of grasses and forbs that require exposure to high light intensities. The grass family is a major group of plants in prairie, as are the legume and aster families. Big bluestem, little bluestem, Indian grass, prairie switch grass, Canada wild rye, prairie cord grass, side-oats grama, and northern dropseed are important grasses. Forbs are flowering herbaceous plants other than the grasslike plants (grasses, sedges, rushes, etc.). Significant legumes include golden cassia, cream wild indigo, Illinois tick trefoil, round-headed bush clover, and purple prairie clover. Members of the aster family include tall coreopsis, pale purple coneflower, downy sunflower, prairie blazing star, prairie dock, compass plant, rigid goldenrod, and sky-blue aster. Species perhaps once common in the prairies of Indiana, but not now, include bluehearts, Hill's thistle, prairie white-fringed orchid (federally endangered), pink milkwort, prairie parsley, and Great Plains ladies' tresses. See Table P-7 for a list of species of prairie plants.

1800. The greatest diversity of native grassland species existed during this time, as most of the landscape was still essentially intact, except for small areas cultivated by Native Americans. The common exotic grassland species had not been introduced at this date.

1900. Because much of the grassland landscape was converted to agriculture by this date, many of the native species were considerably reduced in number, if they were still present at all. Although no grassland species are known to have been extirpated by this date, many were likely becoming seriously threatened. Pasture land was common, given the great number of family farms across the state. This land probably contained some native species, e.g., little bluestem and common purpletop, and non-natives such as Kentucky bluegrass and redtop. The latter two, as well as other exotics, became common along disturbed habitats, such as roadsides, ditches, railroad rights-of-way, etc. Species from native grassland environments that disappeared from the state before 1900 are Mead's milkweed and false bugbane.

2000. By the twenty-first century, practically all of the native grassland in Indiana was gone. Consequently, the diversity and numbers of native grassland species were considerably diminished from those of 1800. In addition to the reduction of habitat, the appearance of invasive exotic species provided competition that negatively impacted the native species. Tall fescue, meadow fescue, and Hungarian brome are now abundant in contemporary pastures and other non-forested uplands. The modern, heavy use of herbicides has also taken its toll on the native flora, especially the native grassland forbs. This is particularly true along the railroad rights-of-way where some of the last remaining native grassland exists. Species from native grassland that became extirpated by 2000 include clustered poppy mallow and western wild lettuce.

See Table P-7 for a list of species of the preserved prairies or historic grasslands.

AMPHIBIANS AND REPTILES. A variety of amphibians and reptiles are associated with grasslands. If wetlands were available for breeding, we would expect among amphibians eastern tiger salamanders and American and Fowler's toads. The assemblage of reptiles associated with grasslands and related habitats is relatively rich. Eastern and ornate box turtles are both found in grasslands and savannas, with their relative abundance dependent upon hydric conditions, tree cover, and soil type. The ornate box turtle predominates in more open, drier areas. The six-lined racerunner and slender glass lizard (western ophisaur) are strongly associated with the open-canopy habitats of grasslands and savannas. Snakes would include the western fox snake, bull snake, hognose snake, plains garter snake, blue racer, and smooth green snake. In moister habitats such as wet prairie, the western fox snake and the eastern massasauga might be found, abundantly so in the past. They would also seasonally use the upland, drier areas nearby. Herpetofauna associated with grasslands are listed in Table H-3.

1800. In the early 1800s, Indiana's grasslands were relatively intact, and a variety of reptiles were quite evident across the landscape. Lizards, such as the six-lined racerunner and western ophisaur, and snakes, such as the western fox snake, bull snake, hognose snake, plains garter snake, blue racer, and smooth green snake, were likely common. The ornate box turtle was also probably common, as was the eastern massasauga in wetter areas of the prairie.

1900. The period from the late 1800s into the early 1900s was likely a period of great decline for grassland amphibians and reptiles. Conversion to agriculture led to immediate habitat loss, while fire suppression facilitated a more gradual but pervasive habitat loss due to succession. The status of most species likely followed the loss of habitat.

2000. By 2000, very little grassland habitat remained, and therefore most grassland herpetofauna have disappeared from most areas where they once occurred. However, some species do appear to be more resilient than others. Fowler's toads, bull snakes, western fox snakes, and prairie kingsnakes appear to cope with agricultural development better than other grassland species. Current programs of prairie restoration may allow the recovery of some of these species.

BIRDS. No other group of birds, with the possible exception of wetland birds, has declined as much as grassland birds following European settlement of Indiana. About half of those species known to breed in the state were listed by IDNR as endangered (e.g., northern harrier, short-eared owl, upland sandpiper, sedge wren, Henslow's sparrow) or of special concern (e.g., western meadowlark) at the start of the twenty-first century. The disruption of grassland bird communities reflects not only the demise of native grasslands, but also changing agricultural practices.

Many of the grassland birds also historically occurred in wet prairies; species more typical of denser and taller grass (such as Henslow's sparrow and sedge wren) would have been relatively more common there than species associated with short grass (see Scott et al. 2002). However, as with the dry prairies, the extant native wet prairie habitats are too rare and fragmented to be of great practical significance to present-day grassland birds.

Seventy-one species of breeding and migratory/wintering birds are associated with grassland habitats in some manner (Tables B-1, B-3). However, only a dozen of the state's present-day breeding species are obligate grassland birds (Table B-3) that are rarely found in other habitats: northern harrier, short-eared owl, upland sandpiper, sedge wren, savannah sparrow, Henslow's sparrow, grasshopper sparrow, eastern meadowlark, western meadowlark, dickcissel, bobolink, and the introduced ring-necked pheasant. A few other obligate species occur as migrants (rough-legged hawk, buff-breasted sandpiper). This section is largely concerned with these obligate grassland species. Such grassland birds were once found mainly in the northwestern and western portions of the state, but can now be found throughout the state where suitable habitat exists as a result of agricultural practices or surface coal mine reclamation. Some grassland species, however, are still limited mainly to the northern half of Indiana (e.g., upland sandpiper, savannah sparrow, western meadowlark, bobolink; Castrale et al. 1998), perhaps reflecting the historical location of prairie habitats in the state.

Besides the obligate grassland species, we recognize three other groupings (Table B-3). Thirty-seven species "use grasslands and other habitats," i.e., make significant use of one or more other habitats, such as row crop fields, developed lands, wetlands, or brushy stages of forest lands (see Table B-1). This is the most numerous group, and such species are often termed "facultative" grassland species in the current literature on grassland birds. Examples include red-winged blackbird (whose primary, highest-density habitat is marsh although it is the most abundant species on grasslands), northern bobwhite, mourning dove (which nests on the ground in grasslands), horned lark, common yellowthroat, and dickcissel. Most facultative species nest in grasslands, but some only forage there during or after the breeding season (red-tailed hawk, American crow, European starling, common grackle). The other groups are species that are characteristically found in large grassland landscapes (and one or more other habitats), but are tied to the presence of shrubs or water. Species requiring shrubs or small trees include eastern kingbird, Bell's vireo, brown thrasher, field sparrow, song sparrow, blue grosbeak, indigo bunting, orchard oriole, and American goldfinch. Those found only near water within grasslands include waterfowl that nest or forage in grasslands (Canada goose, mallard, blue-winged teal) and passerines, such as willow flycatcher and yellow warbler. In fact, several of these species are associated with both shrubs and water (eastern kingbird, willow flycatcher, yellow warbler, song sparrow).

1800. At the dawn of the nineteenth century, Indiana had virtually all of its native grassland habitats and all of its native grassland birds. Most grassland birds occurred historically in dry prairies.

1900. Grassland habitats were not the initial focus of European settlers, and thus the grasslands survived largely intact well into the nineteenth century. However, prairie destruction accelerated toward the latter part of the 1800s, and much of the native wet and dry prairie habitat in Indiana was destroyed by the end of the century. This destruction was an ecological calamity, but it did not have the massive impact on grassland birds that one might expect. The saving grace for many grassland birds was the fact that nineteenth-century agriculture typically involved a great deal of pasture or hayland and fallow fields. This sort of habitat (even if non-native) is suitable for most grassland birds, perhaps with the exception of species like Henslow's sparrow that require relatively undisturbed grasslands. Hence, the initial destruction of native prairie habitats did not destroy grassland bird communities.

In fact, the conversion of forested habitat to agricultural uses undoubtedly created grassland habitat in many regions where it did not exist previously to any significant extent. As a result, grassland birds may have experienced a sort of heyday sometime in the middle third of the nineteenth century as forested habitat was converted (to some extent) to non-native grasslands and before much of the prairie habitat was destroyed. It is perhaps no coincidence that Indiana apparently gained during this time period a few species of North American grassland birds from western states, such as dickcissel and savannah sparrow, as well as some grassland-associated species like lark sparrow and barn owl.

At the close of the nineteenth century, Indiana had all of its native grassland birds, and a few new ones. Most grassland birds were probably holding on reasonably well at this point. The major exception was the greater prairie-chicken, which had become scarce in many parts of its range by the turn of the century (Butler 1898).

2000. Presently, the native dry prairie habitat is of almost no consequence to grassland birds, as virtually all of the (very few) remaining habitat fragments are too small to be attractive to grassland birds (especially those most affected by loss of grassland habitat; see Herkert 1994). The immediate future of grassland birds in Indiana is (sadly) no longer linked to the management of native habitat. This will be the case for the foreseeable future unless efforts to reestablish native grasslands can produce many thousands of hectares of prairies in large parcels. The development of continuous row crop agriculture during the twentieth century, along with the complete destruction of native grassland, had a major impact on Indiana's grassland birds. The effects of changing agricultural practices were particularly severe. Mechanized row crop agriculture consumed many fallow fields, pastures, and hay fields, which reduced those habitats as tractors replaced farm animals as the main source of power. Thus, the non-native grasslands that had helped to sustain grassland birds during much of the nineteenth century were lost in increasing numbers as the twentieth century progressed. The relatively few hay fields and pastures still in existence in the twenty-first century are mostly on farms on which stock is raised, usually cattle for meat or milk, but also to a lesser extent sheep. To make things worse, the remaining hay habitat is cut earlier and more frequently than in the past, often before the first nesting attempt can be completed.

Virtually all grassland birds experienced major declines in abundance during the twentieth century. The greater prairie-chicken diminished rapidly and was largely extirpated by the mid-1900s. The last habitat where they occurred, in Newton County, was first plowed in 1949 (Mumford and Keller 1984). Their demise was probably hastened by brood parasitism and nest destruction by the ring-necked pheasant, whose introduction began in earnest at the start of the century. Many other species declined to low numbers as breeders, including upland sandpiper, northern harrier, and short-eared owl (although the latter two species now winter in the state in substantial numbers). Henslow's sparrow also declined greatly and now breeds in significant numbers only in the reclaimed coal mines of southwestern Indiana (see below) and in the Big Oaks National Wildlife Refuge in the southeastern part of the state. Other grassland species such as dickcissel and grasshopper sparrow are still found locally in some numbers, but are much diminished overall. The only grassland bird still widespread and fairly common (in places) at the beginning of the twenty-first century is the eastern meadowlark, which can exist in marginal grassland habitats.

The only counterexample to this drop in grassland birds is the red-winged blackbird. During the twentieth century, red-winged blackbirds expanded their breeding habitat (from their normal wetland breeding habitat) to include agricultural grasslands. The red-wing became the numerically dominant bird in many of Indiana's grassland habitats (Best et al. 1997; DeVault et al. 2002). This rise in dominance by a "new" grassland species may compound the already troubled situation faced by grassland birds, but the effects of possible competition from red-winged blackbirds on obligate grassland species are not well studied.

During the latter part of the twentieth century, the western meadowlark was verified as breeding in the former prairie regions of northwestern Indiana, but how long this species has been established in Indiana is unclear (it was considered to be a subspecies of the eastern meadowlark until 1908).

MAMMALS. Thirty-seven species of mammals occur in the various grasslands of Indiana (Table M-3), with some species closely related to that habitat: the least shrew, woodchuck (in summer at least), thirteen-lined ground squirrel, Franklin's ground squirrel, plains pocket gopher, western harvest mouse, prairie deer mouse, meadow and prairie voles, southern bog lemming, and perhaps the red fox, least weasel, and badger. The other species listed are common in grasslands but often occur in other habitats as well.

Many of the species listed occur in grasslands throughout the state. The southeastern shrew occurs in the southeastern United States, but in Indiana only in the southwest. The masked shrew is more often in the moist fields of the northern part of the state and is especially common where moss occurs. The short-tailed shrew is much more common in grasslands in northern Indiana, but is more of a woodland species in the south. The least shrew is primarily a grassland species and tolerates dry conditions. The star-nosed mole, which is associated with wet grasslands, occurs only in the northeastern part of the state. Many of the bats are included as they often forage over or along the edge of various open lands. The cottontail rabbit is common in grasslands throughout Indiana and often is seen on lawns.

Three species of squirrels inhabit grasslands: the woodchuck, thirteen-lined ground squirrel, and Franklin's ground squirrel. The woodchuck occurs throughout the state, especially in rolling country. The thirteen-lined ground squirrel occurs in the northern part of the state south to Vigo and Franklin counties. Franklin's ground squirrel once occurred in about 16 northwestern counties, but its range has been shrinking. The thirteen-lined ground squirrel prefers very short grass situations, on golf courses, in cemeteries, along roadsides, and on lawns, where it may often be present in some numbers. Franklin's ground squirrel, on the other hand, prefers dense, tall grass. Also, it is solitary and decreasing in both range and abundance. The best place to look for it today is along railroad rights-of-way or roadsides. It is perhaps most abundant in Benton County, along Highway 52 southwest and just outside of Fowler.

A variety of small mammals characteristically occurs in various grassland habitats. The prairie deer mouse occurs in very sparse grass situations and on sand dunes. It probably originally occurred on the sandy prairies in areas of low ground cover, such as on dunes. Currently, it is very common in cultivated fields. The meadow and prairie voles are dominant small mammals in grasslands, with the meadow vole more abundant in northern Indiana, the prairie vole more abundant to the south. The meadow vole is usually in moist, heavy, grassy vegetation, while the prairie vole is most abundant in drier areas with less total cover, with the vegetation consisting of a greater variety of grass and forb species. The bog lemming is not often taken because it is difficult to catch (it does not readily take bait) and is not very common. It is most often trapped in grassy fields in Indiana, even in dry fields of little bluestem. The meadow jumping mouse is another characteristic mouse of grassy fields in Indiana, although it is usually not very abundant.

The red fox was not originally present, as it did not enter the state until about 1855. The badger is a more recent addition to grasslands also. It is solitary and not very common, yet has been increasing its range southward.

Mammals associated both with wetter grasslands, or wet prairies, and with dry prairies are indicated in Table M-3. Although the mammal communities differ widely, most of the species occur throughout the state. Shrews, other than the least shrew, are often common in wet areas. The masked shrew does not occur in the south-central unglaciated area. The star-nosed mole is characteristic of mucklands associated with wet prairie, but only in a few counties of northeastern Indiana. Meadow voles can be exceedingly common in wet prairies of the north, although they are cyclic, reaching population highs every 3–4 years. In low years, they can be very scarce. Meadow voles are much less abundant in the south. The meadow jumping mouse is often found in wet prairies, not because of the moisture but because of the luxuriant growth of herbaceous vegetation.

A notable species of the dry prairie (Table M-3) is the least shrew, which differs from most shrews in avoiding wet habitats. Ground squirrels (both species) likewise occur in dry areas, with the thirteen-lined most numerous in areas with little cover. Conversely, Franklin's are more solitary and occur in areas with more ground cover. The thirteen-lined ground squirrel occurs in much of northern Indiana, whereas Franklin's occurs only in the northwest. The pocket gopher likewise is found in dry prairie in the prairie lobe of northwestern Indiana (a large area that was originally prairie), centering in Newton County. The prairie vole, as opposed to the meadow vole, is characteristic of dry prairies. The southern bog lemming, despite its name, is characteristic of dry areas.

1800. All of the species listed for grasslands were present in 1800 except for the western harvest mouse, which did not enter the state until about 1969. Many of the species occur in grasslands throughout the state, and their distribution is as indicated in Table M-3.

Most of the mammals indicated as living in wet prairies in Indiana today (Table M-3) were probably living in wet prairies in 1800. The masked shrew was probably in wet prairies throughout the state, except in the unglaciated hill country of southern Indiana. The star-nosed mole probably had a much wider distribution than in 2000, occurring in much of eastern Indiana as indicated by earlier records there.

1900. The natural grasslands were much less extensive in 1900 than they had been in 1800, with many of the prairie areas having been plowed to create farmland. However, the mammal species were quite similar in 1900 to what they had been in 1800 (Table M-3), so many of the comments included for 1800 also apply in 1900. Woodchucks were common in grasslands, especially in rolling country, where they dig prominent burrows. They were often hunted for sport, to prevent livestock from stepping in their burrows and breaking their legs, or sometimes for their hides. The star-nosed mole probably occurred at scattered localities over much of the eastern part of the state. The prairie deer mouse was probably much less common than now, as its current abundance is in cultivated fields. Prairie deer mice occurred in habitats with very sparse grass, especially on sandy prairies and on sand dunes.

Most of the mammals indicated as living in wet prairies in Indiana (Table M-3) were probably there in 1900. The bison and elk were extirpated, wolves were nearly gone, and coyotes were rare.

2000. All species of the original grasslands except for bison, wolves, and elk now occur in grasslands of Indiana. The woodchuck is far less abundant now than formerly because of a decrease in grasslands and possibly also because of increases in coyotes, along with sport shooting. The coyote was apparently scarce in the middle part of the twentieth century but became quite common throughout the state by the mid-1980s. Franklin's ground squirrel has been rapidly decreasing in the last 40 years and is considered endangered in Indiana. The plains pocket gopher occurs in the northwest. It is more restricted in range, occurring primarily in Newton and Jasper counties, but it is doing well, especially in Newton County near Willow Slough Fish and Wildlife Area. The western harvest mouse has rapidly expanded throughout northwestern Indiana. It is still increasing its range and now occurs in at least 18 counties.

The prairie deer mouse was likely much less common originally, since there were no cultivated fields, but it probably occurred in dry prairie situations where there was little vegetative cover, such as on dunes. The bog lemming, despite its name, is not often found in wet grasslands and, surprisingly, is quite often found in dry fields, for example in fields with little bluestem. The house mouse occurs in buildings, but is often found throughout the state in grasslands with good herbaceous ground cover. However, it immediately leaves if the grass is cut or the crop is harvested. It is seldom found in established natural habitats, occurring most often in early seral stages or in disturbed situations. The prairie vole is most common in the southern part of the state, greatly decreasing in the north. Most shrews occur in moist situations, but the least shrew is particularly interesting as it normally occurs in dry grassy areas. Most mammals that occur in prairies (Table M-3) were still present in the early twenty-first century.

Pasture, including Fescue

Pasture is land on which farm animals are put to graze (Figure 5.4). It can be any of several habitats, including sparsely wooded areas, but it is normally thought of as grassland, either native or planted. Depending upon the number of animals using it, it can be hard packed; and, primarily because of this, it is often very poor habitat for many different grassland species that might otherwise occur there.

1800. Most livestock of the Native Americans and the European settlers were free to roam, utilizing forage in native forests and prairies. Cows, sheep, and hogs roamed widely throughout the unfenced native vegetation. Individual domestic animals were ear-notched ("ear-marked") to verify ownership when the animals were rounded up in the fall.

1900. There were 107,887 livestock farms (meaning that most income was derived from domestic livestock) occupying 10,638,358 acres (U.S. Census Bureau 1900). Over 8 million acres of these farms were improved (in crop production), so livestock were grazing most of the unimproved lands, including forests and prairies. Unimproved lands varied by natural region (Table G-3).

2000. There were 1,072,365 acres of pasture on farms in 2002 according to the Indiana Agricultural Statistics, 2003–2004 (Table G-3). This is much less than the 3,955,806 acres shown for pasture/hay by the National Land Cover Data, 1992 (Table G-1). The Indiana Agricultural Statistics estimate is based on a survey of private farmland owners, while the NLCD includes all land in Indiana, including public and private lands not in farms. The NLCD is based on a classification of satellite imagery and may include more than pasture or hay, such as old fields on forest lands.

FLORA. Pasture was more common in the 1800s and early 1900s than in the years approaching and including 2000. With the conversion to row crops, and confinement of livestock, the acreage in pasture has been steadily declining. Whereas the first pastures had native species, Kentucky bluegrass eventually be-

Figure 5.4. Because of trampling, heavily grazed pasture is some of the worst habitat for many species. Photo by James R. Gammon.

came the grass of choice. In the twenty-first century, most pastures are composed of tall fescue, Kentucky bluegrass, orchard grass, and timothy. See Table P-7 for a list of species found in pastures.

Tall fescue and, to a lesser degree, meadow fescue are planted in pastures, recreational areas, highway rights-of-way, and reclamation projects (such as those on mine lands). Areas with monocultures of fescue typically have few species growing in them, in part because of the allelopathic nature of endophytic strains of fescue, which host a fungus (*Acremonium coenophialum*) within the shoot system that secretes various substances (see the "Mammals" section below). See Table P-7 for a list of species found in fescue-dominated areas.

AMPHIBIANS AND REPTILES. While the most intensive grazing practices will restrict herpetofauna to a few resident species, moderate to light grazing may open the vegetative canopy and allow a variety of amphibians and reptiles to persist. Perhaps the biggest factor determining which herpetofauna persist in an area will be the availability of some vegetative and/or rock cover. The loss of shrubs and the grazing of grasses to lawn height will result in the loss of amphibians and reptiles. Extensive areas of fescue are not expected to have resident herpetofauna.

BIRDS. In the nineteenth and early twentieth centuries, pasture lands undoubtedly provided important breeding habitat for grassland birds that are adapted to the more open or short-grass vegetation (e.g., upland sandpiper, killdeer, eastern and western meadowlarks, horned lark, grasshopper sparrow, and savannah sparrow). Pasture lands, while now much diminished, may still provide a favorable breeding habitat for such species. They may be especially important for upland sandpipers, which have declined to very low levels in Indiana, and for vole-hunting barn owls, now restricted to the southern third of the state where pasture is more abundant (Parker and Castrale 1996). However, such pastures must meet several criteria before they might provide habitat for breeding grassland birds: they must have low to moderate grazing pressure, be fairly large in extent (at least 20 ha, preferably much larger), be nonlinear in shape, and be distant from forested habitat. Most of the remaining pasture habitat in Indiana does not meet these criteria; therefore, it is not suitable for most (especially the most beleaguered) grassland birds. However, several large reclaimed coal mines (largely in southwestern Indiana) do contain potentially valuable pasture habitat (see below), particularly for species such as upland sandpiper.

Stands of tall fescue are problematic for all wildlife, including birds. Thus, it is unfortunate that the dominant grass in many non-native grasslands is tall fescue. However, on the reclaimed coal mines, mixtures of tall fescue and smooth brome are productive for breeding birds (Scott et al. 2002).

MAMMALS. Due to soil compaction from domestic livestock, pasture is the most unproductive habitat in the state, other than paved or developed areas, for small mammals. Mammals most likely to be found within pasture lands are the Virginia opossum, the white-footed mouse, the prairie deer mouse, and possibly the house mouse, although the presence of these would depend upon the specific pasture land available, and other species might be present, again depending on the specific type of pasture present and on the adjoining habitats. It is pretty much chance that determines which animals are caught in pasture lands. In 17 randomly selected plots in pasture in Vigo County, Indiana, studied by Whitaker (1962–1965), only 5 individual small mammals were taken: 2 white-footed mice, 1 prairie deer mouse, 1 prairie vole, and 1 least shrew. Deer and coyotes also use pasture lands.

Fescue is notorious for having few mammal inhabitants. We have little data from fescue fields because when we have sampled there, the results were very poor. House mice, prairie or meadow voles, white-footed mice, and cottontail rabbits are the species most likely to be taken in fescue fields, but none prosper there. The reason that the tall fescue is such a poor habitat is that it is infected with the endophytic fungus *Acremonium coenophialum*. This fungus spends its entire life cycle within tall fescue and reproduces by infecting seeds. The seeds later germinate as infected plants. The plants produce alkaloids which may provide an antiherbivory defense for plants through their bitter taste, and may lead to poor reproductive performance and reduced growth rates in some mammals, including prairie voles. Therefore, this habitat has relatively few potential prey organisms; in addition, the fescue itself may taste bad to potential herbivores (Barger and Tannenbaum 1998; Conover 1998; Durham and Tannenbaum 1998). Farmers do not make hay from fescue because it is such a coarse forage that it is almost indigestible.

Hayland

Haylands are mostly composed of grasses and/or legumes that are cut one or more times for livestock food.

1800. A small amount of native grassland may have been cut for hay.

1900. There were 2,360,453 acres producing hay in 1900 (Table G-5). Only 137,721 acres of hay came from native prairie grass, with most of the hayland in cultivated grasses and legumes. Alfalfa and clover were common hayland species. The area in hay varied from 36,447 acres in the Southern Bottomlands region to 915,784 acres in the Central Till Plain region. The presence of hay press barns (buildings in which hay is formed into large bales for shipping) along the Ohio River indicates that Indiana shipped hay to markets downstream.

2000. There were 605,755 acres of hayland in 2000 (Table G-5) with 18,381 acres of native grass cut for hay. Most hayland was in alfalfa (320,210 acres) and tame grasses (25,097 acres). The area in hay varied from 6,457 acres in the Southern Bottomlands region to 148,034 acres in the Central Till Plain region.

FLORA. In addition to weeds, haylands consist mostly of single species crops, such as alfalfa, or some of the grasses mentioned above that are grown in pastures (Figure 5.5). See Table P-7 for a list of species found in haylands.

AMPHIBIANS AND REPTILES. Given their similarity to grassland, several amphibians and reptiles may use hay fields. However, under most circumstances, herpetofauna will not stay very long.

Figure 5.5. Haylands with recently produced bales. Photo by IDNR–*Outdoor Indiana* magazine.

American and Fowler's toads, eastern garter snakes, and racers are among the more likely species to be observed. Unfortunately, hay fields are likely habitat sinks during harvest, as animals that have moved into them likely suffer heavy losses at that time. Stories of snakes bound up in hay bales are common, and individuals seeking refuge beneath the bales are also vulnerable to persecution when the bales are collected.

BIRDS. As with pasture land, haylands (native or otherwise) undoubtedly provided important breeding habitat for just about all grassland birds during the nineteenth and early twentieth centuries. Today, these habitats may be of much more limited value, depending on when the hay is harvested. Historically, hay was not usually harvested in Indiana until early summer, which provided ample time for most birds to successfully raise young from the first breeding attempt. Unfortunately, during the twentieth century, the hay-cutting season began increasingly earlier (especially in alfalfa fields, which are now very common), and today most hay is cut before the first breeding attempt is complete for most grassland birds (with the possible exception of eastern meadowlark). For grassland enrolled in conservation practices by the Natural Resources Conservation Service (NRCS), hay removal is not allowed before midsummer. The present-day short cutting cycle means that subsequent nesting attempts may also be unsuccessful. The unfortunate fact is that many hay fields (if they occur in a landscape context attractive to grassland birds; see the section on pasture habitat above) now function as ecological sinks for many species, especially bobolink (Herkert 1997a).

MAMMALS. Haylands are usually lush meadows with a mammal community most similar to that of dry prairie (both lists are in Table M-3). All of these species are found throughout the state except that the meadow vole is most abundant in the north whereas the prairie vole is most common in the south.

Mined Land

1900. While settlers used native stone for building foundations in the early 1800s, the first organized quarry on record was not established until 1827. It was near Stinesville in southern Indiana (Indiana Limestone Institute 2001). The Indiana Department of Sta-

Figure 5.6. Active mining for coal. Photo by Bruce Kingsbury.

Figure 5.7. Lands mined before 1941 were simply left as they were, forming a washboard-type landscape. Photo by John O. Whitaker, Jr.

Figure 5.8. Lands mined after 1977 have to have the topsoil set aside and replaced, and the original contours have to be resurrected. Most of these lands are now in agricultural fields or in grassland. Photo by Peter Scott.

tistics indicates that there were 2,071 acres of active stone quarries across Indiana in 1900 (Table G-10). Surface or strip-mining for coal (Figure 5.6) has become prevalent in Indiana. It began in the 1920s and has been concentrated in the southwestern portion of the state (Map 5.2) in the Southwestern Lowlands Natural Region. Over 150,000 acres have been mined since that time.

The reclamation of land strip-mined for coal has changed over time, depending on the regulation requirements. Prior to 1941, stripped areas were allowed to recover on their own, with plant colonization related to the nature of the spoil that was deposited at any one place. The land was usually just left alone in the ridges and ravines created by the mining operations (Figure 5.7), although it was often planted with pines. Little variety of plants could occur in stripped areas, because of the poor soils often left at the surface. In 1941, Indiana was the second state to enact reclamation legislation, although it required only the planting of trees with no grading or soil replacement. The land was still left just as it was after mining, with much of the topsoil buried and with the surface often consisting of a washboard-like series of hills and valleys with large deep pits ("last cuts" with high walls). From 1967 to 1977, more stringent state laws required that the land be graded to 33% grade or less, that pits be contoured into more accessible ponds or lakes, and that toxic waste be buried under at least 2 ft of water. This left a series of lower, more rounded hills in a washboard pattern. Finally, on May 13, 1977, the permanent regulatory program implementing section 501(b) of the Surface Mining Control and Reclamation Act (SMCRA) was enacted. It required that the topsoil be set aside and replaced, that the original contours be approximated, and that guidelines regarding water quality, plant diversity, and post-mining land use be adhered to. This completely changed mining practices and the resulting habitats and required a greater diversification of restored conditions, including criteria for wildlife habitat and wetlands. Since 1982, 55,834 strip-mined acres have been reclaimed under these regulations. Much more of the land is now cultivated and much of it is in grassland (Figure 5.8).

2000. On areas strip-mined since 1977 in west-central Indiana, one now finds the full range of grassland small mammals, plus numerous hawks, short-eared owls, and grassland birds, including Henslow's sparrow.

Actively Mined Land

FLORA. Due to the frequent, intense level of disturbance involved with active coal, gravel, or stone mining, few plants other than the very weedy species become established. Examples of these include bouncing bet, cheat grass, northern rush grass, hairy aster, fall panicum, hairy crabgrass, green foxtail, lesser love grass, horseweed, lamb's quarters, common ragweed, and nodding spurge. See Table P-7 for plant species of actively mined lands.

AMPHIBIANS AND REPTILES. Land that is actively being mined will have little value to herpetofauna. With respect to abandoned or reclaimed

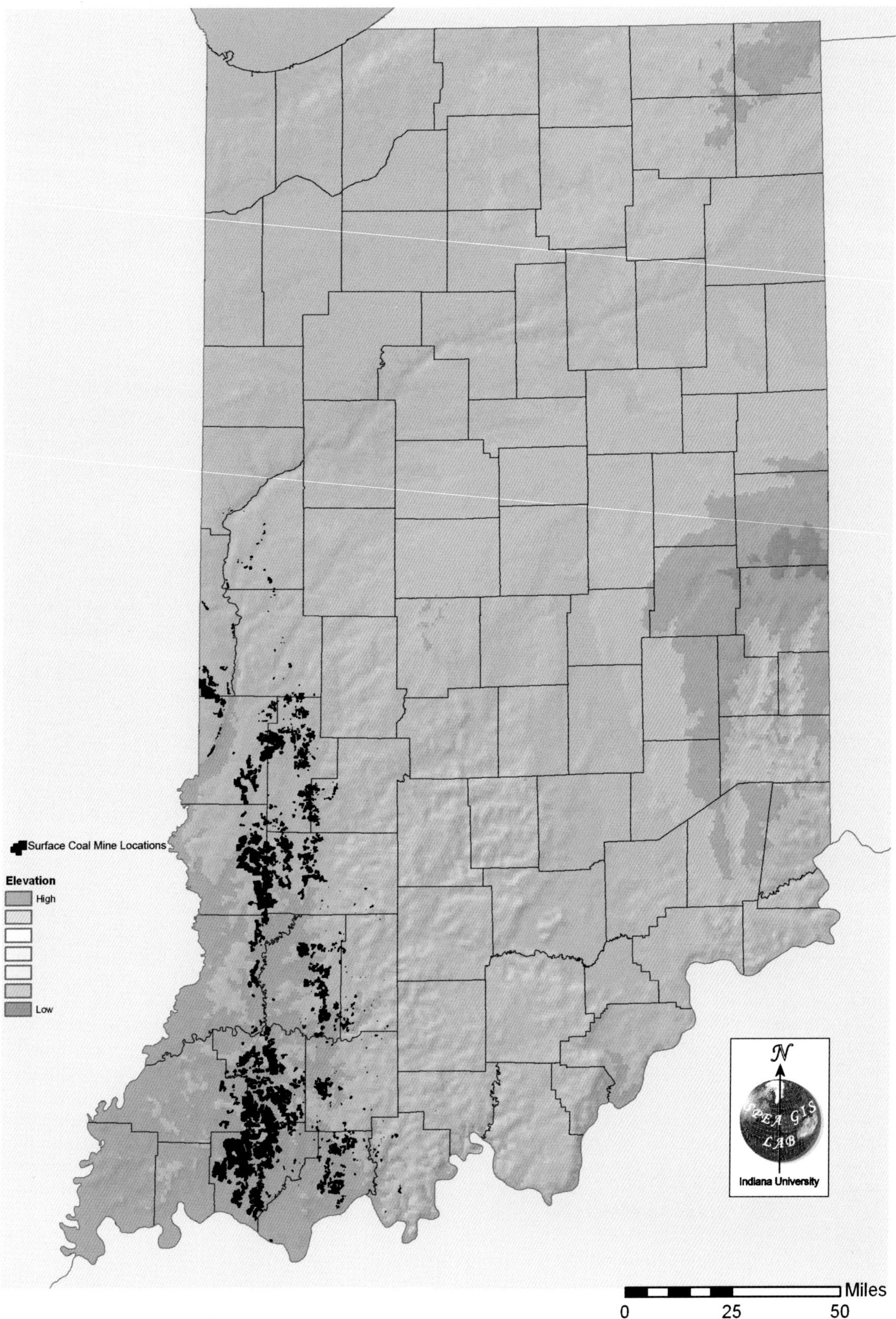

Map 5.2. Surface coal mines of Southern Indiana.
Source: Indiana Geological Survey.

habitat, the herpetofaunal community establishing on reclaimed surface-mining areas will be based on available local colonists and on the morphology and hydrology of the reclamation/restoration. Water and soil must also be of sufficient quality, which for the pre-law (1977) sites is quite variable.

BIRDS. Actively mined areas (prior to any degree of reclamation) are of little value to birds. Any birds present will usually be limited to aerially feeding species, such as swifts and swallows. Among the very few species that might breed in such areas are horned larks and killdeer. Some swallows might also find some opportunities for breeding in such areas.

MAMMALS. Land being actively mined will have little value to mammals since it will not contain adequate cover. Some of the land strip-mined in the early days (before 1967) is nearly barren even today, depending on the soil that was left on the surface. However, land mined since 1967, and especially since 1977, is subject to the updated reclamation laws. These habitats are often much more similar to lands prior to strip-mining and are often in grassland, which is why the major discussion of mining has been included in this chapter.

Land Strip-Mined before 1967

Land mined prior to 1967 (47,738 acres) was primarily planted in trees with no soil replacement. Such land varied, depending mostly upon soil characteristics, but much of this land is like a corrugated series of ridges and valleys, often planted in pines or black locust.

FLORA. In general, terrain strip-mined before 1967 was planted in a mix of tree species, and colonized by native plant species that arrived via windborne propagules or by other vectors, such as the fur of mammals, including many grasses and members of the aster family. In areas of pre-1967 mining activity that have not been extensively revegetated, areas of barren land exist mostly where the soil chemistry is extreme (either highly acidic or mineral-poor) and/or where little or no soil is present. Some of the species tolerant of such conditions include three-awn grass, buttonweed (*Diodia*), partridge pea, Venus's looking glass, common ragweed, broom sedge, Korean clover, silky bush clover, common cinquefoil, yellow sweet clover, annual fleabane, hairy aster, and old-field goldenrod. On more favorable sites, native trees and shrubs can colonize, including sycamore, eastern cottonwood, American elm, hackberry, pin oak, elderberry, blackberry, and common dewberry.

AMPHIBIANS AND REPTILES. Given the susceptibility of amphibians to low pH, many wetlands on old mined areas are depauperate of them. However, not all wetlands appearing after mining have poor water quality. Most of these wetlands also have steep banks and often no littoral zone. This would preclude successful reproduction for most frogs and salamanders. Turtles such as painted turtles and common snapping turtles would be expected in many of the wetlands with reasonable water quality.

Terrestrial habitats in these areas would likely have the species occurring in nearby less-manipulated habitats. Given the dependence of many snakes, such as garter snakes and ribbon snakes, on anurans as prey, upland herpetofaunal diversity and densities are expected to respond to the quality of the wetlands embedded in them.

BIRDS. Pre-1967 mined lands are now covered mainly by forests, some of which have succeeded to sizable hardwood stands. Many such areas were also planted directly in pines, and they now contain some of the largest stands of pines in Indiana. Thus, the birds of pre-1967 mined lands are essentially (depending on the forest cover) as described in the sections on forest birds in chapter 4.

MAMMALS. Many mammals might use or pass through old strip-mined areas, but very few actually live there. The only species of mammal commonly living there are the prairie deer mouse in bare areas, and the white-footed mouse, the prairie vole, and sometimes a few short-tailed shrews if there is enough cover and moisture.

Land Strip-Mined between 1968 and 1977

Some improvements were made in these habitats through changes in strip-mining techniques, but basically the species were the same as in lands strip-mined before 1967.

During this period, spoil piles were graded to approximately 33% grade or less, and the pits were contoured into more accessible ponds or lakes. Also, potentially toxic materials now had to be under at least 2 ft of water or soil. Finally, a more comprehensive revegetation program was introduced.

FLORA. Lands mined after 1967, and especially after 1977, are, paradoxically, much less diverse floristically than lands mined before 1967. While the intent of the newer regulations was to provide for better reclamation, these sites possess substrates that are more compacted than the pre-1967 mined sites, and are commonly planted in a mix of invasive, exotic species that exclude the colonization of native species. Typical species planted include tall fescue, Kentucky bluegrass, smooth brome, orchard grass, reed canary grass, redtop, perennial rye, red clover, sweet clover, Korean clover, alfalfa, and birdsfoot trefoil. Minimal acreage is returned to forest land.

AMPHIBIANS AND REPTILES. The more rounded terrain created during this period improved habitat suitability for herpetofauna. In particular, reduced inclines along the shores of wetlands enhanced the value of them to reproducing amphibians, and thus improved the prey base for reptiles and other wildlife feeding on them.

BIRDS. The situation was essentially as described above for pre-1967 mined areas, unless the areas were reclaimed into grassland habitat (see below).

MAMMALS. The white-footed mouse is the most abundant species of small mammal in this habitat, followed by the prairie deer mouse in the bare areas; a few short-tailed shrews may occur if there is enough cover and moisture.

Land Strip-Mined after 1977

Reclamation practices after 1977 totally changed the character of the land, which now includes some of the most productive grassland in the state, as well as much good farmland. (Agricultural lands are covered in chapter 10.) Topsoil was now stockpiled and reapplied. The original contours had to be restored, and the areas were seeded. This treatment has produced large tracts of grassland (see Figure 5.8) favorable to many vertebrate species. Since 1982, around 55,834 acres have been restored with most being planted in grasses.

FLORA. Most grasses planted on reclaimed mine land are exotic species. The principal ones are tall fescue, Kentucky bluegrass, and Hungarian brome. Silky bush clover is commonly included in the planting mix. It is an invasive species capable of overcoming grass species. See Table P-7 for a list of species found in reclaimed mine lands. The Indiana Department of Natural Resources (IDNR) is converting reclaimed strip-mined land under its management from non-native cool season grasses to warm season grasses as resources permit.

AMPHIBIANS AND REPTILES. The more gentle terrain created during this period improved habitat suitability for herpetofauna. In particular, reduced inclines along the shores of wetlands enhanced the value of them to reproducing amphibians, and thus improved the prey base for reptiles and other wildlife feeding on them.

Surface-mined lands restored after 1977 are much more conducive to supporting herpetofauna, though likely at lower densities than the original countryside. Returning the landscape to its original contours, redistributing topsoil, and defending water quality have all contributed to this success. Most of Indiana's wetlands are naturally shallow, but wetlands established after 1977 on abandoned mine lands were often deep with steep slopes. Post-SMCRA wetlands include more shallow systems, and these will be far more conducive to successful anuran reproduction.

Many areas restored from surface mining are grassland. Unfortunately, due to the limited dispersal capabilities of most amphibians and reptiles, as compared to mammals and birds, the herpetofauna available to exploit such grasslands have been only those species occurring in nearby less-manipulated habitats, which might also use such open areas. However, some amphibians and reptiles do use these lands. In a twenty-first-century study of amphibians on mined lands in Indiana, Timm and Meretsky (2004) provided useful information on species using previously mined areas. They found bullfrog, chorus frog, gray treefrog, cricket frog, Fowler's toad, spring peeper, and even the crawfish frog. The crawfish frogs are of particular importance because they are state-listed and closely associated with the burrows of the more terrestrial, chimney-forming burrowing crayfish. Wetlands associated with grasslands, a common cover type post-mining, suit the crawfish frog nicely. Although their focus was on anurans, Timm and Meretsky (2004) also noted the presence of lesser sirens, (midland) water snakes, red-eared sliders, common snapping turtles, and midland painted turtles. Other species expected on recovering mined areas are listed in Table H-3.

BIRDS. Reclaimed mines (almost entirely in the southwestern part of the state; Brothers 1990) contain large grassland habitats, undoubtedly some of the largest extant grasslands east of the Mississippi (Bajema and Lima 2001). The reclamation of mines into grassland is a direct result of the federal Surface Mining Control and Reclamation Act of 1977. This act did not mandate grasslands nor any other specific type of vegetation; rather, grasses (all non-native) provided the cheapest means of producing a vegetative outcome acceptable under the act. Regardless of the motivations involved, the grasslands of reclaimed mines are now a major refuge for grassland birds in Indiana.

Reclaimed mines attract many of the obligate grassland birds listed in Table B-3. These lands are especially important to grasshopper sparrow and Henslow's sparrow; an appreciable fraction of the global population of the latter species is known to occur in the reclaimed mines of Indiana (Bajema et al. 2001; DeVault et al. 2002). These and other grassland birds breed successfully in the reclaimed mines (Galligan et al. 2006). Northern bobwhites are fairly common in summer, based on the whistle counts of males (DeVault et al. 2002), so the habitat may be important for this declining species. The grassland raptors (northern harrier and short-eared owl) also breed in the reclaimed mines (Castrale et al. 1998), but sparsely, the mines being at the southern limit of their breeding ranges. They winter in reclaimed mines in much larger numbers (P. Scott and S. Lima, unpublished data). The issue of landscape context plays an important role in the attractiveness of these mines to birds. More than just about any other grassland habitat in Indiana, reclaimed mine lands have the "gestalt" of a prairie; that is, they consist of large mosaics of various grassland habitats, often many square kilometers in extent. These reclaimed grasslands also produce habitat of importance to marsh birds and migrating waterfowl (see chapter 6).

MAMMALS. Reclaimed mine lands currently provide large areas of quality grassland and support many of the same species that one finds in other grasslands (Table M-3).

The white-footed mouse was the most abundant species of small mammal in the earlier stripped lands, if adequate cover was present, followed by the prairie deer mouse in the bare areas, and a few short-tailed shrews if enough cover and moisture were present. However, the mammalian fauna since the 1977 changes in the mining laws are the same as those listed for cultivated lands, for old fields, or for whatever habitat was in place after the mining. A comprehensive list of mammals in this habitat is presented in Table M-3. Other lists are presented for cultivated lands (Table M-7). See species lists for other habitats, as appropriate.

However, since most of the reclaimed mine land is in the southwestern part of the state, some of the grassland species are not present (Table M-3). Some species are closely related to grasslands: the least shrew, woodchuck (in summer at least), western harvest mouse, prairie deer mouse, meadow and prairie voles, southern bog lemming, and perhaps the red fox, least weasel, and badger. The other species listed are common in grasslands but are often in other habitats as well.

Many of the species on reclaimed mine lands are those that occur in grasslands, totaling 35 species, as indicated in Table M-3. However, the southeastern shrew occurs in the southwestern third of the state, north to Tippecanoe County. The short-tailed shrew is much more common in grasslands in the north and is more of a woodland species in the south. The least shrew is primarily a grassland species and tolerates quite dry conditions. Many of the bats are included as they often forage over various open lands. The woodchuck digs burrows in grasslands and sometimes occurs in reclaimed mine lands. The prairie deer mouse occurs in areas with sparse ground cover, thus seldom in reclaimed mine areas. The meadow and prairie voles are dominant species in the mine lands, with the meadow vole more abundant in moist, heavy grassy vegetation, whereas the prairie vole is most abundant in drier areas with less ground cover. The bog lemming is not often taken because it is more difficult to catch (it does not readily take bait) and is not very common, but is most often taken in grassy fields in Indiana, even in dry fields of little bluestem. It should inhabit mine lands. The meadow jumping mouse is another characteristic mammal of grassy fields in Indiana and should occur in this habitat. Badgers surely will occur in these areas, but none has been documented as yet. Ron Hellmich of the Natural Heritage Data Center indicated that there are 36 badger records from southwest Indiana. At least 2 road-kill reports occurred near likely mine lands, based on the most recent aerials (2005). Most of our records are road-kill or trapper reports. Hellmich was unable to find anything that would place the badgers directly on reclaimed mine lands, probably because nobody has done surveys on reclaimed mine lands looking for badgers, or for other rare species.

Vegetated Dunes

Vegetated dunes on Lake Michigan begin just beyond the beach. The beach is usually flat and without plants because of the rigors of storms and waves, especially in winter. The first line of dunes is located just above the elevation where the winter storms reach. These usually have beach grass, *Ammophila breviligulata* (Figure 5.9), and prairie sand reed, *Calamovilfa longifolia,* as two of the primary dune-forming grasses. Usually, there are bare sand areas between clumps of these grass species. The cottonwood can also function as a dune-forming tree. Cottonwood trees put out adventitious roots along the trunk, permitting the root system to keep pace with the growth of the developing dune. Cottonwoods produce high, narrow dunes that may become wandering dunes (Figure 5.10) which move inland, especially if beach grass or other plants have not provided sufficient cover when the original tree dies.

A considerable area of vegetated dunes also once occurred in the southwestern part of the state. These were dominated by grasses and scattered groves of small trees. Big bluestem, Indian grass, little bluestem, and side-oats grama were important grasses, and black oak, white oak, chinquapin oak, post oak, and blackjack oak were the dominant trees. Locally, pale hickory occurred on sandy ridgetops.

FLORA. Large areas of sand deposits exist in far northern Indiana and in smaller pockets of southwestern Indiana. An important species of dune habitats that occurs along Lake Michigan is beach grass, which is found only there in Indiana. Also present are prairie sand reed, little bluestem, and Canada wild rye. Dunes there and elsewhere in the state may exhibit beach three-awn grass, arrowfeather, little bluestem, purple love grass, prairie switch grass, sand dropseed, and porcupine grass. Prairie cord grass and blue joint grass are prominent in the swales, as are ephemeral annuals. A prominent example of the dunes and swales type occurs next to Lake Michigan (Lake Michigan Border section of the Northwestern Morainal Natural Region). See Table P-7 for a list of species of vegetated dunes and swales.

AMPHIBIANS AND REPTILES. Indiana lacks herpetofauna specifically adapted to dune habitat, and none would likely occur on open dunes. However, there certainly are several species that exploit the more vegetated areas of dunes and sandy areas associated with the south shore of Lake Michigan. The six-lined racerunner is a common species on the Lake Michigan dunes. The eastern hognose snake is a good example of a species at home in sandy environments, as are the bull snake and the legless lizard. The dunes herpetofaunal community has probably not changed substantively over time. No doubt, however, dunes habitat has been lost to successional advances.

BIRDS. This is a rare habitat in Indiana and is of no special avian concern. No obligate grassland species are likely to breed in such dunes unless the grassland vegetation is unusually dense and the dune field is large in extent (a currently rare situation). The federally endangered piping plover, now a very rare migrant on the Indiana shores of Lake Michigan, uses beaches rather than vegetated dunes.

MAMMALS. Mammals of vegetated dunes are given in Table M-3. All of these species probably occur throughout the state on vegetated dunes except that the thirteen-lined ground squirrel occurs only in the northern half of the state. The meadow vole occurs in the moist depressions between dunes. Its cuttings are often found in these areas, sometimes along with the much longer ones of the meadow jumping mouse. The prairie vole occurs in the drier areas. All of these species probably occurred on the vegetated dunes throughout the time period 1800–2000.

Savanna

Savannas are predominantly prairie mixed with scattered individual trees or groves of trees (Figure 5.11).

Figure 5.9. Beach grass, *Ammophila breviligulata,* is the main grass forming vegetated dunes. Photo by Terry L. Castor.

Figure 5.10. Bare areas left by wandering dunes. Photo by Terry L. Castor.

Figure 5.11. Savanna. Photo by Charles Amlaner.

Low moist areas within savannas are called swales. Savanna vegetation is transitional in type between grassland and forest (Jackson 1997). Thus, information is somewhat duplicated in this section and in the last sub-habitat section of chapter 4.

This habitat type was generally found adjacent to prairies and was maintained by periodic fires, usually set by Native Americans (see Map 1.3). Gordon (1936) mapped just under 4 million acres of oak forest and northern swamp forest which was primarily this habitat type (Table G-14). This habitat type occurred in 7 natural regions in 1800.

FLORA. Grassland savanna habitats are populated by mostly prairie species, as well as some typical of forests (the dominance of which depends on the history of the site and the degree of shading). These environments declined as the state was settled by Europeans and as the fires of the Native Americans were controlled. Only a few scattered parcels of less than a few thousand total acres remained by 2000. Most of the savanna occurred in northwestern Indiana, especially in the Kankakee Sand section of the Grand Prairie Natural Region. Many of the same grasses mentioned above for vegetated dunes can be found here as well. See Table P-7 for a list of species of savanna.

AMPHIBIANS AND REPTILES. Remnant dunes that have not become too overgrown with shrubs and trees may have grassland or savanna habitat on them. Consequently, the herpetofauna in such areas will be dominated by grassland species. The wetlands in the swales between the remnant dunes can be very diverse and can have a rich herpetofaunal diversity. The close proximity of grassland, forest, and a variety of wetlands leads to an even greater potential for biodiversity. Such areas do not have unique species, but rather combinations derived from the communities nearby. Some of the more interesting species include the northern leopard frog, cricket frog, Blanding's and spotted turtles, eastern massasauga, western fox snake, bull snake, and six-lined racerunner.

BIRDS. Savanna habitat can be characterized as largely open woodlands, clearly lacking a closed canopy, in which there are abundant grasses and forbs derived mainly from surrounding prairie habitat. Savannas occur primarily on sandy soils in northern Indiana. Trees there do not grow densely enough for canopy closure, primarily because of the lack of nutrients and water. Fire undoubtedly played a role in the savannas originally. Despite the presence of prairie vegetation, obligate grassland birds are largely absent from savanna habitats (Grundel and Pavlovic 2007a). Simply put, if there is enough tree canopy cover in an area to place it into the category of savanna, no typical grassland birds will breed there (or almost none). Savanna habitats may, however, contain some generalist bird species that sometimes occur in prairie habitat (e.g., field sparrow and common yellowthroat). Red-headed woodpeckers are often found in such habitat when there are dead standing trees. We described the bird species typical of savanna habitats in detail in chapter 4.

MAMMALS. The mammals of the swales and savannas of the Lake Michigan dunes area are the same as those on the vegetated dunes (Table M-3). The two vole species are most abundant in the areas with the heaviest ground cover, and the prairie deer mouse occurs in the areas with very little ground cover.

Farm Bill Program Land: Conservation Reserve Program

The Food Security Act of 1985 contained provisions designed to discourage the conversion of wetlands into non-wetland areas. These provisions, collectively, are commonly referred to as the "swampbuster" provisions (Food Security Act of 1985, Title XII, subtitle C). The swampbuster provisions denied federal farm program benefits to producers who converted wetlands after December 23, 1985. The Food, Agriculture, Conservation, and Trade Act of 1990 strengthened these provisions by making violators ineligible for farm program benefits for that year and subsequent years. The act also created a system for inadvertent violations, allowing farmers to regain lost federal benefits if they restore converted wetlands. The 1996 farm bill (Federal Agriculture Improvement and Reform Act of 1996, P.L. 104-127) contained numerous provisions that purportedly modified the operation of certain agricultural programs. In particular, subtitle C, covering wetland conservation, modified sections 1221 and 1222 (16 U.S.C. 3821 and 3822) of the Food Security Act of 1985 regarding program ineligibility, wetland delineation, and consultation and cooperation requirements, and it clarified the definition of agricultural lands in the memorandum of agreement signed by the Department of the Army, the Department of the Interior, and the Environmental Protection Agency on January 6, 1994. It also authorized the secretary of agriculture to operate a pilot program for the mitigation banking of wetlands to assist persons in increasing the efficiency of agricultural operations while protecting wetland functions and values.

The Conservation Reserve Program (Title XII, 16 U.S.C. 3831) authorizes the federal government to enter into contracts with agricultural producers to remove highly erodible cropland from production, in return for annual rental payments. The Wetlands Reserve Program (16 U.S.C. 3837) authorizes the enrollment of wetlands for protection and restoration through permanent and temporary (30-year) easements.

The CRP allows the federal government to enter into contracts with landowners to establish several different vegetation types, including trees, grasses, and wetland species, to stabilize erosive soils. Establishment of grasses varies from native prairie species to exotic species such as fescue. The acres planted in exotic grass generally include one species, while those planted in native species may include a mixture of species more similar to natural prairie. It needs to be remembered that CRP is not a permanent easement. The land can revert to agriculture at any time.

1800. This program was not present at this time.

1900. This program was not present at this time.

2000. There were 272,494 acres of farmland in various conservation reserve practices in 2000 (Table G-20). Of this, 214,586 acres were in grass, 34,051 in trees, 16,626 in wildlife habitat (including corridor establishment, food plots, water, improving marginal pasture, and restoring rare habitats), and 7,231 acres in wetland restoration. The area planted in grass included 28,448 acres of native prairie grasses. Trees were mostly planted in mixed hardwood plantations (18,547 acres) to control soil erosion. General wildlife habitat, which made up most of the acres planted for wildlife, comprised 11,324 acres. Wetland restoration was the main practice in the wetland category with 6,635 acres restored. These practices varied greatly in acreage by natural region.

There are several different programs under the CRP, including:

CP1. "Plantings of non-native grasses and legumes to reduce soil erosion, improve water quality, and create or enhance wildlife habitat." Introduced grasses were established on 37,412 acres. The area planted to grass varied from 336 in the Northwestern Morainal region to 9,393 acres in the Central Till Plain region (Table G-20).

CP2. "Plantings of native grasses and forbs or legumes to reduce soil erosion, improve water quality, and create or enhance wildlife habitat." Native grasses were established on 28,448 acres. Plantings varied from 857 acres in the Northwestern Morainal region to 7,026 in the Central Till Plain region (Table G-20).

CP10. "Manage existing grass, or grass/legume cover, to reduce soil erosion, improve water quality, and create or enhance wildlife habitat." Non-native grass was planted on 73,214 acres. This practice varied from 1,668 acres in the Northwestern Morainal region to 22,259 acres in the Central Till Plain (Table G-20).

FLORA. Most of the land enrolled in the various farm programs, including the Conservation Reserve Program, has been planted in exotic species, specifically tall fescue and Hungarian brome. Some landowners utilize native warm season grasses, especially big bluestem, little bluestem, Indian grass, and switchgrass. See Table P-7 for a list of species found in farm bill program lands.

AMPHIBIANS AND REPTILES. Since herpetofauna are generally poor colonizers of habitat islands, we would not expect grassland species to usually find and exploit CRP properties. However, this might occur depending on the surrounding landscape matrix. Nevertheless, CRP would commonly benefit local herpetofauna first as habitat superior to crop fields, and as relatively safe open-canopy habitat when planted in grasses. Given these considerations, occupants of CRP lands would be expected to come from, and be strongly influenced by, the available local species. The greatest benefit is derived from the use of native species of grasses and trees.

BIRDS. The most important part of the farm bill programs for bird species is the Conservation Reserve Program, which has produced many thousands of hectares of grassland habitat in Indiana and elsewhere in the Midwest. The majority of CRP land has been committed to non-native grasses (CP1, CP10), which, as mentioned earlier, are not necessarily problematic for grassland birds. A lesser amount of CRP land (CP2) has been planted in a few species of native grasses. This newly created CRP grassland habitat has proven to be of value to many grassland bird species (Johnson and Schwartz 1993; Best et al. 1997; Herkert 1997b; Walk and Warner 2000; Vickery and Herkert 2001). However, as with the newly created grassland habitats in reclaimed coal mines, the CRP grasslands were not created with the goal of producing habitat for grassland birds. Hence, following the discussion above of various grassland types, the value of CRP grassland parcels will vary with their size and shape, management practices (especially haying/mowing operations), the greater landscape context in which they occur, and the specific types of vegetation planted. Generally speaking, grassland birds benefit most when CRP grassland habitat is in large, nonlinear parcels (over 60 ha; Walk and Warner 1999) well away from forested habitat, is planted in a variety of grasses (and perhaps some forbs), and is hayed/mowed infrequently or late in the summer.

MAMMALS. The mammals of the early seral stage fields (Table M-3) are the ones most likely to be here in the beginning, followed by the mammals of mature grasslands later (Table M-3).

Wetlands

6

Wetlands include many habitats and some grade one into the other. In this volume, we have divided wetlands into two chapters. In chapter 7, "Aquatic Systems," are the natural rivers, streams, lakes, and ponds, and also man-made impoundments and reservoirs. Oxbows, backwaters, sloughs, and embayments are also considered in chapter 7. Some overlap with these and the wetlands discussed in this chapter is recognized and speaks to the diversity of wetlands in definition, function, and characteristics.

Wetlands considered in this chapter may be ephemeral or permanent. They consist of swamps, marshes, bogs, fens, potholes, wetlands and ditches of farmed areas, and mudflats. Ephemeral wetlands do not contain permanent populations of fish, although fish may enter them during local flood events. The habitats included in chapter 7 often have submergent vegetation, while those considered in this chapter often have emergent vegetation as well. Swamps are characterized by having trees as their dominant species, although there are also shrub wetlands characterized by such plants as buttonbush. Marshes have abundant emergent herbaceous vegetation such as cattails. Bogs are generally acidic, develop floating masses of vegetation, and have a unique set of plants: sphagnum, cranberry, blueberry, huckleberry, pitcher plant, sundew, bog rosemary, and many others. Potholes are usually small ponds in northern Indiana scoured out by glaciers. Many no longer exist, but many that do are surrounded by croplands. As mentioned above, wetland habitats are often not clearly separated from one another. A lake may have extensive marsh or swamp in its shallower areas. Backwaters of streams and rivers may be choked with aquatic vegetation. The various wetlands, especially those without fish, form some of Indiana's best habitat for many animals, especially amphibians and reptiles.

Most of Indiana's original wetland habitat was located in the recently glaciated northern half of the state, but large and small palustrine (swampy) wetlands were found throughout the state (Map 6.1). Forested palustrine wetlands were also common along big rivers, such as the Wabash. More than a century of drainage to convert wetlands into agricultural land left only a small percentage of the original habitat. However, many wetlands have been restored or created (for the mitigation of losses elsewhere) since the late twentieth century. In this chapter's treatment of present conditions (early twenty-first century), we rarely make distinctions between old, new, and restored wetlands, partly for lack of adequate comparative data. Instead, we concentrate on the differences between ephemeral and permanent wetlands, and on vegetation types, such as forested, shrub-dominated, or herbaceous. However, the accounts for 1800 and 1900 predate conservation efforts, and thus refer to original wetlands.

1800. Wetlands are estimated to have covered 5.6 million acres in Indiana in the late 1700s (Myers 1997). Most wetlands were found within bottomland areas and in upland depressional sites left by glaciation (Table G-22).

1900. Wetlands were not defined by type (see the categories in the next section) in data sources from this time period. Many large wetlands are shown on county maps from 1876 (Table G-22), mainly in the northwestern and northeastern areas of the state. Forests were left uncut in many areas of the state because of wet soil conditions.

2000. The National Wetlands Inventory (1995) found nearly 1 million acres (995,445) of wetlands within Indiana (Table G-21). Wetland types contributing most to this total were palustrine forested (502,000 acres), palustrine emergent (156,000), lacustrine or lake margins (144,000), ponds (95,000), riverine (53,000), and palustrine scrub/shrub (42,000; numbers rounded to the nearest thousand acres).

The Wetlands Reserve Program of the Natural Resources Conservation Service has enrolled 25,000 acres in Indiana since 1994. This voluntary program provides technical and financial support to landowners for the protection, restoration, and enhancement of wetlands.

Flora

The flora of wetland communities can be quite variable, depending on several influencing factors such as substrate type, water level, degree of disturbance, and impact by invasive exotics, among others. In general, native wetlands possess the greatest natural diversity (Table P-8), although not necessarily so. Certain restored or created wetlands could have more species present than would naturally occur at a site. Waterfowl use of wetlands transports seeds and plants, which partially explains the relatively rapid establishment of plants in newly created wetlands even without human planting. Seeds of wetland plants may also survive in the soil of drained wetlands, then germinate after the site is flooded. Wind dispersal is another important vector of seeds of wetland plants. The appendixes for other wetlands types include species that can be found here.

Wetlands today are often restored or created as mitigation of drained wetlands. These wetlands are

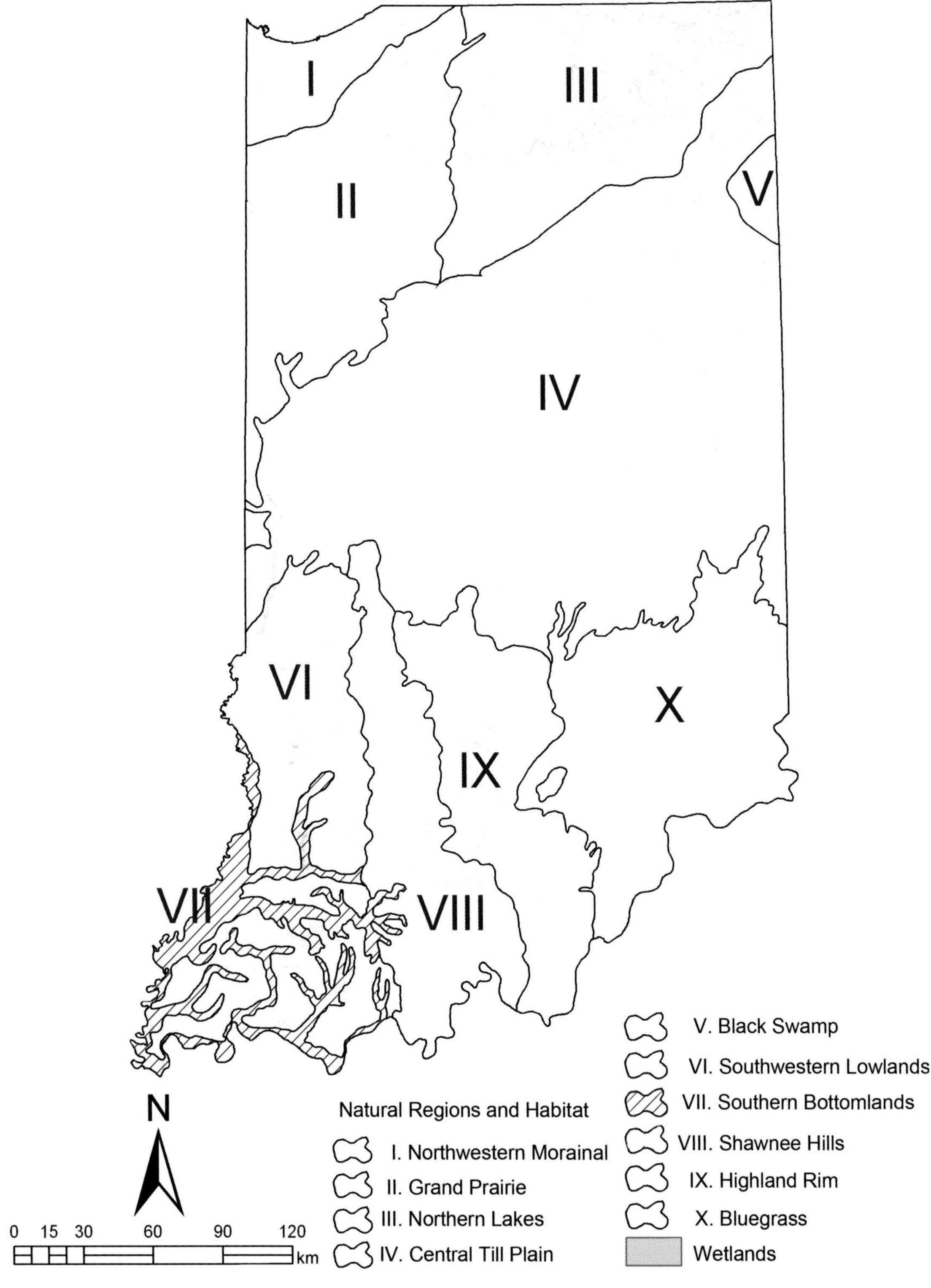

Map 6.1. Wetlands by natural region.

likely to have many of the same species as native systems. However, only those species that are in immediately adjacent habitat will be available to colonize such areas. It will often take special treatment to introduce species where local seed sources are not available.

Wetlands were particularly common in the northern part of the state, especially the Northern Lakes and Grand Prairie natural regions. However, most natural regions had considerable areas of wetland. The flora of wetlands, whether forested or graminoid, consists of species capable of tolerating (or requiring) an extended period of flooding. The area of wetland habitat has been greatly reduced over the past two centuries through ditching and tile drainage. Consequently, many wetland plants perished, and there has been a concomitant reduction in the diversity of native wetland plant species in the state. Part of this reduction is due to the introduction of invasive exotics, especially purple loosestrife and Eurasian strains of common reed and reed canary grass.

1800. The greatest diversity of native wetland plants likely occurred in 1800, for no other reason than that the greatest area and quality of wetlands existed during that time period. The wetland flora was also free of invasive, competitive exotics.

1900. With the advent of new technology and equipment capable of efficiently digging ditches, many wetlands were drained for agricultural production, and consequently, wetland flora was lost in drained areas. Most species persisted in the remaining wetlands and within the drainage ditches (if not too deep and erosive). With hydrological changes, many of the remaining wetlands may have experienced changes in species composition. Species known to have disappeared by 1900 include mare's tail and short-beaked bald rush.

2000. With the continued drainage of wetlands, many wetland plants declined in number and several species were extirpated. Native species that became extirpated between 1900 and 2000 include dragon's mouth orchid, small enchanter's nightshade, northern willow herb, dense cotton grass, reed manna grass, least duckweed, false bearded panic grass, four-angled rose gentian, lance-leaved burhead, Drummond's small-flowered rush, and American brooklime. The widespread use of drainage tile, besides creating larger and deeper drainage ditches, has left but a fraction of the wetlands that occurred in 1800. Consequently, the numbers of wetland plant individuals and species continue to decline. The increase in invasive exotic plants has added to the decline. Purple loosestrife, Eurasian strains of common reed and reed canary grass, and glossy buckthorn are the main species that seriously compete with the native ones.

Fish

Fish communities of wetlands can be highly variable, in some cases temporal in nature, and often are influenced by other aquatic habitats that are in close proximity and by the diversity of plant species. Ephemeral wetlands often do not contain fish or only receive fish when flooded by the surrounding, more permanent, aquatic habitats. The fish communities of these wetlands resemble those from which they came and only survive until the water is depleted. As waters recede, the fish in these habitats provide important food sources for other animals. The construction of levees and other water control structures has altered the timing and periodicity of flood events and how long water remains in many of Indiana's wetland habitats.

More permanent wetlands, especially those associated with big rivers, often have a dichotomy in the species present. Many native species, such as spotted gar, bowfin, cypress minnow, golden shiner, lake chubsucker, the various bullhead species, tadpole madtom, central mudminnow, pirate perch, northern starhead topminnow, blackstripe topminnow, western mosquitofish, flier, warmouth, redspotted sunfish, bluntnose darter, slough darter, and banded pygmy sunfish, desire these habitats and complete their entire life history there. Another group of species, such as paddlefish, longnose and shortnose gar, gizzard shad, the various carpsucker and buffalo species, channel catfish, white bass, yellow bass, bluegill, crappie, sauger, and freshwater drum, simply invade these habitats during periods of high water, then come and go during successive high-water events. Even in these habitats, fish communities can occasionally be completely wiped out in years of extreme drought. Brand-new communities then emerge during the next flood event from the surrounding habitats that persist.

Wetlands associated with lake and riverine habitats can also provide important nursery areas for young fish. Larval and juvenile fish enter these habitats during flood events or as the result of adult fish utilizing them to spawn; juvenile fish then use these wetlands to develop and grow, reentering the associated habitats once they have matured. In wetlands attached to lake habitats, these areas, which are often choked with aquatic vegetation, can provide important refugia for small and young fish to avoid predation.

Many of the fish species that thrive in wetlands are highly tolerant of extreme water quality conditions. Depending on the surrounding land use, wetlands can act as nutrient sinks, becoming choked with vegetation and algae, with extreme daily variability in oxygen levels. Native species, such as bowfin, golden shiner, fathead minnow, the various bullhead species, grass pickerel, central mudminnow, pirate perch, green sunfish, warmouth, bluegill, and largemouth bass, can survive under these conditions and can be found in a variety of wetland habitats across the state. Unfortunately, many of Indiana's wetlands have also become havens for exotic species, such as goldfish, common carp, silver carp, bighead carp, and grass carp, which can survive equally well under these extreme conditions.

1800. Fish assemblages were similar to the present day, excluding the host of exotic species that now persist. Alligator gar, bantam sunfish, and cypress darter, which are all either extirpated or extremely rare, were still present in some of the wetlands of the extreme southwestern portion of the state. Muskellunge likely persisted in the Grand Kankakee Marsh and the near-shore wetland habitats of Lake Michigan in northwestern Indiana.

1900. If not already gone, alligator gar, bantam sunfish, cypress darter, and muskellunge were extremely rare by this point in time. Many of the other species of fish associated with wetlands continued to persist, but in a reduced distribution and in more isolated populations. Some of the first exotic species, mainly common carp, began to appear in the various wetland habitats.

2000. A host of exotic species (grass carp, common carp, silver carp, bighead carp) appeared in the twentieth century and are now present in most of Indiana's wetland habitats. These species are likely negatively impacting the native species co-occurring in these habitats, although this is not yet well understood. Many wetlands have become more tailored for the species most tolerant of extreme conditions.

Amphibians and Reptiles

For the amphibians and reptiles in Indiana, wetlands are one of the more interesting and critical types of habitat. Wetlands are rarely deep and their waters are still, features which promote a diverse array of aquatic plants and animals. Furthermore, they often lack fish, which are the natural predators of amphibian eggs and larvae. This combination of features provides optimum habitat for amphibian reproduction. Unfortunately, wetlands are also particularly vulnerable to drainage and other forms of degradation, and may lack adequate legal protection particularly when small or seasonal in nature—the very ones which are good for amphibians and reptiles.

Most of Indiana's anurans (frogs and toads) live and breed in wetlands. In the shallowest systems, a wide diversity of frogs, such as leopard, chorus, and cricket frogs, breed successfully. Many salamanders use these systems as well. Deeper, permanent wetlands may be less diverse since the eggs and larvae of many salamanders and frogs are lost to predation. Bullfrogs and green frogs often persist, however, as they are more tolerant of fish during reproduction.

Even the more terrestrial amphibians, such as wood frogs and leopard frogs, must breed in wetlands. Consequently, the value of uplands is often tied to the quality of the wetlands embedded within them. This is most clearly observed with respect to most salamander species, which spend much of their lives away from standing water. Aside from some of the plethodontids, which lay their eggs in uplands, the salamanders of Indiana must return to wetlands to reproduce.

Since wetlands are the principal breeding places of many amphibians, they are also the foraging sites for many reptiles. Northern, copperbelly, and diamondback water snakes cruise the shallows in search of adult and larval amphibians. Ribbon snakes and garter snakes search the terrestrial side of the shorelines. While many turtles are associated with the open waters of lakes and streams, some may also be found in wetlands. Blanding's turtles and spotted turtles, both endangered in the state, typify wetland turtles. The more ubiquitous painted turtle may be found even in seasonal wetlands, as might the common snapping turtle. Eastern and ornate box turtles, though considered terrestrial, come to the shallow wetlands to soak, drink, and forage. The amphibians and reptiles associated with wetlands are listed in Table H-4.

1800. Into the early 1800s, the densities of wetland amphibians and reptiles must have been astounding. Given the extent of wetlands prior to European settlement, especially in northeastern and northwestern Indiana, amphibians would have been a dominant component of the vertebrate community.

1900. By the late 1800s and into the early 1900s, the loss of wetlands by ditching and tiling began to take its toll. No wetland species were extirpated regionally, but local extirpations must have grown more common. The emergent problem of the drainage of wetland complexes within an area no doubt began in this era, and it continues today. Loss of connectivity between adjacent wetlands may have been a major factor driving the decline of species such as the copperbelly water snake and Blanding's turtle. The loss of the Grand Kankakee Marsh and the Black Swamp no doubt impacted numerous species.

2000. As wetland losses continue, the amphibians and reptiles relying on them have continued to suffer. Wetland restoration efforts have slowed declines in some areas, but losses are pervasive. Recent awareness of the importance of wetland complexes and the quality of surrounding uplands will likely improve conservation efforts.

In the latter half of the twentieth century and the beginning of the twenty-first century, many of the habitats that remain available to wildlife are managed for them, or at least for select species. One management technique is the drawdown of water bodies during winter, so that the maintenance of levees occurs while migratory waterfowl are absent. Many amphibians and reptiles hibernate in the mud of shallow wetlands, or in soils nearby where the water table is just below the surface of the ground. Examples of mud hibernators include many frogs, such as leopard frogs, green frogs, and bullfrogs, and many turtles, such as painted, spotted, and Blanding's turtles. Examples of soil hibernators include garter snakes, water snakes, racers, and, again, frogs. Access to the water table is often via abandoned crayfish burrows. Hibernating in water prevents desiccation and, perhaps counterintuitively, freezing. Winter disturbances of shallow wetlands, or of areas nearby where the water table is close to the surface, may have catastrophic effects that go well beyond direct mortality. Winter drawdowns may freeze all of the immobile hibernators formerly covered by an insulating "blanket" of water. Drawdowns may impact herpetofauna well up into the drainage if the water table is affected.

Birds

Wetlands are or were a characteristic habitat for 111 species (Table B-4) with three sub-habitats having distinctive groups of birds: forested or shrubby swamps (34 species), marshes (86 species), and mudflats (42 species). Many species utilize both wetlands and aquatic systems (i.e., Lake Michigan, inland lakes, and rivers, including shoreline habitat; see Table B-5). Table B-1 allows comparison of species occurrence in these two major habitat categories. For example, almost all sandpipers using mudflats (a wetlands sub-habitat) in migration also use the shorelines of Lake Michigan or inland lakes, while several ducks, geese, and swans use "big water" rather than wetlands, as do loons, most grebes, and gulls. All herons, bitterns, and egrets characteristically use wetlands, but they also forage along the shorelines of lakes and rivers. Rails are much more associated with wetlands than with lakes or rivers.

This section focuses mainly on the non-forested habitats (forested wetlands are discussed in chapter

4) that are typical of wetlands, especially marshes with relatively shallow, largely permanent water with a combination of open water, some drier areas, and cattails or other reedy emergent vegetation (palustrine emergent wetland). The birds dependent on such palustrine ("marsh-like") wetland habitats for breeding include a wide variety of species from several orders. Virtually all of the rails fall into this category: king rail, Virginia rail, sora, common moorhen, and American coot. Almost all of the herons can be found in such wetlands, but only the 2 bitterns—American and least—critically depend upon them as breeding habitat. Marsh wrens are among the few passerines critically associated with such marsh-like habitats. Black terns are also marsh breeders in Indiana, as are sandhill cranes and pied-billed grebes. These obligate marsh-breeders have undoubtedly been the avian group most severely impacted by the European settlement of Indiana.

1800. Indiana began the nineteenth century with all of its various wetland habitats and wetland bird communities intact and probably near their maximum health and diversity. Most of Indiana's wetland habitat was located in the recently glaciated northern half of the state, but large and small palustrine wetlands were found throughout the state. Forested palustrine wetlands were also common along the big rivers, such as the Wabash. Presumably, almost all of the species known to use Indiana wetlands today were present then, with the exception of mute swan (a European species). The avifauna included some 14 duck or goose species, 10 herons, 4 diurnal raptors, 5 rails, sandhill crane, 29 shorebirds, 4 gulls and terns, 1 owl, 1 nighthawk, 1 kingfisher, 5 icterids (members of the blackbird family), and various species from families not typically associated with wetlands: woodpeckers, flycatchers, a vireo, 2 swallows, a wren, several warblers, and sparrows. Carolina parakeets nested and roosted (in winter) in sycamores in forested swamps along the lower Wabash River, but were extirpated by about 1860 (Butler 1892; McKinley 1976).

1900. Wetland habitats were not the initial focus of European settlers, and thus many wetlands survived well into the twentieth century. However, as with the native prairies, wetland destruction accelerated in the latter part of the 1800s, and much of the wetland habitat in Indiana was destroyed and converted to agricultural use by the end of that century.

The effects of wetland destruction on marsh bird communities were readily apparent by the end of the 1800s (Butler 1898), since, unlike grassland birds, there was no suitable habitat substitute for wetland birds. Nowhere was the effect more dramatic than in the Grand Kankakee Marsh of northwestern Indiana, where drainage efforts accelerated toward the end of the nineteenth century. The demise of much of the Grand Marsh resulted in the loss of whooping cranes, trumpeter swans, and the vast majority of sandhill cranes breeding in Indiana. Several species of ducks that may have bred regularly (e.g., American wigeon, redhead, green-winged teal) were also lost, along with some shorebirds (Wilson's phalarope, lesser yellowlegs, solitary sandpiper) that very rarely (if ever) breed in the state at present. The decay in aquatic habitats in general toward the end of the century also led to the loss of horned grebes and common loons as breeding birds in the state. Virtually all other species of marsh birds undoubtedly declined greatly not only in the Grand Marsh but throughout the state. Canada geese also largely disappeared from Indiana as breeding birds by the end of the century.

The situation faced by marsh birds became even more bleak during the twentieth century. Destruction of the Grand Kankakee Marsh was almost complete with the dredging and channelizing of the Kankakee River by around 1920. Other major wetland wildernesses were also destroyed: the Black Swamp, Great Marsh, and Loblolly Marsh (Limberlost), all in northeastern Indiana. Better and more powerful heavy machinery made it possible during the twentieth century to drain most of the state's wetlands that had survived the nineteenth century.

2000. At the close of the twentieth century, Indiana had little of its original wetlands, and much of the remaining habitat was degraded. Today, the problems include invasive plant species such as purple loosestrife and reed canary grass. Newly created mitigation wetlands and water impoundments have provided only minimal new breeding habitat for wetland birds. As a result, most species of marsh-breeding birds appear to be tenuous in the state; a survey by Chandler and Weiss (1995) of the better remaining wetland habitats in the northern part of the state located strikingly few individuals of obligate marsh-breeding birds. Almost all of the marsh-breeding species mentioned above marked the end of the twentieth century by dominating the IDNR's list of endangered bird species (including both bitterns, marsh wren, black tern, whooping crane, trumpeter swan, and all of the rails except the coot).

There are presently a few bright spots in an otherwise bleak picture for wetland birds. One hopeful sign is the reclaimed coal mines of southwestern Indiana. In addition to creating much habitat for grassland birds after 1977 (see chapter 5), several reclaimed mines contain emergent wetlands of various sizes (see Bajema and Lima 2001) that mimic in some respects the gestalt of the prairie pothole region. A survey of reclaimed mines in the Terre Haute area (Vetter 2004) produced numbers of confirmed and probable breeding attempts by state-endangered marsh birds that were comparable to those produced by the statewide breeding bird atlas project (Castrale et al. 1998). The wetlands in the reclaimed mines are not extensive enough to have a major effect on the situation faced by Indiana's marsh-breeding birds, but Vetter's results suggest that the restoration of wetland/grassland complexes envisioned for the proposed Grand Kankakee Marsh National Wildlife Refuge could ultimately be successful in boosting populations of wetland birds in northwestern Indiana (see also Horstman et al. 1998). The Nature Conservancy is planning to restore several thousand acres of wetland/prairie/savanna habitat in this part of the state. Although that project has not yet been initiated, the Nature Conservancy's Kankakee Sands wetland restoration has attracted rare wetland species, such as Wilson's phalarope, to nest.

The establishment of Goose Pond Fish and Wildlife Area in western Greene County (2005) is another boon for wetland birds. The large area of ponds and marshes—many created by the Natural Resources Conservation Service—in a natural basin which is a historic wetlands area appears capable of supporting large numbers of breeding bitterns, rails, black-necked stilts, and other water birds. Early reports are encouraging (Cole and Sterrenburg 2006; and L. Sterrenburg posts on IN-BIRD-L@listserv.indiana.edu).

Another encouraging development is the establishment of a wintering population of trumpeter swans in western Indiana during the 1990s in the reclaimed coal mines around Terre Haute, where they primarily use large lakes (see chapter 7). These swans breed in the upper Midwest and are the result of an intensive reintroduction program in Wisconsin and Minnesota. Perhaps the only bona fide success story for wetland birds in the twentieth century (some might say a bit too successful) was the reintroduction of the nonmigratory, large midwestern form of the Canada goose (giant Canada goose, *Branta canadensis maxima*) as a breeding bird in Indiana. This species has proven able to breed in a variety of existing wetland habitats.

Mammals

The presence of water of course benefits most species, but there are few mammals of Indiana that can be thought of as residents of wetlands other than the muskrat, beaver, river otter, and, to a lesser degree, mink, star-nosed mole, and swamp rabbit (Table M-4). The muskrat and beaver build lodges when the water is relatively shallow and stable water is present, such as in lakes, ponds, and marshes. However, they often use bank burrows in waterways lacking adequate shallow water, or where flooding often occurs. Dens of river otters are often found along banks and may be in a natural opening or in another animal's burrow or lodge (beaver, muskrat, woodchuck). Dens also may be among tree roots, under brush piles, in hollow stumps or logjams, or in other protected places. The entrance may be above or below the surface of the water, and a den may be used for several years.

The star-nosed mole often lives in mucky situations in northeastern Indiana. Its burrows commonly open at the edge of the water, and it will often enter the water to feed. The swamp rabbit lives in river-bottom woods in southwestern Indiana, primarily in Gibson and nearby counties. It is a good swimmer and often resorts to water. However, during flooding there must be refugia consisting of higher ground that the rabbit can use until the floodwaters recede. The mink is an excellent swimmer and eats many aquatic foods. It therefore spends much time foraging along aquatic areas.

1800. All 6 of the species listed above for aquatic habitats were present in 1800. However, the beaver was very rare at that time because of trapping. The muskrat, river otter, and mink probably occurred throughout the state, while the star-nosed mole probably occurred in about 20 counties of the northeast (although there are early records for Bartholomew County). The swamp rabbit probably occurred from Posey County north along the Wabash to at least Knox and possibly Sullivan and even southern Vigo counties, and to the east along the Ohio River to Spencer County. It may have also occurred up the White and Patoka rivers to the vicinity of Pike, Daviess, and Dubois counties. The river otter was reported by the Prince of Wied to be abundant at New Harmony in 1832–1833. Blatchley reported the otter from Putnam County in 1871. The star-nosed mole and swamp rabbit were probably roughly similar in abundance and range to what they had been before European settlement, although their ranges may have been reduced by 1850 by the draining of wetlands.

1900. The beaver had been long extirpated by 1900. The muskrat occurred wherever there were suitable bodies of water. The mink was still present throughout the state but had been much reduced by trapping and the draining of wetlands. The otter was rare because of trapping, and the last known otter from the state's original population was taken in 1942 at Hovey Lake in Posey County. By 1950, the overall ranges of swamp rabbits and star-nosed moles had declined because of reduced habitat.

The beaver (from Wisconsin and Michigan) was reintroduced in 1935 by the Indiana Department of Natural Resources into the Jasper-Pulaski and Kankakee fish and wildlife areas. By 1938, beavers were present in Jasper, LaPorte, Marshall, Noble, Porter, Pulaski, and Starke counties. Brooks (1959) interviewed all conservation officers in the state in 1955 and estimated that about 2,100 beavers were present in about 400+ beaver colonies located throughout the state.

2000. By 2000, the beaver had become abundant in suitable habitat throughout the state and was often a nuisance. The river otter, reintroduced by IDNR between 1995 and 1999 at 12 sites in northern and southern Indiana, is rapidly expanding its new range. More information is needed, but the star-nosed mole is currently known to occur in only 8 northeastern counties (LaPorte, St. Joseph, Elkhart, LaGrange, Steuben, Kosciusko, Noble, and Allen). Swamp rabbits have been reduced to a population estimated at 80 individuals mostly in the north and south portions of Gibson County, with a few in extreme southern Knox County and a very few at Hovey Lake in Posey County. The muskrat and mink occur throughout the state in suitable habitat. Thus, all aquatic mammal species of the presettlement era are currently present in the state (Table M-4).

Sub-Habitats

Ephemeral Wetlands

Many of these wetlands were on upland-depressional soil profiles with slow to very slow internal drainage. They often dried out in presettlement days in drier years when the vegetation pull on the moisture and atmospheric drying in summer caused the water table to drop below the surface. In some cases, after clearing of the forest but before ditching, the water level actually rose, due to the lack of transpirational pull from the missing trees. The distribution of these original wetlands is apparent in the Central Till Plain region if you fly over the area in the springtime after the soils are plowed, but before crops are planted. The soils of former wetlands (Brookston series) show up as darker from the air due to their higher organic matter from ponding in the depressions. The better-drained soils (Miami series) are much lighter in color, resulting in a strongly mottled landscape pattern.

Ephemeral wetlands hold water periodically, but are dry for part of the year. They include forested, shrubby, and herbaceous situations. They are wet from late fall to late spring in most years, depending on the distribution and occurrence of rainfall.

Ephemeral wetlands are particularly important for reptiles and amphibians. Since the water is not permanent, fish cannot survive except during short-term flooding. Many amphibians can survive and reproduce there, precisely because of the lack of fish, although they must deal with predatory snakes.

Drainage for agriculture and urban development has reduced the acreage of these wetlands since the late 1800s. No good estimates of the extent of these wetlands by natural region were found, but they were most common in the flatter regions of the state.

FLORA. See the general description of wetlands flora above.

FISH. Fish occur in ephemeral wetlands, but only in situations where these habitats are flooded by nearby aquatic habitats that contain fish. The species present would be representative of those found in the contributing habitat. Once the water recedes, the fish no longer persist. The western mosquitofish has been stocked outside of its native range in Indiana within these habitats as an attempt at mosquito control. Early records from the Indiana Department of Conservation (*Year Book* 1921 and following) indicate that fish from these habitats were "salvaged" and returned to nearby waters. Species most commonly saved were game fish species, including bass, other sunfish, and catfish.

AMPHIBIANS AND REPTILES. Ephemeral wetlands, seasonal or temporary, are habitats with some of the greatest herpetofaunal diversity in Indiana (Table H-4). While viewed by some as not wetlands at all because they do not contain water throughout the year, it is this very fact that makes them so valuable to herpetofauna. Most of Indiana's amphibian species must breed in ephemeral wetlands to avoid catastrophic predation by fish.

In the late winter, ambystomatid salamanders emerge from upland forests by the tens, hundreds, or even thousands, and move into ephemeral wetlands to breed. These migrations are often highly synchronized waves of particular species, and as winter winds down, various species initiate the process. What drives these synchronies is incompletely understood, but a combination of warming temperatures and more extensive thawing rains may explain most of what we see.

Most ephemeral wetlands (Figure 6.1) that have trees throughout do not hold water long enough to kill the trees by drowning the roots, especially since wetland trees are adapted to long periods of inundation. Forested wetlands that do not hold water at least

Figure 6.1. Ephemeral wooded wetlands are common breeding areas for *Ambystoma* salamanders and several other amphibians. Photo by Bruce Kingsbury.

Figure 6.2. Shrubby wetlands with beaver lodge. Photo by Scott Johnson.

into late spring have little value as breeding sites for amphibians, although they may be suitable for foraging, rehydration, and other activities. If forested wetlands hold water long enough, typically at least into June or July for most species, then they may provide breeding habitat for a wide variety of amphibians. However, the forest canopy shades the water, cooling it. This slows the development rates of larval amphibians and may prevent them from maturing and metamorphosing in time. Furthermore, transpiration from the trees exceeds the reductions in evaporation due to shading, so the trees speed the drying of the wetland. Many forested wetlands have central treeless areas that hold water for extended periods, and those do provide breeding sites for amphibians.

If these wetlands are not too far from other wetlands, they may be visited by copperbelly water snakes in those areas where the species occurs. Copperbellies have the habit of moving from wetland to wetland, especially if the ponded areas are ephemeral. Blanding's turtles act in the same way, and even such turtle species as painted and snapping may show up in isolated forested pools. Eastern box turtles will also visit them to rest and rehydrate.

Shrubby ephemeral wetlands (Figure 6.2) hold water for much or all of most years, since they have less transpirational pull than trees. They are thus more likely to have resident fish populations, and so are often not as suitable for reproduction for many amphibians. Nevertheless, depending on the conditions in individual wetlands, the species seen in other ephemeral wetlands may also breed in shrub/scrub areas. When fish are abundant, bullfrogs and green frogs may still persist, as will many species of turtle and snake. This is probably because both of these frogs deposit numerous small eggs into a floating mat of algae, etc., thus the eggs and young larvae are difficult to find.

Common snapping turtles may forage in shallow areas, the apex of their shells remaining dry as the rest of them moves along beneath the water, like an iceberg on the prowl. Shrub/scrub habitats offer many snakes both foraging habitat and places to safely rest, in part from the snapping turtles nearby. Water snakes may bask or simply rest on the lower branches of shrubs, or share hummocks with ribbon snakes. Both species forage for prey just on or off shore. In terms of herpetofaunal diversity, shrub/scrub wetlands dominated by buttonbush as opposed to willows appear to be superior. Those sites with clear water and substrates covered with fallen leaves and other organic matter appear to be best as well.

The diversity of the herpetofaunal community of emergent ephemeral wetlands can be quite high. These habitats may be isolated wetlands, but they often encircle other ephemeral or permanent wetlands. If they have standing water, especially if they lack fish, then they may be used as breeding areas for amphib-

Figure 6.3. Cattail wetlands at J. I. Case Park in Terre Haute, Indiana. Photo by Charles Amlaner.

ians. If not, they still provide foraging areas for a wide variety of herpetofauna. Leopard frogs are particularly prominent in such areas. The ease with which many of these areas were drained may help to explain the decline of the northern leopard frog. Blanchard's cricket frogs may be found as well, though far less frequently than before. Many of the more unusual reptiles can be found in emergent ephemeral wetlands. Blanding's and spotted turtles use the puddles and pools, and the eastern massasauga, Kirtland's snake, and Butler's garter snake may join the more common eastern garter snake and northern ribbon snake in some of the permanent wetlands.

Cattail wetlands (Figure 6.3) that are extensive in size tend to have low herpetofaunal diversity in their interior, probably in great part because most contain fish. However, such systems are likely only ephemeral in the broadest sense, often retaining water for many years. Restored and created emergent wetlands are likely to have many of the same species as native systems. However, only those species that are in immediately adjacent habitat will be available to colonize such areas. Reed canary grass (*Phalaris* spp.) may achieve monoculture status in many restored or previously compromised ephemeral wetlands. Given that wildlife biodiversity in monotypic habitats is typically low, it is anticipated that such is the case for herpetofauna in these areas, although this remains to be fully documented.

BIRDS. Few bird species in Indiana are dependent upon ephemeral wetlands for breeding habitat; most marsh birds require wetland habitat that lasts well into the summer for successful breeding. Many of Indiana's birds will nevertheless use such habitats opportunistically, depending on the time of the year.

Flooded bottomland (floodplain) forests can attract large numbers of dabbling ducks (mainly mallards, but also wood ducks) and rusty blackbirds if floods happen to coincide with the spring or fall migrations. The longer-lasting pools following floods (especially if not in fully forested habitat) may contain stranded fish and thus attract large groups of several heron species and fish-eating waterfowl, such as hooded mergansers. Ephemeral flatwood wetlands might also attract American woodcocks.

Non-forested ephemeral wetlands are also used by several species.

Herbaceous ephemeral wetlands attract migratory rails (e.g., sora, yellow rail, Virginia rail), as well as herons and other waders attempting to feed on breeding frogs. Many of the ephemeral wetlands in Indiana form in depressions in agricultural fields (which in many cases were formerly natural wetlands). Such muddy ephemeral habitat can attract a large number and variety of shorebirds (virtually all of those listed in Table B-4) if they occur during the main migration periods in mid-spring and late summer/early fall. An example is the Lye Creek Prairie Burn in

Montgomery County, which is actually a peat depression, where 23 migratory shorebird species have been recorded, including hundreds of American golden-plovers and rarities such as Hudsonian godwit (Murray 2005). Temporarily flooded, recently fallowed (weedy) fields can attract large numbers of migratory dabbling ducks during the fall migration.

MAMMALS. Since the ephemeral wetlands contain water for only part of the year, there are no mammals that are specific to this habitat. However, many mammals will use it during the time that it is covered by water, and therefore mammals of the various subhabitats of the ephemeral wetlands are often the same as at least some of the mammals of other habitats. For example, mammals of the forested ephemeral wetlands are most similar to those of the forested wetlands, and those of the herbaceous ephemeral wetlands are most similar to those of the wet grasslands.

Mammals that might be found in the forested ephemeral wetlands are all of the bat species, swamp rabbit in southwestern Indiana, beaver, white-footed mouse, muskrat, and river otter.

Mammals that might be found in the shrub/scrub ephemeral wetlands are perhaps limited to the beaver, white-footed mouse, muskrat, and river otter.

Permanent Wetlands

For general information, see the discussion at the beginning of the chapter.

FLORA. See the discussion of flora at the beginning of the chapter.

FISH. See the discussion of fish at the beginning of the chapter and also in the sections of chapter 7 dealing with natural lakes and with oxbows, backwaters, sloughs, and embayments.

AMPHIBIANS AND REPTILES. Permanent wetlands include habitats with deeper, long-standing water, and also areas with very shallow water or just saturated soils. The herpetofauna best associated with permanent wetlands are listed in Table H-4. Most types of permanent wetlands do not support the same biodiversity of herpetofauna as do ephemeral wetlands (see Table H-4). The exceptions to this overall pattern are the herbaceous, emergent wetlands, such as fens and wet meadows, which can have a very high diversity of amphibians and reptiles.

In many respects, the composition of the herpetofaunal community in the deeper permanent wetlands is more like that of aquatic systems, such as lakes and rivers (Table H-5), than ephemeral systems, though certainly intermediate. The species needing fish-free environments to breed will drop out, but we would expect more fully aquatic amphibians and reptiles to appear. Likely amphibians include the pervasive green frogs and bullfrogs, and also the mudpuppy and lesser siren. Turtles which generally just get into the southern part of the state, and which utilize these habitats, include the false and Mississippi map turtles and the river cooter. These are the types of areas where we might see alligator snapping turtles, western mud snakes, and possibly western cottonmouth snakes, if they are not already extirpated.

Fens and wet meadows are examples of shallow, permanent, herbaceous wetlands that may have high herpetofaunal biodiversity. Leopard frogs may be extremely abundant. Blanchard's cricket frogs may also be found in some places if the water stays deep enough year after year. Many of Indiana's more unusual reptiles utilize fens and wet meadows. Blanding's and spotted turtles use the puddles and pools, and the eastern massasauga, Kirtland's snake, and Butler's garter snake may join the more common eastern garter snake and northern ribbon snake.

BIRDS. The wetland birds that breed in Indiana require permanent (or nearly permanent) wetland habitat for successful breeding. This is especially true of the obligate marsh-nesting birds discussed above. As mentioned earlier, these sorts of permanent wetlands—with emergent herbaceous vegetation interspersed with areas of open water (Figure 6.4)—have declined greatly in scope, abundance, and quality over the past 200 years. Restored or created permanent wetland habitats have much potential for enhancing these marsh birds, depending on the degree to which these new wetlands can match the vegetative situation in natural wetlands; this is clearly indicated by the situation in reclaimed coal mines (Horstman et al. 1998; Vetter 2004).

As with the various grassland habitats, the landscape context in which such permanent emergent wetlands occur is an important determinant of the birds that they harbor. Wetland habitats embedded within grasslands are most likely to contain marsh birds of management concern; this is undoubtedly a major determinant of the diversity of wetland birds in reclaimed coal mines. Smaller marshes surrounded by forested habitat are likely to have only an occasional sora and many green herons (see Vetter 2004 and references therein), unless they are relatively large (many tens of hectares). Larger wetlands or smaller ones that occur within a larger, cohesive wetland complex are also more valuable to marsh birds than are isolated wetlands. The Grand Kankakee Marsh represented the epitome of such high-quality habitat in Indiana. Projects such as the Nature Conservancy's Kankakee Sands restoration project are important in providing these habitats. That project is restoring 7,200 acres of wetland and prairie in the Grand Prairie Natural Region. An exciting opportunity for large-scale marsh restoration appeared with the IDNR's acquisition in 2005 of the Goose Pond property in Greene County. This property is large enough (several thousands of hectares) and has the right hydrological features to establish an emergent marsh complex with a variety of habitat types, including grasslands. This site should ultimately attract a variety of state-endangered wetland birds.

Permanent, forested wetland habitats were probably locally common in Indiana 200 years ago, especially along the big rivers, but are now rare. Such habitats today are perhaps best represented by the semi-permanent pools of water that exist in the few remaining large tracts of floodplain forest and within flatwood forests across the state. Such areas attract

Figure 6.4. Permanent wetlands: marsh with scattered open water. Photo by Scott Johnson.

breeding wood ducks and hooded mergansers, and may attract the more secretive herons, such as the black-crowned and yellow-crowned night-herons. Forested wetland sites are also valuable for the prothonotary warbler, which is the only passerine in Indiana largely dependent on such habitat for successful breeding.

MAMMALS. Few mammals are aquatic to the point that they can inhabit permanent wetlands. These are primarily the beaver, muskrat, and river otter, although a number of species might visit the edge of the wetlands. Species that are most apt to visit and feed along the wetlands would be the raccoon and mink.

Forested Wetlands

Much more detail is in the forested wetlands section of chapter 4 on forests. Permanently inundated forests, often called swamps, were quite common originally, but are now relatively rare in Indiana. They do occur, however, in southwestern Indiana as cypress swamps, such as at Hovey Lake.

Forested wetlands may be ephemeral or permanent, depending on the depth of the topographic depression. Both can occur along riparian areas or in flatwoods. Permanent wetlands are usually called swamps or fens, categories that have been combined as forested wetlands here. The U.S. Fish and Wildlife Service found 501,637 acres of forested wetlands across Indiana in the 1990s. These wetlands varied from 1,403 acres in the Black Swamp Natural Region to 129,111 acres in the Central Till Plain Natural Region (Table G-21). It also found 53,011 acres of riverine wetlands in the state, some of which are forested.

FLORA. Floodplain forests and shallow depressional forests are examples of ephemeral wetlands, whereas deepwater swamps and seepage swamps (forested fen) are permanent wetlands. The flora is generally similar for both, although in swamps the flora may contain species that are aquatic, e.g., duckweed, featherfoil, and pondweed. Trees that can tolerate longer periods of flooding in swamps include bald cypress, swamp cottonwood, silver maple, red maple, overcup oak, yellow birch, pumpkin ash, and speckled alder. Characteristic herbs include common bur sedge, brome hummock sedge, common wood reed, rice cut grass, white grass, common water hemlock, Canada wood nettle, side-flowering aster, and cardinal flower. See Table P-6 for a list of species for forested wetlands.

FISH. See the oxbows, backwaters, sloughs, and embayments section of chapter 7 for information on fish in these habitats.

AMPHIBIANS AND REPTILES. Forested wetlands are an important group of habitats for amphibians and reptiles. This is the case despite the fact that few herpetofauna are adapted specifically for them. Instead, the biodiversity is generated by multiple users with overlapping interests. There are many types of forested wetlands, the variety largely the consequence of the duration and extent of surface water. Truly permanent forested wetlands have always been relatively uncommon in the state, though the cypress sloughs in southwestern Indiana epitomize what many would think of as forested wetland. Instead, the bulk of forested wetlands are in river floodplains, components of what were once tremendously large, continuous corridors stretching along major rivers, such as the Ohio and Wabash, and also others, like the White and Patoka.

In many respects, the composition of the herpetofaunal community in deeper, permanent forested wetlands is much like that of aquatic systems, such as lakes and rivers (Table H-5). Likely amphibians include the pervasive green frogs and bullfrogs, and also the mudpuppy and lesser siren. Turtles which generally just get into the southern part of the state, and which utilize these habitats, include the false and Mississippi map turtles and the river cooter. These are the types of areas where we might see alligator snapping turtles, western mud snakes, and possibly western cottonmouth snakes, if they are not already extirpated.

The herpetofauna needing fish-free environments to breed will drop out in permanent wetland systems. This will also be the case even in many of the temporary wetlands, either because they only occasionally dry down, or because fish are routinely imported in floodwaters. Consequently, ambystomatid salamanders are generally absent from these habitats. Many frog species may not persist either unless fishless wetlands suitable for breeding are available in the vicinity.

Snake diversity can be quite high, especially in areas where sheet flooding is less pervasive. Wetland associates such as the midland and diamondback water snakes may be found in the forests not too far from open water. The copperbelly water snake may be hundreds of meters from water as it searches for frogs or moves from one body of water to another. Garter snakes and ribbon snakes may also be numerous in forested wetlands. Even upland forest species, such as racers, rat snakes, and kingsnakes, may be found in forested wetlands after the water has withdrawn from some areas. For all of these species, forests with areas of open canopy will have the most snakes and the most species.

BIRDS. Some 34 species of birds characteristically use forested permanent wetlands, mainly for nesting or migration rather than winter habitat (Table B-4). Swamps are attractive to various ducks on migration and provide nesting habitat for wood ducks and hooded mergansers. Indiana's two most common heron species rely on this habitat: great blue herons build rookeries, while green herons nest solitarily. The rare yellow-crowned night-heron is restricted to forested wetlands, and the black-crowned night-heron also uses these areas, but is perhaps more typical of shrubby wetlands. Reintroduced bald eagles nest in these swamp woods as well as along rivers. The extinct Carolina parakeet nested and roosted in wetland sycamores along the Wabash until the mid-nineteenth century. Barred owl and red-shouldered hawk are the characteristic raptors. Certain woodpecker species (red-headed, red-bellied, and pileated) appear to be more common in forested wetlands than in upland forest. Prothonotary warblers occur only in swampy forest, nesting in woodpecker holes in trees. Red-winged blackbirds and common grackles are abundant in migration, and rusty blackbirds travel through forested wetlands to and from their breeding grounds in the swamps and bogs of Canada's boreal forest.

MAMMALS. Few mammals are aquatic to the point that they can inhabit forested permanent wetlands. They are primarily the beaver, muskrat, and river otter, although a number of species might visit the edge of the wetlands. Other species apt to visit and feed along the wetlands are the raccoon and mink.

Permanent Shrub Wetlands

Permanently inundated shrub/scrub areas are atypical for Indiana. Such places are likely ephemeral, though dry-down may take multiple years. Otherwise, the shrubs will not be able to recruit, and will eventually die out, leaving open water.

There were 42,092 acres of shrub/scrub wetlands in Indiana in the 1990s (Table G-21). This wetland type varied from 33 acres in the Black Swamp Natural Region to 15,926 acres in the Northern Lakes Natural Region.

FLORA. Deeper-water shrub wetlands are characterized by buttonbush, swamp rose, and, locally, swamp loosestrife, while various species of shrubby dogwood, shrubby willow, and winterberry are found in shallower wetlands. Shrub thickets are commonly so dense that few other species occur. In some cases, however, the hummocks at the bases of shrubs provide a substrate upon which certain species can grow, e.g., various sedges and grasses, beggar's ticks, and bugleweeds. See Table P-8 for a list of species for shrub/scrub wetlands.

AMPHIBIANS AND REPTILES. Species in shrub areas with water present for many years will likely be a combination of those seen in permanent forested wetlands and, if such habitats are nearby, ephemeral wetlands. See the sections on those habitats for further information.

FISH. Fish species specifically found in shrub wetlands are not well known because these habitats have not been studied specifically for these species. Fish species typical of the other wetland habitats are likely inhabitants, excluding those more adapted to open water. Secretive species that utilize the root systems of shrubs for cover and those able to thrive in shallow water would most likely be able to survive in these habitats. Species such as the tadpole madtom, central mudminnow, pirate perch, western mosquitofish, green sunfish, slough darter, and banded pygmy sunfish would be expected.

BIRDS. Only a few species are characteristic of shrub wetland rather than forested wetland or marsh, so they are grouped with the forested wetland species in Table B-4. Shrub/scrub wetland species include alder flycatcher (Gorney and Casebere 2002), willow flycatcher, and yellow warbler.

MAMMALS. Mammals that inhabit permanent shrub wetlands are the beaver, muskrat, and river otter, although a number of species might visit the edge of such wetlands. Species most apt to visit and feed along the wetlands are the raccoon and mink.

Permanent Herbaceous Wetlands

Herbaceous wetlands include marshes, fens, bogs, and often areas around the margins of lakes or ponds (e.g., sedge meadows). Marshes are open water, usually with relatively good drainage (i.e., often with water normally entering and exiting), and are often characterized by such herbaceous vegetation as cattails, rushes, reeds, and sedges. Bogs are old filled-in lakes, usually acidic in nature, covered wholly or in part with a mat of floating vegetation consisting of heaths, often with cotton grass, pitcher plants, and sundews, and sometimes with some trees. However, there is a "bog" in northern Indiana (Cowles Bog) in which the mat is primarily of cattails. A fen is similar to a bog but is neutral to calcareous (basic) rather than acidic and has an entirely different plant community, more similar to a wet prairie. These wetlands are most common in the glaciated northeastern region of the state. Swinehart and Parker (2001) describe the species composition and successional changes occurring in 16 lake-filled peatlands of northern Indiana.

FLORA. Emergent vegetation typically consists of species that are rooted in a submersed substrate and at least some portions of the plants are emergent (above the water line), although water levels fluctuate greatly and all parts of the plants can be exposed. The type is typically found on lake borders, especially in the Northern Lakes Natural Region, but can be found along bodies of water or in deep marshes throughout the state. This community can be quite diverse in its natural state. Many of the deepwater wetland species occur here, as do many others that require better illumination than what is provided in forested situations. Broad-leaved cattail, pickerel weed, water heartsease, blue joint grass, three-way sedge, common arrowhead, buttonbush, swamp rose, and spatterdock are species that commonly occur here. See Table P-8 for a list of species for emergent wetlands.

Wetland communities composed strictly of herbaceous species are typically found in deep water with emergent vegetation; in wet prairies, bogs, and fens; and on periodically exposed substrates bordering bodies of water, e.g., the shorelines of lakes and rivers. Species are thus similar to those discussed under emergent wetlands, as well as small annuals, such as needle spike rush, blunt spike rush, red-rooted nut sedge, old witch grass, creeping love grass, slender false pimpernel, and clammy hedge hyssop.

A bog is a community consisting of a floating mat (usually partially decomposed sphagnum moss) and is acidic in nature. Some characteristic species of a bog include small shrubs, such as large cranberry and leatherleaf, and mostly herbaceous species, such as round-leaved sundew, pitcher plant, grass pink orchid, regal (royal) fern, buckbean, narrow-leaved cotton grass, and marsh St. John's wort.

A graminoid fen is a saturated peatland dominated mostly by herbaceous vegetation. In Indiana, it typically is alkaline in nature. Characteristic species include fen star sedge, fen panicled sedge, bog lobelia, grass-of-parnassus, narrow-leaved loosestrife, shrubby cinquefoil, queen-of-the-prairie, and Riddell's goldenrod. See Table P-8 for a list of species for herbaceous wetlands.

FISH. Fish of marshes are most similar to those found in natural lakes. See the discussion in the natural lakes section of chapter 7. If any species of fish would be able to survive the bogs and fens of Indiana, it would be the central mudminnow.

AMPHIBIANS AND REPTILES. Of Indiana's habitats, emergent native wetlands such as wet meadows and fens have among the most diverse and interesting herpetofaunal assemblages. Many of the species are not found or are less common in most other habitats. In some respects, the assemblages are similar to those of the ephemeral emergent systems. Leopard frogs and Blanchard's cricket frogs are among the more unusual amphibians, while Blanding's and spotted turtles, the eastern massasauga, Kirtland's snake, and Butler's garter snake are unusual reptiles. The ubiquitous eastern garter snake and northern ribbon snake also use these areas.

Marshes that are extensive in size tend to have low herpetofaunal diversity in their interior, probably because fish are usually present. In terms of amphibians, bullfrogs and green frogs may be the only species to routinely use them, though mudpuppies may cruise unseen underwater. Painted and snapping turtles will also use them. It is also likely that riverine species, such as map turtles and cooters, would use the more open areas. Northern/midland water snakes might also be observed.

Restored and created emergent wetlands are likely to have many of the same species as native systems. However, only those species that are in immediately adjacent habitat will be available to colonize such areas.

BIRDS. Some 30 species of birds nest (or formerly nested) in marshes (Table B-4). By far the most abundant at all seasons (except in winter in the north) is red-winged blackbird. Also common are song sparrow (along the edges of marshes), swamp sparrow (in the far north), and common yellowthroat. Eastern kingbird and tree swallows are characteristic but require a few trees. Common grackles can be abundant if trees are nearby.

Many marsh nesters breed only in this habitat: pied-billed grebe, American and least bittern, king rail, Virginia rail, sora, common moorhen, American coot, sandhill crane, Wilson's phalarope, black tern, and marsh wren. Several are rare and/or restricted to northern Indiana. Among the waterfowl, a handful of dabbling ducks nest in marshes (especially mallard and blue-winged teal), as do Canada geese and,

Figure 6.5. Sandhill cranes. Photo by Marty Jones.

increasingly, the exotic mute swan. Trumpeter swan and whooping crane apparently nested in the Grand Kankakee Marsh in the nineteenth century (Mumford and Keller 1984). Yellow-headed blackbirds nested in Calumet River marshes in the nineteenth century, but have rarely nested in the state in recent decades.

Many more species (86) use marshes during migration or after nesting (Table B-4). The migrants include non-nesting dabbling ducks (gadwall, American wigeon, northern pintail, and green-winged teal) and ruddy duck; most herons, egrets, and night-herons; osprey and northern harrier; non-nesting, very rare rails (yellow rail, black rail); and many sandpipers and other shorebirds. Two nesting rail species (Virginia and sora) are much more common as migrants. The list of 23 shorebird species for Lye Creek Prairie Burn in Montgomery County, a peat depression (Murray 2005), and the rapidly growing list for Goose Pond in Greene County (Lee Sterrenburg et al. on the IN-BIRD archives) indicate how productive central Indiana wetlands can be.

Sandhill cranes are the most spectacular migrants (Figure 6.5) through Indiana marshes (some also nest in northern Indiana), by virtue of their individual size, trumpeting call, and flock size; thousands use Jasper-Pulaski Fish and Wildlife Area for months in the fall and spring. The cranes also forage in various habitats besides the marsh, such as corn fields. Since about 2000, small flocks of juvenile whooping cranes have been guided in the fall from a refuge in Wisconsin to Florida by ultralight aircraft, and they spend nights and days at various wetlands and marshes in Indiana, which is on their historic migration route. The guided cranes return in the spring on their own, and make subsequent fall journeys unaided.

Bird species from more terrestrial families which favor marshes on migration (or for foraging while nesting in a different, nearby habitat) include common nighthawk, various swallows, palm warbler, northern waterthrush, Nelson's sparrow, and common grackle.

MAMMALS. The most characteristic mammal of emergent native wetlands (cattail marsh is probably the most abundant and well-known habitat in this category) is the muskrat, which makes its nest from and feeds heavily on the emergent plant species, especially the cattail. Otters and beavers also occupy marshes. There is usually grassy vegetation around the edges of marshes, and a variety of species of mammals may be found there, such as meadow voles, masked and short-tailed shrews, white-footed mouse, and meadow jumping mouse. Larger mammals of this habitat are the raccoon, mink, and long-tailed weasel. The same group of species probably used this habitat from 1800 through 2000, except that the otter was extirpated from about 1942 until reintroduced in the 1990s.

Other Types of Wetlands

Potholes

Much of Indiana was subjected to several glacial advances, which left ice-block depressions across the landscape that are capable of holding water. Such depressions range from deep kettle lakes to shallow potholes (Figure 6.6) to marshes. Glacially formed potholes originally occurred in a matrix of prairie vegetation, but today are surrounded by cropland, if they survive at all. In the twenty-first century, farm ponds partially substitute for potholes.

FLORA. Potholes possess species like those found in emergent and herbaceous wetlands, plus an assortment of wet prairie species, such as prairie cord grass, blue joint grass, hairy-fruited lake sedge, river bulrush, common mountain mint, marsh blazing star, and New England aster. See the herbaceous and emergent wetland categories in Table P-8 for a list of species for potholes.

FISH. Fish of potholes are most similar to those found in natural lakes. A discussion of these can be found in the natural lakes section of chapter 7. Fish of farm ponds (man-made potholes) include an assemblage of stocked fish, such as largemouth bass, channel catfish, and a combination of other sunfish species (most commonly bluegill and redear sunfish or hybrids). Bait minnows, such as fathead minnow, bluntnose minnow, and golden shiner, are also often stocked as a forage base.

AMPHIBIANS AND REPTILES. Pothole wetlands have diverse assemblages of herpetofauna because they often include many of the ephemeral and permanent wetlands types in one place. Depending on the hydrological nature of the site—particularly how variable the water levels are, and how quick-

Figure 6.6. Pothole at Chain O' Lakes State Park. Photo by IDNR–*Outdoor Indiana* magazine.

ly the water levels change—a pothole may have an open aquatic center surrounded by concentric rings of emergent, shrub/scrub, and forested wetland. Wet meadows, bogs, fens, or seeps may border the pothole, leading to truly high diversity in a relatively small area. See the descriptions and appendixes for the various habitats to get an idea of the species using potholes.

BIRDS. No information seems to be available for birds of potholes in Indiana, but this habitat is highly productive of waterfowl in the northern Great Plains (the Dakotas and Canada). Presumably, such sites would have a subset of the species listed for marshes and aquatic systems.

MAMMALS. Occasionally, muskrats might inhabit potholes, and a number of species (meadow voles, short-tailed shrews, weasels, mink, and others) might inhabit the thick vegetation often found around the edges of potholes. Foxes and skunks are known to be nest predators of waterfowl, and thus might hunt near potholes.

Wetlands of Farmed Areas

This should not be considered to be a separate habitat, but since many wetlands have been drained to produce farmlands, remnants of the wetlands remain, usually as herbaceous or marshy areas in meadows, pastures, or along the edges of ditches or streams.

FLORA. Wetlands that are plowed annually typically possess a small assortment of annual species that grow from seed banks in the soil. Many of the same species found in the exposed substrates of emergent wetland types are also found in farmed wetlands. See Table P-8 for a list of species for farmed wetlands.

FISH. Wetlands of farmed areas, if they contain fish at all, would include some of the more tolerant species found in the nearest permanent aquatic habitats. Many of these areas are likely converted to farm ponds or grass waterways. See the section on potholes for the typical fish species composition of farm ponds.

BIRDS. Wetlands of farmed areas are potentially valuable stopover habitat for migrating shorebirds (plovers and sandpipers). Newly plowed fields wetted by rains are also attractive.

Drained or Ditched Wetlands

Approximately 50% of the cropland in Indiana was drained through sub-surface tiles and ditches in 1998 (Agricultural Drainage 1998). This amounts to 8,055,000 acres, primarily in the northern half of the state.

FLORA. When completely drained, wetlands change in floristic composition. Those species requiring continuously saturated substrates likely perish

Figure 6.7. Ditched wetlands. Photo by Brant Fisher.

first, although as a general rule wetlands are drained for the purpose of conversion to other uses, hence all native species usually perish. Drained wetlands rarely exist for enough time to allow for development of a stable flora, as they are typically converted to agricultural uses. However, such sites have characteristic species that grow in spring before the soil is dry enough to till, e.g., smartweeds. The flora of drained areas not converted to cropland is determined in part by the adaptability and competitive ability of the species currently occupying the site and the seeds available for colonization from adjacent sites. See Table P-8 for a list of species of drained wetlands.

Ditched wetlands (Figure 6.7) can vary in floristic composition, depending on the degree of drainage provided by the ditch. As a general rule, ditching produces compositional changes, and the deeper the ditch (and degree of drainage), the greater the changes. Following the digging of the ditch, some wetland species are able to persist in the channel. The flora of these sites may be similar to the wetland types discussed above. See Table P-8 for those types and for species for ditched wetlands.

FISH. Only the most tolerant species of fish, those able to withstand low dissolved oxygen levels, warm temperatures, and little habitat diversity, are found in these habitats. Spotfin shiner, common carp, striped or common shiner, redfin shiner, bluntnose minnow, fathead minnow, creek chub, white sucker, spotted sucker, the various bullhead species, grass pickerel, central mudminnow, pirate perch, blackstripe topminnow, green sunfish, warmouth, bluegill, largemouth bass, johnny darter, and orangethroat darter are typical. However, if substantial stands of submergent aquatic vegetation are present, the species composition often resembles that of a lake or wetland. Species such as ironcolor shiner, blacknose shiner, weed shiner, and least darter can be found along with the other species in the weedy ditches of northeastern Indiana. Redspotted sunfish, slough darter, and banded pygmy sunfish can be found in these habitats in the southwest. Lake chubsucker, tadpole madtom, and northern starhead topminnow can be found in both locations.

AMPHIBIANS AND REPTILES. The herpetofauna in wetlands damaged by draining or ditching will be relicts of what was there when the system was intact. Changing the hydrology of the site ultimately leads to the rather rapid creation of another habitat. If source populations are available, then the appropriate species will colonize the newly available habitat.

BIRDS. If herbaceous or shrubby successional growth results from draining, some birds of grassland or pioneering forest would be expected (see Table B-2 for forest birds; Table B-3 for grassland birds). If drained wetlands remain open and somewhat wet, they could attract migrating shorebirds. Wilson's snipe takes shelter in ditches during migration.

MAMMALS. Drained wetlands could consist of grassy or weedy fields, shrubland or woodland, or other habitats, including cultivated fields. If so, they could contain the mammals associated with those habitats. See Tables M-3 for grasslands, M-2 for forested lands, and M-7 for cultivated situations.

Mudflats

These habitats generally occur in wetland areas of fluctuating water. Lowered water levels may expose mudflats along streams, lakes, ponds, and impoundments, or in upland depressional areas. Drained farmland may provide exposed mudflats as the water fluctuates following large rainfalls.

FLORA. Areas of recently exposed mud are good environments for the occurrence of annuals that germinate and complete their life cycles in short order. These areas occur along lake and pond borders, stream and river borders, and recently disturbed basins in agricultural fields. The species present are for the most part the same as those for the emergent wetland habitat discussed above. See Table P-8 for species for mudflats.

FISH. Only one species of fish in Indiana could tolerate the extreme conditions of a mudflat. The central mudminnow can bury into the substrate and create a concretion that enables it to survive the temporary loss of water. When water returns, the mud softens and the fish emerges.

AMPHIBIANS AND REPTILES. Mudflats are not inhabited by amphibians and reptiles, although turtle tracks indicate that sometimes individuals pass through them.

BIRDS. Mudflats are an excellent habitat for migrating shorebirds, whether they are along lakes or impoundments, in agricultural fields or grasslands, as long as vegetation is short or absent. Shorebirds of the order Charadriiform (black-bellied plover to long-billed dowitcher, Table B-4) dominate the list; lesser yellowlegs, and solitary, pectoral, least, and semipalmated sandpipers are the most common species. Several dabbling ducks visit mudflats, as do a few herons, American coot, ring-billed gull, common and Forster's terns, European starling, and American pipit.

A recurring complaint of birders during migration season is that mudflats accessible for viewing are hard to find, and that few wetlands or ponds (natural or artificial) are managed to induce shorebirds to rest and feed. The wetlands being restored at Kankakee Sands (Newton County) and Goose Pond (Greene County) are expected to contain attractive mudflats.

MAMMALS. No mammals live on mudflats, but certain species forage there. Visitors might include raccoons, mink, long-tailed weasels, and white-footed mice, as one can see by examining their tracks.

7 Aquatic Systems

Clean fresh water is not only important to fish and wildlife, but a requirement for human survival. At the time of European settlement, Indiana was blessed with an abundance of fresh water and freshwater habitat (Figure 7.1). The state is partly bounded by major water bodies. Lake Michigan forms about 40 mi of the northwest border, the Wabash River (the nation's longest un-dammed river, flowing for a total of 510 mi) forms the western boundary of most of the southern half of Indiana, and the Ohio River forms the entire southern boundary, joining the Wabash at the lowest (345 ft above sea level) and most southwestern point in the state (Map 7.1).

The earliest written descriptions of Indiana's lakes, rivers, and streams remark on the clear water and the abundance and diversity of fish (McCord 1970). Indeed, the origin of the name "Wabash" can be traced through French and English pronunciations to the Miami Indian word *Wah-bah-she-keh,* meaning "pure white," a reference to the limestone river bottom in Huntington County, which is visible through the river's crystal-clear waters. Robert Cavelier de La Salle is credited with the European "discovery" of the Ohio River in 1669–1670. The name "Ohio" is believed to be derived from an Iroquoian word meaning "great river." However, La Salle interpreted "Ohio" as beautiful river, or *la belle rivière* (www.ibiblio.org/eldritch/nhb/S2.HTM). Several of Indiana's interior rivers, such as the White and Whitewater rivers, still reflect the clarity of Indiana streams. All of Indiana's earliest settlements (Ouiatenon, Chippecoke, and Kekionga) were established on major rivers. For the early European explorers and settlers, the major transportation routes were Indiana's waterways and buffalo traces (McCord 1970). As settlers poured into Indiana, the state's rivers, streams, and lakes provided food, power for mills, and transportation for moving grains, livestock, timber, and hay to market (McCord 1970).

As Indiana was settled by Europeans, the surface waters of the state suffered many impacts that made them unrecognizable to Indiana's early settlers. As

Figure 7.1. Clear, freshwater small river in northern Indiana. Photo by Terry L. Castor.

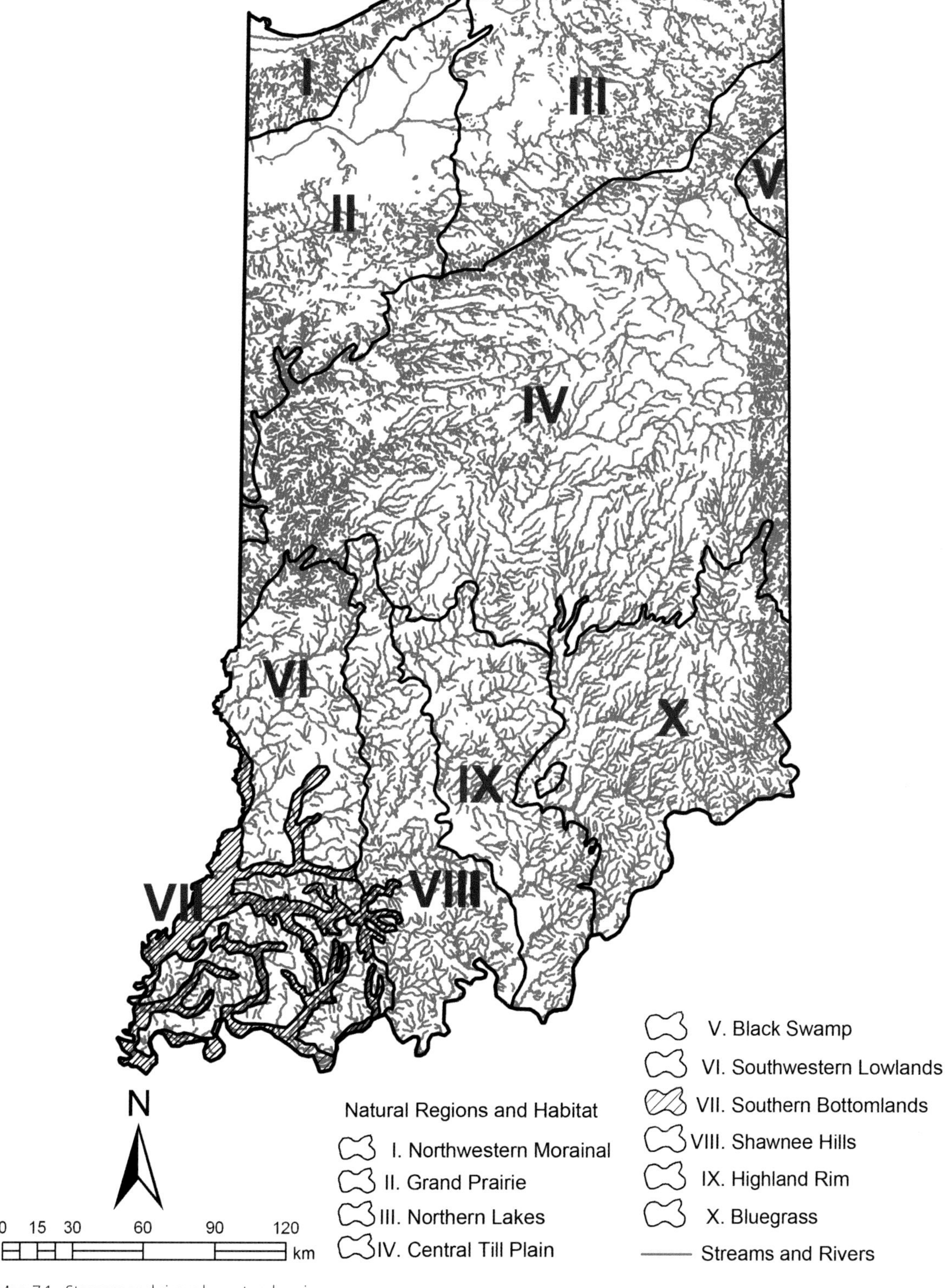

Map 7.1. Streams and rivers by natural region.

the forests were cleared and agricultural fields established, sediments poured into the water, reducing clarity and clogging stream bottoms. Streams were straightened (ditched) to improve drainage, and the tree cover on stream banks was removed. During the nineteenth and early twentieth centuries, Indiana streams received untreated or inadequately treated discharges from industrial and commercial sources and urban sewage. Communities sought to control the natural fluctuations of the rivers and streams. Dams were built to retain water for municipal use or power generation, and levees were built to constrain floodwaters and to secure river bottomland for agriculture. Even the mighty Ohio was dammed, essentially reducing the river to a series of impounded pools, to provide for year-round navigation. These alterations, along with the draining of wetlands that attended many of Indiana's major rivers, had a profound impact on fish and other aquatic-related wildlife populations.

Factors Affecting Water Quality

Terrestrial habitats are described in terms of vegetative cover (e.g., forest or grassland), connectivity, and patch size. Aquatic habitats are described and defined by different parameters; among these are components that are resistant to change, such as the impacts of drainage history, watershed topography, and stream gradient. Many other factors and environmental conditions interact to impact the quality of aquatic habitat and the various aquatic niches available. Some of these are the amount of vegetative cover in the watershed, the type and amount of anthropogenic discharges, and stream channel or lakeshore modifications. Variations in and modifications of these factors have important impacts on aquatic habitat variables, such as dissolved oxygen (and other water chemistry), water temperature, water depth, and stream bottom substrate. Indiana's waters have also been altered by water withdrawals, thermal inputs (hot water discharges), fish management history, and the introduction of exotic species.

Indiana's aquatic habitats are the result of a shared history with much of the midwestern United States (Gerking 1945; Hocutt and Wiley 1986; Burr and Page 1986). Foremost among the factors that shaped the fish assemblages of Indiana were the natural forces that formed the landscape and the series of glacial streams that provided temporary drains, enabling colonization. The most recent glacial event to impact Indiana's aquatic habitats occurred during the Wisconsinan period (Burr and Page 1986). Of particular note among these glacial changes were the formation of the Wabash River and changes in the historic Teays River. The Teays River was a large preglacial river that originated in the Appalachian Mountains and flowed north and west across Ohio into north-central Indiana through the current location of the upper Wabash River valley; however, it continued west, following the Illinois River channel and finally emptying into the Mississippi River near the current mouth of the Illinois River. When the Wisconsinan glacial advance covered the upper Wabash River, the drainage pattern of the Teays River changed drastically, increasing the size of the Ohio River.

Because aquatic organisms are intolerant of drying, their ability to disperse depends upon the continuity of water, that is to say, connected drainages. The geological events that established drainage connections also set aquatic community species composition. Over time, newly connected aquatic communities became stable and self-sustaining.

The scouring of the Great Lakes basin by the Wisconsinan glacier also provided a relatively recent faunal invasion (Gerking 1945; Burr and Page 1986). In addition to creating refugia that provided safety to small stream species in southern Indiana, it caused the formation of the swamps and wetlands of the Patoka, Wabash, and White rivers (Simon et al. 2005).

Beginning in the late twentieth century, there have been massive aquatic community disturbances caused by human-engineered changes in drainage patterns. The sea lamprey and the alewife are Atlantic Ocean species that found their way into Lake Michigan and wreaked havoc on the native aquatic community. Although certain aspects of the spread of these two invasive species remain unclear, the construction of the Welland Ship Canal, which bypasses Niagara Falls between Lake Ontario and Lake Erie, undoubtedly aided their spread to Lake Michigan, with disastrous consequences (Greenberg 2002).

Anthropogenic changes to the landscape that occurred during the late eighteenth and nineteenth centuries were primarily due to the clearing of land for farming during the westward expansion into the Virginia Territory (part of which is now modern Indiana). The clearing of the temperate forests reduced riparian tree canopy cover and elevated stream temperatures. As stream temperatures rose due to the removal of stream-bank vegetation, many streams in central Indiana changed from cool-water streams to warm-water streams. Water temperature influences aquatic community composition as some species are sensitive to water temperature changes. Fish spawning is triggered by water temperature, and temperature impacts dissolved oxygen levels. As stream temperatures rise, a concomitant decrease in dissolved oxygen concentrations occurs. Since no comparative information is available for historical dissolved oxygen levels, the magnitude and extent of dissolved oxygen changes are unknown. However, reduced dissolved oxygen is generally considered to be an environmental stressor for aquatic communities that evolved under higher average dissolved oxygen conditions.

Indiana has seen the wide-scale removal of natural riparian vegetation; stream channelization; the draining of the expansive wetlands of the Black Swamp (Maumee, St. Marys, and St. Joseph rivers), the wetlands along the Grand Kankakee Marsh (Kankakee River) and Great Marsh (Calumet rivers of northwest Indiana), and the riverine wetlands along the Wabash River (southwest Indiana); and the filling of Lake Michigan coastal wetlands. In addition, the damming of the Ohio River has had devastating effects. The loss of wetland habitat has reduced landscape water storage, buffering capacity, and nutrient removal. The construction of the navigation locks and dams on the Ohio River restricted fish movement and caused the loss of creek embayment wetlands. These changes to fish migration caused the extirpation of the Alabama shad and reduction of the American eel, which had indirect effects on mussel species.

The technological revolution of the twentieth century introduced widespread chemical pollution and significant non-point pollutants into watersheds as urban areas expanded. Point source pollution came from expanded sewage discharge, especially during storm events, increased impervious surfaces as roads changed from dirt to concrete, and increases in direct industrial discharges. Anthropogenic changes in urban areas have increased the amount of water that enters streams and retention ponds during storm events. This results in widespread non-point source impacts as road pollutants, such as oil, grease, and polyaromatic hydrocarbons, are washed into stream channels.

The biggest contributors to non-point source water pollution are thought to be agricultural runoff (agricultural chemicals, feedlots, improper manure management), crop field erosion, and erosion from land cleared for development. The impact of non-point pollution is most apparent in streams such as the White River, which was so named because the river was clear and which now runs the color of well-creamed coffee. Today, many of Indiana's rivers and streams carry a significant sediment and nutrient load. Many of the state's waters were previously much

Figure 7.2. Stream carrying heavy silt load during flooding event. Photo by Conestoga-Rovers & Associates (CRA).

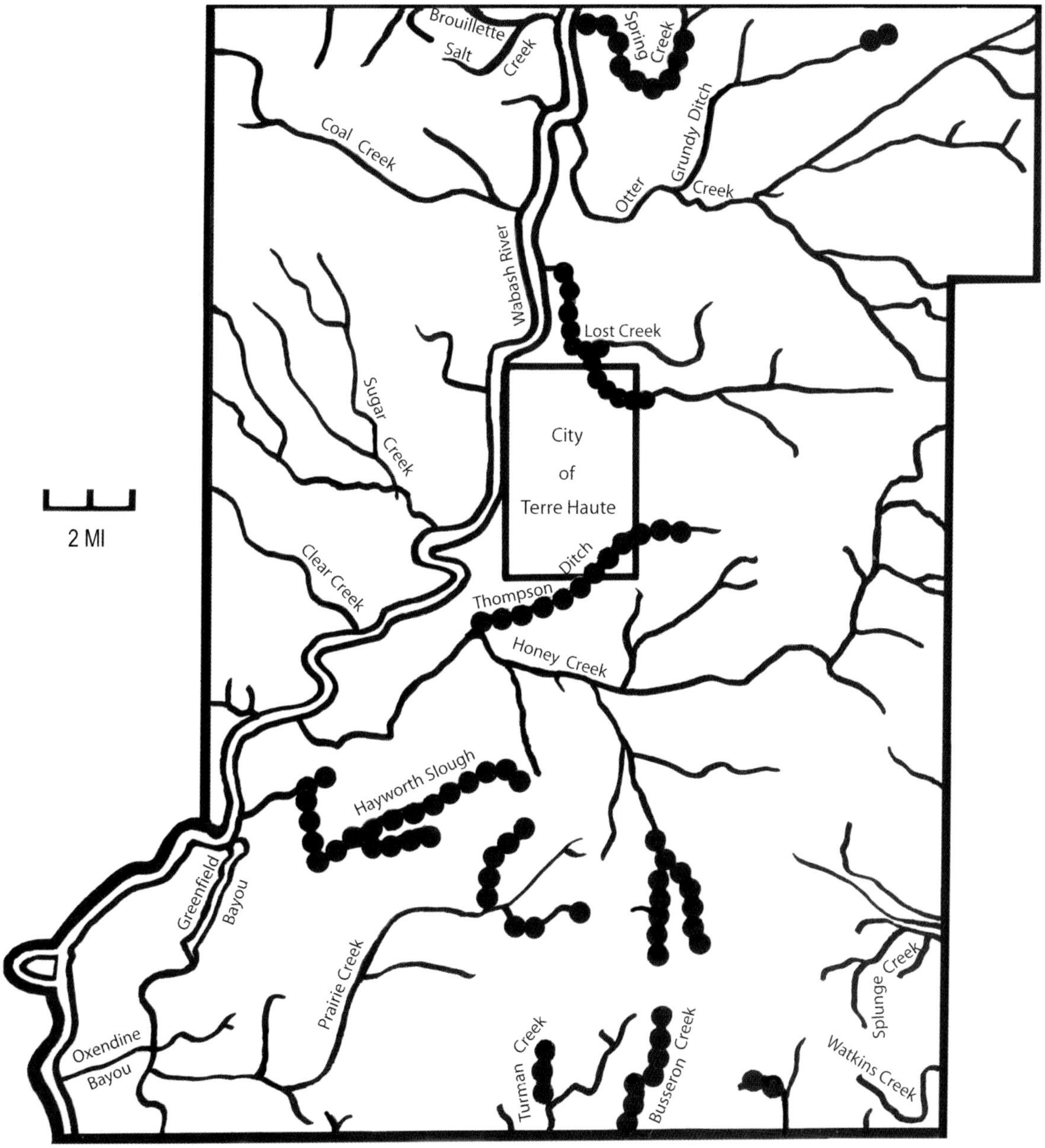

Figure 7.3. Heavily polluted streams of Vigo County, Indiana, 1965. Figure from Whitaker and Wallace 1973.

Figure 7.4. Acid mine drainage. Photo by John O. Whitaker, Jr.

deeper. For example, the Wabash River was clear, commonly reaching depths of 12 ft, and was navigable to Terre Haute (Thomas 1819). Today, the Wabash has a large silt load, primarily due to agriculture and erosion; thus it is always brown and murky and is much shallower. Larger watercraft no longer can navigate the Wabash River as far as Terre Haute.

Most of the small streams still run clear, except during flood events, when they too run brown from carrying heavy silt loads (Figure 7.2). The chemical content of the water throughout the state used to be much better than now, with dissolved oxygen presumably being 8 parts per million (ppm) and higher and the pH presumably around 8 or above. These chemical conditions allowed all permanent waters to have adequate fish populations. Fish populations and biodiversity decrease greatly at lower oxygen and pH levels, and drop out entirely below about 4.5 ppm oxygen and 4.5 pH. Agriculture has contributed to poorer water conditions through silting and presumably also through pollution from escaped manure, fertilizers, and pesticides, although adequate studies on these are lacking.

Not all sediment problems are related to agriculture or development sites. In highly urbanized and industrialized areas, such as northwestern Indiana, toxic river sediments are the result of industrial and municipal discharges. Contaminated sediments are difficult and expensive to remediate and can have negative impacts on aquatic communities for decades.

Mining operations have had a great effect on fish populations, especially in southern Indiana. For example, during the 1960s in Vigo County, fish were absent in whole sections of streams due to mining. In these streams, oxygen content was often zero or nearly so, and pH was very low. Iron in coal deposits, released during mining operations, combined with oxygen, tying up the oxygen and producing acidic conditions. The streams of Vigo County that contained no fish in the late 1960s because of the impacts of mining are shown in Figure 7.3 (Whitaker and Wallace 1973). At times, such streams ran red, orange, green, or black (Figure 7.4). Coal Creek, immediately above the Old Green Valley Mine, contained numerous fish, whereas 10 ft downstream and throughout 5.6 mi of the drainage to the Wabash River, no fish existed. However, there are now mining regulations in place to prevent these negative impacts. The original contours of the land must be retained (or restored), and the topsoil must be replaced. In other words, in the twenty-first century, the land after mining must be much like it was before mining.

All components affecting aquatic species composition, abundance, and distribution are interrelated. Just as the alteration of the factors discussed above has affected species abundance and distribution in the past, changes in these core components will impact aquatic organisms and, ultimately, Indiana's citizens in the future.

Management of Indiana's Water Resources

Nowhere is the dependence of humans on healthy aquatic systems more apparent than in the laws and agencies created to provide for the protection of valued water-related resources. The history of aquatic habitat protection is mainly the history of humanity's realization of society's dependence on an adequate source of clean water. Information on Indiana's water availability and quality is scattered among the various regulatory agencies involved in the management of the state's water. This section is not intended to be an exhaustive guide to Indiana's water management, but rather will introduce the most significant agencies and programs and guide the reader to sources of additional information.

In 1852, the Indiana General Assembly gave city governments the authority to establish local boards of health and to prevent streams being polluted with rubbish, sewage, and dead animals. The Indiana Board of Health (IBH) was established in 1881 and although this preceded the acceptance of the germ theory (officially adopted by the IBH in 1889), water quality, as related to the spread of human disease, was a major concern of the newly established state board (Bennett 1998).

In 1911, the IBH undertook a survey of the Ohio River bordering Indiana. Although several cities were using untreated river water as their municipal water source, the major conclusion was that at no point along the surveyed river was the raw water fit for drinking purposes and that filtration and chemical treatment were required to make the water safe (Bennett 1998). The board of health continued to be the main advocate for clean water in Indiana, and although the control of communicable disease agents began to improve, Indiana's rivers and streams continued to receive anthropogenic inputs.

In 1943, the Stream Pollution Control Law created the Stream Pollution Control Board by which Indiana could control direct discharges into the waters of the state. Through this legislation, Indiana pursued the most horrific pollution cases. However, offending companies often threatened to move to other states with more lenient regulations rather than clean up their operations. Clearly, the "pollute and run" attitude of some companies and the interstate nature of major river systems necessitated more broad-ranging pollution control efforts.

In 1948, Indiana, Illinois, Kentucky, New York, Ohio, Pennsylvania, Tennessee, and West Virginia formed the Ohio River Valley Water Sanitation Commission (ORSANCO) with the expressed mission of controlling future pollution and abating existing pollution from rivers, streams, and other waters. As part of this effort, the signatory states have conducted and continue to conduct biological surveys to determine the status of Ohio River valley resources.

The following decades saw a profusion of state and federal laws intended, at least in some measure, to safeguard the quality, availability, and recreational and aesthetic values of the waters of the state and the nation. These laws include but are not limited to the federal Water Pollution Control Act (Clean Water Act), the Wild and Scenic Rivers Act, the National Environmental Policy Act (NEPA), the Water Resources Planning Act (1965), and the Flood Plain Management Statute (1973). Currently, the water resources of Indiana are managed by the Indiana Department of Natural Resources' (IDNR) Division of Water (created in 1965) and the Indiana Department of Environmental Management (IDEM, created in 1986 to assume some of the responsibilities of the Division of Water, especially relative to water quality).

The Division of Water (DOW) serves as the technical staff of the Natural Resources Commission (NRC). As such, the DOW assists the NRC with its legislative mandate to (1) conduct a continuing assessment of water resources availability, (2) conduct and maintain an inventory of significant withdrawals of surface water and groundwater, and (3) plan for the development and conservation of water resources for beneficial uses. The DOW has additional responsibilities that are limited to the navigable waters of the state, including the regulation of construction activities and mineral extraction, and the protection of cultural resources relative to Indiana's navigable waters. From 1987 to 1996, the DOW completed 5 of 12 regional investigations, providing a description of the availability, distribution, quality, and use of surface and groundwater throughout Indiana (Indiana Department of Natural Resources 1987, 1988, 1990, 1994, 1996). Funding for the remaining 7 regions was not provided.

The DOW works cooperatively with federal agencies, such as the U.S. Geological Survey (USGS). The mission of the USGS is to provide water information that benefits the nation's citizens. The USGS has offices in every state to collectively provide information on the nation's water resources. In Indiana, the DOW supports USGS-monitored stream-gauging stations and groundwater wells. The Indiana USGS office provides information on stream flow at 180 Indiana sites and on water levels in 80 lakes and 90 groundwater observation wells, and it conducts water quality and supply investigations.

The IDEM is responsible for the quality of Indiana's water. Although responsibility for implementation of the federal Clean Water Act lies with the federal Environmental Protection Agency (EPA), the EPA may grant authority to state agencies that have the capability of administering a permit program which will carry out the objectives of the Clean Water Act. In 1973, IDEM received and continues to maintain that authority for Indiana (www.in.gov/idem/permits/water/wastewater/overview). Each state is required by the federal Water Pollution Control Act to prepare and submit every 2 years an assessment of the quality of the state's water resources. These water monitoring and assessment reports (sometimes referred to as 305(b) reports, after the requiring section of the Clean Water Act) provide a historical record of the quality of Indiana's water resources.

The IDNR's Division of Fish and Wildlife has responsibility for the management of the state's fisheries resources. The fish management activities of this agency have been profoundly influenced by the program's funding source. The Sport Fish Restoration Act (SFRA) provided two sources of funding for state agency sport fish management. First, the SFRA (also known as Dingell-Johnson after the co-sponsors) required an excise tax be collected on fishing equipment. The funds generated from this tax were returned to the states based on a formula that considered state size and the number of fishing licenses sold in the state. The federal funds could only be spent on "species of fish which have material value in connection with sport or recreation" (16 U.S.C. 777, sec. 2) and were to be matched by state funds (mainly on a 75% federal and 25% state basis). To ensure that state funds were available for the match, the federal law required each state to adopt assent legislation that provided a "prohibition against the diversion of license fees paid by fishermen for any other purpose than the administration of said State fish and game department" (16 U.S.C. 777). Based on the user-pay/user-benefit model of federal funding, state fish management agencies have focused on a limited number of game fish species. Although the SFRA was amended several times in the last half of the twentieth century, the focus has remained on game fish species with only a slight shift to include boater access, boater safety, aquatic education, angler recruitment, and the management of sewage from boats at large marinas.

Funds for the conservation of nongame fish (i.e., fish not pursued for sport purposes) became available with the passage of the federal Endangered Species Act (ESA) and the Indiana Nongame and Endangered Species Conservation Act (INESCA), both in 1973. Federal ESA expenditures are limited to fish and mussel species of federal interest (i.e., federal endangered, threatened, or candidate species). At the time of this writing, Indiana has never had a native fish species of federal interest. Several species of mussels native to Indiana are on the federal endangered species list or are federal candidate species.

The INESCA established the Nongame Fund, which receives contributions from citizens, mainly through donations of their state income tax refunds. But the total annual contributions to the Nongame Fund have never exceeded $400,000 and have been insufficient to adequately cover the conservation needs of over 70 bird, mammal, amphibian, reptile, fish, mollusk, and crustacean species on the Indiana endangered species list. However, limited surveys and monitoring of fish and mussel distribution and abundance have been accomplished. The federal State Wildlife Grant Program in 2001 provided additional federal funds to the states for the conservation of state-listed species most in need. These SWG funds require non-federal matching funds (usually 50% federal and 50% non-federal). Indiana has received approximately $1 million a year from 2001 to the time of this writing. These moneys have funded distribution and abundance monitoring of nongame fish and freshwater mussel populations as well as nongame fish and mussel life history, genetic, management, and research projects.

The Great Lakes fisheries are managed by the International Joint Commission and the Great Lakes Fisheries Commission. These groups manage the commercial and sport fisheries in Lake Michigan, which are among the most important in Indiana. The collapse of the lake trout fishery from sea lamprey infestation, over-fishing, and the degradation of reef habitats caused the International Joint Commission to institute mechanisms to control sea lamprey. Likewise, the joint commission stocked Pacific salmonids to control the non-indigenous alewife population. The U.S. Fish and Wildlife Service began an extensive effort to control sea lamprey recruitment by targeting ammocoetes and treating natal streams with lampricides. These measures have had a significant impact on reducing sea lamprey abundance and recruitment.

Fish consumption advisories are developed by IDNR, IDEM, and IBH. Since 1972, staff from these agencies have reviewed fish tissue monitoring data, especially for levels of mercury and polychlorinated biphenyls (PCBs), and developed recommendations on where to fish, types of fish to eat, how to prepare fish for cooking, and how to moderate the amount and frequency of fish consumed (www.i.org/isdh/fca/fish_98/fish98.html).

The fragmented focus of the regulatory agencies has limited the systematic monitoring of aquatic communities in Indiana. Fortunately, universities, regulatory agencies (such as IDEM, ORSANCO, the U.S. Army Corps of Engineers, and the EPA), and government-sponsored research programs (such as the USGS, the Mississippi Interstate Cooperative Resource Association, and the U.S. Fish and Wildlife Service) conduct aquatic community assessments, including fish collections, on at least an irregular basis. Additionally, regulatory agencies often require entities that are permitted to discharge pollutants into the waters of the state to measure the impact of their discharge on the receiving water body. Collectively, these efforts provide a useful, albeit incomplete, assessment of Indiana's aquatic communities.

Additional aquatic community data are available as the result of the survey and monitoring activities required as a condition of regulatory permit issuance. Many in-stream activities and discharges are regulated by one or more government agencies. As permits are often based on presumed impacts or permissible discharge quantities, monitoring is often required. For the task of water quality assessment, aquatic community surveys have an advantage over chemical and other abiotic analysis. First, the impacts of water quality insults (chemical, temperature, sediment, or suspended solids) are detectable after the pollutant has moved downstream, settled out, dissipated, or been diluted. Second, the negative impacts to the aquatic community are indicative of potential human or system-wide threats. However, many water bodies receive multiple pollution insults, making direct cause-and-effect determinations difficult and complicating our understanding of the effects of cumulative impacts.

Only recently have fish management activities begun to focus on aquatic habitat. In 1987, Indiana initiated the Lake Enhancement Program to reduce and mitigate sediment and associated nutrient in-flows into Indiana's lakes. Originally housed within the IDNR's Division of Soil Conservation (DSC no longer extant as of 2005), this program sought to help lake conservation groups address lake problems resulting from increased sedimentation. Initially funded as part of the Division of Soil Conservation, in 1989 boat owners were required to pay an additional $5 fee to support this program. In 1991, the original statute was amended to add the words "and river." The Lake and River Enhancement Program moved to the Division of Fish and Wildlife in 2005.

In 2001, the National Fish Habitat Action Plan (NFHAP) was launched to unite partners to restore the nation's waterways and fisheries to healthy and sustainable levels. The NFHAP was modeled after the successful public-private partnership structure of the North American Waterfowl Management Plan. The NFHAP's supporters hope that regional partnerships, also known as joint ventures, will leverage funds and inspire the interest, ownership, and cooperation necessary to restore the nation's fish habitats and declining fisheries.

Another national program that addresses a serious threat to the nation's aquatic resources is the Aquatic Nuisance Species Program. The Indiana Aquatic Nuisance Species Management Plan was approved in 2004, making the state eligible for federal grants. In 2005, the Division of Fish and Wildlife appointed its first full-time aquatic nuisance species coordinator to address this growing and serious threat.

Concerns for water supply and quality have led to a profusion of regulations and regulatory agencies, and, undoubtedly, progress has been made. However, challenges remain, including the widespread use of agricultural, chemical, pharmaceutical, and airborne pollutants (mercury), which end up in Indiana's water supply. Additionally, the uncertain impacts of anticipated climate change will require careful monitoring of the state's water quality and supply.

Indiana Aquatic Habitat Classifications

A classification of the different types of aquatic habitats in Indiana was needed in order to discuss the historical and current conditions of Indiana's aquatic resources. To facilitate the discussion in this chapter, the following simplistic, descriptive categories were developed based on physical aquatic habitat types, drainage relationships, ecoregion classification, and drainage size. "Drainage basin," "drainage area," and "watershed" are all terms given to the land area drained by a particular stream system; generally, the term "watershed" is designated for rivers and all their tributaries (Indiana Department of Natural Resources 1990).

The physical aquatic habitats in Indiana include a variety of freshwater systems that are broadly classified based on water movement. Lentic, or standing water, habitats include wetlands (chapter 6), oxbows, backwaters, sloughs, embayments, natural lakes (including Lake Michigan), and impoundments. The lotic, or flowing water, habitats are separated into three major drainages in Indiana: Great Lakes (Lake Michigan and Lake Erie), Mississippi (Kankakee), and Ohio River. The Ohio River drains approximately three-quarters of Indiana. The diversity of this exceptionally large drainage necessitated further separation. The EPA's ecoregion classification system (Map 7.2; Omernik and Gallant 1988) provided a basis for separating the distinctive southwest portion (Interior River Lowland) of the Ohio River drainage. All lotic habitats were further subdivided by drainage size and separated as headwater streams (< 20 mi^2 drainage area), wadeable/large rivers (≥ 20 mi^2 < 2,000 mi^2), and great rivers (> 1,999 mi^2). A special feature of lotic habitats are sand and gravel bars, which are also discussed in this chapter.

Flora

Aquatic systems are important environments for vascular plants. Natural lakes and ponds, especially those in northern Indiana, contain a diversity of pondweeds, milfoils, waterweeds, duckweeds, hornworts, naiads, and associated other aquatics. These include free-floating species, at the surface or submersed, as well as those rooted in the substrate of the water body. Some rooted species can occur at considerable depths, limited mostly by available light. For Michigan waters, Voss (1972) reports some pondweeds at a depth of 22 ft, although most are in much shallower water.

Streams and rivers are less conducive to the growth of vascular aquatic plants, although many of the species associated with lakes and ponds can occur in slow-moving, high-quality streams and rivers, particularly in quiet backwater areas.

The deterioration of water quality, alteration of water levels, and introduction of non-native invasive species have had deleterious effects on native aquatic species. Siltation, high nutrient input, and excessive turbidity are among the more serious insults. The proliferation of Eurasian water milfoil and beginner's pondweed has provided serious competition for native species. They are also generally indicative of poor water quality, another negative impact.

1800. Submerged aquatic plants were abundant in this time, prior to human-induced water level alterations, pollution, and introduction of invasive exotics.

1900. With the increased use of technology to construct ditches and the input of runoff from agricultural and developed lands, the quality of aquatic communities declined. There was a concomitant decline in the overall population size of aquatic plant species, if not the extirpation of the species themselves. A single species collected in 1880 in LaPorte County, mare's tail (*Hippuris vulgaris*), has not been collected in the state since.

2000. Although the water quality of Indiana's aquatic systems had continued to decline through much of the previous century, advances in controlling non-point source pollution, e.g., conservation tillage, and improved sewage treatment have resulted in cleaner water. Nonetheless, there are now endangered species, including lake cress, least duckweed, pale duckweed, frog's bit, snail-seed pondweed, ribbon-leaved pondweed, Oakes' pondweed, spotted pondweed, and Vasey's pondweed. One semiaquatic plant that has apparently disappeared from the state is dinky duckweed. In the twenty-first century, some exotics are fully established (beginner's pondweed and Eurasian water milfoil). Brazilian waterweed (*Egeria densa*) is becoming established. The Division of Fish and Wildlife initiated an aquatic invasive species program and hired a coordinator in January 2005, and it has an aggressive program to eliminate Brazilian waterweed.

Fish

The aquatic systems of Indiana and the fish that inhabit them are diverse: 211 species of fish have been recorded from the waters of the state. Each unique aquatic system has a characteristic fish assemblage. These communities are formed by the drainage history and specific characteristics of each individual habitat and the specific habitat requirements of the species present.

On a statewide scale, the distribution of fish is first and foremost regulated by the current drainage patterns of the state. Connections between the Great Lakes, Kankakee River (Mississippi River), and Wabash River no longer exist post-glaciation. Except under extreme flooding conditions, or by anthropogenic means, fish can no longer travel between the four major drainages of the state (Lake Michigan, Lake Erie [these are combined in this chapter under Great

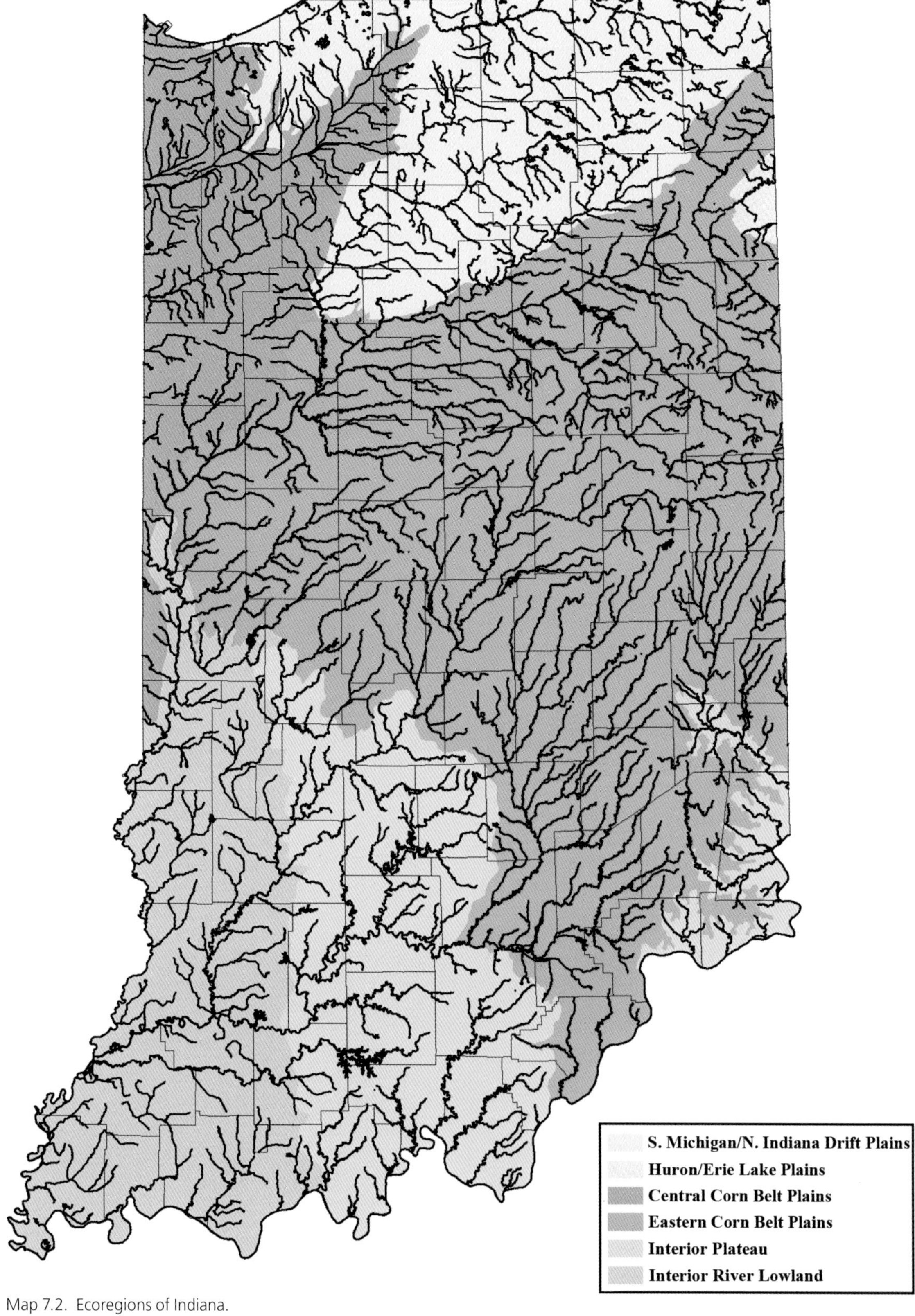

Map 7.2. Ecoregions of Indiana.

Lakes], Kankakee River [Mississippi River], and Ohio River) on their own.

On a local scale, distribution is regulated by the most basic need of all fish—water. Intermittent streams or ephemeral wetlands only contain fish when they hold water and after establishing a connection with local water bodies that contain fish. This most often occurs during periods of high water (flooding). Fish then remain/survive to the extent that water remains or conditions are tolerable.

In addition to water, all fish require oxygen, food, and adequate spawning habitat in order to inhabit and persist in any particular aquatic system. If any of these basic requirements are lacking, as the result of pollution, alteration of the habitat, or other natural or man-made causes, then fish diversity and integrity will be compromised.

Several species of fish in Indiana are not stringent in the habitat they require and can be found generally across Indiana. These species are highly tolerant of a wide range of conditions and are often found in the most degraded habitats. Species such as bluntnose minnow, creek chub, white sucker, yellow bullhead, blackstripe topminnow, green sunfish, bluegill, largemouth bass, and johnny darter can be found statewide and in all types of aquatic habitat.

Many species have unique ecological requirements that limit their distribution. Certain species are more often associated with the lentic, or nonflowing, waters of the state. Lake trout and the coregonid species are restricted to the deep waters of Lake Michigan, while the natural lakes of the northern part of Indiana harbor unique species such as the blackchin shiner, banded killifish, and Iowa darter. Oxbows, backwaters, sloughs, and embayments are naturally, or in some cases man-induced, lentic habitats associated with the wadeable/large/great rivers of the state. Their fish assemblages are normally composed of species that enter from nearby habitats during periods of flooding. Some species, especially in southwestern Indiana, are specific to these habitats, including cypress minnow, western mosquitofish, flier, redspotted sunfish, cypress darter, and banded pygmy sunfish. Manmade lakes, such as impoundments, farm ponds, gravel pits, and retention ponds, rarely contain natural fish communities and are normally dominated by the species stocked for sport fishing. Channel catfish, bluegill, redear sunfish, and largemouth bass can be found in these artificial habitats statewide.

Other species of fish are adapted for life in the lotic, or flowing, waters of the state. Species found in rivers and streams are normally distributed along a gradient of stream size. Southern redbelly dace and redside dace only inhabit small headwater streams that are normally reduced to a series of isolated pools by the fall of each year. These species have very limited ability, if any, to disperse on their own. Species such as shovelnose sturgeon, goldeye, mooneye, skipjack herring, silver chub, river redhorse, blue catfish, and river darter are restricted to the great rivers of the state, utilizing that habitat for all portions of their life history. A large number of species fall somewhere in between, utilizing the wadeable/large rivers but often moving into connected smaller or larger waters during seasonal migrations.

Fish distribution can also be defined in some cases by ecoregion, or areas of the state that contain similar land use, form, vegetation, and soils. Portions of six ecoregions (Central Corn Belt Plains, Southern Michigan/Northern Indiana Drift Plains, Eastern Corn Belt Plains, Huron/Erie Lake Plains, Interior Plateau, and Interior River Lowland) are found in Indiana. Species such as the cypress minnow, spottail darter, and banded pygmy sunfish are only found in extreme southwestern Indiana, within the Interior River Lowland ecoregion. The northern cavefish is only found in the subterranean waters of south-central Indiana, within the Interior Plateau. Characteristic species and assemblages can be assigned to each ecoregion.

1800. Our knowledge of Indiana fish during this time period is limited to the work of Constantine Samuel Rafinesque from the Falls of the Ohio River, Edward Drinker Cope's work on the White River, and Charles Lesueur's studies on the Wabash River and tributaries near New Harmony. Specimens of the alligator gar were known from New Harmony, although food fish were the principal species reported. Descriptions of the now-extirpated popeye shiner were made from the West Fork of the White River near Indianapolis, and brindled madtom, grass pickerel, and river redhorse were also described.

Fish assemblages prior to 1800 would represent the least-impacted conditions; however, little is documented. Overall diversity in the state was actually less than present times, because of the lack of introduced species. Species adapted for wetlands and those requiring the cooler waters of forested landscapes were in greater abundance.

1900. During the latter half of the 1800s, significant land use changes began to occur, as extensive tracts of land were cleared for agriculture, streams were channelized, and wetlands were drained. These changes were so extensive that our knowledge of presettlement fish communities in Indiana is greatly limited. As agricultural, urban, and industrial development increased, so did water quality problems from nonpoint source and untreated point source pollution. Siltation and sedimentation increased, as did stream temperatures, as riparian canopy cover was removed. Many of the largest rivers, such as the Wabash and Ohio rivers, experienced increased sediment loads by the removal of watershed forest. Alligator gar, harelip sucker, several Lake Michigan deepwater cisco species, popeye shiner, crystal darter, saddleback darter, and stargazing darter were seen for the last time in Indiana just prior to or around the beginning of the twentieth century.

2000. The clearing of land and draining of wetlands for agriculture and urban and industrial development continued into the mid-twentieth century. As human populations moved into urban environments, domestic waste and sewage were discharged downstream of the urban areas into rivers and streams. The movement of waste increased biological oxygen demand (BOD), which reduced the dissolved oxygen concentrations of surface waters. The decline of sensitive species by either avoidance or fish kills created large fishless areas. The urban area surrounding Indianapolis was greatly affected, causing most of the West Fork of the White River downstream to be devoid of aquatic life.

The industrial revolution created additional pollution sources, including the runoff of chemicals and the discharge of heavy metals and other manufactured waste products. For example, the Grand Calumet River downstream of Gary is known for its heavy concentration of steel and petrochemical manufacturing. When the river was dredged in the middle of the twentieth century, the river bottom was processed through the steel mills to harvest the iron ore that had become mixed into the river bottom. These contaminants had profound impacts on aquatic life and caused the extirpation of sensitive species in the wetlands along Lake Michigan as the lakefront developed into a significant industrial complex. In southwestern Indiana, the surface mining of coal and the removal of natural gas and crude oil caused significant acidity to affect the surface waters. As a result, many of these streams experienced a drop in pH to acid levels that were toxic to aquatic life. The precipitation of iron and the release of oxidized heavy metals caused acute toxic responses in all aquatic life. Many of these streams have not recovered and still are devoid of life at the beginning of the twenty-first century. These streams have iron precipitates and other flocculents that form a yellow to orange cast in the water. They also have high conductivity and a high concentration of total dissolved solids.

So grievous were the impacts to Indiana's aquatic habitats that, by around the mid-1900s, state and federal regulations were adopted to prevent further damage. By the end of the twentieth century, dramatic improvement had been observed in fish assemblage structure and function in many Indiana watersheds. This improvement can be attributed to improved water quality, habitat stability, and the recolonization of streams due to the restoration of habitats and protection of stream riparian corridors. Much of the improvement is a result of increased point source pollution control, a reduction in non-point source impacts, and the cleanup of Lake Michigan's harbors and embayments. The twentieth century ended with an influx of new invasive aquatic species whose long-term effects may not be known until well into the twenty-first century. Global climate change is also predicted, with unknown consequences to the aquatic systems of Indiana.

The number of species of fish known from Indiana from 1800 to the present is 211 species (Table F-1). Of these, 11 have been extirpated: alligator gar, Alabama shad, popeye shiner, harelip sucker, blackfin cisco, shortnose cisco, shortjaw cisco, southern cavefish, crystal darter, stargazing darter, and saddleback darter. The Great Lakes form of the muskellunge is also considered extirpated, although an Ohio River form of questionable status may still exist in southern Indiana; the stocking of muskellunge has further complicated the current status of this species. Ten species are listed as state endangered and 15 as species of special concern. Also, 22 exotic species have been introduced into Indiana (Table F-1).

Amphibians and Reptiles

Indiana has a variety of aquatic herpetofauna, though many species are more reasonably affiliated with wetlands (discussed elsewhere) than lakes and rivers. Open waters are used by a variety of turtles, including the map and false map turtles, spiny and smooth softshells, midland painted turtle, and snapping turtle. Amphibians are less diverse in the open waters of aquatic systems, although the mudpuppy occurs in lakes and streams. The hellbender no doubt frequented a number of the larger tributaries of the Ohio River, and still persists at least along the lower reaches of the Blue River. Herpetofauna most commonly associated with rivers and lakes are listed in Table H-5.

1800. In the early to mid-1800s, Indiana's aquatic system herpetofauna was what it had been during presettlement times. Beaver trapping, and the ultimate extirpation of this ecosystem engineer in the mid-1800s, ended the impact of this species on the landscape of lakeshores and streams. The small to moderately sized impoundments formed behind beaver dams are a preferred haunt of many amphibians and reptiles, so the loss of beavers was significant. However, no species was entirely reliant on these aquatic features.

1900. As the conversion of land for agricultural use accelerated in the 1800s and into the twentieth century, the effects on aquatic herpetofauna became more pronounced. To some extent, this meant habitat loss, as some bodies of water were drained, but more commonly habitat degradation was the issue. The shorelines of Lake Michigan, other lakes, and streams were modified to meet the needs of farming, industry, and community. Water quality in streams degraded as sediment load increased. This changed the nature of the substrate in many streams, leading to the loss of species such as the hellbender and, to a lesser extent, the mudpuppy.

As human populations grew, lakeshore property became more and more prized for residential areas, first for summer cottages, then for year-round homes. Development just beyond lake and stream shorelines has consequently removed the terrestrial habitat around many lakes, which is needed by many aquatic reptiles to satisfy some of their habitat requirements. Nesting turtles must find sites to lay their eggs. Many semiaquatic snakes and turtles also routinely traverse uplands from one wetland to another. The classic examples include the copperbelly water snake and Blanding's turtle, which use uplands as secondary habitat and move frequently between different wetlands. Development and its associated support structures, such as roads, remove habitat and impose barriers to the movement of herpetofauna.

Shoreline habitat loss, development, and consequent barriers have proved challenging for terrestrial salamanders. Ambystomatid species, such as the spotted salamander, might not breed in lakes or streams, but would do so in peripheral wetlands. Their opportunities to breed are removed when water levels are stabilized, shorelines solidified, wetlands drained and filled, and roads and homes are placed in, on, or around habitat.

An emerging problem across Indiana for lake herpetofauna has been the stabilization of lake levels. It is very common for lake levels to be controlled at an exit point so that the shoreline is predictable for human residents, who then add structures, such as beaches and docks. Stabilizing the level of one lake may stabilize water levels throughout whole networks of lakes, streams, and wetlands. This can have a profound impact on successional processes along the shoreline. Where hydrologic variation once sustained a variety of early successional habitats, competitive terrestrial plants have pushed toward the water's edge, and competitive plants have come to dominate the aquatic side. Consequently, the wetlands along many lakeshores have disappeared or become greatly diminished, and the herpetofauna that once used these areas have diminished as well.

2000. Storm wall placement around lakeshores is another issue, particularly for turtles. Turtles must lay their eggs on land, often using particular areas that have soils and conditions that ease nest digging. Gravid females thus endeavor to come on land and travel to appropriate locations to lay their eggs. Many bodies of water are now ringed extensively by a variety of constructed barriers, storm walls being only one of these. Cement walls and shores covered with rip-rap make it impossible, or at the least very difficult, for the turtles to reach nesting locations. If turtles have used specific areas previously to nest, they may be highly motivated to return to those areas, further complicating matters.

Birds

Aquatic systems—mainly Lake Michigan and inland lakes and rivers—are a characteristic habitat for at least 120 species, if one includes birds of mainly terrestrial families (flycatchers, warblers, etc.) that are common in vegetation along rivers or lake margins (Table B-5). The main groups represented are waterfowl (ducks, geese, swans); loons, grebes, and cormorants; gulls and terns; shorebirds; herons; certain raptors (eagles, ospreys, falcons); kingfishers; and a handful of passerines, such as swallows, phoebes, and waterthrushes. There is much overlap with the bird species of wetlands. Wetlands are distinguished from aquatic systems by being shallow wet habitats with prominent vegetation characteristics. However, there are also differences between the avifauna of these two broad habitat categories (see Table B-1).

The waters and shores of Lake Michigan are especially significant for migratory shorebirds, waterfowl, loons, and grebes that breed in the Arctic or subarctic and winter in the Atlantic Ocean or along its coast. They are also significant for birds that winter on Lake Michigan itself, including species rarely found on large inland lakes, such as greater scaup, glaucous gull, and great black-backed gull.

Inland aquatic habitats in Indiana have been diminished, expanded, and altered to varying degrees, depending on the habitat. Alterations to rivers include extreme channelizing and dredging (Kankakee River); the construction of multiple dams, which created large lakes on rivers such as the Salamonie, Mississinewa, Tippecanoe, Whitewater, and White; the construction of levees rather than dams (Wabash River); and changes in water quality and food webs driven by inputs of agricultural fertilizer (Gammon et al. 1990). Most of the hundreds of natural glacial lakes in the northern third of the state now have developed shorelines and recreational boating that diminish bird use, while others are in relatively natural states. In southwestern Indiana, surface coal mining has created many new lakes.

These changes have reduced naturally flooded areas and riparian forested margins, while expanding large lake and pond habitat for birds in the southern two-thirds of the state. Habitat availability has improved (in the south) for migrating ducks, loons, grebes, cormorants, and gulls, but declined for birds dependent on wild, flooding rivers (rookery sites for herons have been destroyed, for example).

Fall and spring migrations are the times of greatest bird species diversity and abundance in aquatic habitats, especially on Lake Michigan and inland lakes. In the winter, most inland lakes eventually freeze, moving lingering waterfowl south. Lake Michigan hosts an interesting set of wintering ducks and gulls, some of which also frequent large rivers and warm water reservoirs associated with power plants. Currently, the birds of large inland lakes (mostly reservoirs and power plant lakes) and Lake Michigan are much better known than those of rivers, streams, or the natural glacial lakes. The former habitats receive far more attention from birders because of easier access and their known species diversity. Of special note, the Louisiana waterthrush, a summer resident that nests along streams, prefers creeks to larger streams and rivers.

1800. Indiana began the nineteenth century with its various natural aquatic habitats and aquatic bird communities intact. Although no ornithological description exists (to our knowledge), one can imagine the following. The wilderness shoreline of Lake Michigan served as a feeding and resting stopover site for tundra-breeding shorebirds, loons, grebes, and ducks of the Canadian lakes and for land birds, such as warblers breeding in the boreal forest. The 500 glacial lakes in the northeast attracted migratory ducks. The sluggish Kankakee River with its extensive adjacent marshes was a paradise for waterfowl, herons, and rails. Unconstrained large rivers like the Ohio and Wabash flooded seasonally over large areas, with many lazy oxbows in the lower Wabash.

1900. The clearing of forests for farming occurred on a vast scale, no doubt affecting rivers in various ways. The unregulated hunting of birds had major impacts, as indicated by the repeated admonitions in Butler (1898). One riparian species to vanish was the Carolina parakeet, which often roosted in sycamores along rivers.

2000. The construction of man-made lakes, reservoirs, and ponds throughout the twentieth century increased aquatic habitat at inland sites. The contamination of fish with pesticides apparently wreaked havoc with double-crested cormorants in the 1960s and 1970s, but the species rebounded in the 1980s (Bruner 2002). River quality and food webs were affected by agricultural runoff rich in nutrients (e.g., nitrogen-phosphorus-potassium fertilizer) and pesticides.

Mammals

There are few mammals of Indiana that can be thought of as residents of aquatic systems. They are mainly the muskrat, beaver, and river otter and, to a lesser degree, the mink, star-nosed mole (southern edge of continental distribution), and swamp rabbit (northern edge of continental distribution) (Table M-4). The muskrat, beaver, and otter spend much of their time in lakes, ponds, marshes, rivers, and streams. The muskrat and beaver build lodges when the water is relatively shallow and stable water is present, such as in lakes, ponds, and marshes. However, they often use bank burrows along creeks or rivers lacking adequate shallow water, or where flooding often occurs. Dens of river otters are often along banks in a natural opening or in another animal's burrow or lodge (beaver, muskrat, or woodchuck). Dens also may be constructed among tree roots, under a brush pile, in a hollow stump or logjam, or in some other protected place. The entrance may be above or below the surface of the water, and the den may be used for several years.

The star-nosed mole often lives in mucky situations, where its burrows open at the edge of the water, where it feeds. However, it presently occurs only in northeastern Indiana. The swamp rabbit lives in the frequently flooded riverbottom woods of southwestern Indiana, primarily in Gibson, but also in Knox and Posey counties. Although it is a good swimmer, during flooding it is critical that there be refugia of higher ground that the rabbit can use until the floodwaters recede. A major reason the swamp rabbit has declined is because much of its habitat is now farmland or, even if the bottomland woods is still present, the necessary elevated refugia have often been cut and turned into farmland. The mink, an excellent swimmer, spends much time foraging in aquatic areas, although it may resort to woods during the winter when the water is frozen.

1800. All of the species mentioned above were present in 1800. However, the beaver was very rare at that time, because of extensive trapping.

1900. By this date, fur-bearing mammals had taken a major hit. Beaver had long been extirpated. The river otter was reported by the Prince of Wied to be abundant at New Harmony in 1832–1833, and Blatchley reported it from Putnam County in 1871. By 1900, the otter was rare because of unregulated trapping but not entirely extirpated. Though not as rare as otters, mink were also much reduced by unregulated trapping as well as by the drainage of wetlands. The muskrat probably occurred in suitable habitat throughout the state.

The star-nosed mole and swamp rabbit were probably roughly similar in abundance and range to what they had been in 1800. However, their ranges may have been reduced by 1850 due to the drainage of wetlands. Turn-of-the-century records for Bartholomew and Dearborn counties (Butler 1895; True 1896) suggest that the mole's range in 1900 may have been larger than the present 20-county area, perhaps extending through the northern two-thirds of eastern Indiana. The swamp rabbit probably occurred in southwestern counties, from Posey County north along the Wabash to at least Knox and possibly Sullivan and southern Vigo counties; eastward along the Ohio River to Spencer County; and up the White and Patoka rivers to Pike, Daviess, and Dubois counties.

2000. The beaver was reintroduced into Indiana in the 1930s by the Indiana Department of Natural Resources, which obtained beavers from Wisconsin and Michigan and released them in the Jasper-Pulaski and Kankakee fish and wildlife areas in 1935. By 1938, beavers were present in Jasper, LaPorte, Marshall, Noble, Porter, Pulaski, and Starke counties. Other reintroductions were made (some in southern Indiana), and by 1947, an estimated 5,000 beavers were thought to be present in the state (Denny 1952). However, Brooks (1959) interviewed all of the conservation officers in Indiana in 1955 and estimated that about 2,100 beavers were present in about 400+ beaver colonies located throughout the state. By the 1970s and 1980s, major increases occurred; in the twenty-first century, the beaver is abundant in suitable habitat throughout the state, often being a nuisance.

The last-known otter in the state was taken in 1942 at Hovey Lake in Posey County, but between 1995 and 1999, 303 otters from Louisiana were released by IDNR at 12 sites in northern and southern Indiana. They are doing very well, and their range is rapidly increasing in the state.

More information is needed, but the star-nosed mole is currently known to occur in only 8 northeastern counties (LaPorte, St. Joseph, Elkhart, LaGrange, Steuben, Kosciusko, Noble, and Allen). Swamp rabbits have been reduced to a population estimated at 80 individuals mostly in the northern and southern portions of Gibson County (Whitaker and Abrell 1986), but there are a few in extreme southern Knox County, and apparently a very few at Hovey Lake in Posey County. The muskrat and mink occur throughout the state in suitable habitat. Thus, the full complement of aquatic mammals is currently present in the state (Table M-4).

Sub-habitats

Lake Michigan

The entire surface area of Lake Michigan is 22,297 mi^2 with Indiana's portion encompassing 241 mi^2 (Indiana Department of Natural Resources 1994). A 45-mi strip of southern Lake Michigan shoreline is located in northwest Indiana (Figure 7.5). Lake Michigan's aquatic habitats can be divided into deep, off-shore, and shallower, near-shore habitats. (The lake comprises the Lake Michigan Natural Region.) The impacts of Lake Michigan on the surrounding landscape can be seen in its effects on local climate and its ability to drastically alter shoreline areas. The movements of sand as a result of the impacts of storms on Lake Michigan have created extensive upland dunes-and-swales habitat, gravel surf zones that are wave washed, and limited embayments, tributary mouths,

Figure 7.5. Lake Michigan shoreline. Photo by Terry L. Castor.

and harbors that provide submerged vegetation, spawning habitats, and nursery habitats. Pollution, fishing, and non-native introductions have had the greatest effect on the habitats and aquatic communities of Lake Michigan (Greenberg 2002).

FLORA. No known vascular plants are established in the Indiana portion of Lake Michigan. Because its bottom is mostly sand and commonly subjected to strong waves and currents, the environment is not conducive to vascular plant growth.

FISH. Prior to 1800, the Lake Michigan shoreline was natural and included upland habitats principally of dune and swale and oak savanna, while the in-lake habitat was composed of near-shore sand and gravel surf zones and deepwater off-shore areas. Near-shore fish communities were likely dominated by lake sturgeon, emerald shiner, various species of sucker, yellow perch, and walleye, while off-shore areas were dominated by various deepwater cisco species, lake trout, and burbot (Eshenroder et al. 1995).

The bypass of Niagara Falls by the Welland Ship Canal was completed by 1824 (Greenberg 2002). Further developments of this canal provided the means for exotic species to be introduced in the next century. Development and alterations to the Lake Michigan shoreline began in the late 1800s (Indiana Department of Natural Resources 1994). The fish community of Lake Michigan by 1900 was probably very similar to what it was historically; however, commercial fishing was beginning to impact certain species, especially many of the white fish. Lake sturgeon and lake trout were also becoming commercially important (Milner 1874).

By the beginning of the twentieth century, a large portion of the lake's shoreline was filled, creating the U.S. Steel property and the ports and industrial areas of the western shoreline. Dramatic changes in the lakefront occurred during this period, as the shoreline changed from natural coastal wetland habitats composed of marsh wetland vegetation and drier upland black oak savanna to large industrial sites. These industrial areas have been significant pollution sources and have caused the loss of biological integrity in the near-shore areas of Lake Michigan for the last half-century. These industrial changes include landscape degradation, point source pollutant loadings, and wide-scale non-point source runoff of contaminants from industrial properties. These ports and lands were important during the world wars, producing steel and other materials.

Habitat degradation and alteration could have directly contributed to the loss of the Great Lakes muskellunge from Indiana waters. Important connections from the lake to critical spawning wetland habitats were most likely disrupted or the habitats themselves were highly altered or destroyed. The Great Lakes muskellunge was last collected from the Indiana waters of Lake Michigan in the early part of the twentieth century (Meek and Hildebrand 1910).

Even though pollution, habitat destruction, and commercial fishing have certainly had an effect on the fish communities of Lake Michigan, it wasn't until the introduction of non-native species that the fish community was forever changed (Greenberg 2002; Eshenroder et al. 1995). Rainbow smelt, sea lamprey, and alewife all invaded Lake Michigan during the early and middle part of the twentieth century. Alewife directly compete for food with other pelagic fish and are known to consume pelagic larval fish. They have been implicated in the extinction of at least three deepwater cisco species (shortjaw, shortnose, and blackfin cisco are now considered extirpated from the Indiana waters of Lake Michigan; Cudmore-Vokey and Crossman 2000) and the suppression of emerald shiner, lake herring, yellow perch, and deepwater sculpin populations (Eshenroder et al. 1995). The sea lamprey caused the declines of many native species in Lake Michigan, but the most notable was the lake trout. The sea lamprey presumably wiped it out of the lake by the middle of the twentieth century (Greenberg 2002).

A host of other exotic and non-indigenous species have also been accidentally introduced into Lake Michigan, including shortnose gar, American eel, grass carp, pink salmon, goldfish, threespine stickleback, white perch, and round goby (Eshenroder et al. 1995). Other exotic species have been the direct result of intentional stocking efforts, such as Pacific salmonids for alewife control and sport fishing. Simon and Stewart (1999) found that exotic and non-indigenous species represented as much as 80% of the fish fauna in collections made from 1990 to 1997. Round goby was the second most dominant species by number in collections during 1998 along the near-shore areas of Lake Michigan, only behind spottail shiner (Simon 2000).

Introduction of the zebra mussel through the ballast water of transoceanic shipping vessels was first confirmed in the Great Lakes in 1988 and in Lake Michigan in 1989. It has had a deleterious effect on the native plankton community in Lake Michigan, shifting primary production to the benthic layer and increasing water clarity. The long-term effects of this benthic inhabitant on the aquatic communities of Lake Michigan are still relatively uncertain (Greenberg 2002). Other Eurasian species, such as the round goby and rudd, have also been introduced by transoceanic vessels. Significant changes have been proposed in the international shipping laws in an attempt to deter future introductions.

The fish species most commonly associated with the Indiana waters of Lake Michigan are listed in Table F-2; included are 89 species, of which 18 are exotic or non-indigenous.

AMPHIBIANS AND REPTILES. Few amphibians or reptiles actually make their home in the open waters of the lake itself. However, many are found, or at least once were, along its shores. One species that is at home in the lake is the mudpuppy, which apparently was once quite common (Davis and Rice 1883). Divers have found them more than a kilometer offshore, and over 25 m down (A. Resetar, personal communication). The spiny softshell is a strong swimmer and likely exploits areas just off-shore. Species most likely to take up residence in Lake Michigan are listed in Table H-5.

1800. At this time, Lake Michigan was relatively pristine. Unlike today, the shoreline was naturally complex with many bays, river inlets, and shallow wetlands. As a consequence, we expect that many of the species found in other wetlands of the state also occurred along Lake Michigan.

1900. Although the shoreline of Lake Michigan degraded over the 1800s, the composition of the herpetofaunal community was not likely greatly affected, largely because of its paucity to begin with. However, the abundance of many herpetofauna was certainly reduced with the loss of lakeshore habitat.

2000. Despite the changes and loss of habitat along the shoreline, the few species using the open waters of the lake are still extant.

BIRDS. Brock (1997) provides an excellent account of current patterns and historic changes, from which the following paragraphs are mainly derived. Some 88 species (Table B-5) are characteristic lakefront birds in Indiana, feeding in or over the lake or on its beaches, resting on it, or migrating over or along it. Not included are many species that migrate over or around the lake; for them, the lake is an obstacle more than a productive habitat, although they may forage or rest briefly on its shores.

Some 30 waterfowl species occur annually on the lake, based on observations from beaches along the lakefront. Most waterfowl (21 species) occur as migrants in the fall and spring, 7 as wintering birds, and 2 (Canada goose, mallard) as abundant permanent residents. Migrants typically reach peak numbers in late October and early November and are less abundant in the spring. Many pass through the Great Lakes on their way to coastal winter ranges in the mid-Atlantic states, while others are bound for the Gulf of Mexico.

The most common migrant ducks at Lake Michigan, based on Brock's (1997) finding codes, are lesser scaup and red-breasted merganser. Next in abundance are American wigeon, American black duck, blue-winged teal, redhead, and ring-necked duck. The third tier, still common, consists of gadwall, northern shoveler, green-winged teal, canvasback, and hooded merganser. Less common but of interest are the 3 scoters (sea ducks) and tundra swan.

The abundant wintering ducks (besides mallard) are bufflehead, common goldeneye, American black duck, greater scaup, and common merganser. Less common are the long-tailed duck and harlequin duck.

Common loons and horned grebes migrate with waterfowl. Double-crested cormorant is common for extended periods in the fall and spring, and the first nesting in decades was recorded in 2004 (60 pairs in a colony of ring-billed gulls and night-herons; Hedge 2005). Great blue heron is the only heron that commonly feeds along the lakeshore, but black-crowned night-herons have a nesting colony on the lakefront.

Four diurnal raptors, all uncommon or rare, characteristically hunt over Lake Michigan or along the lakefront: osprey, bald eagle, peregrine falcon, and merlin. In addition, turkey vultures scavenge on the shore. Large numbers of hawks (such as broad-winged and red-tailed hawks) pile up along the lakefront in spring because of an aversion to crossing the lake; they migrate east or west along the lakefront to find an overland route north. In the fall, the passage is much less conspicuous at the southern end of Lake Michigan, but the same phenomenon occurs on the north side of Lake Erie.

Nine shorebird species are common along lakefront beaches, all migrants except for the summer resident killdeer. In descending order of abundance (Brock 1997), they are sanderling, semipalmated plover, spotted sandpiper, semipalmated sandpiper, least sandpiper, black-bellied plover, ruddy turnstone, and dunlin. Several shorebirds that are rare in the state occur almost exclusively at Lake Michigan from August to April: willet, red knot, purple sandpiper, red phalarope, and piping plover (which formerly nested and is now only a migrant).

Ring-billed gull is the most abundant gull and is present year-round, breeding in Lake County since 1991 (Brock 1997). Herring gulls are common in the winter, as are Bonaparte's gulls during the winter and migration. Seven other gull species occur annually but are rare. Fall migration brings parasitic jaegers to the southern end of Lake Michigan. Caspian tern is the most common of 4 migrant tern species, occurring in the late summer.

A handful of passerine birds are characteristic of Lake Michigan because they forage on beaches (horned lark, snow bunting) or over the lake (3 swallow species). Bank swallows nest in large colonies in sand banks carved by the lake (Brock 1997).

1800. No information.

1900. Bald eagles nested regularly in the dunes until 1900, when they were extirpated as breeders for many decades.

2000. Absent as breeding birds for most of the century, bald eagles began breeding along the lake after a reintroduction program in the 1980s and 1990s. Piping plovers nested on lakefront beaches from 1897 through 1955; increased human disturbance probably caused their disappearance (Brock 1997). Now federally endangered, the plover occurs only as a rare migrant. Long-tailed duck, a wintering species, declined dramatically from the 1950s (when it was seen daily) to the 1990s (about 10 seen per year). In the 1990s, greater scaup may have benefited from the accidental introduction of zebra mussels, which provided abundant food for the diving mussel-eaters. Gulls did not nest along the lake until 1991, when ring-billed gulls began nesting at Inland Steel (Brock 1997).

MAMMALS. None of the mammals spend much time in Lake Michigan, but beavers, muskrats, river otters, and mink may visit it occasionally, or occur where there are bays, inlets, and shallow wetlands.

1800. Any of the animals mentioned above might have visited the shores of Lake Michigan in the early 1800s.

1900. The beaver was extirpated by 1840, but the other species might have visited Lake Michigan occasionally, although the otter was extirpated in 1942.

2000. The beaver had returned to the state and was increasing by the latter part of the twentieth century, and the otter had been reintroduced, so any of these species might now occasionally visit the shores of Lake Michigan.

Rivers and Streams by Order and Watershed (Altered and Natural)

The rivers and streams of Indiana are very diverse. They vary in geological history, gradient, watershed land use, and extent of alteration, among other characteristics. For strictly aquatic organisms, watershed separation often determines their distribution. Many species are restricted to certain watersheds in the state and cannot normally spread to other watersheds on their own. Aquatic organisms are also influenced by stream size, with certain species restricted to small streams, while others are more adapted to the wadeable/large/great rivers. The ability of species to migrate freely throughout the entire watershed they inhabit, and sometimes to other associated habitats, is often required to complete all phases of their life history.

FLORA. While backwater portions of larger rivers and quiet pools in streams can harbor some species of vascular plants, in general these environments are not high in plant diversity. Some species of pondweeds, such as comb pondweed, can tolerate stream flow, and some plants are found on the edges of these bodies of water, such as riverbank tussock sedge and water willow. Minimal erosion prior to settlement in the early 1800s would have resulted in water of high quality and clarity. Stream and river flow would have likely been more consistent, without the surges and drops of water volume that are experienced today. Consequently, more species might have been able to survive in some of Indiana's rivers and streams, but the actual occurrence is unknown. See Table P-9 for a list of species of rivers and streams.

FISH. Almost 90% of the stream miles in Indiana are associated with headwater streams and wadeable/large rivers. Thus, most stream miles in Indiana are small and rugged habitats for fish species to inhabit. Most of the 211 (Table F-1) species of fish known from Indiana are adapted to the flowing habitats of creeks, streams, and large rivers. Each stream size has characteristic species associated with its thermal regime and various habitat types. For example, altered headwater streams normally possess the most tolerant species, such as bluntnose minnow, creek chub, white sucker, green sunfish, and johnny darter. Other species adapted for cooler water, such as the southern redbelly dace, western blacknose dace, and mottled sculpin, are found in the least-disturbed headwater streams. Fish community diversity increases with stream size. Many of the same families of fish are represented, but species with a wider range of specializations in prey and spawning habitat requirements are found. Wadeable/large rivers include many of the same species found from the smaller streams, but normally see an increase in diversity, adding several more species adapted for life in larger stream habitats. Great rivers, the largest of the lotic systems, possess a unique fauna, including many species that complete all aspects of their life histories within the habitat. Shovelnose sturgeon, goldeye, blue sucker, blue catfish, river redhorse, and river darter are characteristic of the great river habitat.

AMPHIBIANS AND REPTILES. A wide variety of herpetofauna is associated with rivers and streams. However, few species are actually specialized to use them. The hellbender used a variety of the tributaries in southern Indiana, wherever clear waters flowed over a rocky bottom. Most populations are gone now as siltation and other factors have degraded habitat. The green frog and bullfrog are still common along river shorelines. Numerous species of turtles are affiliated with rivers and streams. Some of these, such as common snapping turtles and painted turtles, are found in a wide variety of wetlands and aquatic habitats. However, other species are more narrowly associated with moving water. While the common map turtle may be found in rivers and lakes, many of the other map turtles are mainly associated with rivers and streams. These include the false map turtle and the Mississippi map turtle. Unlike the spiny softshell, the smooth softshell is also more of a river species. The alligator snapping turtle, which may still make it occasionally into the state, used to enter along the Wabash River and other Ohio River tributaries. All of Indiana's water snakes might be found along the shores of rivers and streams.

1800. Through the early 1800s, river herpetofauna were in excellent condition throughout the state.

1900. The herpetofauna of aquatic systems was probably relatively intact well into the 1800s. However, as agricultural development swept across the state, sediment loads increased, and species needing rocky bottoms and clear water, such as the hellbender, declined. With the disappearance of the beaver in the mid-1800s, the small to moderately sized impoundments that were once a natural feature along many streams and tributaries also disappeared. Such beaver ponds are a preferred haunt of many amphibians and reptiles. They also captured much of the sediment heading downstream.

2000. Given the need for rivers and streams as natural drains, most are still present on the landscape, unlike many other wetlands. However, rivers and streams were frequently highly modified as agricultural expansion continued and improvements in technology facilitated draining the landscape. Rivers were straightened and ditched with steep banks. Species such as the alligator snapping turtle, the western mud snake, and most populations of the western cottonmouth disappeared as the river channel was simplified, removing habitat complexities along the shores. Less obvious were the declines of the rest of the riverine herpetofauna. Turtle collection is identified as a cause of the extirpation of alligator snapping turtles from many areas of its range, but collection also became a factor for all turtles. Water pollution in general is anticipated to negatively impact all herpetofauna, but amphibians in particular because of their sensitive skin. With the reintroduction of beavers and their expansion into many areas of the state, beaver impoundments once again have become a part of river and stream landscapes, albeit in a limited fashion.

Patterns observed for the 1900s of habitat decline and the consequent impacts on river herpetofauna likely are still present. The decline of the hellbender continues in the twenty-first century, along with the continued sedimentation of Indiana's waterways. Curiously, the expansion of the zebra mussel may be alleviating the sedimentation problem in many areas, though at substantial cost to a variety of native wildlife. Hopefully, efforts such as the Wetlands Reserve Program, the Conservation Reserve Program, and improvements in soil conservation in farming areas have also reduced sediment loads. The control of point source pollution has also helped with water quality, but non-point source pollution continues to be a concern.

BIRDS. Rivers and streams are significant as feeding and nesting habitat for the riparian bird species discussed in the paragraphs below. Big river systems like the Wabash (with north-south orientations) are also critical migratory corridors for forest species, such as warblers, vireos, and other passerines. Though not well documented, this is obvious when a birder compares riparian habitat with upland areas during migration. The floodplain forests that support the flow of avian migrants have been diminished greatly due to agriculture.

The most common river duck is the wood duck, which nests in tree cavities; females and ducklings are often encountered in the summer. The much rarer hooded merganser also nests along forested streams (Castrale et al. 1998). Almost any migratory duck species might use rivers. In the coldest months, bufflehead, common goldeneye, and common merganser are found along the Wabash River, especially near power plants that discharge warm water. Other characteristic river birds are great blue heron and bald eagle, which nest in trees along rivers and fish in them. Flooded forests are valuable rookery sites for herons, but intensive agriculture keeps them in short supply. Spotted sandpipers, osprey, ring-billed gull, and double-crested cormorant follow rivers during migration. Several birds nest mainly along rivers in vertical banks, on flat shoreline or sandbars, or under bridges, and forage primarily in or over rivers or along their banks. These include killdeer, spotted sandpiper, belted kingfisher, eastern phoebe, 3 swallow species (northern rough-winged, barn, cliff), and Louisiana waterthrush. The waterthrush prefers small streams; along even a modest stream like Big Walnut Creek (Putnam County) it is found mainly at the mouths of tiny tributaries.

A few other species are strongly associated with streamside habitat and are therefore included here, although they nest and forage in trees or vegetation rather than on or over rivers: prothonotary warbler, yellow-throated warbler, and warbling vireo.

The birds of rivers and streams are not as easily monitored as those on inland lakes and Lake Michigan, because road access offers only a narrow view of the habitat. Consequently, the present quality and productivity of riparian habitat for birds are not well known.

1800. See comments in the opening discussion.

1900. Wood ducks were greatly reduced by Butler's (1898) time, being absent from several counties.

2000. With protection and nest box programs, wood ducks recovered dramatically in the twentieth century. Bald eagle reintroduction efforts begun in the 1980s led to the establishment of over 50 nest sites along the Wabash and other rivers, with the number still growing as of 2005 (J. Castrale, personal communication).

MAMMALS. Beavers, muskrats, river otters, and mink spend much time in rivers and streams, and swamp rabbits enter the floodwaters of the woods along the Wabash River in southwestern Indiana. Star-nosed moles occur in muckland along rivers and streams in northeastern Indiana.

1800. There was little clearing of riparian habitat in 1800, so most species associated with rivers and streams were not limited by habitat. The fur trade was beginning to have an impact on mammals such as beaver, muskrat, river otter, and mink.

1900. Riparian areas had been largely cleared for agriculture by 1900, reducing quality habitat for most species using rivers and streams. The beaver became extirpated about 1840, and others were decreasing, but muskrats and mink were still present in rivers and streams. Swamp rabbits occurred in the wooded floodplains along the rivers of southwestern Indiana. Star-nosed moles occurred along rivers and streams in northeastern Indiana.

2000. Riparian habitats, while limited in width along streams and rivers, are in better condition today than in 1900. This has helped to allow the successful reintroduction of the beaver and river otter. The beaver became extirpated about 1840, the river otter by 1942, but by 2000, both had been reintroduced and were doing fine. The beaver is doing well throughout the state, and the river otter is more abundant in the northern and southern parts of the state, where it was released. Muskrats and mink continue to be common in rivers and streams. Swamp rabbits have been greatly reduced because of loss of habitat, and only about 80 individuals survive, mostly in wooded bottoms along the Wabash River mostly in and adjacent to Gibson County. Star-nosed moles occur along rivers and streams in extreme northeastern Indiana.

Great Lakes Drainage (includes Lake Michigan and Lake Erie Tributaries)

The Great Lakes drainage of Indiana can loosely be divided into three major sections: (1) the Maumee River watershed, located in northeastern Indiana and part of the Lake Erie drainage, (2) the St. Joseph River watershed, located in north-central Indiana and flowing into Michigan and part of the Lake Michigan drainage, and (3) the Grand Calumet/Little Calumet/Trail Creek watersheds, located along the southern border of Lake Michigan in northwestern Indiana and part of the Lake Michigan drainage (the Calumet drainage is also connected to the Mississippi River drainage via a man-made canal).

The Maumee River is formed by the confluence of the St. Joseph River and the St. Marys River at Fort Wayne. The St. Joseph River flows southwest into Indiana from Michigan and Ohio, while the St. Marys River flows northwest, originating in Ohio. This confluence once formed the western edge of an expansive wetland/lake plain, known as the Black Swamp. By the late 1800s, the Black Swamp, through extensive deforestation, tiling, and ditching, had been converted to prized farmland. This drainage was once connected to the Wabash River drainage of Indiana through the Wabash and Erie Canal. (More detailed information on the Maumee River basin in Indiana can be found in Indiana Department of Natural Resources 1996.)

The St. Joseph River of the Lake Michigan drainage originates in Michigan, flowing southwest into Indiana until near South Bend, where it heads north again back into Michigan and eventually into Lake Michigan. Major tributaries of the St. Joseph River in Indiana include the Elkhart River, Pigeon River, and Fawn River. Natural lakes and wetlands comprise a majority of the headwaters of the watershed. (More detailed information on the St. Joseph River basin in Indiana can be found in Indiana Department of Natural Resources 1987.)

The area of Indiana directly south of Lake Michigan once contained numerous wetlands, swamps, marshes, and low-gradient rivers. An area once known as the Great Marsh extended from Michigan City west toward the Little Calumet River. The Grand Calumet and Little Calumet rivers were once part of a single river that flowed west into Illinois and then northeast back into Indiana and eventually into Lake Michigan. However, the industrialization and urbanization of the area have led to large-scale modifications, diversions, channelizations, and flow reversals. The formation of new outlets and connections has left this region in its current highly altered state. A connection currently exists between Lake Michigan and the Illinois River (Mississippi River drainage) via the Calumet Sag Channel. (More detailed information on this portion of the Lake Michigan drainage in Indiana can be found in Indiana Department of Natural Resources 1994.)

Headwaters (< 20 mi^2)

Headwater streams of the Great Lakes drainage are of low to medium gradient and are highly associated with the extensive natural lakes and remaining wetlands of the region. They have been extensively channelized, leveed, and modified to maintain agricultural lands (Simon 1991, 1994; Simon and Stewart 1999). Historically, these streams were low gradient, were dominated by sand or muck substrates, and possessed little riffle-run-pool development. The majority of these streams possessed abundant woody debris, decaying leaf packs, and abundant emergent and submergent aquatic plants.

FLORA. While backwater portions of larger rivers and quiet pools in streams can harbor some species of vascular plants, in general these environments are not high in plant diversity. Some species of pondweeds, such as comb pondweed, can tolerate stream flow, and some plants, such as beaked riverbank sedge, riverbank sedge, and water willow, are found on the edges of these bodies of water. Minimal erosion prior to European settlement in the early 1800s resulted in water of high quality and clarity. Stream and river flows were likely more consistent, without the surges and drops of water volume that are experienced today. Consequently, more species might have been able to live in some of Indiana's rivers and streams, but the actual occurrence is unknown. See Table P-9 for a list of species of rivers and streams.

FISH. Fish diversity in the headwater streams of the Great Lakes drainage is low, in part because of the lower overall diversity of the Great Lakes drainage compared to the Ohio River drainage of Indiana, and because of the extensive alterations that have been made to these habitats in the past. Headwaters at one time were highly associated with the wetlands of the region and were dominated by species common to lakes and wetlands. Although many headwater streams of the region are still associated with natural lakes, most have been highly altered and converted to drainage ditches.

Current fish assemblages are dominated by tolerant species and those that enter from associated natural lakes. These species are tolerant of low dissolved oxygen conditions and homogeneous fine-sediment substrates, and are trophic generalists. Fish assemblages here include many of the common species found statewide, such as central stoneroller, bluntnose minnow, striped shiner, common shiner, creek chub, white sucker, yellow bullhead, grass pickerel, green sunfish, bluegill, johnny darter, and blackside darter. Western blacknose dace and mottled sculpin are also present in many of the headwater streams, especially the less degraded ones, with rockier substrates and cooler water temperatures.

The longnose dace is the only native species unique to the headwater streams of the Great Lakes drainage, although it can be found in the wadeable/large/great rivers as well. Direct tributaries of Lake Michigan provide spawning and nursery habitat for the unique, yet invasive sea lamprey. Many of these streams have been treated with lampricides to control sea lamprey recruitment into Lake Michigan. These treatments have likely had a negative impact on the native species of lamprey (northern brook lamprey, American brook lamprey), which are also present in these streams. Attempts have been made over the years to stock many of the cooler headwater streams of the Great Lakes drainage with rainbow trout, brook trout, and brown trout, with various degrees of success (Gerking 1945).

The fish species most commonly associated with the headwater streams of the Great Lakes drainage of Indiana are listed in Table F-2; included are 91 species, of which 11 are exotic or non-indigenous.

AMPHIBIANS AND REPTILES. The headwaters of Indiana streams and rivers draining into the Great Lakes share many species of herpetofauna associated with the lakes and wetlands of the region (Table H-5). These headwaters are frequently highly modified, with some or all streams managed to promote rapid drainage. With the straightening of channels, the imposition of steep banks, the removal of streamside vegetation, and, in some cases, the application of rip-rap to the banks, the habitat components needed by amphibians and reptiles are removed or degraded.

Wadeable/Large Rivers (≥ 20 mi^2 $< 2{,}000$ mi^2)

The wadeable/large rivers of the Great Lakes have been extensively modified in the Huron/Erie Lake Plains ecoregion, but remain fairly natural in the Southern Michigan/Northern Indiana Drift Plains region. Streams remaining in the Central Corn Belt Plains ecoregion have been extensively modified (Simon 1991). The wadeable/large rivers of the Maumee River and Calumet River drainages have been channelized, drained, leveed, and relocated, causing a reversal of flow in the Grand Calumet River, which currently drains away from Lake Michigan. More natural stream channels remain in the St. Joseph River drainage of the Lake Michigan drainage. Little riverine wetland habitat remains in the Maumee River, while extensive tracts of riverine wetland remain in the north and south branches of the Elkhart River and in the Pigeon River. The wadeable/large rivers of the Maumee River and Calumet River drainages are low-gradient streams, are dominated by sand or muck substrates, and possess little riffle-run-pool development. Streams of the St. Joseph River drainage of the Lake Michigan drainage have well-developed riffle-run-pool sequences. All of these streams possess abundant woody debris, decaying leaf packs, and abundant emergent and submergent aquatic plants.

FISH. Extensive channelization, dredging, dam construction, and other habitat modifications have drastically altered many of the wadeable/large rivers of the Great Lakes drainage, especially those of the Maumee River (Lake Erie) and Calumet River drainages. The effects of these practices have also impacted the wadeable/large rivers of the St. Joseph River (Lake Michigan) drainage, but to a lesser extent. Many of these streams still maintain excellent habitat diversity and connections with associated wetlands.

Fish diversity is much lower in the Great Lakes drainage when compared to that of the Ohio River drainage of Indiana; the greatest difference is noticed in the diversity of darter (Percidae family) and minnow (Cyprinidae family) species, which is much higher in the Ohio River drainage. Fish communities of the highly altered wadeable/large rivers of the Great Lakes drainage are dominated by tolerant species, mostly the same tolerant species that are found in the headwater streams. In the less altered areas, hornyhead chub, northern hogsucker, various species of redhorse, mottled sculpin, rock bass, longear sunfish, smallmouth bass, and rainbow darter are more commonly found. Gilt darter was once an inhabitant of the wadeable/large rivers of the Lake Erie drainage but is now extirpated, presumably as a result of habitat alterations and increased urban and non-point source pollution.

Exotic species common to Lake Michigan, such as round goby, white perch, and the various salmonids, can also be found in the wadeable/large rivers of the Great Lakes drainage, especially in the Calumet River drainage, with its close proximity to the lake (Simon et al. 1998). One of the newest invaders to this area is the oriental weatherfish, a highly invasive species from Asia (Simon et al. 2006).

The fish species most commonly associated with the wadeable/large rivers of the Great Lakes drainage of Indiana are listed in Table F-2; included are 102 species, of which 16 are exotic or non-indigenous.

AMPHIBIANS AND REPTILES. The herpetofauna of rivers in this region is not unique to them. All of the species one might encounter are also associated with the lakes and wetlands of the particular area in which the streams occur. Common species include midland painted turtles, common snapping turtles, and northern water snakes. The herpetofauna most likely to be encountered are listed in Table H-5.

Great Rivers (> 1,999 mi^2)

This category includes all of the St. Joseph River in St. Joseph and Elkhart counties, and the lower section of the Maumee River in Allen County.

The St. Joseph River is impacted by the metropolitan areas of South Bend and Mishawaka. The Maumee River is impaired downstream of Fort Wayne, but improves farther east, near the Ohio state line. The St. Joseph and Maumee rivers are large, broad, flat channels with large riffle-run-pool habitat. Little aquatic vegetation occurs in the Maumee River mainstem, while significant amounts of submergent aquatic plants are present in the St. Joseph River. Great river habitats in the St. Joseph and Maumee rivers possess gravel, cobble, and sand substrates. The St. Joseph River has a set of dams that separate the river into a series of pools. The Maumee River has a large riffle, known as Bull Rapids, that possesses large boulder substrates and rapid flows, causing whitewater.

FISH. The great rivers of the Great Lakes drainage of Indiana comprise a very small portion of the entire watershed. The fish assemblages of these areas are similar to those discussed above in the wadeable/large rivers section. Several species of salmonids make an annual run into the St. Joseph River (Lake Michigan drainage) and provide recreational opportunities. The stocking of flathead catfish into the Maumee River for sport fishing purposes has seen dramatic success throughout the watershed.

The fish species most commonly associated with the great rivers of the Great Lakes drainage of Indiana are listed in Table F-2; included are 78 species, of which 8 are exotic or non-indigenous.

AMPHIBIANS AND REPTILES. No big river species of amphibian or reptile make it into Indiana along the Maumee River, the largest river feeding from Indiana into one of the Great Lakes. Common species are the midland painted turtle, common snapping turtle, eastern garter snake, and northern water snake along the shore. The herpetofauna most likely to be encountered are listed in Table H-5.

Kankakee River (Illinois River) Drainage

The Kankakee River drainage of Indiana is located in northwestern Indiana, extending from its headwaters west and southwest of South Bend to the state border between Indiana and Illinois in Lake and Newton counties. Principal tributaries include the Yellow River (which enters the Kankakee River west of Knox, Indiana, in Starke and LaPorte counties) and the Iroquois River (which enters the Kankakee River in Illinois and is situated south of the Kankakee River in Indiana).

Perhaps one of the greatest changes seen among Indiana streams has been in the extensive channelization of this drainage. The Kankakee River drainage, in its current state as rich, agricultural land, barely resembles the massive complex of marshes, swamps, and dunes, collectively known as the Grand Kankakee Marsh, that once covered much of the region. The Kankakee River originally followed a winding 250-mi course through the Grand Kankakee Marsh (which ranged from 3–10 mi wide over its greater than 400,000 acres in northwest Indiana) to a natural bedrock shelf just downstream of the Illinois-Indiana state line at Momence, Illinois. Early European explorers portaged from the Great Lakes through the wetlands of the Grand Kankakee Marsh to enter the Mississippi River drainage. The limited evidence available suggests that the Kankakee River had excellent water quality and supported abundant aquatic life. Wilson and Clark (1912) described a flourishing mussel resource with economic potential greater than agricultural pursuits.

Dynamiting of the bedrock shelf and extensive drainage and channelization projects beginning in the late 1800s forever altered the drainage's landscape, turning it into a network of ditches. The once 250-mi Kankakee River is now a straightened 82-mi course from near South Bend to Momence, Illinois (Indiana Department of Natural Resources 1990). Many oxbows created from the massive ditching effort still remain, giving evidence of its meandering past.

Headwaters (< 20 mi^2)

Historically, the headwaters of the Kankakee River drainage were likely gravel-bottomed, riffle-run-pool streams, surrounded by prairie. Few of these streams remain in an undisturbed state. Currently, most are straightened ditches with grassy banks between fields of row crop agriculture, with silty or sandy substrates. Many possess abundant submerged aquatic vegetation (Simon 1991).

FISH. Spotfin shiner, striped shiner, redfin shiner, silverjaw minnow, sand shiner, bluntnose minnow, creek chub, white sucker, yellow bullhead, grass pickerel, blackstripe topminnow, green sunfish, bluegill, longear sunfish, johnny darter, and blackside darter, all tolerant species common to most headwater streams of Indiana, are also some of the most common species found in the headwater streams and ditches of the Kankakee River drainage. Hornyhead chub is also commonly found, although not a common inhabitant of all headwater streams statewide; it is generally restricted to the northern half of Indiana.

In those streams that still maintain more historical habitat conditions, species such as western blacknose dace and mottled sculpin can also be found. These species are normally associated with cooler water and rockier habitats. Those streams with extensive submerged aquatic vegetation also include species such as golden shiner, ironcolor shiner, blacknose shiner, lake chubsucker, tadpole madtom, central mudminnow, pirate perch, northern starhead topminnow, and least darter. Weed shiner can also be found in these conditions and is unique to the Kankakee River drainage in Indiana (Simon 1991; Seegert 1987).

The fish species most commonly associated with the headwater streams of the Kankakee River drainage of Indiana are listed in Table F-3; included are 83 species, of which 4 are exotic or non-indigenous.

AMPHIBIANS AND REPTILES. The headwaters of Indiana streams and rivers entering the Kankakee River have herpetofauna associated with the lakes and wetlands of the region. The herpetofauna most likely to be encountered are listed in Table H-5. Common species are midland painted turtle, common snapping turtle, and eastern garter snake. Streams are frequently highly modified, with some or all streams managed to promote rapid drainage. The straightening of channels, the imposition of steep banks, the removal of streamside vegetation, and, in some cases, the application of rip-rap to the banks all remove or degrade habitat components selected by amphibians and reptiles.

BIRDS. This river and its marshes were a fabled waterfowl hunting ground in the nineteenth and early twentieth centuries. Nearly a century after its channelization and the conversion of surrounding land to agriculture, the restoration of wetland habitat (but not the aquatic habitat of the river itself) began. In 1996, the USFWS initiated a planning process to begin the establishment of a national wildlife refuge. Although the planning process was approved, no funding has been provided for the establishment of a refuge.

Wadeable/Large Rivers (≥ 20 mi^2 < 2,000 mi^2)

Although nothing remains of the Grand Kankakee Marsh, the wadeable/large rivers (including the mainstem of the Kankakee River) of the Kankakee River drainage probably historically possessed a sand or gravel substrate, had limited woody debris, and were a complex of braided channels with abundant emergent and submergent aquatic vegetation. The Kankakee River, Iroquois River, Yellow River, and other wadeable/large rivers of the Kankakee River drainage currently are mostly straightened ditches with muddy edges and sandy substrates. Even in its current state, the Kankakee River remains unique among Indiana rivers in its low flood peaks and long flood durations; it also maintains a relatively stable low flow as a result of massive groundwater storage and release (Indiana Department of Natural Resources 1990).

FISH. The diversity of fish found in the wadeable/large rivers of the Kankakee River drainage is comparable to that of similar-sized streams of the Great Lakes drainage, but lower than those of the Ohio River drainage. The highly altered rivers of the region have swift currents, steep banks, deep edges, and inverted, sandy/silty, U-shaped mid-channel areas with little habitat diversity. Species that occur are those that can tolerate these conditions. Prior to the channelization and draining of the Grand Kankakee Marsh, the fish community resembled that of a lake or wetland, and was probably composed of many of the species that can now be found in the weedy ditches of the area, as discussed above in the section on headwater fish. A variety of other sunfish would have also been present.

Many of the species found in the headwaters are also common in the wadeable/large rivers; additionally, common carp, quillback, bigmouth buffalo, shorthead redhorse, and largemouth bass can be found. Northern pike and bowfin inhabit the edges or are found in associated weedy backwaters and side channels. Northern brook lamprey, American brook lamprey, northern hogsucker, stonecat, rock bass, smallmouth bass, and banded darter are more commonly found in the less-disturbed areas, like sections of the Yellow River, that still contain wooded riparian areas; have clean, gravel substrate; and have riffle-run-pool complexes.

In spite of the drastic changes to the Kankakee River drainage, only two species are thought to be extirpated. Pallid shiner was last recorded by Gerking (1945) from the Iroquois River. Eigenmann and Beeson (1894) reported muskellunge from English Lake, "which was an expansion of the Kankakee River in Starke County" (Gerking 1945); it was drained and no longer exists. There are no other historical records for muskellunge from central or northern Indiana; the only records are from Lake Michigan and direct tributaries of the Ohio River.

Besides the weed shiner, which was mentioned above in the discussion of headwater fish, the only other species unique to the Kankakee River drainage of Indiana is the bigmouth shiner. It has only ever been collected in Indiana from the mainstem of the Kankakee River near the Indiana-Illinois state line (Simon 1992b), even though it is rather common in the portion of the Kankakee River drainage found in Illinois.

The fish species most commonly associated with the wadeable/large rivers of the Kankakee River drainage of Indiana are listed in Table F-3; included are 98 species, of which 7 are exotic or non-indigenous.

AMPHIBIANS AND REPTILES. Two river species of amphibians and reptiles make their way into Indiana along the Kankakee River: the lesser siren and the eastern mud turtle. Common species include the midland painted turtle, common snapping turtle, and eastern garter snake. The herpetofauna most likely to be encountered are listed in Table H-5.

Ohio River Drainage
Eastern Corn Belt Plains and Interior Plateau Ecoregions

The Eastern Corn Belt Plains (ECBP) ecoregion includes the upper portions of the Wabash River, West

Figure 7.6. Wabash River near Evansville, Indiana. Photo by Qiaho Weng.

Fork of the White River, East Fork of the White River, and Whitewater River drainages within the Ohio River drainage. It encompasses most of central Indiana. The Interior Plateau (IP) extends south from the ECBP to the Ohio River along the southern border of Indiana, but excludes southwest Indiana and the area along the Wabash River to upstream of Terre Haute (Figure 7.6). Portions of the Big Pine Creek, Tippecanoe River, and Eel River watersheds (and some other smaller streams), tributaries of the middle and upper reaches of the Wabash River, reside within the Central Corn Belt Plains and Southern Michigan/Northern Indiana Drift Plains ecoregions. In lieu of creating a separate category, the flora and wildlife of these areas will be considered in this section as part of the aquatic systems within the ECBP/IP.

The following are descriptions of the Eastern Corn Belt Plains and Interior Plateau ecoregions based on Omernik and Gallant (1988).

Eastern Corn Belt Plains

The ECBP consists of extensive cropland agriculture. It is distinguished from more western corn belt regions by its natural forest cover and associated soils. The gently rolling glacial till plain is dissected by moraines, kames, and outwash plains. Elevations range from 600 ft to greater than 1,200 ft. The ECBP typically has low relief, usually less than 50 ft; however, some morainal hills occur in the northern portion of the region near Lake Erie.

Stream valleys are long and sinuous and generally narrow and shallow throughout the 31,800 mi^2 of the ecoregion, which includes portions of Michigan and Ohio. Small streams have narrow valley floors; larger streams have broad valley floors. Precipitation occurs mainly during the growing season and averages from 35 to 40 inches annually.

The ECBP is almost entirely farmland. The major crops produced in the ECBP are corn and soybeans. A total of 75% of the land use is cropland, while the remaining 25% is permanent pasture, small wood lots, or urban. Emphasis on livestock includes the growing of feed grains and hay. Swine, beef and dairy cattle, chickens, and turkeys are raised.

Most of the soils of the ECBP ecoregion developed under the influence of deciduous forest vegetation. The soils are loamy calcareous glacial till, overlain by loess deposits. The soils are lighter in color and more acid than the adjacent Central Corn Belt Plains.

The natural vegetation of the area consisted of diverse hardwood forests, predominantly American beech and sugar maple. A significant amount of white oak, black oak, northern red oak, tulip poplar, hickory, white ash, and black walnut exists. Many of the trees are common in adjacent ecoregions, but most are composed of oak and hickory. Wet sites include white oak, pin oak, northern red oak, tulip poplar, ash, and sweetgum primarily; shingle oak, black oak, and hickory also occur. Silver maple, cottonwood, sycamore, pin oak, elm, swamp white oak, buckeye, hackberry, and sweetgum grow along rivers and stream corridors.

About half the streams of the ecoregion are perennial and many have been channelized. Perennial stream density is approximately 0.5 mi per mi^2. The ecoregion has few reservoirs or natural lakes. Stream quality is highly influenced by the extensive agriculture of the ecoregion.

Interior Plateau

The characteristics of the Interior Plateau ecoregion are transitional between the adjacent Eastern Corn Belt Plains and Western Allegheny Plateau ecoregions. The Interior Plateau includes a till plain of low topographic relief, rolling to moderately dissected basin terrain, and rolling to deeply dissected plateaus. Layers of sandstone, siltstone, shale, and limestone underlie much of the ecoregion, with limestone outcrops and areas pitted with limestone sinks common.

Elevations vary from about 500 ft near the Ohio River to more than 1,000 ft on some of the higher hills of the ecoregion. Local relief is commonly between 100 and 200 ft on the till plains and generally around 400 ft in the more hilly terrain, though relief may exceed 800 ft on some of the steeper hills. Average annual precipitation ranges from 40 to 45 inches and is distributed fairly evenly throughout the growing season, allowing for good crop production.

The Interior Plateau ecoregion is managed for cropland, livestock, pasture, woodland, and forest; the land use varies with local topography. Principal crops include hay, grains, and pasture for livestock, while corn, soybeans, wheat, and tobacco are cultivated to a lesser degree. Beef cattle are the predominant livestock throughout the ecoregion, with dairy cattle and swine well represented. Poultry is raised intensively in some locations. Numerous quarries and gravel pits occur throughout the ecoregion, and some areas have gas and oil fields and coal strip-mines.

Soils of the Interior Plateau formed in residuum from a variety of sedimentary rocks overlain by varying amounts of loess. Like those of the Eastern Corn Belt Plains, many are derived from calcareous loam till with localized mantlings of loess. Soils formed under forest cover tend to be lighter in color, more acidic, and more likely to have a hardpan layer.

Vegetation of the Interior Plateau ranges from hardwood to mixed mesophytic forests. On drier slopes and uplands, forest communities include combinations of oak species and one or more species of hickory. Associated trees include tulip poplar, blackgum, sugar maple, red maple, white ash, green ash, American elm, red elm, basswood, sweetgum, and several pine species. In basins underlain by limestone, forests are composed of blue ash, white ash, American elm, Ohio buckeye, and red mulberry. Flat areas of impervious soils support hydro-mesophytic forest communities of pin oak, Shumard's oak, cherrybark oak, sweetgum, red maple, white elm, and associated species such as swamp white oak, sourgum, white oak, shellbark hickory, beech, and cottonwood.

Most streams are perennial. Stream density over much of the region is approximately 2 mi per mi^2, except in areas containing numerous limestone sinks, where surface streams are much less common. Natural lakes are few, and occur mainly in areas underlain by limestone. Land use impacts on stream quality are mainly from the production of livestock, poultry, and crops. Many rivers have been channelized and/or dammed for flood control.

Headwaters (< 20 mi^2)

Headwater streams of the ECBP/IP can be both perennial and intermittent (Figure 7.7). Many are constructed drainage ditches or altered/channelized streams used to assist in soil drainage in flat, poorly drained areas. Because of their small size, they are less protected and more easily impacted. Headwater streams can be altered by livestock, relocations, and agricultural and impervious surface runoff.

FISH. The clearing of forested riparian corridors and the channelization of many of the headwater streams of the ECBP/IP have resulted in degraded fish communities (Gammon 1976). Fish found in the headwater streams of the ECBP/IP include many of the most common and tolerant species found in Indiana, including central stoneroller, striped shiner, redfin shiner, bluntnose minnow, creek chub, white sucker, creek chubsucker, yellow bullhead, blackstripe topminnow, green sunfish, bluegill, johnny darter, orangethroat darter, and blackside darter.

Redside dace is a rare species of the ECBP/IP. Redside dace is only known from two very small watersheds in the state, both occurring in the ECBP. It inhabits pools of clear, cool streams with rocky bottoms. This species is decreasing across much of its range (Gilbert 1980), presumably as a result of impacts to these habitats.

Although not uncommon in Indiana, the southern redbelly dace is a unique species to headwater streams of the ECBP/IP. Its habitat requirements are specific to high-quality headwater streams; it is an excellent indicator of the condition of this habitat type. Southern redbelly dace requires relatively permanent, clear, and shaded waters with overhanging vegetation (Trautman 1981). Unlike most other small stream fish species, southern redbelly dace does not utilize lower stream sections during the summer months. Once lost from a watershed, it is often unable to recolonize, even if suitable conditions are recovered. Fortunately, southern redbelly dace remains widely distributed within the headwater streams of the ECBP/IP.

The fish species most commonly associated with the headwater streams of the Eastern Corn Belt Plains/Interior Plateau ecoregions of Indiana are listed in Table F-4; included are 107 species, of which 4 are exotic or non-indigenous.

AMPHIBIANS AND REPTILES. The herpetofauna associated with the headwater streams of the Ohio River in the ECBP/IP is simpler than those of the Interior River Lowlands. Downstream, the big river species have already dropped out. Common species include the midland painted turtle, common snapping turtle, and eastern garter snake. Streams are frequently highly modified, with some or all streams managed to promote rapid drainage. The straightening of channels, the imposition of steep banks, the removal of streamside vegetation, and, in some cases,

Figure 7.7. Headwater stream northwest of Attica, Warren County. Photo by Ronald L. Richards

the application of rip-rap to the banks all remove or degrade habitat components selected by amphibians and reptiles.

Wadeable/Large Rivers (≥ 20 mi² < 2,000 mi²)

The wadeable/large rivers of the ECBP/IP contain some of the least-impacted and best-quality streams in Indiana (Figure 7.8), including the Tippecanoe River, Blue River, Whitewater River, and the various tributaries of the Wabash River and the upper East Fork of the White River. Most maintain relatively intact riparian corridors and unsedimented substrates; however, all wadeable/large rivers of the ECBP/IP have been impacted to some extent by human settlement and the resulting urban development, agricultural expansion, and mill and flood control dam construction.

FISH. The wadeable/large rivers of the ECBP/IP contain many unique species (Simon and Dufour 1998) and are some of the most biologically diverse aquatic habitats, for their size, of any in the state (Table F-4). The species common to the headwaters of the ECBP/IP are also found in the wadeable/large rivers of the region. Other common species include spotfin shiner, silverjaw minnow, suckermouth minnow, northern hogsucker, black redhorse, golden redhorse, stonecat, mottled sculpin, rock bass, longear sunfish, smallmouth bass, greenside darter, rainbow darter, fantail darter, logperch, and dusky darter.

Unique species (although most have limited distribution outside or also overlap into the great rivers of the Ohio River drainage) to the ECBP/IP include streamline chub, gravel chub, scarlet shiner, river chub, bigeye shiner, silver shiner, northern studfish, banded sculpin, eastern sand darter, spotted darter, and Tippecanoe darter. The range and abundance of many of these species, among others of the region, seem to at least be remaining stable or in some cases even increasing. This perceived increase may be the result of habitat and water quality improvements, which have afforded these species the opportunity to expand their range. It may also simply be the result of more sampling and more species-specific sampling, which may have uncovered populations that have always existed but just went unnoticed (Fisher 2008).

Although many of the species of the wadeable/large rivers of the ECBP/IP are some of the least impacted in the state, others have not been as fortunate. The popeye shiner, harelip sucker, greater redhorse, bluebreast darter, variegate darter, and gilt darter once inhabited several streams of the region; the bluebreast darter is now limited to only a few, while the greater redhorse, variegate darter, and gilt darter are now only found in single drainages, and the popeye shiner and harelip sucker are extirpated from the entire state. The popeye shiner, brindled madtom, channel darter, and gilt darter were all described from the White River (West Fork) near Indianapolis

Figure 7.8. Wadeable/large river. Photo by James H. Speer.

(Table F-7), but none remain at this location. Urban and industrial pollution, dam construction, and increased sediment loads have impacted this area, as well as all other wadeable/large rivers of the region, at least to some extent.

The fish species most commonly associated with the wadeable/large rivers of the Eastern Corn Belt Plains/Interior Plateau ecoregion of Indiana are listed in Table F-4; included are 150 species, of which 8 are exotic or non-indigenous.

AMPHIBIANS AND REPTILES. Perhaps because of the relatively small size of the tributaries feeding the Ohio River from the Eastern Corn Belt Plains/Interior Plateau ecoregions, the big river species do not get very far north. The ranges of species such as the hellbender, lesser siren, false map turtle, and smooth softshell stay fairly close to the Ohio River. However, the lesser siren is reported from the Wabash River at least as far upstream as Terre Haute. Common species are midland painted turtle, red-eared slider, common snapping turtle, and eastern garter snake. The herpetofauna associated with Indiana's rivers are listed in Table H-5.

Interior River Lowland

The Interior River Lowland (IRL) ecoregion is located in the extreme southwestern portion of Indiana, extending from the confluence of the Wabash and Ohio rivers north to the mouth of Sugar Creek (Parke and Vermillion counties) and east to encompass Big Pigeon Creek, Little Pigeon Creek, and the lower portions of the Patoka River and the West Fork of the White River drainages (Figure 7.9).

The following is a description of the Interior River Lowland ecoregion based on Omernik and Gallant (1988).

The Interior River Lowland has varied land use, including forestry, diverse cropland agriculture, orchards, livestock production, and oil and gas production. The IRL consists of dissected glacial till plain that is covered by a thick loess mantle, rolling narrow ridgetops, and hilly to steep ridge and valley slopes. The IRL elevation ranges from 128.4 to 189.7 m, while local relief varies between 1 m on the till plain to 32.6 m on the rolling ridges, to about 197.6 m on prominent ridges. Stream valleys in the hills are often intermittent, becoming perennial when they reach the valley floor. Large watersheds in the IRL often drain as much as 350 mi^2 throughout the 19,000 mi^2 of the ecoregion. Precipitation occurs mainly during the freeze period and averages from 39 to 46 inches annually. The ecoregion has lakes, reservoirs, and numerous scattered ponds.

The IRL ecoregion supports diverse agricultural endeavors, including feed grains, hay for livestock, and squash and melon production. Some corn, soybeans, and red clover seed are also grown. Undrained soils are used for forage crops, pasture, or timber (almost 35% of the ecoregion is forested). Emphasis is on mixed farming, livestock, and some orcharding, and

Figure 7.9. West Fork of the White River. Photo by Brant Fisher.

some grape vineyards occur on upland sites. Mostly beef cattle, swine, and chickens are raised. Most of the better-drained soils of the ecoregion are generally light in color and moderately acidic.

The natural vegetation of the area consists of oak/hickory forests. White oak, black oak, northern red oak, bitternut hickory, shagbark hickory, tulip poplar, white ash, sugar maple, and black walnut occur on well-drained soils. Pin oak, shingle oak, and sweetgum occur on wet sites. Riparian areas support pin oak, silver maple, cottonwood, willow, sycamore, elm, sweetgum, ash, elm, hackberry, and river birch.

Headwaters (< 20 mi^2)

Both perennial and intermittent streams are common in the IRL ecoregion. Constructed drainage ditches and channelized streams further assist in soil drainage in flat, poorly drained areas. Stream density is approximately 2 mi per mi^2 in the most typical portions of the ecoregion. Most headwater streams are severely impacted in the region.

FISH. Many headwater streams of the IRL dry up during the hottest months, resulting in a series of isolated pools. Because of the extreme nature of these headwater streams, only the most tolerant species can persist in most locations. Common species inhabiting the headwater streams of the IRL include central stoneroller, silverjaw minnow, bluntnose minnow, creek chub, white sucker, yellow bullhead, pirate perch, blackstripe topminnow, western mosquitofish, green sunfish, longear sunfish, and johnny darter. Most of these species are common to headwater streams statewide. Ditched headwater streams of the IRL, if they contain abundant submergent vegetation, will often contain a fish community that resembles that of an oxbow or slough of the ecoregion.

Although occasionally found in the wadeable/large rivers of the IRL, the spottail darter is rather unique to the headwaters of the extreme southern portion of the ecoregion. Southwest Indiana represents the northernmost extent of its range. The spottail darter requires slab-rock habitat for reproduction. This type of habitat is very limited in the southern part of the IRL, as is the spottail darter's distribution.

The fish species most commonly associated with the headwaters of the Interior River Lowland ecoregion of Indiana are listed in Table F-4; included are 90 species, of which 4 are exotic or non-indigenous.

AMPHIBIANS AND REPTILES. The headwater streams of the Ohio River in the Interior River Lowlands will not contain the classic big river species. We would not expect to see the lesser siren, while the mudpuppy persists. Turtles such as the false map turtle and smooth softshell drop out, while the common map turtle might persist. The midland painted turtle will be abundant and will often be joined by the red-eared slider. The midland/northern water snakes will be abundant, but the diamondback water snakes will not be evident. Streams are frequently highly modified, with some or all streams managed to promote rapid drainage. The straightening of channels, the imposition of steep banks, the removal of streamside vegetation, and, in some cases, the application of riprap to the banks all remove or degrade habitat components selected by amphibians and reptiles.

Wadeable/Large Rivers ($\geq$ 20 mi^2 < 2,000 mi^2)

Two types of wadeable/large rivers occur in the Interior River Lowland ecoregion of Indiana. Those in the central and southern portions of the ecoregion tend to have steep, slippery banks with clay, muck, and sand substrates and are composed of primarily run habitat: deeper, flowing water that does not create ripples. Riffles in these streams are created only by accumulations of woody debris. Many that have been extensively modified to drain agricultural areas have stretches with excessive stands of submerged aquatic vegetation. Rivers in the northern portions of the ecoregion tend to contain more riffle-run-pool complexes and have rockier areas along with the clay and sand substrates. The entire ecoregion has been extensively modified by mining, oil and gas exploration, acid mine leachate, and channelization to drain the expansive riverine wetlands of the Wabash River lowland (Simon et al. 2005).

FISH. Many species are, for the most part, limited to the IRL ecoregion of Indiana; southwestern Indiana represents the northern extent of their range. Western mosquitofish, mud darter, bluntnose darter, and slough darter are generally distributed throughout all habitats of the IRL, including the wadeable/large rivers that occur there. Western mosquitofish has been stocked extensively outside the IRL for mosquito control and now has a much wider distribution. Cypress minnow, ribbon shiner, flier, redspotted sunfish, bantam sunfish, and banded pygmy sunfish are more commonly found in the oxbows, backwaters, sloughs, and embayments of the IRL but are also found in those wadeable/large rivers that have abundant submergent aquatic vegetation. Several great river species, such as shovelnose sturgeon, shoal chub, silver chub, emerald shiner, river shiner, channel shiner, bullhead minnow, river carpsucker, and slenderhead darter, can be found in the lowest reaches of the wadeable/large rivers of the IRL.

Many species, although included in Table F-4 as occurring in the wadeable/large rivers of the IRL, are actually rather rare and only occur along the northern and eastern boundaries of the ecoregion, in those streams with rockier substrates. Species such as least brook lamprey, American brook lamprey, bigeye chub, rosyface shiner, black redhorse, brindled madtom, mottled sculpin, banded sculpin, rock bass, smallmouth bass, eastern sand darter, greenside darter, rainbow darter, and fantail darter are found in these peripheral streams. These species are much more common in the streams of the ECBP/IP. The diversity of the wadeable/large rivers in the northernmost section of the IRL is further documented by Whitaker (1976), who collected 57 species over a 12-year period from a single location (at Markle's dam) on Otter Creek, Vigo County.

Simon et al. (1995) investigated the fish fauna of the Patoka River drainage, a more southern wadeable/large river of the IRL, and collected 86 species. Simon et al. (2005), sampling the same locations as those sampled by Simon et al. (1995), found that although the lowest-quality streams had improved, the highest-integrity streams had decreased in quality.

Although many of the newest exotic species of Indiana have entered the state through the great rivers, populations of silver carp, bighead carp, and grass carp have also been found in many of the wadeable/large rivers of the IRL. These invasive species could have devastating effects on the native fish fauna of the state.

The fish species most commonly associated with the wadeable/large rivers of the Interior River Lowland ecoregion of Indiana are listed in Table F-4; included are 109 species, of which 4 are exotic or nonindigenous.

AMPHIBIANS AND REPTILES. For the most part, the amphibians and reptiles found in the larger tributaries of the Ohio River in the Interior River Lowland are much the same as those along the Ohio River itself. The hieroglyphic river cooter only makes it into the lower reaches of the Wabash River, however, and the alligator snapping turtle would have generally followed this pattern prior to extirpation. The false map turtle and smooth softshell get into the heart of Indiana along the Wabash, White, and Patoka rivers. Western mud snake and western cottonmouth, the former likely extirpated, the latter nearly so, would drop out when rivers and streams lost their associated floodplain structure.

Great Rivers (> 1,999 mi^2)

This section includes the Ohio River, the Wabash River upstream to the Mississinewa River, the White River upstream on the West Fork to the Johnson-Morgan county line, and the White River upstream on the East Fork to just south of Columbus (Bartholomew County).

The Ohio River is the largest great river of Indiana (Figure 7.10), forming the southern border of the state. The Wabash River forms the border between Indiana and Illinois for much of its length in southwestern Indiana before it joins with the Ohio River at the extreme southwest tip of the state. Except for the Ohio River, which has been highly altered by the construction of navigational dams, the great rivers of the Ohio River drainage of Indiana still contain fairly good habitat diversity. Each has areas of riffles, runs, and pools that have a variety of bottom substrates, including sand, mud, gravel, cobble, boulder, and bedrock. Sections of each, however, have been altered in some way by dams, levees, dredging, and point and non-point source pollution. A high-gradient drop in the Ohio River does still occur at New Albany, Clark County, forming the Falls of the Ohio. Similar habitats can be found on the White River (Kelly's Ripple, Knox and Gibson counties), on the East Fork of the White River (Hindustan Falls, Martin County), and on the Wabash River (near New Harmony, Posey

Figure 7.10. Ohio River from bluff south of Laconia, Harrison County. Photo by Ronald L. Richards.

County). These, along with other large shoal areas, are important spawning areas for many great river species.

FISH. The great rivers of the Ohio River drainage received significant attention from early ichthyologists. Most of the species originally described from Indiana (Table F-7) were the result of work done by Rafinesque (1820) and Lesueur (1827) during the early nineteenth century in the Ohio River and the Wabash River. Most of these species are still present in Indiana's great rivers, although some inhabit a much smaller range.

The great rivers of the Ohio River drainage presently contain some of the highest fish diversity of any of the aquatic habitats of Indiana (Tables F-2 through F-5). This is presumably the result of the sheer volume of water they possess, the diversity of habitats held within them, and the intimate associations they have with their tributaries, oxbows, backwaters, sloughs, and embayments. A total of 49 species, or nearly a quarter of all the species currently present in Indiana, were collected during a single sampling event from a location on the Wabash River near the mouth of the Tippecanoe River, Tippecanoe County (Fisher et al. 2001).

Many fish species found in the great rivers of the Ohio River drainage are occasional inhabitants, often in close proximity to tributary mouths, oxbows, embayments, sloughs, and backwaters. Other species are specifically associated with great rivers, including species from almost all of the families of fish found in Indiana. The following are the most commonly occurring fish of the great rivers of the Ohio River drainage: chestnut and silver lamprey (as parasitic adults attached to other fish), shovelnose sturgeon, paddlefish, longnose gar, shortnose gar, goldeye, mooneye, skipjack herring, gizzard shad, spotfin shiner, Mississippi silvery minnow, shoal chub, silver chub, emerald shiner, river shiner, ghost shiner, channel shiner, bullhead minnow, river carpsucker, highfin carpsucker, smallmouth buffalo, bigmouth buffalo, black buffalo, river redhorse, blue sucker, blue catfish, channel catfish, mountain madtom, flathead catfish, white bass, spotted bass, slenderhead darter, river darter, sauger, and freshwater drum.

Several exotic species have been introduced into or invaded the great rivers of the Ohio River drainage since the late 1800s. Common carp were first stocked in Indiana waters in 1879 (Greenberg 2002). They were intentionally introduced for recreational fishing opportunities and as a food source. The stocking of hybrid striped bass first occurred in Indiana in 1983; they are annually stocked into several impoundments across the state. Emigrants from these habitats have resulted in substantial populations in the great rivers of the Ohio River drainage. Populations of bighead carp, silver carp, and grass carp are a result of escape from aquaculture facilities in southern parts of the Mississippi River drainage and first appeared in Indiana in the early 1990s. All these exotic species are now common inhabitants of the great rivers of the Ohio River drainage.

The following species no longer inhabit the great rivers of the Ohio River drainage: alligator gar, Alabama shad, northern pike, Ohio River muskellunge, popeye shiner, harelip sucker, crystal darter, variegate darter, gilt darter, saddleback darter, and stargazing darter. Ohio River muskellunge, northern pike, variegate darter, and gilt darter still remain in other portions of the Ohio River drainage in Indiana, while the rest of the listed species are extirpated from the entire state. For many of the darter species, the loss of riffle habitat due to damming and the siltation of existing riffle habitats likely played a role. Great river species such as the northern pike, Ohio River muskellunge, and alligator gar were dependent on seasonally flooded bottomlands for spawning and nursery areas. The loss of these habitats due to flood control measures (levees) or drainage for agricultural purposes certainly affected the reproduction of these species.

The following species still occur in the great rivers of the Ohio River drainage, but at a much-reduced range: lake sturgeon, American eel, northern madtom, western sand darter, and channel darter. Many of the same factors contributing to the loss of the previously discussed species could have contributed to the current status of these species; however, commercial fishing could also be a factor in the reduced range of the lake sturgeon.

At one point, blue suckers were considered imperiled in the great rivers of the Ohio River drainage with documented declines in distribution and abundance (Trautman 1981). Populations have increased greatly since the 1980s, presumably due to cumulative water quality improvements resulting from water quality regulations (Gammon 1995).

The fish species most commonly associated with the great rivers of the Ohio River drainage in Indiana are listed in Table F-4; included are 140 species, of which 10 are exotic or non-indigenous.

AMPHIBIANS AND REPTILES. The herpetofauna of the Ohio River is influenced by the riverine herpetofaunal community to the south. Consequently, the Ohio River and its tributaries have species not found elsewhere in the state. The hellbender is one such example, exploiting those areas with a rocky bottom. Most populations are gone now as siltation and water pollution have degraded the habitat. The green frog and bullfrog are still common along river shorelines. Numerous species of turtles are affiliated with the rivers and streams. Some of these, such as common snapping turtle and painted turtle, are found in a wide variety of wetlands and aquatic habitats. However, other species are more narrowly associated with rivers and streams. While the common map turtle may be found in rivers and lakes, the other species of map turtles are mainly associated with rivers and streams. These include the false map turtle and the Mississippi map turtle. Unlike the spiny softshell, the smooth softshell is also more of a river species. The alligator snapping turtle, which may still make it occasionally into the state, would enter along the Wabash River and other Ohio River tributaries. All of Indiana's water snake species might be found along the shores of rivers and streams.

Oxbows/Backwaters/Sloughs/Embayments

Oxbows, backwaters, sloughs, and embayments are natural and in some cases man-made features of the riverine habitats of the state. Oxbows and sloughs (Figure 7.11) can be formed naturally when meanders of rivers are cut off and isolated or when flood events fill lowland areas of the floodplain. Many oxbows have been created artificially as a result of channelization. Often, these are completely isolated from their original riverine system and don't function naturally. There was extensive loss of oxbow and slough habitat during the latter half of the nineteenth and first half of the twentieth centuries as a result of large-scale draining for agricultural purposes.

Embayments and backwaters form periodically when the tributary mouths flowing into larger rivers are flooded. These can also be formed artificially as the result of impoundments. The many dams along the Ohio River have created permanent embayments at the mouth of each entering tributary.

Oxbows, backwaters, sloughs, and embayments vary highly in their development, structure, and permanency. Most are lake-like and have silty, organic debris substrates. The amount and type of emergent and submergent aquatic vegetation can be highly variable. Some contain extensive stands of trees, shrubs, and other emergent and submergent aquatic plants, while others are completely devoid of any type of aquatic vegetation. Oxbows, backwaters, sloughs, and embayments serve an important function by receiving excess water during flood events and acting as refugia and nursery areas for fish and other aquatic organisms.

FLORA. These aquatic bodies possess waters of varying depths that provide a relatively stable, low-flow environment for aquatic plants. The historic, naturally occurring examples, e.g., the oxbows and natural lakes, typically possess a greater diversity of aquatic plant species than do man-made ones, although highly polluted waters of any type will likely have a reduction in species. Many of Indiana's natural lakes have been significantly altered, either by water level manipulation or by the input of pollutants. In almost any given body of water in the state, many species of pondweeds and other aquatics would have occurred in 1800, only to decline by 1900, and more so by 2000.

In northern Indiana, aquatic bodies have a greater diversity than those in the south, in part because of the greater occurrence of habitat, but also because of their proximity to the region of the continent with some of the greatest diversity of deep freshwater aquatics, i.e., the northern United States and Canada. Most natural lakes in Indiana occur in the Northern Lakes Natural Region, followed by the Northwestern Morainal Natural Region. Very few natural per-

Figure 7.11. Slough. Photo by Qihao Weng.

manent bodies of water occur in the southern part of the state. Oxbow lakes, formed from the cutting off and separation of a river channel from the main flow, are the most common examples, with the largest in the Southern Bottomlands Natural Region. Oxbow lakes typically contain high levels of silt and possess less-transparent water than the high-quality northern Indiana natural lakes. Thus, the plant diversity is not great. Species present may include coontail, yellow water buttercup, Carolina mosquito fern, various species of duckweed and watermeal, water purslane, false mermaid weed, large water starwort, and American pondweed.

Prior to 1900, few if any large human-constructed impoundments of streams and rivers existed, although millponds and small farm ponds abounded. In general, impoundments typically do not have the high degree of plant diversity that natural bodies of water have, although over time diversity may increase as propagules of species are brought in by wildlife, especially waterfowl, or by humans.

See Table P-9 for a list of aquatic plant species found in Indiana's bodies of water.

FISH. Fish communities occurring in the many oxbows, backwaters, sloughs, and embayments of Indiana are highly variable and determined by the system's permanency, degree of connectivity with other habitats, and plant diversity and abundance. The fish community in any given body of water can be diverse under ideal conditions. Hubbs and Lagler (1942) documented over 40 species of fish from Foots Pond, Gibson County.

Many of the fish species found in oxbows, backwaters, sloughs, and embayments are those associated with nearby wadeable/large and great rivers. Inhabitants arrive and leave adventitiously when connections are made during periods of flooding. Large river species, such as paddlefish, various species of carpsucker and buffalo, white bass, white crappie, and freshwater drum, frequently occur. Some of the newest exotic species to invade Indiana's great rivers (silver carp, bighead carp, grass carp) have also found these habitats to be extremely desirable and are now thriving in them. Many of the young of these large river species use the oxbows, backwaters, sloughs, and embayments as nursery areas.

Although no species in Indiana is restricted entirely to living in these habitats, many are highly associated with them, especially in southwestern Indiana, where species such as cypress minnow, western mosquitofish, flier, redspotted sunfish, bantam sunfish, slough darter, cypress darter, and banded pygmy sunfish are only found. Most of these species require extensive submerged aquatic vegetation, so this limits the number of oxbows and sloughs that they can inhabit. Other species, such as spotted gar, bowfin, gizzard shad, common carp, the various bullhead species, warmouth, bluegill, and largemouth bass, are common in these habitats, but they generally inhabit all lake-like habitats.

Alligator gar once inhabited the oxbows, embayments, sloughs, and backwaters along the lower Wabash River, but it is now extirpated. The last record for alligator gar was from the Wabash River near New Harmony near the end of the nineteenth century (Jordan 1890). The bantam sunfish and cypress darter are also extremely rare, if not extirpated. The loss or degradation of the floodplain habitats and changes to the mainstem of the Wabash River likely caused the reduced distribution or extirpation of these species.

The fish species most commonly associated with Indiana's oxbows, backwaters, sloughs, and embayments are listed in Table F-5; included are 99 species, of which 7 are exotic or non-indigenous.

AMPHIBIANS AND REPTILES. The herpetofauna of oxbows is a reflection of both the hydrology of the oxbow itself and the general nature and quality of the habitat around it. Many are still seasonally flooded by the rivers they were once a part of, and many also have ditches to drain them rapidly. The diversity and abundance of amphibians and reptiles may be high if ephemeral emergent and shrub/scrub habitats are pervasive and if terrestrial habitat nearby is of reasonable quality, or may be rather depauperate if banks are steep and water levels fluctuate wildly and/or if the oxbow sits isolated from other natural habitat. Table H-5 lists the herpetofauna associated with rivers. As flooded areas are less influenced by floodwaters and more by surface runoff, species associated with wetlands (Table H-4) will become more typical.

BIRDS. River oxbows and oxbow lakes are prominent in southwestern Indiana along the Patoka, lower White, Wabash, and Ohio rivers. Presumably, they support the usual aquatic bird species, especially nesting wood ducks. Hovey Lake is cited by Mumford and Keller (1984) for the multitudes of mallards and other migrant ducks it supported in the 1940s and 1950s.

Natural Lakes

Natural lakes are lentic water bodies that are greater than 1 ha and were formed by glacial processes. Over 450 natural lakes are found in Indiana. They are restricted to 18 northern counties, with nearly 70% found in Kosciusko, LaGrange, Noble, and Steuben counties. Most are smaller (under 100 acres), although several are larger than 500 acres. They are highly variable in depth, clarity, and fertility. Natural lake habitat includes shallow littoral zones that have a variety of submergent, emergent, and floating aquatic plants. Aquatic plants provide important habitat for spawning and nursery areas for the early life stages of fish and also are important indicators of water quality.

The less-fertile natural lakes tend to have smaller watersheds, are deeper, and contain marl or sand substrates. The more-fertile ones tend to have larger watersheds, are shallower, have dense aquatic vegetation, and contain muck bottoms. All lakes naturally become more fertile over time (eutrophication); however, this process has been greatly accelerated by humans, as a result of increased inputs of nutrients from wastewater disposal, agricultural practices, and runoff from yards. Natural lake habitats have also been altered by uncontrolled drainage, the creation of control structures, excessive shoreline development, and introduced species.

FISH. Many of the best-known and common species of fish from natural lakes are popular sport fish, including northern pike, pumpkinseed, bluegill, redear sunfish, largemouth bass, black crappie, yellow perch, and walleye. Many of these species have been stocked extensively over a long period of time, so determining their natural range in Indiana's natural lakes is difficult. These stockings (and those of various trout species and muskellunge), along with the introduction of invasive species (common carp, white perch, grass carp, zebra mussel) and extensive aquatic plant control, have certainly impacted the native, natural lake fish communities, although these impacts are not well understood.

Natural lakes can be rather diverse, as shown by the over 50 species of fish recorded by Evermann and Clark (1920) in a study of Lake Maxinkuckee, Marshall County, at the beginning of the twentieth century. Several fish species are, for the most part, restricted to natural lakes or associated stream habitats, including pugnose shiner, blackchin shiner, cisco, banded killifish, and Iowa darter. Many of these species are rare and have experienced a reduction in their range. The pugnose shiner was historically known from several natural lakes (Gerking 1945, 1955), but is now possibly extirpated, likely as the result of changes to or losses of native aquatic plant communities and by predation by introduced species. Cisco once inhabited nearly 50 lakes in northern Indiana (Frey 1955), but are now found in less than 20 (Pearson 2001). Cisco require a deep, cold, well-oxygenated layer of water, which has been greatly reduced or eliminated from many lakes as the result of accelerated eutrophication.

The fish species most commonly associated with Indiana's natural lakes are listed in Table F-5; included are 64 species, of which 11 are exotic or non-indigenous.

AMPHIBIANS AND REPTILES. The diversity of amphibians and reptiles of lakes can be quite high, despite the fact that the use of the deeper, open water by these taxa is relatively limited. Table H-5 lists the herpetofauna most likely to be associated with larger bodies of water, such as lakes. Mudpuppies will patrol the substrate of shallow to moderately deep sections, and the strongest swimming species of turtles, such as common map turtles and spiny softshells, are frequently seen away from the shore. Many common species of turtle, such as painted turtle, may also cut across open water, though they have no reason to loiter there. Less obviously, the common musk turtle bulldozes through the muck of the lake bottom in search of invertebrates. It likely does not do so in deep areas, though it may be well away from the shore if the water depth is not more than a meter or two.

Most lake herpetofauna are more reasonably associated with the shoreline and the complexity of habitats located along it. Natural shorelines may have a wide variety of permanent and ephemeral wetland types along them, and the herpetofauna of these habitats is discussed elsewhere. Species such as the northern and midland water snakes and the large ranids, such as the green frog and bullfrog, are among the more visible residents of the lakeshore.

Problems across Indiana for lake herpetofauna include the stabilization of lake levels and storm wall placement (see the discussion above in this chapter). Development just beyond the shoreline has also removed the terrestrial habitat around many lakes. Nesting turtles are not the only aquatic species with a need for a link to terrestrial habitat. Many semiaquatic snakes and turtles routinely traverse uplands from one wetland to another. The classic examples of this are the copperbelly water snake and Blanding's turtle. These species use uplands as secondary habitat and move frequently between different wetlands. Development and the associated support structures, such as roads, remove habitat and impose barriers to the movement of herpetofauna.

Shoreline habitat loss, development, and consequent barriers also prove challenging for terrestrial salamanders. Ambystomatid species, such as the spotted salamander, might not breed in lakes, but would do so in peripheral wetlands. Their opportunities to breed are removed when water levels are stabilized, shorelines solidified, wetlands drained and filled, and roads and homes placed in, on, or around their habitat.

BIRDS. The attractiveness (to people) of northern Indiana's glacial lakes, combined with private ownership of shorelines and boating activity, has made them less productive for birds than they would otherwise be, especially during the summer. However, of 500 or so lakes that exceed 2 ha in size (Frey 1966), a few score have much shoreline in natural condition and parts of the lakes are off-limits to motorized boating (McPherson 2000). Some are nature preserves. One of the southernmost glacial basins in the state, Goose Pond in Greene County, was acquired in the early twenty-first century as a state fish and wildlife conservation area (Indiana Department of Natural Resources 2005). It holds a natural lake, very attractive to ducks, which has resisted many efforts at drainage. Presently, it is a combination of natural lake and impoundments, though impoundments seem to dominate.

Like the impoundments discussed later in this section, natural lakes are of greatest importance to strictly aquatic birds during migration and in early winter. During migration and early winter, lakes such as those in Steuben County are large and deep enough to attract loons, grebes, cormorants, swans, geese, ducks, and gulls (Haw 2005). A relatively small set of species breed on the lakes, although more did so in the past. Present breeding birds of lake edges include species nesting in marsh and cattails (red-winged blackbird, marsh wren, herons, bitterns, and rails), in shrubs or grass (yellow warbler, common yellowthroat, song sparrow), on rocky shore (spotted sandpiper), and in dead snags (tree swallow, red-headed woodpecker).

1800. No information.

1900. Birds were studied from 1899 to 1902 at Lake Maxinkuckee, a 728.4-ha (1,800-acre) lake in Marshall County, during a detailed inventory of fauna and flora (Evermann and Clark 1920). Wild celery beds attracted canvasbacks, which were second only to lesser scaup in abundance among fall migrant ducks. Other common species were redhead, mallard, common merganser, ruddy duck, bufflehead, and common goldeneye. American coot was the most abundant migrant water bird. On the other hand, wood duck had greatly declined as a nesting bird; Canada geese occurred only as migrants (they were common but less abundant than in previous decades); and trumpeter swans were very rare, though still observed.

Green heron and spotted sandpiper nested commonly, while American and least bitterns and sora were fairly common in the summer. Black tern was a common migrant and probably bred. Marsh wren, yellow warbler, common yellowthroat, and red-winged blackbird nested commonly around the lake. The breeding avifauna was similar at lakes in Whitley and Kosciusko counties studied at the same time (Williamson 1900; Littell 1902). Although these particular lakes have not been surveyed recently, the species listed above still occur on undisturbed northern lakes. Canvasback, however, is likely to be uncommon to rare, given its continent-wide decline.

2000. A few nesting species of waterfowl became established or increased: the nonmigratory race of (giant) Canada goose, mute swan (which the state is trying to control), and wood duck.

Impoundments

Impoundments are anthropogenically modified habitats that have resulted from the damming of flowing waters or from excavation during construction or mining operations. These habitats generally are developed on lands that possess steep, forested valleys and have a variety of uses, including flood prevention, recreation, and drinking water supply. Impoundments are highly variable in their size, depth, and water clarity (Figures 7.12 and 7.13). Impoundments can be found statewide, although they are more common in central and southern Indiana.

Beaver dams can also create natural, temporal impoundment situations, especially on smaller streams. Beaver ponds usually possess high BOD from decaying organic matter and the accumulating detritus. The sluggish flow and increased light penetration may increase water temperature, causing dissolved oxygen levels to decrease.

FISH. Impoundments resulting from the damming of flowing waters often initially experience a diverse mixture of fish species from both the original river community and the species stocked into the newly created habitat. The natural riverine and new

Figure 7.12. Impoundment. Photo by Qihao Weng.

lake assemblage of fish flourish as the trophic status of the reservoir is determined. As the impoundment ages, the riverine fish assemblage is eventually lost due to the drastic habitat changes and competition from those species that are more adapted to the lake-like environment.

Dams created to form impoundments on flowing waters often act as barriers to fish movement. Fish characteristic of larger rivers are often found below dams, but not in the watershed above the impoundment. Dams can also keep certain river species from reaching their historic spawning grounds.

Fish species are sometimes removed intentionally from impoundments and their contributing watershed. This occurs either when new impoundments are created or in order to renovate or rehabilitate an impoundment where competition by undesirable species is limiting sport fish potential. In both situations, the entire watershed upstream of the dam that forms the impoundment is treated with rotenone, a chemical that specifically kills fish. The intent is to eliminate all the undesirable species from the watershed prior to stocking the impoundment with desirable game species. Unfortunately, the entire native fish community of the watershed can also be eliminated, unless certain reaches are left untreated; these areas then act as refugia by which the treated reaches can be recolonized.

Fish assemblages of impoundments do not normally represent natural communities of the area, but instead are composed of those stocked and managed for sport fishing opportunities. Common impoundment species, regardless of watershed or ecoregion, include channel catfish, muskellunge, striped bass (and its hybrids), bluegill, redear sunfish, largemouth bass, white crappie, black crappie, and walleye. Other, less-desirable species, such as gizzard shad, common carp, yellow bass, and the various bullhead species, can also thrive in these habitats if they become established. Competition by these species can lead to the renovation of an impoundment, as discussed above.

The fish species most commonly associated with Indiana's impoundments are listed in Table F-5; included are 83 species, of which 12 are exotic or nonindigenous.

AMPHIBIANS AND REPTILES. Given that impoundments frequently are composed of deeper water where it did not previously exist, the herpetofaunal community established there is largely formed via colonization by aquatic and wetland species available from nearby. Potential colonizers will be found in Tables H-4 and H-5. If large rivers or streams were impounded, we might expect the inclusion of species like mudpuppies and map or other turtles. Otherwise, herpetofauna in impoundments would be composed of species from other habitats and include more ubiquitous species, such as painted turtles, common snapping turtles, and garter snakes.

BIRDS. This habitat is very extensive, especially in the central and southern parts of the state, and is much used by migrating waterfowl. Every county has impounded small lakes and ponds, often a large reservoir (some associated with power plants), and sewage ponds (Whitaker and Gummer 2003). Many

Figure 7.13. Small man-made lake. Photo by Charles Amlaner.

impoundments get attention from birders. The electronic archives of IN-BIRD, dating from 1998, contain many daily observation lists from Monroe, Lemon, and Summit lakes; Brookville Reservoir; Muscatatuck Refuge; and other sites. Seasonal reports in the *Indiana Audubon Quarterly* summarize the observations.

The migrating waterfowl that use impoundments are essentially the same as those using natural lakes. At Summit Lake (324 ha = 800 acres, Henry County), 25 species of ducks, swans, geese, and grebes and 17 species of shorebirds regularly occur, most during migration (Pancol 2005). At larger lakes, such as Lake Monroe (4,350 ha = 10,750 acres, mainly in Monroe County), additional species such as loons, gulls, and bald eagles are common in migration.

In contrast, the availability of mudflats and short-grass habitat for migrant sandpipers and other shorebirds varies widely between lakes and between years. Nowadays, birders bemoan the general absence and unpredictability of shorebird habitat.

Power plant reservoirs like Gibson (Gibson County) and Turtle Creek (Sullivan County) have warm water in winter, which helps to retain herons, gulls, ducks, and grebes. Gibson Lake is a nesting site for interior least terns, a federally endangered subspecies.

One other category of artificial lake, although not an impoundment, should be mentioned as significant for aquatic birds in southwestern Indiana: lakes and shallow ponds on former surface coal mines. They attract the same migrant waterfowl as the impoundments, depending on size and productivity (recently created ones are often sterile due to acidity; Frey 1966). Most are set in large grassland landscapes, which appears to make them more attractive to nesting grebes, rails, and bitterns than are lakes in forested, agricultural, or urban areas (Vetter 2004).

Sand/Gravel Bars

FLORA. A special subset of aquatic systems is sand/gravel bars (Figure 7.14). These sites are frequently flooded, but several plant species are adapted to such conditions. Water willow, marsh purslane, beaked tussock sedge, tussock sedge, big bluestem, pale dogwood, Carolina willow, three-square bulrush, and several species of nut sedge are some characteristic species, depending on location.

Rare species associated exclusively with sand/gravel bars in Indiana are sand grape, Short's goldenrod, blue wild indigo, and inland New Jersey tea. See Table P-9 for species of sand and gravel bars.

AMPHIBIANS AND REPTILES. Sand and gravel bars along rivers and streams play several important roles for local herpetofauna. Sandbars are nesting sites for river turtles, such as smooth softshells and map turtles. The substrate is easy for the turtles to dig into, the ground is moist, and the shrub and tree canopy is open, heating the ground and speeding development of the eggs. A wide variety of herpetofauna, largely dependent upon the local community, will exploit sand and gravel bars. Green frogs and leopard frogs may forage on them, while snakes such as garter, ribbon, and water snakes may be out foraging for the frogs. Besides riparian zone manage-

Figure 7.14. Sandbar. Photo by Brant Fisher.

ment that may inhibit sand and gravel bar formation, the other threat to herpetofauna using this habitat is boating. Sand and gravel bars are natural landing and resting points for boaters. Unfortunately, this may discourage turtles from nesting, and may also destroy nests already formed.

BIRDS. Sand and gravel bars along rivers historically provided much breeding habitat for spotted sandpipers, and this species can still be found in the remnants of such habitat. Such areas might also harbor breeding killdeer, as well as a host of other shorebird species during fall and spring migration. Sandbars in major rivers might also have been used as breeding habitat by the least tern, but its status as a breeding bird in Indiana has been unclear prior to recent decades (Castrale et al. 1998). This now federally listed endangered species (interior populations only) might one day breed in such habitat as its population expands from artificial habitat (dikes, fly ash dumps) at the Gibson power plant in Gibson County (DeVault et al. 2006).

MAMMALS. Many mammals might visit sand and gravel bars to forage, but no species of mammal has any strong ties to that habitat.

Barren Lands

8

Barren lands have sparse or no vegetative cover, little or no soil, and exposed rock, sand, and/or minerals. Following a general overview of such lands, we will treat three sub-habitats: sand dunes, rock outcrops and cliffs, and quarries (for rock, sand, and gravel). Such lands have been created both by natural processes (dunes and cliffs) and by human extraction of minerals and energy resources. The regional distribution of barren lands varies depending on the type (Map 8.1). Rock outcrops and cliffs are most common in the south, and sand dunes in the north, while quarries are common throughout the state. The large blocks of land strip-mined for coal in southwestern counties certainly pass through a barren phase, but since 1977 they have typically been revegetated as grasslands. Therefore, they are treated in chapter 5 rather than here. There are many human-generated areas which are far more depauperate of life than are cliffs, dunes, etc. Some of these are interstates and other highways, airports, rooftops, parking lots, shopping malls, and many areas in towns and cities (see chapter 11). The occurrence of species is influenced by whatever pieces of natural habitat are left in these areas, and they will be considered under the various habitats.

Flora

Barren lands include a range of environments for plants, from naturally occurring rock outcrops to severely altered landscapes like those occurring in quarries. If there are common denominators among these habitat types, they might include extreme substrate, excessive insolation, and very high vapor pressure deficits, leading to excessive dryness, a lack of suitable rooting medium, and/or extremes in mineral concentration or pH. The flora associated with natural barren lands is often quite specialized and of restricted occurrence in the state. Adaptations to drought, such as succulence, thick cuticles, light coloration, small needle-like leaves, heavy pubescence, and ephemeral life cycles, are commonly exhibited.

Pioneering species, particularly non-native invasive species, are typical of the human-induced barren lands. Many of these opportunistic species are Eurasian in origin and thrive on, or perhaps require, recent and/or active disturbance.

In relatively stable barren lands where bedrock is at the ground surface, with little to no soil and without dense vegetative cover, the communities are commonly referred to as barrens. Depending on the particular substrate, the flora can be quite diverse and unusual in these natural barrens (Homoya 1994).

Species occurring on rock outcrops are commonly restricted to such environments, and are known as lithophytes. In Indiana, the primary rock outcrops are composed of either sandstone, limestone, or dolomite. In a few places, siltstone and shale rock are the dominant outcrops. Most natural rock outcrops occur in southern Indiana and, to a lesser degree, in west-central Indiana.

Deposits of deep, aeolian sand can produce barren landscapes, particularly where there is active drifting, e.g., the large dunes bordering Lake Michigan. Plants with an affinity for sand are known as psammophytes. Sand and gravel, as well as larger rock sizes, comprise barren land types known as sandbars and gravel washes. Although portions of these communities may have woody growth, the areas most actively swept by floodwaters typically are open and treeless.

1800. Barren lands, as defined in this chapter, were limited in extent in the state during this time. Although there are many references to "barrens" in Indiana by travelers and pioneers in the early 1800s, these examples were typically vegetated with either scrub forest or grassland, and thus are not considered here. Naturally occurring barren lands, such as cliffs, sand dunes, and gravel bars, were more extensive than in later centuries, and thus species associated with such communities were also more numerous.

1900. The late 1800s brought technology capable of both negatively impacting natural barren lands and creating anthropogenic ones. Some bedrock and gravel quarries were located on naturally occurring barren lands, such as limestone glades. In addition, small dams were constructed that flooded streamside gravel and sandbars, and dunes were mined for sand. Areas mined for coal, especially actively mined sites, and the operations associated with them (e.g., slurry ponds, slag piles) created areas of barren land in southwestern Indiana. No plant species documented in natural barren lands in the 1800s were known to have disappeared by 1900.

2000. Barren lands have increased in number and area as new and larger sites have been quarried and mined for coal and minerals, but some naturally occurring barrens were destroyed in the process. Large dams flood many miles of sandbars and gravel wash communities and also reduce the formation of sandbars along streams downstream of the dam. Dune stabilization programs have reduced the area of exposed sand in northern Indiana. During the twentieth century, some species associated with barren lands were extirpated, including Carolina anemone,

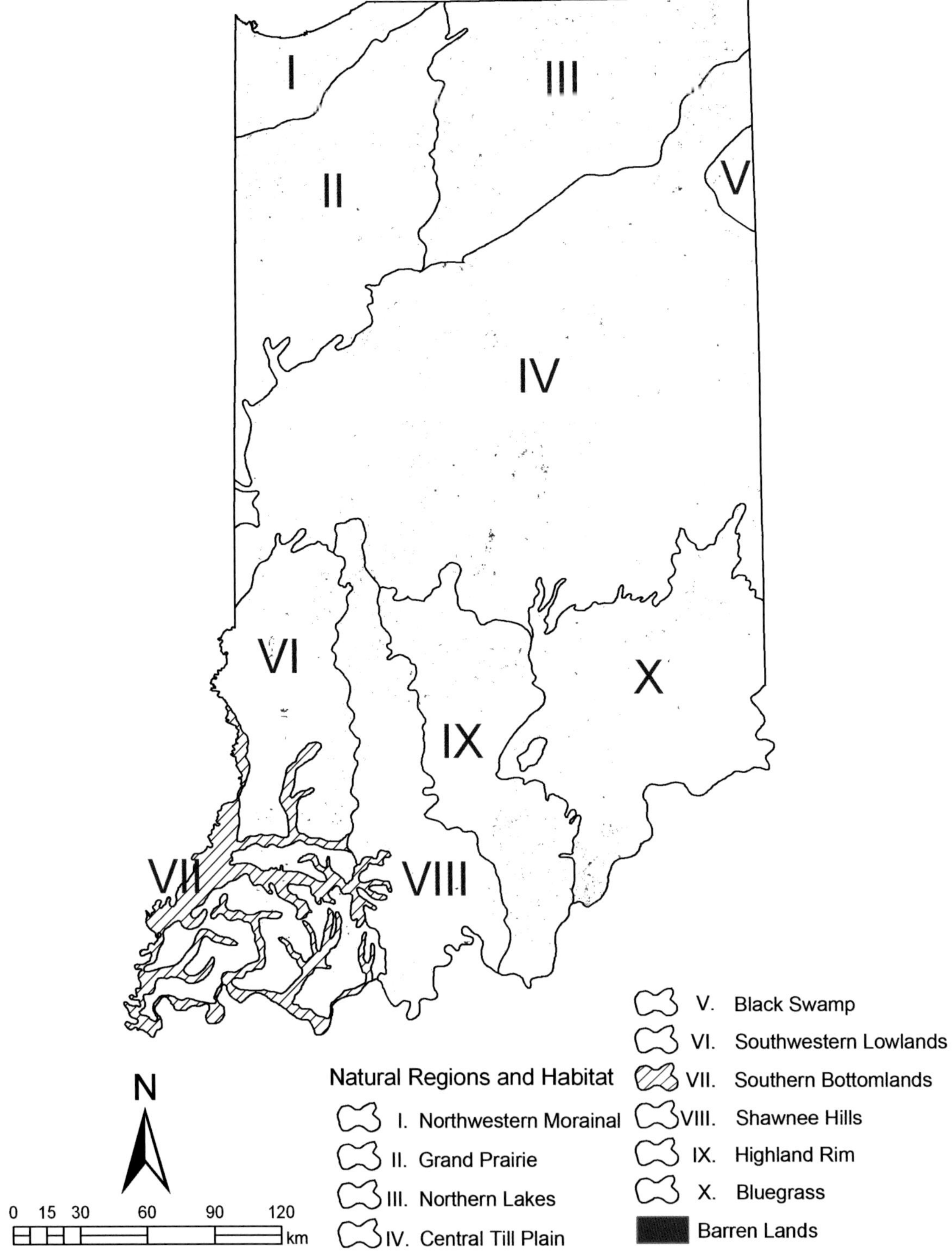

Map 8.1. Barren lands by natural region.

clustered poppy mallow, beard grass, evening primrose, western beard tongue, devil's claw, needle-and-thread, and small skullcap.

Amphibians and Reptiles

Herpetofauna in barren areas are limited in Indiana for several reasons. Given that barren lands were naturally scarce historically, the state lacks amphibians and reptiles specialized for such areas. Herpetofauna generally also require cover to persist in an area, and barren areas by definition have sparse or no cover. Finally, in areas that are being actively manipulated, amphibians and reptiles are vulnerable to human impacts due to their lack of mobility. On the margins of barren areas, we would expect some reptile species from adjacent habitats to take advantage of the open

Figure 8.1. Active dune at Indiana Dunes State Park. Photo by Marion Jackson.

canopy to bask. Also, if there is some cover available, species associated with grasslands and other open habitats, such as whiptail lizards, bull snakes, and western fox snakes, might find success.

Birds

Barren lands have never been a major or important habitat type for Indiana's birds. There are no species that specialize on any such habitat, although killdeer and nighthawks often nest in areas that are essentially barren. Rocky glades and other naturally occurring barrens are generally small in size and surrounded by forest habitat, and thus would be inhabited mainly by birds typical of the forest edge (see chapter 4). Barren areas of recent anthropogenic origin will be devoid of most bird species until they are reclaimed, although some birds, e.g., mourning doves, visit barren areas to obtain grit for crushing seeds in their gizzards. An exception is that sand and gravel pits can provide important nesting substrate for bank swallows. Only 8 bird species are typical of the various barren lands; they are listed in the "Barren Lands" column in Table B-1 and mentioned in the appropriate section below.

Mammals

Barren lands generally have few mammals because nearly all species require adequate cover, and barren lands have relatively little or no cover. A number of species of mammals may pass through barren lands, and Scott Johnson even had bobcats moving through barren lands during his studies of radio-tagged animals. Quarries that have underground portions may be good habitat for cave-loving bats. Some mammals, e.g., cottontails and fox squirrels, do use crushed-limestone-covered roads, apparently to obtain calcium particles, which makes them vulnerable to being killed by vehicles.

Sub-Habitats

Bare (Sand) Dunes

Table G-1 indicates that there were, in 1992, 2,537 acres of bare rock, sand, or clay in the state. Most of the active sand dunes (Figure 8.1) occur at the southern end of Lake Michigan. Most are not bare, although many exposed sand areas occur due to wind. The major dune-stabilizing grass, beach grass, provides good cover where it occurs.

Sand dune soils—mainly vegetated, and therefore not dunes—cover large areas near the southern shore of Lake Michigan. In northwestern Indiana, the Northwestern Morainal Natural Region contains 107,024 acres of dune soils and the Grand Prairie Natural Region has 296,343 acres. In the state's northeastern corner, the Northern Lakes Natural Region has 183,281 acres of dune soils (National Cartography and Geospatial Center 1995). Unfortunately, these figures are not accompanied by data on the vegetative cover of these soils or the converse, barrenness.

We would be remiss if we did not discuss the pioneering ecological studies of plant and animal succession that were made on Indiana's dune soils by Cowles (1899) and Shelford (1912). The successional stages for plants which they elucidated are as follows. As the wind blows off Lake Michigan, sand collects along the shore, allowing dune formation to begin. The lower beach is the area from the water line to the line usually reached by the summer storms; it hosts no permanent plant or animal communities, as the environment is too rigorous. The middle beach environment is less extreme, allowing some annual plants to grow; its upper edge is where the most severe of the summer storms reach. Such storms periodically eliminate plants such as sea rocket, common bugseed, and seaside spurge. Above where severe winter storms reach and the first line of dunes forms is the upper beach, and here plants can persist. The main dune-forming plants, beach grass and sand reed, trap sand and begin the formation of dunes. These dune formers are hardy perennial xerophytes that do not die after their first season. They send out shoots both laterally and downward, trapping wind-blown sand, thereby enabling dunes to grow higher and wider. After such plants form the dunes, others can establish. The newer dunes will generally be the front ones, close to the water; they will have early successional stages, while dunes farther from the water will have older communities. The final stage, once adequate time has elapsed, is often a mature forest community.

Classic succession patterns proceed unless interrupted. Human activity and weather events often intercede, permitting wind or water to return a local area to bare sand, thereby forming a "blowout." When this occurs, the successional process may begin again on that local area. If the bare sand does not become naturally replanted, then sand may continue to blow up and over the dune, accumulating on the far side; a "wandering dune" may result and move inland. Wandering dunes are not stabilized, or captured, by vegetation, permitting the dune to bury other communities, and restarting succession in local areas, thereby complicating the dune vegetation patterns.

FLORA. Most of the bare sand dunes (and associated beach communities) occur in the vicinity of Lake Michigan, but others occur in the substantial sand deposits of northwestern Indiana south of the lake, as well as locally in southwestern Indiana. Species of the more-exposed dunes, as well as in the blowouts of almost pure sand, include beach grass, sea rocket, common bugseed, sand reed, beach wormwood, winged pigweed, sand dropseed, and slender sand sedge. These species, with the exception of the first three, also occur in areas of sand exposed by human disturbance, such as in former sand mines. See Table P-10 for species of bare dunes.

AMPHIBIANS AND REPTILES. Indiana lacks herpetofauna specifically adapted to dune habitat, and none would likely seek out open dunes. However, there certainly are a variety of species that exploit the more vegetated aspects of the dunes and sandy areas associated with the south shore of Lake Michigan. Eastern hognose snakes are a good example of a species at home in sandy environments. The bull snake, six-lined racerunner, and slender glass lizard are other examples. The dunes herpetofaunal community has probably not changed substantially over time. However, although new dunes keep forming, habitat has been lost as succession leads to increases in vegetative cover in the form of shrubs and trees, and as humans build various structures on the dunes. Species most likely found on dunes are listed in Table H-6.

BIRDS. No birds in Indiana are specifically associated with bare dunes habitat, and such habitat in general is of little direct significance to birds. Birds such as gulls do scavenge among the debris deposited along the water's edge. Species that might be present in such habitats include those typical of open, drier grasslands, such as horned larks and possibly vesper or savannah sparrows, but these species would normally occur only on the largest of dune areas. Smaller dune habitats surrounded by forests would most likely be visited by forest edge birds. Such habitat might also be visited by some wintering sparrows.

MAMMALS. Thirteen-lined ground squirrels are not very common on the dunes presently, but possibly were earlier. Prairie deer mice are most common in areas with little ground cover, and are very common year-round in cultivated lands where they exist through plowing and harvesting. One wonders where they occurred when most of the state was covered with forest or prairie—perhaps in sandy dunes areas. The meadow vole occurs only where green herbaceous ground cover is heavy, primarily in the beach grass. White-footed mice are found mostly in the areas with woody vegetation, although they often move through many habitats. Other mammals of the dunes are indicated in Table M-5. The same group of species probably occurred there throughout the time period 1800 through 2000.

Rock Outcrops and Cliffs

Major rock outcrops are found in south-central Indiana with smaller outcrops scattered across the southern parts of the state, primarily within the Bluegrass, Highland Rim, and Shawnee Hills natural regions (Homoya et al. 1985), and in the western portion of the Central Till Plain region. Rock outcrops tend to be relatively small and are patchy in their distribution. The major cliffs in Indiana are along the bluffs of the Ohio River (Figure 8.2), although there are smaller cliffs in many other parts of the state. The most massive rock outcrops occur within the Shawnee Hills region (Figure 8.3) and consist of sandstone cliffs (in the Crawford Upland section) and limestone cliffs (in the Escarpment section). Other natural regions having rock outcrops include the Entrenched Valley section of the Central Till Plain region (e.g., Sugar Creek in Parke County), the Highland Rim region, and the Muscatatuck Flats and Canyons section of the Bluegrass region.

Often associated with cliffs are rock overhangs or rock shelters. These are especially common along the rivers and streams that meander through the southern Hoosier Forest area and along the Ohio River.

Figure 8.2. Cliff at Tobacco Landing. Photo by Scott Johnson.

Figure 8.3. Rock outcrop. Photo by Michael Hamoya.

Overhangs are exactly as the name implies: sections of cliffs that protrude farther out above than below, creating a dry place near the cliff base where many a person, and presumably many animals, have waited out a storm. Evidence of campfires and Native American artifacts attest to their long use by humans, and animal tracks can often be found in the dry, powdery soil below. The little funnels of the ant lion's larvae often dot the floor of such places. Rock shelters are more complicated cliff components where rocks have tumbled or are in such a position as to present a cave-like situation. Again, these can be used by humans and animals, and since they provide much more cover, they can be used more extensively. Phoebes and, sometimes, barn and cliff swallows, among the birds, and wood rats, white-footed mice, bobcats, raccoons, and foxes make use of rock shelters.

FLORA. The cliff flora in Indiana reflects the type of bedrock upon which it grows, i.e., certain species of plants are more or less restricted to different types of rock. Species found mostly on sandstone include marginal shield fern, mountain spleenwort, Bradley's spleenwort, pinnatifid spleenwort, Appalachian filmy fern, common wood fern, French's shooting star, and late alumroot. Species occurring mostly on limestone are wall-rue spleenwort, black-stemmed spleenwort, walking fern, villous alumroot, spreading rockcress, American orpine, Sullivant's coolwort, columbine, and purple cliffbrake. Rare species associated with cliffs include starry cleft phlox, Appalachian filmy fern, Bradley's spleenwort, mountain spleenwort, spreading rockcress, French's shooting star, Forbes' saxifrage, and shoestring fern.

A type of rock outcrop that occurs as exposed fragments or beds of rock is referred to as a rock barrens, or glade. These communities are typically within a forested context on steep slopes. Many species characteristic of prairie may be found growing there, as well as species essentially confined to glades, such as slender heliotrope and straggling St. John's wort. Typical glade plants include little bluestem, Indian grass, prairie dock, rattlesnake master, hoary puccoon, smooth blue aster, and green-flowered milkweed. See Table P-10 for species of cliffs and rock outcrops.

AMPHIBIANS AND REPTILES. Indiana's rock outcrops and cliffs are not extensive, and perhaps no herpetofauna are specialized for their use. Nevertheless, a variety of amphibians and reptiles may use them. Timber rattlesnakes, although they are more reasonably associated with mature hardwood forests in Indiana, use rocky areas for basking, gestation, and, in some areas, hibernation. Openings make forested habitat more amenable to a wide variety of snakes seeking sunshine and to species such as the northern fence lizard.

The green salamander has populations in the bluffs above the Ohio River in southwestern Indiana, far from Appalachia where other populations are found. To the extent that rocky areas are affiliated with caves and springs, the northern dusky salamander and cave salamander are other notable species.

It is likely that rocky outcrops and cliffs have suffered the same fate as many other open areas in becoming covered by shrubs and trees as the consequence of succession. The true extent of such impacts is unknown. Species most likely in rocky areas are listed in Table H-6.

BIRDS. The last-known nesting sites for common ravens were on rock outcrops and cliffs in southern Indiana (Butler 1898), although it is not clear that such areas were always the most important nesting sites for this species. It is also conceivable that peregrine falcons nested in such areas in the past. In the early twenty-first century, a wintering golden eagle has been roosting along a cliff overlooking the rugged valley of Sugar Creek in Parke County. Overall, however, outcrops and cliffs provide no critical or important habitat for any of Indiana's present-day birds.

MAMMALS. Seven species of mammals can be thought of as inhabitants of the rock outcrops and cliffs of Indiana (Table M-5), 6 currently existing in the state, along with the extirpated mountain lion. The only species closely tied to the cliffs is the Allegheny wood rat, as most of the other species can occur in a much greater variety of habitats.

1800. All 7 species of mammals that used cliffs, including the mountain lion, were present in 1800, but the mountain lion was extirpated about 1851. The high cliffs along the Ohio River in southern Indiana are the major haunt of the Allegheny wood rat, now endangered in the state. This wood rat was probably common in 1800 along the cliffs in Perry, Crawford and Harrison counties, and possibly east as far as Jefferson County. It also probably occurred along the streams to the north which had cliffs with crevices and caves. There are fossil deposits as far north as Monroe, Jennings, and extreme southeastern Owen counties. The opossum, white-footed mouse, short-tailed shrew, and raccoon were common on the cliffs, and the bobcat probably occurred there.

1900. Six of the 7 species were present, the mountain lion having vanished. The bobcat was starting to decrease. It is not known how long the Allegheny wood rat inhabited areas north and east of Crawford and Harrison counties, but by 1950 (and possibly much earlier) its range had shrunk to cliff areas in those two counties. Wood rats were documented in Wyandotte Cave (Crawford County) in the late nineteenth century (Cope 1872; Packard 1888) and sporadically in the late twentieth century.

2000. The Allegheny wood rat is now restricted to areas near the cliffs and caves along the Ohio River in Crawford and Harrison counties. Why its range contracted is not known. The opossum, white-footed mouse, short-tailed shrew, and raccoon remain common on the cliffs. The bobcat was quite rare in Indiana during much of the twentieth century, but made a remarkable comeback at the century's end and now uses some cliffs in southern counties.

Quarries

Active quarries generally harbor relatively little biota, but older or abandoned quarries may harbor a num-

Figure 8.4. Quarry at Cape Sandy. Photo by Scott Johnson.

ber of species. Some quarries are open (Figure 8.4) while others are at least partly underground, producing a cave-like environment.

Although European settlers used native stone for building foundations in the early 1800s, the first organized quarry on record was established in 1827 near Stinesville, Monroe County, in southern Indiana (Indiana Limestone Institute 2001). In 1900, according to the *Eighth Biennial Report* of the Indiana Department of Statistics, there were 2,071 acres of active stone quarries statewide (Table G-10).

In 1992, there were 28,177 acres of active quarries and mines (National Land Cover Data 1992; Table G-1). The largest concentration, 14,818 acres, was in the Southwestern Lowlands Natural Region, where surface mining for coal primarily occurs. The Southern Bottomlands region had 3,777 acres, and the Central Till Plain region had 3,366 acres of active quarries. Active quarries occurred in other natural regions as well, but were smaller in extent: less than 3,000 acres in all the other regions combined.

FLORA. Most active quarries in Indiana remove limestone bedrock. Species associated with these active quarries are few, at least in areas with recent disturbance of the surface, but expected ones include northern rush grass, field bindweed, bouncing bet, pineapple weed, cheat grass, white sweet clover, and Kentucky bluegrass. See Table P-10 for species present in quarries.

AMPHIBIANS AND REPTILES. Active quarries, like active mines, are largely unsuitable habitat for herpetofauna. In idle or abandoned areas, snakes such as black rat snakes and timber rattlesnakes might find refuge or perhaps even hibernate among the boulder piles. Species most likely to be found in active quarries are listed in Table H-6.

BIRDS. Active quarries provide little suitable habitat for birds. Inactive portions that contain permanent water might attract some species associated with aquatic and wetland habitats, as is the case for borrow pits on developed lands. Bank and rough-winged swallows, which nest in tunnels in vertical walls of gravel or dirt, are likely nesting species.

MAMMALS. Habitats within quarries vary, and the mammals are those of the habitats which occur in them. One important large quarry in Sellersburg (Clark County) harbors the state's only population of gray bats, *Myotis grisescens*. This quarry includes a lake, at the edge of which are 5 underground entrances to a large underground room, where the bats live. The floor of the cavern is covered with rather deep water, above which the bats live. A few male little brown bats live there in the summer, and a very few pipistrelles and big brown bats hibernate there.

9

Subterranean Systems

 Caves in Indiana (Figure 9.1) are confined for the most part to the Escarpment section of the Shawnee Hills Natural Region and the Mitchell Karst Plain section of the Highland Rim Natural Region, with a small area in the Muscatatuck Flats and Canyons section of the Bluegrass Natural Region (see Map 1.7; Map 9.1). Outside of the karst areas, the groundwater that occurs throughout Indiana in glacial and alluvial plains is also significant. The saturated interstices of the associated soils comprise significant subterranean habitats with simple, but interesting, communities of obligate species. Overall, Indiana is inhabited by a diverse and highly endemic assemblage of obligate subterranean invertebrates (Table I-1). Even greater diversity is exhibited by the group of animals that are non-obligate cavernicoles (cave inhabitants). Peck and Lewis (1978) authored the axiom that the cave fauna of a region potentially include the entire surface fauna, since anything can fall into a hole. That notwithstanding, a list of some of the more significant facultative cavernicoles of Indiana is presented in Table I-2.

Figure 9.1. Sandstone shelter in the Crawford Upland. Photo by Julian J. Lewis.

Karst

The geographic location of Indiana makes it unique in North America as a laboratory for exploring the evolution of subterranean fauna. Understanding the subterranean fauna of Indiana requires knowledge of the regional physiography of the state and its complex history of glaciation. The caves of Indiana are associated with a landform known as "karst," a term derived from the name of the Carso limestone plateau in the former Yugoslavia. In karst topography, surface features like sinkholes, cave entrances, and springs (Figure 9.2) are common (Ford and Williams 1989; White 1988; Jennings 1985). There are relatively few streams above ground, and some disappear and reappear, e.g., the Lost River. While most of the well-known caves of Indiana occur in the south-central karst belt, there is a second karst region in glaciated southeastern Indiana (Powell 1959, 1961; Malott 1932). In addition, throughout Indiana obligate subterranean aquatic invertebrates are found in the saturated interstices of unconsolidated deposits like till and alluvium.

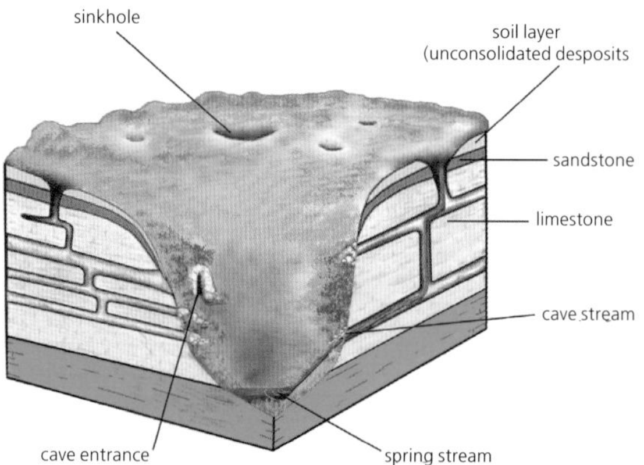

Figure 9.2. Diagram showing karst features. Drawing by Linda Castor.

South-Central Karst

The most prominent karst in Indiana is found in the south-central part of the state, where the Highland Rim section of the Interior Low Plateaus province (defined by Fenneman 1938) extends from the Ohio River to the north of Bloomington (see Map 1.7; Map 9.1). Three geomorphic zones are defined by the Paleozoic rock units on which they are located and the lack of overlying glacial deposits: the Norman Upland, Mitchell Plain, and Crawford Upland. Other geomorphic regions also defined by the underlying Paleozoic strata lie to the east and west. These regions

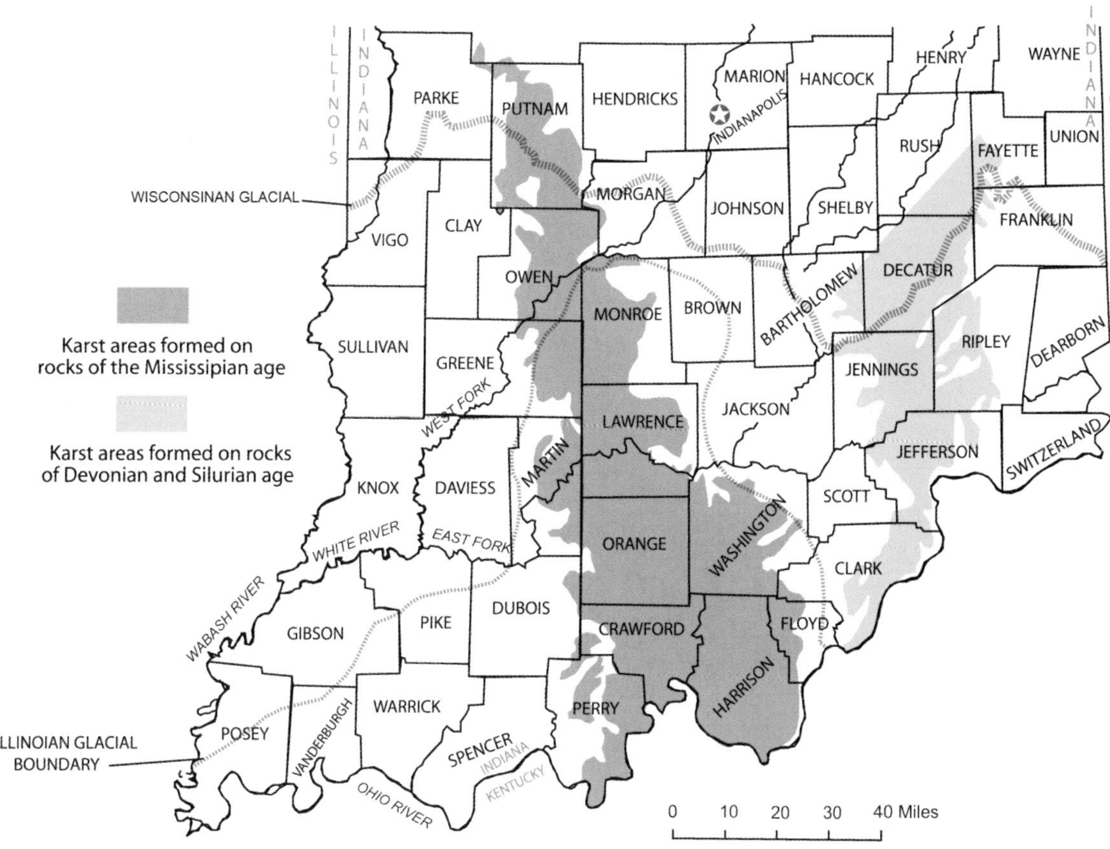

Map 9.1. Karst areas of Southern Indiana.

Figure 9.3. This passage in Binkley Cave is part of a dendritic network that comprises the largest cave system in Indiana. Photo by Dave Everton.

Figure 9.4. In presettlement times, much of the sinkhole-dotted rolling topography of southern Indiana karst probably resembled this scene in Donaldson Woods, Spring Mill State Park. Photo by Julian J. Lewis.

are covered by glacial sediments that are discontinuous and superficial, unlike the deep glacial covering above the bedrock farther to the north (Malott 1922).

The south-central karst (Powell 1961) occurs on the flank of an anticline termed the Cincinnati Arch. On the western side of the anticline, the strata dip toward the Illinois Basin, averaging about 25–30 ft per mi. The eastern boundary of the Highland Rim section in Indiana is the east-facing Knobstone Escarpment, which rises over 300 ft above the adjacent glaciated Scottsburg Lowland. On the west side of the escarpment, the Norman Upland is formed on thick siltstones with thin shale and limestone constituents of the early Mississippian age Borden Formation. Although noncavernous, small seeps and springs are associated with the Norman Upland.

To the west of the Norman Upland lies the Mitchell Plain, a sinkhole plain with karst features so numerous (Figure 9.3) that it is rivaled by few other areas in the United States. Although the presence of karst is based on lithology (Gines and Gines 1992), four factors have combined to make the Mitchell Plain a classic karst region (Palmer 1992): (1) due to the low regional dip, erosion has exposed carbonate rocks over a large continuous area; (2) a humid climate favors solutional processes; (3) the limestones are dense and compact, favoring solution that is concentrated along joints and bedding planes; and (4) base-level streams are deeply incised into the limestones, creating local hydraulic gradients sufficient for karst development over an extensive area.

This broad limestone plateau, bordered on the east and west by highlands of more-resistant rocks, is composed of an assemblage of limestone units of approximately 500 ft in thickness (Moore 1992). These include the limestones of the Ramp Creek, Harrodsburg, and Salem formations (Sanders Group) and of the St. Louis, Ste. Genevieve, and Paoli formations (Blue River Group).

The result is that the Mitchell Plain abounds with karst features (Powell 1992). The most striking feature is the sinkhole plain (Figure 9.4), with thousands of sinkholes dotting the landscape, funneling surface waters to subterranean drainage conduits that, in many cases, are enterable cave passages. Large areas of the Mitchell Plain have hundreds of sinkholes per mi2, with over 1,000 per section in some areas (Malott 1945). Other karst features are also common here, including sinking streams, springs, karst windows, and blind valleys.

The east-facing Chester Escarpment and its dip slope component, the Crawford Upland, are located west of the Mitchell Plain. This upland developed upon a series of interbedded shales, limestones, and sandstones of late Mississippian age (West Baden and Stephensport groups). The surface karst features so common in the Mitchell Plain are mostly absent in the Crawford Upland, except for karst valleys. Some caves divert surface waters from sinkholes on the Mitchell Plain to the west, where they emerge as springs in the Crawford Upland.

Drainage in the southern part of the south-central karst is controlled by the Ohio River. Some streams draining the karst have their headwaters just west of the Knobstone Escarpment, flowing across the Norman Upland until they encounter the carbonate rocks

Figure 9.5. Flat glaciated terrain like this area near Brookston, White County, is characteristic of much of northern Indiana. The mouths of the field drains, like the one shown here, are productive sites for collecting groundwater crustaceans. Photo by Julian J. Lewis.

of middle Mississippian age upon which the karst of the Mitchell Plain has developed. For instance, Buck Creek and Indian Creek head in the Norman Upland, while only the eastern part of the Blue River receives water from there. Much of the flow of the Blue River and all of the Little Blue River come from west of the Norman Upland. In the northern two-thirds of the region, the East Fork and West Fork of the White River are the dominant base-level streams. These rivers originate significantly farther to the east, although two major tributaries, the Patoka and Lost rivers, also begin west of the Knobstone Escarpment.

Southeastern Karst

Although separated from the south-central karst by the relatively short span of the mostly noncavernous Norman Upland and Scottsburg Lowland, some of the differences between the two regions are significant. The southeastern karst region was formed on much older limestones of Silurian and Devonian age. The great continuous thickness of the carbonate rocks seen to the west is diminished, although with typically 100 ft or more of limestone there is more than enough to contain large cave passages (Moore 1992).

The caves of the area have formed in the limestones associated with the Muscatatuck Regional Slope, a physiographic unit characterized by a regional dip afforded by its position on the western side of the Cincinnati Arch. Perhaps the single greatest factor affecting the southeastern karst was its repeated glaciation during the Pleistocene. The entire karst was covered by the Illinoian glaciation, with the subsequent Wisconsinan glaciation advancing to northern Jennings County (Powell 1959).

The effect of glaciation was to carpet the entire southeastern karst with glacial sediments. From a physiographic standpoint, the area is a northerly extension of the Bluegrass region of the Interior Low Plateaus. However, its glacial history has subdued the topography, and the region is classified as part of the Central Lowlands province. The limestone continues to the north, and evidence of paleo-karst and caves has been found in quarries far north of the boundary of the southeastern karst region.

The southeastern karst lacks the deeply incised master streams typical of those that flow through the south-central karst. Most of the known caves occur along stream valleys that have cut through the mantle of glacial sediments. The caves of the area are much shorter on the average than their counterparts in the south-central karst. Cave rooms are smaller and have fewer depositional features. Due to the relative thinness of the overlying rock, multiple entrances are common.

Non-Cave Subterranean Habitats

The majority of Indiana is covered with unconsolidated glacial sediments of Pleistocene age. These deposits frequently contain sand and rounded stones that provide adequate interstices for a unique assemblage of obligate groundwater organisms (Delamare Deboutteville 1960). Unlike caves, this habitat cannot be entered by people. If not for humans' creation of wells, drain tiles, and similar "windows" into groundwater, the existence of this habitat and its fauna might have remained undiscovered.

The primary characteristic of the glacial landform is its flatness. Topographic maps of the area are drawn to show 5-ft contour intervals, and in some areas of northern Indiana the contour lines are few and far between. The area has some of the premier agricultural soil in the United States, but the nearly complete lack of relief has made utilizing it for farming problematic due to the poor drainage. This shortcoming was widely corrected by field drain tiles and ditches beginning in the late 1800s. The tile outlets are typically at the edge of the fields to discharge water into the surface ditches (Figure 9.5). These drain tiles function as small-diameter artificial caves. Groundwater crustaceans living in these shallow, saturated soil interstices find their way into the tiles, and inevitably some are discharged to the surface ditch at the mouths of the spring-like drain tiles.

Wells are also portals into groundwaters. Like field drain tiles, shallow (typically old and hand-dug) wells that penetrate glacial or other sediments allow groundwater animals to disperse into the water column contained by the well. Many of the organisms are tiny, even microscopic, and undoubtedly were consumed unknowingly by those tapping the wells as a water source.

Many classification schemes and their associated terminology have been proposed for groundwater habitats (e.g., Pennak and Ward 1986; Camacho 1992; Bretschko and Klemens 1986). Relevant in the context of the subterranean fauna of Indiana are unconsolidated deposits associated with streams, termed variously as subfluvial, hyporheic, or parafluvial. In the same way that interstices are present in the soils of glacial sediments, the porosity created by sand and gravel beds beneath and to the side of streams creates potential habitat for a wide variety of organisms inhabiting water-saturated interstices (Danielopol 1976). The surface of a stream marks the top of the local water table, but this water table penetrates far beyond the banks of the stream, and the saturated interstitial habitat may extend significant distances beyond as well.

The physical characteristics of this environment include the pore size and surface current, which determines flow rate (Angelier 1962; Danielopol 1976); darkness below about 10 cm (Pennak 1950); and temperature as a function of the surface water (Camacho 1992).

Caves and Cave Features

According to the Indiana Cave Survey, 2,902 caves are currently found in Indiana (http://www.indianacaves.org). Of those, 2,395 occur in the Mitchell Plain and Crawford Upland, fewer than 500 in the southeastern karst, and a smattering in places like Tippecanoe County, along the Wabash River. Some of the most extensive caves in the United States are found in Indiana (Courbon et al. 1989), and all of those are found in the south-central karst (see below). The longest caves, like Binkley Cave (Harrison County),

Table 9.1. The Longest Caves in Indiana

Cave Name	County	Length (mi)
Binkley Cave	Harrison	24.07
Lost River Cave	Orange	21.00
Bluespring Caverns	Lawrence	20.82
Sullivan Cave	Lawrence	9.63
Wyandotte Cave	Crawford	9.20
Whistling Cave	Lawrence	7.81
Reeves Cave	Monroe	4.36
Wayne Cave	Monroe	4.25
Blowing Hole	Harrison	6.57
Saltpeter Cave	Monroe	3.46

Source: Dave Everton, Indiana Cave Survey, unpublished data.

Bluespring Caverns (Lawrence County), and the Lost River cave system (Orange County), originate on the Mitchell Plain, with passages extending toward the edge of the Crawford Upland. These massive cave systems have in common a dendritic series of passages that drain relatively large areas of the sinkhole plain into large trunk stream passages.

Multiple levels are usually present in the larger caves, with dry upper levels representing earlier, now-abandoned routes of the cave streams. At Wyandotte Cave in the Crawford Upland, the entire cave is composed of dry, even dusty, upper-level passages. The only large cave stream known in the vicinity occurs on the opposite side of Sharpe Creek Valley from Wyandotte Cave. The huge passages of Wyandotte are stark remnants of what must have been large stream corridors during the Pleistocene or before.

Large cave systems like these occur near the edge of the Chester Escarpment in Indiana and its continuation into the central Kentucky karst in the Mammoth Cave region. For every large cave system in the south-central Indiana karst, there are dozens of shorter, but still significant caves. These caves may range from a trunk stream passage thousands of feet long to a small, barely enterable crawlway.

Some cave entrances are found in sinkholes where water enters the system. Sinkhole entrances vary from holes barely large enough for entry by humans, to larger sinks where entire surface streams disappear, termed "swallets" or "swallow holes." Under base flow conditions, the entirety of Indian Creek (Harrison County) is a sinking stream, disappearing into inconspicuous holes. For a portion of its length, as the name implies, the Lost River (Orange County) flows entirely underground. A surface dry bed receives overflow, which returns underground in swallow holes along its course, such as Tolliver Swallowhole. The water from these systems ultimately returns to the surface at springs. The largest in Indiana is the rise of Indian Creek at Harrison Spring, located west of Corydon, an alluviated spring 45 ft deep and nearly 100 ft in diameter. Cave divers have explored the spring's conduit system to a depth of 74 ft in passages averaging 65 ft wide.

Other caves may be entered through karst windows, where a section of the cave roof has collapsed, creating a portal into an otherwise continuous cave

Figure 9.6. The Twin Caves' karst window was created by a collapse of the cavern roof. The cave stream emerges from Upper Twin Cave (*bottom*), flows a short distance on the surface, and then sinks underground into the entrance of Lower Twin Cave (*top*). Photo by Julian J. Lewis.

passage. A prominent example occurs in Spring Mill State Park (Lawrence County), where a karst window has created Twin Caves (Figure 9.6). Due to a collapse in part of the Donaldson cave system, water flows from the mouth of Upper Twin Cave and is visible on the surface for about 200 ft, then sinks underground at the opposite end of the karst window at Lower Twin Cave. A second karst window is visible a short distance away where another roof collapse has created the upper and lower Bronson entrances.

Perhaps the largest karst feature in Indiana is Wesley Chapel Gulf in Orange County. Malott (1932) defined a "gulf" as a collapsed sinkhole with steep walls and an alluviated floor. Wesley Chapel Gulf is about 1,000 ft in length and 350 ft wide, enclosing an area of over 6 acres on the bottom. The walls climb to nearly 100 ft, making entry difficult in all but a few spots. The Lost River cave system is enterable at the south end of the gulf. The cavern collapse forming the gulf created a dam that forces the water to resurface in a picturesque rise pool before it sinks again below the entrance to Boiling Springs Cave (an isolated passage of the Lost River cave system).

Vertical dome pits are prominent features of caves in which significant relief occurs between the surface and the base level. These are essentially vertical pipes in which water travels rapidly downward. In Indiana, pits are frequently found along the edge of ridges in the Crawford Upland, where water sitting on the relatively non-permeable sandstone caprock breaches the limestone, then falls vertically. In some cases, dome pits are visible along horizontal passages, where they lead upward from base-level streams or form connections between upper and lower passages. Sometimes, they open directly to the surface, creating large shafts that require rope and vertical gear to enter. Pits from 25 to 100 ft in depth are fairly common in the south-central karst, with Gory Hole (Lawrence County) being the deepest pit in the state at 136 ft (Figure 9.7).

In contrast, only 487 caves are known to occur in the southeastern Indiana karst. The longest cave in the area is Wilson Cave, with over a mile of passages. Caves in this karst belt over 1,000 ft in length are exceptional, and pits of any significant depth are unknown.

The most recognizable features in caves are formations, or speleothems. On the ceilings of caves may hang stalactites that range in size from the aptly named soda straws, the width of a single water drop, to large and frequently complex curtains, or draperies. Some of these draperies form flat, sheet-like formations that are only a few millimeters in thickness. Placing a light behind them allows one to view the "bacon rind" effect caused by the mineral deposition, which produces various gradations of white, orange, yellow, and red. A bizarre permutation of the stalactite is the helictite, which in sites like Wyandotte Cave form extensive displays of strangely twisted, gravity-defying speleothems that grow sideways or even upward.

As the water drips from the ceiling, a stalagmite may form on the floor of the cave. If over the millennia a stalactite and stalagmite finally grow to the point where they connect, a column, or pillar, is created. A similar phenomenon is flowstone, which occurs on walls and floors, where calcite is laid down in broad layers over rock, mudbanks, or other formations. In places like Devil's Graveyard Cave (Harrison County), flowstone mounds may become so large that one has to use a rope to traverse them. Rimstone dams commonly form terraces associated with flowstone, or may bridge entire passages like those in Squire Boone Caverns (Harrison County).

Figure 9.7. This dome pit in a cave in the Hoosier National Forest is about 70 ft in depth. Pits such as this one allow water to rapidly fall toward the base level. Photo by Julian J. Lewis.

Hill (1976) and Hill and Forti (1997) have discussed in detail the mineralogy and creation of these and other related speleothems. In general, their creation is the result of carbonate deposition, with the most common minerals being calcite and aragonite (both are forms of $CaCO_3$). When rainwater combines with carbon dioxide (CO_2), carbonic acid is formed: $H_2O + CO_2 \rightarrow H_2CO_3$. This weak acid dissolves the limestone bedrock as it descends to the water table: $CaCO_3 + H_2CO_3 \rightarrow Ca^{++} + 2(HCO_3)$. When the bicarbonate solution reaches an air-filled cavity, the carbon-dioxide-rich solution typically loses CO_2 to the air until equilibrium is reached. Under these conditions, calcite precipitation occurs: $Ca^{++} + 2(HCO_3) \rightarrow CO_2 + CaCO_3 + H_2O$ (Figure 9.8).

The sulfate deposition of minerals like gypsum ($CaSO_4 \cdot 2H_2O$), mirabilite ($Na_2SO_4 \cdot 10H_2O$), and epsomite ($MgSO_4 \cdot 7H_2O$) accounts for the presence of rarer speleothems that take the form of crusts, needles, or flowers (Hill 1976). These minerals usually occur in drier passages where evaporation creates

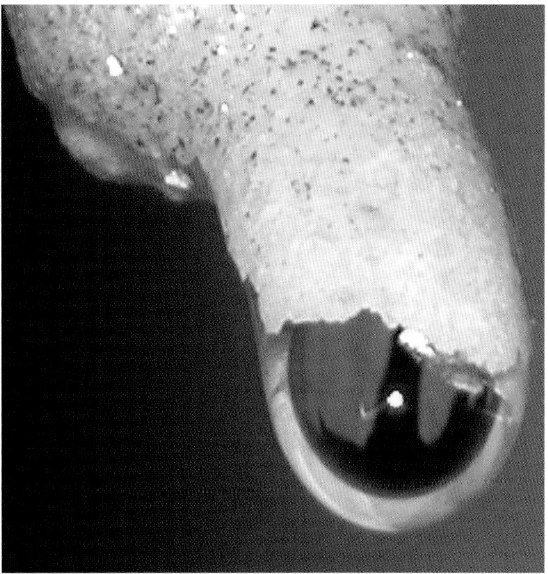

Figure 9.8. The growth of a stalactite occurs as calcite precipitates as almost microscopic crystals at the tip of the speleothem. Photo by Julian J. Lewis.

Figure 9.9. In Indiana, the trechine beetles of the genus *Pseudanophthalmus* are known only from caves. Photo by Julian J. Lewis.

conditions that lead to their precipitation. The earliest record of humans entering an Indiana cave is at Wyandotte Cave, also known as Epsom Salts Cave, where carbon-dating has placed the Native Americans who mined these and other minerals from the cave around 900 BCE (Watson 1974).

Adaptation and Ecological Classification of Subterranean Animals

The average person asked to name an animal living in an Indiana cave usually cites cavefish or bats. In so doing, they describe both ends of the continuum of ecological classification of cavernicoles. The literature is replete with nomenclature for the ecological classification of subterranean organisms. There are classification schemes using a variety of terms, including *troglobite* (Schiner 1854; Racovitza 1907), *stygobite* (Thienemann 1925), *troglomorph* (Christiansen 1962), *stygobiont* (Husmann 1971), and *stygicole* (Chapman 1986). The classification scheme presented here is a synthesis of the terminology in common use, which will be defined below.

Terrestrial Fauna

The tenets of ecological classification include the degree to which an animal is limited to subterranean habitats, the extent of their troglomorphic adaptations, and their evolutionary pathways. The evolution of terrestrial subterranean fauna in Indiana appears to be a product of a climatic-relict model of evolution (Holsinger 2000) and perhaps differs significantly from the evolution of the aquatic counterparts as well as from those occurring in tropical climates. In Indiana, the terrestrial animals that are obligate cavernicoles, or troglobites, are envisioned as relictual species that were "pre-adapted" to the cave environment in the cool, moist, litter habitats of the Appalachian highlands (Barr 1968). During the glacial advances of the Pleistocene, these animals dispersed widely to the lowlands on either side of the Appalachians. When the climatic shift accompanying glaciation reversed, invertebrates like the trechine beetles (*Pseudanoph-*

Table 9.2. Ecological Classification of Subterranean Animals

Classification	Definition
Troglobite	terrestrial, morphologically adapted and restricted to caves, must feed and reproduce in the cave environment
Troglophile	terrestrial, more or less morphologically adapted to caves, not restricted to caves but can feed and reproduce in the cave environment
Trogloxene	terrestrial, not usually morphologically adapted to caves, usually leaves the cave to either feed or reproduce
Stygobite	aquatic, morphologically adapted and restricted to caves, must feed and reproduce in the cave environment
Stygophile	aquatic, more or less morphologically adapted to caves, not restricted to caves but can feed and reproduce in the cave environment
Stygoxene	aquatic, not usually morphologically adapted to caves, usually leaves the cave to either feed or reproduce
Accidental	animals that fall or are washed into caves and usually perish there if unable to escape
Edaphobite	terrestrial, deep-soil inhabitant also occurring in caves
Phreatobite	aquatic, groundwater organism occurring in saturated interstices of non-cave habitats or caves

Figure 9.10. Many relictual troglobites have very limited ranges. The millipede *Pseudotremia cookorum* is known only from caves near Tobacco Landing in southern Harrison County. Photo by Julian J. Lewis.

thalmus, Figure 9.9) and millipedes (*Pseudotremia,* Figure 9.10) found themselves far from their native habitats.

Several survival strategies were available to these animals: (1) follow the glaciers northward to remain in a similar lowland surface habitat; (2) return to the Appalachian highlands; (3) remain and find suitable habitat, e.g., caves (Barr 1968; Holsinger 2000) or superficial underground compartments (Juberthie et al. 1980; Juberthie and Delay 1981); or (4) suffer extinction. Evidence points to the occurrence of large-scale cave invasion, and many species survived in the subterranean environment long after their surface-dwelling ancestors became extinct (Holsinger 1988).

It is of great interest that the pattern of glaciation in Indiana allows reasonable speculation on the timing of the invasion of caves and the evolution of troglobites (Lewis 1983). A crude estimate of the length of time that an animal has lived underground can in some instances be measured as a degree of troglomorphism, that is to say, the expression of "regressive" evolutionary morphological characteristics, such as the loss or reduction of eyes or pigmentation, accompanied by the enhancement of other sensory adaptations. Characterizing this so-called regression is problematic, in that increasing troglomorphism in aquatic isopods produces appendages, for instance antennae, that are more elongate, while in others like millipedes, the antennae become shorter. A growing body of evidence suggests that "regressive evolution" (an archaic term) is in fact selective (Protas et al. 2006).

The karst of southern Indiana can be divided into sections of differing availability for cave colonization. For the terrestrial animals found in Indiana during the Pleistocene, the caves in the south-central karst south of the limit of glaciation were available throughout the Pleistocene as cool, moist refugial habitats. The most troglomorphic troglobites in Indiana occur in caves of the south-central karst (e.g., the Blue River cave millipede, which is white in color as a result of complete depigmentation and has greatly reduced eyes). The richest communities of obligate subterranean species occur in caves of the south-central karst (Table I-3) due to the longer period of time available for cave colonization plus the more extensive size of the caves and therefore the greater breadth of habitats available.

Culver and Sket (2000) defined a global "hotspot" of subterranean biodiversity as being a site with 20 or more troglobites or stygobites. The Binkley, Lost River, and Wyandotte cave systems attain this degree of species richness. The Tincher Karst fauna assemblage also contains over 20 obligate subterranean species, and the Marengo cave system as presently known falls just short. With additional sampling, Marengo Cave will probably be added to this distinctive group. Other prospective candidates, such as Bluespring Caverns, remain mostly unsampled.

The entire southeastern karst region was covered by the Illinoian glacier and was presumably unavailable as a habitat on either the surface or in caves. However, in the southern tip of the karst in Clark County, near the termination of the glacier's travel, the caves are inhabited by the lightly pigmented, small-eyed Indian cave millipede. Although known only from caves, this millipede is only mildly troglomorphic, having probably invaded caves during the Sangamon interglacial stage. The most diverse troglobitic communities in southeastern Indiana are found in the caves of Clark and Jefferson counties (Table I-4; Lewis 1983, 1995, 1996b; Lewis and Lewis 2002), which due to their proximity to the glacial maximum extent would have been the first available for colonization in the glaciated area. Moving to the north, the cave fauna become increasingly depauperate. No species of cave millipede successfully dispersed and survived north of Clark County, although one species of trechine beetle (*Pseudanophthalmus chthonius*) is found in caves as far north as Jennings County.

Figure 9.11. The herald moth (*Scoliopteryx libatrix*) is a common trogloxene in Indiana, where it over-winters in cave entrances. Photo by Julian J. Lewis.

Figure 9.12. The cave cricket, *Ceuthophilus stygius,* is perhaps the most familiar of the invertebrate trogloxenes in Indiana caves. These crickets form clusters near cave entrances, where their droppings contribute to the food chain. Photo by Julian J. Lewis.

Not all animals living in caves are obligate cavernicoles (troglobites) restricted to the subterranean environment. *Troglophiles* are terrestrial animals that can live out their entire life cycles within caves, but are not strikingly troglomorphic and may also be found in suitable surface habitats. The difference between troglophiles and troglobites can be subtle and difficult to ascertain in some instances. The small, darkly pigmented cave dung fly had long been known to occur over much of the eastern United States and had been considered a troglophile. It was not until after Marshall and Peck (1985) studied the species in detail that it was learned that, despite its wide range, this fly was known only from caves (despite searching for it on the surface). Furthermore, compared to related species, it has reduced eyes. Consequently, it was classified as a troglobite.

Conversely, some of the populations of Salisa's cave millipede are rather darkly pigmented and have eyes of moderate size. Formerly considered a troglobite (Lewis 2003), this species has now been found in a surface habitat (Shear et al. 2007).

Bats are the best known examples of *trogloxenes,* animals that may live in caves but must leave to feed or reproduce. Among the invertebrates, the herald moth (*Scoliopteryx libatrix,* Figure 9.11) commonly hibernates in caves. Cave crickets (e.g., *Ceuthophilus stygius,* Figure 9.12) are important to cave communities in their role of importing food to the ecosystem. These insects forage on the surface during the night, then return to contribute nutrients to the cave environment in the form of their droppings as well as, eventually, their carcasses. In a food-poor habitat, a thin veneer of fecal material can be inhabited by a veritable menagerie of invertebrates.

The bottom tier of the ecological pyramid of cave utilization is populated by *accidentals.* The accidental cave fauna potentially include the entire surface fauna, since anything can fall into a cave entrance. As evidenced by the frequency of the shells of the eastern box turtle, some animals fall into caves and are not agile enough to escape, thus becoming part of the food chain.

Aquatic Fauna

The subterranean aquatic fauna is classified in a manner analogous to the terrestrial. In simpler classification schemes, the aquatic species are given the same designations as their terrestrial counterparts, such as troglobite, troglophile, and so forth. But it has become the practice to use the prefix *stygo-* with aquatic taxa, reflecting the differences in evolutionary history between the aquatic and terrestrial groups. Thus, stygobites are obligate aquatic cave inhabitants, but the line of classification in these animals is blurred by the fact that some of the aquatic species, like Packard's groundwater amphipod, seem to inhabit both caves and the interstices of non-cave groundwater habitats. Other crustaceans, like Kendeigh's groundwater isopod, are obligate groundwater inhabitants unknown from caves. Animals such as these can be classified as phreatobites, as they live solely in the saturated interstices of the unconsolidated deposits below the level of the groundwater table. The stygophiles and stygoxenes are aquatic species classified analogously to the terrestrial fauna.

Unlike troglobites, in which a scenario can be deduced that ties the time of cave invasion and degree of troglomorphy to relatively narrow timelines, no such relictual picture can be seen with the aquatic fauna. Most authors (e.g., Barr and Holsinger 1985; Holsinger 1988, 1994, 2000; Lewis and Bowman 1981) now believe that at least some of the fauna inhabiting groundwater far predate the Pleistocene cave invasions theorized for the terrestrial fauna.

Some of the subterranean aquatic crustaceans occurring in Indiana, like the amphipods of the genus *Stygobromus,* are only distantly related taxonomically to surface forms (Holsinger 1988, 1994, 2000).

This freshwater amphipod genus is composed entirely of subterranean species and is a classic example of a relict group that may well have lived in groundwater for millions of years, probably predating the separation of North America from Eurasia by continental drift (Holsinger 1986). Similarly, the isopods of the *Stygius* group have no surviving surface relatives that are recognized as closely related, but some of the subterranean species of the Hobbsi group, like Kendeigh's groundwater isopod, appear to be related to epigean species (Lewis 1982). Among the amphipods of the genus *Crangonyx,* some, like Packard's groundwater amphipod, are clearly troglomorphic. Others, like Barr's cave amphipod, have small but obvious eye remnants. The Indiana cave amphipod, although known only from caves and springs, may in fact not be stygobitic.

First proposed by Howarth (1973, 1981) to explain the evolution of terrestrial troglobites in tropical caves where Pleistocene glacial relictual models seem problematic, the adaptive-shift model may well apply to aquatic subterranean faunas. Rather than invoking isolation as a function of climatic change, the adaptive-shift model views subterranean invasion as a continual process based on a shift into newly developed niches (Holsinger 2000). The evolution of subterranean aquatic species in Indiana probably represents groundwater invasions over a wide range of times. Although the species of *Stygobromus* may not be ancient, the phyletic line leads almost certainly to an ancient inhabitant of groundwater. The more recent invasions may be, as exemplified by Bellés (1991), nonrelictual but rather colonization as a function of opportunism or convenience.

Subterranean Habitats

The cave environment is divided into 4 zones with varying conditions and communities. These are the (1) entrance, (2) twilight zone, (3) variable temperature zone, and (4) constant temperature zone.

The entrance is the area where the surface and subterranean habitats are conjoined and is characterized by the presence of sunlight and green plants. Beyond the entrance is the twilight zone, where light becomes dimmer, finally vanishing as the passage bends beyond the point of penetration of the sun. A variable temperature zone then occurs that is greatly influenced by the influx of surface air into the more-buffered environment of the cave, which theoretically remains near the average regional temperature. In southern Indiana caves, this is usually 54–56°F. The richest communities are frequently found in areas not far from the entrance, since this is where organic debris and nutrients imported by trogloxenes (bats, crickets, wood rats) are most likely to be abundant. Likewise, the environmentally buffered, litter-covered floors of open-air pits may be rich in invertebrates.

Many troglobites are obligate inhabitants of the zone of approximately constant temperature and 100% relative humidity. Air currents flow freely between cave entrances (which may not be large enough for human entry), subjecting the cave to air of low temperature and humidity during the winter, with the opposite occurring during the summer. The "constant temperature zone" of caves is somewhat of a misnomer, since even in the deep interior of Binkley Cave, temperatures vary seasonally by a few degrees and may not even be constant in different parts of the same passage. That notwithstanding, it is safe to say that, in the larger caves, a highly buffered zone usually exists that does not differ greatly from the average regional temperature.

Terrestrial Cave Habitats

In some of the larger Indiana caves, one or more upper levels represent previous drainage corridors from earlier in the Pleistocene (or before). The lowest habitats, adjacent to cave streams, are the riparian corridors. At base-flow conditions, stream-level bars of gravel, sand, silt, and/or mud are barely above the water. Above these stream-level habitats, mudbanks, piles of breakdown (rock that has fallen from the ceiling over long periods of time), and the bedrock passage walls occur. In-flowing streams commonly deposit organic materials, ranging from fine veneers of detritus to leaf packs and logs.

In stream caves, the line between aquatic and terrestrial habitats in the riparian zone is frequently indistinct. Due to frequent flooding, an area that is a terrestrial habitat one day might be completely underwater the next. The only known specimen of the Hudelson cave beetle was collected from what could be characterized as "soupy" mud below a waterfall in Hudelson Cavern, part of the Lost River system in Orange County. The terrestrial isopods, particularly Barr's cave isopod and Elrod's terrestrial isopod are frequently found in semiaquatic organic material.

The ecology of the riparian zone in Indiana caves is relatively complex. In Binkley Cave near the historic entrance along Binkley River Trail, V-shaped mudbanks line the stream passage in many places. A combination of organic debris and a peppering of bat guano form the base of the food chain for microbial decomposers and invertebrate omnivores. Macroscopic growths of bacteria, probably actinomycetes, cover the upper mudbanks and walls with splotches of grays and yellows. Cave diplurans are sometimes found grazing in these areas. The Blue River cave millipede forages on the mudbanks, replaced on the passage walls by Sollman's cave millipede. Earthworms, springtails, and fly larvae living in or on the mudbanks are the prey of the Blue River cave beetle or the occasional Packard's cave pseudoscorpion. Tiny braconid wasps parasitize some of the fly larvae, laying their eggs on them.

The communities and productivity of the upper levels may be starkly different from those of riparian habitats. Much of Wyandotte Cave is very dry, with little importation of nutrients outside of areas where Indiana bats roost. Searching for invertebrate life is almost fruitless, and even baiting produces little evidence of fauna beyond the occasional cave humpbacked fly. In Kentucky, Thomas Poulson has termed the upper levels of the Mammoth Cave system "the great Kentucky desert," and it is safe to say that the same desert occurs to the north in Indiana caves. Only in areas where streams enter through breakdowns or shafts do the communities become noticeably richer.

Aquatic Cave Habitats

As underground drainage conduits, caves channel water from the surface down through the soil into the epikarst, finally reaching a tubular flow system that eventually discharges the water back to the surface at a spring. In the Mitchell Plain, the transit from the surface to base level may be rapid. Sinkholes collect surface sheet flow and funnel the water toward base level with little, if any, interruption or filtration. Many caves in the Mitchell Plain are exceptionally wet and frequently flood to the ceiling when receiving storm waters. Exploration of a cave in this region usually involves wading or even swimming through water that is typically around 54°F and may be considerably colder when receiving snow melt. This and other risks are associated with caving. Persons interested in cave exploration are encouraged to contact the National Speleological Society (www.caves.org), an organization promoting responsible caving and the study, exploration, and conservation of caves and karst.

A variety of aquatic habitats occur between the surface and base level, and all of them are inhabited. The least understood of these as a habitat is the epikarst. This is the zone that is encountered when water seeps through the soil, eventually reaching contact with the underlying rock. In the Mitchell Plain, this is the soil-limestone contact, but in the Crawford Upland, this frequently entails a sandstone caprock that overlies the cave-bearing limestones. The water probably flows along the soil-bedrock contact until it finds a pathway, such as a crack or joint, downward. In the Crawford Upland, where relief is greater and the water travels horizontally along the soil-sandstone contact, deep vertical pits occur on the edge of ridges where the water drops rapidly toward base level.

Observing the fauna of the epikarst is problematic since the habitat cannot be entered directly, but hints of the animals living there can be gleaned from sampling pools and small streams of water dripping from cave ceilings. The fauna of these drip pools reflect its epikarstic origins and are frequently quite different from those seen in nearby cave streams. In Indiana, evidence of the epikarstic fauna was found in 1928 by the Frenchmen Bolivar and Jeannel, who discovered the crustacean now known as Jeannel's groundwater copepod in Marengo Cave. This crustacean remained obscure from the time of its discovery until the 1990s. Lewis (1998) sampled the two large cave streams that flow through Marengo Cave but failed to find the copepod. However, dipping water from the shallow pools on the commercial cave's tourist trails revealed teeming populations of Jeannel's copepod. Continued sampling for epikarstic fauna has revealed some of the rarest animals known from Indiana, including the Indiana groundwater copepod and several species of groundwater amphipods that are new to science and remain undescribed.

In many caves, small streams flow in from side passages or ceiling joints. These streams form a continuum between their surface origins and their ultimate destinations in larger cave streams flowing at base level. These habitats vary in size and the fauna found in them seem to be commensurate with the physical extent of the aquatic environment. Small cave isopods, amphipods, and flatworms, usually less than 10 mm in size, are frequently the only macroscopic inhabitants of shallow pools or streams. When somewhat deeper water is available, stygophilic (*Cambarus laevis*) and stygobitic (*Orconectes inermis,* Figure 9.13) crayfish may join the community. The northern cavefish is usually only present in cave streams with relatively deep pools.

Anyone turning over a stone in an Indiana cave stream is likely to see myriad crustaceans crawling about the underside of the rock. Almost ubiquitous are the northern cave isopod and rotund cave isopod. Accompanying the isopods are usually amphipod crustaceans that are seen flitting about the stream gravels or hiding under stones. Occasionally, Weingartner's cave flatworm is seen on the underside of a rock or gliding along the surface of the water.

Using variations of the method developed by Karaman and Chappuis (Camacho 1992), it is now recognized that aquatic invertebrates partition the cave stream gravel habitat. In this sampling technique, excavating a hole in a gravel bar or sampling the water from the deeper interstices of the gravel will reveal different fauna. Crustaceans like Packard's groundwater amphipod, Jeannel's groundwater ostracod, the Indiana cave copepod, and the Hid-

Figure 9.13. The largest of the invertebrate predators in the aquatic communities of Indiana caves is the cave crayfish, *Orconectes inermis.* Photo by Julian J. Lewis.

Figure 9.14. Jordan's groundwater isopod (*Caecidotea jordani*) is an example of an obligate subterranean animal that does not occur in cave streams, but rather lives in the saturated interstices of soil or gravel. Photo by Julian J. Lewis.

den Spring snail are found in this habitat, mostly to the exclusion of the animals living a few centimeters above them on the surface of the gravels.

Aquatic Non-Cave Subterranean Habitats

Unlike Indiana's caves, which have been visited by biologists for well over a century, there has been a paucity of sampling of other subterranean fauna. Eberly (1965) described Jordan's groundwater isopod (*Caecidotea jordani,* Figure 9.14) as a new species from a seep spring under the biology building on the Indiana University campus in Bloomington. The building had apparently been constructed over this seep so that its water could be used in tanks placed in the sub-basement for holding cavefish. The only other known locality of this species is from a seep emerging from parafluvial gravels along the edge of the Blue River in Crawford County (Lewis 1998). Placed nearby, a Bou-Rouch pumpwell (a sampling well driven to a depth of about a meter in the hyporheic gravels of the river) also produced Jordan's isopod, a bathynellid crustacean that remains undescribed, the Hidden Spring snail, Packard's groundwater amphipod, Yeatman's groundwater copepod, and the Converse groundwater copepod.

Lewis and Bowman (1981) examined thousands of specimens of Kendeigh's groundwater isopod collected from drain tile outlets across Iowa, Illinois, and Indiana. Although known from relatively few sites in Indiana, the range of this species is vast for a subterranean species, and it apparently has little trouble dispersing through glacial sediments. The mucronate groundwater amphipod (Figure 9.15) has a similar range and also occurs across northern Indiana.

A survey of wells on the Big Oaks National Wildlife Refuge (formerly the U.S. Army's Jefferson Proving Ground) in Jefferson, Jennings, and Ripley counties was conducted by Lewis and Lewis (2002). These wells predate the creation of the proving ground, which was decommissioned in the 1990s. All are shallow, typically 10–30 ft in depth, hand-dug, and mostly rock-walled holes penetrating the glacial drift. Sampling revealed the presence of Weingartner's cave flatworm, which is one of the only obligate subterranean species to occur in both the south-central and southeastern karst regions. This species apparently

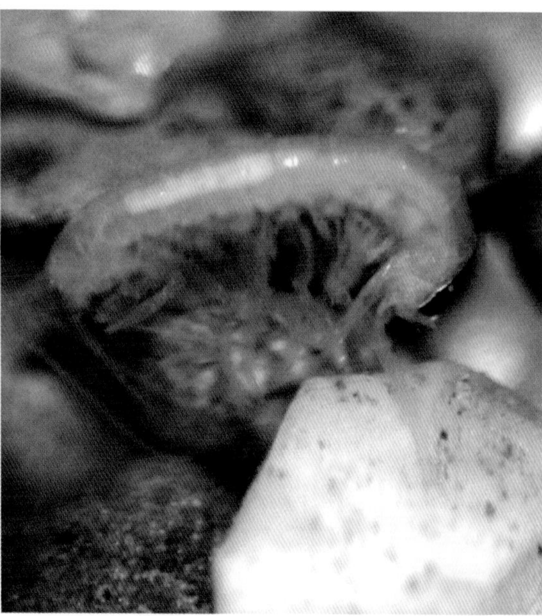

Figure 9.15. The mucronate groundwater amphipod (*Bactrurus mucronatus*) is a common inhabitant of subsurface waters in northern Indiana, where it is frequently found at the mouths of agricultural field drainage systems. Photo by Julian J. Lewis.

disperses readily through cave and non-cave groundwaters, accounting for its relatively wide distribution. To date, Salisa's groundwater copepod and Lewis's groundwater copepod are known only from the groundwaters sampled from wells at Big Oaks.

Subterranean Organisms of Indiana

Flora

Obviously plants do not grow in the depths of caves, and none have been identified in Indiana that have particular affinities to cave entrances. However, plants do play an extremely important role in cave communities. Lacking sunlight and primary plant productivity, nutrients in caves (other than any primary microbial productivity that might occur) must be imported from the surface. The in-flow of organic debris and dissolved organics is of crucial significance to the food chain of caves. The other major source of food in cave ecosystems is imported by trogloxenes. All of the trogloxenes feed in a relatively limited area around the cave entrance, and the presence of undisturbed foraging area is of great importance to animals like cave crickets and wood rats. Although plants do not grow in the darkness of caves, some surface habitats result from the influences the subterranean system has on the topography, i.e., karst. Wetlands and ponds in sinkholes are not uncommon in southern Indiana karst regions. And cave entrances can create a microclimate that benefits certain species. For example, in at least one site, air flow from a cave provides prime habitat for the rare Appalachian filmy fern. Springs and seepage from subterranean systems also provide suitable habitats for certain plants, although no Indiana species is restricted to such environments.

1800. The caves discussed here were largely overlain in presettlement times by virgin deciduous forests in the more rugged terrains, particularly in the Crawford Upland, with barrens ranging from a few to thousands of acres in the Mitchell Plain. The caves of the southeastern karst are found mostly along stream valleys that were forested in presettlement times. The plains of the glaciated areas in the northern part of the state were covered by a mixture of prairie and forest.

1900. By this time, much of the old-growth forest of southern Indiana had been harvested. The steel plow was invented in 1837, to which the prairies of the northern glacial plains subsequently succumbed. Most of the land was in farms and being cultivated by this time. The remaining forests were mostly in poor condition due to harvest, grazing, and repeated fires.

2000. Large areas covered by forest at the time of settlement are now occupied by towns, subdivisions, lawns, parking areas, roads, and a long list of other land applications that are not usable as foraging area for trogloxenes. Sedimentation created by poor land management clogs the interstices of cave stream gravels and creates mud bogs in the riparian zones.

Fish

No comprehensive study of the Indiana fish fauna in karst habitats has been conducted during any time period. Most information is based on anecdotal observations during investigations or explorations of cave or well habitats. All karst fish surveys have been to document the status of northern cavefish (Figure 9.16).

Figure 9.16. The northern cavefish (*Amblyopsis spelaea*) generally occurs in larger cave streams in Indiana's south-central karst area. Photo by Julian J. Lewis.

1800. No information.

1900. The only published study prior to 1900 was Blatchley (1897), which reported on a variety of cave fauna, including the northern cavefish.

2000. The majority of the cavefish surveys were conducted during 1900–1949, primarily by Banta (1907) and Eigenmann (1909), when the Mayfield, Donaldson, and Sibert's Well caves were surveyed. These resulted in the only record of the southern cavefish in the state. There are no additional collections of this species in Indiana, and it is probable that it never really occurred in the state. It is possible that this species was erroneously reported since it has never been collected north of the Ohio River. The most comprehensive study of the distribution of the northern cavefish was conducted by Pearson and Boston (1995). They reported the species to be stable and relatively widespread, occurring from south of the White River to the Ohio River (then south into central Kentucky).

Besides the northern cavefish, only banded sculpin has been regularly documented from Indiana caves during this period. In the main stream of Binkley Cave, Lewis and Sollman (1998) found hundreds of these fish, as well as egg masses. Applying the axiom that anything can fall into a hole, many species of fish that occur in the area accidentally find themselves in caves, including catfish, shiners, bluegills, and sunfish.

Of all the aquatic habitats in the state, the karst habitat is among the least known. This is surprising considering all of the efforts that have been made to protect and manage the northern cavefish (Woods and Inger 1957; Keith 1988; Pearson and Boston 1995). Although the northern cavefish may be a keystone indicator of karst habitats, we need to understand the ecology of the entire karst system and how other non-cavernicole species may use cave systems.

Figure 9.17. The colorful cave salamander (*Eurycea lucifuga*) is found in both caves and surface habitats in southern Indiana. Photo by Julian J. Lewis.

Amphibians and Reptiles

The cave herpetofauna of Indiana is relatively depauperate. None of the classic, highly adapted species seen elsewhere in caves, particularly salamanders, occur in the state. Most species exploiting caves restrict their activities to the twilight zone rather than to areas deep within caves. In Indiana, the aptly named cave salamander (Figure 9.17) is the only salamander that regularly penetrates the dark zone. Both the bright reddish-orange adults and the dark-gray juveniles are found in quiet pools. The longtail salamander also occurs in the dark zone of caves, frequently in the company of cave salamanders. The slimy salamander, zigzag salamander, and northern dusky salamander are examples of species found in caves proper, but usually in the twilight zone. Green salamanders have not been seen in cave systems, but individuals use rock fissures and small caves (not necessarily navigable by humans) as refugia and for nesting.

The pickerel frog is also common around cave and spring entrances where seeps occur. A variety of other frogs and toads are occasionally found in Indiana caves, where they eventually become a nutrient source in the food chain.

Cave names like Turtle Plunge Pit indicate the manner of entry and presumed fate of species like the eastern box turtle. In Fuzzy Hole, a pit with a broad open-air entrance in the Hoosier National Forest, over 20 box turtles were found during one visit; they had survived the 25-ft drop to the floor. More frequently, however, all that remain of the terrapins are their empty shells.

Snakes are not frequently observed in caves by people, but a survey by Richards (1990) revealed the presence of bones from the timber rattlesnake in 32 southern Indiana caves. At some of the sites, only the bones of a single individual were found in the entrance, suggesting casual usage of the cave. At other caves, larger numbers of bones from many individuals beyond the twilight zone indicate the use for longer-term denning. In a cave in Decatur County, the bones of at least 10 rattlesnakes, 2 copperheads, and single individuals of racer, milk snake, and northern water snake were found in a crevice about 50 ft from the entrance.

Today, the timber rattlesnake is listed as an endangered species by the state of Indiana and no recent reports have been made of them occurring in caves, although cracks and fissures are still important for use as dens. See Table H-7 for a list of cave species.

Birds

The eastern phoebe is a common nesting inhabitant of the entrance zone of Indiana caves. The turkey vulture also roosts in cave entrances in bluffs on occasion. Black vultures, which breed in southern Indiana, might also be expected.

Mammals

The numerous caves in Indiana serve at times as shelter for various species of mammals. The most common mammals in caves are bats, but white-footed mice and Allegheny wood rats are also regular inhabitants. Eight of the 12 species of bats found in Indiana are associated with caves. Red and hoary bats are solitary, foliage-living species very seldom associated with caves, although one will occasionally be trapped at a cave entrance or even be found inside. Rafinesque's big-eared bat, now a very rare visitor to Indiana, may have been a resident in the past. Many other mammals occasionally enter caves. Opossums, woodchucks, southern flying squirrels, gray foxes, and raccoons have been documented in caves (and mines) of Indiana. Bobcats probably use cave entrances, rock overhangs, and other such features as resting sites, daytime retreats, and perhaps as observation/vantage points. One of the IDNR staff members on a twenty-first-century bobcat project walked into a deep overhang and spooked a bobcat that was lying there (or perhaps it was vice versa); it was more in the twilight zone than in the deepest, darkest portion of the cave. Also, IDNR personnel periodically saw prey remains, primarily birds, near rock outcrops and overhangs; perhaps bobcats use them as protected places to consume prey. The species most closely associated with caves (and mines) of Indiana are listed in Table M-6.

1800. All of the species listed from caves (Table M-6) were present in 1800 except possibly for the gray bat and big-eared bat. The gray bat is known from Ice Age sediments from Missouri and Illinois, and there are some very large *Myotis* jaws that Richards and McDonald (1991) suspect represent the gray bat from Indiana's Ice Age. Also, it is possible that the big-eared bat was present, as Richards and McDonald (1991) indicate that *Corynorhinus* (species unknown) shows up in several cave deposits. It is not known whether it earlier formed maternity colonies in Indiana. Little brown and Indiana myotis, the eastern pipistrelle, and the big brown bat commonly hibernated in caves in 1800, the first two in large numbers and in large clusters. The southeastern myotis and silver-haired bat probably hibernated in Indiana in small numbers, but as far as we know, neither of these species has ever had young in the state. The northern myotis hibernated in fairly large numbers in certain caves, although probably out of sight in cracks. The big brown bat may have been less abundant in the state than now as most individuals presumably hibernated in hollow trees before many buildings were constructed. However, there are several good U.S. Ice Age fossil localities for the big brown bat, and there are a few undated big brown bat remains from Indiana which Ronald Richards suspects are a few thousand years old. Species present in caves in 1800 are indicated in Table M-6.

The Allegheny wood rat was found in Indiana during different times in the Ice Age and later, and undated remains have been found as far north as Owen County in the main karst area and as far north as Decatur and Shelby counties in the southeastern karst area, i.e., throughout the karst areas of Indiana.

1900. The cave species of mammals in 1900 were likely as they had been in 1800, including all the species in Table M-6 except for the gray bat, which may or may not have been accidental at that time. There have been isolated records of the gray bat, but apparently there were no maternity colonies in Indiana in the nineteenth century; the species moved into the state about 1980. It is possible that Rafinesque's big-eared bat, which is accidental now, may have been present then.

2000. There were two main changes in cave species since 1950 (Table M-6). The southeastern myotis apparently was extirpated by the 1980s. The gray bat, formerly accidental, was found in a cave-like quarry in Sellersburg, Clark County, about 1980. It increased from about 400 individuals to nearly 4,000 by the year 2000, and is still increasing (over 6,000 in 2009). It also occurs in caves at Charlestown, Clark County, and bats have been radio-tracked between the two colonies. The two are only about 5 km apart, and it is likely that only one colony with two roosts is involved. In addition, the Allegheny wood rat is becoming increasingly uncommon and now occupies a very few small caves and crevices of Harrison and Crawford counties.

The big brown bat has increased in number in recent years (Whitaker et al. 2002). Most big brown bats form maternity colonies in buildings and other human structures. A few (less than 15,000) hibernate in caves and mines, but most hibernate in the attics of buildings.

Invertebrates

Invertebrates are generally out of the scope of this work, but are quite well known from caves of Indiana thanks to the efforts of Julian Lewis, and they are included here.

1800. Undoubtedly due to its cryptic nature, nothing was recorded about the subterranean fauna of Indiana at the time of European settlement. Prior to this time, the exploration of caves by Native Americans for the mining of flint, aragonite, and epsomite is well documented in Wyandotte Cave (Munson and Munson 1990). Later, the European settlers frequented the springs emerging from caves for water, and later used them as sources of power for mills and for cool food storage. Unfortunately, none of these people left any record. The subterranean fauna of the state is presumed to have been completely intact at the time of settlement (Tables I-1, I-2).

The nineteenth century was one of discovery, in which our knowledge of the fauna was built on a foundation of several major contributions, punctuated along the way by numerous lesser accounts of new species and other records. This chronology of the invertebrate fauna of Indiana caves is more attuned to the discovery of the fauna rather than changes in their occurrence.

The majority of the early work in southern Indiana caves occurred in Wyandotte Cave or the immediate vicinity in Crawford County. Horn (1871) described the first troglobite new to science from an Indiana cave, the Wyandotte Cave ground beetle. Cope (1871a, 1871b) first referred to the northern cave crayfish in two newspaper articles, then formally described the species the following year (Cope 1872) in his paper on Wyandotte Cave and its fauna. There, he listed 18 taxa from Wyandotte Cave, in addition to the crayfish, including the Blue River cave beetle, cave dipluran, Blue River cave millipede, and the northern cavefish copepod (an ectoparasite of the northern cavefish). Hobbs and Barr (1972) concluded that Cope's (1871b) description of the type locality actually referred to nearby Sibert's Well Cave: "We descended a wall to the water, some twenty feet below the surface, and found it to communicate by a side opening, with a long, low channel, through which flowed a lively stream of very cool water."

Descriptions of two new species of arachnids from Wyandotte Cave were also published: the subterranean sheet-web spider (Emerton 1875) and Packard's cave pseudoscorpion (Hagen 1879; Figure 9.18).

Figure 9.18. Although it was one of the first troglobites to be described from Indiana, Packard's cave pseudoscorpion is extremely rare and remains poorly known.
Photo by Julian J. Lewis.

References to the Erhart cave millipede and Carter cave millipede from Indiana caves were summarized by Hoffman (1958), who found that these were taxonomic mistakes that were repeated many times (Cope 1872; McNeill 1887; Bollman 1888; Blatchley 1897). Shear (1972) finally laid a century of nomenclature errors to rest by coining the name Blue River cave millipede, *Pseudotremia indianae,* for the millipede inhabiting Wyandotte and other caves along the Blue River drainage.

Packard's (1873) note on the cave fauna of Indiana added new records for the taxa described the previous year by Cope, while at the same time generating considerable confusion in the literature. For example, Packard considered, incorrectly, the cave crayfish in Indiana to be the same as *Cambarus* (= *Orconectes*) *pellucidus* in central Kentucky. A garbled record for *Cauloxenus stygius* was reported from "a cave in Bradford, Orleans Co." It is difficult to discern if this record refers to Bradford Cave (from which no cavefish have ever been reported) or perhaps a well in the town of Orleans, Orange County—since there is no Orleans County in Indiana.

McNeill (1887) named the Bollman's cave millipede *Trichopetalum* (= *Conotyla*) *bollmani* in honor of Charles Bollman, a well-known invertebrate zoologist of the time at Indiana University, Bloomington. The species was described from Mayfield's Cave, near Bloomington in Monroe County.

Packard's (1888) treatise on the cave fauna of North America for the National Academy of Sciences was largely based on his work in Kentucky and Indiana caves during 1874 while working for the Kentucky Geological Survey. At that time, for the purpose of comparing the Indiana fauna to that of the Mammoth Cave area, Packard visited several caves in Harrison, Crawford, and Orange counties. His work was based on his personal observations and collections as well as the work of a number of other persons who directed specimens they had collected to him. Packard summarized what was known of 18 caves and their fauna in the south-central karst. The cavernicolous springtail was described as new to science from New Wyandotte Cave (the recently discovered new section) with localities including Bradford Cave (Harrison County) and caves in Kentucky. New records were also presented for many animals listed by previous workers. Packard concluded his study with an analysis of the anatomy of the brain and rudimentary eyes of troglobitic arthropods. He was the first American biologist to attempt to explore beyond the taxonomy of the animals to offer an explanation of their origins.

The single largest contribution to the knowledge of the cave fauna of Indiana during the nineteenth century resulted from an expedition through the caves of the south-central karst by the state geologist, W. S. Blatchley (1897), his son, the artist John B. Peddle, and two other men. Departing on July 4, 1896, for 5 weeks the men rode in a two-horse spring wagon, camping along the way. Starting at Porter's Cave in Owen County, they visited several caves in the vicinity of Bloomington, Monroe County, then continued into Lawrence County to Donnehue's Cave and the caves that are now part of Spring Mill State Park. From there, the band continued to Cave River valley in Washington County, and finished the journey at Wyandotte and surrounding caves in Crawford County. A total of 20 caves was visited, mapped, and sampled for fauna.

Blatchley's collections established the foundation of much of what is known of Indiana's cave fauna. Among his collections were all of the flies commonly found, including descriptions of *Blepharoptera* (= *Aecothea*) *specus* and *Limosina* (= *Spelobia*) *tenebrarum* as species new to science. He listed 13 species of beetles, including collections of eyeless, unpigmented ground beetles that he classified as *Anophthalmus* (= *Pseudanophthalmus*) *tenuis* from Wyandotte and Sibert's Well caves (Crawford County), Shiloh Cave (Lawrence County), and Mayfield's and Truett's caves (Monroe County). Several species of *Pseudanophthalmus* are now recognized from these sites (Barr 1960, see below). Other insects found by Blatchley include the cave cricket, *Ceuthophilus stygius;* and springtail, *Degeeria* (= *Sinella*) *cavernarum.*

The troglobitic millipede fauna of Indiana include two species discussed by Blatchley, the Blue River cave millipede (*Pseudotremia cavernarum* = *indianae*) listed from Wyandotte, Little Wyandotte, Marengo, and Bradford caves, and Bollman's cave millipede (*Conotyla bollmani*) from 7 caves in Owen, Monroe, and Lawrence counties.

1900. In 1907, Arthur M. Banta published what has become a classic account in the annals of cave biology in the United States, *The Fauna of Mayfield's Cave.*

Banta chose this cave because it was less than 5 mi from his laboratory at Indiana University, Bloomington. He visited the cave weekly in 1903–1904, then periodically through 1905. By the time Banta conducted his study, the fauna of the cave had already gained some notoriety. Bollman's cave millipede, *Conotyla bollmani,* was described from Mayfield's Cave by McNeill (1887) as was the subspecies *Cambarus pellucidus testii* (= *Orconectes inermis testii*) by W. P. Hay (1893). Blatchley also visited the cave in 1896 and reported 11 species. Banta prepared a detailed map of the passage with topographic overlay and collected data on temperature, moisture, light, air currents, and food sources. He found that seasonal variations in the temperature in the depths of the cave remained within a narrow range between 10.4 and 12.1°C.

At a time when Banta reported that there were 75 species recorded from about 25 Indiana caves that had been previously sampled, he reported 110 taxa from Mayfield's Cave. He assigned an ecological classification to each species he encountered. In addition to the two species mentioned above, 6 other taxa are recognized today as obligate subterranean animals: Packard's groundwater amphipod, northern cave isopod, subterranean sheet-web spider, cavernicolous springtail, Blue River cave beetle, and cave dung fly.

In 1928, Bolivar and Jeannel visited the United States to participate in the International Congress of Entomology, taking the opportunity to visit and sample caves in Indiana, Kentucky, and Virginia. In Indiana, they visited Donnelson (= Donaldson) Cave in Lawrence County, and Marengo and Wyandotte caves in Crawford County (Bolivar and Jeannel 1931). From these collections, Klie (1931) described 3 ostracod species new to science: Donaldson crayfish ostracod, *Entocythere* (= *Donnaldsoncythere*) *donnaldsonensis;* Marengo cave ostracod, *Candona* (= *Pseudocandona*) *marengoensis;* and Jeannel's cave ostracod, *Candona jeanneli.*

With the onset of World War II came great impacts to the southeastern karst landscape. In Clark County in 1941, the Indiana Army Ammunition Plant (INAAP) was constructed for the production of solid propellants used in artillery shells and naval weapons. The INAAP occupied an area of 10,649 acres and employed over 19,000 workers at the height of production.

The INAAP used a chemical process combining cellulose fibers with a nitric/sulfuric acid mixture to produce nitrocellulose. Acid waste at a pH of 2.3 was discharged at a rate of 22,500 gallons per minute to the karst at a temperature of 80° F. In addition to the nitric/sulfuric acid mixture, particulate nitrocellulose, nitrobenzene, aniline, and domestic sewage were also discharged. The acid dissolved a trench several feet deep into the limestone bedrock of Jenny Lind Run.

A cave system was entered and greatly enlarged by the acid, with sink and discharge points changing as the effects of the dissolution evolved (Wickwire 1947). The subterranean fauna of the cave was extirpated. A study at INAAP 50 years after the discontinuation of the acid discharge revealed that the physical damage to the cave system was permanent, but at least part of the biota had recovered (Lewis 1996a). Of 11 species of troglobites/stygobites known in the immediate vicinity of INAAP, 6 were found by Lewis (1996a) in the nitric acid caves: northern cave isopod, Indian cave millipede, subterranean sheet-web spider, cave dipluran, cave springtail, and cave dung fly. Present in the INAAP's CC Dryer Cave, but missing from the nitric acid cave community, were Weingartner's cave flatworm, Lewis's cave amphipod, and Indiana cave springtail. Semi-quantitative sampling with pitfall traps indicated that the communities in Jenny Lind Run and Ballistics Lab caves, both formerly inundated with the acid, were dominated by a troglophilic cave hump-backed fly, *Megaselia cavernicola.* The CC Dryer and RDX caves, unaffected by acid, were dominated by the troglobitic cave dung fly, *Spelobia tenebrarum.*

At about the same time, the U.S. Army's Jefferson Proving Ground was established, encompassing about 50,000 acres in parts of Jefferson, Jennings, and Ripley counties that were used for the testing of weapons and as a bombing range. At the Jefferson Proving Ground, the karst was bombarded with high explosives that pock-marked the landscape and collapsed parts of at least two caves. In later years, depleted uranium in armor-piercing shells was used, and quantities of this material still remain in the ecosystem. Preliminary indications are that a variety of toxic wastes have extirpated the subterranean aquatic fauna from a portion of the proving ground (Lewis and Lewis 2002). The proving ground was decommissioned in 1995 and rededicated as the Big Oaks National Wildlife Refuge, although the U.S. Air Force still utilizes part of the area as a live-fire target range.

Krekeler (1958) listed 11 species of cave beetle of the genus *Pseudanophthalmus* from Indiana, of which 8 were described as species new to science. Barr (1960), in his analysis of the cave beetles of the genus *Pseudanophthalmus* from the Mitchell Plain, differed with Krekeler's interpretation of the speciation, electing to apply a polytypic species concept rather than regarding each somewhat morphologically different cave population as genetically distinct. In Barr's scenario, most of Krekeler's species were either synonymized or reduced to subspecies, resulting in an interpretation that has remained little changed since that time. The following species were recognized by Barr (1960): (1) *P. eremita* from the type locality at Wyandotte Cave and nearby Langdon's Cave, Harrison County; (2) *P. emersoni* from Donnehue's Cave, Lawrence County; (3) *P. leonae* from Hert Hollow Cave, Lawrence County, described as new by Barr; (4) *P. tenuis,* encompassing 4 subspecies, including *P. jeanneli, P. morrisoni,* and *P. stricticollis* as interpreted by Krekeler (1958), with a range spanning Harrison to Monroe counties; (5) *P. youngi,* including *P. donaldsoni,* from Washington and Lawrence counties; and (6) *P. shilohensis,* including *P. boonensis* and *P. mayfieldensis* of Krekeler (1958), from Lawrence, Monroe, and Owen counties.

On the occasion of the state's sesquicentennial, Krekeler and Williams (1966) presented a list of 30 species of true cave animals of Indiana, adapted from Nicholas (1960). Of these, 8 have since been recognized and placed in synonymy as localized, depigmented populations of common surface species (such as the flatworm *Phagocata subterranea* and millipede *Scytonotus cavernarum*), are clearly epigean (like the amphipod *Crangonyx obliquus*), or do not occur in Indiana (the crayfish *Orconectes pellucidus*). Thus, the list accounts for 22 obligate subterranean species known from Indiana at that time.

By far, the most prominent cave invertebrate in Indiana is the northern cave crayfish, *Orconectes inermis*. In their revision of the cavernicolous *Orconectes*, Hobbs and Barr (1972) redescribed *O. inermis inermis* and *O. inermis testii*. The nominate subspecies occurs from northern Kentucky into the south-central Indiana karst, where it occurs in caves in Crawford, Harrison, Orange, Washington, and Lawrence counties. To the north, it intergrades with *O. inermis testii* in Monroe County. Hobbs and Barr (1972) presented a detailed review of the colorful literature history of the crayfish from the time of its discovery into the twentieth century. Commonly reaching a length of 50–75 mm, the northern cave crayfish is the primary invertebrate predator of Indiana aquatic cave habitats.

Between 1975 and 1982, Lewis (1983) visited 57 caves in the southeastern karst, from which 21 obligate subterranean species were listed. Over half of the taxa were endemic to the area, such as the millipede *Pseudotremia nefanda* described by Shear (1972) from Indian Cave (Clark County), and the 2 cave beetles described by Krekeler (1973), *Pseudanophthalmus chthonius* from caves in Clark, Jefferson, and Jennings counties, and *P. barri* from two caves in Clark County. Lewis (1983) expanded on theories of Barr (1967), Krekeler (1973), and Peck and Lewis (1978) to formulate an explanation of the zoogeography and evolutionary history of the Indiana cave faunas (discussed above). The subterranean isopod from caves along the northern fringe of the southeastern karst discovered by Lewis (1983) was described as the new species *Caecidotea rotunda* by Bowman and Lewis (1984).

In an article primarily concerned with the status of the northern cavefish, Keith (1988) noted that two caves from which the fish were formerly known had been partially or completely destroyed in quarry mining operations. Numerous caves in Indiana (e.g., Vowell Cave) have been discovered and opened in quarries, and many have been impacted.

In a study of the Lost River area for the U.S. Army Corps of Engineers in connection with the possible construction of a flood control dam, the cave fauna of the area was investigated by Lewis (1994). During this project were found 21 obligate subterranean species in the caves of the Lost River drainage, which formed the foundation of this cave system as one of Indiana's hotspots of global subterranean biodiversity (Table I-3).

The subterranean fauna of the southeastern karst belt was again sampled in 1995 by Lewis, who visited 24 caves in and near the Crosley State Fish and Wildlife Area in Jennings County. The following year, Lewis (1996b) visited 55 sites, including 38 caves in Clark and Floyd counties. The most diverse terrestrial cave faunas were found in those caves nearest the Illinoian glacial maximum in Clark County (Table I-4). Indian Cave, formerly with the greatest species richness of any cave in the southeastern karst, was found to have been badly contaminated by domestic septic waste. The stream in Biehle Cave, the most prominent cave in the Crosley Wildlife Area, was found to be similarly polluted due to runoff from a farm animal feeding lot.

In a 3-year bioinventory of subterranean habitats of the Blue River area for the Nature Conservancy, Lewis (1998) sampled 224 sites, including 187 caves and a number of springs, wells, and drain tiles. A total of 358 taxa were recorded, including 66 obligate subterranean species. Many subterranean species new to science were described as an outgrowth of this project, including the Conservation cave millipede (Hoffman and Lewis 1997), Barr's cave amphipod, Indiana cave amphipod (Zhang and Holsinger 2003), Lewis's cave springtail, and Black Medusa cave springtail (Christiansen and Bellinger 1998).

2000. By the end of the twentieth century, the subterranean fauna of the state was reasonably well known and mostly intact despite the sweeping changes in the surface landscape. Almost none of the original forest or prairie that once existed had survived, but the subterranean biota demonstrated a remarkable resilience. As cave exploration became an increasingly popular pastime, vandalism grew to the point that few decorated caves remained intact unless protected from the public. The large-scale destruction of caves and karst was introduced to Indiana as the lands were utilized for military, industrial, and mining applications.

Over 30 years of sampling in hundreds of Indiana caves by Lewis (1983, 1994, 1995, 1996a, 1996b, 1998; Lewis and Lewis 2002; Lewis et al. 2004) has resulted in the discovery of dozens of additional species new to science, as well as the establishment of the ranges of many more. Table I-1 lists all of the obligate subterranean animals recorded from Indiana, of which 69 are known from the south-central karst, 24 from the southeastern karst, and 14 from non-cave groundwater habitats.

The largest change in the fauna of Indiana caves has been the introduction of exotic species. Included among the invasive species recorded are earthworms *Dendrodrilus rubidus, Aporrectodea caliginosa, A. trapezoides, Octolasion tyrtaeum;* millipedes *Oxidus gracilis* and *Ophyiulus gracilis;* terrestrial isopods *Armadillidium nasatum, Porcellionides pruinosis,* and *Haplophthalmus danicus;* and springtail *Entomobrya socia*. It is impossible to date the time or place at which these animals arrived in the United States, although Christiansen (personal communication 2004) noted that *Entomobrya socia* first appeared in collections in the 1970s and probably originated in Asia. The millipede *Oxidus gracilis* can become so dense in caves as to nearly cover the walls and floor and has been found in significant numbers nearly a mile from an entrance in Binkley Cave.

The subterranean fauna of the Big Oaks National Wildlife Refuge was sampled by Lewis and Lewis (2002). Over 30 caves and a dozen wells were sampled there, resulting in the discovery of 83 species (68 of which were invertebrates). Of these, 20 were believed to be obligate subterranean taxa. From this material, Reid (2004) described Salisa's groundwater copepod from a well along Otter Creek, Lewis's groundwater copepod from a well in the Graham and Big creek drainages, and the Indiana cave copepod from gravel interstices in Henry Dilk Falls Cave. In addition, the Converse groundwater copepod was described from the Bou-Rouch pumpwell collections made by Lewis (1998) on a gravel bar along the Blue River in Crawford County.

Koenemann and Holsinger (2001) had the dubious distinction of describing the reclusive groundwater amphipod, *Bactrurus cellulanus,* the first Indiana species to be extirpated from its only known locality at the time of its discovery. The type locality of this species was a seep stream in the basement of Jordan Hall, Indiana University, Bloomington. During a visit to this locality in 1980 to look for Jordan's groundwater isopod, Lewis (1988) found that the habitat had been poisoned with termiticides and no animals were present. Frank Young, on the faculty of the Biology Department, donated a vial of crustaceans that he had collected in 1962, which included the isopod as well as the amphipods. They were the only known specimens of the reclusive groundwater amphipod.

In 2000–2004, Lewis et al. (2004) made 258 trips to 124 caves, springs, wells, and abandoned mines in the Hoosier National Forest for the purpose of sampling the fauna. A total of 54 obligate subterranean (troglobite or stygobite) species were discovered. The karst of the national forest spans an area from the Ohio River in Crawford County to the Deam Wilderness in Monroe County. Within this region, 75 cavernicolous species of significant global rarity were found, including nearly 40 species that were new to science. A high degree of endemicity was found in the area due to the fragmentation of the karst on the western edge of the Crawford Upland, leading to rare species, like Reynold's cave millipede (Lewis 2003), that have been found in only a single cave despite intense searching. A karst island with a unique fauna was created in Monroe County associated with the Mt. Carmel fault zone. Although only a handful of caves are known from this small, isolated karst area, several endemic species have been discovered there, including the Patton Cave pseudoscorpion (*Apochthonius* undescribed species).

Over three-fourths of the species richness of Indiana caves is composed of non-obligate cavernicolous invertebrates, species that are not limited to underground habitats, i.e., troglo/stygophiles. A list of selected taxa is presented in Table I-2, although many more have been found in the caves of the state. Some of these species were first discovered and described from Indiana caves, e.g., the cave funnel-web spider and Stygian rove beetle.

As work continues, the ecological status of some species previously believed to be troglobites is changing. Salisa's cave millipede, *Pseudotremia salisae,* has now been identified from a cave in southern Illinois and from a surface collection in Ohio (Shear et al. 2007). Likewise, specimens of ant beetles found in the twenty-first century in southern Indiana caves compare favorably with the type specimens of *Batrisodes hairstoni* collected from a surface habitat in Clark State Forest. This indicates that Krekeler's cave ant beetle is neither a distinct species nor a troglobite (Chandler and Lewis 2008).

As noted above, some of the troglophiles are of significance to the import of nutrients into cave ecosystems. Cave crickets like *Ceuthophilus stygius* and *C. meridionalis* leave the caves to feed on the surface, where they forage within a radius typically of 100–200 m of the entrance.

Although they do not appear to be morphologically adapted to caves, the gray-handed and Lewis's cave pseudoscorpions are known only from caves in the south-central karst. It seems likely that searching sinkhole floors and other sheltered environments in the southern Indiana karst will reveal other localities for these species. The only known Indiana localities for the southeastern wandering spider and southeastern sac-web spider are caves in the south-central karst.

Part 3.
Man-Made Habitats: Changes over Two Centuries

In this part, we will evaluate flora and wildlife's use of two categories of man-made habitats, agricultural and developed lands. They can hardly be ignored. More than half of Indiana's land is devoted to agriculture, and the quantity was even higher a century ago. The conversion of prior habitat to agriculture has had huge impacts on flora and wildlife, and the present extent and types of agricultural habitats strongly influence wild species. Developed lands consist of residential, commercial, and industrial areas, transportation systems, etc. Such lands include urban forests and golf courses, which support some wildlife populations; structures such as cell and communications towers, which are death traps for migrating birds; and a vast network of paved roads, railroads, utility lines, and rights-of-way, the effects of which extend well beyond the strips of land they occupy. A third significant man-made habitat consists of the large artificial grasslands on reclaimed coal mines in southwestern Indiana, which date to the 1950s. We treat this habitat in chapter 5.

Merging man-made and natural habitats. Photo by IDNR–*Outdoor Indiana* magazine.

Figure 10.1. Benton County farm with freshly plowed field. Photo by Scott Johnson.

Agricultural Habitats 10

The European settlement of Indiana during the agrarian heyday of U.S. history meant that over 90% of Indiana's forests, prairies, and wetlands were converted to agricultural lands by the early twentieth century (Figure 10.1). A substantial amount has since been abandoned and become reforested, but not nearly to the extent that this has happened in the New England states. Indiana's gentle topography and rich soils (especially in the glaciated half of the state) continue to make it productive farmland.

The practice of agriculture and its impacts on adjacent natural lands and wildlife have changed enormously over 200 years. Some sense of this is provided by Kohnke and Robertson's (1966) vivid portrait of the state's first 150 years of agriculture. They describe a typical farm in "the pioneer period" (1816–1865), "the horse and buggy period" (1866–1915), and the "industrialized agriculture era" (1916–1966).

1800. Native Americans were practicing extensive agriculture in Indiana at the time of European settlement. Crop fields were near villages, which in turn were near large streams such as the Wabash River. For example, the central Wabash area near Fort Ouiatenon was home to about 15,000 Native Americans in the late 1700s (Whicker 1916). Crops were grown in naturally open spaces, probably maintained by fire, or in clearings made in the forest. Old clearings were abandoned for newly cleared land as fertility was depleted, leaving forests in all stages of regrowth. Thus, Native Americans had an impact on the seral stage and composition of Indiana's forest through their agricultural activities.

The main crop, corn, was planted in fields as large as 400–500 acres. It was usually planted in hills or rows and kept free of weeds through cultivation. In some cases, only the hills were cultivated with the intervening land left unbroken, while in others intercrops of squash and beans were planted between the hills of corn (Latta 1938).

The first European settlers in Indiana, the French, arrived in the early 1700s. They established trading posts, mainly for furs, near the Indian villages of Kekionga (Fort Wayne), Ouiatenon (near Lafayette), and Chippecoke (Vincennes) (Barnhart and Riker 1971). Vincennes was the first such settlement in Indiana Territory. These families kept large numbers of cattle and hogs in confined pastures and grew wheat, corn, rice, cotton, and tobacco on land close to the fort. In the early 1800s, sheep and horses were found mostly near the larger settlements at Vincennes and Harmony. In 1816, there were 700–800 acres of fenced cropland on the first and second bottoms of the Wabash River near New Harmony. Vineyards were established around 1815 near New Harmony.

The first land purchase from the Native Americans in Indiana Territory occurred in 1795 as part of the Treaty of Greenville. This included a small portion of southeastern Indiana and 16 other small tracts at portages and along river routes, including the Wabash-Maumee portage, Ouiatenon, Clark's Grant (the site of present-day Clarksville), and the Vincennes Tract (land around the existing village of Vincennes). European settlers were already clearing lands adjacent to the Ohio River prior to the Greenville Treaty. The total area of Indiana Territory that was occupied by these settlers outside the Greenville line is unknown, but was relatively small.

The conversion of forest habitats to cropland initially occurred in waves as settlers occupied and then abandoned lands. The first wave of European settlers occupied unpurchased land, built log cabins and cleared small areas of forest for corn and vegetables, and subsisted largely on wild animals. These settlers moved to unoccupied lands as the population increased. The second wave of European settlers expanded the cleared lands of the first wave and eventually moved to occupy new land as the third, more-permanent occupiers of the land moved in.

1900. Following almost a century of forest clearing and swamp draining, the state had become intensely agricultural, with 94% of the land in farms, a total of 21.6 million acres. No natural region was spared: the percentage of land classified as farmland ranged from 81% to 96%, and most of that was "improved," i.e., producing crops or in rotation (Tables G-2, G-3). Of the 16.7 million acres of improved farmland (73% of the state), some 11.4 million acres produced crops that year, primarily corn (4.5 million), wheat (2.9 million), hay (2.4 million), and oats (1.0 million; Tables G-4, G-5). Among the 20 or so minor crops, vegetables (184,000 acres), rye (44,000 acres), barley (26,000 acres), and buckwheat (9,000 acres) were common (Table G-6). The remaining improved farmland (5.3 million acres) was in crop rotation, either fallow or planted to legumes. Our sources for data in 1900, the U.S. Department of Agriculture and Indiana Department of Statistics (see footnotes to cited tables), do not identify the habitat types making up the 4.9 million acres of unimproved farmland. It would likely have been in land too rough to hay, in wetlands, and in forest. Wetlands and prairie would have predominated in the northern counties, forest in the hilly lands of south-central Indiana.

Figure 10.2. Typical Indiana farmland. Photo by Scott Johnson.

There were slightly more than 220,000 farms in the state at this time, a number better comprehended as nearly 2,400 per county. The average farm size was 97 acres. This average varied modestly across the 10 natural regions, from 85 to 139 acres per farm.

2000. Though still the dominant land use in the state (Figure 10.2), farmland dropped substantially to 66% of the state's acreage in 2002, a total of 15.1 million acres (Table G-2). The decline occurred mainly in southern Indiana in the 1920s–1940s. Badly eroded lands there were abandoned and transferred to public ownership, notably becoming Hoosier National Forest and several state parks. This is reflected in the low percentage of county land in farms in the Shawnee Hills region (35%), compared to 76% in the Central Till Plain region (Table G-2).

In 2002, over 83% (12.6 million acres) of classified farmland was cropped (Map 10.1). There were a little over 60,000 farms, less than a third as many as a century earlier, while average farm size had more than doubled, to 250 acres on a statewide basis. Farms were more specialized, and rotation involved switching the crop to be harvested, with fallow years rarely occurring. More than 86% of cropland was either in soybeans, introduced about 1920, or corn (5.8 and 5.4 million acres, respectively; Table G-4). Wheat declined by 90%, to approximately 300,000 acres, and oats declined even more dramatically, from approximately a million acres to slightly under 10,000 (Tables G-4, G-5). Oats, grown as fodder for horses, were much less needed on farms, and Indiana's market share for the hard-seed wheat used in bread had been lost to the northern Great Plains states (Kohnke and Robertson 1966). Hay was produced on about 600,000 acres, roughly a quarter of the acreage used in 1900. New crops included popcorn (69,207 acres) and mint for oils (11,587 acres), as well as soybeans (Table G-6). Rye, barley, and buckwheat were still grown as minor crops. Some 2.1 million farmland acres, consisting mostly of woodland and pasture, were not cropped in 2002 (Table G-3).

About 42% of the farmland was in no-till in 2002. In this farming practice, the land is not plowed and turned over before or after harvesting, but instead is pierced by machinery that makes narrow slits in the earth, in which seeds are planted. The fields are still artificially fertilized, are traversed by heavy machinery, and may have herbicides applied, but soil erosion is reduced. Furthermore, they usually have more vegetative cover in the winter and spring, either in the form of crop residue (for example, corn stubble) or weeds, which can be important for seed-eating birds and mammals (Castrale 1985).

The remainder of this chapter mostly features the vertebrate animals and native plants that use and thrive in agricultural habitats. However, agriculture's dominant presence has many effects on the wildlife species that require natural habitats and are not pre-adapted to exploit agricultural lands. First and foremost, a great deal of natural habitat (forest, grasslands, and wetlands) has simply been lost by conversion to farmlands. However, it is important to remember that agricultural land could be restored to natural habitat much more easily than could urban and suburban development. Second, the remaining areas of natural habitat are much more patchily distributed than in presettlement times, and patches are typically separated by agricultural or developed

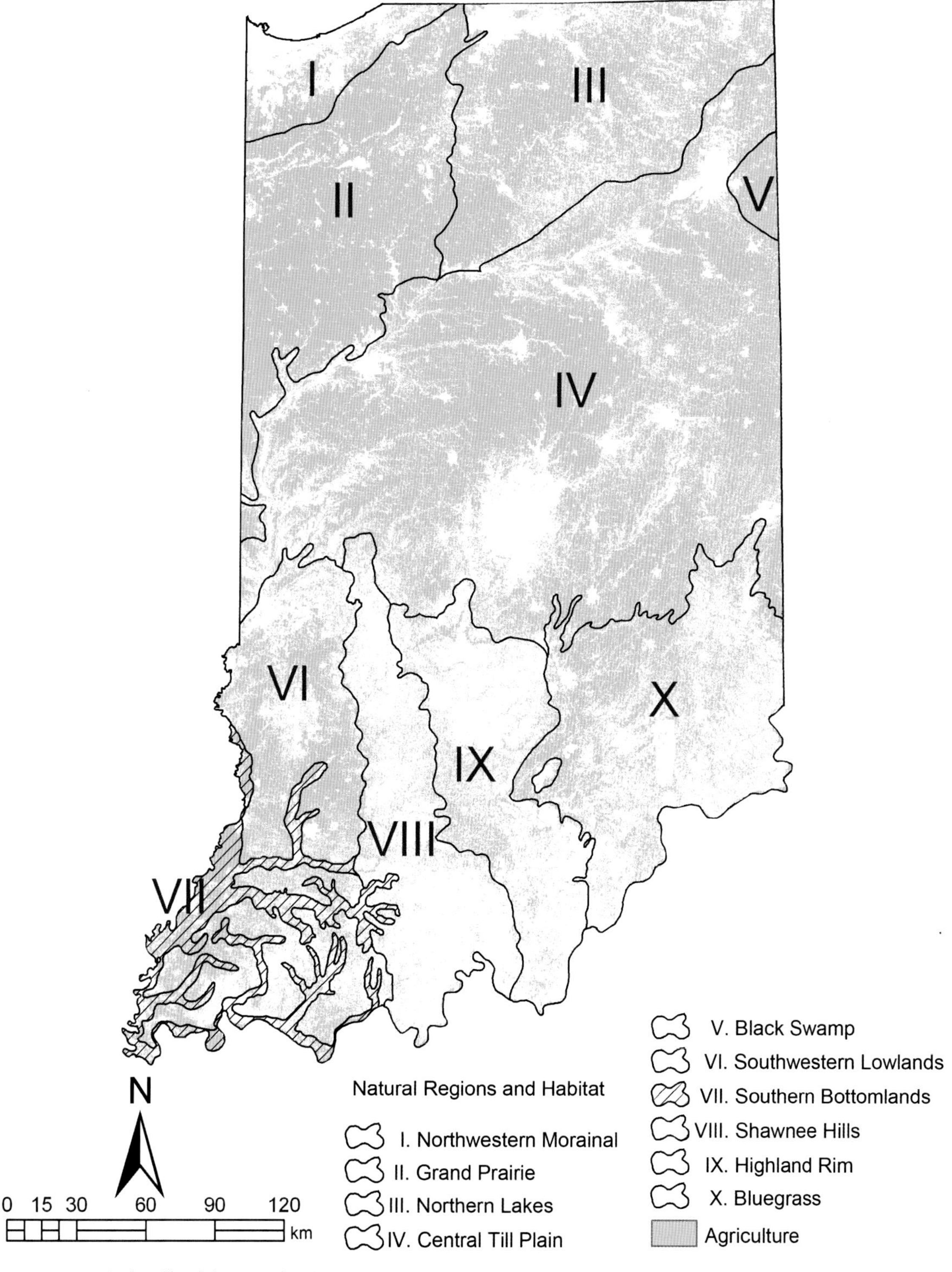

Map 10.1. Agricultural lands by natural region.

lands. It is easy to confuse the effects of habitat loss and of fragmentation (Fahrig 2003).

Among its effects, the fragmentation of natural habitat puts different habitats close together (Figure 10.3). Ecotones (transitional areas between habitats) are often species-rich, and many animals appear to do well in landscapes full of such edges. The benefits of edges were promoted by wildlife managers for many years. Enthusiasm for edges has been tempered by growing awareness of some negative aspects, such as increasing the risk of cowbirds laying eggs in nests of forest birds, or invasion by exotic plants. Thus, the effects are mixed. In the common case of woods bordering cultivated fields, the fields provide rich feeding sites for many woodland mammals and birds (e.g., deer, turkey, mice, sparrows) during crop growth and after harvest. However, harvested fields provide little cover from predators for the mice and sparrows. To cite an example of mixed benefits involving insects, native bees that forage mainly in woods are opportu-

Figure 10.3. Fragmented landscape. Photo by Scott Johnson.

nistic enough to visit spring-flowering weeds in agricultural fields (Dailey and Scott 2006), but the vast field acreage is probably not hospitable for nesting, even for the ground-nesting bee species.

Flora

Several species of plants occur predominantly in agricultural habitats. Typically, these are annuals (as are the crop plants themselves), whose life cycles require frequent disturbance of the substrate, or perennials, whose environment is maintained by mowing, which does not turn over soil.

1800. Most contemporary agricultural weeds in Indiana are introductions from other continents. Although the majority of them arrived with Europeans, some (e.g., carpet weed) may have moved here from Central and South America (Gleason and Cronquist 1991), perhaps with the agricultural activities of Native Americans. In Indiana, carpet weed is found almost exclusively in highly disturbed soils, a condition not common in 1800, except in croplands maintained by Native Americans or in areas of natural erosion. Other species found in early 1800 agricultural sites were the native pioneering ones, and included purslane, charlock, spear grass, little-leaf buttercup, Virginia rockcress, common evening primrose, annual foxtail, horseweed, fall panicum, common ragweed, spotted creeping spurge, little barley, hairy aster, and common pepper cress.

1900. By this time, the composition of agricultural weeds had changed to include Eurasian species. With the increase in commerce within North America as well as with other continents, new plants appeared across the Indiana landscape. Some of these introductions were possibly intentional, such as black mustard, while most were not, usually coming in as contaminated seed with other agricultural products. Some of the more prominent species are field garlic, hairy crabgrass, prickly lettuce, pigeon grass, common morning glory, and common dandelion.

2000. Weeds continue to be a major issue in the agricultural landscape, and the majority have been established in Indiana for a century or more. However, an increasing number of species have established or become much more common since 1900. Some of these include giant foxtail, Johnson grass, henbit, purple dead nettle, and smooth field sow thistle. The native butterweed now commonly colonizes agricultural fields, especially in the southern half of the state.

Amphibians and Reptiles

Herpetofauna are generally not tolerant of the various types of intensive farming practiced today. As a consequence, encounters with species in such areas are largely incidental. Nevertheless, there are several amphibian and reptile species that may persist where less-manipulated refugia are interspersed with agricultural fields. In areas with more extensive refugia, or where farming is less intensive, more species can be found. Hardier species such as American and Fowler's toads and various garter snakes are capable of utilizing these areas. Northern water snakes to the north and the conspecific midland water snake to the south do quite well in drainage ditches in agricultural areas. Painted and snapping turtles also make their way up these ditches and along streams in agricultural areas, as do the green frog and bullfrog. However, by and large, the species encountered in most agricultural areas are simply incidental visitors from more suitable habitat nearby. The species most likely to tolerate agriculture are shown in Table H-8.

Birds

At least 68 bird species currently make (or formerly made) significant use of agricultural habitats (Table B-6). Most published data and recent observations are for row crop and cereal grain fields and open (not confined) feedlots. Orchards, during their nineteenth-century heyday as a bird habitat, attracted many species that are absent from crop fields. The main use of crop fields is for feeding, especially when fields are in stubble from the fall to the late spring; however, insect pests of corn and soybeans attract birds in the summer. A wide taxonomic range of birds use farm fields (e.g., waterfowl, raptors, crows, and sparrows), and there are striking seasonal changes. Quantitative surveys with Indiana data include Castrale (1985) and Best et al. (1997, 1998).

Few birds breed in agricultural fields, but horned larks do so in Indiana by commencing in March, well before tilling and planting. The relatively bare stubble habitat attracts them and other birds that nest in open situations with little or no cover, such as killdeer, mourning dove, vesper sparrow, and (locally in the west and north) lark sparrow. In northwestern Indiana, 20 species commonly visit fields for feeding or other purposes during the summer (Best et al. 1997); in southeastern Indiana, 11 species do so (Castrale 1985). Besides the species listed above, these include northern bobwhite, American crow, barn swallow, American robin, red-winged blackbird, common grackle, and brown-headed cowbird.

In the winter, the characteristic small birds of agricultural fields are horned larks, Lapland longspurs, and (in the snowiest weather) snow buntings. American tree sparrows, dark-eyed juncos, and other sparrows use crop fields less than old fields or grasslands because of a need for cover from predators; however, they forage diligently in fields at the forest-bordered margins. Canada geese and mallards are the main waterfowl in crop fields, which are also important for the relatively rare tundra swan, the (reintroduced) trumpeter swan, the greater white-fronted goose, and the snow goose. Red-tailed hawks, rough-legged hawks, American kestrels, and barn and great horned owls are the primary raptors. Three important game birds feed in crop fields but need adjacent grassland or forest for cover (ring-necked pheasant, wild turkey, northern bobwhite). All three species benefit from well-established fence rows that provide winter and nesting cover. As farm field size has increased, the attractiveness of farm fields for these species has declined. Rock pigeon and mourning dove feed on grain in fields, as do American crows. Very large flocks of American crows use stubble fields as well as other rural habitats during winter days and roost in cities such as Terre Haute (see the Audubon Society's Christmas bird count website, http://www.audubon.org/bird/cbc, Terre Haute count circle). American robins are common in wet fields in early spring. Three nonnative species, the starling, house sparrow, and house finch, forage in feedlots or fields near farm buildings.

One native casualty of the changes in agricultural practices in Indiana has been the barn owl. Barn owls thrived on small, nonmechanized farms, which were common during the late 1800s and early 1900s. They nested primarily in barns, silos, or other farm structures and used hay fields, pastures, wet meadows, and small grain fields as rodent-hunting sites. Barn owls were added to the state's endangered species list in 1984.

Several icterids (blackbirds, grackles, cowbirds, meadowlarks, bobolinks) use crop fields. Brown-headed cowbirds have the strongest year-round preference for the habitat. Large flocks of red-winged blackbirds and common grackles descend on fields in the winter, and both species breed along their edges (blackbirds in grassy strips, grackles in the tree-line belts). Eastern meadowlarks feed in stubble fields in the winter, and breed or at least sing in winter wheat fields in the late spring. Bobolinks use cereal grain fields in migration in the first half of May, when winter wheat is 2–3 ft high. The European starling, a non-icterid, visits fields year-round to feed and, being more hardy, is more abundant in the winter than are blackbirds, grackles, and meadowlarks in the agricultural lands of central and northern Indiana.

During migration, stubble fields attract some interesting species, mainly in the spring when they are likely to be relatively bare. Migrant shorebirds include Wilson's snipe, which rests in fields and ditches during the day, and American golden-plover, especially in northwestern counties along the Illinois border. The agricultural fields of Benton and White counties are prime stopover habitat from late March to early May for golden-plovers on their long journey from South American pampas to Arctic tundra (Greenberg 2005). Adapting to major landscape changes in the region, they now mainly use untilled soybean fields, whereas a few decades ago they used heavily grazed fields (which are uncommon now), and before extensive European settlement, they used prairies in the same area. Other shorebirds also forage and rest in agricultural fields, especially in or around wet patches, including common species such as pectoral sandpiper and lesser yellowlegs and rarer ones such as buff-breasted and Baird's sandpipers (Table B-6).

Sandhill cranes forage frequently in corn stubble fields on their fall and early spring migration. Agricultural fields near wetlands (where cranes roost) are most likely to be used, often by flocks of hundreds. Cranes spend months using such fields near their prime fall stopover site, the Jasper-Pulaski State Fish and Wildlife Area.

Another noteworthy migrant is Smith's longspur, which travels in small flocks in April through west-central Indiana (Parke and Montgomery counties) along the eastern edge of their northward migration path. Vesper and savannah sparrows as well as horned larks occur at the same time, often in weedy foxtail patches in the stubble. Wet fields attract American robin and American pipit. In Butler's (1898) time, the pipit was "familiar to every plowman in early spring." By comparison, the pipit is not commonly reported now, perhaps because little birding is done in the habitat. Northern harriers and short-eared owls regularly hunt or rest in crop fields, but are much more common in grasslands, where barn owls also hunt.

Other species make regular or occasional use of farm fields but are more characteristic of forest or brush and are omitted from Table B-6 (somewhat arbitrarily). For example, from the fall to the spring, downy woodpeckers forage on corn stalks, and northern flickers forage on the ground in stubble. Dark-eyed juncos, American tree sparrows, northern cardinals, and mixed flocks of chickadees and titmice venture into the edges of fields. Hedgerows on farms support northern mockingbird, brown thrasher, and yellow-breasted chat.

Some issues affecting bird use of agricultural habitats are the present pattern of intensive and extensive row crop planting, which leaves only thin strips of grass or trees along the margins; pesticide use; landscape composition (proximity of crop fields to forest, wetlands, grasslands); fallow land; and the Conservation Reserve Program. Best et al. (1995) provide an excellent review of these issues in Iowa, and Warner (1993) discusses the effects of changing agricultural practices on grassland birds in Illinois. Bird use of CRP grasslands is treated under grassland habitat in this book (chapter 5).

Mammals

A number of mammal species may occur in agricultural habitats, but the 29 species in Table M-7 are, or were, the ones most closely associated with these habitats.

The species of mammals vary greatly depending on the type of agricultural use. Deer, raccoons, muskrats, groundhogs, squirrels (fox and gray), and cottontail rabbits will enter row crop fields and feed on the plants. Small mammals found in these fields are mainly the prairie deer mouse and the house mouse, the latter only if adequate ground cover (grasses and forbs) is present. If not, then only the prairie deer mouse is likely. The main predators are the red fox, coyote, and weasel. Skunks and eastern moles often take up residence around farms.

In situations with extensive herbaceous vegetation (especially grasses), a much different fauna may be present, including meadow voles, meadow jumping mice, shrews, and possibly bog lemmings. That community is discussed more fully in chapter 5. All of the species in Table M-7 were present in 1800, but the white-tailed deer had disappeared by 1900. It was reintroduced starting in the 1930s and had spread to all Indiana counties by the latter part of the twentieth century.

Sub-Habitats

Row Crops: Corn, Soybeans

1800. Row crops were limited to a few hundred acres around the villages of Native Americans, permanent settlements such as New Harmony, and along the Ohio River where European settlers were establishing farms. Corn, hemp, rye, wheat, flax, and tobacco were being grown on the first bottom of the Wabash River near New Harmony by 1815. Maize (*Zea mays,*

Figure 10.4. Soybeans, corn, and flatland woods. Photo by John Castrale.

Figure 10.5. Corn. Photo by John Castrale.

Figure 10.6. Corn stubble. Photo by Terry L. Castor.

Figure 10.7. Soybeans. Photo by John Castrale.

early version of modern corn), melons, and pumpkins were cultivated by the Wea and Piankashaw tribes on the Wea Plains along the Wabash River in central Indiana (Barnhart and Riker 1971). Many large Native American villages were greatly diminished by 1800 due to military campaigns. For example, General James Wilkinson destroyed 400–500 acres of corn, gardens, and villages (and killed many of the people) on the Wea Plains in 1791 (Whicker 1916).

1900. Corn was grown on 4.5 million acres. Across the natural regions, the percentage of acreage devoted to it ranged from 17% of improved farmland in the Highland Rim region to 35% in the Grand Prairie region (Table G-4). Soybeans were not grown in Indiana until the early 1900s (Figure 10.4).

2000. Corn was grown on 5.4 million acres (Figures 10.5, 10.6), occupying 25–54% of the cropland. Soybeans (Figure 10.7) were grown on 5.8 million acres, occupying between 28% and 51% of the cropland in different regions. These two crops are typically alternated in successive years.

FLORA. Species found in this environment have life cycles that are attuned to the annual disturbance created by plowing. They are typically non-native species, but a few natives occur. In 1800, most "weeds" were native species, but by 1900 numerous non-natives were likely present, as in 2000. Some of the typical introduced plants include henbit, field cress, yellow rocket, shepherd's purse, sand croton, spear grass, field garlic, common chickweed, rough amaranth, curly dock, purslane, hairy crabgrass, quackgrass, buttonweed (*Abutilon*), flower-of-an-hour, pigeon grass, field thistle, purslane, speedwell, and butterweed. By 2000, some additional weeds on the scene include, among others, purple dead nettle, giant foxtail, musk bristle thistle, Johnson grass, and smooth field sow thistle. See Table P-11 for a list of species of fields with row crops of corn and soybeans.

AMPHIBIANS AND REPTILES. No herpetofauna, except possibly toads, tolerate row crop habitats sufficiently to reside there for long. Any individuals observed are best considered transients.

BIRDS. The general comments at the beginning of this chapter apply primarily to row crops and are repeated here in an abbreviated form. The only common nesters are horned lark (before planting), killdeer, mourning dove, vesper sparrow, and red-winged blackbird. The relatively rare lark sparrow nests in sandy, drier fields on the western edge of the state. Herbivorous insects on crop plants provide a potentially large food resource during the summer for birds breeding adjacent to or in crop fields, although they come with a danger of pesticide consumption (Best 2001). The use of row cropland by birds increases and diversifies taxonomically when fields are in stubble or no-till conditions, from the early fall to the late spring. Certain migrant and wintering waterfowl, raptors, shorebirds, pheasants, turkeys, doves, sparrows, and icterids (i.e., most of the species in Table B-6) feed in fields during those months.

Some differences in use of corn and soybean fields emerged in a Scott County study (Castrale 1985). In the winter, more individuals and species used corn than soybean residue fields. Horned lark and kill-

Figure 10.8. Wheat field. Photo by John O. Whitaker, Jr.

deer preferred the more open soybean residue fields to corn residue fields. Species more common in corn residue were mourning dove, American crow, dark-eyed junco, northern cardinal, eastern meadowlark, and song sparrow.

MAMMALS. The most abundant mammals in row crops are the prairie deer mouse and the house mouse. The prairie deer mouse remains there all year, using the soil as cover. The house mouse is there only when there is adequate ground cover, mostly in the form of heavy grass between the rows and of leaves when plowing or harvesting removes the cover. The white-footed mouse is often found near row crop edges, including young individuals moving through or venturing into that area. Raccoons, deer, foxes, woodchucks, and other species enter row crops, especially corn, to feed (Table M-7). Even muskrats do so, when the corn is near water. Coyotes, deer, and other species use corn fields for cover, and for sites to avoid disturbance by humans, especially later in the growing season when the corn is tall. Since few people willingly enter standing corn prior to harvest, corn fields represent the perfect resting cover for coyotes during the day.

Cereal Grains

1800. Wheat and rye were grown around European settlements in 1800. See discussions above of agriculture in this era.

1900. Wheat (2.9 million acres) and oats (1 million acres) were major crops in 1900 (Tables G-5, G-4). Rye, barley, and buckwheat were grown on 78,301–90,902 acres across the state (the number varies depending on which census is used; Table G-6). Wheat acreage ranged from 6,051 acres in the Northwestern Morainal region to over 1.1 million acres in the Central Till Plain region. Oats varied from 7,741 acres in the Southern Bottomlands region to 326,284 acres in the Central Till Plain region.

2000. All cereal crops covered 619,171 acres in 2002 (Tables G-4, G-5, G-6). Wheat (planted in early winter and harvested in May or June) was grown on 299,873 acres and oats were grown on 11,015 acres. Barley, rye, and buckwheat were grown on the remaining 2,401 acres. Wheat acreage ranged from 3,343 in the Northwestern Morainal region to 109,069 acres in the Central Till Plain region. Oats were primarily grown in the Grand Prairie, Northern Lakes, and Central Till Plain regions.

FLORA. Essentially the same plants that occupy corn and soybean fields also occur in cereal grain fields, except the numbers are perhaps less, as the grain crops are typically established in the fall and early spring, precluding heavy germination of winter annual weeds. Corn cockle was formerly much more common but is now of sparse occurrence in grain fields. Charles Deam reported it as more common before his *Flora of Indiana* (1940), but it apparently declined because of improved threshing machines that better separated the grain from the corn cockle seeds. See Table P-11 for a list of species of fields with cereal grains.

Some weed species have become widespread and troublesome. For instance, the occurrence of butter-

Figure 10.9. Vineyard. Photo by IDNR–*Outdoor Indiana* magazine.

weed has increased dramatically since the 1980s; before that, it was scarce and widely scattered. Butterweed can totally cover huge acreages of crop fields in the spring, turning them a golden yellow before spring tilling.

AMPHIBIANS AND REPTILES. Given that cereal crop fields mimic certain attributes of old-field habitats, some herpetofauna may use them. However, under most circumstances, herpetofauna will not stay for long. American and Fowler's toads, eastern garter snake, and racers are among the more likely species to be observed. Unfortunately, grain fields are likely habitat sinks during harvest, as animals that have moved into them likely suffer heavy losses from direct mortality, subsequent exposure, and predation.

BIRDS. Cereal grains (e.g., winter wheat) attract grassland birds that rarely use corn or soybean fields. These include both obligate grassland species (which are restricted to grasslands, e.g., eastern meadowlark, bobolink, dickcissel, savannah sparrow, grasshopper sparrow) and facultative species (which use other habitats, e.g., red-winged blackbird). Barn owls, which hunt voles in pasture grasslands, might forage there. Such fields are likely to be unproductive nesting habitats (sinks) because of disturbance during nesting and grain harvest in the early summer. The grassland birds attracted to them are more common and successful in less-disturbed grassland habitats, such as CRP fields and reclaimed mines (see chapter 5). We know of no Indiana studies of bird use of winter wheat fields, which is unfortunate since it is an extensive habitat.

In Iowa, cereal grains and row crops had similarly low abundances of breeding birds (Best et al. 1995). Only 2 species were common or abundant in cereal grains (red-winged blackbird, bobolink); 7 species used the habitat "occasionally" (ring-necked pheasant, vesper sparrow, savannah sparrow, meadowlark, common grackle, American goldfinch, house sparrow); and 22 others used it rarely.

MAMMALS. Many mammals, such as white-footed mice and house mice, enter cereal crop fields when the grain is ripe. However, meadow and prairie voles, eastern cottontails, and deer feed on the green vegetation, and thus are much more common in the habitat. All of these species are found throughout the state, except that the meadow vole is more common in the north, and the prairie vole is more common in the south. Harvest mice entered a large rye field at Willow Slough Fish and Wildlife Area from Illinois about 1969, built a huge population, and then spread into several counties of northwestern Indiana. See Table M-7 for a list of 7 mammals closely associated with cereal crops.

Vineyards

1800. Vineyard habitat was rare in Indiana in this period. The first known vineyard in Indiana was established near the settlement called Vevay, located along the Ohio River in Switzerland County in the southeastern corner of the state. Vineyards were established at Vincennes and New Harmony by the early 1800s. Twelve acres of vineyard were established by 1816 at New Harmony on the low hills above the town, which was located on the second terrace of the Wabash River. Vineyards were found in 34 counties in 1860. There were 3,851 acres in vineyards in Indiana in 1880 (Baxevanis 1992), mostly in the southeastern (Ohio, Wayne, and Switzerland) and southwestern (Vanderburgh and Posey) counties of the state.

Figure 10.10. West Orchard in Clay County. Photo by Linda K. Castor.

1900. There were 2.6 million grape vines (acres not given, Table G-6) in the state at this time (U.S. Census Bureau 1900). Grapevines were found in every county, varying from 2,961 in Starke County to 114,629 in Marion County. While we do not have information on the spacing used in 1900, the current spacing most commonly ranges from 605 to 908 vines per acre. The approximate acreage planted to vineyards in 1900 can be estimated by dividing the vines per acre into the total number of vines. For example, the 2.6 million grape vines would equate to a range of 2,863–4,298 acres planted in the state at that time.

2000. Sixteen commercial vineyards covering 199 acres were inventoried across the state in 2000 (Butler and Butler 2001; Table G-7). Numerous other private vineyards (Figure 10.9) also exist, but data were not found in the agricultural census. Sixty-four percent of the commercial vineyards are located in the Bluegrass region. The Highland Rim region has 18% of the commercial vineyards, with the remaining vineyards located in the Central Till Plain, Northern Lakes, Northwestern Morainal, and Shawnee Hills regions.

FLORA. Vineyards are generally highly manicured sites with little plant diversity other than the grapevines and mowed turf between arbors. Tall fescue is the likely turf grass used, but Kentucky bluegrass could also be present. Hairy crabgrass, nimblewill, common dandelion, English plantain, red clover, white clover, and Japanese clover are just a few of the turf weeds expected in such situations. Rough areas along the edges of vineyards include additional species, mostly weeds. See Table P-11 for a list of species of vineyards.

AMPHIBIANS AND REPTILES. No herpetofauna would be anticipated to be resident in intensively managed vineyards. As with other agricultural areas, individuals observed in these areas are likely transients ultimately dependent upon the surrounding residual natural habitat. However, the less intensively managed the area, the more diversity we expect.

BIRDS. Vineyards likely attract the same fruit-eating birds that used orchards in Butler's era (1898). Butler mentioned both habitats when discussing the orchard oriole and a few other species. See the "Orchards" account below. However, vineyards lack trees and are therefore unsuitable nesting habitat for many of the former orchard species. Vineyards may attract aerial insectivores like barn swallows. We know of no recent studies.

MAMMALS. Many species of mammals enter vineyards occasionally, but the 10 species listed in Table M-7 are the most likely to be found there. The 2 species of voles will not be present unless herbaceous ground cover is heavy. All of these species are found throughout the state's vineyards, except that the meadow vole is more common in the north, and the prairie vole in the south. Skunks may enter vineyards to feed on ants or other subterranean insects.

Orchards

1800. Orchards of apples, peaches, pears, and cherries were established near the villages of Vincennes and New Harmony (Latta 1938). About 1,400 acres of orchards and vineyards were established on cleared forest land near New Harmony by 1818 (Butler and Butler 2001).

1900. The number of fruit and nut trees is given in the Twelfth Census of the United States (U.S. Census Bureau 1900; Table G-6). Apples were 61.1% of the 14.1

Figure 10.11. Feedlot. Photo by James R. Gammon.

million trees, peaches were 20.7%, cherries 6.3%, and pears 6.1% (Table G-8). Apricots, plums, and undefined fruits make up the remaining trees. If 400 ft^2 per tree is used to calculate acreage, there were 32,972 acres of fruit and nut orchards in 1900. Land in orchards varied from 406 acres in the Northwestern Morainal region to 10,132 acres in the Central Till Plain region.

2000. There were 5,354 acres in orchards in 2002 (Figure 10.10; Table G-8). This is an underestimate since the acreage for counties with only one grower is not given due to privacy issues. Data were not given by fruit type (U.S. Department of Agriculture 2002). Land in orchards varies from 7 acres in the Southern Bottomlands region to 1,157 acres in the Central Till Plain region. Private orchards where fruit is not sold are excluded.

FLORA. The management of orchards is similar to that of vineyards. See that section for discussion of potential plant species. The orchard flora is likely more varied because orchards are not mowed and manicured as often as are vineyards. See Table P-11 for a list of species of orchards.

AMPHIBIANS AND REPTILES. The considerations regarding herpetofaunal use of orchards are similar to those regarding the use of vineyards. Few, if any, amphibians and reptiles can persist without access to remnants of natural habitat. Generally, the less intensively managed the area, the higher the density of herpetofauna.

BIRDS. The older ornithological literature (e.g., Butler 1898; A. C. Bent's Life History series, ca. 1920) contains frequent references to orchards as bird habitat. They are rarely discussed as bird habitat now because they are less common (note the more than 80% decline in orchard area since 1900 in Indiana) and perhaps less hospitable because of pesticide use.

One of the state's fairly common summering birds was named for its use of this habitat: the orchard oriole. Butler (1898) observed that "the orchard is its home, and not the deep woods"; it nested in apple trees and fed on insects in the orchards. Today, a good place to find this species is on reclaimed strip-mines in small groves of willows or locusts, which shows its preference for trees in an open setting.

Other orchard-frequenting species mentioned by Butler include yellow-billed cuckoo (preying on tent caterpillars in cherry trees), yellow-bellied sapsucker, downy woodpecker, eastern wood-pewee, eastern kingbird, cedar waxwing, field sparrow, Baltimore oriole, American goldfinch, and house sparrow. The now-extinct Carolina parakeet was "very destructive" in the spring, eating leaf buds, blossoms, and young fruit; in the summer, it consumed orchard fruit (apples, grapes, cherries) and grain (wheat). However, they also loved cocklebur seeds and "for this destruction of weed seeds they were held in high regard by farmers" (Butler 1892). Snyder and Russell (1998) endorse McKinley's (1980) conclusion that "shooting to avenge or avert crop depredations was unlikely as the major cause of extinction."

MAMMALS. What applies to vineyards also applies to orchards. The same 10 species of mammals are expected in both areas (Table M-7).

Feedlots and Confined Feeding Operations

1800. There may have been some confined feeding near villages, but the operations were small and limited in number.

1900. There were 91,825 farms reporting domestic animals in barns and enclosures at this time (U.S. Census Bureau 1900). The average number of animals per enclosure was 1.4. This number varied by animal from 1.5 for asses and burros to 20.1 for sheep.

Figure 10.12. Planting corn through no-till methods. Photo by John O. Whitaker, Jr.

2000. Confined feeding operations (Figure 10.11) have been regulated in Indiana since 1971. Any livestock operation with 300 cattle, 600 swine or sheep, or 30,000 fowl requires approval from IDEM for construction and operation. There were 2,998 confined feeding operations in Indiana in January 2001 (http://www.in.gov/idem/4994.htm). These operations are scattered across 9 of the natural regions, but are concentrated in the large Central Till Plain region (Table G-9).

FLORA. Almost no vegetation occurs in feedlots, save for plants toxic to or practically inedible by livestock. Jimsonweed is a common feedlot plant. Other species found in areas frequented by livestock are cheeses or mallows, dog fennel, buffalo bur, catnip, motherwort, and various thistle species. Other species can survive in fence rows, which provide some protection from the livestock. See Table P-11 for a list of species of feedlots. As confined operations are within enclosed buildings, no vascular plants occur there.

AMPHIBIANS AND REPTILES. No herpetofauna are anticipated in feedlots except for transients from more natural habitat remnants nearby.

BIRDS. A small set of species forages in open feedlots: mourning dove, horned lark, European starling, Brewer's blackbird (a rare winter visitor), brown-headed cowbird (see below), and house sparrow. Common grackle and red-winged blackbird are also likely there, especially in the nonbreeding seasons. In winter storms, Lapland longspur and snow bunting are likely to forage there. In confined operations, the expected species are some of those often found around farm buildings: rock pigeon, European starling, house sparrow (all introduced species).

Brown-headed cowbirds are believed to have been associated with large buffalo herds on the Great Plains and were likely an uncommon resident in presettlement Indiana. Their spread to the Midwest was aided by land clearing for agriculture and especially the increase in feedlots. Since the late 1800s, cowbirds have been abundant summer residents. As an obligate brood parasite capable of laying 40 eggs in a breeding season, cowbirds have had a negative impact on the breeding native grassland, forest, and shrubland birds of Indiana.

MAMMALS. Not many wild mammals are found in feedlots. The most likely are the Virginia opossum, Norway rat, house mouse, white-footed mouse, and raccoon. All of these are found throughout the state. Norway rats, house mice, and sometimes white-footed mice are regularly found in farm buildings, as are little brown myotis and big brown bats, which commonly form maternity colonies there.

Residue Management (No-Till) Areas

Fields managed as no-till are not plowed before or after harvesting. Instead, the soil is pierced by machinery that makes narrow slits in the earth, in which seeds are planted. These fields usually have more vegetative cover in the winter and spring, in the form of either crop residue (for example, corn stubble) or weeds.

1800. The agricultural practices of Native Americans were somewhat similar to modern no-till, in that the earth was pierced (with sticks) rather than plowed.

1900. No-till was not practiced until the late 1900s. Crop rotation was a common practice with a cover crop (fallow or legumes) planted on fields in some years to increase soil fertility. This practice increased soil organic matter in a manner similar to no-till.

2000. Modern no-till methods (Figure 10.12) began to be practiced in the 1970s, and by 2000 they were used on 42% of Indiana cropland (Natural Resources Conservation Service; Table G-2). No-till percentages range from 31% in the Grand Prairie region to 53% in the Highland Rim region.

FLORA. Because fields managed as no-till are not plowed following crop harvest in the fall, a prime environment is retained for the germination and growth of winter annuals and early spring species. A sample of these includes henbit, purple dead nettle, common chickweed, mouse-eared cress, silvery cinquefoil, carpet weed, and purslane speedwell. See Table P-11 for a list of species of fields using residue management.

AMPHIBIANS AND REPTILES. The direct influence of no-till farming on herpetofaunal diversity has not been studied. Given the reduced disturbance to the soil as compared to plowing, it seems likely that areas where no-till is practiced will have more amphibians and reptiles, because there is more cover during more of the year. Although this alone would likely not greatly impact herpetofaunal biodiversity, no-till probably benefits herpetofauna in adjacent natural areas compared to tilling because of reduced sedimentary runoff and fewer deaths of transients.

BIRDS. In one Indiana study, no-till corn and soybean fields had more bird activity in the summer than did conventional crop fields (Castrale 1985). Certain species (eastern meadowlark, song sparrow) used no-till fields regularly and conventionally farmed fields rarely. As noted for mammals (below), the greater cover in no-till fields likely makes them more productive for birds that use crop fields, except for bare ground species such as horned lark and killdeer.

MAMMALS. No-till farming provides more cover throughout the year, and thus is more apt to be populated by a greater variety of small mammals than are fields that are tilled. Twelve species that often occur in no-till fields are indicated in Table M-7. The most abundant are the 2 species of *Peromyscus* (mouse), especially *P. maniculatus,* which does fine with no cover. Its food habits in no-till farmland have been studied by Castrale et al. (1987). The presence and abundance of the other species will relate to the amount of ground cover. All are found throughout the state, except that the meadow vole is more common in the north, and the prairie vole is more common in the south. The western harvest mouse is found only in the northwestern part of the state but south of the Kankakee River. In addition, coyotes, red foxes, long-tailed weasels, and raccoons, enter such areas in search of the many small mammals there.

Developed Lands

11

Developed lands are those which have been highly modified by human activities to create urban areas and transportation systems. Their general locations were established by the late 1800s and have expanded to cover around 2 million acres today (see Map 2.4). As with agriculture, development creates new but often ecologically compromised habitats, and diminishes and fragments previously existing habitats.

Following a general overview of developed lands, we will review 8 sub-habitats or structures: urban and suburban forested areas; industrial lands; commercial areas; roads, railroads, and airports; rights-of-way (roadside, railway, utility line); golf courses, soccer fields, and other recreational areas; towers for communication and wind-power generation; and storm-water retention ponds and borrow pits.

1800. Developed lands were limited to a few villages, such as Vincennes and New Harmony. The villages and trails of Native Americans were also present across the state.

1900. In 1901, the *Ninth Biennial Report* of the Indiana Department of Statistics reported that cities and incorporated towns comprised at least 173,976 acres (Table G-11). Another source, the 1876 atlas of Indiana, provides maps of developed lands late in the nineteenth century, although they have not been digitized to quantify the coverage. Most of today's roads and urban areas were present at this time, but were much smaller in area. The non-farmed land was partly in urban areas, partly in transportation systems, and partly held by private individuals as timber land or other non-farm land. The percentage of land in a natural region that was not in private farms (thus potentially "developed") varied from only 4% in the Central Till Plain to 19% in the Northwestern Morainal region.

2000. The National Land Cover Data of 1992 (Table G-1) indicate 911,147 developed acres, mainly in the categories of low- and high-intensity residential areas, commercial and industrial areas, transportation systems, and urban or recreational grasslands (Map 11.1). Urban habitat varied from 4,284 acres in the Black Swamp region to 443,774 acres in the Central Till Plain region. Lands in roads, railroads, and airports are given in Table G-12.

Flora

Developed lands have resulted from human activities that alter the landscape from its original vegetation. In most cases, vegetation associated with developed lands consists of exotic species that have either naturalized into the site or been planted. Much of the developed land has a flora that's more like a European meadow than any community indigenous to North America. Species in this mix have been both intentionally and accidentally introduced. The number of introductions continues to increase, presenting an ever-greater threat to the native flora.

1800. Only a small fraction of the state's landscape was developed, mainly near trails, trade routes, and military forts. Perhaps a few exotics had become established in these areas, but for the most part they were an insignificant part of the flora.

1900. A considerable portion of the state was developed. Land had been cleared for agricultural pursuits, housing, and commerce, and roads and rail lines were built for intra- and interstate travel. The number of exotic species of plants in the state was significant, perhaps over 250. Deam (1940) recorded 302 exotic species by 1940. Most species were innocuous, but some, such as Hungarian brome and Japanese honeysuckle, were just beginning their invasion of the landscape. In addition to Eurasian species, many from western North America were spreading eastward along the railroads and highway rights-of-way. A list of exotics is in Table P-12.

2000. With ever-increasing development on the landscape, particularly urban sprawl, there is a correspondingly smaller area of land for native vegetation. The introduction of more exotic species adds to the threats to native species, given the competition they provide for space and nutrients. The increased use of wide spectrum and broad-leaf spectrum herbicides in vegetation management also has reduced the occurrence of native species. Some of the common invasive exotic plants in developed lands include common teasel, wild parsnip, crown vetch, Kentucky bluegrass, tall fescue, Hungarian brome, Queen Anne's lace, and Japanese chess. See Table P-12 for many more exotics.

Amphibians and Reptiles

In general, the conversion of natural areas for human use removes their value for herpetofauna. Since amphibians and reptiles cannot fly, they are exposed to predators in open areas, and thus are hesitant to use them. On the other hand, because of thermoregulatory requirements, reptiles seek areas with an open canopy to bask. Consequently, if at least some cover is available, reptiles especially may use the fringes of natural habitats, where they contact developed areas. The species most likely to persist in developed habitats are listed in Table H-9.

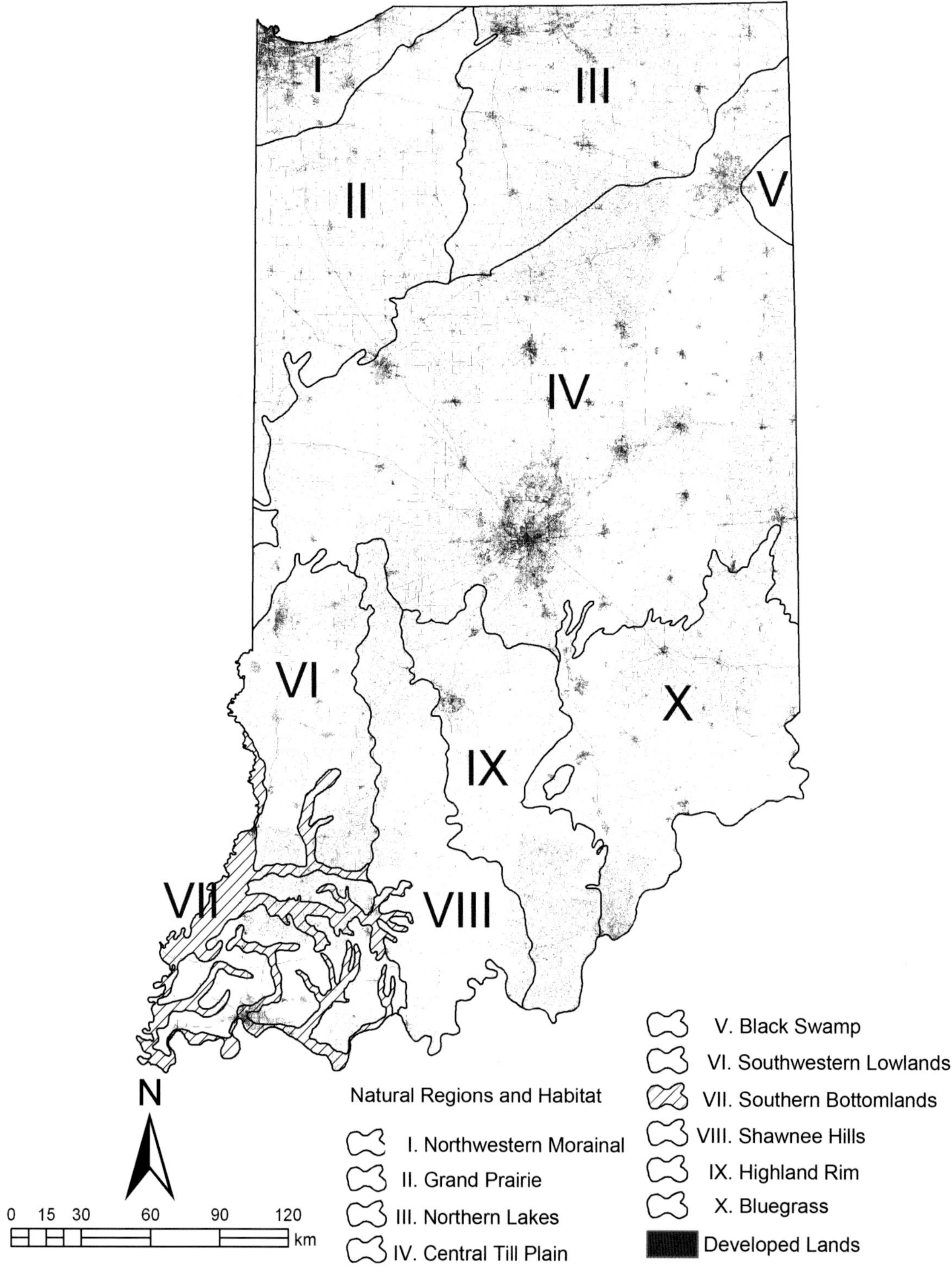

Map. 11.1. Developed lands by natural region.

Birds

1800. No significant urban areas were present.

1900. Butler (1898) had little to say about birds in towns, along roads, or in other developed lands, but much to say about birds in orchards and on other farmland. This reflects the more rural character of Indiana in the nineteenth century as well as his own experience. However, interesting tidbits about city birds are scattered throughout the species accounts; and the lack of information on some now-common urban birds may be good evidence that they had not yet adapted to cities as they have today (e.g., mourning dove and American crow). European starlings did not arrive until 1914 (Mumford and Keller 1984), and rock pigeons, though present, were not discussed by Butler.

The "English sparrow" (house sparrow) was a despised pest in towns, where it drove out purple martins and eastern bluebirds. Forty thousand were trapped in 1886–1887 in Indianapolis some 15 years after being introduced there, with little effect beyond the trapped area. Butler noted that eastern screech-owls "are much more numerous about our towns than they were formerly . . . , feeding on English sparrows" (Butler 1898: 813).

Chipping sparrows, on the other hand, were both welcome and familiar and at least as urban then as now. In the spring, they "at once make themselves at home upon our lawns and . . . come about our doors, upon our porches, and even into our houses, picking up crumbs that have fallen" (Butler 1898: 958–959). Northern cardinals were only slightly less tame. American goldfinches nested among the fruit and shade trees. Barn swallows nested on town buildings as well as on farms. Song sparrows frequented "bushes and hedges along highways" (ibid.: 968). Among the species that sometimes entered towns were warbling vireo, gray catbird, and eastern towhee.

Chimney swifts used "large old-fashioned chimneys . . . in great numbers" and rarely nested in hollow trees, as they had originally. Common nighthawks did not yet nest on rooftops in Indiana, although Butler reported such behavior for Cincinnati and Chicago. American crows did not yet roost in cities in winter, but occupied very large roosts in rural wooded areas; in the twenty-first century, most large roosts are in cities, and crows fly out of town to forage.

Urban hazards to migrating birds were already evident. Butler noted that migrating birds struck buildings due to the confusion of "light towers and other lights in high places."

2000. During the twentieth century, modern developed lands, as defined here, took shape. For birds, as for other wildlife, the impacts of roads are immense, as are commercial and industrial development. Ornithologists interested in habitat use tend to focus on disappearing natural habitats, so the role of developed lands as habitat for birds is understudied. Some structures on developed lands are major sources of mortality (e.g., roads and their fast-moving vehicles), and some of these are unique to flying birds (e.g., plate-glass windows and communication towers).

In terms of habitat use, some birds thrive in developed lands because of their use of man-made structures (a few species), or because lawns, roads, or rooftops offer suitable areas for foraging or other purposes. In general, developed lands favor a subset of species that like open country and tolerate disturbance. Open country conditions are created by lawns in industrial and commercial complexes and by mowing or tree cutting along roads, railroads, utility rights-of-way, and airport runways. However, because city people like trees and their shade, well-maintained urban and suburban forests exist in yards, parks, and along roads. The urban groves of tall trees and shrubbery attract a rich set of migrant warblers and other birds briefly in the spring and a less diverse set of species at other times. Developments like golf courses that incorporate natural habitat can remain productive for many species. Borrow pits (excavated for highway or railroad construction) can become productive wetlands for aquatic birds.

Roads, railroads, and utility lines pass through every habitat. They create openings, perch sites (fences and wires), and potential corridors for nest predators and parasites. Perhaps ironically, roads are used in ornithology to conduct the U.S. Geological Survey's 50-year-old Breeding Bird Survey, a leading source of data on species population changes that has documented serious declines in many species. Although roadsides are certainly occupied by birds, there is a generally negative impact of roads on species composition and abundance. The impact is proportional to traffic volume and detectable up to 1.2 km from the road (Forman and Alexander 1998).

Approximately 175 of Indiana's bird species occur in at least 1 of 8 categories of developed lands (Table B-7). The largest species totals are for urban and suburban forests (63 species) and borrow pits (80 species), reflecting use of those habitats by migrant birds. Habitat use is "probable" for some indicated species, especially for use of borrow pits and golf courses, because there are few or no published data for those habitats in Indiana. Three species occur characteristically in all kinds of developed lands: mourning dove, American robin, and European starling. Six others occur in at least 5 categories: killdeer, American crow, chipping sparrow, song sparrow, common grackle, and American goldfinch.

Mammals

1800. Relatively little urban area was present. Squirrels, raccoons, and rabbits probably were much less common in urban areas than they are now because they were hunted for food.

1900. There was still much less urban area than at present, and probably less urban wildlife, since species such as raccoons and rabbits were hunted for food. Deer had been extirpated. House mice and Norway rats were abundant in old buildings that had cover (trash) and food.

2000. Several species of mammals sometimes occur in urban (even mid-city) and suburban areas. The most common species are indicated in Table M-8. House mice and Norway rats of course populate urban areas, especially run-down areas where trash accumulates. Other common mammals, besides people, are Virginia opossum; short-tailed shrew (if there are moist areas with plenty of detritus); eastern mole; chipmunk; red, fox, and gray squirrels; cottontail rabbit; raccoon; and big and little brown bats. All can exist in close proximity to people and to human structures. Other species, such as skunks, red and gray foxes, coyotes, deer, and even mink can be observed within city limits where suitable habitat is present. Besides the two bat species listed above, the red, hoary, and other bats might occur if enough woods are present. Many bat species are likely to forage in and at the edges of urban woods.

Figure 11.1. Urban forest. Photo by IDNR–*Outdoor Indiana* magazine.

Sub-Habitats

Urban and Suburban Forested Areas

1800. None were present.

1900. City parks may have been the principal wooded areas in towns.

2000. The amount of urban and suburban forest is closely linked to areas defined as "low- or high-intensity residential development" in GIS classifications in 1992 (National Land Cover Data). There were 100,950 acres of high-intensity residential development in 1992 (Table G-1), occupying between 0.3% and 6.3% of the areas of the various natural regions. High-intensity residential development may include scattered trees along streets, in plazas, and in urban parks (Figure 11.1).

Suburban forested habitats are mostly found in low-intensity residential areas where vegetation may account for 20–70% of the land cover, or in parks interspersed through urban developments. There were 455,543 acres of low-intensity residential development across the state in 1992, occupying between 1.6% and 2.9% of the natural regions (National Land Cover Data 1992; Table G-1).

FLORA. Urban forests consist of sites that are either natural forests that have been set aside, such as in parks, or are planted, again usually in park settings. Exotic species are not uncommon, including those that are invasive. Invasive species became a particularly serious problem by the beginning of the twenty-first century, as the plants have become thoroughly established and compete with native species. Some of the more-established species include amur honeysuckle, tartarian honeysuckle, tree-of-heaven, common privet, garlic mustard, and ground ivy. See Table P-12 for a list of plant species of this forest type. Species of the portions of the urban landscape containing native flora can be found in various other appendixes, such as the lists for original forest.

Much of the suburban landscape in Indiana occupies former agricultural land, and thus, few actual forest environments exist. In such places, most of the species present have been planted. Commonly used species include sugar and silver maple, green ash, pin oak, sycamores, sweetgum, Norway maple, Siberian elm, Norway spruce, white pine, and arbor vitae. In some situations, forest preserves consisting of native, original forest are set aside. Composition depends on the site, its disturbance history, and other variables. Invasive, exotic species are commonly a problem in suburban forests, with many of the same species that affect the urban setting. See Table P-12 for a list of species of this forest type. Possible additional species, such as might occur in natural forest remnants, can be found in the plant species list for original forest.

AMPHIBIANS AND REPTILES. Urban forests that are relicts of preexisting habitat will have a simplified herpetofaunal assemblage derived from what was there before. We would expect box turtles to be absent, for example, as well as the big snake species, such as the black rat snake. A vast majority of amphibians and reptiles do not tolerate development which removes existing habitat, and thus the more manipulated the area, or the more it has been restored rather than being original forest, the simpler the herpetofaunal assemblage. Road density also has a negative effect on herpetofauna, as individuals cannot fly or quickly move across roads to avoid traffic. In cases where water is still available for amphibians to breed, some species may persist when all of the others are gone. The species most likely to be found are the American toad and the gray treefrog. The latter may exploit such ephemeral opportunities as nonfunctioning gutters to breed in, so does not need ponds to reproduce. In many neighborhoods, these are the only remaining amphibian or reptile species. The eastern garter snake may also persist in some areas; should more extensive, persistent bodies of water be available, the green frog and bullfrog may be present, as well as the northern/midland water snake and painted turtle. These snakes and Kirtland's snakes would benefit from urban/suburban streams left with some natural forest cover and natural banks. Urban and suburban forests associated with parks and cemeteries often have a very limited understory due to mowing. In these habitats, toads and snakes could benefit from the refugia provided by raised flower beds or the inclusion of rock wall or edging in the landscape. Again, the history and size of a forest tract will greatly influence which species are present.

BIRDS. Urban forests of native and exotic trees attract a small set of familiar species which nest in them or forage for insects, fruits, or seeds and a much larger set of migrant birds that feed and rest in trees, especially in the spring. At least 63 species use urban and suburban forests (Table B-7).

The urban forest is a primary breeding habitat for 7 species: mourning dove, chimney swift, American robin, European starling, chipping sparrow, house finch, and house sparrow. Some of these species are strongly attracted to human structures (dove, swift, starling, house finch, house sparrow), others to open woods (robin, chipping sparrow). But they also make much use of urban trees for nest sites (dove, robin, starling, house finch), foraging (house sparrow, chimney swift), and song perches (chipping sparrow). Another 20 or so species, including many familiar birds of yards and tree-lined streets (blue jay, Carolina wren, house wren, gray catbird, song sparrow, northern cardinal, common grackle, American goldfinch), breed in urban forests as a secondary habitat. Ruby-throated hummingbirds rarely nest in urban or suburban forests because of an apparent requirement for large forest patches as nesting sites. In migration, however, they are common in developed landscapes.

During spring migration, urban trees in parks, alleys, and streets briefly host a rich assortment of northbound neotropical migrants, including many warblers (especially the vociferous Tennessee warbler), rose-breasted grosbeak, Baltimore oriole, least flycatcher, and Swainson's thrush. The migrants feed especially around oak catkins, locust, and tulip poplar flowers. Migrant use of urban forests is much less evident in the fall. American goldfinches seek out the seeds of sweetgum fruits in the fall and winter.

Trees or shrubs with bird-adapted fruits (cultivated crabapples, hawthorns, etc.) attract hordes of American robins and European starlings and smaller numbers of cedar waxwings in the fall and winter. Most wintering Indiana robins are probably found in cities and suburbs, taking advantage of the fruit supply. Such birds promote the spread of the exotic and invasive bush honeysuckle, which reaches high density on neglected urban properties and small wood lots.

In winter, 3 raptor species (Cooper's hawk, sharp-shinned hawk, American kestrel) hunt birds of the urban forest. Twenty-first-century studies in Terre Haute document a substantial density of and season-long home ranges for Cooper's hawks, whose main urban prey are European starlings, mourning doves, and rock pigeons (Roth and Lima 2003).

American crows roost in the winter in cities, sometimes in enormous numbers (e.g., 50,000 in Terre Haute since 1994). They prefer to roost in trees in wooded lots or along streets, although they often gather on rooftops prior to moving to trees at dark. The vast majority fly out of town at dawn to feed in rural areas.

Birds of suburban forested areas are similar to those of urban forests. As tree density and yard and garden sizes increase, the relative abundance of northern cardinals and song sparrows may increase while that of house sparrows and European starlings declines. Common birds of mature wild forest (wood thrush, eastern towhee, eastern wood-pewee, red-eyed vireo) are more likely to be present.

MAMMALS. Several species of mammals occur in urban wooded areas. Those most often occurring even in mid-city urban areas are indicated in Table M-8. House mice and Norway rats populate urban areas but avoid woods. The most-common mammals in urban woods, other than people, are the Virginia opossum, white-footed mouse, short-tailed shrew (in moist areas with plenty of detritus), eastern mole, some of the squirrels, cottontail rabbit, raccoon, and big and little brown bats. In addition, unexpected mammals, such as deer, coyotes, woodchucks, weasels, and mink, have been seen even in Indianapolis.

Coyotes do not generally call when populations are low. Coyote populations in Indiana were increasing in the middle of the twentieth century, yet not until 1985 did Whitaker first hear one howl—it was within the city limits of Terre Haute. Since then, he has heard numerous coyotes in many parts of the state.

With the continued spread of suburbs into the countryside, wild mammals are more commonly found. The most common species are listed in Table M-8 and include Virginia opossum, white-footed mouse, short-tailed shrew, eastern mole (common on lawns as well as in woods), eastern cottontail, eastern chipmunk, gray squirrel, fox squirrel, and raccoon. Striped skunks and white-tailed deer are much less common but occasionally occur if wooded areas are large enough.

Little brown and big brown bats commonly form roosts in buildings, and sometimes under bridges or overpasses. The bats often forage in and at the edges of woods. Prior to 1995, evening bats used buildings as roosts, mostly in the southern part of the state, but the roosts presently known are all in woods, mostly in bottomland floodplains. The big brown bat may have outcompeted the evening bat for urban roosts. Red and sometimes even hoary bats may occur in trees in suburban areas, and may be seen foraging

Figure 11.2. Industrial area along Lake Michigan. Photo by IDNR–*Outdoor Indiana* magazine.

at street lights. In the northern half of the state, red squirrels are often in wooded areas, especially among conifers in suburbs.

Industrial Lands

1800. No industrial land was present

1900. Industrial habitat was primarily found in the larger urban areas of the state (Taylor et al. 1989). Notable concentrations of industry were in Calumet, Fort Wayne, South Bend, Muncie, Indianapolis, Anderson, Lafayette, Evansville, Terre Haute, Bloomington, New Albany, Columbus, Richmond, and Madison.

2000. Some 218,767 acres were classified as commercial, industrial (Figure 11.2), or a transportation route in 1992 (Table G-1). The distribution of such lands by natural region ranged from 1,193 acres in the Black Swamp to 100,581 acres in the Central Till Plain region, accounting for approximately 1% of the land in each region.

FLORA. Typically, there is insufficient available substrate in industrial sites for plants to exist, as structures and pavement dominate. What is available is generally disturbed, either from frequent soil disruption, or from compaction by heavy machinery. Cracks in pavement can provide sites for several plants, as do gravel parking lots and other unpaved areas. Some of the species, both native and introduced, that can survive such rigorous environments include nodding spurge, Queen Anne's lace, three-seeded mercury, white mulberry, Siberian elm, horseweed, hairy crabgrass, stink grass, chicory, and small green foxtail. See Table P-12 for a list of species of industrial areas.

AMPHIBIANS AND REPTILES. Industrial areas are unlikely to have many resident herpetofauna, although remnant patches of nearby habitat may provide immigrants into these areas. If streams or ponds are available, then the most likely species are American toad, eastern garter snake, northern/midland water snake, painted turtle, and perhaps common snapping turtle.

BIRDS. Industrial areas attract, first of all, a few hard-core human-commensal species such as rock pigeon, mourning dove, chimney swift, European starling, and house sparrow. Buildings provide nesting and roosting opportunities: chimneys, cavities, eaves, window ledges, and rooftops (common nighthawks). Smokestacks and other tall industrial structures have served as nest sites for peregrine falcons. The flocks of American crows that roost in the winter in Terre Haute gather on warehouse roofs at dusk, but seem to prefer trees in well-lit areas as their final roost sites. Industrial parks with large mowed lawns and lakes attract Canada goose, mallard, killdeer, European starling, and American robin. Certain sparrows are comfortable in urban commercial settings if a few trees are combined with large mowed lawns (chipping sparrow), or if there is shrubbery along a lake (song sparrow). A total of 18 species are characteristic of industrial and commercial lands (Table B-7).

Several of the above species frequently reach nuisance proportions in cities, and are sometimes the target of control efforts by USDA Wildlife Services. Species posing year-round problems are Canada goose, rock pigeon, and house sparrow. European starling and American crow are problems mainly in their large winter roosts. Starlings have built up in

Figure 11.3. Commercial area. Photo by Qihao Weng.

most large cities, whereas winter crows are concentrated in only a few cities.

MAMMALS. Few mammals occur on the purely industrial lands of Indiana, but they increase with the amount and biodiversity of the land there. Industrial lands with suitable woods and grasslands have many of the species of those habitats. Mammals found on typical industrial lands are listed in Table M-8.

Commercial Areas

FLORA. Commercial areas, such as shopping malls (Figure 11.3), warehouses, etc., have very little native flora. Typical habitats include cracks in pavement, landscaped beds, small areas of lawn, and waste areas. Nonplanted species could include Kentucky bluegrass, lawn weeds such as common dandelion, woolly blue violet, red-stalked plantain, English plantain, ground ivy, corn speedwell, thyme-leaved speedwell, and white clover. See Table P-12 for a list of species of commercial areas.

AMPHIBIANS AND REPTILES. Commercial areas are not expected to have many resident herpetofauna. However, remnant patches of habitat may facilitate immigration into these areas. As with industrial areas, if streams or ponds are available, then the most likely species are the American toad, eastern garter snake, northern/midland water snake, painted turtle, and perhaps common snapping turtle.

BIRDS. The birds of commercial areas are largely the same species listed for industrial areas, because both kinds of development provide similar structures for nesting or roosting and similar foraging opportunities. Thus, 18 species are listed jointly for industrial and commercial lands in Table B-7. Rock pigeon, mourning dove, European starling, and house sparrow are the primary species. Starlings and doves may commute long distances to feeding grounds (for example, to suburbs or agricultural areas) during the day, returning to roost on commercial buildings. House finches may be present; singing males seem to enjoy the echo effect of large buildings. The Eurasian collared dove, recently established in scattered counties, seems to prefer small towns but seeks out utility pole clusters, housetop antennas, and railroad yards in such areas. Another exotic species, the monk parakeet, has been recorded nesting in an electrical substation and in urban forest in Lake County (Marsh 2006).

Commercial urban areas can provide unique habitat opportunities. Between 1991 and 1994, 60 peregrine falcons were released in the commercial districts of Indianapolis, Fort Wayne, South Bend, and Evansville. Peregrine falcons nest on building ledges or use well-placed nest boxes, from which they prey on some of the species mentioned above. Cooper's hawks, however, are a far more common urban raptor, especially in the winter (Roth and Lima 2003); they prey mainly on starlings, but also on doves and pigeons, and sometimes take pigeons from window ledges on tall commercial buildings. Two neotropical migrant species, common nighthawks and chimney swifts, use commercial areas as breeding habitat. Nighthawks nest on rooftops. Swifts use big chimneys for roosting aggregations of hundreds to a few thousand birds in September, prior to migratory departure, and again on their return in April and May,

Figure 11.4. Interstate highway. Photo by Scott Johnson.

prior to dispersing to many smaller chimneys for nesting. Commercial parks are likely to have ponds surrounded by mowed grass, which attract Canada goose and mallard, and song sparrow and chipping sparrow if appropriate shrubs or scattered trees are present. Canada geese can be seen on shopping mall rooftops and parking lots.

The surfaces of tall commercial buildings of urban centers and large cities may be solid or glass-filled. Skyscrapers full of plate glass contribute to a huge window-kill problem, which is considered by some to be the leading source of human-caused mortality for birds in the United States, equaling or exceeding predation by feral cats and easily exceeding the deaths due to high-tension wires, pesticides, cars, and communication towers (Klem 1990; www.sibleyguide.com/mortality.htm). Brightly lit, window-filled buildings confuse birds migrating at night (such as warblers), especially in cloudy, rainy, or windy conditions.

MAMMALS. Few mammals occur on the purely industrial lands of Indiana, but they increase with the amount and biodiversity of the land there. Industrial lands with suitable woods and grasslands have many of the species of those habitats. Mammals found on typical industrial land are listed in Table M-8.

Roads, Railroads, and Airports

1800. Roads were limited and mostly just widened trails through the forest between settlements. Native Americans had extensive trail systems between villages.

1900. The basic network of today's road system was established, but most were still narrow and surfaced with dirt or gravel. The *Ninth Biennial Report* of the Indiana Department of Statistics records 11,694 mi of county gravel roads (Table G-12), an underestimate since data were missing for 19 counties. There were 9,930 mi of railroad.

2000. The road system for cars and trucks is now more than eight times bigger than it was in 1900, reaching 93,607 mi (http://www.in.gov/indot; Table G-12). This figure includes county roads (66,601 mi), city streets (15,791 mi), and state highways (11,215 mi), but does not include interstate highways (1,170 mi; Figure 11.4). Most roads cross rural landscapes (79% of miles), the remainder being urban. Rural roads cover an estimated 738,154 acres, assuming a combined width of 100 ft for roadbed and right-of-way. The system includes 18,125 bridges. The interstate highway system has 37 rest areas. Thirty plantings of native plants and wildflowers are maintained along highways.

In contrast, the total miles of railroad track have declined by nearly 30% in the past century, to 4,686 mi in 2000. The area covered by track bed and right-of-way is approximately 56,800 acres. The state's airports include 1,614 acres of paved runway and 265 acres of turf runway.

FLORA. The discussion of species associated with roads and railways will be confined here to those of the roadbed and railbed, and only touch on those of the rights-of-way (see next section; Figure

Figure 11.5. Railroad right-of-way. Photo by Scott Johnson.

11.5). Roadbed flora is typically sparse (although collectively there can be a high diversity of species), as the sites consist of pavement or gravel, or are heavily compacted. Cracks in pavement and the ballasts of railbeds can offer some rooting medium for plants. Some of the species that can survive here are scouring rush, poison ivy, Virginia creeper, chicory, squirrel-tail grass, lesser love grass, low love grass, hairy crabgrass, common ragweed, crowfoot grass, poison hemlock, common knotweed, green foxtail, hairy aster, dwarf snapdragon, and fetid marigold. See Table P-12 for a list of species of roads and rails.

AMPHIBIANS AND REPTILES. Roads are a major hazard for herpetofauna. Beyond the direct mortality resulting from attempted road crossings and snakes basking on roads, populations also suffer from the isolation and fragmentation of habitat that result when roads divide the countryside. Railroads may block reptiles and amphibians from migrating, as during nesting. Perhaps worse, the animals may succeed in crossing one rail but not the other, eventually dying in between. Trails can also be a problem for these species, as they increase encounter rates with humans. However, given the available cover around trails, reptiles may often use them, or at least their edges, to bask.

Roads create edge in any habitat they pass through. A consequence of this for herpetofauna is that vertebrate predators that hunt along edges will be more likely to encounter the reptiles and amphibians in the surrounding habitat matrix. Furthermore, "subsidized" predators, mostly domestic cats and dogs, will hunt along road corridors and will also more likely be present as a consequence of residences along the road.

BIRDS. Roads have attractions for birds, though only limited species flourish there. The attractions include hunting opportunities, perches (on transmission lines and posts), and nest sites in roadside shrubbery, which tends to be dense because of water runoff. Ten species are characteristic of state or national highways, and 35 species are commonly found along rural roads (Table B-7).

Birds that forage along roads include open-country raptors (red-tailed hawk, American kestrel), scavengers of road-killed animals (turkey vulture, American crow), open-country flycatchers (eastern kingbird), seed eaters (sparrows, mourning dove), and species seeking grit for their gizzards (mourning dove and others). A snowy owl hunted small rodents for days along Interstate 65 in White County before being killed by a truck (Dunning 2005); skulls of 18 voles were found in its pellets, indicating how productive, but hazardous, a highway right-of-way can be for a raptor. Quiet roads adjacent to forest cover are attractive foraging areas for woodland and edge-loving passerines like northern cardinal, dark-eyed junco, indigo bunting, and various sparrows. During winter snowstorms, when agricultural fields are covered but roads and road shoulders have exposed substrates and (apparently) seeds or other food, flocks of horned larks visit county roads, sometimes joined by Lapland longspurs and snow buntings. Lightly traveled country roads through grasslands on reclaimed surface mines are frequented by killdeer and horned larks, and grasshopper sparrows sing from fence posts bordering such roads. The state-endangered loggerhead shrike, in its core range in southwestern Indiana, typically is found along gravel roads with a utility line and a fence line of scattered shrubs, especially in Amish farming neighborhoods (Castrale and Ferchak 2001).

The common grackle is perhaps the most common user of shrubs along busy highways, nesting among them. The rock pigeon and house sparrow nest under bridges. Bridges over large rivers support colonies of cliff swallows, and those over small rivers or creeks are likely to have eastern phoebes or barn swallows.

Roadside transmission wires and poles (for telephone lines or other purposes) are convenient perching sites for birds seeking to rest, survey the landscape for prey, or sing and advertise their territories. Any perching bird of the taxonomic order Passeriformes, which includes roughly half of Indiana's bird species (Table B-1, olive-sided flycatcher through house sparrow), might perch on wires where roads pass through its habitat. In rural areas, for example, male indigo buntings routinely sing from wires. Woodpeckers, hawks, and great horned owls are fond of roadside poles.

Roads are hazards to birds because many are struck by vehicles. Besides direct mortality, vehicle traffic has a depressing effect on the presence and abundance of nesting grassland and forest birds, which is significant for up to 1 km from heavily traveled roads in the eastern United States (Forman and Deblinger 2000).

Roadside habitat is discussed further in the section below on rights-of-way.

MAMMALS. Mammals along roads and trails will be those of the habitats through which the road or trail passes, often grasslands or woodlands. See the accounts for those habitats. Bats often feed on insects that gather in numbers at street lights. However, both lights and traffic noise (light and sound pollution) may deter bats as well as other species from some urban areas.

Many mammals are killed on Indiana's roads. Whitaker and Mumford (2008) list 692 road-kills during 1972–1974, and 2,913 in 2000–2001. The most commonly killed species during the first period were, in descending order, opossum, cottontail, raccoon, striped skunk, and fox squirrel. Thirty years later, the same 5 species were the most common, but the order had changed to raccoon, opossum, fox squirrel, cottontail, and skunk, with white-tailed deer in sixth place. No coyote kills were recorded during the first period, but 26 were counted in the more recent survey.

Rights-of-Way (All Types)

FLORA. Areas of land along railroad tracks, highways, and utility lines provide considerable opportunities for the occurrence of vegetation, both native and exotic. These rights-of-way provide in some cases the last remaining terrain for certain communities, e.g., prairie (see chapter 5 for a list of species of prairie). Unfortunately, the frequent use of herbicides since the mid-twentieth century has caused a major shift of species away from natives to exotic weeds. Thus, the few remaining strips of prairie along railroad rights-of-way are in danger of becoming highly degraded. Rights-of-way that are mowed without herbicide treatment are generally more favorable for native species, especially if the sites were not previously disturbed or planted in exotic species. Most rights-of-way are highly managed with herbicides, however. A classic assortment of species in a contemporary right-of-way includes tall fescue, Kentucky bluegrass, Queen Anne's lace, tall goldenrod, common milkweed, horsetail milkweed, birdsfoot trefoil, hairy aster, wild parsnip, poison hemlock, common ragweed, hairy crabgrass, and white sweet clover. See Table P-12 for a list of species of rights-of-way.

AMPHIBIANS AND REPTILES. In general, rights-of-way are areas of degraded habitat: they are created and maintained by removing natural habitat. However, a common feature of rights-of-way—the lack of a tree and/or shrub canopy—may attract many herpetofauna, for better or worse. Consequently, the manner in which rights-of-way are maintained will influence which species might be present, and also whether or not they act as population sources or sinks for the species involved. Rights-of-way do often provide rather continuous habitat, and thus can be a means through which species can disperse or otherwise move from place to place.

Areas maintained as lawn will generally not have value for reptiles and amphibians. Areas where the vegetation is allowed to become more rank, such as areas treated to remove trees and shrubs but not grass, might have a variety of species present, including some sensitive species. For example, leopard frogs may take advantage of the wet meadows common in low-lying rights-of-way. In southernmost Indiana, even copperbelly water snakes and cricket frogs may use such areas. As is the case with any edge that still confers some element of cover, we anticipate use by a number of local reptiles seeking sites to bask.

If open-canopy maintenance along rights-of-way is performed at inopportune times, then amphibians and reptiles could be negatively impacted, and the sites' attractiveness may become a detriment. An effort should be made to treat these areas in the winter, when amphibians and reptiles are inactive.

Numerous species of medium to large snakes are vulnerable to getting stuck in plastic, large-weave erosion netting and dying a protracted death. Use of such netting should be limited; when unavoidable, the netting should be biodegradable, which would at least shorten the time it is present. Erosion/silt fencing may also be a problem, forming a wall that is impenetrable and insurmountable for herpetofauna.

BIRDS. Rights-of-way along roads, railroads, and airport runways are significant avian habitats, hosting 49 characteristic species (Table B-7). Because much birding is done along country roads, many impressions of species abundance in the state are proba-

Figure 11.6. Power line right-of-way. Photo by Scott Johnson.

bly based on roadside observations. The U.S. Geological Survey's Breeding Bird Survey, over 50 years old and a primary source of information on changes in abundance, is based entirely on roadside counts (50 point counts along 25-mi routes).

Species found along rights-of-way will generally be typical of the habitat through which the road was built, but abundance and species composition are affected by the road's presence. One sees agricultural birds along roads through farmland, grassland birds on roads passing by pastures or through reclaimed mines, and so on for forest, aquatic, and wetland habitats. Telephone and power lines and poles bordering roads offer perch sites that birds appreciate. However, there is a significant and generally negative effect of the road itself—traffic volume and noise—on species presence and abundance when one compares grassland or forest adjacent to roads with similar vegetation distant from roads (Forman and Alexander 1998; Forman et al. 2002). Such effects extend up to 1 km from the road, and thus through and beyond the right-of-way.

Exotic plant species often flourish by roads, in part because they tolerate disturbed soil and also because roadsides are an open, continuous habitat along which to spread. Bush honeysuckle is an increasingly common shrub along many roads at the edges of Indiana towns and along railroad tracks. Its berries, though low in energy value, attract avian frugivores in the fall and winter, mainly American robins, European starlings, eastern bluebirds, cedar waxwings, and hermit thrushes (Ingold and Craycraft 1983). Multiflora rose and autumn olive were planted for a number of years as wildlife habitat, but neither was very satisfactory and should teach us once again that we should not introduce species that are not native to an area.

Rights-of-way along railroad tracks are productive spots for sparrows, robins, doves, and other edge-loving birds. Railroads are typically bordered by weedy herbs (seed sources), shrubs, and small trees. Train traffic probably is less disturbing to birds than heavy auto traffic. Grain spills from railroad cars attract rock pigeons, mourning doves, starlings, house sparrows, and other seed eaters.

Utility rights-of-way (Figure 11.6) have several impacts on birds, based on studies in the eastern United States and elsewhere: they support certain kinds of vegetation (shrubs and herbs rather than trees), bisect and fragment natural habitat into smaller patches, and provide corridors through habitats, increasing access by nest predators, such as blue jays and crows, and by nest parasites, such as cowbirds. If aerial rather than buried transmission lines are involved, as is usual, vegetation must be managed to prevent the growth of trees. Mowing and herbicide treatments encourage the growth of shrubs and herbs; after establishment, shrubs may slow tree colonization and reduce the need for further management. Such vegetation is potentially valuable habitat for shrubland or grassland birds, although use depends on corridor width, with species such as brown thrasher and yellow-breasted chat using only wider corridors (Askins 1994). Rights-of-way offer challenges and opportunities for avian conservation. Consolidating parallel or crossed lines into single wider ones near the edge of forests would increase the value of such areas for shrubland birds and minimize the negative edge and predator-conduit effects on forest birds (Askins 2000).

There has been no analysis in Indiana, apparently, of the habitats traversed by rights-of-way, or of the various vegetation types occurring in them. Such information would be a starting point for assessing the impacts of rights-of-way on Indiana birds. Part of a habitat conservation plan for the Karner blue butterfly involves managing transmission-line vegetation on NIPSCO utility-owned lands in northern Indiana (U.S. Fish and Wildlife Service 2006).

Birds that nest in shrub-dominated rights-of-way in the eastern United States and probably also in Indiana include yellow-billed and black-billed cuckoos, white-eyed vireo, Bell's vireo, brown thrasher, blue-winged warbler, prairie warbler, yellow-breasted chat, indigo bunting, blue grosbeak, and field sparrow. Other, more-generalized species, such as northern cardinal, song sparrow, field sparrow, and eastern towhee, would also be present, as would various wintering sparrows (white-throated, white-crowned, swamp) and dark-eyed juncos. In eastern states such as Pennsylvania, some rights-of-way function as large forest openings, attracting forest game birds, such as ruffed grouse and wild turkey (Bramble et al. 1992).

Rights-of-way at airports consist of frequently mowed, often extensive grassland or other low vegetation. These can support grassland specialist and open country birds year-round. Terre Haute's Hulman Field Airport, for example, has territorial eastern meadowlarks and savannah sparrows in the nesting season, and horned larks and various raptors (northern harrier, rough-legged hawk, red-tailed hawk, American kestrel, short-eared owl) in the winter or during migration. In some parts of the eastern United States, airport grasslands are important habitat for threatened populations of upland sandpiper and bobolink.

MAMMALS. Mammals of rights-of-way vary with the habitat through which they pass, such as woodlands or grasslands; thus, there are no characteristic species of rights-of-way. If the rights-of-way go through woods, then white-footed mice, short-tailed shrews, and other woodland species might be there. Also, bats often forage along edges of woods, especially if an open strip is bordered by woods. If the rights-of-way go through fields, either meadow voles or prairie voles will often be found, depending on whether the meadow is lush or dry, respectively. In northwestern Indiana, Franklin's ground squirrels are sometimes found along rights-of-way, as on Route 52 southeast of Fowler in Benton County. Mounds of pocket gophers are numerous around Willow Slough in Newton County. Thirteen-lined ground squirrels are fairly common on rights-of-way in much of the northern part of the state.

Golf Courses, Soccer Fields, and Other Recreational Areas

1800. None were present.

1900. None were present.

2000. There are now 55,015 acres of municipal, 33,336 acres of commercial, and 47,156 acres of private recreational land across the state (Indiana Department of Natural Resources 2000). Quantities vary greatly from county to county.

FLORA. Soccer fields and other recreational areas are composed mostly of turf grasses. Kentucky bluegrass is common and, possibly, red fescue. Aside from lawn weeds and rough areas, few other species are present, especially native species. See Table P-12 for a list of species of soccer/recreational areas.

With the exception of possible remnant forest land between fairways, golf courses consist mostly of planted turf (Figure 11.7). The usual grass is Kentucky bluegrass, but creeping bent grass, red fescue, and bermuda grass may be found. Tall fescue may be used in rough areas. Lawn weeds are present in courses with less-intense turf management and in unmanicured rough areas. Audubon Society and other nongovernment certification programs have been developed to produce more eco-friendly golf courses. See Table P-12 for a list of species of golf courses.

AMPHIBIANS AND REPTILES. Areas maintained as lawn, such as fairways, greens, soccer fields, etc., will not have value for herpetofauna. However, the hazards typically mixed into golf courses may hold value for local reptiles and amphibians and may provide refugia in urbanized areas where native habitat has become limited. Wetlands in golf courses might very well have green frogs and bullfrogs, and leopard frogs as well if rank fields are available. Northern or midland water snakes may be present, as well as painted turtles, common snapping turtles, and red-eared sliders.

BIRDS. Golf courses are receiving attention as bird habitat, as indicated by Gillihan's book (2000) and a research symposium at the 2003 American Ornithologists' Union meeting, which was followed by articles in *Wildlife Society Bulletin* (e.g., Porter et al. 2005; Rodewald et al. 2005). Golf courses average between 50 and 60 ha (124–148 acres) in size, with 25–40% of the total area in natural habitat or rough, much of it in linear strip fragments (Gange et al. 2003). In Indiana, the natural habitat is likely to be forest, so birds that like forest and adjacent short grass will find it very suitable, for example, eastern bluebird, American robin, and chipping sparrow. Bluebird nest boxes are often placed on golf courses. Red-headed woodpecker, a species of oak savanna and other open habitats with trees, nested successfully on Ohio golf courses that were rich in snags and hard-mast trees (Rodewald et al. 2005).

Besides the birds which benefit from the combination of adjacent habitats, many forest birds (e.g., woodpeckers, flycatchers, chickadees, titmice) use the forest patches. In southwestern Ohio, researchers found that species richness and other diversity measures were correlated with land use in the surround-

Figure 11.7. Golf course.
Photo by IDNR–*Outdoor Indiana* magazine.

ing landscape, that is, more nearby residential development reduced diversity and more nearby natural cover increased it (Porter et al. 2005). Between 40 and 44 species nested on most golf courses, including the most rural ones; this number declined to 34 on a course in the most-developed area. Common breeding species, in approximate descending order of abundance, included American robin, common grackle, brown-headed cowbird, American goldfinch, chipping sparrow, mourning dove, European starling, blue-gray gnatcatcher, eastern bluebird, Canada goose, red-winged blackbird, gray catbird, and song sparrow (Porter et al. 2005).

Grassy fairways, greens, and lakes are a recipe for attracting Canada geese, a major nuisance species because of their excrement and grass consumption. Courses that incorporate more natural rough areas often have fewer problems with geese. Expanses of turf grass also attract European starlings, which grub for soil invertebrates with their powerful head and bill muscles. Killdeer may like the combination of water and very short grass.

Table B-7 lists 35 species likely to be found on at least some golf courses in Indiana. This is a conservative list (restricted to the more common species), since the Ohio study (Porter et al. 2005) found approximately 40 breeding species per surveyed course. Additional species will use such habitat in migration or in the winter.

In evaluating the impact of new golf course construction, an important consideration is the preexisting habitat. If it is an intact woodland or wetland, the golf course will usually degrade the area's value for birds, but the situation is different for agricultural land. Occasionally, contaminated waste areas are converted into environmentally productive golf courses (e.g., Lost Marsh Golf Course in Hammond, Indiana).

Soccer fields, which offer no habitat structure beyond an expanse of turf grass, are attractive to a small set of species, such as Canada geese, killdeer, American robins, and European starlings.

MAMMALS. The common mammals of golf courses will vary depending on the mix of habitats and the locality. In the north, thirteen-lined ground squirrels are sometimes common, and chipmunks, fox squirrels, gray squirrels, cottontails, and eastern moles may be present. In woods or shrubby areas, white-footed mice may be found, along with short-tailed shrews. In grassy areas, voles may be abundant.

Mammals of soccer/recreational areas are apt to be similar to those of golf courses. These sorts of areas are not habitats, but species found there will generally reflect the surrounding habitats, often fields or forest. See the accounts of those habitats.

Towers (Communication or Wind-Power Generation)

Cell towers (Figure 11.8) have rapidly expanded across the state since the 1970s and are still increasing. Wind towers, often in large wind farms, are being built across the country, including a conspicuous installation in Benton County in 2008. Such towers often lead to bird and bat deaths. It has been determined that many of the bats are dying from burst lungs resulting from the low pressure (barotrauma) created at the ends of the moving blades (Baerwald et al. 2008).

FLORA. Areas closely associated with towers typically have little suitable substrate upon which vegetation can develop. Most areas are either paved or graveled, and they are commonly subjected to herbicide application. Typically, any vegetation that does appear will consist of the species similar to those found in industrial areas (Table P-12). See Table P-12 for a list of species of towers.

AMPHIBIANS AND REPTILES. The structure of towers is not anticipated to provide any value to herpetofauna. In fact, the attractiveness of these structures to birds of prey may make them a detriment. The cleared areas around towers are much like rights-of-way in that they provide open-canopy habitat. As with rights-of-way, if tower areas are treated to maintain open canopy at inopportune times, then a variety of amphibians and reptiles could be negatively impacted, and the attractiveness of such sites to these species will be a detriment overall. An effort should be made to manage these areas during the winter or at other times when amphibians and reptiles, as well as other target flora and fauna, are inactive.

BIRDS. Tall communications towers have caused much mortality to migrating birds since they began

Figure 11.8. Communication towers.
Photo by Charles Amlaner.

to be erected in the late 1940s for television broadcasting (Shire et al. 2000). Thus, like plate-glass windows, they are a special hazard to birds, though not for other (non-flying) wildlife. Towers over 200 ft tall must have lights for aviation safety, and this confuses birds flying on nights with fog or low clouds; they circle the towers and hit guy wires or the structure itself (www.towerkill.com). The taller the tower, the greater the mortality. Indiana has its share: as of 1998, there were 587 towers between 200 and 299 ft tall, 479 between 300 and 499 ft tall, and 91 taller than 500 ft, a height distribution typical of national patterns (www.towerkill.com). One can assume that tower mortality in Indiana matches the patterns evident in data gathered in the eastern United States (Shire et al. 2000). Birds most commonly killed are warblers (18%), sparrows (10%), and waterfowl (10%). Communication towers are estimated to kill about as many birds annually in the United States as cars and pesticides (between 5 and 50 million), though fewer than high-tension wires, feral cats, and windows (www.sibleyguides.com/mortality.htm). The explosion in the construction of towers for cellular phones threatens greater rates of mortality for migratory species that are already suffering significant population declines. However, the Communication Tower Working Group, chaired by the U.S. Fish and Wildlife Service, is studying mitigation measures involving tower height, location, and types of lighting (Shire et al. 2000). One option is to prohibit towers along key migratory routes, such as near Hawk Mountain, Pennsylvania.

MAMMALS. There are a few cases of Indiana myotis (an endangered bat species) using telephone poles as roosts, but otherwise there is probably little direct relationship of mammals to poles, towers, etc. However, a swath is often cut below such poles, and this swath completely changes the habitat into open field when power lines go through what were woods. This sort of habitat would then likely contain animals of various types of fields.

In the quest to find new energy sources at the beginning of the twenty-first century, there has been the development of wind towers, or wind farms when in large numbers (Figure 11.9). There is currently only one in Indiana (in Benton County) but more are in the planning stages. Numerous birds have been found dead under these towers, but bats are at even greater risk. The highly migratory bats—the silver-haired, hoary, and red bats—are killed in great numbers at these farms. A number of ideas are being pursued in an effort to find a way to prevent these deaths.

Storm-Water Retention Ponds and Borrow Pits

No data were found on the distribution or number of retention ponds, which have been required for new subdivisions in Indiana since the 1970s. Numerous ponds have also been developed along interstate highways to provide fill for roadbeds (borrow pits; Figure 11.10), especially at overpasses. Many borrow pit ponds and lakes provide excellent fishing, swimming, and ice skating for farm families and other landowners. Along interstate highways especially, some of these areas are developed into campsites and other outdoor recreational uses.

FLORA. Storm-water retention ponds are most commonly associated with new suburban and commercial development. They vary considerably in depth. Most have lawn vegetation adjacent to the ponds, but the immediate pond borders may possess wetland vegetation. Although some wetland vegetation is planted, much of it originates from seed brought in by wind, water in-flow, and waterfowl. Some typical species include broad-leaved cattail, narrow-leaved cattail, common water plantain, common arrowhead, great bulrush, brown fox sedge, blunt spike rush, and swamp milkweed. American pondweed and coontail are submersed aquatics found in some ponds. See Table P-12 for a list of species of storm-water retention ponds.

Areas where soil has been removed for transport and use elsewhere (borrow pits) result in an exposure of subsoil that typically is not optimally conducive to vegetation growth, although some species find the environment to be prime, especially if the substrate is sand. The species associated with actively mined lands could be found here also. In areas where wet sand is exposed, a host of interesting and sometimes rare species can be found, including twisted yellow-eyed grass, round-leaved sundew, lance-leaved violet, appressed bog clubmoss, running ground pine, false

Figure 11.9. The first wind farm in Indiana, Benton County. Photo by Donald Smock.

Figure 11.10. Borrow pit. Soil was taken from the pond area to create the bridge approaches. Photo by John O. Whitaker, Jr.

foxglove, hardhack, and nodding ladies' tresses. Most likely, the plants are the result of seed transport via wind or animals (especially waterfowl). If the site was previously a wetland, then release from a seed bank could account for some of the plants as well. See Table P-12 for a list of species of borrow pits.

FISH. Storm-water retention ponds rarely contain sustaining fish assemblages, due to the high levels of contaminants and fluctuating water levels. Borrow pits usually possess sustaining water levels, but colonization is difficult by most fish, other than by stocking. Virtually no studies of storm-water retention ponds or borrow pits have been conducted in Indiana. Most of these water bodies are privately owned, and if they possess fish they are usually stocked from hatcheries and aquaculture facilities. Species collected from storm-water retention ponds often include mosquitofish, channel catfish, bullheads, and a mixture of black bass and sunfish species (T. P. Simon, unpublished data). None of these assemblages are natural. Sometimes, well-meaning individuals stock their favorite aquarium fish species or other carnivorous fish that have been caught elsewhere in borrow pits. Rarely do these individuals survive, due to the lack of thermal refugia and food resources.

AMPHIBIANS AND REPTILES. In spite of the fact that they appear to provide aquatic habitat, most storm-water retention ponds are not adequately designed to mimic the components of wetlands needed by amphibians and reptiles. While many storm-water retention ponds may be attractive to amphibians and reptiles, they may not retain water long enough for successful reproduction. Consequently, they become a reproductive sink. With improvements in design, it may be possible for storm-water retention ponds to succeed at holding excess runoff and thus provide sites for successful reproduction by amphibians. Under such circumstances, bullfrogs, green frogs, and American toads are the most likely species. If amphibians are able to persist in these sites, then the locations will also have value to reptiles as foraging areas, and northern/midland water snakes and eastern garter snakes might be the most likely reptiles seen.

Borrow pits in and of themselves have little to offer amphibians and reptiles unless they capture water, hold it long enough for amphibians to reproduce (which roadside pits usually do), and either remain fishless or provide enough emergent vegetation to give amphibian eggs and larvae refugia from fish predation. The benefits of these areas, if they hold water, include reproductive sites for amphibians and, consequently, foraging sites for reptiles such as water snakes. Bull and green frogs lay their eggs in floating masses of algae, which are often found in borrow pits.

BIRDS. Storm-water retention ponds are usually too exposed, disturbed, and small to be attractive to wetland or aquatic birds, except perhaps for brief visits for drinking, in which case the likely species would be the birds listed for commercial or industrial lands. However, Canada geese and mallard ducks breed in retention ponds throughout the state.

In contrast, borrow pits along highways can become attractive sites for aquatic birds, because the areas are larger and less disturbed than storm-water ponds, and the pits often fill with water, forming various types of ponds or lakes (deep, shallow, or mudflats). An internet search for "birds and borrow pits" reveals that this is an international phenomenon, with birding reports from the United Kingdom and Australia as well as the midwestern United States (e.g., Illinois, Ohio, Missouri). The aquatic species most often reported are geese, ducks, gulls, terns, and migratory shorebirds. Least terns (an endangered subspecies) nesting in 2005 at a power plant in Spencer County, Indiana, foraged for small fish in borrow pits and other sites (Castrale 2005). A borrow pit lake in Terre Haute near the Interstate 70 bridge supports breeding hooded mergansers, migrating shorebirds, and late summer flocks of egrets and herons. Various swallow species feed on flying insects associated with these water bodies. The bare or scrub lands associated with such pits might be attractive for open and shrubland birds like blue grosbeak. Some 80 aquatic, shrubland, and other species are likely to use borrow pits in Indiana (Table B-7).

MAMMALS. Typical storm-water retention ponds are usually open and have little cover. We would not expect mammals to be generally associated with them, although an occasional muskrat might use one during dispersal. If there is adequate habitat around such a pond, then small mammals of that habitat might be present.

Muskrats might use borrow pits occasionally if there are enough aquatic plants to support them, but otherwise, there are no mammals that would generally make borrow pits their habitat. As borrow pits age and succession occurs around them, more species of mammals, including weasels, mink, and a number of small mammals, could use them. Several other species could live there, depending on the surrounding habitat, such as typical mammals of fields or forest.

Part 4.
Species Concerns: Declining Natives and Invading Exotics

This part begins by summarizing two major wildlife conservation issues: declines in native species diversity and increases in exotic species that have become established since settlement times. We will first discuss native species that have been extirpated, and then those officially recognized at federal or state levels as endangered, threatened, or "to be watched." Exotic species will be enumerated, and some major species problems will be discussed. The final chapter is a contribution to taxonomic history, covering species whose scientific descriptions were based on species taken in Indiana.

Tree-of-heaven and purple loosestrife. Photo by IDNR–*Indiana Outdoor* magazine.

Figure 12.1. Redside dace. Photo by Brant Fisher.

12 Extirpated, Endangered, and Threatened Native Species

The past 200 years of habitat loss and transformation in Indiana have greatly affected the abundance and distribution of its plant and animal species. Numerous species present at the time of European settlement have been extirpated from the state, and many more are greatly reduced. Others that declined badly have recovered, with or without human assistance. Meanwhile, many exotic organisms from other continents have become established, as the next chapter documents.

Here, we will list the species of vascular plants, vertebrate wildlife, and cave invertebrates that have been extirpated (including global extinctions) and those that are presently listed as endangered or threatened at the federal or state levels (see also Whitaker and Gammon 1988). Although most have been mentioned in the habitat-specific histories of chapters 4–11, it is instructive to see them all in one place.

Flora

Currently, there are just under 2,000 native species of vascular plants known to inhabit Indiana (Table P-1), along with almost 900 adventive (exotic) ones. There are 54 that have been extirpated from the state (Table P-13), 2 that are listed as federally endangered, and 3 that are listed as federally threatened. In addition, 209 are listed as state endangered and 90 are listed as state threatened (Table P-13). An additional 130 are on the state "watch list," meaning that they were once on one of the other lists. We know of no Indiana plant species that is now extinct.

The state-determined categories are defined as follows. State-endangered species (SE) are known from 1–5 extant occurrences statewide, threatened species (ST) from 6–10 extant occurrences statewide, and state-rare species (SR) from 11–20 extant occurrences statewide. Extirpated species (SX) are those formerly documented for Indiana, but extant occurrences are unknown. These numbers are guidelines; some deviations may occur. For example, if a species has 12 occurrences (and thus should be placed in the rare category), but has serious threats to its existence, its status might be upgraded. More specifically, there are a sufficient number of occurrences of Canada yew that it should be categorized as state-rare, but because of the intense browsing pressure on it by white-tailed deer, the species has been placed in the state-endangered category.

Fish

There are 200 species of fish currently inhabiting Indiana (Table F-1). Eleven species (and 1 form) have been extirpated from the state; the harelip sucker and shortnose cisco are now considered extinct throughout their ranges, and the blackfin cisco may be extinct. No fish species from Indiana are currently listed federally; however, 10 are state endangered, including the redside dace (Fig 12.1), and 14 (and 1 form) are listed as species of special concern.

Amphibians and Reptiles

Forty species of amphibians and 56 species of reptiles currently inhabit Indiana (Table H-1). Five amphibians—crawfish frog (Figure 12.2), hellbender (Figure 12.3), four-toed salamander, green salamander, and red salamander—are listed as state endangered. Sixteen reptile species (10 snakes and 6 turtles) are state endangered. One reptile, the mud snake, appears to have been extirpated, and another, the alligator snapping turtle, may be as well. The northern populations of the copperbelly water snake (Figure 12.4), federally listed as threatened in 1997, are all but extirpated in northern Indiana, though the state-listed southern populations are more robust. The eastern massasauga is listed as a federal candidate species. The remaining state-listed endangered species are Butler's garter snake, Kirtland's snake, copperbelly water snake, scarlet snake, smooth green snake, southeastern crowned snake, timber rattlesnake, Blanding's turtle, eastern mud turtle, hieroglyphic river cooter, ornate box turtle, and spotted turtle.

Ephemeral wetland habitats are rich in species, but currently no state or federal regulations protect them from conversion to other uses. Given their fre-

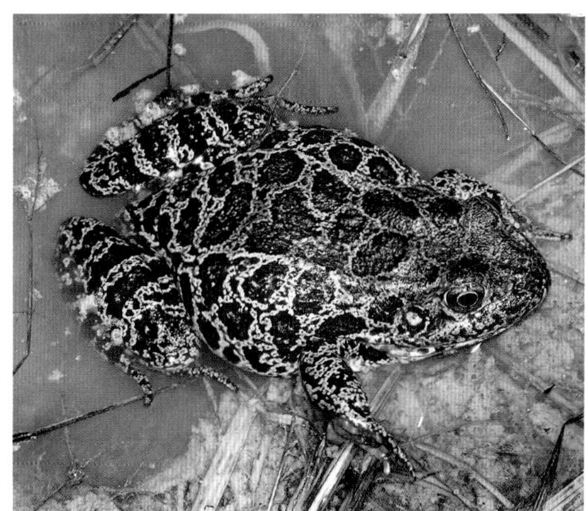

Figure 12.2. Crawfish frog, listed as state endangered. Photo by IDNR–*Outdoor Indiana* magazine.

Figure 12.3. Hellbender, listed as state endangered. Photo by IDNR–*Outdoor Indiana* magazine.

Figure 12.4. Copperbelly water snake, listed as state endangered. Photo by Bruce Kingsbury.

Figure 12.5. Whooping cranes in flight. Photo by IDNR–*Outdoor Indiana* magazine.

quently small size and the ease with which they can be drained, most are already gone. Current federal law is inadequate to protect these wetlands because of their isolated, "non-navigable" nature, and states are grappling with how to fill the gap. The status of many of Indiana's amphibians and reptiles will depend on the outcome of this process.

Birds

The Indiana Bird Records Committee (2005) lists 407 species of birds that have occurred at least once in the state. At least 2 of these species are now globally extinct (see below). Because of avian mobility, approximately 100 species on the state list have occurred accidentally, or occur very irregularly, i.e., rarely more than once every 5 years. Thus, our list of "annually occurring birds of Indiana" contains 309 species (Table B-1), including species that formerly occurred annually and 3 that are now extirpated or extinct.

Either 2 or 3 species that were native and occurred regularly have become globally extinct, depending on the status of the ivory-billed woodpecker in Arkansas and Florida; 4–6 have been extirpated in the state, depending on the strictness of the definition, and on whether one counts the 2 reintroduced species; and 3–5 are federally endangered, depending on whether one counts whooping crane (a "non-essential experimental population" now migrates through the state; Figure 12.5) and Kirtland's warbler (not annually detected in migration). Some 27 species are state endangered, and 13 more are of special concern in the state.

Extinct Birds of Indiana

1. Passenger pigeon: extinct by end of 1800s
2. Carolina parakeet: disappeared about 1860 (Butler 1892; McKinley 1976)
3. Ivory-billed woodpecker (see next section)

A fourth likely species for this list is Eskimo curlew, which is either extinct or has been extremely rare for a century. Its former status in Indiana is uncertain, based on only a few specimens. It was probably a rare migrant, because the normal spring migration was through the Great Plains, and fall migration was through New England and over the Atlantic Ocean to South America (Gill et al. 1998). However, it was considered a common migrant in Illinois and once occurred in the prairies of northwestern Indiana (Mumford and Keller 1984). Its migration companions were American golden-plovers, which continue to use the now-agricultural fields of northwestern Indiana as spring stopover habitat.

Extirpated Birds of Indiana

1. Greater prairie-chicken: Its last active breeding grounds were in Newton County, where breeding ended about 1970 (Mumford and Keller 1984). Presently, the nearest birds are a reintroduced

population in Jasper County in east-central Illinois.

2. Ivory-billed woodpecker: This species has possibly been rediscovered in Arkansas (2005) and the Florida panhandle (2006). We optimistically list it here as well as above.
3. Common raven: It formerly bred in scattered locations in cliffs in southern Indiana, e.g., Dubois and Franklin counties, but disappeared in the 1890s.
4. Bewick's wren: It formerly bred in the state, commonly from about 1860 to 1950. It is now recorded less than annually, the most recent record being a singing adult in Putnam County in July 2006.
5. Bachman's sparrow: It formerly bred on abandoned cultivated fields in southern and central Indiana, reaching peak abundance in the early 1950s, after which it declined rapidly. There was only a single possible breeding record (in Crawford County) during the 5-year breeding bird atlas period of 1985–1990 (Castrale et al. 1998). It is now recorded less than annually.

Extirpated but Reintroduced Birds of Indiana

1. Trumpeter swan: It probably nested in marshes of northwestern Indiana, e.g., at Black Marsh in the Beaver Lake area of Newton County, as late as 1873 (Mumford and Keller 1984). It was likely also a rare migrant. There were no records for over a century. Breeding populations reintroduced to Wisconsin have wintered, since the late 1990s, in west-central Indiana (Vermillion, Parke, Fountain counties) and adjacent Edgar County, Illinois, using large, deep lakes (especially on reclaimed mines) and feeding in corn fields. Many adult and immature birds in these flocks are color banded.
2. Whooping crane: It migrated through the Kankakee River marshes, and may have summered there, although there is no proof of breeding. By 1897, it was a rare migrant and was last seen in 1907 (Mumford and Keller 1984). There were no records for nearly a century, until the midwestern reintroduction program began in Wisconsin. Since 2001, Indiana has been on the fall migration route for small flocks of juvenile cranes fledged in Wisconsin and led south to a Florida refuge by an ultralight glider as a surrogate parent. Limited by the glider's flight capability, the flock proceeds slowly for 2–3 months to winter quarters. In the spring, the young cranes return on their own (much more rapidly) to Wisconsin. In addition, experienced adults make the trip on their own, often as pairs or single birds. One of the guided flock's overnight stops is Muscatatuck National Wildlife Refuge. In the spring, they have been observed there and at Goose Pond Fish and Wildlife Area. The Wisconsin-Florida population numbered 63 birds in 2006; in that summer, the first 2 crane chicks in a century to hatch in the wild in the Midwest did so in Wisconsin.

Figure 12.6. Bald eagle was listed as federally endangered, but has now been delisted. Photo by IDNR–*Outdoor Indiana* magazine.

Figure 12.7. Osprey.
Photo by IDNR–*Outdoor Indiana* magazine.

Figure 12.8. Peregrine falcons formerly nested on cliffs. Now, most nest on buildings. Photo by IDNR–*Outdoor Indiana* magazine.

Figure 12.9. Barn owl.
Photo by IDNR–*Outdoor Indiana* magazine.

Figure 12.10. Bison roamed Indiana in huge numbers prior to European settlement. Photo by IDNR–*Outdoor Indiana* magazine.

Federally Endangered Birds
Occurring Annually in Indiana

1. Least tern (Interior population)
2. Piping plover (Great Lakes population)
3. Whooping crane: "non-essential experimental population" (see above)
4. Kirtland's warbler is occasionally detected (less than annually) in migration in Indiana. Since its breeding grounds are in northern Michigan, it probably passes through Indiana regularly.

Federally Threatened Species
Occurring Annually in Indiana

1. Bald eagle: downgraded from endangered. This species has recovered spectacularly as a breeder since the 1990s, following several years of assisted breeding and fledging (Figure 12.6). Almost 100 pairs now nest on the Wabash, White, and other rivers (J. Castrale, personal communication), and population growth continues.

State-Endangered Bird Species

These are listed on the IDNR website (http://www.in.gov/dnr/fishwild/endangered/birds.htm): trumpeter swan, American bittern, least bittern, black-crowned night-heron, yellow-crowned night-heron, osprey (Figure 12.7), bald eagle, northern harrier, peregrine falcon (Figure 12.8), king rail, Virginia rail, black rail, common moorhen, whooping crane, piping plover, upland sandpiper, least tern, black tern, barn owl (Figure 12.9), short-eared owl, loggerhead shrike, marsh wren, sedge wren, golden-winged warbler, Kirtland's warbler, Henslow's sparrow, yellow-

Figure 12.11. Indiana bat, listed as federally endangered. Photo by Adam Mann.

Figure 12.12. Gray bat, listed as federally endangered. Photo by James Kiser.

Figure 12.13. Cluster of 36,000 Indiana bats in hibernation in Twin Domes Cave. Photo by John O. Whitaker, Jr.

headed blackbird. This group includes a number of species whose breeding status is endangered but that may be fairly common as migrants (e.g., osprey, northern harrier, Virginia rail, black tern, short-eared owl). Peregrine falcons and ospreys have benefited from restoration. Nest platforms have been constructed at lakes in state wildlife areas for ospreys, and nest boxes have been placed on appropriate man-made structures for peregrine falcons.

State Bird Species of Special Concern

These are great egret, sharp-shinned hawk, broad-winged hawk, red-shouldered hawk, Mississippi kite, sandhill crane, common nighthawk, whip-poor-will, black-and-white warbler, cerulean warbler, hooded warbler, worm-eating warbler, and western meadowlark.

Mammals

There are 59 species of mammals currently inhabiting Indiana (Table M-1). Eight additional species have been extirpated from the state, and 6 (2 federal, 4 state) are listed as endangered (Table M-9). Many thousands of bison once inhabited Indiana (Figure 12.10), but these magnificent creatures are now gone. Two federally listed endangered species are currently found in Indiana, the Indiana bat (Figure 12.11) and the gray bat (Figure 12.12). The Indiana bat forms huge clusters in hibernacula (Figure 12.13).

Subterranean Invertebrates

Nearly 100 species of obligate subterranean (including cavernicolous and groundwater) invertebrates are currently known from Indiana. Only one, the groundwater amphipod, *Bactrurus cellulanus,* is suspected to be extinct, although entire communities of species have been extirpated locally. Due to their cryptic nature and the difficulties involved in discovering and monitoring them, entire species may become extinct before they are even described (as was the case with *Bactrurus cellulanus,* which was discovered in a museum collection). None is listed as endangered by the USFWS, although many are on the IDNR Natural Heritage list of threatened and endangered species (Table I-5).

Exotic and Invasive Species

13

Exotic and invasive species are a big conservation problem of our time, a consequence of habitat disturbance, global trade and travel, and the relentless tendency of any species to reproduce to the utmost when given the opportunity (as first pointed out in 1859 by Charles Darwin, who described examples of exotic species explosions in *The Origin of Species*). Since 1800, many organisms have entered or been brought into Indiana and established viable populations. Undoubtedly, many others have entered the state and failed to establish, though this is rarely documented.

Flora

There are about 800 exotic plant species in Indiana, including some highly detrimental invasives; the most troublesome are indicated in Table P-14. Two important exotics are garlic mustard (Figure 13.1) and purple loosestrife (Figure 13.2). The percentage of exotics among the state's vascular plants (approximately 29%) is much higher than for any of the animal groups treated here. Exotic species have been introduced from foreign lands by intentional means, e.g., bringing in plant materials for food, building materials, medicine, ornamental use, etc., and unintentionally, such as weed seeds transported in soil or crop seed mixes. Regardless of the source, some exotics are having a tremendous, negative environmental and economic impact on the state.

Fish

Twenty-two exotic species of fish now inhabit the aquatic systems of Indiana (Table F-6). The striped mullet and inland silverside now occur in the state as the result of natural upstream range expansion on the Ohio River, and could be omitted from the list. They are included because the current, altered state of the Ohio River may have contributed to their range expansion, which might otherwise not have occurred.

Many of the exotic fish species currently found in Indiana, such as common carp, rainbow smelt, the various species of Salmonidae, and striped bass, were intentionally stocked for recreational purposes; alewife was stocked as a forage species. The others have arrived unintentionally, the round goby via the ballast water of transoceanic vessels; the goldfish, grass carp, silver carp, bighead carp (Figure 13.3), and white catfish by escape from private waters. The sea lamprey, threespine stickleback, and white perch arrived through man-made canals/connections between normally disconnected drainages. The rudd arrived as the result of aquarium or bait-bucket release. The oriental weatherfish arrived by the three latter methods.

Many exotic fish species have become invasive, with negative impacts on native species diversity and natural communities. Some, such as sea lamprey, carp, and goldfish, were established over a century ago, while invasions by bighead carp, silver carp, grass carp, white perch, round goby, and oriental weatherfish date from the early 1990s. The highest number of exotic species occurs in Lake Michigan.

Although not exotic to Indiana, a host of native species are now found outside their native ranges; these non-indigenous species can be found in Tables F-2 through F-5, which list the species found in each of the aquatic systems.

Amphibians and Reptiles

Apparently only one species of truly exotic reptile or amphibian has become established in Indiana. The common wall lizard, an exotic from Europe, is clearly resident in at least one location along the Ohio River. It appears to have emigrated from populations upstream around Cincinnati. The red-eared slider, a natural resident in a few Indiana locations, is also now established in a variety of other places; the sources may have been completed science experiments or pets that outlived their entertainment value. Other turtle species populations have likely become established as well, such as the river cooters on the St. Joseph River. Last, the green treefrog has been found in a growing number of locations along the Indiana side of the Ohio River in the vicinity of Evansville. The sheer number of localities and the proximity of natural populations across the river near Henderson, Kentucky, suggest that this species is managing to naturally expand its range into Indiana.

Birds

Eight exotic species have established populations that persist currently, without human help except for ring-necked pheasant. They are listed below in taxonomic order with their source location in parentheses.

1. Mute swan (Europe), well established in Michigan, has increased as a breeding bird in Indiana at an alarming rate in the twenty-first century, spreading from the northern part of the state into the central part.
2. Ring-necked pheasant (Asia), a managed game bird, was introduced to almost all counties, repeatedly in many areas. It is best adapted to the northern half of the state (probably because of climate), using grasslands and agricultural areas.

Figure 13.1. Garlic mustard. Photo by IDNR–*Outdoor Indiana* magazine.

Figure 13.2. Purple loosestrife. Photo by IDNR–*Outdoor Indiana* magazine.

Figure 13.3. Bighead carp, a recent inhabitant of Indiana. Photo by Brant Fisher.

Figure 13.4. Monk parakeet with nesting material. Photo by Marty Jones.

3. Rock pigeon (Europe), known for many years as rock dove, became established in cities and agricultural areas soon after European settlement.
4. Eurasian collared dove (Europe to Bahamas to Florida, 1982) was discovered breeding in Indiana in 2002. It is spreading through the state (there are multiple county records) and is noticed mainly in smaller towns near grain elevators, railroad yards, etc. At present, the largest local populations are about 100 birds.
5. Monk parakeet (South America; imported by pet trade) is presently restricted to Lake County, close to its Chicago stronghold; in the twenty-first century, it has nested in Whiting (Figures 13.4, 13.5).
6. European starling (Europe), introduced in New York City in 1890, expanded across the country, reaching Indiana in 1919. It is one of the most numerous birds in the state and competes with many native species for nest cavities in trees.
7. House finches are native to the southwestern United States, but eastern U.S. populations derive from a colony released in New York in the 1940s. The species established in Indiana in 1976. The rise in house finch numbers on Christmas counts has been paralleled by a decline in numbers of purple finch (a wintering species), although this phenomenon might be restricted to the use of feeders.
8. House sparrows (Europe) were introduced deliberately about 1870 and expanded rapidly in Indi-

Figure 13.5. Monk parakeet nest in Indiana. Photo by IDNR–*Outdoor Indiana* magazine.

ana, as documented and deplored by Butler (1898). They are well established in towns, on farms, and along highways.

Mammals

Exotic mammals currently existing in Indiana are the house mouse, Norway rat, and red fox. The house mouse and Norway rat came in with the early European settlers. The red fox was apparently introduced from Europe into the eastern United States about 1855 for hunting.

Cave Invertebrates

Most of the exotic invertebrates found in Indiana caves are so widespread in surface habitats that it is difficult to tell where they might have originated. The greenhouse millipede, *Oxidus gracilis,* is thought to be native to Japan, but is now essentially worldwide in temperate climates. The social springtail, *Entomobrya socia,* is likewise believed to be Asian. It was first seen in the United States in the 1970s and is spreading.

The largest group of exotics in Indiana caves is the terrestrial isopods. Four non-native species have been recorded to date, and we would expect to find others, considering their love of damp habitats and detritus. As best as can be discerned, these animals originated from Europe, but like other exotics they are so widespread now that their origins are obscure.

Seven exotic species have entered the state: greenhouse millipede (*Oxidus gracilis*); millipede (*Ophyiulus pilosus*); 4 species of terrestrial isopod (*Haplophthalmus danicus, Armadillidium nasatum, Porcellionides pruinosis, Trachelipus rathkei*); and social springtail (*Entomobrya socia*).

14

Vertebrate and Cave Invertebrate Species Described from Indiana

A number of early biologists worked in Indiana and described several species from the state. We will list here the vertebrate and cave invertebrate species that have their type localities in Indiana. An impressive number of fish and cave invertebrate species were described from Indiana—fish because some of America's earliest and most productive ichthyologists worked here, and cave invertebrates because of their high degree of endemism. The information on plants described from Indiana is not readily available and thus has not been included here.

Fish

Thirty-seven species of fish were described from localities in Indiana, out of the 211 fish historically known from the state (17.5%). This is not surprising, as a number of ichthyologists worked in the state throughout the nineteenth century. Samuel Rafinesque described 24 on his own, from a trip in 1818 down the Ohio River and into the lower Wabash River (Rafinesque 1820). Charles Lesueur, Edward Drinker Cope, David Starr Jordan, Herbert E. Copeland, Charles Gilbert, Barton W. Evermann, and Joseph Swain also described fish species from Indiana prior to the beginning of the twentieth century. The type localities and authors for all the fish species described from Indiana are given in Table F-7. Two of these are the shovelnose sturgeon (Figure 14.1) and the greenside darter (Figure 14.2).

Amphibians and Reptiles

A total of 5 presently recognized reptiles and amphibians have their type localities in Indiana: 3 turtles, a snake, and a frog (Table H-10).

Birds

No bird species were originally described from Indiana (American Ornithologists' Union 1998). The 2 closest type localities are those of Henslow's sparrow (Kentucky, opposite Cincinnati, Ohio, described

Figure 14.1. Shovelnose sturgeon. Photo by Brant Fisher.

Figure 14.2. Greenside darter. Photo by Brant Fisher.

1829 by Audubon) and Nelson's sharp-tailed sparrow (Calumet marshes, Cook County, Illinois, 1875). Most Indiana birds have ranges that extend to the Atlantic or Gulf coasts, and were described from the Carolinas, Pennsylvania, or Louisiana, or from wintering grounds in the West Indies or Mexico, or they have Holarctic distributions and were described in Europe (e.g., waterfowl).

Mammals

Two species of mammals were originally described from Indiana: the Indiana myotis, *Myotis sodalis,* described from Wyandotte Cave, Crawford County, by Miller and Allen (1928); and the prairie vole, *Microtus ochrogaster,* described from New Harmony, Posey County, by Wagner (in Schreber 1842).

Cave Invertebrates

A surprising number of cave invertebrates—61 species—have been described from Indiana, as indicated in Table I-6. The majority were described in four periods of discovery: 1871–1897 (15 species), 1929–1933 (8 species), 1958–1973 (16 species), and 1994–2004 (22 species). The types come from approximately 35 localities in 11 counties, with Crawford, Lawrence, and Harrison counties being most productive (22, 11, and 8 types, respectively). The single most productive locality is Wyandotte Cave (Crawford County), where 11 species were described between 1871 and 1998.

Conclusion: Summary and Research Needs

Overview of Habitat Changes

Habitats in Indiana were mostly in native vegetation in 1800 due to the small number of Native Americans and European settlers. While Native Americans were important in disturbing plant and animal communities in Indiana, their estimated population of 20,000 in 1800 means that they were probably growing crops on less than 100,000 acres per year. Their use of fire influenced a much larger area than this. It is important to bear in mind that the landscape in 1800 may still have been recovering from the impacts of much larger Native American populations that were present in the 1400s and 1500s, prior to declines brought on, in part, by diseases acquired from early European visitors and colonists.

The landscape rapidly changed from 1800 to 1900 as settlers poured into the state, cleared forests for agriculture, allowed domestic livestock to roam free, drained wetlands, plowed prairies, and utilized native plants and animals for subsistence. In many ways, the period from 1850 to 1930 was the height of natural resource abuse and habitat destruction in Indiana and the entire Midwest.

The period from the 1930s to the present has, on one hand, been marked by improved management and the recovery of natural resources and habitats with the transfer of private land to public parks, forests, and wildlife refuges. Improved forest and wildlife management, the establishment of natural areas, and environmental regulations have been important in improving the general quality of the Indiana landscape. These improvements have allowed the successful reintroduction of the bald eagle, river otter, wild turkey, beaver, and white-tailed deer, and their expansion within the state indicates that habitats are improving.

On the other hand, the same time period has seen an approximate doubling of the state's human population, sprawling urban and suburban growth, the disappearance of farmland at an alarming rate, and a distancing of citizens from contact with the natural environment in Indiana.

The large increase in use of fossil fuels and chemicals has allowed the support of much larger human populations even while lands were set aside for protection of habitats. The use of these materials has potential impacts on habitats and species that will need to be addressed as they are identified. For example, the impact of DDT on bird reproduction was identified and its use banned. Climate change due to the use of fossil fuels has long-term potential for significant habitat change. The development of better mechanisms for the control of waste products and more efficient use of energy will be necessary for continued restoration of the Indiana landscape.

Forested habitats once covered 20 million acres of Indiana. These habitats were cleared for other uses, primarily agriculture, so that in 1900 only 3.8 million acres remained, of which 2.7 million acres was in poor condition due to poor logging practices, fire, and grazing. Over the twentieth century, the amount of forest rose to 4.5 million acres, most of it in much better condition than in 1900. The increase in forest area from 1900 has been due to a reversion of agriculture land to forest habitat through natural processes and planting. As explained in chapter 10, much of the cropland in the south-central portion of the state was abandoned in the early 1900s and reverted to public ownership. These public lands, managed as state and federal forests, and large areas of private land were allowed to revert to forest or were planted to trees to reduce soil erosion.

Unfortunately, natural habitats are still being compromised today as urban areas expand and individuals develop home sites. Most forest habitats are small woodlands surrounded by areas with other land uses, except those in public ownership, which are usually much larger. Many are changing due to the introduction of exotic species. A lack of disturbance also has caused problems. For example, savannas created by fires set by Native Americans in much of northwestern Indiana have changed to closed-canopy forests due to protection from fire. Prescribed fire is currently being used to reverse these trends.

Grasslands (prairie) have undergone even more extreme changes than forests. In 1800, there were about 1 million acres of grasslands, while only about 1,000 acres of original prairie remained in 2000. Compensating for this somewhat, better reclamation of strip-mined lands in southwestern Indiana has created large areas of grassland habitat, which partially substitute for the loss of prairie, as far as vertebrate wildlife (but not native plants) is concerned. Current interest in prairie restoration will restore small portions of this habitat.

Likewise, wetlands have seen great change. They decreased from about 5.6 million acres in 1800 to about 1 million in 2000. Wetlands have been drained for farmland and development of all kinds. Recent conservation programs have slowed the drainage of wetlands and reestablished some formerly drained ones.

All these factors have changed Indiana from a land of woods, prairies, and wetlands into an agricultural state with many urban communities. Most farmland now produces soybeans and corn with few fields left fallow, since inorganic fertilizers are used to provide the nutrients obtained in the past from cover crops. Today's larger fields mean much less fencerow habitat than formerly. On the other hand, the increased practice of no-till cultivation provides some winter food for wildlife. The state's vast expanses of cropland vary seasonally in their value as food and cover for native species. These cropland areas are interspersed with small fragments of forest, prairie, and wetland with little connectivity, except by riparian zones along streams.

Developed land (homesteads, towns, cities, roads, factories, subdivisions, etc.) expanded from a few thousand acres in 1800 to about 100,000 acres in 1900 and to around 1 million acres in 2000. Currently, Indiana is losing about 100,000 acres of land—mostly farmland—per year to development, which amounts to a county about every 2–3 years.

There have been positive changes across the Indiana landscape since the late twentieth century. Over 30,000 acres of wetlands have been protected or restored since the 1980s. Strip-mined lands are now restored for farming or as grassland through topsoil recovery and grading to natural contours. While many streams and lakes are still impaired due to mercury pollution, they are generally in better condition due to waste treatment and better farming practices, such as no-till. Much of the badly degraded land of the early 1900s has been placed in public ownership for use as state and national parks (23 state parks), forests (18 state forests), reservoirs (9), fish and wildlife areas (16), and museums and state historic sites (18). Consequently, large contiguous areas of native habitat are primarily found in association with state and federal public lands.

Research Needs for the Conservation of Wildlife and Habitats

Fish

The fish fauna has been well studied, enabling a thorough understanding of their ecological relationships across the entire state. The greatest impact on biodiversity has been the loss of riverine wetland habitats along the large water bodies of Lake Michigan and the Ohio and Wabash rivers by filling, channelization, and ditching. Loss of these habitats caused the loss of obligate wetland species. Efforts should be made to restore the habitats and recover these species.

Amphibians and Reptiles

While herpetofauna remain a group of vertebrates that are understudied, great strides have been made in clarifying the ecological requirements of many species. In Indiana, it is clear that the greatest impact to herpetofaunal biodiversity was the loss of most shallow wetland systems, and the degradation of many of those remaining. The extensive loss and degradation of grasslands and open woodlands via agricultural conversion and succession have also been important influences on herpetofaunal diversity in the state.

An emerging pattern for many herpetofauna is that viable populations require much larger landscapes than we might hope, given the resources at our disposal. The necessity of large-scale forest tracts has become evident for a variety of species, including the copperbelly water snake in floodplain forests and the timber rattlesnake in upland forests. Time will likely reveal that far more species and populations are on their way to extirpation unless we can find mechanisms to provide the populations, rather than the individuals, with the landscape they need to persist.

Birds

Habitat use by bird species in Indiana is well known, thanks to decades of fieldwork by birders, which has been distilled and published in state bird books, seasonal reports in national and state birding journals, Christmas and spring bird count summaries, the breeding bird atlas, and so on. We know the basic facts: what species occur in the state, their distribution across counties, habitat affinities, relative abundance, and month-by-month changes in abundance. A few important habitats could use more study, such as successional vegetation in utility rights-of-way, and riparian forest away from roads.

The greatest data need, probably, is for quantitative studies that determine how productive each major habitat (grassland, forest, wetland, etc.) is within the present range of landscape conditions. Natural habitat is now often reduced to strips and patches in agricultural or developed landscapes. Such studies may focus on a single threatened species (e.g., Bajema and Lima 2001), a guild of bird species (e.g., insectivores), or an entire community (Grundel and Pavlovic 2007b). The elements of productivity we would like to see researched include what species occur in the community, their densities (by guild and species), and how the habitat patches contribute (as sources, sinks, etc.) to regional viability of the characteristic native species. For example, which forest species can maintain stable populations when the percentage of forested land in a county is as low as 10%, a common condition in once extensively forested northern Indiana? Because habitat conditions are similar in adjacent midwestern states, coordinated multistate studies are an excellent approach, as pioneered by Robinson et al. (1995) for birds of forest fragments and Best et al. (1997) for agricultural land in the Conservation Reserve Program. Similarly, a 19-site study across several counties in Indiana showed that grasslands on reclaimed surface coal mines were consistently productive for nearly the full native complement of grassland birds (DeVault et al. 2002).

We should maintain a broad perspective and ask what habitats in Indiana are most critical for birds at a continental scale. Our interior, north temperate zone location makes Indiana important for long-distance migratory species, which seek habitat during migration, in the winter, and during the breeding season. Many waterfowl, shorebird, and land bird species migrate through the state. Suitable habitat is scarce for all three groups, which need relatively undisturbed lakes and wetlands, extensive mudflats, and wide corridors of riparian forests, respectively.

Habitat conservation planning is a major preoccupation in bird conservation, as shown by the rapid development of the international Partners in Flight program, which assesses population trends, among other activities. There are many excellent, habitat-specific ideas for bird conservation (see Askins 2000) which can be (and have been) applied in Indiana. The acquisition of Goose Pond State Wildlife Area in Greene County is an excellent example of habitat conservation and restoration at the landscape level. The initial focus on ducks and geese expanded to include shorebirds and marsh birds. The birding community of the region (especially from Bloomington, Monroe County) has been enthusiastically monitoring the productivity of the area at all seasons. In its first 2 years of existence (2007–2008), the Goose Pond Christmas bird count led the state in number of species with 103 and 105 species. Similar exciting restoration efforts and avian monitoring are under way in the Kankakee River area.

Mammals

Challenges at the beginning of the twenty-first century in terms of mammals are to continue to improve the management of many species, to keep watch over all, and to continue to set aside natural lands. Those particularly in need of our help at present, in order of greater concern first, are swamp rabbit, Franklin's ground squirrel, wood rat, bobcat, gray fox, least weasel, badger, long-tailed weasel, star-nosed mole, Indiana myotis, gray myotis, evening bat, pocket gopher, and river otter.

The establishment of large natural areas in Indiana that has occurred in recent years will be of great help for the continued success of mammals as well as other biota. Some of these are Hoosier National Forest, Indiana Dunes National Lakeshore, the extensive grasslands of southern Indiana created after surface mining, Kankakee Sands, and Goose Pond. These have added to the great system of state parks, fish and wildlife areas, and reservoirs established earlier. Other tracts, including smaller ones, are being set aside by the Nature Conservancy, Indiana DNR, and other agencies. Finally, in the twenty-first century a number of land trusts have been formed in Indiana. Land trusts acquire and manage natural lands in local areas as they become available. The best thing we can do for the biota is to set aside patches of natural land, both large and small, and all the organizations mentioned above are doing just that.

Table G-1. Land Use by Natural Region Based on National Land Cover Data, 1992

Highland Rim

Land Use	Acres
open water	22,436.3
low-int. res.	25,147.5
high-int. res	2,535.3
comm./ind./trans.	8,431.8
bare rock/sand/clay	0
quarries/mines	903.9
transitional	1,219.5
deciduous forest	798,539.6
evergreen forest	34,471.2
mixed forest	1,475.0
shrubland	0
grasslands/herbaceous	0
pasture/hay	442,212.5
row crops	389,601.0
small grains	0
urban/rec. grasses	2,934.6
wooded wetlands	4,425.3
emergent herb. wetlands	671.8
Total	**1,735,005.3**

Grand Prairie

Land Use	Acres
open water	12,541.1
low-int. res.	12,102.7
high-int. res	3,735.8
comm./ind./trans.	7,540.2
bare rock/sand/clay	363.7
quarries/mines	497.7
transitional	154.5
deciduous forest	179,187.1
evergreen forest	24,155.6
mixed forest	2,238.8
shrubland	6.2
grasslands/herbaceous	41,840.9
pasture/hay	214,605.3
row crops	1,916,380.7
small grains	1,250.7
urban/rec. grasses	5,187.1
wooded wetlands	43,109.3
emergent herb. wetlands	11,209.0
Total	**2,476,106.3**

Northwestern Morainal

Land Use	Acres
open water	11,992.2
low-int. res.	34,205.5
high-int. res	36,197.1
comm./ind./trans.	33,434.4
bare rock/sand/clay	958.3
quarries/mines	102.0
transitional	0
deciduous forest	87,046.9
evergreen forest	32,632.1
mixed forest	2,885.5
shrubland	969.9
grasslands/herbaceous	22,430.1
pasture/hay	74,969.3
row crops	181,557.3
small grains	412.4
urban/rec. grasses	18,081.2
wooded wetlands	23,752.1
emergent herb. wetlands	10,941.4
Total	**572,567.7**

Central Till Plain

Land Use	Acres
open water	49,760.1
low-int. res.	236,298.9
high-int. res	34,772.4
comm./ind./trans.	100,581.2
bare rock/sand/clay	628.4
quarries/mines	3,366.1
transitional	1,494.1
deciduous forest	654,639.3
evergreen forest	15,525.7
mixed forest	6,843.3
shrubland	39.3
grasslands/herbaceous	12,951.2
pasture/hay	1,140,134.9
row crops	5,767,028.9
small grains	329.0
urban/rec. grasses	72,121.2
wooded wetlands	93,256.6
emergent herb. wetlands	8,389.4
Total	**8,198,159.9**

Table G-1. *continued*

Southwestern Lowlands

Land Use	Acres
open water	32,350.7
low-int. res.	39,196.6
high-int. res	7,912.5
comm./ind./trans.	15,284.5
bare rock/sand/clay	134.0
quarries/mines	14,817.6
transitional	5,592.0
deciduous forest	367,754.7
evergreen forest	35,321.9
mixed forest	17,176.5
shrubland	718.3
grasslands/herbaceous	12,028.4
pasture/hay	674,759.6
row crops	1,085,309.7
small grains	3,003.1
urban/rec. grasses	17,450.6
wooded wetlands	36,081.3
emergent herb. wetlands	3,718.0
Total	**2,368,609.8**

Bluegrass

Land Use	Acres
open water	20,115.5
low-int. res.	39,964.0
high-int. res	3,274.9
comm./ind./trans.	17,312.5
bare rock/sand/clay	0
quarries/mines	2,281.2
transitional	8,037.7
deciduous forest	720,455.8
evergreen forest	36,705.3
mixed forest	3,479.9
shrubland	0
grasslands/herbaceous	0
pasture/hay	829,831.5
row crops	796,469.3
small grains	0
urban/rec. grasses	6,703.7
wooded wetlands	25,859.0
emergent herb. wetlands	532.6
Total	**2,511,023.0**

Southern Bottomlands

Land Use	Acres
no data	8.2
open water	26,817.2
low-int. res.	11,168.4
high-int. res	4,303.1
comm./ind./trans.	5,566.2
bare rock/sand/clay	452.6
quarries/mines	3,777.1
transitional	1,288.5
deciduous forest	124,248.8
evergreen forest	6,842.2
mixed forest	94.9
grassland/herbaceous	1,536.3
pasture/hay	206,532.0
row crops	410,772.2
small grains	3,181.6
urban/rec. grasses	3,311.6
wooded wetlands	45,395.0
emergent herb. wetlands	4,201.7
Total	**859,497.4**

Shawnee Hills

Land Use	Acres
open water	21,438.6
low-int. res.	6,207.9
high-int. res	511.3
comm./ind./trans.	2,195.9
bare rock/sand/clay	0
quarries/mines	1,790.2
transitional	7,450.2
deciduous forest	912,305.0
evergreen forest	38,858.3
mixed forest	1,137.7
shrubland	0
grasslands/herbaceous	0
pasture/hay	353,236.9
row crops	336,931.2
small grains	0
urban/rec. grasses	554.9
wooded wetlands	3,065.1
emergent herb. wetlands	396.1
Total	**1,686,079.3**

Black Swamp

Land Use	Acres
open water	767.2
low-int. res.	2,432.4
high-int. res	423.9
comm./ind./trans.	1,192.6
quarries/mines	183.2
deciduous forest	4,775.4
evergreen forest	49.8
mixed forest	5.3
pasture/hay	19,523.5
row crops	122,384.2
urban/rec. grasses	234.7
wooded wetlands	892.1
emergent herb. wetlands	20.5
Total	**152,884.8**

Northern Lakes

Land Use	Acres
open water	47,432.4
low-int. res.	48,818.6
high-int. res	7,283.2
comm./ind./trans.	27,228.0
quarries/mines	457.9
transitional	641.6
deciduous forest	231,437.2
evergreen forest	3,802.9
mixed forest	558.4
grassland/herbaceous	298.1
pasture/hay	403,835.5
row crops	1,661,535.6
urban/rec. grasses	9,308.1
wooded wetlands	66,782.5
emergent herb. wetlands	19,832.3
Total	**2,529,252.3**

State Totals	
deciduous forest	4,080,389.9
mixed forest	35,895.2
evergreen forest	228,364.8
shrubland	1,733.7
wooded wetlands	342,618.3
grasslands/herbaceous	91,085.0
emergent herb. wetlands	40,080.5
pasture/hay	3,955,805.6
row crops	12,667,970.0
small grains	8,176.6
transitional	25,877.9
urban/rec. grasses	135,887.8
low-int. res.	455,542.5
high-int. res	100,949.5
comm./ind./trans.	218,767.2
open water	245,651.1
bare rock/sand/clay	2,537.1
quarries/mines	28,177.0
no data	8.2
TOTAL	**22,665,517.9**

Note: The NLCD is a cooperative project between the U.S. Geological Survey and the U.S. Environmental Protection Agency.

Table G-2. Land in Farms in 1900 and 2002 and the Percentage of Farmland in No-Till in 2000

		1900	1900	1900	2002	2002	2002	2000
Natural Region County	**County (acres)**	**Farms (number)**	**Farms (acres)**	**Improved (acres)**	**Farms (number)**	**Farms (acres)**	**Cropland (acres)**	**No-Till (%)**
Northwestern Morainal								
Lake	318,070	1,702	233,568	173,841	482	127,782	117,465	40.9
Porter	267,590	1,922	238,783	180,724	606	145,779	133,231	27.4
TOTAL	**585,660**	**3,624**	**472,351**	**354,565**	**1,088**	**273,561**	**250,696**	**34.2**
Average acres/farm			130			251		
Grand Prairie								
Benton	260,038	1,351	249,904	237,650	394	247,998	237,402	40.6
Jasper	358,314	1,870	338,857	235,347	641	280,368	259,680	28.6
LaPorte	382,872	2,613	343,450	261,294	817	243,447	221,809	23.7
Newton	257,183	1,113	245,557	195,190	344	181,557	168,581	32.0
Pulaski	277,553	1,945	241,475	168,358	524	222,797	206,029	34.1
Starke	197,959	1,384	162,224	106,391	518	134,191	116,200	21.8
Vermillion	164,408	1,353	140,984	112,199	221	109,778	96,192	28.7
Warren	233,525	1,506	218,232	185,085	346	166,907	151,809	34.9
White	323,351	2,395	313,194	258,605	589	283,746	259,592	32.3
TOTAL	**2,455,203**	**15,530**	**2,153,877**	**1,760,119**	**4,394**	**1,870,789**	**1,717,294**	**30.7**
Average acres/farm			139			426		
Northern Lakes								
Cass	264,236	2,656	251,591	200,115	717	208,379	186,782	19.3
Elkhart	296,841	3,364	279,019	230,530	1,516	200,879	175,682	32.8
Fulton	235,845	2,464	222,812	173,538	616	192,861	174,478	31.8
Kosciusko	344,002	3,532	322,179	240,069	1,203	262,001	224,999	44.1
LaGrange	242,920	2,145	233,201	176,709	1,551	189,125	153,318	24.2
Marshall	284,354	2,869	262,759	198,378	842	204,322	178,660	15.3
Noble	263,112	2,459	249,812	186,040	1,029	173,298	146,225	51.4
St. Joseph	292,698	2,598	266,707	210,597	855	165,143	148,647	33.7
Steuben	197,583	1,956	185,839	139,657	674	112,729	90,013	55.3
Whitley	214,732	2,113	206,810	154,573	840	172,094	150,359	49.7
TOTAL	**2,636,304**	**26,156**	**2,480,729**	**1,910,206**	**9,843**	**1,880,831**	**1,629,163**	**35.8**
Average acres/farm			95			191		
Central Till Plain								
Adams	217,190	2,462	209,576	170,694	1,296	208,653	199,192	33.2
Allen	420,640	4,362	397,235	294,859	1,550	284,373	256,623	39.6
Blackford	105,662	1,395	103,823	83,555	279	97,009	88,191	62.7
Boone	270,626	3,531	264,150	223,691	672	225,906	212,563	43.2
Carroll	238,245	2,429	231,616	188,340	529	201,683	185,318	13.6
Clinton	259,261	2,974	251,246	218,544	604	244,590	231,157	31.8
DeKalb	232,242	2,578	222,181	173,756	1,000	179,146	153,082	43.5
Delaware	251,707	2,871	246,696	205,970	687	189,573	176,513	59.1
Fountain	253,242	2,225	245,151	196,238	487	205,412	181,922	46.9
Grant	264,979	2,935	248,194	207,474	598	198,446	185,139	47.7
Hamilton	254,682	3,096	243,105	202,912	726	140,448	128,394	31.8
Hancock	195,920	2,215	186,830	157,114	616	161,524	152,369	40.3
Hendricks	261,372	2,867	259,875	194,194	703	182,166	165,835	49.5
Henry	251,473	2,601	245,090	206,739	745	172,963	156,758	48.7
Howard	187,563	2,680	185,082	158,402	536	156,160	147,423	25.1
Huntington	244,860	2,579	233,709	188,330	675	199,773	182,492	56.4
Jay	245,528	2,848	231,150	186,842	857	195,357	173,157	45.3
Johnson	204,924	2,053	194,624	159,269	598	135,178	121,090	31.0
Madison	289,363	3,346	273,956	232,512	807	243,597	228,807	48.2
Marion	253,599	3,437	242,644	199,235	303	23,692	19,531	40.0
Miami	240,396	2,397	232,465	185,621	685	191,369	171,728	28.1
Montgomery	322,887	2,895	311,670	238,954	644	273,426	245,803	46.7
Parke	284,655	2,303	256,647	163,680	470	164,743	123,272	43.6
Putnam	307,399	2,883	301,039	206,070	853	180,544	144,305	55.6
Randolph	289,813	3,448	283,017	227,290	786	257,846	236,943	59.0
Rush	261,301	2,267	254,870	211,724	606	223,527	204,901	42.3
Shelby	264,089	2,807	250,963	218,744	651	199,904	185,044	49.5
Tippecanoe	319,867	2,517	298,842	259,795	705	220,779	200,385	38.7
Tipton	166,646	2,290	162,597	139,370	360	151,647	142,922	22.5
Union	103,391	832	101,710	79,951	262	85,129	72,301	32.6
Wabash	264,429	2,663	253,392	205,686	799	214,703	189,738	30.4
Wayne	258,282	2,583	250,407	200,713	850	170,724	142,423	64.9
Wells	236,774	2,884	232,433	190,475	631	226,294	211,003	40.4
TOTAL	**8,223,007**	**88,253**	**7,905,985**	**6,376,743**	**22,570**	**6,226,573**	**5,616,324**	**42.2**
Average acres/farm			90			276		

		1900	1900	1900	2002	2002	2002	2000
Natural Region County	**County (acres)**	**Farms (number)**	**Farms (acres)**	**Improved (acres)**	**Farms (number)**	**Farms (acres)**	**Cropland (acres)**	**No-Till (%)**
Southwestern Lowlands								
Clay	228,875	2,489	212,036	165,553	555	151,590	125,629	34.4
Daviess	275,621	3,003	259,644	223,610	1,138	206,625	178,718	27.1
Dubois	275,255	2,238	266,195	178,818	758	188,972	140,634	58.3
Greene	346,706	3,549	332,759	269,545	822	170,534	117,715	30.8
Knox	330,134	2,683	305,966	249,603	508	300,136	272,637	31.7
Posey	261,440	2,167	233,797	204,277	396	191,886	174,258	32.6
Spencer	255,159	3,004	246,978	202,799	593	154,895	124,543	62.3
Sullivan	286,205	3,239	272,012	227,785	437	178,617	153,391	38.3
Vanderburgh	150,126	1,970	142,287	120,619	306	82,035	76,068	21.8
Vigo	258,109	2,816	233,996	192,043	476	122,859	104,565	30.8
Warrick	245,807	2,982	236,357	202,705	401	94,441	75,224	40.4
TOTAL	**2,913,437**	**30,140**	**2,742,027**	**2,237,357**	**6,390**	**1,842,590**	**1,543,382**	**37.1**
Average acres/farm			91			288		
Southern Bottomlands								
Gibson	312,822	2,973	278,830	242,145	557	210,989	190,584	31.1
Pike	215,153	2,685	200,724	172,689	288	75,716	63,493	48.4
TOTAL	**527,975**	**5,658**	**479,554**	**414,834**	**845**	**286,705**	**254,077**	**39.8**
Average acres/farm			85			339		
Shawnee Hills								
Crawford	195,636	1,905	177,552	103,112	427	54,950	26,118	
Martin	215,127	1,985	201,006	139,659	350	63,517	42,052	38.7
Orange	255,693	2,392	247,668	160,648	535	106,190	65,520	54.5
Owen	246,514	2,136	246,748	164,439	588	98,679	61,760	56.3
Perry	244,092	2,054	217,316	108,359	470	76,284	39,052	48.5
TOTAL	**1,157,062**	**10,472**	**1,090,290**	**676,217**	**2,370**	**399,620**	**234,502**	**49.5**
Average acres/farm			104			167		
Highland Rim								
Brown	199,849	1,825	178,971	104,504	222	20,390	9,833	
Floyd	94,719	1,213	81,594	53,901	299	24,048	15,632	
Harrison	310,539	3,237	291,587	190,768	1,176	160,251	108,231	60.0
Lawrence	287,252	2,251	266,945	168,575	825	147,295	86,633	42.1
Monroe	252,381	2,242	237,552	149,722	547	60,510	33,755	
Morgan	260,141	2,544	244,694	168,402	690	111,609	88,996	48.3
Washington	329,226	2,948	316,515	218,116	977	180,559	123,355	60.3
TOTAL	**1,734,107**	**16,260**	**1,617,858**	**1,053,988**	**4,736**	**704,662**	**466,435**	**52.7**
Bluegrass								
Bartholomew	260,370	2,431	254,051	202,272	608	160,568	142,687	52.6
Clark	240,025	2,067	216,526	152,648	638	100,602	72,008	53.1
Dearborn	195,336	2,114	182,681	138,129	676	74,042	41,053	34.5
Decatur	238,467	1,944	229,899	184,309	676	206,700	181,234	27.3
Fayette	137,576	1,068	132,695	105,225	424	106,905	84,693	38.6
Franklin	247,042	2,136	240,175	162,983	817	139,464	92,557	44.5
Jackson	325,962	2,813	303,710	209,153	806	206,855	161,732	54.9
Jefferson	231,274	2,529	218,166	146,037	778	109,103	70,292	64.6
Jennings	241,423	2,135	226,014	161,751	669	142,609	108,943	47.9
Ohio	55,503	551	52,436	42,043	213	23,887	13,774	
Bluegrass								
Ripley	285,671	2,935	270,974	199,212	904	173,082	132,766	54.5
Switzerland	141,556	1,802	136,047	110,565	464	60,243	32,065	58.7
TOTAL	**2,722,059**	**25,804**	**2,380,602**	**1,896,329**	**8,060**	**1,573,339**	**1,186,705**	**51.2**
Average acres/farm			92			195		
STATE TOTALS	**22,954,814**	**221,897**	**21,619,623**	**16,680,358**	**60,296**	**15,058,700**	**12,550,891**	**41.5**
Average acres/farm for state			97			250		

Notes: Data for the Black Swamp Natural Region are included in the Central Till Plain and Northern Lakes natural regions. "Improved acres in 1900" includes all farmland used for crops, pasture, and forage.
Sources: U.S. Census Bureau 1900 (vol. 5); U.S. Department of Agriculture 2002; http://www.ia.nrcs.usda.gov/news/newsreleases/2,003/tillage.html.

Table G-3. County Lands Not in Farms; Farmlands Not Cropped, in Forest, or in Pasture; and County Lands in Wetlands (in acres)

Natural Region County	County Land Not in Farms (1900)	Unimproved Farmland (1900)	County Land Not in Farms (2002)	Farmland Not Cropped (2002)	Farm Woodlands (2002)	Farm Pasture (2002)	County Land in Wetlands (1997)
Northwestern Morainal							
Lake	84,502	59,727	190,288	10,317	2,784	2,784	2,2,046
Porter	28,807	58,059	121,811	12,548	5,204	4,893	2,0,661
TOTAL	**113,309**	**117,786**	**312,099**	**22,865**	**7,988**	**7,677**	**4,2,707**
Grand Prairie							
Benton	10,134	12,254	12,040	10,596	2,595	5,408	3,371
Jasper	16,457	103,510	77,946	20,688	9,649	7,957	8,118
LaPorte	39,422	82,156	139,425	21,638	8,654	7,435	20,597
Newton	11,626	50,367	75,626	12,976	4,720	4,758	5,856
Pulaski	36,078	73,117	54,756	16,768	10,019	5,069	11,935
Starke	35,735	55,833	63,768	17,991	10,054	3,175	6,732
Vermillion	23,424	28,785	54,630	13,586	9,838	4,799	1,751
Warren	15,293	33,147	66,618	15,098	6,917	8,063	1,631
White	10,157	54,589	39,605	24,154	8,416	7,418	12,845
TOTAL	**198,326**	**493,758**	**584,414**	**153,495**	**70,862**	**54,082**	**72,836**
Northern Lakes							
Cass	12,645	51,476	55,857	21,597	10,203	10,392	6,631
Elkhart	17,822	48,489	95,962	25,197	10,185	16,641	35,062
Fulton	13,033	48,644	42,984	18,383	9,058	7,150	10,333
Kosciusko	21,823	82,110	82,001	37,002	18,438	15,887	19,842
LaGrange	9,719	56,492	53,795	35,807	15,105	36,647	29,184
Marshall	21,595	64,381	80,032	25,662	13,825	9,446	10,078
Noble	13,300	63,772	89,812	27,073	12,658	10,724	27,244
St. Joseph	25,991	56,110	127,555	16,496	6,974	4,421	19,630
Steuben	11,744	46,182	84,854	22,716	12,266	8,093	21,597
Whitley	7,922	52,237	42,638	21,735	11,898	6,250	7,898
TOTAL	**155,594**	**569,893**	**755,490**	**251,668**	**120,610**	**125,651**	**187,499**
Central Till Plain							
Adams	7,614	38,882	8,537	9,461	9,139	9,062	5,813
Allen	23,405	102,376	136,267	27,750	13,688	11,211	14,489
Blackford	1,839	20,268	8,653	8,818	3,760	1,696	5,475
Boone	6,476	40,459	44,720	13,343	5,133	8,730	3,644
Carroll	6,629	42,276	36,562	16,365	9,246	7,047	4,681
Clinton	8,015	32,702	14,671	13,433	7,122	3,339	5,385
DeKalb	10,061	48,425	53,096	26,064	15,783	6,566	14,313
Delaware	5,011	40,726	62,134	13,060	5,636	5,658	5,984
Fountain	8,091	48,913	47,830	23,490	14,234	14,453	1,836
Grant	16,785	40,720	66,533	13,307	6,343	5,126	7,955
Hamilton	11,577	40,193	114,234	12,054	4,283	7,299	5,883
Hancock	9,090	29,716	34,396	9,155	3,823	5,217	6,612
Hendricks	1,497	65,681	79,206	16,331	6,273	10,881	4,299
Henry	6,383	38,351	78,510	16,205	6,121	10,936	6,494
Howard	2,481	26,680	31,403	8,737	4,912	3,335	4,210
Huntington	11,151	45,379	45,087	17,281	9,464	6,063	9,528
Jay	14,378	44,308	50,171	22,200	13,160	7,426	11,672
Johnson	10,300	35,355	69,746	14,088	6,104	8,132	6,166
Madison	15,407	41,444	45,766	14,790	6,258	7,454	6,491
Marion	10,955	43,409	229,907	4,431	1,929	2,970	6,086
Miami	7,931	46,844	49,027	19,641	9,718	8,498	6,334
Montgomery	11,217	72,716	49,461	27,623	15,629	13,671	3,011
Parke	28,008	92,967	119,912	41,471	30,415	15,349	2,504
Putnam	6,360	94,969	126,855	36,239	23,140	18,693	2,844
Randolph	6,796	55,727	31,967	20,903	11,018	8,994	5,842
Rush	6,431	43,146	37,774	18,626	9,412	11,248	6,426
Shelby	13,126	32,219	64,185	14,860	5,873	9,077	7,896
Tippecanoe	21,025	39,047	99,088	20,394	9,454	9,955	3,681
Tipton	4,049	23,227	14,999	8,725	3,783	2,991	3,962
Union	1,681	21,759	18,262	12,828	6,918	7,870	532
Wabash	11,037	47,706	49,726	24,965	13,360	6,777	8,613
Wayne	7,875	49,694	87,558	28,301	12,463	18,658	1,153
Wells	4,341	41,958	10,480	15,291	6,712	3,550	6,543
TOTAL	**317,022**	**1,528,242**	**2,016,723**	**583,664**	**294,523**	**271,366**	**196,357**

Natural Region County	County Land Not in Farms (1900)	Unimproved Farmland (1900)	County Land Not in Farms (2002)	Farmland Not Cropped (2002)	Farm Woodlands (2002)	Farm Pasture (2002)	County Land in Wetlands (1997)
Southwestern Lowlands							
Clay	16,839	46,483	77,285	25,961	15,782	9,654	2,879
Daviess	15,977	36,034	68,996	27,907	12,169	23,135	5,527
Dubois	9,060	87,377	86,283	48,338	29,970	20,433	9,739
Greene	13,947	63,214	176,172	52,819	27,707	33,932	7,071
Knox	24,168	56,363	29,998	27,499	12,473	11,704	9,208
Posey	27,643	29,520	69,554	17,628	10,203	4,205	15,591
Spencer	8,181	44,179	100,264	30,352	18,307	14,817	5,445
Sullivan	14,193	44,227	107,588	25,226	11,564	11,337	7,298
Vanderburgh	7,839	21,668	68,091	6,967	1,651	2,211	11,089
Vigo	24,113	41,953	135,250	18,294	12,023	6,562	6,371
Warrick	9,450	33,652	151,366	19,217	7,660	7,955	10,163
TOTAL	**171,410**	**504,670**	**1,070,847**	**300,208**	**159,509**	**145,945**	**90,381**
Southern Bottomlands							
Gibson	33,992	36,685	101,833	20,405	9,570	6,635	17,692
Pike	14,429	28,035	139,437	12,223	6,676	5,850	7,444
TOTAL	**48,421**	**64,720**	**241,270**	**32,628**	**16,246**	**12,485**	**25,136**
Shawnee Hills							
Crawford	18,084	74,440	140,686	28,832	19,323	18,317	
Martin	14,121	61,347	151,610	23,465	12,236	14,534	3,211
Orange	8,025	87,020	149,503	40,670	26,424	23,660	5,476
Owen	-234	82,309	147,835	36,919	22,796	19,223	4,266
Perry	26,776	108,957	167,808	37,232	25,989	18,333	3,807
TOTAL	**66,772**	**414,073**	**757,442**	**167,118**	**106,768**	**94,067**	**16,760**
Highland Rim							
Brown	20,878	74,467	179,459	10,557	7,327	4,148	
Floyd	13,125	27,693	70,671	8,416	4,993	5,389	
Harrison	18,952	100,819	150,288	52,020	29,835	35,068	1,755
Lawrence	20,307	98,370	139,957	60,662	32,923	46,312	4,126
Monroe	14,829	87,830	191,871	26,755	16,249	19,370	
Morgan	15,447	76,292	148,532	22,613	11,431	12,387	
Washington	12,711	98,399	148,446	57,204	33,965	39,797	6,030
TOTAL	**116,249**	**563,870**	**1,029,224**	**218,857**	**120,474**	**143,101**	**11,911**
Bluegrass							
Bartholomew	6,325	51,779	99,808	17,881	8,889	8,209	9,441
Clark	23,499	63,878	139,423	28,594	16,560	19,925	5,594
Dearborn	12,655	44,552	121,294	32,990	15,124	25,634	1,672
Decatur	8,568	45,590	31,767	25,466	14,741	13,133	9,099
Fayette	4,881	27,470	30,671	22,212	12,964	13,139	820
Franklin	6,867	77,192	107,578	46,907	28,963	28,990	1,173
Jackson	22,252	94,557	119,107	45,123	29,228	19,417	14,134
Jefferson	13,108	72,129	122,171	38,811	23,764	22,696	10,503
Jennings	15,409	64,263	98,814	33,666	21,571	12,103	14,844
Ohio	3,067	10,393	31,616	10,113	4,931	8,447	
Ripley	14,697	71,762	112,589	40,316	22,532	19,003	8,947
Scott	8,270	31,576	52,569	16,378	10,562	7,572	7,959
Switzerland	5,509	25,482	81,313	28,178	14,958	19,723	1,511
TOTAL	**145,107**	**680,623**	**1,148,720**	**386,635**	**224,787**	**217,991**	**85,697**
STATE TOTALS	**1,332,210**	**4,937,635**	**7,916,229**	**2,117,138**	**1,121,767**	**1,072,365**	**729,284**

Notes: Natural regions include counties with more than 50% of their area in the region. Data for the Black Swamp Natural Region are included in other regions.

Land in 1900 was considered farmland if the operation required the constant services of at least one person.

Land not in farms in 1900 was mostly in roads, urban areas, and private wild lands where the owner was not involved in agricultural production (e.g., forest land).

Unimproved farmland in 1900 included pasture, forest, and wetlands.

Most pasture in 1900 was cultivated grasses and forbs with a small amount in native prairie grass.

Farmland in 2002 was defined as land from which $1,000 of agricultural products, not including timber products, were produced.

County farmland in 2002 was tallied by the location of a farm's headquarters. If farmers owned land in more than one county, all of their land was tallied in the county where they resided.

County land not in farms in 2002 included all other land uses: urban areas, roads, public lands, and private lands not producing $1,000 of agricultural products each year.

Sources: U.S. Census Bureau 1900 (vol. 5); National Wetlands Inventory 1997; Indiana Agricultural Statistics 2003–2004.

Table G-4. Area of Corn, Soybeans, and Oats Planted in 1900 and 2002 by County and Natural Region

Natural Region County	Corn 1900 (acres)	Corn 2002 (acres)	Soybeans* 2002 (acres)	Oats 1900 (acres)	Oats 2002 (acres)
Northwestern Morainal					
Lake	39,339	60,100	58,500	26,474	115
Porter	28,760	62,400	56,800	24,865	267
TOTAL	**68,099**	**122,500**	**115,300**	**51,339**	**382**
Grand Prairie					
Benton	110,057	119,000	113,800	73,343	146
Jasper	73,204	146,000	107,600	43,258	D
LaPorte	54,351	113,000	88,600	18,077	193
Newton	76,280	111,000	77,800	49,953	21
Pulaski	49,514	114,000	88,400	25,963	44
Starke	26,400	59,500	41,500	7,022	46
Vermillion	44,865	34,200	21900	10,358	D
Warren	78,667	87,300	82,700	36,195	303
White	102,444	135,000	120,000	52,475	54
TOTAL	**615,782**	**919,000**	**742,300**	**316,644**	**807**
Northern Lakes					
Cass	62,174	93,000	83,500	7,777	D
Elkhart	41,950	57,600	47,900	12,371	D
Fulton	49,493	87,700	75,000	7,707	D
Kosciusko	53,057	94,300	88,200	13,890	321
LaGrange	35,992	51,100	37,300	6,146	1,140
Marshall	43,846	89,800	75,300	10,571	221
Noble	36,489	61,700	58,900	12,795	156
St. Joseph	39,886	70,800	54,100	9,468	39
Steuben	26,531	35,500	34,500	6,581	150
Whitley	34,906	49,400	70,700	21,393	180
TOTAL	**424,324**	**690,900**	**625,400**	**108,699**	**2,207**
Central Till Plain					
Adams	40,598	65,500	89,300	18,955	1,390
Allen	70,840	76,200	117,900	50,715	1,293
Blackford	26,153	19,600	36,600	3,873	D
Boone	81,472	109,000	112,000	3,297	
Carroll	62,412	99,000	81,100	4,919	18
Clinton	78,353	108,000	101,700	7,515	D
DeKalb	32,357	41,016	68,197	21,661	560
Delaware	61,933	61,100	96,900	4,934	44
Fountain	78,960	97,500	95,800	15,575	27
Grant	65,243	71,000	111,600	7,774	172
Hamilton	67,432	53,300	64,800	4,618	48
Hancock	46,750	69,000	80,600	4,323	149
Hendricks	63,282	59,000	63,700	3,499	D
Henry	57,882	72,700	84,200	2,908	139
Howard	53,326	69,400	71,700	2,624	58
Huntington	52,474	63,700	97,500	27,727	346
Jay	49,417	65,400	99,800	14,001	438
Johnson	51,263	51,800	49,000	1,485	15
Madison	77,244	80,100	100,100	5,183	D
Marion	56,759	7,500	9,200	6,071	D
Miami	54,934	68,600	84,800	6,952	40
Montgomery	83,280	119,000	113,300	6,518	102
Parke	49,786	55,500	69,400	7,544	D
Putnam	55,398	66,600	66,600	4,490	D
Randolph	72,829	83,500	115,500	10,171	186
Rush	67,225	100,000	100,600	1,522	38
Shelby	75,480	97,300	95,600	2,574	193
Tippecanoe	112,547	101,000	95,300	27,472	65
Tipton	53,391	71,500	74,400	1,546	101
Union	23,330	32,400	29,500	731	26
Wabash	53,539	71,200	90,100	22,083	58
Wayne	57,032	59,800	66,300	6,096	107
Wells	51,833	76,200	110,000	16,928	324
TOTAL	**1,984,754**	**2,342,416**	**2,743,097**	**326,284**	**5,937**

Natural Region County	Corn 1900 (acres)	Corn 2002 (acres)	Soybeans* 2002 (acres)	Oats 1900 (acres)	Oats 2002 (acres)
Southwestern Lowlands					
Clay	42,246	53,300	69,900	12,309	D
Daviess	54,161	80,300	60,700	11,081	D
Dubois	30,024	58,100	47,100	9,694	
Greene	58,645	35,000	43,100	12,540	25
Knox	79,296	112,000	119,000	5,443	
Posey	57,379	77,900	91,500	1,632	
Spencer	45,042	56,400	58,400	4,423	
Sullivan	63,356	61,200	73,700	12,842	
Vanderburgh	30,316	34,000	40,200	1,425	
Vigo	60,815	46,100	59,300	12,039	
Warrick	42,541	39,500	38,900	3,685	
TOTAL	**563,821**	**653,800**	**701,800**	**87,113**	**25**
Southern Bottomlands					
Gibson	66,784	85,800	93,600	3,608	D
Pike	39,967	31,500	35,600	4,133	
TOTAL	**106,751**	**117,300**	**129,200**	**7,741**	
Shawnee Hills					
Crawford	20,591	1,869	1,952	4,137	D
Martin	24,966	13,300	13,900	6,970	
Orange	29,940	20,100	18,300	11,524	189
Owen	29,940	14,500	20,800	6,530	D
Perry	24,544	8,900	10,500	2,675	D
TOTAL	**129,981**	**58,669**	**65,452**	**31,836**	**189**
Highland Rim					
Brown	16,238	1,830	1,801	2,079	D
Floyd	9,869	2,601	4,651	1,708	
Harrison	34,247	26,200	27,300	5,783	56
Lawrence	29,420	14,500	20,200	9,891	52
Monroe	23,424	2,689	5,854	5,352	
Morgan	49,506	44,300	46,700	2,906	
Washington	40,724	36,700	41,000	15,262	D
TOTAL	**203,428**	**128,820**	**147,506**	**42,981**	**108**
Bluegrass					
Bartholomew	53,623	58,400	75,100	5,146	
Clark	30,902	15,200	31,400	2,757	D
Dearborn	20,842	6,600	10,200	3,667	8
Decatur	47,502	66,400	77,200	3,343	49
Fayette	25,835	35,500	35,200	1,214	D
Franklin	33,879	33,400	35,000	3,475	43
Jackson	51,094	52,200	78,500	14,344	
Jefferson	29,677	15,500	38,500	1,786	9
Jennings	31,236	30,200	49,300	2,673	
Ohio	6,315	1,441	3,546	219	
Ripley	39,210	32,400	62,200	4,526	43
Scott	18,006	9,100	25,600	937	
Switzerland	17,128	3,230	7,722	661	D
TOTAL	**405,249**	**359,571**	**529,468**	**44,748**	**152**
STATE TOTALS	**4,502,189**	**5,392,976**	**5,799,523**	**1,017,385**	**11,015**
STATE TOTALS B	**4,005,766**			**1,485,604**	

Notes: Data on the Black Swamp Natural Region are included in other regions. *Soybeans were not grown in 1900. D = one farm, data not released.
Sources: U.S. Census Bureau 1900 (vol. 5); U.S. Department of Agriculture 2002; Indiana Department of Statistics 1900 (State Totals B, which reflect acres sown in 1899).

Table G-5. Acreage of Wheat, Vegetables, and Hay by County and Natural Region in 1900 and 2002

Natural Region / County	Wheat 1900 (acres)	Wheat 2002 (acres)	Vegetables 1900 (acres)	Vegetables 2002 (acres)	Hay 1900 (acres)	Hay 2002 (acres)
Northwestern Morainal						
Lake	385	1,381	2,670	1,790	55,965	3,277
Porter	5,666	1,962	2,135	944	39,527	4,479
TOTAL	**6,051**	**3,343**	**4,805**	**2,734**	**95,492**	**7,756**
Grand Prairie						
Benton	67	256	575		16,504	1,256
Jasper	875	1,155	1,859	35	54,231	3,016
LaPorte	44,794	2,341	2,995	2,854	60,090	8,626
Newton	131	1,390	306	49	18,992	1,390
Pulaski	9,932	644	942	D	23,886	2,754
Starke	2,736	721	1,706	532	31,484	2,651
Vermillion	14,637	1,434	892	D	11,279	2,022
Warren	8,189	841	653	D	13,542	3,048
White	6,922	1,543	1,515	66	26,805	3,942
TOTAL	**88,283**	**10,325**	**11,443**	**3,536**	**256,813**	**28,705**
Northern Lakes						
Cass	39,610	1,879	2,617	681	24,321	5,304
Elkhart	51,901	2,154	3,700	1,015	32,254	16,826
Fulton	18,857	1,343	1,943	827	23,991	6,578
Kosciusko	43,734	3,300	4,282	263	34,044	10,828
LaGrange	45,272	2,349	1,899	2,367	26,616	22,945
Marshall	41,677	2,267	2,749	28	25,965	8,107
Noble	45,368	3,258	2,230	58	28,959	10,381
St. Joseph	48,607	1,759	3,359	763	33,400	6,369
Steuben	32,675	2,630	1,879	86	25,415	7,644
Whitley	11,329	6,257	1,856	28	23,086	6,315
TOTAL	**379,030**	**27,196**	**26,514**	**6,116**	**278,051**	**101,297**
Central Till Plain						
Adams	26,430	8,550	1,238	117	29,084	10,187
Allen	3,765	19,586	5,327	694	52,959	9,414
Blackford	14,040	910	710	D	12,178	1,256
Boone	34,900	1,999	1,861	60	34,301	5,089
Carroll	43,643	2,117	1,465	27	19,903	2,414
Clinton	49,265	2,248	1,795	94	21,498	1,255
DeKalb	26,100		2,771		31,206	5,264
Delaware	43,263	1,764	2,462	923	33,896	3,204
Fountain	12,931	1,372	1,437	27	21,120	5,220
Grant	29,396	2,292	2,135	333	30,050	3,639
Hamilton	44,329	1,951	2,567	62	30,490	4,094
Hancock	46,542	2,596	1,423	D	21,171	3,199
Hendricks	44,115	3,730	2,192	46	29,383	5,491
Henry	49,322	2,088	2,747	437	28,950	4,876
Howard	40,789	1,667	2,888	245	20,143	1,804
Huntington	13,613	4,684	1,890	D	28,018	4,625
Jay	34,285	5,547	1,172	D	35,040	6,059
Johnson	39,892	2,041	4,265	80	20,550	5,433
Madison	50,851	1,829	2,044	1,424	36,586	3,358
Marion	49,791	307	8,844	425	37,177	1,302
Miami	33,046	3,255	2,096	9	21,860	5,204
Montgomery	18,034	2,544	1,475	7	29,516	4,624
Parke	18,384	2,772	1,356	231	22,780	5,906
Putnam	28,074	3,026	1,068	29	34,881	9,298
Randolph	51,908	4,230	1,742	471	34,175	3,960
Rush	64,874	4,232	1,400	D	26,490	5,162
Shelby	74,463	2,206	1,692	D	25,360	2,827
Tippecanoe	23,298	4,426	2,369	450	26,744	4,767
Tipton	28,429	1,027	2,346	706	17,226	754
Union	22,850	1,502	709		9,230	2,152
Wabash	11,455	6,189	2,489	256	33,725	4,690
Wayne	47,962	3,342	1,929	147	27,320	8,908
Wells	26,187	3,040	1,769	49	32,774	2,599
TOTAL	**1,146,226**	**109,069**	**73,673**	**7,349**	**915,784**	**148,034**

Natural Region County	Wheat 1900 (acres)	Wheat 2002 (acres)	Vegetables 1900 (acres)	Vegetables 2002 (acres)	Hay 1900 (acres)	Hay 2002 (acres)
Southwestern Lowlands						
Clay	23,086	2,221	1,341	19	21,232	4,261
Daviess	47,368	4,914	1,738	460	24,344	11,691
Dubois	46,590					
Greene	30,686	844	1,642	14	34,909	18,334
Knox	71,382	16,948	4,772	7,252	22,973	4,700
Posey	83,648	30,222	1,565	D	15,900	2,039
Spencer	60,163	4,285	2,400	52	22,966	10,221
Sullivan	35,574	3,975	2,336	1,648	29,996	3,685
Vanderburgh	39,503	6,097	2,770	258	17,064	1,067
Vigo	37,789	1,997	3,072	54	25,463	3,102
Warrick	53,487	2,330	1,880	10	22,242	3,859
TOTAL	**529,276**	**79,671**	**24,917**	**9,767**	**260,659**	**80,420**
Southern Bottomlands						
Gibson	83,038	19,020	3,325	704	18,239	3,859
Pike	44,528	1,366	1,321	26	18,208	2,598
TOTAL	**127,566**	**20,386**	**4,646**		**36,447**	**6,457**
Shawnee Hills						
Crawford	15,346	227	1,394	17	11,953	9,108
Martin	14,714	819	1,052		16,072	6,069
Orange	17,366	2,577	1,235	D	17,548	10,434
Owen	14,428	1,680	778	28	26,609	11,660
Perry	23,938	568	1,290	D	12,144	11,683
TOTAL	**85,792**	**5,871**	**5,749**	**775**	**84,326**	**48,954**
Highland Rim						
Brown	11,206	D	1,153	55	15,096	2,885
Floyd	8,138	404	1,559	173	9,328	3,579
Harrison	46,951	4,004	2,360	121	19,944	22,108
Lawrence	17,573	1,317	1,308	23	25,006	20,935
Monroe	15,118		1,164		26,558	11,268
Morgan	35,628	1,036	1,269	173	22,684	6,103
Washington	26,890	2,026	1,774	613	28,068	20,072
TOTAL	**161,504**	**8,787**	**10,587**	**1,158**	**146,684**	**86,950**
Bluegrass						
Bartholomew	56,899	3,946	2,052	1,212	28,234	3,720
Clark	24,032	3,197	1,932	593	19,981	9,710
Dearborn	27,289	563	1,923	105	29,330	11,328
Decatur	43,750	5,422	941	80	29,896	4,924
Fayette	27,624	1,217	773		11,452	4,917
Franklin	35,653	2,193	1,697	49	20,395	10,712
Jackson	39,347	4,144	2,989	687	30,669	8,808
Jefferson	24,023	2,254	2,075	22	20,405	10,139
Jennings	20,356	1,484	1,260	109	25,853	7,469
Ohio	8,010	D	395	13	7,383	3,803
Ripley	31,762	2,112	1,790	253	34,574	8,523
Scott	14,922	529	1,984	22	10,964	4,106
Switzerland	15,898	535	1,451	23	17,061	9,023
TOTAL	**369,565**	**27,596**	**21,262**	**3,168**	**286,197**	**97,182**
STATE TOTALS	**2,893,293**	**299,873**	**183,596**	**36,606**	**2,360,453**	**605,755**

Notes: Data for the Black Swamp Natural Region are included in other regions. D = one farm, data not released.

Vegetables in 1900 include potatoes, sweet potatoes, onions, and miscellaneous vegetables.

Vegetables in 2002 do not include 2,491 acres of potatoes.

Hay in 1900 includes wild salt/prairie grass (137,721 acres), millet/Hungarian grass (21,273 acres), alfalfa and lucern (844 acres), clover (776,810 acres), other cultivated grasses (1,365,815 acres), and grains (67,757 acres).

Hay in 2002 includes alfalfa (320,210 acres), other tame grasses (250,976 acres), small grains (16,349 acres), and wild grass (18,381 acres).

Sources: U.S. Census Bureau 1900 (vol. 5); U.S. Department of Agriculture 2002.

Table G-6. Other Crops Grown in Indiana in 1900 and 2002

Crop	1900a (acres)	1900 (acres)	2002 (acres)
Sorghum	9,453	3	9,950
Sorghum cane for syrup		7,955	
Broom corn	2,063	815	
Barley	20,865	26,055	1,255
Buckwheat	3,055	8,684	76
Emmer/spelt			268
Popcorn			69,207
Rye	66,982	43,562	1,070
Forage crops		72,194	
Sunflower seed			307
Flaxseed	1,615	171	
Tobacco	13,148	8,219	4,034
Dry edible beans		2,999	1,016
Potatoes	69,768	84,245	2,491
Sweet potatoes	2,950	3,989	5
Peanuts		11	
Seed (grass, clover, vetch)		*	249
Ginseng			8
Mint for oils			11,587
Orchards (fruits and nuts)		35,309	5,354
Berries		13,045	1,226
Cranberries		70	
Nursery, floriculture, sod, vegetable seed		6,285	11,095
Christmas trees			5,630
STATE TOTALS		**516,485**	**124,828**
Maple syrup farms (number of farms)		221,897	
Nut trees (number of trees)		15,774	
Fruit trees (number of trees)		14,123,479	
Grape vines (number of vines)		2,570,579	

Notes: *Seed was present but source did not provide acreage. The fruit trees total includes other trees in addition to the ones specified in the table. Orchard acres in 1900 were estimated using 400 ft2/tree.

Sources: Indiana Department of Statistics 1900 (for 1900a data); U.S. Census Bureau 1900 (vol. 5); U.S. Department of Agriculture 2002.

Table G-7. Major Commercial Vineyards in Indiana in 2000

Name	Town	County	Natural Region	Acres
Chateau Pomije	Guilford	Dearborn	Bluegrass	58.0
Huber Orchard and Winery	Borden	Clark	Bluegrass	37.0
Kauffman Winery	Vernon	Jennings	Bluegrass	8.0
Madison Vineyards	Madison	Jefferson	Bluegrass	9.0
Simmons Winery and Farm Market	Columbus	Bartholomew	Bluegrass	8.5
Villa Milan Vineyard	Milan	Ripley	Bluegrass	7.5
Easley Winery	Indianapolis	Marion	Central Till Plain	18.0
Terre Vin Winery	Rockville	Parke	Central Till Plain	0.1
Wilson Wines	Modoc	Randolph	Central Till Plain	0.7
Butler Winery and Vineyards	Bloomington	Monroe	Highland Rim	4.0
Oliver Winery	Bloomington	Monroe	Highland Rim	21.0
Turtle Run Winery	Corydon	Harrison	Highland Rim	10.0
Satek Winery	Fremont	Steuben	Northern Lakes	2.0
Anderson's Orchard and Winery	Valparaiso	Porter	Northwestern Morainal	10.0
French Lick Wine and Coffee Company	French Lick	Orange	Shawnee Hills	3.0
Winzerwald Winery	Bristow	Perry	Shawnee Hills	2.0
TOTAL ACRES				**198.8**

Note: Numerous other small vineyards are scattered across the state.

Source: Butler and Butler 2001.

Table G-8. Orchards in 1900 and 2002 by County and Natural Region

Natural Region / County	Apples 1900 (# of trees)	Peaches 1900 (# of trees)	Cherries 1900 (# of trees)	Pears 1900 (# of trees)	Total 1900	Orchards 2002 (acres)
Northwestern Morainal						
Lake	63,534	4,154	7,314	2,099	77,101	89
Porter	65,122	15,735	8,585	10,047	99,489	14
TOTALS	**128,656**	**19,889**	**15,899**	**12,146**	**176,590**	**103**
Acres (400 ft²/tree)	**322**	**50**	**4**	**30**	**406**	
Grand Prairie						
Benton	30,984	7,212	7,385	3,909	49,490	
Jasper	43,759	8,418	6,393	4,354	62,924	D
LaPorte	97,412	28,548	7,233	11,196	144,389	556
Newton	18,810	4,753	3,950	892	28,405	D
Pulaski	38,360	3,784	4,217	1,965	48,326	D
Starke	24,216	1,802	2,635	1,006	29,659	14
Vermillion	22,024	11,177	3,831	3,258	40,290	
Warren	31,151	11,654	6,785	3,247	52,837	D
White	59,173	6,925	7,106	5,289	78,493	D
TOTALS	**365,889**	**84,273**	**49,535**	**35,116**	**534,813**	**570**
Acres (400 ft²/tree)	**915**	**211**	**124**	**88**	**1,338**	
Northern Lakes						
Cass	91,911	12,286	15,409	12,502	132,108	60
Elkhart	155,091	27,911	27,856	13,630	224,488	312
Fulton	71,694	4,766	7,212	5,318	88,990	D
Kosciusko	122,592	17,180	9,691	10,274	159,737	44
LaGrange	71,372	23,940	11,595	10,339	117,246	39
Marshall	96,150	7,794	6,670	5,655	116,269	20
Noble	93,975	12,772	9,789	8,308	124,844	59
St. Joseph	93,455	7,566	5,448	9,703	116,172	34
Steuben	90,565	26,573	7,868	9,599	134,605	46
Whitley	75,442	7,201	7,105	5,374	95,122	10
TOTALS	**962,247**	**147,989**	**108,643**	**90,702**	**1,309,581**	**624**
Acres (400 ft2/tree)	**2,406**	**370**	**271**	**227**	**3,274**	
Central Till Plain						
Adams	104,006	7,901	10,134	6,360	128,401	D
Allen	210,750	17,565	19,387	19,598	267,300	89
Blackford	38,977	4,720	5,353	4,496	53,546	D
Boone	68,112	19,898	12,466	9,489	109,965	5
Carroll	76,420	16,821	14,626	9,966	117,833	26
Clinton	72,758	15,787	20,048	11,890	120,483	33
DeKalb	104,083	19,591	10,157	7,801	141,632	30
Delaware	87,383	13,764	16,599	14,814	132,560	26
Fountain	37,912	26,054	9,008	6,579	79,553	D
Grant	82,601	7,449	23,267	16,760	130,077	24
Hamilton	110,684	22,992	24,104	21,459	179,239	44
Hancock	58,138	11,374	10,008	7,032	86,552	62
Hendricks	84,598	22,760	12,334	11,195	130,887	228
Henry	81,441	10,349	15,858	15,143	122,791	113
Howard	87,821	12,838	23,392	15,407	139,458	118
Huntington	93,042	15,903	13,043	14,653	136,641	20
Jay	108,757	8,879	8,660	6,618	132,914	13
Johnson	66,074	15,847	6,203	5,793	93,917	51
Madison	96,465	10,992	20,566	14,454	142,477	19
Marion	96,496	18,508	31,003	41,396	187,403	D
Miami	79,252	10,280	11,771	9,379	110,682	D
Montgomery	53,801	33,249	18,577	6,847	112,474	55
Parke	50,816	18,689	7,851	4,051	81,407	23
Putnam	95,933	45,945	9,623	7,242	158,743	51
Randolph	112,746	11,111	18,101	10,129	152,087	16
Rush	61,295	13,665	11,167	7,092	93,219	D
Shelby	70,411	12,393	10,808	4,984	98,596	D
Tippecanoe	59,678	12,713	13,752	9,881	96,024	62
Tipton	63,632	3,373	11,329	6,823	85,157	10
Union	26,964	4,909	3,826	3,357	39,056	D
Wabash	120,835	10,598	15,814	11,026	158,273	39
Wayne	80,496	11,061	15,159	7,975	114,691	D
Wells	95,135	6,249	9,280	8,461	119,125	D
TOTALS	**2,737,512**	**494,227**	**463,274**	**358,150**	**4,053,163**	**1,157**
Acres (400 ft²/tree)	**6,843**	**1,236**	**1,158**	**895**	**10,132**	

Table G-8. *continued*

Natural Region County	Apples 1900 (# of trees)	Peaches 1900 (# of trees)	Cherries 1900 (# of trees)	Pears 1900 (# of trees)	Total 1900	Orchards 2002 (acres)
Southwestern Lowlands						
Clay	101,598	35,547	8,494	6,553	152,192	D
Daviess	121,765	41,177	8,241	5,567	176,750	49
Dubois	130,365	26,404	4,365	4,057	165,191	
Greene	205,428	66,125	10,792	6,969	289,314	30
Knox	125,536	46,504	8,650	8,058	188,748	123
Posey	69,072	29,132	5,419	22,986	126,609	61
Spencer	107,589	43,885	6,878	13,247	171,599	D
Sullivan	130,180	55,958	9,526	11,247	206,911	D
Vanderburgh	81,397	51,382	9,838	20,194	162,811	164
Vigo	77,164	28,926	8,570	5,377	120,037	35
Warrick	96,297	48,740	8,696	10,270	164,003	D
TOTALS	**1,246,391**	**473,780**	**89,469**	**114,525**	**1,924,165**	**462**
Acres (400 ft²/tree)	**3,116**	**1,184**	**224**	**36**	**4,560**	
Southern Bottomlands						
Gibson	105,051	68,069	5,336	48,931	227,387	7
Pike	92,081	40,574	8,407	6,176	147,238	
TOTALS	**197,132**	**108,643**	**13,743**	**55,107**	**374,625**	**7**
Acres (400 ft²/tree)	**493**	**272**	**34**	**138**	**937**	
Shawnee Hills						
Crawford	180,111	45,040	4,789	3,183	233,123	D
Martin	51,503	35,435	4,741	2,352	94,031	D
Orange	141,443	67,096	9,042	7,543	225,124	16
Owen	111,302	42,246	5,159	4,832	163,539	100
Perry	148,099	41,480	3,541	7,127	200,247	3
TOTALS	**632,458**	**231,297**	**27,272**	**25,037**	**916,064**	**119**
Acres (400 ft²/tree)	**1,581**	**578**	**68**	**63**	**2,290**	
Highland Rim						
Brown	123,103	78,666	5,182	3,885	210,836	4
Floyd	106,570	49,175	5,386	13,616	174,747	17
Harrison	372,839	193,761	6,865	27,887	601,352	288
Lawrence	135,565	45,037	7,608	5,937	194,147	D
Monroe	140,816	62,404	6,472	5,519	215,211	36
Morgan	92,088	53,180	10,155	6,404	151,672	328
Washington	185,477	137,024	8,006	24,596	355,103	41
TOTALS	**1,156,458**	**619,247**	**39,519**	**87,844**	**1,903,068**	**714**
Acres (400 ft2/tree)	**2,891**	**1,548**	**99**	**220**	**4,758**	
Bluegrass						
Bartholomew	105,013	40,410	8,213	5,689	159,325	34
Clark	119,079	258,087	5,715	8,166	391,047	162
Dearborn	85,285	64,755	8,923	10,559	169,522	228
Decatur	56,648	11,879	5,665	3,705	77,897	11
Fayette	26,570	13,790	3,436	2,685	46,481	D
Franklin	90,106	23,986	4,887	4,468	123,447	97
Jackson	135,195	46,209	5,977	9,360	196,741	D
Jefferson	133,627	128,885	6,660	18,273	287,445	74
Jennings	119,947	32,334	6,908	10,172	169,361	42
Ohio	18,461	6,755	262	703	26,181	D
Ripley	134,501	36,198	11,657	6,655	189,011	59
Scott	68,635	29,543	4,208	4,509	106,895	32
Switzerland	102,783	53,350	6,561	4,615	167,309	34
TOTALS	**1,195,850**	**746,181**	**79,072**	**89,559**	**2,110,662**	**773**
Acres (400 ft2/tree)	**2,990**	**1,865**	**198**	**224**	**5,277**	
STATE TOTALS (acres)	**21,557**	**7,314**	**2,180**	**1,921**	**32,972**	**4,529**

Notes: Data from the Black Swamp Natural Region are included in other regions. Counties are placed in the natural region where more than 50% of the county occurs. D = one farm, data not released.
Sources: U.S. Census Bureau 1900 (vol. 5); U.S. Department of Agriculture 2002.

Table G-9. Number of Confined Feeding Operations by County and Natural Region

Natural Region County	
Northwestern Morainal	
Lake	6
Porter	3
TOTAL	**9**
Grand Prairie	
Benton	8
Jasper	53
LaPorte	30
Newton	18
Pulaski	30
Starke	6
Vermillion	5
Warren	8
White	62
TOTAL	**220**
Northern Lakes	
Cass	48
Elkhart	40
Fulton	25
Kosciusko	81
LaGrange	23
Marshall	17
Noble	19
St. Joseph	13
Steuben	4
Whitley	43
TOTAL	**313**
Central Till Plain	
Adams	63
Allen	29
Blackford	8
Boone	23
Carroll	117
Clinton	97
DeKalb	17
Delaware	12
Fountain	6
Grant	25
Hamilton	15
Hancock	24
Hendricks	6
Henry	10
Howard	53
Huntington	30
Jay	70
Johnson	9
Madison	14
Marion	1
Miami	61
Montgomery	32
Parke	9
Putnam	24
Randolph	28
Rush	51
Shelby	21
Tippecanoe	38
Tipton	28
Union	16
Wabash	114
Wayne	10
Wells	31
TOTAL	**1,092**
Southwestern Lowlands	
Clay	15
Daviess	96
Dubois	105
Greene	26
Knox	29
Posey	14
Spencer	34
Sullivan	12
Vanderburgh	2
Vigo	4
Warrick	5
TOTAL	**342**
Southern Bottomlands	
Gibson	22
Pike	8
TOTAL	**30**
Shawnee Hills	
Crawford	4
Martin	34
Orange	9
Owen	3
Perry	11
TOTAL	**61**
Highland Rim	
Brown	1
Floyd	1
Harrison	8
Lawrence	5
Monroe	0
Morgan	6
Washington	37
TOTAL	**58**
Bluegrass	
Bartholomew	12
Clark	3
Dearborn	0
Decatur	82
Fayette	8
Franklin	21
Jackson	28
Jefferson	0
Jennings	8
Ohio	0
Ripley	26
Scott	0
Switzerland	2
TOTAL	**190**

Notes: Counties are included in the natural region in which more than 50% of the land area occurs. The Black Swamp Natural Region, Lake Michigan, and the big rivers are included in other regions.

Source: Indiana Department of Environmental Management 1999.

Table G-10. Stone Quarries in 1900

Kind of Stone	Acres
Oolitic	30
	62
	30
	18
	35
	90
	80
	640
	16
	70
	60
	15
	75
	80
	147
Limestone	104
	3
	256
	154
	100
Sandstone	6
TOTAL	**2,071**

Source: Indiana Department of Statistics 1900.

Table G-11. Cities and Incorporated Towns in 1901

Town	Acres
Alamo	41
Albany	500
Albion	820
Alexandria	1,920
Alton	40
Ambia	60
Amboy	100
Anderson	3,500
Andrews	640
Angola	560
Argos	262
Ashley	nd
Atlanta	190
Attica	nd
Auburn	496
Aurora	nd
Avilla	272
Bainbridge	160
Batesville	nd
Battle Ground	160
Bedford	1,120
Berne	481
Birdseye	nd
Bloomfield	130
Bloomingdale	320
Bloomington	800
Bluffton	nd
Boonville	640
Boston	nd
Boswell	320
Bourbon	160
Bowling Green	80
Bremen	520
Bristol	1,440
Broad Ripple	200
Bronson	40
Brook	160
Brooksburg	30
Brookston	152
Brookville	700
Brownsburg	640
Brownstown	nd
Bryant	160
Bunker Hill	320
Burnettsville	960
Butler	680
Cadiz	160
Cambridge City	nd
Camden	nd
Campbellsburg	640
Cannelburg	180
Cannelton	nd
Carbon	100
Carlisle	nd
Carmel	nd
Carthage	100
Castleton	60
Cayuga	550
Center Point	480
Centerville	400
Chalmers	125
Charlestown	320
Chesterton	nd
Chrisney	200
Churubusco	75
Cicero	nd
Clarks Hill	160
Clarksville	1,000
Clay City	400
Claypool	nd
Clifford	nd
Clinton	nd
Cloverdale	160
Cochran	680
Colfax	111
Columbia City	640
Columbus	1,020
Connersville	1,002
Converse	200
Corydon	275
Covington	640
Crandall	60
Crawfordsville	nd
Crothersville	160
Crown Point	1,175
Culver	160
Cynthiana	40
Dale	414
Dana	160
Danville	nd
Darlington	nd
Decatur	nd
Delphi	400
Dillsboro	229
Dublin	nd
Dunkirk	640
Dunreith	110
Earl Park	800
East Chicago	4,076
East Connersville	nd
East Gernantown	11
Eaton	437
Edinburg	480
Elisabeth	85
Elisabethtown	115
Elkhart	4,500
Ellettsville	210
Elnora	360
Elwood	nd
English	nd
Etna Green	80
Evansville	3,200
Fairmount	680
Farmersburg	nd
Farmland	130
Fishers	nd
Flora	312
Fort Branch	300
Fortville	210
Fountain City	180
Fowler	640
Francesville	240
Frankfort	960
Franklin	nd
Fredericksburg	640
Fremont	640
French Lick	285
Ft. Wayne	3,520
Fulton	45
Garrett	365
Gas City	1,200
Geneva	320
Gentryville	277
Georgetown	13
Goodland	nd
Goshen	nd
Gosport	80
Grandview	640
Greencastle	654
Greendale	900
Greenfield	1,300
Greensboro	113
Greentown	240
Greenville	nd
Greenwood	350
Hagerstown	160
Hamlet	960
Hammond	3,200
Hanover	280
Hardinsburg	2,354
Hartford City	nd
Hartsville	nd
Hazelton	nd
Hebron	160
Hillsboro	nd
Hobart	769
Hope	290
Howell	150
Hudson	nd
Huntingburg	491
Huntington	2,000
Huron	10
Indianapolis	18,016
Ingalls	224
Irvington	650
Jamestown	85
Jasper	400
Jeffersonville	650
Jonesboro	485
Jonesville	39
Judson	75
Kempton	30
Kennard	123
Kentland	400
Kewanna	200
Keystone	45
Kingman	640
Kirklin	134
Knightstown	500
Knightsville	640
Knox	990
Kokomo	1,800
Laconia	25
Ladoga	650
Lafayette	3,840
LaGrange	nd
Lagro	640
Lanesville	31

Town	Acres
Lapel	200
Laporte	nd
Laurel	400
Lawrenceburg	800
Leavenworth	160
Lebanon	720
Leesburg	180
Lewisville	124
Liberty	nd
Ligonier	600
Linden	nd
Linton	nd
Little York	640
Livonia	40
Logansport	2,250
Longview	90
Loogootee	960
Lowell	nd
Lynn	240
Lynnville	50
Macy	40
Madison	nd
Marengo	320
Marion	3,500
Markle	225
Martinsville	700
Mauckport	70
Medaryville	nd
Mellott	240
Mentone	nd
Merom	281
Michigan City	nd
Michigantown	160
Middlebury	nd
Middletown	nd
Milan	360
Milford	nd
Milford Junction	220
Milhousen	720
Millersburg	140
Milton	201
Mishawaka	nd
Mitchell	700
Modoc	nd
Monon	nd
Monroe City	122
Monroeville	240
Monterey	113
Montezuma	nd
Montgomery	nd
Monticello	700
Montpelier	nd
Moorefield	nd
Moores Hill	484
Mooresville	312
Moreland	80
Morocco	175
Morristown	70
Mt. Auburn	nd
Mt. Carmel	nd
Mt. Etna	81
Muncie	nd
Nappanee	nd
Nashville	nd
New Albany	nd
New Amsterdam	nd
New Carlisle	nd
New Castle	1,400
New Harmony	nd
New Haven	350
New Market	105
New Middletown	32
New Palestine	100
New Richmond	120

Town	Acres
New Ross	154
Newburgh	400
Newpoint	80
Newport	198
Noblesville	nd
Normal City	626
North Judson	640
North Liberty	nd
North Manchester	141
North Salem	160
North Vernon	nd
Oakland City	384
Odon	360
Oldenburg	320
Orestes	160
Orleans	nd
Osgood	300
Ossian	160
Otterbein	nd
Owensville	143
Oxford	640
Paoli	nd
Paragon	80
Parker City	278
Patoka	150
Patriot	109
Pendleton	460
Perce	nd
Peru	nd
Petersburg	500
Pierceton	250
Pine Village	75
Poneto	nd
Port Fulton	nd
Portland	nd
Poseyville	153
Princeton	nd
Redkey	640
Remington	480
Rensselaer	nd
Reynolds	nd
Richmond	2,560
Ridgeville	250
Rising Sun	640
River Park	642
Roachdale	160
Roann	nd
Roanoke	331
Rochester	1,030
Rockport	nd
Rockville	600
Rosedale	75
Rossville	212
Royal Center	600
Rushville	700
Russellville	nd
St. Joe	204
St. Leon	404
St. Meinrad	nd
Salamonia	480
Salem	680
Saltillo	734
Scottsburg	640
Sellersburg	nd
Seymour	700
Shelburn	40
Shellbyville	nd
Sheridan	nd
Shirley	210
Shirley City	165
Shoals	nd
Silver Lake	nd
South Bend	4,984.5
South Delphi	80

Town	Acres
South Peru	nd
South Whitley	160
Spencer	320
Spiceland	320
Spring Grove	220
State Line	nd
Staunton	nd
Stinesville	40
Straughns	nd
Sullivan	640
Sulphur Springs	160
Summitville	300
Swayzee	nd
Syracuse	nd
Tell City	416
Tennyson	20
Terre Haute	3,388
Tipton	640
Thorntown	nd
Troy	120
Union City	640
Upland	720
Valparaiso	1,200
Van Buren	nd
Veedersburg	nd
Vera Cruz	80
Vernon	nd
Versailles	63
Vevay	nd
Vincennes	nd
Wabash	3,200
Wakarusa	590
Walkerton	160
Walton	75
Warren	180
Warsaw	nd
Washington	nd
Waterloo	700
Waveland	240
Waynetown	160
West College Corner	100
West Harrison	206
West Lafayette	678
West Lebanon	170
West Madison	57
West Shoals	200
West Terre Haute	100
Westfield	200
Westport	nd
Westville	nd
Wheatfield	80
Whiteland	87
Whitewater	nd
Whiting	1,280
Williamsport	nd
Winamac	550
Winchester	643
Windfall	640
Wingate	160
Winslow	nd
Wolcott	240
Wolcottville	640
Woodruff Place	nd
Worthington	nd
Zionsville	160
TOTAL AREA (all towns)	**173,976**

Note: nd = no data.

Source: Indiana Department of Statistics, Ninth Biennial Report, 1902.

Table G-12. Transportation Systems: Roads, Railroads, and Airports

Roads (2000)	State (miles)	County (miles)	City (miles)
Rural	9,553	60,896	3,215
Urban	1,662	5,705	12,576

Notes: State includes 1,170 miles of interstate highway.
Interstate highways have 37 rest areas.

Railroads	1900	2,000
Miles of main track	7,440	4,686
Miles of side track	2,490	
Estimated acres*	108,327	56,800

Note: *Based on 90 ft right-of-way.

Airports (2000)*	Miles	Acres
Paved runways	67	1,614
Grass runways	22	265

Note: *Estimate based on the longest runway at each airport, 200 ft wide paved and 100 ft wide unpaved.

Natural Region / County	Road Miles 1900	Road Miles 2000
Northwestern Morainal		
Lake	152	2,552
Porter	75	1,274
TOTAL	**227**	**3,826**
Grand Prairie		
Benton	150	835
Jasper	35	1,154
LaPorte	25	1,641
Newton		834
Pulaski		1,006
Starke		840
Vermillion	180	573
Warren	115	682
White	126	1,138
TOTAL	**631**	**8,703**
Northern Lakes		
Cass	133	1,124
Elkhart		1,706
Fulton	35	943
Kosciusko	17	1,509
LaGrange		944
Marshall		1,214
Noble		1,031
St. Joseph		1,998
Steuben		841
Whitley	12	821
TOTAL	**197**	**12,131**
Central Till Plain		
Adams	140	884
Allen	159	2,638
Blackford	118	432
Boone	430	1,091
Carroll	115	914
Clinton	360	999
DeKalb	6	969
Delaware	184	1,361
Fountain	103	879
Grant	375	1,258
Hamilton	400	1,584
Hancock	175	890
Hendricks	171	1,128
Henry	230	1,078
Howard	193	980
Huntington	197	974
Jay	215	932
Johnson	208	985
Madison	280	1,573
Marion	340	3,461
Miami	106	999
Montgomery	550	1,099
Parke	425	878
Putnam	300	965
Randolph	290	1,076
Rush	131	883
Shelby	167	1,026
Tippecanoe	347	1,345
Tipton	240	665
Union	67	325
Wabash	187	972
Wayne	120	1,106
Wells	295	895
TOTAL	**7,624**	**37,244**
Southwestern Lowlands		
Clay	175	870
Daviess		990
Dubois		916
Greene	209	1,149
Knox	48	1,197
Posey	31	875
Spencer		941
Sullivan	215	1,072
Vanderburgh	126	1,146
Vigo	166	1,337
Warrick	29	914
TOTAL	**999**	**11,407**
Southern Bottomlands		
Gibson	30	1,232
Pike		685
TOTAL	**30**	**1,917**
Shawnee Hills		
Crawford		585
Martin	30	472
Orange	88	752
Owen	129	734
Perry		689
TOTAL	**247**	**3,232**
Highland Rim		
Brown	21	455
Floyd	70	542
Harrison	13	1,007
Lawrence	264	927
Monroe	151	991
Morgan	105	931
Washington	66	942
TOTAL	**690**	**5,795**
Bluegrass		
Bartholomew		1,057
Clark		888
Dearborn	40	699
Decatur	87	810
Fayette		483
Franklin	124	751
Jackson	400	1,024
Jefferson	27	742
Jennings	135	778
Ohio		175
Ripley	21	932
Scott	91	453
Switzerland	64	462
TOTAL	**989**	**9,254**
STATE TOTALS	**11,694**	**93,607**
Estimated Total Acres*	141,745	1,135,630

Notes: Data for the Black Swamp Natural Region are included in other regions.
Counties with no data did not report.
*Based on 100 ft right-of-way.

Table G-13. Lindsey Land Cover within Homoya's Natural Regions

Homoya Natural Region	Lindsey Land Cover	Acres
Northwestern Morainal	oak/hickory	324,418.3
	beech/maple	30,275.9
	wetlands	141,760.7
	beech/oak/maple/hickory	0
	dry prairie	75,769.5
TOTAL		**572,224.4**
Grand Prairie	oak/hickory	430,441.9
	beech/maple	91,912.0
	wetlands	1,488,018.9
	beech/oak/maple/hickory	0
	dry prairie	466,021.5
TOTAL		**2,476,394.3**
Northern Lakes	oak/hickory	1,526,918.4
	beech/maple	794,713.8
	wetlands	171,300.3
	beech/oak/maple/hickory	0
	dry prairie	34,538.6
TOTAL		**2,527,471.1**
Central Till Plain	oak/hickory	450,188.4
	beech/maple	7,453,052.0
	wetlands	271,756.3
	beech/oak/maple/hickory	0
	dry prairie	25,334.8
TOTAL		**8,200,331.4**
Black Swamp	oak/hickory	0
	beech/maple	38,684.9
	wetlands	114,158.2
	beech/oak/maple/hickory	0
	dry prairie	0
TOTAL		**152,843.1**
Southwestern Lowlands	oak/hickory	1,464,852.5
	beech/maple	754,508.6
	wetlands	0
	beech/oak/maple/hickory	149,976.4
	dry prairie	0
TOTAL		**2,369,337.5**
Southern Bottomlands	oak/hickory	769,321.9
	beech/maple	9,920.6
	wetlands	0
	beech/oak/maple/hickory	93,977.6
	dry prairie	0
TOTAL		**873,220.1**
Shawnee Hills	oak/hickory	1,051,879.2
	beech/maple	374,058.8
	wetlands	0
	beech/oak/maple/hickory	268,916.1
	dry prairie	0
TOTAL		**1,694,854.1**
Highland Rim	oak/hickory	606,098.3
	beech/maple	264,493.3
	wetlands	0
	beech/oak/maple/hickory	872,120.3
	dry prairie	0
TOTAL		**1,742,711.9**
Bluegrass	oak/hickory	273,759.8
	beech/maple	1,847,859.5
	wetlands	0
	beech/oak/maple/hickory	402,475.3
	dry prairie	0
TOTAL		**2,524,094.7**
TOTAL ACRES		**23,133,482.7**

Sources: Lindsey et al. 1965; Homoya et al. 1985. Data from J. C. Randolph and Richard G. Thurau, SPEA GIS Lab, Indiana University.

Table G-14. Area of Vegetation Types by Natural Region of Indiana Based on Gordon's Map

Homoya Natural Region	Gordon Land Cover	Acres
Northwestern Morainal	beech forest	52,747.6
	oak forest/n. swamp forest	345,368.0
	northern swamp forest	0
	oak forest	0
	prairie grass	174,245.7
	mixed forest	0
	beech/sweetgum	0
	oak forest/s. swamp forest	0
	southern swamp forest	0
	bald cypress	0
Grand Prairie	beech forest	83,484.1
	oak forest/n. swamp forest	956,246.1
	northern swamp forest	0
	oak forest	140,248.4
	prairie grass	1,295,861.5
	mixed forest	0
	beech/sweetgum	0
	oak forest/s. swamp forest	0
	southern swamp forest	0
	bald cypress	0
Northern Lakes	beech forest	76,768.0
	oak forest/n. swamp forest	1,347,724.0
	northern swamp forest	14,343.8
	oak forest	886,474.6
	prairie grass	202,623.3
	mixed forest	0
	beech/sweetgum	0
	oak forest/s. swamp forest	0
	southern swamp forest	0
	bald cypress	0
Central Till Plain	beech forest	2,709,441.5
	oak forest/n. swamp forest	580,255.8
	northern swamp forest	3,017,203.0
	oak forest	1,557,072.0
	prairie grass	336,933.3
	mixed forest	0
	beech/sweetgum	0
	oak forest/s. swamp forest	0
	southern swamp forest	0
	bald cypress	0
Black Swamp	beech forest	0
	oak forest/n. swamp forest	0
	northern swamp forest	135,210.5
	oak forest	17,696.0
	prairie grass	0
	mixed forest	0
	beech/sweetgum	0
	oak forest/s. swamp forest	0
	southern swamp forest	0
	bald cypress	0
Southwestern Lowlands	beech forest	682,487.1
	oak forest/n. swamp forest	467,138.9
	northern swamp forest	100,730.0
	oak forest	342,617.1
	prairie grass	128,962.1
	mixed forest	0
	beech/sweetgum	0
	oak forest/s. swamp forest	471,440.6
	southern swamp forest	173,023.2
	bald cypress	2,914.0
Southern Bottomlands	beech forest	182,738.5
	oak forest/n. swamp forest	46,029.5
	northern swamp forest	0
	oak forest	8,653.4
	prairie grass	11,004.3
	mixed forest	11,748.0
	beech/sweetgum	0
	oak forest/s. swamp forest	246,567.4
	southern swamp forest	316,512.6
	bald cypress	49,736.4
Shawnee Hills	beech forest	204,045.7
	oak forest/n. swamp forest	225,452.1
	northern swamp forest	92,589.4
	oak forest	151,739.8
	prairie grass	4,741.9
	mixed forest	913,055.2
	beech/sweetgum	0
	oak forest/s. swamp forest	86,989.1
	southern swamp forest	16,215.9
	bald cypress	0
Highland Rim	beech forest	553,191.0
	oak forest/n. swamp forest	0
	northern swamp forest	66,533.9
	oak forest	90,616.3
	prairie grass	1,503.4
	mixed forest	1,019,615.5
	beech/sweetgum	11,488.0
	oak forest/s. swamp forest	0
	southern swamp forest	0
	bald cypress	0
Bluegrass	beech forest	1,219,582.1
	oak forest/n. swamp forest	0
	northern swamp forest	207,090.8
	oak forest	223,543.5
	prairie grass	0
	mixed forest	12,231.1
	beech/sweetgum	862,451.3
	oak forest/s. swamp forest	0
	southern swamp forest	0
	bald cypress	0
STATE TOTAL		**23,134,927.3**

Sources: Gordon 1936; Homoya et al. 1985. Data from J. C. Randolph and Richard G. Thurau, SPEA GIS Lab, Indiana University.

Table G-15. Area of Vegetation Types by Natural Region Based on STATSGO Soil Associations

Natural Region	Cover Class	Acres
Northwestern Morainal	forest	344,842.4
	wetland	13,821.4
	prairie/forest	9,304.8
	prairie/wetland	28,770.1
	forest/wetland	66,219.9
	forest/prairie/wetland	108,572.7
TOTAL		**571,531.2**
Grand Prairie	forest	524,525.6
	wetland	336,725.8
	prairie/forest	68,819.9
	prairie/wetland	854,329.9
	forest/wetland	348,277.7
	prairie	36,712.1
	forest/prairie/wetland	305,241.6
	no data	1,014.1
TOTAL		**2,475,646.7**
Northern Lakes	forest	1,436,401.7
	wetland	135,042.2
	prairie/forest	7,984.9
	prairie/wetland	58,833.0
	forest/wetland	805,608.9
	prairie	34,380.7
	forest/prairie/wetland	43,839.6
	no data	5,793.2
TOTAL		**2,527,884.1**
Central Till Plain	forest	2,155,824.4
	wetland	20,941.4
	prairie/wetland	2,680.3
	forest/wetland	5,721,847.5
	prairie	104,422.4
	forest/prairie/wetland	178,894.0
	no data	15,470.9
TOTAL		**8,200,080.8**
Black Swamp	forest	5,496.3
	wetland	3,972.6
	forest/wetland	143,286.8
TOTAL		**152,755.7**
Southwestern Lowlands	forest	1,785,544.7
	wetland	81,867.6
	prairie/forest	1,756.3
	prairie/wetland	38,162.5
	forest/wetland	411,096.5
	prairie	50,934.9
TOTAL		**2,369,362.4**
Southern Bottomlands	forest	340,215.9
	wetland	65,667.0
	prairie/forest	32,332.7
	prairie/wetland	73,408.1
	forest/wetland	359,578.9
	prairie	2,705.4
TOTAL		**873,907.9**
Shawnee Hills	forest	1,521,260.5
	wetland	1,254.8
	prairie/forest	51,318.3
	forest/wetland	116,715.5
	no data	6,435.0
TOTAL		**1,696,984.0**
Highland Rim	forest	1,490,255.1
	wetland	1,518.5
	prairie/forest	51,395.9
	forest/wetland	189,255.1
	no data	11,439.3
TOTAL		**1,743,863.9**
Bluegrass	forest	1,520,767.9
	wetland	2,944.1
	prairie/forest	56,641.5
	forest/wetland	941,216.2
	no data	4,872.0
TOTAL		**2,526,441.6**
STATE TOTAL		**23,138,458.3**

Source: Data from J. C. Randolph and Richard G. Thurau, SPEA GIS Lab, Indiana University.

Table G-16. Quantity and Quality of Timber Land and Number of Trees Planted by Natural Region and County, 1902

Natural Region County	Cultivation Condition (acres)	1st Grade Timber (acres)	2nd Grade Timber (acres)	3rd Grade Timber (acres)	Broken Waste Land (acres)	Trees Planted (number)	Total Farm (acres)
Northwestern Morainal							
Lake	144,199	506	9,181	22,868	11,090	80	215,736
Porter	143,072	732	13,401	22,553	11,854	1,155	206,314
TOTAL	**287,271**	**1,238**	**22,582**	**45,421**	**22,944**	**1,235**	**422,050**
Grand Prairie							
Benton	214,448	315	195	2,188	4,011		221,516
Jasper	204,302	1,157	4,236	77,589	11,790		307,326
LaPorte	181,174	3,652	19,857	35,246	13,777	2,244	382,543
Newton	156,035	3,033	535	28,925	8,978	145	203,837
Pulaski	153,449	830	12,146	46,208	6,614	82	223,990
Starke	73,663	3,277	4,242	37,011	4,726		104,667
Vermillion	98,423	321	1,950	18,532	11,311	114	134,052
Warren	148,246	1,031	4,184	20,510	7,856	6	194,939
White	226,158	519	10,999	29,273	2,128	748	266,348
TOTAL	**1,455,898**	**14,135**	**58,344**	**295,482**	**71,191**	**3,339**	**2,039,218**
Northern Lakes							
Cass	172,306	4,744	14,837	20,875	5,774	6	229,070
Elkhart	181,830	3,122	11,863	18,965	3,946	529	229,161
Fulton	133,019	2,972	10,877	19,551	10,033	339	179,479
Kosciusko	208,145	3,599	12,282	36,152	13,115	410	297,537
LaGrange	146,142	3,157	13,008	16,221	13,491	93	200,115
Marshall	155,237	1,694	14,761	32,375	8,079	174	200,217
Noble	161,091	3,425	16,114	13,358	17,840	477	224,555
St. Joseph	178,601	4,528	11,776	24,908	13,519	905	236,650
Steuben	109,073	1,418	10,695	21,654	11,382	82	159,906
Whitley	141,311	770	8,924	31,083	5,128	44	184,856
TOTAL	**1,586,755**	**29,429**	**125,137**	**235,142**	**102,307**	**3,059**	**2,141,546**
Central Till Plain							
Adams	145,872	1,360	9,976	22,384	2,059	1,593	185,023
Allen	241,500	4,833	19,116	61,668	7,302	327	339,601
Blackford	64,166	1,436	3,257	13,109	1,217		73,474
Boone	190,973	335	2,770	40,446	1,706	116	241,673
Carroll	160,652	4,211	9,317	21,788	5,672	1,301	218,136
Clinton	199,799	1,282	3,597	23,224	1,779	131	239,216
DeKalb	151,381	1,674	10,816	31,434	3,799	162	201,337
Delaware	164,118	809	8,198	22,269	3,250	88	203,288
Fountain	167,074	1,077	5,489	26,426	9,878	414	243,615
Grant	169,188	1,866	7,803	24,036	2,013	820	218,025
Hamilton	181,157	4,745	3,718	20,787	1,735	1,045	222,795
Hancock	151,970	1,822	5,855	14,766	1,524	1,067	176,377
Hendricks	143,034	1,682	2,055	44,437	1,481	58	210,527
Henry	167,448	2,072	10,786	21,535	1,383	11,555	222,120
Howard	142,786	5,787	6,341	13,583	1,651	228	169,879
Huntington	164,071	1,646	11,033	28,605	2,708	93	245,714
Jay	180,565	2,764	10,047	33,479	1,446	116	221,157
Johnson	127,294	963	3,010	35,144	3,640	390	170,183
Madison	185,905	3,532	7,438	23,526	3,065	3,378	220,475
Marion	161,500	1,745	6,336	26,323	4,326	35,723	202,032
Miami	128,171	4,269	9,953	20,717	4,448	3,042	221,545
Montgomery	192,676	2,934	7,291	48,351	4,296	1,218	269,995
Parke	117,719	713	8,522	54,734	24,251	28	228,569
Putnam	143,372	1,153	6,451	84,300	3,263	210	248,614
Randolph	197,112	1,574	12,998	29,835	4,305	850	307,730
Rush	177,795	3,030	4,734	28,931	2,763	847	214,799
Shelby	190,561	4,058	5,868	21,387	3,174	404	226,123
Tippecanoe	196,869	1,388	7,652	19,697	7,512	1,760	281,749
Tipton	114,531	100	4,126	16,574	1,133	231	146,264
Union	67,454	498	1,876	19,952	2,620		93,514
Wabash	154,115	2,692	10,786	27,315	5,240	69	225,851
Wayne	170,378	5,859	6,585	32,080	7,920	515	223,169
Wells	143,519	470	9,870	21,263	2,042	3,150	184,984
TOTAL	**5,254,725**	**74,379**	**243,670**	**974,105**	**134,601**	**70,929**	**7,097,553**

Natural Region County	Cultivation Condition (acres)	1st Grade Timber (acres)	2nd Grade Timber (acres)	3rd Grade Timber (acres)	Broken Waste Land (acres)	Trees Planted (number)	Total Farm (acres)
Southwestern Lowlands							
Clay	122,549	1,191	7,692	24,381	7,945	3,059	174,607
Daviess	186,688	875	8,355	17,209	3,838	341	215,321
Dubois	142,186	17,214	21,821	41,685	11,182		234,294
Greene	204,769	1,846	17,423	31,385	8,316	88	284,970
Knox	177,979	2,534	4,700	28,736	4,736	2,320	239,769
Posey	159,256	1,645	7,431	9,534	6,322	1,002	196,348
Spencer	141,469	5,361	25,358	20,767	9,218	352	200,434
Sullivan	180,127	2,536	3,609	26,833	8,963	1,185	220,973
Vanderburgh	90,367	4,374	1,996	9,642	6,653	13	121,906
Vigo	138,041	758	5,683	18,336	10,734	463	178,308
Warrick	152,275	1,770	5,535	16,670	7,840	70	217,773
TOTAL	**1,695,706**	**40,104**	**109,603**	**245,178**	**85,747**	**8,893**	**2,284,703**
Southern Bottomlands							
Gibson	191,697	3,563	6,034	19,452	2,519	1,788	235,401
Pike	121,035	1,974	6,309	12,552	6,689	4,730	170,609
TOTAL	**312,732**	**5,537**	**12,343**	**32,004**	**9,208**	**6,518**	**406,010**
Shawnee Hills							
Crawford	76,585	1,155	9,356	37,812	14,676	140	151,142
Martin	117,046	3,715	15,855	27,366	11,315	27	180,341
Orange	121,831	7,882	7,747	41,954	10,984		209,886
Owen	105,692	7,264	5,148	69,928	5,707	309	195,211
Perry	80,777	1,169	12,483	44,293	30,164		165,718
TOTAL	**501,931**	**21,185**	**50,589**	**221,353**	**72,846**	**476**	**902,298**
Highland Rim							
Brown	63,939	897	13,748	33,588	7,078		119,651
Floyd	43,169	760	5,190	14,330	7,052	53	70,679
Harrison	157,606	4,123	24,706	47,555	20,379	623	258,426
Lawrence	114,296	8,173	14,118	62,211	8,488	70	206,138
Monroe	152,522	2,793	10,186	52,109	10,273	109	269,515
Morgan	120,655	4,951	12,995	40,141	12,243	3,209	204,118
Washington	168,814	8,016	23,556	44,437	12,235	1,000	265,243
TOTAL	**821,001**	**29,713**	**104,499**	**294,371**	**77,748**	**5,064**	**1,393,770**
Bluegrass							
Bartholomew	163,976	2,849	8,628	32,994	7,307	761	220,671
Clark	106,308	1,538	11,431	36,232	17,327	888	185,417
Dearborn	109,643	4,044	7,778	25,568	9,788	803	183,772
Decatur	155,066	1,691	3,587	25,220	7,002	772	193,111
Fayette	88,897	1,192	7,912	18,037	3,493	145	120,784
Franklin	122,591	3,367	15,033	56,888	12,516	95	227,670
Jackson	157,708	2,777	12,280	48,940	14,279	392	252,667
Jefferson	118,476	1,943	9,027	43,823	10,136	146	192,600
Jennings	129,131	1,351	8,516	42,452	8,067	21	212,928
Ohio	33,725	1,165	1,169	3,651	3,950		42,846
Ripley	164,511	7,274	12,389	40,079	9,875	1,434	231,328
Scott	67,459	445	6,809	17,336	2,371	600	103,736
Switzerland	77,965	4,724	3,180	19,160	10,055	105	114,011
TOTAL	**1,495,456**	**34,360**	**107,739**	**410,380**	**116,166**	**6,162**	**2,281,541**
STATE TOTALS	**13,314,455**	**250,080**	**834,506**	**2,753,456**	**692,738**	**105,675**	**18,968,689**

Notes: Data from the Black Swamp Natural Region are included in other regions. Broken waste land was probably mostly wetlands. These estimates of land in cultivation and total farmland are lower than estimates given in the Twelfth Census of the United States; see Table G-2 and U.S. Census Bureau 1900 (vol. 5).
Source: Indiana Department of Statistics 1901–1902.

Table G-17. Forest Areas by Type and Survey Unit

Forest Survey Unit	Forest Type												
	White Pine	Shortleaf/ Virginia Pine	Eastern Red Cedar	Eastern Red Cedar/ Hardwoods	Oak/Pine	Oak/Hickory	Oak/Gum/ Cypress	Elm/Ash/ Cottonwood	Maple/Beech	Cherry/Ash/ Tulip Poplar	Aspen/Birch	Total	Total All Types
Northern	10,600	100			11,700	329,400	19,100	275,800	387,000	147,600	2,400	812,800	1,183,700
Lower Wabash	10,600	6,200		2,500	21,700	292,600	14,500	164,500	253,200	59,400		477,100	825,200
Knobs	8,700	44,700	24,300	35,800	41,100	821,700	7,800	128,500	537,000	61900	4,800	732,200	1,716,300
Upland Flats			13,200	41,500	2,700	160,000	1,400	91,300	216,700	58,500		366,500	585,300
												State Total	**4,310,500**

Notes: The Northern unit primarily includes the Northwestern Morainal, Grand Prairie, Northern Lakes, Black Swamp, and Central Till Plain natural regions. The Lower Wabash unit primarily includes the Southwestern Lowlands and Southern Bottomlands natural regions. The Knobs unit primarily includes the Shawnee Hills and Highland Rim natural regions. The Upland Flats unit primarily includes the Bluegrass Natural Region.

Source: Schmidt et al. 2000.

Table G-18. Areas of Timber Land by Type and Size Class, 1999–2000

Type	All Stands	Saw Timber	Pole Timber	Sapling/ Seedling
Pine	80,900	61	17,800	1,800
Eastern red cedar	37,400	18,200	19,200	
Eastern red cedar/hardwoods	79,800	37,800	32,500	9,500
Oak/pine	77,100	36,200	27,900	13,100
Oak/hickory	1,603,800	1,195,700	339,300	68,800
Oak/gum/cypress	42,700	29,700	11,800	1,100
Elm/ash/cottonwood	660,100	467,500	156,600	36,000
Maple/beech	1,721,200	1,198,300	413,000	110,000
Cherry/ash/tulip poplar	327,400	173,800	117,200	36,400
Aspen/birch	7,200	7,200		
TOTAL	**4,310,200**	**2,990,661**	**1,018,100**	**240,300**

Source: Schmidt et al. 2000.

Table G-19. Rural and Urban Riparian Areas within the Natural Regions of Indiana

Natural Region	Rural (acres)	Urban (acres)	Total (acres)
Northwestern Morainal	39,107	31,606	70,713
Grand Prairie	381,787	2,980	384,767
Central Till Plain	1,070,488	125,653	1,196,141
Northern Lakes	257,671	16,209	273,880
Black Swamp	24,569	701	25,270
Southwestern Lowlands	516,687	12,930	529,617
Southern Bottomlands	524,823	9,333	534,156
Shawnee Hills	320,528	4,107	324,635
Highland Rim	254,997	3,003	258,000
Bluegrass	557,377	14,017	571,394
TOTAL	**3,948,034**	**220,539**	**4,168,573**

Source: Data from J. C. Randolph and Richard G. Thurau, SPEA GIS Lab, Indiana University.

Table G-20. Acreage of Land in Indiana Placed in Various Conservation Reserve Practices

Natural Region County	Introduced Grass CP1 (acres)	Native Grasses CP2 (acres)	Grass Waterways CP8A (acres)	Established Grass CP10 (acres)	Filterstrip Grass CP13C (acres)	Contour Grass Strips CP15A (acres)	Filter strips CP21 (acres)	Total (acres)
Northwestern Morainal								
Lake	245.2	310.3	75	703.4	5.9	2.3	163.2	1,505.3
Porter	91.1	547.1	28.2	964.3			331.6	1,962.3
TOTAL	**336.3**	**857.4**	**103.2**	**1,667.7**	**5.9**	**2.3**	**494.8**	**3,467.6**
Grand Prairie								
Benton		101.8	325.7	120.1		26	1,451.3	2,024.9
Jasper	94.2	197.2	44.7	76	69.7		2,499.7	2,981.5
LaPorte	230.1	228.6	4.9	863.8	16.2		613.5	1,957.1
Newton		272.7	128	428.7	53.9		1,421.7	2,305
Pulaski	16.7	729.4	9.8	293.8	19		4,448.2	5,516.9
Starke	217.2	3,122.3		1,987.8	43.4		5,032.8	10,403.5
Vermillion	85.2	35.2	86.2	4.9			52.8	264.3
Warren	367.5	428.9	515.6	667.5	7		386.2	2,372.7
White		17.2	201.7	7	8.7		1,620.9	1,855.5
TOTAL	**1,010.9**	**5,133.3**	**1,316.6**	**4,449.6**	**217.9**	**26**	**17,527**	**29,681.4**
Northern Lakes								
Cass	308.8	146.7	278.2	403.1	5.4		1,379.6	2,521.8
Elkhart	45	49	61.5	34.2			128.1	317.8
Fulton	341.4	179.5	34.2	145.3	16.2		852.4	1,569
Kosciusko	1,103.9	459.6	98.1	3,868.3	64.3	4.2	485.2	6,083.6
LaGrange	164.7	87.2	9.7	570.9	41.1	0.8	210.7	1,085.1
Marshall	7.5	828.5	22.1	803.2	24.7	4.8	522.8	2,213.6
Noble	447.5	308	54.1	5,657.4	19.5	7.1	483.9	6,977.5
St. Joseph	267	160.1	4.7	342.9			204.1	978.8
Steuben	2,857	173.4	53.7	7,045.6			828.3	10,958
Whitley	645.5	25.5	211.9	4,022.2	2		468	5,375.1
TOTAL	**5,542.8**	**2,392**	**616.3**	**18,870.9**	**171.2**	**16.9**	**5,095.1**	**38,080.3**
Central Till Plain								
Adams	784.3	196.7	79.6	488.1	31.2		1,049.5	2,629.4
Allen	540.5	55.7	128.1	2,951.7	7.7		1,374.7	5,058.4
Blackford	137.1	139.8	49.6	48.1			305.2	679.8
Boone		12.4	353.8		6		219.1	591.3
Carroll		141.3	199.6	104.5		33.2	384.6	863.2
Clinton	14.5	10.4	155.6	174.2		10.3	416.3	781.3
DeKalb	2,151.3	428.1	40.9	3,352	7.6	2.1	892.1	6,874.1
Delaware	49		84.1	379.4	7.7		398.8	919
Fountain	14.6	155	473.3	273.5	2.5	4.5	367	1,290.4
Grant	163.1	279.1	90.4	187.4		9.8	827.6	1,557.4
Hamilton			11.3				69.4	80.7
Hancock		6.4	40				116.9	163.3
Hendricks	6	6	323.7	39.3			67.1	442.1
Henry	456.1	39.4	101.4	1,011.7			52.5	1,661.1
Howard	1.1	42.3	185.7		5.1	5.1	582	821.3
Huntington	519.6	1,037.8	328.2	453.3		7.1	1,144.8	3,490.8
Jay	662.1	346.8	289.9	1,928.9	19.3		1,424.5	4,671.5
Johnson	100.5		97.6				108.2	306.3
Madison			88.6	57.5			476.4	622.5
Marion			1.2					1.2
Miami	491.5	467.6	383.9	390.9	13		1,110.3	2,857.2
Monroe	374.8		2.8	851.8	43.1		25.2	1,297.7
Montgomery	3.4	410.8	1,290.8	50.1			607.1	2,362.2
Parke	102.4	222.1	470.8	89.3		0.3	392.2	1,277.1
Putnam	139.1	1,395	862	1,132.7	10		394.8	3,933.6
Randolph	85.4	272.4	342.7	328.4			229.7	1,258.6
Rush	0.2		186.3	106			73.6	366.1
Shelby			128.4	76.7			147.2	352.3

Table G-20. *continued*

Natural Region County	Introduced Grass CP1 (acres)	Native Grasses CP2 (acres)	Grass Waterways CP8A (acres)	Established Grass CP10 (acres)	Filterstrip Grass CP13C (acres)	Contour Grass Strips CP15A (acres)	Filter strips CP21 (acres)	Total (acres)
Tippecanoe	12.2	8.9	154.8	48		29.1	457.3	710.3
Tipton			41.5				796.5	838
Union	54.7	50.8	208.1	191.7			29.7	535
Wabash	924.1	836	491	3,832		7	779.2	6,869.3
Wayne	1,556	273.3	625.5	2,972.8	30.3		413.9	5,871.8
Wells	48.9	192.2	133.2	738.5			343.1	1,455.9
TOTAL	**9,392.5**	**7,026.3**	**8,444.4**	**22,258.5**	**183.5**	**108.5**	**16,077**	**63,490.2**
Southwestern Lowlands								
Clay	341.1	167	318.4	1,369.7		38.7	275.4	2,510.3
Daviess	757.1	645.3	81.2	906.5			317.4	2,707.5
Dubois	625	326.7	109.1	1,180.3		1.3	360.3	2,602.7
Greene	612.5	321.5	59.4	924.1			288.6	2,206.1
Knox	69.4	170.6	71.7	104.8			847.9	1,264.4
Posey	151.4	65.8	116.3	27.2	3.1		231.2	595
Spencer	819.1	996.1	71.9	359.2			682.4	2,928.7
Sullivan	493.6	533.9	102.8	509			212.2	1,851.5
Vanderburgh	26.8	35.2	55.1	171.1		3	188	479.2
Vigo	26.9	96.7	128	128.6			49.4	429.6
Warrick	908.2	523	109.8	230.1	13.2		638.8	2,423.1
TOTAL	**4,831.1**	**3,881.8**	**1,223.7**	**5,910.6**	**16.3**	**43**	**4,091.6**	**19,998.1**
Southern Bottomlands								
Gibson	183.8	221.7	132.6	243.4			270.6	1,052.1
Pike	374.6	1,607.9	120.9	292			319	2,714.4
TOTAL	**558.4**	**1,829.6**	**253.5**	**535.4**			**589.6**	**3,766.5**
Shawnee Hills								
Crawford	841.5	7	0.9	1,289.3			87.9	2,226.6
Martin	268.8	42.7	25.9	385.6			116.9	839.9
Orange	769.7	553.2	22.7	2,715.7	178.7		1,432.4	5,672.4
Owen	788.7	262.5	25.4	1,666.4		0.3	821.5	3,564.8
Perry	595.4	157.2	19.7	533.6			128	1,433.9
TOTAL	**3,264.1**	**1,022.6**	**94.6**	**6,590.6**	**178.7**	**0.3**	**2,586.7**	**13,737.6**
Highland Rim								
Brown	21.2		1.5	40.8			97.8	161.3
Floyd	154	20.8		351.1			30.9	556.8
Harrison	1,195.2	482.4	81.7	1,475.9	6		398.7	3,639.9
Lawrence	2,439	610.9	63.7	3,524.3	301.5		991.3	7,930.7
Morgan	49.4	120.5	119.3	330	8.4		97.8	725.4
Washington	2,242	1,292.5	132.5	3,038.5	28		1,151.2	7,884.7
TOTAL	**6,100.8**	**2,527.1**	**398.7**	**8,760.6**	**343.9**		**2,767.7**	**20,898.8**
Bluegrass								
Bartholomew	347.6	218.1	263.8	257.6	90.4		973.8	2,151.3
Clark	470.2	106.9	77.1	305.5			98.6	1,058.3
Dearborn	35.8	4.3	28.3	268.5			5.3	342.2
Decatur	796.9	156.5	570.7	138.7	47.1		863.1	2,573
Fayette	441.2	46.6	203.7	372.7			101.3	1,165.5
Franklin	283.6	358.3	120	906.8	7.6		46.1	1,722.4
Jackson	2,130.2	686.8	77.1	648.8	121.4		923	4,587.3
Jefferson	82.2	62.5	26.1	141.9			20.3	333
Jennings	657.6	363.4	132.7	746.9			296.1	2,196.7
Ohio	12.4	186.7	0.9	146.6			1	347.6
Ripley	167.2	1,162.2	444.9	330.4	14.2		463.2	2,582.1
Scott	763.5	311.3	95.1	411.8		3.7	432.1	2,017.5
Switzerland	185.1	114.4	15.4	26.3			47	388.2
TOTAL	**6,373.5**	**3,778**	**2,055.8**	**4,702.5**	**280.7**	**3.7**	**4,270.9**	**21,465.1**

	Trees	Hardwood Trees	Shelter Belt	Field Windbreak	Filterstrip Trees	Riparian Buffers	Bottomland Wet Trees		Total
Natural Region County	**CP11**	**CP3**	**CP3A**	**CP16, 16A**	**CP5A**	**CP13D**	**CP22**	**CP31**	
Northwestern Morainal									
Lake	95.4		85.6		7.6				188.6
Porter	125.7		151.3		9.5				286.5
TOTAL	**221.1**		**236.9**		**17.1**				**475.1**
Grand Prairie									
Benton		17	17.2	0.4	171.9		8.7		215.2
Jasper		65.5	109.8		7.4	6.1			188.8
LaPorte	110.9	27	212		26		65.7		441.6
Newton	17.1	6.7	57.9		40		12.8		134.5
Pulaski	45		299.8		30.2		4.5		379.5
Starke	160	19.2	452.6	1.3	105.2	6.5	43.7	7.5	796
Vermillion							9.2		9.2
Warren	43.3		340.6		24.5	3.8	12.2		424.4
White					10.8		4		14.8
TOTAL	**376.3**	**135.4**	**1,489.9**	**1.7**	**416**	**16.4**	**160.8**	**7.5**	**2,604**
Northern Lakes									
Cass	207.4		99.6		81.2		21.7		409.9
Elkhart	120.5	12.3	69.6		1.3		1		204.7
Fulton	146.3	22.7	323.4	2.9	6.8		21.6		523.7
Kosciusko	763.6	7	1,911.7	4.9	7.1		21.5		2,715.8
LaGrange	118.7		196.5		11.2				326.4
Marshall	356	97.4	257.5		540.6		50.1		1,301.6
Noble	482.3	48.9	869		56.4		1.8		1,458.4
St. Joseph	185.4	1.5	147.4		18.3		16.3		368.9
Steuben	291.8	0.3	726.1		169.8		114.7		1,302.7
Whitley	266.8				62.8		3.6		333.2
TOTAL	**2,672**	**190.1**	**4,600.8**	**7.8**	**892.7**		**248.7**		**8,945.3**
Central Till Plain									
Adams	21.2		357.5		10				388.7
Allen	58.6		424.8		32.9		42.9		559.2
Blackford	15.8		56.8						72.6
Boone	34.2		25.9		1.6		49.4		111.1
Carroll	28.2		45.9		8.4		240.4		322.9
Clinton	31.8	27	13		4.6		155.4		231.8
DeKalb	422.3		1,711.5		17.7	4.7	7.1		2,163.3
Delaware	28.5		111.1		5.7	4.7	38.6		188.6
Fountain	21.2	1	112.9		6.5		128.3		269.9
Grant	72.5	84	59.7						216.2
Hamilton					9.2		17.3		26.5
Hancock	4.1		2.2	1.6			2.9		10.8
Hendricks		18.7					32.9		51.6
Henry	40.3		58.6				16		114.9
Howard	65	8	29.5		17.9	2.6	81.8		204.8
Huntington	155.2		281.8		40		19.5		496.5
Jay	108.8	12	414.8		8.6		15.9		560.1
Johnson		17	13.7				16.9		47.6
Madison	3				95.6		58.5		157.1
Marion									
Miami	93.8		175.4		69.4		136.4		475
Monroe	18.9	4.2	14.6				1.9		39.6
Montgomery	32.9		441.2		4.9	16	61.3		556.3
Parke	266.6	7	347.8				69.4		690.8
Putnam	58.7	0.5	450.7			15.6	227.8	21.5	774.8
Randolph	47.4		42.5		2.1		13.6		105.6
Rush	6.5		119.1		63.1		24.3		213
Shelby							8.4		8.4

Table G-20. *continued*

	Trees	Hardwood Trees	Shelter Belt	Field Windbreak	Filterstrip Trees	Riparian Buffers	Bottomland Wet Trees		Total
Natural Region County	**CP11**	**CP3**	**CP3A**	**CP16, 16A**	**CP5A**	**CP13D**	**CP22**	**CP31**	
Tippecanoe			98.3		161.2		72.3		331.8
Tipton	5.4			5.5	11.2				22.1
Union	55.5	0.5	36.8		6.1		9.3		108.2
Wabash	145.4		555.6		15.3	7.6	30		753.9
Wayne	142	2.1	495.4		8.6		120.1		768.2
Wells	54.4				2.4		16.3		73.1
TOTAL	**2,038.2**	**182**	**6,497.1**	**7.1**	**603**	**51.2**	**1,714.9**	**21.5**	**11,115**
Southwestern Lowlands									
Clay	36		59				9.4		104.4
Daviess	103.8	35.5	43.9				55.6		238.8
Dubois	148.5	2.5	132.9				81.8		365.7
Greene	44.1		412.7				107.7		564.5
Knox	129.6	31.5	91.7		15.3	21.6	190.3		480
Posey			57.4				0.5		57.9
Spencer	43.5	5.7	158.5				51.6		259.3
Sullivan	136.6		378		1.1		23.2		538.9
Vanderburgh	2.4		9.8						12.2
Vigo	3.7		645.6				6.5		655.8
Warrick		12.4	69.4		1		3.4		86.2
TOTAL	**648.2**	**87.6**	**2,058.9**		**17.4**	**21.6**	**530**		**3,363.7**
Southern Bottomlands									
Gibson	33.3		113		2.3		23.8		
Pike	50	20.8	23.5				85.3		
TOTAL	**83.3**	**20.8**	**136.5**		**2.3**		**109.1**		
Shawnee Hills									
Crawford	43.6		27.8				158.3		229.7
Martin		8.6	282.8				23.8	17.1	332.3
Orange	41		1,328.9				150.8		1,520.7
Owen	107.8	58.8							166.6
Perry		10.8	82.5				1.4		94.7
TOTAL	**359**	**78.2**	**1,722**				**334.3**	**17.1**	**2,344**
Highland Rim									
Brown							10.8		10.8
Floyd			13.3				15.5		28.8
Harrison	203.3		19				262.6		484.9
Lawrence	201.5		411.4			10	117.8		740.7
Morgan	35.3	42.9	55.8		18.7		231.6		384.3
Washington	167.3						217.5		384.8
TOTAL	**607.4**	**42.9**	**499.5**		**18.7**	**10**	**855.8**		**2,034.3**
Bluegrass									
Bartholomew		9.4	75.3		7.7	41.4	52.9		186.7
Clark	37.6		92.3				52.9		182.8
Dearborn			54.1				1.6		55.7
Decatur	25.4		123.1		51.1		157.2		356.8
Fayette	69.3		91.2		0.6	11.5	194.5		367.1
Franklin	83		271.8			4.3	13.7		372.8
Jackson	86.6		219.2		2.4		76.7		384.9
Jefferson	37.5		31.8				3.1		72.4
Jennings	143.2		121	5.7			68.2		338.1
Ohio							5.2		5.2
Ripley	104.6		153.8				104.8		363.2
Scott	9.9		63				25.2		98.1
Switzerland	24.3		7.1				2.4		33.8
TOTAL	**621.4**	**9.4**	**1,303.7**	**5.7**	**61.8**	**57.2**	**758.4**		**2,817.6**

Natural Region County	Wildlife Habitat CP4D	Wildlife Habitat Corridor CP4A, B	Wildlife Food Plot CP12	Wildlife Water CP9	Marginal Pasture Wildlife Habitat CP29	Upland Bird Habitat Buffer CP33	Rare Habitat CP25	Total
Northwestern Morainal								
Lake			3.8	30.9				34.7
Porter	21.5		4	28.8				54.3
TOTAL	**21.5**		**7.8**	**59.7**				**89**
Grand Prairie								
Benton	6.9		3.9	86				96.8
Jasper			12.3	3.7				16
LaPorte	977.5	13.4	19.1	37.7				1,047.7
Newton	58.5		10.2	48				116.7
Pulaski	394	33.4	16.2	62.8				506.4
Starke	525.4		23.1	18.8			4.7	572
Vermillion			3.4					3.4
Warren	18		3.5	53.5				75
White				34.6				34.6
TOTAL	**1,980.3**	**46.8**	**91.7**	**345.1**			**4.7**	**2,468.6**
Northern Lakes								
Cass	335.7	124.6	1.5	117.8				579.6
Elkhart	21.5		3.5	0.5				25.5
Fulton	22.6		4.6	35.5				62.7
Kosciusko	1,012.5		47.7	13				1,073.2
LaGrange	260.3		9.4	1				270.7
Marshall	117.6	4.4	44.8	239.8				406.6
Noble	694.1	15.4	31.2	18.7			19.9	779.3
St. Joseph	160.6		2.9	17.7				181.2
Steuben	1,263.4	34.8	43.4	18.9				1,360.5
Whitley	921	6.1	54	5.4				986.5
TOTAL	**3,888.3**	**179.2**	**189**	**462.9**			**19.9**	**5,725.8**
Central Till Plain								
Adams	15.2	0.5	7	9.2				31.9
Allen	372.1	5	6.5	10				393.6
Blackford	44.2			19.6			2.7	66.5
Boone								
Carroll			0.5	50.1				50.6
Clinton	1.6		0.5					2.1
DeKalb	959.1	2.5	32.7	7.5				1,001.8
Delaware	7.3			17.6	9.6			34.5
Fountain	50.7	1.3	0.8	7				59.8
Grant	4.8	3						7.8
Hamilton				51.4				51.4
Hancock				0.2				0.2
Hendricks	73.5		3.2					76.7
Henry			3.8					3.8
Howard				35.7				35.7
Huntington	34.9		13.6	8.7				57.2
Jay	186.7		4	17.5				208.2
Johnson								
Madison	8.6			8.1				16.7
Marion								
Miami	57	55.3	5.4	70.4				188.1
Monroe	10.1	4.1						14.2
Montgomery	6.3	5.6	8.1	7.7				27.7
Parke	16.3							16.3
Putnam	34.4		27.5					61.9
Randolph			94.4	3.3				97.7
Rush								
Shelby								

Table G-20. *continued*

	Wildlife Habitat	Wildlife Habitat Corridor	Wildlife Food Plot	Wildlife Water	Marginal Pasture Wildlife Habitat	Upland Bird Habitat Buffer	Rare Habitat	Total
Natural Region County	**CP4D**	**CP4A, B**	**CP12**	**CP9**	**CP29**	**CP33**	**CP25**	
Tippecanoe	2.5			13.3				15.8
Tipton				10.1				10.1
Union	1.6		0.7	0.7				3
Wabash	23	6.6	7.6	90.2				127.4
Wayne	41.8	3	8.6					53.4
Wells	321.5	19.9	3					344.4
TOTAL	**2,273.2**	**106.8**	**227.9**	**438.3**	**9.6**		**2.7**	**3,058.5**
Southwestern Lowlands								
Clay	90.6	2.8	13	2				108.4
Daviess	110.7	8.7	27	2.7				149.1
Dubois	175.7	7.1	9.8					192.6
Greene	88		4.9	0.3				93.2
Knox	156.8	11.6	9.9					178.3
Posey	32.2		5.1	11.3				48.6
Spencer	307.1		16.8	5				328.9
Sullivan	65.3		24.3					89.6
Vanderburgh	61.2		1.8					63
Vigo	8.4		1.1					9.5
Warrick	469.7		13.3					483
TOTAL	**1,565.7**	**30.2**	**127**	**21.3**				**1,744.2**
Southern Bottomlands								
Gibson	160.1		7.2	6.3				173.6
Pike	583.5		31.1	23.1				637.7
TOTAL	**743.6**		**38.3**	**29.4**				**811.3**
Shawnee Hills								
Crawford	228.1		9.1					237.2
Martin	1.7		4.4					6.1
Orange	69.1		7.5					76.6
Owen	41.5	38.9	7.8			27.8		116
Perry	183.9		12.3					196.2
TOTAL	**524.3**	**38.9**	**41.1**			**27.8**		**632.1**
Highland Rim								
Brown	139.8			5				144.8
Floyd			3.1					3.1
Harrison	41.1		37.2					78.3
Lawrence	649.7		8.9	59.5				718.1
Morgan								
Washington	171.9		39.7	52.2				263.8
TOTAL	**1,002.5**		**88.9**	**116.7**				**1,208.1**
Bluegrass								
Bartholomew	4.7	0.5	6.3	15.7				27.2
Clark			5.9	10				15.9
Dearborn	5.8		0.4					6.2
Decatur	156	3.8	13.1	11.2				184.1
Fayette	2		1.1					3.1
Franklin		20.8	3.8					24.6
Jackson	236		24.8		2.5			263.3
Jefferson	48.6		0.7					49.3
Jennings	155.9	2.3	13.3	23.9				195.4
Ohio			3.3					3.3
Ripley	95.7		9.1					104.8
Scott	0.5		5.1	5				10.6
Switzerland	29.2							
TOTAL	**734.4**	**27.4**	**86.9**	**65.8**	**2.5**			**887.8**

	Wetland Restoration	Farmable Wetland	Farmable Wetland Buffer	Marginal Pasture Wetland Buffer	Total
Natural Region County	**CP23**	**CP27**	**CP28**	**CP30**	
Northwestern Morainal					
Lake	129.3				129.3
Porter	130.3				130.3
TOTAL	**234.7**				**259.6**
Grand Prairie					
Benton		5.2	4.8		10
Jasper	10.4				10.4
LaPorte	698.4	3.7	5.9		708
Newton	300.4	1.9	3.9		306.2
Pulaski	279				279
Starke	1,641.4	10.1	18.8		1,670.3
Vermillion					
Warren					
White	24				24
TOTAL	**2,953.6**	**20.9**	**33.4**		**3,007.9**
Northern Lakes					
Cass	136	13	54.8	8	211.8
Elkhart	10.2				10.2
Fulton	256.5				256.5
Kosciusko	1,031.3	5	12.9		1,049.2
LaGrange	12.5				12.5
Marshall	480.1	2	2		484.1
Noble	190.3				190.3
St. Joseph	19.8				19.8
Steuben	207.9				207.9
Whitley	109.1	19	37.4		165.5
TOTAL	**2,344.6**	**20**	**69.7**	**8**	**2,607.8**
Central Till Plain					
Adams					
Allen	77.2				77.2
Blackford		1.9	1.5		3.4
Boone					
Carroll	1.3		23.6		24.9
Clinton					
DeKalb	150.8				150.8
Delaware	27.8				27.8
Fountain	16.7				16.7
Grant	8				8
Hamilton	33.9				33.9
Hancock					
Hendricks	1				1
Henry					
Howard					
Huntington					
Jay	39.9	22.8	53.5		116.2
Johnson					
Madison	13	5.6	14.8		33.4
Marion					
Miami	139.1	25.3	64.7		229.1
Monroe					
Montgomery	19.9				19.9
Parke					
Putnam					
Randolph	6				6
Rush					
Shelby					

Table G-20. *continued*

	Wetland Restoration	Farmable Wetland	Farmable Wetland Buffer	Marginal Pasture Wetland Buffer	Total
Natural Region County	**CP23**	**CP27**	**CP28**	**CP30**	
Tippecanoe	210.8				210.8
Tipton					
Union					
Wabash					
Wayne	17				17
Wells					
TOTAL	**762.4**	**55.6**	**158.1**		**976.1**
Southwestern Lowlands					
Clay	9.1				9.1
Daviess		3	0.4		3.4
Dubois	2.9				2.9
Greene					
Knox		5	5.3		10.3
Posey					
Spencer					
Sullivan					
Vanderburgh					
Vigo					
Warrick					
TOTAL	**12**	**8**	**5.7**		**25.7**
Southern Bottomlands					
Gibson					
Pike					
TOTAL					
Shawnee Hills					
Crawford					
Martin					
Orange	18.9				18.9
Owen					
Perry					
TOTAL	**18.9**				**18.9**
Highland Rim					
Brown					
Floyd					
Harrison					
Lawrence	244.2				244.2
Morgan					
Washington	30.1				30.1
TOTAL	**274.3**				**274.3**
Bluegrass					
Bartholomew					
Clark		26.1			26.1
Dearborn					
Decatur					
Fayette					
Franklin	18.1				18.1
Jackson	16.2				16.2
Jefferson					
Jennings					
Ohio					
Ripley					
Scott					
Switzerland					
TOTAL	**34.3**	**26.1**			**60.4**

Note: Data from the Black Swamp Natural Region are included in other regions.
Source: Unpublished data from Farm Service Agency State Office, Indianapolis, Indiana.

Table G-21. U.S. Fish and Wildlife Service's National Wetlands Inventory within Homoya's Natural Regions

Natural Region	NWI Category	Acres
Highland Rim	lacustrine	18,469.4
	palustrine emergent	2,792.2
	palustrine forested	19,356.7
	palustrine scrub/shrub	1,023.9
	palustrine submergent	103.6
	ponds	8,870.6
	riverine	2,238.0
	uplands	1,691,022.1
Northwestern Morainal	lacustrine	5,393.1
	palustrine emergent	15,582.9
	palustrine forested	20,598.8
	palustrine open water	147.7
	palustrine scrub/shrub	3,604.3
	palustrine submergent	892.2
	ponds	3,907.0
	riverine	721.5
	uplands	518,706.3
Grand Prairie	lacustrine	6,776.3
	palustrine emergent	25,493.2
	palustrine forested	38,657.4
	palustrine open water	97.6
	palustrine scrub/shrub	3,510.7
	palustrine submergent	497.5
	ponds	3,262.7
	riverine	2,726.8
	uplands	2,394,088.6
Northern Lakes	lacustrine	36,346.3
	palustrine emergent	68,769.1
	palustrine forested	77,771.0
	palustrine scrub/shrub	15,925.6
	palustrine submergent	864.2
	ponds	10,364.0
	riverine	2,505.9
	uplands	2,312,868.9
	no data	304.0
Central Till Plain	lacustrine	23,868.4
	palustrine emergent	25,962.5
	palustrine forested	129,110.6
	palustrine open water	1.1
	palustrine scrub/shrub	5,431.3
	palustrine submergent	365.6
	ponds	20,351.3
	riverine	19,391.9
	uplands	7,971,178.0
Black Swamp	lacustrine	15.4
	palustrine emergent	114.8
	palustrine forested	1,402.6
	palustrine scrub/shrub	33.4
	ponds	192.4
	riverine	484.6
	uplands	150,597.2
Southwestern Lowlands	lacustrine	11,490.9
	palustrine emergent	5,094.8
	palustrine forested	56,924.6
	palustrine scrub/shrub	2,586.4
	palustrine submergent	252.0
	ponds	24,652.8
	riverine	4,294.7
	uplands	2,262,909.9
Southern Bottomlands	lacustrine	9,989.9
	palustrine emergent	7,009.6
	palustrine forested	76,720.1
	palustrine scrub/shrub	5,329.2
	palustrine submergent	429.2
	ponds	6,436.8
	riverine	11,548.9
	uplands	749,924.9
Shawnee Hills	lacustrine	17,776.2
	palustrine emergent	1,919.0
	palustrine forested	13,156.6
	palustrine scrub/shrub	727.5
	palustrine submergent	35.1
	ponds	5,815.2
	riverine	3,285.4
	uplands	1,654,232.1
Bluegrass	lacustrine	13,839.6
	palustrine emergent	3,205.8
	palustrine forested	67,938.7
	palustrine scrub/shrub	3,919.3
	palustrine submergent	192.8
	ponds	11,064.3
	riverine	5,813.6
	uplands	2,419,483.9
STATE TOTAL		**23,120,766.6**

Wetland Type	State Total Acres
Lacustrine	143,965
Palustrine emergent	155,944
Palustrine forested	501,637
Palustrine scrub/shrub	42,092
Palustrine open water	246
Palustrine submergent	3,632
Ponds	94,917
Riverine	53,011
TOTAL WETLANDS	**995,445**

Table G-22. Distribution of Lakes, Wetlands, and Prairies on 1876 Maps of Indiana Counties

Region County	Lakes	Wetlands	Prairies	Notes
Northwest				
Fulton	yes+	yes++		
Jasper	yes	yes++		
LaPorte	yes+			
Lake	yes	yes++	yes+	
Marshall	yes+	yes++		
Newton	yes	yes++	yes	
Porter		yes++	yes	
Pulaski				
Starke	yes	yes++		
Northeast				
Allen		yes	yes++	
DeKalb	yes	yes		
Elkhart	yes			
Kosciusko	yes++	yes+	yes+	
LaGrange	yes	yes++		
Noble	yes++	yes++		
St. Joseph	yes			
Steuben	yes++	yes	yes	
Whitley	yes			
West-Central				
Benton		yes+		forest groves shown
Boone			yes	
Carroll		yes		
Clinton			yes+	
Fountain			yes	
Montgomery			yes	
Tippecanoe			yes+	
Warren			yes ++	
White				
North-Central				
Cass	yes	yes		
Grant				
Hamilton				
Howard				
Huntington	yes		yes	
Madison				
Miami				
Tipton		yes	yes	
Wabash	yes		yes	
East-Central				
Adams			yes	
Blackford		yes	yes	
Delaware		yes		
Henry				
Jay		yes		
Randolph				
Wayne				
Wells			yes	
Southwest-Central				
Clay				
Greene		yes	yes	
Owen				
Parke				
Putnam				
Sullivan	yes	yes	yes	
Vermillion	yes		yes++	
Vigo				
Central				
Bartholomew				
Brown				
Hancock				
Hendricks				
Johnson				
Marion				
Morgan				
Shelby				
Southeast-Central				
Dearborn				
Decatur				
Fayette				
Franklin				
Jennings				
Ripley				
Rush				
Union				
Southwest				
Daviess	yes			
Gibson	yes	yes		
Knox	yes	yes		
Pike	yes			
Posey	yes	yes		
Spencer		yes		
Vanderburgh	yes	yes		
Warrick				
South-Central				
Crawford				
Dubois	yes			
Jackson				
Lawrence				caves shown
Martin				
Monroe				
Orange				
Perry				
Southeast				
Clark				
Floyd				
Harrison				
Jefferson				
Ohio				
Scott				
Switzerland				
Washington				

Note: yes = present, yes+ = common, yes++ = abundant.
Source: Historical Atlas of Indiana Counties 1876.

Soils

Table S-1. U.S. Soil Taxonomy

Soil Series	Description	Parent Material	Agricultural Crops	Native Vegetation	Taxonomic Family	Reference
Alford	Deep, well-drained, gently sloping to moderately steep soils	Formed in more than 5 ft of loess	Corn, soybeans, small grains, meadow, pasture; well suited to orchards; erosion and runoff are major hazards	Maple, tulip poplar, oak, hickory	Fine-silty, mixed, mesic Typic Hapludalfs	Kelly 1974
Ashkum	Poorly drained, moderately slow permeability	Ground moraines and end moraine; Colluvium and underlying till; toeslopes	Corn, oats, pasture	Marsh grasses and sedges	Fine, mixed, superactive, mesic Typic Endoaquolls	Calsyn 2004
Ava	Gently sloping, deep, and moderately well-drained on knolls, ridgetops, and breaks along drainage ways and uplands	Moderately well-drained soils on convex ridges and side slopes of drainage ways on till plains	Corn, soybeans, small grains; tall fescue	White oak, northern red oak, tulip poplar, black walnut	Fine-silty, mixed, mesic Typic Fragiudalfs	McCarter 1982
Avonburg	Very deep, somewhat poorly drained	Loess and the underlying paleosol in till	Corn, soybeans	Bald cypress, Norway spruce, eastern cottonwood, black chokeberry, hawthorn, eastern red cedar, eastern white pine, green ash, pin oak, dogwood, hazelnut	Fine-silty, mixed, active, mesic Aeric Fragic Glossaqualfs	http://www2.ftw.nrcs.usda.gov/osd/dat/A/AVONBURG.html
Barry	Very deep, poorly drained	Till and moraines on flats and swales	Corn, oats; good for grain crops and grassland habitat; fair for woodland	Deciduous forest	Fine-loamy, mixed, superactive, mesic Typic Argiaquolls	Jackson 2004
Baxter	Steep, well-drained; moderately permeable with low available moisture capacity and low natural fertility; medium to very strongly acidic	Limestone with some chert	Timber with some pasture	Oak, hickory, elm, maple, beech, ironwood, persimmon, dogwood, hackberry, black walnut, eastern red cedar, shortleaf pine, Virginia pine	Fine, mixed, mesic Typic Paleudults	Gilbert 1971
Bedford	Very deep, moderately well-drained	Hills underlain with limestone; loess, loamy material, and a paleosol in clay-like residuum	Mainly corn	Northern red oak, Virginia pine, tulip poplar, white oak, sugar maple	Fine-silty, mixed, active mesic Oxyaquic Fragiudalfs	Nagel 1998
Berks	Moderately deep, well-drained, steep and very steep on uplands	Weathered sandstone, siltstone, shale	Well suited to trees; erosion and runoff are limitations to this soil	Mixed hardwoods	Loamy-skeletal, mixed, mesic Typic Dystrochrepts	Wingard 1975
Birds	Poorly drained, moderate permeablity	Formed in back swamps and floodplains; fine-silty alluvium	Prime farmland when drained; corn	Bald cypress, black gum, bur oak, green ash, overcup oak, pin oak, red maple, shellbark hickory, silver maple, swamp white oak, sweetgum	Fine-silty, mixed, superactive, nonacid, mesic Typic Fluvaquents	Wigginton and Marshall 2004
Blount	Somewhat poorly drained, moderate available water capacity	Till plains	Corn, pasture	Northern red oak, white oak, green ash, bur oak, pin oak	Fine, illitic, mesic Aeric Epiaqualfs	NRCS 2002

Table S-1. *continued*

Soil Series	Description	Parent Material	Agricultural Crops	Native Vegetation	Taxonomic Family	Reference
Bonnell	Deep, steep, and well-drained; on slopes bordering stream valleys of the Illinoian till plain	Loess or loamy materials and the underlying till	Not prime farmland	Mixed hardwood forest	Fine, mixed, active, mesic Typic Hapludalfs	http://ortho.ftw.nrcs.usda.gov/osd/dat/B/BONNELL.html
Bonnie	Deep, poorly drained	Alluvium in bottomlands	Corn, soybeans	Water-tolerant trees	Fine-silty, mixed, acid Typic Fragiudalfs	Kelly 1974
Brookston	Poorly drained, high available water capacity	Till plains	Corn, winter wheat, soybeans	White oak, northern red oak, sweetgum, pin oak	Fine-loamy, mixed, superactive, mesic Typic Argiaquolls	NRCS 2002
Cincinnati	Deep, well-drained, moderately sloping to strongly sloping, on uplands	Formed in loess with underlying glacial till	Suitable for corn, soybeans, small grains, meadow, pasture; Christmas trees because the soil makes them slow growing	Northern red oak, white oak, black walnut, black cherry, sugar maple, white ash, tulip poplar	Fine-silty, mixed, active, mesic Oxyaquic Fragiudalfs	http://www2.ftw.nrcs.usda.gov/osd/dat/C/CINCINNATI.html
Cobbsfork	Very deep, poorly drained	Loess and a paleosol in till	Woods	Mixed hardwood forest	Fine-silty, mixed, active, mesic Fragic Glossaqualfs	http://www2.ftw.nrcs.usda.gov/osd/dat/C/COBBSFORK.html
Coloma	Somewhat excessively drained with low available water capacity	Moraines and outwash plains	Some corn; low productivity, good for conifers but very poor for wetlands	White oak, northern red oak	Mixed, mesic Lamellic Udipsamments	NRCS 2002
Crider	Very deep, well-drained, moderately permeable, on uplands	Formed in a mantle of loess and underlying limestone residuum	Mostly crops (corn, small grains, soybeans, tobacco, hay) or pasture	Mixed hardwoods	Fine-silty, mixed, mesic Typic Paleudalfs	Wingard 1975
Crosby	Nearly level to gently sloping, deep, somewhat poorly drained	Thin mantle of loess over loamy glacial till; broad till plains and moraines	Corn, pasture, hay	White oak, pin oak, tulip poplar, northern red oak	Fine, mixed, mesic Aeric Ochraqualfs	Neely 1987
Crosier	Somewhat poorly drained, high available water capacity	Till plains	Corn and pasture with some winter wheat	Northern red oak, tulip poplar	Fine-loamy, mixed, active, mesic Aeric Epiaqualfs	NRCS 2002
Drummer	Deep topsoil with high organic matter content; poorly drained	Loess over loamy outwash; flats and depressions on outwash plains and toeslopes	Very good for corn; also winter wheat, soybeans, pasture	Was under prairie grass in Illinois; pin oak, white oak	Fine-silty, mixed, superactive, mesic Typic Endoaquolls	Wigginton and Clark 2003
Eden	Moderately deep, well-drained, slowly permeable; on hillsides and narrow crests of ridges on uplands	Formed in residuum of interbedded soft, calcareous shale and limestone bedrock	Pasture and hay. Some ridgetops used for tobacco, corn, small grains	Bald cypress, eastern cottonwood, eastern white pine, white ash	Fine, mixed, active, mesic Typic Hapludalfs	Nagel and Marshall 2007
Edenton	Moderately deep, well-drained	Formed in till and underlying residuum from clayey shale with thin strata of limestone and, in places, a mantle of loess	Permanent pasture or woodland	Hardwood forest	Fine-loamy, mixed, superactive, mesic Typic Hapludalfs	http://ortho.ftw.nrcs.usda.gov/osd/dat/E/EDENTON.html
Fincastle	Deep, somewhat poorly drained, nearly level, on uplands; high available water capacity, slow permeability	2–3 ft of loess over till	Suitable for all crops grown in the county	Mixed hardwoods	Fine-silty, mixed, mesic, Aeric Ochraqualfs	Montgomery 1974
Gilford	Very deep, poorly drained or very poorly drained; permeability is moderately rapid in surface layer and subsoil and rapid in substratum	Outwash plains and floodplain steps; soils formed in loam over sandy sediments	Corn, wetland vegetation, animals, hardwood trees	Bigtooth aspen, eastern white pine, pin oak, red maple	Coarse-loamy, mixed, superactive, mesic Typic Endoaquolls	NRCS 2003

Soil Series	Description	Parent Material	Agricultural Crops	Native Vegetation	Taxonomic Family	Reference
Gilpin	Moderately deep, well-drained, steep, on uplands	Formed on weathering sandstone, siltstone, shale	Pasture and trees; runoff and susceptibility to erosion are the main limitations	Mixed hardwoods	Fine-loamy, mixed, mesic Typic Hapludults	Wingard 1975
Glynwood	Moderately well-drained, moderate available water capacity	Till plains	Corn	White oak, white ash, black cherry, red maple, slippery elm, northern red oak, black oak	Fine, illitic, mesic Awuic Hapludalfs	NRCS 2002
Haymond	Deep, well-drained, nearly level	Formed in alluvium on bottomlands	Corn, soybeans, alfalfa; flooding is problem	Mixed hardwoods	Coarse-silty, mixed, mesic dystric Fluventic Eutrochrepts	Kelly 1974
Hickory	Deep, well-drained, moderately steep to very steep, on uplands	0–18 inches of loess and underlying till	Pasture or woods due to much runoff and risk of erosion	Deciduous forest	Fine-loamy, mixed, active, mesic Typic Hapludalfs	http://www2.ftw.nrcs.usda.gov/osd/dat/H/HICKORY.html
Hosmer	Deep, well-drained, nearly level to strongly sloping	4–8 ft of loess over sandstone and shale bedrock, Illinoian till, or stratified lake sediments on uplands	Corn, soybeans, small grains, meadow, pasture; not well suited for alfalfa	Upland oaks, tulip poplar, Virginia pine, white pine	Fine-silty, mixed, mesic Typic Fragiudalfs	Kelly 1974
Houghton	Very poorly drained, very high available water capacity	Outwash plains and moraines; organic herbaceous materials; in depressions	Undrained, not good for agriculture; when drained, can be good for corn and moderate for soybeans, winter wheat, grass/legume hay, pasture	Silver maple, white ash, red maple, green ash, eastern arbor vitae, tamarack, quaking aspen, black willow	Euic, mesic Typic Haplosaprists	NRCS 2002
Hoytville	Very poorly drained, deep or very deep to dense till	Formed in till that has been leveled by wave action; found on lake plains	Corn, soybeans, wheat	Deciduous swamp forest, primarily swamp white oak, bur oak, pin oak, elm, hickory, ash, cottonwood, basswood, and soft maple with some marsh grasses	Fine, illitic, mesic Mollic Epiaqualfs	http://www2.ftw.nrcs.usda.gov/os/d/dat/H/HOYTVILLE.html
Iona	Deep, moderately well-drained, nearly level or gently sloping	Formed in more than 5 ft of loess	Corn, soybeans, small grains, meadow, pasture	Mixed hardwoods, upland oaks, tulip poplar, white pine	Fine-silty, mixed, acid Typic Hapludalfs	Kelly 1974
Kalamazoo	Very deep, well-drained; moderate permeability in upper loamy materials and rapid permeability in lower sandy materials; slopes range from 0 to 18%	Formed in loamy outwash overlying sand, loamy sand, or in sand and gravel outwash on outwash plains, terraces, valley trains, and low-lying moraines	Mostly corn, wheat, soybeans, hay; a small part is in pasture; some areas adjacent to the larger cities are idle cropland	Northern red oak, hickory	Fine-loamy, mixed, semiactive, mesic Typic Hapludalfs	NCSS 2005a
Markham	Moderately well-drained, slow permeability	Ground moraines and end moraines; thin mantle of loess or other silty material and underlying till	Corn, oats	Northern red oak, black cherry, shagbark hickory, white oak	Fine, illitic, mesic Oxyaquic Hapludalfs	Deniger 2003a
Maumee	Very deep, poorly drained and very poorly drained; rapid permeability	Outwash plains and lake plains; formed in sandy sediments in depressions	Corn, wetland vegetation, hardwood trees	Bigtooth aspen, eastern white pine, pin oak, silver maple	Sandy, mixed, mesic Typic Endoaquolls	NRCS 2003
Miami	Deep, moderately well-drained; high available water capacity on uplands	Moraines	Corn, winter wheat	White oak, sweetgum, tulip poplar	Fine-loamy, mixed, active, mesic Oxyaquic Hapludalfs	NRCS 2002
Miamian	Very deep, well-drained	Formed in a thin layer of loess and the underlying loamy till, which is high in lime content	Corn, soybeans, winter wheat	White oak, maple, elm, ash, hickory	Fine, mixed, active, mesic Oxyaquic Hapludalfs	USDA 2005

Table S-1. *continued*

Soil Series	Description	Parent Material	Agricultural Crops	Native Vegetation	Taxonomic Family	Reference
Morley	Deep, well-drained on knobs and ridges; some shrink and swell	Till plains and moraines	Corn, soybeans, small grains, pasture, hay, woodlands	White oak, northern red oak, tulip poplar, black walnut, bur oak, shagbark hickory	Fine, illitic, mesic Typic Hapludalfs	Neely 1987
Nappanee	Very deep, somewhat poorly drained; moderately deep or deep to dense till	Formed in till that has been leveled by wave action on lake plains or in till on moraines	Corn, oats, wheat, soybeans, clover, alfalfa	American beech, red maple, pin oak, American basswood, American elm	Fine, illitic, mesic Aeric Epiaqualfs	http://www2.ftw.nrcs.usda.gov/osd/dat/N/NAPPANEE.html
Nolin	Deep, well-drained, nearly level	Formed in alluvium on bottomlands	Corn, soybeans, alfalfa, although hazards from flooding	Mixed hardwoods, tulip poplar, white pine	Fine-silty, mixed, mesic dystric Fluventic Eutrochrepts	Kelly 1974
Oshtemo	Well-drained, low available water capacity	Moraines	Corn, herbs, hardwoods, conifers; very poor for wetlands	White oak, red pine, eastern white pine	Coarse-loamy, mixed, active, mesic Typic Hapludalfs	NRCS 2002
Parr	Moderately well-drained, moderate permeability	Ground moraines and end moraines; mantle of loess or other silty material over underlying till	Corn, also winter wheat and oats	Walnut, black gum, green ash, northern red oak, pin oak, tulip poplar	Fine-loamy, mixed, active, mesic Oxyaquic Argiudolls	Deniger 2003b
Petrolia	Deep, poorly drained, nearly level	Formed in alluvium on bottomlands	Corn, soybeans, meadow, pasture; also alfalfa and small grains, but susceptible to flooding in winter and spring	Pin oak, sweetgum, tulip poplar, Virginia pine, white pine	Fine-silty, mixed, nonacid, mesic Fluventic Haplaquepts	Kelly 1974
Pewamo	Very deep, poorly and very poorly drained	Formed in clay-like till or lacustrine material on ground moraines, lake plains, or depressional areas of end moraines	Corn, soybeans, small grains, hay; areas with poor drainage have permanent pasture or forest	Red maple, American elm, white ash, American basswood	Fine, mixed, mesic Typic Argiaquolls	USDA 2005
Riddles	Well-drained, high available water capacity	Till plains and moraines	Corn and pasture	White oak, sweetgum, tulip poplar, northern red oak	Fine-loamy, mixed, active, mesic Typic Hapludalfs	NRCS 2002
Rossmoyne	Deep, moderately well-drained	Loess and the underlying Illinoian glacial till on till plains	Corn, soybeans, winter wheat	Pin oak, eastern white pine	Fine-silty, mixed, active, mesic Aquic Fragiudalfs	Nickell 1987
Saybrook	Very deep, moderately well-drained; moderate permeability	Loess over glacial till	Corn, oats	Eastern white pine, pin oak	Fine-silty, mixed, mesic Oxyaquic Argiudolls	Treater and Walker 2001
Sparta	Excessively drained, low available water capacity	Terrace side slopes, eolian deposits	Pasture and hay; poor as cropland, moderate for woodlands	Black oak, eastern white pine	Sandy, mixed, mesic Entic Hapludolls	Treater and Walker 2001
Spinks	Very deep, well-drained	Sandy glacial till or glacial outwash on dunes and on foot slopes of moraines, till plains, outwash plains, beach ridges, lake plains	Mostly hay or pasture; some corn, wheat, oats, soybeans, orchards	Hardwoods, mostly oaks, hickories	Sandy, mixed, mesic Psammentic Hapludalfs	NOSS 2005
Stendal	Deep, somewhat poorly drained	Alluvium on bottomlands	Corn, soybeans, meadow, pasture	Hardwood forest	Fine-silty, mixed, acid, mesic aeric Fluventic Haplaquepts	Kelly 1974
Switzerland	Well-drained; usually with high relief	Fossiliferous limestone and pale olive calcareous soft clay shale	Best for grass and meadow	Deciduous forest of oak, maple, hickory, poplar, beech, basswood		Lindsey 1966

Soil Series	Description	Parent Material	Agricultural Crops	Native Vegetation	Taxonomic Family	Reference
Sylvan	Very deep, well-drained, permeable; on till plains and high stream terraces on till plains	Loess	Steeper slopes wooded or used for pasture; less sloping areas used for corn, soybeans, small grains, forage	Hardwoods	Fine-silty, mixed, superactive, mesic Typic Hapludalfs	http://www2.ftw.nrcs.usda.gov/osd/dat/S/SYLVAN.html
Treaty	Silty clay loam, on a plane slope of less than 1%, in a cultivated field	Till	Corn, winter wheat, soybeans	Wetlands, pin oak	Fine-silty, mixed, superactive, mesic Typic Argiaquolls	Wigginton and Clark 2003
Wawasee	Deep, well-drained, moderately permeable	Formed in glacial till on moraines and till plains; upland soils have slopes ranging from 0 to 18%	Corn, soybeans, small grains, and hay or pasture	Beech, maple, hickory	Fine-loamy, mixed, active, mesic Typic Hapludalfs	NCSS 2005b
Wellston	Moderately deep, well-drained, moderately sloping to strongly sloping, on uplands	Formed on loess and in material weathered from sandstone, siltstone, shale	Small grains, hay, pasture with occasional corn and soybeans	Mixed hardwoods	Fine-silty, mixed, mesic Ultic Hapludalfs	Wingard 1975
Zanesville	Deep, well-drained, moderately sloping; very firm and brittle fragipan at 24 inches depth	Formed on loess and underlying sandstone, siltstone, shale on uplands	Suitable to most crops in the area	Mixed hardwoods	Fine-silty, mixed, mesic Typic Fragiudalfs	Wingard 1975

Notes: NCSS = National Cooperative Soil Survey; NOSS = Northwest Ohio Soil Survey; NRCS = Natural Resources Conservation Service; USDA = U.S. Department of Agriculture.

Source: Soil Survey Staff 1999.

APPENDIXES

Plants

Table P-1. Vascular Plants Occurring in Indiana Listed by Common Name

Common Name	Scientific Name[a]	Coefficient[b]
Adam-and-Eve	*Aplectrum hyemale*	7
Adam's needle	*YUCCA FLACCIDA*	
Alder buckthorn	*Rhamnus alnifolia*	10
Alfalfa	*MEDICAGO SATIVA s. SATIVA*	
Alkali grass	*PUCCINELLIA DISTANS*	
Alkali yellowtops	*FLAVERIA CAMPESTRIS*	
Allegheny barberry	*Berberis canadensis*	10
Allegheny chinquapin	*Castanea pumila*	10
Allegheny spurge	*Pachysandra procumbens*	9
Allegheny vine	*Adlumia fungosa*	10
Alsike clover	*TRIFOLIUM HYBRIDUM*	
American beak grass	*Diarrhena americana*	5
American beech	*Fagus grandifolia*	8
American bellflower	*Campanulastrum americanum* (= *Campanula americanum*)	4
American bindweed	*Calystegia sepium* (including subspecies)	1
American brooklime	*Veronica americana*	10
American burnet	*Sanguisorba canadensis*	10
American bur reed	*Sparganium americanum*	10
American chestnut	*Castanea dentata*	10
American columbo	*Frasera caroliniensis*	8
American dragonhead	*DRACOCEPHALUM PARVIFLORUM*	
American elm	*Ulmus americana*	3
American filbert	*Corylus americana*	4
American fly honeysuckle	*Lonicera canadensis*	10
American germander	*Teucrium canadense v. canadense*	3
American gromwell	*Lithospermum latifolium*	7
American holly	*ILEX OPACA*	
American hops	*Humulus lupulus v. pubescens*	5
American hops	*Humulus lupulus v. lupuloides*	5
American larch	*Larix laricina*	10
American linden	*Tilia americana v. americana*	5
American lotus	*Nelumbo lutea*	4
American mountain ash	*Sorbus decora*	10
American orpine	*Hylotelephium telephioides* (= *Sedum telephioides*)	10
American pennyroyal	*Hedeoma pulegioides*	3
American pennywort	*Hydrocotyle americana*	10
American plum	*Prunus americana*	4
American pondweed	*Potamogeton nodosus*	4
American spikenard	*Aralia racemosa*	8
American storax	*Styrax americana*	8
American sweet flag	*Acorus americanus*	10
American vetch	*Vicia americana*	6
American water plantain	*Alisma triviale*	2
American wormseed	*DYSPHANIA AMBROSIOIDES* (= *CHENOPODIUM AMBROSIOIDES*)	
Amur honeysuckle	*LONICERA MAACKII*	
Angel's trumpet	*DATURA WRIGHTII*	
Angled spike rush	*Eleocharis quadrangulata*	4
Angle-fruited milk vine	*Gonolobus suberosa*	7
Angle-stemmed primrose willow	*Ludwigia leptocarpa*	
Anise root	*Osmorhiza longistylis*	3
Annual bedstraw	*Galium aparine*	1
Annual bluegrass	*POA ANNUA*	
Annual fleabane	*Erigeron annuus*	0
Annual foxtail	*Alopecurus carolinianus*	0
Annual purple bladderwort	*Utricularia resupinata*	10
Annual wild buckwheat	*ERIOGONUM ANNUUM*	
Annual wormwood	*ARTEMISIA ANNUA*	
Appalachian filmy fern	*Trichomanes boschianum*	10
Apple	*MALUS DOMESTICA*	
Apple mint	*MENTHA SUAVEOLENS*	
Apple-of-Peru	*NICANDRA PHYSALODES*	
Appressed bog clubmoss	*Lycopodiella subappressa*	7
Arbor vitae	*Thuja occidentalis*	10
Arching dewberry	*Rubus sec. Flagellares: R. enslenii*	5
Aromatic aster	*Symphyotrichum oblongifolium*	9
Aromatic sumac	*Rhus aromatica v. aromatica*	7
Arrow arum	*Peltandra virginica*	6
Arrowfeather	*Aristida purpurascens*	7
Arrowgrass	*Scheuchzeria palustris*	10
Arrow-leaved aster	*Symphyotrichum urophyllum*	4
Arrow-leaved tear-thumb	*Persicaria sagittata*	4
Arrow-leaved violet	*Viola sagittata v. sagittata*	6
Arum-leaved arrowhead	*Sagittaria cuneata*	3
Ascendent-flowered dewberry	*Rubus sec. Flagellares: R. meracus*	5
Ashe's panic grass	*Dichanthelium commutatum s. ashei*	7
Ashy hydrangea	*Hydrangea cinerea*	7
Atlantic star sedge	*Carex atlantica s. atlantica*	10
Atlantic white cedar	*CHAMAECYPARIS THYOIDES*	
Atlantic wormseed	*CHENOPODIUM ANTHELMINTICUM*	
Aunt Lucy	*Ellisia nyctelea*	5
Autumn bent grass	*Agrostis perennans*	2
Autumn bluegrass	*Poa autumnalis*	7
Autumn olive	*ELAEAGNUS UMBELLATA*	
Autumn sedge	*Fimbristylis autumnalis*	3
Autumn willow	*Salix serissima*	10
Awned bent grass	*Agrostis elliottiana*	2
Awned flat sedge	*Cyperus squarrosus*	2
Awned graceful sedge	*Carex davisii*	3
Awned oval sedge	*Carex straminea*	10
Awned wheat grass	*Elymus trachycaulus s. subsecundus* (= *Agropyron trachycaulum*)	8
Axil flower	*Mecardonia acuminata*	10
Bachelor's button	*CENTAUREA CYANUS*	
Bailey's dogwood	*Cornus baileyi*	9
Bald cypress	*Taxodium distichum*	10
Baldwin's fimbristylis	*Fimbristylis annua*	10
Baldwin's ironweed	*VERNONIA BALDWINII*	
Ball mustard	*NESLIA PANICULATA*	
Balloon vine	*CARDIOSPERMUM HALICACABUM*	
Balsam poplar	*Populus balsamifera*	10
Balsam ragwort	*Packera paupercula*	3

Common Name	Scientific Name[a]	Coefficient[b]
Bare-stemmed tick trefoil	*Desmodium nudiflorum*	5
Barnaby's thistle	*CENTAUREA SOLSTITIALIS*	
Barnyard grass	*ECHINOCHLOA CRUS-GALLI*	
Barren strawberry	*Waldsteinia fragarioides*	9
Basil bee balm	*Monarda clinopodia*	7
Basil thyme	*ACINOS ARVENSIS*	
Basket oak	*Quercus michauxii*	7
Basket willow	*SALIX VIMINALIS*	
Bastard toadflax	*Comandra umbellata*	7
Bay-leaved willow	*SALIX PENTANDRA*	
Beach grass	*Ammophila breviligulata*	10
Beach pea	*Lathyrus japonicus v. maritimus*	10
Beach sumac	*Rhus aromatica v. arenaria*	10
Beach three-awn grass	*Aristida tuberculosa*	10
Beach wormwood	*Artemisia campestris s. caudata*	5
Beaked black snakeroot	*Sanicula trifoliata*	8
Beaked corn salad	*Valerianella radiata*	1
Beaked panic grass	*Panicum anceps*	3
Beaked tussock sedge	*Carex torta*	9
Beaked willow	*Salix bebbiana*	7
Beak-seeded knotweed	*Polygonum achoreum*	0
Bearberry	*Arctostaphylos uva-ursi*	10
Beard grass	*Gymnopogon ambiguus*	10
Bearded panic grass	*Dichanthelium boscii*	4
Bearded sprangle top	*LEPTOCHLOA FUSCA s. FASCICULARIS*	
Beardless wild rye	*Elymus submuticus*	3
Bear's foot	*Smallanthus uvedalia* (= *Polymnia uvedalia*)	5
Bebb's oval sedge	*Carex bebbii*	7
Beech drops	*Epifagus virginiana*	8
Beech wood sedge	*Carex laxiflora*	7
Beefsteak plant	*PERILLA FRUTESCENS* (including 1 variety)	
Beggar's lice	*LAPPULA SQUARROSA*	
Beginner's pondweed	*POTAMOGETON CRISPUS*	
Belvedere summer cypress	*KOCHIA SCOPARIA*	
Bent bracted sedge	*Carex retroflexa*	4
Bent-seeded hop sedge	*Carex tuckermanii*	10
Bermuda grass	*CYNODON DACTYLON*	
Bessey's false foxglove	*Agalinis tenuifolia v. macrophylla*	4
Bessey's sand cherry	*Prunus pumila v. besseyi*	8
Bicknell's oval sedge	*Carex bicknellii*	9
Bicknell's panic grass	*Dichanthelium bicknellii* (*nomen nudum*)	10
Biennial gaura	*Gaura biennis*	3
Biennial wormwood	*ARTEMISIA BIENNIS*	
Big baby's breath	*GYPSOPHILA SCORZONERIFOLIA*	
Big bluestem grass	*Andropogon gerardii*	5
Big-fruited hawthorn	*Crataegus series Tenuifoliae: C. macrosperma*	5
Big-leaved aster	*Eurybia macrophylla*	7
Big shellbark hickory	*Carya laciniosa*	8
Bigtooth aspen	*Populus grandidentata*	4
Biltmore's hawthorn	*Crataegus series Intricatae: C. biltmoreana*	4
Birdseed grass	*PHALARIS CANARIENSIS*	
Bird's-eye speedwell	*VERONICA PERSICA*	
Birdsfoot trefoil	*LOTUS CORNICULATUS*	
Bird's foot violet	*Viola pedata*	9
Bird's rape	*BRASSICA RAPA*	
Birthwort	*Aristolochia serpentaria*	8
Bishop's cap	*Mitella diphylla*	7
Bitter dock	*RUMEX OBTUSIFOLIUS*	
Bitternut hickory	*Carya cordiformis*	5
Bittersweet nightshade	*SOLANUM DULCAMARA*	
Bitterweed	*Helenium amarum*	0
Black alder	*ALNUS GLUTINOSA*	

Common Name	Scientific Name[a]	Coefficient[b]
Black ash	*Fraxinus nigra*	7
Blackberry lily	*BELAMCANDA CHINENSIS*	
Black bindweed	*FALLOPIA CONVOLVULUS*	
Black blueberry	*Vaccinium fuscatum*	9
Black chokeberry	*Photinia melanocarpa*	8
Black cohosh	*Cimicifuga rubifolia*	10
Black-eyed pea	*VIGNA UNGUICULATA*	
Black-eyed Susan	*Rudbeckia hirta v. pulcherrima*	2
Black-eyed Susan	*Rudbeckia hirta v. hirta*	2
Black-fruited spike rush	*Eleocharis melanocarpa*	10
Black grass	*JUNCUS COMPRESSUS*	
Black gum	*Nyssa sylvatica*	5
Black haw	*Viburnum prunifolium*	4
Black henbane	*HYOSCYAMUS NIGER*	
Black hickory	*Carya texana*	10
Black huckleberry	*Gaylussacia baccata*	7
Blackjack oak	*Quercus marilandica*	7
Black locust	*Robinia pseudoacacia*	1
Black maple	*Acer saccharum s. nigrum*	6
Black medick	*MEDICAGO LUPULINA*	
Black mustard	*BRASSICA NIGRA*	
Black nightshade	*Solanum ptycanthum*	0
Black oak	*Quercus velutina*	4
Black oat grass	*Piptochaetium avenaceum* (= *Stipa avenacea*)	10
Black quillwort	*Isoetes melanopoda*	4
Black raspberry	*Rubus occidentalis*	1
Black-seeded rice grass	*Piptatherum racemosa*	8
Black snakeroot	*Sanicula marilandica*	6
Black spleenwort	*Asplenium resiliens*	10
Black swallow-wort	*VINCETOXICUM NIGRUM*	
Black walnut	*Juglans nigra*	2
Black willow	*Salix nigra*	3
Bladder campion	*SILENE VULGARIS*	
Bladdernut	*Staphylea trifolia*	5
Blade duckweed	*Wolffiella gladiata*	5
Blazing star	*Liatris squarrosa*	5
Blighted goldenrod	*Solidago sphacelata*	8
Bloodleaf	*Iresine rhizomatosa*	10
Bloodroot	*Sanguinaria canadensis*	5
Bloody cranesbill	*GERANIUM SANGUINEUM*	
Blue ash	*Fraxinus quadrangulata*	7
Bluebead	*Clintonia borealis*	10
Blue beech	*Carpinus caroliniana s. virginiana*	5
Bluebottle	*MUSCARI NEGLECTUM*	
Blue cohosh	*Caulophyllum thalictroides*	8
Blue curls	*Trichostema dichotomum*	4
Bluedevil	*ECHIUM PUSTULATUM*	
Blue-eyed Mary	*Collinsia verna*	6
Blue-eyed pearlwort	*SAGINA PROCUMBENS*	
Blue hearts	*Buchnera americana*	8
Blue hosta	*HOSTA VENTRICOSA*	
Blue joint grass	*Calamagrostis canadensis*	5
Blue-leaved willow	*Salix myricoides*	9
Blue lettuce	*Lactuca floridana*	5
Blue phlox	*Phlox divaricata* (including 1 subspecies)	5
Blue sage	*SALVIA AZUREA v. GRANDIFLORA*	
Blue sedge	*Carex glaucodea*	3
Blue star	*Amsonia tabernaemontana v. salicifolia*	5
Bluestem goldenrod	*Solidago caesia*	7
Blue toadflax	*Nuttallanthus canadensis* (= *Linaria canadensis*)	2
Bluets	*Houstonia caerulea* (= *Hedyotis caerulea*)	4
Blue vervain	*Verbena hastata* (including 1 variety)	3
Bluevine	*Cynanchum laeve*	1

Table P-1. *continued*

Common Name	Scientific Name[a]	Coefficient[b]
Blue water iris	*Iris brevicaulis*	9
Blue waxweed	*Cuphea viscosissima*	4
Blue wild indigo	*Baptisia australis*	10
Blunt-flowered dodder	*CUSCUTA OBTUSIFLORA v. GLANDULOSA*	
Blunt-leaf sandwort	*Moehringia lateriflora* (= *Arenaria lateriflora*)	6
Blunt-leaved senna	*Senna obtusifolia*	0
Blunt-leaved spurge	*Euphorbia obtusata*	3
Blunt mountain mint	*Pycnanthemum muticum*	0
Blunt-scaled oak sedge	*Carex albicans v. albicans*	6
Blunt-scaled wood sedge	*Carex albursina*	7
Blunt spike rush	*Eleocharis obtusa*	1
Bog bedstraw	*Galium labradoricum*	10
Bog bladderwort	*Utricularia geminiscapa*	10
Bog clearweed	*Pilea fontana*	5
Bog clubmoss	*Lycopodiella inundata* (= *Lycopodium inundatum*)	7
Bog goldenrod	*Solidago uliginosa*	10
Bog lobelia	*Lobelia kalmii*	10
Bog panicled sedge	*Carex diandra*	10
Bog reed grass	*Calamagrostis stricta s. inexpansa*	7
Bog rosemary	*Andromeda polifolia v. glaucophylla*	10
Bog spike rush	*Eleocharis robbinsii*	10
Bog willow	*Salix pedicellaris*	10
Border privet	*LIGUSTRUM OBTUSIFOLIUM*	
Boston ivy	*PARTHENOCISSUS TRICUSPIDATA*	
Bottlebrush grass	*Elymus hystrix* (including 1 variety)	5
Bottlebrush sedge	*Carex lurida*	4
Bouncing bet	*SAPONARIA OFFICINALIS*	
Boxelder	*Acer negundo* (including varieties)	1
Boxwood knotweed	*Polygonum aviculare s. buxiforme*	0
Bracken fern	*Pteridium aquilinum v. latiusculum*	5
Bracted green orchid	*Coeloglossum viride* (= *Habenaria viridis*)	7
Bracted water willow	*Dicliptera brachiata*	10
Bradford pear	*PYRUS CALLERYANA*	
Bradley's spleenwort	*Asplenium bradleyi*	10
Branched bur reed	*Sparganium androcladum*	9
Branched horseweed	*Conyza ramosissima*	0
Brazilian waterweed	*EGERIA DENSA*	
Bridal wreath	*SPIRAEA PRUNIFOLIA*	
Bristleless dark-green bulrush	*Scirpus georgianus*	3
Bristly aster	*Symphyotrichum puniceum*	7
Bristly blackberry	*Rubus sec. Tholiformes: R. missouricus*	5
Bristly cattail sedge	*Carex frankii*	2
Bristly crowfoot	*Ranunculus pensylvanicus*	6
Bristly foxtail grass	*SETARIA VERTICILLATA*	
Bristly green brier	*Smilax hispida*	3
Bristly locust	*ROBINIA HISPIDA*	
Bristly sarsaparilla	*Aralia hispida*	10
Bristly sedge	*Carex comosa*	6
Bristly sunflower	*Helianthus hirsutus*	5
Bristly wood grass	*Brachyelytrum aristosum*	10
Brittle naiad	*NAJAS MINOR*	
Broad beech fern	*Phegopteris hexagonoptera*	7
Broad-leaved cattail	*Typha latifolia*	1
Broad-leaved cow wheat	*Melampyrum lineare v. latifolium*	10
Broad-leaved goldenrod	*Solidago flexicaulis*	6
Broad-leaved oval sedge	*Carex tribuloides v. tribuloides*	5
Broad-leaved panic grass	*Dichanthelium latifolium*	6
Broad-leaved panicled sedge	*Carex decomposita*	10
Broad-leaved pepper cress	*LEPIDIUM LATIFOLIUM*	

Common Name	Scientific Name[a]	Coefficient[b]
Broad-leaved purple coneflower	*Echinacea purpurea*	6
Broad-leaved small pondweed	*Potamogeton pusillus s. tennuissimus*	4
Broad-leaved speedwell	*VERONICA AUSTRIACA s. TEUCRIUM*	
Broad-leaved spiderwort	*Tradescantia subaspera*	4
Broad-leaved wild rice	*Zizania aquatica v. aquatica*	10
Broad-leaved wood sedge	*Carex platyphylla*	10
Brome hummock sedge	*Carex bromoides*	10
Bronze fern	*Botrychium dissectum*	3
Broom corn millet	*PANICUM MILIACEUM*	
Broom panic grass	*Dichanthelium scoparium*	5
Broom sedge	*Andropogon virginicus*	1
Broomweed	*AMPHIACHYRIS DRACUNCULOIDES*	
Brown beak rush	*Rhynchospora capitellata*	6
Brown-eyed Susan	*Rudbeckia triloba*	3
Brown fox sedge	*Carex vulpinoidea*	2
Brown-fruited rush	*Juncus pelocarpus*	10
Brown-headed fox sedge	*Carex alopecoidea*	7
Brownish sedge	*Carex brunnescens s. sphaerostachya*	10
Brown-rayed knapweed	*CENTAUREA JACEA*	
Buckbean	*Menyanthes trifoliata*	10
Buckley's goldenrod	*Solidago buckleyi*	10
Buckwheat	*FAGOPYRUM ESCULENTUM*	
Buffalo berry	*Shepherdia canadensis*	10
Buffalo bur	*SOLANUM ROSTRATUM*	
Buffalo clover	*Trifolium reflexum*	8
Buffalo currant	*RIBES AUREUM v. VILLOSUM*	
Bugleweed	*Lycopus virginicus*	5
Bulb bitter cress	*Cardamine bulbosa*	4
Bulblet-bearing water hemlock	*Cicuta bulbifera*	8
Bulblet bladder fern	*Cystopteris bulbifera*	9
Bulbous bluegrass	*POA BULBOSA* (including 1 subspecies)	
Bulbous buttercup	*RANUNCULUS BULBOSUS*	
Bulbous wood rush	*Luzula bulbosa*	6
Bull brier	*Smilax bona-nox*	5
Bullhead lily	*Nuphar variegata*	8
Bull thistle	*CIRSIUM VULGARE*	
Bulrush	*Scirpus expansus*	10
Bunchberry	*Cornus canadensis*	10
Bunch flower	*Melanthium virginicum*	10
Bur buttercup	*RANUNCULUS TESTICULATUS* (= *CERATOCEPHALUS TESTICULATUS*)	
Bur chervil	*ANTHRISCUS CAUCALIS*	
Bur cucumber	*Sicyos angulatus*	3
Bur oak	*Quercus macrocarpa*	5
Bushy aster	*Symphyotrichum dumosum* (including 1 variety)	4
Bushy knotweed	*Polygonum ramosissimum*	4
Bushy pinweed	*Lechea stricta*	10
Butter-and-eggs	*LINARIA VULGARIS*	
Buttercup phacelia	*Phacelia ranunculacea*	10
Butterfly pea	*Clitoria mariana*	10
Butterflyweed	*Asclepias tuberosa* (including 1 variety)	4
Butternut	*Juglans cinerea*	5
Butterweed	*Packera glabella*	0
Buttonbush	*Cephalanthus occidentalis*	5
Buttonbush dodder	*Cuscuta cephalanthi*	5
Buttonweed	*Diodia teres*	2
Buttonweed	*ABUTILON THEOPHRASTI*	
California rose	*CALYSTEGIA PELLITA*	
Camphor weed	*Pluchea camphorata*	5
Camphorweed	*HETEROTHECA SUBAXILLARIS*	
Canada blueberry	*Vaccinium myrtilloides*	10
Canada clearweed	*Pilea pumila*	2

Common Name	Scientific Name[a]	Coefficient[b]
Canada goldenrod	*Solidago canadensis* (including 1 subspecies)	0
Canada hawkweed	*Hieracium umbellatum*	5
Canada lily	*Lilium canadense*	7
Canada mayflower	*Maianthemum canadense*	8
Canada plum	*Prunus nigra*	8
Canada summer bluet	*Houstonia canadensis*	10
Canada violet	*Viola canadensis*	8
Canada waterleaf	*Hydrophyllum canadense*	8
Canada wild ginger	*Asarum canadense*	5
Canada wild rye	*Elymus canadensis*	5
Canada wood nettle	*Laportea canadensis*	2
Canada yew	*Taxus canadensis*	10
Canadian black snakeroot	*Sanicula canadensis* (including 1 variety)	2
Canadian bluegrass	*POA COMPRESSA*	
Canadian milk vetch	*Astragalus canadensis*	9
Canadian rush	*Juncus canadensis*	7
Canadian St. John's wort	*Hypericum canadense*	8
Cancer root	*Orobanche uniflora*	6
Cancer root	*Conopholis americana*	8
Cancer weed	*Salvia lyrata*	3
Candle anemone	*Anemone cylindrica*	7
Caraway	*CARUM CARVI*	
Cardinal flower	*Lobelia cardinalis*	4
Carey's heartsease	*Persicaria careyi*	10
Carey's wood sedge	*Carex careyana*	9
Carolina anemone	*Anemone caroliniana*	10
Carolina buckthorn	*Frangula caroliniana* (= *Rhamnus caroliniana*)	4
Carolina cranesbill	*Geranium carolinianum*	2
Carolina figwort	*Cabomba caroliniana*	2
Carolina mosquito fern	*Azolla caroliniana*	4
Carolina panic grass	*Dichanthelium dichotomum s.yadkinense*	8
Carolina phlox	*Phlox carolina s. angusta*	5
Carolina thistle	*Cirsium carolinianum*	10
Carolina willow	*Salix caroliniana*	8
Carpet bugle	*AJUGA REPTANS*	
Carpet weed	*MOLLUGO VERTICILLATA*	
Castor bean	*RICINUS COMMUNIS*	
Catbird grape	*Vitis palmata*	6
Cat brier	*Smilax rotundifolia*	4
Catchfly grass	*Leersia lenticularis*	5
Catesby's hedge bindweed	*Calystegia catesbiana*	8
Catnip	*NEPETA CATARIA*	
Cat's foot	*Antennaria neglecta*	3
Celandine	*CHELIDONIUM MAJUS*	
Celandine poppy	*Stylophorum diphyllum*	7
Chaffweed	*Anagallis minima*	3
Charlock	*SINAPIS ARVENSIS*	
Cheat grass	*BROMUS TECTORUM*	
Checkerberry	*Gaultheria procumbens*	8
Cheeses	*MALVA NEGLECTA*	
Cherrybark oak	*Quercus pagoda*	5
Chestnut sedge	*Fimbristylis puberula*	10
Chickasaw plum	*PRUNUS ANGUSTIFOLIA*	
Chicory	*CICHORIUM INTYBUS*	
Chick-pea milk vetch	*ASTRAGALUS CICER*	
Chinese fountain grass	*PENNISETUM ALOPECUROIDES*	
Chinese silver grass	*MISCANTHUS SINENSIS*	
Chinese yam	*DIOSCOREA POLYSTACHYA*	
Chinquapin oak	*Quercus muhlenbergii*	4
Chocolate vine	*AKEBIA QUINATA*	
Christmas fern	*Polystichum acrostichoides*	5
Cigar tree	*Catalpa speciosa*	0
Ciliate crabgrass	*DIGITARIA CILIARIS*	
Cinnamon fern	*Osmunda cinnamomea*	9
Cinnamon willow herb	*Epilobium coloratum*	3
Citronella horse balm	*Collinsonia canadensis*	8
City goosefoot	*CHENOPODIUM URBICUM*	
Clammy chickweed	*CERASTIUM GLOMERATUM*	
Clammy cudweed	*Pseudognaphalium macounii*	2
Clammy false foxglove	*Aureolaria pedicularia* (including varieties)	7
Clammy ground cherry	*Physalis heterophylla*	3
Clammy hedge hyssop	*Gratiola neglecta*	4
Clammy locust	*ROBINIA VISCOSA*	
Clammy weed	*Polanisia dodecandra s. dodecandra*	1
Clammy weed	*Polanisia dodecandra s. trachysperma*	1
Clasping mullein	*VERBASCUM PHLOMOIDES*	
Clasping pepperwort	*LEPIDIUM PERFOLIATUM*	
Clasping St. John's wort	*Hypericum gymnanthum*	4
Cleft phlox	*Phlox bifida s. bifida*	7
Cleft violet	*Viola palmata* (including 1 variety)	5
Cliff adder's tongue fern	*Ophioglossum engelmannii*	10
Cliff clubmoss	*Huperzia porophila*	10
Cliff onion	*ALLIUM STELLATUM*	
Climbing bittersweet	*Celastrus scandens*	2
Climbing dayflower	*COMMELINA DIFFUSA*	
Climbing dogbane	*Trachelospermum difforme*	8
Climbing false buckwheat	*Fallopia scandens v. scandens*	0
Climbing false buckwheat	*Fallopia scandens v. cristata*	0
Climbing false buckwheat	*FALLOPIA SCANDENS v. DUMETORUM*	
Climbing fern	*Lygodium palmatum*	6
Climbing hempweed	*Mikania scandens*	7
Climbing milkweed	*Matelea obliqua*	10
Clingman's hedge nettle	*Stachys clingmanii*	10
Clinton's wood fern	*Dryopteris clintoniana*	10
Closed gentian	*Gentiana andrewsii*	4
Clustered black snakeroot	*Sanicula odorata*	2
Clustered broom rape	*Orobanche fasciculata*	10
Clustered false foxglove	*Agalinis fasciculata*	3
Clustered poppy mallow	*Callirhoë triangulata*	10
Clustered wild bean	*Strophostyles umbellata*	4
Coastal sandbur	*Cenchrus spinifex*	0
Cocklebur	*Xanthium strumarium*	0
Cocks comb	*CELOSIA CRISTATA*	
Cockspur grass	*Echinochloa walteri*	5
Cock-spur hawthorn	*Crataegus series Crus-galli: C. crus-galli*	4
Coffee senna	*SENNA OCCIDENTALIS*	
Colic root	*Aletris farinosa*	9
Colorado bluestem	*PASCOPYRUM SMITHII* (= *AGROPYRON SMITHII*)	
Colt's foot	*TUSSILAGO FARFARA*	
Columbine	*Aquilegia canadensis*	5
Comb-leaved cow wheat	*Melampyrum lineare v. pectinatum*	10
Comb pondweed	*Stuckenia pectinata* (= *Potamogeton pectinatus*)	3
Common alder	*Alnus serrulata*	6
Common arrowhead	*Sagittaria latifolia*	3
Common baby's breath	*GYPSOPHILA PANICULATA*	
Common balm	*MELISSA OFFICINALIS*	
Common barberry	*BERBERIS VULGARIS*	
Common barley	*HORDEUM VULGARE*	
Common beech sedge	*Carex communis*	8
Common beggar's ticks	*Bidens frondosa*	1
Common blackberry	*Rubus sec. Alleghenienses: R. allegheniensis*	2
Common bladderwort	*Utricularia macrorhiza*	5
Common blue-eyed grass	*Sisyrinchium albidum*	4
Common bog arrow grass	*Triglochin maritima*	10
Common boneset	*Eupatorium perfoliatum*	4
Common buckthorn	*RHAMNUS CATHARTICA*	
Common bugseed	*Corispermum pallasii*	3
Common burdock	*ARCTIUM MINUS*	
Common bur reed	*Sparganium eurycarpum*	5
Common bur sedge	*Carex grayi*	5

Table P-1. *continued*

Common Name	Scientific Name[a]	Coefficient[b]
Common carrion flower	*Smilax lasioneura*	4
Common catalpa	*CATALPA BIGNONIOIDES*	
Common cattail sedge	*Carex typhina*	7
Common centaury	*CENTAURIUM ERYTHRACEA*	
Common chickweed	*STELLARIA MEDIA s. MEDIA*	
Common choke cherry	*Prunus virginiana* (including 1 variety)	3
Common cinquefoil	*Potentilla simplex*	2
Common comfrey	*SYMPHYTUM OFFICINALE*	
Common dandelion	*TARAXACUM OFFICINALE*	
Common dayflower	*COMMELINA COMMUNIS*	
Common dewberry	*Rubus sec. Flagellares: R. flagellaris*	2
Common dodder	*Cuscuta gronovii* (including 1 variety)	2
Common elderberry	*Sambucus nigra s. canadensis*	2
Common evening primrose	*Oenothera biennis*	0
Common fig	*FICUS CARICA*	
Common flax	*LINUM USITATISSIMUM*	
Common flowering quince	*CHAENOMELES SPECIOSA*	
Common fly honeysuckle	*LONICERAx MUENDENIENSIS*	
Common forget-me-not	*MYOSOTIS SCORPIOIDES*	
Common fox sedge	*Carex stipata v. stipata*	2
Common fragile fern	*Cystopteris protrusa*	4
Common gaura	*Gaura longiflora*	3
Common goat's beard	*TRAGOPOGON PRATENSIS*	
Common grape hyacinth	*MUSCARI BOTRYOIDES*	
Common gray sedge	*Carex grisea*	3
Common groundsel	*SENECIO VULGARIS*	
Common hops	*HUMULUS LUPULUS v. LUPULUS*	
Common hop sedge	*Carex lupulina*	4
Common horehound	*MARRUBIUM VULGARE*	
Common horsetail	*Equisetum arvense*	1
Common hound's tongue	*CYNOGLOSSUM OFFICINALE*	
Common ironweed	*Vernonia fasciculata*	5
Common juniper	*Juniperus communis v. depressa*	10
Common knotweed	*POLYGONUM AVICULARE* (including subspecies)	
Common lake sedge	*Carex lacustris*	7
Common matrimony vine	*LYCIUM BARBARUM*	
Common milfoil	*Achillea millefolium*	0
Common milkweed	*Asclepias syriaca*	1
Common morning glory	*IPOMOEA PURPUREA*	
Common mountain mint	*Pycnanthemum virginianum*	5
Common mouse-ear chickweed	*CERASTIUM FONTANUM s. VULGARE*	
Common naiad	*Najas flexilis*	5
Common ninebark	*Physocarpus opulifolius* (including 1 variety)	7
Common nipplewort	*LAPSANA COMMUNIS*	
Common pepper cress	*Lepidium virginicum*	0
Common periwinkle	*VINCA MINOR*	
Common plantain	*PLANTAGO MAJOR v. MAJOR*	
Common polypody	*Polypodium virginianum*	10
Common pondweed	*Potamogeton natans*	8
Common privet	*LIGUSTRUM VULGARE*	
Common purpletop	*Tridens flavus*	1
Common ragweed	*Ambrosia artemisiifolia v. elatior*	0
Common red raspberry	*RUBUS IDAEUS v. IDAEUS*	
Common reed	*Phragmites australis*	0
Common rockrose	*Helianthemum canadense*	7
Common rush	*Juncus effusus*	3
Common rusty nut sedge	*Cyperus odoratus*	1
Common sand bracted sedge	*Carex muehlenbergii v. muehlenbergii*	5
Common satin grass	*Muhlenbergia frondosa*	3
Common sneezeweed	*Helenium autumnale*	3
Common sow thistle	*SONCHUS OLERACEUS*	
Common speedwell	*VERONICA OFFICINALIS v. OFFICINALIS*	
Common spiderwort	*Tradescantia ohiensis*	3
Common St. John's wort	*HYPERICUM PERFORATUM*	
Common star of Bethlehem	*ORNITHOGALUM UMBELLATUM*	
Common stiff sedge	*Carex tetanica*	9
Common streambank chervil	*Chaerophyllum procumbens v. procumbens*	2
Common sunflower	*HELIANTHUS ANNUUS*	
Common tansy	*TANACETUM VULGARE*	
Common teasel	*DIPSACUS FULLONUM*	
Common tussock sedge	*Carex stricta*	5
Common valerian	*Valeriana edulis v. ciliata*	10
Common water hemlock	*Cicuta maculata* (including 1 variety)	6
Common water horehound	*Lycopus americanus*	3
Common water hyacinth	*EICHHORNIA CRASSIPES*	
Common water plantain	*Alisma subcordatum*	2
Common waterweed	*Elodea canadensis*	3
Common white violet	*Viola striata*	4
Common whitlow cress	*Draba reptans*	2
Common wild comfrey	*Cynoglossum virginianum v. virginianum*	5
Common wild yam	*Dioscorea villosa*	4
Common wood fern	*Dryopteris intermedia*	10
Common wood reed	*Cinna arundinacea*	4
Common wood rush	*Luzula echinata*	6
Common wood rush	*Luzula multiflora*	6
Common wood sedge	*Carex blanda*	1
Common woodsia	*Woodsia obtusa s. obtusa*	4
Common woolly sedge	*Carex pellita*	2
Common wormwood	*ARTEMISIA ABSINTHIUM*	
Common yellow lake sedge	*Carex utriculata*	8
Compact dodder	*Cuscuta compacta*	10
Compass plant	*Silphium laciniatum*	10
Concealed sedge	*Carex cumberlandensis*	8
Coontail	*Ceratophyllum demersum*	1
Coralberry	*Symphoricarpos orbiculatus*	1
Cordroot sedge	*Carex chordorrhiza*	10
Corn	*ZEA MAYS*	
Corn chamomile	*ANTHEMIS ARVENSIS*	
Corn cockle	*AGROSTEMA GITHAGO*	
Corn gromwell	*BUGLOSSOIDES ARVENSE (= LITHOSPERMUM ARVENSE)*	
Corn poppy	*PAPAVER RHOEAS*	
Corn salad	*Valerianella umbilicata*	5
Corn speedwell	*VERONICA ARVENSIS*	
Corn spurrey	*SPERGULA ARVENSIS*	
Costmary	*TANACETUM BALSAMITA*	
Cottonweed	*FROELICHIA GRACILIS*	
Cottonweed	*Froelichia floridana v. campestris*	5
Cowbane	*Oxypolis rigidior*	7
Cow herb	*VACCARIA HISPANICA*	
Cow parsnip	*Heracleum sphondylium s. montanum*	6
Cowslip	*Caltha palustris*	7
Cow vetch	*VICIA CRACCA*	
Crack willow	*SALIX FRAGILIS*	
Crane-fly orchid	*Tipularia discolor*	4
Cranesbill	*GERANIUM AEQUALE*	
Crape myrtle	*LAGERSTROEMIA INDICA*	
Crawford's oval sedge	*Carex crawfordii*	9
Cream wild indigo	*Baptisia bracteata v. leucophaea*	10
Creeping bent grass	*AGROSTIS STOLONIFERA*	
Creeping bracted sedge	*Carex socialis*	8
Creeping burhead	*Echinodorus cordifolius*	10
Creeping bush clover	*Lespedeza repens*	6
Creeping buttercup	*RANUNCULUS REPENS*	
Creeping cotoneaster	*COTONEASTER ADPRESSUS*	

Common Name	Scientific Name[a]	Coefficient[b]
Creeping cucumber	*Melothria pendula*	3
Creeping love grass	*Eragrostis hypnoides*	3
Creeping primrose willow	*Ludwigia peploides s. glabrescens*	2
Creeping smartweed	*PERSICARIA CAESPITOSA*	
Creeeping vervain	*Verbena bracteata*	0
Creeping wood sorrel	*OXALIS CORNICULATA*	
Creeping yellow cress	*RORIPPA SYLVESTRIS*	
Crested anoda	*ANODA CRISTATA*	
Crested coralroot	*Hexalectris spicata*	10
Crested dog-tail grass	*CYNOSURUS CRISTATUS*	
Crested oval sedge	*Carex cristatella*	3
Crested wheat grass	*AGROPYRON DESERTORUM*	
Crested wheat grass	*AGROPYRON CRISTATUM s. PECTINATUM*	
Crested wood fern	*Dryopteris cristata*	10
Crimson clover	*TRIFOLIUM INCARNATUM*	
Crooked aster	*Symphyotrichum prenanthoides*	8
Cross milkwort	*Polygala cruciata v. aquilonia*	10
Cross vine	*Bignonia capreolata*	7
Crowded oval sedge	*Carex cumulata*	10
Crowfoot fox sedge	*Carex crus-corvi*	6
Crowfoot grass	*ELEUSINE INDICA*	
Crown vetch	*CORONILLA VARIA*	
Crow poison	*Nothoscordum bivalve*	6
Cuckoo flower	*Cardamine pratensis*	10
Cucumber magnolia	*Magnolia acuminata*	10
Culver's root	*Veronicastrum virginicum*	8
Cup plant	*Silphium perfoliatum*	4
Cupseed	*Calycocarpum lyonii*	7
Curly dock	*RUMEX CRISPUS*	
Curly-styled bracted sedge	*Carex rosea*	5
Curlytop lady's thumb	*Persicaria lapathifolia*	0
Cursed crowfoot	*Ranunculus sceleratus*	3
Curtis's mouse-ear chickweed	*CERASTIUM PUMILUM*	
Cusped bluegrass	*Poa cuspidata*	10
Cut-leaved blackberry	*RUBUS sec. SYLVATICI: R. LACINIATUS*	
Cut-leaved prairie dock	*Silphium terebinthinaceum v. pinnatifidum*	6
Cut-leaved teasel	*DIPSACUS LACINIATUS*	
Cylindrical blazing star	*Liatris cylindracea*	10
Cypress spurge	*EUPHORBIA CYPARISSIAS*	
Daffodil	*NARCISSUS PSEUDONARCISSUS*	
Dahurian buckthorn	*RHAMNUS DAVURICA s. NIPPONICA*	
Dainties	*Phyllanthus caroliniensis*	5
Daisy fleabane	*Erigeron strigosus*	2
Daisy-leaf grape fern	*Botrychium matricariifolium*	4
Dalmation toadflax	*LINARIA DALMATICA s. MACEDONICA*	
Dame's rocket	*HESPERIS MATRONALIS*	
Dark-green bulrush	*Scirpus atrovirens*	4
Dark green carrion flower	*Smilax pulverulenta*	5
Dark-scaled sedge	*Carex buxbaumii*	10
David's spurge	*EUPHORBIA DAVIDII*	
Deam's beard tongue	*Penstemon deamii*	5
Deam's coneflower	*Rudbeckia fulgida v. deamii*	10
Deam's dayflower	*Commelina erecta v. deamii*	7
Deam's dewberry	*Rubus sec. Flagellares: R. deamii*	5
Deam's prairie phlox	*Phlox pilosa s. deamii*	6
Deam's rockcress	*Arabis missouriensis*	10
Deam's rosin weed	*Silphium integrifolium v. deamii*	7
Deam's wild-indigo	*Baptisia x serenae*	10
Declined trillium	*Trillium flexipes*	5
Deerberry	*Vaccinium stamineum*	4
Deer-tongue grass	*Dichanthelium clandestinum*	3
Deer vetch	*LOTUS UNIFOLIOLATUS*	
Deflexed bottlebrush sedge	*Carex retrorsa*	10
Dense cotton grass	*Eriophorum vaginatum*	10
Deptford pink	*DIANTHUS ARMERIA*	
Devil's claw	*PROBOSCIDEA LOUISIANICA*	
Devil's paint brush	*HIERACIUM AURANTIACUM*	
Devil's walking stick	*Aralia spinosa*	5
Dewberry	*Rubus sec. Tholiformes: R. impar*	5
Dill	*ANETHUM GRAVEOLENS*	
Dinky duckweed	*Lemna minuta*	3
Ditch stonecrop	*Penthorum sedoides*	2
Dittany	*Cunila origanoides*	5
Divided crinkleroot	*Cardamine dissecta*	8
Dogbane	*Apocynum cannabinum*	2
Dog fennel	*ANTHEMIS COTULA*	
Dog mint	*Clinopodium vulgare*	2
Dog mustard	*ERUCASTRUM GALLICUM*	
Dog rose	*ROSA CANINA*	
Dog violet	*Viola labradorica*	8
Doll's-eyes	*Actaea pachypoda*	7
Dotted hawthorn	*Crataegus series Punctatae: C. punctata*	2
Doubleclaw	*PROBOSCIDEA PARVIFLORA*	
Doubtful mouse-ear-chickweed	*CERASTIUM DUBIUM*	
Downy arrowwood	*Viburnum molle*	10
Downy arrowwood	*Viburnum rafinesquianum*	7
Downy cinquefoil	*POTENTILLA INTERMEDIA*	
Downy corymbose dewberry	*Rubus sec. Flagellares: R. curtipes*	5
Downy false foxglove	*Aureolaria virginica*	8
Downy gentian	*Gentiana puberulenta*	10
Downy green sedge	*Carex swanii*	4
Downy hawthorn	*Crataegus series Molles: C. mollis*	2
Downy incised dewberry	*Rubus sec. Tholiformes: R. aboriginum*	5
Downy lens grass	*Paspalum setaceum v. stramineum*	3
Downy lobelia	*Lobelia puberula v. simulans*	5
Downy racemose dewberry	*Rubus sec. Tholiformes: R. satis*	5
Downy skullcap	*Scutellaria incana*	4
Downy Solomon's seal	*Polygonatum pubescens*	8
Downy sunflower	*Helianthus mollis*	9
Downy wafer ash	*Ptelea trifoliata v. mollis*	6
Downy willow herb	*Epilobium strictum*	10
Downy yellow violet	*Viola pubescens* (including varieties)	5
Dragon's mouth	*Arethusa bulbosa*	10
Drummond's aster	*Symphyotrichum drummondii*	4
Drummond's half-chaff sedge	*Lipocarpha drummondii* (= *Hemicarpha drummondii*)	10
Drummond's red maple	*Acer rubrum v. drummondii*	5
Drummond's rockcress	*Arabis drummondii*	10
Dudley's rush	*Juncus dudleyi*	2
Dune goldenrod	*Solidago simplex v. gillmanii*	10
Dune sand cherry	*Prunus pumila v. pumila*	10
Dune thistle	*Cirsium pitcheri*	10
Dune willow	*Salix cordata*	10
Dutch crocus	*CROCUS VERNUS*	
Dutchman's breeches	*Dicentra cucullaria*	6
Dutchman's pipe	*Aristolochia tomentosa*	7
Dwarf bindweed	*Calystegia spithamaea*	8
Dwarf birch	*Betula pumila*	10
Dwarf bird's-eye speedwell	*VERONICA POLITA*	
Dwarf bracted sedge	*Carex leavenworthii*	1
Dwarf bur reed	*Sparganium emersum*	8
Dwarf chinquapin oak	*Quercus prinoides*	10
Dwarf crested iris	*Iris cristata*	7
Dwarf ginseng	*Panax trifolius*	9
Dwarf grape fern	*Botrychium simplex*	6
Dwarf grass pink orchid	*Calopogon oklahomensis*	10
Dwarf hackberry	*Celtis tenuifolia*	8
Dwarf honeysuckle	*Diervilla lonicera*	9

Table P-1. *continued*

Common Name	Scientific Name[a]	Coefficient[b]
Dwarf iris	*IRIS PUMILA*	
Dwarf larkspur	*Delphinium tricorne*	5
Dwarf mallow	*MALVA PUSILLA*	
Dwarf plantain	*Plantago virginica*	2
Dwarf raspberry	*Rubus pubescens*	10
Dwarf snapdragon	*CHAENORRHINUM MINUS*	
Dwarf St. John's wort	*Hypericum mutilum*	4
Dwarf sumac	*Rhus copallina v. latifolia*	3
Eared false foxglove	*Agalinis auriculata*	8
Early buttercup	*Ranunculus fascicularis*	6
Early coralroot	*Corallorhiza trifida*	10
Early cudweed	*Gamochaeta purpurea* (= *Gnaphalium purpureum*)	0
Early dark-green bulrush	*Scirpus hattorianus*	3
Early fen sedge	*Carex crawei*	10
Early figwort	*Scrophularia lanceolata*	5
Early goldenrod	*Solidago juncea*	3
Early horse gentian	*Triosteum aurantiacum* (including varieties)	5
Early ladies' tresses	*Spiranthes lucida*	10
Early-leaved brome	*Bromus latiglumis*	6
Early low blueberry	*Vaccinium angustifolium*	5
Early meadow rue	*Thalictrum dioicum*	7
Early oak sedge	*Carex umbellata*	5
Early saxifrage	*Saxifraga virginiensis*	7
Early white-haired panic grass	*Dichanthelium ovale s. praecocius*	10
Early wild rose	*Rosa blanda* (including 1 variety)	4
Early winter cress	*BARBAREA VERNA*	
Earthnut vetchling	*LATHYRUS TUBEROSUS*	
Eastern blue-eyed grass	*Sisyrinchium atlanticum*	10
Eastern cottonwood	*Populus deltoides*	1
Eastern poison ivy	*Toxicodendron radicans s. negundo*	1
Eastern prickly pear	*Opuntia humifusa*	2
Eastern red cedar	*Juniperus virginiana*	2
Eastern redbud	*Cercis canadensis*	3
Eastern sand cherry	*Prunus pumila v. susquehanae*	8
Eastern sea rocket	*CAKILE EDENTULA v. EDENTULA*	
Ebony spleenwort	*Asplenium platyneuron*	3
Eel grass	*Vallisneria americana*	7
Eggleston's violet	*Viola egglestonii*	10
Elecampane	*INULA HELENIUM*	
Elephant's foot	*Elephantopus carolinianus*	5
Elliott's broom sedge	*Andropogon gyrans*	3
Elliptic-leaved blackberry	*Rubus sec. Allegheniensis: R. alumnus*	2
Elm-leaved goldenrod	*Solidago ulmifolia*	5
Enchanter's nightshade	*Circaea lutetiana s. canadensis*	2
Engelmann's quillwort	*Isoetes engelmannii*	10
Engelmann's spike rush	*Eleocharis engelmannii*	4
English daisy	*BELLIS PERENNIS*	
English ivy	*HEDERA HELIX*	
English plantain	*PLANTAGO LANCEOLATA*	
Erect knotweed	*Polygonum erectum*	0
Erect primrose willow	*Ludwigia decurrens*	4
Eurasian paper birch	*BETULA PUBESCENS*	
European bellflower	*CAMPANULA RAPUNCULOIDES*	
European columbine	*AQUILEGIA VULGARIS*	
European corn salad	*VALERIANELLA LOCUSTA*	
European elderberry	*SAMBUCUS NIGRA s. NIGRA*	
European fly honeysuckle	*LONICERA XYLOSTEUM*	
European gooseberry	*RIBES UVA-CRISPA v. SATIVUM*	
European gromwell	*LITHOSPERMUM OFFICINALE*	
European high-bush cranberry	*VIBURNUM OPULUS v. OPULUS*	
European lake sedge	*CAREX ACUTIFORMIS*	
European meadowsweet	*FILIPENDULA ULMARIA*	
European mountain ash	*SORBUS AUCUPARIA*	
European smoketree	*COTINUS COGGYGRIA*	
European sweet flag	*ACORUS CALAMUS*	
European vervain	*VERBENA OFFICINALIS*	
European water clover	*MARSILEA QUADRIFOLIA*	
European water horehound	*LYCOPUS EUROPAEUS*	
European water milfoil	*MYRIOPHYLLUM SPICATUM*	
European white birch	*BETULA PENDULA*	
Evening primrose	*Oenothera triloba*	10
Everlasting pea	*LATHYRUS LATIFOLIUS*	
Expressway aster	*SYMPHYOTRICHUM SUBULATUM*	
Expressway sedge	*CAREX PRAEGRACILIS*	
Fairground grass	*SCLEROCHLOA DURA*	
Fairy wand	*Chamaelirium luteum*	8
Fall coralroot	*Corallorhiza odontorhiza* (including 1 variety)	3
Fall panicum	*Panicum dichotomiflorum* (including 1 subspecies)	0
Fall witch grass	*Digitaria cognata* (= *Leptoloma cognatum*)	2
False aloe	*Manfreda virginica* (= *Agave virginica*)	8
False arrowfeather	*Aristida longespica v. geniculata*	8
False asphodel	*Triantha glutinosa* (= *Tofieldia glutinosa*)	10
False aster	*Boltonia asteroides v. recognita*	5
False bearded panic grass	*Dichanthelium mattamuskeetense*	5
False boneset	*Brickellia eupatorioides* (= *Kuhnia eupatoriodes*) (including 1 variety)	8
False bristly sedge	*Carex pseudocyperus*	10
False bugbane	*Cimicifuga racemosa*	9
False bugbane	*Trautvetteria caroliniensis*	10
False dandelion	*Pyrrhopappus carolinianus*	2
False foxglove	*Agalinis purpurea*	6
False foxglove	*Agalinis paupercula* (including 1 variety)	7
False foxtail	*CRYPSIS SCHOENOIDES*	
False golden ragwort	*Packera pseudaurea v. semicordata*	4
False golden sedge	*Carex garberi*	10
False grass sedge	*Carex timida*	9
False gray sedge	*Carex amphibola*	8
False green flat sedge	*Cyperus pseudovegetus*	3
False heather	*Hudsonia tomentosa*	10
False hellebore	*Melanthium woodii* (= *Veratrum woodii*)	7
False indigo bush	*Amorpha fruticosa*	3
False loosestrife	*Ludwigia polycarpa*	4
False loosestrife	*Ludwigia glandulosa*	3
False melic grass	*Schizachne purpurascens*	10
False mermaid weed	*Floerkea proserpinacoides*	5
False mermaid weed	*Proserpinaca palustris* (including 1 variety)	4
False nettle	*Boehmeria cylindrica* (including 1 variety)	3
False pennyroyal	*Isanthus brachiatus* (= *Trichostema brachiatum*)	4
False pimpernel	*Lindernia dubia v. dubia*	3
False rue anemone	*Enemion biternatum* (= *Isopyrum biternatum*)	5
False rusty nut sedge	*Cyperus engelmannii*	3
False spiraea	*SORBARIA SORBIFOLIA*	
False sunflower	*Heliopsis helianthoides* (including 1 variety)	4
False white-haired panic grass	*Dichanthelium ovale s. pseudopubescens*	6
False wild stonecrop	*SEDUM SPURIUM*	

Common Name	Scientific Name[a]	Coefficient[b]
Fame flower	*Phemeranthus rugospermus (= Talinum rugospermum)*	10
Farkleberry	*Vaccinium arboreum*	8
Fat-hen saltbush	*ATRIPLEX PATULA*	
Featherbells	*Stenanthium gramineum*	8
Feathered amaranth	*CELOSIA ARGENTEA*	
Featherfoil	*Hottonia inflata*	9
Feathery false Solomon's seal	*Maianthemum racemosum (= Smilacina racemosa)*	4
Fen betony	*Pedicularis lanceolata*	6
Fen panicled sedge	*Carex prairea*	10
Fen star sedge	*Carex sterilis*	9
Fen thistle	*Cirsium muticum*	8
Fen willow herb	*Epilobium leptophyllum*	10
Fern-leaf verbena	*GLANDULARIA BIPINNATIFIDA (= VERBENA BIPINNATIFIDA)*	
Fern pondweed	*Potamogeton robbinsii*	10
Fescue oval sedge	*Carex festucacea*	6
Fetid marigold	*DYSSODIA PAPPOSA*	
Feverfew	*TANACETUM PARTHENIUM*	
Few-flowered bog sedge	*Carex pauciflora*	10
Few-flowered nut rush	*Scleria pauciflora v. caroliniana*	4
Few-flowered panic grass	*Dichanthelium oligosanthes v. oligosanthes*	8
Few-flowered spike rush	*Eleocharis quinqueflora*	10
Few-flowered tick trefoil	*Desmodium pauciflorum*	8
Few-fruited gray sedge	*Carex oligocarpa*	8
Few-nerved wood sedge	*Carex leptonervia*	8
Field bindweed	*CONVOLVULUS ARVENSIS*	
Field chickweed	*Cerastium arvense v. villosum*	6
Field cress	*LEPIDIUM CAMPESTRE*	
Field dodder	*Cuscuta campestris*	1
Field garlic	*ALLIUM VINEALE*	
Field hawkweed	*HIERACIUM CAESPITOSUM*	
Field hedge parsley	*TORILIS ARVENSIS s. ARVENSIS*	
Field milkwort	*Polygala sanguinea*	4
Field nut sedge	*Cyperus esculentus v. leptostachyus*	0
Field oval sedge	*Carex molesta*	2
Field penny cress	*THLASPI ARVENSE*	
Field pumpkin	*CUCURBITA PEPO v. OVIFERA*	
Field sorrel	*RUMEX ACETOSELLA*	
Field thistle	*CIRSIUM ARVENSE*	
Fine-leaved sheep fescue	*FESTUCA FILIFORMIS*	
Fireberry hawthorn	*Crataegus series Rotundifoliae: C. chrysocarpa*	6
Fire pink	*Silene virginica*	7
Fireweed	*Erechtites hieracifolia*	2
Fireweed	*Chamerion angustifolium s. circumvagum (= Epilobium angustifolium)*	3
Firewheels	*GAILLARDIA PULCHELLA*	
Five-leaved aralia	*ELEUTHEROCOCCUS PENTAPHYLLUS*	
Five leaves	*Isotria verticillata*	7
Flat-fruited hawthorn	*Crataegus series Pruinosae: C. platycarpa*	7
Flat-leaved bladderwort	*Utricularia intermedia*	8
Flat-spiked gray sedge	*Carex planispicata*	7
Flat-stemmed pondweed	*Potamogeton zosteriformis*	8
Flat-stemmed spike rush	*Eleocharis compressa*	10
Flat-top aster	*Doellingeria umbellata (= Aster umbellatus)*	8
Flax-leaved aster	*Ionactis linariifolius (= Aster linariifolius)*	9
Fleshy hawthorn	*Crataegus series Macracanthae: C. succulenta*	6
Flixweed	*DESCURAINIA SOPHIA*	
Floating bladderwort	*Utricularia radiata*	10
Floating bur reed	*Sparganium natans*	10
Floating manna grass	*Glyceria septentrionalis*	7
Florida crown grass	*Paspalum floridanum*	2
Flowering dogwood	*Cornus florida*	4
Flowering rush	*BUTOMUS UMBELLATUS*	
Flowering spurge	*Euphorbia corollata*	4
Flowering wintergreen	*Polygala paucifolia*	10
Flower-of-an-hour	*HIBISCUS TRIONUM*	
Fluellin	*KICKXIA ELATINE*	
Fly honeysuckle	*LONICERAx XYLOSTEOIDES*	
Fly honeysuckle	*LONICERAx MINUTIFLORA*	
Fly honeysuckle	*LONICERAx MUSCAVIENSIS*	
Fog fruit	*Phyla lanceolata*	2
Follicle sedge	*Carex folliculata*	10
Fool's parsley	*AETHUSA CYNAPIUM*	
Foothill bedstraw	*CRUCIATA PEDEMONTANUM (= GALIUM PEDEMONTANUM)*	
Forbes' saxifrage	*Saxifraga pensylvanica v. forbesii*	10
Forked aster	*Eurybia furcata (= Aster furcatus)*	10
Forked catchfly	*SILENE DICHOTOMA*	
Forked duckweed	*Lemna trisulca*	6
Forked panic grass	*Dichanthelium dichotomum s. dichotomum*	5
Forked-tip three-awn grass	*ARISTIDA BASIRAMEA*	
Four-angled rose gentian	*Sabatia campanulata*	10
Four-leaf yam	*Dioscorea quaternata*	5
Four o'clock	*MIRABILIS JALAPA*	
Four-rowed bead grass	*Paspalum pubiflorum*	3
Four-seeded vetch	*VICIA TETRASPERMA*	
Fowl bluegrass	*Poa palustris*	6
Fowl manna grass	*Glyceria striata*	4
Foxglove beard tongue	*Penstemon digitalis*	4
Fox grape	*Vitis labrusca*	6
Foxtail	*Alopecurus aequalis*	6
Foxtail millet	*SETARIA ITALICA*	
Foxtail prairie clover	*DALEA LEPORINA*	
Fragrant water lily	*Nymphaea odorata s. tuberosa*	6
Fraser's St. John's wort	*Triadenum fraseri*	8
French grass	*Orbexilum onobrychis (= Psoralea onobrychis)*	4
French rose	*ROSA GALLICA*	
French's shooting star	*Dodecatheon frenchii*	10
Fries's pondweed	*Potamogeton friesii*	10
Fringed bindweed	*Fallopia cilinodis (= Polygonum cilinode)*	10
Fringed brome	*Bromus ciliatus*	10
Fringed gentian	*Gentianopsis crinita*	8
Fringed loosestrife	*Lysimachia ciliata*	4
Fringed phlox	*Phlox amplifolia*	8
Fringed puccoon	*Lithospermum incisum*	10
Fringed sedge	*Carex crinita*	8
Frog's bit	*Limnobium spongia*	10
Frosted hawthorn	*Crataegus series Pruinosae: C. pruinosa*	5
Frost grape	*Vitis vulpina*	3
Frostweed	*Verbesina virginica*	3
Fuller's bristly dewberry	*Rubus sec. Setosi: R. fulleri*	9
Fumitory	*FUMARIA OFFICINALIS*	
Gama grass	*Tripsacum dactyloides*	2
Garden annual stonecrop	*HYLOTELEPHIUM ERYTHROSTICTUM*	
Garden asparagus	*ASPARAGUS OFFICINALIS*	
Garden bleeding-hearts	*DICENTRA SPECTABILIS*	
Garden chamomile	*CHAMAEMELUM NOBILE*	
Garden heliotrope	*VALERIANA OFFICINALIS*	
Garden lettuce	*LACTUCA SATIVA*	
Garden loosestrife	*LYSIMACHIA VULGARIS*	

Table P-1. *continued*

Common Name	Scientific Name[a]	Coefficient[b]
Garden onion	*ALLIUM CEPA*	
Garden petunia	*PETUNIA x ATKINSIANA*	
Garden phlox	*Phlox paniculata*	3
Garden pink	*DIANTHUS PLUMARIUS*	
Garden snowberry	*SYMPHORICARPOS ALBUS v. LAEVIGATUS*	
Garlic	*ALLIUM SATIVUM*	
Garlic mustard	*ALLIARIA PETIOLATA*	
Gattinger's hawthorn	*Crataegus series Pruinosae: C. gattingeri*	5
Gattinger's panic grass	*Panicum gattingeri*	3
German chamomile	*MATRICARIA CHAMOMILLA*	
Germander speedwell	*VERONICA CHAMAEDRYS*	
German iris	*IRIS GERMANICA*	
Geyer's spurge	*Chamaesyce geyeri*	10
Giant cane	*Arundinaria gigantea*	5
Giant chickweed	*MYOSOTON AQUATICUM*	
Giant foxtail grass	*SETARIA FABERI*	
Giant green foxtail grass	*SETARIA VIRIDIS v. MAJOR*	
Giant ragweed	*Ambrosia trifida*	0
Giant St. John's wort	*Hypericum pyramidatum*	10
Ginseng	*Panax quinquefolius*	7
Glade fern	*Diplazium pycnocarpon (= Athyrium pycnocarpon)*	9
Glade mallow	*Napaea dioica*	3
Glaucous campion	*SILENE CSEREI*	
Glaucous tick trefoil	*Desmodium laevigatum*	5
Glaucous white lettuce	*Prenanthes racemosa*	10
Globe beak rush	*Rhynchospora recognita*	10
Globe-fruit primrose willow	*Ludwigia sphaerocarpa*	10
Globose watermeal	*Wolffia columbiana*	5
Glossy buckthorn	*FRANGULA ALNUS (= RHAMNUS FRANGULA)*	
Goat's rue	*Tephrosia virginiana*	7
Goat's beard	*Aruncus dioicus*	7
Golden alexanders	*Zizia aurea*	7
Golden aster	*Heterotheca camporum v. camporum (= Chrysopsis camporum)*	4
Golden bell	*FORSYTHIA x INTERMEDIA*	
Golden cassia	*Chamaecrista fasciculata (= Cassia fasciculata)*	2
Golden cattail sedge	*Carex aureolensis*	10
Golden coreopsis	*COREOPSIS TINCTORIA*	
Golden ragwort	*Packera aurea*	4
Golden rain tree	*KOELREUTERIA PANICULATA*	
Golden saxifrage	*Chrysosplenium americanum*	10
Golden seal	*Hydrastis canadensis*	7
Golden sedge	*Carex aurea*	9
Golden-seeded spike rush	*Eleocharis elliptica*	10
Golden St. John's wort	*Hypericum frondosum*	10
Goldie fern	*Dryopteris goldiana*	9
Gold-of-pleasure	*CAMELINA SATIVA*	
Goldthread	*Coptis trifolia*	10
Goose-neck loosestrife	*LYSIMACHIA CLETHROIDES*	
Goutweed	*AEGOPODIUM PODAGRARIA*	
Grainless field sorrel	*RUMEX HASTATULUS*	
Grape honeysuckle	*Lonicera reticulata*	8
Grass beak rush	*Rhynchospora globularis*	10
Grass-leaved arrowhead	*Sagittaria graminea*	9
Grass-leaved goldenrod	*Euthamia graminifolia*	3
Grass-leaved orach	*ATRIPLEX LITTORALIS*	
Grass-leaved pondweed	*Potamogeton gramineus*	7
Grass-leaved rush	*Juncus marginatus*	4
Grass-of-parnassus	*Parnassia glauca*	10
Grass pink orchid	*Calopogon tuberosus*	10
Grass sedge	*Carex jamesii*	4
Gray beak rush	*Rhynchospora fusca*	10
Gray birch	*Betula populifolia*	10
Gray bog sedge	*Carex canescens s. disjuncta*	10
Gray dogwood	*Cornus racemosa*	2
Gray germander	*Teucrium canadense v. occidentale*	3

Common Name	Scientific Name[a]	Coefficient[b]
Grayish evening primrose	*Oenothera villosa*	0
Gray mouse-ear chickweed	*CERASTIUM BRACHYPETALUM*	
Gray polypody	*Pleopeltis polypodioides v. michauxiana (= Polypodium polypodioides)*	10
Gray poplar	*POPULUS x CANESCENS*	
Gray willow	*SALIX CINEREA*	
Great angelica	*Angelica atropurpurea*	6
Great blue lobelia	*Lobelia siphilitica*	3
Great bulrush	*Schoenoplectus tabernaemontani (= Scirpus validus)*	4
Great burdock	*ARCTIUM LAPPA*	
Great chickweed	*Stellaria pubera*	7
Great duckweed	*Spirodela polyrhiza*	5
Greater hop sedge	*Carex gigantea*	10
Greater nodding fescue	*Festuca paradoxa*	10
Great fox sedge	*Carex stipata v. maxima*	5
Great globe thistle	*ECHINOPS SPHAEROCEPHALUS*	
Great hawthorn	*Crataegus series Punctatae: C. grandis*	5
Great Indian plantain	*Arnoglossum reniforme*	8
Great knapweed	*CENTAUREA SCABIOSA*	
Great Lakes corn salad	*Valerianella chenopodifolia*	5
Great Lakes sea rocket	*Cakile edentula v. lacustris*	10
Great Plains flat sedge	*Cyperus lupulinus s. macilentus*	4
Great Plains ladies' tresses	*Spiranthes magnicamporum*	10
Great spike rush	*Eleocharis palustris*	8
Great tickseed	*COREOPSIS MAJOR*	
Great water dock	*Rumex orbiculatus v. borealis*	7
Great waterleaf	*Hydrophyllum appendiculatum*	6
Great white lettuce	*Prenanthes crepidinea*	7
Great yellow wood sorrel	*Oxalis grandis*	8
Grecian foxglove	*DIGITALIS LANATA*	
Green adder's mouth	*Malaxis unifolia*	10
Green amaranth	*AMARANTHUS HYBRIDUS*	
Green ash	*Fraxinus pennsylvanica v. lanceolata*	1
Green brier	*Smilax glauca*	4
Green dragon	*Arisaema dracontium*	5
Greene's rush	*Juncus greenei*	8
Green-flowered milkweed	*Asclepias viridiflora*	9
Green-flowered tick trefoil	*Desmodium viridiflorum*	4
Green-fringed orchid	*Platanthera lacera*	4
Green hawthorn	*Crataegus series Virides: C. viridis*	7
Green-headed fox sedge	*Carex conjuncta*	6
Green hellebore	*HELLEBORUS VIRIDIS*	
Green milkweed	*Asclepias viridis*	10
Green orchid	*Platanthera huronensis*	10
Green shinleaf	*Pyrola chlorantha*	10
Green thread	*THELESPERMA MEGAPOTAMICUM*	
Green twayblade	*Liparis loeselii*	4
Green violet	*Hybanthus concolor*	6
Green yellow sedge	*Carex viridula*	8
Grooved yellow flax	*Linum sulcatum*	10
Ground cedar	*Lycopodium tristachyum*	10
Ground ivy	*GLECHOMA HEDERACEA*	
Ground nut	*Apios americana*	3
Ground pine	*Lycopodium obscurum*	6
Grove bluegrass	*Poa alsodes*	8
Gum plant	*GRINDELIA SQUARROSA*	
Hackberry	*Celtis occidentalis*	3
Hair beak rush	*Rhynchospora capillacea*	10
Hair bladderwort	*Utricularia subulata*	10
Hair grass	*Agrostis hyemalis*	2
Hair grass	*Muhlenbergia capillaris*	10

Common Name	Scientific Name[a]	Coefficient[b]
Hair sedge	*Bulbostylis capillaris*	4
Hair spike rush	*Eleocharis microcarpa v. filiculmis*	10
Hair star sedge	*Carex atlantica s. capillacea*	10
Hairy aster	*Symphyotrichum pilosum v. pilosum*	0
Hairy beard tongue	*Penstemon hirsutus*	5
Hairy bedstraw	*Galium pilosum*	5
Hairy bitter cress	*CARDAMINE HIRSUTA*	
Hairy bracted tick trefoil	*Desmodium cuspidatum v. longifolium*	6
Hairy brome	*BROMUS COMMUTATUS*	
Hairy bush clover	*Lespedeza hirta*	7
Hairy buttercup	*RANUNCULUS SARDOUS*	
Hairy crabgrass	*DIGITARIA SANGUINALIS*	
Hairy false golden aster	*HETEROTHECA CAMPORUM v. GLANDULISSIMA*	
Hairy-fruited lake sedge	*Carex trichocarpa*	4
Hairy gentian	*Gentiana villosa*	3
Hairy gray sedge	*Carex hitchcockiana*	8
Hairy green sedge	*Carex hirsutella*	3
Hairy ground cherry	*Physalis pubescens* (including 1 variety)	3
Hairy hawkweed	*Hieracium gronovii*	5
Hairy-leaved lake sedge	*Carex atherodes*	6
Hairy lens grass	*Paspalum setaceum v. muhlenbergii* (and additional varieties)	3
Hairy lip fern	*Cheilanthes lanosa*	10
Hairy marsh yellow cress	*Rorippa palustris s. hispida*	2
Hairy meadow parsnip	*Thaspium barbinode*	7
Hairy mountain mint	*Pycnanthemum verticillatum v. pilosum*	4
Hairy nightshade	*SOLANUM PHYSALIFOLIUM*	
Hairy pinweed	*Lechea mucronata*	7
Hairy puccoon	*Lithospermum caroliniense v. croceum*	8
Hairy rockcress	*Arabis hirsuta v. pycnocarpa*	5
Hairy rose mallow	*Hibiscus moscheutos v. occidentalis*	4
Hairy ruellia	*Ruellia humilis*	5
Hairy-seeded nut rush	*Scleria muhlenbergii*	10
Hairy skullcap	*Scutellaria elliptica v. hirsuta*	5
Hairy spicebush	*Lindera benzoin*	5
Hairy spurge	*Chamaesyce vermiculata*	0
Hairy sweet cicely	*Osmorhiza claytonii*	3
Hairy tick trefoil	*Desmodium ciliare*	3
Hairy white goldenrod	*Solidago hispida*	8
Hairy wild lettuce	*Lactuca hirsuta*	10
Hairy wild licorice	*Galium circaezans v. hypomalacum*	5
Hairy willow herb	*EPILOBIUM HIRSUTUM*	
Hairy wood rush	*Luzula acuminata*	10
Hairy wood sedge	*Carex hirtifolia*	5
Halberd-leaved orach	*ATRIPLEX PROSTRATA*	
Halberd-leaved rose mallow	*Hibiscus laevis*	4
Halberd-leaved tear-thumb	*Persicaria arifolia*	10
Hall's tufted bulrush	*Schoenoplectus hallii*	7
Handsome Harry	*Rhexia virginica*	5
Harbinger of spring	*Erigenia bulbosa*	5
Hard fescue	*FESTUCA OVINA*	
Hardhack	*Spiraea tomentosa*	4
Harebell	*Campanula rotundifolia*	8
Hare's-ear mustard	*CONRINGIA ORIENTALIS*	
Harvey's buttercup	*Ranunculus harveyi*	8
Hashish	*CANNABIS SATIVA*	
Hawkbit	*LEONTODON TARAXACOIDES*	
Hawkins's oak	*Quercus x hawkinsiae*	4
Hawk's beard	*CREPIS PULCHRA*	
Hawk's beard	*CREPIS CAPILLARIS*	
Hawkweed mustard	*ERYSIMUM HIERACIFOLIUM*	
Hawthorn-of-the-hills	*Crataegus series Punctatae: C. collina*	5
Hay-scented fern	*Dennstaedtia punctilobula*	10
Hazel dodder	*Cuscuta coryli*	7
Hard-stemmed bulrush	*Schoenoplectus acutus* (= *Scirpus acutus*)	5
Heart-leaved aster	*Symphyotrichum cordifolium*	5
Heart-leaved hedge nettle	*Stachys cordata*	7
Heart-leaved meadow parsnip	*Zizia aptera*	10
Heart-leaved plantain	*Plantago cordata*	10
Heart-leaved skullcap	*Scutellaria ovata*	7
Heart-leaved willow	*Salix eriocephala*	4
Heath aster	*Symphyotrichum ericoides v. ericoides*	4
Hedge apple	*MACLURA POMIFERA*	
Hedgehog club rush	*Cyperus echinatus*	4
Hedge mustard	*SISYMBRIUM OFFICINALE*	
Helleborine orchid	*EPIPACTIS HELLEBORINE*	
Heller's old-field balsam	*Pseudognaphalium helleri s. micradenium* (= *Gnaphalium helleri*)	10
Hemlock	*Tsuga canadensis*	10
Hemlock panic grass	*Dichanthelium acuminatum s. columbianum* (= *Panicum columbianum*)	8
Hemlock parsley	*Conioselinum chinense*	10
Hen-and-chickens	*SEMPERVIVUM TECTORUM*	
Henbit	*LAMIUM AMPLEXICAULE*	
Herb Robert	*Geranium robertianum*	4
Hickey's clubmoss	*Lycopodium hickeyi*	6
High-bush blackberry	*Rubus sec. Arguti: R. argutus*	3
High-bush blueberry	*Vaccinium corymbosum*	9
High-bush cranberry	*Viburnum opulus v. americanum*	10
High mallow	*MALVA SYLVESTRIS*	
Hill's oak	*Quercus ellipsoidalis*	4
Hillside strawberry	*Fragaria vesca s. americana*	10
Hill's thistle	*Cirsium hillii*	10
Hispid swamp buttercup	*Ranunculus hispidus v. caricetorum*	10
Hoary alyssum	*BERTEROA INCANA*	
Hoary beard tongue	*Penstemon canescens*	7
Hoary cinquefoil	*POTENTILLA INCLINATA*	
Hoary cress	*CARDARIA DRABA*	
Hoary fog fruit	*PHYLA CUNEIFOLIA*	
Hoary puccoon	*Lithospermum canescens*	10
Hoary sedge	*Carex canescens s. canescens*	10
Hoary tick trefoil	*Desmodium canescens*	3
Hoary vervain	*Verbena stricta*	4
Hoary willow	*Salix candida*	10
Hog peanut	*Amphicarpaea bracteata v. comosa*	5
Hog peanut	*Amphicarpaea bracteata v. bracteata*	5
Hogwort	*CROTON CAPITATUS* (including 1 variety)	
Hollow Joe Pye weed	*Eupatoriadelphus fistulosus* (= *Eupatorium fistulosum*)	4
Hollyhock	*ALCEA ROSEA*	
Holly-leaved naiad	*NAJAS MARINA*	
Holms' hawthorn	*Crataegus series Coccineae: C. holmsiana*	5
Honesty	*LUNARIA ANNUA*	
Honewort	*Cryptotaenia canadensis*	3
Honey locust	*Gleditsia triacanthos*	1
Hooded ladies' tresses	*Spiranthes romanzoffiana*	10
Hooked buttercup	*Ranunculus recurvatus*	5
Hooked monkshood	*Aconitum uncinatum*	9
Hooker's orchid	*Platanthera hookeri*	10
Hop hornbeam	*Ostrya virginiana*	5
Horned beak rush	*Rhynchospora macrostachya*	10
Horned bladderwort	*Utricularia cornuta*	10
Horned pondweed	*Zannichellia palustris*	6

Table P-1. *continued*

Common Name	Scientific Name[a]	Coefficient[b]
Horse chestnut	*AESCULUS HIPPOCASTANUM*	
Horsemint	*Monarda punctata v. villicaulis*	4
Horse nettle	*Solanum carolinense*	0
Horse radish	*ARMORACIA RUSTICANA*	
Horsetail milkweed	*Asclepias verticillata*	5
Horsetail spike rush	*Eleocharis equisetoides*	10
Horseweed	*Conyza canadensis*	0
Humped bladderwort	*Utricularia gibba*	4
Hungarian brome	*BROMUS INERMIS*	
Hybrid alfalfa	*MEDICAGO x VARIA*	
Hybrid alpine rush	*Juncus x alpiniformis*	4
Hybrid black willow	*Salix x glatfelteri*	4
Hybrid cattail	*TYPHA x GLAUCA*	
Hybrid crack willow	*SALIX x RUBENS*	
Hybrid dwarf birch	*Betula x purpusii*	10
Hybrid fly honeysuckle	*LONICERAx NOTHA*	
Hybrid sumac	*Rhus x pulvinata*	1
Hyssop hedge nettle	*Stachys hyssopifolia*	8
Hyssop-leaved boneset	*Eupatorium hyssopifolium*	2
Ice cream grass	*ERAGROSTIS TRICHODES*	
Illinois bundle flower	*Desmanthus illinoensis*	3
Illinois carrion flower	*Smilax illinoensis*	6
Illinois hawthorn	*Crataegus series Pruinosae: C. prona*	5
Illinois pondweed	*Potamogeton illinoensis*	7
Illinois tick trefoil	*Desmodium illinoense*	5
Illinois wood sorrel	*Oxalis illinoensis*	9
Ill-scented trillium	*TRILLIUM ERECTUM v. ERECTUM*	
Indiana dewberry	*Rubus sec. Flagellares: R. centralis*	5
Indian balsam	*IMPATIENS GLANDULIFERA*	
Indian cucumber root	*Medeola virginiana*	7
Indian grass	*Sorghastrum nutans*	4
Indian heliotrope	*HELIOTROPIUM INDICUM*	
Indian hemp	*Apocynum sibiricum*	2
Indian mustard	*BRASSICA JUNCEA*	
Indian paintbrush	*Castilleja coccinea*	10
Indian physic	*Gillenia stipulata*	6
Indian pink	*Spigelia marilandica*	8
Indian pipe	*Monotropa uniflora*	7
Indian strawberry	*DUCHESNEA INDICA*	
Indian tobacco	*Lobelia inflata*	3
Indian turnip	*Arisaema triphyllum*	4
Indian wood oats	*Chasmanthium latifolium*	4
Inland meadow beauty	*Rhexia mariana v. interior*	2
Inland New Jersey tea	*Ceanothus herbaceus*	10
Inland rush	*Juncus interior*	3
Interior horned beak rush	*Rhynchospora corniculata*	3
Intermediate dogbane	*Apocynum x floribundum*	6
Interrupted fern	*Osmunda claytoniana*	8
Iowa crab	*Malus ioensis*	3
Italian rye grass	*LOLIUM MULTIFLORUM*	
Itch-grass	*ROTTBOELLIA COCHINCHINENSIS*	
Ithaca blackberry	*Rubus sec. Flagellares: R. ithacanus*	5
Ivory sedge	*Carex eburnea*	10
Ivy-leaved morning glory	*IPOMOEA HEDERACEA*	
Ivy-leaved speedwell	*VERONICA HEDERIFOLIA*	
Jack oak	*Quercus imbricaria*	3
Jack pine	*Pinus banksiana*	10
Jacob's ladder	*Polemonium reptans v. reptans*	5
Jagged chickweed	*HOLOSTEUM UMBELLATUM*	
Japanese barberry	*BERBERIS THUNBERGII*	
Japanese chaff flower	*ACHYRANTHES JAPONICA*	
Japanese chess	*BROMUS JAPONICUS*	
Japanese hedge parsley	*TORILIS JAPONICA*	
Japanese honeysuckle	*LONICERA JAPONICA*	
Japanese hops	*HUMULUS JAPONICUS*	
Japanese knotweed	*FALLOPIA JAPONICA*	
Japanese lawn grass	*ZOYSIA JAPONICA*	
Japanese lespedeza	*KUMMEROWIA STRIATA*	
Japanese mazus	*MAZUS PUMILUS*	
Japanese meadowsweet	*SPIRAEA JAPONICA*	
Japanese rose	*KERRIA JAPONICA*	
Japanese rose	*ROSA MULTIFLORA*	
Japanese snowball bush	*VIBURNUM PLICATUM*	
Japanese spindle tree	*EUONYMUS HAMILTONIANA*	
Japanese spurge	*PACHYSANDRA TERMINALIS*	
Jerusalem artichoke	*Helianthus tuberosus*	2
Jerusalem oak	*DYSPHANIA BOTRYS (= CHENOPODIUM BOTRYS)*	
Jesup's horsetail	*Equisetum x mackaii*	10
Jetbead	*RHODOTYPOS SCANDENS*	
Jimsonweed	*DATURA STRAMONIUM*	
Johnny-jump-up	*VIOLA TRICOLOR*	
Johnson grass	*SORGHUM HALEPENSE*	
Jointed goat grass	*AEGILOPS CYLINDRICA*	
Jointed rush	*Juncus articulatus*	4
Joint rush	*Juncus nodosus*	5
Jointweed	*Polygonella articulata*	10
Joliet horsetail	*Equisetum x ferrissii*	2
Juneberry	*Amelanchier arborea*	6
June grass	*Koeleria macrantha*	8
Kalm's St. John's wort	*Hypericum kalmianum*	10
Kankakee mallow	*Iliamna rivularis*	10
Kansas mugwort	*ARTEMISIA CARRUTHII*	
Kellogg's hawthorn	*Crataegus series Molles: C. kelloggii*	5
Kenilworth ivy	*CYMBALARIA MURALIS*	
Kentucky bluegrass	*POA PRATENSIS*	
Kentucky coffee tree	*Gymnocladus dioica*	4
Kentucky wisteria	*Wisteria frutescens*	4
King devil	*HIERACIUM PILOSELLOIDES*	
Kinnickinnick dewberry	*Rubus sec. Flagellares: R. multifer*	5
Kiss-me-over-the-garden-gate	*PERSICARIA ORIENTALE*	
Kitten tails	*Besseya bullii*	8
Knawel	*SCLERANTHUS ANNUUS*	
Knee spike rush	*Eleocharis geniculata*	10
Knobbed hop sedge	*Carex lupuliformis*	10
Knotweed dodder	*Cuscuta polygonorum*	5
Korean clover	*KUMMEROWIA STIPULACEA (= LESPEDEZA STIPULACEA)*	
Kral's sedge	*Carex kraliana*	8
Kudzu	*PUERARIA MONTANA v. LOBATA*	
Lace grass	*Eragrostis capillaris*	5
Lady fern	*Athyrium filix-femina s. angustum*	6
Lady's thumb	*PERSICARIA VULGARIS*	
Lake cress	*Armoracia lacustris*	8
Lake shore rush	*Juncus balticus*	6
Lamb's quarters	*CHENOPODIUM ALBUM v. ALBUM*	
Lance-fruited oval sedge	*Carex scoparia*	4
Lanceleaf ragweed	*AMBROSIA BIDENTATA*	
Lance-leaved buckthorn	*Rhamnus lanceolata* (including 1 subspecies)	4
Lance-leaved burhead	*Echinodorus berteroi*	10
Lance-leaved ground cherry	*Physalis virginiana*	3
Lance-leaved loosestrife	*Lysimachia lanceolata*	7
Lance-leaved violet	*Viola lanceolata*	7
Lance-leaved wild licorice	*Galium lanceolatum*	7
Large buttonweed	*Diodia virginiana*	2
Large cranberry	*Vaccinium macrocarpon*	10
Large flower bellwort	*Uvularia grandiflora*	7
Large-flowered beard tongue	*PENSTEMON GRANDIFLORUS*	
Large-flowered coreopsis	*COREOPSIS GRANDIFLORA v. HARVEYANA*	

Common Name	Scientific Name[a]	Coefficient[b]
Large-flowered evening primrose	OENOTHERA GLAZIOVIANA	
Large-flowered periwinkle	VINCA MAJOR	
Large-fruited star sedge	*Carex echinata*	10
Large houstonia	*Houstonia purpurea* (including 1 variety)	6
Large-leaf waterleaf	*Hydrophyllum macrophyllum*	7
Large-leaved pondweed	*Potamogeton amplifolius*	10
Large-leaved shinleaf	*Pyrola elliptica*	8
Large-leaved storax	*Styrax grandifolia*	10
Large passion flower	*Passiflora incarnata*	4
Large plantain-leaved pussytoes	*Antennaria parlinii s. parlinii*	3
Large plantain-leaved pussytoes	*Antennaria parlinii s. fallax*	3
Large poverty rush	*Juncus anthelatus*	0
Large-seeded mercury	*Acalypha deamii*	5
Large water starwort	*Callitriche heterophylla*	3
Large white trillium	*Trillium grandiflorum*	8
Large-whorled mallow	MALVA VERTICILLATA	
Large yellow fox sedge	*Carex annectens*	3
Large yellow lady's slipper	*Cypripedium parviflorum v. pubescens*	8
Large yellow sedge	*Carex flava*	10
Late alumroot	*Heuchera parviflora* (including 1 variety)	10
Late boneset	*Eupatorium serotinum*	0
Late figwort	*Scrophularia marilandica*	5
Late goldenrod	*Solidago gigantea*	4
Late horse gentian	*Triosteum perfoliatum*	5
Late low blueberry	*Vaccinium pallidum*	5
Late meadow rue	*Thalictrum pubescens*	6
Lawn prunella	PRUNELLA VULGARIS s. VULGARIS	
Lawn water pennywort	HYDROCOTYLE SIBTHORPIOIDES	
Lead-colored stiff sedge	*Carex livida v. grayana*	10
Lead plant	*Amorpha canescens*	9
Leafy phacelia	*Phacelia bipinnatifida*	6
Leafy pondweed	*Potamogeton foliosus*	4
Leafy satin grass	*Muhlenbergia mexicana*	4
Leafy spurge	EUPHORBIA ESULA	
Leafy wool grass	*Scirpus polyphyllus*	10
Least duckweed	*Lemna perpusilla*	10
Leather flower	*Clematis pitcheri*	4
Leatherflower	*Clematis viorna*	8
Leatherleaf	*Chamaedaphne calyculata*	10
Leatherwood	*Dirca palustris*	8
Leek sedge	*Carex prasina*	10
Lemon day lily	HEMEROCALLIS LILIOASPHODELUS	
Lens-podded hoary cress	CARDARIA CHALAPENSIS	
Lentil	LENS CULINARIS	
Lesquereaux's mustard	*Physaria globosa* (= *Lesquerella globosa*)	5
Lesser celandine	RANUNCULUS FICARIA	
Lesser love grass	ERAGROSTIS MINOR	
Lesser salt spurrey	SPERGULARIA SALINA	
Licorice milkvetch	ASTRAGALUS GLYCYPHYLLOS	
Lilac	SYRINGA VULGARIS	
Lilac sage	SALVIA VERTICILLATA	
Lily-of-the-valley	CONVALLARIA MAJALIS	
Limber honeysuckle	*Lonicera dioica* (including 1 variety)	8
Lineless squill	HYACINTHOIDES NONSCRIPTA (= SCILLA NONSCRIPTA)	
Lion's foot	*Prenanthes alba*	5
Lion's tail	CHAITURUS MARRUBIASTRUM (= LEONURUS MARRUBIASTRUM)	
Little barley	*Hordeum pusillum*	0
Little bluestem grass	*Schizachyrium scoparium* (= *Andropogon scoparius*)	4
Little hop clover	TRIFOLIUM DUBIUM	
Little ladies' tresses	*Spiranthes tuberosa*	3
Little-leaf buttercup	*Ranunculus abortivus*	0
Live-forever	HYLOTELEPHIUM TELEPHIUM s. TELEPHIUM	
Lizard's tail	*Saururus cernuus*	4
Log fern	*Dryopteris celsa*	10
Lombardy poplar	POPULUS NIGRA	
Long-awned bracted sedge	*Carex gravida*	5
Long-awned wood grass	*Brachyelytrum erectum*	6
Long-beaked bald rush	*Rhynchospora scirpoides*	10
Long-beaked sedge	*Carex sprengelii*	8
Long-bearded hawkweed	*Hieracium longipilum*	5
Long-bracted spiderwort	*Tradescantia bracteata*	0
Long-bracted tussock sedge	*Carex aquatilis v. substricta*	8
Long-flowered tobacco	NICOTIANA LONGIFLORA	
Long-fruited oval sedge	*Carex albolutescens*	9
Long-headed coneflower	RATIBIDA COLUMNIFERA	
Long-headed poppy	PAPAVER DUBIUM	
Long-leaved ammannia	*Ammannia coccinea*	2
Long-leaved bluets	*Houstonia longifolia*	7
Long-leaved ground cherry	PHYSALIS LONGIFOLIA v. LONGIFOLIA	
Long-leaved panic grass	*Panicum rigidulum s. pubescens*	10
Long-leaved speedwell	VERONICA LONGIFOLIA	
Long's oval sedge	*Carex longii*	5
Long-scaled green sedge	*Carex bushii*	7
Long-scaled manna grass	*Glyceria acutiflora*	10
Long-scaled nut sedge	*Cyperus strigosus*	0
Long-scaled tussock sedge	*Carex haydenii*	8
Long-spurred violet	*Viola rostrata*	8
Long-stalked cranesbill	GERANIUM COLUMBIANUM	
Long-stalked hummock sedge	*Carex pedunculata*	10
Long-stalked panic grass	*Dichanthelium perlongum*	10
Long-stalked starwort	*Stellaria longipes*	10
Long-stoloned oak sedge	*Carex inops s. heliophila*	10
Loogootee dewberry	*Rubus sec. Flagellares: R. griseus*	10
Loose-flowered panic grass	*Dichanthelium laxiflorum*	5
Loose-headed bracted sedge	*Carex sparganioides*	4
Loose-headed oval sedge	*Carex projecta*	7
Loosestrife	*Lysimachia hybrida*	10
Lopseed	*Phryma leptostachya*	4
Lovage	*Ligusticum canadense*	10
Love-in-a-mist	NIGELLA DAMASCENA	
Love-lies-bleeding	AMARANTHUS CRUENTUS	
Low calamint	*Clinopodium arkansanum* (= *Satureja arkansanum*)	10
Low cudweed	GNAPHALIUM ULIGINOSUM	
Low forked chickweed	*Paronychia fastigiata* (including 1 variety)	6
Low hop clover	TRIFOLIUM CAMPESTRE	
Lowland beard tongue	*Penstemon alluviorum*	4
Low nut rush	*Scleria verticillata*	10
Low shadbush	*Amelanchier spicata*	9
Lucretia dewberry	*Rubus sec. Flagellares: R. roribaccus*	5
Lyme grass	LEYMUS ARENARIUS	
Lyre-leaved rockcress	*Arabidopsis lyrata* (= *Arabis lyrata*)	7
Mackay's fragile fern	*Cystopteris tenuis*	10
Mad-dog skullcap	*Scutellaria lateriflora*	4
Maidenhair fern	*Adiantum pedatum*	7
Maidenhair spleenwort	*Asplenium trichomanes*	10
Maltese cross	LYCHNIS CHALCEDONICA	
Manchurian honeysuckle	LONICERA RUPRECHTIANA	
Maple-leaved arrowwood	*Viburnum acerifolium*	8
Maple-leaved goosefoot	*Chenopodium simplex*	3
Mare's tail	*Hippuris vulgaris*	10
Margaret's hawthorn	*Crataegus series Rotundifoliae: C. margaretta*	5

Table P-1. *continued*

Common Name	Scientific Name[a]	Coefficient[b]
Marginal shield fern	*Dryopteris marginalis*	8
Marsh bellflower	*Campanula aparinoides*	8
Marsh blazing star	*Liatris spicata*	8
Marsh bluegrass	*Poa paludigena*	10
Marsh blue violet	*Viola cucullata*	9
Marsh cinquefoil	*Comarum palustre* (= *Potentilla palustris*)	9
Marsh club moss	*Selaginella apoda*	4
Marsh elder	*Iva annua* (including 1 variety)	0
Marsh fleabane	*Erigeron philadelphicus*	3
Marsh hedge nettle	*Stachys tenuifolia v. hispida*	4
Marsh purslane	*Ludwigia palustris*	3
Marsh shield fern	*Thelypteris palustris v. pubescens*	7
Marsh skullcap	*Scutellaria galericulata*	4
Marsh speedwell	*Veronica scutellata*	9
Marsh St. John's wort	*Triadenum tubulosum*	8
Marsh St. John's wort	*Triadenum walteri*	8
Marsh St. John's wort	*Triadenum virginicum*	10
Marsh valerian	*Valeriana uliginosa*	10
Marsh vetchling	*Lathyrus palustris*	7
Marsh wild timothy	*Muhlenbergia glomerata*	10
Marsh yellow cress	*Rorippa palustris s. fernaldiana*	2
Maryland senna	*Senna marilandica*	4
Masterwort	*PEUCEDANUM OSTRUTHIUM*	
Mat panic grass	*Dichanthelium meridionale*	7
Mat sandbur	*Cenchrus longispinus*	0
Matted spike rush	*Eleocharis intermedia*	10
Maximilian's sunflower	*HELIANTHUS MAXIMILIANII*	
May apple	*Podophyllum peltatum*	3
Meadow anemone	*Anemone canadensis*	4
Meadow barley	*HORDEUM BRACHYANTHERUM*	
Meadow beauty	*Rhexia mariana v. mariana*	5
Meadow fescue	*SCHEDONORUS PRATENSIS*	
Meadow foxtail	*ALOPECURUS PRATENSIS*	
Meadowsweet	*Spiraea alba*	4
Meadow willow	*Salix petiolaris*	6
Mead's milkweed	*Asclepias meadii*	10
Mead's stiff sedge	*Carex meadii*	7
Merrybells	*Uvularia sessilifolia*	6
Mexican dock	*Rumex salicifolius v. Mexicanus*	1
Mexican prickly poppy	*ARGEMONE MEXICANA*	
Miami mist	*Phacelia purshii*	3
Michigan lily	*Lilium michiganense*	5
Midland bracted sedge	*Carex mesochorea*	2
Midland sand sedge	*Cyperus x mesochorus*	4
Mild water pepper	*Persicaria hydropiperoides*	3
Milk thistle	*SILYBUM MARIANUM*	
Miniature beefsteak plant	*MOSLA DIANTHERA*	
Minor smartweed	*PERSICARIA MINOR*	
Mississippi milk pea	*Galactia volubilis*	9
Missouri goldenrod	*Solidago missouriensis*	4
Missouri gooseberry	*Ribes missouriense*	3
Missouri goosefoot	*Chenopodium album v. missouriense*	0
Missouri gourd	*CUCURBITA FOETIDISSIMA*	
Missouri ironweed	*Vernonia missurica*	4
Missouri oval sedge	*Carex missouriensis*	10
Missouri small skullcap	*Scutellaria parvula v. missouriensis*	5
Missouri violet	*Viola missouriensis*	3
Mistflower	*Conoclinium coelestinum* (= *Eupatorium coelestinum*)	2
Mistletoe	*Phoradendron leucarpum*	3
Moccasin flower	*Cypripedium acaule*	10
Mockernut hickory	*Carya tomentosa*	6
Monarda	*Monarda bradburiana*	7
Moneywort	*LYSIMACHIA NUMMULARIA*	
Monkey flower	*Mimulus ringens*	4
Moonseed	*Menispermum canadense*	3
Morrow's honeysuckle	*LONICERA MORROWII*	
Moss phlox	*PHLOX SUBULATA s. SUBULATA*	
Moss rose	*PORTULACA GRANDIFLORA*	
Mossy stonecrop	*SEDUM ACRE*	
Motherwort	*LEONURUS CARDIACA*	
Moth mullein	*VERBASCUM BLATTARIA*	
Mountain blue-eyed grass	*Sisyrinchium montanum*	10
Mountain chestnut oak	*Quercus montana*	7
Mountain holly	*Ilex mucronata* (= *Nemopanthus mucronata*)	10
Mountain laurel	*Kalmia latifolia*	10
Mountain mint	*Pycnanthemum pycnanthemoides*	4
Mountain phlox	*Phlox ovata*	9
Mountain spleenwort	*Asplenium montanum*	10
Mountain winter aconite	*ERANTHIS HYEMALIS*	
Mouse-eared cress	*ARABIDOPSIS THALIANA*	
Mouse-eared whitlow cress	*DRABA VERNA*	
Mousetail	*Myosurus minimus*	0
Mousetail fescue	*VULPIA MYUROS*	
Muck sedge	*Carex limosa*	10
Mud plantain	*Heteranthera reniformis*	10
Mugwort	*ARTEMISIA VULGARIS*	
Mulberry weed	*FATOUA VILLOSA*	
Mullein foxglove	*Dasistoma macrophylla*	5
Mullein pink	*LYCHNIS CORONARIA*	
Munro grass	*Panicum rigidulum s. rigidulum*	4
Musk bristle thistle	*CARDUUS NUTANS*	
Musk mallow	*MALVA MOSCHATA*	
Naked-fruited lamb's quarters	*CHENOPODIUM STRICTUM*	
Nannyberry	*Viburnum lentago*	5
Narrow-fruited pinweed	*Lechea racemulosa*	8
Narrow-leaved bluets	*Stenaria nigricans* (= *Hedyotis nigricans*)	9
Narrow-leaved cattail	*TYPHA ANGUSTIFOLIA*	
Narrow-leaved cattail sedge	*Carex squarrosa*	4
Narrow-leaved cotton grass	*Eriophorum angustifolium*	10
Narrow-leaved cow wheat	*Melampyrum lineare v. lineare*	10
Narrow-leaved hawk's beard	*CREPIS TECTORUM*	
Narrow-leaved loosestrife	*Lysimachia quadriflora*	9
Narrow-leaved marsh elder	*IVA ANGUSTIFOLIA*	
Narrow-leaved oval sedge	*Carex tribuloides v. sangamonensis*	5
Narrow-leaved pinweed	*Lechea tenuifolia*	4
Narrow-leaved sundew	*Drosera intermedia*	10
Narrow-leaved sunflower	*Helianthus angustifolius*	10
Narrow-leaved umbrellawort	*MIRABILIS LINEARIS*	
Narrow-leaved Venus's-looking glass	*TRIODANIS LEPTOCARPA*	
Narrow-leaved vervain	*Verbena simplex*	4
Narrow-leaved vetch	*VICIA SATIVA s. NIGRA*	
Narrow-leaved white-top aster	*Sericocarpus linifolius* (= *Aster solidagineus*)	7
Narrow-leaved wild rice	*Zizania palustris* (including 1 variety)	10
Narrow-leaved wood sedge	*Carex digitalis* (including 1 variety)	7
Narrow-leaved woolly sedge	*Carex lasiocarpa s. americana*	10
Narrow melic grass	*Melica mutica*	6
Narrow-racemed blackberry	*Rubus sec. Arguti: R. ablatus*	4
Needle-and-thread	*HESPEROSTIPA COMATA* (= *STIPA COMATA*)	
Needle spike rush	*Eleocharis acicularis*	2
Nelson's horsetail	*Equisetum x nelsonii*	10
Nepalese browntop	*MICROSTEGIUM VIMINEUM*	
Nerveless sand bracted sedge	*Carex muehlenbergii v. enervis*	5
Netted chainfern	*Woodwardia areolata*	6

Common Name	Scientific Name[a]	Coefficient[b]
Netted nut rush	*Scleria reticularis*	10
Nettle-leaved goosefoot	*CHENOPODIUM MURALE*	
New England aster	*Symphyotrichum novae-angliae*	3
New Jersey tea	*Ceanothus americanus*	8
New Mexican love grass	*ERAGROSTIS MEXICANA*	
New York fern	*Thelypteris noveboracensis*	5
Night-flowering catchfly	*SILENE NOCTIFLORA*	
Nimblewill	*Muhlenbergia schreberi*	0
Nippled watermeal	*Wolffia braziliensis*	6
Nits-and-lice	*Hypericum drummondii*	4
Nodding brome	*BROMUS SQUARROSUS*	
Nodding bur marigold	*Bidens cernua*	2
Nodding chickweed	*Cerastium nutans v. nutans*	0
Nodding evening primrose	*Oenothera nutans*	0
Nodding fescue	*Festuca subverticillata*	4
Nodding ladies' tresses	*Spiranthes cernua*	3
Nodding pogonia	*Triphora trianthophora s. trianthophora*	9
Nodding spurge	*Chamaesyce nutans*	0
Nodding star of Bethlehem	*ORNITHOGALUM NUTANS*	
Nodding trillium	*Trillium cernuum*	10
Nodding wild onion	*Allium cernuum*	4
Northern adder's tongue fern	*Ophioglossum pusillum*	10
Northern bedstraw	*Galium boreale*	7
Northern bitter cress	*Cardamine douglassii*	5
Northern blue violet	*Viola nephrophylla*	8
Northern bog orchid	*Platanthera aquilonis*	10
Northern bugleweed	*Lycopus uniflorus*	5
Northern cranesbill	*Geranium bicknellii*	9
Northern dropseed	*Sporobolus heterolepis*	10
Northern gooseberry	*Ribes hirtellum*	10
Northern grape fern	*Botrychium multifidum*	10
Northern manna grass	*Glyceria borealis*	10
Northern panic grass	*Dichanthelium boreale*	10
Northern prairie phlox	*Phlox pilosa s. fulgida*	6
Northern red currant	*RIBES RUBRUM*	
Northern red oak	*Quercus rubra*	4
Northern rush grass	*Sporobolus vaginiflorus*	1
Northern sedge	*Carex arctata*	10
Northern St. John's wort	*Hypericum boreale*	8
Northern tubercled orchid	*Platanthera flava v. herbiola*	7
Northern weak sedge	*Carex debilis v. rudgei*	10
Northern wild comfrey	*Cynoglossum virginianum v. boreale*	10
Northern willow herb	*Epilobium ciliatum*	3
Norway maple	*ACER PLATANOIDES*	
Notched spike rush	*Eleocharis bifida*	10
Nottoway valley brome	*Bromus nottowayanus*	7
Nuttall's poverty weed	*MONOLEPIS NUTTALLIANA*	
Nuttall's tick trefoil	*Desmodium nuttallii*	4
Oakes' evening primrose	*Oenothera oakesiana*	10
Oakes' pondweed	*Potamogeton oakesianus*	10
Oak-leaved goosefoot	*CHENOPODIUM GLAUCUM*	
Oak-leaved hydrangea	*HYDRANGEA QUERCIFOLIA*	
Oak-leaved privet	*LIGUSTRUM OVALIFOLIUM*	
Oats	*AVENA SATIVA*	
Obe-wan-conobea	*Leucospora multifida*	3
Obovate beak grass	*Diarrhena obovata*	5
Ohio buckeye	*Aesculus glabra*	5
Ohio goldenrod	*Solidago ohioensis*	10
Ohio horse mint	*Blephilia ciliata*	7
Oklahoma bracted sedge	*Carex oklahomensis*	5
Old-fashioned wigela	*WEIGELA FLORIDA*	
Old-field balsam	*Pseudognaphalium obtusifolium*	2
Old-field goldenrod	*Solidago nemoralis* (including 1 subspecies)	3
Old field panic grass	*Dichanthelium acuminatum s. implicatum*	2
Old plainsman	*Hymenopappus scabiosaeus*	8
Old witch grass	*Panicum capillare*	0
One-flowered leavenworthia	*Leavenworthia uniflora*	10

Common Name	Scientific Name[a]	Coefficient[b]
Oneida grape fern	*Botrychium oneidense*	9
One-rowed yellowcress	*RORIPPA MICROPHYLLA*	
One-sided shinleaf	*Orthilia secunda* (= *Pyrola secunda*)	10
Ontario aster	*Symphyotrichum ontarionis*	5
Orange coneflower	*Rudbeckia fulgida v. fulgida*	5
Orange day lily	*HEMEROCALLIS FULVA*	
Orange-eyed butterfly bush	*BUDDLEJA DAVIDII*	
Orange-fringed orchid	*Platanthera ciliaris*	9
Orange grass	*Hypericum gentianoides*	4
Orchard grass	*DACTYLIS GLOMERATA*	
Oregano	*ORIGANUM VULGARE*	
Oregon holly grape	*BERBERIS REPENS* (= *MAHONIA REPENS*)	
Oriental bittersweet	*CELASTRUS ORBICULATA*	
Oriental poppy	*PAPAVER ORIENTALE*	
Ostrich fern	*Matteuccia struthiopteris v. pensylvanica*	9
Oval ladies' tresses	*Spiranthes ovalis v. erostellata*	3
Oval spike rush	*Eleocharis ovata*	10
Overcup oak	*Quercus lyrata*	7
Ox-eye daisy	*LEUCANTHEMUM VULGARE* (= *CHRYSANTHEMUM LEUCANTHEMUM*)	
Oyster salsify	*TRAGOPOGON PORRIFOLIUS*	
Ozark ironweed	*VERNONIA ARKANSANA*	
Pagoda dogwood	*Cornus alternifolia*	8
Painted leaf	*Euphorbia cyathophora*	0
Painted sedge	*Carex picta*	7
Pale alyssum	*ALYSSUM ALYSSOIDES*	
Pale avens	*Geum virginianum*	5
Pale beard tongue	*Penstemon pallidus*	5
Pale corydalis	*Corydalis flavula*	3
Pale dock	*Rumex altissimus*	2
Pale dogwood	*Cornus obliqua*	5
Pale duckweed	*Lemna valdiviana*	10
Pale false foxglove	*Agalinis skinneriana*	10
Pale gentian	*Gentiana alba*	10
Pale hickory	*Carya pallida*	10
Pale Indian plantain	*Arnoglossum atriplicifolium* (= *Cacalia atriplicifolia*)	6
Pale leafcup	*Polymnia canadensis*	3
Pale-leaved sunflower	*Helianthus strumosus*	5
Pale manna grass	*Torreyochloa pallida* (= *Glyceria pallida*)	10
Pale narrow-leaved goosefoot	*Chenopodium pallescens*	3
Paleolithic oak	*Quercus x palaeolithicola*	4
Pale poppy mallow	*CALLIRHOË ALCAEODIES*	
Pale purple coneflower	*Echinacea pallida*	10
Pale sedge	*Carex granularis*	2
Pale spiked lobelia	*Lobelia spicata* (including varieties)	7
Pale sunflower	*Helianthus decapetalus*	5
Pale touch-me-not	*Impatiens pallida*	4
Pale umbrellawort	*MIRABILIS ALBIDA*	
Pale vetchling	*Lathyrus ochroleucus*	10
Panicled aster	*Symphyotrichum lanceolatum* (including 2 varieties)	3
Panicled hawkweed	*Hieracium paniculatum*	8
Panicled hydrangea	*HYDRANGEA PANICULATA*	
Panicled screwstem	*Bartonia paniculata*	5
Panicled tick trefoil	*Desmodium paniculatum*	2
Papaw	*Asimina triloba*	6
Paper birch	*Betula papyrifera*	7
Paper mulberry	*BROUSSONETIA PAPYRIFERA*	
Parisian bedstraw	*GALIUM DIVARICATUM*	
Partridge berry	*Mitchella repens*	8
Pasture rose	*Rosa carolina*	4
Pasture thistle	*Cirsium discolor*	3
Path rush	*Juncus tenuis*	0
Patience dock	*RUMEX PATIENTIA*	
Peach	*PRUNUS PERSICA*	

Table P-1. *continued*

Common Name	Scientific Name[a]	Coefficient[b]
Peach-leaved willow	*Salix amygdaloides*	4
Pear	*PYRUS COMMUNIS*	
Pearl yarrow	*ACHILLEA PTARMICA*	
Pearly everlasting	*Anaphalis margaritacea*	3
Pecan	*Carya illinoinensis*	4
Peking cotoneaster	*COTONEASTER ACUTIFOLIA*	
Pencil flower	*Stylosanthes biflora*	5
Pennsylvania bitter cress	*Cardamine pensylvanica*	2
Pennsylvania oak sedge	*Carex pensylvanica*	5
Pennsylvania pellitory	*Parietaria pensylvanica*	1
Pennywort	*Obolaria virginica*	4
Peppermint	*MENTHA x PIPERITA*	
Perennial duckweed	*Lemna turionifera*	3
Perennial foxtail grass	*Setaria parviflora*	2
Perennial rye grass	*LOLIUM PERENNE*	
Perfoliate bellwort	*Uvularia perfoliata*	7
Perfoliate penny cress	*THLASPI PERFOLIATUM*	
Perfumed cherry	*PRUNUS MAHALEB*	
Perplexing tick trefoil	*Desmodium perplexum*	3
Persimmon	*Diospyros virginiana*	2
Peruvian daisy	*GALINSOGA QUADRIRADIATA*	
Peruvian ground cherry	*PHYSALIS PERUVIANA*	
Petioled sunflower	*HELIANTHUS PETIOLARIS*	
Petty spurge	*EUPHORBIA PEPLUS*	
Philadelphia panic grass	*Panicum philadelphicum*	4
Phlox-leaved aster	*Symphyotrichum phlogifolium*	6
Pickerel weed	*Pontederia cordata*	5
Pigeon grass	*SETARIA PUMILA s. PUMILA*	
Pignut hickory	*Carya glabra*	4
Pin cherry	*Prunus pensylvanica*	2
Pineapple weed	*MATRICARIA DISCOIDEA*	
Pinesap	*Monotropa hypopitys*	8
Pink corydalis	*Corydalis sempervirens*	9
Pink-flowered skeleton weed	*LYGODESMIA JUNCEA*	
Pink milkwort	*Polygala incarnata*	5
Pink shinleaf	*Pyrola asarifolia*	10
Pink thoroughwort	*Fleischmannia incarnata* (= *Eupatorium incarnatum*)	5
Pink turtlehead	*Chelone obliqua v. speciosa*	8
Pink valerian	*Valeriana pauciflora*	7
Pinkweed	*Persicaria pensylvanica*	0
Pinnatifid spleenwort	*Asplenium pinnatifidum*	10
Pin oak	*Quercus palustris*	3
Pipes	*Equisetum fluviatile*	10
Pipewort	*Eriocaulon aquaticum*	10
Pipsissewa	*Chimaphila umbellata s. cisatlantica*	10
Pitcher plant	*Sarracenia purpurea s. gibbosa*	10
Pitch pine	*PINUS RIGIDA*	
Pitseed goosefoot	*Chenopodium berlandieri v. bushianum*	0
Pitseed goosefoot	*Chenopodium berlandieri v. macrocalycium*	0
Pitseed goosefoot	*Chenopodium berlandieri v. zschackii*	0
Plains blackberry	*Rubus sec. Arguti: R. laudatus*	5
Plains bluegrass	*POA ARIDA*	
Plains oval sedge	*Carex brevior*	4
Plains three awn grass	*Aristida oligantha*	2
Plait-leaved dewberry	*Rubus sec. Flagellares: R. plicatifolius*	4
Plantain-leaved wood sedge	*Carex plantaginea*	10
Plume grass	*SACCHARUM RAVENNAE*	
Plume poppy	*MACLEAYA CORDATA*	
Poet's narcissus	*NARCISSUS POETICUS*	
Pointed tick trefoil	*Desmodium glutinosum*	6
Poison hemlock	*CONIUM MACULATUM*	
Poison ivy	*Toxicodendron radicans s. radicans*	1
Poison sumac	*Toxicodendron vernix*	10
Poke milkweed	*Asclepias exaltata*	8
Pokeweed	*Phytolacca americana v. americana*	0
Poor Joe	*Plantago aristata*	0
Poor man's weatherglass	*ANAGALLIS ARVENSIS*	
Porcupine grass	*Hesperostipa spartea* (= *Stipa spartea*)	8
Porcupine sedge	*Carex hystericina*	5
Post oak	*Quercus stellata*	5
Potato dwarf dandelion	*Krigia dandelion*	8
Poverty brome	*BROMUS STERILIS*	
Poverty grass	*Aristida dichotoma*	2
Poverty oat grass	*Danthonia spicata*	3
Prairie alumroot	*Heuchera richardsonii*	8
Prairie blazing star	*Liatris pycnostachya*	10
Prairie brome	*Bromus kalmii*	10
Prairie cinquefoil	*Potentilla arguta*	10
Prairie cord grass	*Spartina pectinata*	4
Prairie coreopsis	*Coreopsis palmata*	10
Prairie cup grass	*ERIOCHLOA CONTRACTA*	
Prairie dock	*Silphium terebinthinaceum v. terebinthinaceum*	6
Prairie dodder	*Cuscuta pentagona*	5
Prairie gray sedge	*Carex conoidea*	10
Prairie ground cherry	*PHYSALIS HISPIDA*	
Prairie hummock sedge	*Carex richardsonii*	10
Prairie Indian plantain	*Arnoglossum plantagineum*	10
Prairie lily	*Lilium philadelphicum*	10
Prairie meadow sage	*SALVIA PRATENSIS*	
Prairie milkweed	*Asclepias sullivantii*	8
Prairie obedient plant	*Physostegia virginiana v. arenaria*	5
Prairie panic grass	*Dichanthelium leibergii*	10
Prairie parsley	*Polytaenia nuttallii*	10
Prairie ragwort	*Packera plattensis*	5
Prairie rose	*Rosa setigera* (including 1 variety)	4
Prairie sand reed	*Calamovilfa longifolia v. magna*	9
Prairie satin grass	*Muhlenbergia cuspidata*	10
Prairie star sedge	*Carex interior*	8
Prairie sundrops	*Oenothera pilosella*	4
Prairie sunflower	*Helianthus pauciflorus s. pauciflorus*	4
Prairie switch grass	*Panicum virgatum*	4
Prairie tea	*CROTON MONANTHOGYNUS*	
Prairie violet	*Viola pedatifida*	9
Prairie wedge grass	*Sphenopholis obtusata v. obtusata*	5
Prairie white-fringed orchid	*Platanthera leucophaea*	10
Prairie willow	*Salix humilis* (including 1 variety)	5
Pretty pinweed	*Lechea pulchella*	7
Prickly ash	*Zanthoxylum americanum*	3
Prickly lettuce	*LACTUCA SERRIOLA*	
Prickly sedge	*CAREX SPICATA*	
Prickly sida	*SIDA SPINOSA*	
Prickly sow thistle	*SONCHUS ASPER*	
Prickly wild gooseberry	*Ribes cynosbati*	4
Primrose-leaved violet	*Viola primulifolia*	10
Primrose peerless	*NARCISSUS x MEDIOLUTEUS*	
Princess tree	*PAULOWNIA TOMENTOSA*	
Prostrate amaranth	*AMARANTHUS BLITOIDES*	
Pumpkin ash	*Fraxinus profunda*	8
Puncture vine	*TRIBULUS TERRESTRIS*	
Purple avens	*Geum rivale*	10
Purple bergamot	*MONARDA MEDIA*	
Purple bladderwort	*Utricularia purpurea*	10
Purple chokeberry	*Photinia floribunda* (= *Aronia floribunda*)	8
Purple cliffbrake	*Pellaea atropurpurea*	10
Purple daisy	*Symphyotrichum patens*	6
Purple dead nettle	*LAMIUM PURPUREUM*	

Common Name	Scientific Name[a]	Coefficient[b]
Purple duckweed	*Lemna obscura*	3
Purple flowering raspberry	*Rubus odoratus*	6
Purple-fringed orchid	*Platanthera psycodes*	10
Purple fringeless orchid	*Platanthera peramoena*	4
Purple giant hyssop	*Agastache scrophulariifolia*	4
Purple-headed sneezeweed	*Helenium flexuosum*	3
Purple Joe Pye weed	*Eupatoriadelphus purpureus*	5
Purple loosestrife	*LYTHRUM SALICARIA*	
Purple love grass	*Eragrostis spectabilis*	3
Purple meadow rue	*Thalictrum dasycarpum*	4
Purple milkweed	*Asclepias purpurascens*	7
Purple milkwort	*Polygala polygama*	7
Purple poppy mallow	*CALLIRHOË INVOLUCRATA*	
Purple prairie clover	*Dalea purpurea*	10
Purple rockcress	*Arabis x divaricarpa*	5
Purple rocket	*CHORISPORA TENELLA*	
Purple sandgrass	*Triplasis purpurea*	5
Purple-sheathed graceful sedge	*Carex gracillima*	7
Purplestemmed tickseed	*Bidens connata*	2
Purple twayblade	*Liparis liliifolia*	3
Pursh's tufted bulrush	*Schoenoplectus purshianus* (including 1 variety)	4
Purslane	*PORTULACA OLERACEA*	
Pussytoes	*Antennaria plantaginifolia*	3
Pussy willow	*Salix discolor*	3
Quackgrass	*ELYMUS REPENS* (= *AGROPYRON REPENS*)	
Quaking aspen	*Populus tremuloides*	2
Queen Anne's lace	*DAUCUS CAROTA*	
Queen-of-the-prairie	*Filipendula rubra*	9
Quill oval sedge	*Carex tenera v. echinodes*	8
Rabbit-foot clover	*TRIFOLIUM ARVENSE*	
Raccoon grape	*Ampelopsis cordata*	3
Radish	*RAPHANUS SATIVUS*	
Ragged evening primrose	*Oenothera laciniata*	2
Rag sumpweed	*IVA XANTHIFOLIA*	
Rattlebox	*CROTALARIA SAGITTALIS*	
Rattlesnake chess	*BROMUS BRIZIFORMIS*	
Rattlesnake fern	*Botrychium virginianum*	4
Rattlesnake manna grass	*Glyceria canadensis*	10
Rattlesnake master	*Eryngium yuccifolium*	10
Rattlesnake plantain	*Goodyera pubescens*	5
Rattlesnake weed	*Hieracium venosum*	10
Rayless aster	*BRACHYACTIS CILIATA s. ANGUSTA* (= *ASTER BRACHYACTIS*)	
Rectangular-sinused hedge bindweed	*Calystegia silvatica s. fraterniflora*	1
Recurved blackberry	*Rubus sec. Arguti: R. recurvans*	5
Red ash	*Fraxinus pennsylvanica v. pennsylvanica*	3
Red baneberry	*Actaea rubra*	9
Red-berried elderberry	*Sambucus racemosa v. pubens*	8
Red-brown panic grass	*Dichanthelium acuminatum s. leucothrix*	10
Red buckeye	*AESCULUS PAVIA*	
Red bulrush	*Scirpus pendulus*	2
Red catchfly	*SILENE DIOICA* (= *LYCHNIS DIOICA*)	
Red clover	*TRIFOLIUM PRATENSE*	
Red fescue	*FESTUCA RUBRA*	
Red hawthorn	*Crataegus series Intricatae: C. rubella*	6
Redhead grass	*Potamogeton richardsonii*	10
Red hemp nettle	*GALEOPSIS LADANUM*	
Red maple	*Acer rubrum v. trilobum*	5
Red maple	*Acer rubrum v. rubrum*	5
Red morning glory	*IPOMOEA COCCINEA*	
Red mulberry	*Morus rubra*	4
Red osier dogwood	*Cornus sericea*	4
Red raspberry	*Rubus idaeus v. strigosus*	4

Common Name	Scientific Name[a]	Coefficient[b]
Red-rooted nut sedge	*Cyperus erythrorhizos*	1
Red-rooted spike rush	*Eleocharis erythropoda*	2
Red-seeded dandelion	*TARAXACUM LAEVIGATUM*	
Red soapwort	*SAPONARIA OCYMOIDES*	
Red sprangle top	*Leptochloa panicea s. brachiata*	4
Red-stalked plantain	*Plantago rugelii* (including 1 variety)	0
Redtop	*AGROSTIS GIGANTEA*	
Red trillium	*Trillium recurvatum*	4
Reed bent grass	*Calamagrostis porteri s. insperata*	10
Reed canary grass	*PHALARIS ARUNDINACEA*	
Reed manna grass	*Glyceria grandis*	5
Regal fern	*Osmunda regalis v. spectabilis*	8
Reversed clover	*TRIFOLIUM RESUPINATUM*	
Rhubarb	*RHEUM RHABARBICUM*	
Ribbon-leaved pondweed	*Potamogeton epihydrus*	10
Rice cut grass	*Leersia oryzoides*	2
Richardson's rush	*Juncus alpinoarticulatus*	6
Riddell's goldenrod	*Solidago riddellii*	9
Rigid goldenrod	*Solidago rigida* (including 1 subspecies)	7
Ringed panic grass	*Dichanthelium annulum*	10
Riverbank grape	*Vitis riparia*	1
Riverbank tussock sedge	*Carex emoryi*	7
Riverbank wild rye	*Elymus riparius*	5
River birch	*Betula nigra*	2
River bulrush	*Bolboschoenus fluviatilis* (= *Scirpus fluviatilis*)	4
Roadside penny cress	*THLASPI ALLIACEUM*	
Robin's plantain	*Erigeron pulchellus*	8
Rock elm	*Ulmus thomasii*	10
Rocket larkspur	*CONSOLIDA AJACIS* (= *DELPHINIUM AJACIS*)	
Rock goldenrod	*Solidago rupestris*	10
Rock jasmine	*Androsace occidentalis*	4
Rockrose	*Helianthemum bicknellii*	7
Rock sandwort	*Minuartia michauxii* (= *Arenaria stricta*)	10
Rock satin grass	*Muhlenbergia sobolifera*	5
Rock selaginella	*Selaginella rupestris*	10
Rock skullcap	*Scutellaria saxatilis*	10
Rockspray cotoneaster	*COTONEASTER HORIZONTALIS*	
Rocky Mountain beeplant	*CLEOME SERRULATA*	
Rocky Mountain locust	*ROBINIA NEOMEXICANA*	
Rocky Mountain sage	*SALVIA REFLEXA*	
Rocky stonecrop	*SEDUM REFLEXUM*	
Rope dodder	*Cuscuta glomerata*	8
Rose blackberry	*Rubus sec. Allegheniensis: R. rosa*	5
Rose gentian	*Sabatia angularis*	3
Rose-of-Sharon	*HIBISCUS SYRIACUS*	
Rose pogonia	*Pogonia ophioglossoides*	10
Rosette goldenrod	*Solidago squarrosa*	10
Rose verbena	*GLANDULARIA CANADENSIS*	
Rosin weed	*Silphium integrifolium v. integrifolium*	7
Rosin weed	*Silphium asteriscus v. trifoliatum*	8
Rough avens	*Geum laciniatum* (including 1 variety)	3
Rough barnyard grass	*Echinochloa muricata* (including 1 variety)	1
Rough bedstraw	*Galium asprellum*	7
Rough bent grass	*Agrostis scabra*	5
Rough blazing star	*Liatris aspera* (including 1 variety)	8
Rough bluegrass	*POA TRIVIALIS*	
Rough buttercup	*Ranunculus hispidus v. hispidus*	7

Table P-1. *continued*

Common Name	Scientific Name[a]	Coefficient[b]
Rough cinquefoil	*Potentilla norvegica* (including 1 subspecies)	0
Rough clustered sedge	*Carex cephaloidea*	6
Rough dropseed	*Sporobolus compositus*	1
Rough forget-me-not	*MYOSOTIS ARVENSIS*	
Rough goldenrod	*Solidago rugosa* (including 1 variety)	6
Rough hawkweed	*Hieracium scabrum*	5
Rough hedge nettle	*Stachys aspera*	0
Rough-leaved dogwood	*Cornus drummondii*	2
Rough-leaved goldenrod	*Solidago patula*	8
Rough-leaved rice grass	*Oryzopsis asperifolia*	10
Rough marbleseed	*Onosmodium molle s. hispidissimum*	2
Rough Mexican clover	*RICHARDIA SCABRA*	
Rough pennyroyal	*Hedeoma hispida*	2
Rough pigweed	*AMARANTHUS RETROFLEXUS*	
Rough rush grass	*Sporobolus clandestinus*	5
Rough sand sedge	*Cyperus schweinitzii*	5
Rough sedge	*Carex scabrata*	10
Rough water horehound	*LYCOPUS ASPER*	
Rough water milfoil	*Myriophyllum pinnatum*	10
Rough white lettuce	*Prenanthes aspera*	9
Round-fruited hedge hyssop	*Gratiola virginiana*	4
Round-fruited panic grass	*Dichanthelium sphaerocarpon*	5
Round-fruited St. John's wort	*Hypericum sphaerocarpum*	7
Round-headed bush clover	*Lespedeza capitata*	4
Round-headed rush	*Juncus scirpoides*	9
Round-leaved dogwood	*Cornus rugosa*	10
Round-leaved hepatica	*Anemone americana* (= *Hepatica americana*)	8
Round-leaved orchid	*Platanthera orbiculata*	10
Round-leaved ragwort	*Packera obovata*	7
Round-leaved serviceberry	*Amelanchier sanguinea*	10
Round-leaved shinleaf	*Pyrola americana*	8
Round-leaved spurge	*Chamaesyce serpens*	0
Round-leaved sundew	*Drosera rotundifolia*	9
Round-leaved thoroughwort	*Eupatorium rotundifolium*	2
Round-leaved tick trefoil	*Desmodium rotundifolium*	5
Round-leaved woolly croton	*CROTON LINDHEIMERIANUS*	
Round-stemmed false foxglove	*Agalinis gattingeri*	7
Royal catchfly	*Silene regia*	6
Rue anemone	*Thalictrum thalictroides*	7
Running bog sedge	*Carex oligosperma*	10
Running buffalo clover	*Trifolium stoloniferum*	3
Running ground pine	*Lycopodium clavatum*	4
Running marsh sedge	*Carex sartwellii*	7
Running savanna sedge	*Carex siccata*	8
Running strawberry bush	*Euonymus obovata*	7
Rush aster	*Symphyotrichum boreale* (= *Aster borealis*)	10
Rushfoil	*Croton willdenowii*	4
Russian knapweed	*ACROPTILON REPENS* (= *CENTAUREA REPENS*)	
Russian olive	*ELAEAGNUS ANGUSTIFOLIA*	
Russian thistle	*SALSOLA TRAGUS*	
Rusty cotton grass	*Eriophorum virginicum*	10
Rusty nannyberry	*Viburnum rufidulum*	8
Rye	*SECALE CEREALE*	
Rye brome	*BROMUS SECALINUS*	
Salad burnet	*SANGUISORBA MINOR*	
Saltmarsh rush	*JUNCUS GERARDII*	
Salt meadow grass	*Leptochloa panicoides*	10
Sampson's snakeroot	*Orbexilum pedunculatum*	7
Sandbar love grass	*Eragrostis frankii*	2
Sandbar willow	*Salix interior*	1
Sand bluestem grass	*ANDROPOGON HALLII*	
Sand chickweed	*STELLARIA MEDIA s. PALLIDA*	
Sand coreopsis	*Coreopsis lanceolata*	5
Sand croton	*Croton glandulosus v. septentrionalis*	0
Sand dropseed	*Sporobolus cryptandrus*	4
Sand goat's beard	*TRAGOPOGON DUBIUS*	
Sand grape	*Vitis rupestris*	10
Sand lily	*MENTZELIA DECAPETALA*	
Sand milkweed	*Asclepias amplexicaulis*	7
Sand panic grass	*Dichanthelium acuminatum s. spretum*	10
Sand prairie phlox	*Phlox pilosa s. pilosa*	6
Sand primrose	*Oenothera clelandii*	4
Sand rocket	*DIPLOTAXIS TENUIFOLIA*	
Sand spurrey	*SPERGULARIA RUBRA*	
Sand St. John's wort	*Hypericum majus*	6
Sand violet	*Viola sagittata v. ovata*	6
Sassafras	*Sassafras albidum*	1
Satin-flowered sand spurrey	*SPERGULARIA MARITIMA*	
Savanna blazing star	*Liatris scariosa v. nieuwlandii*	9
Saw-toothed buckthorn	*RHAMNUS ARGUTUS v. VELUTINA*	
Saw-toothed oak	*QUERCUS ACUTISSIMA*	
Sawtooth sunflower	*Helianthus grosseserratus*	3
Scaly mild water pepper	*Persicaria opelousana*	10
Scarlet bedstraw	*GAURA COCCINEA*	
Scarlet bee-balm	*MONARDA DIDYMA*	
Scarlet loosestrife	*Ammannia robusta*	2
Scarlet oak	*Quercus coccinea*	7
Scentless chamomile	*TRIPLEUROSPERMUM PERFORATA*	
Scentless mock orange	*PHILADELPHUS INODORUS*	
Scorpion grass	*Myosotis macrosperma*	2
Scotch cotton thistle	*ONOPORDUM ACANTHIUM*	
Scotch pine	*PINUS SYLVESTRIS*	
Scotch rose	*ROSA SPINOSISSIMA*	
Scott's spleenwort	*Asplenium x ebenoides*	10
Scratch grass	*MUHLENBERGIA ASPERIFOLIA*	
Scribner's panic grass	*Dichanthelium oligosanthes v. scribnerianum*	6
Scrub pine	*Pinus virginiana*	5
Scurfy pea	*Psoralidium tenuiflorum* (= *Psoralea tenuiflora*)	10
Sea blite	*SUAEDA CALCEOLIFORMIS*	
Seaside goldenrod	*SOLIDAGO SEMPERVIRENS*	
Seaside spurge	*Chamaesyce polygonifolia*	10
Seedbox	*Ludwigia alternifolia*	3
Self heal	*Prunella vulgaris s. lanceolata*	1
Seneca snakeroot	*Polygala senega*	8
Sensitive fern	*Onoclea sensibilis*	4
Sessile-flowered cress	*Rorippa sessiliflora*	3
Sessile-leaved tick trefoil	*Desmodium sessilifolium*	6
Sessile trillium	*Trillium sessile*	4
Sessile water horehound	*Lycopus amplectens*	10
Shadbush	*Amelanchier interior*	8
Shadbush	*Amelanchier laevis*	8
Shagbark hickory	*Carya ovata*	4
Sharp-fruited rush	*Juncus acuminatus*	4
Sharp-lobed hepatica	*Anemone acutiloba* (= *Hepatica acutiloba*)	8
Sharp-scaled oak sedge	*Carex albicans v. emmonsii*	5
Sheep fescue	*FESTUCA TRACHYPHYLLA*	
Shepherd's cress	*TEESDALIA NUDICAULIS*	
Shepherd's purse	*CAPSELLA BURSA-PASTORIS*	
Sheviak's yellow lady's slipper	*Cypripedium parviflorum v. makasin*	10
Shining aster	*Symphyotrichum firmum*	4
Shining bedstraw	*Galium concinnum*	5
Shining-branched hawthorn	*Crataegus series Coccineae: C. coruscа*	5
Shining bur sedge	*Carex intumescens*	8
Shining clubmoss	*Huperzia lucidula* (= *Lycopodium lucidulum*)	5

Common Name	Scientific Name[a]	Coefficient[b]
Shining flat sedge	*Cyperus bipartitus*	3
Shining panic grass	*Dichanthelium lucidum*	10
Shining wedge grass	*Sphenopholis nitida*	8
Shining willow	*Salix lucida*	10
Shoestring fern	*Vittaria appalachiana*	10
Shooting star	*Dodecatheon meadia*	7
Shore St. John's wort	*Hypericum adpressum*	10
Short-beaked arrowleaf	*Sagittaria brevirostra*	3
Short-beaked bald rush	*Rhynchospora nitens*	10
Short-fruited rush	*Juncus brachycarpus*	4
Short-fruited whitlow grass	*Draba brachycarpa*	2
Short-headed bracted sedge	*Carex cephalophora*	3
Short-headed rush	*Juncus brachycephalus*	7
Short-horned rice grass	*Piptatherum pungens* (= *Oryzopsis pungens*)	10
Short-leaved satin grass	*Muhlenbergia bushii*	6
Short-pedicelled chickweed	*CERASTIUM NUTANS v. BRACHYPODUM*	
Short-pointed flat sedge	*Cyperus acuminatus*	2
Short's aster	*Symphyotrichum shortii*	6
Short-scaled green sedge	*Carex caroliniana*	7
Short's goldenrod	*Solidago shortii*	10
Short's sedge	*Carex shortiana*	3
Short's streambank chervil	*Chaerophyllum procumbens v. shortii*	10
Short-stalked bedstraw	*Galium brevipes*	10
Showy annual stonecrop	*HYLOTELEPHIUM SPECTABILE*	
Showy beard tongue	*PENSTEMON COBAEA v. PURPUREUS*	
Showy centaury	*CENTAURIUM PULCHELLUM*	
Showy evening primrose	*OENOTHERA SPECIOSA*	
Showy fly honeysuckle	*LONICERA x BELLA*	
Showy goldenrod	*Solidago speciosa* (including 1 variety)	7
Showy lady's slipper	*Cypripedium reginae*	10
Showy obedient plant	*Physostegia virginiana v. speciosa*	5
Showy orchis	*Galearis spectabilis* (= *Orchis spectabilis*)	7
Showy ragged evening primrose	*OENOTHERA GRANDIS*	
Showy tick trefoil	*Desmodium canadense*	3
Shrubby bush clover	*LESPEDEZA THUNBERGII*	
Shrubby cinquefoil	*Dasiphora fruticosa s. floribunda* (= *Potentilla fruticosa*)	9
Shrubby St. John's wort	*Hypericum dolabriforme*	10
Shrubby St. John's wort	*Hypericum prolificum*	4
Shrubby sundrops	*Oenothera fruticosa*	10
Shumard's oak	*Quercus shumardii v. shumardii*	7
Shumard's oak	*Quercus shumardii v. schneckii*	7
Siberian elm	*ULMUS PUMILA*	
Siberian squill	*SCILLA SIBIRICA*	
Sicklepod	*Arabis canadensis*	6
Side-flowering aster	*Symphyotrichum lateriflorum* (including 1 variety)	3
Side-flowering rush	*Juncus secundus*	3
Side-oats grama	*Bouteloua curtipendula*	7
Silk tree	*ALBIZIA JULIBRISSIN*	
Silky aster	*Symphyotrichum sericeum*	10
Silky bent grass	*APERA INTERRUPTA*	
Silky bush clover	*LESPEDEZA CUNEATA*	
Silky dogwood	*Cornus amomum*	10
Silky wild rye	*Elymus villosus* (including 1 variety)	4
Silky willow	*Salix sericea*	6
Silver bluestem	*Andropogon ternarius*	3
Silver hair grass	*AIRA CARYOPHYLLAEA*	
Silver-leaved nightshade	*SOLANUM ELAEAGNIFOLIUM*	
Silver maple	*Acer saccharinum*	1
Silver plume grass	*Saccharum alopecuroides*	3
Silverrod	*Solidago bicolor*	8
Silverweed	*Argentina anserina* (= *Potentilla anserina*)	4
Silvery cinquefoil	*POTENTILLA ARGENTEA*	
Silvery spleenwort	*Deparia acrostichoides* (= *Athyrium thelypterioides*)	8
Six-sided stonecrop	*SEDUM SEXANGULARE*	
Six-weeks fescue	*Vulpia octoflora* (including 1 variety)	1
Skeleton weed	*CHONDRILLA JUNCEA*	
Skunk cabbage	*Symplocarpus foetidus*	8
Sky-blue aster	*Symphyotrichum oolentangiense*	8
Sleepy catchfly	*Silene antirrhina*	0
Slender beard tongue	*PENSTEMON GRACILIS v. WISCONSINENSIS*	
Slender bog arrow grass	*Triglochin palustris*	10
Slender bracken fern	*Pteridium aquilinum v. pseudocaudatum*	10
Slender bush clover	*Lespedeza virginica*	4
Slender corydalis	*CORYDALIS MICRANTHA*	
Slender cotton grass	*Eriophorum gracile*	10
Slender crabgrass	*Digitaria filiformis*	10
Slender false foxglove	*Agalinis tenuifolia* (includes 2 varieties)	4
Slender false pimpernel	*Lindernia dubia v. anagallidea*	3
Slender gaura	*Gaura filipes*	10
Slender green sedge	*Carex virescens*	8
Slender heliotrope	*Heliotropium tenellum*	10
Slender knotweed	*Polygonum tenue*	4
Slender ladies' tresses	*Spiranthes lacera v. lacera*	10
Slender ladies' tresses	*Spiranthes lacera v. gracilis*	3
Slender-leaf collomia	*COLLOMIA LINEARIS*	
Slender-leaved goldenrod	*Euthamia caroliniana*	10
Slender-leaved panic grass	*Dichanthelium linearifolium*	7
Slender milkwort	*Polygala ambigua*	4
Slender mountain mint	*Pycnanthemum tenuifolium*	4
Slender naiad	*Najas gracillima*	10
Slender oval sedge	*Carex tenera v. tenera*	8
Slender panic grass	*Panicum flexile*	5
Slender sand sedge	*Cyperus lupulinus s. lupulinus*	4
Slender sandwort	*Minuartia patula* (= *Arenaria patula*)	10
Slender satin grass	*Muhlenbergia tenuiflora*	7
Slender sedge	*Carex leptalea*	8
Slender spike rush	*Eleocharis tenuis v. verrucosa*	5
Slender spike rush	*Eleocharis tenuis v. pseudoptera*	5
Slender three-awn grass	*Aristida ramosissima*	5
Slender three-seeded mercury	*Acalypha gracilens*	3
Slender toothwort	*Cardamine angustata*	5
Slender water milfoil	*Myriophyllum tenellum*	10
Slender waterweed	*Elodea nuttallii*	4
Slender wedge grass	*Sphenopholis obtusata v. major*	3
Slender wheat grass	*Elymus trachycaulus s. trachycaulus*	8
Slender wood sedge	*Carex gracilescens*	5
Slender yellow flax	*Linum virginianum*	4
Slimpod rush	*Juncus diffusissimus*	4
Slippery elm	*Ulmus rubra*	3
Small bedstraw	*Galium trifidum*	8
Small bladderwort	*Utricularia minor*	10
Small bluets	*HOUSTONIA PUSILLA*	
Small bugseed	*Corispermum americanum*	3
Small burhead	*Echinodorus tenellus*	10
Small carp grass	*ARTHRAXON HISPIDUS*	
Small clubmoss	*Selaginella eclipes*	10
Small cranberry	*Vaccinium oxycoccos*	10
Small duckweed	*Lemna minor*	3
Small enchanter's nightshade	*Circaea alpina*	10

Table P-1. *continued*

Common Name	Scientific Name[a]	Coefficient[b]
Small-flowered bitter cress	*Cardamine parviflora v. arenicola*	2
Small-flowered coneflower	*Rudbeckia fulgida v. umbrosa*	10
Small-flowered crowfoot	*Ranunculus micranthus*	4
Small-flowered evening primrose	*Oenothera parviflora*	2
Small-flowered forget-me-not	*MYOSOTIS STRICTA*	
Small-flowered gaura	*GAURA MOLLIS*	
Small-flowered half-chaff sedge	*Lipocarpha micrantha*	3
Small-flowered sweetbrier	*ROSA MICRANTHA*	
Small-flowered yellow wood sorrel	*Oxalis fontana* (including 1 variety)	0
Small forget-me-not	*Myosotis laxa*	10
Small-fringed gentian	*Gentianopsis virgata*	8
Small-fruited blue violet	*Viola hirsutula*	10
Small-fruited false flax	*CAMELINA MICROCARPA*	
Small-fruited panic grass	*Dichanthelium polyanthes*	5
Small-fruited panic grass	*Dichanthelium dichotomum s. microcarpon*	4
Small geranium	*GERANIUM PUSILLUM*	
Small green foxtail grass	*SETARIA VIRIDIS v. VIRIDIS*	
Small green wood orchid	*Platanthera clavellata*	9
Small horse gentian	*Triosteum angustifolium*	6
Small love grass	*Eragrostis pectinacea*	0
Small morning glory	*Ipomoea lacunosa*	2
Small mouse-ear chickweed	*CERASTIUM SEMIDECANDRUM*	
Small passion flower	*Passiflora lutea*	7
Small pepper cress	*LEPIDIUM DENSIFLORUM*	
Small pinweed	*Lechea minor*	8
Small plantain	*Plantago pusilla*	2
Small pondweed	*Potamogeton pusillus s. pusillus*	4
Small pussytoes	*Antennaria howellii s. canadensis*	3
Small pussytoes	*Antennaria howellii s. neodioica*	3
Small rush grass	*Sporobolus neglectus*	1
Small scouring rush	*Equisetum variegatum*	10
Small skullcap	*Scutellaria parvula v. parvula*	5
Small Solomon's seal	*Polygonatum biflorum*	4
Small spearwort	*Ranunculus pusillus*	9
Small spike rush	*Eleocharis parvula*	10
Small's ragwort	*Packera anonyma* (= *Senecio anonymus*)	2
Small's snakeroot	*Sanicula smallii*	10
Small sundrops	*Oenothera perennis*	5
Small white aster	*Symphyotrichum racemosum*	4
Small wild bean	*Strophostyles leiosperma*	4
Small wood sunflower	*Helianthus microcephalus*	8
Small wormseed mustard	*ERYSIMUM INCONSPICUUM*	
Small yellow flax	*Linum medium v. texanum*	4
Small yellow sedge	*Carex cryptolepis*	10
Smartweed	*Persicaria punctata*	3
Smith's tufted bulrush	*Schoenoplectus smithii* (including 1 variety)	5
Smooth arrowwood	*VIBURNUM RECOGNITUM*	
Smooth beard tongue	*Penstemon calycosus*	4
Smooth blue aster	*Symphyotrichum laeve*	10
Smooth bracted tick trefoil	*Desmodium cuspidatum v. cuspidatum*	6
Smooth buttonweed	*Spermacoce glabra*	3
Smooth chess	*BROMUS RACEMOSUS*	
Smooth cliffbrake	*Pellaea glabella*	10
Smooth clustered sedge	*Carex aggregata*	2
Smooth crabgrass	*DIGITARIA ISCHAEMUM*	
Smooth creeping spurge	*Chamaesyce glyptosperma*	2
Smooth false foxglove	*Aureolaria flava* (including 1 variety)	7
Smooth field sow thistle	*SONCHUS ARVENSIS s. ULIGINOSUS*	
Smooth-flowered wild rye	*Elymus glabriflorus* (including 1 variety)	3
Smooth forked aster	*Eurybia schreberi*	10
Smooth-fruited oak sedge	*Carex tonsa v. tonsa*	9
Smooth gaura	*STENOSIPHON LINIFOLIUS*	
Smooth ground cherry	*Physalis longifolia v. subglabrata*	0
Smooth lens grass	*Paspalum laeve*	2
Smooth Peruvian daisy	*GALINSOGA PARVIFLORA*	
Smooth phlox	*Phlox glaberrima* (including subspecies)	5
Smooth pigweed	*AMARANTHUS POWELLII*	
Smooth purslane speedwell	*Veronica peregrina s. peregrina*	0
Smooth rockcress	*Arabis laevigata*	5
Smooth ruellia	*Ruellia strepens*	4
Smooth sand sedge	*Cyperus houghtonii*	4
Smooth satin grass	*Muhlenbergia glabriflora*	8
Smooth scaleseed	*SPERMOLEPIS INERMIS*	
Smooth scouring rush	*Equisetum laevigatum*	2
Smooth-seeded nut rush	*Scleria oligantha*	10
Smooth-sheathed fox sedge	*Carex laevivaginata*	7
Smooth sumac	*Rhus glabra*	1
Smooth swamp buttercup	*Ranunculus hispidus v. nitidus*	5
Smooth tick trefoil	*Desmodium glabellum*	3
Smooth wafer ash	*Ptelea trifoliata v. trifoliata*	4
Smooth white aster	*Symphyotrichum pilosum v. pringlei*	5
Smooth white goldenrod	*Solidago erecta*	8
Smooth white violet	*Viola pallens*	10
Smooth white violet	*Viola blanda*	8
Smooth wild licorice	*Galium circaezans v. circaezans*	7
Smooth woolly panic grass	*Dichanthelium acuminatum s. lindheimeri*	5
Snailseed	*Cocculus carolinus*	6
Snailseed pondweed	*Potamogeton bicupulatus*	10
Snowdrop	*GALANTHUS NIVALIS*	
Snowflake	*LEUCOJUM AESTIVUM*	
Snow-on-the-mountain	*EUPHORBIA MARGINATA*	
Snow trillium	*Trillium nivale*	8
Snowy catchfly	*Silene nivea*	7
Soapwort gentian	*Gentiana saponaria*	6
Soft agrimony	*Agrimonia pubescens*	5
Soft chess	*BROMUS HORDEACEUS*	
Soldier rush	*Juncus militaris*	10
Solid-stemmed burnet saxifrage	*PIMPINELLA SAXIFRAGA*	
Solitary cat's foot	*Antennaria solitaria*	10
Sorghum	*SORGHUM BICOLOR*	
Soulard's crab-apple	*MALUS SOULARDII*	
Sour cherry	*PRUNUS CERASUS*	
Sourwood	*Oxydendron arboreum*	8
Southern adder's tongue fern	*Ophioglossum vulgatum*	4
Southern arrowleaf	*Sagittaria australis*	5
Southern arrowwood	*Viburnum dentatum*	6
Southern blazing star	*Liatris squarrulosa*	9
Southern blue flag	*Iris virginica*	5
Southern broom rape	*Orobanche ludoviciana*	4
Southern buckthorn	*Sideroxylon lycioides* (= *Bumelia lycioides*)	10
Southern hop sedge	*Carex louisianica*	8
Southern lady fern	*Athyrium filix-femina s. asplenioides*	6
Southern lake sedge	*Carex hyalinolepis*	3
Southern naiad	*Najas guadalupensis* (including 1 subspecies)	5
Southern red oak	*Quercus falcata*	5
Southern small skullcap	*Scutellaria parvula v. australis*	5
Southern tubercled orchid	*Platanthera flava v. flava*	7
Southern yellow flax	*Linum intercursum*	10
Soybean	*GLYCINE MAX*	
Spanish needles	*Bidens bipinnata*	0
Sparse-lobed grape fern	*Botrychium biternatum*	4
Spatterdock	*Nuphar advena*	6

Common Name	Scientific Name[a]	Coefficient[b]
Spear grass	*Poa chapmaniana*	0
Spearmint	*MENTHA SPICATA*	
Spearwort	*Ranunculus laxicaulis*	6
Spearwort	*Ranunculus ambigens*	10
Speckled alder	*Alnus incana s. rugosa*	9
Spider brake	*PTERIS MULTIFIDA*	
Spider flower	*CLEOME HASSLERIANA*	
Spider lily	*Hymenocallis occidentalis*	9
Spiked water milfoil	*Myriophyllum sibiricum*	7
Spinulose wood fern	*Dryopteris carthusiana*	6
Spiny cocklebur	*XANTHIUM SPINOSUM*	
Spiny coontail	*Ceratophyllum echinatum*	10
Spiny pigweed	*AMARANTHUS SPINOSUS*	
Spotted cat's ear	*HYPOCHAERIS RADICATA*	
Spotted coralroot	*Corallorhiza maculata* (including 1 variety)	7
Spotted creeping spurge	*Chamaesyce maculata*	0
Spotted Joe Pye weed	*Eupatoriadelphus maculatus*	5
Spotted knapweed	*CENTAUREA STOEBE s. MICRANTHOS*	
Spotted pondweed	*Potamogeton pulcher*	10
Spotted St. John's wort	*Hypericum punctatum*	3
Spotted touch-me-not	*Impatiens capensis*	2
Spotted watermeal	*Wolffia borealis*	4
Spotted wintergreen	*Chimaphila maculata*	4
Spreading dogbane	*Apocynum androsaemifolium*	6
Spreading oval sedge	*Carex normalis*	3
Spreading rockcress	*Arabis patens*	10
Spreading sedge	*Carex laxiculmis v. copulata*	5
Spreading spurge	*Chamaesyce humistrata*	0
Spreading star thistle	*CENTAUREA DIFFUSA*	
Spreading tick trefoil	*Desmodium humifusum*	10
Spring avens	*Geum vernum*	1
Spring beauty	*Claytonia virginica*	2
Spring coralroot	*Corallorhiza wisteriana*	6
Spring ladies' tresses	*Spiranthes vernalis*	3
Spring speedwell	*VERONICA VERNA*	
Spurred butterfly-pea	*CENTROSEMA VIRGINIANUM*	
Squirrel corn	*Dicentra canadensis*	7
Squirrel-tail grass	*HORDEUM JUBATUM*	
St. Andrew's cross	*Hypericum hypericoides s. multicaule*	4
Staghorn sumac	*Rhus typhina*	2
Stalked dodder	*Cuscuta cuspidata*	10
Stalked great chickweed	*Stellaria corei*	9
Stalked hawthorn	*Crataegus series Coccineae: C. pedicellata*	7
Stalked water horehound	*Lycopus rubellus*	8
Stalked wool grass	*Scirpus pedicellatus*	7
Stalk-fruited panic grass	*Panicum rigidulum s. elongatum*	4
Standing cypress	*IPOMOPSIS RUBRA*	
Star cleft phlox	*Phlox bifida s. stellaria*	9
Starflower	*Trientalis borealis*	10
Starry campion	*Silene stellata*	5
Starry false Solomon's seal	*Maianthemum stellatum* (= *Smilacina stellatum*)	6
Starry rosinweed	*SILPHIUM ASTERISCUS v. ASTERISCUS*	
Star tickseed	*COREOPSIS PUBESCENS*	
Starved panic grass	*Dichanthelium depauperatum*	6
Starwort	*STELLARIA GRAMINEA*	
Steele's dewberry	*Rubus sec. Flagellares: R. steelei*	5
Stickseed	*Hackelia virginiana*	0
Stiff arrowhead	*Sagittaria rigida*	10
Stiff aster	*Solidago ptarmicoides*	10
Stiff bedstraw	*Galium tinctorium*	6
Stiff dogwood	*Cornus foemina*	5
Stiff gentian	*Gentianella quinquefolia s. occidentalis*	5
Stiff pondweed	*Potamogeton strictifolius*	10
Stiff sunflower	*Helianthus pauciflorus s. subrhomboideus*	4
Stiff tick trefoil	*Desmodium obtusum*	3
Stiff yellow flax	*Linum striatum*	5
Stink grass	*ERAGROSTIS CILIANENSIS*	
Stinking goosefoot	*CHENOPODIUM VULVARIA*	
Stitchwort	*Stellaria longifolia*	7
Storksbill	*ERODIUM CICUTARIUM*	
Stout blue-eyed grass	*Sisyrinchium angustifolium*	3
Stout rush	*Juncus nodatus*	7
Straight-styled bracted sedge	*Carex radiata*	4
Strawberry blite	*Chenopodium capitatum*	5
Strawberry bush	*Euonymus americana*	8
Strawberry tomato	*Physalis grisea*	4
Straw oval sedge	*Carex suberecta*	5
Streambank hedge nettle	*Stachys tenuifolia v. tenuifolia*	4
Striped toadflax	*LINARIA REPENS*	
Stueve's bush clover	*Lespedeza stuevei*	10
Sugarberry	*Celtis laevigata*	7
Sugar hawthorn	*Crataegus series Macracanthae: C. calpodendron*	7
Sugar maple	*Acer saccharum* (includes 2 subspecies)	4
Sulfur cinquefoil	*POTENTILLA RECTA*	
Sullivant's coolwort	*Sullivantia sullivantii*	10
Sullivant's orange coneflower	*Rudbeckia fulgida v. sullivantii*	8
Summer grape	*Vitis aestivalis* (including 1 variety)	4
Summer savory	*SATUREJA HORTENSIS*	
Sunshine rose	*Rosa arkansana v. suffulta*	4
Superb lily	*Lilium superbum*	8
Swamp agrimony	*Agrimonia parviflora*	4
Swamp bead grass	*Paspalum repens*	7
Swamp beggar's ticks	*Bidens discoidea*	5
Swamp candles	*Lysimachia terrestris*	8
Swamp cottonwood	*Populus heterophylla*	8
Swamp dock	*Rumex verticillatus*	5
Swamp holly	*Ilex decidua*	6
Swamp loosestrife	*Decodon verticillatus*	8
Swamp marigold	*Bidens aristosa*	1
Swamp milkweed	*Asclepias incarnata*	4
Swamp oval sedge	*Carex muskingumensis*	6
Swamp privet	*Forestiera acuminata*	8
Swamp rose mallow	*Hibiscus moscheutos v. moscheutos*	4
Swamp saxifrage	*Saxifraga pensylvanica v. pensylvanica*	10
Swamp smartweed	*Persicaria setacea*	10
Swamp star sedge	*Carex seorsa*	10
Swamp tickseed	*Bidens comosa*	2
Swamp white oak	*Quercus bicolor*	7
Swampy dewberry	*Rubus sec. Hispidus: R. hispidus*	6
Swampy rose	*Rosa palustris*	5
Sweet alyssum	*LOBULARIA MARITIMA*	
Sweet autumn virgin's bower	*CLEMATIS TERNIFLORA*	
Sweet black-eyed Susan	*Rudbeckia subtomentosa*	7
Sweet blue violet	*VIOLA ODORATA*	
Sweetbrier	*ROSA EGLANTERIA*	
Sweet cherry	*PRUNUS AVIUM*	
Sweet fennel	*FOENICULUM VULGARE*	
Sweet fern	*Comptonia peregrina*	8
Sweet grass	*Hierochloë odorata*	10
Sweetgum	*Liquidambar styraciflua*	4
Sweet Indian plantain	*Hasteola suaveolens* (= *Cacalia suaveolens*)	7
Sweet iris	*IRIS PALLIDA*	
Sweet mock orange	*PHILADELPHUS CORONARIUS*	

Table P-1. *continued*

Common Name	Scientific Name[a]	Coefficient[b]
Sweet scent	*PLUCHEA ODORATA v. SUCCULENTA*	
Sweet-scented bedstraw	*Galium triflorum*	5
Sweet sultan	*AMBERBOA MOSCHATA* (= *CENTAUREA MOSCHATA*)	
Sweet vernal grass	*ANTHOXANTHUM ODORATUM*	
Sweet William	*DIANTHUS BARBATUS*	
Sweet William catchfly	*SILENE ARMERIA*	
Swollen duckweed	*Lemna gibba*	10
Sycamore	*Platanus occidentalis*	3
Synandra	*Synandra hispidula*	5
Tall agrimony	*Agrimonia gryposepala*	2
Tall alum-root	*Heuchera americana* (including 1 variety)	7
Tall anemone	*Anemone virginiana*	4
Tall beggar's ticks	*Bidens vulgata*	0
Tall blue lettuce	*Lactuca biennis*	2
Tall boneset	*Eupatorium altissimum*	1
Tall buttercup	*RANUNCULUS ACRIS*	
Tall coreopsis	*Coreopsis tripteris*	8
Tall cotton grass	*Eriophorum viridicarinatum*	10
Tall fescue	*SCHEDONORUS ARUNDINACEUS* (= *FESTUCA ELATIOR*)	
Tall forked chickweed	*Paronychia canadensis*	6
Tall goldenrod	*Solidago altissima* (including 1 subspecies)	0
Tall green milkweed	*Asclepias hirtella*	6
Tall hedge mustard	*SISYMBRIUM LOESELII*	
Tall ironweed	*Vernonia gigantea*	2
Tall melic grass	*Melica nitens*	9
Tall nettle	*URTICA DIOICA s. DIOICA*	
Tall nut rush	*Scleria triglomerata*	10
Tall oat grass	*ARRHENATHERUM ELATIUS*	
Tall scouring rush	*Equisetum hyemale s. affine*	2
Tall stinging nettle	*Urtica dioica s. gracilis*	1
Tall sunflower	*Helianthus giganteus*	6
Tall swamp marigold	*Bidens coronata*	5
Tall thistle	*Cirsium altissimum*	4
Tall waterhemp	*Amaranthus tuberculatus*	1
Tall white lettuce	*Prenanthes altissima* (including 1 variety)	5
Tall white orchid	*Platanthera dilatata*	10
Tall wood sorrel	*Oxalis stricta*	0
Tall yellow iris	*IRIS PSEUDACORUS*	
Tamarisk water hemp	*Amaranthus rudis*	0
Tansy mustard	*DESCURAINIA PINNATA v. BRACHYCARPA*	
Tansy ragwort	*SENECIO JACOBAEA*	
Tartarian blue lettuce	*LACTUCA TATARICA v. PULCHELLUM*	
Tartarian honeysuckle	*LONICERA TATARICA*	
Tarweed	*MADIA SATIVA*	
Tatarian aster	*ASTER TATARICUS*	
Tennessee bladder fern	*Cystopteris tennesseensis*	10
Tennessee milk vetch	*Astragalus tennesseensis*	10
Terrestrial water starwort	*Callitriche terrestris*	2
Texas bracted sedge	*Carex texensis*	0
Thicket bean	*Phaseolus polystachios*	5
Thicket creeper	*Parthenocissus vitacea*	2
Thicket parsley	*Perideridia americana*	9
Thick-stalked arrowhead	*Sagittaria montevidensis s. calycina*	6
Thin-leaved milkweed	*Asclepias perennis*	8
Thoroughwax	*BUPLEURUM ROTUNDIFOLIUM*	
Three-awn grass	*Aristida longespica v. longespica*	2
Three-leaved stonecrop	*Sedum ternatum*	8
Three-nerved duckweed	*Lemna aequinoctialis*	5
Three-seeded bog sedge	*Carex trisperma*	10
Three-seeded mercury	*Acalypha rhomboidea*	0
Three-seeded mercury	*Acalypha ostryifolia*	0
Three-seeded mercury	*Acalypha virginica*	0
Three-square bulrush	*Schoenoplectus pungens*	3
Three-veined narrow-leaved goosefoot	*Chenopodium pratericola*	3
Three-way sedge	*Dulichium arundinaceum*	10
Thyme	*THYMUS PRAECOX s. ARCTICUS*	
Thyme-leaved sandwort	*ARENARIA SERPYLLIFOLIA*	
Thyme-leaved speedwell	*VERONICA SERPYLLIFOLIA*	
Tiger lily	*LILIUM LANCIFOLIUM*	
Timothy grass	*PHLEUM PRATENSE*	
Tinted spurge	*Euphorbia commutata*	5
Toad rush	*Juncus bufonius*	2
Tomatillo	*PHYSALIS PHILADELPHICA v. IMMACULATA*	
Tomato	*SOLANUM LYCOPERSICUM*	
Toothed cress	*Arabis shortii*	5
Toothed evening primrose	*CALYLOPHUS SERRULATUS*	
Toothed flat sedge	*Cyperus dentatus*	10
Toothed spurge	*Euphorbia dentata* (= *Poinsettia dentata*)	0
Toothed St. John's wort	*Hypericum virgatum*	9
Toothwort	*Cardamine concatenata*	4
Torrey's amaranth	*AMARANTHUS ARENICOLA*	
Torrey's bulrush	*Schoenoplectus torreyi*	10
Torrey's mountain mint	*Pycnanthemum torrei*	3
Torrey's rush	*Juncus torreyi*	3
Tower mustard	*Arabis glabra*	3
Tragia	*Tragia cordata*	8
Trailing arbutus	*Epigaea repens*	9
Trailing bush clover	*Lespedeza procumbens*	6
Trailing ground pine	*Lycopodium digitatum*	2
Trailing pearlwort	*Sagina decumbens*	0
Trailing wild bean	*Strophostyles helvola*	3
Trampled dewberry	*Rubus sec. Flagellares: R. depavitus*	5
Treacle mustard	*ERYSIMUM REPANDUM*	
Tree ground pine	*Lycopodium dendroideum*	10
Tree hawthorn	*Crataegus series Crus-galli: C. arborea*	10
Tree-of-heaven	*AILANTHUS ALTISSIMA*	
Trifling hawthorn	*Crataegus series Intricatae: C. intricata*	5
Trumpet creeper	*Campsis radicans*	1
Trumpet honeysuckle	*LONICERA SEMPERVIRENS*	
Tuckerman's panic grass	*Panicum tuckermanii*	10
Tufted flat sedge	*Kyllinga pumila* (= *Cyperus tenuifolius*)	0
Tufted hair grass	*Deschampsia cespitosa*	10
Tufted lake sedge	*Carex vesicaria*	10
Tufted loosestrife	*Lysimachia thyrsiflora*	7
Tulip poplar	*Liriodendron tulipifera*	4
Tumble mustard	*SISYMBRIUM ALTISSIMUM*	
Tumbleweed	*Amaranthus albus*	0
Turnip	*BRASSICA NAPUS*	
Twig rush	*Cladium mariscoides*	10
Twinflower	*Linnaea borealis s. longifolia*	10
Twinleaf	*Jeffersonia diphylla*	7
Twisted yellow-eyed grass	*Xyris torta*	9
Two-colored bush clover	*LESPEDEZA BICOLOR*	
Two-flower false dandelion	*Krigia biflora*	5
Two-flowered rush	*Juncus biflorus*	4
Two-leaved toothwort	*Cardamine diphylla*	8
Two-seeded hawthorn	*Crataegus series Punctatae: C. disperma*	4
Two-seeded sedge	*Carex disperma*	10
Tyrol knapweed	*CENTAUREA NIGRESCENS*	
Umbrella flat sedge	*Cyperus diandrus*	6
Umbrella magnolia	*Magnolia tripetala*	10
Umbrella sedge	*Fuirena pumila*	10

Common Name	Scientific Name[a]	Coefficient[b]
Uncut hawthorn	*Crataegus series Macracanthae: C. incaedua*	5
Upland boneset	*Eupatorium sessilifolium*	6
Upland dewberry	*Rubus sec. Flagellares: R. invisus*	5
Upland wild timothy	*MUHLENBERGIA RACEMOSA*	
Upright carrion flower	*Smilax ecirrhata*	5
Upright yellow wood sorrel	*Oxalis florida s. prostrata*	0
Variable panic grass	*Dichanthelium commutatum s. commutatum*	7
Variegated milkweed	*Asclepias variegata*	8
Various-leaved water milfoil	*Myriophyllum heterophyllum*	7
Vasey's pondweed	*Potamogeton vaseyi*	10
Veiny pea	*Lathyrus venosus*	10
Veiny skullcap	*Scutellaria nervosa*	5
Velvet bent-grass	*AGROSTIS CANINA*	
Velvet blackberry	*Rubus sec. Arguti: R. frondosus*	4
Velvet grass	*HOLCUS LANATUS*	
Velvety white vervain	*Verbena urticifolia v. leiocarpa*	3
Venus's looking glass	*Triodanis perfoliata*	2
Vervain mallow	*MALVA ALCEA*	
Villous alumroot	*Heuchera villosa*	10
Violet bush clover	*Lespedeza violacea*	5
Violet cress	*Iodanthus pinnatifidus*	6
Violet wood sorrel	*Oxalis violacea*	7
Viper's bugloss	*ECHIUM VULGARE*	
Virginia bluebells	*Mertensia virginica*	6
Virginia chainfern	*Woodwardia virginica*	10
Virginia creeper	*Parthenocissus quinquefolia*	2
Virginia dayflower	*Commelina virginica*	6
Virginia dwarf dandelion	*Krigia virginica*	4
Virginia knotweed	*Tovara virginiana (= Polygonum virginianum)*	3
Virginia mallow	*Sida hermaphrodita*	4
Virginia obedient plant	*Physostegia virginiana v. virginiana*	5
Virginia rockcress	*Sibara virginica*	0
Virginia spiderwort	*Tradescantia virginiana*	7
Virginia waterleaf	*Hydrophyllum virginianum*	4
Virginia wild rye	*Elymus virginicus* (including 1 variety)	3
Virginia willow	*Itea virginica*	10
Virgin's bower	*Clematis virginiana*	3
Viscid field sow thistle	*SONCHUS ARVENSIS s. ARVENSIS*	
Viscid grass-leaved goldenrod	*Euthamia gymnospermoides*	5
Viscid purslane speedwell	*Veronica peregrina s. xalapensis*	5
Wahoo	*Euonymus atropurpurea*	5
Walking fern	*Asplenium rhizophyllum (= Camptosorus rhizophyllus)*	10
Wall rocket	*DIPLOTAXIS MURALIS*	
Wall-rue spleenwort	*Asplenium ruta-muraria*	10
Wand-like bush clover	*Lespedeza frutescens*	5
Wand mullein	*VERBASCUM VIRGATUM*	
Wart cress	*CORONOPUS DIDYMUS*	
Warty panic grass	*Panicum verrucosum*	9
Washington DC dewberry	*Rubus sec. Flagellares: R. celer*	4
Washington hawthorn	*CRATAEGUS series CORDATAE: C. PHAENOPYRUM*	
Water arum	*Calla palustris*	10
Water bulrush	*Schoenoplectus subterminalis*	10
Water cress	*RORIPPA NASTURTIUM-AQUATICUM*	
Water heartsease	*Persicaria amphibia v. emersa (= Polygonum coccineum)*	4
Water hyssop	*Bacopa rotundifolia*	4

Common Name	Scientific Name[a]	Coefficient[b]
Water knotweed	*Persicaria amphibia v. stipulacea*	4
Water locust	*Gleditsia aquatica*	8
Water marigold	*Magalodonta beckii (= Bidens beckii)*	10
Watermelon	*CITRULLUS LANATUS*	
Water mint	*MENTHA AQUATICA*	
Water parsnip	*Sium suave*	5
Water pennywort	*Hydrocotyle umbellata*	7
Water pepper	*PERSICARIA HYDROPIPER*	
Water pimpernel	*Samolus valerandi*	5
Water purslane	*Didiplis diandra*	6
Watershield	*Brasenia schreberi*	4
Water speedwell	*Veronica anagallis-aquatica*	5
Water star grass	*Heteranthera dubia*	4
Water-thread pondweed	*Potamogeton diversifolius*	4
Water willow	*Justicia americana*	6
Wavy-leaved aster	*Symphyotrichum undulatum*	7
Wavy-leaved thistle	*CIRSIUM UNDULATUM*	
Wavy-stemmed bitter cress	*CARDAMINE FLEXUOSA*	
Waxy meadow rue	*Thalictrum revolutum*	5
Wayfaring tree	*VIBURNUM LANTANA*	
Weak bluegrass	*Poa saltuensis*	8
Weak sedge	*Carex debilis v. debilis*	6
Weak-stemmed wood sedge	*Carex laxiculmis v. laxiculmis*	7
Weedy dwarf dandelion	*Krigia caespitosa*	1
Weeping forsythia	*FORSYTHIA SUSPENSA*	
Weft fern	*Trichomanes intricatum*	10
Western beard tongue	*Penstemon tubaeflorus*	10
Western poison ivy	*Toxicodendron rydbergii*	7
Western ragweed	*AMBROSIA PSILOSTACHYA*	
Western sunflower	*Helianthus occidentalis*	9
Western wallflower	*Erysimum capitatum*	3
Western wild lettuce	*Lactuca ludoviciana*	10
Wheat	*TRITICUM AESTIVUM*	
Wheelwort	*Rotala ramosior*	2
Whiplash hawkweed	*HIERACIUM FLAGELLARE*	
White adder's-mouth orchid	*Malaxis monophyllos v. brachypoda*	10
White adder's tongue	*Erythronium albidum*	3
White ash	*Fraxinus americana*	4
White avens	*Geum canadense*	1
White basswood	*Tilia americana v. heterophylla*	5
White beak rush	*Rhynchospora alba*	10
White bedstraw	*GALIUM MOLLUGO*	
White camass	*Zigadenus elegans*	10
White campion	*SILENE LATIFOLIA s. ALBA (= LYCHNIS ALBA)*	
White clover	*TRIFOLIUM REPENS*	
White forget-me-not	*Myosotis verna*	3
White fringe tree	*CHIONANTHUS VIRGINICUS*	
White grass	*Leersia virginica*	4
White-haired panic grass	*Dichanthelium ovale s. villosissimum*	6
White lady's slipper	*Cypripedium candidum*	10
White mulberry	*MORUS ALBA*	
White mustard	*SINAPIS ALBA (= BRASSICA HIRTA)*	
White oak	*Quercus alba*	5
White pine	*Pinus strobus*	5
White poplar	*POPULUS ALBA*	
White prairie clover	*Dalea candida*	10
White prickly poppy	*ARGEMONE POLYANTHEMOS*	
White sage	*ARTEMISIA LUDOVICIANA*	
White snakeroot	*Ageratina altissima (= Eupatorium rugosum)*	2
White-stemmed pondweed	*Potamogeton praelongus*	10
White stonecrop	*SEDUM ALBUM*	
White swallow-wort	*VINCETOXICUM HIRUNDINARIA*	
White sweet clover	*MELILOTUS ALBA*	

Table P-1. *continued*

Common Name	Scientific Name[a]	Coefficient[b]
White thoroughwort	*Eupatorium album*	4
White turtlehead	*Chelone glabra*	7
White vervain	*Verbena urticifolia v. urticifolia*	3
White water crowfoot	*Ranunculus aquatilis v. diffusus*	7
White wild indigo	*Baptisia alba v. macrophylla*	6
White willow	*SALIX ALBA*	
Whorled loosestrife	*Lysimachia quadrifolia*	6
Whorled milkweed	*Asclepias quadrifolia*	8
Whorled milkwort	*Polygala verticillata v. isocycla*	4
Whorled milkwort	*Polygala verticillata v. verticillata*	4
Whorled plantain	*PLANTAGO PSYLLIUM*	
Whorled tickseed	*COREOPSIS VERTICILLATA*	
Whorled water milfoil	*Myriophyllum verticillatum*	10
Wicket spike rush	*Eleocharis rostellata*	10
Wide-leaved lamb's quarters	*Chenopodium opulifolium*	0
Widow's cross	*SEDUM PULCHELLUM*	
Wilcox's panic grass	*Dichanthelium wilcoxianum*	10
Wild bergamot	*Monarda fistulosa* (including 1 variety)	3
Wild black cherry	*Prunus serotina*	1
Wild black currant	*Ribes americanum*	5
Wild chervil	*Chaerophyllum tainturieri*	1
Wild chives	*ALLIUM SCHOENOPRASUM*	
Wild cucumber	*Echinocystis lobata*	3
Wild four o'clock	*MIRABILIS NYCTAGINEA*	
Wild garlic	*Allium canadense*	1
Wild geranium	*Geranium maculatum*	4
Wild golden glow	*Rudbeckia laciniata*	3
Wild goose plum	*Prunus hortulana*	4
Wild hyacinth	*Camassia angusta*	10
Wild hyacinth	*Camassia scilloides*	5
Wild hydrangea	*Hydrangea arborescens*	7
Wild leek	*Allium tricoccum v. tricoccum*	7
Wild leek	*Allium tricoccum v. burdickii*	6
Wild lettuce	*Lactuca canadensis*	2
Wild licorice	*GLYCYRRHIZA LEPIDOTA*	
Wild lupine	*Lupinus perennis*	7
Wild madder	*Galium obtusum*	5
Wild mint	*Mentha arvensis v. villosa*	4
Wild oats	*AVENA FATUA*	
Wild pansy	*VIOLA ARVENSIS*	
Wild pansy	*VIOLA BICOLOR*	
Wild parsnip	*PASTINACA SATIVA*	
Wild petunia	*Ruellia caroliniensis*	6
Wild plum	*Prunus Mexicana*	4
Wild quinine	*Parthenium integrifolium*	9
Wild radish	*RAPHANUS RAPHANISTRUM*	
Wild rape	*RAPISTRUM RUGOSUM*	
Wild sage	*SALVIA NEMOROSA*	
Wild sarsaparilla	*Aralia nudicaulis*	7
Wild senna	*Senna hebecarpa* (= *Cassia hebecarpa*)	4
Wild sensitive plant	*Chamaecrista nictitans*	2
Wild strawberry	*Fragaria virginiana* (including 1 subspecies)	2
Wild sweet crab	*Malus coronaria*	5
Wild sweet potato	*Ipomoea pandurata*	3
Wild sweet William	*Phlox maculata* (including 1 subspecies)	8
Willdenow's grass sedge	*Carex willdenowii*	8
Willow aster	*Symphyotrichum praealtum* (including 1 variety)	6
Willow-leaved lettuce	*LACTUCA SALIGNA*	
Windmill grass	*CHLORIS VERTICILLATA*	
Wineberry	*RUBUS PHOENICOLASIUS*	
Winecup	*CALLIRHOË DIGITATA*	
Winged elm	*Ulmus alata*	7
Winged euonymus	*EUONYMUS ALATA*	
Winged loosestrife	*Lythrum alatum*	5
Winged monkey flower	*Mimulus alatus*	4
Winged oval sedge	*Carex alata*	10
Winged pigweed	*Cycloloma atriplicifolium*	2
Wingstem	*Verbesina alternifolia*	3
Winterberry	*EUONYMUS BUNGEANA*	
Winterberry	*Ilex verticillata*	8
Wintercreeper	*EUONYMUS FORTUNEI*	
Winter grape	*Vitis cinerea* (including 1 variety)	4
Winter vetch	*VICIA VILLOSA s. VILLOSA*	
Wirtgen's bedstraw	*GALIUM WIRTGENII*	
Witch hazel	*Hamamelis virginiana*	5
Witch rod	*Viburnum nudum v. cassinoides*	8
Wolfberry	*SYMPHORICARPOS OCCIDENTALIS*	
Wolf's bluegrass	*Poa wolfii*	9
Wolf's spike rush	*Eleocharis wolfii*	8
Wood anemone	*Anemone quinquefolia*	7
Wood angelica	*Angelica venenosa*	8
Wood betony	*Pedicularis canadensis*	6
Wood millet	*Milium effusum v. cisatlanticum*	10
Wood mint	*Blephilia hirsuta*	5
Wood vetch	*Vicia caroliniana*	7
Woodland agrimony	*Agrimonia rostellata*	5
Woodland bluegrass	*Poa sylvestris*	5
Woodland bluegrass	*POA NEMORALIS*	
Woodland blue violet	*Viola affinis*	2
Woodland brome	*Bromus pubescens*	4
Woodland catchfly	*Silene ovata*	7
Woodland goosefoot	*Chenopodium standleyanum*	5
Woodland satin grass	*Muhlenbergia sylvatica*	7
Woodland sunflower	*Helianthus divaricatus*	5
Wood's stiff sedge	*Carex woodii*	8
Wool grass	*Scirpus cyperinus*	4
Woolly blue violet	*Viola sororia*	1
Woolly hedge nettle	*STACHYS BYZANTINA*	
Woolly mullein	*VERBASCUM THAPSUS*	
Woolly panic grass	*Dichanthelium acuminatum s. fasculatum*	2
Woolly plantain	*PLANTAGO PATAGONICA*	
Woolly-pod vetch	*VICIA VILLOSA s. VARIA*	
Wormseed mustard	*ERYSIMUM CHEIRANTHOIDES*	
Woundwort	*Stachys pilosa v. arenicola*	5
Wrinkled gray sedge	*Carex corrugata*	7
Wrinkle-fruited oak sedge	*Carex tonsa v. rugosperma*	9
Wrinkle-sheathed spike rush	*Eleocharis flavescens v. olivacea*	10
Yankee blackberry	*Rubus sec. Arguti: R. abactus*	5
Yellow adder's tongue	*Erythronium americanum*	5
Yellow alfalfa	*MEDICAGO SATIVA s. FALCATA*	
Yellow avens	*Geum aleppicum*	5
Yellow birch	*Betula alleghaniensis*	10
Yellow buckeye	*Aesculus flava*	10
Yellow coneflower	*Ratibida pinnata*	5
Yellow crownbeard	*Verbesina helianthoides*	7
Yellow-eyed grass	*Xyris difformis*	10
Yellow false foxglove	*Aureolaria grandiflora v. pulchra*	7
Yellow flat sedge	*Cyperus flavescens*	3
Yellow floatingheart	*NYMPHOIDES PELTATA*	
Yellow giant hyssop	*Agastache nepetoides*	4
Yellow-green catchfly	*SILENE CHLORANTHA*	
Yellow hop clover	*TRIFOLIUM AUREUM*	
Yellow ladies' tresses	*Spiranthes ochroleuca*	4
Yellow meadow parsnip	*Thaspium trifoliatum v. aureum*	5
Yellow pimpernel	*Taenidia integerrima*	7

Common Name	Scientific Name[a]	Coefficient[b]
Yellow rocket	*BARBAREA VULGARIS*	
Yellow screwstem	*Bartonia virginica*	5
Yellow spring bedstraw	*GALIUM VERUM*	
Yellow star grass	*Hypoxis hirsuta*	7
Yellow stiff aster	*Solidago x lutescens*	10
Yellow stonecrop	*SEDUM SARMENTOSUM*	
Yellow sweet clover	*MELILOTUS OFFICINALIS*	
Yellow water buttercup	*Ranunculus flabellaris*	7
Yellow wild indigo	*Baptisia tinctoria*	10
Yellowwood	*Cladrastis kentuckea*	10
Yerba de tajo	*Eclipta prostrata*	3

Notes: [a] Scientific names in all capital letters are exotic species.
[b] Coefficient of conservatism. The values, ranging from 0 to 10, are an estimate of the fidelity of an individual species to an undisturbed plant community that characterized the region before European settlement.

Table P-2. Vascular Plants Occurring in Indiana Listed by Scientific Name

Scientific Name[a]	Common Name	Coefficient[b]
ABUTILON THEOPHRASTI	Buttonweed	
Acalypha deamii	Large-seeded mercury	5
Acalypha gracilens	Slender three-seeded mercury	3
Acalypha ostryifolia	Three-seeded mercury	0
Acalypha rhomboidea	Three-seeded mercury	0
Acalypha virginica	Three-seeded mercury	0
Acer negundo (including varieties)	Boxelder	1
ACER PLATANOIDES	Norway maple	
Acer rubrum v. drummondii	Drummond's red maple	5
Acer rubrum v. rubrum	Red maple	5
Acer rubrum v. trilobum	Red maple	5
Acer saccharinum	Silver maple	1
Acer saccharum (includes 2 subspecies)	Sugar maple	4
Acer saccharum s. nigrum	Black maple	6
Achillea millefolium	Common milfoil	0
ACHILLEA PTARMICA	Pearl yarrow	
ACHYRANTHES JAPONICA	Japanese chaff flower	
ACINOS ARVENSIS	Basil thyme	
Aconitum uncinatum	Hooked monkshood	9
Acorus americanus	American sweet flag	10
ACORUS CALAMUS	European sweet flag	
ACROPTILON REPENS (= *CENTAUREA REPENS*)	Russian knapweed	
Actaea pachypoda	Doll's-eyes	7
Actaea rubra	Red baneberry	9
Adiantum pedatum	Maidenhair fern	7
Adlumia fungosa	Allegheny vine	10
AEGILOPS CYLINDRICA	Jointed goat grass	
AEGOPODIUM PODAGRARIA	Goutweed	
Aesculus flava	Yellow buckeye	10
Aesculus glabra	Ohio buckeye	5
AESCULUS HIPPOCASTANUM	Horse chestnut	
AESCULUS PAVIA	Red buckeye	
AETHUSA CYNAPIUM	Fool's parsley	
Agalinis auriculata	Eared false foxglove	8
Agalinis fasciculata	Clustered false foxglove	3
Agalinis gattingeri	Round-stemmed false foxglove	7
Agalinis paupercula (including 1 variety)	False foxglove	7
Agalinis purpurea	False foxglove	6
Agalinis skinneriana	Pale false foxglove	10
Agalinis tenuifolia (includes 2 varieties)	Slender false foxglove	4
Agalinis tenuifolia v. macrophylla	Bessey's false foxglove	4
Agastache nepetoides	Yellow giant hyssop	4
Agastache scrophulariifolia	Purple giant hyssop	4
Agave virginica. See *Manfreda virginica*		
Ageratina altissima (= *Eupatorium rugosum*)	White snakeroot	2
Agrimonia gryposepala	Tall agrimony	2
Agrimonia parviflora	Swamp agrimony	4
Agrimonia pubescens	Soft agrimony	5
Agrimonia rostellata	Woodland agrimony	5
AGROPYRON CRISTATUM s. PECTINATUM	Crested wheat grass	
AGROPYRON DESERTORUM	Crested wheat grass	
AGROPYRON REPENS. See *ELYMUS REPENS*		
AGROPYRON SMITHII. See *PASCOPYRUM SMITHII*		
Agropyron trachycaulum. See *Elymus trachycaulus*		
AGROSTEMA GITHAGO	Corn cockle	
AGROSTIS CANINA	Velvet bent-grass	
Agrostis elliottiana	Awned bent grass	2
AGROSTIS GIGANTEA	Redtop	
Agrostis hyemalis	Hair grass	2
Agrostis perennans	Autumn bent grass	2
Agrostis scabra	Rough bent grass	5
AGROSTIS STOLONIFERA	Creeping bent grass	
AILANTHUS ALTISSIMA	Tree-of-heaven	
AIRA CARYOPHYLLAEA	Silver hair grass	
AJUGA REPTANS	Carpet bugle	
AKEBIA QUINATA	Chocolate vine	
ALBIZIA JULIBRISSIN	Silk tree	
ALCEA ROSEA	Hollyhock	
Aletris farinosa	Colic root	9
Alisma subcordatum	Common water plantain	2
Alisma triviale	American water plantain	2
ALLIARIA PETIOLATA	Garlic mustard	
Allium canadense	Wild garlic	1
ALLIUM CEPA	Garden onion	
Allium cernuum	Nodding wild onion	4
ALLIUM SATIVUM	Garlic	
ALLIUM SCHOENOPRASUM	Wild chives	
ALLIUM STELLATUM	Cliff onion	
Allium tricoccum v. burdickii	Wild leek	6
Allium tricoccum v. tricoccum	Wild leek	7
ALLIUM VINEALE	Field garlic	
ALNUS GLUTINOSA	Black alder	
Alnus incana s. rugosa	Speckled alder	9
Alnus serrulata	Common alder	6
Alopecurus aequalis	Foxtail	6
Alopecurus carolinianus	Annual foxtail	0
ALOPECURUS PRATENSIS	Meadow foxtail	
ALYSSUM ALYSSOIDES	Pale alyssum	
Amaranthus albus	Tumbleweed	0
AMARANTHUS ARENICOLA	Torrey's amaranth	
AMARANTHUS BLITOIDES	Prostrate amaranth	
AMARANTHUS CRUENTUS	Love-lies-bleeding	
AMARANTHUS HYBRIDUS	Green amaranth	
AMARANTHUS POWELLII	Smooth pigweed	
AMARANTHUS RETROFLEXUS	Rough pigweed	
Amaranthus rudis	Tamarisk water hemp	0
AMARANTHUS SPINOSUS	Spiny pigweed	
Amaranthus tuberculatus	Tall waterhemp	1
AMBERBOA MOSCHATA (= *CENTAUREA MOSCHATA*)	Sweet sultan	
Ambrosia artemisiifolia v. elatior	Common ragweed	0
AMBROSIA BIDENTATA	Lanceleaf ragweed	
AMBROSIA PSILOSTACHYA	Western ragweed	
Ambrosia trifida	Giant ragweed	0
Amelanchier arborea	Juneberry	6
Amelanchier interior	Shadbush	8
Amelanchier laevis	Shadbush	8
Amelanchier sanguinea	Round-leaved serviceberry	10
Amelanchier spicata	Low shadbush	9
Ammannia coccinea	Long-leaved ammannia	2
Ammannia robusta	Scarlet loosestrife	2
Ammophila breviligulata	Beach grass	10
Amorpha canescens	Lead plant	9
Amorpha fruticosa	False indigo bush	3
Ampelopsis cordata	Raccoon grape	3
AMPHIACHYRIS DRACUNCULOIDES	Broomweed	
Amphicarpaea bracteata v. bracteata	Hog peanut	5
Amphicarpaea bracteata v. comosa	Hog peanut	5
Amsonia tabernaemontana v. salicifolia	Blue star	5
ANAGALLIS ARVENSIS	Poor man's weatherglass	
Anagallis minima	Chaffweed	3
Anaphalis margaritacea	Pearly everlasting	3
Andromeda polifolia v. glaucophylla	Bog rosemary	10
Andropogon gerardii	Big bluestem grass	5
Andropogon gyrans	Elliott's broom sedge	3
ANDROPOGON HALLII	Sand bluestem grass	
Andropogon scoparius. See *Schizachyrium scoparium*		
Andropogon ternarius	Silver bluestem	3
Andropogon virginicus	Broom sedge	1

Scientific Name[a]	Common Name	Coefficient[b]
Androsace occidentalis	Rock jasmine	4
Anemone acutiloba (= Hepatica acutiloba)	Sharp-lobed hepatica	8
Anemone americana (= Hepatica americana)	Round-leaved hepatica	8
Anemone canadensis	Meadow anemone	4
Anemone caroliniana	Carolina anemone	10
Anemone cylindrica	Candle anemone	7
Anemone quinquefolia	Wood anemone	7
Anemone virginiana	Tall anemone	4
Anemonella thalictroides. See Thalictrum thalictroides		
ANETHUM GRAVEOLENS	Dill	
Angelica atropurpurea	Great angelica	6
Angelica venenosa	Wood angelica	8
ANODA CRISTATA	Crested anoda	
Antennaria howellii s. canadensis	Small pussytoes	3
Antennaria howellii s. neodioica	Small pussytoes	3
Antennaria neglecta	Cat's foot	3
Antennaria parlinii s. fallax	Large plantain-leaved pussytoes	3
Antennaria parlinii s. parlinii	Large plantain-leaved pussytoes	3
Antennaria plantaginifolia	Pussytoes	3
Antennaria solitaria	Solitary cat's foot	10
ANTHEMIS ARVENSIS	Corn chamomile	
ANTHEMIS COTULA	Dog fennel	
ANTHOXANTHUM ODORATUM	Sweet vernal grass	
ANTHRISCUS CAUCALIS	Bur chervil	
APERA INTERRUPTA	Silky bent grass	
Apios americana	Ground nut	3
Aplectrum hyemale	Adam-and-Eve	7
Apocynum androsaemifolium	Spreading dogbane	6
Apocynum cannabinum	Dogbane	2
Apocynum sibiricum	Indian hemp	2
Apocynum x floribundum	Intermediate dogbane	6
Aquilegia canadensis	Columbine	5
AQUILEGIA VULGARIS	European columbine	
Arabidopsis lyrata (= Arabis lyrata)	Lyre-leaved rockcress	7
ARABIDOPSIS THALIANA	Mouse-eared cress	
Arabis canadensis	Sicklepod	6
Arabis drummondii	Drummond's rockcress	10
Arabis glabra	Tower mustard	3
Arabis hirsuta v. pycnocarpa	Hairy rockcress	5
Arabis laevigata	Smooth rockcress	5
Arabis lyrata. See Arabidopsis lyrata		
Arabis missouriensis	Deam's rockcress	10
Arabis patens	Spreading rockcress	10
Arabis shortii	Toothed cress	5
Arabis x divaricarpa	Purple rockcress	5
Aralia hispida	Bristly sarsaparilla	10
Aralia nudicaulis	Wild sarsaparilla	7
Aralia racemosa	American spikenard	8
Aralia spinosa	Devil's walking stick	5
ARCTIUM LAPPA	Great burdock	
ARCTIUM MINUS	Common burdock	
Arctostaphylos uva-ursi	Bearberry	10
Arenaria lateriflora. See Moehringia lateriflora		
Arenaria patula. See Minuartia patula		
ARENARIA SERPYLLIFOLIA	Thyme-leaved sandwort	
Arenaria stricta. See Minuartia michauxii		
Arethusa bulbosa	Dragon's mouth	10
ARGEMONE MEXICANA	Mexican prickly poppy	
ARGEMONE POLYANTHEMOS	White prickly poppy	
Argentina anserina (= Potentilla anserina)	Silverweed	4
Arisaema dracontium	Green dragon	5
Arisaema triphyllum	Indian turnip	4
ARISTIDA BASIRAMEA	Forked-tip three-awn grass	
Aristida dichotoma	Poverty grass	2
Aristida longespica v. geniculata	False arrowfeather	8
Aristida longespica v. longespica	Three-awn grass	2
Aristida oligantha	Plains three awn grass	2
Aristida purpurascens	Arrowfeather	7
Aristida ramosissima	Slender three-awn grass	5
Aristida tuberculosa	Beach three-awn grass	10
Aristolochia serpentaria	Birthwort	8
Aristolochia tomentosa	Dutchman's pipe	7
Armoracia lacustris	Lake cress	8
ARMORACIA RUSTICANA	Horse radish	
Arnoglossum atriplicifolium (= Cacalia atriplicifolia)	Pale Indian plantain	6
Arnoglossum plantagineum	Prairie Indian plantain	10
Arnoglossum reniforme	Great Indian plantain	8
Aronia. See 2 species of Photinia		
ARRHENATHERUM ELATIUS	Tall oat grass	
ARTEMISIA ABSINTHIUM	Common wormwood	
ARTEMISIA ANNUA	Annual wormwood	
ARTEMISIA BIENNIS	Biennial wormwood	
Artemisia campestris s. caudata	Beach wormwood	5
ARTEMISIA CARRUTHII	Kansas mugwort	
ARTEMISIA LUDOVICIANA	White sage	
ARTEMISIA VULGARIS	Mugwort	
ARTHRAXON HISPIDUS	Small carp grass	
Aruncus dioicus	Goat's beard	7
Arundinaria gigantea	Giant cane	5
Asarum canadense	Canada wild ginger	5
Asclepias amplexicaulis	Sand milkweed	7
Asclepias exaltata	Poke milkweed	8
Asclepias hirtella	Tall green milkweed	6
Asclepias incarnata	Swamp milkweed	4
Asclepias meadii	Mead's milkweed	10
Asclepias perennis	Thin-leaved milkweed	8
Asclepias purpurascens	Purple milkweed	7
Asclepias quadrifolia	Whorled milkweed	8
Asclepias sullivantii	Prairie milkweed	8
Asclepias syriaca	Common milkweed	1
Asclepias tuberosa (including 1 variety)	Butterflyweed	4
Asclepias variegata	Variegated milkweed	8
Asclepias verticillata	Horsetail milkweed	5
Asclepias viridiflora	Green-flowered milkweed	9
Asclepias viridis	Green milkweed	10
Asimina triloba	Papaw	6
ASPARAGUS OFFICINALIS	Garden asparagus	
Asplenium bradleyi	Bradley's spleenwort	10
Asplenium montanum	Mountain spleenwort	10
Asplenium pinnatifidum	Pinnatifid spleenwort	10
Asplenium platyneuron	Ebony spleenwort	3
Asplenium resiliens	Black spleenwort	10
Asplenium rhizophyllum (= Camptosorus rhizophyllus)	Walking fern	10
Asplenium ruta-muraria	Wall-rue spleenwort	10
Asplenium trichomanes	Maidenhair spleenwort	10
Asplenium x ebenoides	Scott's spleenwort	10
Aster. See also 3 species of Eurybia and 27 species of Symphyotrichum		
ASTER CILIATA. See BRACHYACTIS CILIATA		
Aster linariifolius. See Ionactis linariifolius		
Aster solidagineus. See Sericocarpus linifolius		
ASTER TATARICUS	Tatarian aster	
Aster umbellatus. See Doellingeria umbellata		
Astragalus canadensis	Canadian milk vetch	9
ASTRAGALUS CICER	Chick-pea milk vetch	
ASTRAGALUS GLYCYPHYLLOS	Licorice milkvetch	
Astragalus tennesseensis	Tennessee milk vetch	10
Athyrium filix-femina s. angustum	Lady fern	6

Table P-2. *continued*

Scientific Name[a]	Common Name	Coefficient[b]
Athyrium filix-femina s. asplenioides	Southern lady fern	6
Athyrium pycnocarpon. See *Diplazium pycnocarpon*		
Athyrium thelypterioides. See *Deparia acrostichoides*		
ATRIPLEX LITTORALIS	Grass-leaved orach	
ATRIPLEX PATULA	Fat-hen saltbush	
ATRIPLEX PROSTRATA	Halberd-leaved orach	
Aureolaria flava (including 1 variety)	Smooth false foxglove	7
Aureolaria grandiflora v. pulchra	Yellow false foxglove	7
Aureolaria pedicularia (including varieties)	Clammy false foxglove	7
Aureolaria virginica	Downy false foxglove	8
AVENA FATUA	Wild oats	
AVENA SATIVA	Oats	
Azolla caroliniana	Carolina mosquito fern	4
Bacopa rotundifolia	Water hyssop	4
Baptisia alba v. macrophylla	White wild indigo	6
Baptisia australis	Blue wild indigo	10
Baptisia bracteata v. leucophaea	Cream wild indigo	10
Baptisia tinctoria	Yellow wild indigo	10
Baptisia x serenae	Deam's wild-indigo	10
BARBAREA VERNA	Early winter cress	
BARBAREA VULGARIS	Yellow rocket	
Bartonia paniculata	Panicled screwstem	5
Bartonia virginica	Yellow screwstem	5
BELAMCANDA CHINENSIS	Blackberry lily	
BELLIS PERENNIS	English daisy	
Berberis canadensis	Allegheny barberry	10
BERBERIS REPENS (= *MAHONIA REPENS*)	Oregon holly grape	
BERBERIS THUNBERGII	Japanese barberry	
BERBERIS VULGARIS	Common barberry	
BERTEROA INCANA	Hoary alyssum	
Besseya bullii	Kitten tails	8
Betula alleghaniensis	Yellow birch	10
Betula nigra	River birch	2
Betula papyrifera	Paper birch	7
BETULA PENDULA	European white birch	
Betula populifolia	Gray birch	10
BETULA PUBESCENS	Eurasian paper birch	
Betula pumila	Dwarf birch	10
Betula x purpusii	Hybrid dwarf birch	10
Bidens aristosa	Swamp marigold	1
Bidens beckii. See *Magalodonta beckii*		
Bidens bipinnata	Spanish needles	0
Bidens cernua	Nodding bur marigold	2
Bidens comosa	Swamp tickseed	2
Bidens connata	Purplestemmed tickseed	2
Bidens coronata	Tall swamp marigold	5
Bidens discoidea	Swamp beggar's ticks	5
Bidens frondosa	Common beggar's ticks	1
Bidens vulgata	Tall beggar's ticks	0
Bignonia capreolata	Cross vine	7
Blephilia ciliata	Ohio horse mint	7
Blephilia hirsuta	Wood mint	5
Boehmeria cylindrica (including 1 variety)	False nettle	3
Bolboschoenus fluviatilis (= *Scirpus fluviatilis*)	River bulrush	4
Boltonia asteroides v. recognita	False aster	5
Botrychium biternatum	Sparse-lobed grape fern	4
Botrychium dissectum	Bronze fern	3
Botrychium matricariifolium	Daisy-leaf grape fern	4
Botrychium multifidum	Northern grape fern	10
Botrychium oneidense	Oneida grape fern	9
Botrychium simplex	Dwarf grape fern	6
Botrychium virginianum	Rattlesnake fern	4
Bouteloua curtipendula	Side-oats grama	7
BRACHYACTIS CILIATA s. ANGUSTA (= *ASTER BRACHYACTIS*)	Rayless aster	
Brachyelytrum aristosum	Bristly wood grass	10
Brachyelytrum erectum	Long-awned wood grass	6
Brasenia schreberi	Watershield	4
BRASSICA HIRTA. See *SINAPIS ALBA*		
BRASSICA JUNCEA	Indian mustard	
BRASSICA NAPUS	Turnip	
BRASSICA NIGRA	Black mustard	
BRASSICA RAPA	Bird's rape	
Brickellia eupatorioides (= *Kuhnia eupatoriodes*) (including 1 variety)	False boneset	8
BROMUS BRIZIFORMIS	Rattlesnake chess	
Bromus ciliatus	Fringed brome	10
BROMUS COMMUTATUS	Hairy brome	
BROMUS HORDEACEUS	Soft chess	
BROMUS INERMIS	Hungarian brome	
BROMUS JAPONICUS	Japanese chess	
Bromus kalmii	Prairie brome	10
Bromus latiglumis	Early-leaved brome	6
Bromus nottowayanus	Nottoway valley brome	7
Bromus pubescens	Woodland brome	4
BROMUS RACEMOSUS	Smooth chess	
BROMUS SECALINUS	Rye brome	
BROMUS SQUARROSUS	Nodding brome	
BROMUS STERILIS	Poverty brome	
BROMUS TECTORUM	Cheat grass	
BROUSSONETIA PAPYRIFERA	Paper mulberry	
Buchnera americana	Blue hearts	8
BUDDLEJA DAVIDII	Orange-eyed butterfly bush	
BUGLOSSOIDES ARVENSE (= *LITHOSPERMUM ARVENSE*)	Corn gromwell	
Bulbostylis capillaris	Hair sedge	4
Bumelia lycioides. See *Sideroxylon lycioides*		
BUPLEURUM ROTUNDIFOLIUM	Thoroughwax	
BUTOMUS UMBELLATUS	Flowering rush	
Cabomba caroliniana	Carolina figwort	2
Cacalia. See 3 species of *Arnoglossum*		
Cacalia suaveolens. See *Hasteola suaveolens*		
CAKILE EDENTULA v. EDENTULA	Eastern sea rocket	
Cakile edentula v. lacustris	Great Lakes sea rocket	10
Calamagrostis canadensis	Blue joint grass	5
Calamagrostis porteri s. insperata	Reed bent grass	10
Calamagrostis stricta s. inexpansa	Bog reed grass	7
Calamovilfa longifolia v. magna	Prairie sand reed	9
Calla palustris	Water arum	10
CALLIRHOË ALCAEODIES	Pale poppy mallow	
CALLIRHOË DIGITATA	Winecup	
CALLIRHOË INVOLUCRATA	Purple poppy mallow	
Callirhoë triangulata	Clustered poppy mallow	10
Callitriche heterophylla	Large water starwort	3
Callitriche terrestris	Terrestrial water starwort	2
Calopogon oklahomensis	Dwarf grass pink orchid	10
Calopogon tuberosus	Grass pink orchid	10
Caltha palustris	Cowslip	7
Calycocarpum lyonii	Cupseed	7
CALYLOPHUS SERRULATUS	Toothed evening primrose	
Calystegia catesbiana	Catesby's hedge bindweed	8
CALYSTEGIA PELLITA	California rose	
Calystegia sepium (including subspecies)	American bindweed	1
Calystegia silvatica s. fraterniflora	Rectangular-sinused hedge bindweed	1
Calystegia spithamaea	Dwarf bindweed	8
Camassia angusta	Wild hyacinth	10
Camassia scilloides	Wild hyacinth	5
CAMELINA MICROCARPA	Small-fruited false flax	

Scientific Name[a]	Common Name	Coefficient[b]
CAMELINA SATIVA	Gold-of-pleasure	
Campanula aparinoides	Marsh bellflower	8
CAMPANULA RAPUNCULOIDES	European bellflower	
Campanula rotundifolia	Harebell	8
Campanulastrum americanum (= *Campanula americanum*)	American bellflower	4
Campsis radicans	Trumpet creeper	1
Camptosorus rhizophyllus. See *Asplenium rhizophyllum*		
CANNABIS SATIVA	Hashish	
CAPSELLA BURSA-PASTORIS	Shepherd's purse	
Cardamine angustata	Slender toothwort	5
Cardamine bulbosa	Bulb bitter cress	4
Cardamine concatenata	Toothwort	4
Cardamine diphylla	Two-leaved toothwort	8
Cardamine dissecta	Divided crinkleroot	8
Cardamine douglassii	Northern bitter cress	5
CARDAMINE FLEXUOSA	Wavy-stemmed bitter cress	
CARDAMINE HIRSUTA	Hairy bitter cress	
Cardamine parviflora v. arenicola	Small-flowered bitter cress	2
Cardamine pensylvanica	Pennsylvania bitter cress	2
Cardamine pratensis	Cuckoo flower	10
CARDARIA CHALAPENSIS	Lens-podded hoary cress	
CARDARIA DRABA	Hoary cress	
CARDIOSPERMUM HALICACABUM	Balloon vine	
CARDUUS NUTANS	Musk bristle thistle	
CAREX ACUTIFORMIS	European lake sedge	
Carex aggregata	Smooth clustered sedge	2
Carex alata	Winged oval sedge	10
Carex albicans v. albicans	Blunt-scaled oak sedge	6
Carex albicans v. emmonsii	Sharp-scaled oak sedge	5
Carex albolutescens	Long-fruited oval sedge	9
Carex albursina	Blunt-scaled wood sedge	7
Carex alopecoidea	Brown-headed fox sedge	7
Carex amphibola	False gray sedge	8
Carex annectens	Large yellow fox sedge	3
Carex aquatilis v. substricta	Long-bracted tussock sedge	8
Carex arctata	Northern sedge	10
Carex atherodes	Hairy-leaved lake sedge	6
Carex atlantica s. atlantica	Atlantic star sedge	10
Carex atlantica s. capillacea	Hair star sedge	10
Carex aurea	Golden sedge	9
Carex aureolensis	Golden cattail sedge	10
Carex bebbii	Bebb's oval sedge	7
Carex bicknellii	Bicknell's oval sedge	9
Carex blanda	Common wood sedge	1
Carex brevior	Plains oval sedge	4
Carex bromoides	Brome hummock sedge	10
Carex brunnescens s. sphaerostachya	Brownish sedge	10
Carex bushii	Long-scaled green sedge	7
Carex buxbaumii	Dark-scaled sedge	10
Carex canescens s. canescens	Hoary sedge	10
Carex canescens s. disjuncta	Gray bog sedge	10
Carex careyana	Carey's wood sedge	9
Carex caroliniana	Short-scaled green sedge	7
Carex cephaloidea	Rough clustered sedge	6
Carex cephalophora	Short-headed bracted sedge	3
Carex chordorrhiza	Cordroot sedge	10
Carex communis	Common beech sedge	8
Carex comosa	Bristly sedge	6
Carex conjuncta	Green-headed fox sedge	6
Carex conoidea	Prairie gray sedge	10
Carex corrugata	Wrinkled gray sedge	7
Carex crawei	Early fen sedge	10
Carex crawfordii	Crawford's oval sedge	9
Carex crinita	Fringed sedge	8
Carex cristatella	Crested oval sedge	3
Carex crus-corvi	Crowfoot fox sedge	6
Carex cryptolepis	Small yellow sedge	10
Carex cumberlandensis	Concealed sedge	8
Carex cumulata	Crowded oval sedge	10

Scientific Name[a]	Common Name	Coefficient[b]
Carex davisii	Awned graceful sedge	3
Carex debilis v. debilis	Weak sedge	6
Carex debilis v. rudgei	Northern weak sedge	10
Carex decomposita	Broad-leaved panicled sedge	10
Carex diandra	Bog panicled sedge	10
Carex digitalis (including 1 variety)	Narrow-leaved wood sedge	7
Carex disperma	Two-seeded sedge	10
Carex eburnea	Ivory sedge	10
Carex echinata	Large-fruited star sedge	10
Carex emoryi	Riverbank tussock sedge	7
Carex festucacea	Fescue oval sedge	6
Carex flava	Large yellow sedge	10
Carex folliculata	Follicle sedge	10
Carex frankii	Bristly cattail sedge	2
Carex garberi	False golden sedge	10
Carex gigantea	Greater hop sedge	10
Carex glaucodea	Blue sedge	3
Carex gracilescens	Slender wood sedge	5
Carex gracillima	Purple-sheathed graceful sedge	7
Carex granularis	Pale sedge	2
Carex gravida	Long-awned bracted sedge	5
Carex grayi	Common bur sedge	5
Carex grisea	Common gray sedge	3
Carex haydenii	Long-scaled tussock sedge	8
Carex hirsutella	Hairy green sedge	3
Carex hirtifolia	Hairy wood sedge	5
Carex hitchcockiana	Hairy gray sedge	8
Carex hyalinolepis	Southern lake sedge	3
Carex hystericina	Porcupine sedge	5
Carex inops s. heliophila	Long-stoloned oak sedge	10
Carex interior	Prairie star sedge	8
Carex intumescens	Shining bur sedge	8
Carex jamesii	Grass sedge	4
Carex kraliana	Kral's sedge	8
Carex lacustris	Common lake sedge	7
Carex laevivaginata	Smooth-sheathed fox sedge	7
Carex lasiocarpa s. americana	Narrow-leaved woolly sedge	10
Carex laxiculmis v. copulata	Spreading sedge	5
Carex laxiculmis v. laxiculmis	Weak-stemmed wood sedge	7
Carex laxiflora	Beech wood sedge	7
Carex leavenworthii	Dwarf bracted sedge	1
Carex leptalea	Slender sedge	8
Carex leptonervia	Few-nerved wood sedge	8
Carex limosa	Muck sedge	10
Carex livida v. grayana	Lead-colored stiff sedge	10
Carex longii	Long's oval sedge	5
Carex louisianica	Southern hop sedge	8
Carex lupuliformis	Knobbed hop sedge	10
Carex lupulina	Common hop sedge	4
Carex lurida	Bottlebrush sedge	4
Carex meadii	Mead's stiff sedge	7
Carex mesochorea	Midland bracted sedge	2
Carex missouriensis	Missouri oval sedge	10
Carex molesta	Field oval sedge	2
Carex muehlenbergii v. enervis	Nerveless sand bracted sedge	5
Carex muehlenbergii v. muehlenbergii	Common sand bracted sedge	5
Carex muskingumensis	Swamp oval sedge	6
Carex normalis	Spreading oval sedge	3
Carex oklahomensis	Oklahoma bracted sedge	5
Carex oligocarpa	Few-fruited gray sedge	8
Carex oligosperma	Running bog sedge	10
Carex pauciflora	Few-flowered bog sedge	10
Carex pedunculata	Long-stalked hummock sedge	10
Carex pellita	Common woolly sedge	2
Carex pensylvanica	Pennsylvania oak sedge	5
Carex picta	Painted sedge	7
Carex planispicata	Flat-spiked gray sedge	7
Carex plantaginea	Plantain-leaved wood sedge	10

Table P-2. *continued*

Scientific Name[a]	Common Name	Coefficient[b]
Carex platyphylla	Broad-leaved wood sedge	10
CAREX PRAEGRACILIS	Expressway sedge	
Carex prairea	Fen panicled sedge	10
Carex prasina	Leek sedge	10
Carex projecta	Loose-headed oval sedge	7
Carex pseudocyperus	False bristly sedge	10
Carex radiata	Straight-styled bracted sedge	4
Carex retroflexa	Bent bracted sedge	4
Carex retrorsa	Deflexed bottlebrush sedge	10
Carex richardsonii	Prairie hummock sedge	10
Carex rosea	Curly-styled bracted sedge	5
Carex sartwellii	Running marsh sedge	7
Carex scabrata	Rough sedge	10
Carex scoparia	Lance-fruited oval sedge	4
Carex seorsa	Swamp star sedge	10
Carex shortiana	Short's sedge	3
Carex siccata	Running savanna sedge	8
Carex socialis	Creeping bracted sedge	8
Carex sparganioides	Loose-headed bracted sedge	4
CAREX SPICATA	Prickly sedge	
Carex sprengelii	Long-beaked sedge	8
Carex squarrosa	Narrow-leaved cattail sedge	4
Carex sterilis	Fen star sedge	9
Carex stipata v. maxima	Great fox sedge	5
Carex stipata v. stipata	Common fox sedge	2
Carex straminea	Awned oval sedge	10
Carex stricta	Common tussock sedge	5
Carex suberecta	Straw oval sedge	5
Carex swanii	Downy green sedge	4
Carex tenera v. echinodes	Quill oval sedge	8
Carex tenera v. tenera	Slender oval sedge	8
Carex tetanica	Common stiff sedge	9
Carex texensis	Texas bracted sedge	0
Carex timida	False grass sedge	9
Carex tonsa v. rugosperma	Wrinkle-fruited oak sedge	9
Carex tonsa v. tonsa	Smooth-fruited oak sedge	9
Carex torta	Beaked tussock sedge	9
Carex tribuloides v. sangamonensis	Narrow-leaved oval sedge	5
Carex tribuloides v. tribuloides	Broad-leaved oval sedge	5
Carex trichocarpa	Hairy-fruited lake sedge	4
Carex trisperma	Three-seeded bog sedge	10
Carex tuckermanii	Bent-seeded hop sedge	10
Carex typhina	Common cattail sedge	7
Carex umbellata	Early oak sedge	5
Carex utriculata	Common yellow lake sedge	8
Carex vesicaria	Tufted lake sedge	10
Carex virescens	Slender green sedge	8
Carex viridula	Green yellow sedge	8
Carex vulpinoidea	Brown fox sedge	2
Carex willdenowii	Willdenow's grass sedge	8
Carex woodii	Wood's stiff sedge	8
Carpinus caroliniana s. virginiana	Blue beech	5
CARUM CARVI	Caraway	
Carya cordiformis	Bitternut hickory	5
Carya glabra	Pignut hickory	4
Carya illinoinensis	Pecan	4
Carya laciniosa	Big shellbark hickory	8
Carya ovata	Shagbark hickory	4
Carya pallida	Pale hickory	10
Carya texana	Black hickory	10
Carya tomentosa	Mockernut hickory	6
Cassia. See 2 species of *Chamaecrista* and 4 species of *Senna*		
Castanea dentata	American chestnut	10
Castanea pumila	Allegheny chinquapin	10
Castilleja coccinea	Indian paintbrush	10
CATALPA BIGNONIOIDES	Common catalpa	
Catalpa speciosa	Cigar tree	0
Caulophyllum thalictroides	Blue cohosh	8
Ceanothus americanus	New Jersey tea	8
Ceanothus herbaceus	Inland New Jersey tea	10
CELASTRUS ORBICULATA	Oriental bittersweet	
Celastrus scandens	Climbing bittersweet	2
CELOSIA ARGENTEA	Feathered amaranth	
CELOSIA CRISTATA	Cocks comb	
Celtis laevigata	Sugarberry	7
Celtis occidentalis	Hackberry	3
Celtis tenuifolia	Dwarf hackberry	8
Cenchrus longispinus	Mat sandbur	0
Cenchrus spinifex	Coastal sandbur	0
CENTAUREA CYANUS	Bachelor's button	
CENTAUREA DIFFUSA	Spreading star thistle	
CENTAUREA JACEA	Brown-rayed knapweed	
CENTAUREA MOSCHATA. See *AMBERBOA MOSCHATA*		
CENTAUREA NIGRESCENS	Tyrol knapweed	
CENTAUREA REPENS. See *ACROPTILON REPENS*		
CENTAUREA SCABIOSA	Great knapweed	
CENTAUREA SOLSTITIALIS	Barnaby's thistle	
CENTAUREA STOEBE s. MICRANTHOS	Spotted knapweed	
CENTAURIUM ERYTHRACEA	Common centaury	
CENTAURIUM PULCHELLUM	Showy centaury	
CENTROSEMA VIRGINIANUM	Spurred butterfly-pea	
Cephalanthus occidentalis	Buttonbush	5
Cerastium arvense v. villosum	Field chickweed	6
CERASTIUM BRACHYPETALUM	Gray mouse-ear chickweed	
CERASTIUM DUBIUM	Doubtful mouse-ear-chickweed	
CERASTIUM FONTANUM s. VULGARE	Common mouse-ear chickweed	
CERASTIUM GLOMERATUM	Clammy chickweed	
CERASTIUM NUTANS v. BRACHYPODUM	Short-pedicelled chickweed	
Cerastium nutans v. nutans	Nodding chickweed	0
CERASTIUM PUMILUM	Curtis's mouse-ear chickweed	
CERASTIUM SEMIDECANDRUM	Small mouse-ear chickweed	
CERATOCEPHALUS TESTICULATUS. See *RANUNCULUS TESTICULATUS*		
Ceratophyllum demersum	Coontail	1
Ceratophyllum echinatum	Spiny coontail	10
Cercis canadensis	Eastern redbud	3
CHAENOMELES SPECIOSA	Common flowering quince	
CHAENORRHINUM MINUS	Dwarf snapdragon	
Chaerophyllum procumbens v. procumbens	Common streambank chervil	2
Chaerophyllum procumbens v. shortii	Short's streambank chervil	10
Chaerophyllum tainturieri	Wild chervil	1
CHAITURUS MARRUBIASTRUM (= *LEONURUS MARRUBIASTRUM*)	Lion's tail	
Chamaecrista fasciculata (= *Cassia fasciculata*)	Golden cassia	2
Chamaecrista nictitans	Wild sensitive plant	2
CHAMAECYPARIS THYOIDES	Atlantic white cedar	
Chamaedaphne calyculata	Leatherleaf	10
Chamaelirium luteum	Fairy wand	8
CHAMAEMELUM NOBILE	Garden chamomile	
Chamaesyce geyeri	Geyer's spurge	10
Chamaesyce glyptosperma	Smooth creeping spurge	2
Chamaesyce humistrata	Spreading spurge	0
Chamaesyce maculata	Spotted creeping spurge	0
Chamaesyce nutans	Nodding spurge	0
Chamaesyce polygonifolia	Seaside spurge	10
Chamaesyce serpens	Round-leaved spurge	0
Chamaesyce vermiculata	Hairy spurge	0
Chamerion angustifolium s. circumvagum (= *Epilobium angustifolium*)	Fireweed	3
Chasmanthium latifolium	Indian wood oats	4

Scientific Name[a]	Common Name	Coefficient[b]
Cheilanthes lanosa	Hairy lip fern	10
CHELIDONIUM MAJUS	Celandine	
Chelone glabra	White turtlehead	7
Chelone obliqua v. speciosa	Pink turtlehead	8
CHENOPODIUM ALBUM v. ALBUM	Lamb's quarters	
Chenopodium album v. missouriense	Missouri goosefoot	0
CHENOPODIUM AMBROSIOIDES. See DYSPHANIA AMBROSIOIDES		
CHENOPODIUM ANTHELMINTICUM	Atlantic wormseed	
Chenopodium berlandieri v. bushianum	Pitseed goosefoot	0
Chenopodium berlandieri v. macrocalycium	Pitseed goosefoot	0
Chenopodium berlandieri v. zschackii	Pitseed goosefoot	0
CHENOPODIUM BOTRYS. See DYSPHANIA BOTRYS		
Chenopodium capitatum	Strawberry blite	5
CHENOPODIUM GLAUCUM	Oak-leaved goosefoot	
CHENOPODIUM MURALE	Nettle-leaved goosefoot	
Chenopodium opulifolium	Wide-leaved lamb's quarters	0
Chenopodium pallescens	Pale narrow-leaved goosefoot	3
Chenopodium pratericola	Three-veined narrow-leaved goosefoot	3
Chenopodium simplex	Maple-leaved goosefoot	3
Chenopodium standleyanum	Woodland goosefoot	5
CHENOPODIUM STRICTUM	Naked-fruited lamb's quarters	
CHENOPODIUM URBICUM	City goosefoot	
CHENOPODIUM VULVARIA	Stinking goosefoot	
Chimaphila maculata	Spotted wintergreen	4
Chimaphila umbellata s. cisatlantica	Pipsissewa	10
CHIONANTHUS VIRGINICUS	White fringe tree	
CHLORIS VERTICILLATA	Windmill grass	
CHONDRILLA JUNCEA	Skeleton weed	
CHORISPORA TENELLA	Purple rocket	
CHRYSANTHEMUM LEUCANTHEMUM. See LEUCANTHEMUM VULGARE		
Chrysopsis camporum. See Heterotheca camporum		
Chrysosplenium americanum	Golden saxifrage	10
CICHORIUM INTYBUS	Chicory	
Cicuta bulbifera	Bulblet-bearing water hemlock	8
Cicuta maculata (including 1 variety)	Common water hemlock	6
Cimicifuga racemosa	False bugbane	9
Cimicifuga rubifolia	Black cohosh	10
Cinna arundinacea	Common wood reed	4
Circaea alpina	Small enchanter's nightshade	10
Circaea lutetiana s. canadensis	Enchanter's nightshade	2
Cirsium altissimum	Tall thistle	4
CIRSIUM ARVENSE	Field thistle	
Cirsium carolinianum	Carolina thistle	10
Cirsium discolor	Pasture thistle	3
Cirsium hillii	Hill's thistle	10
Cirsium muticum	Fen thistle	8
Cirsium pitcheri	Dune thistle	10
CIRSIUM UNDULATUM	Wavy-leaved thistle	
CIRSIUM VULGARE	Bull thistle	
CITRULLUS LANATUS	Watermelon	
Cladium mariscoides	Twig rush	10
Cladrastis kentuckea	Yellowwood	10
Claytonia virginica	Spring beauty	2
Clematis pitcheri	Leather flower	4
CLEMATIS TERNIFLORA	Sweet autumn virgin's bower	
Clematis viorna	Leatherflower	8
Clematis virginiana	Virgin's bower	3
CLEOME HASSLERIANA	Spider flower	
CLEOME SERRULATA	Rocky Mountain beeplant	
Clinopodium arkansanum (= Satureja arkansanum)	Low calamint	10
Clinopodium vulgare	Dog mint	2
Clintonia borealis	Bluebead	10
Clitoria mariana	Butterfly pea	10
Cocculus carolinus	Snailseed	6
Coeloglossum viride (= Habenaria viridis)	Bracted green orchid	7
Collinsia verna	Blue-eyed Mary	6
Collinsonia canadensis	Citronella horse balm	8
COLLOMIA LINEARIS	Slender-leaf collomia	
Comandra umbellata	Bastard toadflax	7
Comarum palustre (= Potentilla palustris)	Marsh cinquefoil	9
COMMELINA COMMUNIS	Common dayflower	
COMMELINA DIFFUSA	Climbing dayflower	
Commelina erecta v. deamii	Deam's dayflower	7
Commelina virginica	Virginia dayflower	6
Comptonia peregrina	Sweet fern	8
Conioselinum chinense	Hemlock parsley	10
CONIUM MACULATUM	Poison hemlock	
Conoclinium coelestinum (= Eupatorium coelestinum)	Mistflower	2
Conopholis americana	Cancer root	8
CONRINGIA ORIENTALIS	Hare's-ear mustard	
CONSOLIDA AJACIS (= DELPHINIUM AJACIS)	Rocket larkspur	
CONVALLARIA MAJALIS	Lily-of-the-valley	
CONVOLVULUS ARVENSIS	Field bindweed	
Conyza canadensis	Horseweed	0
Conyza ramosissima	Branched horseweed	0
Coptis trifolia	Goldthread	10
Corallorhiza maculata (including 1 variety)	Spotted coralroot	7
Corallorhiza odontorhiza (including 1 variety)	Fall coralroot	3
Corallorhiza trifida	Early coralroot	10
Corallorhiza wisteriana	Spring coralroot	6
COREOPSIS GRANDIFLORA v. HARVEYANA	Large-flowered coreopsis	
Coreopsis lanceolata	Sand coreopsis	5
COREOPSIS MAJOR	Great tickseed	
Coreopsis palmata	Prairie coreopsis	10
COREOPSIS PUBESCENS	Star tickseed	
COREOPSIS TINCTORIA	Golden coreopsis	
Coreopsis tripteris	Tall coreopsis	8
COREOPSIS VERTICILLATA	Whorled tickseed	
Corispermum americanum	Small bugseed	3
Corispermum pallasii	Common bugseed	3
Cornus alternifolia	Pagoda dogwood	8
Cornus amomum	Silky dogwood	10
Cornus baileyi	Bailey's dogwood	9
Cornus canadensis	Bunchberry	10
Cornus drummondii	Rough-leaved dogwood	2
Cornus florida	Flowering dogwood	4
Cornus foemina	Stiff dogwood	5
Cornus obliqua	Pale dogwood	5
Cornus racemosa	Gray dogwood	2
Cornus rugosa	Round-leaved dogwood	10
Cornus sericea	Red osier dogwood	4
CORONILLA VARIA	Crown vetch	
CORONOPUS DIDYMUS	Wart cress	
Corydalis flavula	Pale corydalis	3
CORYDALIS MICRANTHA	Slender corydalis	
Corydalis sempervirens	Pink corydalis	9
Corylus americana	American filbert	4
COTINUS COGGYGRIA	European smoketree	
COTONEASTER ACUTIFOLIA	Peking cotoneaster	
COTONEASTER ADPRESSUS	Creeping cotoneaster	
COTONEASTER HORIZONTALIS	Rockspray cotoneaster	

Table P-2. *continued*

Scientific Name[a]	Common Name	Coefficient[b]
Crataegus series Coccineae: C. corusca	Shining-branched hawthorn	5
Crataegus series Coccineae: C. holmsiana	Holms' hawthorn	5
Crataegus series Coccineae: C. pedicellata	Stalked hawthorn	7
CRATAEGUS series CORDATAE: C. PHAENOPYRUM	Washington hawthorn	
Crataegus series Crus-galli: C. arborea	Tree hawthorn	10
Crataegus series Crus-galli: C. crus-galli	Cock-spur hawthorn	4
Crataegus series Intricatae: C. biltmoreana	Biltmore's hawthorn	4
Crataegus series Intricatae: C. intricata	Trifling hawthorn	5
Crataegus series Intricatae: C. rubella	Red hawthorn	6
Crataegus series Macracanthae: C. calpodendron	Sugar hawthorn	7
Crataegus series Macracanthae: C. incaedua	Uncut hawthorn	5
Crataegus series Macracanthae: C. succulenta	Fleshy hawthorn	6
Crataegus series Molles: C. kelloggii	Kellogg's hawthorn	5
Crataegus series Molles: C. mollis	Downy hawthorn	2
Crataegus series Pruinosae: C. gattingeri	Gattinger's hawthorn	5
Crataegus series Pruinosae: C. platycarpa	Flat-fruited hawthorn	7
Crataegus series Pruinosae: C. prona	Illinois hawthorn	5
Crataegus series Pruinosae: C. pruinosa	Frosted hawthorn	5
Crataegus series Punctatae: C. collina	Hawthorn-of-the-hills	5
Crataegus series Punctatae: C. disperma	Two-seeded hawthorn	4
Crataegus series Punctatae: C. grandis	Great hawthorn	5
Crataegus series Punctatae: C. punctata	Dotted hawthorn	2
Crataegus series Rotundifoliae: C. chrysocarpa	Fireberry hawthorn	6
Crataegus series Rotundifoliae: C. margaretta	Margaret's hawthorn	5
Crataegus series Tenuifoliae: C. macrosperma	Big-fruited hawthorn	5
Crataegus series Virides: C. viridis	Green hawthorn	7
CREPIS CAPILLARIS	Hawk's beard	
CREPIS PULCHRA	Hawk's beard	
CREPIS TECTORUM	Narrow-leaved hawk's beard	
CROCUS VERNUS	Dutch crocus	
CROTALARIA SAGITTALIS	Rattlebox	
CROTON CAPITATUS (including 1 variety)	Hogwort	
Croton glandulosus v. septentrionalis	Sand croton	0
CROTON LINDHEIMERIANUS	Round-leaved woolly croton	
CROTON MONANTHOGYNUS	Prairie tea	
Croton willdenowii	Rushfoil	4
CRUCIATA PEDEMONTANUM (= *GALIUM PEDEMONTANUM*)	Foothill bedstraw	
CRYPSIS SCHOENOIDES	False foxtail	
Cryptotaenia canadensis	Honewort	3
CUCURBITA FOETIDISSIMA	Missouri gourd	
CUCURBITA PEPO v. OVIFERA	Field pumpkin	
Cunila origanoides	Dittany	5
Cuphea viscosissima	Blue waxweed	4
Cuscuta campestris	Field dodder	1
Cuscuta cephalanthi	Buttonbush dodder	5
Cuscuta compacta	Compact dodder	10
Cuscuta coryli	Hazel dodder	7
Cuscuta cuspidata	Stalked dodder	10
Cuscuta glomerata	Rope dodder	8
Cuscuta gronovii (including 1 variety)	Common dodder	2
CUSCUTA OBTUSIFLORA v. GLANDULOSA	Blunt-flowered dodder	
Cuscuta pentagona	Prairie dodder	5
Cuscuta polygonorum	Knotweed dodder	5
Cycloloma atriplicifolium	Winged pigweed	2
CYMBALARIA MURALIS	Kenilworth ivy	
Cynanchum laeve	Bluevine	1
CYNODON DACTYLON	Bermuda grass	
CYNOGLOSSUM OFFICINALE	Common hound's tongue	
Cynoglossum virginianum v. boreale	Northern wild comfrey	10
Cynoglossum virginianum v. virginianum	Common wild comfrey	5
CYNOSURUS CRISTATUS	Crested dog-tail grass	
Cyperus acuminatus	Short-pointed flat sedge	2
Cyperus bipartitus	Shining flat sedge	3
Cyperus dentatus	Toothed flat sedge	10
Cyperus diandrus	Umbrella flat sedge	6
Cyperus echinatus	Hedgehog club rush	4
Cyperus engelmannii	False rusty nut sedge	3
Cyperus erythrorhizos	Red-rooted nut sedge	1
Cyperus esculentus v. leptostachyus	Field nut sedge	0
Cyperus flavescens	Yellow flat sedge	3
Cyperus houghtonii	Smooth sand sedge	4
Cyperus lupulinus s. lupulinus	Slender sand sedge	4
Cyperus lupulinus s. macilentus	Great Plains flat sedge	4
Cyperus odoratus	Common rusty nut sedge	1
Cyperus pseudovegetus	False green flat sedge	3
Cyperus schweinitzii	Rough sand sedge	5
Cyperus squarrosus	Awned flat sedge	2
Cyperus strigosus	Long-scaled nut sedge	0
Cyperus tenuifolius. See *Kyllinga pumila*		
Cyperus x mesochorus	Midland sand sedge	4
Cypripedium acaule	Moccasin flower	10
Cypripedium candidum	White lady's slipper	10
Cypripedium parviflorum v. makasin	Sheviak's yellow lady's slipper	10
Cypripedium parviflorum v. pubescens	Large yellow lady's slipper	8
Cypripedium reginae	Showy lady's slipper	10
Cystopteris bulbifera	Bulblet bladder fern	9
Cystopteris protrusa	Common fragile fern	4
Cystopteris tennesseensis	Tennessee bladder fern	10
Cystopteris tenuis	Mackay's fragile fern	10
DACTYLIS GLOMERATA	Orchard grass	
Dalea candida	White prairie clover	10
DALEA LEPORINA	Foxtail prairie clover	
Dalea purpurea	Purple prairie clover	10
Danthonia spicata	Poverty oat grass	3
Dasiphora fruticosa s. floribunda (= *Potentilla fruticosa*)	Shrubby cinquefoil	9
Dasistoma macrophylla	Mullein foxglove	5
DATURA STRAMONIUM	Jimsonweed	
DATURA WRIGHTII	Angel's trumpet	
DAUCUS CAROTA	Queen Anne's lace	
Decodon verticillatus	Swamp loosestrife	8
DELPHINIUM AJACIS. See *CONSOLIDA AJACIS*		
Delphinium tricorne	Dwarf larkspur	5
Dennstaedtia punctilobula	Hay-scented fern	10
Deparia acrostichoides (= *Athyrium thelypterioides*)	Silvery spleenwort	8
Deschampsia cespitosa	Tufted hair grass	10
DESCURAINIA PINNATA v. BRACHYCARPA	Tansy mustard	
DESCURAINIA SOPHIA	Flixweed	
Desmanthus illinoensis	Illinois bundle flower	3

Scientific Name[a]	Common Name	Coefficient[b]
Desmodium canadense	Showy tick trefoil	3
Desmodium canescens	Hoary tick trefoil	3
Desmodium ciliare	Hairy tick trefoil	3
Desmodium cuspidatum v. cuspidatum	Smooth bracted tick trefoil	6
Desmodium cuspidatum v. longifolium	Hairy bracted tick trefoil	6
Desmodium glabellum	Smooth tick trefoil	3
Desmodium glutinosum	Pointed tick trefoil	6
Desmodium humifusum	Spreading tick trefoil	10
Desmodium illinoense	Illinois tick trefoil	5
Desmodium laevigatum	Glaucous tick trefoil	5
Desmodium marilandicum	Small-leaved tick trefoil	3
Desmodium nudiflorum	Bare-stemmed tick trefoil	5
Desmodium nuttallii	Nuttall's tick trefoil	4
Desmodium obtusum	Stiff tick trefoil	3
Desmodium paniculatum	Panicled tick trefoil	2
Desmodium pauciflorum	Few-flowered tick trefoil	8
Desmodium perplexum	Perplexing tick trefoil	3
Desmodium rotundifolium	Round-leaved tick trefoil	5
Desmodium sessilifolium	Sessile-leaved tick trefoil	6
Desmodium viridiflorum	Green-flowered tick trefoil	4
DIANTHUS ARMERIA	Deptford pink	
DIANTHUS BARBATUS	Sweet William	
DIANTHUS PLUMARIUS	Garden pink	
Diarrhena americana	American beak grass	5
Diarrhena obovata	Obovate beak grass	5
Dicentra canadensis	Squirrel corn	7
Dicentra cucullaria	Dutchman's breeches	6
DICENTRA SPECTABILIS	Garden bleeding-hearts	
Dichanthelium acuminatum s. columbianum (= *Panicum columbianum*)	Hemlock panic grass	8
Dichanthelium acuminatum s. fasculatum	Woolly panic grass	2
Dichanthelium acuminatum s. implicatum	Old field panic grass	2
Dichanthelium acuminatum s. leucothrix	Red-brown panic grass	10
Dichanthelium acuminatum s. lindheimeri	Smooth woolly panic grass	5
Dichanthelium acuminatum s. spretum	Sand panic grass	10
Dichanthelium annulum	Ringed panic grass	10
Dichanthelium bicknellii (*nomen nudum*)	Bicknell's panic grass	10
Dichanthelium boreale	Northern panic grass	10
Dichanthelium boscii	Bearded panic grass	4
Dichanthelium clandestinum	Deer-tongue grass	3
Dichanthelium commutatum s. ashei	Ashe's panic grass	7
Dichanthelium commutatum s. commutatum	Variable panic grass	7
Dichanthelium depauperatum	Starved panic grass	6
Dichanthelium dichotomum s. dichotomum	Forked panic grass	5
Dichanthelium dichotomum s. microcarpon	Small-fruited panic grass	4
Dichanthelium dichotomum s.yadkinense	Carolina panic grass	8
Dichanthelium latifolium	Broad-leaved panic grass	6
Dichanthelium laxiflorum	Loose-flowered panic grass	5
Dichanthelium leibergii	Prairie panic grass	10
Dichanthelium linearifolium	Slender-leaved panic grass	7
Dichanthelium lucidum	Shining panic grass	10
Dichanthelium mattamuskeetense	False bearded panic grass	5
Dichanthelium meridionale	Mat panic grass	7
Dichanthelium oligosanthes v. oligosanthes	Few-flowered panic grass	8
Dichanthelium oligosanthes v. scribnerianum	Scribner's panic grass	6
Dichanthelium ovale s. praecocius	Early white-haired panic grass	10
Dichanthelium ovale s. pseudopubescens	False white-haired panic grass	6
Dichanthelium ovale s. villosissimum	White-haired panic grass	6
Dichanthelium perlongum	Long-stalked panic grass	10
Dichanthelium polyanthes	Small-fruited panic grass	5
Dichanthelium scoparium	Broom panic grass	5
Dichanthelium sphaerocarpon	Round-fruited panic grass	5
Dichanthelium wilcoxianum	Wilcox's panic grass	10
Dicliptera brachiata	Bracted water willow	10
Didiplis diandra	Water purslane	6
Diervilla lonicera	Dwarf honeysuckle	9
DIGITALIS LANATA	Grecian foxglove	
DIGITARIA CILIARIS	Ciliate crabgrass	
Digitaria cognata (= *Leptoloma cognatum*)	Fall witch grass	2
Digitaria filiformis	Slender crabgrass	10
DIGITARIA ISCHAEMUM	Smooth crabgrass	
DIGITARIA SANGUINALIS	Hairy crabgrass	
Diodia teres	Buttonweed	2
Diodia virginiana	Large buttonweed	2
DIOSCOREA POLYSTACHYA	Chinese yam	
Dioscorea quaternata	Four-leaf yam	5
Dioscorea villosa	Common wild yam	4
Diospyros virginiana	Persimmon	2
Diplazium pycnocarpon (= *Athyrium pycnocarpon*)	Glade fern	9
DIPLOTAXIS MURALIS	Wall rocket	
DIPLOTAXIS TENUIFOLIA	Sand rocket	
DIPSACUS FULLONUM	Common teasel	
DIPSACUS LACINIATUS	Cut-leaved teasel	
Dirca palustris	Leatherwood	8
Dodecatheon frenchii	French's shooting star	10
Dodecatheon meadia	Shooting star	7
Doellingeria umbellata (= *Aster umbellatus*)	Flat-top aster	8
Draba brachycarpa	Short-fruited whitlow grass	2
Draba reptans	Common whitlow cress	2
DRABA VERNA	Mouse-eared whitlow cress	
DRACOCEPHALUM PARVIFLORUM	American dragonhead	
Drosera intermedia	Narrow-leaved sundew	10
Drosera rotundifolia	Round-leaved sundew	9
Dryopteris carthusiana	Spinulose wood fern	6
Dryopteris celsa	Log fern	10
Dryopteris clintoniana	Clinton's wood fern	10
Dryopteris cristata	Crested wood fern	10
Dryopteris goldiana	Goldie fern	9
Dryopteris intermedia	Common wood fern	10
Dryopteris marginalis	Marginal shield fern	8
DUCHESNEA INDICA	Indian strawberry	
Dulichium arundinaceum	Three-way sedge	10
DYSPHANIA AMBROSIOIDES (= *CHENOPODIUM AMBROSIOIDES*)	American wormseed	
DYSPHANIA BOTRYS (= *CHENOPODIUM BOTRYS*)	Jerusalem oak	
DYSSODIA PAPPOSA	Fetid marigold	
Echinacea pallida	Pale purple coneflower	10
Echinacea purpurea	Broad-leaved purple coneflower	6
ECHINOCHLOA CRUS-GALLI	Barnyard grass	
Echinochloa muricata (including 1 variety)	Rough barnyard grass	1
Echinochloa walteri	Cockspur grass	5
Echinocystis lobata	Wild cucumber	3
Echinodorus berteroi	Lance-leaved burhead	10
Echinodorus cordifolius	Creeping burhead	10
Echinodorus tenellus	Small burhead	10
ECHINOPS SPHAEROCEPHALUS	Great globe thistle	
ECHIUM PUSTULATUM	Bluedevil	
ECHIUM VULGARE	Viper's bugloss	
Eclipta prostrata	Yerba de tajo	3
EGERIA DENSA	Brazilian waterweed	

Table P-2. *continued*

Scientific Name[a]	Common Name	Coefficient[b]
EICHHORNIA CRASSIPES	Common water hyacinth	
ELAEAGNUS ANGUSTIFOLIA	Russian olive	
ELAEAGNUS UMBELLATA	Autumn olive	
Eleocharis acicularis	Needle spike rush	2
Eleocharis bifida	Notched spike rush	10
Eleocharis compressa	Flat-stemmed spike rush	10
Eleocharis elliptica	Golden-seeded spike rush	10
Eleocharis engelmannii	Engelmann's spike rush	4
Eleocharis equisetoides	Horsetail spike rush	10
Eleocharis erythropoda	Red-rooted spike rush	2
Eleocharis flavescens v. olivacea	Wrinkle-sheathed spike rush	10
Eleocharis geniculata	Knee spike rush	10
Eleocharis intermedia	Matted spike rush	10
Eleocharis melanocarpa	Black-fruited spike rush	10
Eleocharis microcarpa v. filiculmis	Hair spike rush	10
Eleocharis obtusa	Blunt spike rush	1
Eleocharis ovata	Oval spike rush	10
Eleocharis palustris	Great spike rush	8
Eleocharis parvula	Small spike rush	10
Eleocharis quadrangulata	Angled spike rush	4
Eleocharis quinqueflora	Few-flowered spike rush	10
Eleocharis robbinsii	Bog spike rush	10
Eleocharis rostellata	Wicket spike rush	10
Eleocharis tenuis v. pseudoptera	Slender spike rush	5
Eleocharis tenuis v. verrucosa	Slender spike rush	5
Eleocharis wolfii	Wolf's spike rush	8
Elephantopus carolinianus	Elephant's foot	5
ELEUSINE INDICA	Crowfoot grass	
ELEUTHEROCOCCUS PENTAPHYLLUS	Five-leaved aralia	
Ellisia nyctelea	Aunt lucy	5
Elodea canadensis	Common waterweed	3
Elodea nuttallii	Slender waterweed	4
Elymus canadensis	Canada wild rye	5
Elymus glabriflorus (including 1 variety)	Smooth-flowered wild rye	3
Elymus hystrix (including 1 variety)	Bottlebrush grass	5
ELYMUS REPENS (= *AGROPYRON REPENS*)	Quackgrass	
Elymus riparius	Riverbank wild rye	5
Elymus submuticus	Beardless wild rye	3
Elymus trachycaulus s. subsecundus (= *Agropyron trachycaulum*)	Awned wheat grass	8
Elymus trachycaulus s. trachycaulus	Slender wheat grass	8
Elymus villosus (including 1 variety)	Silky wild rye	4
Elymus virginicus (including 1 variety)	Virginia wild rye	3
Enemion biternatum (= *Isopyrum biternatum*)	False rue anemone	5
Epifagus virginiana	Beech drops	8
Epigaea repens	Trailing arbutus	9
Epilobium angustifolium. See *Chamerion angustifolium s. circumvagum*		
Epilobium ciliatum	Northern willow herb	3
Epilobium coloratum	Cinnamon willow herb	3
EPILOBIUM HIRSUTUM	Hairy willow herb	
Epilobium leptophyllum	Fen willow herb	10
Epilobium strictum	Downy willow herb	10
EPIPACTIS HELLEBORINE	Helleborine orchid	
Equisetum arvense	Common horsetail	1
Equisetum fluviatile	Pipes	10
Equisetum hyemale s. affine	Tall scouring rush	2
Equisetum laevigatum	Smooth scouring rush	2
Equisetum variegatum	Small scouring rush	10
Equisetum x ferrissii	Joliet horsetail	2
Equisetum x mackaii	Jesup's horsetail	10
Equisetum x nelsonii	Nelson's horsetail	10
Eragrostis capillaris	Lace grass	5
ERAGROSTIS CILIANENSIS	Stink grass	
Eragrostis frankii	Sandbar love grass	2
Eragrostis hypnoides	Creeping love grass	3
ERAGROSTIS MEXICANA	New Mexican love grass	
ERAGROSTIS MINOR	Lesser love grass	
Eragrostis pectinacea	Small love grass	0
Eragrostis spectabilis	Purple love grass	3
ERAGROSTIS TRICHODES	Ice cream grass	
ERANTHIS HYEMALIS	Mountain winter aconite	
Erechtites hieracifolia	Fireweed	2
Erigenia bulbosa	Harbinger of spring	5
Erigeron annuus	Annual fleabane	0
Erigeron philadelphicus	Marsh fleabane	3
Erigeron pulchellus	Robin's plantain	8
Erigeron strigosus	Daisy fleabane	2
Eriocaulon aquaticum	Pipewort	10
ERIOCHLOA CONTRACTA	Prairie cup grass	
ERIOGONUM ANNUUM	Annual wild buckwheat	
Eriophorum angustifolium	Narrow-leaved cotton grass	10
Eriophorum gracile	Slender cotton grass	10
Eriophorum vaginatum	Dense cotton grass	10
Eriophorum virginicum	Rusty cotton grass	10
Eriophorum viridicarinatum	Tall cotton grass	10
ERODIUM CICUTARIUM	Storksbill	
ERUCASTRUM GALLICUM	Dog mustard	
Eryngium yuccifolium	Rattlesnake master	10
Erysimum capitatum	Western wallflower	3
ERYSIMUM CHEIRANTHOIDES	Wormseed mustard	
ERYSIMUM HIERACIFOLIUM	Hawkweed mustard	
ERYSIMUM INCONSPICUUM	Small wormseed mustard	
ERYSIMUM REPANDUM	Treacle mustard	
Erythronium albidum	White adder's tongue	3
Erythronium americanum	Yellow adder's tongue	5
EUONYMUS ALATA	Winged euonymus	
Euonymus americana	Strawberry bush	8
Euonymus atropurpurea	Wahoo	5
EUONYMUS BUNGEANA	Winterberry	
EUONYMUS FORTUNEI	Wintercreeper	
EUONYMUS HAMILTONIANA	Japanese spindle tree	
Euonymus obovata	Running strawberry bush	7
Eupatoriadelphus fistulosus (= *Eupatorium fistulosum*)	Hollow Joe Pye weed	4
Eupatoriadelphus maculatus	Spotted Joe Pye weed	5
Eupatoriadelphus purpureus	Purple Joe Pye weed	5
Eupatorium. See also 3 species of *Eupatoriadelphus*		
Eupatorium album	White thoroughwort	4
Eupatorium altissimum	Tall boneset	1
Eupatorium coelestinum. See *Conoclinium coelestinum*		
Eupatorium hyssopifolium	Hyssop-leaved boneset	2
Eupatorium incarnatum. See *Fleischmannia incarnata*		
Eupatorium perfoliatum	Common boneset	4
Eupatorium rotundifolium	Round-leaved thoroughwort	2
Eupatorium rugosum. See *Ageratina altissima*		
Eupatorium serotinum	Late boneset	0
Eupatorium sessilifolium	Upland boneset	6
Euphorbia commutata	Tinted spurge	5
Euphorbia corollata	Flowering spurge	4
Euphorbia cyathophora	Painted leaf	0
EUPHORBIA CYPARISSIAS	Cypress spurge	
EUPHORBIA DAVIDII	David's spurge	
Euphorbia dentata (= *Poinsettia dentata*)	Toothed spurge	0
EUPHORBIA ESULA	Leafy spurge	
EUPHORBIA MARGINATA	Snow-on-the-mountain	
Euphorbia obtusata	Blunt-leaved spurge	3
EUPHORBIA PEPLUS	Petty spurge	
Eurybia furcata (= *Aster furcatus*)	Forked aster	10
Eurybia macrophylla	Big-leaved aster	7
Eurybia schreberi	Smooth forked aster	10
Euthamia caroliniana	Slender-leaved goldenrod	10
Euthamia graminifolia	Grass-leaved goldenrod	3
Euthamia gymnospermoides	Viscid grass-leaved goldenrod	5

Scientific Name[a]	Common Name	Coefficient[b]
FAGOPYRUM ESCULENTUM	Buckwheat	
Fagus grandifolia	American beech	8
Fallopia cilinodis (= *Polygonum cilinode*)	Fringed bindweed	10
FALLOPIA CONVOLVULUS	Black bindweed	
FALLOPIA JAPONICA	Japanese knotweed	
Fallopia scandens v. cristata	Climbing false buckwheat	0
FALLOPIA SCANDENS v. DUMETORUM	Climbing false buckwheat	
Fallopia scandens v. scandens	Climbing false buckwheat	0
FATOUA VILLOSA	Mulberry weed	
FESTUCA ELATIOR. See *SCHEDONORUS ARUNDINACEUS*		
FESTUCA FILIFORMIS	Fine-leaved sheep fescue	
FESTUCA OVINA	Hard fescue	
Festuca paradoxa	Greater nodding fescue	10
FESTUCA PRATENSIS. See *SCHEDONORUS PRATENSIS*		
FESTUCA RUBRA	Red fescue	
Festuca subverticillata	Nodding fescue	4
FESTUCA TRACHYPHYLLA	Sheep fescue	
FICUS CARICA	Common fig	
Filipendula rubra	Queen-of-the-prairie	9
FILIPENDULA ULMARIA	European meadowsweet	
Fimbristylis annua	Baldwin's fimbristylis	10
Fimbristylis autumnalis	Autumn sedge	3
Fimbristylis puberula	Chestnut sedge	10
FLAVERIA CAMPESTRIS	Alkali yellowtops	
Fleischmannia incarnata (= *Eupatorium incarnatum*)	Pink thoroughwort	5
Floerkea proserpinacoides	False mermaid weed	5
FOENICULUM VULGARE	Sweet fennel	
Forestiera acuminata	Swamp privet	8
FORSYTHIA SUSPENSA	Weeping forsythia	
FORSYTHIA x INTERMEDIA	Golden bell	
Fragaria vesca s. americana	Hillside strawberry	10
Fragaria virginiana (including 1 subspecies)	Wild strawberry	2
FRANGULA ALNUS (= *RHAMNUS FRANGULA*)	Glossy buckthorn	
Frangula caroliniana (= *Rhamnus caroliniana*)	Carolina buckthorn	4
Frasera caroliniensis	American columbo	8
Fraxinus americana	White ash	4
Fraxinus nigra	Black ash	7
Fraxinus pennsylvanica v. lanceolata	Green ash	1
Fraxinus pennsylvanica v. pennsylvanica	Red ash	3
Fraxinus profunda	Pumpkin ash	8
Fraxinus quadrangulata	Blue ash	7
Froelichia floridana v. campestris	Cottonweed	5
FROELICHIA GRACILIS	Cottonweed	
Fuirena pumila	Umbrella sedge	10
FUMARIA OFFICINALIS	Fumitory	
GAILLARDIA PULCHELLA	Firewheels	
Galactia volubilis	Mississippi milk pea	9
GALANTHUS NIVALIS	Snowdrop	
Galearis spectabilis (= *Orchis spectabilis*)	Showy orchis	7
GALEOPSIS LADANUM	Red hemp nettle	
GALINSOGA PARVIFLORA	Smooth Peruvian daisy	
GALINSOGA QUADRIRADIATA	Peruvian daisy	
Galium aparine	Annual bedstraw	1
Galium asprellum	Rough bedstraw	7
Galium boreale	Northern bedstraw	7
Galium brevipes	Short-stalked bedstraw	10
Galium circaezans v. circaezans	Smooth wild licorice	7
Galium circaezans v. hypomalacum	Hairy wild licorice	5
Galium concinnum	Shining bedstraw	5
GALIUM DIVARICATUM	Parisian bedstraw	
Galium labradoricum	Bog bedstraw	10
Galium lanceolatum	Lance-leaved wild licorice	7
GALIUM MOLLUGO	White bedstraw	
Galium obtusum	Wild madder	5
GALIUM PEDEMONTANUM. See *CRUCIATA PEDEMONTANUM*		
Galium pilosum	Hairy bedstraw	5
Galium tinctorium	Stiff bedstraw	6
Galium trifidum	Small bedstraw	8
Galium triflorum	Sweet-scented bedstraw	5
GALIUM VERUM	Yellow spring bedstraw	
GALIUM WIRTGENII	Wirtgen's bedstraw	
Gamochaeta purpurea (= *Gnaphalium purpureum*)	Early cudweed	0
Gaultheria procumbens	Checkerberry	8
Gaura biennis	Biennial gaura	3
GAURA COCCINEA	Scarlet bedstraw	
Gaura filipes	Slender gaura	10
Gaura longiflora	Common gaura	3
GAURA MOLLIS	Small-flowered gaura	
Gaylussacia baccata	Black huckleberry	7
Gentiana alba	Pale gentian	10
Gentiana andrewsii	Closed gentian	4
Gentiana puberulenta	Downy gentian	10
Gentiana saponaria	Soapwort gentian	6
Gentiana villosa	Hairy gentian	3
Gentianella quinquefolia s. occidentalis	Stiff gentian	5
Gentianopsis crinita	Fringed gentian	8
Gentianopsis virgata	Small-fringed gentian	8
GERANIUM AEQUALE	Cranesbill	
Geranium bicknellii	Northern cranesbill	9
Geranium carolinianum	Carolina cranesbill	2
GERANIUM COLUMBIANUM	Long-stalked cranesbill	
Geranium maculatum	Wild geranium	4
GERANIUM PUSILLUM	Small geranium	
Geranium robertianum	Herb robert	4
GERANIUM SANGUINEUM	Bloody cranesbill	
Geum aleppicum	Yellow avens	5
Geum canadense	White avens	1
Geum laciniatum (including 1 variety)	Rough avens	3
Geum rivale	Purple avens	10
Geum vernum	Spring avens	1
Geum virginianum	Pale avens	5
Gillenia stipulata	Indian physic	6
GLANDULARIA BIPINNATIFIDA (= *VERBENA BIPINNATIFIDA*)	Fern-leaf verbena	
GLANDULARIA CANADENSIS	Rose verbena	
GLECHOMA HEDERACEA	Ground ivy	
Gleditsia aquatica	Water locust	8
Gleditsia triacanthos	Honey locust	1
Glyceria acutiflora	Long-scaled manna grass	10
Glyceria borealis	Northern manna grass	10
Glyceria canadensis	Rattlesnake manna grass	10
Glyceria grandis	Reed manna grass	5
Glyceria pallida. See *Torreyochloa pallida v. pallida*		
Glyceria septentrionalis	Floating manna grass	7
Glyceria striata	Fowl manna grass	4
GLYCINE MAX	Soybean	
GLYCYRRHIZA LEPIDOTA	Wild licorice	
Gnaphalium. See also 3 species of *Pseudognaphalium*		
Gnaphalium purpureum. See *Gamochaeta purpurea*		
GNAPHALIUM ULIGINOSUM	Low cudweed	
Gonolobus suberosa	Angle-fruited milk vine	7
Goodyera pubescens	Rattlesnake plantain	5
Gratiola neglecta	Clammy hedge hyssop	4
Gratiola virginiana	Round-fruited hedge hyssop	4
GRINDELIA SQUARROSA	Gum plant	
Gymnocladus dioica	Kentucky coffee tree	4
Gymnopogon ambiguus	Beard grass	10

Table P-2. *continued*

Scientific Name[a]	Common Name	Coefficient[b]
GYPSOPHILA PANICULATA	Common baby's breath	
GYPSOPHILA SCORZONERIFOLIA	Big baby's breath	
Habenaria viridis. See *Coeloglossum viride*		
Hackelia virginiana	Stickseed	0
Hamamelis virginiana	Witch hazel	5
Hasteola suaveolens (= *Cacalia suaveolens*)	Sweet Indian plantain	7
Hedeoma hispida	Rough pennyroyal	2
Hedeoma pulegioides	American pennyroyal	3
HEDERA HELIX	English ivy	
Hedyotis. See 5 species of *Houstonia*		
Hedyotis nigricans. See *Stenaria nigricans*		
Helenium amarum	Bitterweed	0
Helenium autumnale	Common sneezeweed	3
Helenium flexuosum	Purple-headed sneezeweed	3
Helianthemum bicknellii	Rockrose	7
Helianthemum canadense	Common rockrose	7
Helianthus angustifolius	Narrow-leaved sunflower	10
HELIANTHUS ANNUUS	Common sunflower	
Helianthus decapetalus	Pale sunflower	5
Helianthus divaricatus	Woodland sunflower	5
Helianthus giganteus	Tall sunflower	6
Helianthus grosseserratus	Sawtooth sunflower	3
Helianthus hirsutus	Bristly sunflower	5
HELIANTHUS MAXIMILIANII	Maximilian's sunflower	
Helianthus microcephalus	Small wood sunflower	8
Helianthus mollis	Downy sunflower	9
Helianthus occidentalis	Western sunflower	9
Helianthus pauciflorus s. pauciflorus	Prairie sunflower	4
Helianthus pauciflorus s. subrhomboideus	Stiff sunflower	4
HELIANTHUS PETIOLARIS	Petioled sunflower	
Helianthus strumosus	Pale-leaved sunflower	5
Helianthus tuberosus	Jerusalem artichoke	2
Heliopsis helianthoides (including 1 variety)	False sunflower	4
HELIOTROPIUM INDICUM	Indian heliotrope	
Heliotropium tenellum	Slender heliotrope	10
HELLEBORUS VIRIDIS	Green hellebore	
HEMEROCALLIS FULVA	Orange day lily	
HEMEROCALLIS LILIOASPHODELUS	Lemon day lily	
Hemicarpha. See 2 species of *Lipocarpha*		
Hepatica. See 2 species of *Anemone*		
Heracleum sphondylium s. montanum	Cow parsnip	6
HESPERIS MATRONALIS	Dame's rocket	
HESPEROSTIPA COMATA (= *STIPA COMATA*)	Needle-and-thread	
Hesperostipa spartea (= *Stipa spartea*)	Porcupine grass	8
Heteranthera dubia	Water star grass	4
Heteranthera reniformis	Mud plantain	10
Heterotheca camporum v. camporum (= *Chrysopsis camporum*)	Golden aster	4
HETEROTHECA CAMPORUM v. GLANDULISSIMA	Hairy false golden aster	
HETEROTHECA SUBAXILLARIS	Camphorweed	
Heuchera americana (including 1 variety)	Tall alum-root	7
Heuchera parviflora (including 1 variety)	Late alumroot	10
Heuchera richardsonii	Prairie alumroot	8
Heuchera villosa	Villous alumroot	10
Hexalectris spicata	Crested coralroot	10
Hibiscus laevis	Halberd-leaved rose mallow	4
Hibiscus moscheutos v. moscheutos	Swamp rose mallow	4
Hibiscus moscheutos v. occidentalis	Hairy rose mallow	4
HIBISCUS SYRIACUS	Rose-of-Sharon	
HIBISCUS TRIONUM	Flower-of-an-hour	
HIERACIUM AURANTIACUM	Devil's paint brush	
HIERACIUM CAESPITOSUM	Field hawkweed	
HIERACIUM FLAGELLARE	Whiplash hawkweed	
Hieracium gronovii	Hairy hawkweed	5
Hieracium longipilum	Long-bearded hawkweed	5
Hieracium paniculatum	Panicled hawkweed	8
HIERACIUM PILOSELLOIDES	King devil	
Hieracium scabrum	Rough hawkweed	5
Hieracium umbellatum	Canada hawkweed	5
Hieracium venosum	Rattlesnake weed	10
Hierochloë odorata	Sweet grass	10
Hippuris vulgaris	Mare's tail	10
HOLCUS LANATUS	Velvet grass	
HOLOSTEUM UMBELLATUM	Jagged chickweed	
HORDEUM BRACHYANTHERUM	Meadow barley	
HORDEUM JUBATUM	Squirrel-tail grass	
Hordeum pusillum	Little barley	0
HORDEUM VULGARE	Common barley	
HOSTA VENTRICOSA	Blue hosta	
Hottonia inflata	Featherfoil	9
Houstonia caerulea (= *Hedyotis caerulea*)	Bluets	4
Houstonia canadensis	Canada summer bluet	10
Houstonia longifolia	Long-leaved bluets	7
Houstonia purpurea (including 1 variety)	Large houstonia	6
HOUSTONIA PUSILLA	Small bluets	
Hudsonia tomentosa	False heather	10
HUMULUS JAPONICUS	Japanese hops	
Humulus lupulus v. lupuloides	American hops	5
HUMULUS LUPULUS v. LUPULUS	Common hops	
Humulus lupulus v. pubescens	American hops	5
Huperzia lucidula (= *Lycopodium lucidulum*)	Shining clubmoss	5
Huperzia porophila	Cliff clubmoss	10
HYACINTHOIDES NONSCRIPTA (= *SCILLA NONSCRIPTA*)	Lineless squill	
Hybanthus concolor	Green violet	6
Hydrangea arborescens	Wild hydrangea	7
Hydrangea cinerea	Ashy hydrangea	7
HYDRANGEA PANICULATA	Panicled hydrangea	
HYDRANGEA QUERCIFOLIA	Oak-leaved hydrangea	
Hydrastis canadensis	Golden seal	7
Hydrocotyle americana	American pennywort	10
HYDROCOTYLE SIBTHORPIOIDES	Lawn water pennywort	
Hydrocotyle umbellata	Water pennywort	7
Hydrophyllum appendiculatum	Great waterleaf	6
Hydrophyllum canadense	Canada waterleaf	8
Hydrophyllum macrophyllum	Large-leaf waterleaf	7
Hydrophyllum virginianum	Virginia waterleaf	4
HYLOTELEPHIUM ERYTHROSTICTUM	Garden annual stonecrop	
HYLOTELEPHIUM SPECTABILE	Showy annual stonecrop	
Hylotelephium telephioides (= *Sedum telephioides*)	American orpine	10
HYLOTELEPHIUM TELEPHIUM s. TELEPHIUM	Live-forever	
Hymenocallis occidentalis	Spider lily	9
Hymenopappus scabiosaeus	Old plainsman	8
HYOSCYAMUS NIGER	Black henbane	
Hypericum adpressum	Shore St. John's wort	10
Hypericum boreale	Northern St. John's wort	8
Hypericum canadense	Canadian St. John's wort	8
Hypericum dolabriforme	Shrubby St. John's wort	10
Hypericum drummondii	Nits-and-lice	4
Hypericum frondosum	Golden St. John's wort	10
Hypericum gentianoides	Orange grass	4
Hypericum gymnanthum	Clasping St. John's wort	4
Hypericum hypericoides s. multicaule	St. Andrew's cross	4

Scientific Name[a]	Common Name	Coefficient[b]
Hypericum kalmianum	Kalm's St. John's wort	10
Hypericum majus	Sand St. John's wort	6
Hypericum mutilum	Dwarf St. John's wort	4
HYPERICUM PERFORATUM	Common St. John's wort	
Hypericum prolificum	Shrubby St. John's wort	4
Hypericum punctatum	Spotted St. John's wort	3
Hypericum pyramidatum	Giant St. John's wort	10
Hypericum sphaerocarpum	Round-fruited St. John's wort	7
Hypericum virgatum	Toothed St. John's wort	9
HYPOCHAERIS RADICATA	Spotted cat's ear	
Hypoxis hirsuta	Yellow star grass	7
Ilex decidua	Swamp holly	6
Ilex mucronata (= *Nemopanthus mucronata*)	Mountain holly	10
ILEX OPACA	American holly	
Ilex verticillata	Winterberry	8
Iliamna rivularis	Kankakee mallow	10
Impatiens capensis	Spotted touch-me-not	2
IMPATIENS GLANDULIFERA	Indian balsam	
Impatiens pallida	Pale touch-me-not	4
INULA HELENIUM	Elecampane	
Iodanthus pinnatifidus	Violet cress	6
Ionactis linariifolius (= *Aster linariifolius*)	Flax-leaved aster	9
IPOMOEA COCCINEA	Red morning glory	
IPOMOEA HEDERACEA	Ivy-leaved morning glory	
Ipomoea lacunosa	Small morning glory	2
Ipomoea pandurata	Wild sweet potato	3
IPOMOEA PURPUREA	Common morning glory	
IPOMOPSIS RUBRA	Standing cypress	
Iresine rhizomatosa	Bloodleaf	10
Iris brevicaulis	Blue water iris	9
Iris cristata	Dwarf crested iris	7
IRIS GERMANICA	German iris	
IRIS PALLIDA	Sweet iris	
IRIS PSEUDACORUS	Tall yellow iris	
IRIS PUMILA	Dwarf iris	
Iris virginica	Southern blue flag	5
Isanthus brachiatus (= *Trichostema brachiatum*)	False pennyroyal	4
Isoetes engelmannii	Engelmann's quillwort	10
Isoetes melanopoda	Black quillwort	4
Isopyrum biternatum. See *Enemion biternatum*		
Isotria verticillata	Five leaves	7
Itea virginica	Virginia willow	10
IVA ANGUSTIFOLIA	Narrow-leaved marsh elder	
Iva annua (including 1 variety)	Marsh elder	0
IVA XANTHIFOLIA	Rag sumpweed	
Jeffersonia diphylla	Twinleaf	7
Juglans cinerea	Butternut	5
Juglans nigra	Black walnut	2
Juncus acuminatus	Sharp-fruited rush	4
Juncus alpinoarticulatus	Richardson's rush	6
Juncus anthelatus	Large poverty rush	0
Juncus articulatus	Jointed rush	4
Juncus balticus	Lake shore rush	6
Juncus biflorus	Two-flowered rush	4
Juncus brachycarpus	Short-fruited rush	4
Juncus brachycephalus	Short-headed rush	7
Juncus bufonius	Toad rush	2
Juncus canadensis	Canadian rush	7
JUNCUS COMPRESSUS	Black grass	
Juncus diffusissimus	Slimpod rush	4
Juncus dudleyi	Dudley's rush	2
Juncus effusus	Common rush	3
JUNCUS GERARDII	Saltmarsh rush	
Juncus greenei	Greene's rush	8
Juncus interior	Inland rush	3
Juncus marginatus	Grass-leaved rush	4
Juncus militaris	Soldier rush	10
Juncus nodatus	Stout rush	7

Scientific Name[a]	Common Name	Coefficient[b]
Juncus nodosus	Joint rush	5
Juncus pelocarpus	Brown-fruited rush	10
Juncus scirpoides	Round-headed rush	9
Juncus secundus	Side-flowering rush	3
Juncus tenuis	Path rush	0
Juncus torreyi	Torrey's rush	3
Juncus x alpiniformis	Hybrid alpine rush	4
Juniperus communis v. depressa	Common juniper	10
Juniperus virginiana	Eastern red cedar	2
Justicia americana	Water willow	6
Kalmia latifolia	Mountain laurel	10
KERRIA JAPONICA	Japanese rose	
KICKXIA ELATINE	Fluellin	
KOCHIA SCOPARIA	Belvedere summer cypress	
Koeleria macrantha	June grass	8
KOELREUTERIA PANICULATA	Golden rain tree	
Krigia biflora	Two-flower false dandelion	5
Krigia caespitosa	Weedy dwarf dandelion	1
Krigia dandelion	Potato dwarf dandelion	8
Krigia virginica	Virginia dwarf dandelion	4
Kuhnia eupatoriodes. See *Brickellia eupatorioides*		
KUMMEROWIA STIPULACEA (= *LESPEDEZA STIPULACEA*)	Korean clover	
KUMMEROWIA STRIATA	Japanese lespedeza	
Kyllinga pumila (= *Cyperus tenuifolius*)	Tufted flat sedge	0
Lactuca biennis	Tall blue lettuce	2
Lactuca canadensis	Wild lettuce	2
Lactuca floridana	Blue lettuce	5
Lactuca hirsuta	Hairy wild lettuce	10
Lactuca ludoviciana	Western wild lettuce	10
LACTUCA SALIGNA	Willow-leaved lettuce	
LACTUCA SATIVA	Garden lettuce	
LACTUCA SERRIOLA	Prickly lettuce	
LACTUCA TATARICA v. PULCHELLUM	Tartarian blue lettuce	
LAGERSTROEMIA INDICA	Crape myrtle	
LAMIUM AMPLEXICAULE	Henbit	
LAMIUM PURPUREUM	Purple dead nettle	
Laportea canadensis	Canada wood nettle	2
LAPPULA SQUARROSA	Beggar's lice	
LAPSANA COMMUNIS	Common nipplewort	
Larix laricina	American larch	10
Lathyrus japonicus v. maritimus	Beach pea	10
LATHYRUS LATIFOLIUS	Everlasting pea	
Lathyrus ochroleucus	Pale vetchling	10
Lathyrus palustris	Marsh vetchling	7
LATHYRUS TUBEROSUS	Earthnut vetchling	
Lathyrus venosus	Veiny pea	10
Leavenworthia uniflora	One-flowered leavenworthia	10
Lechea minor	Small pinweed	8
Lechea mucronata	Hairy pinweed	7
Lechea pulchella	Pretty pinweed	7
Lechea racemulosa	Narrow-fruited pinweed	8
Lechea stricta	Bushy pinweed	10
Lechea tenuifolia	Narrow-leaved pinweed	4
Leersia lenticularis	Catchfly grass	5
Leersia oryzoides	Rice cut grass	2
Leersia virginica	White grass	4
Lemna aequinoctialis	Three-nerved duckweed	5
Lemna gibba	Swollen duckweed	10
Lemna minor	Small duckweed	3
Lemna minuta	Dinky duckweed	3
Lemna obscura	Purple duckweed	3
Lemna perpusilla	Least duckweed	10
Lemna trisulca	Forked duckweed	6
Lemna turionifera	Perennial duckweed	3
Lemna valdiviana	Pale duckweed	10
LENS CULINARIS	Lentil	
LEONTODON TARAXACOIDES	Hawkbit	
LEONURUS CARDIACA	Motherwort	

Table P-2. *continued*

Scientific Name[a]	Common Name	Coefficient[b]
LEONURUS MARRUBIASTRUM. See *CHAITURUS MARRUBIASTRUM*		
LEPIDIUM CAMPESTRE	Field cress	
LEPIDIUM DENSIFLORUM	Small pepper cress	
LEPIDIUM LATIFOLIUM	Broad-leaved pepper cress	
LEPIDIUM PERFOLIATUM	Clasping pepperwort	
Lepidium virginicum	Common pepper cress	0
LEPTOCHLOA FUSCA s. *FASCICULARIS*	Bearded sprangle top	
Leptochloa panicea s. *brachiata*	Red sprangle top	4
Leptochloa panicoides	Salt meadow grass	10
Leptoloma cognatum. See *Digitaria cognata*		
LESPEDEZA BICOLOR	Two-colored bush clover	
Lespedeza capitata	Round-headed bush clover	4
LESPEDEZA CUNEATA	Silky bush clover	
Lespedeza frutescens	Wand-like bush clover	5
Lespedeza hirta	Hairy bush clover	7
Lespedeza procumbens	Trailing bush clover	6
Lespedeza repens	Creeping bush clover	6
LESPEDEZA STIPULACEA. See *KUMMEROWIA STIPULACEA*		
LESPEDEZA STRIATA. See *KUMMEROWIA STRIATA*		
Lespedeza stuevei	Stueve's bush clover	10
LESPEDEZA THUNBERGII	Shrubby bush clover	
Lespedeza violacea	Violet bush clover	5
Lespedeza virginica	Slender bush clover	4
Lesquerella globosa. See *Physaria globosa*		
LEUCANTHEMUM VULGARE (= *CHRYSANTHEMUM LEUCANTHEMUM*)	Ox-eye daisy	
LEUCOJUM AESTIVUM	Snowflake	
Leucospora multifida	Obe-wan-conobea	3
LEYMUS ARENARIUS	Lyme grass	
Liatris aspera (including 1 variety)	Rough blazing star	8
Liatris cylindracea	Cylindrical blazing star	10
Liatris pycnostachya	Prairie blazing star	10
Liatris scariosa v. *nieuwlandii*	Savanna blazing star	9
Liatris spicata	Marsh blazing star	8
Liatris squarrosa	Blazing star	5
Liatris squarrulosa	Southern blazing star	9
Ligusticum canadense	Lovage	10
LIGUSTRUM OBTUSIFOLIUM	Border privet	
LIGUSTRUM OVALIFOLIUM	Oak-leaved privet	
LIGUSTRUM VULGARE	Common privet	
Lilium canadense	Canada lily	7
LILIUM LANCIFOLIUM	Tiger lily	
Lilium michiganense	Michigan lily	5
Lilium philadelphicum	Prairie lily	10
Lilium superbum	Superb lily	8
Limnobium spongia	Frog's bit	10
Linaria canadensis. See *Nuttallanthus canadensis*		
LINARIA DALMATICA s. *MACEDONICA*	Dalmation toadflax	
LINARIA REPENS	Striped toadflax	
LINARIA VULGARIS	Butter-and-eggs	
Lindera benzoin	Hairy spicebush	5
Lindernia dubia v. *anagallidea*	Slender false pimpernel	3
Lindernia dubia v. *dubia*	False pimpernel	3
Linnaea borealis s. *longifolia*	Twinflower	10
Linum intercursum	Southern yellow flax	10
Linum medium v. *texanum*	Small yellow flax	4
Linum striatum	Stiff yellow flax	5
Linum sulcatum	Grooved yellow flax	10
LINUM USITATISSIMUM	Common flax	
Linum virginianum	Slender yellow flax	4
Liparis liliifolia	Purple twayblade	3
Liparis loeselii	Green twayblade	4
Lipocarpha drummondii (= *Hemicarpha drummondii*)	Drummond's half-chaff sedge	10
Lipocarpha micrantha	Small-flowered half-chaff sedge	3
Liquidambar styraciflua	Sweetgum	4
Liriodendron tulipifera	Tulip poplar	4
LITHOSPERMUM ARVENSE. See *BUGLOSSOIDES ARVENSE*		
Lithospermum canescens	Hoary puccoon	10
Lithospermum caroliniense v. *croceum*	Hairy puccoon	8
Lithospermum incisum	Fringed puccoon	10
Lithospermum latifolium	American gromwell	7
LITHOSPERMUM OFFICINALE	European gromwell	
Lobelia cardinalis	Cardinal flower	4
Lobelia inflata	Indian tobacco	3
Lobelia kalmii	Bog lobelia	10
Lobelia puberula v. *simulans*	Downy lobelia	5
Lobelia siphilitica	Great blue lobelia	3
Lobelia spicata (including varieties)	Pale spiked lobelia	7
LOBULARIA MARITIMA	Sweet alyssum	
LOLIUM MULTIFLORUM	Italian rye grass	
LOLIUM PERENNE	Perennial rye grass	
Lonicera canadensis	American fly honesuckle	10
Lonicera dioica (including 1 variety)	Limber honeysuckle	8
LONICERA JAPONICA	Japanese honeysuckle	
LONICERA MAACKII	Amur honeysuckle	
LONICERA MORROWII	Morrow's honeysuckle	
Lonicera reticulata	Grape honeysuckle	8
LONICERA RUPRECHTIANA	Manchurian honeysuckle	
LONICERA SEMPERVIRENS	Trumpet honeysuckle	
LONICERA TATARICA	Tartarian honeysuckle	
LONICERA XYLOSTEUM	European fly honeysuckle	
LONICERA x *BELLA*	Showy fly honeysuckle	
LONICERA x *MINUTIFLORA*	Fly honeysuckle	
LONICERA x *MUENDENIENSIS*	Common fly honeysuckle	
LONICERA x *MUSCAVIENSIS*	Fly honeysuckle	
LONICERA x *NOTHA*	Hybrid fly honeysuckle	
LONICERA x *XYLOSTEOIDES*	Fly honeysuckle	
LOTUS CORNICULATUS	Birdsfoot trefoil	
LOTUS UNIFOLIOLATUS	Deer vetch	
Ludwigia alternifolia	Seedbox	3
Ludwigia decurrens	Erect primrose willow	4
Ludwigia glandulosa	False loosestrife	3
Ludwigia leptocarpa	Angle-stemmed primrose willow	
Ludwigia palustris	Marsh purslane	3
Ludwigia peploides s. *glabrescens*	Creeping primrose willow	2
Ludwigia polycarpa	False loosestrife	4
Ludwigia sphaerocarpa	Globe-fruit primrose willow	10
LUNARIA ANNUA	Honesty	
Lupinus perennis	Wild lupine	7
Luzula acuminata	Hairy wood rush	10
Luzula bulbosa	Bulbous wood rush	6
Luzula echinata	Common wood rush	6
Luzula multiflora	Common wood rush	6
LYCHNIS. See also 2 species of *SILENE*		
LYCHNIS CHALCEDONICA	Maltese cross	
LYCHNIS CORONARIA	Mullein pink	
LYCIUM BARBARUM	Common matrimony vine	
Lycopodiella inundata (= *Lycopodium inundatum*)	Bog clubmoss	7
Lycopodiella subappressa	Appressed bog clubmoss	7
Lycopodium. See also 2 species of *Huperzia* and 2 species of *Lycopodiella*		
Lycopodium clavatum	Running ground pine	4
Lycopodium dendroideum	Tree ground pine	10
Lycopodium digitatum	Trailing ground pine	2
Lycopodium hickeyi	Hickey's clubmoss	6
Lycopodium obscurum	Ground pine	6
Lycopodium tristachyum	Ground cedar	10
Lycopus americanus	Common water horehound	3
Lycopus amplectens	Sessile water horehound	10

Scientific Name[a]	Common Name	Coefficient[b]
LYCOPUS ASPER	Rough water horehound	
LYCOPUS EUROPAEUS	European water horehound	
Lycopus rubellus	Stalked water horehound	8
Lycopus uniflorus	Nothern bugleweed	5
Lycopus virginicus	Bugleweed	5
LYGODESMIA JUNCEA	Pink-flowered skeleton weed	
Lygodium palmatum	Climbing fern	6
Lysimachia ciliata	Fringed loosestrife	4
LYSIMACHIA CLETHROIDES	Goose-neck loosestrife	
Lysimachia hybrida	Loosestrife	10
Lysimachia lanceolata	Lance-leaved loosestrife	7
LYSIMACHIA NUMMULARIA	Moneywort	
Lysimachia quadriflora	Narrow-leaved loosestrife	9
Lysimachia quadrifolia	Whorled loosestrife	6
Lysimachia terrestris	Swamp candles	8
Lysimachia thyrsiflora	Tufted loosestrife	7
LYSIMACHIA VULGARIS	Garden loosestrife	
Lythrum alatum	Winged loosestrife	5
LYTHRUM SALICARIA	Purple loosestrife	
MACLEAYA CORDATA	Plume poppy	
MACLURA POMIFERA	Hedge apple	
MADIA SATIVA	Tarweed	
Magalodonta beckii (= *Bidens beckii*)	Water marigold	10
Magnolia acuminata	Cucumber magnolia	10
Magnolia tripetala	Umbrella magnolia	10
MAHONIA REPENS. See *BERBERIS REPENS*		
Maianthemum canadense	Canada mayflower	8
Maianthemum racemosum (= *Smilacina racemosa*)	Feathery false Solomon's seal	4
Maianthemum stellatum (= *Smilacina stellatum*)	Starry false Solomon's seal	6
Malaxis monophyllos v. brachypoda	White adder's-mouth orchid	10
Malaxis unifolia	Green adder's mouth	10
Malus coronaria	Wild sweet crab	5
MALUS DOMESTICA	Apple	
Malus ioensis	Iowa crab	3
MALUS SOULARDII	Soulard's crab-apple	
MALVA ALCEA	Vervain mallow	
MALVA MOSCHATA	Musk mallow	
MALVA NEGLECTA	Cheeses	
MALVA PUSILLA	Dwarf mallow	
MALVA SYLVESTRIS	High mallow	
MALVA VERTICILLATA	Large-whorled mallow	
Manfreda virginica (= *Agave virginica*)	False aloe	8
MARRUBIUM VULGARE	Common horehound	
MARSILEA QUADRIFOLIA	European water clover	
Matelea obliqua	Climbing milkweed	10
MATRICARIA CHAMOMILLA	German chamomile	
MATRICARIA DISCOIDEA	Pineapple weed	
Matteuccia struthiopteris v. pensylvanica	Ostrich fern	9
MAZUS PUMILUS	Japanese mazus	
Mecardonia acuminata	Axil flower	10
Medeola virginiana	Indian cucumber root	7
MEDICAGO LUPULINA	Black medick	
MEDICAGO SATIVA s. FALCATA	Yellow alfalfa	
MEDICAGO SATIVA s. SATIVA	Alfalfa	
MEDICAGO x VARIA	Hybrid alfalfa	
Melampyrum lineare v. latifolium	Broad-leaved cow wheat	10
Melampyrum lineare v. lineare	Narrow-leaved cow wheat	10
Melampyrum lineare v. pectinatum	Comb-leaved cow wheat	10
Melanthium virginicum	Bunch flower	10
Melanthium woodii (= *Veratrum woodii*)	False hellebore	7
Melica mutica	Narrow melic grass	6
Melica nitens	Tall melic grass	9
MELILOTUS ALBA	White sweet clover	
MELILOTUS OFFICINALIS	Yellow sweet clover	
MELISSA OFFICINALIS	Common balm	
Melothria pendula	Creeping cucumber	3
Menispermum canadense	Moonseed	3
MENTHA x PIPERITA	Peppermint	
MENTHA AQUATICA	Water mint	
Mentha arvensis v. villosa	Wild mint	4
MENTHA SPICATA	Spearmint	
MENTHA SUAVEOLENS	Apple mint	
MENTZELIA DECAPETALA	Sand lily	
Menyanthes trifoliata	Buckbean	10
Mertensia virginica	Virginia bluebells	6
MICROSTEGIUM VIMINEUM	Nepalese browntop	
Mikania scandens	Climbing hempweed	7
Milium effusum v. cisatlanticum	Wood millet	10
Mimulus alatus	Winged monkey flower	4
Mimulus ringens	Monkey flower	4
Minuartia michauxii (= *Arenaria stricta*)	Rock sandwort	10
Minuartia patula (= *Arenaria patula*)	Slender sandwort	10
MIRABILIS ALBIDA	Pale umbrellawort	
MIRABILIS JALAPA	Four o'clock	
MIRABILIS LINEARIS	Narrow-leaved umbrellawort	
MIRABILIS NYCTAGINEA	Wild four o'clock	
MISCANTHUS SINENSIS	Chinese silver grass	
Mitchella repens	Partridge berry	8
Mitella diphylla	Bishop's cap	7
Moehringia lateriflora (= *Arenaria lateriflora*)	Blunt-leaf sandwort	6
MOLLUGO VERTICILLATA	Carpet weed	
Monarda bradburiana	Monarda	7
Monarda clinopodia	Basil bee balm	7
MONARDA DIDYMA	Scarlet bee-balm	
Monarda fistulosa (including 1 variety)	Wild bergamot	3
MONARDA MEDIA	Purple bergamot	
Monarda punctata v. villicaulis	Horsemint	4
MONOLEPIS NUTTALLIANA	Nuttall's poverty weed	
Monotropa hypopitys	Pinesap	8
Monotropa uniflora	Indian pipe	7
MORUS ALBA	White mulberry	
Morus rubra	Red mulberry	4
MOSLA DIANTHERA	Miniature beefsteak plant	
MUHLENBERGIA ASPERIFOLIA	Scratch grass	
Muhlenbergia bushii	Short-leaved satin grass	6
Muhlenbergia capillaris	Hair grass	10
Muhlenbergia cuspidata	Prairie satin grass	10
Muhlenbergia frondosa	Common satin grass	3
Muhlenbergia glabriflora	Smooth satin grass	8
Muhlenbergia glomerata	Marsh wild timothy	10
Muhlenbergia mexicana	Leafy satin grass	4
MUHLENBERGIA RACEMOSA	Upland wild timothy	
Muhlenbergia schreberi	Nimblewill	0
Muhlenbergia sobolifera	Rock satin grass	5
Muhlenbergia sylvatica	Woodland satin grass	7
Muhlenbergia tenuiflora	Slender satin grass	7
MUSCARI BOTRYOIDES	Common grape hyacinth	
MUSCARI NEGLECTUM	Bluebottle	
MYOSOTIS ARVENSIS	Rough forget-me-not	
Myosotis laxa	Small forget-me-not	10
Myosotis macrosperma	Scorpion grass	2
MYOSOTIS SCORPIOIDES	Common forget-me-not	
MYOSOTIS STRICTA	Small-flowered forget-me-not	
Myosotis verna	White forget-me-not	3
MYOSOTON AQUATICUM	Giant chickweed	
Myosurus minimus	Mousetail	0
Myriophyllum heterophyllum	Various-leaved water milfoil	7
Myriophyllum pinnatum	Rough water milfoil	10
Myriophyllum sibiricum	Spiked water milfoil	7
MYRIOPHYLLUM SPICATUM	European water milfoil	
Myriophyllum tenellum	Slender water milfoil	10
Myriophyllum verticillatum	Whorled water milfoil	10
Najas flexilis	Common naiad	5
Najas gracillima	Slender naiad	10

Table P-2. *continued*

Scientific Name[a]	Common Name	Coefficient[b]
Najas guadalupensis (including 1 subspecies)	Southern naiad	5
NAJAS MARINA	Holly-leaved naiad	
NAJAS MINOR	Brittle naiad	
Napaea dioica	Glade mallow	3
NARCISSUS POETICUS	Poet's narcissus	
NARCISSUS PSEUDONARCISSUS	Daffodil	
NARCISSUS x MEDIOLUTEUS	Primrose peerless	
Nelumbo lutea	American lotus	4
Nemopanthus mucronata. See *Ilex mucronata*		
NEPETA CATARIA	Catnip	
NESLIA PANICULATA	Ball mustard	
NICANDRA PHYSALODES	Apple-of-peru	
NICOTIANA LONGIFLORA	Long-flowered tobacco	
NIGELLA DAMASCENA	Love-in-a-mist	
Nothoscordum bivalve	Crow poison	6
Nuphar advena	Spatterdock	6
Nuphar variegata	Bullhead lily	8
Nuttallanthus canadensis (= *Linaria canadensis*)	Blue toadflax	2
Nymphaea odorata s. tuberosa	Fragrant water lily	6
NYMPHOIDES PELTATA	Yellow floatingheart	
Nyssa sylvatica	Black gum	5
Obolaria virginica	Pennywort	4
Oenothera biennis	Common evening primrose	0
Oenothera clelandii	Sand primrose	4
Oenothera fruticosa	Shrubby sundrops	10
OENOTHERA GLAZIOVIANA	Large-flowered evening primrose	
OENOTHERA GRANDIS	Showy ragged evening primrose	
Oenothera laciniata	Ragged evening primrose	2
Oenothera nutans	Nodding evening primrose	0
Oenothera oakesiana	Oakes' evening primrose	10
Oenothera parviflora	Small-flowered evening primrose	2
Oenothera perennis	Small sundrops	5
Oenothera pilosella	Prairie sundrops	4
OENOTHERA SPECIOSA	Showy evening primrose	
Oenothera triloba	Evening primrose	10
Oenothera villosa	Grayish evening primrose	0
Onoclea sensibilis	Sensitive fern	4
ONOPORDUM ACANTHIUM	Scotch cotton thistle	
Onosmodium molle s. hispidissimum	Rough marbleseed	2
Ophioglossum engelmannii	Cliff adder's tongue fern	10
Ophioglossum pusillum	Northern adder's tongue fern	10
Ophioglossum vulgatum	Southern adder's tongue fern	4
Opuntia humifusa	Eastern prickly pear	2
Orbexilum onobrychis (= *Psoralea onobrychis*)	French grass	4
Orbexilum pedunculatum	Sampson's snakeroot	7
Orchis spectabilis. See *Galearis spectabilis*		
ORIGANUM VULGARE	Oregano	
ORNITHOGALUM NUTANS	Nodding star of Bethlehem	
ORNITHOGALUM UMBELLATUM	Common star of Bethlehem	
Orobanche fasciculata	Clustered broom rape	10
Orobanche ludoviciana	Southern broom rape	4
Orobanche uniflora	Cancer root	6
Orthilia secunda (= *Pyrola secunda*)	One-sided shinleaf	10
Oryzopsis. See 2 species of *Piptatherum*		
Oryzopsis asperifolia	Rough-leaved rice grass	10
Osmorhiza claytonii	Hairy sweet cicely	3
Osmorhiza longistylis	Anise root	3
Osmunda cinnamomea	Cinnamon fern	9
Osmunda claytoniana	Interrupted fern	8
Osmunda regalis v. spectabilis	Regal fern	8
Ostrya virginiana	Hop hornbeam	5
OXALIS CORNICULATA	Creeping wood sorrel	
Oxalis florida s. prostrata	Upright yellow wood sorrel	0
Oxalis fontana (including 1 variety)	Small-flowered yellow wood sorrel	0
Oxalis grandis	Great yellow wood sorrel	8
Oxalis illinoensis	Illinois wood sorrel	9
Oxalis stricta	Tall wood sorrel	0
Oxalis violacea	Violet wood sorrel	7
Oxydendron arboreum	Sourwood	8
Oxypolis rigidior	Cowbane	7
Pachysandra procumbens	Allegheny spurge	9
PACHYSANDRA TERMINALIS	Japanese spurge	
Packera anonyma (= *Senecio anonymus*)	Small's ragwort	2
Packera aurea	Golden ragwort	4
Packera glabella	Butterweed	0
Packera obovata	Round-leaved ragwort	7
Packera paupercula	Balsam ragwort	3
Packera plattensis	Prairie ragwort	5
Packera pseudaurea v. semicordata	False golden ragwort	4
Panax quinquefolius	Ginseng	7
Panax trifolius	Dwarf ginseng	9
Panicum. See also *Dichanthelium*		
Panicum anceps	Beaked panic grass	3
Panicum capillare	Old witch grass	0
Panicum dichotomiflorum (including 1 subspecies)	Fall panicum	0
Panicum flexile	Slender panic grass	5
Panicum gattingeri	Gattinger's panic grass	3
PANICUM MILIACEUM	Broom corn millet	
Panicum philadelphicum	Philadelphia panic grass	4
Panicum rigidulum s. elongatum	Stalk-fruited panic grass	4
Panicum rigidulum s. pubescens	Long-leaved panic grass	10
Panicum rigidulum s. rigidulum	Munro grass	4
Panicum tuckermanii	Tuckerman's panic grass	10
Panicum verrucosum	Warty panic grass	9
Panicum virgatum	Prairie switch grass	4
PAPAVER DUBIUM	Long-headed poppy	
PAPAVER ORIENTALE	Oriental poppy	
PAPAVER RHOEAS	Corn poppy	
Parietaria pensylvanica	Pennsylvania pellitory	1
Parnassia glauca	Grass-of-parnassus	10
Paronychia canadensis	Tall forked chickweed	6
Paronychia fastigiata (including 1 variety)	Low forked chickweed	6
Parthenium integrifolium	Wild quinine	9
Parthenocissus quinquefolia	Virginia creeper	2
PARTHENOCISSUS TRICUSPIDATA	Boston ivy	
Parthenocissus vitacea	Thicket creeper	2
PASCOPYRUM SMITHII (= *AGROPYRON SMITHII*)	Colorado bluestem	
Paspalum floridanum	Florida crown grass	2
Paspalum laeve	Smooth lens grass	2
Paspalum pubiflorum	Four-rowed bead grass	3
Paspalum repens	Swamp bead grass	7
Paspalum setaceum v. muhlenbergii (and additional varieties)	Hairy lens grass	3
Paspalum setaceum v. stramineum	Downy lens grass	3
Passiflora incarnata	Large passion flower	4
Passiflora lutea	Small passion flower	7
PASTINACA SATIVA	Wild parsnip	
PAULOWNIA TOMENTOSA	Princess tree	
Pedicularis canadensis	Wood betony	6
Pedicularis lanceolata	Fen betony	6
Pellaea atropurpurea	Purple cliffbrake	10
Pellaea glabella	Smooth cliffbrake	10
Peltandra virginica	Arrow arum	6
PENNISETUM ALOPECUROIDES	Chinese fountain grass	
Penstemon alluviorum	Lowland beard tongue	4
Penstemon calycosus	Smooth beard tongue	4
Penstemon canescens	Hoary beard tongue	7

Scientific Name[a]	Common Name	Coefficient[b]
PENSTEMON COBAEA v. PURPUREUS	Showy beard tongue	
Penstemon deamii	Deam's beard tongue	5
Penstemon digitalis	Foxglove beard tongue	4
PENSTEMON GRACILIS v. WISCONSINENSIS	Slender beard tongue	
PENSTEMON GRANDIFLORUS	Large-flowered beard tongue	
Penstemon hirsutus	Hairy beard tongue	5
Penstemon pallidus	Pale beard tongue	5
Penstemon tubaeflorus	Western beard tongue	10
Penthorum sedoides	Ditch stonecrop	2
Perideridia americana	Thicket parsley	9
PERILLA FRUTESCENS (including 1 variety)	Beefsteak plant	
Persicaria amphibia v. emersa (= *Polygonum coccineum*)	Water heartsease	4
Persicaria amphibia v. stipulacea	Water knotweed	4
Persicaria arifolia	Halberd-leaved tear-thumb	10
PERSICARIA CAESPITOSA	Creeping smartweed	
Persicaria careyi	Carey's heartsease	10
PERSICARIA HYDROPIPER	Water pepper	
Persicaria hydropiperoides	Mild water pepper	3
Persicaria lapathifolia	Curlytop lady's thumb	0
PERSICARIA MINOR	Minor smartweed	
Persicaria opelousana	Scaly mild water pepper	10
PERSICARIA ORIENTALE	Kiss-me-over-the-garden-gate	
Persicaria pensylvanica	Pinkweed	0
Persicaria punctata	Smartweed	3
Persicaria sagittata	Arrow-leaved tear-thumb	4
Persicaria setacea	Swamp smartweed	10
PERSICARIA VULGARIS	Lady's thumb	
PETUNIA x ATKINSIANA	Garden petunia	
PEUCEDANUM OSTRUTHIUM	Masterwort	
Phacelia bipinnatifida	Leafy phacelia	6
Phacelia purshii	Miami mist	3
Phacelia ranunculacea	Buttercup phacelia	10
PHALARIS ARUNDINACEA	Reed canary grass	
PHALARIS CANARIENSIS	Birdseed grass	
Phaseolus polystachios	Thicket bean	5
Phegopteris hexagonoptera	Broad beech fern	7
Phemeranthus rugospermus (= *Talinum rugospermum*)	Fame flower	10
PHILADELPHUS CORONARIUS	Sweet mock orange	
PHILADELPHUS INODORUS	Scentless mock orange	
PHLEUM PRATENSE	Timothy grass	
Phlox amplifolia	Fringed phlox	8
Phlox bifida s. bifida	Cleft phlox	7
Phlox bifida s. stellaria	Star cleft phlox	9
Phlox carolina s. angusta	Carolina phlox	5
Phlox divaricata (including 1 subspecies)	Blue phlox	5
Phlox glaberrima (including subspecies)	Smooth phlox	5
Phlox maculata (including 1 subspecies)	Wild sweet William	8
Phlox ovata	Mountain phlox	9
Phlox paniculata	Garden phlox	3
Phlox pilosa s. deamii	Deam's prairie phlox	6
Phlox pilosa s. fulgida	Northern prairie phlox	6
Phlox pilosa s. pilosa	Sand prairie phlox	6
PHLOX SUBULATA s. SUBULATA	Moss phlox	
Phoradendron leucarpum	Mistletoe	3
Photinia floribunda (= *Aronia floribunda*)	Purple chokeberry	8
Photinia melanocarpa	Black chokeberry	8
Phragmites australis	Common reed	0
Phryma leptostachya	Lopseed	4
PHYLA CUNEIFOLIA	Hoary fog fruit	
Phyla lanceolata	Fog fruit	2
Phyllanthus caroliniensis	Dainties	5
Physalis grisea	Strawberry tomato	4
Physalis heterophylla	Clammy ground cherry	3
PHYSALIS HISPIDA	Prairie ground cherry	
PHYSALIS LONGIFOLIA v. LONGIFOLIA	Long-leaved ground cherry	
Physalis longifolia v. subglabrata	Smooth ground cherry	0
PHYSALIS PERUVIANA	Peruvian ground cherry	
PHYSALIS PHILADELPHICA v. IMMACULATA	Tomatillo	
Physalis pubescens (including 1 variety)	Hairy ground cherry	3
Physalis virginiana	Lance-leaved ground cherry	3
Physaria globosa (= *Lesquerella globosa*)	Lesquereaux's mustard	5
Physocarpus opulifolius (including 1 variety)	Common ninebark	7
Physostegia virginiana v. arenaria	Prairie obedient plant	5
Physostegia virginiana v. speciosa	Showy obedient plant	5
Physostegia virginiana v. virginiana	Virginia obedient plant	5
Phytolacca americana v. americana	Pokeweed	0
Pilea fontana	Bog clearweed	5
Pilea pumila	Canada clearweed	2
PIMPINELLA SAXIFRAGA	Solid-stemmed burnet saxifrage	
Pinus banksiana	Jack pine	10
PINUS RIGIDA	Pitch pine	
Pinus strobus	White pine	5
PINUS SYLVESTRIS	Scotch pine	
Pinus virginiana	Scrub pine	5
Piptatherum pungens (= *Oryzopsis pungens*)	Short-horned rice grass	10
Piptatherum racemosa	Black-seeded rice grass	8
Piptochaetium avenaceum (= *Stipa avenacea*)	Black oat grass	10
Plantago aristata	Poor Joe	0
Plantago cordata	Heart-leaved plantain	10
PLANTAGO LANCEOLATA	English plantain	
PLANTAGO MAJOR v. MAJOR	Common plantain	
PLANTAGO PATAGONICA	Woolly plantain	
PLANTAGO PSYLLIUM	Whorled plantain	
Plantago pusilla	Small plantain	2
Plantago rugelii (including 1 variety)	Red-stalked plantain	0
Plantago virginica	Dwarf plantain	2
Platanthera aquilonis	Northern bog orchid	10
Platanthera ciliaris	Orange-fringed orchid	9
Platanthera clavellata	Small green wood orchid	9
Platanthera dilatata	Tall white orchid	10
Platanthera flava v. flava	Southern tubercled orchid	7
Platanthera flava v. herbiola	Northern tubercled orchid	7
Platanthera hookeri	Hooker's orchid	10
Platanthera huronensis	Green orchid	10
Platanthera lacera	Green-fringed orchid	4
Platanthera leucophaea	Prairie white-fringed orchid	10
Platanthera orbiculata	Round-leaved orchid	10
Platanthera peramoena	Purple fringeless orchid	4
Platanthera psycodes	Purple-fringed orchid	10
Platanus occidentalis	Sycamore	3
Pleopeltis polypodioides v. michauxiana (= *Polypodium polypodioides*)	Gray polypody	10
Pluchea camphorata	Camphor weed	5
PLUCHEA ODORATA v. SUCCULENTA	Sweet scent	
Poa alsodes	Grove bluegrass	8
POA ANNUA	Annual bluegrass	
POA ARIDA	Plains bluegrass	
Poa autumnalis	Autumn bluegrass	7
POA BULBOSA (including 1 subspecies)	Bulbous bluegrass	
Poa chapmaniana	Spear grass	0
POA COMPRESSA	Canadian bluegrass	
Poa cuspidata	Cusped bluegrass	10
POA NEMORALIS	Woodland bluegrass	
Poa paludigena	Marsh bluegrass	10

Table P-2. *continued*

Scientific Name[a]	Common Name	Coefficient[b]
Poa palustris	Fowl bluegrass	6
POA PRATENSIS	Kentucky bluegrass	
Poa saltuensis	Weak bluegrass	8
Poa sylvestris	Woodland bluegrass	5
POA TRIVIALIS	Rough bluegrass	
Poa wolfii	Wolf's bluegrass	9
Podophyllum peltatum	May apple	3
Pogonia ophioglossoides	Rose pogonia	10
Poinsettia dentata. See *Euphorbia dentata*		
Polanisia dodecandra s. dodecandra	Clammy weed	1
Polanisia dodecandra s. trachysperma	Clammy weed	1
Polemonium reptans v. reptans	Jacob's ladder	5
Polygala ambigua	Slender milkwort	4
Polygala cruciata v. aquilonia	Cross milkwort	10
Polygala incarnata	Pink milkwort	5
Polygala paucifolia	Flowering wintergreen	10
Polygala polygama	Purple milkwort	7
Polygala sanguinea	Field milkwort	4
Polygala senega	Seneca snakeroot	8
Polygala verticillata v. isocycla	Whorled milkwort	4
Polygala verticillata v. verticillata	Whorled milkwort	4
Polygonatum biflorum	Small Solomon's seal	4
Polygonatum pubescens	Downy Solomon's seal	8
Polygonella articulata	Jointweed	10
Polygonum. See also 6 species of *Fallopia* and 16 species of *Persicaria*		
Polygonum achoreum	Beak-seeded knotweed	0
POLYGONUM AVICULARE (including subspecies)	Common knotweed	
Polygonum aviculare s. buxiforme	Boxwood knotweed	0
Polygonum erectum	Erect knotweed	0
Polygonum ramosissimum	Bushy knotweed	4
Polygonum tenue	Slender knotweed	4
Polygonum virginianum. See *Tovara virginiana*		
Polymnia canadensis	Pale leafcup	3
Polymnia uvedalia. See *Smallanthus uvedalia*		
Polypodium virginianum	Common polypody	10
Polystichum acrostichoides	Christmas fern	5
Polytaenia nuttallii	Prairie parsley	10
Pontederia cordata	Pickerel weed	5
POPULUS ALBA	White poplar	
Populus balsamifera	Balsam poplar	10
Populus deltoides	Eastern cottonwood	1
Populus grandidentata	Bigtooth aspen	4
Populus heterophylla	Swamp cottonwood	8
POPULUS NIGRA	Lombardy poplar	
Populus tremuloides	Quaking aspen	2
POPULUS x CANESCENS	Gray poplar	
PORTULACA GRANDIFLORA	Moss rose	
PORTULACA OLERACEA	Purslane	
Potamogeton amplifolius	Large-leaved pondweed	10
Potamogeton bicupulatus	Snailseed pondweed	10
POTAMOGETON CRISPUS	Beginner's pondweed	
Potamogeton diversifolius	Water-thread pondweed	4
Potamogeton epihydrus	Ribbon-leaved pondweed	10
Potamogeton foliosus	Leafy pondweed	4
Potamogeton friesii	Fries's pondweed	10
Potamogeton gramineus	Grass-leaved pondweed	7
Potamogeton illinoensis	Illinois pondweed	7
Potamogeton natans	Common pondweed	8
Potamogeton nodosus	American pondweed	4
Potamogeton oakesianus	Oakes' pondweed	10
Potamogeton pectinatus. See *Stuckenia pectinata*		
Potamogeton praelongus	White-stemmed pondweed	10
Potamogeton pulcher	Spotted pondweed	10
Potamogeton pusillus s. pusillus	Small pondweed	4
Potamogeton pusillus s. tennuissimus	Broad-leaved small pondweed	4
Potamogeton richardsonii	Redhead grass	10
Potamogeton robbinsii	Fern pondweed	10
Potamogeton strictifolius	Stiff pondweed	10
Potamogeton vaseyi	Vasey's pondweed	10
Potamogeton zosteriformis	Flat-stemmed pondweed	8
Potentilla anserina. See *Argentina anserina*		
POTENTILLA ARGENTEA	Silvery cinquefoil	
Potentilla arguta	Prairie cinquefoil	10
Potentilla fruticosa. See *Dasiphora fruticosa s. floribunda*		
POTENTILLA INCLINATA	Hoary cinquefoil	
POTENTILLA INTERMEDIA	Downy cinquefoil	
Potentilla norvegica (including 1 subspecies)	Rough cinquefoil	0
Potentilla palustris. See *Comarum palustre*		
POTENTILLA RECTA	Sulfur cinquefoil	
Potentilla simplex	Common cinquefoil	2
Prenanthes alba	Lion's foot	5
Prenanthes altissima (including 1 variety)	Tall white lettuce	5
Prenanthes aspera	Rough white lettuce	9
Prenanthes crepidinea	Great white lettuce	7
Prenanthes racemosa	Glaucous white lettuce	10
PROBOSCIDEA LOUISIANICA	Devil's claw	
PROBOSCIDEA PARVIFLORA	Doubleclaw	
Proserpinaca palustris (including 1 variety)	False mermaidweed	4
Prunella vulgaris s. lanceolata	Self heal	1
PRUNELLA VULGARIS s. VULGARIS	Lawn prunella	
Prunus americana	American plum	4
PRUNUS ANGUSTIFOLIA	Chickasaw plum	
PRUNUS AVIUM	Sweet cherry	
PRUNUS CERASUS	Sour cherry	
Prunus hortulana	Wild goose plum	4
PRUNUS MAHALEB	Perfumed cherry	
Prunus Mexicana	Wild plum	4
Prunus nigra	Canada plum	8
Prunus pensylvanica	Pin cherry	2
PRUNUS PERSICA	Peach	
Prunus pumila v. besseyi	Bessey's sand cherry	8
Prunus pumila v. pumila	Dune sand cherry	10
Prunus pumila v. susquehanae	Eastern sand cherry	8
Prunus serotina	Wild black cherry	1
Prunus virginiana (including 1 variety)	Common choke cherry	3
Pseudognaphalium helleri s. micradenium (= *Gnaphalium helleri*)	Heller's old-field balsam	10
Pseudognaphalium macounii	Clammy cudweed	2
Pseudognaphalium obtusifolium	Old-field balsam	2
Psoralea. See 2 species of *Orbexilum* and 1 species of *Psoralidium*		
Psoralidium tenuiflorum (= *Psoralea tenuiflora*)	Scurfy pea	10
Ptelea trifoliata v. mollis	Downy wafer ash	6
Ptelea trifoliata v. trifoliata	Smooth wafer ash	4
Pteridium aquilinum v. latiusculum	Bracken fern	5
Pteridium aquilinum v. pseudocaudatum	Slender bracken fern	10
PTERIS MULTIFIDA	Spider brake	
PUCCINELLIA DISTANS	Alkali grass	
PUERARIA MONTANA v. LOBATA	Kudzu	
Pycnanthemum muticum	Blunt mountain mint	0
Pycnanthemum pycnanthemoides	Mountain mint	4
Pycnanthemum tenuifolium	Slender mountain mint	4
Pycnanthemum torrei	Torrey's mountain mint	3
Pycnanthemum verticillatum v. pilosum	Hairy mountain mint	4

Scientific Name[a]	Common Name	Coefficient[b]
Pycnanthemum virginianum	Common mountain mint	5
Pyrola americana	Round-leaved shinleaf	8
Pyrola asarifolia	Pink shinleaf	10
Pyrola chlorantha	Green shinleaf	10
Pyrola elliptica	Large-leaved shinleaf	8
Pyrola secunda. See *Orthilia secunda*		
Pyrrhopappus carolinianus	False dandelion	2
PYRUS CALLERYANA	Bradford pear	
PYRUS COMMUNIS	Pear	
QUERCUS ACUTISSIMA	Saw-toothed oak	
Quercus alba	White oak	5
Quercus bicolor	Swamp white oak	7
Quercus coccinea	Scarlet oak	7
Quercus ellipsoidalis	Hill's oak	4
Quercus falcata	Southern red oak	5
Quercus imbricaria	Jack oak	3
Quercus lyrata	Overcup oak	7
Quercus macrocarpa	Bur oak	5
Quercus marilandica	Blackjack oak	7
Quercus michauxii	Basket oak	7
Quercus montana	Mountain chestnut oak	7
Quercus muhlenbergii	Chinquapin oak	4
Quercus pagoda	Cherrybark oak	5
Quercus palustris	Pin oak	3
Quercus prinoides	Dwarf chinquapin oak	10
Quercus rubra	Northern red oak	4
Quercus shumardii v. schneckii	Shumard's oak	7
Quercus shumardii v. shumardii	Shumard's oak	7
Quercus stellata	Post oak	5
Quercus velutina	Black oak	4
Quercus x hawkinsiae	Hawkins's oak	4
Quercus x palaeolithicola	Paleolithic oak	4
Ranunculus abortivus	Little-leaf buttercup	0
RANUNCULUS ACRIS	Tall buttercup	
Ranunculus ambigens	Spearwort	10
Ranunculus aquatilis v. diffusus	White water crowfoot	7
RANUNCULUS BULBOSUS	Bulbous buttercup	
Ranunculus fascicularis	Early buttercup	6
RANUNCULUS FICARIA	Lesser celandine	
Ranunculus flabellaris	Yellow water buttercup	7
Ranunculus harveyi	Harvey's buttercup	8
Ranunculus hispidus v. caricetorum	Hispid swamp buttercup	10
Ranunculus hispidus v. hispidus	Rough buttercup	7
Ranunculus hispidus v. nitidus	Smooth swamp buttercup	5
Ranunculus laxicaulis	Spearwort	6
Ranunculus micranthus	Small-flowered crowfoot	4
Ranunculus pensylvanicus	Bristly crowfoot	6
Ranunculus pusillus	Small spearwort	9
Ranunculus recurvatus	Hooked buttercup	5
RANUNCULUS REPENS	Creeping buttercup	
RANUNCULUS SARDOUS	Hairy buttercup	
Ranunculus sceleratus	Cursed crowfoot	3
RANUNCULUS TESTICULATUS (= CERATOCEPHALUS TESTICULATUS)	Bur buttercup	
RAPHANUS RAPHANISTRUM	Wild radish	
RAPHANUS SATIVUS	Radish	
RAPISTRUM RUGOSUM	Wild rape	
RATIBIDA COLUMNIFERA	Long-headed coneflower	
Ratibida pinnata	Yellow coneflower	5
Rhamnus alnifolia	Alder buckthorn	10
RHAMNUS ARGUTUS v. VELUTINA	Saw-toothed buckthorn	
Rhamnus caroliniana. See *Frangula caroliniana*		
RHAMNUS CATHARTICA	Common buckthorn	
RHAMNUS DAVURICA s. NIPPONICA	Dahurian buckthorn	
RHAMNUS FRANGULA. See *FRANGULA ALNUS*		
Rhamnus lanceolata (including 1 subspecies)	Lance-leaved buckthorn	4
RHEUM RHABARBICUM	Rhubarb	

Scientific Name[a]	Common Name	Coefficient[b]
Rhexia mariana v. interior	Inland meadow beauty	2
Rhexia mariana v. mariana	Meadow beauty	5
Rhexia virginica	Handsome Harry	5
RHODOTYPOS SCANDENS	Jetbead	
Rhus aromatica v. arenaria	Beach sumac	10
Rhus aromatica v. aromatica	Aromatic sumac	7
Rhus copallina v. latifolia	Dwarf sumac	3
Rhus glabra	Smooth sumac	1
Rhus typhina	Staghorn sumac	2
Rhus x pulvinata	Hybrid sumac	1
Rhynchospora alba	White beak rush	10
Rhynchospora capillacea	Hair beak rush	10
Rhynchospora capitellata	Brown beak rush	6
Rhynchospora corniculata	Interior horned beak rush	3
Rhynchospora fusca	Gray beak rush	10
Rhynchospora globularis	Grass beak rush	10
Rhynchospora macrostachya	Horned beak rush	10
Rhynchospora nitens	Short-beaked bald rush	10
Rhynchospora recognita	Globe beak rush	10
Rhynchospora scirpoides	Long-beaked bald rush	10
Ribes americanum	Wild black currant	5
RIBES AUREUM v. VILLOSUM	Buffalo currant	
Ribes cynosbati	Prickly wild gooseberry	4
Ribes hirtellum	Northern gooseberry	10
Ribes missouriense	Missouri gooseberry	3
RIBES RUBRUM	Northern red currant	
RIBES UVA-CRISPA v. SATIVUM	European gooseberry	
RICHARDIA SCABRA	Rough Mexican clover	
RICINUS COMMUNIS	Castor bean	
ROBINIA HISPIDA	Bristly locust	
ROBINIA NEOMEXICANA	Rocky Mountain locust	
Robinia pseudoacacia	Black locust	1
ROBINIA VISCOSA	Clammy locust	
RORIPPA MICROPHYLLA	One-rowed yellowcress	
RORIPPA NASTURTIUM-AQUATICUM	Water cress	
Rorippa palustris s. fernaldiana	Marsh yellow cress	2
Rorippa palustris s. hispida	Hairy marsh yellow cress	2
Rorippa sessiliflora	Sessile-flowered cress	3
RORIPPA SYLVESTRIS	Creeping yellow cress	
Rosa arkansana v. suffulta	Sunshine rose	4
Rosa blanda (including 1 variety)	Early wild rose	4
ROSA CANINA	Dog rose	
Rosa carolina	Pasture rose	4
ROSA EGLANTERIA	Sweetbrier	
ROSA GALLICA	French rose	
ROSA MICRANTHA	Small-flowered sweetbrier	
ROSA MULTIFLORA	Japanese rose	
Rosa palustris	Swampy rose	5
Rosa setigera (including 1 variety)	Prairie rose	4
ROSA SPINOSISSIMA	Scotch rose	
Rotala ramosior	Wheelwort	2
ROTTBOELLIA COCHINCHINENSIS	Itch-grass	
RUBUS IDAEUS v. IDAEUS	Common red raspberry	
Rubus idaeus v. strigosus	Red raspberry	4
Rubus occidentalis	Black raspberry	1
Rubus odoratus	Purple flowering raspberry	6
RUBUS PHOENICOLASIUS	Wineberry	
Rubus pubescens	Dwarf raspberry	10
Rubus sec. Allegheniensis: R. allegheniensis	Common blackberry	2
Rubus sec. Allegheniensis: R. alumnus	Elliptic-leaved blackberry	2
Rubus sec. Allegheniensis: R. rosa	Rose blackberry	5
Rubus sec. Arguti: R. abactus	Yankee blackberry	5
Rubus sec. Arguti: R. ablatus	Narrow-racemed blackberry	4
Rubus sec. Arguti: R. argutus	High-bush blackberry	3
Rubus sec. Arguti: R. frondosus	Velvet blackberry	4
Rubus sec. Arguti: R. laudatus	Plains blackberry	5
Rubus sec. Arguti: R. recurvans	Recurved blackberry	5
Rubus sec. Flagellares: R. celer	Washington DC dewberry	4
Rubus sec. Flagellares: R. centralis	Indiana dewberry	5

Table P-2. *continued*

Scientific Name[a]	Common Name	Coefficient[b]
Rubus sec. Flagellares: R. curtipes	Downy corymbose dewberry	5
Rubus sec. Flagellares: R. deamii	Deam's dewberry	5
Rubus sec. Flagellares: R. depavitus	Trampled dewberry	5
Rubus sec. Flagellares: R. enslenii	Arching dewberry	5
Rubus sec. Flagellares: R. flagellaris	Common dewberry	2
Rubus sec. Flagellares: R. griseus	Loogootee dewberry	10
Rubus sec. Flagellares: R. invisus	Upland dewberry	5
Rubus sec. Flagellares: R. ithacanus	Ithaca blackberry	5
Rubus sec. Flagellares: R. meracus	Ascendent-flowered dewberry	5
Rubus sec. Flagellares: R. multifer	Kinnickinnick dewberry	5
Rubus sec. Flagellares: R. plicatifolius	Plait-leaved dewberry	4
Rubus sec. Flagellares: R. roribaccus	Lucretia dewberry	5
Rubus sec. Flagellares: R. steelei	Steele's dewberry	5
Rubus sec. Hispidus: R. hispidus	Swampy dewberry	6
Rubus sec. Setosi: R. fulleri	Fuller's bristly dewberry	9
RUBUS sec. SYLVATICI: R. LACINIATUS	Cut-leaved blackberry	
Rubus sec. Tholiformes: R. aboriginum	Downy incised dewberry	5
Rubus sec. Tholiformes: R. impar	Dewberry	5
Rubus sec. Tholiformes: R. missouricus	Bristly blackberry	5
Rubus sec. Tholiformes: R. satis	Downy racemose dewberry	5
Rudbeckia fulgida v. deamii	Deam's coneflower	10
Rudbeckia fulgida v. fulgida	Orange coneflower	5
Rudbeckia fulgida v. sullivantii	Sullivant's orange coneflower	8
Rudbeckia fulgida v. umbrosa	Small-flowered coneflower	10
Rudbeckia hirta v. hirta	Black-eyed Susan	2
Rudbeckia hirta v. pulcherrima	Black-eyed Susan	2
Rudbeckia laciniata	Wild golden glow	3
Rudbeckia subtomentosa	Sweet black-eyed Susan	7
Rudbeckia triloba	Brown-eyed Susan	3
Ruellia caroliniensis	Wild petunia	6
Ruellia humilis	Hairy ruellia	5
Ruellia strepens	Smooth ruellia	4
RUMEX ACETOSELLA	Field sorrel	
Rumex altissimus	Pale dock	2
RUMEX CRISPUS	Curly dock	
RUMEX HASTATULUS	Grainless field sorrel	
RUMEX OBTUSIFOLIUS	Bitter dock	
Rumex orbiculatus v. borealis	Great water dock	7
RUMEX PATIENTIA	Patience dock	
Rumex salicifolius v. Mexicanus	Mexican dock	1
Rumex verticillatus	Swamp dock	5
Sabatia angularis	Rose gentian	3
Sabatia campanulata	Four-angled rose gentian	10
Saccharum alopecuroides	Silver plume grass	3
SACCHARUM RAVENNAE	Plume grass	
Sagina decumbens	Trailing pearlwort	0
SAGINA PROCUMBENS	Blue-eyed pearlwort	
Sagittaria australis	Southern arrowleaf	5
Sagittaria brevirostra	Short-beaked arrowleaf	3
Sagittaria cuneata	Arum-leaved arrowhead	3
Sagittaria graminea	Grass-leaved arrowhead	9
Sagittaria latifolia	Common arrowhead	3
Sagittaria montevidensis s. calycina	Thick-stalked arrowhead	6
Sagittaria rigida	Stiff arrowhead	10
SALIX ALBA	White willow	
Salix amygdaloides	Peach-leaved willow	4
Salix bebbiana	Beaked willow	7
Salix candida	Hoary willow	10
Salix caroliniana	Carolina willow	8
SALIX CINEREA	Gray willow	
Salix cordata	Dune willow	10
Salix discolor	Pussy willow	3
Salix eriocephala	Heart-leaved willow	4
SALIX FRAGILIS	Crack willow	
Salix humilis (including 1 variety)	Prairie willow	5
Salix interior	Sandbar willow	1

Scientific Name[a]	Common Name	Coefficient[b]
Salix lucida	Shining willow	10
Salix myricoides	Blue-leaved willow	9
Salix nigra	Black willow	3
Salix pedicellaris	Bog willow	10
SALIX PENTANDRA	Bay-leaved willow	
Salix petiolaris	Meadow willow	6
Salix sericea	Silky willow	6
Salix serissima	Autumn willow	10
SALIX VIMINALIS	Basket willow	
Salix x glatfelteri	Hybrid black willow	4
SALIX x RUBENS	Hybrid crack willow	
SALSOLA TRAGUS	Russian thistle	
SALVIA AZUREA v. GRANDIFLORA	Blue sage	
Salvia lyrata	Cancer weed	3
SALVIA NEMOROSA	Wild sage	
SALVIA PRATENSIS	Prairie meadow sage	
SALVIA REFLEXA	Rocky Mountain sage	
SALVIA VERTICILLATA	Lilac sage	
Sambucus nigra s. canadensis	Common elderberry	2
SAMBUCUS NIGRA s. NIGRA	European elderberry	
Sambucus racemosa v. pubens	Red-berried elderberry	8
Samolus valerandi	Water pimpernel	5
Sanguinaria canadensis	Bloodroot	5
Sanguisorba canadensis	American burnet	10
SANGUISORBA MINOR	Salad burnet	
Sanicula canadensis (including 1 variety)	Canadian black snakeroot	2
Sanicula marilandica	Black snakeroot	6
Sanicula odorata	Clustered black snakeroot	2
Sanicula smallii	Small's snakeroot	10
Sanicula trifoliata	Beaked black snakeroot	8
SAPONARIA OCYMOIDES	Red soapwort	
SAPONARIA OFFICINALIS	Bouncing bet	
Sarracenia purpurea s. gibbosa	Pitcher plant	10
Sassafras albidum	Sassafras	1
Satureja arkansanum. See *Clinopodium arkansanum*		
SATUREJA HORTENSIS	Summer savory	
Saururus cernuus	Lizard's tail	4
Saxifraga pensylvanica v. forbesii	Forbes' saxifrage	10
Saxifraga pensylvanica v. pensylvanica	Swamp saxifrage	10
Saxifraga virginiensis	Early saxifrage	7
SCHEDONORUS ARUNDINACEUS (= FESTUCA ELATIOR)	Tall fescue	
SCHEDONORUS PRATENSIS	Meadow fescue	
Scheuchzeria palustris	Arrowgrass	10
Schizachne purpurascens	False melic grass	10
Schizachyrium scoparium (= *Andropogon scoparius*)	Little bluestem grass	4
Schoenoplectus acutus (= *Scirpus acutus*)	Heard-stemmed bulrush	5
Schoenoplectus hallii	Hall's tufted bulrush	7
Schoenoplectus pungens	Three-square bulrush	3
Schoenoplectus purshianus (including 1 variety)	Pursh's tufted bulrush	4
Schoenoplectus smithii (including 1 variety)	Smith's tufted bulrush	5
Schoenoplectus subterminalis	Water bulrush	10
Schoenoplectus tabernaemontani (= *Scirpus validus*)	Great bulrush	4
Schoenoplectus torreyi	Torrey's bulrush	10
SCILLA NONSCRIPTA. See *HYACINTHOIDES NONSCRIPTA*		
SCILLA SIBIRICA	Siberian squill	
Scirpus. See also 8 species of *Schoenoplectus*		
Scirpus atrovirens	Dark-green bulrush	4
Scirpus cyperinus	Wool grass	4
Scirpus expansus	Bulrush	10
Scirpus fluviatilis. See *Bolboschoenus fluviatilis*		

Scientific Name[a]	Common Name	Coefficient[b]
Scirpus georgianus	Bristleless dark-green bulrush	3
Scirpus hattorianus	Early dark-green bulrush	3
Scirpus pedicellatus	Stalked wool grass	7
Scirpus pendulus	Red bulrush	2
Scirpus polyphyllus	Leafy wool grass	10
SCLERANTHUS ANNUUS	Knawel	
Scleria muhlenbergii	Hairy-seeded nut rush	10
Scleria oligantha	Smooth-seeded nut rush	10
Scleria pauciflora v. caroliniana	Few-flowered nut rush	4
Scleria reticularis	Netted nut rush	10
Scleria triglomerata	Tall nut rush	10
Scleria verticillata	Low nut rush	10
SCLEROCHLOA DURA	Fairground grass	
Scrophularia lanceolata	Early figwort	5
Scrophularia marilandica	Late figwort	5
Scutellaria elliptica v. hirsuta	Hairy skullcap	5
Scutellaria galericulata	Marsh skullcap	4
Scutellaria incana	Downy skullcap	4
Scutellaria lateriflora	Mad-dog skullcap	4
Scutellaria nervosa	Veiny skullcap	5
Scutellaria ovata	Heart-leaved skullcap	7
Scutellaria parvula v. australis	Southern small skullcap	5
Scutellaria parvula v. missouriensis	Missouri small skullcap	5
Scutellaria parvula v. parvula	Small skullcap	5
Scutellaria saxatilis	Rock skullcap	10
SECALE CEREALE	Rye	
SEDUM ACRE	Mossy stonecrop	
SEDUM ALBUM	White stonecrop	
SEDUM PULCHELLUM	Widow's cross	
SEDUM REFLEXUM	Rocky stonecrop	
SEDUM SARMENTOSUM	Yellow stonecrop	
SEDUM SEXANGULARE	Six-sided stonecrop	
SEDUM SPURIUM	False wild stonecrop	
Sedum telephioides. See *Hylotelephium telephioides*		
Sedum ternatum	Three-leaved stonecrop	8
Selaginella apoda	Marsh club moss	4
Selaginella eclipes	Small clubmoss	10
Selaginella rupestris	Rock selaginella	10
SEMPERVIVUM TECTORUM	Hen-and-chickens	
Senecio. See also 7 species of *Packera*		
SENECIO JACOBAEA	Tansy ragwort	
SENECIO VULGARIS	Common groundsel	
Senna hebecarpa (= *Cassia hebecarpa*)	Wild senna	4
Senna marilandica	Maryland senna	4
Senna obtusifolia	Blunt-leaved senna	0
SENNA OCCIDENTALIS	Coffee senna	
Sericocarpus linifolius (= *Aster solidagineus*)	Narrow-leaved white-top aster	7
SETARIA FABERI	Giant foxtail grass	
SETARIA ITALICA	Foxtail millet	
Setaria parviflora	Perennial foxtail grass	2
SETARIA PUMILA s. PUMILA	Pigeon grass	
SETARIA VERTICILLATA	Bristly foxtail grass	
SETARIA VIRIDIS v. MAJOR	Giant green foxtail grass	
SETARIA VIRIDIS v. VIRIDIS	Small green foxtail grass	
Shepherdia canadensis	Buffalo berry	10
Sibara virginica	Virginia rockcress	0
Sicyos angulatus	Bur cucumber	3
Sida hermaphrodita	Virginia mallow	4
SIDA SPINOSA	Prickly sida	
Sideroxylon lycioides (= *Bumelia lycioides*)	Southern buckthorn	10
Silene antirrhina	Sleepy catchfly	0
SILENE ARMERIA	Sweet William catchfly	
SILENE CHLORANTHA	Yellow-green catchfly	
SILENE CSEREI	Glaucous campion	
SILENE DICHOTOMA	Forked catchfly	
SILENE DIOICA (= *LYCHNIS DIOICA*)	Red catchfly	
SILENE LATIFOLIA s. ALBA (= *LYCHNIS ALBA*)	White campion	
Silene nivea	Snowy catchfly	7
SILENE NOCTIFLORA	Night-flowering catchfly	
Silene ovata	Woodland catchfly	7
Silene regia	Royal catchfly	6
Silene stellata	Starry campion	5
Silene virginica	Fire pink	7
SILENE VULGARIS	Bladder campion	
SILPHIUM ASTERISCUS v. ASTERISCUS	Starry rosinweed	
Silphium asteriscus v. trifoliatum	Rosin weed	8
Silphium integrifolium v. deamii	Deam's rosin weed	7
Silphium integrifolium v. integrifolium	Rosin weed	7
Silphium laciniatum	Compass plant	10
Silphium perfoliatum	Cup plant	4
Silphium terebinthinaceum v. pinnatifidum	Cut-leaved prairie dock	6
Silphium terebinthinaceum v. terebinthinaceum	Prairie dock	6
SILYBUM MARIANUM	Milk thistle	
SINAPIS ALBA (= *BRASSICA HIRTA*)	White mustard	
SINAPIS ARVENSIS	Charlock	
SISYMBRIUM ALTISSIMUM	Tumble mustard	
SISYMBRIUM LOESELII	Tall hedge mustard	
SISYMBRIUM OFFICINALE	Hedge mustard	
Sisyrinchium albidum	Common blue-eyed grass	4
Sisyrinchium angustifolium	Stout blue-eyed grass	3
Sisyrinchium atlanticum	Eastern blue-eyed grass	10
Sisyrinchium montanum	Mountain blue-eyed grass	10
Sium suave	Water parsnip	5
Smallanthus uvedalia (= *Polymnia uvedalia*)	Bear's foot	5
Smilacina. See 2 species of *Maianthemum*		
Smilax bona-nox	Bull brier	5
Smilax ecirrhata	Upright carrion flower	5
Smilax glauca	Green brier	4
Smilax hispida	Bristly green brier	3
Smilax illinoensis	Illinois carrion flower	6
Smilax lasioneura	Common carrion flower	4
Smilax pulverulenta	Dark green carrion flower	5
Smilax rotundifolia	Cat brier	4
Solanum carolinense	Horse nettle	0
SOLANUM DULCAMARA	Bittersweet nightshade	
SOLANUM ELAEAGNIFOLIUM	Silver-leaved nightshade	
SOLANUM LYCOPERSICUM	Tomato	
SOLANUM PHYSALIFOLIUM	Hairy nightshade	
Solanum ptycanthum	Black nightshade	0
SOLANUM ROSTRATUM	Buffalo bur	
Solidago altissima (including 1 subspecies)	Tall goldenrod	0
Solidago bicolor	Silverrod	8
Solidago buckleyi	Buckley's goldenrod	10
Solidago caesia	Bluestem goldenrod	7
Solidago canadensis (including 1 subspecies)	Canada goldenrod	0
Solidago erecta	Smooth white goldenrod	8
Solidago flexicaulis	Broad-leaved goldenrod	6
Solidago gigantea	Late goldenrod	4
Solidago hispida	Hairy white goldenrod	8
Solidago juncea	Early goldenrod	3
Solidago missouriensis	Missouri goldenrod	4
Solidago nemoralis (including 1 subspecies)	Old-field goldenrod	3
Solidago ohioensis	Ohio goldenrod	10
Solidago patula	Rough-leaved goldenrod	8
Solidago ptarmicoides	Stiff aster	10
Solidago riddellii	Riddell's goldenrod	9
Solidago rigida (including 1 subspecies)	Rigid goldenrod	7

Table P-2. *continued*

Scientific Name[a]	Common Name	Coefficient[b]
Solidago rugosa (including 1 variety)	Rough goldenrod	6
Solidago rupestris	Rock goldenrod	10
SOLIDAGO SEMPERVIRENS	Seaside goldenrod	
Solidago shortii	Short's goldenrod	10
Solidago simplex v. gillmanii	Dune goldenrod	10
Solidago speciosa (including 1 variety)	Showy goldenrod	7
Solidago sphacelata	Blighted goldenrod	8
Solidago squarrosa	Rosette goldenrod	10
Solidago uliginosa	Bog goldenrod	10
Solidago ulmifolia	Elm-leaved goldenrod	5
Solidago x lutescens	Yellow stiff aster	10
SONCHUS ARVENSIS s. ARVENSIS	Viscid field sow thistle	
SONCHUS ARVENSIS s. ULIGINOSUS	Smooth field sow thistle	
SONCHUS ASPER	Prickly sow thistle	
SONCHUS OLERACEUS	Common sow thistle	
SORBARIA SORBIFOLIA	False spiraea	
SORBUS AUCUPARIA	European mountain ash	
Sorbus decora	American mountain ash	10
Sorghastrum nutans	Indian grass	4
SORGHUM BICOLOR	Sorghum	
SORGHUM HALEPENSE	Johnson grass	
Sparganium americanum	American bur reed	10
Sparganium androcladum	Branched bur reed	9
Sparganium emersum	Dwarf bur reed	8
Sparganium eurycarpum	Common bur reed	5
Sparganium natans	Floating bur reed	10
Spartina pectinata	Prairie cord grass	4
SPERGULA ARVENSIS	Corn spurrey	
SPERGULARIA MARITIMA	Satin-flowered sand spurrey	
SPERGULARIA RUBRA	Sand spurrey	
SPERGULARIA SALINA	Lesser salt spurrey	
Spermacoce glabra	Smooth buttonweed	3
SPERMOLEPIS INERMIS	Smooth scaleseed	
Sphenopholis nitida	Shining wedge grass	8
Sphenopholis obtusata v. major	Slender wedge grass	3
Sphenopholis obtusata v. obtusata	Prairie wedge grass	5
Spigelia marilandica	Indian pink	8
Spiraea alba	Meadowsweet	4
SPIRAEA JAPONICA	Japanese meadowsweet	
SPIRAEA PRUNIFOLIA	Bridal wreath	
Spiraea tomentosa	Hardhack	4
Spiranthes cernua	Nodding ladies' tresses	3
Spiranthes lacera v. gracilis	Slender ladies' tresses	3
Spiranthes lacera v. lacera	Slender ladies' tresses	10
Spiranthes lucida	Early ladies' tresses	10
Spiranthes magnicamporum	Great Plains ladies' tresses	10
Spiranthes ochroleuca	Yellow ladies' tresses	4
Spiranthes ovalis v. erostellata	Oval ladies' tresses	3
Spiranthes romanzoffiana	Hooded ladies' tresses	10
Spiranthes tuberosa	Little ladies' tresses	3
Spiranthes vernalis	Spring ladies' tresses	3
Spirodela polyrhiza	Great duckweed	5
Sporobolus clandestinus	Rough rush grass	5
Sporobolus compositus	Rough dropseed	1
Sporobolus cryptandrus	Sand dropseed	4
Sporobolus heterolepis	Northern dropseed	10
Sporobolus neglectus	Small rush grass	1
Sporobolus vaginiflorus	Northern rush grass	1
Stachys aspera	Rough hedge nettle	0
STACHYS BYZANTINA	Woolly hedge nettle	
Stachys clingmanii	Clingman's hedge nettle	10
Stachys cordata	Heart-leaved hedge nettle	7
Stachys hyssopifolia	Hyssop hedge nettle	8
Stachys pilosa v. arenicola	Woundwort	5
Stachys tenuifolia v. hispida	Marsh hedge nettle	4
Stachys tenuifolia v. tenuifolia	Streambank hedge nettle	4
Staphylea trifolia	Bladdernut	5
Stellaria corei	Stalked great chickweed	9
STELLARIA GRAMINEA	Starwort	
Stellaria longifolia	Stitchwort	7
Stellaria longipes	Long-stalked starwort	10
STELLARIA MEDIA s. MEDIA	Common chickweed	
STELLARIA MEDIA s. PALLIDA	Sand chickweed	
Stellaria pubera	Great chickweed	7
Stenanthium gramineum	Featherbells	8
Stenaria nigricans (= *Hedyotis nigricans*)	Narrow-leaved bluets	9
STENOSIPHON LINIFOLIUS	Smooth gaura	
Stipa. See 2 species of *Hesperostipa*		
Stipa avenacea. See *Piptochaetium avenaceum*		
Strophostyles helvola	Trailing wild bean	3
Strophostyles leiosperma	Small wild bean	4
Strophostyles umbellata	Clustered wild bean	4
Stuckenia pectinata (= *Potamogeton pectinatus*)	Comb pondweed	3
Stylophorum diphyllum	Celandine poppy	7
Stylosanthes biflora	Pencil flower	5
Styrax americana	American storax	8
Styrax grandifolia	Large-leaved storax	10
SUAEDA CALCEOLIFORMIS	Sea blite	
Sullivantia sullivantii	Sullivant's coolwort	10
SYMPHORICARPOS ALBUS v. LAEVIGATUS	Garden snowberry	
SYMPHORICARPOS OCCIDENTALIS	Wolfberry	
Symphoricarpos orbiculatus	Coralberry	1
Symphyotrichum boreale (= *Aster borealis*)	Rush aster	10
SYMPHYOTRICHUM CILIATUM. See *BRACHYACTIS CILIATA*		
Symphyotrichum cordifolium	Heart-leaved aster	5
Symphyotrichum drummondii	Drummond's aster	4
Symphyotrichum dumosum (including 1 variety)	Bushy aster	4
Symphyotrichum ericoides v. ericoides	Heath aster	4
Symphyotrichum firmum	Shining aster	4
Symphyotrichum laeve	Smooth blue aster	10
Symphyotrichum lanceolatum (including 2 varieties)	Panicled aster	3
Symphyotrichum lateriflorum (including 1 variety)	Side-flowering aster	3
Symphyotrichum novae-angliae	New England aster	3
Symphyotrichum oblongifolium	Aromatic aster	9
Symphyotrichum ontarionis	Ontario aster	5
Symphyotrichum oolentangiense	Sky-blue aster	8
Symphyotrichum patens	Purple daisy	6
Symphyotrichum phlogifolium	Phlox-leaved aster	6
Symphyotrichum pilosum v. pilosum	Hairy aster	0
Symphyotrichum pilosum v. pringlei	Smooth white aster	5
Symphyotrichum praealtum (including 1 variety)	Willow aster	6
Symphyotrichum prenanthoides	Crooked aster	8
Symphyotrichum puniceum	Bristly aster	7
Symphyotrichum racemosum	Small white aster	4
Symphyotrichum sericeum	Silky aster	10
Symphyotrichum shortii	Short's aster	6
SYMPHYOTRICHUM SUBULATUM	Expressway aster	
Symphyotrichum undulatum	Wavy-leaved aster	7
Symphyotrichum urophyllum	Arrow-leaved aster	4
SYMPHYTUM OFFICINALE	Common comfrey	
Symplocarpus foetidus	Skunk cabbage	8
Synandra hispidula	Synandra	5
SYRINGA VULGARIS	Lilac	
Taenidia integerrima	Yellow pimpernel	7
Talinum rugospermum. See *Phemeranthus rugospermus*		
TANACETUM BALSAMITA	Costmary	
TANACETUM PARTHENIUM	Feverfew	
TANACETUM VULGARE	Common tansy	
TARAXACUM LAEVIGATUM	Red-seeded dandelion	

Scientific Name[a]	Common Name	Coefficient[b]
TARAXACUM OFFICINALE	Common dandelion	
Taxodium distichum	Bald cypress	10
Taxus canadensis	Canada yew	10
TEESDALIA NUDICAULIS	Shepherd's cress	
Tephrosia virginiana	Goat's rue	7
Teucrium canadense v. canadense	American germander	3
Teucrium canadense v. occidentale	Gray germander	3
Thalictrum dasycarpum	Purple meadow rue	4
Thalictrum dioicum	Early meadow rue	7
Thalictrum pubescens	Late meadow rue	6
Thalictrum revolutum	Waxy meadow rue	5
Thalictrum thalictroides	Rue anemone	7
Thaspium barbinode	Hairy meadow parsnip	7
Thaspium trifoliatum v. aureum	Yellow meadow parsnip	5
THELESPERMA MEGAPOTAMICUM	Green thread	
Thelypteris noveboracensis	New York fern	5
Thelypteris palustris v. pubescens	Marsh shield fern	7
THLASPI ALLIACEUM	Roadside penny cress	
THLASPI ARVENSE	Field penny cress	
THLASPI PERFOLIATUM	Perfoliate penny cress	
Thuja occidentalis	Arbor vitae	10
THYMUS PRAECOX s. ARCTICUS	Thyme	
Tilia americana v. americana	American linden	5
Tilia americana v. heterophylla	White basswood	5
Tipularia discolor	Crane-fly orchid	4
Tofieldia glutinosa. See *Trianthus glutinosa*		
TORILIS ARVENSIS s. ARVENSIS	Field hedge parsley	
TORILIS JAPONICA	Japanese hedge parsley	
Torreyochloa pallida (= *Glyceria pallida*)	Pale manna grass	10
Tovara virginiana (= *Polygonum virginianum*)	Virginia knotweed	3
Toxicodendron radicans s. negundo	Eastern poison ivy	1
Toxicodendron radicans s. radicans	Poison ivy	1
Toxicodendron rydbergii	Western poison ivy	7
Toxicodendron vernix	Poison sumac	10
Trachelospermum difforme	Climbing dogbane	8
Tradescantia bracteata	Long-bracted spiderwort	0
Tradescantia ohiensis	Common spiderwort	3
Tradescantia subaspera	Broad-leaved spiderwort	4
Tradescantia virginiana	Virginia spiderwort	7
Tragia cordata	Tragia	8
TRAGOPOGON DUBIUS	Sand goat's beard	
TRAGOPOGON PORRIFOLIUS	Oyster salsify	
TRAGOPOGON PRATENSIS	Common goat's beard	
Trautvetteria caroliniensis	False bugbane	10
Triadenum fraseri	Fraser's St. John's wort	8
Triadenum tubulosum	Marsh St. John's wort	8
Triadenum virginicum	Marsh St. John's wort	10
Triadenum walteri	Marsh St. John's wort	8
Triantha glutinosa (= *Tofieldia glutinosa*)	False asphodel	10
TRIBULUS TERRESTRIS	Puncture vine	
Trichomanes boschianum	Appalachian filmy fern	10
Trichomanes intricatum	Weft fern	10
Trichostema brachiatum. See *Isanthus brachiatus*		
Trichostema dichotomum	Blue curls	4
Tridens flavus	Common purpletop	1
Trientalis borealis	Starflower	10
TRIFOLIUM ARVENSE	Rabbit-foot clover	
TRIFOLIUM AUREUM	Yellow hop clover	
TRIFOLIUM CAMPESTRE	Low hop clover	
TRIFOLIUM DUBIUM	Little hop clover	
TRIFOLIUM HYBRIDUM	Alsike clover	
TRIFOLIUM INCARNATUM	Crimson clover	
TRIFOLIUM PRATENSE	Red clover	
Trifolium reflexum	Buffalo clover	8
TRIFOLIUM REPENS	White clover	
TRIFOLIUM RESUPINATUM	Reversed clover	
Trifolium stoloniferum	Running buffalo clover	3
Triglochin maritima	Common bog arrow grass	10
Triglochin palustris	Slender bog arrow grass	10
Trillium cernuum	Nodding trillium	10
TRILLIUM ERECTUM v. ERECTUM	Ill-scented trillium	
Trillium flexipes	Declined trillium	5
Trillium grandiflorum	Large white trillium	8
Trillium nivale	Snow trillium	8
Trillium recurvatum	Red trillium	4
Trillium sessile	Sessile trillium	4
TRIODANIS LEPTOCARPA	Narrow-leaved Venus's-looking glass	
Triodanis perfoliata	Venus's looking glass	2
Triosteum angustifolium	Small horse gentian	6
Triosteum aurantiacum (including varieties)	Early horse gentian	5
Triosteum perfoliatum	Late horse gentian	5
Triphora trianthophora s. trianthophora	Nodding pogonia	9
Triplasis purpurea	Purple sandgrass	5
TRIPLEUROSPERMUM PERFORATA	Scentless chamomile	
Tripsacum dactyloides	Gama grass	2
TRITICUM AESTIVUM	Wheat	
Tsuga canadensis	Hemlock	10
TUSSILAGO FARFARA	Colt's foot	
TYPHA ANGUSTIFOLIA	Narrow-leaved cattail	
Typha latifolia	Broad-leaved cattail	1
TYPHA x GLAUCA	Hybrid cattail	
Ulmus alata	Winged elm	7
Ulmus americana	American elm	3
ULMUS PUMILA	Siberian elm	
Ulmus rubra	Slippery elm	3
Ulmus thomasii	Rock elm	10
URTICA DIOICA s. DIOICA	Tall nettle	
Urtica dioica s. gracilis	Tall stinging nettle	1
Utricularia cornuta	Horned bladderwort	10
Utricularia geminiscapa	Bog bladderwort	10
Utricularia gibba	Humped bladderwort	4
Utricularia intermedia	Flat-leaved bladderwort	8
Utricularia macrorhiza	Common bladderwort	5
Utricularia minor	Small bladderwort	10
Utricularia purpurea	Purple bladderwort	10
Utricularia radiata	Floating bladderwort	10
Utricularia resupinata	Annual purple bladderwort	10
Utricularia subulata	Hair bladderwort	10
Uvularia grandiflora	Large flower bellwort	7
Uvularia perfoliata	Perfoliate bellwort	7
Uvularia sessilifolia	Merrybells	6
VACCARIA HISPANICA	Cow herb	
Vaccinium angustifolium	Early low blueberry	5
Vaccinium arboreum	Farkleberry	8
Vaccinium corymbosum	High-bush blueberry	9
Vaccinium fuscatum	Black blueberry	9
Vaccinium macrocarpon	Large cranberry	10
Vaccinium myrtilloides	Canada blueberry	10
Vaccinium oxycoccos	Small cranberry	10
Vaccinium pallidum	Late low blueberry	5
Vaccinium stamineum	Deerberry	4
Valeriana edulis v. ciliata	Common valerian	10
VALERIANA OFFICINALIS	Garden heliotrope	
Valeriana pauciflora	Pink valerian	7
Valeriana uliginosa	Marsh valerian	10
Valerianella chenopodifolia	Great Lakes corn salad	5
VALERIANELLA LOCUSTA	European corn salad	
Valerianella radiata	Beaked corn salad	1
Valerianella umbilicata	Corn salad	5
Vallisneria americana	Eel grass	7
Veratrum woodii. See *Melanthium woodii*		
VERBASCUM BLATTARIA	Moth mullein	
VERBASCUM PHLOMOIDES	Clasping mullein	
VERBASCUM THAPSUS	Woolly mullein	
VERBASCUM VIRGATUM	Wand mullein	
VERBENA BIPINNATIFIDA. See *GLANDULARIA BIPINNATIFIDA*		

Table P-2. *continued*

Scientific Name[a]	Common Name	Coefficient[b]
Verbena bracteata	Creeeping vervain	0
Verbena hastata (including 1 variety)	Blue vervain	3
VERBENA OFFICINALIS	European vervain	
Verbena simplex	Narrow-leaved vervain	4
Verbena stricta	Hoary vervain	4
Verbena urticifolia v. leiocarpa	Velvety white vervain	3
Verbena urticifolia v. urticifolia	White vervain	3
Verbesina alternifolia	Wingstem	3
Verbesina helianthoides	Yellow crownbeard	7
Verbesina virginica	Frostweed	3
VERNONIA ARKANSANA	Ozark ironweed	
VERNONIA BALDWINII	Baldwin's ironweed	
Vernonia fasciculata	Common ironweed	5
Vernonia gigantea	Tall ironweed	2
Vernonia missurica	Missouri ironweed	4
Veronica americana	American brooklime	10
Veronica anagallis-aquatica	Water speedwell	5
VERONICA ARVENSIS	Corn speedwell	
VERONICA AUSTRIACA s. TEUCRIUM	Broad-leaved speedwell	
VERONICA CHAMAEDRYS	Germander speedwell	
VERONICA HEDERIFOLIA	Ivy-leaved speedwell	
VERONICA LONGIFOLIA	Long-leaved speedwell	
VERONICA OFFICINALIS v. OFFICINALIS	Common speedwell	
Veronica peregrina s. peregrina	Smooth purslane speedwell	0
Veronica peregrina s. xalapensis	Viscid purslane speedwell	5
VERONICA PERSICA	Bird's-eye speedwell	
VERONICA POLITA	Dwarf bird's-eye speedwell	
Veronica scutellata	Marsh speedwell	9
VERONICA SERPYLLIFOLIA	Thyme-leaved speedwell	
VERONICA VERNA	Spring speedwell	
Veronicastrum virginicum	Culver's root	8
Viburnum acerifolium	Maple-leaved arrowwood	8
Viburnum dentatum	Southern arrowwood	6
VIBURNUM LANTANA	Wayfaring tree	
Viburnum lentago	Nannyberry	5
Viburnum molle	Downy arrowwood	10
Viburnum nudum v. cassinoides	With rod	8
Viburnum opulus v. americanum	High-bush cranberry	10
VIBURNUM OPULUS v. OPULUS	European high-bush cranberry	
VIBURNUM PLICATUM	Japanese snowball bush	
Viburnum prunifolium	Black haw	4
Viburnum rafinesquianum	Downy arrowwood	7
VIBURNUM RECOGNITUM	Smooth arrowwood	
Viburnum rufidulum	Rusty nannyberry	8
Vicia americana	American vetch	6
Vicia caroliniana	Wood vetch	7
VICIA CRACCA	Cow vetch	
VICIA SATIVA s. NIGRA	Narrow-leaved vetch	
VICIA TETRASPERMA	Four-seeded vetch	
VICIA VILLOSA s. VARIA	Woolly-pod vetch	
VICIA VILLOSA s. VILLOSA	Winter vetch	
VIGNA UNGUICULATA	Black-eyed pea	
VINCA MAJOR	Large-flowered periwinkle	
VINCA MINOR	Common periwinkle	
VINCETOXICUM HIRUNDINARIA	White swallow-wort	
VINCETOXICUM NIGRUM	Black swallow-wort	
Viola affinis	Woodland blue violet	2
VIOLA ARVENSIS	Wild pansy	
VIOLA BICOLOR	Wild pansy	
Viola blanda	Smooth white violet	8

Scientific Name[a]	Common Name	Coefficient[b]
Viola canadensis	Canada violet	8
Viola cucullata	Marsh blue violet	9
Viola egglestonii	Eggleston's violet	10
Viola hirsutula	Small-fruited blue violet	10
Viola labradorica	Dog violet	8
Viola lanceolata	Lance-leaved violet	7
Viola missouriensis	Missouri violet	3
Viola nephrophylla	Northern blue violet	8
VIOLA ODORATA	Sweet blue violet	
Viola pallens	Smooth white violet	10
Viola palmata (including 1 variety)	Cleft violet	5
Viola pedata	Bird's foot violet	9
Viola pedatifida	Prairie violet	9
Viola primulifolia	Primrose-leaved violet	10
Viola pubescens (including varieties)	Downy yellow violet	5
Viola rostrata	Long-spurred violet	8
Viola sagittata v. ovata	Sand violet	6
Viola sagittata v. sagittata	Arrow-leaved violet	6
Viola sororia	Woolly blue violet	1
Viola striata	Common white violet	4
VIOLA TRICOLOR	Johnny-jump-up	
Vitis aestivalis (including 1 variety)	Summer grape	4
Vitis cinerea (including 1 variety)	Winter grape	4
Vitis labrusca	Fox grape	6
Vitis palmata	Catbird grape	6
Vitis riparia	Riverbank grape	1
Vitis rupestris	Sand grape	10
Vitis vulpina	Frost grape	3
Vittaria appalachiana	Shoestring fern	10
VULPIA MYUROS	Mousetail fescue	
Vulpia octoflora (including 1 variety)	Six-weeks fescue	1
Waldsteinia fragarioides	Barren strawberry	9
WEIGELA FLORIDA	Old-fashioned wigela	
Wisteria frutescens	Kentucky wisteria	4
Wolffia borealis	Spotted watermeal	4
Wolffia braziliensis	Nippled watermeal	6
Wolffia columbiana	Globose watermeal	5
Wolffiella gladiata	Blade duckweed	5
Woodsia obtusa s. obtusa	Common woodsia	4
Woodwardia areolata	Netted chainfern	6
Woodwardia virginica	Virginia chainfern	10
XANTHIUM SPINOSUM	Spiny cocklebur	
Xanthium strumarium	Cocklebur	0
Xyris difformis	Yellow-eyed grass	10
Xyris torta	Twisted yellow-eyed grass	9
YUCCA FLACCIDA	Adam's needle	
Zannichellia palustris	Horned pondweed	6
Zanthoxylum americanum	Prickly ash	3
ZEA MAYS	Corn	
Zigadenus elegans	White camass	10
Zizania aquatica v. aquatica	Broad-leaved wild rice	10
Zizania palustris (including 1 variety)	Narrow-leaved wild rice	10
Zizia aptera	Heart-leaved meadow parsnip	10
Zizia aurea	Golden alexanders	7
ZOYSIA JAPONICA	Japanese lawn grass	

Notes: [a] Scientific names in all capital letters are exotic species.
[b] Coefficient of conservatism. The values, ranging from 0 to 10, are an estimate of the fidelity of an individual species to an undisturbed plant community that characterized the region before European settlement.

Table P-3. Plant Species in Deciduous Forests

Common Name	Scientific Name
Adam-and-Eve	*Aplectrum hyemale*
Allegheny spurge	*Pachysandra procumbens*
American beak grass	*Diarrhena americana*
American beech	*Fagus grandifolia*
American bellflower	*Campanulastrum americanum* (= *Campanula americanum*)
American chestnut	*Castanea dentata*
American columbo	*Frasera caroliniensis*
American elm	*Ulmus americana*
American filbert	*Corylus americana*
American gromwell	*Lithospermum latifolium*
American hops	*Humulus lupulus v. pubescens*
American linden	*Tilia americana v. americana*
American pennyroyal	*Hedeoma pulegioides*
American storax	*Styrax americana*
Amur honeysuckle	*LONICERA MAACKII*
Anise root	*Osmorhiza longistylis*
Aromatic sumac	*Rhus aromatica v. aromatica*
Arrow arum	*Peltandra virginica*
Autumn bent grass	*Agrostis perennans*
Autumn bluegrass	*Poa autumnalis*
Autumn olive	*ELAEAGNUS UMBELLATA*
Awned graceful sedge	*Carex davisii*
Bare-stemmed tick trefoil	*Desmodium nudiflorum*
Barren strawberry	*Waldsteinia fragarioides*
Basil bee balm	*Monarda clinopodia*
Basket oak	*Quercus michauxii*
Bastard toadflax	*Comandra umbellata*
Beaked black snakeroot	*Sanicula trifoliata*
Bearded panic grass	*Dichanthelium boscii*
Bear's foot	*Smallanthus uvedalia* (= *Polymnia uvedalia*)
Beech drops	*Epifagus virginiana*
Beech wood sedge	*Carex laxiflora*
Big-leaved aster	*Eurybia macrophylla*
Big shellbark hickory	*Carya laciniosa*
Bigtooth aspen	*Populus grandidentata*
Bishop's cap	*Mitella diphylla*
Bitternut hickory	*Carya cordiformis*
Bittersweet nightshade	*SOLANUM DULCAMARA*
Black ash	*Fraxinus nigra*
Black chokeberry	*Photinia melanocarpa*
Black cohosh	*Cimicifuga rubifolia*
Black gum	*Nyssa sylvatica*
Black hickory	*Carya texana*
Black huckleberry	*Gaylussacia baccata*
Blackjack oak	*Quercus marilandica*
Black maple	*Acer saccharum s. nigrum*
Black oak	*Quercus velutina*
Black oat grass	*Piptochaetium avenaceum* (= *Stipa avenacea*)
Black-seeded rice grass	*Piptatherum racemosa*
Black snakeroot	*Sanicula marilandica*
Black walnut	*Juglans nigra*
Bladdernut	*Staphylea trifolia*
Blighted goldenrod	*Solidago sphacelata*
Bloodleaf	*Iresine rhizomatosa*
Bloodroot	*Sanguinaria canadensis*
Blue ash	*Fraxinus quadrangulata*
Blue beech	*Carpinus caroliniana s. virginiana*
Blue cohosh	*Caulophyllum thalictroides*
Bluets	*Houstonia caerulea* (= *Hedyotis caerulea*)
Blue-eyed Mary	*Collinsia verna*
Blue lettuce	*Lactuca floridana*
Blue phlox	*Phlox divaricata* (including 1 subspecies)
Blue sedge	*Carex glaucodea*
Blue star	*Amsonia tabernaemontana v. salicifolia*
Bluestem goldenrod	*Solidago caesia*
Blunt-scaled oak sedge	*Carex albicans v. albicans*
Blunt-scaled wood sedge	*Carex albursina*
Bottlebrush grass	*Elymus hystrix* (including 1 variety)
Bottlebrush sedge	*Carex lurida*
Boxelder	*Acer negundo* (including varieties)
Bracted green orchid	*Coeloglossum viride* (= *Habenaria viridis*)
Bristly cattail sedge	*Carex frankii*
Bristly sunflower	*Helianthus hirsutus*
Broad beech fern	*Phegopteris hexagonoptera*
Broad-leaved goldenrod	*Solidago flexicaulis*
Broad-leaved oval sedge	*Carex tribuloides v. tribuloides*
Broad-leaved spiderwort	*Tradescantia subaspera*
Broad-leaved wood sedge	*Carex platyphylla*
Bronze fern	*Botrychium dissectum*
Brown-eyed Susan	*Rudbeckia triloba*
Buckley's goldenrod	*Solidago buckleyi*
Buffalo clover	*Trifolium reflexum*
Bulb bitter cress	*Cardamine bulbosa*
Bulbous wood rush	*Luzula bulbosa*
Bull brier	*Smilax bona-nox*
Buttercup phacelia	*Phacelia ranunculacea*
Butterfly pea	*Clitoria mariana*
Butternut	*Juglans cinerea*
Canada clearweed	*Pilea pumila*
Canada lily	*Lilium canadense*
Canada violet	*Viola canadensis*
Canada waterleaf	*Hydrophyllum canadense*
Canada wild ginger	*Asarum canadense*
Canada wood nettle	*Laportea canadensis*
Canada yew	*Taxus canadensis*
Canadian black snakeroot	*Sanicula canadensis* (including 1 variety)
Canadian bluegrass	*POA COMPRESSA*
Cardinal flower	*Lobelia cardinalis*
Carolina buckthorn	*Frangula caroliniana* (= *Rhamnus caroliniana*)
Carolina panic grass	*Dichanthelium dichotomum s.yadkinense*
Cat brier	*Smilax rotundifolia*
Cat's foot	*Antennaria neglecta*
Celandine poppy	*Stylophorum diphyllum*
Checkerberry	*Gaultheria procumbens*
Cherrybark oak	*Quercus pagoda*
Chinquapin oak	*Quercus muhlenbergii*
Cigar tree	*Catalpa speciosa*
Cleft phlox	*Phlox bifida s. bifida*
Cleft violet	*Viola palmata* (including 1 variety)
Climbing bittersweet	*Celastrus scandens*
Climbing dayflower	*COMMELINA DIFFUSA*
Climbing fern	*Lygodium palmatum*
Climbing hempweed	*Mikania scandens*
Common beech sedge	*Carex communis*
Common blackberry	*Rubus sec. Allegheniensis: R. allegheniensis*
Common burdock	*ARCTIUM MINUS*
Common bur sedge	*Carex grayi*
Common chickweed	*STELLARIA MEDIA s. MEDIA*
Common cinquefoil	*Potentilla simplex*
Common dayflower	*COMMELINA COMMUNIS*
Common dodder	*Cuscuta gronovii* (including 1 variety)
Common elderberry	*Sambucus nigra s. canadensis*
Common forget-me-not	*MYOSOTIS SCORPIOIDES*
Common fragile fern	*Cystopteris protrusa*
Common hops	*HUMULUS LUPULUS v. LUPULUS*
Common hop sedge	*Carex lupulina*
Common horsetail	*Equisetum arvense*
Common privet	*LIGUSTRUM VULGARE*
Common star of Bethlehem	*ORNITHOGALUM UMBELLATUM*
Common streambank chervil	*Chaerophyllum procumbens v. procumbens*
Common water hemlock	*Cicuta maculata* (including 1 variety)
Common wild comfrey	*Cynoglossum virginianum v. virginianum*
Common wild yam	*Dioscorea villosa*
Common wood reed	*Cinna arundinacea*
Common wood rush	*Luzula echinata*
Common wood sedge	*Carex blanda*
Concealed sedge	*Carex cumberlandensis*

Table P-3. *continued*

Common Name	Scientific Name
Crane-fly orchid	*Tipularia discolor*
Creeping bracted sedge	*Carex socialis*
Creeping bush clover	*Lespedeza repens*
Crested coralroot	*Hexalectris spicata*
Crow poison	*Nothoscordum bivalve*
Cucumber magnolia	*Magnolia acuminata*
Cupseed	*Calycocarpum lyonii*
Dame's rocket	*HESPERIS MATRONALIS*
Deam's beard tongue	*Penstemon deamii*
Declined trillium	*Trillium flexipes*
Deerberry	*Vaccinium stamineum*
Devil's walking stick	*Aralia spinosa*
Dittany	*Cunila origanoides*
Dog mint	*Clinopodium vulgare*
Doll's-eyes	*Actaea pachypoda*
Downy arrowwood	*Viburnum molle*
Downy false foxglove	*Aureolaria virginica*
Downy green sedge	*Carex swanii*
Downy skullcap	*Scutellaria incana*
Downy Solomon's seal	*Polygonatum pubescens*
Downy yellow violet	*Viola pubescens* (including varieties)
Dutchman's breeches	*Dicentra cucullaria*
Dwarf crested iris	*Iris cristata*
Dwarf ginseng	*Panax trifolius*
Dwarf larkspur	*Delphinium tricorne*
Early figwort	*Scrophularia lanceolata*
Early horse gentian	*Triosteum aurantiacum* (including varieties)
Early-leaved brome	*Bromus latiglumis*
Early low blueberry	*Vaccinium angustifolium*
Early oak sedge	*Carex umbellata*
Early saxifrage	*Saxifraga virginiensis*
Eastern cottonwood	*Populus deltoides*
Eastern redbud	*Cercis canadensis*
Elephant's foot	*Elephantopus carolinianus*
Elm-leaved goldenrod	*Solidago ulmifolia*
Enchanter's nightshade	*Circaea lutetiana s. canadensis*
Fairy wand	*Chamaelirium luteum*
Fall coralroot	*Corallorhiza odontorhiza* (including 1 variety)
False grass sedge	*Carex timida*
False hellebore	*Melanthium woodii* (= *Veratrum woodii*)
False loosestrife	*Ludwigia glandulosa*
False melic grass	*Schizachne purpurascens*
False mermaid weed	*Floerkea proserpinacoides*
False rue anemone	*Enemion biternatum* (= *Isopyrum biternatum*)
Farkleberry	*Vaccinium arboreum*
Featherbells	*Stenanthium gramineum*
Feathery false Solomon's seal	*Maianthemum racemosum* (= *Smilacina racemosa*)
Fen betony	*Pedicularis lanceolata*
Few-flowered tick trefoil	*Desmodium pauciflorum*
Field sorrel	*RUMEX ACETOSELLA*
Fire pink	*Silene virginica*
Fireweed	*Erechtites hieracifolia*
Five leaves	*Isotria verticillata*
Flat-spiked gray sedge	*Carex planispicata*
Flowering dogwood	*Cornus florida*
Forked aster	*Eurybia furcata* (= *Aster furcatus*)
Forked panic grass	*Dichanthelium dichotomum s. dichotomum*
Four-leaf yam	*Dioscorea quaternata*
Fowl manna grass	*Glyceria striata*
Fringed loosestrife	*Lysimachia ciliata*
Fringed phlox	*Phlox amplifolia*
Garden phlox	*Phlox paniculata*
Garlic mustard	*ALLIARIA PETIOLATA*
Giant cane	*Arundinaria gigantea*
Giant ragweed	*Ambrosia trifida*
Ginseng	*Panax quinquefolius*
Glade fern	*Diplazium pycnocarpon* (= *Athyrium pycnocarpon*)
Glaucous tick trefoil	*Desmodium laevigatum*
Goat's beard	*Aruncus dioicus*
Golden ragwort	*Packera aurea*
Golden rain tree	*KOELREUTERIA PANICULATA*
Golden seal	*Hydrastis canadensis*
Goldie fern	*Dryopteris goldiana*
Grass sedge	*Carex jamesii*
Great burdock	*ARCTIUM LAPPA*
Great chickweed	*Stellaria pubera*
Greater hop sedge	*Carex gigantea*
Great Indian plantain	*Arnoglossum reniforme*
Great waterleaf	*Hydrophyllum appendiculatum*
Great white lettuce	*Prenanthes crepidinea*
Great yellow wood sorrel	*Oxalis grandis*
Green adder's mouth	*Malaxis unifolia*
Green ash	*Fraxinus pennsylvanica v. lanceolata*
Green brier	*Smilax glauca*
Green-fringed orchid	*Platanthera lacera*
Green violet	*Hybanthus concolor*
Ground ivy	*GLECHOMA HEDERACEA*
Ground pine	*Lycopodium obscurum*
Grove bluegrass	*Poa alsodes*
Hackberry	*Celtis occidentalis*
Hair grass	*Agrostis hyemalis*
Hairy bedstraw	*Galium pilosum*
Hairy bush clover	*Lespedeza hirta*
Hairy gentian	*Gentiana villosa*
Hairy gray sedge	*Carex hitchcockiana*
Hairy hawkweed	*Hieracium gronovii*
Hairy skullcap	*Scutellaria elliptica v. hirsuta*
Hairy spicebush	*Lindera benzoin*
Hairy sweet cicely	*Osmorhiza claytonii*
Hairy white goldenrod	*Solidago hispida*
Harbinger of spring	*Erigenia bulbosa*
Harvey's buttercup	*Ranunculus harveyi*
Heart-leaved skullcap	*Scutellaria ovata*
Hedge apple	*MACLURA POMIFERA*
Helleborine orchid	*EPIPACTIS HELLEBORINE*
Hoary beard tongue	*Penstemon canescens*
Hog peanut	*Amphicarpaea bracteata v. bracteata*
Hollow Joe Pye weed	*Eupatoriadelphus fistulosus* (= *Eupatorium fistulosum*)
Honewort	*Cryptotaenia canadensis*
Honey locust	*Gleditsia triacanthos*
Hooked monkshood	*Aconitum uncinatum*
Hop hornbeam	*Ostrya virginiana*
Illinois wood sorrel	*Oxalis illinoensis*
Indian cucumber root	*Medeola virginiana*
Indian heliotrope	*HELIOTROPIUM INDICUM*
Indian physic	*Gillenia stipulata*
Indian pink	*Spigelia marilandica*
Indian tobacco	*Lobelia inflata*
Indian turnip	*Arisaema triphyllum*
Indian wood oats	*Chasmanthium latifolium*
Interrupted fern	*Osmunda claytoniana*
Ivory sedge	*Carex eburnea*
Jack oak	*Quercus imbricaria*
Japanese barberry	*BERBERIS THUNBERGII*
Japanese honeysuckle	*LONICERA JAPONICA*
Japanese hops	*HUMULUS JAPONICUS*
Jetbead	*RHODOTYPOS SCANDENS*
Juneberry	*Amelanchier arborea*
Kentucky bluegrass	*POA PRATENSIS*
Kentucky coffee tree	*Gymnocladus dioica*
Kentucky wisteria	*Wisteria frutescens*
Kral's sedge	*Carex kraliana*
Lady fern	*Athyrium filix-femina s. angustum*
Large flower bellwort	*Uvularia grandiflora*
Large-leaf waterleaf	*Hydrophyllum macrophyllum*
Large-leaved shinleaf	*Pyrola elliptica*
Large-leaved storax	*Styrax grandifolia*
Large white trillium	*Trillium grandiflorum*
Late horse gentian	*Triosteum perfoliatum*
Late low blueberry	*Vaccinium pallidum*
Leafy phacelia	*Phacelia bipinnatifida*

Common Name	Scientific Name
Leather flower	*Clematis pitcheri*
Leatherwood	*Dirca palustris*
Leek sedge	*Carex prasina*
Lizard's tail	*Saururus cernuus*
Long-awned wood grass	*Brachyelytrum erectum*
Long-fruited oval sedge	*Carex albolutescens*
Long-scaled green sedge	*Carex bushii*
Long-spurred violet	*Viola rostrata*
Long-stalked hummock sedge	*Carex pedunculata*
Loose-flowered panic grass	*Dichanthelium laxiflorum*
Lopseed	*Phryma leptostachya*
Mad-dog skullcap	*Scutellaria lateriflora*
Maidenhair fern	*Adiantum pedatum*
Maple-leaved arrowwood	*Viburnum acerifolium*
Marsh fleabane	*Erigeron philadelphicus*
Marsh St. John's wort	*Triadenum tubulosum*
Marsh St. John's wort	*Triadenum walteri*
Maryland senna	*Senna marilandica*
May apple	*Podophyllum peltatum*
Miami mist	*Phacelia purshii*
Michigan lily	*Lilium michiganense*
Missouri violet	*Viola missouriensis*
Mockernut hickory	*Carya tomentosa*
Monarda	*Monarda bradburiana*
Moneywort	*LYSIMACHIA NUMMULARIA*
Monkey flower	*Mimulus ringens*
Moonseed	*Menispermum canadense*
Mountain chestnut oak	*Quercus montana*
Mountain laurel	*Kalmia latifolia*
Mountain mint	*Pycnanthemum pycnanthemoides*
Mountain phlox	*Phlox ovata*
Narrow-fruited pinweed	*Lechea racemulosa*
Narrow-leaved cattail sedge	*Carex squarrosa*
Narrow-leaved cow wheat	*Melampyrum lineare v. lineare*
Narrow-leaved pinweed	*Lechea tenuifolia*
Narrow-leaved white-top aster	*Sericocarpus linifolius* (= *Aster solidagineus*)
Narrow-leaved wood sedge	*Carex digitalis* (including 1 variety)
Narrow melic grass	*Melica mutica*
Nepalese browntop	*MICROSTEGIUM VIMINEUM*
Netted chainfern	*Woodwardia areolata*
New York fern	*Thelypteris noveboracensis*
Nodding fescue	*Festuca subverticillata*
Nodding pogonia	*Triphora trianthophora s. trianthophora*
Northern bitter cress	*Cardamine douglassii*
Northern red oak	*Quercus rubra*
Northern tubercled orchid	*Platanthera flava v. herbiola*
Nottoway valley brome	*Bromus nottowayanus*
Ohio buckeye	*Aesculus glabra*
Ohio horse mint	*Blephilia ciliata*
Oneida grape fern	*Botrychium oneidense*
Ostrich fern	*Matteuccia struthiopteris v. pensylvanica*
Painted sedge	*Carex picta*
Pale avens	*Geum virginianum*
Pale corydalis	*Corydalis flavula*
Pale hickory	*Carya pallida*
Pale leafcup	*Polymnia canadensis*
Pale touch-me-not	*Impatiens pallida*
Panicled hawkweed	*Hieracium paniculatum*
Panicled tick trefoil	*Desmodium paniculatum*
Papaw	*Asimina triloba*
Partridge berry	*Mitchella repens*
Pasture thistle	*Cirsium discolor*
Pecan	*Carya illinoinensis*
Pennsylvania oak sedge	*Carex pensylvanica*
Pennywort	*Obolaria virginica*
Perfoliate bellwort	*Uvularia perfoliata*
Persimmon	*Diospyros virginiana*
Pignut hickory	*Carya glabra*
Pinesap	*Monotropa hypopitys*
Pink valerian	*Valeriana pauciflora*
Pin oak	*Quercus palustris*
Plantain-leaved wood sedge	*Carex plantaginea*
Pointed tick trefoil	*Desmodium glutinosum*
Poison ivy	*Toxicodendron radicans s. radicans*
Pokeweed	*Phytolacca americana v. americana*
Post oak	*Quercus stellata*
Poverty oat grass	*Danthonia spicata*
Prairie parsley	*Polytaenia nuttallii*
Prairie wedge grass	*Sphenopholis obtusata v. obtusata*
Prickly ash	*Zanthoxylum americanum*
Princess tree	*PAULOWNIA TOMENTOSA*
Purple chokeberry	*Photinia floribunda* (= *Aronia floribunda*)
Purple-fringed orchid	*Platanthera psycodes*
Purple fringeless orchid	*Platanthera peramoena*
Purple Joe Pye weed	*Eupatoriadelphus purpureus*
Purple twayblade	*Liparis liliifolia*
Pussytoes	*Antennaria plantaginifolia*
Quaking aspen	*Populus tremuloides*
Rattlesnake fern	*Botrychium virginianum*
Rattlesnake plantain	*Goodyera pubescens*
Rattlesnake weed	*Hieracium venosum*
Red ash	*Fraxinus pennsylvanica v. pennsylvanica*
Red-berried elderberry	*Sambucus racemosa v. pubens*
Red maple	*Acer rubrum v. rubrum*
Red morning glory	*IPOMOEA COCCINEA*
Red mulberry	*Morus rubra*
Red trillium	*Trillium recurvatum*
Regal fern	*Osmunda regalis v. spectabilis*
Riverbank wild rye	*Elymus riparius*
River birch	*Betula nigra*
Robin's plantain	*Erigeron pulchellus*
Rock satin grass	*Muhlenbergia sobolifera*
Rough-leaved rice grass	*Oryzopsis asperifolia*
Round-fruited panic grass	*Dichanthelium sphaerocarpon*
Round-leaved hepatica	*Anemone americana* (= *Hepatica americana*)
Round-leaved orchid	*Platanthera orbiculata*
Round-leaved ragwort	*Packera obovata*
Round-leaved shinleaf	*Pyrola americana*
Round-leaved tick trefoil	*Desmodium rotundifolium*
Running buffalo clover	*Trifolium stoloniferum*
Running ground pine	*Lycopodium clavatum*
Running savanna sedge	*Carex siccata*
Running strawberry bush	*Euonymus obovata*
Rusty nannyberry	*Viburnum rufidulum*
Sampson's snakeroot	*Orbexilum pedunculatum*
Sassafras	*Sassafras albidum*
Scarlet oak	*Quercus coccinea*
Scorpion grass	*Myosotis macrosperma*
Seneca snakeroot	*Polygala senega*
Sensitive fern	*Onoclea sensibilis*
Sessile trillium	*Trillium sessile*
Shagbark hickory	*Carya ovata*
Sharp-lobed hepatica	*Anemone acutiloba* (= *Hepatica acutiloba*)
Shining bedstraw	*Galium concinnum*
Shining bur sedge	*Carex intumescens*
Shining clubmoss	*Huperzia lucidula* (= *Lycopodium lucidulum*)
Shining panic grass	*Dichanthelium lucidum*
Shining wedge grass	*Sphenopholis nitida*
Shooting star	*Dodecatheon meadia*
Short-headed bracted sedge	*Carex cephalophora*
Short's aster	*Symphyotrichum shortii*
Short's streambank chervil	*Chaerophyllum procumbens v. shortii*
Showy orchis	*Galearis spectabilis* (= *Orchis spectabilis*)
Shumard's oak	*Quercus shumardii v. shumardii*
Side-flowering aster	*Symphyotrichum lateriflorum* (including 1 variety)
Silky wild rye	*Elymus villosus* (including 1 variety)
Silver maple	*Acer saccharinum*
Silverrod	*Solidago bicolor*
Silvery spleenwort	*Deparia acrostichoides* (= *Athyrium thelypterioides*)

Table P-3. *continued*

Common Name	Scientific Name
Slender green sedge	*Carex virescens*
Slender satin grass	*Muhlenbergia tenuiflora*
Small carp grass	*ARTHRAXON HISPIDUS*
Small-flowered crowfoot	*Ranunculus micranthus*
Small-fruited panic grass	*Dichanthelium dichotomum s. microcarpon*
Small green wood orchid	*Platanthera clavellata*
Small horse gentian	*Triosteum angustifolium*
Small morning glory	*Ipomoea lacunosa*
Small passion flower	*Passiflora lutea*
Small Solomon's seal	*Polygonatum biflorum*
Small spearwort	*Ranunculus pusillus*
Small wood sunflower	*Helianthus microcephalus*
Smooth beard tongue	*Penstemon calycosus*
Smooth false foxglove	*Aureolaria flava* (including 1 variety)
Smooth forked aster	*Eurybia schreberi*
Smooth ruellia	*Ruellia strepens*
Smooth-seeded nut rush	*Scleria oligantha*
Smooth swamp buttercup	*Ranunculus hispidus v. nitidus*
Smooth white goldenrod	*Solidago erecta*
Smooth wild licorice	*Galium circaezans v. circaezans*
Snow trillium	*Trillium nivale*
Soft agrimony	*Agrimonia pubescens*
Sourwood	*Oxydendron arboreum*
Southern adder's tongue fern	*Ophioglossum vulgatum*
Southern blazing star	*Liatris squarrulosa*
Southern hop sedge	*Carex louisianica*
Southern red oak	*Quercus falcata*
Southern tubercled orchid	*Platanthera flava v. flava*
Sparse-lobed grape fern	*Botrychium biternatum*
Spider lily	*Hymenocallis occidentalis*
Spinulose wood fern	*Dryopteris carthusiana*
Spotted touch-me-not	*Impatiens capensis*
Spotted wintergreen	*Chimaphila maculata*
Spreading tick trefoil	*Desmodium humifusum*
Squirrel corn	*Dicentra canadensis*
St. Andrew's cross	*Hypericum hypericoides s. multicaule*
Stalked great chickweed	*Stellaria corei*
Stalked water horehound	*Lycopus rubellus*
Standing cypress	*IPOMOPSIS RUBRA*
Starved panic grass	*Dichanthelium depauperatum*
Stickseed	*Hackelia virginiana*
Stiff gentian	*Gentianella quinquefolia s. occidentalis*
Strawberry bush	*Euonymus americana*
Sugarberry	*Celtis laevigata*
Sugar maple	*Acer saccharum* (includes 2 subspecies)
Summer grape	*Vitis aestivalis* (including 1 variety)
Superb lily	*Lilium superbum*
Swamp agrimony	*Agrimonia parviflora*
Swamp cottonwood	*Populus heterophylla*
Swamp dock	*Rumex verticillatus*
Swamp holly	*Ilex decidua*
Swamp white oak	*Quercus bicolor*
Swampy dewberry	*Rubus sec. Hispidus: R. hispidus*
Sweetgum	*Liquidambar styraciflua*
Sweet Indian plantain	*Hasteola suaveolens* (= *Cacalia suaveolens*)
Sweet-scented bedstraw	*Galium triflorum*
Sycamore	*Platanus occidentalis*
Synandra	*Synandra hispidula*
Tall blue lettuce	*Lactuca biennis*
Tall melic grass	*Melica nitens*
Tall scouring rush	*Equisetum hyemale s. affine*
Tall thistle	*Cirsium altissimum*
Tartarian honeysuckle	*LONICERA TATARICA*
Terrestrial water starwort	*Callitriche terrestris*
Thicket bean	*Phaseolus polystachios*
Thicket parsley	*Perideridia americana*
Three-leaved stonecrop	*Sedum ternatum*
Toothwort	*Cardamine concatenata*
Trailing arbutus	*Epigaea repens*
Trailing bush clover	*Lespedeza procumbens*
Trailing ground pine	*Lycopodium digitatum*
Trumpet creeper	*Campsis radicans*
Tulip poplar	*Liriodendron tulipifera*
Twinleaf	*Jeffersonia diphylla*
Two-flower false dandelion	*Krigia biflora*
Two-leaved toothwort	*Cardamine diphylla*
Upland boneset	*Eupatorium sessilifolium*
Variegated milkweed	*Asclepias variegata*
Veiny pea	*Lathyrus venosus*
Violet bush clover	*Lespedeza violacea*
Violet wood sorrel	*Oxalis violacea*
Virginia bluebells	*Mertensia virginica*
Virginia creeper	*Parthenocissus quinquefolia*
Virginia dayflower	*Commelina virginica*
Virginia knotweed	*Tovara virginiana* (= *Polygonum virginianum*)
Virginia waterleaf	*Hydrophyllum virginianum*
Virginia wild rye	*Elymus virginicus* (including 1 variety)
Wahoo	*Euonymus atropurpurea*
Water locust	*Gleditsia aquatica*
Water parsnip	*Sium suave*
Water purslane	*Didiplis diandra*
Weak sedge	*Carex debilis v. debilis*
Weak-stemmed wood sedge	*Carex laxiculmis v. laxiculmis*
White adder's tongue	*Erythronium albidum*
White ash	*Fraxinus americana*
White basswood	*Tilia americana v. heterophylla*
White grass	*Leersia virginica*
White mulberry	*MORUS ALBA*
White oak	*Quercus alba*
White snakeroot	*Ageratina altissima* (= *Eupatorium rugosum*)
White vervain	*Verbena urticifolia v. urticifolia*
Whorled milkweed	*Asclepias quadrifolia*
Wild cucumber	*Echinocystis lobata*
Wild garlic	*Allium canadense*
Wild geranium	*Geranium maculatum*
Wild golden glow	*Rudbeckia laciniata*
Wild hydrangea	*Hydrangea arborescens*
Wild leek	*Allium tricoccum v. burdickii*
Wild leek	*Allium tricoccum v. tricoccum*
Wild lettuce	*Lactuca canadensis*
Wild madder	*Galium obtusum*
Wild petunia	*Ruellia caroliniensis*
Wild quinine	*Parthenium integrifolium*
Wild sensitive plant	*Chamaecrista nictitans*
Willdenow's grass sedge	*Carex willdenowii*
Winged elm	*Ulmus alata*
Winged euonymus	*EUONYMUS ALATA*
Winged monkey flower	*Mimulus alatus*
Wingstem	*Verbesina alternifolia*
Wintercreeper	*EUONYMUS FORTUNEI*
Witch hazel	*Hamamelis virginiana*
With rod	*Viburnum nudum v. cassinoides*
Wolf's bluegrass	*Poa wolfii*
Wolf's spike rush	*Eleocharis wolfii*
Wood anemone	*Anemone quinquefolia*
Wood angelica	*Angelica venenosa*
Wood betony	*Pedicularis canadensis*
Woodland agrimony	*Agrimonia rostellata*
Woodland brome	*Bromus pubescens*
Woodland sunflower	*Helianthus divaricatus*
Wood mint	*Blephilia hirsuta*
Wood's stiff sedge	*Carex woodii*
Woolly blue violet	*Viola sororia*
Yellow adder's tongue	*Erythronium americanum*
Yellow crownbeard	*Verbesina helianthoides*
Yellow meadow parsnip	*Thaspium trifoliatum v. aureum*
Yellow pimpernel	*Taenidia integerrima*
Yellow star grass	*Hypoxis hirsuta*
Yellowwood	*Cladrastis kentuckea*

Note: Scientific names in all capital letters are exotic species.

Table P-4. Vascular Plants in the Developmental Stages of Forests

Common Name	Scientific Name	Pre-Forest Land	Early Successional Land	Early Forest	Pole Forest
Alfalfa	*MEDICAGO SATIVA s. SATIVA*		X		
Alsike clover	*TRIFOLIUM HYBRIDUM*		X		
American bellflower	*Campanulastrum americanum* (= *Campanula americanum*)				X
American bindweed	*Calystegia sepium* (including subspecies)		X		
American elm	*Ulmus americana*			X	X
American hops	*Humulus lupulus v. pubescens*			X	
American pennyroyal	*Hedeoma pulegioides*				X
Annual bluegrass	*POA ANNUA*	X			
Annual fleabane	*Erigeron annuus*		X		
Annual foxtail	*Alopecurus carolinianus*	X	X		
Autumn olive	*ELAEAGNUS UMBELLATA*			X	X
Autumn sedge	*Fimbristylis autumnalis*		X		
Awned bent grass	*Agrostis elliottiana*		X		
Barnyard grass	*ECHINOCHLOA CRUS-GALLI*		X		
Beaked corn salad	*Valerianella radiata*		X		
Belvedere summer cypress	*KOCHIA SCOPARIA*	X	X		
Big shellbark hickory	*Carya laciniosa*				X
Bigtooth aspen	*Populus grandidentata*			X	X
Black-eyed Susan	*Rudbeckia hirta v. hirta*		X	X	
Black gum	*Nyssa sylvatica*				X
Black medick	*MEDICAGO LUPULINA*		X		
Black mustard	*BRASSICA NIGRA*	X			
Black oak	*Quercus velutina*				X
Black quillwort	*Isoetes melanopoda*		X	X	X
Black snakeroot	*Sanicula marilandica*				X
Black walnut	*Juglans nigra*				X
Blue cohosh	*Caulophyllum thalictroides*			X	X
Blue lettuce	*Lactuca floridana*				X
Blue toadflax	*Nuttallanthus canadensis* (= *Linaria canadensis*)	X	X		
Bluevine	*Cynanchum laeve*		X	X	X
Bouncing bet	*SAPONARIA OFFICINALIS*		X		
Boxelder	*Acer negundo* (including varieties)			X	X
Bristly cattail sedge	*Carex frankii*		X	X	X
Bristly foxtail grass	*SETARIA VERTICILLATA*	X	X		
Bronze fern	*Botrychium dissectum*		X	X	X
Broom panic grass	*Dichanthelium scoparium*		X	X	
Broom sedge	*Andropogon virginicus*		X		
Buffalo bur	*SOLANUM ROSTRATUM*		X		
Bulbous bluegrass	*POA BULBOSA* (including 1 subspecies)	X	X		
Bulbous buttercup	*RANUNCULUS BULBOSUS*		X		
Bull thistle	*CIRSIUM VULGARE*		X		
Bur buttercup	*RANUNCULUS TESTICULATUS* (= *CERATOCEPHALUS TESTICULATUS*)	X			
Bur oak	*Quercus macrocarpa*				X
Bushy aster	*Symphyotrichum dumosum* (including 1 variety)		X		
Butterflyweed	*Asclepias tuberosa* (including 1 variety)		X		
Buttonweed	*Diodia teres*		X		
Canadian black snakeroot	*Sanicula canadensis* (including 1 variety)				X
Canadian bluegrass	*POA COMPRESSA*		X		
Cardinal flower	*Lobelia cardinalis*			X	X
Catnip	*NEPETA CATARIA*		X		
Cat's foot	*Antennaria neglecta*		X		
Celandine	*CHELIDONIUM MAJUS*				X
Cheat grass	*BROMUS TECTORUM*	X	X		
Cherrybark oak	*Quercus pagoda*				X
Chicory	*CICHORIUM INTYBUS*	X	X		
Chinese silver grass	*MISCANTHUS SINENSIS*		X		
Chinquapin oak	*Quercus muhlenbergii*				X
Cigar tree	*Catalpa speciosa*			X	X
Climbing fern	*Lygodium palmatum*				X
Clustered false foxglove	*Agalinis fasciculata*		X		
Clustered wild bean	*Strophostyles umbellata*		X		
Common blackberry	*Rubus sec. Allegheniensis: R. allegheniensis*		X	X	X
Common buckthorn	*RHAMNUS CATHARTICA*				X

Table P-4. *continued*

Common Name	Scientific Name	Pre-Forest Land	Early Successional Land	Early Forest	Pole Forest
Common chickweed	*STELLARIA MEDIA s. MEDIA*	X	X	X	X
Common cinquefoil	*Potentilla simplex*		X	X	X
Common dandelion	*TARAXACUM OFFICINALE*	X	X		
Common dayflower	*COMMELINA COMMUNIS*				X
Common dewberry	*Rubus sec. Flagellares: R. flagellaris*		X		
Common evening primrose	*Oenothera biennis*	X	X		
Common goat's beard	*TRAGOPOGON PRATENSIS*	X	X		
Common groundsel	*SENECIO VULGARIS*		X		
Common milfoil	*Achillea millefolium*		X		
Common milkweed	*Asclepias syriaca*		X		
Common morning glory	*IPOMOEA PURPUREA*		X		
Common mouse-ear chickweed	*CERASTIUM FONTANUM s. VULGARE*		X		
Common pepper cress	*Lepidium virginicum*	X	X		
Common purpletop	*Tridens flavus*		X	X	
Common ragweed	*Ambrosia artemisiifolia v. elatior*	X			
Common sneezeweed	*Helenium autumnale*		X		
Common sow thistle	*SONCHUS OLERACEUS*	X	X		
Common St. John's wort	*HYPERICUM PERFORATUM*		X		
Common streambank chervil	*Chaerophyllum procumbens v. procumbens*				X
Common sunflower	*HELIANTHUS ANNUUS*		X		
Common wood sedge	*Carex blanda*			X	X
Common woodsia	*Woodsia obtusa s. obtusa*		X	X	X
Corn cockle	*AGROSTEMA GITHAGO*	X	X		
Corn speedwell	*VERONICA ARVENSIS*	X			
Crested oval sedge	*Carex cristatella*		X	X	
Cupseed	*Calycocarpum lyonii*				X
Curly dock	*RUMEX CRISPUS*		X		
Daisy fleabane	*Erigeron strigosus*		X		
Deptford pink	*DIANTHUS ARMERIA*		X	X	
Dogbane	*Apocynum cannabinum*		X	X	
Dog mint	*Clinopodium vulgare*		X		
Downy lobelia	*Lobelia puberula v. simulans*		X		
Dwarf plantain	*Plantago virginica*		X		
Early goldenrod	*Solidago juncea*		X	X	
Eastern cottonwood	*Populus deltoides*		X	X	X
Eastern redbud	*Cercis canadensis*			X	X
Elephant's foot	*Elephantopus carolinianus*			X	X
Elliott's broom sedge	*Andropogon gyrans*		X		
English plantain	*PLANTAGO LANCEOLATA*	X	X		
Fall coralroot	*Corallorhiza odontorhiza* (including 1 variety)				X
Fall panicum	*Panicum dichotomiflorum* (including 1 subspecies)	X	X		
Fall witch grass	*Digitaria cognata* (= *Leptoloma cognatum*)		X		
False dandelion	*Pyrrhopappus carolinianus*		X		
False sunflower	*Heliopsis helianthoides* (including 1 variety)		X		
Fat-hen saltbush	*ATRIPLEX PATULA*		X		
Few-flowered nut rush	*Scleria pauciflora v. caroliniana*		X		
Field bindweed	*CONVOLVULUS ARVENSIS*	X	X		
Field cress	*LEPIDIUM CAMPESTRE*	X	X		
Field garlic	*ALLIUM VINEALE*	X	X		
Field hedge parsley	*TORILIS ARVENSIS s. ARVENSIS*	X	X		
Field milkwort	*Polygala sanguinea*		X		
Field nut sedge	*Cyperus esculentus v. leptostachyus*		X		
Field penny cress	*THLASPI ARVENSE*	X	X		
Field sorrel	*RUMEX ACETOSELLA*	X	X	X	X
Field thistle	*CIRSIUM ARVENSE*		X		
Fireweed	*Erechtites hieracifolia*	X	X	X	
Flat-top aster	*Doellingeria umbellata* (= *Aster umbellatus*)				X
Flowering dogwood	*Cornus florida*				X
Flower-of-an-hour	*HIBISCUS TRIONUM*	X			
Foothill bedstraw	*CRUCIATA PEDEMONTANUM* (= *GALIUM PEDEMONTANUM*)	X	X		
Forked panic grass	*Dichanthelium dichotomum s. dichotomum*				X
Foxglove beard tongue	*Penstemon digitalis*		X	X	X
Garlic mustard	*ALLIARIA PETIOLATA*		X	X	X
Giant foxtail grass	*SETARIA FABERI*	X	X		

Common Name	Scientific Name	Pre-Forest Land	Early Successional Land	Early Forest	Pole Forest
Glaucous tick trefoil	*Desmodium laevigatum*				X
Golden cassia	*Chamaecrista fasciculata* (= *Cassia fasciculata*)		X	X	X
Golden ragwort	*Packera aurea*				X
Gray dogwood	*Cornus racemosa*			X	X
Great white lettuce	*Prenanthes crepidinea*				X
Green ash	*Fraxinus pennsylvanica v. lanceolata*			X	X
Green-flowered tick trefoil	*Desmodium viridiflorum*		X		
Green-fringed orchid	*Platanthera lacera*		X	X	X
Green twayblade	*Liparis loeselii*		X	X	X
Ground cedar	*Lycopodium tristachyum*				X
Ground pine	*Lycopodium obscurum*				X
Hackberry	*Celtis occidentalis*			X	X
Hair grass	*Agrostis hyemalis*		X	X	X
Hairy aster	*Symphyotrichum pilosum v. pilosum*		X		
Hairy buttercup	*RANUNCULUS SARDOUS*		X		
Hairy crabgrass	*DIGITARIA SANGUINALIS*	X	X		
Hairy false golden aster	*HETEROTHECA CAMPORUM v. GLANDULISSIMA*		X		
Hairy green sedge	*Carex hirsutella*		X	X	
Hairy tick trefoil	*Desmodium ciliare*		X		
Hedge mustard	*SISYMBRIUM OFFICINALE*	X			
Henbit	*LAMIUM AMPLEXICAULE*	X	X		
Hoary alyssum	*BERTEROA INCANA*		X		
Hoary beard tongue	*Penstemon canescens*				X
Honey locust	*Gleditsia triacanthos*				X
Hop hornbeam	*Ostrya virginiana*				X
Horse nettle	*Solanum carolinense*		X		
Horseweed	*Conyza canadensis*	X	X		
Hungarian brome	*BROMUS INERMIS*		X		
Hyssop-leaved boneset	*Eupatorium hyssopifolium*		X		
Indian tobacco	*Lobelia inflata*			X	X
Ivy-leaved morning glory	*IPOMOEA HEDERACEA*	X	X		
Jack oak	*Quercus imbricaria*				X
Jagged chickweed	*HOLOSTEUM UMBELLATUM*	X	X		
Japanese chess	*BROMUS JAPONICUS*	X	X		
Japanese honeysuckle	*LONICERA JAPONICA*		X	X	X
Japanese hops	*HUMULUS JAPONICUS*		X		
Japanese lespedeza	*KUMMEROWIA STRIATA*	X	X		
Jerusalem artichoke	*Helianthus tuberosus*			X	
Johnson grass	*SORGHUM HALEPENSE*	X	X		
Kentucky bluegrass	*POA PRATENSIS*	X	X	X	X
Kentucky coffee tree	*Gymnocladus dioica*				X
Knawel	*SCLERANTHUS ANNUUS*	X	X		
Korean clover	*KUMMEROWIA STIPULACEA* (= *LESPEDEZA STIPULACEA*)	X	X		
Lance-leaved buckthorn	*Rhamnus lanceolata* (including 1 subspecies)		X	X	
Large passion flower	*Passiflora incarnata*		X		
Late boneset	*Eupatorium serotinum*		X		
Little barley	*Hordeum pusillum*	X	X		
Little bluestem grass	*Schizachyrium scoparium* (= *Andropogon scoparius*)		X		
Little-leaf buttercup	*Ranunculus abortivus*	X	X	X	X
Long-leaved ammannia	*Ammannia coccinea*	X	X		
Long-scaled nut sedge	*Cyperus strigosus*	X	X		
Lopseed	*Phryma leptostachya*				X
Low hop clover	*TRIFOLIUM CAMPESTRE*	X	X		
Marsh fleabane	*Erigeron philadelphicus*		X	X	X
Mat sandbur	*Cenchrus longispinus*	X	X		
Meadow fescue	*SCHEDONORUS PRATENSIS*		X		
Miami mist	*Phacelia purshii*				X
Michigan lily	*Lilium michiganense*				X
Mistflower	*Conoclinium coelestinum* (= *Eupatorium coelestinum*)		X		
Moneywort	*LYSIMACHIA NUMMULARIA*	X	X	X	X
Moonseed	*Menispermum canadense*				X
Moth mullein	*VERBASCUM BLATTARIA*	X	X		
Narrow-leaved pinweed	*Lechea tenuifolia*				X
Narrow-leaved sunflower	*Helianthus angustifolius*		X		

Table P-4. *continued*

Common Name	Scientific Name	Pre-Forest Land	Early Successional Land	Early Forest	Pole Forest
Nepalese browntop	*MICROSTEGIUM VIMINEUM*		X	X	X
Night-flowering catchfly	*SILENE NOCTIFLORA*	X	X		
Nimblewill	*Muhlenbergia schreberi*		X		
Nits-and-lice	*Hypericum drummondii*		X		
Nodding brome	*BROMUS SQUARROSUS*	X	X		
Nodding fescue	*Festuca subverticillata*				X
Northern red oak	*Quercus rubra*				X
Northern rush grass	*Sporobolus vaginiflorus*		X		
Old-field goldenrod	*Solidago nemoralis* (including 1 subspecies)		X	X	
Old witch grass	*Panicum capillare*		X		
Oneida grape fern	*Botrychium oneidense*				X
Orchard grass	*DACTYLIS GLOMERATA*		X		
Ox-eye daisy (= *CHRYSANTHEMUM LEUCANTHEMUM*)	*LEUCANTHEMUM VULGARE*	X			
Pale avens	*Geum virginianum*			X	X
Pale corydalis	*Corydalis flavula*				X
Panicled tick trefoil	*Desmodium paniculatum*		X	X	X
Paper birch	*Betula papyrifera*			X	X
Pasture rose	*Rosa carolina*		X		
Pearly everlasting	*Anaphalis margaritacea*		X		
Perennial rye grass	*LOLIUM PERENNE*	X	X		
Persimmon	*Diospyros virginiana*			X	X
Pignut hickory	*Carya glabra*				X
Pink thoroughwort	*Fleischmannia incarnata* (= *Eupatorium incarnatum*)		X		
Pinkweed	*Persicaria pensylvanica*		X		
Pin oak	*Quercus palustris*				X
Plains three awn grass	*Aristida oligantha*		X		
Poison hemlock	*CONIUM MACULATUM*	X	X		
Poison ivy	*Toxicodendron radicans s. radicans*				X
Pokeweed	*Phytolacca americana v. americana*	X	X	X	X
Poor Joe	*Plantago aristata*	X	X		
Post oak	*Quercus stellata*				X
Poverty grass	*Aristida dichotoma*		X	X	
Poverty oat grass	*Danthonia spicata*		X		
Prairie tea	*CROTON MONANTHOGYNUS*		X		
Prickly lettuce	*LACTUCA SERRIOLA*	X	X		
Prickly sida	*SIDA SPINOSA*	X	X		
Prickly sow thistle	*SONCHUS ASPER*	X	X		
Princess tree	*PAULOWNIA TOMENTOSA*				X
Puncture vine	*TRIBULUS TERRESTRIS*	X	X		
Purple dead nettle	*LAMIUM PURPUREUM*	X	X		
Purple fringeless orchid	*Platanthera peramoena*		X	X	X
Purple-headed sneezeweed	*Helenium flexuosum*		X		
Purple love grass	*Eragrostis spectabilis*		X		
Purple twayblade	*Liparis liliifolia*				X
Purslane	*PORTULACA OLERACEA*	X	X		
Quackgrass	*ELYMUS REPENS* (= *AGROPYRON REPENS*)		X		
Quaking aspen	*Populus tremuloides*				X
Queen Anne's lace	*DAUCUS CAROTA*		X		
Ragged evening primrose	*Oenothera laciniata*		X		
Red ash	*Fraxinus pennsylvanica v. pennsylvanica*			X	X
Red clover	*TRIFOLIUM PRATENSE*		X		
Red maple	*Acer rubrum v. rubrum*				X
Red raspberry	*Rubus idaeus v. strigosus*		X	X	
Red-stalked plantain	*Plantago rugelii* (including 1 variety)	X	X		
River birch	*Betula nigra*			X	X
Rose gentian	*Sabatia angularis*		X	X	
Rough cinquefoil	*Potentilla norvegica* (including 1 subspecies)		X		
Rough marbleseed	*Onosmodium molle s. hispidissimum*		X		
Round-leaved thoroughwort	*Eupatorium rotundifolium*		X		
Round-stemmed false foxglove	*Agalinis gattingeri*		X		
Running ground pine	*Lycopodium clavatum*				X
Rushfoil	*Croton willdenowii*		X		
Sand goat's beard	*TRAGOPOGON DUBIUS*	X	X		

Common Name	Scientific Name	Pre-Forest Land	Early Successional Land	Early Forest	Pole Forest
Sassafras	*Sassafras albidum*			X	X
Sawtooth sunflower	*Helianthus grosseserratus*		X		
Scorpion grass	*Myosotis macrosperma*		X		
Scrub pine	*Pinus virginiana*				X
Sensitive fern	*Onoclea sensibilis*			X	X
Shagbark hickory	*Carya ovata*				X
Shepherd's purse	*CAPSELLA BURSA-PASTORIS*	X	X		
Silky bush clover	*Lespedeza virginica*		X		
Silver bluestem	*Andropogon ternarius*		X		
Silver maple	*Acer saccharinum*			X	X
Silvery cinquefoil	*POTENTILLA ARGENTEA*	X	X		
Sleepy catchfly	*Silene antirrhina*	X	X		
Slender bush clover	*Lespedeza virginica*		X	X	
Slender false foxglove	*Agalinis tenuifolia* (includes 2 varieties)		X		
Slender mountain mint	*Pycnanthemum tenuifolium*		X	X	
Slender three-seeded mercury	*Acalypha gracilens*		X	X	
Slender yellow flax	*Linum virginianum*		X		
Slippery elm	*Ulmus rubra*			X	X
Small-flowered crowfoot	*Ranunculus micranthus*				X
Small-fruited panic grass	*Dichanthelium polyanthes*			X	X
Small green foxtail grass	*SETARIA VIRIDIS v. VIRIDIS*	X	X		
Small-leaved tick trefoil	*Desmodium marilandicum*		X		
Small love grass	*Eragrostis pectinacea*	X	X		
Small yellow flax	*Linum medium v. texanum*		X		
Smooth beard tongue	*Penstemon calycosus*		X	X	X
Smooth field sow thistle	*SONCHUS ARVENSIS s. ULIGINOSUS*	X	X		
Smooth purslane speedwell	*Veronica peregrina s. peregrina*	X	X		
Southern adder's tongue fern	*Ophioglossum vulgatum*				X
Southern red oak	*Quercus falcata*				X
Sparse-lobed grape fern	*Botrychium biternatum*		X		
Spear grass	*Poa chapmaniana*	X	X		
Spearwort	*Ranunculus laxicaulis*				X
Spiny cocklebur	*XANTHIUM SPINOSUM*	X	X		
Spotted St. John's wort	*Hypericum punctatum*		X		
Spring beauty	*Claytonia virginica*				X
Squirrel-tail grass	*HORDEUM JUBATUM*	X	X		
St. Andrew's cross	*Hypericum hypericoides s. multicaule*		X		
Stickseed	*Hackelia virginiana*				X
Stink grass	*ERAGROSTIS CILIANENSIS*	X	X		
Sugar maple	*Acer saccharum* (includes 2 subspecies)				X
Sulfur cinquefoil	*POTENTILLA RECTA*	X	X		
Summer grape	*Vitis aestivalis* (including 1 variety)				X
Swamp marigold	*Bidens aristosa*		X		
Swampy dewberry	*Rubus sec. Hispidus: R. hispidus*				X
Sweetgum	*Liquidambar styraciflua*			X	X
Sycamore	*Platanus occidentalis*			X	X
Tall boneset	*Eupatorium altissimum*		X		
Tall buttercup	*RANUNCULUS ACRIS*		X		
Tall fescue	*SCHEDONORUS ARUNDINACEUS* (= *FESTUCA ELATIOR*)	X	X		
Tall goldenrod	*Solidago altissima* (including 1 subspecies)	X	X	X	
Three-awn grass	*Aristida longespica v. longespica*		X		
Thyme-leaved speedwell	*VERONICA SERPYLLIFOLIA*	X	X		
Timothy grass	*PHLEUM PRATENSE*		X		
Toothed spurge	*Euphorbia dentata* (= *Poinsettia dentata*)		X		
Torrey's mountain mint	*Pycnanthemum torrei*		X	X	
Trailing ground pine	*Lycopodium digitatum*		X	X	X
Tree hawthorn	*Crataegus series Crus-galli: C. arborea*			X	
Trumpet creeper	*Campsis radicans*		X	X	X
Tulip poplar	*Liriodendron tulipifera*			X	X
Two-colored bush clover	*LESPEDEZA BICOLOR*		X	X	
Venus's looking glass	*Triodanis perfoliata*	X	X		
Virginia creeper	*Parthenocissus quinquefolia*				X
Virginia dwarf dandelion	*Krigia virginica*	X	X		
Virginia knotweed	*Tovara virginiana* (= *Polygonum virginianum*)				X

Table P-4. *continued*

Common Name	Scientific Name	Pre-Forest Land	Early Successional Land	Early Forest	Pole Forest
Virginia wild rye	*Elymus virginicus* (including 1 variety)				X
Viscid field sow thistle	*SONCHUS ARVENSIS s. ARVENSIS*	X			
Wahoo	*Euonymus atropurpurea*				X
White ash	*Fraxinus americana*			X	X
White clover	*TRIFOLIUM REPENS*	X	X		
White grass	*Leersia virginica*				X
White mulberry	*MORUS ALBA*			X	X
White oak	*Quercus alba*				X
White sweet clover	*MELILOTUS ALBA*		X		
White thoroughwort	*Eupatorium album*		X		
Wild bergamot	*Monarda fistulosa* (including 1 variety)		X		
Wild garlic	*Allium canadense*	X	X	X	
Wild lettuce	*Lactuca canadensis*		X	X	X
Wild parsnip	*PASTINACA SATIVA*		X		
Wild sensitive plant	*Chamaecrista nictitans*		X		
Wild strawberry	*Fragaria virginiana* (including 1 subspecies)		X	X	
Wild sweet potato	*Ipomoea pandurata*		X		
Windmill grass	*CHLORIS VERTICILLATA*		X		
Wingstem	*Verbesina alternifolia*				X
Winter vetch	*VICIA VILLOSA s. VILLOSA*	X			
Wood betony	*Pedicularis canadensis*				X
Woolly blue violet	*Viola sororia*	X	X	X	X
Woolly mullein	*VERBASCUM THAPSUS*	X	X		
Yellow ladies' tresses	*Spiranthes ochroleuca*		X		
Yellow sweet clover	*MELILOTUS OFFICINALIS*		X		

Note: Scientific names in all capital letters are exotic species.

Table P-5. Plant Species of Mature or High-Canopy Forest

		Deciduous							Conifer	
Common Name	**Scientific Name**	**Oak/Pine**	**Oak/Hickory**	**Oak/Gum/Cypress**	**Elm/Ash/Cottonwood**	**Maple/Beech**	**Cherry/Ash/Poplar**	**Aspen/Birch**	**Shortleaf/Virginia Pine**	**Eastern Red Cedar**
Adam-and-Eve	*Aplectrum hyemale*		X			X	X			
Allegheny barberry	*Berberis canadensis*		X							
Allegheny spurge	*Pachysandra procumbens*					X	X			
American beak grass	*Diarrhena americana*		X			X	X			
American beech	*Fagus grandifolia*					X				
American bellflower	*Campanulastrum americanum* (= *Campanula americanum*)	X	X	X	X	X				
American chestnut	*Castanea dentata*	X	X						X	
American columbo	*Frasera caroliniensis*		X							
American elm	*Ulmus americana*				X	X	X			
American filbert	*Corylus americana*		X							
American fly honeysuckle	*Lonicera canadensis*		X		X	X				
American gromwell	*Lithospermum latifolium*		X			X	X			
American hops	*Humulus lupulus v. pubescens*		X		X					
American linden	*Tilia americana v. americana*		X			X	X			
American pennyroyal	*Hedeoma pulegioides*	X	X						X	X
American storax	*Styrax americana*		X	X						
Amur honeysuckle	*LONICERA MAACKII*		X			X	X	X		X
Anise root	*Osmorhiza longistylis*		X			X	X			
Aromatic sumac	*Rhus aromatica v. aromatica*		X							X
Autumn bent grass	*Agrostis perennans*	X	X			X		X		
Autumn bluegrass	*Poa autumnalis*		X		X	X				
Autumn olive	*ELAEAGNUS UMBELLATA*		X			X		X		
Bald cypress	*Taxodium distichum*			X						
Bare-stemmed tick trefoil	*Desmodium nudiflorum*	X	X				X		X	
Barren strawberry	*Waldsteinia fragarioides*		X			X				
Basil bee balm	*Monarda clinopodia*		X			X	X			
Basket oak	*Quercus michauxii*		X	X						
Bastard toadflax	*Comandra umbellata*	X	X							
Beach sumac	*Rhus aromatica v. arenaria*	X	X							
Beaked black snakeroot	*Sanicula trifoliata*					X	X			
Bearberry	*Arctostaphylos uva-ursi*	X								
Bearded panic grass	*Dichanthelium boscii*	X	X			X	X		X	
Bear's foot	*Smallanthus uvedalia* (= *Polymnia uvedalia*)		X			X	X			
Beech wood sedge	*Carex laxiflora*		X			X	X			
Beefsteak plant	*PERILLA FRUTESCENS* (including 1 variety)		X		X	X				
Bicknell's panic grass	*Dichanthelium bicknellii* (*nomen nudum*)	X	X							
Big-leaved aster	*Eurybia macrophylla*	X	X			X	X			
Big shellbark hickory	*Carya laciniosa*		X	X						
Bigtooth aspen	*Populus grandidentata*		X			X	X	X		
Bird's foot violet	*Viola pedata*	X	X							
Bishop's cap	*Mitella diphylla*		X			X	X			
Bitternut hickory	*Carya cordiformis*		X			X	X			
Black ash	*Fraxinus nigra*				X					
Black chokeberry	*Photinia melanocarpa*		X							
Black cohosh	*Cimicifuga rubifolia*					X	X			
Black gum	*Nyssa sylvatica*	X	X	X					X	
Black hickory	*Carya texana*		X							
Black huckleberry	*Gaylussacia baccata*	X	X						X	
Blackjack oak	*Quercus marilandica*	X	X						X	
Black maple	*Acer saccharum s. nigrum*					X	X			
Black oak	*Quercus velutina*	X	X						X	
Black oat grass	*Piptochaetium avenaceum* (= *Stipa avenacea*)		X							
Black quillwort	*Isoetes melanopoda*		X	X						
Black-seeded rice grass	*Piptatherum racemosa*					X	X			
Black snakeroot	*Sanicula marilandica*		X		X					
Black walnut	*Juglans nigra*		X		X	X	X			
Bladdernut	*Staphylea trifolia*		X			X	X			
Blighted goldenrod	*Solidago sphacelata*	X	X							X
Bloodleaf	*Iresine rhizomatosa*			X	X					
Bloodroot	*Sanguinaria canadensis*		X			X	X			
Blue ash	*Fraxinus quadrangulata*		X			X				X
Blue beech	*Carpinus caroliniana s. virginiana*		X		X	X				

Table P-5. *continued*

Common Name	Scientific Name	Deciduous							Conifer	
		Oak/Pine	Oak/Hickory	Oak/Gum/Cypress	Elm/Ash/Cottonwood	Maple/Beech	Cherry/Ash/Poplar	Aspen/Birch	Shortleaf/Virginia Pine	Eastern Red Cedar
Blue cohosh	*Caulophyllum thalictroides*					X	X			
Blue-eyed Mary	*Collinsia verna*				X	X	X			
Blue lettuce	*Lactuca floridana*		X		X	X	X			
Blue phlox	*Phlox divaricata* (including 1 subspecies)		X			X	X			
Blue sedge	*Carex glaucodea*	X	X							
Blue star	*Amsonia tabernaemontana v. salicifolia*			X	X					
Bluestem goldenrod	*Solidago caesia*		X			X	X			
Bluets	*Houstonia caerulea* (= *Hedyotis caerulea*)	X	X			X	X		X	
Blunt-scaled oak sedge	*Carex albicans v. albicans*	X	X							
Blunt-scaled wood sedge	*Carex albursina*		X			X	X			
Bottlebrush grass	*Elymus hystrix* (including 1 variety)		X			X	X			
Bottlebrush sedge	*Carex lurida*		X	X	X					
Boxelder	*Acer negundo* (including varieties)		X	X	X	X	X	X		
Bracted green orchid	*Coeloglossum viride* (= *Habenaria viridis*)					X	X			
Bristly cattail sedge	*Carex frankii*			X	X			X		
Bristly sunflower	*Helianthus hirsutus*	X	X			X	X			
Broad beech fern	*Phegopteris hexagonoptera*		X			X	X			
Broad-leaved goldenrod	*Solidago flexicaulis*		X			X	X			
Broad-leaved oval sedge	*Carex tribuloides v. tribuloides*		X	X	X					
Broad-leaved spiderwort	*Tradescantia subaspera*		X	X		X	X			
Broad-leaved wood sedge	*Carex platyphylla*	X	X			X			X	
Bronze fern	*Botrychium dissectum*		X	X	X	X	X	X		
Brown-eyed Susan	*Rudbeckia triloba*				X		X			
Buffalo clover	*Trifolium reflexum*	X	X							
Bulb bitter cress	*Cardamine bulbosa*			X	X			X		
Bulbous wood rush	*Luzula bulbosa*		X							
Bull brier	*Smilax bona-nox*		X							
Bur oak	*Quercus macrocarpa*		X	X	X					
Buttercup phacelia	*Phacelia ranunculacea*		X	X	X					
Butterfly pea	*Clitoria mariana*		X							
Butternut	*Juglans cinerea*		X			X	X			
Buttonbush	*Cephalanthus occidentalis*			X						
Camphor weed	*Pluchea camphorata*		X	X	X					
Canada blueberry	*Vaccinium myrtilloides*	X	X							
Canada clearweed	*Pilea pumila*		X	X	X	X	X	X		
Canada lily	*Lilium canadense*		X			X				
Canada mayflower	*Maianthemum canadense*		X			X		X		
Canada violet	*Viola canadensis*		X			X	X			
Canada waterleaf	*Hydrophyllum canadense*					X	X			
Canada wild ginger	*Asarum canadense*		X			X	X			
Canada wood nettle	*Laportea canadensis*		X	X	X	X	X			
Canada yew	*Taxus canadensis*	X				X				
Canadian black snakeroot	*Sanicula canadensis* (including 1 variety)		X	X	X	X	X	X		
Canadian bluegrass	*POA COMPRESSA*	X	X						X	
Cardinal flower	*Lobelia cardinalis*			X	X					
Carey's wood sedge	*Carex careyana*					X	X			
Carolina anemone	*Anemone caroliniana*		X							
Carolina buckthorn	*Frangula caroliniana* (= *Rhamnus caroliniana*)		X							X
Carolina mosquito fern	*Azolla caroliniana*			X						
Carolina panic grass	*Dichanthelium dichotomum s. yadkinense*		X							
Carolina thistle	*Cirsium carolinianum*	X	X						X	
Catbird grape	*Vitis palmata*			X						
Cat brier	*Smilax rotundifolia*	X	X						X	X
Cat's foot	*Antennaria neglecta*		X							
Celandine	*CHELIDONIUM MAJUS*				X	X	X			
Celandine poppy	*Stylophorum diphyllum*		X			X	X			
Checkerberry	*Gaultheria procumbens*	X	X					X		
Cherrybark oak	*Quercus pagoda*		X	X	X					
Chinquapin oak	*Quercus muhlenbergii*	X	X			X	X			X
Cigar tree	*Catalpa speciosa*			X	X					
Cinnamon fern	*Osmunda cinnamomea*		X					X		
Cleft phlox	*Phlox bifida s. bifida*	X	X						X	
Cleft violet	*Viola palmata* (including 1 variety)	X	X			X	X		X	

Common Name	Scientific Name	Deciduous							Conifer	
		Oak/Pine	Oak/Hickory	Oak/Gum/Cypress	Elm/Ash/Cottonwood	Maple/Beech	Cherry/Ash/Poplar	Aspen/Birch	Shortleaf/Virginia Pine	Eastern Red Cedar
Climbing bittersweet	*Celastrus scandens*	X	X						X	X
Climbing dayflower	*COMMELINA DIFFUSA*			X	X					
Climbing dogbane	*Trachelospermum difforme*			X	X					
Climbing hempweed	*Mikania scandens*			X	X					
Climbing milkweed	*Matelea obliqua*		X							X
Common beech sedge	*Carex communis*		X			X	X			
Common buckthorn	*RHAMNUS CATHARTICA*	X	X					X		
Common bur sedge	*Carex grayi*		X	X	X					
Common cattail sedge	*Carex typhina*		X	X	X					
Common chickweed	*STELLARIA MEDIA s. MEDIA*		X	X	X	X	X	X		
Common cinquefoil	*Potentilla simplex*	X	X						X	X
Common dayflower	*COMMELINA COMMUNIS*		X		X	X	X			
Common elderberry	*Sambucus nigra s. canadensis*		X	X	X	X	X	X		
Common fragile fern	*Cystopteris protrusa*		X			X	X			
Common hop sedge	*Carex lupulina*		X	X	X					
Common privet	*LIGUSTRUM VULGARE*		X			X	X			
Common star of Bethlehem	*ORNITHOGALUM UMBELLATUM*				X	X	X			
Common streambank chervil	*Chaerophyllum procumbens v. procumbens*		X	X	X	X	X			
Common water hemlock	*Cicuta maculata* (including 1 variety)		X	X	X					
Common white violet	*Viola striata*		X	X	X	X	X			
Common wild comfrey	*Cynoglossum virginianum v. virginianum*	X	X			X	X		X	
Common wild yam	*Dioscorea villosa*	X	X						X	X
Common wood reed	*Cinna arundinacea*		X	X	X					
Common wood rush	*Luzula echinata*		X			X	X			
Common wood sedge	*Carex blanda*		X	X	X	X	X	X		
Common woodsia	*Woodsia obtusa s. obtusa*	X	X						X	X
Concealed sedge	*Carex cumberlandensis*					X	X			
Coralberry	*Symphoricarpos orbiculatus*	X	X						X	X
Cowbane	*Oxypolis rigidior*			X	X					
Crane-fly orchid	*Tipularia discolor*		X			X	X			
Creeping bracted sedge	*Carex socialis*		X	X	X					
Creeping bush clover	*Lespedeza repens*	X	X						X	
Crested coralroot	*Hexalectris spicata*		X							X
Cross vine	*Bignonia capreolata*		X	X						
Crow poison	*Nothoscordum bivalve*		X							X
Cucumber magnolia	*Magnolia acuminata*					X	X			
Cup plant	*Silphium perfoliatum*				X					
Cupseed	*Calycocarpum lyonii*			X						
Cusped bluegrass	*Poa cuspidata*	X	X							
Deam's beard tongue	*Penstemon deamii*	X	X						X	
Deam's rockcress	*Arabis missouriensis*		X							
Declined trillium	*Trillium flexipes*		X			X	X			
Deerberry	*Vaccinium stamineum*	X	X						X	
Devil's walking stick	*Aralia spinosa*	X	X			X			X	
Dittany	*Cunila origanoides*	X	X						X	
Dogbane	*Apocynum cannabinum*	X	X						X	X
Dog mint	*Clinopodium vulgare*		X							X
Doll's-eyes	*Actaea pachypoda*		X			X	X			
Downy arrowwood	*Viburnum molle*		X			X	X			
Downy false foxglove	*Aureolaria virginica*	X	X						X	
Downy green sedge	*Carex swanii*	X	X			X			X	
Downy skullcap	*Scutellaria incana*	X	X			X	X		X	X
Downy Solomon's seal	*Polygonatum pubescens*					X	X			
Downy yellow violet	*Viola pubescens* (including varieties)		X	X	X	X	X			
Dutchman's breeches	*Dicentra cucullaria*		X			X	X			
Dutchman's pipe	*Aristolochia tomentosa*			X	X					
Dwarf chinquapin oak	*Quercus prinoides*		X							
Dwarf crested iris	*Iris cristata*		X			X				
Dwarf ginseng	*Panax trifolius*		X			X		X		
Dwarf larkspur	*Delphinium tricorne*		X			X	X			
Early figwort	*Scrophularia lanceolata*		X							
Early horse gentian	*Triosteum aurantiacum* (including varieties)		X							
Early-leaved brome	*Bromus latiglumis*		X		X	X				

Table P-5. *continued*

		Deciduous							Conifer	
Common Name	**Scientific Name**	**Oak/Pine**	**Oak/Hickory**	**Oak/Gum/Cypress**	**Elm/Ash/Cottonwood**	**Maple/Beech**	**Cherry/Ash/Poplar**	**Aspen/Birch**	**Shortleaf/Virginia Pine**	**Eastern Red Cedar**
Early low blueberry	*Vaccinium angustifolium*		X							
Early oak sedge	*Carex umbellata*	X	X						X	
Early saxifrage	*Saxifraga virginiensis*		X			X	X			
Eastern cottonwood	*Populus deltoides*				X					
Eastern redbud	*Cercis canadensis*		X			X	X			X
Eastern red cedar	*Juniperus virginiana*		X							X
Elephant's foot	*Elephantopus carolinianus*		X			X				
Elm-leaved goldenrod	*Solidago ulmifolia*	X	X						X	
Enchanter's nightshade	*Circaea lutetiana s. canadensis*		X		X	X	X	X		
European corn salad	*VALERIANELLA LOCUSTA*				X					
Fairy wand	*Chamaelirium luteum*		X			X				
Fall coralroot	*Corallorhiza odontorhiza* (including 1 variety)		X	X		X	X	X		
False bugbane	*Cimicifuga racemosa*					X	X			
False grass sedge	*Carex timida*		X			X				
False hellebore	*Melanthium woodii* (= *Veratrum woodii*)		X			X	X			
False melic grass	*Schizachne purpurascens*		X							
False mermaid weed	*Floerkea proserpinacoides*		X		X	X	X			
False mermaidweed	*Proserpinaca palustris* (including 1 variety)			X	X					
False rue anemone	*Enemion biternatum* (= *Isopyrum biternatum*)				X	X	X			
Farkleberry	*Vaccinium arboreum*		X							
Featherbells	*Stenanthium gramineum*		X							
Featherfoil	*Hottonia inflata*			X						
Feathery false Solomon's seal	*Maianthemum racemosum* (= *Smilacina racemosa*)		X			X	X			
Field sorrel	*RUMEX ACETOSELLA*	X	X						X	
Fire pink	*Silene virginica*		X			X	X			
Fireweed	*Erechtites hieracifolia*		X			X	X			
Five leaves	*Isotria verticillata*		X							
Flat-spiked gray sedge	*Carex planispicata*		X							X
Flat-top aster	*Doellingeria umbellata* (= *Aster umbellatus*)	X	X		X			X		
Flowering dogwood	*Cornus florida*	X	X						X	
Follicle sedge	*Carex folliculata*							X		
Forked aster	*Eurybia furcata* (= *Aster furcatus*)		X			X				
Forked panic grass	*Dichanthelium dichotomum s. dichotomum*	X	X						X	
Four-leaf yam	*Dioscorea quaternata*	X	X			X	X		X	X
Fowl manna grass	*Glyceria striata*		X	X	X			X		
Fringed loosestrife	*Lysimachia ciliata*		X	X	X					
Fringed phlox	*Phlox amplifolia*		X			X	X			
Frog's bit	*Limnobium spongia*			X	X					
Frost grape	*Vitis vulpina*		X	X	X	X	X			
Garden phlox	*Phlox paniculata*				X					
Garlic mustard	*ALLIARIA PETIOLATA*		X		X	X	X			
Giant cane	*Arundinaria gigantea*			X	X					
Giant ragweed	*Ambrosia trifida*			X	X					
Ginseng	*Panax quinquefolius*		X			X	X			
Glade fern	*Diplazium pycnocarpon* (= *Athyrium pycnocarpon*)					X	X			
Glaucous tick trefoil	*Desmodium laevigatum*		X							
Globose watermeal	*Wolffia columbiana*			X						
Goat's rue	*Tephrosia virginiana*	X	X						X	
Goat's beard	*Aruncus dioicus*	X				X	X			
Golden cassia	*Chamaecrista fasciculata* (= *Cassia fasciculata*)	X	X						X	
Golden cattail sedge	*Carex aureolensis*			X						
Golden ragwort	*Packera aurea*		X	X	X	X	X			
Golden seal	*Hydrastis canadensis*		X			X	X			
Goldie fern	*Dryopteris goldiana*					X	X			
Goldthread	*Coptis trifolia*		X		X			X		
Grass sedge	*Carex jamesii*		X			X	X			
Gray dogwood	*Cornus racemosa*		X		X	X	X	X		
Great chickweed	*Stellaria pubera*		X			X	X			
Greater hop sedge	*Carex gigantea*			X						
Great Indian plantain	*Arnoglossum reniforme*		X			X	X			
Great waterleaf	*Hydrophyllum appendiculatum*		X			X	X			
Great white lettuce	*Prenanthes crepidinea*				X					
Great yellow wood sorrel	*Oxalis grandis*	X	X							

Common Name	Scientific Name	Deciduous							Conifer	
		Oak/Pine	Oak/Hickory	Oak/Gum/Cypress	Elm/Ash/Cottonwood	Maple/Beech	Cherry/Ash/Poplar	Aspen/Birch	Shortleaf/Virginia Pine	Eastern Red Cedar
Green adder's mouth	*Malaxis unifolia*		X							
Green ash	*Fraxinus pennsylvanica v. lanceolata*				X					
Green brier	*Smilax glauca*	X	X						X	X
Green-flowered tick trefoil	*Desmodium viridiflorum*	X	X						X	
Green-fringed orchid	*Platanthera lacera*		X	X	X			X		
Green twayblade	*Liparis loeselii*							X		
Green violet	*Hybanthus concolor*		X			X	X			
Ground cedar	*Lycopodium tristachyum*		X							
Ground nut	*Apios americana*				X					
Ground pine	*Lycopodium obscurum*	X						X		
Grove bluegrass	*Poa alsodes*					X	X	X		
Hackberry	*Celtis occidentalis*		X	X	X					
Hair grass	*Agrostis hyemalis*	X	X						X	
Hairy bedstraw	*Galium pilosum*	X	X						X	
Hairy bush clover	*Lespedeza hirta*	X	X						X	
Hairy gentian	*Gentiana villosa*		X							X
Hairy gray sedge	*Carex hitchcockiana*		X			X	X			
Hairy hawkweed	*Hieracium gronovii*	X	X						X	
Hairy ruellia	*Ruellia humilis*		X							
Hairy skullcap	*Scutellaria elliptica v. hirsuta*		X			X	X			
Hairy spicebush	*Lindera benzoin*		X	X	X	X	X			
Hairy sweet cicely	*Osmorhiza claytonii*		X			X	X			
Hairy white goldenrod	*Solidago hispida*	X	X							
Harbinger of spring	*Erigenia bulbosa*		X		X	X	X			
Harebell	*Campanula rotundifolia*		X							
Harvey's buttercup	*Ranunculus harveyi*	X	X							
Heart-leaved skullcap	*Scutellaria ovata*		X			X	X			
Hedge apple	*MACLURA POMIFERA*		X		X	X	X			
Helleborine orchid	*EPIPACTIS HELLEBORINE*		X			X				
Hemlock	*Tsuga canadensis*		X			X				
Hoary beard tongue	*Penstemon canescens*		X			X	X			
Hog peanut	*Amphicarpaea bracteata v. bracteata*	X	X	X	X	X	X	X	X	
Honewort	*Cryptotaenia canadensis*		X	X	X	X	X			
Honey locust	*Gleditsia triacanthos*		X	X	X					
Hooked monkshood	*Aconitum uncinatum*		X			X				
Hooker's orchid	*Platanthera hookeri*	X				X				
Hop hornbeam	*Ostrya virginiana*	X	X						X	X
Illinois wood sorrel	*Oxalis illinoensis*					X	X			
Indian cucumber root	*Medeola virginiana*		X			X	X			
Indian heliotrope	*HELIOTROPIUM INDICUM*			X	X					
Indian physic	*Gillenia stipulata*	X	X						X	
Indian pink	*Spigelia marilandica*		X							
Indian tobacco	*Lobelia inflata*		X			X	X			
Indian turnip	*Arisaema triphyllum*		X		X	X	X			
Indian wood oats	*Chasmanthium latifolium*		X	X	X	X	X			
Interrupted fern	*Osmunda claytoniana*		X			X				
Ivory sedge	*Carex eburnea*		X			X				
Jack oak	*Quercus imbricaria*		X	X	X					
Jack pine	*Pinus banksiana*	X								
Japanese barberry	*BERBERIS THUNBERGII*		X			X	X			
Japanese honeysuckle	*LONICERA JAPONICA*	X	X			X	X		X	X
Jetbead	*RHODOTYPOS SCANDENS*	X	X			X	X			
Juneberry	*Amelanchier arborea*	X	X			X	X		X	
Kentucky coffee tree	*Gymnocladus dioica*				X	X	X			
Kentucky wisteria	*Wisteria frutescens*		X	X	X					
Kitten tails	*Besseya bullii*		X							
Knobbed hop sedge	*Carex lupuliformis*			X	X					
Kral's sedge	*Carex kraliana*		X			X	X			
Lady fern	*Athyrium filix-femina s. angustum*		X			X	X			
Large flower bellwort	*Uvularia grandiflora*					X	X			
Large-leaf waterleaf	*Hydrophyllum macrophyllum*					X	X			
Large-leaved shinleaf	*Pyrola elliptica*	X	X			X		X		
Large-leaved storax	*Styrax grandifolia*		X							

Table P-5. *continued*

Common Name	Scientific Name	Deciduous							Conifer	
		Oak/Pine	Oak/Hickory	Oak/Gum/Cypress	Elm/Ash/Cottonwood	Maple/Beech	Cherry/Ash/Poplar	Aspen/Birch	Shortleaf/Virginia Pine	Eastern Red Cedar
Large white trillium	*Trillium grandiflorum*		X			X	X			
Late horse gentian	*Triosteum perfoliatum*		X							
Late low blueberry	*Vaccinium pallidum*	X	X						X	
Leafy phacelia	*Phacelia bipinnatifida*		X			X	X			
Leather flower	*Clematis pitcheri*			X	X					
Leatherwood	*Dirca palustris*		X			X	X			
Leek sedge	*Carex prasina*					X				
Little-leaf buttercup	*Ranunculus abortivus*		X			X	X			
Lizard's tail	*Saururus cernuus*		X	X	X					
Long-awned wood grass	*Brachyelytrum erectum*	X	X			X	X		X	
Long-scaled green sedge	*Carex bushii*		X							
Long-spurred violet	*Viola rostrata*	X				X	X			
Long-stalked hummock sedge	*Carex pedunculata*	X	X			X				
Loose-flowered panic grass	*Dichanthelium laxiflorum*	X	X							
Lopseed	*Phryma leptostachya*		X			X	X			
Lovage	*Ligusticum canadense*		X							
Mad-dog skullcap	*Scutellaria lateriflora*		X	X	X					
Maidenhair fern	*Adiantum pedatum*		X			X	X			
Maple-leaved arrowwood	*Viburnum acerifolium*		X			X	X			
Marsh fleabane	*Erigeron philadelphicus*		X			X	X			
Marsh St. John's wort	*Triadenum tubulosum*		X	X	X					
Marsh St. John's wort	*Triadenum walteri*		X	X	X					
Maryland senna	*Senna marilandica*		X		X					
May apple	*Podophyllum peltatum*		X		X	X	X			
Miami mist	*Phacelia purshii*		X		X	X				
Michigan lily	*Lilium michiganense*					X	X			
Missouri violet	*Viola missouriensis*		X	X	X					
Mockernut hickory	*Carya tomentosa*		X							
Monarda	*Monarda bradburiana*		X							
Moneywort	*LYSIMACHIA NUMMULARIA*		X	X	X	X	X	X		
Monkey flower	*Mimulus ringens*			X	X					
Moonseed	*Menispermum canadense*		X	X	X	X	X	X		
Mountain chestnut oak	*Quercus montana*	X	X						X	
Mountain laurel	*Kalmia latifolia*		X							
Mountain mint	*Pycnanthemum pycnanthemoides*		X							
Mountain phlox	*Phlox ovata*		X			X				
Narrow-fruited pinweed	*Lechea racemulosa*	X	X						X	
Narrow-leaved cattail sedge	*Carex squarrosa*		X	X	X					
Narrow-leaved cow wheat	*Melampyrum lineare v. lineare*		X							
Narrow-leaved pinweed	*Lechea tenuifolia*	X	X						X	
Narrow-leaved white-top aster	*Sericocarpus linifolius* (= *Aster solidagineus*)	X	X						X	
Narrow-leaved wood sedge	*Carex digitalis* (including 1 variety)	X	X			X			X	
Narrow melic grass	*Melica mutica*		X			X				
Nepalese browntop	*MICROSTEGIUM VIMINEUM*		X	X	X	X	X			
Netted chainfern	*Woodwardia areolata*			X						
New York fern	*Thelypteris noveboracensis*		X			X		X		
Nodding fescue	*Festuca subverticillata*		X		X	X	X	X		
Nodding pogonia	*Triphora trianthophora s. trianthophora*		X			X	X			
Nodding wild onion	*Allium cernuum*		X							X
Northern bitter cress	*Cardamine douglassii*		X			X	X			
Northern grape fern	*Botrychium multifidum*		X							
Northern red oak	*Quercus rubra*		X			X	X			
Northern tubercled orchid	*Platanthera flava v. herbiola*		X		X			X		
Northern weak sedge	*Carex debilis v. rudgei*				X	X	X	X		
Nottoway valley brome	*Bromus nottowayanus*		X			X	X			
Ohio buckeye	*Aesculus glabra*		X			X	X			
Ohio horse mint	*Blephilia ciliata*		X			X				X
Oneida grape fern	*Botrychium oneidense*		X		X	X		X		
Orange coneflower	*Rudbeckia fulgida v. fulgida*		X							
Orange-fringed orchid	*Platanthera ciliaris*	X	X							
Ostrich fern	*Matteuccia struthiopteris v. pensylvanica*		X		X	X				
Overcup oak	*Quercus lyrata*			X						
Painted sedge	*Carex picta*		X			X				

Common Name	Scientific Name	Deciduous							Conifer	
		Oak/Pine	Oak/Hickory	Oak/Gum/Cypress	Elm/Ash/Cottonwood	Maple/Beech	Cherry/Ash/Poplar	Aspen/Birch	Shortleaf/Virginia Pine	Eastern Red Cedar
Pale avens	*Geum virginianum*		X		X	X	X			
Pale corydalis	*Corydalis flavula*		X	X	X	X	X			
Pale hickory	*Carya pallida*		X							
Pale Indian plantain	*Arnoglossum atriplicifolium* (= *Cacalia atriplicifolia*)	X	X						X	X
Pale leafcup	*Polymnia canadensis*		X			X				X
Pale touch-me-not	*Impatiens pallida*		X	X	X	X	X	X		
Panicled hawkweed	*Hieracium paniculatum*	X	X						X	
Panicled tick trefoil	*Desmodium paniculatum*		X			X	X			
Papaw	*Asimina triloba*		X			X	X			
Paper birch	*Betula papyrifera*							X		
Partridge berry	*Mitchella repens*	X	X			X		X		
Pasture thistle	*Cirsium discolor*	X	X						X	X
Pecan	*Carya illinoinensis*		X	X	X					
Pennsylvania oak sedge	*Carex pensylvanica*	X	X			X				
Pennywort	*Obolaria virginica*		X			X	X			
Perfoliate bellwort	*Uvularia perfoliata*		X							
Persimmon	*Diospyros virginiana*	X	X	X					X	X
Pignut hickory	*Carya glabra*	X	X						X	
Pinesap	*Monotropa hypopitys*	X				X		X		
Pink valerian	*Valeriana pauciflora*		X		X	X	X			
Pin oak	*Quercus palustris*		X	X						
Pipsissewa	*Chimaphila umbellata s. cisatlantica*		X							
Plantain-leaved wood sedge	*Carex plantaginea*		X			X	X			
Pointed tick trefoil	*Desmodium glutinosum*		X			X	X			
Poison ivy	*Toxicodendron radicans s. radicans*	X	X	X	X	X	X	X	X	X
Pokeweed	*Phytolacca americana v. americana*	X	X	X	X	X	X	X	X	X
Post oak	*Quercus stellata*		X							X
Poverty oat grass	*Danthonia spicata*	X	X						X	X
Prairie parsley	*Polytaenia nuttallii*		X							
Prairie wedge grass	*Sphenopholis obtusata v. obtusata*	X	X						X	
Prickly ash	*Zanthoxylum americanum*		X			X	X			
Princess tree	*PAULOWNIA TOMENTOSA*	X	X			X	X			
Purple chokeberry	*Photinia floribunda* (= *Aronia floribunda*)		X							
Purple fringeless orchid	*Platanthera peramoena*		X	X	X					
Purple Joe Pye weed	*Eupatoriadelphus purpureus*		X			X	X			
Purple milkweed	*Asclepias purpurascens*	X	X							
Purple twayblade	*Liparis liliifolia*		X			X	X			
Pussytoes	*Antennaria plantaginifolia*	X	X			X			X	
Quaking aspen	*Populus tremuloides*		X					X		
Rattlesnake fern	*Botrychium virginianum*		X	X	X	X	X	X		
Rattlesnake plantain	*Goodyera pubescens*		X			X	X	X		
Rattlesnake weed	*Hieracium venosum*	X	X						X	
Red ash	*Fraxinus pennsylvanica v. pennsylvanica*				X					
Red-berried elderberry	*Sambucus racemosa v. pubens*				X	X				
Red maple	*Acer rubrum v. rubrum*	X	X	X	X	X		X	X	
Red mulberry	*Morus rubra*		X	X	X	X	X			
Red trillium	*Trillium recurvatum*		X			X	X			
Reed bent grass	*Calamagrostis porteri s. insperata*	X							X	
Regal fern	*Osmunda regalis v. spectabilis*		X	X				X		
Riverbank wild rye	*Elymus riparius*		X		X	X	X			
River birch	*Betula nigra*			X	X			X		
Robin's plantain	*Erigeron pulchellus*		X							
Rock satin grass	*Muhlenbergia sobolifera*		X			X				X
Rosette goldenrod	*Solidago squarrosa*	X							X	
Rosin weed	*Silphium asteriscus v. trifoliatum*		X							X
Rough-leaved rice grass	*Oryzopsis asperifolia*		X							
Rough white lettuce	*Prenanthes aspera*		X							X
Round-fruited panic grass	*Dichanthelium sphaerocarpon*		X							
Round-leaved dogwood	*Cornus rugosa*					X				
Round-leaved hepatica	*Anemone americana* (= *Hepatica americana*)		X			X				
Round-leaved orchid	*Platanthera orbiculata*					X				
Round-leaved ragwort	*Packera obovata*		X			X				
Round-leaved serviceberry	*Amelanchier sanguinea*		X							

Table P-5. *continued*

Common Name	Scientific Name	Deciduous							Conifer	
		Oak/Pine	Oak/Hickory	Oak/Gum/Cypress	Elm/Ash/Cottonwood	Maple/Beech	Cherry/Ash/Poplar	Aspen/Birch	Shortleaf/Virginia Pine	Eastern Red Cedar
Round-leaved shinleaf	*Pyrola americana*	X	X							
Round-leaved tick trefoil	*Desmodium rotundifolium*	X	X						X	
Running buffalo clover	*Trifolium stoloniferum*				X	X	X			
Running savanna sedge	*Carex siccata*		X							
Running strawberry bush	*Euonymus obovata*		X			X	X			
Rusty nannyberry	*Viburnum rufidulum*		X							X
Sampson's snakeroot	*Orbexilum pedunculatum*		X							
Sassafras	*Sassafras albidum*	X	X							
Scarlet oak	*Quercus coccinea*	X	X							
Scorpion grass	*Myosotis macrosperma*		X			X	X			
Scrub pine	*Pinus virginiana*	X							X	
Seneca snakeroot	*Polygala senega*		X							
Sensitive fern	*Onoclea sensibilis*		X	X	X			X		
Sessile trillium	*Trillium sessile*		X		X	X	X			
Shagbark hickory	*Carya ovata*		X			X				
Sharp-lobed hepatica	*Anemone acutiloba* (= *Hepatica acutiloba*)		X			X	X			
Shining bedstraw	*Galium concinnum*	X	X			X	X			
Shining bur sedge	*Carex intumescens*		X	X	X					
Shining clubmoss	*Huperzia lucidula* (= *Lycopodium lucidulum*)		X			X	X	X		
Shining panic grass	*Dichanthelium lucidum*				X					
Shining wedge grass	*Sphenopholis nitida*	X	X						X	
Shooting star	*Dodecatheon meadia*	X	X							X
Short-headed bracted sedge	*Carex cephalophora*	X	X			X	X			
Short's aster	*Symphyotrichum shortii*	X	X			X	X			
Short's streambank chervil	*Chaerophyllum procumbens v. shortii*				X	X	X			
Showy orchis	*Galearis spectabilis* (= *Orchis spectabilis*)		X			X	X			
Shumard's oak	*Quercus shumardii v. shumardii*		X	X						
Side-flowering aster	*Symphyotrichum lateriflorum* (including 1 variety)		X	X	X	X	X			
Silky wild rye	*Elymus villosus* (including 1 variety)		X			X	X			
Silver maple	*Acer saccharinum*				X		X			
Silverrod	*Solidago bicolor*	X	X						X	
Silvery spleenwort	*Deparia acrostichoides* (= *Athyrium thelypterioides*)		X			X	X			
Skunk cabbage	*Symplocarpus foetidus*				X					
Slender green sedge	*Carex virescens*	X								
Slender knotweed	*Polygonum tenue*	X	X						X	
Slender-leaved panic grass	*Dichanthelium linearifolium*		X							
Slender satin grass	*Muhlenbergia tenuiflora*		X			X	X			
Slippery elm	*Ulmus rubra*				X	X	X			
Small-flowered crowfoot	*Ranunculus micranthus*		X	X	X	X	X			
Small-fruited panic grass	*Dichanthelium dichotomum s. microcarpon*	X	X						X	
Small-fruited panic grass	*Dichanthelium polyanthes*		X			X	X			
Small horse gentian	*Triosteum angustifolium*	X	X						X	X
Small morning glory	*Ipomoea lacunosa*		X	X	X					
Small passion flower	*Passiflora lutea*		X			X	X			
Small Solomon's seal	*Polygonatum biflorum*		X			X	X			
Small spearwort	*Ranunculus pusillus*			X	X					
Small's snakeroot	*Sanicula smallii*		X							
Small wood sunflower	*Helianthus microcephalus*		X							
Smooth beard tongue	*Penstemon calycosus*		X		X	X				
Smooth false foxglove	*Aureolaria flava* (including 1 variety)	X	X						X	
Smooth forked aster	*Eurybia schreberi*		X			X	X			
Smooth ruellia	*Ruellia strepens*			X	X					
Smooth-seeded nut rush	*Scleria oligantha*		X							
Smooth white goldenrod	*Solidago erecta*	X	X						X	
Smooth wild licorice	*Galium circaezans v. circaezans*	X	X			X	X			
Snow trillium	*Trillium nivale*		X			X				
Soft agrimony	*Agrimonia pubescens*		X			X				
Solitary cat's foot	*Antennaria solitaria*	X	X						X	
Sourwood	*Oxydendron arboreum*		X							
Southern adder's tongue fern	*Ophioglossum vulgatum*		X	X	X	X	X	X		
Southern blazing star	*Liatris squarrulosa*		X							
Southern blue flag	*Iris virginica*			X	X					
Southern hop sedge	*Carex louisianica*		X	X	X	X				

Common Name	Scientific Name	Deciduous							Conifer	
		Oak/Pine	Oak/Hickory	Oak/Gum/Cypress	Elm/Ash/Cottonwood	Maple/Beech	Cherry/Ash/Poplar	Aspen/Birch	Shortleaf/Virginia Pine	Eastern Red Cedar
Southern red oak	*Quercus falcata*		X							
Southern tubercled orchid	*Platanthera flava v. flava*		X		X					
Sparse-lobed grape fern	*Botrychium biternatum*		X	X	X	X				
Spinulose wood fern	*Dryopteris carthusiana*		X		X	X	X	X		
Spotted touch-me-not	*Impatiens capensis*		X		X	X	X			
Spotted wintergreen	*Chimaphila maculata*	X	X						X	
Spreading tick trefoil	*Desmodium humifusum*		X							
Spring beauty	*Claytonia virginica*		X		X	X	X	X		
Squirrel corn	*Dicentra canadensis*					X	X			
St. Andrew's cross	*Hypericum hypericoides s. multicaule*	X	X						X	
Stalked great chickweed	*Stellaria corei*					X	X			
Starved panic grass	*Dichanthelium depauperatum*	X	X						X	
Stickseed	*Hackelia virginiana*	X	X	X	X	X	X	X	X	X
Stiff gentian	*Gentianella quinquefolia s. occidentalis*		X							X
Strawberry bush	*Euonymus americana*		X	X	X	X				
Sugarberry	*Celtis laevigata*			X	X					
Sugar maple	*Acer saccharum* (includes 2 subspecies)		X			X	X			
Summer grape	*Vitis aestivalis* (including 1 variety)	X	X			X	X		X	
Superb lily	*Lilium superbum*		X			X				
Swamp agrimony	*Agrimonia parviflora*			X	X			X		
Swamp beggar's ticks	*Bidens discoidea*			X	X					
Swamp cottonwood	*Populus heterophylla*			X	X					
Swamp dock	*Rumex verticillatus*			X	X					
Swamp holly	*Ilex decidua*		X	X	X					
Swamp oval sedge	*Carex muskingumensis*			X	X					
Swamp white oak	*Quercus bicolor*		X	X	X					
Swampy dewberry	*Rubus sec. Hispidus: R. hispidus*		X			X		X		
Swampy rose	*Rosa palustris*			X	X					
Sweetgum	*Liquidambar styraciflua*		X	X	X					
Sweet-scented bedstraw	*Galium triflorum*		X			X	X			
Sycamore	*Platanus occidentalis*			X	X					
Synandra	*Synandra hispidula*		X		X	X	X			
Tall agrimony	*Agrimonia gryposepala*		X		X	X				
Tall blue lettuce	*Lactuca biennis*				X		X			
Tall melic grass	*Melica nitens*		X							
Tall scouring rush	*Equisetum hyemale s. affine*				X					
Tall thistle	*Cirsium altissimum*		X		X	X	X			
Tartarian honeysuckle	*LONICERA TATARICA*		X		X	X	X	X		X
Terrestrial water starwort	*Callitriche terrestris*		X	X		X	X			
Thicket bean	*Phaseolus polystachios*		X							
Thin-leaved milkweed	*Asclepias perennis*			X	X					
Three-leaved stonecrop	*Sedum ternatum*		X			X	X			
Three-seeded mercury	*Acalypha rhomboidea*			X	X	X	X			
Toothwort	*Cardamine concatenata*		X			X	X			
Tragia	*Tragia cordata*		X							X
Trailing arbutus	*Epigaea repens*		X			X				
Trailing bush clover	*Lespedeza procumbens*	X	X						X	
Trailing ground pine	*Lycopodium digitatum*		X			X		X		
Tree-of-heaven	*AILANTHUS ALTISSIMA*		X			X	X			X
Trumpet creeper	*Campsis radicans*		X	X	X					
Tulip poplar	*Liriodendron tulipifera*					X	X			
Twinleaf	*Jeffersonia diphylla*		X			X	X			
Two-flower false dandelion	*Krigia biflora*	X	X						X	
Two-leaved toothwort	*Cardamine diphylla*		X			X	X			
Umbrella magnolia	*Magnolia tripetala*		X			X				
Upland boneset	*Eupatorium sessilifolium*	X	X						X	
Variegated milkweed	*Asclepias variegata*		X							
Veiny pea	*Lathyrus venosus*	X	X						X	
Venus's looking glass	*Triodanis perfoliata*	X	X							
Violet bush clover	*Lespedeza violacea*	X	X			X	X		X	
Violet wood sorrel	*Oxalis violacea*	X	X			X			X	
Virginia bluebells	*Mertensia virginica*			X	X	X	X			
Virginia creeper	*Parthenocissus quinquefolia*	X	X	X	X	X	X	X	X	X

Table P-5. *continued*

Common Name	Scientific Name	Oak/Pine	Oak/Hickory	Oak/Gum/Cypress	Elm/Ash/Cottonwood	Maple/Beech	Cherry/Ash/Poplar	Aspen/Birch	Shortleaf/Virginia Pine	Eastern Red Cedar
		Deciduous							Conifer	
Virginia dayflower	*Commelina virginica*		X	X	X					
Virginia knotweed	*Tovara virginiana* (= *Polygonum virginianum*)		X		X	X	X			
Virginia waterleaf	*Hydrophyllum virginianum*		X			X	X	X		
Virginia wild rye	*Elymus virginicus* (including 1 variety)			X	X	X	X			
Virginia willow	*Itea virginica*			X	X					
Wahoo	*Euonymus atropurpurea*		X		X	X	X			
Water purslane	*Didiplis diandra*			X	X					
Weak sedge	*Carex debilis v. debilis*		X			X				
Weak-stemmed wood sedge	*Carex laxiculmis v. laxiculmis*				X	X	X			
White adder's tongue	*Erythronium albidum*		X		X	X	X			
White ash	*Fraxinus americana*		X			X	X			
White basswood	*Tilia americana v. heterophylla*		X		X	X	X			
White grass	*Leersia virginica*		X	X	X	X	X			
White mulberry	*MORUS ALBA*		X		X	X	X			
White oak	*Quercus alba*	X	X			X			X	
White pine	*Pinus strobus*	X								
Whorled milkweed	*Asclepias quadrifolia*		X			X				
Wild cucumber	*Echinocystis lobata*				X					
Wild garlic	*Allium canadense*			X	X					
Wild geranium	*Geranium maculatum*		X			X	X			
Wild golden glow	*Rudbeckia laciniata*				X					
Wild hydrangea	*Hydrangea arborescens*		X			X	X			
Wild leek	*Allium tricoccum v. burdickii*		X			X	X			
Wild leek	*Allium tricoccum v. tricoccum*		X			X	X			
Wild lettuce	*Lactuca canadensis*		X							
Wild madder	*Galium obtusum*		X	X	X	X	X	X		
Wild petunia	*Ruellia caroliniensis*		X							X
Wild quinine	*Parthenium integrifolium*		X							
Wild sensitive plant	*Chamaecrista nictitans*	X	X						X	X
Wild strawberry	*Fragaria virginiana* (including 1 subspecies)		X							
Willdenow's grass sedge	*Carex willdenowii*	X	X						X	
Winged elm	*Ulmus alata*	X	X	X					X	
Winged euonymus	*EUONYMUS ALATA*		X		X	X	X			
Winged monkey flower	*Mimulus alatus*			X	X					
Winged pigweed	*Cycloloma atriplicifolium*		X							
Wingstem	*Verbesina alternifolia*		X		X					
Winterberry	*Ilex verticillata*			X	X			X		
Wintercreeper	*EUONYMUS FORTUNEI*		X	X	X	X	X	X		
Witch hazel	*Hamamelis virginiana*	X	X			X	X	X		
With rod	*Viburnum nudum v. cassinoides*		X					X		
Wolf's bluegrass	*Poa wolfii*		X	X		X				
Wood anemone	*Anemone quinquefolia*		X			X		X		
Wood angelica	*Angelica venenosa*		X							
Wood betony	*Pedicularis canadensis*		X							
Woodland agrimony	*Agrimonia rostellata*	X	X			X			X	X
Woodland brome	*Bromus pubescens*	X	X			X			X	X
Woodland sunflower	*Helianthus divaricatus*	X	X			X	X		X	
Wood millet	*Milium effusum v. cisatlanticum*				X	X				
Wood mint	*Blephilia hirsuta*					X	X			
Wood's stiff sedge	*Carex woodii*		X			X	X			
Woolly blue violet	*Viola sororia*		X	X	X	X	X	X		
Yellow adder's tongue	*Erythronium americanum*		X		X	X	X			
Yellow buckeye	*Aesculus flava*					X	X			
Yellow crownbeard	*Verbesina helianthoides*	X	X						X	X
Yellow ladies' tresses	*Spiranthes ochroleuca*		X							
Yellow meadow parsnip	*Thaspium trifoliatum v. aureum*	X	X						X	X
Yellow pimpernel	*Taenidia integerrima*		X			X				
Yellow star grass	*Hypoxis hirsuta*	X	X						X	
Yellowwood	*Cladrastis kentuckea*		X			X				
Yerba de tajo	*Eclipta prostrata*			X	X					

Note: Scientific names in all capital letters are exotic species.

Table P-6. Plant Species of Various Forest Communities

Common Name	Scientific Name	Original Forest	Old Forest	Upland Forest	Floodplain Forest	Forested Wetlands	Flatwood Forest	Riparian Wooded Corridor
Adam-and-Eve	*Aplectrum hyemale*	X	X	X			X	
Alder buckthorn	*Rhamnus alnifolia*					X		
Allegheny barberry	*Berberis canadensis*	X	X	X				
Allegheny spurge	*Pachysandra procumbens*	X	X	X				
American beak grass	*Diarrhena americana*	X	X	X				
American beech	*Fagus grandifolia*	X	X	X				
American bellflower	*Campanulastrum americanum* (= *Campanula americanum*)	X	X	X	X		X	
American chestnut	*Castanea dentata*	X	X	X				
American columbo	*Frasera caroliniensis*	X	X	X				
American elm	*Ulmus americana*	X	X	X	X		X	X
American filbert	*Corylus americana*	X	X	X			X	
American gromwell	*Lithospermum latifolium*	X	X	X				
American hops	*Humulus lupulus v. pubescens*	X	X	X				
American larch	*Larix laricina*	X	X			X		
American linden	*Tilia americana v. americana*	X	X	X				
American pennyroyal	*Hedeoma pulegioides*	X	X	X				
American storax	*Styrax americana*	X	X	X	X	X		X
Amur honeysuckle	*LONICERA MAACKII*		X	X	X		X	X
Angle-stemmed primrose willow	*Ludwigia leptocarpa*	X	X		X	X		
Anise root	*Osmorhiza longistylis*	X	X	X				
Arbor vitae	*Thuja occidentalis*	X	X			X		
Aromatic sumac	*Rhus aromatica v. aromatica*	X	X	X				
Arrow arum	*Peltandra virginica*	X	X		X	X		
Atlantic star sedge	*Carex atlantica s. atlantica*	X	X			X		
Autumn bent grass	*Agrostis perennans*	X	X	X				
Autumn bluegrass	*Poa autumnalis*	X	X	X	X	X		
Autumn olive	*ELAEAGNUS UMBELLATA*		X	X			X	
Awned graceful sedge	*Carex davisii*	X	X	X	X			X
Bald cypress	*Taxodium distichum*	X	X		X	X		
Baldwin's fimbristylis	*Fimbristylis annua*	X	X				X	
Bare-stemmed tick trefoil	*Desmodium nudiflorum*	X	X	X				
Barren strawberry	*Waldsteinia fragarioides*	X	X	X				
Basil bee balm	*Monarda clinopodia*	X	X	X				
Basket oak	*Quercus michauxii*	X	X		X		X	
Bastard toadflax	*Comandra umbellata*	X	X	X				
Beaked black snakeroot	*Sanicula trifoliata*	X	X	X				
Beaked corn salad	*Valerianella radiata*	X	X		X			X
Bearded panic grass	*Dichanthelium boscii*	X	X	X				
Bear's foot	*Smallanthus uvedalia* (= *Polymnia uvedalia*)	X	X	X				
Beech drops	*Epifagus virginiana*	X	X	X				
Beech wood sedge	*Carex laxiflora*	X	X	X				
Beefsteak plant	*PERILLA FRUTESCENS* (including 1 variety)		X	X	X			X
Bent-seeded hop sedge	*Carex tuckermanii*	X	X			X		
Bicknell's panic grass	*Dichanthelium bicknellii* (*nomen nudum*)	X	X	X				
Big-leaved aster	*Eurybia macrophylla*	X	X	X				
Big shellbark hickory	*Carya laciniosa*	X	X		X	X	X	
Bigtooth aspen	*Populus grandidentata*	X	X	X				
Bird's foot violet	*Viola pedata*	X	X	X				
Bishop's cap	*Mitella diphylla*	X	X	X			X	
Bitternut hickory	*Carya cordiformis*	X	X	X	X			X
Bittersweet nightshade	*SOLANUM DULCAMARA*		X	X				
Black ash	*Fraxinus nigra*	X	X			X		
Black chokeberry	*Photinia melanocarpa*	X	X	X	X		X	
Black cohosh	*Cimicifuga rubifolia*	X	X	X				
Black gum	*Nyssa sylvatica*	X	X	X	X		X	
Black hickory	*Carya texana*	X	X	X				
Black huckleberry	*Gaylussacia baccata*	X	X	X				
Blackjack oak	*Quercus marilandica*	X	X	X				
Black maple	*Acer saccharum s. nigrum*	X	X	X				
Black oak	*Quercus velutina*	X	X	X				
Black oat grass	*Piptochaetium avenaceum* (= *Stipa avenacea*)	X	X	X				
Black quillwort	*Isoetes melanopoda*	X	X	X			X	
Black-seeded rice grass	*Piptatherum racemosa*	X	X	X				

Table P-6. *continued*

Common Name	Scientific Name	Original Forest	Old Forest	Upland Forest	Floodplain Forest	Forested Wetlands	Flatwood Forest	Riparian Wooded Corridor
Black snakeroot	*Sanicula marilandica*	X	X		X			
Black walnut	*Juglans nigra*	X	X	X	X			X
Bladdernut	*Staphylea trifolia*	X	X	X				
Blighted goldenrod	*Solidago sphacelata*	X	X	X				
Bloodleaf	*Iresine rhizomatosa*	X	X		X	X		
Bloodroot	*Sanguinaria canadensis*	X	X	X				
Blue ash	*Fraxinus quadrangulata*	X	X	X				
Bluebead	*Clintonia borealis*	X	X			X		
Blue beech	*Carpinus caroliniana s. virginiana*	X	X	X	X			X
Blue cohosh	*Caulophyllum thalictroides*	X	X	X				
Blue-eyed Mary	*Collinsia verna*	X	X		X			
Blue lettuce	*Lactuca floridana*	X	X	X	X			
Blue phlox	*Phlox divaricata* (including 1 subspecies)	X	X	X				X
Blue sedge	*Carex glaucodea*	X	X	X				
Blue star	*Amsonia tabernaemontana v. salicifolia*	X	X		X	X		
Bluestem goldenrod	*Solidago caesia*	X	X	X				
Bluets	*Houstonia caerulea* (= *Hedyotis caerulea*)	X	X	X				
Blue water iris	*Iris brevicaulis*	X	X		X	X		
Blunt-scaled oak sedge	*Carex albicans v. albicans*	X	X	X				
Blunt-scaled wood sedge	*Carex albursina*	X	X	X				
Bog clubmoss	*Lycopodiella inundata* (= *Lycopodium inundatum*)	X	X			X	X	
Bottlebrush grass	*Elymus hystrix* (including 1 variety)	X	X	X	X			
Bottlebrush sedge	*Carex lurida*	X	X		X	X		X
Boxelder	*Acer negundo* (including varieties)	X	X		X		X	X
Bracted green orchid	*Coeloglossum viride* (= *Habenaria viridis*)	X	X	X				
Bracted water willow	*Dicliptera brachiata*	X	X		X	X		
Bristly aster	*Symphyotrichum puniceum*	X	X			X		
Bristly cattail sedge	*Carex frankii*	X	X	X	X			X
Bristly sunflower	*Helianthus hirsutus*	X	X	X				
Broad beech fern	*Phegopteris hexagonoptera*	X	X	X				
Broad-leaved cow wheat	*Melampyrum lineare v. latifolium*	X	X	X			X	
Broad-leaved goldenrod	*Solidago flexicaulis*	X	X	X				
Broad-leaved oval sedge	*Carex tribuloides v. tribuloides*	X	X		X			
Broad-leaved panicled sedge	*Carex decomposita*	X	X			X		
Broad-leaved spiderwort	*Tradescantia subaspera*	X	X	X	X			X
Broad-leaved wood sedge	*Carex platyphylla*	X	X	X				
Brome hummock sedge	*Carex bromoides*	X	X		X	X		
Bronze fern	*Botrychium dissectum*	X	X	X	X		X	X
Brown-eyed Susan	*Rudbeckia triloba*	X	X		X			X
Buckley's goldenrod	*Solidago buckleyi*	X	X				X	
Buffalo clover	*Trifolium reflexum*	X	X	X			X	
Bulb bitter cress	*Cardamine bulbosa*	X	X		X	X		X
Bulblet-bearing water hemlock	*Cicuta bulbifera*	X	X			X		
Bulbous wood rush	*Luzula bulbosa*	X	X	X				
Bull brier	*Smilax bona-nox*	X	X	X				
Bunchberry	*Cornus canadensis*	X	X			X		
Bur oak	*Quercus macrocarpa*	X	X	X	X	X		X
Buttercup phacelia	*Phacelia ranunculacea*	X	X	X	X			
Butterfly pea	*Clitoria mariana*	X	X	X				
Butternut	*Juglans cinerea*	X	X	X				
Buttonbush	*Cephalanthus occidentalis*	X	X		X	X		
Camphor weed	*Pluchea camphorata*	X	X		X	X		X
Canada blueberry	*Vaccinium myrtilloides*	X	X	X			X	
Canada clearweed	*Pilea pumila*	X	X		X	X		X
Canada lily	*Lilium canadense*	X	X	X				
Canada violet	*Viola canadensis*	X	X	X				
Canada waterleaf	*Hydrophyllum canadense*	X	X	X				
Canada wild ginger	*Asarum canadense*	X	X	X				
Canada wood nettle	*Laportea canadensis*	X	X	X	X		X	
Canada yew	*Taxus canadensis*	X	X	X				
Canadian black snakeroot	*Sanicula canadensis* (including 1 variety)	X	X	X	X		X	X
Cardinal flower	*Lobelia cardinalis*	X	X		X	X		
Carey's wood sedge	*Carex careyana*	X	X	X				

Common Name	Scientific Name	Original Forest	Old Forest	Upland Forest	Floodplain Forest	Forested Wetlands	Flatwood Forest	Riparian Wooded Corridor
Carolina buckthorn	*Frangula caroliniana* (= *Rhamnus caroliniana*)	X	X	X				
Carolina mosquito fern	*Azolla caroliniana*	X	X			X		
Carolina panic grass	*Dichanthelium dichotomum s.yadkinense*	X	X	X				
Catbird grape	*Vitis palmata*				X	X		
Cat brier	*Smilax rotundifolia*	X	X	X				
Cat's foot	*Antennaria neglecta*	X	X	X				
Celandine poppy	*Stylophorum diphyllum*	X	X	X				
Checkerberry	*Gaultheria procumbens*	X	X	X				
Cherrybark oak	*Quercus pagoda*	X	X		X			
Chinquapin oak	*Quercus muhlenbergii*	X	X	X				
Cigar tree	*Catalpa speciosa*	X	X		X			
Cinnamon fern	*Osmunda cinnamomea*	X	X			X		
Clasping St. John's wort	*Hypericum gymnanthum*	X	X				X	
Cleft phlox	*Phlox bifida s. bifida*	X	X	X				
Cleft violet	*Viola palmata* (including 1 variety)	X	X	X				
Climbing bittersweet	*Celastrus scandens*	X	X	X				
Climbing dayflower	*COMMELINA DIFFUSA*		X		X	X		X
Climbing dogbane	*Trachelospermum difforme*	X	X		X	X		
Climbing fern	*Lygodium palmatum*	X	X				X	
Climbing hempweed	*Mikania scandens*	X	X		X	X		
Clinton's wood fern	*Dryopteris clintoniana*	X	X			X		
Common beech sedge	*Carex communis*	X	X	X				
Common blackberry	*Rubus sec. Allegheniensis: R. allegheniensis*	X	X	X				
Common buckthorn	*RHAMNUS CATHARTICA*		X					
Common burdock	*ARCTIUM MINUS*		X		X			X
Common bur sedge	*Carex grayi*	X	X		X	X		
Common cattail sedge	*Carex typhina*	X	X		X	X		
Common chickweed	*STELLARIA MEDIA s. MEDIA*		X	X	X		X	X
Common cinquefoil	*Potentilla simplex*	X	X	X				
Common dayflower	*COMMELINA COMMUNIS*		X	X	X		X	
Common dodder	*Cuscuta gronovii* (including 1 variety)	X	X		X	X		X
Common elderberry	*Sambucus nigra s. canadensis*	X	X	X	X		X	
Common forget-me-not	*MYOSOTIS SCORPIOIDES*		X		X			
Common fox sedge	*Carex stipata v. stipata*	X	X			X		
Common fragile fern	*Cystopteris protrusa*	X	X	X	X			
Common gray sedge	*Carex grisea*	X	X	X	X			X
Common hops	*HUMULUS LUPULUS v. LUPULUS*		X	X	X			
Common hop sedge	*Carex lupulina*	X	X		X	X	X	
Common horsetail	*Equisetum arvense*	X	X		X			X
Common privet	*LIGUSTRUM VULGARE*		X	X				
Common rockrose	*Helianthemum canadense*	X	X	X				
Common star of Bethlehem	*ORNITHOGALUM UMBELLATUM*		X	X	X		X	
Common streambank chervil	*Chaerophyllum procumbens v. procumbens*	X	X	X	X			X
Common water hemlock	*Cicuta maculata* (including 1 variety)	X	X		X	X		
Common water plantain	*Alisma subcordatum*	X	X		X	X		
Common white violet	*Viola striata*	X	X		X		X	X
Common wild comfrey	*Cynoglossum virginianum v. virginianum*	X	X	X				
Common wild yam	*Dioscorea villosa*	X	X	X	X			
Common wood reed	*Cinna arundinacea*	X	X		X		X	X
Common wood rush	*Luzula echinata*	X	X	X				
Common wood sedge	*Carex blanda*	X	X	X	X		X	X
Common woodsia	*Woodsia obtusa s. obtusa*	X	X	X				
Compact dodder	*Cuscuta compacta*	X	X		X		X	
Concealed sedge	*Carex cumberlandensis*	X	X	X				
Coralberry	*Symphoricarpos orbiculatus*	X	X	X				
Cowbane	*Oxypolis rigidior*	X	X		X	X	X	
Crane-fly orchid	*Tipularia discolor*	X	X	X				
Creeping bracted sedge	*Carex socialis*	X	X		X	X		
Creeping bush clover	*Lespedeza repens*	X	X	X				
Crested coralroot	*Hexalectris spicata*	X	X	X				
Crested wood fern	*Dryopteris cristata*	X	X			X	X	
Crooked aster	*Symphyotrichum prenanthoides*	X	X		X			X
Cross vine	*Bignonia capreolata*	X	X		X	X	X	X

Table P-6. *continued*

Common Name	Scientific Name	Original Forest	Old Forest	Upland Forest	Floodplain Forest	Forested Wetlands	Flatwood Forest	Riparian Wooded Corridor
Crow poison	*Nothoscordum bivalve*	X	X	X				
Cucumber magnolia	*Magnolia acuminata*	X	X	X				
Cup plant	*Silphium perfoliatum*	X	X		X			X
Cupseed	*Calycocarpum lyonii*	X	X		X	X		X
Dainties	*Phyllanthus caroliniensis*	X	X		X		X	
Dame's rocket	*HESPERIS MATRONALIS*		X		X			
Dark-green bulrush	*Scirpus atrovirens*	X	X		X	X		
Deam's beard tongue	*Penstemon deamii*	X	X	X				
Deam's rockcress	*Arabis missouriensis*	X	X	X				
Declined trillium	*Trillium flexipes*	X	X	X				
Deerberry	*Vaccinium stamineum*	X	X	X				
Deer-tongue grass	*Dichanthelium clandestinum*	X	X	X	X			
Devil's walking stick	*Aralia spinosa*	X	X	X				
Dittany	*Cunila origanoides*	X	X	X				
Dog mint	*Clinopodium vulgare*	X	X	X				
Doll's-eyes	*Actaea pachypoda*	X	X	X				
Downy arrowwood	*Viburnum molle*	X	X	X				
Downy false foxglove	*Aureolaria virginica*	X	X	X				
Downy green sedge	*Carex swanii*	X	X	X				
Downy skullcap	*Scutellaria incana*	X	X	X			X	
Downy Solomon's seal	*Polygonatum pubescens*	X	X	X				
Downy yellow violet	*Viola pubescens* (including varieties)	X	X	X	X			X
Dutchman's breeches	*Dicentra cucullaria*	X	X	X				
Dutchman's pipe	*Aristolochia tomentosa*	X	X	X	X	X		X
Dwarf crested iris	*Iris cristata*	X	X	X	X			
Dwarf ginseng	*Panax trifolius*	X	X	X			X	
Dwarf larkspur	*Delphinium tricorne*	X	X	X	X			
Early coralroot	*Corallorhiza trifida*	X	X			X		
Early figwort	*Scrophularia lanceolata*	X	X	X				
Early horse gentian	*Triosteum aurantiacum* (including varieties)	X	X	X				
Early-leaved brome	*Bromus latiglumis*	X	X		X			
Early low blueberry	*Vaccinium angustifolium*	X	X	X				
Early oak sedge	*Carex umbellata*	X	X	X				
Early saxifrage	*Saxifraga virginiensis*	X	X	X				
Eastern cottonwood	*Populus deltoides*	X	X		X			X
Eastern redbud	*Cercis canadensis*	X	X	X				
Eastern red cedar	*Juniperus virginiana*	X	X	X				
Elephant's foot	*Elephantopus carolinianus*	X	X	X	X			
Elm-leaved goldenrod	*Solidago ulmifolia*	X	X	X				
Enchanter's nightshade	*Circaea lutetiana s. canadensis*	X	X	X	X			
Engelmann's quillwort	*Isoetes engelmannii*	X	X		X	X		X
European corn salad	*VALERIANELLA LOCUSTA*		X		X			X
European high-bush cranberry	*VIBURNUM OPULUS v. OPULUS*		X			X		X
Fairy wand	*Chamaelirium luteum*	X	X	X				
Fall coralroot	*Corallorhiza odontorhiza* (including 1 variety)	X	X	X	X			
False bugbane	*Cimicifuga racemosa*	X	X	X				
False grass sedge	*Carex timida*	X	X	X				
False hellebore	*Melanthium woodii* (= *Veratrum woodii*)	X	X	X				
False loosestrife	*Ludwigia glandulosa*	X	X		X		X	
False melic grass	*Schizachne purpurascens*	X	X	X				
False mermaid weed	*Floerkea proserpinacoides*	X	X	X	X			
False mermaidweed	*Proserpinaca palustris* (including 1 variety)	X	X		X	X		
False rue anemone	*Enemion biternatum* (= *Isopyrum biternatum*)	X	X	X	X			X
Farkleberry	*Vaccinium arboreum*	X	X	X				
Featherbells	*Stenanthium gramineum*	X	X	X				
Featherfoil	*Hottonia inflata*	X	X			X		
Feathery false Solomon's seal	*Maianthemum racemosum* (= *Smilacina racemosa*)	X	X	X				
Fen betony	*Pedicularis lanceolata*	X	X			X		
Few-flowered tick trefoil	*Desmodium pauciflorum*	X	X	X	X		X	
Field sorrel	*RUMEX ACETOSELLA*		X	X				
Fire pink	*Silene virginica*	X	X	X				
Fireweed	*Erechtites hieracifolia*	X	X	X				
Five leaves	*Isotria verticillata*	X	X	X				

Common Name	Scientific Name	Original Forest	Old Forest	Upland Forest	Floodplain Forest	Forested Wetlands	Flatwood Forest	Riparian Wooded Corridor
Flat-spiked gray sedge	*Carex planispicata*	X	X	X				
Flat-top aster	*Doellingeria umbellata* (= *Aster umbellatus*)	X	X			X	X	
Flowering dogwood	*Cornus florida*	X	X	X				
Fog fruit	*Phyla lanceolata*	X	X		X			X
Follicle sedge	*Carex folliculata*	X	X			X		
Forked aster	*Eurybia furcata* (= *Aster furcatus*)	X	X	X				X
Forked panic grass	*Dichanthelium dichotomum s. dichotomum*	X	X	X				
Four-leaf yam	*Dioscorea quaternata*	X	X	X				
Fowl manna grass	*Glyceria striata*	X	X		X	X	X	X
Fox grape	*Vitis labrusca*	X	X				X	
Fringed loosestrife	*Lysimachia ciliata*	X	X		X	X		X
Fringed phlox	*Phlox amplifolia*	X	X	X				
Fringed sedge	*Carex crinita*	X	X		X	X		
Frog's bit	*Limnobium spongia*	X	X			X		
Frost grape	*Vitis vulpina*	X	X	X	X		X	X
Garden phlox	*Phlox paniculata*	X	X		X			X
Garlic mustard	*ALLIARIA PETIOLATA*		X	X	X		X	X
Giant cane	*Arundinaria gigantea*	X	X		X			X
Giant ragweed	*Ambrosia trifida*	X	X		X			
Giant St. John's wort	*Hypericum pyramidatum*	X	X		X	X		X
Ginseng	*Panax quinquefolius*	X	X	X				
Glade fern	*Diplazium pycnocarpon* (= *Athyrium pycnocarpon*)	X	X	X				
Glade mallow	*Napaea dioica*	X	X		X			X
Glaucous tick trefoil	*Desmodium laevigatum*	X	X	X				
Globose watermeal	*Wolffia columbiana*	X	X			X		
Glossy buckthorn	*FRANGULA ALNUS* (= *RHAMNUS FRANGULA*)	X			X			
Goat's beard	*Aruncus dioicus*	X	X	X				
Golden cassia	*Chamaecrista fasciculata* (= *Cassia fasciculata*)	X	X					
Golden cattail sedge	*Carex aureolensis*	X	X		X	X		
Golden ragwort	*Packera aurea*	X	X	X	X		X	
Golden rain tree	*KOELREUTERIA PANICULATA*			X				
Golden seal	*Hydrastis canadensis*	X	X	X				
Goldie fern	*Dryopteris goldiana*	X	X	X				
Goldthread	*Coptis trifolia*	X	X			X		
Grass sedge	*Carex jamesii*	X	X	X				
Great angelica	*Angelica atropurpurea*	X	X			X		
Great chickweed	*Stellaria pubera*	X	X	X				
Great duckweed	*Spirodela polyrhiza*	X	X			X		
Greater hop sedge	*Carex gigantea*	X	X		X	X		
Greater nodding fescue	*Festuca paradoxa*	X	X				X	
Great Indian plantain	*Arnoglossum reniforme*	X	X	X				
Great waterleaf	*Hydrophyllum appendiculatum*	X	X	X				
Great white lettuce	*Prenanthes crepidinea*	X	X		X			X
Great yellow wood sorrel	*Oxalis grandis*	X	X	X				
Green adder's mouth	*Malaxis unifolia*	X	X	X				
Green ash	*Fraxinus pennsylvanica v. lanceolata*	X	X		X			X
Green brier	*Smilax glauca*	X	X	X				
Green-flowered tick trefoil	*Desmodium viridiflorum*	X	X	X				
Green-fringed orchid	*Platanthera lacera*	X	X	X	X	X	X	
Green twayblade	*Liparis loeselii*	X	X			X		
Green violet	*Hybanthus concolor*	X	X	X				
Ground ivy	*GLECHOMA HEDERACEA*		X	X	X			X
Ground nut	*Apios americana*	X	X					X
Ground pine	*Lycopodium obscurum*	X	X				X	
Grove bluegrass	*Poa alsodes*	X	X	X	X		X	
Hackberry	*Celtis occidentalis*	X	X		X			X
Hair grass	*Agrostis hyemalis*	X	X	X			X	
Hair star sedge	*Carex atlantica s. capillacea*	X	X			X		
Hairy bedstraw	*Galium pilosum*	X	X	X				
Hairy bush clover	*Lespedeza hirta*	X	X	X				
Hairy gentian	*Gentiana villosa*	X	X	X				
Hairy gray sedge	*Carex hitchcockiana*	X	X	X				
Hairy hawkweed	*Hieracium gronovii*	X	X	X				

Table P-6. *continued*

Common Name	Scientific Name	Original Forest	Old Forest	Upland Forest	Floodplain Forest	Forested Wetlands	Flatwood Forest	Riparian Wooded Corridor
Hairy skullcap	*Scutellaria elliptica v. hirsuta*	X	X	X				
Hairy spicebush	*Lindera benzoin*	X	X	X				X
Hairy sweet cicely	*Osmorhiza claytonii*	X	X	X				
Hairy white goldenrod	*Solidago hispida*	X	X	X				
Halberd-leaved tear-thumb	*Persicaria arifolia*	X	X			X		
Handsome Harry	*Rhexia virginica*	X	X			X	X	
Harbinger of spring	*Erigenia bulbosa*	X	X	X	X			X
Hardhack	*Spiraea tomentosa*	X	X			X	X	
Harvey's buttercup	*Ranunculus harveyi*	X	X	X				
Heart-leaved skullcap	*Scutellaria ovata*	X	X	X				
Hedge apple	*MACLURA POMIFERA*			X	X			X
Helleborine orchid	*EPIPACTIS HELLEBORINE*		X	X				
Hemlock	*Tsuga canadensis*	X	X	X				
Hemlock parsley	*Conioselinum chinense*	X	X			X		
High-bush cranberry	*Viburnum opulus v. americanum*	X	X		X	X		
Hispid swamp buttercup	*Ranunculus hispidus v. caricetorum*	X	X		X	X		
Hoary beard tongue	*Penstemon canescens*	X	X	X				
Hog peanut	*Amphicarpaea bracteata v. bracteata*	X	X	X	X	X	X	X
Hollow Joe Pye weed	*Eupatoriadelphus fistulosus* (= *Eupatorium fistulosum*)	X	X	X	X			X
Honewort	*Cryptotaenia canadensis*	X	X	X	X		X	X
Honey locust	*Gleditsia triacanthos*	X	X	X	X			X
Hooked monkshood	*Aconitum uncinatum*	X	X	X				
Hooker's orchid	*Platanthera hookeri*	X	X	X				
Hop hornbeam	*Ostrya virginiana*	X	X	X				
Humped bladderwort	*Utricularia gibba*	X	X			X		
Hyssop hedge nettle	*Stachys hyssopifolia*	X	X			X		
Illinois wood sorrel	*Oxalis illinoensis*	X	X	X				
Indian cucumber root	*Medeola virginiana*	X	X	X				
Indian heliotrope	*HELIOTROPIUM INDICUM*		X		X			X
Indian physic	*Gillenia stipulata*	X	X	X				
Indian pink	*Spigelia marilandica*	X	X		X		X	
Indian tobacco	*Lobelia inflata*	X	X	X			X	
Indian turnip	*Arisaema triphyllum*	X	X	X	X			X
Indian wood oats	*Chasmanthium latifolium*	X	X	X	X			X
Interior horned beak rush	*Rhynchospora corniculata*	X	X		X	X	X	
Interrupted fern	*Osmunda claytoniana*	X	X	X				
Ivory sedge	*Carex eburnea*	X	X	X				
Jack oak	*Quercus imbricaria*	X	X	X	X			X
Japanese barberry	*BERBERIS THUNBERGII*		X	X	X			
Japanese chaff flower	*ACHYRANTHES JAPONICA*		X		X			
Japanese honeysuckle	*LONICERA JAPONICA*		X	X				
Japanese hops	*HUMULUS JAPONICUS*				X			
Jerusalem artichoke	*Helianthus tuberosus*	X	X		X			
Jetbead	*RHODOTYPOS SCANDENS*		X	X				
Juneberry	*Amelanchier arborea*	X	X	X				
Kentucky bluegrass	*POA PRATENSIS*		X	X				
Kentucky coffee tree	*Gymnocladus dioica*	X	X	X	X		X	X
Kentucky wisteria	*Wisteria frutescens*	X	X		X			X
Knobbed hop sedge	*Carex lupuliformis*	X	X		X	X		
Kral's sedge	*Carex kraliana*	X	X	X				
Lady fern	*Athyrium filix-femina s. angustum*	X	X	X				
Lance-leaved violet	*Viola lanceolata*	X	X				X	
Large flower bellwort	*Uvularia grandiflora*	X	X	X			X	
Large-leaf waterleaf	*Hydrophyllum macrophyllum*	X	X	X			X	
Large-leaved shinleaf	*Pyrola elliptica*	X	X	X				
Large-leaved storax	*Styrax grandifolia*	X	X	X				
Large white trillium	*Trillium grandiflorum*	X	X	X			X	
Late goldenrod	*Solidago gigantea*	X	X		X			X
Late horse gentian	*Triosteum perfoliatum*	X	X	X				
Late low blueberry	*Vaccinium pallidum*	X	X	X				
Leafy phacelia	*Phacelia bipinnatifida*	X	X	X				
Leafy wool grass	*Scirpus polyphyllus*	X	X			X	X	
Leather flower	*Clematis pitcheri*	X	X		X			X

Common Name	Scientific Name	Original Forest	Old Forest	Upland Forest	Floodplain Forest	Forested Wetlands	Flatwood Forest	Riparian Wooded Corridor
Leatherwood	*Dirca palustris*	X	X	X				
Leek sedge	*Carex prasina*	X	X	X		X		
Lesser celandine	*RANUNCULUS FICARIA*		X		X	X		
Little-leaf buttercup	*Ranunculus abortivus*	X	X	X	X		X	
Lizard's tail	*Saururus cernuus*	X	X		X	X		
Log fern	*Dryopteris celsa*	X	X			X		
Long-awned wood grass	*Brachyelytrum erectum*	X	X	X				
Long-fruited oval sedge	*Carex albolutescens*	X	X			X	X	
Long-scaled green sedge	*Carex bushii*	X	X	X			X	
Long-spurred violet	*Viola rostrata*	X	X	X				
Long-stalked hummock sedge	*Carex pedunculata*	X	X	X				
Loose-flowered panic grass	*Dichanthelium laxiflorum*	X	X	X				
Lopseed	*Phryma leptostachya*	X	X	X			X	
Mad-dog skullcap	*Scutellaria lateriflora*	X	X		X	X	X	
Maidenhair fern	*Adiantum pedatum*	X	X	X				
Maple-leaved arrowwood	*Viburnum acerifolium*	X	X	X				
Marsh bluegrass	*Poa paludigena*	X	X			X		
Marsh fleabane	*Erigeron philadelphicus*	X	X	X	X		X	
Marsh shield fern	*Thelypteris palustris v. pubescens*	X	X		X	X		
Marsh St. John's wort	*Triadenum tubulosum*	X	X		X	X		
Marsh St. John's wort	*Triadenum walteri*	X	X		X	X		X
Maryland senna	*Senna marilandica*	X	X	X	X			
May apple	*Podophyllum peltatum*	X	X	X	X		X	
Meadow beauty	*Rhexia mariana v. mariana*	X	X				X	
Miami mist	*Phacelia purshii*	X	X	X	X			
Michigan lily	*Lilium michiganense*	X	X	X		X	X	
Missouri violet	*Viola missouriensis*	X	X		X			
Moccasin flower	*Cypripedium acaule*	X	X			X		
Mockernut hickory	*Carya tomentosa*	X	X	X				
Monarda	*Monarda bradburiana*	X	X	X				
Moneywort	*LYSIMACHIA NUMMULARIA*		X	X	X	X	X	X
Monkey flower	*Mimulus ringens*	X	X		X	X	X	
Moonseed	*Menispermum canadense*	X	X	X	X		X	X
Mountain chestnut oak	*Quercus montana*	X	X	X				
Mountain laurel	*Kalmia latifolia*	X	X	X				
Mountain mint	*Pycnanthemum pycnanthemoides*	X	X	X				
Mountain phlox	*Phlox ovata*	X	X	X				
Nannyberry	*Viburnum lentago*	X	X			X		
Narrow-fruited pinweed	*Lechea racemulosa*	X	X	X				
Narrow-leaved cattail sedge	*Carex squarrosa*	X	X		X	X	X	
Narrow-leaved cow wheat	*Melampyrum lineare v. lineare*	X	X	X				
Narrow-leaved pinweed	*Lechea tenuifolia*	X	X	X				
Narrow-leaved sunflower	*Helianthus angustifolius*	X	X				X	
Narrow-leaved white-top aster	*Sericocarpus linifolius* (= *Aster solidagineus*)	X	X	X				
Narrow-leaved wood sedge	*Carex digitalis* (including 1 variety)	X	X	X				
Narrow melic grass	*Melica mutica*	X	X	X				
Nepalese browntop	*MICROSTEGIUM VIMINEUM*		X	X	X	X	X	X
Netted chainfern	*Woodwardia areolata*	X	X		X	X		
New Jersey tea	*Ceanothus americanus*	X	X	X				
New York fern	*Thelypteris noveboracensis*	X	X	X			X	
Nippled watermeal	*Wolffia braziliensis*	X	X			X		
Nits-and-lice	*Hypericum drummondii*	X	X	X				
Nodding fescue	*Festuca subverticillata*	X	X	X	X		X	X
Nodding pogonia	*Triphora trianthophora s. trianthophora*	X	X	X				
Nodding trillium	*Trillium cernuum*	X	X			X		
Northern bitter cress	*Cardamine douglassii*	X	X	X				
Northern grape fern	*Botrychium multifidum*	X	X	X				
Northern red oak	*Quercus rubra*	X	X	X			X	
Northern tubercled orchid	*Platanthera flava v. herbiola*	X	X		X	X		
Northern weak sedge	*Carex debilis v. rudgei*	X	X				X	
Nottoway valley brome	*Bromus nottowayanus*	X	X	X				X
Ohio buckeye	*Aesculus glabra*	X	X	X				
Ohio horse mint	*Blephilia ciliata*	X	X	X				

Table P-6. *continued*

Common Name	Scientific Name	Original Forest	Old Forest	Upland Forest	Floodplain Forest	Forested Wetlands	Flatwood Forest	Riparian Wooded Corridor
Oneida grape fern	*Botrychium oneidense*	X	X			X	X	
Orange coneflower	*Rudbeckia fulgida v. fulgida*	X	X	X				
Orange grass	*Hypericum gentianoides*	X	X	X				
Ostrich fern	*Matteuccia struthiopteris v. pensylvanica*	X	X	X	X			X
Overcup oak	*Quercus lyrata*	X	X		X	X		
Painted sedge	*Carex picta*	X	X	X				
Pale avens	*Geum virginianum*	X	X		X			X
Pale corydalis	*Corydalis flavula*	X	X	X	X			
Pale hickory	*Carya pallida*	X	X	X				
Pale Indian plantain	*Arnoglossum atriplicifolium* (= *Cacalia atriplicifolia*)	X	X	X				
Pale leafcup	*Polymnia canadensis*	X	X	X				
Pale touch-me-not	*Impatiens pallida*	X	X	X	X	X	X	X
Panicled hawkweed	*Hieracium paniculatum*	X	X	X				
Panicled screwstem	*Bartonia paniculata*	X	X				X	
Panicled tick trefoil	*Desmodium paniculatum*	X	X	X				
Papaw	*Asimina triloba*	X	X	X				
Paper birch	*Betula papyrifera*	X	X				X	
Partridge berry	*Mitchella repens*	X	X	X			X	
Pasture thistle	*Cirsium discolor*	X	X	X				
Pecan	*Carya illinoinensis*	X	X		X	X		X
Pennsylvania oak sedge	*Carex pensylvanica*	X	X	X				
Pennywort	*Obolaria virginica*	X	X	X				
Perfoliate bellwort	*Uvularia perfoliata*	X	X	X				
Persimmon	*Diospyros virginiana*	X	X	X	X		X	
Pignut hickory	*Carya glabra*	X	X	X				
Pinesap	*Monotropa hypopitys*	X	X	X				
Pink thoroughwort	*Fleischmannia incarnata* (= *Eupatorium incarnatum*)	X	X		X			
Pink turtlehead	*Chelone obliqua v. speciosa*	X	X		X	X		
Pink valerian	*Valeriana pauciflora*	X	X	X	X			
Pin oak	*Quercus palustris*	X	X		X	X	X	X
Pipes	*Equisetum fluviatile*	X	X			X		
Plantain-leaved wood sedge	*Carex plantaginea*	X	X	X				
Pointed tick trefoil	*Desmodium glutinosum*	X	X	X				
Poison ivy	*Toxicodendron radicans s. radicans*	X	X	X	X	X	X	X
Pokeweed	*Phytolacca americana v. americana*	X	X	X	X		X	X
Post oak	*Quercus stellata*	X	X	X			X	
Poverty oat grass	*Danthonia spicata*	X	X	X				
Prairie parsley	*Polytaenia nuttallii*	X	X	X				
Prairie wedge grass	*Sphenopholis obtusata v. obtusata*	X	X	X				
Prickly ash	*Zanthoxylum americanum*	X	X	X			X	
Princess tree	PAULOWNIA TOMENTOSA		X	X				
Pumpkin ash	*Fraxinus profunda*	X	X		X	X		
Purple chokeberry	*Photinia floribunda* (= *Aronia floribunda*)	X	X		X	X		
Purple-fringed orchid	*Platanthera psycodes*	X	X		X	X		
Purple fringeless orchid	*Platanthera peramoena*	X	X		X	X	X	
Purple Joe Pye weed	*Eupatoriadelphus purpureus*	X	X	X				
Purple loosestrife	LYTHRUM SALICARIA	X	X		X	X		
Purple milkweed	*Asclepias purpurascens*	X	X	X			X	
Purple twayblade	*Liparis liliifolia*	X	X	X				
Pussytoes	*Antennaria plantaginifolia*	X	X	X				
Quaking aspen	*Populus tremuloides*	X	X	X		X	X	
Rattlesnake fern	*Botrychium virginianum*	X	X	X	X		X	X
Rattlesnake plantain	*Goodyera pubescens*	X	X	X				
Rattlesnake weed	*Hieracium venosum*	X	X	X				
Red ash	*Fraxinus pennsylvanica v. pennsylvanica*	X	X		X			X
Red-berried elderberry	*Sambucus racemosa v. pubens*	X	X	X	X	X		
Red maple	*Acer rubrum v. rubrum*	X	X	X	X	X		
Red morning glory	IPOMOEA COCCINEA				X			
Red mulberry	*Morus rubra*	X	X	X	X		X	
Red trillium	*Trillium recurvatum*	X	X	X				
Reed bent grass	*Calamagrostis porteri s. insperata*	X	X	X				
Regal fern	*Osmunda regalis v. spectabilis*	X	X		X	X		
Rice cut grass	*Leersia oryzoides*	X	X		X	X		

Common Name	Scientific Name	Original Forest	Old Forest	Upland Forest	Floodplain Forest	Forested Wetlands	Flatwood Forest	Riparian Wooded Corridor
Riverbank wild rye	*Elymus riparius*	X	X		X			X
River birch	*Betula nigra*	X	X		X			X
Robin's plantain	*Erigeron pulchellus*	X	X	X				
Rock satin grass	*Muhlenbergia sobolifera*	X	X	X				
Rosette goldenrod	*Solidago squarrosa*	X	X	X				
Rough-leaved goldenrod	*Solidago patula*	X	X		X	X		
Rough-leaved rice grass	*Oryzopsis asperifolia*	X	X	X				
Round-fruited panic grass	*Dichanthelium sphaerocarpon*	X	X	X			X	
Round-leaved dogwood	*Cornus rugosa*	X	X	X				
Round-leaved hepatica	*Anemone americana* (= *Hepatica americana*)	X	X	X				
Round-leaved orchid	*Platanthera orbiculata*	X	X	X			X	
Round-leaved ragwort	*Packera obovata*	X	X	X				
Round-leaved shinleaf	*Pyrola americana*	X	X	X				
Round-leaved tick trefoil	*Desmodium rotundifolium*	X	X	X				
Running buffalo clover	*Trifolium stoloniferum*	X	X	X	X			
Running ground pine	*Lycopodium clavatum*	X	X	X			X	
Running savanna sedge	*Carex siccata*	X	X	X				
Running strawberry bush	*Euonymus obovata*	X	X	X				
Rushfoil	*Croton willdenowii*	X	X				X	
Rusty nannyberry	*Viburnum rufidulum*	X	X	X				
Sampson's snakeroot	*Orbexilum pedunculatum*	X	X	X			X	
Sassafras	*Sassafras albidum*	X	X	X			X	
Scarlet oak	*Quercus coccinea*	X	X	X				
Scorpion grass	*Myosotis macrosperma*	X	X	X				
Scotch pine	*PINUS SYLVESTRIS*			X				
Scrub pine	*Pinus virginiana*	X	X	X				
Seneca snakeroot	*Polygala senega*	X	X	X				
Sensitive fern	*Onoclea sensibilis*	X	X		X		X	
Sessile trillium	*Trillium sessile*	X	X	X				
Shagbark hickory	*Carya ovata*	X	X	X			X	
Sharp-lobed hepatica	*Anemone acutiloba* (= *Hepatica acutiloba*)	X	X	X				
Sheviak's yellow lady's slipper	*Cypripedium parviflorum v. makasin*	X	X			X		
Shining bedstraw	*Galium concinnum*	X	X	X				
Shining bur sedge	*Carex intumescens*	X	X		X		X	
Shining clubmoss	*Huperzia lucidula* (= *Lycopodium lucidulum*)	X	X	X				
Shining panic grass	*Dichanthelium lucidum*	X	X			X		
Shining wedge grass	*Sphenopholis nitida*	X	X	X				
Shooting star	*Dodecatheon meadia*	X	X	X				
Short-headed bracted sedge	*Carex cephalophora*	X	X	X				
Short's aster	*Symphyotrichum shortii*	X	X	X				
Short's streambank chervil	*Chaerophyllum procumbens v. shortii*	X	X	X	X			
Showy lady's slipper	*Cypripedium reginae*	X	X			X		
Showy orchis	*Galearis spectabilis* (= *Orchis spectabilis*)	X	X	X				
Shumard's oak	*Quercus shumardii v. shumardii*	X	X	X	X			
Side-flowering aster	*Symphyotrichum lateriflorum* (including 1 variety)	X	X		X			
Silky wild rye	*Elymus villosus* (including 1 variety)	X	X	X				
Silver maple	*Acer saccharinum*	X	X		X	X		
Silverrod	*Solidago bicolor*	X	X	X				
Silvery spleenwort	*Deparia acrostichoides* (= *Athyrium thelypterioides*)	X	X	X				
Skunk cabbage	*Symplocarpus foetidus*	X	X		X	X		
Slender green sedge	*Carex virescens*	X	X	X				
Slender-leaved panic grass	*Dichanthelium linearifolium*	X	X	X				
Slender satin grass	*Muhlenbergia tenuiflora*	X	X	X				
Slender sedge	*Carex leptalea*	X	X			X		
Slippery elm	*Ulmus rubra*	X	X	X	X			
Small carp grass	*ARTHRAXON HISPIDUS*				X			
Small-flowered crowfoot	*Ranunculus micranthus*	X	X	X	X		X	
Small forget-me-not	*Myosotis laxa*	X	X			X		
Small-fruited panic grass	*Dichanthelium dichotomum s. microcarpon*	X	X	X	X		X	X
Small-fruited panic grass	*Dichanthelium polyanthes*	X	X	X	X			
Small green wood orchid	*Platanthera clavellata*	X	X		X	X		
Small horse gentian	*Triosteum angustifolium*	X	X	X				
Small morning glory	*Ipomoea lacunosa*	X	X		X			X

Table P-6. *continued*

Common Name	Scientific Name	Original Forest	Old Forest	Upland Forest	Floodplain Forest	Forested Wetlands	Flatwood Forest	Riparian Wooded Corridor
Small passion flower	*Passiflora lutea*	X	X	X				
Small Solomon's seal	*Polygonatum biflorum*	X	X	X				
Small spearwort	*Ranunculus pusillus*	X	X		X	X	X	
Small's snakeroot	*Sanicula smallii*	X	X	X				
Small wood sunflower	*Helianthus microcephalus*	X	X	X				
Smooth beard tongue	*Penstemon calycosus*	X	X	X	X			X
Smooth false foxglove	*Aureolaria flava* (including 1 variety)	X	X	X				
Smooth forked aster	*Eurybia schreberi*	X	X	X				
Smooth ruellia	*Ruellia strepens*	X	X	X	X	X		X
Smooth satin grass	*Muhlenbergia glabriflora*	X	X		X		X	
Smooth-seeded nut rush	*Scleria oligantha*	X	X	X				
Smooth swamp buttercup	*Ranunculus hispidus v. nitidus*	X	X		X	X		X
Smooth white goldenrod	*Solidago erecta*	X	X	X				
Smooth white violet	*Viola blanda*	X	X	X			X	
Smooth wild licorice	*Galium circaezans v. circaezans*	X	X	X				
Snow trillium	*Trillium nivale*	X	X	X				
Soft agrimony	*Agrimonia pubescens*	X	X	X				
Solitary cat's foot	*Antennaria solitaria*	X	X	X				
Sourwood	*Oxydendron arboreum*	X	X	X				
Southern adder's tongue fern	*Ophioglossum vulgatum*	X	X	X	X		X	
Southern blazing star	*Liatris squarrulosa*	X	X	X				
Southern blue flag	*Iris virginica*	X	X		X	X		
Southern hop sedge	*Carex louisianica*	X	X		X	X	X	
Southern red oak	*Quercus falcata*	X	X	X				
Southern tubercled orchid	*Platanthera flava v. flava*	X	X		X	X		
Sparse-lobed grape fern	*Botrychium biternatum*	X	X	X	X	X	X	
Spearwort	*Ranunculus laxicaulis*	X	X		X			
Speckled alder	*Alnus incana s. rugosa*	X	X			X		
Spider lily	*Hymenocallis occidentalis*	X	X		X	X		
Spinulose wood fern	*Dryopteris carthusiana*	X	X		X	X	X	
Spotted touch-me-not	*Impatiens capensis*	X	X	X	X	X	X	X
Spotted wintergreen	*Chimaphila maculata*	X	X	X				
Spreading tick trefoil	*Desmodium humifusum*	X	X	X				
Spring beauty	*Claytonia virginica*	X	X	X	X		X	
Squirrel corn	*Dicentra canadensis*	X	X	X				
St. Andrew's cross	*Hypericum hypericoides s. multicaule*	X	X	X				
Stalked great chickweed	*Stellaria corei*	X	X	X				
Stalked water horehound	*Lycopus rubellus*	X	X			X		
Standing cypress	*IPOMOPSIS RUBRA*				X			X
Starved panic grass	*Dichanthelium depauperatum*	X	X	X				
Stickseed	*Hackelia virginiana*	X	X	X	X		X	X
Stiff gentian	*Gentianella quinquefolia s. occidentalis*	X	X	X				
Stiff yellow flax	*Linum striatum*	X	X	X			X	
Strawberry bush	*Euonymus americana*	X	X	X	X	X		
Sugarberry	*Celtis laevigata*	X	X		X	X		
Sugar maple	*Acer saccharum* (includes 2 subspecies)	X	X	X				
Summer grape	*Vitis aestivalis* (including 1 variety)	X	X	X				
Superb lily	*Lilium superbum*	X	X	X				
Swamp agrimony	*Agrimonia parviflora*	X	X		X	X		X
Swamp beggar's ticks	*Bidens discoidea*	X	X			X		
Swamp cottonwood	*Populus heterophylla*	X	X		X	X		
Swamp dock	*Rumex verticillatus*	X	X		X	X		
Swamp holly	*Ilex decidua*	X	X		X	X	X	X
Swamp loosestrife	*Decodon verticillatus*	X	X			X		
Swamp oval sedge	*Carex muskingumensis*	X	X		X			X
Swamp privet	*Forestiera acuminata*	X	X		X	X		
Swamp saxifrage	*Saxifraga pensylvanica v. pensylvanica*	X	X			X		
Swamp star sedge	*Carex seorsa*	X	X		X	X		
Swamp white oak	*Quercus bicolor*	X	X		X	X		
Swampy dewberry	*Rubus sec. Hispidus: R. hispidus*	X	X	X			X	
Swampy rose	*Rosa palustris*	X	X			X		
Sweetgum	*Liquidambar styraciflua*	X	X		X		X	
Sweet Indian plantain	*Hasteola suaveolens* (= *Cacalia suaveolens*)	X	X		X	X		

Common Name	**Scientific Name**	**Original Forest**	**Old Forest**	**Upland Forest**	**Floodplain Forest**	**Forested Wetlands**	**Flatwood Forest**	**Riparian Wooded Corridor**
Sweet-scented bedstraw	*Galium triflorum*	X	X	X				
Sycamore	*Platanus occidentalis*	X	X		X			X
Synandra	*Synandra hispidula*	X	X	X	X			X
Tall agrimony	*Agrimonia gryposepala*	X	X	X			X	
Tall blue lettuce	*Lactuca biennis*	X	X		X			
Tall melic grass	*Melica nitens*	X	X	X				
Tall scouring rush	*Equisetum hyemale s. affine*	X	X		X			
Tall stinging nettle	*Urtica dioica s. gracilis*	X	X		X			X
Tall thistle	*Cirsium altissimum*	X	X	X				
Tartarian honeysuckle	*LONICERA TATARICA*		X	X	X		X	X
Terrestrial water starwort	*Callitriche terrestris*	X	X	X				
Thicket bean	*Phaseolus polystachios*	X	X	X				
Thicket parsley	*Perideridia americana*	X	X		X		X	
Thin-leaved milkweed	*Asclepias perennis*	X	X		X	X		
Three-leaved stonecrop	*Sedum ternatum*	X	X	X				
Three-seeded mercury	*Acalypha rhomboidea*	X	X		X			X
Toothwort	*Cardamine concatenata*	X	X	X	X			
Tragia	*Tragia cordata*	X	X	X				
Trailing arbutus	*Epigaea repens*	X	X	X				
Trailing bush clover	*Lespedeza procumbens*	X	X	X				
Trailing ground pine	*Lycopodium digitatum*	X	X	X				
Tree-of-heaven	*AILANTHUS ALTISSIMA*			X				
Trumpet creeper	*Campsis radicans*	X	X	X	X		X	
Tulip poplar	*Liriodendron tulipifera*	X	X	X			X	
Twinleaf	*Jeffersonia diphylla*	X	X	X				
Two-flower false dandelion	*Krigia biflora*	X	X	X				
Two-leaved toothwort	*Cardamine diphylla*	X	X	X				
Umbrella flat sedge	*Cyperus diandrus*	X	X		X			
Umbrella magnolia	*Magnolia tripetala*	X	X	X				
Upland boneset	*Eupatorium sessilifolium*	X	X	X				
Variegated milkweed	*Asclepias variegata*	X	X	X				
Veiny pea	*Lathyrus venosus*	X	X	X				
Venus's looking glass	*Triodanis perfoliata*	X	X					
Violet bush clover	*Lespedeza violacea*	X	X	X				
Violet wood sorrel	*Oxalis violacea*	X	X	X				
Virginia bluebells	*Mertensia virginica*	X	X		X			
Virginia chainfern	*Woodwardia virginica*	X	X			X		
Virginia creeper	*Parthenocissus quinquefolia*	X	X	X	X		X	X
Virginia dayflower	*Commelina virginica*	X	X		X			
Virginia knotweed	*Tovara virginiana* (= *Polygonum virginianum*)	X	X	X	X		X	
Virginia mallow	*Sida hermaphrodita*	X	X					X
Virginia waterleaf	*Hydrophyllum virginianum*	X	X	X	X		X	X
Virginia wild rye	*Elymus virginicus* (including 1 variety)	X	X		X			X
Virginia willow	*Itea virginica*	X	X		X	X	X	
Wahoo	*Euonymus atropurpurea*	X	X	X	X			X
Water locust	*Gleditsia aquatica*	X	X		X	X		
Water parsnip	*Sium suave*	X	X		X	X		
Water purslane	*Didiplis diandra*	X	X		X	X		
Weak sedge	*Carex debilis v. debilis*	X	X				X	
Weak-stemmed wood sedge	*Carex laxiculmis v. laxiculmis*	X	X	X	X			
White adder's-mouth orchid	*Malaxis monophyllos v. brachypoda*	X	X			X		
White adder's tongue	*Erythronium albidum*	X	X	X	X		X	X
White ash	*Fraxinus americana*	X	X	X				
White basswood	*Tilia americana v. heterophylla*	X	X	X			X	
White grass	*Leersia virginica*	X	X	X	X		X	X
White mulberry	*MORUS ALBA*			X			X	X
White oak	*Quercus alba*	X	X	X			X	
White pine	*Pinus strobus*	X	X	X				
White snakeroot	*Ageratina altissima* (= *Eupatorium rugosum*)	X	X	X				
White vervain	*Verbena urticifolia v. urticifolia*	X	X		X		X	
Whorled milkweed	*Asclepias quadrifolia*	X	X	X				
Wild cucumber	*Echinocystis lobata*	X	X		X	X		X
Wild garlic	*Allium canadense*	X	X		X			

Table P-6. *continued*

Common Name	Scientific Name	Original Forest	Old Forest	Upland Forest	Floodplain Forest	Forested Wetlands	Flatwood Forest	Riparian Wooded Corridor
Wild geranium	*Geranium maculatum*	X	X	X				
Wild golden glow	*Rudbeckia laciniata*	X	X		X			X
Wild hydrangea	*Hydrangea arborescens*	X	X	X				
Wild leek	*Allium tricoccum v. burdickii*	X	X	X				
Wild leek	*Allium tricoccum v. tricoccum*	X	X	X				
Wild lettuce	*Lactuca canadensis*	X	X	X				
Wild madder	*Galium obtusum*	X	X		X			X
Wild petunia	*Ruellia caroliniensis*	X	X	X				
Wild quinine	*Parthenium integrifolium*	X	X				X	
Wild sensitive plant	*Chamaecrista nictitans*	X	X	X				
Wild sweet William	*Phlox maculata* (including 1 subspecies)	X	X				X	
Willdenow's grass sedge	*Carex willdenowii*	X	X	X				
Winged elm	*Ulmus alata*	X	X	X	X			
Winged euonymus	*EUONYMUS ALATA*		X	X				
Winged monkey flower	*Mimulus alatus*	X	X		X	X	X	X
Winged pigweed	*Cycloloma atriplicifolium*	X	X					
Wingstem	*Verbesina alternifolia*	X	X		X			X
Winterberry	*Ilex verticillata*	X	X		X	X		
Wintercreeper	*EUONYMUS FORTUNEI*		X	X	X			X
Witch hazel	*Hamamelis virginiana*	X	X	X				X
With rod	*Viburnum nudum v. cassinoides*	X	X			X		
Wolf's bluegrass	*Poa wolfii*	X	X	X				
Wolf's spike rush	*Eleocharis wolfii*	X	X			X	X	
Wood anemone	*Anemone quinquefolia*	X	X	X				
Wood angelica	*Angelica venenosa*	X	X	X				
Wood betony	*Pedicularis canadensis*	X	X	X				
Woodland agrimony	*Agrimonia rostellata*	X	X	X				
Woodland brome	*Bromus pubescens*	X	X	X				
Woodland sunflower	*Helianthus divaricatus*	X	X	X				
Wood millet	*Milium effusum v. cisatlanticum*	X	X			X		
Wood mint	*Blephilia hirsuta*	X	X	X				
Wood's stiff sedge	*Carex woodii*	X	X	X				
Woolly blue violet	*Viola sororia*	X	X	X	X	X	X	X
Yellow adder's tongue	*Erythronium americanum*	X	X	X				
Yellow birch	*Betula alleghaniensis*	X	X			X		
Yellow buckeye	*Aesculus flava*	X	X					
Yellow crownbeard	*Verbesina helianthoides*	X	X	X				
Yellow ladies' tresses	*Spiranthes ochroleuca*	X	X					
Yellow meadow parsnip	*Thaspium trifoliatum v. aureum*	X	X	X				
Yellow pimpernel	*Taenidia integerrima*	X	X	X				
Yellow screwstem	*Bartonia virginica*	X	X			X		
Yellow star grass	*Hypoxis hirsuta*	X	X	X				
Yellow water buttercup	*Ranunculus flabellaris*	X	X			X		
Yellowwood	*Cladrastis kentuckea*	X	X	X				
Yerba de tajo	*Eclipta prostrata*	X	X		X			

Note: Scientific names in all capital letters are exotic species.

Table P-7. Plant Species of Grasslands, including Savanna

Common Name	Scientific Name	Prairies	Historic Grasslands	Pastures	Fescue Fields	Hay Lands	Actively Mined Lands	Reclaimed Mine Lands	Vegetated Dunes/Swales	Savannas	Farm Bill Program Lands
Alfalfa	MEDICAGO SATIVA s. SATIVA			X	X	X	X	X			X
Allegheny vine	*Adlumia fungosa*									X	
Alsike clover	TRIFOLIUM HYBRIDUM			X	X	X	X	X			X
American bindweed	*Calystegia sepium* (including subspecies)			X	X			X			X
American filbert	*Corylus americana*		X						X	X	
American hops	*Humulus lupulus v. pubescens*										
American pennyroyal	*Hedeoma pulegioides*									X	
Amur honeysuckle	LONICERA MAACKII						X				
Annual bluegrass	POA ANNUA			X	X	X	X	X			X
Annual fleabane	*Erigeron annuus*			X			X	X			X
Appressed bog clubmoss	*Lycopodiella subappressa*		X						X		
Arrowfeather	*Aristida purpurascens*	X	X						X	X	
Arrow-leaved violet	*Viola sagittata v. sagittata*		X							X	
Autumn olive	ELAEAGNUS UMBELLATA							X		X	
Autumn sedge	*Fimbristylis autumnalis*								X		
Awned bent grass	*Agrostis elliottiana*			X							X
Axil flower	*Mecardonia acuminata*								X		
Barnyard grass	ECHINOCHLOA CRUS-GALLI			X			X	X			X
Bastard toadflax	*Comandra umbellata*										
Beach grass	*Ammophila breviligulata*								X		
Beach pea	*Lathyrus japonicus v. maritimus*								X		
Beach sumac	*Rhus aromatica v. arenaria*								X		
Beach three-awn grass	*Aristida tuberculosa*								X		
Beach wormwood	*Artemisia campestris s. caudata*								X		
Bearberry	*Arctostaphylos uva-ursi*								X	X	
Beard grass	*Gymnopogon ambiguus*								X		
Beggar's lice	LAPPULA SQUARROSA			X							
Belvedere summer cypress	KOCHIA SCOPARIA						X	X			
Bessey's sand cherry	*Prunus pumila v. besseyi*		X						X	X	
Bicknell's oval sedge	*Carex bicknellii*	X	X						X	X	
Big bluestem grass	*Andropogon gerardii*	X	X						X	X	X
Birdsfoot trefoil	LOTUS CORNICULATUS			X							
Bird's foot violet	*Viola pedata*								X		
Blackberry lily	BELAMCANDA CHINENSIS						X				
Black chokeberry	*Photinia melanocarpa*									X	
Black-eyed Susan	*Rudbeckia hirta v. hirta*	X							X	X	
Black hickory	*Carya texana*									X	
Blackjack oak	*Quercus marilandica*									X	
Black medick	MEDICAGO LUPULINA			X	X	X	X	X			X
Black mustard	BRASSICA NIGRA						X				X
Black oak	*Quercus velutina*									X	
Black oat grass	*Piptochaetium avenaceum* (= *Stipa avenacea*)		X							X	
Blazing star	*Liatris squarrosa*								X	X	
Blue curls	*Trichostema dichotomum*		X						X	X	
Blue hearts	*Buchnera americana*	X	X						X	X	
Blue joint grass	*Calamagrostis canadensis*	X	X						X		
Blue toadflax	*Nuttallanthus canadensis* (= *Linaria canadensis*)								X	X	
Bluevine	*Cynanchum laeve*				X						X
Bouncing bet	SAPONARIA OFFICINALIS			X	X		X	X			X
Boxwood knotweed	*Polygonum aviculare s. buxiforme*						X				
Bristly foxtail grass	SETARIA VERTICILLATA			X	X		X	X			X
Bristly locust	ROBINIA HISPIDA						X				
Bristly sarsaparilla	*Aralia hispida*								X		
Broom sedge	*Andropogon virginicus*	X	X	X	X		X		X	X	
Brown beak rush	*Rhynchospora capitellata*	X	X						X		
Buffalo berry	*Shepherdia canadensis*									X	
Buffalo bur	SOLANUM ROSTRATUM			X	X			X			X
Bulbous bluegrass	POA BULBOSA (including 1 subspecies)			X	X			X			X
Bulbous buttercup	RANUNCULUS BULBOSUS			X							
Bull thistle	CIRSIUM VULGARE	X		X	X	X	X	X			X
Bunch flower	*Melanthium virginicum*	X	X								
Bur oak	*Quercus macrocarpa*									X	
Bushy aster	*Symphyotrichum dumosum* (including 1 variety)								X	X	
Butter-and-eggs	LINARIA VULGARIS			X							

Table P-7. *continued*

Common Name	Scientific Name	Prairies	Historic Grasslands	Pastures	Fescue Fields	Hay Lands	Actively Mined Lands	Reclaimed Mine Lands	Vegetated Dunes/Swales	Savannas	Farm Bill Program Lands
Butterflyweed	*Asclepias tuberosa* (including 1 variety)	X		X				X		X	
Butterweed	*Packera glabella*						X				
Canada wild rye	*Elymus canadensis*	X	X						X	X	
Canadian bluegrass	*POA COMPRESSA*	X		X	X		X	X	X	X	X
Canadian rush	*Juncus canadensis*								X		
Canadian St. John's wort	*Hypericum canadense*								X		
Carolina anemone	*Anemone caroliniana*								X		
Catnip	*NEPETA CATARIA*			X	X		X	X			
Cat's foot	*Antennaria negletca*										
Cheat grass	*BROMUS TECTORUM*						X				X
Checkerberry	*Gaultheria procumbens*								X		
Cheeses	*MALVA NEGLECTA*						X				
Cherrybark oak	*Quercus pagoda*									X	
Chestnut sedge	*Fimbristylis puberula*								X		
Chicory	*CICHORIUM INTYBUS*			X	X		X	X			X
Cigar tree	*Catalpa speciosa*						X				
Clasping St. John's wort	*Hypericum gymnanthum*								X		
Cleft phlox	*Phlox bifida s. bifida*		X						X	X	
Climbing bittersweet	*Celastrus scandens*									X	
Clustered broom rape	*Orobanche fasciculata*								X		
Clustered false foxglove	*Agalinis fasciculata*									X	
Clustered poppy mallow	*Callirhoë triangulata*								X		
Clustered wild bean	*Strophostyles umbellata*								X	X	
Colic root	*Aletris farinosa*		X						X		
Common blackberry	*Rubus sec. Allegheniensis: R. allegheniensis*								X		
Common blue-eyed grass	*Sisyrinchium albidum*	X	X							X	
Common boneset	*Eupatorium perfoliatum*			X				X		X	
Common buckthorn	*RHAMNUS CATHARTICA*			X							
Common burdock	*ARCTIUM MINUS*						X				
Common catalpa	*CATALPA BIGNONIOIDES*						X				
Common chickweed	*STELLARIA MEDIA s. MEDIA*			X	X		X	X			X
Common cinquefoil	*Potentilla simplex*	X					X				
Common dandelion	*TARAXACUM OFFICINALE*			X	X	X	X	X			X
Common dayflower	*COMMELINA COMMUNIS*						X				
Common dewberry	*Rubus sec. Flagellares: R. flagellaris*			X			X		X		
Common evening primrose	*Oenothera biennis*			X	X		X	X			X
Common goat's beard	*TRAGOPOGON PRATENSIS*			X	X	X	X	X			X
Common groundsel	*SENECIO VULGARIS*							X			X
Common hops	*HUMULUS LUPULUS v. LUPULUS*										X
Common ironweed	*Vernonia fasciculata*	X								X	
Common juniper	*Juniperus communis v. depressa*								X		
Common milfoil	*Achillea millefolium*				X						X
Common milkweed	*Asclepias syriaca*	X		X	X		X	X	X		X
Common morning glory	*IPOMOEA PURPUREA*				X		X	X			X
Common mouse-ear chickweed	*CERASTIUM FONTANUM s. VULGARE*						X				X
Common pepper cress	*Lepidium virginicum*			X	X	X	X	X			X
Common plantain	*PLANTAGO MAJOR v. MAJOR*						X				
Common purpletop	*Tridens flavus*	X		X	X			X			
Common ragweed	*Ambrosia artemisiifolia v. elatior*						X				
Common reed	*Phragmites australis*	X					X				
Common rockrose	*Helianthemum canadense*		X						X	X	
Common sand bracted sedge	*Carex muehlenbergii v. muehlenbergii*		X						X	X	
Common sow thistle	*SONCHUS OLERACEUS*			X	X	X	X	X			X
Common spiderwort	*Tradescantia ohiensis*	X	X						X	X	
Common St. John's wort	*HYPERICUM PERFORATUM*			X			X	X			
Common sunflower	*HELIANTHUS ANNUUS*						X				X
Common teasel	*DIPSACUS FULLONUM*						X				
Common tussock sedge	*Carex stricta*	X	X						X		
Common water plantain	*Alisma subcordatum*									X	
Common whitlow cress	*Draba reptans*	X								X	
Compass plant	*Silphium laciniatum*	X	X								
Coralberry	*Symphoricarpos orbiculatus*									X	
Corn cockle	*AGROSTEMA GITHAGO*										X
Corn speedwell	*VERONICA ARVENSIS*			X		X	X	X			X

Common Name	Scientific Name	Prairies	Historic Grasslands	Pastures	Fescue Fields	Hay Lands	Actively Mined Lands	Reclaimed Mine Lands	Vegetated Dunes/Swales	Savannas	Farm Bill Program Lands
Cottonweed	*Froelichia floridana v. campestris*								X	X	
Cream wild indigo	*Baptisia bracteata v. leucophaea*	X	X								
Crested oval sedge	*Carex cristatella*									X	
Crowded oval sedge	*Carex cumulata*								X		
Crowfoot grass	*ELEUSINE INDICA*						X				
Crown vetch	*CORONILLA VARIA*			X	X		X	X			
Culver's root	*Veronicastrum virginicum*	X	X						X	X	
Curly dock	*RUMEX CRISPUS*			X	X	X	X	X			X
Cut-leaved prairie dock	*Silphium terebinthinaceum v. pinnatifidum*	X									
Cut-leaved teasel	*DIPSACUS LACINIATUS*						X				
Cylindrical blazing star	*Liatris cylindracea*	X	X							X	
Daisy fleabane	*Erigeron strigosus*	X		X							
Deam's dayflower	*Commelina erecta v. deamii*								X	X	
Deam's rockcress	*Arabis missouriensis*										
Deer-tongue grass	*Dicanthelium clandestinum*								X		
Deptford pink	*DIANTHUS ARMERIA*			X	X		X	X			X
Dogbane	*Apocynum cannabinum*	X			X						
Dog mint	*Clinopodium vulgare*								X		
Downy gentian	*Gentiana puberulenta*	X	X								
Downy lobelia	*Lobelia puberula v. simulans*									X	
Downy skullcap	*Scutellaria incana*									X	
Downy sunflower	*Helianthus mollis*	X	X						X	X	
Dune goldenrod	*Solidago simplex v. gillmanii*								X		
Dune sand cherry	*Prunus pumila v. pumila*								X		
Dune thistle	*Cirsium pitcheri*								X		
Dune willow	*Salix cordata*								X		
Dwarf bindweed	*Calystegia spithamaea*	X	X							X	
Dwarf chinquapin oak	*Quercus prinoides*									X	
Eared false foxglove	*Agalinis auriculata*	X	X								
Early fen sedge	*Carex crawei*		X						X		
Early figwort	*Scrophularia lanceolata*		X							X	
Early low blueberry	*Vaccinium angustifolium*									X	
Eastern blue-eyed grass	*Sisyrinchium atlanticum*								X		
Eastern cottonwood	*Populus deltoides*							X			
Eastern prickly pear	*Opuntia humifusa*								X		
Eastern sand cherry	*Prunus pumila v. susquehanae*		X						X	X	
English plantain	*PLANTAGO LANCEOLATA*			X	X		X	X			X
Elliott's broom sedge	*Andropogon gyrans*									X	
European sweet flag	*ACORUS CALAMUS*			X							
Expressway sedge	*CAREX PRAEGRACILIS*						X		X		
Fall panicum	*Panicum dichotomiflorum* (including 1 subspecies)				X		X	X			X
Fall witch grass	*Digitaria cognata* (= *Leptoloma cognatum*)	X	X						X	X	
False boneset	*Brickellia eupatorioides* (= *Kuhnia eupatoriodes*) (including 1 variety)	X	X							X	
False dandelion	*Pyrrhopappus carolinianus*								X	X	
False foxglove	*Agalinis purpurea*		X							X	
False green flat sedge	*Cyperus pseudovegetus*		X						X		
False heather	*Hudsonia tomentosa*								X		
False sunflower	*Heliopsis helianthoides* (including 1 variety)	X	X						X	X	
Fame flower	*Phemeranthus rugospermus* (= *Talinum rugospermum*)								X		
Fat-hen saltbush	*ATRIPLEX PATULA*						X	X			X
Featherbells	*Stenanthium gramineum*									X	
Fen betony	*Pedicularis lanceolata*								X		
Few-flowered nut rush	*Scleria pauciflora v. caroliniana*		X						X	X	
Few-flowered panic grass	*Dichanthelium oligosanthes v. oligosanthes*	X	X						X	X	
Field bindweed	*CONVOLVULUS ARVENSIS*			X	X	X	X	X			X
Field cress	*LEPIDIUM CAMPESTRE*			X	X	X	X	X			X
Field garlic	*ALLIUM VINEALE*			X	X	X		X			X
Field hedge parsley	*TORILIS ARVENSIS s. ARVENSIS*			X	X	X	X	X			X
Field milkwort	*Polygala sanguinea*								X	X	
Field nut sedge	*Cyperus esculentus v. leptostachyus*			X	X	X		X			X
Field penny cress	*THLASPI ARVENSE*			X	X	X	X	X			X
Field sorrel	*RUMEX ACETOSELLA*			X				X	X	X	X

Table P-7. *continued*

Common Name	Scientific Name	Prairies	Historic Grasslands	Pastures	Fescue Fields	Hay Lands	Actively Mined Lands	Reclaimed Mine Lands	Vegetated Dunes/Swales	Savannas	Farm Bill Program Lands
Field thistle	*CIRSIUM ARVENSE*	X		X	X	X	X	X	X		X
Flat-top aster	*Doellingeria umbellata* (= *Aster umbellatus*)										
Flax-leaved aster	*Ionactis linariifolius* (= *Aster linariifolius*)		X							X	
Floating bladderwort	*Utricularia radiata*								X		
Flowering dogwood	*Cornus florida*									X	
Flowering spurge	*Euphorbia corollata*	X	X							X	
Flower-of-an-hour	*HIBISCUS TRIONUM*							X			X
Foothill bedstraw	*CRUCIATA PEDEMONTANUM* (= *GALIUM PEDEMONTANUM*)							X		X	
Four-angled rose gentian	*Sabatia campanulata*		X						X		
Foxglove beard tongue	*Penstemon digitalis*									X	
French grass	*Orbexilum onobrychis* (= *Psoralea onobrychis*)	X								X	
Fringed brome	*Bromus ciliatus*	X	X							X	
Fringed gentian	*Gentianopsis crinita*								X		
Fringed puccoon	*Lithospermum incisum*	X	X								
Garden asparagus	*ASPARAGUS OFFICINALIS*						X				
Giant foxtail grass	*SETARIA FABERI*			X	X	X	X	X			X
Glaucous campion	*SILENE CSEREI*						X				
Globe-fruit primrose willow	*Ludwigia sphaerocarpa*								X		
Goat's rue	*Tephrosia virginiana*		X						X	X	
Golden aster	*Heterotheca camporum v. camporum* (= *Chrysopsis camporum*)	X						X	X		
Golden cassia	*Chamaecrista fasciculata* (= *Cassia fasciculata*)	X	X						X	X	
Grass-leaved goldenrod	*Euthamia graminifolia*	X	X						X	X	
Grass pink orchid	*Calopogon tuberosus*	X	X						X		
Gray dogwood	*Cornus racemosa*	X									
Great Plains ladies' tresses	*Spiranthes magnicamporum*	X	X							X	
Green brier	*Smilax glauca*									X	
Green-flowered milkweed	*Asclepias viridiflora*	X	X							X	
Green-flowered tick trefoil	*Desmodium viridiflorum*									X	
Green-fringed orchid	*Platanthera lacera*	X	X						X	X	
Green orchid	*Platanthera huronensis*									X	
Green twayblade	*Liparis loeselii*								X		
Ground cedar	*Lycopodium tristachyum*									X	
Hair bladderwort	*Utricularia subulata*								X		
Hair grass	*Agrostis hyemalis*									X	X
Hair sedge	*Bulbostylis capillaris*								X		
Hairy aster	*Symphyotrichum pilosum v. pilosum*			X	X		X	X			X
Hairy buttercup	*RANUNCULUS SARDOUS*			X							
Hairy crabgrass	*DIGITARIA SANGUINALIS*			X	X	X	X	X			X
Hairy false golden aster	*HETEROTHECA CAMPORUM v. GLANDULISSIMA*	X							X	X	
Hairy-fruited lake sedge	*Carex trichocarpa*	X	X						X		
Hairy green sedge	*Carex hirsutella*									X	
Hairy lens grass	*Paspalum setaceum v. muhlenbergii* (and additional varieties)							X	X		
Hairy puccoon	*Lithospermum caroliniense v. croceum*		X						X	X	
Hairy ruellia	*Ruellia humilis*	X	X						X	X	
Hairy tick trefoil	*Desmodium ciliare*									X	
Hall's tufted bulrush	*Schoenoplectus hallii*		X						X		
Handsome Harry	*Rhexia virginica*		X						X		
Hardhack	*Spiraea tomentosa*									X	
Harebell	*Campanula rotundifolia*									X	
Heath aster	*Symphyotrichum ericoides v. ericoides*	X									
Hedge apple	*MACLURA POMIFERA*			X							
Hedge mustard	*SISYMBRIUM OFFICINALE*			X	X	X	X	X			X
Henbit	*LAMIUM AMPLEXICAULE*			X	X	X	X	X			X
Hill's thistle	*Cirsium hillii*	X	X							X	
Hoary alyssum	*BERTEROA INCANA*					X					X
Hoary puccoon	*Lithospermum canescens*	X	X							X	
Hogwort	*CROTON CAPITATUS* (including 1 variety)			X			X				
Hollow Joe Pye weed	*Eupatoriadelphus fistolusus* (= *Eupatorium fistulosum*)									X	
Horned bladderwort	*Utricularia cornuta*								X		
Horsemint	*Monarda punctata v. villicaulis*		X						X	X	

Common Name	Scientific Name	Prairies	Historic Grasslands	Pastures	Fescue Fields	Hay Lands	Actively Mined Lands	Reclaimed Mine Lands	Vegetated Dunes/Swales	Savannas	Farm Bill Program Lands
Horse nettle	*Solanum carolinense*			X	X	X	X	X			X
Horsetail milkweed	*Asclepias verticillata*	X	X						X	X	
Horseweed	*Conyza canadensis*						X				
Hungarian brome	*BROMUS INERMIS*	X		X	X	X	X	X	X		X
Hyssop hedge nettle	*Stachys hyssopifolia*								X		
Illinois tick trefoil	*Desmodium illinoense*	X									
Indian grass	*Sorghastrum nutans*	X	X						X	X	X
Indian mustard	*BRASSICA JUNCEA*						X				
Indian paintbrush	*Castilleja coccinea*	X							X	X	
Inland New Jersey tea	*Ceanothus herbaceus*								X	X	
Ivy-leaved morning glory	*IPOMOEA HEDERACEA*			X	X	X		X			X
Jagged chickweed	*HOLOSTEUM UMBELLATUM*			X	X	X	X	X			
Japanese chess	*BROMUS JAPONICUS*			X		X	X	X			X
Japanese honeysuckle	*LONICERA JAPONICA*						X				
Japanese lespedeza	*KUMMEROWIA STRIATA*			X			X	X			X
Japanese rose	*ROSA MULTIFLORA*			X						X	
Jerusalem artichoke	*Helianthus tuberosus*	X		X				X			
Jimsonweed	*DATURA STRAMONIUM*			X							
Johnson grass	*SORGHUM HALEPENSE*			X	X	X	X	X			X
June grass	*Koeleria macrantha*									X	
Kankakee mallow	*Iliamna rivularis*								X		
Kentucky bluegrass	*POA PRATENSIS*	X		X	X		X	X	X	X	X
Kitten tails	*Besseya bullii*									X	
Knawel	*SCLERANTHUS ANNUUS*			X	X		X	X			X
Korean clover	*KUMMEROWIA STIPULACEA* (= *LESPEDEZA STIPULACEA*)			X			X	X			X
Lamb's quarters	*CHENOPODIUM ALBUM v. ALBUM*						X				
Lance-leaved violet	*Viola lanceolata*		X						X		
Late boneset	*Eupatorium serotinum*			X	X		X	X	X		X
Late horse gentian	*Triosteum perfoliatum*								X	X	
Lead plant	*Amorpha canescens*	X	X								
Leafy spurge	*EUPHORBIA ESULA*			X							
Lesser love grass	*ERAGROSTIS MINOR*						X				
Little barley	*Hordeum pusillum*						X	X			X
Little bluestem grass	*Schizachyrium scoparium* (= *Andropogon scoparius*)	X	X						X	X	X
Little-leaf buttercup	*Ranunculus abortivus*						X				
Long-awned bracted sedge	*Carex gravida*	X	X						X	X	
Long-bearded hawkweed	*Hieracium longipilum*		X						X	X	
Long-leaved ammannia	*Ammannia coccinea*								X		
Long-scaled nut sedge	*Cyperus strigosus*			X	X	X	X	X			X
Long-stoloned oak sedge	*Carex inops s. heliophila*								X		
Loosestrife	*Lysimachia hybrida*								X		
Lovage	*Ligusticum canadense*									X	
Low calamint	*Clinopodium arkansanum* (= *Satureja arkansanum*)									X	
Low hop clover	*TRIFOLIUM CAMPESTRE*			X	X	X	X	X			X
Marsh blazing star	*Liatris spicata*	X	X						X	X	
Marsh elder	*Iva annua* (including 1 variety)						X				
Marsh shield fern	*Thelypteris palustris v. pubescens*								X		
Maryland senna	*Ssenna marilandica*									X	
Mat sandbur	*Cenchrus longispinus*	X	X						X	X	
Meadow anemone	*Anemone canadensis*									X	
Meadow beauty	*Rhexia mariana v. mariana*		X						X		
Meadow fescue	*SCHEDONORUS PRATENSIS*			X	X		X	X			X
Meadowsweet	*Spiraea alba*	X	X						X		
Mead's milkweed	*Asclepias meadii*	X	X								
Mississippi milk pea	*Galactia volubilis*		X						X		
Missouri goldenrod	*Solidago missouriensis*	X									
Missouri ironweed	*Vernonia missurica*			X							
Mistflower	*Conoclinium coelestinum* (= *Eupatorium coelestinum*)			X	X						
Mockernut hickory	*Carya tomentosa*										
Moth mullein	*VERBASCUM BLATTARIA*			X	X	X	X	X			X
Motherwort	*LEONURUS CARDIACA*						X				
Musk bristle thistle	*CARDUUS NUTANS*				X		X	X			X

Table P-7. *continued*

Common Name	Scientific Name	Prairies	Historic Grasslands	Pastures	Fescue Fields	Hay Lands	Actively Mined Lands	Reclaimed Mine Lands	Vegetated Dunes/Swales	Savannas	Farm Bill Program Lands
Narrow-leaved cattail	*TYPHA ANGUSTIFOLIA*									X	
Narrow-leaved pinweed	*Lechea tenuifolia*										
New Jersey tea	*Ceanothus americanus*	X	X						X	X	
Night-flowering catchfly	*SILENE NOCTIFLORA*			X		X	X	X			X
Nimblewill	*Muhlenbergia schreberi*			X	X	X	X	X			X
Nodding brome	*BROMUS SQUARROSUS*								X		
Nodding spurge	*Chamaesyce nutans*						X				
Nodding wild onion	*Allium cernuum*	X	X							X	
Northern dropseed	*Sporobolus heterolepis*	X	X								
Northern rush grass	*Sporobolus vaginiflorus*						X			X	
Ohio goldenrod	*Solidago ohioensis*	X	X								
Ohio horse mint	*Blephilia ciliata*	X									
Oklahoma bracted sedge	*Carex oklahomensis*		X						X		
Old-field goldenrod	*Solidago nemoralis* (including 1 subspecies)			X	X		X		X		
Old plainsman	*Hymenopappus scabiosaeus*									X	
Old witch grass	*Panicum capillare*						X				X
Orange coneflower	*Rudbeckia fulgida v. fulgida*										
Orange day lily	*HEMEROCALLIS FULVA*						X				
Orange grass	*Hypericum gentianoides*		X						X		
Orchard grass	*DACTYLIS GLOMERATA*			X		X		X			X
Pale false foxglove	*Agalinis skinneriana*	X	X							X	
Pale gentian	*Gentiana alba*	X								X	
Pale hickory	*Carya pallida*									X	
Pale Indian plantain	*Arnoglossum atriplicifolium* (= *Cacalia atriplicifolia*)		X						X	X	
Pale purple coneflower	*Echinacea pallida*	X	X								
Pale spiked lobelia	*Lobelia spicata* (including varieties)	X	X						X	X	
Pale vetchling	*Lathyrus ochroleucus*		X						X	X	
Panicled tick trefoil	*Desmodium paniculatum*								X		
Paper birch	*Betula papyrifera*								X		
Pasture rose	*Rosa carolina*	X							X	X	
Pencil flower	*Stylosanthes biflora*								X		
Pennsylvania oak sedge	*Carex pensylvanica*		X							X	
Perennial rye grass	*LOLIUM PERENNE*				X						
Pineapple weed	*MATRICARIA DISCOIDEA*						X				
Pink corydalis	*Corydalis sempervirens*									X	
Pink milkwort	*Polygala incarnata*	X									
Pink thoroughwort	*Fleischmannia incarnata* (= *Eupatorium incarnatum*)			X							
Pinkweed	*Persicaria pensylvanica*	X		X			X	X			X
Poison hemlock	*CONIUM MACULATUM*			X	X		X	X			X
Poison ivy	*Toxicodendron radicans s. radicans*						X				
Pokeweed	*Phytolacca americana v. americana*				X		X	X			X
Poor Joe	*Plantago aristata*						X	X			X
Porcupine grass	*Hesperostipa spartea* (= *Stipa spartea*)	X							X		
Post oak	*Quercus stellata*									X	
Potato dwarf dandelion	*Krigia dandelion*								X	X	
Poverty grass	*Aristida dichotoma*									X	
Poverty oat grass	*Danthonia spicata*		X						X		
Prairie alumroot	*Heuchera richardsonii*	X									
Prairie blazing star	*Liatris pycnostachya*	X	X								
Prairie brome	*Bromus kalmii*	X	X							X	
Prairie cinquefoil	*Potentilla arguta*	X									
Prairie cord grass	*Spartina pectinata*	X	X						X		
Prairie coreopsis	*Coreopsis palmata*	X	X							X	
Prairie dock	*Silphium terebinthinaceum v. terebinthinaceum*	X	X								
Prairie hummock sedge	*Carex richardsonii*								X		
Prairie lily	*Lilium philadelphicum*	X	X							X	
Prairie milkweed	*Asclepias sullivantii*	X	X								
Prairie panic grass	*Dichanthelium leibergii*	X									
Prairie parsley	*Polytaenia nuttallii*	X									
Prairie sand reed	*Calamovilfa longifolia v. magna*								X	X	
Prairie satin grass	*Muhlenbergia cuspidata*	X	X								
Prairie sunflower	*Helianthus pauciflorus s. pauciflorus*	X	X								
Prairie switch grass	*Panicum virgatum*	X	X						X	X	X
Prairie violet	*Viola pedatifida*	X	X								

Common Name	Scientific Name	Prairies	Historic Grasslands	Pastures	Fescue Fields	Hay Lands	Actively Mined Lands	Reclaimed Mine Lands	Vegetated Dunes/Swales	Savannas	Farm Bill Program Lands
Prairie white-fringed orchid	*Platanthera leucophaea*	X	X								
Prairie willow	*Salix humilis* (including 1 variety)	X	X						X	X	
Prickly lettuce	*LACTUCA SERRIOLA*			X	X	X	X	X			X
Prickly sida	*SIDA SPINOSA*			X	X	X	X	X			X
Prickly sow thistle	*SONCHUS ASPER*			X		X	X				
Primrose-leaved violet	*Viola primulifolia*								X		
Puncture vine	*TRIBULUS TERRESTRIS*			X		X	X	X			X
Purple daisy	*Symphyotrichum patens*		X						X		
Purple dead nettle	*LAMIUM PURPUREUM*			X		X	X	X			X
Purple loosestrife	*LYTHRUM SALICARIA*									X	
Purple love grass	*Eragrostis spectabilis*	X	X						X	X	
Purple meadow rue	*Thalictrum dasycarpum*								X		
Purple milkweed	*Asclepias purpurascens*	X									
Purple milkwort	*Polygala polygama*		X						X	X	
Purple poppy mallow	*CALLIRHOË INVOLUCRATA*								X		
Purple prairie clover	*Dalea purpurea*	X	X							X	
Purple twayblade	*Liparis liliifolia*									X	
Purslane	*PORTULACA OLERACEA*			X	X		X	X			X
Pussytoes	*Antennaria plantaginifolia*									X	
Quackgrass	*ELYMUS REPENS* (= *AGROPYRON REPENS*)			X	X		X	X			X
Quaking aspen	*Populus tremuloides*									X	
Queen Anne's lace	*DAUCUS CAROTA*	X		X	X	X	X	X			X
Rattlesnake master	*Eryngium yuccifolium*	X	X							X	
Red clover	*TRIFOLIUM PRATENSE*			X	X	X	X	X			X
Red-stalked plantain	*Plantago rugelii* (including 1 variety)				X		X	X			X
Reed canary grass	*PHALARIS ARUNDINACEA*			X							
Regal fern	*Osmunda regalis v. spectabilis*		X						X		
Rigid goldenrod	*Solidago rigida* (including 1 subspecies)	X	X							X	
Robin's plantain	*Erigeron pulchellus*									X	
Rockrose	*Helianthemum bicknellii*		X						X	X	
Rock selaginella	*Selaginella rupestris*								X		
Rose gentian	*Sabatia angularis*		X							X	
Rosin weed	*Silphium integrifolium v. integrifolium*	X	X						X	X	
Rosin weed	*Silphium asteriscus v. trifoliatum*									X	
Rough barnyard grass	*Echinochloa muricata* (including 1 variety)						X				
Rough blazing star	*Liatris aspera* (including 1 variety)	X	X						X	X	
Rough cinquefoil	*Potentilla norvegica* (including 1 subspecies)			X	X		X	X			X
Rough-leaved rice grass	*Oryzopsis asperifolia*								X		
Rough marbleseed	*Onosmodium molle s. hispidissimum*			X							
Rough pennyroyal	*Hedeoma hispida*								X		
Rough pigweed	*AMARANTHUS RETROFLEXUS*						X				
Rough rush grass	*Sporobolus clandestinus*	X							X	X	
Rough sand sedge	*Cyperus schweinitzii*		X						X	X	
Rough white lettuce	*Prenanthes aspera*									X	
Round-fruited St. John's wort	*Hypericum sphaerocarpum*								X	X	
Round-headed bush clover	*Lespedeza capitata*	X	X						X	X	
Round-headed rush	*Juncus scirpoides*								X		
Round-leaved thoroughwort	*Eupatorium rotundifolium*									X	
Round-stemmed false foxglove	*Agalinis gattingeri*								X	X	
Royal catchfly	*Silene regia*	X	X						X	X	
Rue anemone	*Thalictrum thalictroides*		X							X	
Running savanna sedge	*Carex siccata*									X	
Russian thistle	*SALSOLA TRAGUS*						X				
Sampson's snakeroot	*Orbexilum pedunculatum*								X		
Sand coreopsis	*Coreopsis lanceolata*	X	X						X	X	
Sand croton	*Croton glandulosus v. septentrionalis*						X				
Sand dropseed	*Sporobolus cryptandrus*	X							X	X	
Sand goat's beard	*TRAGOPOGON DUBIUS*			X	X		X	X			X
Sand milkweed	*Asclepias amplexicaulis*		X						X	X	
Sand prairie phlox	*Phlox pilosa s. pilosa*	X	X						X	X	
Sand primrose	*Oenothera clelandii*								X		
Sand violet	*Viola sagittata v. ovata*		X						X	X	
Sassafras	*Sassafras albidum*										
Savanna blazing star	*Liatris scariosa v. nieuwlandii*		X						X	X	

Table P-7. *continued*

Common Name	Scientific Name	Prairies	Historic Grasslands	Pastures	Fescue Fields	Hay Lands	Actively Mined Lands	Reclaimed Mine Lands	Vegetated Dunes/Swales	Savannas	Farm Bill Program Lands
Sawtooth sunflower	*Helianthus grosseserratus*	X	X						X	X	
Scribner's panic grass	*Dichanthelium oligosanthes v. scribnerianum*		X						X	X	
Scurfy pea	*Psoralidium tenuiflorum (= Psoralea tenuiflora)*								X		
Sessile-leaved tick trefoil	*Desmodium sessilifolium*	X	X						X	X	
Shepherd's purse	*CAPSELLA BURSA-PASTORIS*			X	X	X	X	X	X		X
Shooting star	*Dodecatheon meadia*	X									
Shore St. John's wort	*Hypericum adpressum*		X						X		
Showy tick trefoil	*Desmodium canadense*	X									
Side-oats grama	*Bouteloua curtipendula*	X	X						X	X	
Silky aster	*Symphyotrichum sericeum*	X	X						X	X	
Silky bush clover	*LESPEDEZA CUNEATA*			X	X		X	X			X
Silver bluestem	*Andropogon ternarius*									X	
Silvery cinquefoil	*POTENTILLA ARGENTEA*			X	X			X			X
Sky-blue aster	*Symphyotrichum oolentangiense*	X								X	
Sleepy catchfly	*Silene antirrhina*						X	X			X
Slender bush clover	*Lespedeza virginica*		X						X	X	
Slender crabgrass	*Digitaria filiformis*								X		
Slender false foxglove	*Agalinis tenuifolia* (includes 2 varieties)									X	
Slender knotweed	*Polygonum tenue*								X	X	
Slender ladies' tresses	*Spiranthes lacera v. lacera*								X	X	
Slender-leaved panic grass	*Dichanthelium linearifolium*		X							X	
Slender mountain mint	*Pycnanthemum tenuifolium*	X	X						X	X	
Slender yellow flax	*Linum virginianum*		X						X	X	
Small burhead	*Echinodorus tenellus*								X		
Small-flowered half-chaff sedge	*Lipocarpha micrantha*	X							X	X	
Small green foxtail grass	*SETARIA VIRIDIS v. VIRIDIS*			X	X	X	X	X			X
Small horse gentian	*Triosteum angustifolium*									X	
Small-leaved tick trefoil	*Desmodium marilandicum*									X	
Small love grass	*Eragrostis pectinacea*			X	X	X	X	X			X
Small sundrops	*Oenothera perennis*	X	X						X	X	
Small wild bean	*Strophostyles leiosperma*		X						X	X	
Small wood sunflower	*Helianthus microcephalus*									X	
Small yellow flax	*Linum medium v. texanum*		X						X	X	
Small yellow sedge	*Carex cryptolepis*								X		
Smooth beard tongue	*Penstemon calycosus*									X	
Smooth blue aster	*Symphyotrichum laeve*	X	X								
Smooth field sow thistle	*SONCHUS ARVENSIS s. ULIGINOSUS*			X	X	X	X	X			X
Smooth-fruited oak sedge	*Carex tonsa v. tonsa*		X						X	X	
Smooth phlox	*Phlox glaberrima* (including subspecies)	X	X							X	
Smooth purslane speedwell	*Veronica peregrina s. peregrina*			X	X	X	X	X			X
Southern red oak	*Quercus falcata*									X	
Spanish needles	*Bidens bipinnata*						X				
Spear grass	*Poa chapmaniana*							X			X
Spiny cocklebur	*XANTHIUM SPINOSUM*			X	X	X	X	X			X
Spotted creeping spurge	*Chamaesyce maculata*						X				
Spotted knapweed	*CENTAUREA STOEBE s. MICRANTHOS*			X							
Squirrel-tail grass	*HORDEUM JUBATUM*						X	X			X
St. Andrew's cross	*Hypericum hypericoides s. multicaule*									X	
Stiff aster	*Solidago ptarmicoides*									X	
Stiff gentian	*Gentianella quinquefolia s. occidentalis*									X	
Stink grass	*ERAGROSTIS CILIANENSIS*			X	X	X	X	X			X
Storksbill	*ERODIUM CICUTARIUM*						X				
Sulfur cinquefoil	*POTENTILLA RECTA*			X							
Sullivant's orange coneflower	*Rudbeckia fulgida v. sullivantii*									X	
Swamp milkweed	*Asclepias incarnata*									X	
Sweet grass	*Hierochloë odorata*	X									
Tall boneset	*Eupatorium altissimum*	X		X	X		X	X			
Tall buttercup	*RANUNCULUS ACRIS*			X	X						
Tall coreopsis	*Coreopsis tripteris*	X	X						X	X	
Tall fescue	*SCHEDONORUS ARUNDINACEUS (= FESTUCA ELATIOR)*		X	X		X	X			X	
Tall goldenrod	*Solidago altissima* (including 1 subspecies)			X	X		X	X			X
Tall green milkweed	*Asclepias hirtella*	X							X	X	
Tall nut rush	*Scleria triglomerata*	X							X	X	

Common Name	Scientific Name	Prairies	Historic Grasslands	Pastures	Fescue Fields	Hay Lands	Actively Mined Lands	Reclaimed Mine Lands	Vegetated Dunes/Swales	Savannas	Farm Bill Program Lands
Tansy mustard	*DESCURAINIA PINNATA v. BRACHYCARPA*								X		
Tartarian honeysuckle	*LONICERA TATARICA*						X				
Three-awn grass	*Aristida longespica v. longespica*						X				
Three-square bulrush	*Schoenoplectus pungens*									X	
Thyme-leaved sandwort	*ARENARIA SERPYLLIFOLIA*						X				
Thyme-leaved speedwell	*VERONICA SERPYLLIFOLIA*			X	X	X		X			X
Timothy grass	*PHLEUM PRATENSE*			X	X	X	X	X			X
Toothed flat sedge	*Cyperus dentatus*								X		
Toothed spurge	*Euphorbia dentata* (= *Poinsettia dentata*)			X			X	X			X
Tragia	*Tragia cordata*									X	
Tumble mustard	*SISYMBRIUM ALTISSIMUM*			X							
Twig rush	*Cladium mariscoides*		X						X		
Twisted yellow-eyed grass	*Xyris torta*								X		
Two-colored bush clover	*LESPEDEZA BICOLOR*							X			X
Venus's looking glass	*Triodanis perfoliata*						X		X	X	
Virginia chainfern	*Woodwardia virginica*								X		
Virginia dwarf dandelion	*Krigia virginica*								X	X	
Virginia obedient plant	*Physostegia virginiana v. virginiana*	X	X							X	
Warty panic grass	*Panicum verrucosum*								X		
Waxy meadow rue	*Thalictrum revolutum*	X	X							X	
Western beard tongue	*Penstemon tubaeflorus*	X	X							X	
Western sunflower	*Helianthus occidentalis*	X	X						X	X	
Western wallflower	*Erysimum capitatum*	X									
Western wild lettuce	*Lactuca ludoviciana*	X	X								
White clover	*TRIFOLIUM REPENS*			X	X	X	X	X			X
White lady's slipper	*Cypripedium candidum*	X									
White oak	*Quercus alba*									X	
White prairie clover	*Dalea candida*	X	X							X	
White sweet clover	*MELILOTUS ALBA*			X	X	X	X	X			X
White thoroughwort	*Eupatorium album*									X	
White vervain	*Verbena urticifolia v. urticifolia*	X								X	
White wild indigo	*Baptisia alba v. macrophylla*	X	X						X	X	
Wild bergamot	*Monarda fistulosa* (including 1 variety)	X	X						X	X	
Wild four o'clock	*MIRABILIS NYCTAGINEA*			X			X				
Wild garlic	*Allium canadense*	X								X	
Wild hyacinth	*Camassia angusta*	X	X								
Wild lettuce	*Lactuca canadensis*	X		X							
Wild lupine	*Lupinus perennis*		X						X	X	
Wild parsnip	*PASTINACA SATIVA*			X	X			X			X
Wild petunia	*Ruellia caroliniensis*									X	
Wild quinine	*Parthenium integrifolium*	X	X								
Wild sensitive plant	*Chamaecrista nictitans*		X						X	X	
Wild strawberry	*Fragaria virginiana* (including 1 subspecies)	X	X	X					X	X	
Wild sweet potato	*Ipomoea pandurata*		X						X		
Willdenow's grass sedge	*Carex willdenowii*									X	
Willow aster	*Symphyotrichum praealtum* (including 1 variety)	X	X							X	
Windmill grass	*CHLORIS VERTICILLATA*			X					X		
Winged loosestrife	*Lythrum alatum*									X	
Winged oval sedge	*Carex alata*	X							X		
Winged pigweed	*Cycloloma atriplicifolium*									X	
Winter vetch	*VICIA VILLOSA s. VILLOSA*			X	X	X	X	X			X
Wolf's spike rush	*Eleocharis wolfii*								X		
Wood angelica	*Angelica venenosa*								X	X	
Wood betony	*Pedicularis canadensis*		X						X	X	
Wool grass	*Scirpus cyperinus*								X		
Woolly mullein	*VERBASCUM THAPSUS*			X	X		X	X			X
Wrinkle-fruited oak sedge	*Carex tonsa v. rugosperma*								X		
Yellow coneflower	*Ratibida pinnata*	X	X						X	X	
Yellow-eyed grass	*Xyris difformis*		X						X		
Yellow rocket	*BARBAREA VULGARIS*						X				
Yellow sweet clover	*MELILOTUS OFFICINALIS*			X	X	X	X	X			X
Yellow wild indigo	*Baptisia tinctoria*								X		

Note: Scientific names in all capital letters are exotic species.

Table P-8. Plant Species of Wetlands

Common Name	Scientific Name	Forested Wetlands (Ephemeral and Permanent)	Shrub/Scrub Wetlands (Ephemeral and Permanent)	Emergent Wetlands (Ephemeral and Permanent)	Herbaceous Wetlands (Ephemeral and Permanent)	Farmed Wetlands	Drained Wetlands	Ditched Wetlands	Mudfdlats
Alder buckthorn	*Rhamnus alnifolia*		X	X	X				
American brooklime	*Veronica americana*	X							
American burnet	*Sanguisorba canadensis*				X				
American bur reed	*Sparganium americanum*			X					
American filbert	*Corylus americana*		X						
American larch	*Larix laricina*	X							
American lotus	*Nelumbo lutea*			X					
American sweet flag	*Acorus americanus*			X	X				
Angled spike rush	*Eleocharis quadrangulata*			X	X				
Angle-stemmed primrose willow	*Ludwigia leptocarpa*			X	X		X	X	X
Annual purple bladderwort	*Utricularia resupinata*				X				
Appressed bog clubmoss	*Lycopodiella subappressa*				X				
Arbor vitae	*Thuja occidentalis*	X							
Arrow arum	*Peltandra virginica*	X		X					
Arrowgrass	*Scheuchzeria palustris*				X				
Arrow-leaved tear-thumb	*Persicaria sagittata*	X	X	X					
Atlantic star sedge	*Carex atlantica s. atlantica*	X							
Autumn sedge	*Fimbristylis autumnalis*				X			X	X
Axil flower	*Mecardonia acuminata*				X				X
Bald cypress	*Taxodium distichum*	X							
Barnyard grass	*ECHINOCHLOA CRUS-GALLI*				X	X	X	X	X
Bent-seeded hop sedge	*Carex tuckermanii*	X							
Bishop's cap	*Mitella diphylla*	X							
Bittersweet nightshade	*SOLANUM DULCAMARA*		X	X	X	X	X	X	
Black ash	*Fraxinus nigra*	X							
Black chokeberry	*Photinia melanocarpa*	X	X						
Bluebead	*Clintonia borealis*	X							
Blue joint grass	*Calamagrostis canadensis*			X	X				
Blue star	*Amsonia tabernaemontana v. salicifolia*			X					
Blue water iris	*Iris brevicaulis*			X					
Blunt spike rush	*Eleocharis obtusa*				X	X	X	X	X
Bog bladderwort	*Utricularia geminiscapa*				X				
Bog clubmoss	*Lycopodiella inundata (= Lycopodium inundatum)*				X				X
Bog goldenrod	*Solidago uliginosa*				X				
Bog lobelia	*Lobelia kalmii*				X				
Bog rosemary	*Andromeda polifolia v. glaucophylla*				X				
Bottlebrush sedge	*Carex lurida*				X				
Bracted water willow	*Dicliptera brachiata*	X							
Branched bur reed	*Sparganium androcladum*			X					
Bristly aster	*Symphyotrichum puniceum*	X		X	X				
Bristly cattail sedge	*Carex frankii*				X				
Bristly sedge	*Carex comosa*		X	X					
Broad-leaved cattail	*Typha latifolia*		X	X	X		X	X	X
Broad-leaved panicled sedge	*Carex decomposita*	X	X						
Broad-leaved wild rice	*Zizania aquatica v. aquatica*			X					
Brome hummock sedge	*Carex bromoides*	X							
Brown beak rush	*Rhynchospora capitellata*				X				
Brown fox sedge	*Carex vulpinoidea*				X				
Buckbean	*Menyanthes trifoliata*				X				
Bulb bitter cress	*Cardamine bulbosa*	X							
Bulblet-bearing water hemlock	*Cicuta bulbifera*	X	X	X					
Bullhead lily	*Nuphar variegata*		X	X	X				
Bunchberry	*Cornus canadensis*	X							
Bunch flower	*Melanthium virginicum*				X				
Buttonbush	*Cephalanthus occidentalis*	X	X	X					
Buttonbush dodder	*Cuscuta cephalanthi*		X						
Canada wood nettle	*Laportea canadensis*	X							
Canadian bluegrass	*POA COMPRESSA*						X	X	
Canadian rush	*Juncus canadensis*				X				
Canadian St. John's wort	*Hypericum canadense*				X				X
Cardinal flower	*Lobelia cardinalis*	X		X	X			X	
Carolina mosquito fern	*Azolla caroliniana*	X	X						X

Common Name	Scientific Name	Forested Wetlands (Ephemeral and Permanent)	Shrub/Scrub Wetlands (Ephemeral and Permanent)	Emergent Wetlands (Ephemeral and Permanent)	Herbaceous Wetlands (Ephemeral and Permanent)	Farmed Wetlands	Drained Wetlands	Ditched Wetlands	Mudfdlats
Catbird grape	*Vitis palmata*	X	X						
Catchfly grass	*Leersia lenticularis*		X	X					
Cinnamon fern	*Osmunda cinnamomea*	X							
Cinnamon willow herb	*Epilobium coloratum*		X	X	X				
Clammy hedge hyssop	*Gratiola neglecta*				X	X	X	X	X
Clasping St. John's wort	*Hypericum gymnanthum*				X				X
Climbing dayflower	*COMMELINA DIFFUSA*	X					X	X	
Climbing dogbane	*Trachelospermum difforme*	X							
Climbing hempweed	*Mikania scandens*	X							
Clinton's wood fern	*Dryopteris clintoniana*	X							
Closed gentian	*Gentiana andrewsii*				X				
Colic root	*Aletris farinosa*				X				X
Common arrowhead	*Sagittaria latifolia*		X	X	X		X	X	X
Common beggar's ticks	*Bidens frondosa*		X	X	X				
Common bog arrow grass	*Triglochin maritima*				X				
Common boneset	*Eupatorium perfoliatum*				X				
Common bur reed	*Sparganium eurycarpum*			X	X				
Common bur sedge	*Carex grayi*	X							
Common forget-me-not	*MYOSOTIS SCORPIOIDES*			X	X				
Common fox sedge	*Carex stipata v. stipata*	X	X	X	X				
Common hop sedge	*Carex lupulina*	X							
Common horsetail	*Equisetum arvense*				X		X	X	
Common lake sedge	*Carex lacustris*		X	X	X				
Common ninebark	*Physocarpus opulifolius* (including 1 variety)		X						
Common reed	*Phragmites australis*			X	X		X	X	
Common rush	*Juncus effusus*			X	X		X	X	X
Common spiderwort	*Tradescantia ohiensis*				X				
Common tussock sedge	*Carex stricta*			X	X				
Common valerian	*Valeriana edulis v. ciliata*				X				
Common water hemlock	*Cicuta maculata* (including 1 variety)	X	X						
Common water plantain	*Alisma subcordatum*			X	X	X	X	X	X
Common wood reed	*Cinna arundinacea*	X							
Common yellow lake sedge	*Carex utriculata*			X					
Cowbane	*Oxypolis rigidior*	X	X						
Creeping bracted sedge	*Carex socialis*	X							
Creeping love grass	*Eragrostis hypnoides*				X				X
Creeping primrose willow	*Ludwigia peploides s. glabrescens*			X	X			X	X
Creeping yellow cress	*RORIPPA SYLVESTRIS*						X	X	X
Crested oval sedge	*Carex cristatella*				X				
Crested wood fern	*Dryopteris cristata*	X	X	X	X				
Dainties	*Phyllanthus caroliniensis*								X
Dark-green bulrush	*Scirpus atrovirens*				X		X	X	
Dark-scaled sedge	*Carex buxbaumii*			X	X				
Dense cotton grass	*Eriophorum vaginatum*				X				
Ditch stonecrop	*Penthorum sedoides*			X	X		X	X	X
Dragon's mouth	*Arethusa bulbosa*				X				
Drummond's half-chaff sedge	*Lipocarpha drummondii* (= *Hemicarpha drummondii*)				X				X
Dutchman's pipe	*Aristolochia tomentosa*	X							
Dwarf birch	*Betula pumila*		X		X				
Dwarf ginseng	*Panax trifolius*	X							
Early coralroot	*Corallorhiza trifida*	X							
Early ladies' tresses	*Spiranthes lucida*				X				
Eastern blue-eyed grass	*Sisyrinchium atlanticum*				X				
Eastern sea rocket	*CAKILE EDENTULA v. EDENTULA*				X				
Engelmann's spike rush	*Eleocharis engelmannii*				X	X		X	X
Erect primrose willow	*Ludwigia decurrens*			X	X			X	X
European high-bush cranberry	*VIBURNUM OPULUS v. OPULUS*	X	X						
European sweet flag	*ACORUS CALAMUS*			X	X		X	X	
False asphodel	*Triantha glutinosa* (= *Tofieldia glutinosa*)				X				
False bristly sedge	*Carex pseudocyperus*		X	X	X				
False foxglove	*Agalinis purpurea*				X				X
False green flat sedge	*Cyperus pseudovegetus*			X	X				X

Table P-8. *continued*

Common Name	Scientific Name	Forested Wetlands (Ephemeral and Permanent)	Shrub/Scrub Wetlands (Ephemeral and Permanent)	Emergent Wetlands (Ephemeral and Permanent)	Herbaceous Wetlands (Ephemeral and Permanent)	Farmed Wetlands	Drained Wetlands	Ditched Wetlands	Mudfdlats
False loosestrife	*Ludwigia glandulosa*			X	X		X	X	X
False mermaidweed	*Proserpinaca palustris* (including 1 variety)	X	X	X	X				
False pimpernel	*Lindernia dubia v. dubia*				X	X	X	X	X
False rusty nut sedge	*Cyperus engelmannii*			X	X	X	X	X	X
Featherfoil	*Hottonia inflata*	X	X						
Fen betony	*Pedicularis lanceolata*	X			X				
Fen panicled sedge	*Carex prairea*				X				
Fen star sedge	*Carex sterilis*				X				
Fen thistle	*Cirsium muticum*		X	X	X				
Fen willow herb	*Epilobium leptophyllum*				X				
Few-flowered bog sedge	*Carex pauciflora*				X				
Five leaves	*Isotria verticillata*				X				
Flat-leaved bladderwort	*Utricularia intermedia*			X	X				
Flat-top aster	*Doellingeria umbellata* (= *Aster umbellatus*)		X		X				
Floating bladderwort	*Utricularia radiata*			X					
Floating manna grass	*Glyceria septentrionalis*	X	X	X	X				
Fog fruit	*Phyla lanceolata*				X				
Follicle sedge	*Carex folliculata*	X							
Fowl bluegrass	*Poa palustris*			X					
Fowl manna grass	*Glyceria striata*	X	X	X	X				
Fringed brome	*Bromus ciliatus*			X	X				
Fringed gentian	*Gentianopsis crinita*				X				
Fringed loosestrife	*Lysimachia ciliata*	X							
Fringed sedge	*Carex crinita*	X	X						
Frog's bit	*Limnobium spongia*	X	X						
Garden loosestrife	*LYSIMACHIA VULGARIS*				X			X	X
Giant chickweed	*MYOSOTON AQUATICUM*				X		X	X	
Giant ragweed	*Ambrosia trifida*						X	X	
Giant St. John's wort	*Hypericum pyramidatum*				X				
Glaucous white lettuce	*Prenanthes racemosa*				X				
Globe-fruit primrose willow	*Ludwigia sphaerocarpa*				X				
Globose watermeal	*Wolffia columbiana*	X							
Glossy buckthorn	*FRANGULA ALNUS* (= *RHAMNUS FRANGULA*)	X	X						
Golden saxifrage	*Chrysosplenium americanum*	X							
Goldthread	*Coptis trifolia*	X							
Grass-leaved arrowhead	*Sagittaria graminea*			X					
Grass-leaved goldenrod	*Euthamia graminifolia*			X	X				
Grass-of-parnassus	*Parnassia glauca*				X				
Grass pink orchid	*Calopogon tuberosus*				X				
Gray dogwood	*Cornus racemosa*		X						
Great angelica	*Angelica atropurpurea*			X	X				
Great blue lobelia	*Lobelia siphilitica*			X	X		X	X	
Great bulrush	*Schoenoplectus tabernaemontani* (= *Scirpus validus*)			X	X		X	X	X
Great duckweed	*Spirodela polyrhiza*	X							
Greater hop sedge	*Carex gigantea*	X							
Great spike rush	*Eleocharis palustris*			X	X				X
Great water dock	*Rumex orbiculatus v. borealis*			X					
Green-fringed orchid	*Platanthera lacera*	X	X	X	X		X	X	
Green orchid	*Platanthera huronensis*				X				
Green twayblade	*Liparis loeselii*	X			X				
Green yellow sedge	*Carex viridula*				X				
Grove bluegrass	*Poa alsodes*	X							
Hair beak rush	*Rhynchospora capillacea*				X				
Hair bladderwort	*Utricularia subulata*				X				
Hair sedge	*Bulbostylis capillaris*				X				X
Hair star sedge	*Carex atlantica s. capillacea*	X							
Hairy crabgrass	*DIGITARIA SANGUINALIS*							X	
Hairy-fruited lake sedge	*Carex trichocarpa*				X				
Hairy rose mallow	*Hibiscus moscheutos v. occidentalis*		X						
Hairy-seeded nut rush	*Scleria muhlenbergii*			X	X				X
Halberd-leaved rose mallow	*Hibiscus laevis*		X						
Halberd-leaved tear-thumb	*Persicaria arifolia*	X	X						

Common Name	Scientific Name	Forested Wetlands (Ephemeral and Permanent)	Shrub/Scrub Wetlands (Ephemeral and Permanent)	Emergent Wetlands (Ephemeral and Permanent)	Herbaceous Wetlands (Ephemeral and Permanent)	Farmed Wetlands	Drained Wetlands	Ditched Wetlands	Mudfdlats
Hall's tufted bulrush	*Schoenoplectus hallii*				X	X			X
Handsome Harry	*Rhexia virginica*				X				
Hardhack	*Spiraea tomentosa*				X				
Heard-stemmed bulrush	*Schoenoplectus acutus* (= *Scirpus acutus*)			X	X			X	X
Hemlock parsley	*Conioselinum chinense*	X			X				
High-bush blueberry	*Vaccinium corymbosum*		X						
High-bush cranberry	*Viburnum opulus v. americanum*	X							
Hispid swamp buttercup	*Ranunculus hispidus v. caricetorum*	X							
Hoary willow	*Salix candida*		X						
Hollow Joe Pye weed	*Eupatoriadelphus fistulosus* (= *Eupatorium fistulosum*)		X				X	X	
Hooded ladies' tresses	*Spiranthes romanzoffiana*				X				
Horned beak rush	*Rhynchospora macrostachya*				X				X
Horned bladderwort	*Utricularia cornuta*				X				
Humped bladderwort	*Utricularia gibba*	X	X						
Hungarian brome	*BROMUS INERMIS*						X	X	
Indian paintbrush	*Castilleja coccinea*				X				
Inland meadow beauty	*Rhexia mariana v. interior*				X				
Interior horned beak rush	*Rhynchospora corniculata*	X	X	X	X				
Interrupted fern	*Osmunda claytoniana*	X							
Japanese hops	*HUMULUS JAPONICUS*				X	X	X		
Kentucky bluegrass	*POA PRATENSIS*				X	X	X	X	
Knobbed hop sedge	*Carex lupuliformis*	X							
Lance-leaved buckthorn	*Rhamnus lanceolata* (including 1 subspecies)		X						
Lance-leaved violet	*Viola lanceolata*				X				X
Large buttonweed	*Diodia virginiana*				X				X
Large cranberry	*Vaccinium macrocarpon*				X				
Large yellow sedge	*Carex flava*				X				
Lead-colored stiff sedge	*Carex livida v. grayana*				X				
Leafy wool grass	*Scirpus polyphyllus*	X							
Leather flower	*Clematis pitcheri*		X						
Leatherleaf	*Chamaedaphne calyculata*		X		X				
Leek sedge	*Carex prasina*	X							
Lesser celandine	*RANUNCULUS FICARIA*	X							
Lizard's tail	*Saururus cernuus*	X	X	X	X				
Log fern	*Dryopteris celsa*	X							
Long-beaked bald rush	*Rhynchospora scirpoides*								X
Long-bracted tussock sedge	*Carex aquatilis v. substricta*			X	X				
Long-leaved ammannia	*Ammannia coccinea*				X	X	X	X	X
Long-scaled manna grass	*Glyceria acutiflora*		X						
Low calamint	*Clinopodium arkansanum* (= *Satureja arkansanum*)				X				
Low nut rush	*Scleria verticillata*				X				
Mad-dog skullcap	*Scutellaria lateriflora*	X	X						
Marsh bellflower	*Campanula aparinoides*			X	X				
Marsh blazing star	*Liatris spicata*				X				
Marsh bluegrass	*Poa paludigena*	X			X				
Marsh cinquefoil	*Comarum palustre* (= *Potentilla palustris*)			X	X				
Marsh purslane	*Ludwigia palustris*				X		X	X	X
Marsh shield fern	*Thelypteris palustris v. pubescens*			X	X				
Marsh skullcap	*Scutellaria galericulata*		X	X	X				
Marsh St. John's wort	*Triadenum tubulosum*	X							
Marsh St. John's wort	*Triadenum virginicum*			X	X				
Marsh St. John's wort	*Triadenum walteri*	X							
Marsh valerian	*Valeriana uliginosa*				X				
Marsh vetchling	*Lathyrus palustris*			X	X				
Marsh yellow cress	*Rorippa palustris s. fernaldiana*				X	X	X	X	X
Meadow anemone	*Anemone canadensis*				X				
Meadow beauty	*Rhexia mariana v. mariana*				X				
Meadowsweet	*Spiraea alba*		X	X					
Mild water pepper	*Persicaria hydropiperoides*			X	X				
Moccasin flower	*Cypripedium acaule*	X							
Moneywort	*LYSIMACHIA NUMMULARIA*	X	X	X	X		X	X	X
Monkey flower	*Mimulus ringens*	X	X	X	X		X	X	X

Table P-8. *continued*

Common Name	Scientific Name	Forested Wetlands (Ephemeral and Permanent)	Shrub/Scrub Wetlands (Ephemeral and Permanent)	Emergent Wetlands (Ephemeral and Permanent)	Herbaceous Wetlands (Ephemeral and Permanent)	Farmed Wetlands	Drained Wetlands	Ditched Wetlands	Mudfdlats
Nannyberry	*Viburnum lentago*	X	X						
Narrow-leaved cattail	*TYPHA ANGUSTIFOLIA*			X	X		X	X	
Narrow-leaved cattail sedge	*Carex squarrosa*	X							
Narrow-leaved cotton grass	*Eriophorum angustifolium*				X				
Narrow-leaved loosestrife	*Lysimachia quadriflora*				X				
Narrow-leaved sundew	*Drosera intermedia*				X				
Narrow-leaved wild rice	*Zizania palustris* (including 1 variety)			X					
Narrow-leaved woolly sedge	*Carex lasiocarpa s. americana*			X	X				
Needle spike rush	*Eleocharis acicularis*			X	X		X	X	X
Nepalese browntop	*MICROSTEGIUM VIMINEUM*	X	X	X	X	X	X	X	
Netted chainfern	*Woodwardia areolata*	X							
Netted nut rush	*Scleria reticularis*				X				
Nippled watermeal	*Wolffia braziliensis*	X							
Nits-and-lice	*Hypericum drummondii*								X
Nodding wild onion	*Allium cernuum*				X				
Northern blue violet	*Viola nephrophylla*				X				
Northern bog orchid	*Platanthera aquilonis*	X			X				
Northern dropseed	*Sporobolus heterolepis*				X				
Northern panic grass	*Dichanthelium boreale*				X				
Northern tubercled orchid	*Platanthera flava v. herbiola*				X				
Obe-wan-conobea	*Leucospora multifida*			X	X				
Ohio goldenrod	*Solidago ohioensis*				X				
Oklahoma bracted sedge	*Carex oklahomensis*				X				
Old witch grass	*Panicum capillare*				X				X
Oneida grape fern	*Botrychium oneidense*	X							
Orange-fringed orchid	*Platanthera ciliaris*				X				
Overcup oak	*Quercus lyrata*	X							
Pale dogwood	*Cornus obliqua*		X						
Pale manna grass	*Torreyochloa pallida* (= *Glyceria pallida*)	X	X	X					
Pale touch-me-not	*Impatiens pallida*	X			X				
Pecan	*Carya illinoinensis*	X							
Pickerel weed	*Pontederia cordata*			X					
Pink turtlehead	*Chelone obliqua v. speciosa*	X							
Pinkweed	*Persicaria pensylvanica*				X				
Pipes	*Equisetum fluviatile*	X		X				X	
Pipewort	*Eriocaulon aquaticum*								X
Pitcher plant	*Sarracenia purpurea s. gibbosa*				X				
Poison ivy	*Toxicodendron radicans s. radicans*	X							
Poison sumac	*Toxicodendron vernix*	X	X						
Porcupine sedge	*Carex hystericina*			X	X				
Prairie cord grass	*Spartina pectinata*			X	X				
Prairie Indian plantain	*Arnoglossum plantagineum*				X				
Prairie star sedge	*Carex interior*				X				
Pumpkin ash	*Fraxinus profunda*	X							
Purple chokeberry	*Photinia floribunda* (= *Aronia floribunda*)	X	X						
Purple-fringed orchid	*Platanthera psycodes*	X	X						
Purple fringeless orchid	*Platanthera peramoena*	X		X	X		X	X	
Purple-headed sneezeweed	*Helenium flexuosum*				X		X	X	
Purple loosestrife	*LYTHRUM SALICARIA*		X	X	X		X	X	
Purple meadow rue	*Thalictrum dasycarpum*			X	X		X	X	
Purslane	*PORTULACA OLERACEA*				X	X	X	X	X
Queen-of-the-prairie	*Filipendula rubra*				X				
Rattlesnake manna grass	*Glyceria canadensis*		X	X	X				
Red-berried elderberry	*Sambucus racemosa v. pubens*	X							
Red maple	*Acer rubrum v. rubrum*	X							
Red osier dogwood	*Cornus sericea*		X	X					
Red-rooted nut sedge	*Cyperus erythrorhizos*			X	X		X	X	X
Reed canary grass	*PHALARIS ARUNDINACEA*		X	X	X		X	X	
Regal fern	*Osmunda regalis v. spectabilis*	X							
Rice cut grass	*Leersia oryzoides*	X		X	X		X	X	
Riddell's goldenrod	*Solidago riddellii*				X				
River bulrush	*Bolboschoenus fluviatilis* (= *Scirpus fluviatilis*)			X	X				

Common Name	Scientific Name	Forested Wetlands (Ephemeral and Permanent)	Shrub/Scrub Wetlands (Ephemeral and Permanent)	Emergent Wetlands (Ephemeral and Permanent)	Herbaceous Wetlands (Ephemeral and Permanent)	Farmed Wetlands	Drained Wetlands	Ditched Wetlands	Mudflats
Rose pogonia	*Pogonia ophioglossoides*				X				
Rough barnyard grass	*Echinochloa muricata* (including 1 variety)				X	X	X	X	X
Rough-leaved goldenrod	*Solidago patula*	X	X	X	X				
Round-headed rush	*Juncus scirpoides*				X				
Round-leaved sundew	*Drosera rotundifolia*				X				X
Running bog sedge	*Carex oligosperma*				X				
Running marsh sedge	*Carex sartwellii*			X	X				
Rush aster	*Symphyotrichum boreale* (= *Aster borealis*)				X				
Rusty cotton grass	*Eriophorum virginicum*				X				
Salt meadow grass	*Leptochloa panicoides*				X				X
Seedbox	*Ludwigia alternifolia*			X	X		X	X	
Sensitive fern	*Onoclea sensibilis*			X	X		X	X	X
Sessile-flowered cress	*Rorippa sessiliflora*				X	X	X	X	X
Sheviak's yellow lady's slipper	*Cypripedium parviflorum v. makasin*	X							
Shining aster	*Symphyotrichum firmum*			X	X				
Shining panic grass	*Dichanthelium lucidum*	X							
Shining willow	*Salix lucida*		X						
Shore St. John's wort	*Hypericum adpressum*				X				
Short's sedge	*Carex shortiana*			X	X		X	X	
Showy lady's slipper	*Cypripedium reginae*	X			X				
Shrubby cinquefoil	*Dasiphora fruticosa s. floribunda* (= *Potentilla fruticosa*)				X				
Side-flowering aster	*Symphyotrichum lateriflorum* (including 1 variety)	X							
Silver maple	*Acer saccharinum*	X							
Skunk cabbage	*Symplocarpus foetidus*	X	X		X				
Slender bog arrow grass	*Triglochin palustris*				X				
Slender cotton grass	*Eriophorum gracile*				X				
Slender false foxglove	*Agalinis tenuifolia* (includes 2 varieties)				X				X
Slender false pimpernel	*Lindernia dubia v. anagallidea*				X	X	X	X	X
Slender panic grass	*Panicum flexile*				X				
Slender sedge	*Carex leptalea*	X			X				
Slimpod rush	*Juncus diffusissimus*				X	X	X	X	X
Small burhead	*Echinodorus tenellus*								X
Small carp grass	*ARTHRAXON HISPIDUS*				X			X	
Small clubmoss	*Selaginella eclipes*				X				
Small cranberry	*Vaccinium oxycoccos*				X				
Small enchanter's nightshade	*Circaea alpina*	X							
Small-flowered half-chaff sedge	*Lipocarpha micrantha*								X
Small forget-me-not	*Myosotis laxa*	X							
Small-fringed gentian	*Gentianopsis virgata*				X				
Small green wood orchid	*Platanthera clavellata*	X							
Small yellow sedge	*Carex cryptolepis*				X				
Smartweed	*Persicaria punctata*			X	X				
Smith's tufted bulrush	*Schoenoplectus smithii* (including 1 variety)			X	X				X
Smooth swamp buttercup	*Ranunculus hispidus v. nitidus*	X							
Snailseed pondweed	*Potamogeton bicupulatus*			X					
Southern blue flag	*Iris virginica*	X		X	X				
Southern lake sedge	*Carex hyalinolepis*			X	X		X	X	
Spatterdock	*Nuphar advena*			X					
Spearwort	*Ranunculus laxicaulis*				X				X
Speckled alder	*Alnus incana s. rugosa*	X	X						
Spider lily	*Hymenocallis occidentalis*	X							
Spotted Joe Pye weed	*Eupatoriadelphus maculatus*			X	X				
Spotted touch-me-not	*Impatiens capensis*	X							
Stalked water horehound	*Lycopus rubellus*	X	X						
Stiff arrowhead	*Sagittaria rigida*			X					
Straw oval sedge	*Carex suberecta*				X				
Sullivant's orange coneflower	*Rudbeckia fulgida v. sullivantii*				X				
Swamp agrimony	*Agrimonia parviflora*			X	X				
Swamp beggar's ticks	*Bidens discoidea*	X	X						
Swamp candles	*Lysimachia terrestris*			X					
Swamp cottonwood	*Populus heterophylla*	X							
Swamp dock	*Rumex verticillatus*	X	X	X					

Table P-8. *continued*

Common Name	Scientific Name	Forested Wetlands (Ephemeral and Permanent)	Shrub/Scrub Wetlands (Ephemeral and Permanent)	Emergent Wetlands (Ephemeral and Permanent)	Herbaceous Wetlands (Ephemeral and Permanent)	Farmed Wetlands	Drained Wetlands	Ditched Wetlands	Mudflats
Swamp loosestrife	*Decodon verticillatus*	X							
Swamp milkweed	*Asclepias incarnata*			X	X			X	
Swamp privet	*Forestiera acuminata*	X							
Swamp rose mallow	*Hibiscus moscheutos v. moscheutos*		X						
Swamp saxifrage	*Saxifraga pensylvanica v. pensylvanica*	X	X		X				
Swamp star sedge	*Carex seorsa*	X							
Swampy rose	*Rosa palustris*	X	X	X					
Sweet grass	*Hierochloë odorata*				X				
Sweet Indian plantain	*Hasteola suaveolens* (= *Cacalia suaveolens*)			X	X				
Tall cotton grass	*Eriophorum viridicarinatum*				X				
Tall white orchid	*Platanthera dilatata*				X				
Thick-stalked arrowhead	*Sagittaria montevidensis s. calycina*			X					X
Three-seeded bog sedge	*Carex trisperma*	X	X		X				
Three-square bulrush	*Schoenoplectus pungens*			X	X				X
Three-way sedge	*Dulichium arundinaceum*		X	X	X				
Toad rush	*Juncus bufonius*				X	X	X	X	
Toothed flat sedge	*Cyperus dentatus*				X				
Torrey's rush	*Juncus torreyi*			X	X				
Tufted hair grass	*Deschampsia cespitosa*				X				
Twig rush	*Cladium mariscoides*				X				
Twisted yellow-eyed grass	*Xyris torta*				X				X
Two-flowered rush	*Juncus biflorus*				X	X	X	X	X
Umbrella flat sedge	*Cyperus diandrus*								X
Umbrella sedge	*Fuirena pumila*				X				X
Virginia chainfern	*Woodwardia virginica*	X							
Virginia willow	*Itea virginica*	X	X						
Warty panic grass	*Panicum verrucosum*				X				X
Water arum	*Calla palustris*	X		X	X				
Water bulrush	*Schoenoplectus subterminalis*			X					
Water cress	*RORIPPA NASTURTIUM-AQUATICUM*			X	X				
Water heartsease	*Persicaria amphibia v. emersa* (= *Polygonum coccineum*)		X	X	X				
Water hyssop	*Bacopa rotundifolia*			X	X				X
Water locust	*Gleditsia aquatica*	X							
Water marigold	*Magalodonta beckii* (= *Bidens beckii*)			X					
Water parsnip	*Sium suave*	X	X	X	X				
Water pennywort	*Hydrocotyle umbellata*				X				X
Water willow	*Justicia americana*			X					
Waxy meadow rue	*Thalictrum revolutum*				X				
Wheelwort	*Rotala ramosior*				X		X	X	X
White adder's-mouth orchid	*Malaxis monophyllos v. brachypoda*	X							
White beak rush	*Rhynchospora alba*				X				
White camass	*Zigadenus elegans*				X				
White grass	*Leersia virginica*	X							
White lady's slipper	*Cypripedium candidum*				X				
White pine	*Pinus strobus*	X							
White vervain	*Verbena urticifolia v. urticifolia*				X				
Wicket spike rush	*Eleocharis rostellata*				X				
Wild bergamot	*Monarda fistulosa* (including 1 variety)				X				
Wild sweet William	*Phlox maculata* (including 1 subspecies)			X	X				
Winged loosestrife	*Lythrum alatum*				X				
Winged monkey flower	*Mimulus alatus*	X	X	X	X		X	X	X
Winged oval sedge	*Carex alata*				X				
Winterberry	*Ilex verticillata*	X	X						
With rod	*Viburnum nudum v. cassinoides*	X							
Wolf's spike rush	*Eleocharis wolfii*	X			X				
Wood millet	*Milium effusum v. cisatlanticum*	X							
Wool grass	*Scirpus cyperinus*			X	X				
Yellow birch	*Betula alleghaniensis*	X							
Yellow-eyed grass	*Xyris difformis*								X
Yellow screwstem	*Bartonia virginica*	X			X				
Yellow water buttercup	*Ranunculus flabellaris*	X	X						

Note: Scientific names in all capital letters are exotic species.

Table P-9. Plant Species of Aquatic Systems and Sandbars

Common Name	Scientific Name	Rivers/Streams	Oxbows/Lakes	Sand/Gravel Bars
American bindweed	*Calystegia sepium* (including subspecies)			X
American lotus	*Nelumbo lutea*		X	
American pondweed	*Potamogeton nodosus*	X	X	
Angled spike rush	*Eleocharis quadrangulata*		X	
Angle-stemmed primrose willow	*Ludwigia leptocarpa*			X
Annual purple bladderwort	*Utricularia resupinata*		X	
Balloon vine	*CARDIOSPERMUM HALICACABUM*			X
Barnyard grass	*ECHINOCHLOA CRUS-GALLI*			X
Beaked corn salad	*Valerianella radiata*			X
Beaked tussock sedge	*Carex torta*			X
Beefsteak plant	*PERILLA FRUTESCENS* (including 1 variety)			X
Beginner's pondweed	*POTAMOGETON CRISPUS*		X	
Big bluestem grass	*Andropogon gerardii*			X
Blade duckweed	*Wolffiella gladiata*		X	
Blue wild indigo	*Baptisia australis*			X
Brazilian waterweed	*EGERIA DENSA*		X	
Bristly cattail sedge	*Carex frankii*			X
Brittle naiad	*NAJAS MINOR*		X	
Broad-leaved small pondweed	*Potamogeton pusillus s. tennuissimus*		X	
Brown fox sedge	*Carex vulpinoidea*			X
Buttonbush	*Cephalanthus occidentalis*		X	
Canada clearweed	*Pilea pumila*			X
Carolina figwort	*Cabomba caroliniana*		X	
Carolina mosquito fern	*Azolla caroliniana*		X	
Carolina willow	*Salix caroliniana*			X
Clammy hedge hyssop	*Gratiola neglecta*			X
Clammy weed	*Polanisia dodecandra s. dodecandra*			X
Climbing dayflower	*COMMELINA DIFFUSA*			X
Comb pondweed	*Stuckenia pectinata* (= *Potamogeton pectinatus*)	X	X	
Common bladderwort	*Utricularia macrorhiza*		X	
Common dodder	*Cuscuta gronovii* (including 1 variety)			X
Common horsetail	*Equisetum arvense*			X
Common naiad	*Najas flexilis*	X	X	
Common ninebark	*Physocarpus opulifolius* (including 1 variety)			X
Common pondweed	*Potamogeton natans*		X	
Common satin grass	*Muhlenbergia frondosa*			X
Common waterweed	*Elodea canadensis*	X	X	
Coontail	*Ceratophyllum demersum*	X	X	
Creeping burhead	*Echinodorus cordifolius*		X	
Creeping love grass	*Eragrostis hypnoides*			X
Creeping primrose willow	*Ludwigia peploides s. glabrescens*		X	
Crooked aster	*Symphyotrichum prenanthoides*			X
Crown vetch	*CORONILLA VARIA*			X
Deer-tongue grass	*Dichanthelium clandestinum*			X
Dinky duckweed	*Lemna minuta*		X	
Dwarf crested iris	*Iris cristata*			X
Early ladies' tresses	*Spiranthes lucida*			X
Early-leaved brome	*Bromus latiglumis*			X
Eel grass	*Vallisneria americana*	X	X	
Engelmann's quillwort	*Isoetes engelmannii*	X	X	
Erect primrose willow	*Ludwigia decurrens*		X	
European water milfoil	*MYRIOPHYLLUM SPICATUM*	X	X	
False mermaidweed	*Proserpinaca palustris* (including 1 variety)		X	
Featherfoil	*Hottonia inflata*		X	
Fern pondweed	*Potamogeton robbinsii*		X	
Flat-stemmed pondweed	*Potamogeton zosteriformis*		X	
Fog fruit	*Phyla lanceolata*			X
Forked aster	*Eurybia furcata* (= *Aster furcatus*)			X
Forked duckweed	*Lemna trisulca*		X	
Fragrant water lily	*Nymphaea odorata s. tuberosa*	X	X	
Fries's pondweed	*Potamogeton friesii*		X	
Frost grape	*Vitis vulpina*			X
Garden loosestrife	*LYSIMACHIA VULGARIS*			X
Garden phlox	*Phlox paniculata*			X
Globose watermeal	*Wolffia columbiana*		X	
Grass-leaved pondweed	*Potamogeton gramineus*	X	X	
Great blue lobelia	*Lobelia siphilitica*			X

Table P-9. *continued*

Common Name	Scientific Name	Rivers/Streams	Oxbows/Lakes	Sand/Gravel Bars
Great duckweed	*Spirodela polyrhiza*		X	
Great white lettuce	*Prenanthes crepidinea*			X
Green amaranth	*AMARANTHUS HYBRIDUS*			X
Ground ivy	*GLECHOMA HEDERACEA*			X
Ground nut	*Apios americana*			X
Heart-leaved plantain	*Plantago cordata*	X		
Holly-leaved naiad	*NAJAS MARINA*		X	
Honewort	*Cryptotaenia canadensis*			X
Horned beak rush	*Rhynchospora macrostachya*		X	
Horned pondweed	*Zannichellia palustris*		X	
Horsetail spike rush	*Eleocharis equisetoides*		X	
Humped bladderwort	*Utricularia gibba*		X	
Illinois bundle flower	*Desmanthus illinoensis*			X
Illinois pondweed	*Potamogeton illinoensis*		X	
Inland New Jersey tea	*Ceanothus herbaceus*			X
Japanese chaff flower	*ACHYRANTHES JAPONICA*			X
Japanese hops	*HUMULUS JAPONICUS*			X
Jerusalem artichoke	*Helianthus tuberosus*			X
Lake cress	*Armoracia lacustris*	X	X	
Lance-leaved burhead	*Echinodorus berteroi*		X	
Large buttonweed	*Diodia virginiana*			X
Large-leaved pondweed	*Potamogeton amplifolius*		X	
Large water starwort	*Callitriche heterophylla*	X	X	
Late goldenrod	*Solidago gigantea*			X
Leafy pondweed	*Potamogeton foliosus*		X	
Least duckweed	*Lemna perpusilla*		X	
Long-beaked bald rush	*Rhynchospora scirpoides*		X	
Long-scaled nut sedge	*Cyperus strigosus*			X
Mare's tail	*Hippuris vulgaris*	X	X	
Marsh purslane	*Ludwigia palustris*	X	X	X
Moneywort	*LYSIMACHIA NUMMULARIA*			X
Needle spike rush	*Eleocharis acicularis*		X	
Nippled watermeal	*Wolffia braziliensis*		X	
Nodding bur marigold	*Bidens cernua*			X
Nodding spurge	*Chamaesyce nutans*			X
Oakes' pondweed	*Potamogeton oakesianus*		X	
Old witch grass	*Panicum capillare*			X
Pale dogwood	*Cornus obliqua*			X
Pale duckweed	*Lemna valdiviana*		X	
Perennial duckweed	*Lemna turionifera*		X	
Pink thoroughwort	*Fleischmannia incarnata* (= *Eupatorium incarnatum*)			X
Pipewort	*Eriocaulon aquaticum*		X	
Prairie switch grass	*Panicum virgatum*			X
Purple bladderwort	*Utricularia purpurea*		X	
Purple duckweed	*Lemna obscura*		X	
Purple loosestrife	*LYTHRUM SALICARIA*			X
Purslane	*PORTULACA OLERACEA*			X
Redhead grass	*Potamogeton richardsonii*		X	
Red morning glory	*IPOMOEA COCCINEA*			X
Red-rooted nut sedge	*Cyperus erythrorhizos*			X
Red-rooted spike rush	*Eleocharis erythropoda*			X
Ribbon-leaved pondweed	*Potamogeton epihydrus*	X	X	
Riverbank tussock sedge	*Carex emoryi*			X
Riverbank wild rye	*Elymus riparius*			X
River birch	*Betula nigra*			X
Rough barnyard grass	*Echinochloa muricata* (including 1 variety)			X
Rough water milfoil	*Myriophyllum pinnatum*		X	
Running buffalo clover	*Trifolium stoloniferum*			X
Salt meadow grass	*Leptochloa panicoides*		X	
Sandbar love grass	*Eragrostis frankii*			X
Sand grape	*Vitis rupestris*			X
Short's goldenrod	*Solidago shortii*			X
Slender naiad	*Najas gracillima*		X	
Slender water milfoil	*Myriophyllum tenellum*		X	
Slender waterweed	*Elodea nuttallii*		X	
Small carp grass	*ARTHRAXON HISPIDUS*			X
Small duckweed	*Lemna minor*		X	

Common Name	Scientific Name	Rivers/Streams	Oxbows/Lakes	Sand/Gravel Bars
Small love grass	*Eragrostis pectinacea*			X
Small morning glory	*Ipomoea lacunosa*			X
Small pondweed	*Potamogeton pusillus s. pusillus*	X	X	
Snailseed pondweed	*Potamogeton bicupulatus*		X	
Southern naiad	*Najas guadalupensis* (including 1 subspecies)	X	X	
Spatterdock	*Nuphar advena*	X	X	
Spiked water milfoil	*Myriophyllum sibiricum*		X	
Spiny coontail	*Ceratophyllum echinatum*		X	
Spotted pondweed	*Potamogeton pulcher*		X	
Spotted watermeal	*Wolffia borealis*		X	
Standing cypress	*IPOMOPSIS RUBRA*			X
Stiff pondweed	*Potamogeton strictifolius*		X	
Swollen duckweed	*Lemna gibba*		X	
Tall scouring rush	*Equisetum hyemale s. affine*			X
Three-nerved duckweed	*Lemna aequinoctialis*		X	
Three-square bulrush	*Schoenoplectus pungens*			X
Various-leaved water milfoil	*Myriophyllum heterophyllum*		X	
Vasey's pondweed	*Potamogeton vaseyi*		X	
Water bulrush	*Schoenoplectus subterminalis*		X	
Water heartsease	*Persicaria amphibia v. emersa* (= *Polygonum coccineum*)		X	
Water marigold	*Magalodonta beckii* (= *Bidens beckii*)		X	
Water purslane	*Didiplis diandra*		X	
Watershield	*Brasenia schreberi*		X	
Water star grass	*Heteranthera dubia*	X	X	
Water-thread pondweed	*Potamogeton diversifolius*	X	X	
Water willow	*Justicia americana*	X		X
White-stemmed pondweed	*Potamogeton praelongus*		X	
White water crowfoot	*Ranunculus aquatilis v. diffusus*		X	
Whorled water milfoil	*Myriophyllum verticillatum*		X	
Wild cucumber	*Echinocystis lobata*			X
Wingstem	*Verbesina alternifolia*			X
Wolf's bluegrass	*Poa wolfii*			X
Yellow floatingheart	*NYMPHOIDES PELTATA*		X	
Yellow water buttercup	*Ranunculus flabellaris*		X	

Note: Scientific names in all capital letters are exotic species.

Table P-10. Plant Species of Barren Lands

Common Name	Scientific Name	Active Quarries	Bare Dunes	Cliffs/Rock Outcrops
Alfalfa	*MEDICAGO SATIVA s. SATIVA*	X		
Alsike clover	*TRIFOLIUM HYBRIDUM*	X		
American beak grass	*Diarrhena americana*			X
American filbert	*Corylus americana*			X
American orpine	*Hylotelephium telephioides* (= *Sedum telephioides*)			X
American pennywort	*Hydrocotyle americana*			X
Amur honeysuckle	*LONICERA MAACKII*	X		
Annual bluegrass	*POA ANNUA*	X		
Annual fleabane	*Erigeron annuus*	X		
Appalachian filmy fern	*Trichomanes boschianum*			X
Aromatic aster	*Symphyotrichum oblongifolium*			X
Aromatic sumac	*Rhus aromatica v. aromatica*			X
Arrowfeather	*Aristida purpurascens*			X
Arrow-leaved violet	*Viola sagittata v. sagittata*		X	X
Autumn bent grass	*Agrostis perennans*			X
Barnyard grass	*ECHINOCHLOA CRUS-GALLI*	X		
Barren strawberry	*Waldsteinia fragarioides*			X
Beach grass	*Ammophila breviligulata*		X	
Beach pea	*Lathyrus japonicus v. maritimus*		X	
Beach sumac	*Rhus aromatica v. arenaria*		X	
Beach three-awn grass	*Aristida tuberculosa*		X	
Beach wormwood	*Artemisia campestris s. caudata*		X	
Beard grass	*Gymnopogon ambiguus*		X	
Belvedere summer cypress	*KOCHIA SCOPARIA*	X		
Bicknell's panic grass	*Dichanthelium bicknellii* (*nomen nudum*)			X
Big bluestem grass	*Andropogon gerardii*			X
Bird's foot violet	*Viola pedata*			X
Bishop's cap	*Mitella diphylla*			X
Blackberry lily	*BELAMCANDA CHINENSIS*	X		
Black chokeberry	*Photinia melanocarpa*			X
Black-eyed Susan	*Rudbeckia hirta v. hirta*			X
Black huckleberry	*Gaylussacia baccata*			X
Blackjack oak	*Quercus marilandica*			X
Black medick	*MEDICAGO LUPULINA*	X		
Black mustard	*BRASSICA NIGRA*	X		
Black spleenwort	*Asplenium resiliens*			X
Blazing star	*Liatris squarrosa*			X
Blighted goldenrod	*Solidago sphacelata*			X
Blue ash	*Fraxinus quadrangulata*			X
Blue curls	*Trichostema dichotomum*		X	X
Blue toadflax	*Nuttallanthus canadensis* (= *Linaria canadensis*)		X	
Bluets	*Houstonia caerulea* (= *Hedyotis caerulea*)			X
Blunt-scaled oak sedge	*Carex albicans v. albicans*			X
Bouncing bet	*SAPONARIA OFFICINALIS*	X		
Boxwood knotweed	*Polygonum aviculare s. buxiforme*	X		
Bradley's spleenwort	*Asplenium bradleyi*			X
Bristly foxtail grass	*SETARIA VERTICILLATA*	X		
Bristly locust	*ROBINIA HISPIDA*	X		
Bristly sarsaparilla	*Aralia hispida*		X	
Broom sedge	*Andropogon virginicus*			X
Buffalo clover	*Trifolium reflexum*			X
Bulblet bladder fern	*Cystopteris bulbifera*			X
Bull brier	*Smilax bona-nox*			X
Bull thistle	*CIRSIUM VULGARE*	X		
Butterfly pea	*Clitoria mariana*			X
Butterflyweed	*Asclepias tuberosa* (including 1 variety)		X	X
Butterweed	*Packera glabella*	X		
Buttonweed	*Diodia teres*			X
Canadian bluegrass	*POA COMPRESSA*	X		X
Carolina buckthorn	*Frangula caroliniana* (= *Rhamnus caroliniana*)			X
Carolina thistle	*Cirsium carolinianum*			X
Cat brier	*Smilax rotundifolia*			X
Catnip	*NEPETA CATARIA*	X		
Cheat grass	*BROMUS TECTORUM*	X	X	
Cheeses	*MALVA NEGLECTA*	X		

Common Name	Scientific Name	Active Quarries	Bare Dunes	Cliffs/Rock Outcrops
Chicory	*CICHORIUM INTYBUS*	X		
Chinquapin oak	*Quercus muhlenbergii*			X
Cigar tree	*Catalpa speciosa*	X		
Cliff adder's tongue fern	*Ophioglossum engelmannii*			X
Cliff clubmoss	*Huperzia porophila*			X
Climbing milkweed	*Matelea obliqua*			X
Clustered broom rape	*Orobanche fasciculata*		X	
Clustered poppy mallow	*Callirhoë triangulata*		X	
Columbine	*Aquilegia canadensis*			X
Common blue-eyed grass	*Sisyrinchium albidum*			X
Common bugseed	*Corispermum pallasii*		X	
Common burdock	*ARCTIUM MINUS*	X		
Common catalpa	*CATALPA BIGNONIOIDES*	X		
Common chickweed	*STELLARIA MEDIA s. MEDIA*	X		
Common dandelion	*TARAXACUM OFFICINALE*	X		X
Common dayflower	*COMMELINA COMMUNIS*	X		X
Common evening primrose	*Oenothera biennis*	X		
Common goat's beard	*TRAGOPOGON PRATENSIS*	X		
Common juniper	*Juniperus communis v. depressa*		X	
Common milkweed	*Asclepias syriaca*	X		
Common morning glory	*IPOMOEA PURPUREA*	X		
Common mouse-ear chickweed	*CERASTIUM FONTANUM s. VULGARE*	X		
Common ninebark	*Physocarpus opulifolius* (including 1 variety)			X
Common pepper cress	*Lepidium virginicum*	X		
Common plantain	*PLANTAGO MAJOR v. MAJOR*	X		
Common polypody	*Polypodium virginianum*			X
Common ragweed	*Ambrosia artemisiifolia v. elatior*	X		X
Common reed	*Phragmites australis*	X		
Common rockrose	*Helianthemum canadense*		X	X
Common sow thistle	*SONCHUS OLERACEUS*	X		
Common spiderwort	*Tradescantia ohiensis*			X
Common St. John's wort	*HYPERICUM PERFORATUM*	X	X	
Common sunflower	*HELIANTHUS ANNUUS*	X		
Common teasel	*DIPSACUS FULLONUM*	X		
Common whitlow cress	*Draba reptans*		X	X
Common wood fern	*Dryopteris intermedia*			X
Common woodsia	*Woodsia obtusa s. obtusa*			X
Corn speedwell	*VERONICA ARVENSIS*	X		
Cottonweed	*Froelichia floridana v. campestris*		X	
Crested coralroot	*Hexalectris spicata*			X
Crowfoot grass	*ELEUSINE INDICA*	X		
Crow poison	*Nothoscordum bivalve*			X
Crown vetch	*CORONILLA VARIA*	X		X
Curly dock	*RUMEX CRISPUS*	X		
Cut-leaved teasel	*DIPSACUS LACINIATUS*	X		
Cylindrical blazing star	*Liatris cylindracea*			X
Deam's dayflower	*Commelina erecta v. deamii*		X	
Deerberry	*Vaccinium stamineum*			X
Deptford pink	*DIANTHUS ARMERIA*	X		
Dittany	*Cunila origanoides*			X
Dogbane	*Apocynum cannabinum*			X
Dune goldenrod	*Solidago simplex v. gillmanii*		X	
Dune sand cherry	*Prunus pumila v. pumila*		X	
Dune thistle	*Cirsium pitcheri*		X	
Dwarf bindweed	*Calystegia spithamaea*			X
Dwarf crested iris	*Iris cristata*			X
Dwarf hackberry	*Celtis tenuifolia*			X
Early fen sedge	*Carex crawei*			X
Early oak sedge	*Carex umbellata*			X
Early saxifrage	*Saxifraga virginiensis*			X
Eastern prickly pear	*Opuntia humifusa*		X	
Eastern redbud	*Cercis canadensis*			X
Eastern red cedar	*Juniperus virginiana*			X
Eggleston's violet	*Viola egglestonii*			X
English plantain	*PLANTAGO LANCEOLATA*	X		

Table P-10. *continued*

Common Name	Scientific Name	Active Quarries	Bare Dunes	Cliffs/Rock Outcrops
Expressway sedge	*CAREX PRAEGRACILIS*	X		
Fairy wand	*Chamaelirium luteum*			X
Fall panicum	*Panicum dichotomiflorum* (including 1 subspecies)	X		
Fall witch grass	*Digitaria cognata* (= *Leptoloma cognatum*)		X	
False aloe	*Manfreda virginica* (= *Agave virginica*)			X
False boneset	*Brickellia eupatorioides* (= *Kuhnia eupatoriodes*) (including 1 variety)			X
False heather	*Hudsonia tomentosa*		X	
Fame flower	*Phemeranthus rugospermus* (= *Talinum rugospermum*)		X	
Farkleberry	*Vaccinium arboreum*			X
Fat-hen saltbush	*ATRIPLEX PATULA*	X		
Few-flowered nut rush	*Scleria pauciflora v. caroliniana*			X
Field bindweed	*CONVOLVULUS ARVENSIS*	X		
Field cress	*LEPIDIUM CAMPESTRE*	X		
Field hedge parsley	*TORILIS ARVENSIS s. ARVENSIS*	X		
Field milkwort	*Polygala sanguinea*			X
Field penny cress	*THLASPI ARVENSE*	X		
Field sorrel	*RUMEX ACETOSELLA*		X	X
Field thistle	*CIRSIUM ARVENSE*	X		
Flowering spurge	*Euphorbia corollata*			X
Foothill bedstraw	*CRUCIATA PEDEMONTANUM* (= *GALIUM PEDEMONTANUM*)		X	
Forbes' saxifrage	*Saxifraga pensylvanica v. forbesii*			X
Four-leaf yam	*Dioscorea quaternata*			X
French's shooting star	*Dodecatheon frenchii*			X
Garden asparagus	*ASPARAGUS OFFICINALIS*	X		
Giant foxtail grass	*SETARIA FABERI*	X		
Glaucous campion	*SILENE CSEREI*	X		
Goat's rue	*Tephrosia virginiana*		X	X
Golden aster	*Heterotheca camporum v. camporum* (= *Chrysopsis camporum*)		X	
Gray polypody	*Pleopeltis polypodioides v. michauxiana* (= *Polypodium polypodioides*)			X
Greater nodding fescue	*Festuca paradoxa*			X
Great Lakes sea rocket	*Cakile edentula v. lacustris*		X	
Great Plains ladies' tresses	*Spiranthes magnicamporum*		X	X
Green brier	*Smilax glauca*			X
Green-flowered milkweed	*Asclepias viridiflora*			X
Green milkweed	*Asclepias viridis*			X
Grooved yellow flax	*Linum sulcatum*			X
Ground cedar	*Lycopodium tristachyum*		X	
Hair grass	*Agrostis hyemalis*			X
Hair grass	*Muhlenbergia capillaris*			X
Hairy aster	*Symphyotrichum pilosum v. pilosum*	X		
Hairy beard tongue	*Penstemon hirsutus*			X
Hairy bedstraw	*Galium pilosum*			X
Hairy crabgrass	*DIGITARIA SANGUINALIS*	X		
Hairy false golden aster	*HETEROTHECA CAMPORUM v. GLANDULISSIMA*		X	
Hairy gentian	*Gentiana villosa*			X
Hairy lip fern	*Cheilanthes lanosa*			X
Hairy puccoon	*Lithospermum caroliniense v. croceum*		X	
Hairy ruellia	*Ruellia humilis*			X
Harebell	*Campanula rotundifolia*			X
Hay-scented fern	*Dennstaedtia punctilobula*			X
Heart-leaved meadow parsnip	*Zizia aptera*			X
Hedge mustard	*SISYMBRIUM OFFICINALE*	X		
Henbit	*LAMIUM AMPLEXICAULE*	X		
Hillside strawberry	*Fragaria vesca s. americana*			X
Hoary puccoon	*Lithospermum canescens*			X
Hogwort	*CROTON CAPITATUS* (including 1 variety)	X		X
Hooked monkshood	*Aconitum uncinatum*			X
Hop hornbeam	*Ostrya virginiana*			X
Horsemint	*Monarda punctata v. villicaulis*		X	
Horse nettle	*Solanum carolinense*	X		
Horseweed	*Conyza canadensis*	X		
Hungarian brome	*BROMUS INERMIS*	X		
Indian grass	*Sorghastrum nutans*			X
Indian mustard	*BRASSICA JUNCEA*	X		
Ivory sedge	*Carex eburnea*			X

Common Name	Scientific Name	Active Quarries	Bare Dunes	Cliffs/Rock Outcrops
Jack pine	*Pinus banksiana*		X	
Jagged chickweed	*HOLOSTEUM UMBELLATUM*	X		
Japanese chess	*BROMUS JAPONICUS*	X	X	
Japanese honeysuckle	*LONICERA JAPONICA*	X		X
Japanese lespedeza	*KUMMEROWIA STRIATA*	X		
Johnson grass	*SORGHUM HALEPENSE*	X		
Jointweed	*Polygonella articulata*		X	
Juneberry	*Amelanchier arborea*			X
Kenilworth ivy	*CYMBALARIA MURALIS*			X
Kentucky bluegrass	*POA PRATENSIS*	X		
Knawel	*SCLERANTHUS ANNUUS*		X	
Korean clover	*KUMMEROWIA STIPULACEA* (= *LESPEDEZA STIPULACEA*)	X		
Lady fern	*Athyrium filix-femina s. angustum*			X
Lamb's quarters	*CHENOPODIUM ALBUM v. ALBUM*	X		
Large passion flower	*Passiflora incarnata*			X
Late alumroot	*Heuchera parviflora* (including 1 variety)			X
Late boneset	*Eupatorium serotinum*	X		
Little barley	*Hordeum pusillum*	X		
Little bluestem grass	*Schizachyrium scoparium* (= *Andropogon scoparius*)			X
Little-leaf buttercup	*Ranunculus abortivus*	X		
Long-scaled nut sedge	*Cyperus strigosus*	X		
Long-stalked hummock sedge	*Carex pedunculata*			X
Lovage	*Ligusticum canadense*			X
Low hop clover	*TRIFOLIUM CAMPESTRE*	X		
Lyme grass	*LEYMUS ARENARIUS*		X	
Mackay's fragile fern	*Cystopteris tenuis*			X
Maidenhair fern	*Adiantum pedatum*			X
Maidenhair spleenwort	*Asplenium trichomanes*			X
Marginal shield fern	*Dryopteris marginalis*			X
Marsh blazing star	*Liatris spicata*			X
Marsh elder	*Iva annua* (including 1 variety)	X		
Maryland senna	*Senna marilandica*			X
Mat sandbur	*Cenchrus longispinus*		X	
Meadow fescue	*SCHEDONORUS PRATENSIS*	X		
Mississippi milk pea	*Galactia volubilis*			X
Moneywort	*LYSIMACHIA NUMMULARIA*			X
Mossy stonecrop	*SEDUM ACRE*		X	X
Motherwort	*LEONURUS CARDIACA*	X		
Moth mullein	*VERBASCUM BLATTARIA*	X		
Mountain chestnut oak	*Quercus montana*			X
Mountain laurel	*Kalmia latifolia*			X
Mountain spleenwort	*Asplenium montanum*			X
Musk bristle thistle	*CARDUUS NUTANS*	X		
Narrow-fruited pinweed	*Lechea racemulosa*			X
Narrow-leaved bluets	*Stenaria nigricans* (= *Hedyotis nigricans*)			X
Narrow-leaved pinweed	*Lechea tenuifolia*			X
Netted chainfern	*Woodwardia areolata*			X
New Jersey tea	*Ceanothus americanus*			X
Night-flowering catchfly	*SILENE NOCTIFLORA*	X		
Nimblewill	*Muhlenbergia schreberi*	X		
Nits-and-lice	*Hypericum drummondii*			X
Nodding brome	*BROMUS SQUARROSUS*		X	
Nodding spurge	*Chamaesyce nutans*	X		X
Nodding wild onion	*Allium cernuum*			X
Northern rush grass	*Sporobolus vaginiflorus*	X		X
Notched spike rush	*Eleocharis bifida*			X
Obe-wan-conobea	*Leucospora multifida*			X
Ohio horse mint	*Blephilia ciliata*			X
Old-field goldenrod	*Solidago nemoralis* (including 1 subspecies)	X	X	X
Old witch grass	*Panicum capillare*	X		
One-flowered leavenworthia	*Leavenworthia uniflora*			X
Orange coneflower	*Rudbeckia fulgida v. fulgida*			X
Orange day lily	*HEMEROCALLIS FULVA*	X		
Orange grass	*Hypericum gentianoides*			X
Pale gentian	*Gentiana alba*			X

Table P-10. *continued*

Common Name	Scientific Name	Active Quarries	Bare Dunes	Cliffs/Rock Outcrops
Pale Indian plantain	*Arnoglossum atriplicifolium* (= *Cacalia atriplicifolia*)			X
Pale leafcup	*Polymnia canadensis*			X
Pale spiked lobelia	*Lobelia spicata* (including varieties)			X
Pasture rose	*Rosa carolina*			X
Pasture thistle	*Cirsium discolor*			X
Pencil flower	*Stylosanthes biflora*			X
Pineapple weed	*MATRICARIA DISCOIDEA*	X		
Pinkweed	*Persicaria pensylvanica*	X		
Pinnatifid spleenwort	*Asplenium pinnatifidum*			X
Plains three awn grass	*Aristida oligantha*			X
Plantain-leaved wood sedge	*Carex plantaginea*			X
Poison hemlock	*CONIUM MACULATUM*	X		
Poison ivy	*Toxicodendron radicans s. radicans*	X		X
Pokeweed	*Phytolacca americana v. americana*	X		
Poor Joe	*Plantago aristata*	X	X	
Potato dwarf dandelion	*Krigia dandelion*		X	
Poverty grass	*Aristida dichotoma*			X
Poverty oat grass	*Danthonia spicata*			X
Prairie dock	*Silphium terebinthinaceum v. terebinthinaceum*			X
Prairie panic grass	*Dichanthelium leibergii*			X
Prairie sand reed	*Calamovilfa longifolia v. magna*		X	
Prairie tea	*CROTON MONANTHOGYNUS*	X		X
Prairie willow	*Salix humilis* (including 1 variety)			X
Prickly ash	*Zanthoxylum americanum*			X
Prickly lettuce	*LACTUCA SERRIOLA*	X		
Prickly sida	*SIDA SPINOSA*	X		
Prickly sow thistle	*SONCHUS ASPER*	X		
Puncture vine	*TRIBULUS TERRESTRIS*	X		
Purple chokeberry	*Photinia floribunda* (= *Aronia floribunda*)			X
Purple cliffbrake	*Pellaea atropurpurea*			X
Purple daisy	*Symphyotrichum patens*			X
Purple dead nettle	*LAMIUM PURPUREUM*	X		
Purple flowering raspberry	*Rubus odoratus*			X
Purple milkwort	*Polygala polygama*		X	
Purple poppy mallow	*CALLIRHOË INVOLUCRATA*		X	
Purple prairie clover	*Dalea purpurea*			X
Purple sandgrass	*Triplasis purpurea*		X	
Purslane	*PORTULACA OLERACEA*	X		X
Quackgrass	*ELYMUS REPENS* (= *AGROPYRON REPENS*)	X		
Queen Anne's lace	*DAUCUS CAROTA*	X		
Ragged evening primrose	*Oenothera laciniata*		X	
Rattlesnake master	*Eryngium yuccifolium*			X
Rattlesnake plantain	*Goodyera pubescens*			X
Red clover	*TRIFOLIUM PRATENSE*	X		
Red-stalked plantain	*Plantago rugelii* (including 1 variety)	X		
Rigid goldenrod	*Solidago rigida* (including 1 subspecies)			X
Rock jasmine	*Androsace occidentalis*		X	X
Rockrose	*Helianthemum bicknellii*		X	X
Rock sandwort	*Minuartia michauxii* (= *Arenaria stricta*)		X	X
Rock satin grass	*Muhlenbergia sobolifera*			X
Rock selaginella	*Selaginella rupestris*		X	X
Rock skullcap	*Scutellaria saxatilis*			X
Rosin weed	*Silphium asteriscus v. trifoliatum*			X
Rough barnyard grass	*Echinochloa muricata* (including 1 variety)	X		
Rough blazing star	*Liatris aspera* (including 1 variety)			X
Rough cinquefoil	*Potentilla norvegica* (including 1 subspecies)	X		
Rough pigweed	*AMARANTHUS RETROFLEXUS*	X		
Rough sand sedge	*Cyperus schweinitzii*		X	
Rough white lettuce	*Prenanthes aspera*			X
Round-fruited panic grass	*Dichanthelium sphaerocarpon*			X
Round-fruited St. John's wort	*Hypericum sphaerocarpum*			X
Round-leaved serviceberry	*Amelanchier sanguinea*			X
Running strawberry bush	*Euonymus obovata*			X
Russian thistle	*SALSOLA TRAGUS*	X	X	
Rusty nannyberry	*Viburnum rufidulum*			X

Common Name	Scientific Name	Active Quarries	Bare Dunes	Cliffs/Rock Outcrops
Sand croton	*Croton glandulosus v. septentrionalis*	X		
Sand dropseed	*Sporobolus cryptandrus*		X	
Sand goat's beard	*TRAGOPOGON DUBIUS*	X	X	
Sand milkweed	*Asclepias amplexicaulis*		X	
Sand prairie phlox	*Phlox pilosa s. pilosa*			X
Scorpion grass	*Myosotis macrosperma*			X
Scott's spleenwort	*Asplenium x ebenoides*			X
Seaside spurge	*Chamaesyce polygonifolia*		X	
Seneca snakeroot	*Polygala senega*			X
Shepherd's purse	*CAPSELLA BURSA-PASTORIS*	X		
Shining clubmoss	*Huperzia lucidula* (= *Lycopodium lucidulum*)			X
Shining panic grass	*Dichanthelium lucidum*			X
Shining wedge grass	*Sphenopholis nitida*			X
Shoestring fern	*Vittaria appalachiana*			X
Shooting star	*Dodecatheon meadia*			X
Shrubby St. John's wort	*Hypericum dolabriforme*			X
Side-oats grama	*Bouteloua curtipendula*			X
Silky bush clover	*LESPEDEZA CUNEATA*	X		X
Sleepy catchfly	*Silene antirrhina*	X	X	
Slender bush clover	*Lespedeza virginica*			X
Slender false foxglove	*Agalinis tenuifolia* (includes 2 varieties)			X
Slender gaura	*Gaura filipes*		X	X
Slender heliotrope	*Heliotropium tenellum*			X
Slender knotweed	*Polygonum tenue*		X	X
Slender mountain mint	*Pycnanthemum tenuifolium*			X
Slender sand sedge	*Cyperus lupulinus s. lupulinus*		X	
Slender yellow flax	*Linum virginianum*			X
Small-fruited panic grass	*Dichanthelium dichotomum s. microcarpon*			X
Small green foxtail grass	*SETARIA VIRIDIS v. VIRIDIS*	X		
Small horse gentian	*Triosteum angustifolium*			X
Small love grass	*Eragrostis pectinacea*	X		
Small mouse-ear chickweed	*CERASTIUM SEMIDECANDRUM*		X	
Small skullcap	*Scutellaria parvula v. parvula*			X
Small wild bean	*Strophostyles leiosperma*			X
Smooth blue aster	*Symphyotrichum laeve*			X
Smooth cliffbrake	*Pellaea glabella*			X
Smooth field sow thistle	*SONCHUS ARVENSIS s. ULIGINOSUS*	X		
Smooth phlox	*Phlox glaberrima* (including subspecies)			X
Smooth purslane speedwell	*Veronica peregrina s. peregrina*	X		
Smooth rockcress	*Arabis laevigata*			X
Smooth-seeded nut rush	*Scleria oligantha*			X
Snow trillium	*Trillium nivale*			X
Sourwood	*Oxydendron arboreum*			X
Southern buckthorn	*Sideroxylon lycioides* (= *Bumelia lycioides*)			X
Spanish needles	*Bidens bipinnata*	X		
Spiny cocklebur	*XANTHIUM SPINOSUM*	X		
Spotted creeping spurge	*Chamaesyce maculata*	X		
Spreading rockcress	*Arabis patens*			X
Squirrel-tail grass	*HORDEUM JUBATUM*	X		
Star cleft phlox	*Phlox bifida s. stellaria*			X
Stiff gentian	*Gentianella quinquefolia s. occidentalis*			X
Stink grass	*ERAGROSTIS CILIANENSIS*	X		
Storksbill	*ERODIUM CICUTARIUM*	X		
Sullivant's coolwort	*Sullivantia sullivantii*			X
Tall boneset	*Eupatorium altissimum*	X		
Tall coreopsis	*Coreopsis tripteris*			X
Tall fescue	*SCHEDONORUS ARUNDINACEUS* (= *FESTUCA ELATIOR*)	X		
Tall goldenrod	*Solidago altissima* (including 1 subspecies)	X		
Tall melic grass	*Melica nitens*			X
Tall wood sorrel	*Oxalis stricta*	X		
Tartarian honeysuckle	*LONICERA TATARICA*	X		X
Tennessee bladder fern	*Cystopteris tennesseensis*			X
Tennessee milk vetch	*Astragalus tennesseensis*			X
Three-awn grass	*Aristida longespica v. longespica*			X
Three-leaved stonecrop	*Sedum ternatum*			X

Table P-10. *continued*

Common Name	Scientific Name	Active Quarries	Bare Dunes	Cliffs/Rock Outcrops
Thyme-leaved sandwort	*ARENARIA SERPYLLIFOLIA*	X		
Timothy grass	*PHLEUM PRATENSE*	X		
Toothed spurge	*Euphorbia dentata* (= *Poinsettia dentata*)	X		
Tragia	*Tragia cordata*			X
Trailing bush clover	*Lespedeza procumbens*			X
Tree ground pine	*Lycopodium dendroideum*			X
Tree-of-heaven	*AILANTHUS ALTISSIMA*			X
Tufted hair grass	*Deschampsia cespitosa*			X
Two-flower false dandelion	*Krigia biflora*			X
Umbrella magnolia	*Magnolia tripetala*			X
Venus's looking glass	*Triodanis perfoliata*		X	X
Villous alumroot	*Heuchera villosa*			X
Virginia dwarf dandelion	*Krigia virginica*		X	
Virginia obedient plant	*Physostegia virginiana v. virginiana*			X
Walking fern	*Asplenium rhizophyllum* (= *Camptosorus rhizophyllus*)			X
Wall-rue spleenwort	*Asplenium ruta-muraria*			X
Weft fern	*Trichomanes intricatum*			X
Western beard tongue	*Penstemon tubaeflorus*		X	
Western wallflower	*Erysimum capitatum*			X
White camass	*Zigadenus elegans*			X
White clover	*TRIFOLIUM REPENS*	X		
White snakeroot	*Ageratina altissima* (= *Eupatorium rugosum*)			X
White sweet clover	*MELILOTUS ALBA*	X		
Wild bergamot	*Monarda fistulosa* (including 1 variety)		X	
Wild four o'clock	*MIRABILIS NYCTAGINEA*	X		
Wild lupine	*Lupinus perennis*		X	
Wild petunia	*Ruellia caroliniensis*			X
Wild sweet potato	*Ipomoea pandurata*			X
Willdenow's grass sedge	*Carex willdenowii*			X
Winged elm	*Ulmus alata*			X
Winged pigweed	*Cycloloma atriplicifolium*		X	
Winter vetch	*VICIA VILLOSA s. VILLOSA*	X		
Wolf's bluegrass	*Poa wolfii*			X
Wood angelica	*Angelica venenosa*			X
Wood betony	*Pedicularis canadensis*			X
Woolly mullein	*VERBASCUM THAPSUS*	X		
Wrinkle-fruited oak sedge	*Carex tonsa v. rugosperma*		X	
Yellow coneflower	*Ratibida pinnata*			X
Yellow rocket	*BARBAREA VULGARIS*	X		
Yellow star grass	*Hypoxis hirsuta*			X
Yellow sweet clover	*MELILOTUS OFFICINALIS*	X		

Note: Scientific names in all capital letters are exotic species.

Table P-11. Plant Species of Agricultural Lands

Common Name	Scientific Name	Corn/ Soybeans	Cereal Grains	Vineyards	Orchards	Feedlots	Residue Management Lands
Alfalfa	*MEDICAGO SATIVA s. SATIVA*			X	X		
American bindweed	*Calystegia sepium* (including subspecies)	X	X	X	X		X
American sweet flag	*Acorus americanus*	X		X			
Annual bluegrass	*POA ANNUA*	X	X	X	X		X
Annual fleabane	*Erigeron annuus*						X
Annual foxtail	*Alopecurus carolinianus*	X	X				
Apple	*MALUS DOMESTICA*				X		
Awned bent grass	*Agrostis elliottiana*						X
Barnyard grass	*ECHINOCHLOA CRUS-GALLI*					X	
Black medick	*MEDICAGO LUPULINA*	X	X	X	X	X	X
Black mustard	*BRASSICA NIGRA*	X	X			X	X
Blue toadflax	*Nuttallanthus canadensis* (= *Linaria canadensis*)	X					
Bluevine	*Cynanchum laeve*			X	X		X
Bristly foxtail grass	*SETARIA VERTICILLATA*	X	X				
Broom corn millet	*PANICUM MILIACEUM*		X				X
Buffalo bur	*SOLANUM ROSTRATUM*					X	
Bulbous bluegrass	*POA BULBOSA* (including 1 subspecies)			X	X		
Butterweed	*Packera glabella*	X	X				X
Buttonweed	*ABUTILON THEOPHRASTI*	X					
Canadian bluegrass	*POA COMPRESSA*			X	X		
Carolina cranesbill	*Geranium carolinianum*	X	X				
Carpet weed	*MOLLUGO VERTICILLATA*	X	X				X
Catnip	*NEPETA CATARIA*			X	X	X	
Charlock	*SINAPIS ARVENSIS*	X	X				X
Cheat grass	*BROMUS TECTORUM*	X	X				X
Cheeses	*MALVA NEGLECTA*	X	X			X	X
Chicory	*CICHORIUM INTYBUS*			X	X	X	
Common burdock	*ARCTIUM MINUS*					X	
Common chickweed	*STELLARIA MEDIA s. MEDIA*	X	X	X	X	X	X
Common dandelion	*TARAXACUM OFFICINALE*	X	X	X	X	X	X
Common dayflower	*COMMELINA COMMUNIS*			X	X		
Common dewberry	*Rubus sec. Flagellares: R. flagellaris*			X	X		
Common goat's beard	*TRAGOPOGON PRATENSIS*	X	X	X	X		X
Common groundsel	*SENECIO VULGARIS*	X	X	X			X
Common horehound	*MARRUBIUM VULGARE*					X	
Common milfoil	*Achillea millefolium*			X	X		
Common milkweed	*Asclepias syriaca*			X	X		
Common morning glory	*IPOMOEA PURPUREA*	X	X			X	X
Common pepper cress	*Lepidium virginicum*	X	X	X	X	X	X
Common plantain	*PLANTAGO MAJOR v. MAJOR*			X	X		
Common purpletop	*Tridens flavus*			X	X		
Common ragweed	*Ambrosia artemisiifolia v. elatior*	X	X	X	X		X
Common sow thistle	*SONCHUS OLERACEUS*	X	X				X
Common star of Bethlehem	*ORNITHOGALUM UMBELLATUM*			X	X		
Corn	*ZEA MAYS*	X					
Corn cockle	*AGROSTEMA GITHAGO*		X				
Corn speedwell	*VERONICA ARVENSIS*	X	X	X		X	X
Curly dock	*RUMEX CRISPUS*	X	X			X	X
Deptford pink	*DIANTHUS ARMERIA*			X	X		
Dog fennel	*ANTHEMIS COTULA*					X	
English plantain	*PLANTAGO LANCEOLATA*			X	X		
Fall panicum	*Panicum dichotomiflorum* (including 1 subspecies)	X	X			X	X
Field bindweed	*CONVOLVULUS ARVENSIS*	X	X	X	X	X	X
Field cress	*LEPIDIUM CAMPESTRE*	X		X			X
Field garlic	*ALLIUM VINEALE*	X	X	X	X		X
Field nut sedge	*Cyperus esculentus v. leptostachyus*	X	X				X
Field penny cress	*THLASPI ARVENSE*	X	X	X	X	X	X
Field thistle	*CIRSIUM ARVENSE*			X	X	X	X
Flower-of-an-hour	*HIBISCUS TRIONUM*	X	X				X
Giant foxtail grass	*SETARIA FABERI*	X	X				
Hair grass	*Agrostis hyemalis*						X
Hairy aster	*Symphyotrichum pilosum v. pilosum*			X	X		
Hairy bitter cress	*CARDAMINE HIRSUTA*	X	X				
Hairy crabgrass	*DIGITARIA SANGUINALIS*	X	X	X	X	X	X
Hedge mustard	*SISYMBRIUM OFFICINALE*	X	X	X			X
Henbit	*LAMIUM AMPLEXICAULE*	X	X	X	X	X	X
Horse nettle	*Solanum carolinense*	X	X			X	

Table P-11. *continued*

Common Name	Scientific Name	Corn/ Soybeans	Cereal Grains	Vineyards	Orchards	Feedlots	Residue Management Lands
Horseweed	*Conyza canadensis*	X	X			X	X
Hungarian brome	*BROMUS INERMIS*			X	X		
Indian strawberry	*DUCHESNEA INDICA*			X	X		
Ivy-leaved morning glory	*IPOMOEA HEDERACEA*	X	X				X
Jagged chickweed	*HOLOSTEUM UMBELLATUM*	X	X	X	X		X
Japanese lespedeza	*KUMMEROWIA STRIATA*			X			
Japanese rose	*ROSA MULTIFLORA*			X	X		
Jimsonweed	*DATURA STRAMONIUM*					X	
Johnson grass	*SORGHUM HALEPENSE*	X	X	X	X		X
Kentucky bluegrass	*POA PRATENSIS*			X	X		
Lamb's quarters	*CHENOPODIUM ALBUM v. ALBUM*	X	X	X	X	X	X
Late boneset	*Eupatorium serotinum*						X
Little barley	*Hordeum pusillum*	X	X			X	X
Little-leaf buttercup	*Ranunculus abortivus*	X	X				X
Long-scaled nut sedge	*Cyperus strigosus*	X	X				X
Marsh elder	*Iva annua* (including 1 variety)	X	X				X
Meadow fescue	*SCHEDONORUS PRATENSIS*			X	X		
Motherwort	*LEONURUS CARDIACA*			X	X	X	
Moth mullein	*VERBASCUM BLATTARIA*			X	X		
Mouse-eared cress	*ARABIDOPSIS THALIANA*	X	X				X
Mousetail	*Myosurus minimus*	X	X				X
Night-flowering catchfly	*SILENE NOCTIFLORA*	X	X	X	X		X
Nimblewill	*Muhlenbergia schreberi*			X	X		
Oats	*AVENA SATIVA*		X				
Orchard grass	*DACTYLIS GLOMERATA*			X	X		
Ox-eye daisy	*LEUCANTHEMUM VULGARE* (= *CHRYSANTHEMUM LEUCANTHEMUM*)			X	X		
Pear	*PYRUS COMMUNIS*				X		
Pigeon grass	*SETARIA PUMILA s. PUMILA*	X					
Pineapple weed	*MATRICARIA DISCOIDEA*					X	
Pinkweed	*Persicaria pensylvanica*	X	X			X	X
Poison hemlock	*CONIUM MACULATUM*					X	
Pokeweed	*Phytolacca americana v. americana*					X	
Prickly lettuce	*LACTUCA SERRIOLA*	X	X	X	X	X	X
Prickly sida	*SIDA SPINOSA*	X	X	X	X	X	X
Prickly sow thistle	*SONCHUS ASPER*	X	X	X	X	X	X
Puncture vine	*TRIBULUS TERRESTRIS*	X	X	X	X	X	X
Purple dead nettle	*LAMIUM PURPUREUM*	X	X	X	X	X	X
Purslane	*PORTULACA OLERACEA*	X	X	X	X	X	X
Quackgrass	*ELYMUS REPENS* (= *AGROPYRON REPENS*)	X	X	X	X	X	X
Queen Anne's lace	*DAUCUS CAROTA*			X	X		
Ragged evening primrose	*Oenothera laciniata*	X					
Red clover	*TRIFOLIUM PRATENSE*			X	X		
Rough cinquefoil	*Potentilla norvegica* (including 1 subspecies)	X	X				X
Rough pigweed	*AMARANTHUS RETROFLEXUS*	X	X				X
Russian thistle	*SALSOLA TRAGUS*	X	X				
Rye	*SECALE CEREALE*		X				
Sand croton	*Croton glandulosus v. septentrionalis*	X	X				X
Shepherd's purse	*CAPSELLA BURSA-PASTORIS*	X	X	X	X	X	X
Silvery cinquefoil	*POTENTILLA ARGENTEA*						X
Sleepy catchfly	*Silene antirrhina*	X	X				X
Small-fruited false flax	*CAMELINA MICROCARPA*	X	X				
Small green foxtail grass	*SETARIA VIRIDIS v. VIRIDIS*	X		X	X		X
Small love grass	*Eragrostis pectinacea*	X	X	X		X	X
Small mouse-ear chickweed	*CERASTIUM SEMIDECANDRUM*	X	X				
Smooth field sow thistle	*SONCHUS ARVENSIS s. ULIGINOSUS*	X	X	X	X	X	X
Smooth pigweed	*AMARANTHUS POWELLII*	X	X				X
Smooth purslane speedwell	*Veronica peregrina s. peregrina*	X	X			X	X
Sorghum	*SORGHUM BICOLOR*	X	X				X
Soybean	*GLYCINE MAX*	X	X				X
Spanish needles	*Bidens bipinnata*	X	X			X	
Spear grass	*Poa chapmaniana*	X	X		X		
Spearmint	*MENTHA SPICATA*	X	X				X
Spiny cocklebur	*XANTHIUM SPINOSUM*	X	X	X	X	X	X
Spotted creeping spurge	*Chamaesyce maculata*	X	X				X
Stink grass	*ERAGROSTIS CILIANENSIS*	X	X	X	X	X	X

Common Name	Scientific Name	Corn/ Soybeans	Cereal Grains	Vineyards	Orchards	Feedlots	Residue Management Lands
Tall fescue	*SCHEDONORUS ARUNDINACEUS (= FESTUCA ELATIOR)*			X	X		
Tall goldenrod	*Solidago altissima* (including 1 subspecies)			X	X		
Tall hedge mustard	*SISYMBRIUM LOESELII*					X	
Tall wood sorrel	*Oxalis stricta*	X	X	X	X		X
Tansy mustard	*DESCURAINIA PINNATA v. BRACHYCARPA*	X	X				
Timothy grass	*PHLEUM PRATENSE*			X	X		
Tumble mustard	*SISYMBRIUM ALTISSIMUM*	X	X				
Virginia rockcress	*Sibara virginica*	X					
Wheat	*TRITICUM AESTIVUM*		X				
White clover	*TRIFOLIUM REPENS*			X	X		
White sweet clover	*MELILOTUS ALBA*	X	X	X	X		X
Wild garlic	*Allium canadense*	X	X				X
Winter vetch	*VICIA VILLOSA s. VILLOSA*			X	X		
Yellow rocket	*BARBAREA VULGARIS*	X					
Yellow sweet clover	*MELILOTUS OFFICINALIS*	X	X	X	X		X

Note: Scientific names in all capital letters are exotic species.

Table P-12. Plant Species of Developed Lands

Common Name	Scientific Name	Urban Forests	Suburban Forests	Industrial Lands	Commercial	Roads/Rails	Rights-of-Way	Soccer/Recreational Lands	Golf Courses	Towers	Storm-water Retention Ponds	Borrow Pits
Alfalfa	*MEDICAGO SATIVA s. SATIVA*			X	X	X	X	X	X	X	X	X
Alkali grass	*PUCCINELLIA DISTANS*				X	X	X				X	X
Alsike clover	*TRIFOLIUM HYBRIDUM*			X	X	X	X	X	X	X	X	X
American bindweed	*Calystegia sepium* (including subspecies)			X		X	X			X	X	X
Amur honeysuckle	*LONICERA MAACKII*	X	X	X	X	X	X	X	X	X	X	X
Angled spike rush	*Eleocharis quadrangulata*											X
Annual bluegrass	*POA ANNUA*	X	X	X	X	X	X	X	X	X	X	X
Annual fleabane	*Erigeron annuus*			X		X						
Appressed bog clubmoss	*Lycopodiella subappressa*											X
Arbor vitae	*Thuja occidentalis*		X									
Barnyard grass	*ECHINOCHLOA CRUS-GALLI*										X	X
Beefsteak plant	*PERILLA FRUTESCENS* (including 1 variety)					X	X					
Beggar's lice	*LAPPULA SQUARROSA*					X						
Belvedere summer cypress	*KOCHIA SCOPARIA*			X	X	X	X	X	X	X	X	X
Bermuda grass	*CYNODON DACTYLON*				X	X	X	X	X	X	X	
Birdsfoot trefoil	*LOTUS CORNICULATUS*					X	X					
Bittersweet nightshade	*SOLANUM DULCAMARA*	X	X			X	X	X	X	X	X	X
Bitterweed	*Helenium amarum*					X	X					
Blackberry lily	*BELAMCANDA CHINENSIS*			X	X	X	X					
Black-eyed Susan	*Rudbeckia hirta v. hirta*						X					
Black medick	*MEDICAGO LUPULINA*			X	X	X	X	X	X	X	X	
Black mustard	*BRASSICA NIGRA*			X	X	X	X					
Bladder campion	*SILENE VULGARIS*				X	X	X					
Blue hosta	*HOSTA VENTRICOSA*	X	X									
Bluevine	*Cynanchum laeve*			X	X	X	X		X	X	X	
Blunt-leaved senna	*Senna obtusifolia*					X	X					
Blunt spike rush	*Eleocharis obtusa*										X	
Border privet	*LIGUSTRUM OBTUSIFOLIUM*	X	X									
Boston ivy	*PARTHENOCISSUS TRICUSPIDATA*					X	X					
Bouncing bet	*SAPONARIA OFFICINALIS*			X	X	X	X					
Boxwood knotweed	*Polygonum aviculare s. buxiforme*			X	X	X	X	X	X	X		
Bradford pear	*PYRUS CALLERYANA*	X	X			X	X					
Bristly foxtail grass	*SETARIA VERTICILLATA*			X	X	X	X	X	X	X	X	X
Bristly locust	*ROBINIA HISPIDA*					X	X					
Broad-leaved cattail	*Typha latifolia*										X	X
Broom corn millet	*PANICUM MILIACEUM*			X								
Broom sedge	*Andropogon virginicus*						X					
Brown beak rush	*Rhynchospora capitellata*											X
Brown fox sedge	*Carex vulpinoidea*						X				X	X
Buffalo bur	*SOLANUM ROSTRATUM*					X	X					
Bulbous bluegrass	*POA BULBOSA* (including 1 subspecies)			X	X	X	X	X	X	X	X	X
Bull thistle	*CIRSIUM VULGARE*			X	X	X	X	X	X	X	X	X
Bur buttercup	*RANUNCULUS TESTICULATUS* (= *CERATOCEPHALUS TESTICULATUS*)			X	X	X	X	X	X	X		
Butter-and-eggs	*LINARIA VULGARIS*					X	X					
Butterflyweed	*Asclepias tuberosa* (including 1 variety)						X					
Butterweed	*Packera glabella*			X	X	X	X				X	X
Buttonweed	*Diodia teres*					X	X					X
Canadian bluegrass	*POA COMPRESSA*			X	X	X	X	X	X	X	X	X
Caraway	*CARUM CARVI*					X						
Carolina cranesbill	*Geranium carolinianum*			X		X	X					
Carpet bugle	*AJUGA REPTANS*				X							
Carpet weed	*MOLLUGO VERTICILLATA*					X	X					
Catnip	*NEPETA CATARIA*			X	X	X	X	X	X	X		
Cheat grass	*BROMUS TECTORUM*			X	X	X	X					
Cheeses	*MALVA NEGLECTA*	X	X	X	X	X	X	X	X	X	X	X
Chicory	*CICHORIUM INTYBUS*			X		X	X	X	X	X	X	X
Chinese silver grass	*MISCANTHUS SINENSIS*			X	X	X	X					
Cigar tree	*Catalpa speciosa*			X	X		X					
Clammy hedge hyssop	*Gratiola neglecta*											X
Clammy weed	*Polanisia dodecandra s. dodecandra*											X
Clasping St. John's wort	*Hypericum gymnanthum*						X					X
Colic root	*Aletris farinosa*											X
Common arrowhead	*Sagittaria latifolia*										X	

Common Name	Scientific Name	Urban Forests	Suburban Forests	Industrial Lands	Commercial	Roads/Rails	Rights-of-Way	Soccer/Recreational Lands	Golf Courses	Towers	Storm-water Retention Ponds	Borrow Pits
Common barley	*HORDEUM VULGARE*			X		X	X					
Common blackberry	*Rubus sec. Allegheniensis: R. allegheniensis*						X					
Common boneset	*Eupatorium perfoliatum*						X					
Common buckthorn	*RHAMNUS CATHARTICA*	X	X			X	X					
Common burdock	*ARCTIUM MINUS*			X	X	X	X					
Common catalpa	*CATALPA BIGNONIOIDES*			X	X	X	X					
Common chickweed	*STELLARIA MEDIA s. MEDIA*	X	X	X	X	X	X	X	X	X	X	X
Common dandelion	*TARAXACUM OFFICINALE*			X	X	X	X	X	X	X	X	X
Common dayflower	*COMMELINA COMMUNIS*			X	X	X	X	X	X	X		
Common evening primrose	*Oenothera biennis*			X	X	X	X				X	X
Common fig	*FICUS CARICA*	X	X									
Common flax	*LINUM USITATISSIMUM*			X	X	X	X					
Common forget-me-not	*MYOSOTIS SCORPIOIDES*	X	X									
Common goat's beard	*TRAGOPOGON PRATENSIS*			X	X	X	X	X	X	X	X	X
Common grape hyacinth	*MUSCARI BOTRYOIDES*	X	X									
Common groundsel	*SENECIO VULGARIS*			X	X	X	X	X	X	X		
Common hops	*HUMULUS LUPULUS v. LUPULUS*					X	X					
Common horehound	*MARRUBIUM VULGARE*						X					
Common horsetail	*Equisetum arvense*						X					X
Common knotweed	*POLYGONUM AVICULARE* (including subspecies)			X	X	X	X					
Common matrimony vine	*LYCIUM BARBARUM*					X	X					
Common milfoil	*Achillea millefolium*			X	X		X	X	X	X		
Common milkweed	*Asclepias syriaca*			X	X	X	X		X	X		
Common morning glory	*IPOMOEA PURPUREA*					X	X					
Common mouse-ear chickweed	*CERASTIUM FONTANUM s. VULGARE*			X	X	X	X	X	X	X		
Common pepper cress	*Lepidium virginicum*			X	X	X	X	X	X	X	X	X
Common periwinkle	*VINCA MINOR*	X	X		X							
Common plantain	*PLANTAGO MAJOR v. MAJOR*	X	X	X	X	X	X	X	X	X	X	X
Common privet	*LIGUSTRUM VULGARE*	X	X									
Common purpletop	*Tridens flavus*					X	X					
Common ragweed	*Ambrosia artemisiifolia v. elatior*			X	X	X	X			X		
Common reed	*Phragmites australis*			X		X	X				X	X
Common sow thistle	*SONCHUS OLERACEUS*			X	X	X	X	X		X	X	X
Common St. John's wort	*HYPERICUM PERFORATUM*			X	X	X	X					
Common star of Bethlehem	*ORNITHOGALUM UMBELLATUM*		X	X	X	X	X	X	X	X	X	X
Common sunflower	*HELIANTHUS ANNUUS*			X	X	X	X	X		X	X	X
Common teasel	*DIPSACUS FULLONUM*			X	X	X	X			X		X
Common water plantain	*Alisma subcordatum*										X	
Common whitlow cress	*Draba reptans*					X						
Corn speedwell	*VERONICA ARVENSIS*			X	X	X	X	X	X	X	X	X
Cottonweed	*FROELICHIA GRACILIS*					X						
Creeping bent grass	*AGROSTIS STOLONIFERA*								X			
Creeping love grass	*Eragrostis hypnoides*											X
Creeping primrose willow	*Ludwigia peploides s. glabrescens*										X	X
Creeping smartweed	*PERSICARIA CAESPITOSA*	X	X									
Crested oval sedge	*Carex cristatella*						X					
Crowfoot grass	*ELEUSINE INDICA*			X	X	X	X	X	X		X	X
Crown vetch	*CORONILLA VARIA*			X	X	X	X		X	X		X
Curly dock	*RUMEX CRISPUS*				X	X	X	X	X	X	X	X
Cut-leaved teasel	*DIPSACUS LACINIATUS*			X	X	X	X			X		X
Cypress spurge	*EUPHORBIA CYPARISSIAS*	X	X									
Daffodil	*NARCISSUS PSEUDONARCISSUS*	X	X		X		X					
Daisy fleabane	*Erigeron strigosus*					X	X					
Dame's rocket	*HESPERIS MATRONALIS*	X	X				X					
Deam's beard tongue	*Penstemon deamii*						X					
Deptford pink	*DIANTHUS ARMERIA*			X	X	X	X					
Dogbane	*Apocynum cannabinum*					X	X			X		
Dwarf snapdragon	*CHAENORRHINUM MINUS*					X	X					
Eastern prickly pear	*Opuntia humifusa*						X					
Eastern red cedar	*Juniperus virginiana*						X					
Engelmann's spike rush	*Eleocharis engelmannii*											X
English ivy	*HEDERA HELIX*	X	X		X							

Table P-12. *continued*

Common Name	Scientific Name	Urban Forests	Suburban Forests	Industrial Lands	Commercial	Roads/Rails	Rights-of-Way	Soccer/Recreational Lands	Golf Courses	Towers	Storm-water Retention Ponds	Borrow Pits
English plantain	*PLANTAGO LANCEOLATA*			X	X	X	X	X	X	X	X	X
European corn salad	*VALERIANELLA LOCUSTA*	X	X									
European high-bush cranberry	*VIBURNUM OPULUS v. OPULUS*	X	X									
European meadowsweet	*FILIPENDULA ULMARIA*	X	X									
European mountain ash	*SORBUS AUCUPARIA*	X	X									
Everlasting pea	*LATHYRUS LATIFOLIUS*					X	X					
Expressway sedge	*CAREX PRAEGRACILIS*			X	X	X	X					
Fairground grass	*SCLEROCHLOA DURA*							X				
Fall panicum	*Panicum dichotomiflorum* (including 1 subspecies)			X	X	X	X				X	X
False foxglove	*Agalinis purpurea*											X
Fat-hen saltbush	*ATRIPLEX PATULA*			X	X	X	X					
Fetid marigold	*DYSSODIA PAPPOSA*					X						
Field bindweed	*CONVOLVULUS ARVENSIS*			X	X	X	X	X	X	X	X	X
Field cress	*LEPIDIUM CAMPESTRE*			X	X	X	X	X	X	X	X	
Field garlic	*ALLIUM VINEALE*			X	X	X	X	X	X			
Field hedge parsley	*TORILIS ARVENSIS s. ARVENSIS*			X	X	X	X	X	X	X	X	X
Field nut sedge	*Cyperus esculentus v. leptostachyus*			X	X	X	X	X	X	X	X	X
Field penny cress	*THLASPI ARVENSE*			X	X	X	X	X	X	X	X	X
Field sorrel	*RUMEX ACETOSELLA*					X	X					X
Field thistle	*CIRSIUM ARVENSE*			X	X	X	X	X	X	X	X	X
Florida crown grass	*Paspalum floridanum*						X					
Foothill bedstraw	*CRUCIATA PEDEMONTANUM* (= *GALIUM PEDEMONTANUM*)			X	X	X	X			X		
Gama grass	*Tripsacum dactyloides*						X					
Garden asparagus	*ASPARAGUS OFFICINALIS*			X	X	X	X					
Garden loosestrife	*LYSIMACHIA VULGARIS*	X	X									
Garlic mustard	*ALLIARIA PETIOLATA*	X	X									
German iris	*IRIS GERMANICA*		X									
Giant foxtail grass	*SETARIA FABERI*			X	X	X	X	X	X	X	X	X
Giant ragweed	*Ambrosia trifida*			X								
Glaucous campion	*SILENE CSEREI*			X	X	X	X					
Glossy buckthorn	*FRANGULA ALNUS* (= *RHAMNUS FRANGULA*)	X	X									
Golden bell	*FORSYTHIA x INTERMEDIA*	X	X									
Golden cassia	*Chamaecrista fasciculata* (= *Cassia fasciculata*)						X					
Golden rain tree	*KOELREUTERIA PANICULATA*	X	X									
Goose-neck loosestrife	*LYSIMACHIA CLETHROIDES*	X	X									
Great bulrush	*Schoenoplectus tabernaemontani* (= *Scirpus validus*)										X	
Green ash	*Fraxinus pennsylvanica v. lanceolata*		X									
Green hellebore	*HELLEBORUS VIRIDIS*	X	X									
Ground ivy	*GLECHOMA HEDERACEA*	X	X	X	X	X	X	X	X	X	X	X
Hair sedge	*Bulbostylis capillaris*											X
Hairy aster	*Symphyotrichum pilosum v. pilosum*			X	X	X	X			X	X	X
Hairy brome	*BROMUS COMMUTATUS*			X	X	X	X					
Hairy buttercup	*RANUNCULUS SARDOUS*						X					
Hairy crabgrass	*DIGITARIA SANGUINALIS*			X	X	X	X	X	X	X	X	X
Hairy false golden aster	*HETEROTHECA CAMPORUM v. GLANDULISSIMA*						X					
Hard fescue	*FESTUCA OVINA*	X	X						X			
Hardhack	*Spiraea tomentosa*											X
Hedge apple	*MACLURA POMIFERA*					X	X					
Hedge mustard	*SISYMBRIUM OFFICINALE*			X	X	X	X					
Henbit	*LAMIUM AMPLEXICAULE*			X	X	X	X	X	X	X	X	X
Hoary alyssum	*BERTEROA INCANA*					X	X					
Hogwort	*CROTON CAPITATUS* (including 1 variety)					X						
Horse nettle	*Solanum carolinense*			X	X	X	X					
Horsetail milkweed	*Asclepias verticillata*					X	X					
Horseweed	*Conyza canadensis*			X	X	X	X			X	X	X
Hungarian brome	*BROMUS INERMIS*			X	X	X	X		X	X	X	X
Indian mustard	*BRASSICA JUNCEA*			X	X	X	X					
Indian strawberry	*DUCHESNEA INDICA*				X		X	X	X			
Ivy-leaved morning glory	*IPOMOEA HEDERACEA*			X		X	X					

Common Name	Scientific Name	Urban Forests	Suburban Forests	Industrial Lands	Commercial	Roads/Rails	Rights-of-Way	Soccer/Recreational Lands	Golf Courses	Towers	Storm-water Retention Ponds	Borrow Pits
Jagged chickweed	*HOLOSTEUM UMBELLATUM*			X	X	X	X	X	X	X	X	X
Japanese barberry	*BERBERIS THUNBERGII*	X	X									
Japanese chess	*BROMUS JAPONICUS*			X	X	X	X					
Japanese honeysuckle	*LONICERA JAPONICA*	X	X	X		X	X	X	X	X	X	X
Japanese lespedeza	*KUMMEROWIA STRIATA*					X	X					
Japanese rose	*ROSA MULTIFLORA*					X	X		X	X		
Japanese spindle tree	*EUONYMUS HAMILTONIANA*		X									
Jerusalem artichoke	*Helianthus tuberosus*						X					
Jetbead	*RHODOTYPOS SCANDENS*	X	X				X					
Jimsonweed	*DATURA STRAMONIUM*			X	X	X	X					
Johnson grass	*SORGHUM HALEPENSE*			X	X	X	X	X	X	X	X	X
Kankakee mallow	*Iliamna rivularis*						X					
Kentucky bluegrass	*POA PRATENSIS*	X	X	X	X	X	X	X	X	X	X	X
Knawel	*SCLERANTHUS ANNUUS*			X	X	X	X	X	X	X		
Korean clover	*KUMMEROWIA STIPULACEA* (= *LESPEDEZA STIPULACEA*)					X						
Kudzu	*PUERARIA MONTANA v. LOBATA*						X					
Lamb's quarters	*CHENOPODIUM ALBUM v. ALBUM*			X	X	X	X			X	X	X
Lance-leaved violet	*Viola lanceolata*											X
Large passion flower	*Passiflora incarnata*						X					
Late boneset	*Eupatorium serotinum*			X	X	X	X				X	X
Lawn prunella	*PRUNELLA VULGARIS s. VULGARIS*			X	X	X	X	X	X	X	X	X
Leafy spurge	*EUPHORBIA ESULA*					X	X					
Lesquereaux's mustard	*Physaria globosa* (= *Lesquerella globosa*)						X					
Lesser love grass	*ERAGROSTIS MINOR*					X						
Lilac	*SYRINGA VULGARIS*	X	X									
Little-leaf buttercup	*Ranunculus abortivus*			X	X	X						
Long-leaved ammannia	*Ammannia coccinea*											X
Long-scaled nut sedge	*Cyperus strigosus*			X	X	X	X		X	X	X	X
Low hop clover	*TRIFOLIUM CAMPESTRE*			X	X	X	X	X	X	X	X	X
Marsh elder	*Iva annua* (including 1 variety)			X	X	X	X					
Mat sandbur	*Cenchrus longispinus*			X		X						X
Meadow fescue	*SCHEDONORUS PRATENSIS*			X	X	X	X	X	X	X	X	X
Miniature beefsteak plant	*MOSLA DIANTHERA*					X	X					
Moneywort	*LYSIMACHIA NUMMULARIA*	X	X								X	X
Mossy stonecrop	*SEDUM ACRE*				X							
Motherwort	*LEONURUS CARDIACA*	X	X	X	X	X	X	X	X	X	X	X
Moth mullein	*VERBASCUM BLATTARIA*			X	X	X	X	X	X	X	X	X
Mouse-eared cress	*ARABIDOPSIS THALIANA*					X						
Mugwort	*ARTEMISIA VULGARIS*					X						
Mulberry weed	*FATOUA VILLOSA*	X	X									
Musk bristle thistle	*CARDUUS NUTANS*			X	X	X	X			X		X
Narrow-leaved cattail	*TYPHA ANGUSTIFOLIA*			X			X				X	X
Narrow-leaved hawk's beard	*CREPIS TECTORUM*			X	X	X	X					
Nepalese browntop	*MICROSTEGIUM VIMINEUM*	X	X				X					
Night-flowering catchfly	*SILENE NOCTIFLORA*			X	X	X	X	X	X	X	X	X
Nimblewill	*Muhlenbergia schreberi*			X	X	X	X	X	X			
Nits-and-lice	*Hypericum drummondii*											X
Nodding brome	*BROMUS SQUARROSUS*					X	X					
Nodding ladies' tresses	*Spiranthes cernua*											X
Nodding spurge	*Chamaesyce nutans*			X	X	X	X	X	X	X		
Northern rush grass	*Sporobolus vaginiflorus*			X		X	X					
Norway maple	*ACER PLATANOIDES*		X									
Oats	*AVENA SATIVA*					X						
Old-field goldenrod	*Solidago nemoralis* (including 1 subspecies)						X					
Old witch grass	*Panicum capillare*			X	X	X	X					
Orange day lily	*HEMEROCALLIS FULVA*	X	X	X	X	X	X		X	X		
Orange grass	*Hypericum gentianoides*						X					
Orchard grass	*DACTYLIS GLOMERATA*			X	X	X	X					
Ox-eye daisy	*LEUCANTHEMUM VULGARE* (= *CHRYSANTHEMUM LEUCANTHEMUM*)			X	X	X	X	X	X	X	X	
Panicled tick trefoil	*Desmodium paniculatum*						X					
Perennial rye grass	*LOLIUM PERENNE*	X	X	X	X	X	X	X	X	X	X	
Peruvian daisy	*GALINSOGA QUADRIRADIATA*			X	X	X	X					

Table P-12. *continued*

Common Name	Scientific Name	Urban Forests	Suburban Forests	Industrial Lands	Commercial	Roads/Rails	Rights-of-Way	Soccer/Recreational Lands	Golf Courses	Towers	Storm-water Retention Ponds	Borrow Pits
Petioled sunflower	*HELIANTHUS PETIOLARIS*					X						
Pineapple weed	*MATRICARIA DISCOIDEA*			X	X	X	X			X		
Pinkweed	*Persicaria pensylvanica*			X	X	X	X					
Pin oak	*Quercus palustris*		X									
Poet's narcissus	*NARCISSUS POETICUS*	X	X									
Poison hemlock	*CONIUM MACULATUM*			X	X	X	X			X		
Pokeweed	*Phytolacca americana v. americana*			X	X	X	X					
Poor Joe	*Plantago aristata*			X	X	X	X					
Prairie tea	*CROTON MONANTHOGYNUS*					X	X					
Prickly lettuce	*LACTUCA SERRIOLA*			X	X	X	X	X	X	X	X	X
Prickly sida	*SIDA SPINOSA*			X	X	X	X	X	X	X	X	X
Prickly sow thistle	*SONCHUS ASPER*			X	X	X	X	X	X	X	X	X
Princess tree	*PAULOWNIA TOMENTOSA*	X	X	X	X	X	X					
Puncture vine	*TRIBULUS TERRESTRIS*			X	X	X	X	X	X	X	X	X
Purple dead nettle	*LAMIUM PURPUREUM*			X	X	X	X	X	X	X	X	X
Purple loosestrife	*LYTHRUM SALICARIA*										X	X
Purslane	*PORTULACA OLERACEA*	X	X	X	X	X	X	X	X	X	X	X
Quackgrass	*ELYMUS REPENS* (= *AGROPYRON REPENS*)			X	X	X	X		X	X	X	X
Queen Anne's lace	*DAUCUS CAROTA*			X	X	X	X	X		X	X	X
Red clover	*TRIFOLIUM PRATENSE*			X	X	X	X	X	X	X	X	X
Red fescue	*FESTUCA RUBRA*	X	X						X			
Red morning glory	*IPOMOEA COCCINEA*					X	X					
Red raspberry	*Rubus idaeus v. strigosus*						X					
Red-stalked plantain	*Plantago rugelii* (including 1 variety)			X	X	X	X	X	X	X		X
Reed canary grass	*PHALARIS ARUNDINACEA*					X	X				X	X
Rock jasmine	*Androsace occidentalis*			X	X	X						X
Rose blackberry	*Rubus sec. Allegheniensis: R. rosa*						X					
Rose-of-Sharon	*HIBISCUS SYRIACUS*	X	X		X		X					
Rough cinquefoil	*Potentilla norvegica* (including 1 subspecies)			X	X	X	X					
Rough pigweed	*AMARANTHUS RETROFLEXUS*			X	X	X	X					
Round-leaved sundew	*Drosera rotundifolia*											X
Running buffalo clover	*Trifolium stoloniferum*		X									
Running ground pine	*Lycopodium clavatum*											X
Russian thistle	*SALSOLA TRAGUS*			X	X	X	X			X		X
Rye	*SECALE CEREALE*					X	X					
Sand croton	*Croton glandulosus v. septentrionalis*			X		X	X					
Sand goat's beard	*TRAGOPOGON DUBIUS*			X	X	X	X					
Sawtooth sunflower	*Helianthus grosseserratus*						X					
Scotch pine	*PINUS SYLVESTRIS*	X	X									
Sea blite	*SUAEDA CALCEOLIFORMIS*						X					
Shepherd's purse	*CAPSELLA BURSA-PASTORIS*			X	X	X	X	X	X	X		
Short's sedge	*Carex shortiana*						X					
Showy evening primrose	*OENOTHERA SPECIOSA*					X	X					
Siberian elm	*ULMUS PUMILA*	X	X	X	X	X	X	X	X	X	X	X
Silk tree	*ALBIZIA JULIBRISSIN*						X					
Silky bush clover	*LESPEDEZA CUNEATA*			X	X	X	X			X		X
Silver maple	*Acer saccharinum*		X									
Silvery cinquefoil	*POTENTILLA ARGENTEA*			X	X	X	X	X	X	X	X	X
Sleepy catchfly	*Silene antirrhina*			X	X	X	X					
Slender corydalis	*CORYDALIS MICRANTHA*					X						
Small-flowered forget-me-not	*MYOSOTIS STRICTA*			X	X	X	X	X	X	X	X	X
Small-fruited false flax	*CAMELINA MICROCARPA*			X		X						
Small geranium	*GERANIUM PUSILLUM*				X	X	X	X	X	X		
Small green foxtail grass	*SETARIA VIRIDIS v. VIRIDIS*			X	X	X	X	X	X	X	X	X
Small love grass	*Eragrostis pectinacea*			X	X	X	X	X	X	X	X	X
Small mouse-ear chickweed	*CERASTIUM SEMIDECANDRUM*				X	X	X					
Small wild bean	*Strophostyles leiosperma*						X					
Smooth field sow thistle	*SONCHUS ARVENSIS s. ULIGINOSUS*			X	X	X	X	X	X	X	X	X
Smooth Peruvian daisy	*GALINSOGA PARVIFLORA*			X	X	X	X					
Smooth purslane speedwell	*Veronica peregrina s. peregrina*			X	X	X	X			X	X	X
Snowdrop	*GALANTHUS NIVALIS*	X	X									
Snow-on-the-mountain	*EUPHORBIA MARGINATA*	X	X									

Common Name	Scientific Name	Urban Forests	Suburban Forests	Industrial Lands	Commercial	Roads/Rails	Rights-of-Way	Soccer/Recreational Lands	Golf Courses	Towers	Storm-water Retention Ponds	Borrow Pits
Sorghum	*SORGHUM BICOLOR*			X		X	X					
Spanish needles	*Bidens bipinnata*			X		X	X					
Spearmint	*MENTHA SPICATA*					X	X					
Spiny cocklebur	*XANTHIUM SPINOSUM*			X	X	X	X	X	X	X	X	X
Spotted creeping spurge	*Chamaesyce maculata*			X	X	X	X			X		X
Spotted knapweed	*CENTAUREA STOEBE s. MICRANTHOS*					X						
Squirrel-tail grass	*HORDEUM JUBATUM*			X	X	X	X	X	X	X	X	X
Starwort	*STELLARIA GRAMINEA*				X		X	X	X			
Stink grass	*ERAGROSTIS CILIANENSIS*			X	X		X	X	X	X	X	X
Storksbill	*ERODIUM CICUTARIUM*			X	X	X	X	X	X	X	X	X
Sulfur cinquefoil	*POTENTILLA RECTA*				X	X	X					
Swamp milkweed	*Asclepias incarnata*										X	
Sweetgum	*Liquidambar styraciflua*		X									
Tall boneset	*Eupatorium altissimum*					X	X					
Tall buttercup	*RANUNCULUS ACRIS*					X	X					
Tall fescue	*SCHEDONORUS ARUNDINACEUS* (= *FESTUCA ELATIOR*)			X	X	X	X	X	X	X	X	X
Tall goldenrod	*Solidago altissima* (including 1 subspecies)			X	X	X	X				X	X
Tall scouring rush	*Equisetum hyemale s. affine*					X	X					
Tall wood sorrel	*Oxalis stricta*			X	X	X	X	X	X	X		X
Tansy mustard	*DESCURAINIA PINNATA v. BRACHYCARPA*					X	X					
Tartarian honeysuckle	*LONICERA TATARICA*	X	X	X	X	X	X	X	X	X	X	X
Thicket bean	*Phaseolus polystachios*						X					
Three-seeded mercury	*Acalypha rhomboidea*			X								
Thyme-leaved sandwort	*ARENARIA SERPYLLIFOLIA*			X	X	X	X					
Thyme-leaved speedwell	*VERONICA SERPYLLIFOLIA*			X	X	X	X	X	X	X	X	X
Timothy grass	*PHLEUM PRATENSE*			X	X	X	X	X	X	X	X	X
Toothed spurge	*Euphorbia dentata* (= *Poinsettia dentata*)			X	X	X	X			X		
Treacle mustard	*ERYSIMUM REPANDUM*					X	X					
Tree-of-heaven	*AILANTHUS ALTISSIMA*	X		X	X					X		
Tumble mustard	*SISYMBRIUM ALTISSIMUM*			X	X	X	X					
Twisted yellow-eyed grass	*Xyris torta*											X
Weeping forsythia	*FORSYTHIA SUSPENSA*	X	X									
Western ragweed	*AMBROSIA PSILOSTACHYA*					X	X					
Wheat	*TRITICUM AESTIVUM*			X	X	X	X					
Wheelwort	*Rotala ramosior*											X
White bedstraw	*GALIUM MOLLUGO*			X	X	X	X					
White clover	*TRIFOLIUM REPENS*			X	X	X	X	X	X	X	X	X
White mulberry	*MORUS ALBA*	X	X	X	X	X	X					
White pine	*Pinus strobus*		X									
White sage	*ARTEMISIA LUDOVICIANA*					X						
White snakeroot	*Ageratina altissima* (= *Eupatorium rugosum*)	X	X			X	X					X
White sweet clover	*MELILOTUS ALBA*			X	X	X	X	X	X	X	X	X
Wild chervil	*Chaerophyllum tainturieri*					X	X					
Wild four o'clock	*MIRABILIS NYCTAGINEA*			X	X	X	X					
Wild oats	*AVENA FATUA*					X						
Wild parsnip	*PASTINACA SATIVA*			X		X	X			X		
Willow-leaved lettuce	*LACTUCA SALIGNA*					X	X					
Windmill grass	*CHLORIS VERTICILLATA*			X	X	X	X					
Winged euonymus	*EUONYMUS ALATA*	X	X									
Winged monkey flower	*Mimulus alatus*											X
Winged pigweed	*Cycloloma atriplicifolium*											X
Winter vetch	*VICIA VILLOSA s. VILLOSA*			X	X	X	X	X	X	X	X	X
Winterberry	*EUONYMUS BUNGEANA*	X	X									
Wintercreeper	*EUONYMUS FORTUNEI*	X	X									
Woolly blue violet	*Viola sororia*			X	X		X	X	X		X	
Woolly mullein	*VERBASCUM THAPSUS*			X	X	X	X			X		X
Yellow rocket	*BARBAREA VULGARIS*			X	X	X	X					
Yellow sweet clover	*MELILOTUS OFFICINALIS*			X	X	X	X	X	X	X	X	X

Note: Scientific names in all capital letters are exotic species.

Table P-13. Endangered, Threatened, and Rare Plants

Common Name	Scientific Name	Status
Alderleaf buckthorn	*Rhamnus alnifolia*	WL
Allegheny spurge	*Pachysandra procumbens*	SE
Allegheny stonecrop	*Sedum telephioides*	SR
Alumroot	*Heuchera parviflora v. rugelii*	WL
Amazon sprangle-top	*Leptochloa panicoides*	SE
American barberry	*Berberis canadensis*	SE
American chestnut	*Castanea dentata*	WL
American cow-wheat	*Melampyrum lineare*	SR
American fly honeysuckle	*Lonicera canadensis*	SX
American frog's bit	*Limnobium spongia*	SE
American ginseng	*Panax quinquefolius*	WL
American golden saxifrage	*Chrysosplenium americanum*	ST
American lotus	*Nelumbo lutea*	WL
American manna grass	*Glyceria grandis*	SX
American mistletoe	*Phoradendron serotinum*	WL
American pinesap	*Monotropa hypopithys*	WL
American scheuchzeria	*Scheuchzeria palustris ssp. americana*	SE
American sea rocket	*Cakile edentula v. lacustris*	WL
American snowbell	*Styrax americanus*	WL
American speedwell	*Veronica americana*	SX
American water pennywort	*Hydrocotyle americana*	SE
American wintergreen	*Pyrola rotundifolia v. americana*	SR
American yew	*Taxus canadensis*	SE
Angle pod	*Gonolobus obliquus*	SR
Angular-fruited milkvine	*Gonolobus gonocarpos*	WL
Annual fimbry	*Fimbristylis annua*	SE
Appalachian bugbane	*Cimicifuga rubifolia*	SE
Appalachian quillwort	*Isoetes engelmannii*	SE
Appalachian vittaria	*Vittaria appalachiana*	SR
Aromatic aster	*Aster oblongifolius*	SR
Atlantic sedge	*Carex atlantica ssp. atlantica*	ST
Autumn willow	*Salix serissima*	ST
Awned sedge	*Carex atherodes*	SE
Axil flower	*Mecardonia acuminata*	SE
Bald cypress	*Taxodium distichum*	ST
Balsam poplar	*Populus balsamifera*	SX
Baltic rush	*Juncus balticus v. littoralis*	SR
Barren strawberry	*Waldsteinia fragarioides*	SR
Bayonet rush	*Juncus militaris*	SE
Beach peavine	*Lathyrus maritimus v. glaber*	SE
Beach sumac	*Rhus aromatica v. arenaria*	SR
Bearberry	*Arctostaphylos uva-ursi*	SR
Bebb's sedge	*Carex bebbii*	ST
Beck water marigold	*Bidens beckii*	ST
Bellwort	*Uvularia perfoliata*	SE
Bicknell northern crane's bill	*Geranium bicknellii*	SE
Bicknell's panic grass	*Panicum bicknellii*	SE
Biltmore hawthorn	*Crataegus biltmoreana*	SE
Black bugbane	*Cimicifuga racemosa*	WL
Blackfoot quillwort	*Isoetes melanopoda*	ST
Black-fruit mountain ricegrass	*Oryzopsis racemosa*	SR
Black-fruited spike rush	*Eleocharis melanocarpa*	ST
Black hickory	*Carya texana*	SE
Black sedge	*Carex arctata*	SE
Blackseed needlegrass	*Stipa avenacea*	SR
Black-stem spleenwort	*Asplenium resiliens*	SE
Blood witchgrass	*Panicum wilcoxianum*	SR
Bluegrass	*Poa cuspidata*	SX
Bluehearts	*Buchnera americana*	SE
Blue monkshood	*Aconitum uncinatum*	SE
Blue scorpion-weed	*Phacelia ranunculacea*	SE
Blunt-leaf senna	*Senna obtusifolia*	SR
Bluntleaf spurge	*Euphorbia obtusata*	SE
Blunt-lobe grape-fern	*Botrychium oneidense*	WL
Bog bluegrass	*Poa paludigena*	WL
Bog rosemary	*Andromeda glaucophylla*	SR
Bracken fern	*Pteridium aquilinum v. pseudocaudatum*	SX
Bradley's spleenwort	*Asplenium bradleyi*	SE
Branching bur-reed	*Sparganium androcladum*	ST
Bristly foxtail	*Setaria geniculata*	SE
Bristly sarsaparilla	*Aralia hispida*	SE
Bristly-stalk sedge	*Carex leptalea*	WL
Broadleaf beard grass	*Gymnopogon ambiguus*	SX
Broadwing sedge	*Carex alata*	WL
Broom panic grass	*Panicum scoparium*	SE
Brown-fruited rush	*Juncus pelocarpus*	SE
Brownish sedge	*Carex brunnescens*	SE
Buckbean	*Menyanthes trifoliata*	WL
Buckley's goldenrod	*Solidago buckleyi*	SE
Buckthorn	*Bumelia lycioides*	SE
Buffalo clover	*Trifolium reflexum v. glabrum*	SE
Bulrush	*Scirpus expansus*	SE
Bunchberry	*Cornus canadensis*	SE
Burhead	*Echinodorus berteroi*	SX
Bush's sedge	*Carex bushii*	ST
Butternut	*Juglans cinerea*	WL
Buttonweed	*Diodia virginiana*	WL
Calamint	*Satureja glabella v. angustifolia*	SE
Canada buffalo-berry	*Shepherdia canadensis*	SX
Canada burnet	*Sanguisorba canadensis*	SE
Canada lily	*Lilium canadense*	SR
Capitate spike rush	*Eleocharis geniculata*	ST
Carey's smartweed	*Polygonum careyi*	ST
Carolina anemone	*Anemone caroliniana*	SX
Carolina buckthorn	*Rhamnus caroliniana*	WL
Carolina fimbry	*Fimbristylis puberula*	SE
Carolina mosquito fern	*Azolla caroliniana*	ST
Carolina panic grass	*Panicum yadkinense*	SE
Carolina spider lily	*Hymenocallis occidentalis*	WL
Carolina tassel rue	*Trautvetteria caroliniensis*	SX
Carolina thistle	*Cirsium carolinianum*	SR
Carolina willow	*Salix caroliniana*	WL
Carolina woollywhite	*Hymenopappus scabiosaeus*	SE
Carolina yellow-eyed grass	*Xyris difformis*	ST
Catbird grape	*Vitis palmata*	SR
Cattail gay feather	*Liatris pycnostachya*	ST
Chamomile grape fern	*Botrychium matricariifolium*	SR
Cherrybark oak	*Quercus falcata v. pagodifolia*	WL
Clasping-leaved St. John's wort	*Hypericum gymnanthum*	SE
Cleft phlox	*Phlox bifida ssp. stellaria*	SE
Climbing dogbane	*Trachelospermum difforme*	SR
Climbing fern	*Lygodium palmatum*	SE
Climbing fumatory	*Adlumia fungosa*	SX
Climbing hempweed	*Mikania scandens*	SE
Clingman hedge nettle	*Stachys clingmanii*	SE
Clinton lily	*Clintonia borealis*	SE
Clinton wood fern	*Dryopteris clintoniana*	SX
Cluster fescue	*Festuca paradoxa*	ST
Clustered broom rape	*Orobanche fasciculata*	SE
Clustered foxglove	*Agalinis fasciculata*	WL
Clustered poppy mallow	*Callirhoe triangulata*	SX
Clustered sedge	*Carex cumulata*	SE
Common mare's tail	*Hippuris vulgaris*	SX
Commons' panic grass	*Panicum commonsianum v. addisonii*	SE
Coneflower	*Rudbeckia fulgida v. umbrosa*	SE
Coppery St. John's wort	*Hypericum denticulatum*	ST
Crawe sedge	*Carex crawei*	ST
Cream wild indigo	*Baptisia leucophaea*	WL
Creeping bur-head	*Echinodorus cordifolius*	SE
Creeping cucumber	*Melothria pendula*	SE
Creeping sedge	*Carex chordorrhiza*	SE
Creeping St. John's wort	*Hypericum adpressum*	SE
Crested coralroot	*Hexalectris spicata*	SR
Crow poison	*Nothoscordum bivalve*	SR
Cuckoo flower	*Cardamine pratensis v. palustris*	WL
Cucumber magnolia	*Magnolia acuminata*	SE
Cupseed	*Calycocarpum lyonii*	ST
Cusp dodder	*Cuscuta cuspidata*	SX
Cutleaf water milfoil	*Myriophyllum pinnatum*	SE
Cylindric-fruited seedbox	*Ludwigia glandulosa*	ST
Cyperus-like sedge	*Carex pseudocyperus*	SE
Cypress-knee sedge	*Carex decomposita*	ST
Deam's beard tongue	*Penstemon deamii*	SR

Common Name	Scientific Name	Status
Deam's dewberry	*Rubus deamii*	SX
Deciduous holly	*Ilex decidua*	WL
Deep-root clubmoss	*Lycopodium tristachyum*	SR
Dense cotton grass	*Eriophorum spissum*	SX
Devil's bit	*Chamaelirium luteum*	SE
Dewberry	*Rubus impar*	SX
Divided toothwort	*Dentaria multifida*	SE
Downy gentian	*Gentiana puberulenta*	ST
Downy panic grass	*Panicum subvillosum*	SE
Downy yellow violet	*Viola pubescens*	WL
Drummond's hemicarpha	*Hemicarpha drummondii*	SX
Drummond's rockcress	*Arabis drummondii*	SE
Dune thistle	*Cirsium pitcheri*	LT, ST
Dwarf chinquapin oak	*Quercus prinoides*	SE
Dwarf dandelion	*Krigia oppositifolia*	ST
Dwarf ginseng	*Panax trifolius*	WL
Dwarf umbrella sedge	*Fuirena pumila*	ST
Ear-leaf foxglove	*Agalinis auriculata*	ST
Early coralroot	*Corallorhiza trifida v. verna*	SX
Eastern bee-balm	*Monarda bradburiana*	SE
Eastern bloodleaf	*Iresine rhizomatosa*	SR
Eastern eulophus	*Perideridia americana*	SE
Eastern featherbells	*Stenanthium gramineum*	ST
Eastern hay-scented fern	*Dennstaedtia punctilobula*	WL
Eastern hemlock	*Tsuga canadensis*	WL
Eastern jointweed	*Polygonella articulata*	SR
Eastern milk pea	*Galactia volubilis v. mississippiensis*	WL
Eastern white pine	*Pinus strobus*	SR
Ebony sedge	*Carex eburnea*	SR
Eggleston's violet	*Viola egglestonii*	SE
Elk sedge	*Carex garberi*	ST
Elliptical rushfoil	*Crotonopsis elliptica*	SE
Elliptical-leaf wintergreen	*Pyrola elliptica*	WL
Elliptic-leaved blackberry	*Rubus alumnus*	SX
False asphodel	*Tofieldia glutinosa*	SR
False bearded panic grass	*Panicum mattamuskeetense*	SX
False hellebore	*Veratrum woodii*	WL
False hop sedge	*Carex lupuliformis*	SR
Farkleberry	*Vaccinium arboreum*	WL
Featherfoil	*Hottonia inflata*	ST
Few-flower nut rush	*Scleria pauciflora*	WL
Few-flower spike rush	*Eleocharis pauciflora*	WL
Few-flowered scurf pea	*Psoralea tenuiflora*	SX
Filmy fern	*Trichomanes boschianum*	SE
Fineberry hawthorn	*Crataegus chrysocarpa*	SE
Finely-nerved sedge	*Carex leptonervia*	SE
Fire cherry	*Prunus pensylvanica*	SR
Fireweed	*Epilobium angustifolium*	SE
Flatleaf bladderwort	*Utricularia intermedia*	WL
Flatleaf pondweed	*Potamogeton robbinsii*	SR
Fleabane	*Conyza canadensis v. pusilla*	SX
Fleshy hawthorn	*Crataegus succulenta*	SR
Forbes' saxifrage	*Saxifraga forbesii*	SE
Forked aster	*Aster furcatus*	SR
Forked bluecurl	*Trichostema dichotomum*	SR
Foxtail sedge	*Carex alopecoidea*	SE
French's shooting star	*Dodecatheon frenchii*	SR
Fries' pondweed	*Potamogeton friesii*	ST
Fringed black bindweed	*Polygonum cilinode*	SE
Gay-wing milkwort	*Polygala paucifolia*	SE
Glade mallow	*Napaea dioica*	SR
Globe beaked rush	*Rhynchospora recognita*	SE
Globe-fruited false loosestrife	*Ludwigia sphaerocarpa*	SE
Golden alexanders	*Zizia aptera*	SR
Golden cattail sedge	*Carex aureolensis*	SE
Golden-fruited sedge	*Carex aurea*	SR
Golden seal	*Hydrastis canadensis*	WL
Golden St. John's wort	*Hypericum frondosum*	SX
Goldthread	*Coptis trifolia v. groenlandica*	WL
Goose-foot corn-salad	*Valerianella chenopodiifolia*	SE
Grand hawthorn	*Crataegus grandis*	SE
Grassleaf ladies' tresses	*Spiranthes vernalis*	WL
Gray beard tongue	*Penstemon canescens*	SE
Gray birch	*Betula populifolia*	SE
Great Plains ladies' tresses	*Spiranthes magnicamporum*	SE
Great St. John's wort	*Hypericum pyramidatum*	ST
Green adder's mouth	*Malaxis unifolia*	SE
Green flat sedge	*Cyperus pseudovegetus*	SR
Green hawthorn	*Crataegus viridis*	ST
Green milkweed	*Asclepias viridis*	SE
Green-fringe orchis	*Platanthera lacera*	WL
Greenish-flowered wintergreen	*Pyrola virens*	SX
Green-keeled cotton grass	*Eriophorum viridicarinatum*	SR
Grooved yellow flax	*Linum sulcatum*	SR
Ground juniper	*Juniperus communis*	SR
Grove meadow grass	*Poa alsodes*	SR
Gyandotte beauty	*Synandra hispidula*	WL
Hairy alumroot	*Heuchera villosa*	WL
Hairy-fruit sedge	*Carex trichocarpa*	WL
Hairy-fruited hibiscus	*Hibiscus moscheutos ssp. lasiocarpos*	SE
Hairy golden aster	*Chrysopsis villosa*	ST
Hairy goldenrod	*Solidago hispida*	WL
Hairy lipfern	*Cheilanthes lanosa*	SR
Hairy valerian	*Valeriana edulis*	SE
Hairy willow herb	*Epilobium ciliatum*	SX
Hairy woodrush	*Luzula acuminata*	SE
Hall's bulrush	*Scirpus hallii*	SE
Harvey's buttercup	*Ranunculus harveyi*	SE
Heartleaf willow	*Salix cordata*	ST
Heart-leaved noseburn	*Tragia cordata*	WL
Heart-leaved plantain	*Plantago cordata*	SE
Heavy sedge	*Carex gravida*	SE
Hemlock panic grass	*Panicum columbianum*	SR
Hemlock parsley	*Conioselinum chinense*	SE
Herb Robert	*Geranium robertianum*	ST
Hickey's clubmoss	*Lycopodium hickeyi*	SR
Hidden-fruited bladderwort	*Utricularia geminiscapa*	SE
High-bush cranberry	*Viburnum opulus v. americanum*	SE
Hill's thistle	*Cirsium hillii*	SE
Holly-leaved naiad	*Najas marina*	WL
Hooded ladies' tresses	*Spiranthes romanzoffiana*	ST
Hooker's orchid	*Platanthera hookeri*	SX
Horned bladderwort	*Utricularia cornuta*	ST
Horned pondweed	*Zannichellia palustris*	SR
Horse-tail spike rush	*Eleocharis equisetoides*	SE
Houghton's nut sedge	*Cyperus houghtonii*	SE
Howe sedge	*Carex atlantica ssp. capillacea*	SE
Illinois blackberry	*Rubus centralis*	SE
Illinois hawthorn	*Crataegus prona*	SE
Illinois pinweed	*Lechea racemulosa*	SE
Illinois wood sorrel	*Oxalis illinoensis*	WL
Jack pine	*Pinus banksiana*	SR
Jointed rush	*Juncus articulatus*	SE
Kalm St. John's wort	*Hypericum kalmianum*	WL
Kankakee globe mallow	*Iliamna remota*	SE
Kellogg hawthorn	*Crataegus kelloggii*	SE
Kentucky wisteria	*Wisteria macrostachya*	SR
Kitten tails	*Besseya bullii*	SE
Lake cress	*Armoracia aquatica*	SE
Lance-leaved buckthorn	*Rhamnus lanceolata*	WL
Large cranberry	*Vaccinium macrocarpon*	WL
Large-flower false false foxglove	*Aureolaria grandiflora v. pulchra*	SX
Large-leaf snowbell	*Styrax grandifolius*	SE
Large-leaved phlox	*Phlox amplifolia*	SR
Large marsh St. John's wort	*Triadenum tubulosum*	WL
Large roundleaf orchid	*Platanthera orbiculata*	SX
Large sedge	*Carex gigantea*	ST
Large-seeded forget-me-not	*Myosotis macrosperma*	WL
Large whorled pogonia	*Isotria verticillata*	WL
Large yellow lady's slipper	*Cypripedium calceolus v. pubescens*	WL
Leafy northern green orchis	*Platanthera hyperborea*	ST
Leafy white orchis	*Platanthera dilatata*	SE
Least duckweed	*Lemna minima*	SE
Least grape fern	*Botrychium simplex*	SE

Table P-13. *continued*

Common Name	Scientific Name	Status
Leathery grape fern	*Botrychium multifidum v. intermedium*	SX
Ledge spike moss	*Selaginella rupestris*	ST
Leiberg's witchgrass	*Panicum leibergii*	ST
Lesquereux's mustard	*Lesquerella globosa*	FC, SE
Lesser bladderwort	*Utricularia minor*	ST
Lesser ladies' tresses	*Spiranthes ovalis*	WL
Limestone adder's tongue	*Ophioglossum engelmannii*	SR
Little bur-head	*Echinodorus parvulus*	SE
Little-headed nut rush	*Scleria oligantha*	WL
Little ladies' tresses	*Spiranthes tuberosa*	WL
Little prickly sedge	*Carex echinata*	SE
Livid sedge	*Carex livida*	SE
Loesel's twayblade	*Liparis loeselii*	WL
Log fern	*Dryopteris celsa*	SE
Long-awn hairgrass	*Muhlenbergia capillaris*	SE
Longbeak arrowhead	*Sagittaria australis*	SR
Long-beaked baldrush	*Psilocarya scirpoides*	ST
Long-bract green orchis	*Coeloglossum viride v. virescens*	ST
Long-leaved panic grass	*Panicum longifolium*	SX
Long sedge	*Carex folliculata*	SR
Longstalk sedge	*Carex pedunculata*	SR
Louisiana broom rape	*Orobanche ludoviciana*	SE
Louisiana sedge	*Carex louisianica*	WL
Louisiana unicorn plant	*Proboscidea louisianica*	SX
Marram grass	*Ammophila breviligulata*	WL
Marsh arrowgrass	*Triglochin palustris*	SR
Marsh valerian	*Valeriana uliginosa*	SE
Maryland butterfly-pea	*Clitoria mariana*	WL
Maryland meadow beauty	*Rhexia mariana v. mariana*	ST
Matted broomspurge	*Euphorbia serpens*	SE
Meadow spike-moss	*Selaginella apoda*	WL
Mead's milkweed	*Asclepias meadii*	LT, SRE
Mercury	*Acalypha deamii*	SR
Michaux leavenworthia	*Leavenworthia uniflora*	SE
Michaux's stitchwort	*Arenaria stricta*	SR
Minute duckweed	*Lemna perpusilla*	SX
Mississippi buttercup	*Ranunculus laxicaulis*	SE
Missouri rockcress	*Arabis missouriensis v. deamii*	SE
Mountain holly	*Nemopanthus mucronatus*	WL
Mountain laurel	*Kalmia latifolia*	WL
Mountain phlox	*Phlox ovata*	SE
Mountain spleenwort	*Asplenium montanum*	SE
Mud sedge	*Carex limosa*	SE
Narrowleaf aster	*Aster solidagineus*	WL
Narrowleaf summer bluets	*Houstonia nigricans*	SR
Narrow-leaved cotton grass	*Eriophorum angustifolium*	SR
Narrow-leaved puccoon	*Lithospermum incisum*	SE
Narrow melic grass	*Melica mutica*	WL
Netted chainfern	*Woodwardia areolata*	SR
Nodding rattlesnake root	*Prenanthes crepidinea*	WL
Nodding trillium	*Trillium cernuum v. macranthum*	SE
Nondo lovage	*Ligusticum canadense*	SE
Northeastern bladderwort	*Utricularia resupinata*	SX
Northeastern smartweed	*Polygonum hydropiperoides v. opelousanum*	ST
Northern appressed bog clubmoss	*Lycopodiella subappressa*	SE
Northern bog clubmoss	*Lycopodiella inundata*	SE
Northern bush honeysuckle	*Diervilla lonicera*	SR
Northern catalpa	*Catalpa speciosa*	SR
Northern gama grass	*Tripsacum dactyloides*	WL
Northern mountain ash	*Sorbus decora*	SX
Northern pitcher plant	*Sarracenia purpurea*	WL
Northern white cedar	*Thuja occidentalis*	SE
Northern wild raisin	*Viburnum cassinoides*	SE
Northern witchgrass	*Panicum boreale*	SR
Nuttall pondweed	*Potamogeton epihydrus*	SE
Oakes' pondweed	*Potamogeton oakesianus*	SE
Oklahoma sedge	*Carex oklahomensis*	SE
One-sided wintergreen	*Pyrola secunda*	SX
Orange coneflower	*Rudbeckia fulgida v. fulgida*	WL
Ostrich fern	*Matteuccia struthiopteris*	SR
Ovate catchfly	*Silene ovata*	SE
Overcup oak	*Quercus lyrata*	WL
Pale corydalis	*Corydalis sempervirens*	ST
Pale duckweed	*Lemna valdiviana*	SE
Pale false foxglove	*Agalinis skinneriana*	ST
Pale green orchis	*Platanthera flava v. herbiola*	WL
Pale vetchling peavine	*Lathyrus ochroleucus*	SE
Paper birch	*Betula papyrifera*	WL
Partridge pea	*Cassia fasciculata v. robusta*	WL
Pink lady's slipper	*Cypripedium acaule*	WL
Pink milkwort	*Polygala incarnata*	SE
Pink thoroughwort	*Eupatorium incarnatum*	ST
Pink wintergreen	*Pyrola asarifolia*	SE
Pipewort	*Eriocaulon aquaticum*	SE
Pipsissewa	*Chimaphila umbellata ssp. cisatlantica*	ST
Pitcher leather flower	*Clematis pitcheri*	SR
Pitcher's stitchwort	*Arenaria patula*	SE
Plains muhlenbergia	*Muhlenbergia cuspidata*	SE
Prairie fame flower	*Talinum rugospermum*	ST
Prairie goldenrod	*Solidago ptarmicoides*	SR
Prairie gray sedge	*Carex conoidea*	ST
Prairie parsley	*Polytaenia nuttallii*	SE
Prairie redroot	*Ceanothus herbaceus*	SE
Prairie rocket wallflower	*Erysimum capitatum*	ST
Prairie violet	*Viola pedatifida*	ST
Prairie white-fringed orchid	*Platanthera leucophaea*	LT, SE
Pretty sedge	*Carex woodii*	WL
Prickly hornwort	*Ceratophyllum echinatum*	SR
Primrose-leaf violet	*Viola primulifolia*	ST
Primrose willow	*Ludwigia decurrens*	WL
Purple avens	*Geum rivale*	SE
Purple bladderwort	*Utricularia purpurea*	SR
Purple flowering raspberry	*Rubus odoratus*	ST
Purple fringeless orchis	*Platanthera peramoena*	WL
Purple oat	*Schizachne purpurascens*	SE
Purple passion flower	*Passiflora incarnata*	SR
Pursh buttercup	*Ranunculus pusillus*	SE
Queen-of-the-prairie	*Filipendula rubra*	WL
Rattlesnake hawkweed	*Hieracium venosum*	WL
Red baneberry	*Actaea rubra*	SR
Red-berried moonseed	*Cocculus carolinus*	WL
Redhead grass	*Potamogeton richardsonii*	SR
Reed bent grass	*Calamagrostis porteri ssp. insperata*	ST
Resurrection fern	*Polypodium polypodioides*	SR
Reticulated nut rush	*Scleria reticularis*	ST
Retrorse sedge	*Carex retrorsa*	SE
Richardson's sedge	*Carex richardsonii*	ST
Ridged yellow flax	*Linum striatum*	WL
Ringed panic grass	*Panicum annulum*	SE
Robbins' spike rush	*Eleocharis robbinsii*	SR
Rock clubmoss	*Huperzia porophila*	WL
Rock skullcap	*Scutellaria saxatilis*	SE
Rose pogonia	*Pogonia ophioglossoides*	WL
Rose turtlehead	*Chelone obliqua v. speciosa*	WL
Rough rattlesnake-root	*Prenanthes aspera*	SR
Rough sedge	*Carex scabrata*	SE
Roundleaf dogwood	*Cornus rugosa*	SR
Roundleaf sundew	*Drosera rotundifolia*	WL
Roundleaf water hyssop	*Bacopa rotundifolia*	ST
Round-leaved boneset	*Eupatorium rotundifolium*	WL
Round-stem foxglove	*Agalinis gattingeri*	WL
Royal catchfly	*Silene regia*	ST
Running buffalo clover	*Trifolium stoloniferum*	LE, SE
Running pine	*Lycopodium clavatum*	WL
Running serviceberry	*Amelanchier humilis*	SE
Rushlike aster	*Aster borealis*	SR
Sand grape	*Vitis rupestris*	SE
Sand heather	*Hudsonia tomentosa*	ST
Sand hickory	*Carya pallida*	SE
Sandplain flax	*Linum intercursum*	SE
Saw greenbrier	*Smilax bona-nox*	WL
Scaly gay feather	*Liatris squarrosa*	WL
Scarlet hawthorn	*Crataegus pedicellata*	ST

Common Name	Scientific Name	Status
Schreber aster	*Aster schreberi*	SE
Scirpus-like rush	*Juncus scirpoides*	ST
Seabeach needlegrass	*Aristida tuberculosa*	SR
Seaside spurge	*Euphorbia polygonifolia*	SR
Secund rush	*Juncus secundus*	SE
Sessile-leaved bugleweed	*Lycopus amplectens*	SE
Sewing needle grass	*Stipa comata*	SX
Shaggy false gromwell	*Onosmodium hispidissimum*	SE
Sharp-scaled manna grass	*Glyceria acutiflora*	SE
Shining clubmoss	*Lycopodium lucidulum*	WL
Shining ladies' tresses	*Spiranthes lucida*	SR
Shining panic grass	*Panicum lucidum*	SE
Short-beaked bald rush	*Psilocarya nitens*	SX
Short-bristle horned rush	*Rhynchospora corniculata v. interior*	ST
Short-point flat sedge	*Cyperus acuminatus*	SE
Short's goldenrod	*Solidago shortii*	LE, SE
Showy lady's slipper	*Cypripedium reginae*	WL
Showy meadow beauty	*Rhexia mariana v. interior*	WL
Silky dogwood	*Cornus amomum ssp. amomum*	SE
Silver bluestem	*Andropogon ternarius*	WL
Silverweed	*Potentilla anserina*	ST
Single-head pussytoes	*Antennaria solitaria*	WL
Slender cotton grass	*Eriophorum gracile*	ST
Slender heliotrope	*Heliotropium tenellum*	ST
Slender marsh pink	*Sabatia campanulata*	SX
Slender mountain ricegrass	*Oryzopsis pungens*	SX
Slender pondweed	*Potamogeton pusillus*	WL
Slender-stalked gaura	*Gaura filipes*	ST
Slender water milfoil	*Myriophyllum tenellum*	SE
Slick-seed wild bean	*Strophostyles leiosperma*	ST
Slim-spike three-awn grass	*Aristida intermedia*	SR
Small bristleberry	*Rubus setosus*	SE
Small cranberry	*Vaccinium oxycoccos*	ST
Small enchanter's nightshade	*Circaea alpina*	SX
Smaller forget-me-not	*Myosotis laxa*	ST
Small floating manna grass	*Glyceria borealis*	SE
Small-fruited spike rush	*Eleocharis microcarpa*	SE
Small green woodland orchis	*Platanthera clavellata*	WL
Small purple-fringe orchis	*Platanthera psycodes*	SR
Small skullcap	*Scutellaria parvula v. parvula*	SX
Small's ragwort	*Senecio anonymus*	WL
Small's snakeroot	*Sanicula smallii*	SR
Small sundrops	*Oenothera perennis*	SR
Small swollen bladderwort	*Utricularia radiata*	SE
Small white lady's slipper	*Cypripedium candidum*	WL
Small yellow lady's slipper	*Cypripedium calceolus v. parviflorum*	SR
Smith's bulrush	*Scirpus smithii*	SE
Smooth gooseberry	*Ribes hirtellum*	WL
Smooth tick trefoil	*Desmodium laevigatum*	WL
Smooth veiny pea	*Lathyrus venosus*	ST
Smooth white violet	*Viola blanda*	WL
Snail-seed pondweed	*Potamogeton bicupulatus*	SE
Social sedge	*Carex socialis*	SR
Soft-leaf arrowwood	*Viburnum molle*	SR
Soft-leaf sedge	*Carex disperma*	SE
Sourwood	*Oxydendrum arboreum*	SR
Southern dewberry	*Rubus enslenii*	SE
Southern rein orchid	*Platanthera flava v. flava*	SE
Southern skullcap	*Scutellaria parvula v. australis*	WL
Southern wood violet	*Viola hirsutula*	SX
Sparse-lobe grape fern	*Botrychium biternatum*	WL
Speckled alder	*Alnus rugosa*	WL
Spoon-leaved sundew	*Drosera intermedia*	SR
Spotted pondweed	*Potamogeton pulcher*	SE
Spotted wintergreen	*Chimaphila maculata*	WL
Spreading rockcress	*Arabis patens*	SE
Stemless evening primrose	*Oenothera triloba*	SX
Sticky goldenrod	*Solidago simplex v. gillmanii*	ST
Stout-ragged goldenrod	*Solidago squarrosa*	SE
Straggling St. John's wort	*Hypericum dolabriforme*	SR
Straight-leaf pondweed	*Potamogeton strictifolius*	ST
Straw sedge	*Carex straminea*	ST

Common Name	Scientific Name	Status
Strict blue-eyed grass	*Sisyrinchium montanum*	SE
Striped gentian	*Gentiana villosa*	SE
Sullivantia	*Sullivantia sullivantii*	ST
Swamp smartweed	*Polygonum hydropiperoides v. setaceum*	SE
Swamp sunflower	*Helianthus angustifolius*	SE
Swamp pink	*Arethusa bulbosa*	SX
Sweet fern	*Comptonia peregrina*	WL
Sword bogmat	*Wolffiella gladiata*	SE
Tall beaked rush	*Rhynchospora macrostachya*	SR
Tall bush clover	*Lespedeza stuevei*	SX
Tall meadow rue	*Thalictrum pubescens*	ST
Tall millet grass	*Milium effusum*	SR
Tamarack	*Larix laricina*	WL
Tennessee milk vetch	*Astragalus tennesseensis*	SRE
Texas bracted sedge	*Carex texensis*	WL
Thicket sedge	*Carex abscondita*	WL
Thinleaf sedge	*Carex sparganioides v. cephaloidea*	SE
Thread-like naiad	*Najas gracillima*	ST
Three-flower melic grass	*Melica nitens*	ST
Three-seed sedge	*Carex trisperma*	WL
Timid sedge	*Carex timida*	SE
Toothed sedge	*Cyperus dentatus*	SE
Torrey's bulrush	*Scirpus torreyi*	SE
Tower mustard	*Arabis glabra*	WL
Trailing arbutus	*Epigaea repens*	WL
Trampled dewberry	*Rubus depavitus*	SX
Tree clubmoss	*Lycopodium obscurum*	SR
Tree hawthorn	*Crataegus arborea*	SE
Treelike clubmoss	*Lycopodium dendroideum*	SE
Trifling hawthorn	*Crataegus intricata*	SR
Tube penstemon	*Penstemon tubaeflorus*	SX
Tufted hair grass	*Deschampsia cespitosa*	SR
Turk's cap lily	*Lilium superbum*	WL
Twinflower	*Linnaea borealis*	SX
Twining bartonia	*Bartonia paniculata*	WL
Two-leaf toothwort	*Dentaria diphylla*	WL
Umbrella magnolia	*Magnolia tripetala*	SE
Upright pinweed	*Lechea stricta*	SX
Variegated horsetail	*Equisetum variegatum*	SE
Vasey's pondweed	*Potamogeton vaseyi*	SE
Velvet-leaf blueberry	*Vaccinium myrtilloides*	SE
Velvety tick trefoil	*Desmodium viridiflorum*	WL
Virginia bunchflower	*Melanthium virginicum*	SE
Virginia mallow	*Sida hermaphrodita*	SE
Virginia pine	*Pinus virginiana*	WL
Virginia saxifrage	*Saxifraga virginiensis*	WL
Virginia tuberose	*Agave virginica*	WL
Virginia willow	*Itea virginica*	SE
Wall rue spleenwort	*Asplenium ruta-muraria*	SR
Walter's St. John's wort	*Triadenum walteri*	WL
Warty panic grass	*Panicum verrucosum*	ST
Water bulrush	*Scirpus subterminalis*	SR
Water locust	*Gleditsia aquatica*	SE
Water purslane	*Didiplis diandra*	SE
Waxy-leaved aster	*Aster undulatus*	WL
Weak stellate sedge	*Carex seorsa*	SR
Weak-stalk bulrush	*Scirpus purshianus*	SR
Western lettuce	*Lactuca ludoviciana*	SX
Western rock jasmine	*Androsace occidentalis*	ST
Western silvery aster	*Aster sericeus*	SR
White camas	*Zigadenus elegans v. glaucus*	SR
White crownbeard	*Verbesina virginica*	SE
White-edge sedge	*Carex debilis v. rudgei*	SR
White-grained mountain ricegrass	*Oryzopsis asperifolia*	SE
White milkweed	*Asclepias variegata*	WL
White-stem pondweed	*Potamogeton praelongus*	ST
White thoroughwort	*Eupatorium album*	ST
Whorled water milfoil	*Myriophyllum verticillatum*	SR
Wild basil	*Satureja vulgaris v. neogaea*	ST
Wild calla	*Calla palustris*	SE
Wild chervil	*Chaerophyllum procumbens v. shortii*	ST

Table P-13. *continued*

Common Name	Scientific Name	Status
Wild false indigo	*Baptisia australis*	SR
Wild hyacinth	*Camassia angusta*	SE
Wild mudwort	*Dicliptera brachiata*	SE
Wild sensitive plant	*Cassia nictitans*	WL
Winged cudweed	*Gnaphalium macounii*	SX
Wolf bluegrass	*Poa wolfii*	SR
Wolf spike rush	*Eleocharis wolfii*	SR
Woodland pinkroot	*Spigelia marilandica*	SE
Woodland strawberry	*Fragaria vesca v. americana*	SE
Woollybeard grass	*Erianthus alopecuroides*	WL
Woolly Dutchman's pipe	*Aristolochia tomentosa*	WL
Yellow buckeye	*Aesculus octandra*	WL
Yellow-fringe orchis	*Platanthera ciliaris*	SE
Yellow gentian	*Gentiana alba*	SR
Yellow nodding ladies' tresses	*Spiranthes ochroleuca*	ST
Yellow sedge	*Carex flava*	ST
Yellow wild indigo	*Baptisia tinctoria*	WL
Yellowwood	*Cladrastis lutea*	ST
Zigzag bladderwort	*Utricularia subulata*	ST

Notes: FC = federal candidate; LT = federally listed as threatened; LE = federally listed as endangered; SX = state extirpated; SE = state endangered; ST = state threatened; SR = state rare; WL = state watch list; SRE = state reintroduced (for rare species that have been intentionally reintroduced, such as *Asclepias meadii*).

Table P-14. Invasive Exotic Plants in Indiana Natural Areas

Common Name	Scientific Name	Comments
Amur bush honeysuckle	*Lonicera maackii*	
Beefsteak mint	*Perilla frutescens*	
Bicolor lespedeza	*Lespedeza bicolor*	
Bittersweet nightshade	*Solanum dulcamara*	
Black alder	*Alnus glutinosa*	
Black locust	*Robinia pseudo-acacia*	in areas other than Ohio River counties (apparently native along the Ohio River)
Bull thistle	*Cirsium vulgare*	
Burning bush	*Euonymus alatus*	
Callery pear	*Pyrus calleryana*	
Canada bluegrass	*Poa compressa*	
Canada thistle	*Cirsium arvense*	
Chaff flower	*Achyranthes japonica*	
Cheat brome	*Bromus spp.*	
Chinese silver grass	*Miscanthus sinensis*	
Chinese wisteria	*Wisteria sinensis*	
Cinnamon vine	*Dioscorea polystachya*	
Coltsfoot	*Tussilago farfara*	
Common buckthorn	*Rhamnus cathartica*	
Common chickweed	*Stellaria media*	
Common day lily	*Hemerocallis fulva*	
Common privet	*Ligustrum spp.*	
Common reed	*Phragmites australis*	introduced lineage
Creeping bent grass	*Agrostis stolonifera*	
Crown vetch	*Coronilla varia*	
Curly muckweed	*Potamogeton crispus*	
Dame's rocket	*Hesperis matronalis*	
English ivy	*Hedera helix*	
European water milfoil	*Myriophyllum spicatum*	
Garden loosestrife	*Lysimachia vulgaris*	
Garlic mustard	*Alliaria petiolata*	
Glossy buckthorn	*Rhamnus frangula*	
Greater periwinkle	*Vinca major*	
Ground ivy	*Glechoma hederacea*	
Hairy joint grass	*Arthraxon hispidus*	

Table P-14. *continued*

Common Name	Scientific Name	Comments
High-bush cranberry	*Viburnum opulus* (= *v. Trilobum v. Opulus*)	
Japanese barberry	*Berberis thunbergii*	
Japanese honeysuckle	*Lonicera japonica*	
Japanese hops	*Humulus japonicus*	
Japanese knotweed	*Polygonum cuspidatum*	
Japanese lespedeza	*Kummerowia striata* (= *lespedeza striata*)	
Johnson grass	*Sorghum halapense*	
Kentucky bluegrass	*Poa pratensis*	
Korean lespedeza	*Kummerowia stipulacea* (= *lespedeza stipulacea*)	
Kudzu vine	*Pueraria lobata*	
Leafy spurge	*Euphorbia esula*	
Meadow fescue	*Schedonorus pratensis* (= *festuca pratensis*)	
Moneywort	*Lysimachia nummularia*	
Multiflora rose	*Rosa multiflora*	
Musk thistle	*Carduus nutans*	
Myrtle (= periwinkle)	*Vinca minor*	
Osage orange	*Maclura pomifera*	
Ox-eye daisy	*Leucanthemum vulgare* (= *chrysanthemum leucanthemum*)	
Perfumed cherry	*Prunus mahaleb*	
Princess tree	*Paulownia tomentosa*	
Purple loosestrife	*Lythrum salicaria*	
Reed canary grass	*Phalaris arundinacea*	apparent introduced lineage
Round-leaved bittersweet	*Celastrus orbiculatus*	
Sheep sorrel	*Rumex acetosella*	
Silky bush clover	*Lespedeza cuneata*	
Smooth brome	*Bromus inermis*	
Star thistle (= knapweed)	*Centaurea spp.*	
Stilt grass	*Microstegium vimineus*	
Tall fescue	*Schedonorus phoenix* (= *festuca elatior*)	
Tartarian bush honeysuckle	*Lonicera tatarica* (and related species and hybrids)	
Teasel	*Dipsacus sylvestris, d. Laciniatus*	
Tree-of-heaven	*Ailanthus altissima*	
White clover	*Trifolium repens*	
White sweet clover	*Melilotus alba*	
Wild parsnip	*Pastinaca sativa*	
Wineberry	*Rubus phoenicolasius*	
Winter creeper	*Euonymus fortunei*	
Yellow sweet clover	*Melilotus officinalis*	

Note: This table contains most of the troublesome non-native plants that have been observed occurring in natural communities. Some are more invasive than others, but all can spread into natural communities and compete with native flora. Thus, their use in landscaping and revegetation projects should be avoided or limited when possible. Other invasive exotics may have not yet been noted in natural communities.

APPENDIXES

Fishes

Table F-1. Checklist of the Fish of Indiana, by Order and Family

Scientific Name	Common Name	Range	Relative Abundance	Status
Petromyzontiformes: Petromyzontidae (Lampreys)				
Ichthyomyzon bdellium (Jordan)	Ohio lamprey	W,S	R	
I. castaneus Girard	chestnut lamprey	SW	O	
I. fossor Reighard and Cummins,	northern brook lamprey	NE	R	SE
I. unicuspis Hubbs and Trautman	silver lamprey	W,S		O
Lampetra aepyptera (Abbott)	least brook lamprey	SW	R	
L. appendix (DeKay)	American brook lamprey	NW	O	
Petromyzon marinus Linnaeus	sea lamprey	NW	O	I
Acipenseriformes: Acipenseridae (Sturgeons)				
Acipenser fulvescens Rafinesque	lake sturgeon	W,S	R	SE
Scaphirhynchus platorynchus (Rafinesque)	shovelnose sturgeon	W,SE	O	
Acipenseriformes: Polyodontidae (Paddlefish)				
Polyodon spathula (Walbaum)	paddlefish	W,SE	O	
Lepisosteiformes: Lepisosteidae (Gars)				
Lepisosteus oculatus Winchell	spotted gar	NE,SW	O	
L. osseus Linnaeus	Longnose gar	IN	C	
L. platostomus Rafinesque	shortnose gar	W,S	O	
Amiiformes: Amiidae (Bowfins)				
Amia calva Linnaeus	bowfin	N,S	O	
Hiodontiformes: Hiodontidae (Mooneyes)				
Hiodon alosoides (Rafinesque)	goldeye	S	O	
H. tergisus (Lesueur)	mooneye	W,S	O	
Anguilliformes: Anguillidae (Freshwater Eels)				
Anguilla rostrata (Lesueur)	American eel	W,S	R	
Clupeiformes: Clupeidae (Herrings)				
Alosa chrysochloris (Rafinesque)	skipjack herring	W,S	C	
A. pseudoharengus (Wilson)	alewife	NW	A	I
Dorosoma cepedianum (Lesueur)	gizzard shad	IN	A	
D. petenense (Günther)	threadfin shad	S	C	
Cypriniformes: Cyprinidae (Carps and Minnows)				
Campostoma anomalum (Rafinesque)	central stoneroller	IN	A	
C. oligolepis Hubbs and Greene	largescale stoneroller	N	A	
Carassius auratus (Linnaeus)	goldfish	IN	C	I
Clinostomus elongatus (Kirtland)	redside dace	E	R	SE
Couesius plumbeus (Agassiz)	lake chub	NW	R	
Ctenopharyngodon idella Valenciennes	grass carp	NW,CT	O	I
Cyprinella lutrensis (Baird and Girard)	red shiner	NW	O	
C. spiloptera Cope	spotfin shiner	IN	A	
C. whipplei Girard	steelcolor shiner	CT,S	C	
Cyprinus carpio Linnaeus	common carp	IN	A	I
Erimystax dissimilis (Kirtland)	streamline chub	NW	R	
E. x-punctatus (Hubbs and Crowe)	gravel chub	W	R	
Hybognathus hayi Jordan	cypress minnow	SW	R	
H. nuchalis Agassiz	Mississippi silvery minnow	S,CT,SW	C	
Hybopsis amblops (Rafinesque)	bigeye chub	NW	C	
H. amnis (Hubbs and Greene)	pallid shiner	W	R	SE
Hypophthalmichthys molitrix (Valenciennes)	silver carp	SE,SW	R	I
H. nobilis (Richardson)	bighead carp	SW	O	I
Luxilus chrysocephalus Rafinesque	striped shiner	IN	A	
L. cornutus (Mitchill)	common shiner	N	O	
Lythrurus fasciolaris (Gilbert)	scarlet shiner	SE	C	
L. fumeus (Evermann)	ribbon shiner	SW	R	
L. umbratilis (Girard)	redfin shiner	W,CT	C	

Scientific Name	Common Name	Range	Relative Abundance	Status
Macrhybopsis hyostoma (Gilbert)	shoal chub	W,S	O	
M. storeriana (Kirtland)	silver chub	W	C	
Nocomis biguttatus (Kirtland)	hornyhead chub	N	C	
N. micropogon (Cope)	river chub	NE,CT		C
Notemigonus crysoleucas (Mitchill)	golden shiner	IN	C	
Notropis anogenus Forbes,	pugnose shiner	NE	R	SC
N. atherinoides Rafinesque	emerald shiner	IN	A	
N. blennius (Girard)	river shiner	W,S	C	
N. boops (Gilbert)	bigeye shiner	CT	C	
N. buccatus (Cope)	silverjaw minnow	IN	C	
N. buchanani (Meek)	ghost shiner	NW,S	O	
N. chalybaeus (Cope)	ironcolor shiner	NW	O	
N. dorsalis (Agassiz)	bigmouth shiner	NW	R	SC
N. heterodon (Cope)	blackchin shiner	N	R	
N. heterolepis Eigenmann and Eigenmann	blacknose shiner	N	R	
N. hudsonius (Clinton)	spottail shiner	NW	A	
N. photogenis (Cope)	silver shiner	CT,SE	O	
N. rubellus (Agassiz)	rosyface shiner	N,CT	C	
N. shumardi (Girard)	silverband shiner	SW	C	
N. stramineus (Cope)	sand shiner	IN	A	
N. texanus (Girard)	Weed shiner	NW	R	
N. volucellus (Cope)	mimic shiner	E,CT,S		O
N. wickliffi Trautman	channel shiner	S	C	
Opsopoeodus emiliae Hay	pugnose minnow	N,SW	R	
Phenacobius mirabilis (Girard)	suckermouth minnow	CT,S	C	
Phoxinus erythrogaster (Rafinesque)	southern redbelly dace	NW,CT	O	
Pimephales notatus (Rafinesque)	bluntnose minnow	IN	A	
P. promelas Rafinesque	fathead minnow	N,SE	C	
P. vigilax (Baird and Girard)	bullhead minnow	W,S	O	
Rhinichthys cataractae (Valenciennes)	longnose dace	N	O	SC
R. obtusus Agassiz	western blacknose dace	NW,CT,SE	C	
Scardinius erythrophthalmus (Linnaeus)	rudd	NW	R	I
Semotilus atromaculatus (Mitchill)	creek chub	IN	A	
Cypriniformes: Catostomidae (Suckers)				
Carpiodestcarpio (Rafinesque)	river carpsucker	W,S	C	
C. cyprinus (Lesueur)	quillback	IN	C	
C. velifer (Rafinesque)	highfin carpsucker	W,S	O	
Catostomus catostomus (Forster)	Longnose sucker	NW	R	SC
C. commersonii (Lacepede)	white sucker	IN	A	
Cycleptus elongatus (Lesueur)	blue sucker	CT,S	O	
Erimyzon oblongus (Mitchill)	creek chubsucker	NW,CT,SW	O	
E. sucetta (Lacepede)	lake chubsucker	N	O	
Hypentelium nigricans (Lesueur)	northern hogsucker	N,CT	C	
Ictiobus bubalus (Rafinesque)	smallmouth buffalo	W,S	C	
1. cyprinellus (Valenciennes)	bigmouth buffalo	W,S	O	
I. niger (Rafinesque)	black buffalo	NW,S	R	
Minytrema melanops (Rafinesque)	spotted sucker	NE,CT		C
Moxostoma anisurum (Rafinesque)	silver redhorse	N,CT	C	
M. breviceps (Cope)	smallmouth redhorse	S	C	
M. carinatum (Cope)	river redhorse	CT	O	
M. duquesnei (Lesueur)	black redhorse	CT	C	
M. erythrurum (Rafinesque)	golden redhorse	IN	A	
M. macrolepidotum (Lesueur)	shorthead redhorse	IN	A	
M. valenciennesi Jordan	greater redhorse	N	R	SE
Cypriniformes: Cobitidae (Loaches)				
Misgurnus anguillicaudatus (Cantor)	oriental weatherfish	NW	O	I
Siluriformes: Ictaluridae (North American Catfish)				
Ameiurus catus (Linnaeus)	white catfish	S	O	I
A. melas (Rafinesque)	black bullhead	IN	A	
A. natalis (Lesueur)	yellow bullhead	IN	A	
A. nebulosus (Lesueur)	brown bullhead	S	C	
Ictalurus furcatus (Lesueur)	blue catfish	S	O	
I. punctatus (Rafinesque)	channel catfish	IN	C	
Noturus eleutherus Jordan	mountain madtom	W,CT	O	
N. flavus Rafinesque	stonecat	IN	C	
N. gyrinus (Mitchill)	tadpole madtom	IN	C	
N. miurus Jordan	brindled madtom	CT	O	
N. nocturnus Jordan and Gilbert	freckled madtom	W	O	
N. stigmosus Taylor,	northern madtom	WC	R	SC
Pylodictis olivaris (Rafinesque)	flathead catfish	IN	C	

Table F-1. *continued*

Scientific Name	Common Name	Range	Relative Abundance	Status
Esociformes: Esocidae (Pikes)				
Esox americanus Gmelin	grass pickerel	IN	C	
E. lucius Linnaeus	northern pike	N		
E. masquinongy Mitchill	muskellunge	S	Ra	
Esociformes: Umbridae (Mudminnows)				
Umbra limi (Kirtland)	central mudminnow	N	A	
Salmoniformes: Osmeridae (Smelts)				
Osmerus mordax (Mitchill)	rainbow smelt	NW	C	I
Salmoniformes: Salmonidae (Trouts and Salmons)				
Coregonus artedi Lesueur	cisco	NW	R	SC
C. clupeaformis (Mitchill)	lake whitefish	NW	C	SC
C. hoyi (Gill)	bloater	NW	R	
C. kiyi (Koelz)	kiyi	NW	R	
Oncorhynchus kisutch (Walbaum)	coho salmon	NW	C	I
O. mykiss (Walbaum)	rainbow trout	N	C	I
O. tshawytscha (Walbaum)	chinook salmon	NW	C	I
Salmo salar Linnaeus	Atlantic salmon	NW	O	I
S. trutta Linnaeus	brown trout	N	C	I
Salvelinus fontinalis (Mitchill)	brook trout	NW	R	
S. namaycush (Walbaum)	lake trout	NW	O	
Percopsiformes: Percopsidae (Trout-Perches)				
Percopsis omiscomaycus (Walbaum)	trout-perch	NW,S	R	SC
Percopsiformes: Aphredoderidae (Pirate Perches)				
Aphredoderus sayanus (Gilliams)	pirate perch	N,SW	C	
Percopsiformes: Amblyopsidae (Cavefish)				
Amblyopsis spelaea DeKay	northern cavefish	S	R	SE
Gadiformes: Gadidae (Cods)				
Lota lota (Linnaeus)	burbot	NW,SE	O	
Mugiliformes: Mugilidae (Mullets)				
Mugil cephalus Linnaeus	striped mullet	S	R	I
Atheriniformes: Atherinidae (New World Silversides)				
Labidesthes sicculus (Cope)	brook silverside	IN	C	
Menidia beryllina (Cope)	inland silverside	S	R	I
Cyprinodontiformes: Fundulidae (Topminnows)				
Fundulus catenatus (Storer)	northern studfish	CT	C	
F. diaphanus (Lesueur)	banded killifish	N	C	
F. dispar (Agassiz)	northern starhead topminnow	NW	C	
F. notatus (Rafinesque)	blackstripe topminnow	IN	A	
F. olivaceus (Storer)	blackspotted topminnow	W,NE	R	
Cyprinodontiformes: Poeciliidae (Livebearers)				
Gambusia affinis (Baird and Girard)	western mosquitofish	W	O	
Gasterosteiformes: Gasterosteidae (Sticklebacks)				
Culaea inconstans Kirtland	brook stickleback	N,SE	C	
Gasterosteus aculeatus Linnaeus	threespine stickleback	NW	O	I
Pungitius pungitius (Linnaeus)	ninespine stickleback	NW	O	
Scorpaeniformes: Cottidae (Sculpins)				
Cottus bairdii (Girard)	mottled sculpin	IN	C	
C. carolinae (Gill)	banded sculpin	S,CT	O	
C. cognatus Richardson	slimy sculpin	NW	R	SC
Myoxocephalus thompsonii (Girard)	deepwater sculpin	NW	R	
Perciformes: Moronidae (Temperate Basses)				
Morone americana (Gmelin)	white perch	NW	R	I
M. chrysops (Rafinesque)	white bass	W	C	
M. mississippiensis Jordan and Eigenmann	yellow bass	W,S	O	I
M. saxatilis (Walbaum)	striped bass	S	O	
Perciformes: Centrarchidae (Sunfish)				
Ambloplites rupestris (Rafinesque)	rock bass	IN	C	
Centrarchus macropterus (Lacepede)	flier	SW	O	
Lepomis cyanellus Rafinesque	green sunfish	IN	A	
L. gibbosus (Linnaeus)	pumpkinseed	IN	C	

Scientific Name	Common Name	Range	Relative Abundance	Status
L. gulosus (Cuvier)	warmouth	N	C	
L. humilis (Girard)	orangespotted sunfish	N	O	
L. macrochirus Rafinesque	bluegill	IN	A	
L. megalotis (Rafinesque)	longear sunfish	IN	A	
L. microlophus (Günther)	redear sunfish	N,S	C	
L. miniatus Jordan,	redspotted sunfish	SW	R	
L. symmetricus Forbes,	bantam sunfish	W	R	SE
Micropterus dolomieu Lacepede,	smallmouth bass	IN	A	
M. punctulatus (Rafinesque)	spotted bass	S	A	
M. salmoides (Lacepede)	largemouth bass	IN	A	
Pomoxis annularis Rafinesque,	white crappie	IN	C	
P. nigromaculatus (Lesueur)	black crappie	IN	C	
Perciformes: Percidae (Perches)				
Ammocrypta clara Jordan and Meek	western sand darter	NW,S	O	
A. pellucida (Agassiz)	eastern sand darter	CT,SW	O	
Etheostoma asprigene (Forbes)	mud darter	S	C	
E. blennioides Rafinesque,	greenside darter	CT,E	C	
E. caeruleum Storer,	rainbow darter	N,CT	C	
E. camurum (Cope)	bluebreast darter	CT	R	
E. chlorosoma (Hay)	bluntnose darter	W	R	
E. exile (Girard)	Iowa darter	N	O	
E. flabellare Rafinesque,	fantail darter	E,CT	C	
E. gracile (Girard)	slough darter	SW	O	
E. histrio (Jordan and Gilbert)	harlequin darter	S	R	
E. maculatum Kirtland	spotted darter	CT	R	SC
E. microperca Jordan and Gilbert	least darter	N	C	
E. nigrum Rafinesque	johnny darter	IN	A	
E. proeliare (Hay)	cypress darter	SW	R	
E. spectabile (Agassiz)	orangethroat darter	CT	A	
E. squamiceps Jordan,	spottail darter	SW	R	
E. tippecanoe Jordan and Evermann	Tippecanoe darter	CT	R	SC
E. variatum Kirtland	variegate darter	SE	R	SE
E. zonale (Cope)	banded darter	NW,SE	C	
Perca flavescens (Mitchill)	yellow perch	N	C	
Percina caprodes (Rafinesque)	logperch	IN	C	
P. copelandi (Jordan)	channel darter	CT	R	SE
P. evides (Jordan and Copeland)	gilt darter	CT	O	SE
P. maculata (Girard)	blackside darter	IN	C	
P. phoxocephala (Nelson)	slenderhead darter	CT	C	
P. sciera (Swain)	dusky darter	CT	C	
P. shumardi (Girard)	river darter	CT,S	O	
Sander canadensis (Griffith and Smith)	sauger	W,S	C	
S. vitreus (Mitchill)	walleye	IN	C	
Perciformes: Sciaenidae (Drums and Croakers)				
Aplodinotus grunniens Rafinesque	freshwater drum	IN	C	
Perciformes: Elassomatidae (Pygmy Sunfish)				
Elassoma zonatum Jordan	banded pygmy sunfish	SW	R	SC
Perciformes: Gobiidae (Gobies)				
Apollonia melanostomus (Pallas)	round goby	NW	A	I
Extirpated				
Atractosteus spatula (Lacepede)	alligator gar	S		EX
Alosa alabamae (Jordan and Evermann)	Alabama shad	SW		EX
Notropis ariommus (Cope)	popeye shiner	W,CT		EX
Moxostoma lacerum (Jordan and Brayton)	harelip sucker	C		EX
Esox masquinongy Mitchill	Great Lakes muskellunge	N		EXa
Coregonus nigripinnis (Gill)	blackfin cisco	NW		EX
C. reighardi (Koelz)	shortnose cisco	NW		EX
C. zenithicus (Jordan and Evermann)	shortjaw cisco	NW		EX
Typhlichthys subterraneus Girard,	southern cavefish	S		EX
Crystallaria asprella Jordan,	crystal darter	S		EX
Percina uranidea (Jordan and Gilbert)b	stargazing darter	SW		EX
P. vigil (Hoy)	saddleback darter	SW		EX

Notes: Range is indicated as statewide (IN), north (N), south (S), west (W), east (E), central (CT), or various combinations. General abundance is listed roughly as abundant (A), common (C), occasional (O), or rare (R). State designations are state endangered (SE), special concern (SC), or extirpated (EX). I indicates introduced or exotic species.

a *Esox masquinongy* from the Great Lakes is extirpated, but another Ohio River form of questionable status exists.

b It is questionable whether *Percina uranidea* ever existed in Indiana. It is likely that samples were confused between Indiana and Arkansas specimens or that the species is *P. vigil*.

Table F-2. Fish Occurring in Indiana in Lake Michigan and in the Headwaters, Wadeable/ Large Rivers, and Great Rivers of the Great Lakes Drainage, by Order and Family

Species	Lake Michigan	Headwaters	Wadeable/Large Rivers	Great Rivers
Ichthyomyzon castaneus	N	N	N	N
I. fossor		N	N	
I. unicuspis	N			
Lampetra appendix		N	N	
Petromyzon marinus	I	I	I	
Acipenser fulvescens	N			
Lepisosteus oculatus		N	N	
L. osseus	N	N	N	N
Amia calva	N	N	N	N
Hiodon tergisus	N			
Anguilla rostrata	NI			
Alosa chrysochloris	NI			
A. pseudoharengus	I		I	
Dorosoma cepedianum	NI	NI	NI	NI
Campostoma anomalum		N	N	N
C. oligolepis		N	N	
Carassius auratus	I	I	I	
Cousesius plumbeus	N			
Ctenopharyngodon idella			I	
Cyprinella spiloptera	N	N	N	N
Cyprinus carpio	I	I	I	I
Hybopsis amblops			N	N
Luxilus chrysocephalus		N	N	N
L. cornutus	N	N	N	N
Lythrurus umbratilis		N	N	N
Nocomis biguttatus		N	N	N
N. micropogon		N	N	N
Notemigonus crysoleucus	N	N	N	N
Notropis anogenus		N		
N. atherinoides	N	N	N	N
N. buccatus		N	N	N
N. chalybaeus		N		
N. heterolepis		N		
N. hudsonius	N	N	N	N
N. photogenis		N	N	
N. rubellus	N	N	N	N
N. stramineus	N	N	N	N
N. volucellus	N	N	N	N
Opsopoeodus emiliae			N	
Phenacobius mirabilis		N	N	N
Pimephales notatus	N	N	N	N
P. promelas	N	N	N	N
Rhinichthys cataractae	N	N	N	N
R. obtusus	N	N	N	N
Scardinius erythrophthalmus	I		I	
Semotilus atromaculatus	N	N	N	N
Carpiodes cyprinus	N	N	N	N
Catostomus catostomus	N			
C. commersonii	N	N	N	N
Erimyzon oblongus		N	N	
E. sucetta	N	N	N	
Hypentelium nigricans		N	N	N
Minytrema melanops		N	N	N
Moxostoma anisurum	N	N	N	N
M. carinatum			N	N
M. duquesnei		N	N	N
M. erythrurum	N	N	N	N
M. macrolepidotum	N	N	N	N
M. valenciennesi			N	N
Misgurnus anguillicaudatus			I	
Ameiurus melas	N	N	N	N
A. natalis	N	N	N	N
A. nebulosus	N	N	N	N

Species	Lake Michigan	Headwaters	Wadeable/Large Rivers	Great Rivers
Ictalurus punctatus	N	N	N	N
Noturus flavus		N	N	N
N. gyrinus	N	N	N	N
N. miurus		N		N
Pylodictis olivaris				NI
Esox americanus	N	N	N	N
E. lucius	N	N	N	N
E. masquinongy	N			N
Umbra limi	N	N	N	N
Osmerus mordax	I			
Coregonus artedi	N			
C. clupeaformis	N			
C. hoyi	N			
C. kiyi	N			
C. nigripinnis	N			
C. reighardi	N			
C. zenithicus	N			
Oncorhynchus kisutch	I	I	I	I
O. mykiss	I	I	I	I
O. tshawytscha	I	I	I	I
Salmo salar		I	I	
S. trutta	I	I	I	I
Salvelinus fontinalis	N	NI		
S. namaycush	N			
Percopsis omiscomaycus	N			
Aphredoderus sayanus		N	N	N
Lota lota	N		N	
Labidesthes sicculus	N	N	N	N
Fundulus diaphanus	N	N	N	
F. dispar		N	N	
F. notatus		N	N	N
Gambusia affinis	NI			
Culaea inconstans	N	N	N	
Gasterosteus aculeatus	I			
Pungitius pungitius	N		N	
Cottus bairdii	N	N	N	N
C. cognatus	N			
Myoxocephalus thompsonii	N			
Morone americana	I		I	
M. chrysops	N			
M. mississippiensis				
M. saxatilis				
Ambloplites rupestris	N	N	N	N
Lepomis cyanellus	N	N	N	N
L. gibbosus	N	N	N	N
L. gulosus		N	N	
L. humilis		N	N	N
L. macrochirus	N	N	N	N
L. megalotis	N	N	N	N
L. microlophus	NI	NI	NI	NI
Micropterus dolomieu	N	N	N	N
M. salmoides	N	N	N	N
Pomoxis annularis	N	N	N	N
P. nigromaculatus	N	N	N	N
Ammocrypta pellucida			N	N
Etheostoma blennioides		N	N	N
E. caeruleum		N	N	N
E. exile	N	N	N	
E. flabellare		N	N	

Table F-2. *continued*

Species	Lake Michigan	Headwaters	Wadeable/Large Rivers	Great Rivers
E. microperca		N		
E. nigrum	N	N	N	N
E. spectabile		N	N	
Perca flavescens	N	N	N	N
Percina caprodes	N	N	N	N
P. evides			N	
P. maculata	N	N	N	N
P. sciera		N	N	N
Sander canadensis			N	N
S. vitreus	N		N	N
Aplodinotus grunniens	N		N	N
Apollonia melanostomus	I	N	I	
Total Number of Species	**89**	**91**	**102**	**78**
Total Number of NI/I Species	**18**	**11**	**16**	**8**
Total Number of Native Species	**71**	**80**	**86**	**70**

Note: Fish are categorized as occurring naturally (N), as non-indigenous (NI), or as introduced (I).

Table F-3. Fish Occurring in Indiana in the Headwaters and Wadeable/Large Rivers of the Kankakee River Drainage, by Order and Family

Species	Headwaters	Wadeable/ Large Rivers
Ichthyomyzon fossor	N	N
I. unicuspis		N
Lampetra appendix	N	N
Lepisosteus osseus	N	
Amia calva	N	N
Anguilla rostrata		N
Dorosoma cepedianum	N	N
Campostoma anomalum	N	N
C. oligolepis	N	N
Carassius auratus		I
Cyprinella lutrensis	N	N
C. spiloptera	N	N
C. whipplei	N	N
Cyprinus carpio	I	I
Luxilus chrysocephalus	N	N
L. cornutus	N	N
Lythrurus umbratilis	N	N
Macrhybopsis storeriana		N
Nocomis biguttatus	N	N
Notemigonus crysoleucus	N	N
Notropis atherinoides		N
N. buccatus	N	N
N. chalybaeus	N	N
N. dorsalis		N
N. heterolepis	N	N
N. hudsonius	N	N
N. rubellus	N	N
N. stramineus	N	N
N. texanus	N	N
N. volucellus	N	N
Opsopoeodus emiliae		N
Phenacobius mirabilis	N	N
Phoxinus erythrogaster	N	
Pimephales notatus	N	N
P. promelas	N	N
P. vigilax		N
Rhinichthys obtusus	N	N
Semotilus atromaculatus	N	N
Carpiodes carpio		N
C. cyprinus	N	N
C. velifer		N
Catostomus commersonii	N	N
Erimyzon oblongus	N	N
E. sucetta	N	N
Hypentelium nigricans	N	N
Ictiobus bubalus	N	N
I. cyprinellus	N	N
I. niger		N
Minytrema melanops	N	N
Moxostoma anisurum	N	N
M. carinatum		N
M. duquesnei	N	N
M. erythrurum	N	N
M. macrolepidotum	N	N
M. valenciennesi		N
Ameiurus melas	N	N
A. natalis	N	N
A. nebulosus	N	N
Ictalurus punctatus	N	N
Noturus flavus	N	N
N. gyrinus	N	N
Pylodictis olivaris		N
Esox americanus	N	N
E. lucius	N	N
E. masquinongy		N
Umbra limi	N	N
Oncorhynchus mykiss	I	I
Salmo trutta		I
Aphredoderus sayanus	N	N
Labidesthes sicculus	N	N
Fundulus dispar	N	N
F. notatus	N	N
Gambusia affinis		NI
Culaea inconstans	N	N
Cottus bairdii	N	N
Morone americana	I	I
M. chrysops		N
Ambloplites rupestris	N	N
Lepomis cyanellus	N	N
L. gibbosus	N	N
L. gulosus	N	N
L. humilis	N	N
L. macrochirus	N	N
L. megalotis	N	N
L. microlophus	NI	NI
Micropterus dolomieu	N	N
M. salmoides	N	N
Pomoxis annularis	N	N
P. nigromaculatus	N	N
Etheostoma caeruleum	N	N
E. chlorosoma	N	N
E. exile	N	
E. flabellare	N	
E. microperca	N	N
E. nigrum	N	N
E. spectabile	N	
E. zonale	N	N
Perca flavescens	N	N
Percina caprodes	N	N
P. maculata	N	N
P. phoxocephala	N	N
Sander vitreus		N
Aplodinotus grunniens		N
Total Number of Species	**83**	**98**
Total Number of NI/I Species	**4**	**7**
Total Number of Native Species	**79**	**91**

Note: Fish are categorized as occurring naturally (N), as non-indigenous (NI), or as introduced (I).

Table F-4. Fish Occurring in Indiana in the Headwaters and Wadeable/Large Streams of the Eastern Corn Belt Plains (ECBP)/Interior Plateau (IP), the Headwaters and Wadeable/Large Rivers of the Interior River Lowland (IRL), and the Great Rivers of the Ohio River Drainage, by Order and Family

Species	Headwaters ECBP/IP	Wadeable/Large Rivers ECBP/IP	Headwaters IRL	Wadeable/Large Rivers IRL	Great Rivers Ohio River Drainage
Ichthyomyzon bdellium	N	N			
I. castaneusw	N	N	N	N	N
I. fossor	N	N			
I. unicuspis	N	N		N	N
Lampetra aepyptera	N	N	N	N	
L. appendix	N	N	N	N	
Acipenser fulvescens					N
Scaphirhynchus platorynchus		N		N	N
Polyodon spathula		N			N
Atractosteus spatula					N
Lepisosteus oculatus		N	N	N	N
L. osseus	N	N	N	N	N
L. platostomus		N	N	N	N
Amia calva	N	N	N	N	N
Hiodon alosoides					N
H. tergisus		N			N
Anguilla rostrata		N			N
Alosa alabamae					N
A. chrysochloris		N			N
A. pseudoharengus					I
Dorosoma cepedianum	N	N	N	N	N
D. petenense	N	N	N	N	N
Campostoma anomalum	N	N	N	N	N
Carassius auratus	I	I			I
Clinostomus elongatus	N	N			
Ctenopharyngodon idella			I	I	I
Cyprinella spiloptera	N	N	N	N	N
C. whipplei	N	N	N	N	N
Cyprinus carpio	I	I	I	I	I
Erimystax dissimilis		N			N
E. x-punctatus		N			N
Hybognathus hayi				N	
H. nuchalis	N	N	N	N	N
Hybopsis amblops	N	N		N	N
H. amnis	N	N			
Hypophthalmichthys molitrix		I	I	I	I
H. nobilis		I	I	I	I
Luxilus chrysocephalus	N	N	N	N	N
L. cornutus	N	N			
Lythrurus fasciolaris	N	N			
L. fumeus	N	N	N	N	
L. umbratilis	N	N	N	N	N
Macrhybopsis hyostoma		N		N	N
M. storeriana		N		N	N
Nocomis biguttatus	N	N			N
N. micropogon	N	N			N
Notemigonus crysoleucus	N	N	N	N	
Notropis ariommus		N			N
N. atherinoides	N	N	N	N	N
N. blennius	N	N	N	N	N
N. boops	N	N			N
N. buccatus	N	N	N	N	N
N. buchanani		N			N
N. chalybaeus	N	N			
N. heterodon	N				
N. heterolepis	N	N			
N. hudsonius		N			N
N. photogenis	N	N			N
N. rubellus	N	N		N	N
N. shumardi					N
N. stramineus	N	N	N	N	N
N. volucellus	N	N	N		N
N. wickliffi		N		N	N
Opsopoeodus emiliae	N	N	N	N	N
Phenacobius mirabilis	N	N	N	N	N
Phoxinus erythrogaster	N	N	N		

Species	Headwaters ECBP/IP	Wadeable/Large Rivers ECBP/IP	Headwaters IRL	Wadeable/Large Rivers IRL	Great Rivers Ohio River Drainage
Pimephales notatus	N	N	N	N	N
P. promelas	N	N	N	N	
P. vigilax		N		N	N
Rhinichthys obtusus	N	N	N		N
Semotilus atromaculatus	N	N	N	N	N
Carpiodes carpio	N	N	N	N	N
C. cyprinus	N	N	N	N	N
C. velifer		N		N	N
Catostomus commersonii	N	N	N	N	N
Cycleptus elongatus		N			N
Erimyzon oblongus	N	N	N	N	N
E. sucetta	N	N	N	N	
Hypentelium nigricans	N	N	N	N	N
Ictiobus bubalus	N	N	N	N	N
I. cyprinellus	N	N	N	N	N
I. niger		N		N	N
Minytrema melanops	N	N	N	N	N
Moxostoma anisurum	N	N	N	N	N
M. breviceps					N
M. carinatum		N			N
M. duquesnei	N	N	N	N	N
M. erythrurum	N	N	N	N	N
M. lacerum		N			N
M. macrolepidotum	N	N	N	N	N
M. valenciennesi		N			N
Ameiurus catus					I
A. melas	N	N	N	N	N
A. natalis	N	N	N	N	N
A. nebulosus	N	N	N	N	
Ictalurus furcatus					N
I. punctatus	N	N	N	N	N
Noturus eleutherus		N			N
N. flavus	N	N			N
N. gyrinus	N	N	N	N	N
N. miurus	N	N	N	N	N
N. nocturnus		N		N	N
N. stigmosus					N
Pylodictis olivaris		N		N	N
Esox americanus	N	N	N	N	N
E. lucius	N	N			N
E. masquinongy		N			N
Umbra limi	N	N	N	N	N
Oncorhynchus mykiss		I			
Salmo trutta		I			
Percopsis omiscomaycus		N			
Aphredoderus sayanus	N	N	N	N	
Amblyopsis spelaea		N			
Lota lota					N
Mugil cephalus					I
Labidesthes sicculus	N	N	N	N	N
Menidia beryllina					I
Fundulus catenatus	N	N			
F. dispar	N	N	N	N	
F. notatus	N	N	N	N	N
F. olivaceus			N		
Gambusia affinis	NI	NI	N	N	N
Culaea inconstans	N	N			
Cottus bairdii	N	N	N	N	N
C. carolinae	N	N		N	N
Morone chrysops	N	N		N	N
M. mississippiensis	N	N		N	N
M. saxatilis		I			I

Table F-4. *continued*

Species	Headwaters ECBP/IP	Wadeable/Large Rivers ECBP/IP	Headwaters IRL	Wadeable/Large Rivers IRL	Great Rivers Ohio River Drainage
Ambloplites rupestris	N	N	N	N	N
Centrarchus macropterus	N	N	N	N	
Lepomis cyanellus	N	N	N	N	N
L. gibbosus	N	N			
L. gulosus	N	N	N	N	N
L. humilis	N	N	N	N	N
L. macrochirus	N	N	N	N	N
L. megalotis	N	N	N	N	N
L. microlophus	NI	NI	N	N	N
L. miniatus			N	N	
L. symmetricus				N	
Micropterus dolomieu	N	N	N	N	N
M. punctulatus	N	N	N	N	N
M. salmoides	N	N	N	N	N
Pomoxis annularis	N	N	N	N	N
P. nigromaculatus	N	N	N	N	N
Ammocrypta clara					N
A. pellucida		N		N	N
Crystallaria asprella					N
Etheostoma asprigene	N	N	N	N	N
E. blennioides	N	N	N	N	N
E. caeruleum	N	N	N	N	N
E. camurum		N			N
E. chlorosoma			N	N	
E. exile	N	N			
E. flabellare	N	N	N	N	N
E. gracile			N	N	N
E. histrio		N		N	N
E. maculatum		N			N
E. microperca	N	N			
E. nigrum	N	N	N	N	N
E. proeliare			N	N	
E. spectabile	N	N	N	N	N
E. squamiceps			N	N	
E. tippecanoe		N			N
E. variatum		N			N
E. zonale	N	N			
Perca flavescens	N	N			
Percina caprodes	N	N	N	N	N
P. copelandi					N
P. evides		N			N
P. maculata	N	N	N	N	N
P. phoxocephala		N		N	N
P. sciera	N	N	N	N	N
P. shumardi		N		N	N
P. uranidea					N
P. vigil					N
Sander canadensis		N		N	N
S. vitreus		N		N	N
Aplodinotus grunniens	N	N	N	N	N
Elassoma zonatum			N	N	
Total Number of Species	**107**	**150**	**90**	**109**	**140**
Total Number of NI/I Species	**4**	**8**	**4**	**4**	**10**
Total Number of Native Species	**103**	**142**	**86**	**105**	**130**

Note: Fish are categorized as occurring naturally (N), as non-indigenous (NI), or as introduced (I).

Table F-5. Fish Occurring in Indiana in Oxbows/Backwaters/Sloughs/Embayments, Natural Lakes, Impoundments, and Caves, by Order and Family

Species	Oxbows, Backwaters, Sloughs, Embayments	Natural Lakes	Impoundments	Caves
Ichthyomyzon castaneus	N	N	N	
I. unicuspis	N	N	N	
Acipenser fulvescens		N		
Polyodon spathula	N		N	
Atractosteus spatula	N			
Lepisosteus oculatus	N	N	N	
L. osseus	N	N	N	
L. platostomus	N		N	
Amia calva	N	N	N	
Alosa chrysochloris	N			
A. pseudoharengus			I	
Dorosoma cepedianum	N	N	N	
D. petenense	N		NI	
Campostoma anomalum	N		N	
Carassius auratus	I	I	I	
Ctenopharyngodon idella	I	I	I	
Cyprinella spiloptera	N	N	N	
C. whipplei	N		N	
Cyprinus carpio	I	I	I	
Hybognathus hayi	N			
H. nuchalis	N		N	
Hybopsis amblops			N	
Hypophthalmichthys molitrix	I		I	
H. nobilis	I		I	
Luxilus chrysocephalus	N		N	
L. cornutus		N		
Lythrurus fumeus	N			
L. umbratilis	N		N	
Notemigonus crysoleucus	N	N	N	
Notropis anogenus		N		
N. atherinoides	N	N	N	
N. blennius	N		N	
N. boops	N			
N. buccatus	N			
N. chalybaeus		N		
N. heterodon		N		
N. heterolepis		N		
N. hudsonius		N	N	
N. stramineus	N	N	N	
N. texanus		N		
N. volucellus		N	N	
Opsopoeodus emiliae	N	N		
Pimephales notatus	N	N	N	
P. promelas	N	N	N	NI
P. vigilax	N		N	
Scardinius erythrophthalmus		I		
Semotilus atromaculatus	N	N	N	
Carpiodes carpio	N		N	
C. cyprinus	N	N	N	
C. velifer	N		N	
Catostomus commersonii	N	N	N	
Erimyzon oblongus	N		N	
E. sucetta	N	N	N	
Hypentelium nigricans	N		N	
Ictiobus bubalus	N		N	
I. cyprinellus	N	N	N	
I. niger	N		N	
Minytrema melanops	N	N	N	
Moxostoma anisurum	N		N	
M. duquesnei	N		N	
M. erythrurum	N	N	N	

Table F-5. *continued*

Species	Oxbows, Backwaters, Sloughs, Embayments	Natural Lakes	Impoundments	Caves
M. macrolepidotum	N	N	N	
Ameiurus catus			I	
A. melas	N	N	N	
A. natalis	N	N	N	
A. nebulosus	N	N	N	
Ictalurus punctatus	N	N	N	
Noturus flavus			N	
N. gyrinus	N	N	N	
Pylodictis olivaris	N		N	
Esox americanus	N	N	N	
E. lucius	N	N	N	
E. masquinongy		N	NI	
Umbra limi	N	N	N	
Osmerus mordax		I		
Coregonus artedi		N		
Oncorhynchus mykiss		I		
Salmo trutta		I		
Salvelinus namaycush		NI		
Aphredoderus sayanus	N	N	N	
Amblyopsis spelaea				N
Typhlichthys subterraneus				N
Labidesthes sicculus	N	N	N	
Menidia beryllina	I			
Fundulus diaphanus		N	N	
F. dispar	N	N	N	
F. notatus	N	N	N	
Gambusia affinis	N		NI	
Culaea inconstans		N		
Gasterosteus aculeatus				
Pungitius pungitius		N		
Cottus carolinae				N
Morone americana		I		
M. chrysops	N	N	N	
M. mississippiensis	N		N	
M. saxatilis	I		I	
Ambloplites rupestris	N	N	N	
Centrarchus macropterus	N			
Lepomis cyanellus	N	N	N	NI
L. gibbosus	N	N	N	
L. gulosus	N	N	N	
L. humilis	N		N	
L. macrochirus	N	N	N	
L. megalotis	N	N	N	
L. microlophus	N	NI	NI	
L. miniatus	N	NI		
L. symmetricus	N			
Micropterus dolomieu		N	N	
M. punctulatus	N		N	
M. salmoides	N	N	N	
Pomoxis annularis	N	N	N	
P. nigromaculatus	N	N	N	
Etheostoma asprigene	N		N	
E. caeruleum			N	
E. chlorosoma	N			
E. exile		N	N	
E. gracile	N		N	
E. microperca	N	N	N	
E. nigrum	N	N	N	

Species	Oxbows, Backwaters, Sloughs, Embayments	Natural Lakes	Impoundments	Caves
E. proeliare	N			
E. spectabile	N		N	
Perca flavescens		N	N	
Percina caprodes	N	N	N	
P. maculatae	N		N	
P. phoxocephala	N		N	
P. sciera	N			
P. shumardi	N			
Sander canadensis	N		N	
S. vitreus	N	N	N	
Aplodinotus grunniens	N		N	
Elassoma zonatum	N			
Total Number of Species	**99**	**75**	**95**	**5**
Total Number of NI/I Species	**7**	**11**	**12**	**2**
Total Number of Native Species	**92**	**64**	**83**	**3**

Note: Fish are categorized as occurring naturally (N), as non-indigenous (NI), or as introduced (I)

Table F-6. Exotic Fish Species Occurring in Indiana Waters, by Order and Family

	Range	Relative Abundance
Petromyzontiformes: Petromyzontidae		
Petromyzon marinus Linnaeus, sea lamprey	NW	O
Clupeiformes: Clupeidae		
Alosa psuedoharengus (Wilson), alewife	NW	A
Cypriniformes: Cyprinidae		
Carassius auratus (Linnaeus), goldfish	IN	C
Ctenopharyngodon idella Valenciennes, grass carp	NW,CT	O
Cyprinus carpio Linnaeus, common carp	IN	A
Hypophthalmichthys molitrix (Valenciennes), silver carp	SE,SW	R
Hypophthalmichthys nobilis (Richardson), bighead carp	SW	O
Scardinius erythrophthalmus (Linnaeus), rudd	NW	O
Cypriniformes: Cobitidae		
Misgurnus anguillicaudatus (Cantor), oriental weatherfish	NW	C
Siluriformes: Ictaluridae		
Ameiurus catus (Linnaeus), white catfish	CT,S	O
Salmoniformes: Osmeridae		
Osmerus mordax (Mitchill), rainbow smelt	NW	C
Salmoniformes: Salmonidae		
Oncorhynchus kisutch (Walbaum), coho salmon	NW	C
Oncorhynchus mykiss (Walbaum), rainbow trout	N	C
Oncorhynchus tshawytscha (Walbaum), chinook salmon	NW	C
Salmo salar Linnaeus, Atlantic salmon	NW	O
Salmo trutta Linnaeus, brown trout	N	C
Mugiliformes: Mugilidae		
Mugil cephalus Linnaeus, striped mullet	S	R
Atheriniformes: Atherinidae		
Menidia beryllina (Cope), inland silverside	S	R
Gasterosteiformes: Gasterosteidae		
Gasterosteus aculeatus Linnaeus, threespine stickleback	NW	O
Perciformes: Moronidae		
Morone americana (Gmelin), white perch	NW	R
Morone saxatilis (Walbaum), striped bass	S	O
Perciformes: Gobiidae		
Apollonia melanostomus (Pallas), round goby	NW	A

Note: Range is indicated as statewide (IN), north (N), south (S), west (W), east (E), central (CT), and various combinations of these. Relative abundance is indicated as abundant (A), common (C), occasional (O), or rare (R).

Table F-7. Type Localities of Fish Species Described from Indiana

Species	Author	Specific Locality
Scaphirhynchus platorynchus	Rafinesque 1820	No specific locality; Ohio, Wabash, and Cumberland rivers; seldom reaching as high as Pittsburgh; also in Mississippi and Missouri rivers
Lepisosteus platostomus	Rafinesque 1820	Ohio River
Hiodon alosoides	Rafinesque 1819	Ohio River (probably Falls of the Ohio at Louisville, Ky.)
Alosa chrysochloris	Rafinesque 1820	Ohio River
Hybopsis amblops	Rafinesque 1820	Falls of the Ohio River at Louisville, Ky.
Macrhybopsis hyostoma	Gilbert 1884	East Fork of White River, at Bedford, Lawrence County
Notropis ariommus	Cope 1867	White River near Indianapolis, Marion County
Notropis boops	Gilbert 1884	Salt Creek, Brown County
Pimephales notatus	Rafinesque 1820	Ohio River
Carpiodes carpio	Rafinesque 1820	Falls of the Ohio River, below Louisville, Ky.
Carpiodes velifer	Rafinesque 1820	Ohio River
Cycleptus elongatus	Lesueur 1817	Ohio River
Ictiobus bubalus	Rafinesque 1818	Ohio River
Ictiobus niger	Rafinesque 1819	Ohio River
Minytrema melanops	Rafinesque 1820	Ohio River, at Louisville, Ky.
Moxostoma anisurum	Rafinesque 1820	Ohio River and its large tributaries
Moxostoma carinatum	Cope 1870	Wabash River at Lafayette
Ameiurus melas	Rafinesque 1820	Ohio River
Ictalurus punctatus	Rafinesque 1818	Ohio River
Noturus flavus	Rafinesque 1818	Falls of the Ohio River
Noturus miurus	Jordan 1877	White River near Indianapolis
Pylodictis olivaris	Rafinesque 1818	Ohio River
Esox americanus vermiculatus	Lesueur 1846	Tributaries of Wabash River near New Harmony
Coregonus reighardi	Koetz 1924	Lake Michigan off Michigan City
Morone chrysops	Rafinesque 1820	Falls of Ohio, Ohio River at Louisville, Ky.
Lepomis cyanellus	Rafinesque 1819	Ohio River
Lepomis macrochirus	Rafinesque 1819	Ohio River
Micropterus punctulatus	Rafinesque 1819	Ohio River
Pomoxis nigromaculatus	Lesueur 1829	Wabash River
Etheostoma blennioides	Rafinesque 1819	Falls of the Ohio River below Louisville, Ky.
Etheostoma flabellare	Rafinesque 1819	Ohio River
Etheostoma tippecanoe	Jordan and Evermann 1890	Tippecanoe River at Marshland
Percina caprodes	Rafinesque 1818	Ohio River (presumably in vicinity of Louisville, Ky.)
Percina copelandi	Jordan 1877	White River, 8 km N of Indianapolis
Percina evides	Jordan and Copeland 1877	White River near Indianapolis
Percina sciera	Swain 1883	Bean Blossom Creek, tributary of White River, 9 km N Bloomington, Monroe County
Aplodinotus grunniens	Rafinesque 1819	Ohio River

APPENDIXES

Amphibians and Reptiles

Table H-1. Herpetofaunal Species Presently or Recently Occurring in Indiana (96 Species), by Order and Family

Common Name	Scientific Name	Range	Primary Habitats	Critical Habitat	Indiana Status
Anura: Bufonidae					
American toad	*Bufo americanus*	IN	generalist	shallow wetlands	
Fowler's toad	*Bufo fowleri*	IN	grassland, savanna, old field	shallow wetlands	
Anura: Hylidae					
Cricket frog	*Acris crepitans*	IN	forest near wetlands	well-vegetated shallow permanent wetlands	SC
Cope's gray treefrog	*Hyla chrysoscelis*	IN	forest	shallow seasonal wetlands	
Green treefrog	*Hyla cinerea*	SW2	forest	shallow wetlands	
Eastern gray treefrog	*Hyla versicolor*	IN	forest	shallow seasonal wetlands	
Spring peeper	*Pseudacris crucifer*	IN	forest	shallow seasonal wetlands	
Western chorus frog	*Pseudacris triseriata*	IN	grassland, savanna, old field	shallow seasonal wetlands	
Anura: Pelobatidae					
Eastern spadefoot	*Scaphiopus holbrookii*	S	lowland forest, grassland	shallow seasonal wetlands, loose soils	SC
Anura: Ranidae					
Crawfish frog	*Rana areolata*	SE,SW	native and restored grasslands	large-diameter crayfish burrows	SE
Plains leopard frog	*Rana blairi*	NW	wet meadows and grasslands	shallow wetlands and streams	SC
Bullfrog	*Rana catesbeiana*	IN	permanent water		
Green frog	*Rana clamitans*	IN	permanent water		
Pickerel frog	*Rana palustris*	IN1	grasslands near seeps	seeps	
Northern leopard frog	*Rana pipiens*	N	wet meadows, grasslands	shallow wetlands and streams	SC
Southern leopard frog	*Rana sphenocephala (utricularia)*	S	aquatic habitats, wetlands	shallow wetlands and streams	
Wood frog	*Rana sylvatica*	IN1	forest	shallow seasonal wetlands	
Caudata: Ambystomatidae					
Streamside salamander	*Ambystoma barbouri*	SE	forest	small rocky streams	
Jefferson's salamander	*Ambystoma jeffersonianum*	S	forest	shallow seasonal wetlands	
Blue-spotted salamander	*Ambystoma laterale*	N	forest	shallow seasonal wetlands	SC
Spotted salamander	*Ambystoma maculatum*	IN	forest	shallow seasonal wetlands	
Marbled salamander	*Ambystoma opacum*	NE,NW,S	forest	shallow seasonal wetlands	
Mole salamander	*Ambystoma talpoideum*	SW2	forest	shallow seasonal wetlands	
Smallmouth salamander	*Ambystoma texanum*	IN	forest	shallow seasonal wetlands	
Eastern tiger salamander	*Ambystoma tigrinum*	IN	forest, prairie	shallow seasonal wetlands, loose soils	
Caudata: Cryptobranchidae					
Hellbender	*Cryptobranchus alleganiensis*	S	large streams	clear, rocky streams	SE
Caudata: Plethodontidae					
Green salamander	*Aneides aeneus*	SC	forest with rocks	rock outcrops with moist deep crevices	SE
Northern dusky salamander	*Desmognathus fuscus*	SE	forest with rocks	hillside springs, small rocky streams	
Southern two-lined salamander	*Eurycea cirrigera*	IN	forest near streams	semi-permanent to permanent rocky streams	
Long-tailed salamander	*Eurycea longicauda*	S	forest near streams	rocky streams and springs	
Cave salamander	*Eurycea lucifuga*	S	forest with rocks	springs, spring-fed streams, caves	
Four-toed salamander	*Hemidactylium scutatum*	N,SC	bog, forest	sphagnum and tamarack bogs, springs	SE
Redback salamander	*Plethodon cinereus*	IN1	forest	moist, but not wet, areas in forest	
Northern zigzag salamander	*Plethodon dorsalis*	S	forest with rocks	moist, but not wet, areas in forest	
Northern ravine salamander	*Plethodon electromorphus*	SE	forest with rocks	drier areas with loose soil	
Northern slimy salamander	*Plethodon glutinosus*	S	forest with rocks	moist, but not wet, areas in forest	
Red salamander	*Pseudotriton ruber*	SC	forest	small permanent streams	SE

Caudata: Proteidae					
Common mudpuppy	*Necturus maculosus*	IN	lakes, streams	silt-free areas required for nesting	SC
Caudata: Salamandridae					
Eastern newt	*Notophthalmus viridescens*	N,S	forest	shallow wetlands	
Caudata: Sirenidae					
Lesser siren	*Siren intermedia*	W	shallow aquatic habitats	well-vegetated with mucky bottom	
Testudines: Chelydridae					
Common snapping turtle	*Chelydra serpentina*	IN	aquatic and wetland habitats		
Alligator snapping turtle	*Macroclemys temminckii*	SW	rivers, shallow permanent aquatic systems	deeper muddy pockets	SE
Testudines: Emydidae					
Midland painted turtle	*Chrysemys picta marginata*	IN	aquatic and wetland habitats		
Spotted turtle	*Clemmys guttata*	N	very shallow wetlands and aquatic habitats	wetland complexes in intact upland matrix	SE
Blanding's turtle	*Emydoidea blandingii*	N	very shallow wetlands and aquatic habitats	wetland complexes in intact upland matrix	SE
Common map turtle	*Graptemys geographica*	IN	lakes, rivers, streams		
Mississippi map turtle	*Graptemys geographica kohnii*		rivers		
Ouachita map turtle	*Graptemys ouachitensis*		rivers, streams		
False map turtle	*Graptemys pseudogeographica*	S	rivers, streams		
Hieroglyphic river cooter	*Pseudemys concinna hieroglyphica*	SW	rivers, streams		SE
Eastern box turtle	*Terrapene carolina*	IN	forested habitats		SC
Ornate box turtle	*Terrapene ornata*	NW,SW	sandy grassland and savanna		SE
Red-eared slider	*Trachemys scripta elegans*	NW,S,W	permanent water bodies		
Testudines:Kinosternidae					
Eastern mud turtle	*Kinosternon subrubrum*	NW,SW	shallow water bodies		SE
Common musk turtle	*Sternotherus odoratus*	IN	permanent, shallow water bodies		
Testudines:Trionychidae					
Smooth softshell	*Apalone mutica*	S	rivers	clear water and sandy substrate	
Spiny softshell	*Apalone spinifera*	IN	lakes, rivers, streams	muddy/sandy substrate	
Squamata: Anguidae					
Slender glass lizard	*Ophisaurus attenuatus*	NW	grassland, savanna	loose soils	
Squamata: Lacertidae					
Common wall lizard	*Podarcis muralis*	SC3	open rocky habitat		
Squamata: Phrynosomatidae					
Eastern fence lizard	*Sceloporus undulatus*	S	forested areas	open, sunny gaps	
Squamata: Scincidae					
Five-lined skink	*Eumeces fasciatus*	IN	forest		
Broadhead skink	*Eumeces laticeps*	S	forest	open, sunny gaps	
Ground skink	*Scincella lateralis*	S	forest	open, sunny gaps	
Squamata: Teiidae					
Six-lined racerunner	*Cnemidophorus sexlineatus*	NW,SW	open habitats	loose soils	
Squamata: Colubridae					
Eastern worm snake	*Carphophis amoenus*	S	forest		
Scarlet snake	*Cemophora coccinea*	SC	forest		SE
Kirtland's snake	*Clonophis kirtlandii*	IN4	moist, grassy areas	nearby aquatic habitat	SE
Racer	*Coluber constrictor*	IN	open and forested habitats	areas with open canopy	
Ringneck snake	*Diadophis punctatus*	IN1	forested habitats		
Rat snake	*Elaphe obsoleta*	IN	forested habitats	areas with open canopy	

Table H-1. *continued*

Common Name	Scientific Name	Range	Primary Habitats	Critical Habitat	Indiana Status
Fox snake	*Elaphe vulpina*	NW	open, grassy areas		
Western mud snake	*Farancia abacura reinwardtii*	SW	floodplain wetlands	wetland complexes in intact forest matrix	SC
Eastern hognose snake	*Heterodon platirhinos*	IN	grassland, open woodland		
Prairie kingsnake	*Lampropeltis calligaster*	W	open, grassy areas		
Common kingsnake	*Lampropeltis getula*	SW	forest, grassland		
Milk snake	*Lampropeltis triangulum*	N,SW	forest, grassland		
Copperbelly water snake	*Nerodia erythrogaster neglecta*	NW,SE	shallow wetlands in forest	wetland complexes in intact forest matrix, large-diameter crayfish burrows	SE (northern population), SE, FT (northern population)
Diamondback water snake	*Nerodia rhombifer*	SW	shallow aquatic habitats	permanent water	
Northern water snake	*Nerodia sipedon*	IN	aquatic habitats and wetlands		
Rough green snake	*Opheodrys aestivus*	S	open habitats		SC
Smooth green snake	*Opheodrys vernalis*	NW	grassland, woodland		SE
Bull snake	*Pituophis catenifer*	NW5	open habitats	loose soils	
Queen snake	*Regina septemvittata*	IN1,4	open habitats	large-diameter crayfish burrows	
Brown snake	*Storeria dekayi*	IN	forest, grassland	avoids driest areas	
Red-bellied snake	*Storeria occipitomaculata*	N,SW	forest		
Southeastern crowned snake	*Tantilla coronata*	SC	open forest	dry rocky slopes	SE
Eastern ribbon snake	*Thamnophis sauritus*	NE,SE,W,SW6	areas associated with aquatic habitats	adjacent to aquatic or wetland habitats	
Butler's garter snake	*Thamnophis butleri*	NE	open, moist, grassy areas	large-diameter crayfish burrows	SE
Western ribbon snake	*Thamnophis proximus*	NW,SW	open forest	adjacent to aquatic or wetland habitats	SC
Plains garter snake	*Thamnophis radix*	NW	open, moist, prairie areas	adjacent to aquatic or wetland habitats	
Common garter snake	*Thamnophis sirtalis*	IN	variety of moist habitats	adjacent to aquatic or wetland habitats	
Smooth earth snake	*Virginia valeriae*	SC	forest		
Squamata: Viperidae					
Northern copperhead	*Agkistrodon contortrix*	S	forest		
Cottonmouth	*Agkistrodon piscivorus*	SW	permanent forested wetlands	shallow wetlands and swamps near uplands for hibernation	SE
Timber rattlesnake	*Crotalus horridus*	S	forest	extensive forest tracts, rocky areas to hibernate	SE
Eastern massasauga	*Sistrurus catenatus*	N	moist, open areas	saturated soils nearby, large-diameter crayfish burrows	SE, FC
Possibly Extirpated Reptiles					
Western mud snake	*Farancia abacura*				
Alligator snapping turtle	*Macroclemys temmincki*				
Species Likely Introduced into Indiana by Humans					
Common wall lizard	*Podarcis muralis*				
Species Native to Indiana for Which Localities Have Likely Been Expanded by Humans					
Red-eared slider	*Trachemys scripta elegans*				
River cooter (in northern Indiana)	*Pseudemys concinna*				

Notes: IN = statewide distribution; N = northern distribution; NW = northwestern distribution, C = central distribution, etc.; 1 = absent from some prairie areas; 2 = restricted to vicinity of Evansville; 3 = restricted to Falls of the Ohio State Park; 4 = absent from SW lowlands; 5 = also single record in historic SW plains; 6 = patchy (complex) distribution; SE = state endangered; FC = federal candidate; FT = federally threatened; SC = state species of concern.

Table H-2. Herpetofauna Associated with Forests

Common Name	Scientific Name	Range
American toad	*Bufo americanus*	IN
Fowler's toad	*Bufo fowleri*	IN
Cope's gray treefrog	*Hyla chrysoscelis*	IN
Green treefrog	*Hyla cinerea*	SW[2]
Eastern gray treefrog	*Hyla versicolor*	IN
Spring peeper	*Pseudacris crucifer*	IN
Western chorus frog	*Pseudacris triseriata*	IN
Pickerel frog	*Rana palustris*	IN[1]
Northern leopard frog	*Rana pipiens*	N
Southern leopard frog	*Rana sphenocephala (utricularia)*	S
Wood frog	*Rana sylvatica*	IN[1]
Streamside salamander	*Ambystoma barbouri*	SE
Jefferson's salamander	*Ambystoma jeffersonianum*	S
Blue-spotted salamander	*Ambystoma laterale*	N
Spotted salamander	*Ambystoma maculatum*	IN
Marbled salamander	*Ambystoma opacum*	NE,NW,S
Mole salamander	*Ambystoma talpoideum*	SW[2]
Smallmouth salamander	*Ambystoma texanum*	IN
Eastern tiger salamander	*Ambystoma tigrinum*	IN
Green salamander	*Aneides aeneus*	SC
Northern dusky salamander	*Desmognathus fuscus*	SE
Southern two-lined salamander	*Eurycea cirrigera*	IN
Long-tailed salamander	*Eurycea longicauda*	S
Cave salamander	*Eurycea lucifuga*	S
Four-toed salamander	*Hemidactylium scutatum*	N,SC
Eastern newt	*Notophthalmus viridescens*	N,S
Redback salamander	*Plethodon cinereus*	IN
Northern zigzag salamander	*Plethodon dorsalis*	S
Northern ravine salamander	*Plethodon electromorphus*	SE
Northern slimy salamander	*Plethodon glutinosus*	S
Red salamander	*Pseudotriton ruber*	SC
Eastern box turtle	*Terrapene carolina*	
Five-lined skink	*Eumeces fasciatus*	IN
Broadhead skink	*Eumeces laticeps*	S
Eastern fence lizard	*Sceloporus undulatus*	S
Ground skink	*Scincella lateralis*	SW
Northern copperhead	*Agkistrodon contortrix*	S
Eastern worm snake	*Carphophis amoenus*	S
Scarlet snake	*Cemophora coccinea*	SC
Racer	*Coluber constrictor*	IN
Timber rattlesnake	*Crotalus horridus*	S
Ringneck snake	*Diadophis punctatus*	IN[1]
Rat snake	*Elaphe obsoleta*	IN
Common kingsnake	*Lampropeltis getula*	SW
Milk snake	*Lampropeltis triangulum*	N,SW
Rough green snake	*Opheodrys aestivus*	S
Brown snake	*Storeria dekayi*	IN
Red-bellied snake	*Storeria occipitomaculata*	N,SW
Southeastern crowned snake	*Tantilla coronata*	SC
Western ribbon snake	*Thamnophis proximus*	NW,SW
Eastern ribbon snake	*Thamnophis sauritus*	NE,SE,W,SW[6]
Common garter snake	*Thamnophis sirtalis*	IN
Smooth earth snake	*Virginia valeriae*	SC

Notes: IN = statewide distribution; N = northern distribution; NW = northwestern distribution, C = central distribution, etc.; [1] = absent from some prairie areas; [2] = restricted to vicinity of Evansville; [3] = restricted to Falls of the Ohio State Park; [4] = absent from SW lowlands; [5] = also single record in historic SW plains; [6] = patchy (complex) distribution.

Table H-3. Herpetofauna Associated with Grasslands, including Savanna

Common Name	Scientific Name	Range	Grassland	Savanna	Recovering Mine Land
Cricket frog	*Acris crepitans*	IN	X	X	X
American toad	*Bufo americanus*	IN		X	X
Fowler's toad	*Bufo fowleri*	IN	X	X	X
Cope's gray treefrog	*Hyla chrysoscelis*	IN		X	X
Eastern gray treefrog	*Hyla versicolor*	IN		X	X
Spring peeper	*Pseudacris crucifer*	IN	X	X	X
Western chorus frog	*Pseudacris triseriata*	IN	X	X	X
Crawfish frog	*Rana areolata*	SE,SW	X	X	X
Plains leopard frog	*Rana blairi*	NW	X	X	
Bullfrog	*Rana catesbeiana*	IN			X
Green frog	*Rana clamitans*	IN			X
Northern leopard frog	*Rana pipiens*	N	X	X	X
Southern leopard frog	*Rana sphenocephala (utricularia)*	S			X
Eastern spadefoot	*Scaphiopus holbrookii*	S	X	X	X
Eastern tiger salamander	*Ambystoma tigrinum*	IN	X	X	X
Redback salamander	*Plethodon cinereus*	IN1			X
Spiny softshell	*Apalone spinifera*	IN			X
Common snapping turtle	*Chelydra serpentina*	IN			X
Midland painted turtle	*Chrysemys picta marginata*	IN			X
Common musk turtle	*Sternotherus odoratus*	IN			X
Ornate box turtle	*Terrapene ornata*	NW,SW	X	X	
Red-eared slider	*Trachemys scripta elegans*	NW,S,W			X
Six-lined racerunner	*Cnemidophorus sexlineatus*	NW,SW	X	X	X
Five-lined skink	*Eumeces fasciatus*	IN	X	X	X
Slender glass lizard	*Ophisaurus attenuatus*	NW	X	X	
Eastern fence lizard	*Sceloporus undulatus*	S	X	X	X
Northern copperhead	*Agkistrodon contortrix*	S			X
Kirtland's snake	*Clonophis kirtlandii*	IN4	X	X	X
Racer	*Coluber constrictor*	IN	X	X	X
Rat snake	*Elaphe obsoleta*	IN		X	X
Fox snake	*Elaphe vulpina*	NW	X	X	X
Eastern hognose snake	*Heterodon platirhinos*	IN	X	X	X
Prairie kingsnake	*Lampropeltis calligaster*	W	X	X	
Common kingsnake	*Lampropeltis getula*	SW	X	X	X
Milk snake	*Lampropeltis triangulum*	N,SW	X	X	X
Copperbelly water snake	*Nerodia erythrogaster neglecta*	NW,SE			X
Northern water snake	*Nerodia sipedon*	IN			X
Rough green snake	*Opheodrys aestivus*	S			X
Smooth green snake	*Opheodrys vernalis*	NW	X	X	
Bull snake	*Pituophis catenifer*	NW5	X	X	
Eastern massasauga	*Sistrurus catenatus*	N		X	
Brown snake	*Storeria dekayi*	IN	X	X	
Red-bellied snake	*Storeria occipitomaculata*	N,SW	X	X	
Butler's garter snake	*Thamnophis butleri*	NE	X	X	
Western ribbon snake	*Thamnophis proximus*	NW, SW	X	X	X
Plains garter snake	*Thamnophis radix*	NW	X	X	
Eastern ribbon snake	*Thamnophis sauritus*	NE,SE,W,SW6	X	X	X
Common garter snake	*Thamnophis sirtalis*	IN	X	X	X

Notes: IN = statewide distribution; N = northern distribution; NW = northwestern distribution, C = central distribution, etc.; 1 = absent from some prairie areas; 2 = restricted to vicinity of Evansville; 3 = restricted to Falls of the Ohio State Park; 4 = absent from SW lowlands; 5 = also single record in historic SW plains; 6 = patchy (complex) distribution.

Table H-4. Herpetofauna Associated with Wetlands

Common Name	Scientific Name	Range	Ephemeral Wetlands	Permanent Wetlands
Cricket frog	*Acris crepitans*	IN		X
American toad	*Bufo americanus*	IN	X	X
Fowler's toad	*Bufo fowleri*	IN	X	
Cope's gray treefrog	*Hyla chrysoscelis*	IN	X	
Green treefrog	*Hyla cinerea*	SW2	X	X
Eastern gray treefrog	*Hyla versicolor*	IN	X	
Spring peeper	*Pseudacris crucifer*	IN	X	
Western chorus frog	*Pseudacris triseriata*	IN	X	X
Crawfish frog	*Rana areolata*	SW	X	
Plains leopard frog	*Rana blairi*	NW	X	X
Bullfrog	*Rana catesbeiana*	IN		X
Green frog	*Rana clamitans*	IN	X	
Pickerel frog	*Rana palustris*	IN1		X
Northern leopard frog	*Rana pipiens*	N	X	X
Southern leopard frog	*Rana sphenocephala (utricularia)*	S	X	X
Wood frog	*Rana sylvatica*	IN1	X	
Eastern spadefoot	*Scaphiopus holbrookii*	S	X	
Jefferson's salamander	*Ambystoma jeffersonianum*	S	X	
Blue-spotted salamander	*Ambystoma laterale*	N	X	
Spotted salamander	*Ambystoma maculatum*	IN	X	X
Marbled salamander	*Ambystoma opacum*	NE,NW,S	X	
Mole salamander	*Ambystoma talpoideum*	SW2	X	X
Smallmouth salamander	*Ambystoma texanum*	IN	X	
Eastern tiger salamander	*Ambystoma tigrinum*	IN	X	X
Northern dusky salamander	*Desmognathus fuscus*	SE		X
Four-toed salamander	*Hemidactylium scutatum*	N,SC	X	
Common mudpuppy	*Necturus maculosus*	IN		X
Eastern newt	*Notophthalmus viridescens*	N,S	X	X
Lesser Siren	*Siren intermedia*	W		X
Common snapping turtle	*Chelydra serpentina*	IN	X	X
Midland painted turtle	*Chrysemys picta marginata*	IN	X	X
Spotted turtle	*Clemmys guttata*	N	X	X
Blanding's turtle	*Emydoidea blandingii*	N	X	X
Eastern mud turtle	*Kinosternon subrubrum*	NW,SW	X	X
Common musk turtle	*Sternotherus odoratus*	IN	X	X
Red-eared slider	*Trachemys scripta elegans*	NW,S,W	X	X
Cottonmouth	*Agkistrodon piscivorus*	SW		X
Kirtland's snake	*Clonophis kirtlandii*	IN4	X	X
Western mud snake	*Farancia abacura reinwardtii*	SW		X
Common kingsnake	*Lampropeltis getula*	SW	X	
Copperbelly water snake	*Nerodia erythrogaster neglecta*	NW,SE	X	X
Diamondback water snake	*Nerodia rhombifer*	SW		X
Northern water snake	*Nerodia sipedon*	IN	X	X
Queen snake	*Regina septemvittata*	IN1,4		X
Eastern massasauga	*Sistrurus catenatus*	N	X	X
Butler's garter snake	*Thamnophis butleri*	NE	X	X
Western ribbon snake	*Thamnophis proximus*	NW,SW	X	X
Plains garter snake	*Thamnophis radix*	NW	X	X
Eastern ribbon snake	*Thamnophis sauritus*	NE, SE,W,SW6	X	X
Common garter snake	*Thamnophis sirtalis*	IN	X	X

Notes: IN = statewide distribution; N = northern distribution; NW = northwestern distribution, C = central distribution, etc.; 1 = absent from some prairie areas; 2 = restricted to vicinity of Evansville; 3 = restricted to Falls of the Ohio State Park; 4 = absent from SW lowlands; 5 = also single record in historic SW plains; 6 = patchy (complex) distribution.

Table H-5. Herpetofauna Associated with Aquatic Systems

Common Name	Scientific Name	Range	Riverine	Large water Bodies
Cricket frog	*Acris crepitans*	IN		
Bullfrog	*Rana catesbeiana*	IN	X	X
Green frog	*Rana clamitans*	IN	X	X
Hellbender	*Cryptobranchus alleganiensis*	S	X	
Common mudpuppy	*Necturus maculosus*	IN	X	X
Lesser Siren	*Siren intermedia*	W		
Smooth softshell	*Apalone mutica*	S	X	
Spiny softshell	*Apalone spinifera*	IN	X	X
Common snapping turtle	*Chelydra serpentina*	IN	X	X
Midland painted turtle	*Chrysemys picta marginata*		X	X
Blanding's turtle	*Emydoidea blandingii*	N	X	
Common map turtle	*Graptemys geographica*	IN	X	X
Mississippi map turtle	*Graptemys geographica kohnii*		X	
Ouachita map turtle	*Graptemys ouachitensis*		X	
False map turtle	*Graptemys pseudogeographica*	S	X	
Eastern mud turtle	*Kinosternon subrubrum*	NW,SW		X
Alligator snapping turtle	*Macroclemys temminckii*	SW	X	X
Hieroglyphic river cooter	*Pseudemys concinna heiroglyphica*	SW	X	
Common musk turtle	*Sternotherus odoratus*	IN	X	X
Red-eared slider	*Trachemys scripta elegans*	NW,S,W	X	X
Snakes (Squamata)				
Diamondback water snake	*Nerodia rhombifer*	SW	X	X
Northern water snake	*Nerodia sipedon*	IN	X	X
Queen snake	*Regina septemvittata*	IN1,4	X	

Notes: IN = statewide distribution; N = northern distribution; NW = northwestern distribution, C = central distribution, etc.; 1 = absent from some prairie areas; 2 = restricted to vicinity of Evansville; 3 = restricted to Falls of the Ohio State Park; 4 = absent from SW lowlands; 5 = also single record in historic SW plains; 6 = patchy (complex) distribution.

Table H-6. Herpetofauna Associated with Barren Lands

Common Name	Scientific Name	Range	Dunes	Cliffs/Outcrops	Quarries
Cricket frog	*Acris crepitans*	IN			X
American toad	*Bufo americanus*	IN			X
Fowler's toad	*Bufo fowleri*	IN	X		X
Cope's gray treefrog	*Hyla chrysoscelis*	IN			X
Eastern gray treefrog	*Hyla versicolor*	IN			X
Western chorus frog	*Pseudacris triseriata*	IN			X
Bullfrog	*Rana catesbeiana*	IN			X
Green frog	*Rana clamitans*	IN			X
Pickerel frog	*Rana palustris*	IN1			X
Northern leopard frog	*Rana pipiens*	N			X
Southern leopard frog	*Rana sphenocephala (utricularia)*	S			X
Green salamander	*Aneides aeneus*	SC		X	
Northern dusky salamander	*Desmognathus fuscus*	SE		X	
Long-tailed salamander	*Eurycea longicauda*	S			X
Cave salamander	*Eurycea lucifuga*	S		X	X
Northern zigzag salamander	*Plethodon dorsalis*	S		X	
Common snapping turtle	*Chelydra serpentina*	IN			X
Midland painted turtle	*Chrysemys picta marginata*	IN			X
Red-eared slider	*Trachemys scripta elegans*	NW,S,W			X
Six-lined racerunner	*Cnemidophorus sexlineatus*	NW,SW	X	X	
Five-lined skink	*Eumeces fasciatus*	IN			X
Broadhead skink	*Eumeces laticeps*	S		X	X
Slender glass lizard	*Ophisaurus attenuatus*	NW	X		
Eastern fence lizard	*Sceloporus undulatus*	S		X	X
Northern copperhead	*Agkistrodon contortrix*	S		X	X
Racer	*Coluber constrictor*	IN	X		X
Timber rattlesnake	*Crotalus horridus*	S		X	
Ringneck snake	*Diadophis punctatus*	IN1			X
Rat snake	*Elaphe obsoleta*	IN			X
Eastern hognose snake	*Heterodon platirhinos*	IN	X		
Common kingsnake	*Lampropeltis getula*	SW			X
Milk snake	*Lampropeltis triangulum*	N,SW			X
Northern water snake	*Nerodia sipedon*	IN			X
Bull snake	*Pituophis catenifer*	NW5	X		
Brown snake	*Storeria dekayi*	IN			X
Common garter snake	*Thamnophis sirtalis*	IN			X

Notes: IN = statewide distribution; N = northern distribution; NW = northwestern distribution, C = central distribution, etc.; 1 = absent from some prairie areas; 2 = restricted to vicinity of Evansville; 3 = restricted to Falls of the Ohio State Park; 4 = absent from SW lowlands; 5 = also single record in historic SW plains; 6 = patchy (complex) distribution.

Table H-7. Herpetofauna Associated with Caves

Common Name	Scientific Name	Range
Green salamander	*Aneides aeneus*	SC
Northern dusky salamander	*Desmognathus fuscus*	SE
Cave salamander	*Eurycea lucifuga*	S
Northern zigzag salamander	*Plethodon dorsalis*	S
Northern slimy salamander	*Plethodon glutinosus*	S
Northern copperhead	*Agkistrodon contortrix*	S
Timber rattlesnake	*Crotalus horridus*	S
Rat snake	*Elaphe obsoleta*	IN

Notes: IN = statewide distribution; N = northern distribution; NW = northwestern distribution, C = central distribution, etc.

Table H-8. Herpetofauna of Agricultural Habitats

Common Name	Scientific Name	Range
American toad	*Bufo americanus*	IN
Fowler's toad	*Bufo fowleri*	IN
Cope's gray treefrog	*Hyla chrysoscelis*	IN
Eastern gray treefrog	*Hyla versicolor*	IN
Western chorus frog	*Pseudacris triseriata*	IN
Plains leopard frog	*Rana blairi*	IN1
Bullfrog	*Rana catesbeiana*	IN
Green frog	*Rana clamitans*	IN
Northern leopard frog	*Rana pipiens*	N
Southern leopard frog	*Rana sphenocephala (utricularia)*	S
Five-lined skink	*Eumeces fasciatus*	IN
Slender glass lizard	*Ophisaurus attenuatus*	NW
Racer	*Coluber constrictor*	IN
Rat snake	*Elaphe obsoleta*	IN
Fox snake	*Elaphe vulpina*	NW
Eastern hognose snake	*Heterodon platirhinos*	IN
Prairie kingsnake	*Lampropeltis calligaster*	W
Milk snake	*Lampropeltis triangulum*	N,SW
Bull snake	*Pituophis catenifer*	NW5
Common garter snake	*Thamnophis sirtalis*	IN

Notes: IN = statewide distribution; N = northern distribution; NW = northwestern distribution, C = central distribution, etc.; 1 = absent from some prairie areas; 2 = restricted to vicinity of Evansville; 3 = restricted to Falls of the Ohio State Park; 4 = absent from SW lowlands; 5 = also single record in historic SW plains; 6 = patchy (complex) distribution.

Table H-9. Herpetofauna Associated with Developed Lands

Common Name	Scientific Name	Range
American toad	*Bufo americanus*	IN
Cope's gray treefrog	*Hyla chrysoscelis*	IN
Eastern gray treefrog	*Hyla versicolor*	IN
Western chorus frog	*Pseudacris triseriata*	IN
Bullfrog	*Rana catesbeiana*	IN
Green frog	*Rana clamitans*	IN
Common snapping turtle	*Chelydra serpentina*	IN
Midland painted turtle	*Chrysemys picta marginata*	IN
Red-eared slider	*Trachemys scripta elegans*	NW,S,W
Kirtland's snake	*Clonophis kirtlandii*	IN4
Northern water snake	*Nerodia sipedon*	IN
Brown snake	*Storeria dekayi*	IN
Butler's garter snake	*Thamnophis butleri*	NE
Plains garter snake	*Thamnophis radix*	NW
Common garter snake	*Thamnophis sirtalis*	IN

Notes: IN = statewide distribution; N = northern distribution; NW = northwestern distribution, C = central distribution, etc.; 1 = absent from some prairie areas; 2 = restricted to vicinity of Evansville; 3 = restricted to Falls of the Ohio State Park; 4 = absent from SW lowlands; 5 = also single record in historic SW plains; 6 = patchy (complex) distribution.

Table H-10. Currently Recognized Species of Reptiles and Amphibians Having Their Type Localities in Indiana

Common Name	Scientific Name	Type Locality
Smooth softshell	*Apalone mutica* (Lesueur 1827)	Wabash River at New Harmony
Spiny softshell	*Apalone spinifer* (Lesueur 1827)	Wabash River at New Harmony
False map turtle	*Graptemys pseudogeographica* (Gray 1831)	Wabash River at New Harmony
Western chorus frog	*Pseudacris triseriata* (Wied-Neuwied 1839)	Rush Creek, 4 miles south of New Harmony
Butler's garter snake	*Thamnophis butleri* (Cope 1888)	Richmond, Wayne County

Table B-1. Annually Occurring Birds of Indiana as of 2000

		Habitat							Seasonality, Abundance[a]		
Common Name	**Scientific Name**	**Agricultural**	**Aquatic Systems**	**Barren Lands**	**Developed Lands[b]**	**Forest Lands[c]**	**Grasslands**	**Wetlands**	**Nest**	**Migration**	**Winter**
Greater white-fronted goose	*Anser albifrons*	X	X				X	X		R	R
Snow goose	*Chen caerulescens*	X	X				X	X		U	R
Ross's goose	*Chen rossii*		X					X		R	R
Cackling goose	*Branta hutchinsii*		X					X		R	R
Canada goose	*Branta canadensis*	X	X		X		X	X	C	C	C
Mute swan	*Cygnus olor*		X		X			X	U		U
Trumpeter swan	*Cygnus buccinator*	X	X					X	EX	RI	RI
Tundra swan	*Cygnus columbianus*	X	X							U	U
Wood duck	*Aix sponsa*		X		X	X		X	C	C	R
Gadwall	*Anas strepera*		X		X			X		C	R
American wigeon	*Anas americana*		X		X			X		C	R
American black duck	*Anas rubripes*	X	X		X			X	R	U	U
Mallard	*Anas platyrhynchos*	X	X		X		X	X	C	C	C
Blue-winged teal	*Anas discors*		X		X		X	X	U	C	
Northern shoveler	*Anas clypeata*		X		X			X	R	C	U
Northern pintail	*Anas acuta*		X		X			X		C	R
Green-winged teal	*Anas crecca*		X		X			X	R	C	R
Canvasback	*Aythya valisineria*		X		X					U	R
Redhead	*Aythya americana*		X		X			X	R	C	U
Ring-necked duck	*Aythya collaris*		X		X			X	R	C	R
Greater scaup	*Aythya marila*		X								R
Lesser scaup	*Aythya affinis*		X		X					C	R
Harlequin duck	*Histrionicus histrionicus*		X								R
Surf scoter	*Melanitta perspicillata*		X							R	
White-winged scoter	*Melanitta fusca*		X							R	
Black scoter	*Melanitta nigra*		X							R	
Long-tailed duck	*Clangula hyemalis*		X							R	
Bufflehead	*Bucephala albeola*		X		X					C	U
Common goldeneye	*Bucephala clangula*		X		X					C	U
Hooded merganser	*Lophodytes cucullatus*		X		X	X		X	U	C	U
Common merganser	*Mergus merganser*		X		X					U	U
Red-breasted merganser	*Mergus serrator*		X		X					U	U
Ruddy duck	*Oxyura jamaicensis*		X		X			X		C	R
Northern bobwhite	*Colinus virginianus*	X			X	X	X		U		U
Ring-necked pheasant	*Phasianus colchicus*	X					X		C	C	C
Ruffed grouse	*Bonasa umbellus*				X	X			R		R
Greater prairie-chicken	*Tympanuchus cupido*						X		EX		EX
Wild turkey	*Meleagris gallopavo*	X			X	X			C		C
Red-throated loon	*Gavia stellata*		X							R	
Common loon	*Gavia immer*		X		X					U	
Pied-billed grebe	*Podilymbus podiceps*		X		X			X	U	C	R
Horned grebe	*Podiceps auritus*		X		X					U	
Red-necked grebe	*Podiceps grisegena*		X							R	
Eared grebe	*Podiceps nigricollis*		X							R	R
Western grebe	*Aechmophorus occidentalis*		X							R	R
American white pelican	*Pelecanus erythrorhynchos*		X							R	
Double-crested cormorant	*Phalacrocorax auritus*		X		X			X	U	C	R
American bittern	*Botaurus lentiginosus*		X					X	U	U	
Least bittern	*Ixobrychus exilis*		X					X	U	U	
Great blue heron	*Ardea herodias*		X		X	X		X	C	C	R
Great egret	*Ardea alba*		X		X			X	R	U	

Table B-1. *continued*

Common Name	Scientific Name	Habitat							Seasonality, Abundance[a]		
		Agricultural	Aquatic Systems	Barren Lands	Developed Lands[b]	Forest Lands[c]	Grasslands	Wetlands	Nest	Migration	Winter
Snowy egret	*Egretta thula*							X		R	
Little blue heron	*Egretta caerulea*							X		R	
Cattle egret	*Bubulcus ibis*						X	X		R	
Green heron	*Butorides virescens*		X		X	X		X	C	C	
Black-crowned night-heron	*Nycticorax nycticorax*		X					X	U	U	
Yellow-crowned night-heron	*Nyctanassa violacea*		X			X		X	R	R	
Black vulture	*Coragyps atratus*				X	X			U	U	
Turkey vulture	*Cathartes aura*	X	X		X	X	X		C	C	U
Osprey	*Pandion haliaetus*		X		X			X	R	U	
Mississippi kite	*Ictinia mississippiensis*					X			R	R	
Bald eagle	*Haliaeetus leucocephalus*		X		X	X		X	U	U	U
Northern harrier	*Circus cyaneus*	X			X		X	X	R	C	
Sharp-shinned hawk	*Accipiter striatus*				X	X			R	C	C
Cooper's hawk	*Accipiter cooperii*				X	X	X		U	C	C
Northern goshawk	*Accipiter gentilis*					X				R	R
Red-shouldered hawk	*Buteo lineatus*				X	X		X	C		C
Broad-winged hawk	*Buteo platypterus*					X			R	U	
Red-tailed hawk	*Buteo jamaicensis*	X			X	X	X		C	C	C
Rough-legged hawk	*Buteo lagopus*	X			X		X			U	R
Golden eagle	*Aquila chrysaetos*			X		X				R	R
American kestrel	*Falco sparverius*	X			X	X	X		C	U	C
Merlin	*Falco columbarius*		X							R	
Peregrine falcon	*Falco peregrinus*		X		X					R	R
Yellow rail	*Coturnicops noveboracensis*						X	X		R	
Black rail	*Laterallus jamaicensis*							X		R	
King rail	*Rallus elegans*							X	R	R	
Virginia rail	*Rallus limicola*		X					X	R	U	
Sora	*Porzana carolina*		X					X	R	C	
Common moorhen	*Gallinula chloropus*		X					X	R	R	
American coot	*Fulica americana*		X		X			X	U	C	U
Sandhill crane	*Grus canadensis*	X					X	X	R	C	
Whooping crane	*Grus americana*							X	EX	RI	
Black-bellied plover	*Pluvialis squatarola*		X					X		U	
American golden-plover	*Pluvialis dominica*	X					X	X		U	
Semipalmated plover	*Charadrius semipalmatus*		X		X			X		C	
Piping plover	*Charadrius melodus*		X							R	
Killdeer	*Charadrius vociferus*	X	X	X	X		X	X	C	C	U
Black-necked stilt	*Himantopus mexicanus*							X	R	R	
American avocet	*Recurvirostra americana*		X					X		R	
Spotted sandpiper	*Actitis macularius*		X	X	X			X	C	C	
Solitary sandpiper	*Tringa solitaria*		X		X			X		C	
Greater yellowlegs	*Tringa melanoleuca*		X		X			X		U	
Willet	*Catoptrophorus semipalmatus*		X					X		R	
Lesser yellowlegs	*Tringa flavipes*	X	X		X			X		C	
Upland sandpiper	*Bartramia longicauda*				X		X		R	R	
Hudsonian godwit	*Limosa haemastica*							X		R	
Marbled godwit	*Limosa fedoa*		X					X		R	
Ruddy turnstone	*Arenaria interpres*		X					X		U	
Red knot	*Calidris canutus*		X					X		R	
Sanderling	*Calidris alba*		X					X		U	
Semipalmated sandpiper	*Calidris pusilla*		X		X			X		C	
Western sandpiper	*Calidris mauri*		X					X		R	
Least sandpiper	*Calidris minutilla*		X		X			X		C	
White-rumped sandpiper	*Calidris fuscicollis*		X					X		R	
Baird's sandpiper	*Calidris bairdii*	X	X					X		R	
Pectoral sandpiper	*Calidris melanotos*	X	X		X		X	X		C	
Purple sandpiper	*Calidris maritima*		X							R	
Dunlin	*Calidris alpina*		X		X			X		U	
Stilt sandpiper	*Calidris himantopus*		X		X			X		U	
Buff-breasted sandpiper	*Tryngites subruficollis*	X					X	X		R	
Short-billed dowitcher	*Limnodromus griseus*		X		X			X		U	
Long-billed dowitcher	*Limnodromus scolopaceus*		X					X		R	
Wilson's snipe	*Gallinago delicata*	X			X			X		C	

		Habitat							Seasonality, Abundance[a]		
Common Name	**Scientific Name**	**Agricultural**	**Aquatic Systems**	**Barren Lands**	**Developed Lands[b]**	**Forest Lands[c]**	**Grasslands**	**Wetlands**	**Nest**	**Migration**	**Winter**
American woodcock	*Scolopax minor*					X	X	X	U	U	
Wilson's phalarope	*Phalaropus tricolor*							X	R	R	
Red-necked phalarope	*Phalaropus lobatus*							X		R	
Red phalarope	*Phalaropus fulicarius*		X							R	
Black-legged kittiwake	*Rissa tridactyla*		X							R	
Bonaparte's gull	*Chroicocephalus philadelphia*		X		X					U	U
Little gull	*Hydrocoloeus minutus*		X							R	
Laughing gull	*Leucophaeus atricilla*		X							R	
Franklin's gull	*Leucophaeus pipixcan*		X							R	
Ring-billed gull	*Larus delawarensis*	X	X		X			X	U	C	C
Herring gull	*Larus argentatus*		X		X					U	U
Thayer's gull	*Larus thayeri*		X								R
Glaucous gull	*Larus hyperboreus*		X								R
Great black-backed gull	*Larus marinus*		X								R
Least tern	*Sterna antillarum*		X	X	X				R	R	
Caspian tern	*Hydroprogne caspia*		X		X					U	
Black tern	*Chlidonias niger*		X		X			X	R	U	
Common tern	*Sterna hirundo*		X		X			X		U	
Forster's tern	*Sterna forsteri*		X		X			X		U	
Parasitic jaeger	*Stercorarius parasiticus*		X							R	
Rock pigeon	*Columba livia*	X			X				C		C
Eurasian collared dove	*Streptopelia decaocto*				X				R		R
Mourning dove	*Zenaida macroura*	X			X	X	X		C		C
Passenger pigeon	*Ectopistes migratorius*					X			EX	EX	
Monk parakeet	*Myiopsitta monachus*				X				R		R
Carolina parakeet	*Conuropsis carolinensis*	X				X		X	EX	EX	EX
Yellow-billed cuckoo	*Coccyzus americanus*	X			X	X			C	C	
Black-billed cuckoo	*Coccyzus erythropthalmus*				X	X			U	U	
Barn owl	*Tyto alba*	X					X		R		R
Eastern screech-owl	*Megascops asio*				X	X			C		C
Great horned owl	*Bubo virginianus*	X			X	X	X		C		C
Snowy owl	*Bubo scandiacus*	X			X					R	R
Barred owl	*Strix varia*				X	X		X	C		C
Long-eared owl	*Asio otus*					X			R	R	R
Short-eared owl	*Asio flammeus*	X			X		X		R	U	U
Northern saw-whet owl	*Aegolius acadicus*					X				R	R
Common nighthawk	*Chordeiles minor*				X		X	X	C	C	
Chuck-will's-widow	*Caprimulgus carolinensis*					X			R	R	
Whip-poor-will	*Caprimulgus vociferus*				X	X			U	U	
Chimney swift	*Chaetura pelagica*				X	X			C	C	
Ruby-throated hummingbird	*Archilochus colubris*				X	X			C	C	
Belted kingfisher	*Megaceryle alcyon*		X		X			X	U	U	U
Red-headed woodpecker	*Melanerpes erythrocephalus*		X		X	X		X	C	C	U
Red-bellied woodpecker	*Melanerpes carolinus*				X	X		X	C		C
Yellow-bellied sapsucker	*Sphyrapicus varius*	X			X	X				C	R
Downy woodpecker	*Picoides pubescens*	X			X	X			C		C
Hairy woodpecker	*Picoides villosus*				X	X			U		U
Northern flicker	*Colaptes auratus*				X	X	X		C	C	C
Pileated woodpecker	*Dryocopus pileatus*				X	X		X	C		C
Ivory-billed woodpecker	*Campephilus principalis*					X			EX	EX	
Olive-sided flycatcher	*Contopus cooperi*					X				R	
Eastern wood-pewee	*Contopus virens*	X			X	X			C	C	
Yellow-bellied flycatcher	*Empidonax flaviventris*					X				R	
Acadian flycatcher	*Empidonax virescens*					X			C	U	
Alder flycatcher	*Empidonax alnorum*		X					X	R	R	
Willow flycatcher	*Empidonax traillii*		X				X	X	C	U	
Least flycatcher	*Empidonax minimus*				X	X			R	C	
Eastern phoebe	*Sayornis phoebe*		X		X	X		X	C	C	R
Great crested flycatcher	*Myiarchus crinitus*				X	X			C	C	
Eastern kingbird	*Tyrannus tyrannus*	X			X	X	X	X	C	C	
Loggerhead shrike	*Lanius ludovicianus*				X	X	X		R	R	R
Northern shrike	*Lanius excubitor*					X	X			R	R
White-eyed vireo	*Vireo griseus*				X	X			C	C	

Table B-1. *continued*

		Habitat							Seasonality, Abundance[a]		
Common Name	**Scientific Name**	**Agricultural**	**Aquatic Systems**	**Barren Lands**	**Developed Lands[b]**	**Forest Lands[c]**	**Grasslands**	**Wetlands**	**Nest**	**Migration**	**Winter**
Bell's vireo	*Vireo bellii*				X	X	X		U	R	
Yellow-throated vireo	*Vireo flavifrons*					X			U	U	
Blue-headed vireo	*Vireo solitarius*				X	X				U	
Warbling vireo	*Vireo gilvus*		X		X	X		X	C	C	
Philadelphia vireo	*Vireo philadelphicus*					X				R	
Red-eyed vireo	*Vireo olivaceus*				X	X			C	C	
Blue jay	*Cyanocitta cristata*				X	X			C	C	C
American crow	*Corvus brachyrhynchos*	X	X		X	X	X		C	C	C
Fish crow	*Corvus ossifragus*		X			X				R	R
Common raven	*Corvus corax*			X					EX		EX
Horned lark	*Eremophila alpestris*	X	X	X	X		X		C	C	C
Purple martin	*Progne subis*	X						X	U	U	
Tree swallow	*Tachycineta bicolor*		X		X			X	C	C	
Northern rough-winged swallow	*Stelgidopteryx serripennis*		X	X	X				C	C	
Bank swallow	*Riparia riparia*		X	X	X				U	U	
Cliff swallow	*Petrochelidon pyrrhonota*		X		X				C	C	
Barn swallow	*Hirundo rustica*	X	X		X		X		C	C	
Carolina chickadee	*Poecile carolinensis*				X	X			C		C
Black-capped chickadee	*Poecile atricapillus*				X	X			C		C
Tufted titmouse	*Baeolophus bicolor*				X	X			C		C
Red-breasted nuthatch	*Sitta canadensis*				X	X				U	R
White-breasted nuthatch	*Sitta carolinensis*				X	X			C		C
Brown creeper	*Certhia americana*					X			R	C	U
Carolina wren	*Thryothorus ludovicianus*				X	X			C		C
Bewick's wren	*Thryomanes bewickii*					X			EX		
House wren	*Troglodytes aedon*				X	X			C	C	
Winter wren	*Troglodytes troglodytes*					X				U	U
Sedge wren	*Cistothorus platensis*						X		U	U	
Marsh wren	*Cistothorus palustris*		X					X	U	U	
Golden-crowned kinglet	*Regulus satrapa*					X				U	U
Ruby-crowned kinglet	*Regulus calendula*				X	X				C	R
Blue-gray gnatcatcher	*Polioptila caerulea*				X	X			C	C	
Eastern bluebird	*Sialia sialis*				X	X	X		C		C
Veery	*Catharus fuscescens*					X			R	U	
Gray-cheeked thrush	*Catharus minimus*					X				U	
Swainson's thrush	*Catharus ustulatus*				X	X				C	
Hermit thrush	*Catharus guttatus*				X	X				U	R
Wood thrush	*Hylocichla mustelina*				X	X			C	U	
American robin	*Turdus migratorius*	X			X	X	X		C	C	C
Gray catbird	*Dumetella carolinensis*				X	X			C	C	
Northern mockingbird	*Mimus polyglottos*				X	X	X		U		U
Brown thrasher	*Toxostoma rufum*				X	X	X		C	R	R
European starling	*Sturnus vulgaris*	X			X	X	X	X	C	C	C
American pipit	*Anthus rubescens*	X					X	X		U	
Cedar waxwing	*Bombycilla cedrorum*	X			X	X			C	C	U
Blue-winged warbler	*Vermivora pinus*				X	X			U	U	
Golden-winged warbler	*Vermivora chrysoptera*					X			R	R	
Tennessee warbler	*Vermivora peregrina*				X	X				C	
Orange-crowned warbler	*Vermivora celata*					X				U	
Nashville warbler	*Vermivora ruficapilla*				X	X				C	
Northern parula	*Parula americana*					X			U	U	
Yellow warbler	*Dendroica petechia*		X		X		X	X	C	C	
Chestnut-sided warbler	*Dendroica pensylvanica*				X	X			R	U	
Magnolia warbler	*Dendroica magnolia*				X	X				C	
Cape May warbler	*Dendroica tigrina*				X	X				U	
Black-throated blue warbler	*Dendroica caerulescens*					X				R	
Yellow-rumped warbler	*Dendroica coronata*				X	X				C	R
Black-throated green warbler	*Dendroica virens*				X	X			R	C	
Blackburnian warbler	*Dendroica fusca*				X	X				U	
Yellow-throated warbler	*Dendroica dominica*		X			X			C	U	
Pine warbler	*Dendroica pinus*					X			U	R	
Prairie warbler	*Dendroica discolor*				X	X			C	U	
Palm warbler	*Dendroica palmarum*				X	X		X		C	
Bay-breasted warbler	*Dendroica castanea*				X	X				C	

Common Name	Scientific Name	Habitat							Seasonality, Abundance[a]		
		Agricultural	Aquatic Systems	Barren Lands	Developed Lands[b]	Forest Lands[c]	Grasslands	Wetlands	Nest	Migration	Winter
Blackpoll warbler	*Dendroica striata*				X	X				C	
Cerulean warbler	*Dendroica cerulea*					X			U	U	
Black-and-white warbler	*Mniotilta varia*				X	X			R	C	
American redstart	*Setophaga ruticilla*				X	X			U	C	
Prothonotary warbler	*Protonotaria citrea*		X			X		X	U	U	
Worm-eating warbler	*Helmitheros vermivorum*					X			U	R	
Ovenbird	*Seiurus aurocapilla*				X	X			C	C	
Northern waterthrush	*Seiurus noveboracensis*				X	X		X		U	
Louisiana waterthrush	*Seiurus motacilla*		X			X			C	U	
Kentucky warbler	*Oporornis formosus*					X			C	U	
Connecticut warbler	*Oporornis agilis*					X				R	
Mourning warbler	*Oporornis philadelphia*					X				R	
Common yellowthroat	*Geothlypis trichas*		X		X	X	X	X	C	C	
Hooded warbler	*Wilsonia citrina*					X			R	R	
Wilson's warbler	*Wilsonia pusilla*					X				U	
Canada warbler	*Wilsonia canadensis*					X			R	R	
Yellow-breasted chat	*Icteria virens*				X	X			C	C	
Eastern towhee	*Pipilo erythrophthalmus*				X	X			C	U	R
Bachman's sparrow	*Aimophila aestivalis*					X			EX	EX	
American tree sparrow	*Spizella arborea*				X	X	X			C	C
Chipping sparrow	*Spizella passerina*				X	X	X		C	C	R
Clay-colored sparrow	*Spizella pallida*					X				R	
Field sparrow	*Spizella pusilla*	X			X	X	X		C	U	U
Vesper sparrow	*Pooecetes gramineus*	X			X		X		U	U	
Lark sparrow	*Chondestes grammacus*	X			X		X		R	R	
Savannah sparrow	*Passerculus sandwichensis*	X		X	X		X		U	C	
Grasshopper sparrow	*Ammodramus savannarum*	X			X		X		C	C	
Henslow's sparrow	*Ammodramus henslowii*						X		U	U	
Le Conte's sparrow	*Ammodramus leconteii*						X			R	
Nelson's sparrow	*Ammodramus nelsoni*							X		R	
Fox sparrow	*Passerella iliaca*					X				U	U
Song sparrow	*Melospiza melodia*	X	X		X	X	X	X	C		C
Lincoln's sparrow	*Melospiza lincolnii*					X		X		U	
Swamp sparrow	*Melospiza georgiana*		X		X	X		X	U	C	C
White-throated sparrow	*Zonotrichia albicollis*				X	X				C	C
White-crowned sparrow	*Zonotrichia leucophrys*				X	X				C	C
Dark-eyed junco	*Junco hyemalis*	X			X	X				C	C
Lapland longspur	*Calcarius lapponicus*	X			X		X			U	U
Smith's longspur	*Calcarius pictus*	X					X			R	
Snow bunting	*Plectrophenax nivalis*	X	X		X		X			R	R
Summer tanager	*Piranga rubra*					X			U	U	
Scarlet tanager	*Piranga olivacea*					X			C	C	
Northern cardinal	*Cardinalis cardinalis*	X			X	X			C		C
Rose-breasted grosbeak	*Pheucticus ludovicianus*				X	X			U	C	
Blue grosbeak	*Passerina caerulea*				X	X	X		U	U	
Indigo bunting	*Passerina cyanea*	X			X	X	X		C	C	
Dickcissel	*Spiza americana*	X					X		C	C	
Bobolink	*Dolichonyx oryzivorus*	X					X		U	C	
Red-winged blackbird	*Agelaius phoeniceus*	X	X		X		X	X	C	C	C
Eastern meadowlark	*Sturnella magna*	X			X		X		C	C	R
Western meadowlark	*Sturnella neglecta*						X		R		
Yellow-headed blackbird	*Xanthocephalus xanthocephalus*							X	R	R	
Rusty blackbird	*Euphagus carolinus*		X			X		X		U	
Brewer's blackbird	*Euphagus cyanocephalus*	X			X		X			R	
Common grackle	*Quiscalus quiscula*	X			X	X	X	X	C	C	U
Brown-headed cowbird	*Molothrus ater*	X			X	X	X		C	C	U
Orchard oriole	*Icterus spurius*	X				X	X		C	C	
Baltimore oriole	*Icterus galbula*	X			X	X		X	C	C	
Pine grosbeak	*Pinicola enucleator*					X				R	R
Purple finch	*Carpodacus purpureus*					X				U	U
House finch	*Carpodacus mexicanus*	X			X	X			C		C
Red crossbill	*Loxia curvirostra*					X				R	
White-winged crossbill	*Loxia leucoptera*					X				R	

Table B-1. *continued*

Common Name	Scientific Name	Habitat: Agricultural	Aquatic Systems	Barren Lands	Developed Lands[b]	Forest Lands[c]	Grasslands	Wetlands	Seasonality, Abundance[a]: Nest	Migration	Winter
Common redpoll	*Acanthis flammea*					X				R	
Pine siskin	*Spinus pinus*					X			R	U	R
American goldfinch	*Spinus tristis*	X			X	X	X		C	C	C
Evening grosbeak	*Coccothraustes vespertinus*					X				R	R
House sparrow	*Passer domesticus*	X			X				C		C
TOTAL SPECIES		**68**	**125**	**9**	**175**	**156**	**71**	**111**			

Notes: Species (*N* = 309) which are (or formerly were) observed most years in Indiana, their characteristic habitat use, seasonal status, and abundance.a Abbreviations: C = common, U = uncommon, R = rare, EX = extirpated, RI = reintroduced. Taxonomic order follows American Ornithologists' Union (1998), as supplemented (Chesser et al. 2009).

[a] Using habitat categories as defined in this book. Assignments are based mainly on habitat and abundance notes in Mumford and Keller (1984), Keller et al. (1986), Castrale et al. (1998), and Robinson (1996).

[b] Includes urban and suburban forest, roads, utility rights-of-way, industrial/commercial, and other categories.

[c] Includes early successional shrublands, open oak savanna, mature mesic forest, floodplain forest, and other categories.

Table B-2. Birds of Forest Lands

Common Name	Scientific Name	Pioneering/ Shrubland/ Savanna/Open woods	Mature Forest			Seasonality, Abundancea		
			Conifer	Hardwoods/Upland Deciduous	Floodplain/Wet Woods/ Riparian	Nest	Migration	Winter
Wood duck	*Aix sponsa*				1	C	C	R
Hooded merganser	*Lophodytes cucullatus*				1	U	C	U
Northern bobwhite	*Colinus virginianus*	1				U		U
Ruffed grouse	*Bonasa umbellus*			1		R		R
Wild turkey	*Meleagris gallopavo*			1		C		C
Great blue heron	*Ardea herodias*			2	1	C	C	R
Green heron	*Butorides virescens*				1	C		
Yellow-crested night-heron	*Nyctanassa violacea*				1	R		
Black vulture	*Coragyps atratus*			1		R	R	
Turkey vulture	*Cathartes aura*	2	2	1		C	C	U
Mississippi kite	*Ictinia mississippiensis*			1		R	R	
Bald eagle	*Haliaeetus leucocephalus*				1	U		U
Sharp-shinned hawk	*Accipiter striatus*	2	1	2		R	C	C
Cooper's hawk	*Accipiter cooperii*	2	2	1		U	C	C
Northern goshawk	*Accipiter gentilis*			1			R	R
Red-shouldered hawk	*Buteo lineatus*	2		2	1	C		C
Broad-winged hawk	*Buteo platypterus*	2		1		R	U	
Red-tailed hawk	*Buteo jamaicensis*	2	2	1		C	C	C
Golden eagle	*Aquila chrysaetos*			1			R	R
American kestrel	*Falco sparverius*	1				C		C
American woodcock	*Scolopax minor*	1		2	2	U	U	
Mourning dove	*Zenaida macroura*	1		2		C		C
Passenger pigeon	*Ectopistes migratorius*			1		EX	EX	
Carolina parakeet	*Conuropsis carolinensis*	2			1	EX	EX	EX
Yellow-billed cuckoo	*Coccyzus americanus*	2		1	2	C	C	
Black-billed cuckoo	*Coccyzus erythropthalmus*	1		2		U	U	
Eastern screech-owl	*Megascops asio*		2	1	2	C		C
Great horned owl	*Bubo virginianus*	2	2	1		C		C
Barred owl	*Strix varia*		2	2	1	C		C
Long-eared owl	*Asio otus*	2	1			R	R	R
Northern saw-whet owl	*Aegolius acadicus*	2	1				R	R
Chuck-will's-widow	*Caprimulgus carolinensis*	1		2		R	R	
Whip-poor-will	*Caprimulgus vociferus*	1		2		U	U	
Chimney swift	*Chaetura pelagica*			1		C	C	
Ruby-throated hummingbird	*Archilochus colubris*	2		1	2	C	C	
Red-headed woodpecker	*Melanerpes erythrocephalus*	1		2	2	C	C	U
Red-bellied woodpecker	*Melanerpes carolinus*			1	2	C		C
Yellow-bellied sapsucker	*Sphyrapicus varius*		2	1	2		C	R
Downy woodpecker	*Picoides pubescens*	2	2	1	2	C		C
Hairy woodpecker	*Picoides villosus*			1	2	U		U
Northern flicker	*Colaptes auratus*	1		2		C	C	C
Pileated woodpecker	*Dryocopus pileatus*			1	2	C		C
Ivory-billed woodpecker	*Campephilus principalis*			1	2	EX	EX	
Olive-sided flycatcher	*Contopus cooperi*			1			R	
Eastern wood-pewee	*Contopus virens*	2		1		C	C	
Yellow-bellied flycatcher	*Empidonax flaviventris*	2		1			R	
Acadian flycatcher	*Empidonax virescens*			1	2	C	U	
Least flycatcher	*Empidonax minimus*	1				R	C	
Eastern phoebe	*Sayornis phoebe*			2	1	C	C	R
Great crested flycatcher	*Myiarchus crinitus*			1	2	C	C	
Eastern kingbird	*Tyrannus tyrannus*	1				U	U	
Loggerhead shrike	*Lanius ludovicianus*	1				R	R	R
Northern shrike	*Lanius excubitor*	1					R	R
White-eyed vireo	*Vireo griseus*	1		2		C	C	
Bell's vireo	*Vireo bellii*	1				U	R	
Yellow-throated vireo	*Vireo flavifrons*			1		U	U	
Blue-headed vireo	*Vireo solitarius*	2	2	1			U	
Warbling vireo	*Vireo gilvus*	2		2	1	C	C	
Philadelphia vireo	*Vireo philadelphicus*			1	2		R	
Red-eyed vireo	*Vireo olivaceus*			1	2	C	C	
Blue jay	*Cyanocitta cristata*	2		1	2	C	C	C
American crow	*Corvus brachyrhynchos*	2		1	2	C	C	C
Fish crow	*Corvus ossifragus*				1		R	R

Table B-2. *continued*

Common Name	Scientific Name	Pioneering/ Shrubland/ Savanna/Open woods	Mature Forest: Conifer	Mature Forest: Hardwoods/Upland Deciduous	Mature Forest: Floodplain/Wet Woods/ Riparian	Seasonality, Abundancea: Nest	Seasonality, Abundancea: Migration	Seasonality, Abundancea: Winter
Carolina chickadee	*Poecile carolinensis*	2		1	2	C		C
Black-capped chickadee	*Poecile atricapillus*	2		1	2	C		C
Tufted titmouse	*Baeolophus bicolor*	2		1	2	C		C
Red-breasted nuthatch	*Sitta canadensis*		1				U	R
White-breasted nuthatch	*Sitta carolinensis*	1	2	2	2	C		C
Brown creeper	*Certhia americana*			2	1	R	C	U
Carolina wren	*Thryothorus ludovicianus*	2		2	1	C		C
Bewick's wren	*Thryomanes bewickii*	1				EX		
House wren	*Troglodytes aedon*	2			1	C	C	
Winter wren	*Troglodytes troglodytes*	2	2	2	1		U	U
Golden-crowned kinglet	*Regulus satrapa*		1	2			U	U
Ruby-crowned kinglet	*Regulus calendula*	2	2	1	2		C	R
Blue-gray gnatcatcher	*Polioptila caerulea*	2		1	2	C	C	
Eastern bluebird	*Sialia sialis*	1		2		C		C
Veery	*Catharus fuscescens*		2	2	1	R	U	
Gray-cheeked thrush	*Catharus minimus*			1			U	
Swainson's thrush	*Catharus ustulatus*	2		1			C	
Hermit thrush	*Catharus guttatus*	1	2	2			U	R
Wood thrush	*Hylocichla mustelina*			1	2	C	U	
American robin	*Turdus migratorius*	1		2		C	C	C
Gray catbird	*Dumetella carolinensis*	2		1		C	C	
Northern mockingbird	*Mimus polyglottos*	1				C		U
Brown thrasher	*Toxostoma rufum*	1				C	R	R
European starling	*Sturnus vulgaris*	1		2		C	C	C
Cedar waxwing	*Bombycilla cedrorum*	1		2		C	C	U
Blue-winged warbler	*Vermivora pinus*	1		2		U	U	
Golden-winged warbler	*Vermivora chrysoptera*	2			1	R	R	
Tennessee warbler	*Vermivora peregrina*	2	2	1	2		C	
Orange-crowned warbler	*Vermivora celata*	1		2			U	
Nashville warbler	*Vermivora ruficapilla*	1		2			C	
Northern parula	*Parula americana*		2	2	1	U	U	
Yellow warbler	*Dendroica petechia*	2			1	U	U	
Chestnut-sided warbler	*Dendroica pensylvanica*	1				R	U	
Magnolia warbler	*Dendroica magnolia*	2	2	1			C	
Cape May warbler	*Dendroica tigrina*		2	1	2		U	
Black-throated blue warbler	*Dendroica caerulescens*			1	2		R	
Yellow-rumped warbler	*Dendroica coronata*	2	2	1	2		C	U
Black-throated green warbler	*Dendroica virens*		1	2	2	R	C	
Blackburnian warbler	*Dendroica fusca*	2	2	1			U	
Yellow-throated warbler	*Dendroica dominica*			2	1	C	U	
Pine warbler	*Dendroica pinus*		1			U	R	
Prairie warbler	*Dendroica discolor*	1				C	U	
Palm warbler	*Dendroica palmarum*	1			2		C	
Bay-breasted warbler	*Dendroica castanea*			2	1		C	
Blackpoll warbler	*Dendroica striata*			1			C	
Cerulean warbler	*Dendroica cerulea*			1	2	U	U	
Black-and-white warbler	*Mniotilta varia*			1		R	C	
American redstart	*Setophaga ruticilla*	2		2	1	U	C	
Prothonotary warbler	*Protonotaria citrea*				1	U	U	
Worm-eating warbler	*Helmitheros vermivorum*			1		U	R	
Ovenbird	*Seiurus aurocapilla*			1		C	C	
Northern waterthrush	*Seiurus noveboracensis*	2			1		U	
Louisiana waterthrush	*Seiurus motacilla*				1	C	U	
Kentucky warbler	*Oporornis formosus*			1	2	C	U	
Connecticut warbler	*Oporornis agilis*	2			1		R	
Mourning warbler	*Oporornis philadelphia*	2		1			R	
Common yellowthroat	*Geothlypis trichas*	1			2	C	C	
Hooded warbler	*Wilsonia citrina*			1		R	R	
Wilson's warbler	*Wilsonia pusilla*	1		2	2		U	
Canada warbler	*Wilsonia canadensis*			2	1	R	R	
Yellow-breasted chat	*Icteria virens*	1				C	C	
Eastern towhee	*Pipilo erythrophthalmus*	1		2		C	U	R
Bachman's sparrow	*Aimophila aestivalis*	1				EX	EX	

Common Name	Scientific Name	Pioneering/ Shrubland/ Savanna/Open woods	Mature Forest: Conifer	Mature Forest: Hardwoods/Upland Deciduous	Mature Forest: Floodplain/Wet Woods/ Riparian	Seasonality, Abundance[a]: Nest	Seasonality, Abundance[a]: Migration	Seasonality, Abundance[a]: Winter
American tree sparrow	*Spizella arborea*	1					C	C
Chipping sparrow	*Spizella passerina*	2	1			C	C	R
Clay-colored sparrow	*Spizella pallida*	1					R	
Field sparrow	*Spizella pusilla*	1				C	U	U
Fox sparrow	*Passerella iliaca*	1		2			U	U
Song sparrow	*Melospiza melodia*	1			2	C		C
Lincoln's sparrow	*Melospiza lincolnii*	1					U	
Swamp sparrow	*Melospiza georgiana*	2			1	U	C	C
White-throated sparrow	*Zonotrichia albicollis*	2		1			C	C
White-crowned sparrow	*Zonotrichia leucophrys*	1					C	C
Dark-eyed junco	*Junco hyemalis*	1	2	2			C	C
Summer tanager	*Piranga rubra*	2		1		U	U	
Scarlet tanager	*Piranga olivacea*			1	2	C	C	
Northern cardinal	*Cardinalis cardinalis*	1		2	2	C		C
Rose-breasted grosbeak	*Pheucticus ludovicianus*	2		1	2	U	C	
Blue grosbeak	*Passerina caerulea*	1				U	U	
Indigo bunting	*Passerina cyanea*	1		2		C	C	
Rusty blackbird	*Euphagus carolinus*	2			1		U	R
Common grackle	*Quiscalus quiscula*	1	2		2	C	C	U
Brown-headed cowbird	*Molothrus ater*	2		1		C	C	U
Orchard oriole	*Icterus spurius*	1				C	C	
Baltimore oriole	*Icterus galbula*	1			2	C	C	
Pine grosbeak	*Pinicola enucleator*		1				R	R
Purple finch	*Carpodacus purpureus*	2		1			U	U
House finch	*Carpodacus mexicanus*	1				C		C
Red crossbill	*Loxia curvirostra*		1				R	
White-winged crossbill	*Loxia leucoptera*		1				R	
Pine siskin	*Spinus pinus*	1	2			R	U	R
American goldfinch	*Spinus tristis*	1		2	2	C	C	C
Evening grosbeak	*Coccothraustes vespertinus*			1			R	R
TOTAL SPECIES USING HABITAT (as primary or secondary)		**99**	**34**	**104**	**71**		**129**	**73**
Species using habitat as primary one		**52**	**11**	**63**	**30**			

Notes: Species ($N = 156$) which characteristically use (or formerly used) early successional or mature forest habitats, their seasonal status, and present abundance. Abbreviations: 1 = primary habitat, 2 = secondary habitat, C = common, U = uncommon, R = rare, EX = extirpated.

[a] In forested habitats; some species are more common in other habitats (see Table B-1).

Table B-3. Birds of Grasslands

Common Name	Scientific Name	Obligate (restricted to grassland)	Use Grasslands and Other Habitats	Require Shrubs	Near Water	Seasonality, Abundance			
						Nest	Summer*	Migration	Winter
Greater white-fronted goose	*Anser albifrons*				X			R	R
Snow goose	*Chen caerulescens*				X			U	R
Canada goose	*Branta canadensis*				X	C		C	C
Mallard	*Anas platyrhynchos*				X	U		C	C
Blue-winged teal	*Anas discors*				X	U		U	
Northern bobwhite	*Colinus virginianus*		X			U			U
Ring-necked pheasant	*Phasianus colchicus*	X				C			C
Greater prairie-chicken	*Tympanuchus cupido*	X				EX			EX
Cattle egret	*Bubulcus ibis*		X					R	
Turkey vulture	*Cathartes aura*		X				C	C	U
Northern harrier	*Circus cyaneus*	X				R		C	U
Cooper's hawk	*Accipiter cooperii*		X				U	U	U
Red-tailed hawk	*Buteo jamaicensis*		X				C	C	C
Rough-legged hawk	*Buteo lagopus*	X						U	R
American kestrel	*Falco sparverius*		X				U	U	U
Yellow rail	*Coturnicops noveboracensis*		X					R	
Sandhill crane	*Grus canadensis*		X			R		C	
American golden-plover	*Pluvialis dominica*		X					U	
Killdeer	*Charadrius vociferus*		X			C		C	U
Upland sandpiper	*Bartramia longicauda*	X				R		R	
Pectoral sandpiper	*Calidris melanotos*		X					C	
Buff-breasted sandpiper	*Tryngites subruficollis*	X						R	
American woodcock	*Scolopax minor*		X			U		U	
Mourning dove	*Zenaida macroura*		X			C			C
Barn owl	*Tyto alba*		X				R		R
Great horned owl	*Bubo virginianus*		X				U		U
Short-eared owl	*Asio flammeus*	X				R		U	U
Common nighthawk	*Chordeiles minor*		X			R	U	C	
Northern flicker	*Colaptes auratus*		X				U	U	U
Willow flycatcher	*Empidonax traillii*				X	U		U	
Eastern kingbird	*Tyrannus tyrannus*			X		C		C	
Loggerhead shrike	*Lanius ludovicianus*		X			R		R	R
Northern shrike	*Lanius excubitor*		X					R	R
Bell's vireo	*Vireo bellii*			X		U		R	
American crow	*Corvus brachyrhynchos*		X				U	C	C
Horned lark	*Eremophila alpestris*		X			U		U	U
Barn swallow	*Hirundo rustica*		X				C	C	
Sedge wren	*Cistothorus platensis*	X				U		U	
Eastern bluebird	*Sialia sialis*		X				U		U
American robin	*Turdus migratorius*			X		U		C	U
Northern mockingbird	*Mimus polyglottos*			X		U			U
Brown thrasher	*Toxostoma rufum*			X		C		R	R
European starling	*Sturnus vulgaris*		X				C	C	U
American pipit	*Anthus rubescens*		X					U	
Yellow warbler	*Dendroica petechia*				X	U		U	
Common yellowthroat	*Geothlypis trichas*		X			C		C	
American tree sparrow	*Spizella arborea*		X					U	U
Chipping sparrow	*Spizella passerina*			X		U		U	
Field sparrow	*Spizella pusilla*			X		C		U	U
Vesper sparrow	*Pooecetes gramineus*		X			U		U	
Lark sparrow	*Chondestes grammacus*		X			R		R	
Savannah sparrow	*Passerculus sandwichensis*	X				U		C	
Grasshopper sparrow	*Ammodramus savannarum*	X				C		C	
Henslow's sparrow	*Ammodramus henslowii*	X				U		U	
Le Conte's sparrow	*Ammodramus leconteii*		X					R	
Song sparrow	*Melospiza melodia*			X		U			U
Lapland longspur	*Calcarius lapponicus*		X					U	U
Smith's longspur	*Calcarius pictus*		X					R	
Snow bunting	*Plectrophenax nivalis*		X					R	R
Blue grosbeak	*Passerina caerulea*			X		U		U	
Indigo bunting	*Passerina cyanea*			X		U		U	
Dickcissel	*Spiza americana*	X				C		C	
Bobolink	*Dolichonyx oryzivorus*	X				U		C	
Red-winged blackbird	*Agelaius phoeniceus*		X			C		C	R

Common Name	Scientific Name	Obligate (restricted to grassland)	Use Grasslands and Other Habitats	Require Shrubs	Near Water	Seasonality, Abundance			
						Nest	Summer*	Migration	Winter
Eastern meadowlark	*Sturnella magna*	X				C		C	R
Western meadowlark	*Sturnella neglecta*	X				R			
Brewer's blackbird	*Euphagus cyanocephalus*		X					R	
Common grackle	*Quiscalus quiscula*		X				U	C	U
Brown-headed cowbird	*Molothrus ater*		X			R		U	U
Orchard oriole	*Icterus spurius*			X		U		U	
American goldfinch	*Spinus tristis*			X		C		C	C
TOTAL SPECIES		**15**	**37**	**12**	**7**				

Notes: Species (*N* = 71) which characteristically use grasslands, their seasonal status, and present abundance in that habitat. Abbreviations: C = common, U = uncommon, R = rare, EX = extirpated.

*Does not nest in habitat but forages there in summer.

Table B-4. Birds of Wetlands

		Forested/Shrubby Swamp			Herbaceous (marsh)			Mudflats
Common Name	**Scientific Name**	**Nest**	**Migration**	**Winter**	**Nest**	**Migration**	**Winter**	**Migration**
Greater white-fronted goose	*Anser albifrons*					R	R	
Snow goose	*Chen caerulescens*					U	R	
Ross's goose	*Chen rossii*					R	R	
Cackling goose	*Branta hutchinsii*					R	R	
Canada goose	*Branta canadensis*				C	C	C	
Mute swan	*Cygnus olor*				R	R	R	
Trumpeter swan	*Cygnus buccinator*				EX	EX, RI	EX, RI	
Wood duck	*Aix sponsa*	C	C		U	C		
Gadwall	*Anas strepera*					C		
American wigeon	*Anas americana*					C		
American black duck	*Anas rubripes*				R	U	U	U
Mallard	*Anas platyrhynchos*		C	C	C	C	C	C
Blue-winged teal	*Anas discors*		U		U	C		C
Northern shoveler	*Anas clypeata*				R	C	R	U
Northern pintail	*Anas acuta*		U			U		
Green-winged teal	*Anas crecca*					C	R	C
Redhead	*Aythya americana*				R	U		
Ring-necked duck	*Aythya collaris*					C	R	
Hooded merganser	*Lophodytes cucullatus*	U	U			U	R	
Ruddy duck	*Oxyura jamaicensis*					C		
Pied-billed grebe	*Podilymbus podiceps*				U	C	R	
Double-crested cormorant	*Phalacrocorax auritus*	R	U					
American bittern	*Botaurus lentiginosus*				U	U		
Least bittern	*Ixobrychus exilis*				U	U		
Great blue heron	*Ardea herodias*	C	C	R		C	R	C
Great egret	*Ardea alba*		U			U		
Snowy egret	*Egretta thula*					R		
Little blue heron	*Egretta caerulea*		R			R		
Cattle egret	*Bubulcus ibis*					R		
Green heron	*Butorides virescens*	C	C			U		U
Black-crested night-heron	*Nycticorax nycticorax*	R	U			R		
Yellow-crested night-heron	*Nyctanassa violacea*	R	R			R		
Osprey	*Pandion haliaetus*		U			U		
Bald eagle	*Haliaeetus leucocephalus*	U	U	R				
Northern harrier	*Circus cyaneus*					U	U	
Red-shouldered hawk	*Buteo lineatus*	C		C				
Yellow rail	*Coturnicops noveboracensis*					R		
Black rail	*Laterallus jamaicensis*					R		
King rail	*Rallus limicola*				R	R		
Virginia rail	*Rallus limicola*				U	U	R	
Sora	*Porzana carolina*				U	C		
Common moorhen	*Gallinula chloropus*				R	R		
American coot	*Fulica americana*				U	C	R	U
Sandhill crane	*Grus canadensis*				R	C	U	
Whooping crane	*Grus americana*				EX	EX, RI		
Black-bellied plover	*Pluvialis squatarola*							U
American golden-plover	*Pluvialis dominica*							U
Semipalmated plover	*Charadrius semipalmatus*							U
Killdeer	*Charadrius vociferus*				C	C	R	C
Black-necked stilt	*Himantopus mexicanus*				R	R		R
American avocet	*Recurvirostra americana*					R		R
Spotted sandpiper	*Actitis macularius*				R	U		U
Solitary sandpiper	*Tringa solitaria*					C		C
Greater yellowlegs	*Tringa melanoleuca*					U		U
Willet	*Catoptrophorus semipalmatus*							R
Lesser yellowlegs	*Tringa flavipes*					C		C
Hudsonian godwit	*Limosa haemastica*					R		R
Marbled godwit	*Limosa fedoa*					R		R
Ruddy turnstone	*Arenaria interpres*					R		R
Red knot	*Calidris canutus*							R
Sanderling	*Calidris alba*							R
Semipalmated sandpiper	*Calidris pusilla*					U		C
Western sandpiper	*Calidris mauri*					R		R
Least sandpiper	*Calidris minutilla*					C		C
White-rumped sandpiper	*Calidris fuscicollis*					R		R
Baird's sandpiper	*Calidris bairdii*							R
Pectoral sandpiper	*Calidris melanotos*					C		C
Dunlin	*Calidris alpina*					U		U

		Forested/Shrubby Swamp			Herbaceous (marsh)			Mudflats
Common Name	**Scientific Name**	**Nest**	**Migration**	**Winter**	**Nest**	**Migration**	**Winter**	**Migration**
Stilt sandpiper	*Calidris himantopus*					U		U
Buff-breasted sandpiper	*Tryngites subruficollis*							R
Short-billed dowitcher	*Limnodromus griseus*					U		U
Long-billed dowitcher	*Limnodromus scolopaceus*					R		R
Wilson's snipe	*Gallinago delicata*					C		
American woodcock	*Scolopax minor*	U	U					
Wilson's phalarope	*Phalaropus tricolor*				R	R		R
Red-necked phalarope	*Phalaropus lobatus*					R		R
Ring-billed gull	*Larus delawarensis*							U
Black tern	*Chlidonias niger*				R	U		
Common tern	*Sterna hirundo*							R
Forster's tern	*Sterna forsteri*							U
Carolina parakeet	*Conuropsis carolinensis*	EX	EX					
Barred owl	*Strix varia*	C		C				
Common nighthawk	*Chordeiles minor*					C		
Belted kingfisher	*Megaceryle alcyon*		C			C		
Red-headed woodpecker	*Melanerpes erythrocephalus*	U		U				
Red-bellied woodpecker	*Melanerpes carolinensis*	C		C				
Pileated woodpecker	*Dryocopus pileatus*	U		U				
Alder flycatcher	*Empidonax alnorum*	R	R		R	R		
Willow flycatcher	*Empidonax traillii*	C	C		C	C		
Eastern phoebe	*Sayornis phoebe*				U	U		
Eastern kingbird	*Tyrannus tyrannus*				C	C		
Warbling vireo	*Vireo gilvus*	C	C					
Purple martin	*Progne subis*					U		
Tree swallow	*Tachycineta bicolor*	C	C			C		
Marsh wren	*Cistothorus palustris*				U	U		
European starling	*Sturnus vulgaris*	C						C
American pipit	*Anthus rubescens*							U
Yellow warbler	*Dendroica petechia*	C	C		C	C		
Palm warbler	*Dendroica palmarum*					C		
Prothonotary warbler	*Protonotaria citrea*	U	U					
Northern waterthrush	*Seiurus noveboracensis*		U			U		
Common yellowthroat	*Geothlypis trichas*				C	C		
Nelson's sparrow	*Ammodramus nelsoni*					R		
Song sparrow	*Melospiza melodia*	C	C	C	C	C	C	
Lincoln's sparrow	*Melospiza lincolnii*		U					
Swamp sparrow	*Melospiza georgiana*	U	C	U	U	C	U	
Red-winged blackbird	*Agelaius phoeniceus*	C	C	C	C	C	C	
Yellow-headed blackbird	*Xanthocephalus xanthocephalus*					R		
Rusty blackbird	*Euphagus carolinus*		U			U		
Common grackle	*Quiscalus quiscula*	C	C	U		C		
Baltimore oriole	*Icterus galbula*	U	U			U		
TOTAL SPECIES (per season)		**27**	**31**	**12**	**30**	**86**	**23**	**42**
TOTAL SPECIES (per habitat)			**34**			**86**		**42**

Notes: Species ($N = 111$) which characteristically use or formerly used wetland habitats, their seasonal status, and present abundance. Abbreviations: C = common, U = uncommon, R = rare, EX = extirpated, RI = reintroduced.

Table B-5. Birds of Aquatic Systems

		Lake Michigan			Rivers			Inland Lakes		
Common Name	**Scientific Name**	**Nest**	**Migration**	**Winter**	**Nest**	**Migration**	**Winter**	**Nest**	**Migration**	**Winter**
Greater white-fronted goose	*Anser albifrons*								R	R
Snow goose	*Chen caerulescens*		R						U	R
Ross's goose	*Chen rossii*								R	R
Cackling goose	*Branta hutchinsii*								R	R
Canada goose	*Branta canadensis*	C		C		C		C	C	C
Mute swan	*Cygnus olor*							U	U	U
Trumpeter swan	*Cygnus buccinator*								R	R
Tundra swan	*Cygnus columbianus*		R						R	R
Wood duck	*Aix sponsa*				C	C	R	C	C	R
Gadwall	*Anas strepera*		C	R		U			C	R
American wigeon	*Anas americana*		C			U			C	
American black duck	*Anas rubripes*		C	U		U			C	U
Mallard	*Anas platyrhynchos*	C	C	C		C	C	C	C	C
Blue-winged teal	*Anas discors*		C			U			C	
Northern shoveler	*Anas clypeata*		C			U			C	
Northern pintail	*Anas acuta*		U			U			C	
Green-winged teal	*Anas crecca*		C			U			C	
Canvasback	*Aythya valisineria*		U	R		U			U	
Redhead	*Aythya americana*		C	R		U			C	
Ring-necked duck	*Aythya collaris*		C			U			C	
Greater scaup	*Aythya marila*			C						
Lesser scaup	*Aythya affinis*		C	R		U			C	
Harlequin duck	*Histrionicus histrionicus*			R						
Surf scoter	*Melanitta perspicillata*		U						R	
White-winged scoter	*Melanitta fusca*		U							
Black scoter	*Melanitta nigra*		U							
Long-tailed duck	*Clangula hyemalis*		R							
Bufflehead	*Bucephala albeola*			C			U		C	C
Common goldeneye	*Bucephala clangula*			C			U		C	C
Hooded merganser	*Lophodytes cucullatus*		U		U	C	C	U	C	R
Common merganser	*Mergus merganser*			C			U		U	U
Red-breasted merganser	*Mergus serrator*		C						U	
Ruddy duck	*Oxyura jamaicensis*		U						C	
Red-throated loon	*Gavia stellata*		R						R	
Common loon	*Gavia immer*		C						U	
Pied-billed grebe	*Podilymbus podiceps*		C			U		U	C	
Horned grebe	*Podiceps auritus*		C						C	U
Red-necked grebe	*Podiceps grisegena*		R							
Eared grebe	*Podiceps nigricollis*		R							
Western grebe	*Aechmophorus occidentalis*		R							
American white pelican	*Pelecanus erythrorhynchos*		R						R	
Double-crested cormorant	*Phalacrocorax auritus*	R	C			U			C	
American bittern	*Botaurus lentiginosus*							U	U	
Least bittern	*Ixobrychus exilis*							U	U	
Great blue heron	*Ardea herodias*	C	C		C		R	C		R
Great egret	*Ardea alba*	R	U			U			U	
Green heron	*Butorides virescens*	U	U		U			C		
Black-crested night-heron	*Nycticorax nycticorax*	U				U		R		
Yellow-crested night-heron	*Nyctanassa violacea*					R				
Turkey vulture	*Cathartes aura*	U	U							
Osprey	*Pandion haliaetus*		U			R			U	
Bald eagle	*Haliaeetus leucocephalus*	R	U	R	U		U	U		
Merlin	*Falco columbarius*		R							
Peregrine falcon	*Falco peregrinus*	U	U							
Virginia rail	*Rallus limicola*							R	U	
Sora	*Porzana carolina*							U	U	
Common moorhen	*Gallinula chloropus*							R		
American coot	*Fulica americana*		U					U	C	
Black-bellied plover	*Pluvialis squatarola*		U						U	
Semipalmated plover	*Charadrius semipalmatus*		C						U	
Piping plover	*Charadrius melodus*		R							
Killdeer	*Charadrius vociferus*		C		U	C		U		
American avocet	*Recurvirostra americana*		R						R	
Spotted sandpiper	*Actitis macularius*	U	C		U	C		U	C	
Solitary sandpiper	*Tringa solitaria*								C	
Greater yellowlegs	*Tringa melanoleuca*		U						U	
Willet	*Catoptrophorus semipalmatus*		R							
Lesser yellowlegs	*Tringa flavipes*								C	

Common Name	Scientific Name	Lake Michigan			Rivers			Inland Lakes		
		Nest	Migration	Winter	Nest	Migration	Winter	Nest	Migration	Winter
Marbled godwit	*Limosa fedoa*		R							
Ruddy turnstone	*Arenaria interpres*		U						R	
Red knot	*Calidris canutus*		R							
Sanderling	*Calidris alba*		C						R	
Semipalmated sandpiper	*Calidris pusilla*		C						C	
Western sandpiper	*Calidris mauri*		R							
Least sandpiper	*Calidris minutilla*		C						C	
White-rumped sandpiper	*Calidris fuscicollis*		R							
Baird's sandpiper	*Calidris bairdii*		R						R	
Pectoral sandpiper	*Calidris melanotos*		R						C	
Purple sandpiper	*Calidris maritima*		R	R						
Dunlin	*Calidris alpina*		C						C	
Stilt sandpiper	*Calidris himantopus*		R						R	
Short-billed dowitcher	*Limnodromus griseus*		R						U	
Long-billed dowitcher	*Limnodromus scolopaceus*		R						R	
Red phalarope	*Phalaropus fulicarius*		R							
Black-legged kittiwake	*Rissa tridactyla*		R	R						
Bonaparte's gull	*Chroicocephalus philadelphia*		C	R					C	C
Little gull	*Hydrocoloeus minutus*		R	R						
Laughing gull	*Leucophaeus atricilla*		R							
Franklin's gull	*Leucophaeus pipixcan*		R							
Ring-billed gull	*Larus delawarensis*	C	C	C		C	C		C	C
Herring gull	*Larus argentatus*		C	C					R	R
Thayer's gull	*Larus thayeri*		R	R						
Glaucous gull	*Larus hyperboreus*		U	U						
Great black-backed gull	*Larus marinus*		R	R						
Least tern	*Sterna antillarum*				R			R		
Caspian tern	*Sterna caspia*		C						U	
Black tern	*Chlidonias niger*		R					R	U	
Common tern	*Sterna hirundo*		U						U	
Forster's tern	*Sterna forsteri*		U						U	
Parasitic jaeger	*Stercorarius parasiticus*		R							
Belted kingfisher	*Ceryle alcyon*				C		R		U	R
Red-headed woodpecker	*Melanerpes erythrocephalus*							U		U
Alder flycatcher	*Empidonax alnorum*				R	R				
Willow flycatcher	*Empidonax traillii*				U	U		C		
Eastern phoebe	*Sayornis phoebe*				U			U		
Warbling vireo	*Vireo gilvus*				C			C		
American crow	*Corvus americanus*					C	C		C	C
Fish crow	*Corvus ossifragus*					R				
Horned lark	*Eremophila alpestris*		C	U						
Tree swallow	*Tachycineta bicolor*		C					C		
Northern rough-winged swallow	*Stelgidopteryx serripennis*		U		C				C	
Bank swallow	*Riparia riparia*	C	C		U					
Cliff swallow	*Petrochelidon pyrrhonota*				U			U		
Barn swallow	*Hirundo rustica*								C	
Marsh wren	*Cistothorus palustris*							U		
Yellow warbler	*Dendroica petechia*							C		
Yellow-throated warbler	*Dendroica dominica*				C					
Prothonotary warbler	*Protonotaria citrea*				U					
Louisiana waterthrush	*Seiurus motacilla*				U					
Common yellowthroat	*Geothlypis trichas*							C		
Song sparrow	*Melospiza melodia*							C		U
Swamp sparrow	*Melospiza georgiana*								U	U
Snow bunting	*Plectrophenax nivalis*		U							
Red-winged blackbird	*Agelaius phoeniceus*							C		
Rusty blackbird	*Euphagus carolinus*								U	
TOTAL SPECIES		**13**	**82**	**23**	**19**	**28**	**11**	**31**	**71**	**26**

Notes: Species (N = 125) which characteristically use aquatic habitats (lakes, rivers, and shorelines), their seasonal status, and present abundance. Abbreviations: C = common, U = uncommon, R = rare. Wetlands are a separate habitat category in this book (see Table B-4).

Table B-6. Birds of Agricultural Lands

						Seasonality, Abundance			
Common Name	**Scientific Name**	**Row Crops**	**Cereal Grains**	**Orchards[a]**	**Feedlots[b]**	**Nest**	**Summer[c]**	**Migration**	**Winter**
Greater white-fronted goose	*Anser albifrons*	X						R	R
Snow goose	*Chen caerulescens*	X						U	R
Canada goose	*Branta canadensis*	X					C	C	C
Trumpeter swan	*Cygnus buccinator*	X							RI
Tundra swan	*Cygnus columbianus*	X							R
American black duck	*Anas rubripes*	X							U
Mallard	*Anas platyrhynchos*	X						C	C
Northern bobwhite	*Colinus virginianus*	X					U		U
Ring-necked pheasant	*Phasianus colchicus*	X					C		C
Wild turkey	*Meleagris gallopavo*	X					C		C
Turkey vulture	*Cathartes aura*	X					C	C	U
Northern harrier	*Circus cyaneus*	X	X					R	
Red-tailed hawk	*Buteo jamaicensis*	X					C	C	C
Rough-legged hawk	*Buteo lagopus*	X	X					U	R
American kestrel	*Falco sparverius*	X					U	U	U
Sandhill crane	*Grus canadensis*	X						C	
American golden-plover	*Pluvialis dominica*	X						C	
Killdeer	*Charadrius vociferus*	X				C		C	R
Lesser yellowlegs	*Tringa flavipes*	X						C	
Baird's sandpiper	*Calidris bairdii*	X						R	
Pectoral sandpiper	*Calidris melanotos*	X						C	
Buff-breasted sandpiper	*Tryngites subruficollis*	X						R	
Wilson's snipe	*Gallinago delicata*	X						C	
Ring-billed gull	*Larus delawarensis*	X						U	U
Rock pigeon	*Columba livia*	X			X	C			C
Mourning dove	*Zenaida macroura*	X			X	C			C
Carolina parakeet	*Conuropsis carolinensis*			X			EX	EX	
Yellow-billed cuckoo	*Coccyzus americanus*			X			C	C	
Barn owl	*Tyto alba*	X	X			R			R
Great horned owl	*Bubo virginianus*	X					C		C
Snowy owl	*Bubo scandiacus*	X						R	R
Short-eared owl	*Asio flammeus*	X	X					R	R
Yellow-bellied sapsucker	*Sphyrapicus varius*			X				C	
Downy woodpecker	*Picoides pubescens*			X		C			C
Eastern wood-pewee	*Contopus virens*			X		C		C	
Eastern kingbird	*Tyrannus tyrannus*			X		C		C	
American crow	*Corvus brachyrhynchos*	X	X				C	C	C
Horned lark	*Eremophila alpestris*	X			X	C		C	C
Purple martin	*Progne subis*	X					U	U	
Barn swallow	*Hirundo rustica*	X					C	C	
American robin	*Turdus migratorius*	X					C	C	R
European starling	*Sturnus vulgaris*	X			X		C	C	C
American pipit	*Anthus rubescens*	X						U	
Cedar waxwing	*Bombycilla cedrorum*			X			U	C	R
Field sparrow	*Spizella pusilla*			X		C		U	R
Vesper sparrow	*Pooecetes gramineus*	X				C		U	
Lark sparrow	*Chondestes grammacus*	X				R		R	
Savannah sparrow	*Passerculus sandwichensis*	X	X			U		C	
Grasshopper sparrow	*Ammodramus savannarum*		X			R		R	
Song sparrow	*Melospiza melodia*	X				U		U	C
Dark-eyed junco	*Junco hyemalis*	X						C	C
Lapland longspur	*Calcarius lapponicus*	X						U	U
Smith's longspur	*Calcarius pictus*	X						R	
Snow bunting	*Plectrophenax nivalis*	X						R	R
Northern cardinal	*Cardinalis cardinalis*	X					C		C
Indigo bunting	*Passerina cyanea*	X					C	C	
Dickcissel	*Spiza americana*		X			U		U	
Bobolink	*Dolichonyx oryzivorus*		X			R		U	

Common Name	Scientific Name	Row Crops	Cereal Grains	Orchards[a]	Feedlots[b]	Seasonality, Abundance: Nest	Summer[c]	Migration	Winter
Red-winged blackbird	*Agelaius phoeniceus*	X	X		X	C		C	C
Eastern meadowlark	*Sturnella magna*	X	X			C		C	R
Brewer's blackbird	*Euphagus cyanocephalus*				X			R	R
Common grackle	*Quiscalus quiscula*	X			X	C		C	U
Brown-headed cowbird	*Molothrus ater*	X			X		C	C	U
Orchard oriole	*Icterus spurius*			X		C		C	
Baltimore oriole	*Icterus galbula*			X		U		U	
House finch	*Carpodacus mexicanus*	X					U		U
American goldfinch	*Spinus tristis*	X	X	X		C		C	C
House sparrow	*Passer domesticus*	X			X	C			C
TOTAL SPECIES		**54**	**12**	**11**	**9**	**23**	**20**	**54**	**42**

Notes: Species ($N = 68$) which make (or formerly made) significant use of agricultural habitats and their seasonal abundance. Fields contain growing crops in some seasons, and are bare, plowed, or in stubble condition at other times. Abbreviations: C = common, U = uncommon, R = rare, EX = extirpated, RI = reintroduced.

[a] Species listed are those that were common in the late nineteenth century (Butler 1898), when orchard lands were most widespread.

[b] Open or confined.

[c] Does not nest in habitat but forages there in summer.

Table B-7. Birds of Developed Lands

Common Name	Scientific Name	Urban/Suburban Forests	Industrial/ Commercial	Roads/Highways	Roads/Rural	Rights-of-Way (utility, etc.)	Golf Courses	Borrow Pits
Canada goose	*Branta canadensis*		X				X	X
Mute swan	*Cygnus olor*						X	X
Wood duck	*Aix sponsa*							X
Gadwall	*Anas strepera*							X
American wigeon	*Anas americana*							X
American black duck	*Anas rubripes*							X
Mallard	*Anas platyrhynchos*		X				X	X
Blue-winged teal	*Anas discors*							X
Northern shoveler	*Anas clypeata*							X
Northern pintail	*Anas acuta*							X
Green-winged teal	*Anas crecca*							X
Canvasback	*Aythya valisineria*							X
Redhead	*Aythya americana*							X
Ring-necked duck	*Aythya collaris*							X
Lesser scaup	*Aythya affinis*							X
Bufflehead	*Bucephala albeola*							X
Common goldeneye	*Bucephala clangula*							X
Hooded merganser	*Lophodytes cucullatus*							X
Common merganser	*Mergus merganser*							X
Red-breasted merganser	*Mergus serrator*							X
Ruddy duck	*Oxyura jamaicensis*							X
Northern bobwhite	*Colinus virginianus*					X		
Ruffed grouse	*Bonasa umbellus*					X		
Wild turkey	*Meleagris gallopavo*					X		
Common loon	*Gavia immer*							X
Pied-billed grebe	*Podilymbus podiceps*							X
Horned grebe	*Podiceps auritus*							X
Double-crested cormorant	*Phalacrocorax auritus*							X
Great blue heron	*Ardea herodias*							X
Great egret	*Ardea alba*							X
Green heron	*Butorides virescens*							X
Black vulture	*Coragyps atratus*			X				
Turkey vulture	*Cathartes aura*			X				X
Osprey	*Pandion haliaetus*							X
Bald eagle	*Haliaeetus leucocephalus*							X
Northern harrier	*Circus cyaneus*					X		
Sharp-shinned hawk	*Accipiter striatus*	X						
Cooper's hawk	*Accipiter cooperii*	X	X					
Red-shouldered hawk	*Buteo lineatus*				X			
Red-tailed hawk	*Buteo jamaicensis*			X	X	X		
Rough-legged hawk	*Buteo lagopus*					X		
American kestrel	*Falco sparverius*	X		X	X	X		
Peregrine falcon	*Falco peregrinus*		X					
American coot	*Fulica americana*							X
Semipalmated plover	*Charadrius semipalmatus*							X
Killdeer	*Charadrius vociferus*		X		X	X	X	X
Spotted sandpiper	*Actitis macularius*							X
Solitary sandpiper	*Tringa solitaria*							X
Greater yellowlegs	*Tringa melanoleuca*							X
Lesser yellowlegs	*Tringa flavipes*							X
Upland sandpiper	*Bartramia longicauda*				X			
Semipalmated sandpiper	*Calidris pusilla*							X
Least sandpiper	*Calidris minutilla*							X
Pectoral sandpiper	*Calidris melanotos*							X
Dunlin	*Calidris alpina*							X
Stilt sandpiper	*Calidris himantopus*							X
Short-billed dowitcher	*Limnodromus griseus*							X
Wilson's snipe	*Gallinago delicata*							X
Bonaparte's gull	*Chroicocephalus philadelphia*							X
Ring-billed gull	*Larus delawarensis*							X
Herring gull	*Larus argentatus*							X
Least tern	*Sterna antillarum*							X
Caspian tern	*Sterna caspia*							X
Black tern	*Chlidonias niger*							X
Common tern	*Sterna hirundo*							X
Forster's tern	*Sterna forsteri*							X
Rock pigeon	*Columba livia*		X	X		X		X

Common Name	Scientific Name	Urban/Suburban Forests	Industrial/ Commercial	Roads/Highways	Roads/Rural	Rights-of-Way (utility, etc.)	Golf Courses	Borrow Pits
Eurasian collared dove	*Streptopelia decaocto*	X	X					
Mourning dove	*Zenaida macroura*	X	X	X	X	X	X	X
Monk parakeet	*Myiopsitta monachus*	X	X					
Yellow-billed cuckoo	*Coccyzus americanus*					X		
Black-billed cuckoo	*Coccyzus erythropthalmus*					X		
Eastern screech-owl	*Megascops asio*	X				X		
Great horned owl	*Bubo virginianus*				X	X		
Snowy owl	*Bubo scandiacus*			X				
Barred owl	*Strix varia*	X				X		
Short-eared owl	*Asio flammeus*					X		
Common nighthawk	*Chordeiles minor*		X					X
Whip-poor-will	*Caprimulgus vociferus*				X			
Chimney swift	*Chaetura pelagica*	X	X					
Ruby-throated hummingbird	*Archilochus colubris*	X						
Belted kingfisher	*Megaceryle alcyon*							X
Red-headed woodpecker	*Melanerpes erythrocephalus*						X	
Red-bellied woodpecker	*Melanerpes carolinus*	X			X		X	
Yellow-bellied sapsucker	*Sphyrapicus varius*	X						
Downy woodpecker	*Picoides pubescens*						X	
Hairy woodpecker	*Picoides villosus*						X	
Northern flicker	*Colaptes auratus*	X			X		X	
Pileated woodpecker	*Dryocopus pileatus*						X	
Eastern wood-pewee	*Contopus virens*					X	X	
Least flycatcher	*Empidonax minimus*	X						
Eastern phoebe	*Sayornis phoebe*				X			X
Great crested flycatcher	*Myiarchus crinitus*	X				X		
Eastern kingbird	*Tyrannus tyrannus*				X			
Loggerhead shrike	*Lanius ludovicianus*				X			
White-eyed vireo	*Vireo griseus*					X		
Bell's vireo	*Vireo bellii*					X		
Blue-headed vireo	*Vireo solitarius*	X						
Warbling vireo	*Vireo gilvus*							X
Red-eyed vireo	*Vireo olivaceus*	X						
Blue jay	*Cyanocitta cristata*	X				X	X	X
American crow	*Corvus brachyrhynchos*	X	X	X		X	X	X
Horned lark	*Eremophila alpestris*				X	X		X
Tree swallow	*Tachycineta bicolor*						X	
Northern rough-winged swallow	*Stelgidopteryx serripennis*							X
Bank swallow	*Riparia riparia*							X
Cliff swallow	*Petrochelidon pyrrhonota*							X
Barn swallow	*Hirundo rustica*				X		X	
Carolina chickadee	*Poecile carolinensis*	X					X	
Black-capped chickadee	*Poecile atricapillus*	X					X	
Tufted titmouse	*Baeolophus bicolor*	X					X	
Red-breasted nuthatch	*Sitta canadensis*	X						
White-breasted nuthatch	*Sitta carolinensis*	X					X	
Carolina wren	*Thryothorus ludovicianus*	X					X	
House wren	*Troglodytes aedon*	X						X
Ruby-crowned kinglet	*Regulus calendula*	X						
Blue-gray gnatcatcher	*Polioptila caerulea*						X	
Eastern bluebird	*Sialia sialis*	X				X	X	
Swainson's thrush	*Catharus ustulatus*	X						
Hermit thrush	*Catharus guttatus*					X		
Wood thrush	*Hylocichla mustelina*	X						
American robin	*Turdus migratorius*	X	X	X	X	X	X	X
Gray catbird	*Dumetella carolinensis*	X					X	
Northern mockingbird	*Mimus polyglottos*				X		X	
Brown thrasher	*Toxostoma rufum*	X				X		
European starling	*Sturnus vulgaris*	X	X	X	X	X	X	X
Cedar waxwing	*Bombycilla cedrorum*	X				X		
Blue-winged warbler	*Vermivora pinus*					X		
Tennessee warbler	*Vermivora peregrina*	X						
Nashville warbler	*Vermivora ruficapilla*	X						
Yellow warbler	*Dendroica petechia*	X						X
Chestnut-sided warbler	*Dendroica pensylvanica*	X						
Magnolia warbler	*Dendroica magnolia*	X						
Cape May warbler	*Dendroica tigrina*	X						

Table B-7. *continued*

Common Name	Scientific Name	Urban/Suburban Forests	Industrial/ Commercial	Roads/Highways	Roads/Rural	Rights-of-Way (utility, etc.)	Golf Courses	Borrow Pits
Yellow-rumped warbler	*Dendroica coronata*	X						
Black-throated green warbler	*Dendroica virens*	X						
Blackburnian warbler	*Dendroica fusca*	X						
Prairie warbler	*Dendroica discolor*					X		
Palm warbler	*Dendroica palmarum*	X						
Bay-breasted warbler	*Dendroica castanea*	X						
Blackpoll warbler	*Dendroica striata*	X						
Black-and-white warbler	*Mniotilta varia*	X						
American redstart	*Setophaga ruticilla*	X						
Ovenbird	*Seiurus aurocapilla*	X						
Northern waterthrush	*Seiurus noveboracensis*							X
Common yellowthroat	*Geothlypis trichas*	X				X		X
Yellow-breasted chat	*Icteria virens*					X		
Eastern towhee	*Pipilo erythrophthalmus*	X				X		
American tree sparrow	*Spizella arborea*					X		
Chipping sparrow	*Spizella passerina*	X	X		X	X	X	
Field sparrow	*Spizella pusilla*					X		X
Vesper sparrow	*Pooecetes gramineus*				X			
Lark sparrow	*Chondestes grammacus*				X			
Savannah sparrow	*Passerculus sandwichensis*					X		
Grasshopper sparrow	*Ammodramus savannarum*				X			
Song sparrow	*Melospiza melodia*	X	X		X	X	X	X
Swamp sparrow	*Melospiza georgiana*					X		
White-throated sparrow	*Zonotrichia albicollis*	X				X		
White-crowned sparrow	*Zonotrichia leucophrys*				X	X		
Dark-eyed junco	*Junco hyemalis*	X			X	X		
Lapland longspur	*Calcarius lapponicus*				X			
Snow bunting	*Plectrophenax nivalis*				X			
Northern cardinal	*Cardinalis cardinalis*	X			X	X	X	
Rose-breasted grosbeak	*Pheucticus ludovicianus*	X						
Blue grosbeak	*Passerina caerulea*				X	X		X
Indigo bunting	*Passerina cyanea*				X	X		X
Red-winged blackbird	*Agelaius phoeniceus*				X		X	X
Eastern meadowlark	*Sturnella magna*					X		
Common grackle	*Quiscalus quiscula*	X		X	X		X	X
Brown-headed cowbird	*Molothrus ater*				X	X	X	
Baltimore oriole	*Icterus galbula*	X						X
House finch	*Carpodacus mexicanus*	X	X				X	X
American goldfinch	*Spinus tristis*	X			X	X	X	X
House sparrow	*Passer domesticus*	X	X		X			
SPECIES PER HABITAT		**63**	**18**	**11**	**35**	**49**	**35**	**80**

Notes: Species (*N* = 174) which characteristically use various developed lands, or are expected to do so. See Table B-1 for seasonal status and abundance.

APPENDIXES

Mammals

Table M-1. Mammal Species of Indiana, by Order and Family

Common Name	Scientific Name	Range	1800	1900	2000	Critical Habitat	Status	Reason for Decline
Didelphimorphia: Didelphidae								
Virginia opossum	*Didelphis virginiana*	IN	A	A	A	mixed		
Soricomorpha: Soricidae								
Masked shrew	*Sorex cinereus*	IN	A	A	C	mixed, wetlands		
Smoky shrew	*Sorex fumeus*	SCT	O	O	O	woods		
Pygmy shrew	*Sorex hoyi*	SCT	O	O	O	woods		
Southeastern shrew	*Sorex longirostris*	S	C	C	C	mixed, wetlands		
Short-tailed shrew	*Blarina brevicauda*	IN	A	A	A	mixed, woods		
Least shrew	*Cryptotis parva*	IN	O	O	O	grasslands		
Soricomorpha: Talpidae								
Eastern mole	*Scalopus aquaticus*	IN	A	A	A	mixed		
Star-nosed mole	*Condylura cristata*	NE	O	O	R	wetlands	SC	habitat loss
Chiroptera: Vespertilionidae								
Southeastern myotis	*Myotis austroriparius*	SCT	R	R	EX		SE	unknown
Eastern small-footed myotis[a]	*Myotis leibii*	SCT						
Little brown myotis	*Myotis lucifugus*	IN	R	R	C	human structures		
Gray myotis	*Myotis grisescens*	S			R	wet cave	FE	habitat loss
Northern myotis	*Myotis septentrionalis*	IN	C	C	C	woods		
Indiana myotis	*Myotis sodalis*	IN	O?	O?	O	mixed	FE	habitat loss
Silver-haired bat	*Lasionycteris noctivagans*	IN	M	M	M	woods		
Eastern pipistrelle	*Perimyotis subflavus*	S	O	O	C	woods, caves		
Big brown bat	*Eptesicus fuscus*	IN	C?	C?	A	human structures		human presence
Evening bat	*Nycticeius humeralis*	S			O	bottomland woods		habitat loss
Rafinesque's big-eared bat	*Corynorhinus rafinesquii*	SCT	R	R	R	caves	SC	
Red bat	*Lasiurus borealis*	IN	A	A	A	woods		habitat loss
Hoary bat	*Lasiurus cinereus*	IN	O	O	O	woods		habitat loss
Cingulata: Dasypodidae								
Armadillo[a]	*Dasypus novemcinctus*							
Lagomorpha: Leporidae								
Swamp rabbit	*Sylvilagus aquaticus*	SW	O	O	R	bottomland woods	SE	habitat loss, hunting
Eastern cottontail	*Sylvilagus floridanus*	IN	A	A	C	mixed		
Rodentia: Sciuridae								
Eastern chipmunk	*Tamias striatus*	IN	A	A	A	woods		
Woodchuck	*Marmota monax*	IN	O	C	EX	meadows		habitat loss
Thirteen-lined ground squirrel	*Spermophilus tridecemlineatus*	N	O	O	C	open, short grass		habitat loss
Franklin's ground squirrel	*Spermophilus franklinii*	NW	O	O	R	grassy fields	SE	habitat loss
Gray squirrel	*Sciurus carolinensis*	IN	C	C	C	woods		habitat loss
Fox squirrel	*Sciurus niger*	IN	C	C	A	open woods		habitat loss
Red squirrel	*Tamiasciurus hudsonicus*	N	C	C	C	woods		habitat loss
Southern flying squirrel	*Glaucomys volans*	IN	C	C	C	woods		habitat loss
Rodentia: Geomyidae								
Plains pocket gopher	*Geomys bursarius*	NW	C	C	C	prairies	SC	habitat loss
Rodentia: Castoridae								
American beaver	*Castor canadensis*	IN	C	EX	C	wetlands		
Rodentia: Cricetidae: Neotominae								
Western harvest mouse	*Reithrodontomys megalotis*	NW	not present	not present	C	early stage grasslands		
Prairie deer mouse	*Peromyscus maniculatus*	IN	O	O	C	farmlands, woods		
White-footed mouse	*Peromyscus leucopus*	IN	A	A	A			
Allegheny wood rat	*Neotoma magister*	S	O	O	R		SE	habitat loss, raccoon nematodes

Table M-1. continued

Common Name	Scientific Name	Range	1800	1900	2000	Critical Habitat	Status	Reason for Decline
Rodentia: Cricetidae: Arvicolinae								
Meadow vole	*Microtus pennsylvanicus*	IN	C	C	C	moist grasslands		
Prairie vole	*Microtus ochrogaster*	IN	C	C	C	dry grasslands		
Woodland vole	*Microtus pinetorum*	IN	O	O	O	woods		
Muskrat	*Ondatra zibethicus*	IN	A	A	A	wetlands		
Southern bog lemming	*Synaptomys cooperi*	IN	O	O	O	grasslands		
Rodentia: Muridae								
Norway rat	*Rattus norvegicus*	IN		A	A	buildings		
House mouse	*Mus musculus*	IN	A	A	A	buildings, grasslands		
Rodentia: Dipodidae: Zapodinae								
Meadow jumping mouse	*Zapus hudsonius*	IN	O	O	O	moist grasslands		habitat loss
Carnivora: Canidae								
Coyote	*Canis latrans*	IN	O?	O	C			
Red fox	*Vulpes vulpes*	IN		C	O	mixed		
Gray fox	*Urocyon cinereoargenteus*	IN	C	C	O	woodlands		
Carnivora: Procyonidae								
Raccoon	*Procyon lotor*	IN	A	A	A	woods, mixed		
Carnivora: Mustelidae								
River otter	*Lontra canadensis*	IN	O	O	R	wetlands		trapping
Least weasel	*Mustela nivalis*	N	R	R	R	grassy, mixed		
Long-tailed weasel	*Mustela frenata*	IN	C	C	O	woodlands, mixed		
Mink	*Mustela vison*	IN	O	O	O	wetlands		
Badger	*Taxidea taxus*	IN	R	R	R	grassy fields	SC	habitat loss
Carnivora: Mephitidae								
Striped skunk	*Mephitis mephitis*	IN			C	mixed		habitat loss
Carnivora: Felidae								
Bobcat	*Lynx rufus*	IN	O	O	R	woodlands	SC	habitat loss
Artiodactyla: Cervidae								
White-tailed deer	*Odocoileus virginianus*	IN	C	EX	A	mixed		hunting, habitat

Extirpated Species

Common Name	Scientific Name	Range	1800	1900	Year Extirpated	Reason for Extirpation
Porcupine	*Erethizon dorsatum*	N	R	R	1918	eradicated by humans
Black rat	*Rattus rattus*	?	R	EX	1845	eradicated by humans; competition with Norway rat
Gray wolf	*Canis lupus*	IN	R	R	1908	eradicated by humans
Black bear	*Ursus americanus*	IN	R	EX	1850	Hunting
Fisher	*Martes pennanti*	IN	R	EX	1859	Trapping
Mountain lion	*Felis concolor*	IN	O	EX	1851	Hunting
Wapiti or American elk	*Cervus canadensis*	IN	R	EX	1830	Hunting
Bison	*Bos bison*	IN	R	EX	1830	Hunting

Species Introduced into Indiana by Humans

House mouse, *Mus musculus* (with first European settlers)
Black rat, *Rattus rattus* (with first European settlers s)
Norway rat, *Rattus norvegicus* (about 1827 with first European settlers)
Red fox, *Vulpes vulpes* (about 1855)

Notes: IN = throughout the state, S = south, CT = central, etc.; A = abundant, C = common, O = occasional, U = uncommon, R = rare, M = migrant, EX = extirpated; SE = state endangered, SC = state concern, FE = federally endangered.
[a] These two species were unknown in Indiana until after 2000 (see the end of chapter 3).

Table M-2. Mammals of Forest Lands

Common Name	Scientific Name	Range	Oak/Gum/ Cypress	Pine	Forested Uplands	Forested Wetlands/ Riparian Corridors	Plantations
Virginia opossum	*Didelphis virginiana*	IN	X	X	X	X	X
Masked shrew	*Sorex cinereus*	IN	X		X	X	X
Smoky shrew	*Sorex fumeus*	SCT			X		
Pygmy shrew	*Sorex hoyi*	SCT			X		
Southeastern shrew	*Sorex longirostris*	S			X	X	X
Short-tailed shrew	*Blarina brevicauda*	IN	X	X	X	X	X
Eastern mole	*Scalopus aquaticus*	IN			X	X	X
Star-nosed mole	*Condylura cristata*	NE				X	
Southeastern myotis	*Myotis austroriparius*	SCT	X		X	X	
Little brown myotis	*Myotis lucifugus*	IN				X	
Gray myotis	*Myotis grisescens*	S				X	
Northern myotis	*Myotis septentrionalis*	IN	X		X	X	
Indiana myotis	*Myotis sodalis*	IN	X		X	X	
Silver-haired bat	*Lasionycteris noctivagans*	IN	X		X	X	
Eastern pipistrelle	*Perimyotis subflavus*	S	X		X	X	
Big brown bat	*Eptesicus fuscus*	IN				X	
Evening bat	*Nycticeius humeralis*	S	X		X	X	
Red bat	*Lasiurus borealis*	IN	X		X	X	
Hoary bat	*Lasiurus cinereus*	IN	X		X	X	
Swamp rabbit	*Sylvilagus aquaticus*	SW	X			X	
Eastern cottontail	*Sylvilagus floridanus*	IN		X	X	X	X
Eastern chipmunk	*Tamias striatus*	IN		X	X	X	
Woodchuck	*Marmota monax*	IN			X		X
Gray squirrel	*Sciurus carolinensis*	IN	X	X	X	X	
Fox squirrel	*Sciurus niger*	IN		X	X	X	
Red squirrel	*Tamiasciurus hudsonicus*	N		X	X	X	
Southern flying squirrel	*Glaucomys volans*	IN	X	X	X	X	
Plains pocket gopher	*Geomys bursarius*	NW					X
American beaver	*Castor canadensis*	IN				X	
Western harvest mouse	*Reithrodontomys megalotis*	NW					X
Prairie deer mouse	*Peromyscus maniculatus*	IN					X
White-footed mouse	*Peromyscus leucopus*	IN	X	X	X	X	X
Allegheny wood rat	*Neotoma magister*	S			X		
Meadow vole	*Microtus pennsylvanicus*	IN					X
Prairie vole	*Microtus ochrogaster*	IN					X
Woodland vole	*Microtus pinetorum*	IN			X	X	
Muskrat	*Ondatra zibethicus*	IN				X	
Southern bog lemming	*Synaptomys cooperi*	IN			X	X	X
Meadow jumping mouse	*Zapus hudsonius*	IN	X		X	X	X
Coyote	*Canis latrans*	IN			X	X	X
Red fox	*Vulpes vulpes*	IN				X	X
Gray fox	*Urocyon cinereoargenteus*	IN	X		X	X	
Raccoon	*Procyon lotor*	IN	X	X	X	X	X
River otter	*Lontra canadensis*	IN	X			X	
Least weasel	*Mustela nivalis*	N			X		X
Long-tailed weasel	*Mustela frenata*	IN	X		X	X	X
Mink	*Mustela vison*	IN	X			X	X
Badger	*Taxidea taxus*	IN					X
Striped skunk	*Mephitis mephitis*	IN	X			X	X
Bobcat	*Lynx rufus*	IN	X		X	X	
White-tailed deer	*Odocoileus virginianus*	IN	X		X	X	X
Extirpated Species		**Year Extirpated**					
Porcupine	*Erethizon dorsatum*	1918					
Gray wolf	*Canis lupus*	1908					
Black bear	*Ursus americanus*	1850					
Fisher	*Martes pennanti*	1859					
Mountain lion	*Felis concolor*	1851					
Wapiti or American elk	*Cervus canadensis*	1830					
Bison	*Bos bison*	1830					

Note: IN = throughout the state, S = south, CT = central, etc.

Table M-3. Mammals of Grasslands, including Savanna

Common Name	Scientific Name	Range	Wet Prairies	Dry Prairies	Hay Lands	Reclaimed Mine Lands	Vegetated Dunes	Early Seral Stage Fields
Virginia opossum	*Didelphis virginiana*	IN	X	X	X	X	X	X
Masked shrew	*Sorex cinereus*	IN	X		X	X		X
Southeastern shrew	*Sorex longirostris*	S	X			X		
Short-tailed shrew	*Blarina brevicauda*	IN	X			X		X
Least shrew	*Cryptotis parva*	IN		X		X		X
Eastern mole	*Scalopus aquaticus*	IN		X		X	X	X
Star-nosed mole	*Condylura cristata*	NE	X					
Little brown myotis	*Myotis lucifugus*	IN	X			X		
Northern myotis	*Myotis septentrionalis*	IN						
Indiana myotis	*Myotis sodalis*	IN				X		
Silver-haired bat	*Lasionycteris noctivagans*	IN						
Eastern pipistrelle	*Perimyotis subflavus*	S				X		
Big brown bat	*Eptesicus fuscus*	IN				X		
Evening bat	*Nycticeius humeralis*	S						
Red bat	*Lasiurus borealis*	IN				X		
Hoary bat	*Lasiurus cinereus*	IN				X		
Eastern cottontail	*Sylvilagus floridanus*	IN	X	X	X	X	X	X
Eastern chipmunk	*Tamias striatus*	IN						
Woodchuck	*Marmota monax*	IN		X	X	X		
Thirteen-lined ground squirrel	*Spermophilus tridecemlineatus*	N		X		X	X	
Franklin's ground squirrel	*Spermophilus franklinii*	NW		X				
Gray squirrel	*Sciurus carolinensis*	IN						
Fox squirrel	*Sciurus niger*	IN						
Red squirrel	*Tamiasciurus hudsonicus*	N						
Southern flying squirrel	*Glaucomys volans*	IN						
Plains pocket gopher	*Geomys bursarius*	NW		X				
American beaver	*Castor canadensis*	IN						
Western harvest mouse	*Reithrodontomys megalotis*	NW		X		X		X
Prairie deer mouse	*Peromyscus maniculatus*	IN		X		X	X	X
White-footed mouse	*Peromyscus leucopus*	IN	X		X	X	X	X
Meadow vole	*Microtus pennsylvanicus*	IN	X		X	X	X	X
Prairie vole	*Microtus ochrogaster*	IN		X	X	X	X	X
Woodland vole	*Microtus pinetorum*	IN						
Muskrat	*Ondatra zibethicus*	IN				X		
Southern bog lemming	*Synaptomys cooperi*	IN		X	X	X		X
House mouse	*Mus musculus*	IN		X	X	X	X	X
Meadow jumping mouse	*Zapus hudsonius*	IN	X		X	X	X	
Coyote	*Canis latrans*	IN			X	X		
Red fox	*Vulpes vulpes*	IN			X	X		
Gray fox	*Urocyon cinereoargenteus*	IN						
Raccoon	*Procyon lotor*	IN	X			X	X	X
Least weasel	*Mustela nivalis*	N			X	X		X
Long-tailed weasel	*Mustela frenata*	IN	X		X	X		X
Mink	*Mustela vison*	IN	X			X		
Badger	*Taxidea taxus*	IN		X		X	X	
Striped skunk	*Mephitis mephitis*	IN				X		
Bobcat	*Lynx rufus*	IN						
White-tailed deer	*Odocoileus virginianus*	IN				X	X	X

Extirpated Species		Year Extirpated
Gray wolf	*Canis lupus*	1908
Fisher	*Martes pennanti*	1859
Mountain lion	*Felis concolor*	1851
Wapiti or American elk	*Cervus canadensis*	1830
Bison	*Bos bison*	1830

Note: IN = throughout the state, S = south, CT = central, etc.

Table M-4. Mammals of Aquatic Systems and Wetlands

Common Name	Scientific Name	Range
Star-nosed mole	*Condylura cristata*	NE
Swamp rabbit	*Sylvilagus aquaticus*	SW
American beaver	*Castor canadensis*	IN
Muskrat	*Ondatra zibethicus*	IN
River otter	*Lontra canadensis*	IN
Mink	*Mustela vison*	IN

Note: IN = throughout the state, S = south, CT = central, etc.

Table M-5. Mammals of Barren Lands

Common Name	Scientific Name	Range	Dunes	Cliffs
Virginia opossum	*Didelphis virginiana*	IN		X
Short-tailed shrew	*Blarina brevicauda*	IN	X	X
Eastern cottontail	*Sylvilagus floridanus*	IN	X	
Thirteen-lined ground squirrel	*Spermophilus tridecemlineatus*	N	X	
Prairie deer mouse	*Peromyscus maniculatus*	IN	X	
White-footed mouse	*Peromyscus leucopus*	IN	X	X
Allegheny wood rat	*Neotoma magister*	S		X
Meadow vole	*Microtus pennsylvanicus*	IN	X	
Meadow jumping mouse	*Zapus hudsonius*	IN	X	
Raccoon	*Procyon lotor*	IN		X
Bobcat	*Lynx rufus*	IN		X
Extirpated Species		**Year Extirpated**		
Mountain lion	*Felis concolor*	1851		

Note: IN = throughout the state, S = south, CT = central, etc.

Table M-6. Mammals of Subterranean Habitats

Common Name	Scientific Name	Range
Southeastern myotis	*Myotis austroriparius*	SCT
Little brown myotis	*Myotis lucifugus*	IN
Gray myotis	*Myotis grisescens*	S
Northern myotis	*Myotis septentrionalis*	IN
Indiana myotis	*Myotis sodalis*	IN
Silver-haired bat	*Lasionycteris noctivagans*	IN
Eastern pipistrelle	*Perimyotis subflavus*	S
Big brown bat	*Eptesicus fuscus*	IN
White-footed mouse	*Peromyscus leucopus*	IN
Allegheny wood rat	*Neotoma magister*	S

Note: IN = throughout the state, S = south, CT = central, etc.

Table M-7. Mammals of Agricultural Habitats

Common Name	Scientific Name	Range	Row Crops	Cereal Grain Crops	Vineyards/ Orchards	No-Till
Virginia opossum	*Didelphis virginiana*	IN			X	
Eastern mole	*Scalopus aquaticus*	IN	X			
Little brown myotis	*Myotis lucifugus*	IN				
Big brown bat	*Eptesicus fuscus*	IN				
Eastern cottontail	*Sylvilagus floridanus*	IN	X	X	X	
Eastern chipmunk	*Tamias striatus*	IN				
Woodchuck	*Marmota monax*	IN	X			
Thirteen-lined ground squirrel	*Spermophilus tridecemlineatus*	N				
Franklin's ground squirrel	*Spermophilus franklinii*	NW				
Fox squirrel	*Sciurus niger*	IN			X	
Plains pocket gopher	*Geomys bursarius*	NW				
American beaver	*Castor canadensis*	IN				
Western harvest mouse	*Reithrodontomys megalotis*	NW		X		X
Prairie deer mouse	*Peromyscus maniculatus*	IN	X			X
White-footed mouse	*Peromyscus leucopus*	IN	X	X		X
Meadow vole	*Microtus pennsylvanicus*	IN		X	X	X
Prairie vole	*Microtus ochrogaster*	IN		X	X	X
Muskrat	*Ondatra zibethicus*	IN	X			
Norway rat	*Rattus norvegicus*	IN				
Black rat	*Rattus rattus*	?				
House mouse	*Mus musculus*	IN	X	X		X
Meadow jumping mouse	*Zapus hudsonius*	IN				
Coyote	*Canis latrans*	IN				X
Red fox	*Vulpes vulpes*	IN			X	X
Raccoon	*Procyon lotor*	IN	X		X	X
Long-tailed weasel	*Mustela frenata*	IN			X	X
Mink	*Mustela vison*	IN				
Badger	*Taxidea taxus*	IN				
Striped skunk	*Mephitis mephitis*	IN			X	X
White-tailed deer	*Odocoileus virginianus*	IN	X	X	X	X

Note: IN = throughout the state, S = south, CT = central, etc.

Table M-8. Mammals of Developed Lands

Common Name	Scientific Name	Range	Urban Areas	Suburban Areas	Industrial Lands
Virginia opossum	*Didelphis virginiana*	IN	X	X	X
Masked shrew	*Sorex cinereus*	IN		X	
Southeastern shrew	*Sorex longirostris*	S		X	
Short-tailed shrew	*Blarina brevicauda*	IN	X	X	
Eastern mole	*Scalopus aquaticus*	IN	X	X	X
Little brown myotis	*Myotis lucifugus*	IN	X	X	X
Indiana myotis	*Myotis sodalis*	IN		X	
Silver-haired bat	*Lasionycteris noctivagans*	IN		X	
Eastern pipistrelle	*Perimyotis subflavus*	S		X	
Big brown bat	*Eptesicus fuscus*	IN	X	X	X
Evening bat	*Nycticeius humeralis*	S		X	
Red bat	*Lasiurus borealis*	IN		X	
Hoary bat	*Lasiurus cinereus*	IN		X	
Eastern cottontail	*Sylvilagus floridanus*	IN	X	X	
Eastern chipmunk	*Tamias striatus*	IN	X	X	
Gray squirrel	*Sciurus carolinensis*	IN	X	X	
Fox squirrel	*Sciurus niger*	IN	X	X	
Red squirrel	*Tamiasciurus hudsonicus*	N	X	X	
Southern flying squirrel	*Glaucomys volans*	IN		X	
Prairie deer mouse	*Peromyscus maniculatus*	IN			X
White-footed mouse	*Peromyscus leucopus*	IN	X	X	X
Norway rat	*Rattus norvegicus*	IN	X	X	X
House mouse	*Mus musculus*	IN	X	X	X
Raccoon	*Procyon lotor*	IN	X	X	X
Striped skunk	*Mephitis mephitis*	IN		X	
White-tailed deer	*Odocoileus virginianus*	IN		X	

Note: IN = throughout the state, S = south, CT = central, etc.

Table M-9. Status of Various Mammals of Indiana

Extirpated Species	Range	1800	1900	Year Extirpated	Reason for Extirpation
Porcupine, *Erethizon dorsatum*	N	R	R	1918	eradicated by humans
Black rat, *Rattus rattus*	?	R	EX	1845	eradicated by humans; competition with Norway rat
Gray wolf, *Canis lupus*	IN	R	R	1908	eradicated by humans
Black bear, *Ursus americanus*	IN	R	EX	1850	hunting
Fisher, *Martes pennanti*	IN	R	EX	1859	trapping
Mountain lion, *Felis concolor*	IN	O	EX	1851	hunting
Wapiti or American elk, *Cervus canadensis*	IN	R	EX	1830	hunting
Bison, *Bos bison*	IN	R	EX	1830	hunting

Federally Endangered
Gray bat, *Myotis grisescens*
Indiana bat, *Myotis sodalis*
State Endangered
Evening bat, *Nycticeius humeralis*
Swamp rabbit, *Sylvilagus aquaticus*
Franklin's ground squirrel, *Spermophilus franklinii*
Allegheny woodrat, *Neotoma magister*
State Protected Nongame
River otter, *Lontra canadensis*
American badger, *Taxidea taxus*
Bobcat, *Lynx rufus*
State Special Concern
Pygmy shrew, *Sorex hoyi*
Smoky shrew, *Sorex fumeus*
Star-nosed mole, *Condylura cristata*
Southeastern bat, *Myotis austroriparius* (probably extirpated)
Little brown bat, *Myotis lucifugus*
Northern bat, *Myotis septentrionalis*
Silver-haired bat, *Lasionycteris noctivagans*
Big brown bat, *Eptesicus fuscus*
Eastern pipistrelle, *Perimyotis subflavus*
Red bat, *Lasiurus borealis*
Hoary bat, *Lasiurus cinereus*
Rafinesque's big-eared bat, *Corynorhinus rafinesquii*
Northern pocket gopher, *Geomys bursarius*
Least weasel, *Mustela nivalis*
Long-tailed weasel, *Mustela frenata*

APPENDIXES

Invertebrates

Table I-1. Obligate Subterranean Invertebrates of Indiana

Common Name	Scientific Name	South-Central Karst	Southeastern Karst	Non-Karst Groundwaters
Spiral cave snail	*Antroselates spiralis*			
Hidden Spring snail	*Fontigens cryptica*	X	X	X
Weingartner's cave flatworm	*Sphalloplana weingartneri*	X	X	
Chandler's groundwater flatworm	*Sphalloplana chandleri*	X		
Jeannel's cave ostracod	*Pseudocandona jeanneli*	X		X
Marengo cave ostracod	*Pseudocandona marengoensis*	X		
HNF cave ostracod	*Pseudocandona* undescribed sp.	X		
Barr's cave crayfish ostracod	*Sagittocythere barri*	X		
Donaldson's cave copepod	*Megacyclops donnaldsoni*	X		
Campground cave copepod.	*Megacyclops* undescribed sp	X		
Jeannel's groundwater copepod	*Diacyclops jeanneli*	X		X
Indiana groundwater copepod	*Diacyclops indianensis*		X	X
Converse groundwater copepod	*Diacyclops conversus*			X
Yeatman's groundwater copepod	*Diacyclops yeatmani*			X
Salisa's groundwater copepod	*Diacyclops salisae*			X
Lewis's groundwater copepod	*Diacyclops lewisi*			X
Indiana groundwater copepod	*Rheocyclops indiana*	X		X
Northern cavefish copepod	*Cauloxenus stygius*	X		
Mucronate groundwater amphipod	*Bactrurus mucronatus*			X
Reclusive groundwater amphipod	*Bactrurus cellulanus*			X
Mackin's cave amphipod	*Styobromus mackini*		X	
Devil's graveyard cave amphipod	*Styobromus* undescribed sp. 1	X		
Ladder cave amphipod	*Styobromus* undescribed sp. 2	X		
IUS groundwater amphipod	*Styobromus* undescribed sp. 3			X
Barr's cave amphipod	*Crangonyx barri*	X		
Packard's groundwater amphipod	*Crangonyx packardi*	X	X	X
Indiana cave amphipod	*Crangonyx indianensis*	X		
Lewis's cave amphipod	*Crangonyx lewisi*		X	
Jordan's groundwater isopod	*Caecidotea jordani*	X		X
IUS groundwater isopod	*Caecidotea teresae*			X
Kendeigh's groundwater isopod	*Caecidotea kendeighi*			X
Northern cave isopod	*Caecidotea stygia*	X	X	
Rotund cave isopod	*Caecidotea rotunda*		X	
Barr's cave isopod	*Miktoniscus barri*	X		
Northern cave crayfish	*Orconectes inermis Bathynellid* undescribed sp.	X		
Subterranean sheet-web spider	*Phanetta subterranea*	X	X	
Cavernicolous sheet-web spider	*Porrhomma cavernicola*	X	X	
Cave sheet-web spider	*Islandiana cavicola*	X		
Cave sheet-web spider	*Islandiana* undescribed sp.		X	
Cave sheet-web spider	*Oreonetides* undescribed sp.	X	X	
Indiana cave pseudoscorpion	*Apochthonius indianensis*	X		
Limekiln hollow cave pseudoscorpion	*Apochthonius* undescribed sp. 1	X		
Patton Cave pseudoscorpion	*Apochthonius* undescribed sp. 2	X		
Packard's cave pseudoscorpion	*Kleptochthonius packardi*	X		
Holsinger's cave pseudoscorpion	*Hesperochernes holsingeri*		X	
Southeastern cave pseudoscorpion	*Hesperochernes mirabilis*	X	X	
Borden's pit cave pseudoscorpion	*Chitrella* undescribed sp.	X		
Blue River cave millipede	*Pseudotremia indianae*	X		
Black's cave millipede	*Pseudotremia blacki*	X		
Pursell's cave millipede	*Pseudotremia purselli*	X		
Cook's cave millipede	*Pseudotremia cookorum*	X		
Conservation cave millipede	*Pseudotremia conservata*	X		
Burns' cave millipede	*Pseudotremia burnsorum*	X		
Reynold's cave millipede	*Pseudotremia reynoldsae*	X		
Indian cave millipede	*Pseudotremia nefanda*		X	
Bollman's cave millipede	*Conotyla bollmani*	X		
Sollman's cave millipede	*Scoterpes sollmani*	X		
Cavernicolous springtail	*Sinella cavernarum*	X	X	
Indiana cave springtail	*Sinella alata*	X	X	
Saltpeter cave springtail	*Sinella* undescribed sp.	X		

Common Name	Scientific Name	South-Central Karst	Southeastern Karst	Non-Karst Groundwaters
Fountain cave springtail	*Pseudosinella fonsa*	X	X	
Undescribed springtail	*Pseudosinella* undescribed sp.	X	X	
Relict cave springtail	*Tomocerus missus*	X		
Wyandotte cave springtail	*Hypogastrura lucifuga*	X		
Benign cave springtail	*Isotoma* undescribed sp.	X		
Undescribed springtail	*Onychiurus* undescribed sp.	X		
Cave springtail	*Onychiurus* undescribed sp. 2		X	
Lewis's cave springtail	*Arrhopalites lewisi*	X		
Black Medusa cave springtail	*Arrhopalites ater*	X		
Two year cave springtail	*Arrhopalites bimus*	X		
Carolyn's cave springtail	*Arrhopalites carolynae*	X		
Undescribed springtail	*Arrhopalites* undescribed sp. 1	X		
Ollie Wilson cave springtail	*Arrhopalites* undescribed sp. 2		X	
Gray's cave springtail	*Arrhopalites* undescribed sp. 3		X	
Indiana cave dipluran	*Litocampa* undescribed sp.	X	X	
Potato run cave dipluran	*Eumesocampa* undescribed sp.	X		
Blue River cave ground beetle	*Pseudanophthalmus tenuis*	X		
Wyandotte cave ground beetle	*Pseudanophthalmus eremita*	X		
Marengo cave ground beetle	*Pseudanophthalmus stricticollis*	X		
Young's cave ground beetle	*Pseudanophthalmus youngi*	X		
Leona's cave ground beetle	*Pseudanophthalmus leonae*	X		
Emerson's cave ground beetle	*Pseudanophthalmus emersoni*	X		
Shiloh cave ground beetle	*Pseudanophthalmus shilohensis*	X		
Morrison's cave ground beetle	*Pseudanophthalmus morrisoni*	X		
Barr's cave ground beetle	*Pseudanophthalmus barri*		X	
Cave ground beetle	*Pseudanophthalmus chthonius*		X	
Lost River cave ground beetle	*Pseudanophthalmus* undescribed sp. 1	X		
Vowell cave ground beetle	*Pseudanophthalmus* undescribed sp. 2	X		
Patton cave ground beetle	*Pseudanophthalmus* undescribed sp. 3	X		
Mayfield's cave ground beetle	*Pseudanophthalmus* undescribed sp. 4	X		
Cave dung fly	*Spelobia tenebrarum*	X	X	

Table I-2. Selected Non-Obligate Subterranean Invertebrates of Indiana

Common Name	Scientific Name
Slender spring flatworm	*Phagocata gracilis*
Terrestrial snail	*Carychium exile*
Alternate disc snail	*Anguispira alternate*
Koch's terrestrial snail	*Anguispira kochi*
Carnivorous forest snail	*Haplotrema concavum*
Inflected three-toothed snail	*Inflectarius inflectus*
Terrestrial snail	*Patera laevior*
Common three-toothed snail	*Triodopsis tridentata*
Minute terrestrial snail	*Punctum minutissimum*
Arboreal terrestrial snail	*Zonitoides arboreus*
Robust copepod	*Acanthocyclops robustus*
Nearctic copepod	*Diacyclops nearcticus*
Bluegrass spring isopod	*Lirceus fontinalis*
Elrod's terrestrial isopod	*Ligidium elrodi*
Lesser spring isopod	*Gammarus minus*
Karst crayfish	*Cambarus laevis*
Cave funnel-web spider	*Calymmaria persica*
Pallid funnel-web spider	*Cicurina pallida*
Southeastern wandering spider	*Anahita punctulata*
Southeastern sac-web spider	*Talanites echinus*
Sheet-web spider	*Bathyphantes albiventris*
Sheet-web spider	*Centromerus latidens*
Sheet-web spider	*Centromerus cornupalpis*
Sheet-web spider	*Eperigone maculate*
Tennessee liocranid spider	*Liocranoides tennesseensis*
Carter's cave spider	*Nesticus carteri*
Fishing spider	*Dolomedes scriptus*
Fishing spider	*Dolomedes vittatus*
Cave orb weaver	*Meta ovalis*
American house spider	*Achaearanea tepidariorum*
Gray-handed pseudoscorpion	*Kleptochthonius griseomanus*
Lewis's cave pseudoscorpion	*Kleptochthonius lewisorum*
Cavernicolous harvestman	*Sabacon cavicolens*
Golden cave harvestman	*Erebomaster flavescens*
Forest harvestman	*Leiobunum elegans*
Salisa's cave millipede	*Pseudotremia salisae*
Leach's millipede	*Euryurus leachii*
Granulated millipede	*Scytonotus granulatus*
Lesser cave-loving millipede	*Cambala minor*
Hilly springtail	*Pseudosinella collina*
Toothed springtail	*Hypogastrura denticulate*
White springtail	*Folsomia candida*
Star springtail	*Folsomia stella*
Anglican springtail	*Isotoma anglicana*
Remarkable springtail	*Isotoma notabilis*
Truncate springtail	*Isotoma truncata*
Two-toothed springtail	*Tomocerus bidentata*
Dubious springtail	*Tomocerus dubius*
Golden springtail	*Tomocerus flavescens*
Glistening springtail	*Onychiurus reluctus*
Pygmy springtail	*Arrhopalites pygmaeus*
Southern cave cricket	*Ceuthophilus meridionalis*
Stygian cave cricket	*Ceuthophilus stygius*
Slender ground beetle	*Platynus tenuicollis*
Round fungus beetle	*Catops gratiosus*
Cave ant beetle	*Batrisodes hairstoni*
Rove beetle	*Aleochara lucifuga*
Rove beetle	*Atheta annexa*
Cave-loving rove beetle	*Atheta troglophila*
Rove beetle	*Aloconota laurentiana*
Rove beetle	*Lesteva pallipes*
Rove beetle	*Quedium erythrogaster*
Spelean rove beetle	*Quedius spelaeus*
Herald moth	*Scoliopteryx libatrix*
Mosquito	*Anopheles punctipennis*
Mosquito	*Culex pipiens*
Heleomyzid fly	*Amoebaleria defessa*
Heleomyzid fly	*Aecothea specus*
Heleomyzid fly	*Heleomyza brachypterna*
Cavernicolous fungus gnat	*Macrocera nobilis*
Cave hump-backed fly	*Megaselia cavernicola*
Stygian rove beetle	*Quedius spelaeus*

Table I-3. South-Central Indiana Karst: Species Richness of Cave Systems

	Binkley/Blowing Hole System (Harrison County) 22 species	Sharpe Creek Valley/Blue River (Wyandotte) (Crawford County) 28 species	Lost River System (Orange County) 21 species	Tincher Karst System (Lawrence County) 21 species
Snails	*Antroselates spiralis* (Spiral cave snail)	*Antroselates spiralis* (Spiral cave snail)		
		Fontigens cryptica (Hidden Spring snail)		
Flatworms	*Sphalloplana weingartneri* (Weingartner's cave flatworm)	*Sphalloplana weingartneri* (Weingartner's cave flatworm)	*Sphalloplana weingartneri* (Weingartner's cave flatworm)	*Sphalloplana weingartneri* (Weingartner's cave flatworm)
Crustaceans		*Sagittocythere barri* (Barr's cave crayfish ostracod)		
		Pseudocandona jeanneli (Jeannel's groundwater copepod)		*Pseudocandona jeanneli* (Jeannel's groundwater copepod)
		Megacyclops donnaldsoni (Donaldson's cave copepod)	*Diacyclops jeanneli* (Jeannel's groundwater copepod)	
		Diacyclops yeatmani (Yeatman's groundwater copepod)	*Rheocyclops indiana* (Indiana groundwater copepod)	
		Cauloxenus stygius (Northern cavefish copepod)	*Cauloxenus stygius* (Northern cavefish copepod)	
	Crangonyx barri (Barr's cave amphipod)	*Crangonyx barri* (Barr's cave amphipod)	*Crangonyx indianensis* (Indiana cave amphipod)	
	Styobromus undescribed sp. 1 (Devil's graveyard cave amphipod)	*Crangonyx packardi* (Packard's groundwater amphipod)	*Crangonyx packardi* (Packard's groundwater amphipod)	*Crangonyx packardi* (Packard's groundwater amphipod)
	Caecidotea stygia (Northern cave isopod)	*Caecidotea stygia* (Northern cave isopod)	*Caecidotea stygia* (Northern cave isopod)	*Caecidotea stygia* (Northern cave isopod)
		Caecidotea jordani (Jordan's groundwater isopod)		
		Bathynellid undescribed sp. (bathynellid)		
	Orconectes inermis (Northern cave crayfish)	*Orconectes inermis* (Northern cave crayfish)	*Orconectes inermis* (Northern cave crayfish)	*Orconectes inermis* (Northern cave crayfish)
Spiders	*Phanetta subterranea* (Subterranean sheet-web spider)	*Phanetta subterranea* (Subterranean sheet-web spider)	*Phanetta subterranea* (Subterranean sheet-web spider)	*Phanetta subterranea* (Subterranean sheet-web spider)
			Porrhomma cavernicola (Cavernicolous sheet-web spider)	*Porrhomma cavernicola* (Cavernicolous sheet-web spider)
				Oreonitides undescribed sp. (cave sheet-web spider)
Pseudoscorpions	*Kleptochthonius packardi* (Packard's cave pseudoscorpion)	*Kleptochthonius packardi* (Packard's cave pseudoscorpion)		*Kleptochthonius packardi* (Packard's cave pseudoscorpion)
				Apochthonius indianensis (Indiana cave pseudoscorpion)
Millipedes	*Pseudotremia indianae* (Blue River cave millipede)	*Pseudotremia indianae* (Blue River cave millipede)	*Conotyla bollmani* (Bollman's cave millipede)	*Conotyla bollmani* (Bollman's cave millipede)
	Scoterpes sollmani (Sollman's cave millipede)	*Scoterpes sollmani* (Sollman's cave millipede)		

Table I-3. *continued*

	Binkley/Blowing Hole System (Harrison County) 22 species	Sharpe Creek Valley/Blue River (Wyandotte) (Crawford County) 28 species	Lost River System (Orange County) 21 species	Tincher Karst System (Lawrence County) 21 species
Springtails	*Sinella cavernarum* (Cavernicolous springtail)	*Sinella cavernarum* (Cavernicolous springtail)		*Sinella cavernarum* (Cavernicolous springtail)
	Sinella alata (Indiana cave springtail)		*Sinella alata* (Indiana cave springtail)	
		Sinella undescribed sp. (cave springtail)		
	Pseudosinella fonsa (Fountain cave springtail)			*Pseudosinella fonsa* (Fountain cave springtail)
				Pseudosinella undescribed sp. (cave springtail)
	Arrhopalites lewisi (Lewis's cave springtail)	*Arrhopalites lewisi* (Lewis's cave springtail)	*Arrhopalites bimus* (Two year cave springtail)	*Arrhopalites* undescribed sp. 2 (cave springtail)
	Arrhopalites undescribed sp. 1 (cave springtail)		*Arrhopaliates carolynae* (Carolyn's cave springtail)	
	Tomocerus missus (Relict cave springtail)			*Tomocerus missus* (Relict cave springtail)
	Onychiurus undescribed sp. (cave springtail)	*Onychiurus* undescribed sp. (cave springtail)	*Onychiurus* undescribed sp. (cave springtail)	*Onychiurus* undescribed sp. (cave springtail)
		Hypogastrura lucifuga (Wyandotte cave springtail)		
Diplurans	*Litocampa* undescribed sp. 1 (cave dipluran)	*Litocampa* undescribed sp. 1 (cave dipluran)	*Litocampa* undescribed sp. 1 (cave dipluran)	
Beetles	*Pseudanophthalmus tenuis* (Blue (River cave ground beetle)	*Pseudanophthalmus tenuis* (Blue River (Cave ground beetle)	*Pseudanophthalmus stricticollis* (Marengo cave ground beetle)	*Pseudanophthalmus stricticollis* (Marengo cave ground beetle)
		Pseudanophthalmus eremita (Wyandotte cave ground beetle)	*Pseudanophthalmus youngi* (Young's cave ground beetle)	
			Pseudanophthalmus undescribed sp.	
				Batrisodes undescribed sp. (cave ant beetle)
Flies	*Spelobia tenebrarum* (Cave dung fly)	*Spelobia tenebrarum* (Cave dung fly)	*Spelobia tenebrarum* (Cave dung fly)	*Spelobia tenebrarum* (Cave dung fly)
Cavefish	*Amblyopsis spelaea* (Northern cavefish)	*Amblyopsis spelaea* (Northern cavefish)	*Amblyopsis spelaea* (Northern cavefish)	*Amblyopsis spelaea* (Northern cavefish)

Table I-4. Southeastern Indiana Karst: Species Richness of Selected Caves

	Indian Cave (Clark County) 9 species	Wilson Cave (Jefferson County) 7 species	Grays Cave (Jefferson County) 9 species	Bernice Chandler Cave (Ripley County) 7 species
Flatworms			*Sphalloplana weingartneri* (Weingartner's cave flatworm)	*Sphalloplana weingartneri* (Weingartner's cave flatworm)
Crustaceans	*Crangonyx packardi* (Packard's groundwater amphipod)	*Crangonyx packardi* (Packard's groundwater amphipod)	*Crangonyx packardi* (Packard's groundwater amphipod)	*Crangonyx packardi* (Packard's groundwater amphipod)
	Styobromus mackini (Mackin's groundwater amphipod)	*Crangonyx lewisi* (Lewis's cave amphipod)		*Crangonyx lewisi* (Lewis's cave amphipod)
	Caecidotea stygia (Northern cave isopod)	*Caecidotea stygia* (Northern cave isopod)	*Caecidotea stygia* (Northern cave isopod)	*Caecidotea rotunda* (Rotund cave isopod)
Spiders	*Phanetta subterranea* (Subterranean sheet-web spider)	*Phanetta subterranea* (Subterranean sheet-web spider)	*Phanetta subterranea* (Subterranean sheet-web spider)	*Phanetta subterranea* (Subterranean sheet-web spider)
			Oreonetides undescribed sp. (cave sheet-web spider)	
Pseudoscorpions		*Hesperochernes holsingeri* (Holsinger's cave pseudoscorpion)		
Millipedes	*Pseudotremia nefanda* (Indian cave millipede)			
Springtails	*Sinella alata* (Indiana cave springtail)		*Sinella alata* (Indiana cave springtail)	
			Arrhopalites undescribed sp. (cave springtail)	*Pseudosinella* undescribed sp. (cave springtail)
Beetles	*Pseudanophthalmus barri* Barr's cave beetle)			
	Pseudanophthalmus chthonius (Muscatatuck cave beetle)	*Pseudanophthalmus chthonius* (Muscatatuck cave beetle)	*Pseudanophthalmus chthonius* (Muscatatuck cave beetle)	*Pseudanophthalmus chthonius* (Muscatatuck cave beetle)
Flies	*Spelobia tenebrarum* (Cave dung fly)	*Spelobia tenebrarum* (Cave dung fly)	*Spelobia tenebrarum* (Cave dung fly)	*Spelobia tenebrarum* (Cave dung fly)

Table I-5. Indiana Department of Natural Resources' Natural Heritage Program List of Endangered, Threatened, and Rare Cave Invertebrates

Common Name	Scientific Name
State Endangered Species Category S1 (5 or fewer populations in Indiana)	
Chandler's cave flatworm	*Sphalloplana chandleri*
Millipede	*Pseudopolydesmus collinus*
TNC cave millipede	*Pseudotremia conservata*
Black's cave millipede	*Pseudotremia blacki*
Pursell's cave millipede	*Pseudotremia purselli*
Burns' cave millipede	*Pseudotremia burnsorum*
Cook's cave millipede	*Pseudotremia cookorum*
Salisa's cave millipede	*Pseudotremia salisae*
Reynold's cave millipede	*Pseudotremia reynoldsae*
Sollman's cave millipede	*Scoterpes sollmani*
groundwater amphipod	*Bactrurus cellulanus*
Ohio cave amphipod	*Crangonyx ohioensis*
Bousfield's spring amphipod	*Gammarus bousfieldi*
Mackin's cave amphipod	*Styobromus mackini*
IUS groundwater amphipod	*Styobromus* undescribed sp. 1
Devil's graveyard cave amphipod	*Styobromus* undescribed sp. 2
Ladder cave amphipod	*Styobromus* undescribed sp. 3
Base Line Barrens groundwater amphipod	*Styobromus* undescribed sp. 4
Jordan's groundwater isopod	*Caecidotea jordani*
IUS groundwater isopod	*Caecidotea teresae*
Morrison's cave copepod	*Bryocamptus morrisoni morrisoni*
Donaldson's cave copepod	*Megacyclops donnaldsoni*
Cave copepod	*Megacyclops* undescribed sp.
Indiana groundwater copepod	*Rheocyclops indiana*
Yeatman's groundwater copepod	*Diacyclops yeatmani*
Salisa's groundwater copepod	*Diacyclops salisae*
Lewis's groundwater copepod	*Diacyclops lewisi*
Indiana groundwater copepod	*Diacyclops indianensis*
Blue River groundwater copepod	*Diacyclops conversus*
Burns Hollow groundwater copepod	*Diacyclops* undescribed sp.
Jeannel's groundwater ostracod	*Pseudocandona jeanelli*
Marengo cave ostracod	*Pseudocandona marengoensis*
Groundwater ostracod	*Pseudocandona* undescribed sp.
Donaldson Cave water mite	*Hamohalacarus subterraneus*
Cave sheet-web spider	*Islandiana cavealis*
Wandering spider	*Anahita punctulata*
Sac-web spider	*Talanites echinus*
Liocranid spider	*Liocranoides tennesseensis*
Cave sheet-web spider	*Oreonetides* undescribed sp.
Indiana cave pseudoscorpion	*Apochthonius indianensis*
Patton Cave pseudoscorpion	*Apochthonius* undescribed sp. 1
Vowell Cave pseudoscorpion	*Apochthonius* undescribed sp. 2
Packard's cave pseudoscorpion	*Kleptochthonius packardi*
Gray-handed pseudoscorpion	*Kleptochthonius griseomanus*
Lewis's pseudoscorpion	*Kleptochthonius lewisorum*
Holsinger's cave pseudoscorpion	*Hesperochernes holsingeri*
Cave pseudoscorpion	*Chitrella* undescribed sp.
Hidden Spring snail	*Fontigens cryptica*
Springtail	*Arrhopalites bimus*
Carolyn's cave springtail	*Arrhopalites carolynae*
Wyandotte cave springtail	*Hypogastrura lucifuga*
Truncated springtail	*Isotoma truncata*
Ancestral springtail	*Sinella avita*
Barr's cave springtail	*Sinella barri*
Saltpeter cave springtail	*Sinella* undescribed sp.
Krekeler's cave ant beetle	*Batrisodes krekeleri*
Barr's cave ground beetle	*Pseudanophthalmus barri*
Emerson's cave ground beetle	*Pseudanophthalmus emersoni*
Wyandotte cave ground beetle	*Pseudanophthalmus eremita*
Leona's cave ground beetle	*Pseudanophthalmus leonae*
Shiloh cave ground beetle	*Pseudanophthalmus shilohensis shilohensis*
Monroe cave ground beetle	*Pseudanophthalmus shilohensis mayfieldensis*
Hudelson cave ground beetle	*Pseudanophthalmus* undescribed sp. 1
Vowell cave ground beetle	*Pseudanophthalmus* undescribed sp. 2
Patton cave ground beetle	*Pseudanophthalmus* undescribed sp. 3
Buddha cave ground beetle	*Pseudanophthalmus* undescribed sp. 4
Mayfield's cave ground beetle	*Pseudanophthalmus* undescribed sp. 5
State Threatened Species Category S2 (6–10 known populations in Indiana)	
Clark cave millipede	*Pseudotremia nefanda*
Anomolus amphipod	*Crangonyx anomalus*
Lewis's cave amphipod	*Crangonyx lewisi*
Jeannel's groundwater copepod	*Diacyclops jeanneli*
Black Medusa cave springtail	*Arrhopalites ater*
Lewis's cave springtail	*Arrhopalites lewisi*
Fountain cave springtail	*Pseudosinella fonsa*
Cave dipluran	*Litocampa* undescribed sp.
State Rare Species Category S2 (11–19 known populations in Indiana)	
Cave crayfish	*Orconectes inermis testii*
Barr's cave amphipod	*Crangonyx barri*
Northeastern cave isopod	*Caecidotea rotunda*
Shaggy cave snail	*Antroselates spiralis*
Hilly springtail	*Pseudosinella collina*
Cave ground beetle	*Pseudanophthalmus chthonius*
Young's cave ground beetle	*Pseudanophthalmus youngi*
State Watch List Categories S3 (20–99 known populations) and S4 (more than 100 known populations)	
Weingartner's cave flatworm	*Sphalloplana weingartneri*
Bollman's cave millipede	*Conotyla bollmani*
Blue River cave millipede	*Pseudotremia indianae*
Cave crayfish	*Orconectes inermis inermis*
Packard's groundwater amphipod	*Crangonyx packardi*
Indiana cave amphipod	*Crangonyx indianensis*
Dentate amphipod	*Synurella dentata*
Barr's terrestrial isopod	*Miktoniscus barri*
Northern cavefish commensal copepod	*Cauloxenus stygius*
Donaldson cave ostracod	*Donnalsoncythere donnaldsonensis*
Barr's commensal cave ostracod	*Sagittocythere barri*
Southeastern cave pseudoscorpion	*Hesperochernes mirabilis*
Springtail	*Arrhopalites benitus*
Flaming springtail	*Dicyrtoma flamea*
Primitive springtail	*Folsomia prima*
Humped springtail	*Hypogastrura gibbosus*
Helen's springtail	*Hypogastrura helena*
Bristly springtail	*Hypogastrura horrida*
Maheux springtail	*Hypogastrura maheuxi*
Girded springtail	*Hypogastrura succinea*
Springtail	*Isotoma anglicana*
Blue springtail	*Isotoma caeruleatra*
Christiansen's springtail	*Isotoma christianseni*
Dark springtail	*Isotoma nigrifrons*
Nixon's springtail	*Isotoma nixoni*
Springtail	*Isotoma torildae*
Petit springtail	*Isotomiella minor*
Fallen springtail	*Onychiurus casus*
Springtail	*Onychiurus reluctus*
Slender springtail	*Onychiurus subtenuis*
Barber's springtail	*Sensillanura barberi*
Blind springtail	*Sensillanura caeca*
Indiana cave springtail	*Sinella alata*
Springtail	*Sminthurides hypogramme*
Weichsel's springtail	*Sminthurides weichseli*
Elongate springtail	*Tomocerus elongatus*
Layered springtail	*Tomocerus lamelliferus*
Relict cave springtail	*Tomocerus missus*
Cavernicolous springtail	*Sinella cavernarum*
Rove beetle	*Aleochara lucifuga*
Rove beetle	*Atheta annexa*
Light shunning rove beetle	*Atheta lucifuga*
Slender cave ground beetle	*Pseudanophthalmus tenuis*
Marengo cave ground beetle	*Pseudanophthalmus stricticollis*
Slender cave ground beetle	*Pseudanophthalmus tenuis*
Marengo cave ground beetle	*Pseudanophthalmus stricticollis*

Table I-6. Subterranean Invertebrates with Their Type Localities in Indiana

Common Name	Scientific Name	Type Locality
Hidden Spring snail	*Fontigens cryptic* (Hubricht 1963)	spring near Bethlehem, Clark County
Weingartner's cave flatworm	*Sphalloplana weingartneri* (Kenk 1970)	Donaldson Cave System, Lawrence County
Jeannel's cave ostracod	*Pseudocandona jeanneli* (Klie 1931)	Donaldson Cave, Lawrence County
Marengo cave ostracod	*Pseudocandona marengoensisi* (Klie 1931)	Marengo Cave, Crawford County
Donaldson crayfish ostracod	*Donnaldsoncythere donnaldsonensis* (Klie 1931)	Donaldson Cave, Lawrence County
Morrison's cave copepod	*Bryocamptus morrisoni morrisoni* (Chappuis 1929)	Donaldson Cave, Lawrence County
Jeannel's groundwater copepod	*Diacyclops jeanneli* (Chappuis 1929)	Marengo Cave, Crawford County
Indiana cave copepod	*Diacyclops indianensis* (Reid 2004)	Henry Dilk Falls Cave, Jefferson County
Converse groundwater copepod	*Diacyclops converses* (Reid 2004)	Bou-Rouch pumpwell on Blue River, Crawford County
Salisa's groundwater copepod	*Diacyclops salisae* (Reid 2004)	well, Jennings County
Lewis's groundwater copepod	*Diacyclops lewisi* (Reid 2004)	well, Jennings County
Donaldson's cave copepod	*Megacyclops donnaldsoni* (Chappuis 1929)	Donaldson Cave, Lawrence County
Indiana groundwater copepod	*Rheocyclops indiana* (Reid et al. 1999)	Ladder Cave, Washington County
Northern cavefish copepod	*Cauloxenus stygius* (Cope 1872)	Sibert's Well Cave, Crawford County
Reclusive groundwater amphipod	*Bactrurus cellulanus* (Koenemann and Holsinger 2001)	seep spring, Monroe County
Lewis's cave amphipod	*Crangonyx lewisi* (Zhang and Holsinger 2003)	Crosley Canyon Cave, Jennings County
Packard's groundwater amphipod	*Crangonyx packardi* (Smith 1888)	well, Orange County
Indiana cave amphipod	*Crangonyx indianensis* (Zhang and Holsinger 2003)	Ray's Cave, Greene County
Jordan's groundwater isopod	*Caecidotea jordani* (Eberly 1965)	seep spring, Monroe County
IUS groundwater isopod	*Caecidotea teresae* (Lewis 1982)	drain tile, Floyd County
Elrod's terrestrial isopod	*Ligidium elrodii* (Packard 1873)	Elrod Cave, Orange County
Barr's cave isopod	*Miktoniscus barri* (Vandel 1965)	Marengo Cave, Crawford County (co-type),
Cave crayfish	*Orconectes inermis* (Cope 1871a)	Sibert's Well Cave, Crawford County
Cave crayfish	*Orconectes inermis testii* (Hay 1891)	Mayfield's Cave, Monroe County
Subterranean sheet-web spider	*Phanetta subterranean* (Emerton 1875)	Wyandotte Cave, Crawford County (co-type),
Cave orb weaver	*Meta ovalis* (Gertsch 1933)	Marengo Cave, Crawford County
Indiana cave pseudoscorpion	*Apochthonius indianensis* (Muchmore 1967)	Donaldson Cave, Lawrence County
Packard's cave pseudoscorpion	*Kleptochthonius packardi* (Hagen 1879)	Wyandotte Cave, Crawford County
Gray-handed pseudoscorpion	*Kleptochthonius griseomanus* (Muchmore 2000)	Indian Cave, Crawford County
Lewis's cave pseudoscorpion	*Kleptochthonius lewisorum* (Muchmore 2000)	Binkley Cave, Harrison County
Holsinger's cave pseudoscorpion	*Hesperochernes holsingeri* (Muchmore 1994)	Wilson Cave, Jefferson County
Golden cave harvestman	*Erebomaster flavescens* (Cope 1872)	Wyandotte Cave, Crawford County
Lesser cave-loving millipede	*Cambala minor* (Bollman 1888)	Bloomington, Monroe County
Blue River cave millipede	*Pseudotremia indianae* (Hoffman 1958)	Wyandotte Cave, Crawford County
Black's cave millipede	*Pseudotremia blacki* (Lewis 2000a)	Tabler Spring Cave, Harrison County
Indian cave millipede	*Pseudotremia nefanda* (Shear 1972)	Indian Cave, Clark County
Pursell's cave millipede	*Pseudotremia purselli* (Lewis 2000a)	South Fork Cave, Harrison County
Salisa's cave millipede	*Pseudotremia salisae* (Lewis 2000a)	Heron Cave, Crawford County
Cook's cave millipede	*Pseudotremia cookorum* (Lewis 2000a)	Little Mouth Cave, Harrison County
Conservation cave millipede	*Pseudotremia conservata* (Hoffman and Lewis 1997)	Seven Springs Cave, Harrison County
Burns' cave millipede	*Pseudotremia burnsorum* (Lewis 2000a)	Wallier Cave, Harrison County
Reynold's cave millipede	*Pseudotremia reynoldsae* (Lewis 2003)	Megenity Peccary Cave, Crawford County
Sollman's cave millipede	*Scoterpes sollmani* (Lewis 2000b)	Binkley Cave, Harrison County
Cavernicolous springtail	*Sinella cavernarum* (Packard 1888)	Wyandotte Cave, Crawford County
Indiana cave springtail	*Sinella alata* (Christiansen 1960)	Mays Cave, Monroe County
Fountain cave springtail	*Pseudosinella fonsa* (Christiansen and Bellinger 1996)	Peyton Spring Cave, Clark County
Wyandotte cave springtail	*Hypogastrura lucifuga* (Packard 1888)	Wyandotte Cave, Crawford County
Lewis's cave springtail	*Arrhopalites lewisi* (Christiansen and Bellinger 1998)	Wyandotte Cave, Crawford County
Black Medusa cave springtail	*Arrhopalites ater* (Christiansen and Bellinger 1998)	Black Medusa Cave, Harrison County
Two year cave springtail	*Arrhopalites bimus* (Christiansen 1966)	Shiloh Cave, Lawrence County
Barr's cave ground beetle	*Pseudanophthalmus barri* (Krekeler 1973)	Indian Cave, Clark County
Cave ground beetle	*Pseudanophthalmus chthonius* (Krekeler 1973)	Wilson Cave, Jefferson County
Blue River cave ground beetle	*Pseudanophthalmus tenuis* (Horn 1871)	Wyandotte Cave, Crawford County
Wyandotte cave ground beetle	*Pseudanophthalmus eremite* (Horn 1871)	Wyandotte Cave, Crawford County
Marengo cave ground beetle	*Pseudanophthalmus stricticollis* (Jeannel 1931)	Marengo Cave, Crawford County
Young's cave ground beetle	*Pseudanophthalmus youngi* (Krekeler 1958)	Clifty Caves, Washington County
Leona's cave ground beetle	*Pseudanophthalmus leonae* (Barr 1960)	Hert Farm Cave, Lawrence County
Emerson's cave ground beetle	*Pseudanophthalmus emersoni* (Krekeler 1958)	Donnehue's Cave, Lawrence County
Shiloh cave ground beetle	*Pseudanophthalmus shilohensis* (Krekeler 1958)	Shiloh Cave, Lawrence County
Krekeler's cave ant beetle	*Batrisodes krekeleri* (Park 1960)	Cave Spring Cave, Clark County
Spelean rove beetle	*Quedius spelaeus* (Horn 1871)	Wyandotte Cave, Crawford County
Cave dung fly	*Spelobia tenebrarum* (Aldrich 1897)	Wyandotte Cave, Crawford County

ASTER Mapping

Methods Used to Create Maps Generated Using ASTER

(Maps 1.8, 4.1, 5.1, 6.1, 7.1, 8.1, 10.1, 11.1)

Dr. Qihao Weng, Coordinator of Habitat Mapping

Graduate Student Participants: Guiying Li, Bingqing Liang, Hua Liu, Xiefei Hu, Derrick Burch, and Jacqueline Schubring

Objective

The major goal of the habitat-mapping portion of this Indiana Department of Natural Resources project was to produce a digital habitat (land use/land cover) map for the state of Indiana based on satellite imagery, digital aerial photos, and other geospatial data sources, and to build a GIS database that can be used for natural resource management and biodiversity preservation and restoration. Terra's Advanced Spaceborne Thermal Emission and Reflection Radiometer (ASTER) images were the primary data source for habitat mapping. A total of 7 habitat types—agriculture, aquatic systems, barren land, developed land, forest land, grassland, and wetland—were delineated from the satellite imagery.

Data and Procedures for Delineating Habitat Types

Data

ASTER is an advanced, multispectral sensor covering a wide spectral region from visible to thermal infrared with 14 spectral bands with high spatial, spectral, and radiometric resolution. Table A-1 gives information on ASTER. Near infrared bands (3B and 3N) are stereo pair images from which a digital elevation model (DEM) can be generated; thermal bands can be used to produce detailed maps of surface temperature and emissivity. In this project, VNIR (bands 1, 2, 3) and SWIR (bands 4, 5, 6, 7, 8, 9) bands were used to produce a land use and land cover map.

Procedures

Geometric Correction. ASTER images were acquired through the Earth Observing System Data Gateway of NASA. The data (level 1B) have been radiometrically and geometrically corrected. However, we performed our own geometric correction in order to get geometric accuracy to the level needed for this project. Topographic maps (1:24000) were downloaded from the Indiana Spatial Data Portal and used as reference maps. For each image scene, at least 30 ground control points were selected for registration, and the nearest resampling method was applied to resample the original VNIR and SWIR images. The root mean square errors had to be less than 0.5 pixel.

Table A-1. Spectral Characteristics of ASTER Bands

Subsystem	Band No.	Spectral Range (μm)	Spatial Resolution (m)	Quantization Level
VNIR	1	0.52–0.60	15	8 bits
	2	0.63–0.69		
	3N	0.78–0.86		
	3B	0.78–0.86		
SWIR	4	1.60–1.70	30	8 bits
	5	2.145–2.185		
	6	2.185–2.225		
	7	2.235–2.285		
	8	2.295–2.365		
	9	2.360–2.430		
TIR	10	8.125–8.475	90	12 bits
	11	8.475–8.825		
	12	8.925–9.275		
	13	10.25–10.95		
	14	10.95–11.65		

Image Development

Remotely sensed image data are often highly correlated between the adjacent spectral wavebands, and this will slow the processing if all bands are used. Principal component analysis (PCA) was used to identify which bands out of the original 9 bands contained more information. Usually, the first three principal components can explain 99% of all variance of the original data. Based on the PCA results, 5–6 bands were selected for further image analysis.

Image Classification

An unsupervised image classification algorithm was used to produce 50 clusters. Then, we labeled each spectral cluster based on (1) general knowledge of the reflectance characteristics of typical ground features; (2) the shapes of features; and (3) image textures and locations. Digital aerial photographs taken in 2003 and the National Land Cover Data of 1992 were also used as references. Following the first unsupervised classification, if we could not label all clusters precisely, we then masked out the labeled clusters and ran a second unsupervised classification. This process continued until all clusters were identified.

Post-Classification Refinement

Post-classification refinement was applied to minimize the impact of spectral confusion among the habitat classes. We used a spatial filter and image neighborhood function to refine the map, based on aerial photographs and other references.

Accuracy Assessment

We performed an accuracy assessment for the final land use/cover (habitat) map (Map 1.8). Table A-2 shows the result of the accuracy assessment. Aerial photographs (2003) were used as reference data, with 50 points randomly selected for each habitat class. A total accuracy of 80.86% was achieved, which is acceptable according to the national standard set by the U.S. Geological Survey. Producer's accuracy refers to the probability of a reference pixel being correctly classified. User's accuracy refers to the probability that a pixel classified on a map represents the actual class on the ground. Kappa coefficient expresses the proportionate reduction in error generated by a classification process compared with the error of a completely random classification. For instance, a value of 0.91 means that the classification process is avoiding 91 percent of the errors that a completely random classification would generate.

Table A-2. Accuracy Assessment and Error Matrix

Class Name	Reference Totals	Classified Totals	Number Correct	Producer's Accuracy (%)	User's Accuracy (%)	Kappa Coefficient
Agriculture	62	50	40	64.52	80	0.7569
Aquatic Systems	45	50	45	100	90	0.8852
Barren Lands	49	50	46	93.88	92	0.9070
Developed Lands	31	50	28	90.32	56	0.5172
Forest Lands	65	50	46	70.77	92	0.9018
Grasslands	58	50	38	65.52	76	0.7123
Wetlands	40	50	40	100	80	0.7742
TOTALS	**350**	**350**	**283**			**0.7767**

Table A-3. Distribution of Habitat Types by Natural Region as Indicated on Map 1.8

Natural Region	Image Class Type	Area (km²)	Percentage	Natural Region	Image Class Type	Area (km²)	Percentage
	Agriculture	6,574.17	64.21		Agriculture	21,689.54	65.35
	Aquatic Systems	170.92	1.67		Aquatic Systems	296.78	0.89
	Barren Lands	20.51	0.20		Barren Lands	60.74	0.18
Northwestern Morainal	Developed Lands	462.53	4.52	**Southwestern Lowlands**	Developed Lands	1,574.33	4.74
	Forest Lands	1,460.19	14.26		Forest Lands	4,560.22	13.74
	Grasslands	1,253.08	12.24		Grasslands	4,870.60	14.67
	Wetlands	297.14	2.9		Wetlands	139.41	0.42
	Agriculture	526.28	85.30		Agriculture	4,828.84	50.31
	Aquatic Systems	1.94	0.31		Aquatic Systems	146.32	1.52
	Barren Lands	0.80	0.13		Barren Lands	20.21	0.21
Grand Prairie	Developed Lands	10.63	1.72	**Southern Bottomlands**	Developed Lands	273.85	2.85
	Forest Lands	29.04	4.69		Forest Lands	2,545.64	26.52
	Grasslands	43.13	6.97		Grasslands	1,646.58	17.15
	Wetlands	7.09	1.15		Wetlands	137.33	1.43
	Agriculture	1,727.07	48.74		Agriculture	1,074.29	15.63
	Aquatic Systems	147.75	4.17		Aquatic Systems	99.75	1.45
	Barren Lands	1.12	0.03		Barren Lands	13.13	0.19
Northern Lakes	Developed Lands	84.90	2.40	**Shawnee Hills**	Developed Lands	90.37	1.31
	Forest Lands	858.53	24.23		Forest Lands	3,907.53	56.86
	Grasslands	612.25	17.28		Grasslands	1,628.64	23.70
	Wetlands	112.03	3.16		Wetlands	58.84	0.86
	Agriculture	911.50	39.21		Agriculture	1,567.74	22.21
	Aquatic Systems	37.64	1.62		Aquatic Systems	100.60	1.42
	Barren Lands	4.90	0.21		Barren Lands	19.69	0.28
Central Till Plain	Developed Lands	338.52	14.56	**Highland Rim**	Developed Lands	179.60	2.54
	Forest Lands	466.87	20.08		Forest Lands	3,480.50	49.30
	Grasslands	558.62	24.03		Grasslands	1,653.56	23.42
	Wetlands	6.89	0.30		Wetlands	58.35	0.83
	Agriculture	8,472.98	84.51		Agriculture	4,202.90	41.06
	Aquatic Systems	40.59	0.40		Aquatic Systems	123.47	1.21
	Barren Lands	11.91	0.12		Barren Lands	25.83	0.25
Black Swamp	Developed Lands	236.53	2.36	**Bluegrass**	Developed Lands	271.04	2.65
	Forest Lands	710.34	7.09		Forest Lands	3,692.97	36.08
	Grasslands	532.01	5.31		Grasslands	1,909.64	18.66
	Wetlands	21.54	0.21		Wetlands	9.11	0.09

Glossary

ADVENTIVE Not native; a species that has moved in from somewhere else; used especially in botany

ALLELOPATHIC Chemical secretions of plants or their fungal associates that poison or reduce the growth rates of competitors, usually other plant species

AMMOCETES Larval stages of lamprey

ANNUAL Plant which grows from seeds each year

ANTICLINE A fold of stratified rock that bows up in the center and has its oldest rocks at its core.

BEACH Especially the sandy shore of Lake Michigan, an area washed by wave action, which thus lacks plant growth; also can be found on smaller lakes or streams

BENTHIC Bottom levels of a body of water

BIENNIAL Plant which grows for two years, producing roots, stems, and leaves the first year, and flowers and fruit the second year

BIODIVERSITY The number of species present in a situation

BIOTIC INTEGRITY The capacity of an area to support and maintain an appropriate diversity of organisms to allow for a functional adaptive system comparable to natural habitat of the same type

BLIND VALLEY A valley formed from a stream that has dissolved away bedrock leaving behind steep walls at its head

BOG A pond or lake overgrown with or covered by a floating mat of vegetation, usually including many plants of the heath family (Ericaceae)

BORROW PIT Pond often left along highways when earth is removed ("borrowed") to use for building bridges or other needs

BRAKE A clump of brush or other vegetation

BREEDING BIRD A species which has its young in the state as opposed to one which merely migrates through

CHANNELIZE To straighten, deepen, or widen a ditch or creek to assist rapid drainage of the land

CONSERVATION TILLAGE Utilization of erosion control measures, including no-till farming

COOL-WATER STREAM Stream with temperatures between 22–26° C

CP1 Plantings of non-native grasses and legumes to reduce soil erosion, improve water quality, and create or enhance wildlife habitat

CP2 Plantings of native grasses and forbs or legumes to reduce soil erosion, improve water quality, and create or enhance wildlife habitat

CP10 Managing existing grass or grass/legume cover to reduce soil erosion, improve water quality, and create or enhance wildlife habitat

DIP SLOPE The erosion surface of a tilted geologic bed. It gets its name from how geologists measure the strike (direction of the axial plane) and dip (angle of the plane from horizontal) of geological units.

DUNE Rounded hill or ridge of sand formed by blowing wind; may be "captured" by *Ammophila* (beach grass) or other dune-forming plants

EARLY SERAL Early community in the successional series

EARLY SUCCESSIONAL Early community in the successional series, such as annual forb or grass stages

ECOLOGICAL SINK An area in which organisms fail to adequately survive and/or reproduce, therefore the population relies on immigration from source populations to maintain population numbersecological trap: See *ecological sink*

ECOREGION A major area of similar ecological characteristics, such as a desert or an eastern deciduous forest

EDAPHIC Relating to or determined by conditions of the soil

ENDOPHYTIC A plant or other organism that grows within a plant, such as the fungus in certain strains of fescue

EPHEMERAL Existing for a brief time; ephemeral ponds or streams dry up in summer, ephemeral annuals last a short time

EPIKARST The interval below the soil and above the bedrock, consisting of a network of intersecting fissures and cavities that collect and transport surface water and nutrients underground

ESCARPMENT A long cliff or steep slope separating two comparatively level surfaces; resulting from erosion or faulting, typically demarcates the boundary of two physiographic regions

EXOTIC A species not native to the place where found. See also *non-indigenous*

EXTINCT A species no longer present anywhere

EXTIRPATED A species no longer present in certain areas, but still present elsewhere

FEN A wetland community where groundwater flows to the surface in a diffuse manner. The seepage is commonly through an organic substrate, such as peat, muck, or marl.

FIRST BOTTOM The floodplain terrace immediately adjacent to the stream channel

FIRST TERRACE See *terrace*

FORBS Herbaceous (nonwoody) plants other than ferns and their allies and the grasslike (graminoid) plants (grasses, sedges, rushes, etc.) and related groups, i.e., generally the flowering plants

FRAGIPAN A formally defined diagnostic subsurface horizon in the U.S. Soil Taxonomy that is more than 15 cm thick and undergoes brittle failure when struck; usually impedes root penetration

GRAMINOID Grasslike plant

GREAT RIVER Larger river, too large to sample with seine and hip boots

HALOPHYTIC Growing in salt-impregnated soils

HAY PRESS BARN Where hay is formed into large bales for shipping

HYDRIC A moist environment; soils that are sufficiently wet in the upper part to develop anaerobic conditions during the growing season

HYPORHEIC A groundwater habitat below a surface stream

ICTERID A member of the blackbird family, i.e., blackbird, grackle, cowbird, meadowlark, bobolink

ILLINOIAN GLACIAL PERIOD Era from about 300,000 to about 130,000 years ago

IMPROVED FARMLAND Privately owned land that has been cleared of native vegetation and placed under cultivation; part of this land is often planted with legumes or left fallow each year to improve fertility

INDIGENOUS Native or naturally occurring

KAME A ridge formed by stratified glacial drift

KARST A three-dimensional landscape shaped by the dissolution of soluble layers of bedrock, usually carbonate rock such as limestone or dolomite. These landscapes display distinctive surface features and underground drainages, and in some examples there may be little or no surface drainage. Some areas of karst topography are underlain by thousands of caves.

KARST WINDOW A site where part of a cave has lost its roof, making a portion of the subterranean stream visible from the surface

LANDSAT Land observation satellite systems; a program of earth-observing satellite missions jointly managed by NASA and the U.S. Geological Survey since 1972

LARGE RIVER Non-wadeable river, as opposed to one you can walk across

LEGUME A member of the pea family (Leguminosae)

LENTIC Related to or living in still waters (lakes or ponds)

LITHOLOGY The physical character of a rock formation described in terms of its structure, texture, color, and mineral composition

LITHOPHYTE Plant that grows on rock or stone

LOTIC Related to or living in moving water

MARSH Shallow wetland with emergent herbaceous plants, usually dominated by cattails or graminoid (grasslike) plants

MESIC Habitat with an intermediate supply of water, not excessively wet or dry

METAPOPULATION A series of populations of a species in which some populations are permanent, while others are not but are repopulated periodically from the permanent ones

MIGRATORY CORRIDOR A band of vegetation used commonly by migrating organisms, such as woodlands along major rivers running north-south

MYOTIS Bats of the genus *Myotis,* which contains a large number of closely related species, including 5 of the 12 bats of Indiana. Although they are often called "bats," the preferred common name for the organisms in this genus is myotis.

NON-INDIGENOUS A species that is not native to the area identified

NON-OBLIGATE A species that may use, but does not require, some specific habitat, e.g., non-obligate grassland birds

NON-POINT SOURCE POLLUTION Pollution (of air, rivers, etc.) that comes from automobiles, farms, or other sources, but no single point of origin can be traced; generally, pollution by private individuals

NO-TILL Farmland which is not plowed before planting. A seed drill is used to insert the seeds directly into the soil.

OBLIGATE A species that requires some specific situation or habitat, e.g., obligate grassland birds

OLD FIELD Field allowed to lie fallow; usually contains a mixture of grasses and forbs

PALUSTRINE From the Latin word *palus,* or marsh. Wetlands within this category include inland emergent vegetation such as marshes and swamps as well as bogs and fens.

PANNE Small pool of water in the flatlands behind the first row of dunes (rare, but can be found on Lake Michigan in Indiana)

PARAFLUVIAL A groundwater habitat adjacent to a surface stream

PASTURE Land on which animals graze

PERENNIAL A plant that lives for more than two years, typically lasting year after year

POINT SOURCE POLLUTION Pollution coming from an identifiable, usually large source such as a utility plant, university, or business

PRAIRIE LOBE (PRAIRIE PENINSULA) An area projecting eastward from Illinois into northwest Indiana (Newton, Benton, Jasper, White, and other counties) which was originally tallgrass prairie. It is now almost entirely cultivated and includes some of the prime black soils of the country.

PRIORITY BLOCK An area measuring approximately 9 square miles, approximately one-sixth of a USGS 7.5-minute topographic map. Indiana contains approximately 680 topographic maps of this size, and thus 680 priority blocks.

REFUGIA Area in which organisms can survive poor conditions such as flooding; for example, swamp rabbits need raised areas

RIFFLES Area of rough water in a stream, usually caused by underwater rocks

RIVER BOTTOM The Wabash in particular, but other rivers also, were much larger as the glaciers receded, and they lowered by intervals, leaving terraces; the present level is the first bottom, or simply the bottom, the second level is the second bottom, etc. The lowest bottom often floods and is called the floodplain. See also *terrace*

ROW CROPS Crops which are planted in rows far apart, such as corn and soybeans, as opposed to wheat and rye, which are planted close together thus basically covering the area

SANGAMON INTERGLACIAL PERIOD Between the Illinoian and Wisconsinan glaciations

SAVANNA An area usually of sandy soil that contains mostly grassland but has trees occurring sporadically

SECOND BOTTOM The second floodplain terrace away from the stream channel and adjacent to the first bottom

SECOND TERRACE See *terrace*

SEDIMENT LOAD Sand or silt carried in water

SERAL STAGE One of the habitats in a series, such as old field or brushy field, as a system moves toward its ecological climax

SHEET FLOODING Flooding from a river or stream which leads to a mobile sheet of water across an area, typically the floodplain. Sheet flooding can be erosive due to the current and may also lead to substantial deposits of sediment in areas outside of the normal banks of the river.

SINK A habitat where a species does not produce enough young to increase the population. See *source*

SINKHOLE A hole in the ground formed by water running into a cave system; also called simply a "sink"

SOURCE A population that survives and produces enough young to populate other areas

SPOIL Mixed soil deposited on the surface after coal extraction, as occurred prior to 1977. Current laws require that topsoil be set aside and replaced in the original contours after mining is completed.

SUBFLUVIAL A groundwater habitat below a surface stream

SUCCESSION Natural changes in community composition over time

SWALE A low tract of land, especially when moist or marshy; a long, narrow, usually shallow trough between ridges on a beach, running parallel to the coastline; a shallow, trough-like depression that carries water mainly during rainstorms or snow melts

SWAMP Shallow water with emergent woody vegetation (trees)

SYSTEMATICS The procedure of taxonomy or the science relating to the classification and nomenclature of organisms

TAXA Unspecified taxonomic categories, e.g., the taxa of plants

TAXONOMY The formal and orderly classification of plants and animals according to their presumed natural relationships and origins

TECHNICAL ADVISORY COMMITTEE A group of individuals appointed by the IDNR who make recommendations concerning the status of and actions toward mammals, birds, herps, fish, etc.

TERRACE Rivers were much larger during glacial meltdown, then receded by intervals, leaving terraces. The main river now flows in the bottom proper; the first terrace marks an earlier bottom; and the second terrace represents a still earlier bottom.

TYPE LOCALITY The specific location where a new species is first described, e.g., Wyandotte Cave for *Myotis sodalis*

UNIMPROVED FARMLAND Privately owned land that has not been cleared of native vegetation, including forest, prairie, and wetlands. Most of this land has been grazed by domestic livestock each year.

WADEABLE STREAM Smaller stream that does not require boats to sample

WEED A plant growing in a location where it is not wanted

WISCONSINAN GLACIAL PERIOD Era from about 80,000 years ago to about 10,000 years ago

XERIC Very dry environment; desert

Bibliography

Agricultural drainage: Water quality impacts and subsurface drainage studies in the Midwest. 1998. *Ohio State University Extension Bulletin* 871-98. http://ohioline.osu.edu/b871.

Aldrich, J. M. 1897. A collection of Diptera from Indiana caves. In W. S. Blatchley, *The fauna of Indiana caves. Indiana Department of Geological and Natural Resources Annual Report* (1896) 21: 175–212.

Aldrich, J. R., J. A. Bacone, and M. D. Hutchison. 1982. Limestone glades of Harrison County, Indiana. *Proceedings of the Indiana Academy of Science* 91: 480–485.

Allen, A. W., and M. W. Vandever. 2003. *A national survey of Conservation Reserve Program (CRP) participants on environmental effects, wildlife issues, and vegetation management on program lands.* U.S. Geological Survey, Biological Science Report 2003-0001.

American Ornithologists' Union. 1998. *Check-list of North American birds,* 7th ed. Washington, D.C.: American Ornithologists' Union.

Angelier, E. 1962. Remarques sur la repartition de la faune dans le milieu interstitial hyporhéique. *Zoologischer Anzeiger* 168(7–10): 352–355.

Aquilani, S. M., T. E. Morrell, and D. C. LeBlanc. 2003. Breeding bird communities in burned and unburned sites in a mature Indiana oak forest. *Proceedings of the Indiana Academy of Science* 112: 186–191.

Askins, R. A. 1994. Open corridors in a heavily forested landscape: Impact on shrubland and forest-interior birds. *Wildlife Society Bulletin* 22: 339–347.

———. 2000. *Restoring North America's birds: Lessons from landscape ecology.* New Haven, Conn.: Yale University Press.

Bacone, J. A., L. A. Casebere, and M. D. Hutchinson. 1984. Glades of the Knobstone Escarpment in Indiana. *Proceedings of the Indiana Academy of Science* 93: 303–307.

Baerwald, E. F., G. H. D'Amours, B. J. Klug, and R. M. R. Barclay. 2008. Barotrauma is a significant cause of bat fatalities at wind turbines. *Current Biology* 18(16): R695–696.

Bajema, R. A., T. L. DeVault, P. E. Scott, and S. L. Lima. 2001. Reclaimed coal mine grasslands and their significance for Henslow's sparrows in the American Midwest. *Auk* 118: 422–431.

Bajema, R. A., and S. L. Lima. 2001. Landscape-level analyses of Henslow's sparrow (*Ammodramus henslowii*) abundance in reclaimed coal mine grasslands. *American Midland Naturalist* 145: 288–298.

Banta, A. M. 1907. The fauna of Mayfield's Cave. *Carnegie Institute of Washington Publications* 67: 5–114.

Barger, J. L., and M. G. Tannenbaum. 1998. Consumption of endophyte-infected fescue seeds and osmoregulation in white-footed mice. *Journal of Mammalogy* 79: 464–474.

Barnes, W. 2005. *Natural resources and the Great Depression in Martin County and south-central Indiana: The memoirs of William B. Barnes Sr.* Indianapolis: Indiana Historical Bureau.

Barnhart, J. D., and D. L. Riker. 1971. *Indiana to 1816: The colonial period.* Indianapolis: Indiana Historical Bureau and Indiana Historical Society.

Barr, T. C. 1960. A synopsis of the cave beetles of the genus *Pseudanophthalmus* of the Mitchell Plain in southern Indiana (Coleoptera, Carabidae). *American Midland Naturalist* 63(2): 307–320.

———. 1967. Ecological studies in the Mammoth Cave system of Kentucky: I. The biota. *International Journal of Speleology* 3: 147–204.

———. 1968. Cave ecology and the evolution of troglobites. *Evolutionary Biology* 2: 35–102.

Barr, T. C., and J. R. Holsinger. 1985. Speciation in cave faunas. *Annual Review of Ecology and Systematics* 16: 313–337.

Baxevanis, J. J. 1992. *The wine regions of Indiana: Geographical reflections and appraisals.* Stroudsbury, Pa.: Vinifera Wine Growers Journal.

Bellés, X. 1991. Survival, opportunism and convenience in the processes of cave colonization by terrestrial faunas. Pp. 325–335 in J. D. Ross and N. Prat, eds., *Homage to Ramon Margalef; or, Why there is such pleasure in studying nature.* Barcelona, Spain: University of Barcelona Press.

Bennett, P. J., ed. 1998. *Indiana Historian* (March).

Bent, A. C. 1919–1968. *Life histories of North American birds.* 21 vols. Various publishers.

Best, L. B. 2001. Temporal patterns of bird abundance in cornfield edges during the breeding season. *American Midland Naturalist* 146: 94–104.

Best, L. B., H. Campa, K. E. Kemp, R. J. Robel, M. R. Ryan, J. A. Savidge, H. P. Weeks Jr., and S. R. Winterstein. 1997. Bird abundance and nesting in CRP fields and cropland in the Midwest: a regional approach. *Wildlife Society Bulletin* 25: 864–877.

———. 1998. Avian abundance in CRP fields and crop fields during winter in the Midwest. *American Midland Naturalist* 139: 311–324.

Best, L. B., K. E. Freemark, J. J. Dinsmore, and M. Camp. 1995. A review and synthesis of habitat use by breeding birds in agricultural landscapes of Iowa. *American Midland Naturalist* 134: 1–29.

Betz, R. F. 1978. The prairies of Indiana. Pp. 25–31 in D. C. Glenn-Lewin and R. Q. Landers, eds., *Proceedings of the Fifth Midwest Prairie Conference.* Ames: Iowa State University Press.

Blatchley, W. S. 1897. Indiana caves and their fauna. Pp. 120–212 in *Twenty-First Report of the Indiana state geologist for 1896*. Indianapolis: Indiana State Geologist.

———. 1938. *The fishes of Indiana*. Indianapolis, Ind.: Nature Publishing.

Bolivar, C., and R. Jeannel. 1931. Campagne spéleologique dans l'Amérique du Nord. *Archives de Zoologie Expérimentale et Générale* 71: 294–316.

Bollman, C. H. 1888. Catalog of the myriapods of Indiana. *Proceedings of the U.S. National Museum* 11: 403–410.

Bowman, T. E., and J. J. Lewis. 1984. *Caecidotea rotunda*, a new troglobitic asellid from Indiana and Ohio (Crustacea: Isopoda: Asellidae). *Proceedings of the Biological Society of Washington* 97(2): 425–431.

Brack, V., Jr., S. A. Johnson, and R. K. Dunlap. 2003. Wintering populations of bats in Indiana, with emphasis on the endangered Indiana *Myotis*, *Myotis sodalis*. *Proceedings of the Indiana Academy of Science* 112: 61–74.

Brack, V., Jr., and R. E. Mumford. 1984. The distribution of *Pipistrellus subflavus* and the limit of the Wisconsinan glaciation: An interface. *American Midland Naturalist* 112: 397–401.

Brack, V., Jr., R. E. Mumford, and V. R. Holmes. 1984. The gray bat (*Myotis grisescens*) in Indiana. *American Midland Naturalist* 111: 205.

Brady, N. C., and R. R. Weil. 2002. *The nature and properties of soils*, 13th ed. Upper Saddle River, N.J.: Prentice Hall.

Bramble, W. C., R. H. Yahner, and W. R. Byrnes. 1992. Breeding-bird population changes following right-of-way maintenance treatments. *Journal of Arboriculture* 18: 23–32.

Brawn, J. D., S. K. Robinson, and F. R. Thompson. 2001. The role of disturbance in the ecology and conservation of birds. *Annual Review of Ecology and Systematics* 32: 251–276.

Bretschko, G., and W. E. Klemens. 1986. Quantitative methods and aspects in the study of the interstitial fauna of running waters. *Stygologia* 24 (2): 297–316.

Brittain, R. 2008. Characterizing northern saw-whet owl (*Aegolius acadicus*) winter habitats in south-central Indiana. *Proceedings of the Indiana Academy of Science* 117: 71–80.

Brock, K. J. 1997. *Birds of the Indiana dunes*, 2nd ed. Michigan City, Ind.: Shirley Heinze Environmental Fund.

———. 2006. *Brock's birds of Indiana*. CD (ISBN 1-4243-0568-3). Distributed by Amos Butler Audubon Society, Indianapolis, Ind.

Brooks, D. M. 1959. *Fur animals of Indiana*. Pittman-Robertson Bulletin no. 4.

Brothers, T. S. 1990. Surface-mine grasslands. *Geographical Review* 80: 209–225.

Bruner, A. W. 2002. From the archives: Part 3. Procellariformes and Pelecaniformes. *Indiana Audubon Quarterly* 80: 69–81.

Burr, B. M., and L. M. Page. 1986. Zoogeography of fishes of the lower Ohio–upper Mississippi basin. Pp. 287–324 in C. H. Hocutt and E. O. Wiley, eds., *The zoogeography of North American freshwater fishes*. New York: Wiley.

Burr, B. M., and M. L. Warren Jr. 1986. *A distributional atlas of Kentucky fishes*. Kentucky Nature Preserves Commission, Scientific and Technical Series, no. 4.

Busacca, J. 1975. Distribution and biology of *Amoebaleria defessa* (Osten-Sacken) and *Heleomyza brachypterna* (Loew) (Diptera: Heleomyzidae) in an Indiana cave. *NSS Bulletin* 37(1): 5–8.

Butler, A. W. 1892. Notes on the range and habits of the Carolina parakeet. *Auk* 9: 49–56.

———. 1895. The mammals of Indiana. *Proceedings of the Indiana Academy of Science* 4:81–86.

———. 1898. The birds of Indiana. Pp. 575–1187 in *22nd Annual Report*, Indiana Department of Geology and Natural Resources.

Butler, J. L., and J. J. Butler. 2001. *Indiana wine: A history*. Bloomington: Indiana University Press.

Cain, S. A. 1928. Plant succession and ecological history of a central Indiana swamp. *Botanical Gazette* 86: 384–401.

Caldwell, R. S., C. K. Smith, and J. O. Whitaker Jr. 1982. First records of the smoky shrew, *Sorex fumeus*, and the pygmy shrew, *Microsorex hoyi*, from Indiana. *Proceedings of the Indiana Academy of Science* 91: 606–608.

Calsyn, D. E. 2004. *Soil survey of Ford County, Illinois*. USDA, Natural Resources Conservation Service. http://soils.usda.gov.

Camacho, A. I. 1992. Sampling the subterranean biota. Pp. 133–168 in A. I.Camacho, ed., *The natural history of biospeleology*. Madrid: Museu Nacional de Ciencias Naturales.

Case, D. J., and Associates. 2005. *Indiana Comprehensive Wildlife Strategy*. Mishawaka, Ind.: D. J. Case and Associates.

Castrale, J. S. 1985. Responses of wildlife to various tillage conditions. *Transactions of the North American Wildlife and Natural Resources Conference* 50: 142–156.

———. 2005. *Occurrence of federally listed birds in Indiana*. www.isco.purdue.edu/pesticide/endangered_birds.pdf.

Castrale, J. S., and A. Ferchak. 2001. Survey of loggerhead shrikes in their primary range in Indiana, 1999–2000. *Indiana Audubon Quarterly* 79: 147–162.

Castrale, J. S., E. M. Hopkins, and C. E. Keller, eds. 1998. *Atlas of breeding birds of Indiana*. Indianapolis: Indiana Department of Natural Resources.

Castrale, J. S., R. T. Spear, and J. O. Whitaker Jr. 1987. Influence of tillage practices on the diets of deer mice. *Proceedings of the Indiana Academy of Science* 97: 527–534.

Chandler, C. R., and R. A. Weiss. 1995. *Status and distribution of marsh-nesting birds in northern Indiana*. Indiana Department of Natural Resources, Special Project Final Report.

Chandler, D. S., and J. J. Lewis. 2008. Notes on the cave-associated Pselaphinae (Staphylinidae) of Indiana. *Coleopterists Bulletin* 62(1): 114–119.

Chapman, P. 1986. Proposal to abandon the Schiner-Racovitza classsification for animals found in caves. *Proceedings of the Ninth International Congress of Speleology* 2: 179–182.

Chappuis, P. A. 1929. Copépodes cavernicoles de l'Amérique du Nord: Note préliminaire. *Bulletin de la Société des Sciences de Cluj* (Romania) 4: 51–57.

Chesser, R. T., R. C. Banks, F. K. Barker, C. Cicero, J. L. Dunn, A. W. Kratter, I. J. Lovette, P. C. Rasmussen, J. V. Remsen Jr., J. D. Rising, D. F. Stotz, and K. Winker. 2009. Fiftieth supplement to the American Ornithologists' Union *Check-list of North American birds. Auk* 126: 705–714.

Christiansen, K. 1960. The genus *Sinella Brook* (Collembola: Entomobryidae) in nearctic caves. *Annals of the Entomological Society of America* 53(4): 481–491.

———. 1962. Proposition pour la classification des animaux cavernicoles. *Spelunca-Memoires* 2: 76–78.

———. 1966. The genus *Arrhopalites* (Collembola: Sminthuridae) in the United States and Canada. *International Journal of Speleology* 2: 43–73.

Christiansen, K., and P. Bellinger. 1996. Cave *Pseudosinella* and *Oncopodura* new to science. *Journal of Cave and Karst Studies* 58(1): 38–53.

———. 1998. *The Collembola of North America, north of the Rio Grande*: part 4. *Families Neelidae, Sminthuridae, Mackenziellidae, Glossary, Bibliography, Index.* Grinnell, Iowa: Grinnell College.

Clapp, A. 1852. A synopsis; or, Systematic catalogue of the indigenous and naturalized, flowering and filicoid (exogens, endogens, and acrogens) medicinal plants of the United States. *Transactions of the American Medical Association* 5: 659–906.

Clark, D. L. 1987. *Entrepreneurs in hardwoods: A study of small business strategies.* Indianapolis, Ind.: White Arts.

Cole, J., and L. Sterrenburg. 2006. A brief analysis of the avian response to the Goose Pond/Beehunter Marsh restoration in Greene County, Indiana. *Indiana Audubon Quarterly* 84: 7–20.

Conant, R., and J. T. Collins. 1991. *A field guide to reptiles and amphibians: Eastern and central North America*. Boston: Houghton Mifflin.

Conover, M. R. 1998. Impact of consuming tall fescue leaves with the endophytic fungus, *Acremonium coenophialum,* on meadow voles. *Journal of Mammalogy* 79: 457–463.

Cope, E. D. 1868. Synopsis of the Cyprinidae of Pennsylvania. *Transactions of the American Philosophical Society* 13: 351–410.

———. 1870. A partial synopsis of the fishes of the fresh waters of North Carolina. *Proceedings of the American Philosophical Society* 11: 448–495.

———. 1871a. Wyandotte Cave and its life. *Indianapolis Journal* (5 Sept.): 4.

———. 1871b. Life in the Wyandotte Cave. *Annals and Magazine of Natural History,* ser. 4, 8(47): 368–370. Reprinted from *Indianapolis Journal,* 5 Sept.

———. 1872. On the Wyandotte Cave and its fauna. *American Naturalist* 6: 109–116.

Cope, J. B., A. R. Richter, and R. S. Mills. 1974. A summer concentration of the Indiana bat, *Myotis sodalis,* in Wayne County, Indiana. *Proceedings of the Indiana Academy of Science* 83: 482–484.

Cope, J. B., J. O. Whitaker Jr., and S. L. Gummer. 1991. Duration of bat colonies in Indiana. *Proceedings of the Indiana Academy of Science* 99: 199–201.

Coulter, J. M., S. Coulter, and C. R. Barnes. 1881. *Catalogue of the phanerogamous and vascular cryptogamous plants of Indiana.* Crawfordsville, Ind.: Review Steam Book and Job Printers.

Courbon, P., C. Chabert, P. Bosted, and K. Lindsley. 1989. *Atlas of the great caves of the world.* St. Louis, Mo.: Cave.

Cowles, H. C. 1899. The ecological relations of the vegetation on the sand dunes of Lake Michigan. *Botanical Gazette* 27: 95–391.

Crandall, R. M., and R. W. Dolan. 1997. Floristic investigation of the Crooked Creek community, Juan Solomon Park, Indianapolis, Ind. *Proceedings of the Indiana Academy of Science* 106: 1–23.

Crankshaw, W. B., S. A. Qadir, and A. A. Lindsey. 1965. Edaphic controls of tree species in presettlement Indiana. *Ecology* 46: 688–698.

Cudmore, W. W. 1985. The present distribution and status of the eastern woodrat, *Neotoma floridana,* in Indiana. *Proceedings of the Indiana Academy of Science* 94: 621–627.

Cudmore, W. W., and J. O. Whitaker Jr. 1984. The distribution of the smoky shrew, *Sorex fumeus,* and the pygmy shrew, *Microsorex hoyi,* in Indiana with notes on the distribution of other shrews. *Proceedings of the Indiana Academy of Science* 93: 469–474.

Cudmore-Vokey, B., and E. J. Crossman. 2000. *Checklists of the fish fauna of the Laurentian Great Lakes and their connecting channels.* Toronto, Ont.: Canadian Manuscript Report of Fisheries and Aquatic Sciences (2550).

Culver, D. C. 1982. *Cave life: Evolution and ecology.* Cambridge, Mass.: Harvard University Press.

Culver, D. C., and B. Sket. 2000. Hotspots of subterranean biodiversity in caves and wells. *Journal of Cave and Karst Studies* 62(1): 11–17.

Dailey, T. B. 2003. Nest box use and nesting success of house wrens (*Troglodytes aedon*) in a midwestern wetland park. *Ohio Journal of Science* 103: 25–28.

Dailey, T. B., and P. E. Scott. 2006. Spring nectar sources for solitary bees and flies in a landscape of deciduous forest and agricultural fields: Production, variability, and consumption. *Journal of the Torrey Botanical Society* 133: 535–547.

Danielopol, D. L. 1976. The distribution of the fauna in the interstitial habitats of riverine sediments of the Danube and the Piesting (Austria). *International Journal of Speleology* 8: 23–51.

Davis, N. S., Jr., and F. L. Rice. 1883. List of Batrachia and Reptilia of Illinois. *Bulletin of the Chicago Academy of Science* 1(3): 25–32.

Deam, C. C. 1940. *Flora of Indiana.* Indianapolis, Ind.: Department of Conservation.

Delamare Deboutteville, C. 1960. *Biologie des eaux souterraines littorals et continentals.* Paris: Hermann.

Denevan, W. M. 1992. The pristine myth: The landscape of the Americas in 1492. *Annals of the Association of American Geographers* 82(3): 369–385.

Deniger, J. A. 2003a. *Soil survey of DeKalb County, Illinois.* USDA, Natural Resources Conservation Service. *http://soils.usda.gov.*

———. 2003b. *Soil survey of Kane County, Illinois.* USDA, Natural Resources Conservation Service. http://soils.usda.gov.

Denny, R. N. 1952. *A summary of North American beaver management, 1946–1948.* Denver: Colorado Game and Fish Department.

DeVault, T. L., M. B. Douglas, J. S. Castrale, C. E. Mills, T. Hayes, and O. E. Rhodes Jr. 2006. Nesting success and status of the least tern breeding colony at Gibson Lake in southwestern Indiana. *Proceedings of the Indiana Academy of Science* 115: 53–59.

DeVault, T. L., P. E. Scott, R. A. Bajema, and S. L. Lima. 2002. Breeding bird communities of reclaimed coal-mine grasslands in the American Midwest. *Journal of Field Ornithology* 73: 268–275.

Dunning, J. B., Jr. 2005. Snowy owl in White County, July–August 2004. *Indiana Audubon Quarterly* 83: 105–110.

Durham, W. F., and M. G. Tannenbaum. 1998. Effects of endophyte consumption on food intake, growth, and reproduction in prairie voles. *Canadian Journal of Zoology* 76: 960–969.

Eberly, W. R. 1965. A new troglobitic isopod (Asellidae) from southern Indiana. *Proceedings of the Indiana Academy of Science* 75: 286–288.

Eigenmann, C. H. 1909. *Cave vertebrates of America: A study in degenerative evolution.* Washington, D.C.: Carnegie Institution of Washington.

Eigenmann, C. H., and C. H. Beeson. 1894. Fishes of Indiana. *Proceedings of the Indiana Academy of Science* 9: 76–108.

———. 1905. The fishes of Indiana. Pp. 113–157 in *Biennial Report of the Commissioner of Fisheries and Game for Indiana, 1903–04.*

Elrod, M. N., and E. S. McIntire. 1876. Orange County. Pp. 203–239 in *Indiana Geological Survey, Seventh Annual Report.*

Emerton, J. H. 1875. Notes on spiders from caves in Kentucky, Virginia and Indiana. *American Naturalist* 9: 278–281.

Engels, W. L. 1931. Long-tailed shrews in northern Indiana. *Journal of Mammalogy* 12: 312.

———. 1933. Notes on the mammals of St. Joseph County, Indiana. *American Midland Naturalist* 14: 1–16.

Eshenroder, R. L., M. E. Holey, T. K. Gorenflo, and R. D. Clark Jr. 1995. *Fish-community objectives for Lake Michigan.* Great Lakes Fishery Commission, Special Publication 95-3.

Evermann, B. W. 1886. A list of the fishes observed in the vicinity of Brookville, Franklin County, Indiana. *Bulletin of the Brookville Society of Natural History* 1–11.

———. 1888. The occurrence in Indiana of the star-nosed mole (*Condylura cristata* L.). *American Naturalist* 22: 359.

Evermann, B. W., and A. W. Butler. 1894a. Bibliography of Indiana mammals. *Proceedings of the Indiana Academy of Science* 3: 120–124.

———. 1894b. Preliminary list of Indiana mammals. *Proceedings of the Indiana Academy of Science* 3: 124–139.

Evermann, B. W., and H. W. Clark. 1908. Lake Cicott, Indiana, and notes on the flora and fauna. *Proceedings of the Biological Society of Washington* 11: 213–218.

———. 1910. Fletcher Lakes, Indiana, and its flora and fauna. *Proceedings of the Biological Society of Washington* 13: 81–88.

———. 1911. Notes on the mammals of the Lake Maxinkuckee region. *Proceedings of the Washington Academy of Science* 13:1–34.

———. 1920. *Lake Maxinkuckee: A physical and biological survey,* vols. 1 and 2. Indiana Department of Conservation Publication no. 7.

Fahrig, L. 2003. Effects of habitat fragmentation on biodiversity. *Annual Review of Ecology, Evolution, and Systematics* 34: 487–515.

Fenneman, N. M. 1938. *Physiography of the eastern United States.* New York: McGraw-Hill.

Fernald, M. L. 1950. *Gray's' manual of botany,* 8th ed. New York: American Book Co. 1632 pp.

Fisher, B. E. 2008. Current status and distribution of Indiana's seven endangered darter species (Percidae). *Proceedings of the Indiana Academy of Science.* 117(2): 167–192.

Fisher, B. E., S. P. Wente, T. P. Simon, and A. Spacie. 2001. The fishes of Tippecanoe County, Indiana. *Proceedings of the Indiana Academy of Science* 107: 151–166.

Forbes, S. A., and R. E. Richardson. 1920. The fishes of Illinois. *Natural History Survey of Illinois* 3: 1–357.

Ford, D. C., and P. W. Williams. 1989. *Karst geomorphology and hydrology.* London: Unwin Hyman.

Ford, S. D. 1977. Range, distribution, and habitat of the western harvest mouse, *Reithrodontomys megalotis,* in Indiana. *American Midland Naturalist* 98: 422–432.

Forman, R. T. T., and L. E. Alexander. 1998. Roads and their major ecological effects. *Annual Review of Ecology and Systematics* 29: 207–231.

Forman, R. T. T., and R. D. Deblinger. 2000. The ecological road-effect zone of a Massachusetts (USA) suburban highway. *Conservation Biology* 14: 36–46.

Forman, R. T. T., B. Reineking, and A. M. Hersperger. 2002. Road traffic and nearby grassland bird patterns in a suburbanizing landscape. *Environmental Management* 29: 782–800.

Franzmeier, D. P., G. C. Steinhardt, H. R. Sinclair, and W. D. Hosteter. 1989. *Taxonomic and environmental factor keys to the soils of Indiana.* West Lafayette, Ind.: Purdue University Cooperative Extension Service (AY-249).

Freeman, W. H. 1908. *Eighth annual report.* Indianapolis, Ind.: State Board of Forestry.

French, T. W. 1984. Dietary overlap of *Sorex longirostris* and *S. cinereus* in hardwood floodplain habitats in Vigo County, Indiana. *American Midland Naturalist* 111: 41–46.

Frey, D. G. 1955. Distributional ecology of the cisco, *Coregonus artedii,* in Indiana. *Investigations of Indiana Lakes and Streams* 4: 177–228.

———. 1966. Limnology. Pp. 297–320 in A. A. Lindsey, ed., *Natural features of Indiana*. Indianapolis: Indiana Academy of Science.

Friesner, R. C., and J. E. Potzger. 1946. The Cabin Creek raised bog, Randolph County, Indiana. *Butler University Botanical Studies* 8: 24–43.

Galligan, E. W., T. L. DeVault, and S. L. Lima. 2006. Nesting success of grassland and savanna birds on reclaimed midwestern coal mines. *Wilson Journal of Ornithology* 118: 537–546.

Gammon, J. R. 1964. The distribution of fishes in Putnam County, Indiana, and vicinity. *Proceedings of the Indiana Academy of Science* 74: 353–364.

———. 1976. The status of Indiana streams and fish from 1800 to 1900. *Proceedings of the Indiana Academy of Science* 86: 209–216.

———. 1995. *The Wabash River ecosystem: II. Final report for Eli Lilly and Company and PSI Energy.* Indianapolis, Ind.

Gammon, J. R., and R. S. Benda. 1967. The fish populations of Big Walnut Creek. *Proceedings of the Indiana Academy of Science* 77: 193–205.

Gammon, J. R., Gammon C. W., and M. K. Schmid. 1990. Land-use influence on fish communities in central Indiana streams. Pp. 111–120 in *Proceedings of the 1990 Midwest Pollution Control Biologists meeting.* www.epa.gov.

Gange, A. C., D. E. Lindsay, and J. M. Schofield. 2003. The ecology of golf courses. *Biologist* 50: 63–68.

Gerking, S. D. 1945. Distribution of the fishes of Indiana. *Investigations of Indiana Lakes and Streams* 3: 1–137.

———. 1955. Key to the fishes of Indiana. *Investigations of Indiana Lakes and Streams* 4(2): 49–86.

Gertsch, W. J. 1933. Diagnosis of new American spiders. *American Museum Novitates* 637: 1–14.

Gibson, J., J. G. Palis, S. E. Gibson, and B. A. Kingsbury. 2005. *Composition and abundance of amphibians and reptiles among two habitat types in the German Ridge unit of Hoosier National Forest, Indiana: Final Report to the U.S. Forest Service.*

Gilbert, C. H. 1884. A list of the fishes observed in the East Fork of White River, Indiana, with descriptions of two new species. *Proceedings of the U.S. National Museum* 7: 199–205.

———. 1980. *Clinostomus elongatus* (Kirtland), redside dace. P. 148 in D. S. Lee et al., eds., *Atlas of North American freshwater fishes.* Raleigh: North Carolina State Museum of Natural History.

Gilbert, F. L. 1971. *Soil survey of Dent County, Missouri.* USDA, Soil Conservation Service. http://soils .usda.gov.

Gill, R. E., Jr., P. Canevari, and E. H. Iversen. 1998. Eskimo curlew (*Numenius borealis*). In A. Poole and F. Gill, eds., *The birds of North America.* Philadelphia, Pa.: Birds of North America.

Gillihan, S. W. 2000. *Bird conservation on golf courses: A design and management manual.* Chelsea, Mich.: Ann Arbor Press.

Gines, A., and J. Gines. 1992. Karst phenomena and biospeleological environments. Pp. 27–53 in A. I. Camacho, ed., *The natural history of biospeleology.* Madrid: Museu Nacional de Ciencias Naturales.

Gleason, H. A., and A. Cronquist. 1991. *Manual of vascular plants of northeastern United States and adjacent Canada,* 2nd ed. Bronx, N.Y.: New York Botanical Garden.

Gordon, R. B. 1936. A preliminary vegetation map of Indiana. *American Midland Naturalist* 17: 866–877.

Gorney, D., and L. A. Casebere. 2002. Alder flycatcher: First confirmed nesting record and its status in Indiana. *Indiana Audubon Quarterly* 80: 11–19.

Greenberg, J. 2005. There's gold in those fields: Agricultural fields along the borders of Illinois and Indiana are where to find American golden-plover each spring. *Birder's World* (April): 40–45.

Greenberg, J. R. 2002. *A natural history of the Chicago region.* Chicago: University of Chicago Press.

Grundel, R., and N. B. Pavlovic. 2007a. Distinctiveness, use, and value of midwestern oak savannas and woodlands as avian habitats. *Auk* 124: 969–985.

———. 2007b. Response of bird species densities to habitat structure and fire history along a midwestern open-forest gradient. *Condor* 109: 734–749.

Guo, Y., R. Amundson, P. Gong, and R. Ahrens. 2003. Taxonomic structure, distribution, and abundance of soils in the USA. *Soil Science Society of America Journal* 67: 1507–1516.

Hagen, H. 1879. Hoehlen-Chelifer in Nord-America. *Zoologischer Anzeiger* 2: 399–400.

Hahn, W. L. 1907. Notes on the mammals of the Kankakee Valley. *Proceedings of the U.S. National Museum* 32: 455–464.

———. 1909. The mammals of Indiana. In *33rd annual report: Indiana Department of Geology and Natural Resources.*

Hall, E. R. 1981. *The mammals of North America.* 2 vols. New York: Wiley.

Hamel, P. B. 1998. Cerulean warbler (*Dendroica cerulea*). In A. Poole and F. Gill, eds., *The birds of North America.* Philadelphia, Pa.: Birds of North America.

Harding, J. H. 1997. *Amphibians and reptiles of the Great Lakes region.* Ann Arbor: University of Michigan Press.

Harper, D. 1981. *Trends in underground coal mining in Indiana.* Department of Natural Resources, Geological Survey Occasional Paper, no. 33. Bloomington, Ind.

Harrison, T., and P. F. Hickie. 1931. Indiana's swamp rabbit. *Journal of Mammalogy* 12: 319–320.

Haw, J. 2005. Steuben County lakes. *Online Birding Guide.* http://www.indianaaudubon.org/guide/sites/ steuben.htm.

Hay, O. P. 1894. The lamprey and fishes of Indiana. *Indiana Department of Geology and Natural Resources* 19: 146–296.

Hay, W. P. 1891. The crustacea of Indiana. *Proceedings of the Indiana Academy of Science* 147–151.

———. 1893. Observations on the blind crayfishes of Indiana, with a description of a new subspecies: *Cambarus pellucidus testii. Proceedings of the U.S. National Museum* 16 (935): 283–286.

Haymond, R. 1870. Mammals found at present time in Franklin County, Indiana. Pp 203–208 in

First annual report, Indiana Geological Survey. Indianapolis: Indiana Geological Survey.

Hedge, R. L. 2005. Field notes, summer 2004. *Indiana Audubon Quarterly* 83: 114–139.

Herkert, J. R. 1994. The effects of habitat fragmentation on midwestern grassland bird communities. *Ecological Applications* 4: 461–471.

———. 1997a. Bobolink *Dolichonyx oryzivorus* population decline in agricultural landscapes in the midwestern USA. *Biological Conservation* 80: 107–112.

———. 1997b. Population trends of the Henslow's sparrow in relation to the Conservation Reserve Program in Illinois, 1975–1995. *Journal of Field Ornithology* 68: 235–244.

———. 1998. Breeding birds of the midwestern grassland-forest transition zone: Who were they and where are they now? *U.S. Environmental Protection Agency.* http://www.epa.gov/glnpo/oak/proceedings/herkert.html.

Hickie, P. F., and T. Harrison. 1930. The Alleghany [*sic*] wood rat in Indiana. *American Midland Naturalist* 12: 169–174.

Hill, C. A. 1976. *Cave minerals.* Huntsville, Ala.: National Speleological Society.

Hill, C. A., and P. Forti. 1997. *Cave minerals of the world,* 2nd ed. Huntsville, Ala.: National Speleological Society.

Historical atlas of Indiana counties. 1876. Chicago: Baskin, Forster.

Hobbs, H. H., Jr., and T. C. Barr. 1972. Origins and affinities of the troglobitic crayfishes of North America (Decapoda: Astacidae). II: Genus *Orconectes. Smithsonian Contributions to Zoology* 105: 1–84.

Hocutt, C. H., and E. O. Wiley. 1986. *The zoogeography of North American freshwater fishes.* New York: Wiley.

Hoffman, R. L. 1958. On the identity of *Pseudotremia cavernarum* Cope, a poorly known American chordumoid diplopod. *Proceedings of the Biological Society of Washington* 71: 113–118.

Hoffman, R. L., and J. J. Lewis. 1997. *Pseudotremia conservata,* a new cleidogonid milliped (Diplopoda: Chordeumatida), with a synopsis of the cavernicolous millipeds of Indiana. *Myriapodologica* 4(13): 107–119.

Hoffmeister, D. F. 1989. *Mammals of Illinois.* Urbana: University of Illinois Press.

Holsinger, J. R. 1986. Zoogeographic patterns of North American subterranean amphipod crustaceans. Pp. 85–106 in R. H. Gore and K. L. Heck, eds., *Crustacean biogeography.* Rotterdam: Balkema.

———. 1988. Troglobites: The evolution of cave-dwelling organisms. *American Scientist* 76: 147–153.

———. 1994. Pattern and process in the biogeography of subterranean amphipods. *Hydrobiologica* 287: 131–145.

———. 2000. Ecological derivation, colonization and speciation. Pp. 399–415 in H. Wilkens, D. C. Culver, and W. F. Humphreys, eds., *Ecosystems of the world,* vol. 30: *Subterranean ecosystems.* Amsterdam: Elsevier.

Homoya, M. A. 1985. Map showing the natural regions of Indiana. *Proceedings of the Indiana Academy of Science* 94: pl. 1.

———. 1993. *Orchids of Indiana.* Bloomington: Indiana University Press.

———. 1994. Indiana Barrens: Classification and description. *Castanea* 59(3): 204–213.

———. 1997. Land of the cliff dwellers: The Shawnee Hills natural region. Pp. 172–176 in M. T. Jackson, ed., *The natural heritage of Indiana.* Bloomington: Indiana University Press.

Homoya, M. A., D. B. Abrell, J. R. Aldrich, and T. W. Post. 1985. The natural regions of Indiana. *Proceedings of the Indiana Academy of Science* 94: 245–268.

Homoya, M. A., and C. L. Hedge. 1983. The upland sinkhole swamps and ponds of Harrison County, Indiana. *Proceedings of the Indiana Academy of Science* 92: 383–387.

Horn, G. H. 1871. Descriptions of new Coleoptera of the United States, with notes on known species. *Transactions of the American Entomological Society* 3: 325–344.

Horstman, A. J., J. R. Nawrot, and A. Woolf. 1998. Mine-associated wetlands as avian habitat. *Wetlands* 18: 298–304.

Howarth, F. G. 1973. The cavernicolous fauna of Hawaiian lava tubes. 1: Introduction. *Pacific Insects* 15(1): 139–151.

———. 1981. Community structure and niche differentiation in Hawaiian lava tubes. Pp. 318–336 in D. Mueller-Dombois, K. W. Bridges, and H. L. Carson, eds., *Island ecosystems: Biological organization in selected Hawaiian communities.* Stroudsburg, Pa.: Hutchinson Ross.

Hubbs, C. L., and K. F. Lagler. 1942. Annotated list of the fishes of Foots Pond, Gibson County, Indiana. *Investigations of Indiana Lakes and Streams* 2: 73–83.

Hubricht, L. 1963. New species of Hydrobiidae. *Nautilus* 76(4): 138–140.

Humphrey, S. R., and J. B. Cope. 1976. Population ecology of the little brown bat, *Myotis lucifugus,* in Indiana and north-central Kentucky. American Society of Mammalogists, Special Publication no. 4.

———. 1977. Survival rates of the endangered Indiana bat, *Myotis sodalis. Journal of Mammalogy* 58: 32–36.

Humphrey, S. R., A. R. Richter, and J. B. Cope. 1977. Summer habitat and ecology of the endangered Indiana bat, *Myotis sodalis. Journal of Mammalogy* 58: 334–346.

Husmann, S. 1971. Ecological studies on freshwater meiobenthon in layers of sand and gravel. *Smithsonian Contributions to Zoology* 76: 161–169.

Indiana Agricultural Statistics. 2003–2004. Purdue University College of Agriculture. www.nass.usda.gov/in.

Indiana Bird Records Committee. 2005. *Official state bird checklist.* http://www.indianaaudubon.org/ibrc/offcklst.htm.

Indiana Department of Environmental Management. 1999. *Confined feeding operations in Indiana.* http://www.in.gov/idem/4994.htm.

Indiana Department of Natural Resources. 1987. *Water resource availability in the St. Joseph River basin,*

Indiana. Indianapolis, Ind.: Division of Water, Water Resource Assessment (87-1).

———. 1988. *Water resource availability in the Whitewater River basin, Indiana*. Indianapolis, Ind.: Division of Water, Water Resource Assessment (88-2).

———. 1990. *Water resource availability in the Kankakee River basin, Indiana*. Indianapolis, Ind.: Division of Water, Water Resource Assessment (90-3).

———. 1994. *Water resource availability in the Lake Michigan region, Indiana*. Indianapolis, Ind.: Division of Water, Water Resource Assessment (94-4).

———. 1996. *Water resource availability in the Maumee River basin, Indiana*. Indianapolis, Ind.: Division of Water, Water Resource Assessment (96-5).

———. 2000. *Statewide Comprehensive Outdoor Recreation Plan*. Division of Outdoor Recreation, Indianapolis, Ind.

———. 2005. Goose Pond project. http://www.in.gov/dnr/fishwild/goosepond.

Indiana Department of Statistics. 1900. *Eighth biennial report*, vol. 14. Indianapolis, Ind.

———. 1901–1902. *Ninth biennial report*, vol 15. Indianapolis, Ind.

Indiana Limestone Institute. 2001. *History of Indiana limestone*. www.reidpres.com/limestone.htm.

Indiana Natural Heritage Data Center. 2005. http://www.in.gov/dnr/naturepreserve/4746.htm.

Ingold, J. L., and M. J. Craycraft. 1983. Avian frugivory on honeysuckle (*Lonicera*) in southwestern Ohio in fall. *Ohio Journal of Science* 83: 256–258.

Jackson, M. T. 2004. *101 trees of Indiana: A field guide*. Bloomington: Indiana University Press.

Jackson, M. T., ed. 1997. *The natural heritage of Indiana*. Bloomington: Indiana University Press.

Jackson, M. T., and P. R. Allen. 1969. Detailed studies of old-growth forest in Versailles State Park, Indiana. *Proceedings of the Indiana Academy of Science* 78: 210–230.

Jackson, T. C. 2004. *Soil survey of Wright County, Minnesota*. USDA, Natural Resources Conservation Service. http://soils.usda.gov.

Jeannel, R. 1931. Révision des Trechinae de l'Amérique du nord. *Archives de Zoologie Expérimentale et Générale* 71: 403–499.

Jenkins, O. P. 1887. List of fishes collected in Vigo County in 1885 and 1886. *Hoosier Naturalist* 2: 93–96.

Jennings, J. N. 1985. *Karst geomorphology*. Oxford: Basil Blackwell

Johnson, D. H., and M. D. Schwartz. 1993. The Conservation Reserve Program and grassland birds. *Conservation Biology* 7: 934–937.

Johnson, H. 1978. *A home in the woods: Pioneer life in Indiana*. Bloomington: Indiana University Press.

Johnson, S. A. 2002. Reassessment of the Allegheny woodrat (*Neotoma magister*) in Indiana. *Proceedings of the Indiana Academy of Science* 111: 56–66.

Johnson, S. A., and K. A. Berkley. 1999a. Restoring river otters in Indiana. *Wildlife Society Bulletin* 27: 419–427.

Johnson, S. A., V. Brack Jr., and R. E. Rolley. 1998. Overwinter weight loss of Indiana bats (*Myotis sodalis*) from hibernacula subject to human visitation. *American Midland Naturalist* 139: 255–261.

Johnson, S. A., and J. Choromanski-Norris. 1992. Reduction in the range of the Franklin's ground squirrel (*Spermophilus franklinii*). *American Midland Naturalist* 128: 325–331.

Jordan, D. S. 1877. On the fishes of northern Indiana. *Proceedings of the Academy of Natural Sciences at Philadelphia* 29: 42–104.

———. 1878. Catalogue of the fishes of Indiana. In *Report of the Indiana State Board of Agriculture 1877*.

———. 1890. Report of explorations made during the summer and autumn of 1888, in the Alleghany region of Virginia, North Carolina and Tennessee, and in western Indiana, with an account of the fishes found in each of the river basins of those regions. *Bulletin of the U.S. Fish Commission* 8: 97–173.

———. 1896–1900. The fishes of North and Middle America. *Bulletin of the U.S. National Museum*, no. 47.

Jordan, D. S., and H. W. Clark. 1930. Checklist of the fishes and fish-like vertebrates of North and Middle America north of the northern boundary of Venezuela and Colombia. *Report of the U.S. Commission of Fisheries* 2: 1–670.

Jordan, D. S., and B. W. Evermann. 1896. The food fishes of Indiana. *Report of the Indiana State Board of Agriculture* 28: 156–173.

Jordan, D. S., and C. H. Gilbert. 1877. Catalogue of the fishes of Indiana. *Indiana Farmer* 12(3) (January): 2.

Juberthie, C., and B. Delay. 1981. Ecological and biological implications of the existence of a superficial underground compartment. *Proceedings of the Eighth International Congress of Speleology* 1: 203–206.

Juberthie, C., B. Delay, and M. Bouillon. 1980. Extension du milieu souterrain en zone non calcaire: Description d'un nouveau milieu et de son peuplement par les coléoptères troglobies. *Mémoires Biolspéleoligique* 7: 19–52.

Keith, J. H. 1988. Distribution of the northern cavefish, *Amblyopsis spelaea* DeKay, in Indiana and Kentucky and recommendations for its protection. *Natural Areas Journal* 8(2): 69–79.

Keller, B. L., and C. J. Krebs. 1970. *Microtus* population biology: III. Reproductive changes in fluctuating populations of *M. ochrogaster* and *M. pennsylvanicus* in southern Indiana, 1965–67. *Ecological Monographs* 40: 263–294.

Keller, C. E., S. A. Keller, and T. C. Keller. 1986. *Indiana birds and their haunts*, 2nd ed. Bloomington: Indiana University Press.

Kelly, L. A. 1974. *Soil survey of Daviess County, Indiana*. USDA, Soil Conservation Service. http://soils.usda.gov.

Kenk, R. 1970. Freshwater triclads (Turbellaria) of North America: III. *Sphalloplana weingartneri*, new species, from a cave in Indiana. *Proceedings of the Biological Society of Washington* 83(29): 313–320.

Kirkpatrick, C. M. 1943. Rafinesque's bat in Indiana. *American Midland Naturalist* 29: 797.

———. 1948. Some notes on Indiana mammals. *American Midland Naturalist* 39: 128–136.

Kirkpatrick, R. D. 1961. New observations of Indiana swamp rabbits. *Journal of Mammalogy* 42: 99–100.

Klem, D., Jr. 1990. Collisions between birds and windows: Mortality and prevention. *Journal of Field Ornithology* 61: 120–128.

Klie, W. 1931. Campagne speologique de C. Bolivar et R. Jeannel dans l'Amerique du Nord (1928): 3. Crustaces ostracods. *Biospeologica: Archives de Zoologie Expérimentale et Générale* 71: 333–334.

Koelz, W. 1929. Coregonid fishes of the Great Lakes. *Bulletin of the U.S. Bureau of Fisheries* 43(pt. 2): 297–643.

Koenemann, S., and J. R. Holsinger. 2001. Systematics of the North American subterranean amphipod genus *Bactrurus* (Crangonyctidae). *Beaufortia* 51(1): 1–56.

Kohnke, H., and L. S. Robertson. 1966. Changing patterns in agriculture. Pp. 519–531 in A. A. Lindsey, ed., *Natural features of Indiana*. Indianapolis: Indiana Academy of Science.

Kolozsvary, M. B., and R. K. Swihart. 1999. Habitat fragmentation and the distribution of amphibians: Patch and landscape correlates in farmland. *Canadian Journal of Zoology* 77: 1288–1299.

Krebs, C. J., B. L. Keller, and J. H. Myers. 1971. *Microtus* population densities and soil nutrients in southern Indiana grasslands. *Ecology* 52: 660–663.

Krekeler, C. H. 1958. Speciation in cave beetles of the genus *Pseudanophthalmus* (Coleoptera, Carabidae). *American Midland Naturalist* 59(1): 167–189.

———. 1973. Cave beetles of the genus *Pseudanophthalmus* (Coleoptera, Carabidae) from the Kentucky bluegrass and vicinity. *Fieldiana Zoology* 62(4): 35–83.

Krekeler, C. H., and E. C. Williams. 1966. Cave fauna. Pp. 390–400 in A. A. Lindsey, ed., *Natural features of Indiana*. Indianapolis: Indiana Academy of Science.

Kurta, A. 1995. *Mammals of the Great Lakes region*, rev. ed. Ann Arbor: University of Michigan Press.

Lagler, K. F., and M. J. Lagler. 1942. A summer creel census for Foot's Pond, Indiana. *Investigations of Indiana Lakes and Streams* 2: 111–115.

Lannoo, M. J., ed. 1998. *Status and conservation of midwestern amphibians*. Iowa City: University of Iowa Press.

———. 2005. *Amphibian declines: The conservation status of United States species*. Berkeley: University of California Press.

Latta, W. C. 1938. *Outline history of Indiana agriculture*. West Lafayette, Ind.: Purdue University Press.

Lehman, L. E. 1982. Indiana fur harvests, 1700–1980. Pittman-Robertson Bulletin no. 13.

Leibacher, B., and J. O. Whitaker Jr. 1998. Distribution of the western harvest mouse, *Reithrodontomys megalotis*, in Indiana. *Proceedings of the Indiana Academy of Science* 107: 167–170.

Lesueur, C. A. 1827. *American ichthyology; or, Natural history of the fishes of North America, with coloured figures from drawings executed from nature*. New Harmony, Ind.

Lewis, J. J. 1982. A diagnosis of the *Hobbsi* group, with descriptions of *Caecidotea teresae*, n. sp., and *C. macropropoda* Chase and Blair (Crustacea: Isopoda: Asellidae). *Proceedings of the Biological Society of Washington* 95(2): 338–346.

———. 1983. The obligatory subterranean invertebrates of glaciated southeastern Indiana. *NSS Bulletin* 45: 34–40.

———. 1988. The systematic, zoogeography and life history of the troglobitic isopods of the interior plateaus of the eastern United States. Ph.D. diss., Department of Biology, University of Louisville.

———. 1994. *Lost River cave and karst biological survey*. Final Report, U.S. Army Corps of Engineers, Louisville District (DACW27-94-M-0110).

———. 1995. *Inventory of the troglobitic fauna of the Crosley State Fish and Wildlife Area, Jennings County, Indiana*. Special Project of the Nongame and Endangered Wildlife Program, Indiana Department of Natural Resources.

———. 1996a. The devastation and recovery of caves and karst affected by industrialization. Pp. 214–227 in *Proceedings of the 1995 National Cave Management Symposium*. Mitchell, Ind.

———. 1996b. *Inventory of the subterranean biota threatened by the urbanization of Clark and Floyd counties, Indiana*. Final Report, Nongame and Endangered Wildlife Program, Indiana Department of Natural Resources.

———. 1996c. Cave bioinventory as a management tool. Pp. 228–236 in *Proceedings of the 1995 National Cave Management Symposium*. Mitchell, Ind.

———. 1998. *The subterranean fauna of the Blue River area*. Final Report, Nature Conservancy, Indianapolis.

———. 2000a. Five new species of *Pseudotremia* from caves in the Blue River area of southern Indiana (Diplopoda: Chordeumatida: Cleidogonidae). *Myriapodologica* 6(6): 55–68.

———. 2000b. *Scoterpes sollmani*, a new species of subterranean milliped from the Blue River basin of southern Indiana (Diplopoda: Chordeumatida: Trichopetalidae). *Myriapodologica* 6(13): 115–120.

———. 2003. *Pseudotremia reynoldsae*, a new species of troglobitic millipede (Diplopoda: Chordeumatida: Cleidogonidae), with a synopsis of the cavernicolous millipeds of the Hoosier National Forest in Indiana. *Proceedings of the Indiana Academy of Science* 112(1): 36–42.

Lewis, J. J., and T. E. Bowman. 1981. The subterranean asellids (*Caecidotea*) of Illinois (Crustacea: Isopoda: Asellidae). *Smithsonian Contributions to Zoology* 335: 1–66.

Lewis, J. J., R. Burns, and S. Lewis. 2004. *The subterranean fauna of the Hoosier National Forest*. Final report, Hoosier National Forest, U.S. Department of Agriculture, Forest Service.

Lewis, J. J., and S. T. Lewis. 2002. *The subterranean fauna of the Big Oaks National Wildlife Refuge*. U.S. Department of the Interior, Fish and Wildlife Service, Indiana Department of Natural Resources, Natural Heritage Program.

Lewis, J. J., and T. P. Sollman. 1998. *Groundwater monitoring in significant aquatic caves that lie beneath impending residential developments in the Blue River basin of southern Indiana*. Final report, Ohio River Valley Ecosystem, U.S. Fish and Wildlife Service and Indiana Karst Conservancy.

Lindley, H., ed. 1916. *Indiana as seen by early travelers: A collection of reprints from books of travel, letters and diaries prior to 1830.* Indianapolis: Indiana Historical Commission.

Lindsay, D. M. 1956a. Additional records of *Nycticeius* in Indiana. *Journal of Mammalogy* 37: 282.

———. 1956b. Some bat records from southeastern Indiana. *Journal of Mammalogy* 37: 543–545.

———. 1960. Mammals of Ripley and Jefferson counties, Indiana. *Journal of Mammalogy* 41: 253–262.

Lindsey, A. A. 1961. Vegetation of the drainage-aeration classes of northern Indiana soils in 1830. *Ecology* 42: 432–436.

———. 1962. Analysis of an original forest of the lower Wabash floodplain and upland. *Proceedings of the Indiana Academy of Science* 72: 282–287.

———. 1973. Tornado tracks in the presettlement forests of Indiana. *Proceedings of the Indiana Academy of Science* 82: 181.

Lindsey, A. A., ed. 1966. *Natural features of Indiana.* Indianapolis: Indiana Academy of Science.

Lindsey, A. A., W. B. Crankshaw, and S. A. Qadir. 1965. Soil relations and distribution map of the vegetation of presettlement Indiana. *Botanical Gazette* 126: 155–163.

Lindsey, A. A., R. O. Petty, D. K. Sterling, and W. Van Asdall. 1961. Vegetation and environment along the Wabash and Tippecanoe rivers. *Ecological Monographs* 31: 105–156.

Lindsey, A. A., D. V. Schmelz, and S. A. Nichols. 1969. *Natural areas in Indiana and their preservation: Indiana natural areas survey.* West Lafayette, Ind.: Purdue University Press.

Littell, C. G. 1902. The birds of Winona Lake. *Proceedings of the Indiana Academy of Science* 10: 134–158.

LoGiudice, K. 2006. Toward a synthetic view of extinction: A history lesson from a North American rodent. *BioScience* 56: 687–693.Lyon, M. W., Jr. 1923. Notes on the mammals of the dune region of Porter County, Indiana. *Proceedings of the Indiana Academy of Science* 31: 209–221.

———. 1936. Mammals of Indiana. *American Midland Naturalist* 17: 1–384.

———. 1942. Additions to the mammals of Indiana. *American Midland Naturalist* 27: 790–791.

Madej, R. F. 1994. *Aneides aeneus* (green salamander). *Herpetological Review* 25: 31.

Malott, C. A. 1922. The physiography of Indiana. Pp. 59–256 in *Handbook of Indiana geology,* pt. 2. Indiana Department of Conservation Publication 21.

———. 1932. Lost River at Wesley Chapel Gulf, Orange County, Indiana. *Proceedings of the Indiana Academy of Science* 41: 285–316.

———. 1945. Significant features of the Indiana karst. *Proceedings of the Indiana Academy of Science* 54: 8–24.

Marquis, R. J., and C. J. Whelan. 1994. Insectivorous birds increase growth of white oak through consumption of leaf-chewing insects. *Ecology* 75: 2007–2014.

Marsh, C. 2006. Monk parakeet: First state breeding records and expansion into northwest Indiana. *Indiana Audubon Quarterly* 84: 1–6.

Marshall, S. A., and S. B. Peck. 1985. The origin and relationships of *Spelobia tenebrarum* Aldrich, a troglobitic, eastern North American sphaerocerid fly. *Canadian Entomologist* 117: 1013–1015.

Maxwell, R. H., and W. E. Thomas. 2003. Distribution records of southern Indiana vascular plants. *Proceedings of the Indiana Academy of Science* 112: 22–28.

McCarter, P. 1982. *Soil survey of Clay County, Indiana.* USDA, Soil Conservation Service. http://soils.usda.gov.

McCord, S. S. 1970. *Travel accounts of Indiana 1679–1961.* Indianapolis: Indiana Library and Historical Board.

McKinley, D. 1976. The Carolina parakeet in Indiana. *Indiana Audubon Quarterly* 54: 97–107.

———. 1980. The balance of decimating factors and recruitment in extinction of the Carolina parakeet. *Indiana Audubon Quarterly* 58(1): 8–18; (2): 50–61; (3) 103–114.

McNeill, J. 1887. Descriptions of twelve new species of Myriapoda, chiefly from Indiana. *Proceedings of the U.S. National Museum* 10: 328–334.

McPherson, A. 2000. *Paddle Indiana: An access guide to canoeing and kayaking Indiana's lakes and streams.* Bloomington, Ind.: J. L. Waters.

Meek, S. E. 1908. List of fishes known to occur in the waters of Indiana. Pp. 134–171 in *Biennial report, Indiana Commission of Fish and Game 1907–1908.*

Meek, S. E., and S. F. Hildebrand. 1910. A synoptic list of the fishes known to occur within fifty miles of Chicago. Field Museum of Natural History, zoological series, 7(9): 223–338.

Miller, G. S., Jr., and G. M. Allen. 1928. The American bats of the genera *Myotis* and *Pizonyx. Bulletin of the U.S. National Museum,* no. 144.

Milner, J. W. 1874. Report on fisheries of the Great Lakes: The results of inquiries prosecuted in 1871 and 1872. Supplementary paper in U.S. Commission of Fish and Fisheries, *Report of the Commissioner for 1872 and 1873.*

Minton, S. A. 2001. *Amphibians and reptiles of Indiana,* 2nd ed. Indianapolis: Indiana Academy of Science.

Moenkhaus, W. J. 1896. Notes on a collection of fishes of Dubois County, Indiana. *Proceedings of the Indiana Academy of Science* 11: 159–162.

Montgomery, R. H. 1974. *Soil survey of Vigo County, Indiana.* USDA, Soil Conservation Service. http://soils.usda.gov.

Moore, M. C. 1992. Stratigraphy and lithology of the karst-bearing units. Pp. 11–13 in G. T. Rea, ed., *Caving in the heartland.* Huntsville, Ala.: National Speleological Society.

Morgan, F. 1968. Effects of effluent on the fish population of Mill Creek, Rochester, Indiana. *Proceedings of the Indiana Academy of Science* 78: 202.

Muchmore, W. B. 1967. New cave pseudoscorpions of the genus *Apochthonius* (Arachnida: Chelonethida). *Ohio Journal of Science* 67(2): 89–95.

———. 1994. Some pseudoscorpions (Arachnida: Pseudoscorpionida) from caves in Ohio and Indiana, U.S.A. *Transactions of the American Microscopical Society* 113(3): 316–324.

———. 2000. New species and records of *Kleptochthonius* from Indiana (Pseudoscorpionida, Chthoniidae). *Journal of Arachnology* 28: 293–299.

Mumford, R. E. 1953. Status of *Nycticeius humeralis* in Indiana. *Journal of Mammalogy* 34: 121–122.

———. 1964. Distribution and status of the Chiroptera of Indiana. *American Midland Naturalist* 72: 473–489.

———. 1969. *Distribution of the mammals of Indiana.* Indianapolis: Indiana Academy of Science.

Mumford, R. E., and C. O. Handley Jr. 1956. Notes on the mammals of Jackson County, Indiana. *Journal of Mammalogy* 37: 407–412.

Mumford, R. E., and C. E. Keller. 1984. *The birds of Indiana.* Bloomington: Indiana University Press.

Mumford, R. E., and C. L. Rippy. 1963. The southeastern shrew (*Sorex longirostris*) in Indiana. *Proceedings of the Indiana Academy of Science* 72: 340–341.

Munson, P. J., and C. A. Munson. 1990. The prehistoric and early historic archaeology of Wyandotte Cave and other caves in southern Indiana. *Indiana Historical Society,* prehistory research series 7(1): 1–101.

Murray, C. 2005. The Burn. *Online Birding Guide.* http://www.indianaaudubon.org/guide/sites/theburn.htm.

Myers, E. 1997. An endangered natural resource: Wetlands. Pp. 67–76 in M. T. Jackson, ed., *The natural heritage of Indiana.* Bloomington: Indiana University Press.

Nagel, B. G. 1998. *Soil survey of Scott County, Indiana.* Natural Resources Conservation Service. http://soils.usda.gov.

Nagel, B. G., and D. L. Marshall. 2007. *Soil survey of Clark County, Indiana.* Natural Resources Conservation Service. http://soils.usda.gov.

National Cartography and Geospatial Center. 1995. *State soil geographic database (STATSGO).* http://www.ncgc.nrcs.usda.gov/branch/ssb/products/statsgo.

National Cooperative Soil Survey. 2005a. *Wawasee soil series.* http://ortho.ftw.nrcs.usda.gov/osd/dat/W/WAWASEE.html.

———. 2005b. *Kalamazoo soil series.* http://lter.kbs.msu.edu/Soil/Characterization/KalamazooCached.htm.

National Land Cover Data. 1992. U.S. Environmental Protection Agency. www.epa.gov/mrlc/nlcd.html.

National Wetlands Inventory. 1997. http://www.fws.gov/wetlands.

Natural Resources Conservation Service. 1998. *Soil survey of Scott County, Indiana.* USDA, Soil Conservation Service. http://soils.usda.gov.

———. 2002. *Soil survey of Elkhart County, Indiana.* USDA, Soil Conservation Service. http://soils.usda.gov.

———. 2003. *Soil survey of Pulaski County, Indiana.* USDA, Soil Conservation Service. http://soils.usda.gov.

Neely, T. 1987. *Soil survey of Randolph County, Indiana.* USDA, Soil Conservation Service. http://soils.usda.gov.

Nicholas, Brother G. 1960. Checklist of the macroscopic troglobitic organisms of the United States. *American Midland Naturalist* 64(1): 123–160.

Nichols, D. A. 2008. A commercial embassy in the old Northwest: The U.S. Indian trading factory at Fort Wayne, 1803–1812. *Ohio Valley History* 8(4): 1–16.

Nickell, A. K. 1987. *Soil survey of Switzerland County, Indiana.* USDA, Soil Conservation Service. http://soils.usda.gov.

Nieuwland, J. A., and T. Just. 1931. New and interesting plant records from northern Indiana. *American Midland Naturalist* 12: 217–223.

Nolan, V., Jr. 1978. *The ecology and behavior of the prairie warbler Dendroica discolor.* Ornithological Monographs, no. 26. American Ornithologists' Union.

Northwest Ohio Soil Survey. 2005. *Spinks soil series.* http://www2.wcoil.com/~rfrobb/spinks2.html.

Nupp, T. E., and R. K. Swihart. 2001. Assessing competition between forest rodents in a fragmented landscape of midwestern USA. *Mammalian Biology* 66: 345–356.

Nuzzo, V. A. 1986. Extent and status of Midwest oak savanna: Presettlement and 1985. *Natural Areas Journal* 6: 6–36.

Omernik, J. M., and A. L. Gallant. 1988. *Ecoregions of the upper Midwest states.* Corvallis, Ore.: U.S. Environmental Protection Agency (EPA/600/3-88/037).

Overlease, W., and E. Overlease. 2007. *100 years of change in the distribution of common Indiana weeds.* West Lafayette, Ind.: Purdue University Press.

Packard, A. S. 1873. On the cave fauna of Indiana. Pp. 93–97 in *Fifth annual report of the Peabody Academy of Science.* Boston: Peabody Academy of Science.

Packard, A. S., ed. 1888. The cave fauna of North America, with remarks on the anatomy of the brain and origin of the blind species. *Memoirs of the National Academy of Sciences* 4: 1–156.

Palmer, A. N. 1992. The south-central karst area of Indiana: An introduction. P. 2 in G. T. Rea, ed., *Caving in the heartland.* Huntsville, Ala.: National Speleological Society.

Pancol, S. 2005. Summit Lake State Park. *Online Birding Guide.* http://www.indianaaudubon.org/guide/sites/summitlk.htm.

Park, O. 1960. Cavernicolous pselaphid beetles of the United States. *American Midland Naturalist* 64(1): 66–104.

Parker, A. R., and J. S. Castrale. 1996. Nesting by barn owls in Indiana. *Proceedings of the Indiana Academy of Science* 105: 21–28.

Parker, G. R. 1997. The wave of settlement. Pp. 369–381 in M. T. Jackson, ed., *The natural heritage of Indiana.* Bloomington: Indiana University Press.

Pearson, J. 2001. *Cisco population status and management in Indiana.* Columbia City: Indiana Division of Fish and Wildlife.

Pearson, W. D., and C. H. Boston. 1995. Distribution and status of the northern cavefish, *Amblyopsis spelaea.* Final report, Nongame and Endangered Wildlife Program, Indiana Department of Natural Resources.

Peattie, D. C. 1930. *Flora of the Indiana dunes.* Chicago: Field Museum of Natural History.

Peck, S. B., and J. J. Lewis. 1978. Zoogeography and evolution of the subterranean invertebrate fauna of Illinois and southeastern Missouri. *NSS Bulletin* 40: 39–63.

Pennak, R. W. 1950. Comparative ecology of the interstitial fauna of freshwater and marine beaches. *Annales Biology* 27(6): 449–480.

Pennak, R. W., and J. V. Ward. 1986. Interstitial fauna communities of the hyporheic and adjacent groundwater biotopes of a Colorado mountain range. *Archives Hydrobiology Supplement* 74(3): 356–396.

Pepoon, H. S. 1927. *An annotated flora of the Chicago area.* Chicago: Chicago Academy of Sciences.

Petranka, J. W. 1998. *Salamanders of the United States and Canada.* Washington, D.C.: Smithsonian Institution Press.

Petty, R. O., and M. T. Jackson. 1966. Plant communities. Pp. 264–296 in A. A. Lindsey, ed., *Natural features of Indiana*. Indianapolis: Indiana Academy of Science.

Porter, E. E., J. Bulluck, and R. B. Blair. 2005. Multiple spatial-scale assessment of the conservation value of golf courses for breeding birds in southwestern Ohio. *Wildlife Society Bulletin* 33: 494–506.

Potzger, J. E. 1934. A notable case of bog formation. *American Midland Naturalist* 15: 567–580.

Potzger, J. E., M. E. Potzger, and J. McCormick. 1956. The forest primeval of Indiana as recorded in the original U.S. Land Survey and an evaluation of previous interpretations of Indiana vegetation. *Butler University Botanical Studies* 13: 95–111.

Powell, R. L. 1959. Limestone caverns and natural bridges of southeastern Indiana. *Bloomington Indiana Grotto Newsletter* 2(1): 1–7.

———. 1961. *Caves of Indiana.* Indiana Geologic Survey, circular 8.

———. 1992. Physiography and development of the south-central karst. Pp. 2–9 in G. T. Rea, ed., *Caving in the heartland.* Huntsville, Ala.: National Speleological Society.

Protas, M. E., C. Hersey, D. Kochanek, Y. Zhou, H. Wilkens, W. R. Jeffery, L. I. Zon, R. Borowsky, and C. Tabin. 2006. Genetic analysis of cavefish reveals molecular convergence in the evolution of albinism. *Nature Genetics* 38: 107–111.

Qadir, S. A. 1964. A study of edaphic controls of tree species in presettlement forests of northern Indiana. Ph.D. diss., Department of Biological Sciences, Purdue University.

Racovitza, E. G. 1907. Essai sur les problemes biospeologiques. *Archives Zoologie Experimentale et Generale* (Biospeologica I), ser. 43, 6: 371–488.

Rafinesque, C. S. 1820. *Ichthyologia Ohioensis, or, Natural history of the fishes inhabiting the River Ohio and its tributary streams.* Cleveland, Ohio: Burrows, 1899.

Rand, A. L., and A. S. Rand. 1951. Mammal bones from dunes south of Lake Michigan. *American Midland Naturalist* 46: 649–659.

Reid, J. W. 2004. New records and new species of the genus *Diacyclops* (Crustacea: Copepoda) from subterranean habitats in southern Indiana, USA. *Jeffersoniana* 12: 65.

Reid, J. W., D. L. Strayer, J. V. McArthur, S. E. Stibbe, and J. J. Lewis. 1999. *Rheocyclops,* a new genus of copepods from the southeastern and central U.S.A. (Copepoda: Cyclopoida: Cyclopidae). *Journal of Crustacean Biology* 19(2): 384–396.

Richards, R. L. 1990. Quaternary distribution of the timber rattlesnake (*Crotalus horridus*) in southern Indiana. *Proceedings of the Indiana Academy of Science* 99(1): 113–122.

Richards, R. L., and J. N. McDonald. 1991. New records of Harlan's muskox (*Bootherium bombifrons*) and an associated fauna from the late Pleistocene of Indiana. *Proceedings of the Indiana Academy of Science* 99: 211–228.

Richards, R. L., and J. O. Whitaker Jr. 1997. Indiana's vertebrate fauna: Origins and change. Pp. 144–156 in M. T. Jackson, ed., *The natural heritage of Indiana*. Bloomington: Indiana University Press.

Richter, A. R., D. A. Seerley, J. B. Cope, and J. H. Keith. 1978. A newly discovered concentration of hibernating Indiana bats, *Myotis sodalis,* in southern Indiana. *Journal of Mammalogy* 59: 191.

Ricketts, T. H., E. Dinerstein, D. M. Olson, et al. 1999. *Terrestrial ecoregions of North America: A conservation assessment.* Washington, D.C.: Island.

Ridgway, R. 1872a. Notes on the vegetation of the lower Wabash Valley. *American Naturalist* 6: 658–665.

———. 1872b. Notes on the vegetation of the lower Wabash Valley: II. Peculiar features of the bottomlands. *American Naturalist* 6: 724–732.

Robinson, S. K., F. Thompson, T. Donovan, D. Whitehead, and J. Faaborg. 1995. Regional forest fragmentation and the nesting success of migratory birds. *Science* 267(5206): 1987–1990.

Robinson, W. D. 1996. *Southern Illinois birds: An annotated list and site guide.* Carbondale: Southern Illinois University Press.

Rodewald, P. G., M. J. Santiago, and A. D. Rodewald. 2005. Habitat use of breeding red-headed woodpeckers on golf courses in Ohio. *Wildlife Society Bulletin* 33: 448–453.

Roth, T. C., and S. L. Lima. 2003. Hunting behavior and diet of Cooper's hawks: An urban view of the small-bird-in-winter paradigm. *Condor* 105: 478–483.

Rothrock, P. E. 2004. *Floristic quality assessment in Indiana: The concept, use, and development of coefficients of conservatism.* Final Report for ARN A305-4-53, EPA Wetland Program Development Grant CD975586-01. http://www.ingov/idem/water/planbr/401/publications.html.

Rothrock, P. E., H. Starcs, R. Dunbar, and R. L. Hedge. 1993. The vascular flora of Mounds State Park, Madison County, Indiana. *Proceedings of the Indiana Academy of Science* 102: 161–199.

Ruch, D. G., B. G. Torke, C. R. Reidy, K. S. Badger, and P. E. Rothrock. 2002. The flora and vegetational communities of Wilbur Wright Fish and Wildlife Area, Henry County, Indiana. *Proceedings of the Indiana Academy of Science* 111: 147–176.

Schiner, J. R. 1854. Fauna der Adelsberger-Luegr: Und Magdalenen Grotte. Pp. 231–272 in A. Schmidt, ed., *Die Grotten und Hohlen von Adelsberg, Lueg, Planina und Loos.* Vienna: Braumuller. Cited in Racovitza (1907).

Schmelz, D. V., and A. A. Lindsey. 1970. Relationships among the forest types of Indiana. *Ecology* 51: 620–629.

Schmidt, T. L., M. H. Hansen, and J. A. Solomakos. 2000. *Indiana's forests in 1998*. St. Paul, Minn.: U.S. Department of Agriculture, Forest Service, North Central Research Station. Resource Bulletin NC-196.

Schneck, J. 1876. Catalogue of the flora of the Wabash Valley below the mouth of White River, and observations thereon. Pp. 504–579 in *Seventh annual report of the Geological Survey of Indiana*, vol. 7.

Schreber, J. C. D. 1842. Die Säugthiere in Abbildungen nach der Natur, mit Beschreibunger von dr. Johann Andreas Wagner. *Supplementband* 3: 359.

Scott, P. E., T. L. DeVault, R. A. Bajema, and S. L. Lima. 2002. Grassland vegetation and bird abundances on reclaimed midwestern coal mines. *Wildlife Society Bulletin* 30: 1006–1014.

Seegert, G. 1987. *Distribution of fishes in the Kankakee River basin of Indiana*. Final Report to the Nongame and Endangered Wildlife Program, Division of Fish and Wildlife, Indiana Department of Natural Resources.

Sever, D. M., and D. Duff. 1985. Survey of the fishes of the Kingsbury State Fish and Wildlife Area, LaPorte County, Indiana. *Proceedings of the Indiana Academy of Science* 94: 673–679.

Shannon, W. P. 1887. *A list of fishes of Decatur County, Indiana: The fishes inhabiting Clifty Creek within the borders of Decatur County*. Greensburg, Ind.

Shear, W. A. 1972. Studies in the milliped order Chordeumida (Diplopoda): A revision of the family Cleidogonidae and a reclassification of the order Chordeumida in the New World. *Bulletin of the Museum of Comparative Zoology* 144: 151–352.

Shear, W. A., J. J. Lewis, and M. Farfan. 2007. Diplopoda, Chordeumatida, Cleidogonidae, *Pseudotremia salisae* Lewis: Distribution extension north of the Ohio River in Ohio and Illinois, U.S.A. *Check List 2007* 3(1): 67–69.

Sheldon, R. 1997. *Jefferson Proving Ground karst study*. Report to Jefferson Proving Ground.

Shelford, V. E. 1912. Ecological succession: IV. Vegetation and control of land animal communities. *Biological Bulletin* 23: 59–99.

Shire, G. G., K. Brown, and G. Winegrad. 2000. Communication towers: A deadly hazard to birds. *American Bird Conservancy*. http://www.abcbirds.org/newsandreports/towerkillweb.PDF.

Shoemaker, H. H. 1942. The fishes of Wayne County, Indiana. *Investigations of Indiana Lakes and Streams* 2(14): 268–296.

Simon, T. P. 1991. *Development of index of biotic integrity expectations for the ecoregions of Indiana: I. Central corn belt plain*. Chicago: U.S. Environmental Protection Agency (EPA 905/9-91/025).

———. 1992a. *Biological criteria development for large rivers with an emphasis on an assessment of the White River drainage, Indiana*. Chicago: U.S. Environmental Protection Agency (EPA 905/R-92/006).

———. 1992b. New ichthyofaunal records for the Calumet, Kankakee, and Iroquois drainages of Indiana. *Proceedings of the Indiana Academy of Science* 101: 279–291.

———. 1993a. Assessment of the range of the threatened eastern sand darter *Ammocrypta pellucida* (Putnam) in the Maumee River drainage, Indiana. *Proceedings of the Indiana Academy of Science* 102: 139–145.

———. 1993b. *An assessment of remaining populations of the endangered harlequin darter, Etheostoma histrio Jordan, in the White River drainage*. Indianapolis: Indiana Department of Natural Resources Nongame Grants Program.

———. 1994. *Development of index of biotic integrity expectations for the ecoregions of Indiana: II. Huron-Erie lake plain*. Chicago: U.S. Environmental Protection Agency (EPA 905/R-92/007).

———. 1998. Development of fish community reference conditions for dunal, palustrine wetlands along the southern shore of Lake Michigan. *Aquatic Ecosystem Health and Management* 1: 57–70.

———. 2000. *Survey of rare Indiana fishes including the longnose dace Rhinichthys cataractae (Valenciennes), slimy sculpin Cottus cognatus Richardson, trout-perch Percopsis omiscomaycus (Walbaum), and longnose sucker Catostomus catostomus (Forster) in the nearshore zone of Lake Michigan*. Indianapolis: Indiana Department of Natural Resources, Division of Fish and Wildlife, Nongame Grants Program.

———. 2003. *Evaluation of fish assemblages in the fish kill zone: Muncie to Indianapolis*. Bloomington, Ind.: U.S. Fish and Wildlife Service.

Simon, T. P., G. Bright, F. Veraldi, J. R. Smith, and J. R. Stahl. 2006. New records for the alien oriental weatherfish, *Misgurnus anguillicaudatus*, in the Lake Michigan basin, Indiana (Cypriniformes: Cobitidae). *Proceedings of the Indiana Academy of Science* 115(1): 32–36.

Simon, T. P., and R. L. Dufour. 1998. Development of index of biotic integrity expectations for the ecoregions of Indiana: V. Eastern corn belt plain. Chicago: U.S. Environmental Protection Agency (EPA 905/R-96/003).

Simon, T. P., R. L. Dufour, and B. E. Fisher. 2005. Changes in the biological integrity of fish assemblages in the Patoka River drainage as a result of anthropogenic disturbance from 1888 to 2001. Pp. 383–398 in J. N. Rinne, R. M. Hughes, and B. Calamusso, eds., *Historical changes in large river fish assemblages of the Americas*. Bethesda, Md.: American Fisheries Society.

Simon, T. P., R. Jankowski, and C. Morris. 2000. Modification of an index of biotic integrity for vernal ponds and small palustrine wetlands using amphibians, crayfish, and fish assemblages along southern Lake Michigan. *Aquatic Ecosystem Health and Management* 3: 407–418.

Simon, T. P., and A. Kiley. 1993. Rediscovery of the endangered harlequin darter, *Etheostoma histrio* Jordan and Gilbert, in the White River drainage, Indiana. *Proceedings of the Indiana Academy of Science* 102: 279–281.

Simon, T. P., P. B. Moy, and D. Barnes. 1998. New faunal records for exotic fish species in the southern Lake Michigan drainage, Indiana. *Proceedings of the Indiana Academy of Science* 107: 61–70.

Simon, T. P., S. A. Sobiech, T. H. Cervone, and N. E. Morales. 1995. Historical and present distribution of fishes in the Patoka River drainage: Pike, Gibson, and Dubois counties, Indiana. *Proceedings of the Indiana Academy of Science* 104: 193–206.

Simon, T. P., and J. R. Stahl. 1998. Development of index of biotic integrity expectations for the Wabash River. Chicago: U.S. Environmental Protection Agency (EPA 905/R-96/005).

Simon, T. P., and P. M. Stewart. 1998. Validation of an index of biotic integrity for evaluating dunal palustrine wetlands with emphasis on the Grand Calumet lagoons. *Aquatic Ecosystem Health and Management* 1: 71–82.

———. 1999. Structure and function of fish communities in the southern Lake Michigan basin with emphasis on restoration of native fish communities. *Natural Areas Journal* 19: 142–154.

———. 2006. *Coastal wetlands of the Laurentian Great Lakes: Health, habitat, and indicators.* Bloomington, Ind.: AuthorHouse.

Simon, T. P., J. O. Whitaker Jr., J. S. Castrale, and S. A. Minton. 1992. Checklist of the vertebrates of Indiana. *Proceedings of the Indiana Academy of Science* 101: 95–126.

———. 2002. Revised checklist of the vertebrates of Indiana. *Proceedings of the Indiana Academy of Science* 111: 182–214.

Skinner, A. A., and R. M. Lehtinen. 2006. The enigmatic decline of Blanchard's cricket frog (*Acris crepitans blanchardi*): A test of the habitat acidification hypothesis. *Copeia* 2006: 159–167.

Smith, S. I. 1888. *Crangonyx packardi.* Pp. 35–36 in A. S. Packard, ed., The cave fauna of North America, with remarks on the anatomy of the brain and origin of the blind species. *Memoirs of the National Academy of Sciences* 4.

Snyder, N. F. R., and K. Russell. 1998. Carolina parakeet (*Conuropsis carolinensis*). In A. Poole and F. Gill, eds., *The birds of North America.* Philadelphia, Pa.: Birds of North America.

Soil Survey Staff. 1999. *Soil Taxonomy: A basic system of soil classification for making and interpreting soil surveys,* 2nd ed. Washington, D.C.: U.S. Government Printing Office.

Spetich, M. A., G. R. Parker, and E. J. Gustafson. 1997. Spatial and temporal relationships of old-growth and secondary forests in Indiana. *Natural Areas Journal* 17: 118–130.

Stewart, P. M., and J. T. Butcher. 1996. *Ecology of the great marsh, Indiana Dunes National Lakeshore.* Porter, Ind.: National Park Service, Indiana Dunes National Lakeshore.

Swain, J. 1883. A description of a new species of *Hadropterus* (*Hadropterus scierus*) from southern Indiana. *Proceedings of the U.S. National Museum* 6: 252.

Swinehart, A. L., and G. R. Parker. 2001. The structure and composition of vegetation in the lake-fill peatlands of Indiana. *Proceedings of the Indiana Academy of Science* 110: 51–78.

Swink, F., and G. Wilhelm. 1994. *Plants of the Chicago region,* 4th ed. Indianapolis: Indiana Academy of Science.

Taylor, R. M., Jr., E. W. Stevens, M. A. Ponder, and P. Brockman. 1989. *Indiana: A new historical guide.* Indianapolis: Indiana Historical Society.

Temple, S. A. 1998. Surviving where ecosystems meet: Ecotonal animal communities of midwestern oak savannas and woodlands. *Transactions of the Wisconsin Academy of Sciences, Arts and Letters* 86: 207–222.

Terrel, T. L. 1972. The swamp rabbit (*Sylvilagus aquaticus*) in Indiana. *American Midland Naturalist* 87: 283–295.

Thienemann, R. 1925. *Die Binnengewasser Mitteleuropas,* vol. 1. Stuttgart.

Thomas, D. 1819. Travels through the western country in the summer of 1816. Reprinted in H. Lindley, ed., *Indiana as seen by early travelers: A collection of reprints from books of travel, letters and diaries prior to 1830.* Indianapolis: Indiana Historical Commission, 1916.

Thompson, F. R., III, ed. 2004. *The Hoosier-Shawnee ecological assessment.* USDA, Forest Service. North Central Research Station General Tech Report NC-244.

Timm, A., and V. Meretsky. 2004. Anuran habitat use on abandoned and reclaimed mining areas of southwestern Indiana. *Proceedings of the Indiana Academy of Science* 113(2): 140–146.

Tormoehlen, B., J. Gallion, and T. L. Schmidt. 2000. *Forests of Indiana: A 1998 overview.* USDA, Forest Service (NA-TP-03-00).

Trautman, M. B. 1981. *The fishes of Ohio.* Columbus: Ohio State University Press.

Treater, W. M., and W. B. Walker. 2001. *Soil survey of Marshall County, Illinois.* USDA, Natural Resources Conservation Service. http://soils.usda.gov.

True, F. W. 1896. A revision of the American moles. *Proceedings of the U.S. National Museum* 19: 1–112.

U.S. Census Bureau. 1900. *Twelfth census of the United States.* http://www.census.gov/prod/www/abs/decennial/1900.html.

U.S. Department of Agriculture. 1981. *Land resource regions and major land resource areas of the United States.* Washington, D.C.: U.S. Government Printing Office.

———. 2002. *Indiana state and county data: Census of agriculture* (National Agricultural Statistics Service, AC-02-A-14).

———. 2005. *Web soil survey.* http://websoilsurvey.nrcs.usda.gov.

U.S. Fish and Wildlife Service. 2006. *Service approves plan from NIPSCO and IAWC to conserve endangered Karner blue butterfly.* www.fws.gov/midwest/News/Release06-25.html.

U.S. Geological Survey. 2006. *North American breeding bird survey: Route level analysis of land cover, bird abundance, and population change.* http://www.mbr-pwrc.usgs.gov/cgi-bin/rtena04a.pl?35.

Vandel, A. 1965. Les *Trichoniscidae cavernicoles* (Isopoda Terrestria: Crustacea) de l'Amérique du Nord. *Annales de Spéléologie* 20(3): 347–389.

Van Kley, J. E., and G. R. Parker. 1993. An ecological classification system for the central hardwoods region: The Hoosier National Forest. Pp. 308–326 in *Proceedings, Ninth Central Hardwood Forest Conference.* USDA, Forest Service. North Central Forest Experiment Station General Technical Report NC-161.

Veilleux, J. P., J. O. Whitaker Jr., and E. A. Vincent. 1998. Mammals of the Newport chemical depot, Vermillion County, Indiana. *Proceedings of the Indiana Academy of Science* 107: 91–104.

Vetter, W. E. 2004. Determinants of marshbird occurrence in reclaimed coal mines. M.S. thesis, Department of Ecology and Organismal Biology, Indiana State University.

Vickery, P. D., and J. R. Herkert. 2001. Recent advances in grassland bird research: Where do we go from here? *Auk* 118: 11–15.

Voss, E. G. 1972. *Michigan flora: Part 1. Gymnosperms and monocots.* Ann Arbor: Cranbrook Institute of Science and University of Michigan Herbarium.

Walk, J. W., and R. E. Warner. 1999. Effects of habitat area on the occurrence of grassland birds in Illinois. *American Midland Naturalist* 141: 339–344.

———. 2000. Grassland management for the conservation of songbirds in the midwestern USA. *Biological Conservation* 94: 165–172.

Warner, R. E. 1993. Agricultural land use and grassland habitat in Illinois: Future shock for midwestern birds? *Conservation Biology* 8: 147–156.

Watson, P. J. 1974. Wyandotte Cave. In P. J. Watson, ed., *Archaeology of the Mammoth Cave area.* St. Louis, Mo.: Cave.

Webster, J. D. 1998. Biogeographic analysis of breeding bird distribution in Indiana. Pp. 21–24 in J. C. Castrale, E. M. Hopkins, and C. E. Keller, eds., *Atlas of breeding birds of Indiana.* Indianapolis: Indiana Department of Natural Resources.

Whicker, J. W. 1916. *Historical sketches of the Wabash Valley.* Attica, Ind.: Privately published.

Whitaker, J. O., Jr. 1967. Habitat and reproduction of some of the small mammals of Vigo County, Indiana, with a list of mammals known to occur there. C. C. Adams Center for Ecological Studies, Western Michigan University, Occasional Papers no. 16.

———. 1976. Fish community changes at one Vigo County, Indiana, locality over a twelve year period. *Proceedings of the Indiana Academy of Science* 85: 191–207.

Whitaker, J. O., Jr., and B. Abrell. 1986. The swamp rabbit, *Sylvilagus aquaticus,* in Indiana, 1984–85. *Proceedings of the Indiana Academy of Science* 95: 563–570.

Whitaker, J. O., Jr., V. Brack Jr., and J. B. Cope. 2002. Are bats in Indiana declining? *Proceedings of the Indiana Academy of Science* 111: 95–106.

Whitaker, J. O., Jr., and J. R. Gammon. 1988. *Endangered and threatened vertebrate animals of Indiana: Their distribution and abundance.* Indianapolis: Indiana Academy of Science.

Whitaker, J. O., Jr., J. Gibble and E. Kjellmark. 1994. *Mammals of Indiana Dunes National Lakeshore.* U.S. Department of the Interior, National Park Service.

Whitaker, J. O., Jr., and S. L. Gummer. 2001. Bats of the Wabash and Ohio river basins of southwestern Indiana. *Proceedings of the Indiana Academy of Science* 110: 126–140.

———. 2003. Birds of the Brazil sewage lagoons, Clay County, Indiana. *Indiana Audubon Quarterly* 81: 226–232.

Whitaker, J. O., Jr., and W. J. Hamilton Jr. 1998. *Mammals of the eastern United States.* Ithaca, N.Y.: Cornell University Press.

Whitaker, J. O., Jr., and R. E. Mumford. 1972. Ecological studies of *Reithrodontomys megalotis* in Indiana. *Journal of Mammalogy* 53: 850–860.

———. 2008. *Mammals of Indiana.* Bloomington: Indiana University Press.

Whitaker, J. O., Jr., and L. J. Rissler. 1992a. Seasonal activity of bats at Copperhead Cave. *Proceedings of the Indiana Academy of Science* 101: 127–134.

———. 1992b. Winter activity of bats at a mine entrance in Vermillion County, Indiana. *American Midland Naturalist* 127: 52–59.

———. 1993. Do bats feed in winter? *American Midland Naturalist* 129: 200–203.

Whitaker, J. O., Jr., and D. C. Wallace. 1973. Fishes of Vigo County, Indiana. *Proceedings of the Indiana Academy of Science* 82: 450–464.

White, W. B. 1988. *Geomorphology and hydrology of Karst terrains.* Oxford: Oxford University Press.

Wickwire, G. T. 1947. Accelerated erosion due to industrial waste. *Proceedings of the Indiana Academy of Science* 57: 163–168.

Wigginton, M., and B. Clark. 2003. *Soil survey of Fountain County, Indiana.* USDA, Natural Resources Conservation Service. http://soils.usda.gov.

Wigginton, M., and D. Marshall. 2004. *Soil survey of Bartholomew County, Indiana.* USDA, Natural Resources Conservation Service. http://soils.usda.gov.

Williams, R. N., and B. J. MacGowan. 2004. Geographic distribution, *Ambystoma talpoideum. Herpetological Review* 35: 279.

Williamson, E. B. 1900. Biological conditions of Round and Shriner lakes, Whitley County, Ind. *Proceedings of the Indiana Academy of Science* 8: 151–155.

Will-Wolf, S., and F. Stearns. 1999. Dry soil oak savanna in the Great Lakes region. Pp. 135–154 in R. C. Anderson, J. S. Fralish, and J. M. Baskin, eds., *Savannas, barrens, and rock outcrop plant communities of North America.* New York: Cambridge University Press.

Wilson, C. B., and H. W. Clark. 1912. *The mussel fauna of the Kankakee Basin.* Report and Special Papers of the U.S. Fish Commission. Bureau of Fisheries Document no. 758. Washington, D.C.

Wilson, J. S. 2003. *Indiana atlas.* Austin, Tex.: Greenleaf.

Wilson, N. A. 1960. A northernmost record of *Plecotus rafinesquii* Lesson (Mammalia, Chiroptera). *American Midland Naturalist* 64: 500.

Wingard, R. C. 1975. *Soil survey of Crawford County, Indiana.* USDA, Natural Resources Conservation Service. http://soils.usda.gov.

Woodall, C., D. Johnson, J. Gallion, C. Perry, B. Butler, R. Piva, E. Jepsen, D. Nowak, and P. Marshall. 2005. *Indiana's forests 1999–2003*, pt. A. USDA, Forest Service, North Central Research Station (NC-253A).

Woods, A. J., J. M. Omernik, C. S. Brockman, T. D. Gerber, W. D. Hosteter, and S. H. Azevedo. 1998. Ecoregions of Indiana and Ohio (map poster). Reston, Va.: U.S. Geological Survey.

Woods, L. P., and R. F. Inger. 1957. The cave, spring and swamp fishes of the family Amblopsidae of central and eastern United States. *American Midland Naturalist* 58(1): 232–256.

Yatskievych, G., and K. M. Yatskievych. 1987. A floristic survey of the Yellow Birch Ravine Nature Preserve, Crawford County, Indiana. *Proceedings of the Indiana Academy of Science* 96: 435–445.

Year book of the state of Indiana for the year 1920. 1921. Fort Wayne, Ind.: Fort Wayne Printing.

Zhalnin, A. V. 2004. Delineation and spatial analysis of ecological classification units for the Hoosier National Forest. Ph.D. diss., Department of Forestry and Natural Resources, Purdue University.

Zhang, J., and J. R. Holsinger. 2003. Systematics of the freshwater amphipod genus *Crangonyx* (Crangonyctidae) in North America. *Virginia Museum of Natural History Memoir* 6.

Zollner, P. A. 2000. Comparing the landscape level perceptual abilities of forest sciurids in fragmented agricultural landscapes. *Landscape Ecology* 15: 523–533.

Index

Note: Species in the major taxonomic groups—flora, fish, amphibians and reptiles, birds, mammals, and invertebrates—are listed in separate indexes following the general index. Page numbers in italics refer to pages with illustrations.

General

Flora

Note: Scientific names of plants are cross-listed with common names in Tables P-1 and P-2.

Fish

Note: Scientific names corresponding to these common names are found in Table F-1. The remaining tables (except F-6) use only scientific names and are thus not found in this index.

Amphibians and Reptiles

Birds

Mammals

Invertebrates

Books in the

Indiana Natural Science Series

Mammals of Indiana, Revised and Enlarged Edition
by John O. Whitaker Jr. and Russell E. Mumford

Indiana's Weather and Climate by John E. Oliver

Mammals of Indiana: A Field Guide
by John O. Whitaker Jr.

Habitats and Ecological Communities of Indiana: Presettlement to Present
edited by John O. Whitaker Jr. and Charles J. Amlaner

The Essential Knobstone Trail: A Forgotten History of Indiana's Longest Footpath
by Nathan Strange

Field Guide to the Fishes of Indiana
by Thomas P. Simon,
Illustrations by Joseph R. Tomelleri

Field Guide to the Common Wildflowers of Indiana: With Associated Plants of Indiana's Upland Forests
by Michael A. Homoya

Photo by Angela Chamberlain.

Photo by John Lesku.

Volume Editors

John O. Whitaker, Jr., received his Ph.D. from Cornell University in 1962 and has been a professor of biology at Indiana State University since then. He is the founder and director of the ISU Center for North American Bat Research and Conservation. Whitaker has expansive knowledge of the plant and animal associations in all of the major habitats of Indiana, having worked throughout the state studying vertebrates, particularly mammals, for nearly 50 years. He is an author of *Keys to the Vertebrates of the Eastern United States*, *The Audubon Guide to Mammals of North America*, *Mammals of the Eastern United States*, *Mammals of Indiana* (the revised and enlarged edition), *Mammals of Indiana: A Field Guide*, and more than 380 scientific papers.

Charles J. Amlaner, Jr., received his Ph.D. from Oxford University in animal behavior. For the past 30 years, he and members of his Animal Sleep Research Group have been studying the evolutionary significance of sleep in animals. He is also known for his work in radio tracking and biotelemetry on free-ranging animals. Amlaner chaired the Zoology, Life Sciences, and Ecology and Organismal Biology departments at the University of Arkansas (Fayetteville) and Indiana State University. He has served as a commissioner and science advisor to the Arkansas Game and Fish Commission and as an advisory board member to the Indiana Department of Natural Resources. He currently serves as the vice president of research and as dean of the Graduate College at Kennesaw State University, Kennesaw, Georgia.

Associate Editors

Marion T. Jackson received his Ph.D. in plant ecology at Purdue University in 1964. He accepted a position at Indiana State University that same year. He has served as chair of the Indiana chapter of the Nature Conservancy and is the editor of *The Natural Heritage of Indiana* and the author of *101 Trees of Indiana*.

George R. Parker, professor emeritus, retired from Purdue University in 2007 after 37 years of teaching and research on midwestern forest ecosystems. He taught various courses, including conservation of natural resources, dendrology, and forest ecosystems. He and his graduate students have published on many different topics, including ecological classification systems and long-term change in old growth forests.

Peter E. Scott received his Ph.D. from Louisiana State University in 1995 and joined the biology faculty at Indiana State University that same year. An ornithologist, he has studied grassland birds of reclaimed mines and coordinates breeding bird atlas research. He also studies the pollination of wildflowers and their interactions with native bee species.